# SOMETHING ABOUT THE AUTHOR®

Something about
the Author *was named
an* **"Outstanding
Reference Source,"**
*the highest honor given
by the American
Library Association
Reference and Adult
Services Division.*

ISSN 0276-816X

# SOMETHING ABOUT THE AUTHOR®

**Facts and Pictures about Authors
and Illustrators of Books for Young People**

# volume 177

THOMSON

GALE

Detroit • New York • San Francisco • New Haven, Conn. • Waterville, Maine • London

# Something about the Author, Volume 177

**Project Editor**
Lisa Kumar

**Editorial**
Amy Elisabeth Fuller, Michelle Kazensky, Mary Ruby, Robert James Russell, Amanda D. Sams

**Permissions**
Margaret Chamberlain-Gaston, Andrew Specht, Jhanay Williams

**Imaging and Multimedia**
Leitha Etheridge-Sims, Lezlie Light

**Composition and Electronic Capture**
Tracey L. Matthews

**Manufacturing**
Drew Kalasky

**Product Manager**
Peg Knight

LIBRARY OF CONGRESS CATALOG CARD NUMBER 62-52046

ISBN-13: 978-0-7876-8801-1
ISBN-10: 0-7876-8801-0
ISSN 0276-816X

This title is also available as an e-book.
ISBN-13: 978-1-4144-2941-0, ISBN-10: 1-4144-2941-X
Contact your Thomson Gale sales representative for ordering information.

Printed in the United States of America
10 9 8 7 6 5 4 3 2 1

# Contents

Authors in Forthcoming Volumes . . . . . . . . . . . . . . ix

Introduction . . . . . . . . . . . . . . . . . . . xi

SATA Product Advisory Board . . . . . . . . . . . . . . xiii

Illustrations Index . . . . . . . . . . . . . . . . 207

Author Index . . . . . . . . . . . . . . . . . . . 237

## A

Abercrombie, Lynn
 *See* Sorrells, Walter . . . . . . . . . . . . . . . . 179

Abolafia, Yossi
 *See* Abulafia, Yossi . . . . . . . . . . . . . . . . 1

Abulafia, Yossi 1944- . . . . . . . . . . . . . . . . 1

Agonito, Joseph . . . . . . . . . . . . . . . . . . 4

Agonito, Rosemary . . . . . . . . . . . . . . . . . 4

Allen, Jonathan 1957- . . . . . . . . . . . . . . . . 6

Allen, Jonathan Dean
 *See* Allen, Jonathan . . . . . . . . . . . . . . . . 6

Arzoumanian, Alik . . . . . . . . . . . . . . . . . 12

## B

Baicker-McKee, Carol 1958- . . . . . . . . . . . . . . 14

Barry, Dan 1958- . . . . . . . . . . . . . . . . . . 15

Bell, Siobhán . . . . . . . . . . . . . . . . . . . 17

Bertrand, Diane Gonzales 1956- . . . . . . . . . . . . 17

Birmingham, Ruth
 *See* Sorrells, Walter . . . . . . . . . . . . . . . . 179

Bond, Higgins 1951- . . . . . . . . . . . . . . . . . 21

Brisson, Pat 1951- . . . . . . . . . . . . . . . . . 24

Buckley, Michael . . . . . . . . . . . . . . . . . . 30

Butts, Ed 1951- . . . . . . . . . . . . . . . . . . 32

Butts, Edward P.
 *See* Butts, Ed . . . . . . . . . . . . . . . . . . 32

## C

Cabrera, Cozbi A. 1963- . . . . . . . . . . . . . . . . 34

Carey, Ernestine Gilbreth 1908-2006
 *Obituary Notice* . . . . . . . . . . . . . . . . . 35

Chamberlin, Mary 1960- . . . . . . . . . . . . . . . 35

Chamberlin, Rich . . . . . . . . . . . . . . . . . . 38

Chamberlin, Richard
 *See* Chamberlin, Rich . . . . . . . . . . . . . . . . 38

Cooley, Regina Françoise 1940- . . . . . . . . . . . . 38

Cooper, Dutch
 *See* Kuyper, Sjoerd . . . . . . . . . . . . . . . . 100

Crawley, Dave . . . . . . . . . . . . . . . . . . . 39

## D

Daly, Jude 1951- . . . . . . . . . . . . . . . . . . 42

Dandi
 *See* Mackall, Dandi Daley . . . . . . . . . . . . . . 123

Demers, Dominique 1956- . . . . . . . . . . . . . . . 44

Dray, Matt 1967- . . . . . . . . . . . . . . . . . . 46

Dray, Matthew Frederick
 *See* Dray, Matt . . . . . . . . . . . . . . . . . . 46

Dreyer, Ellen . . . . . . . . . . . . . . . . . . . 48

## F

Fancher, Lou 1960- . . . . . . . . . . . . . . . . . 50

Fellows, Stan 1957- . . . . . . . . . . . . . . . . . 53

Fellows, Stanley
 *See* Fellows, Stan . . . . . . . . . . . . . . . . . 53

Fisher, Valorie . . . . . . . . . . . . . . . . . . 54

Florian, Douglas 1950- . . . . . . . . . . . . . . . . 56

Frazier, Craig 1955- . . . . . . . . . . . . . . . . . 62

## G

Gardner, Sally . . . . . . . . . . . . . . . . . . . 65

Gerritsen, Paula 1956- . . . . . . . . . . . . . . . . 68

Gilpin, Stephen . . . . . . . . . . . . . . . . . . 70

**H**

Hamilton, Emma Walton 1962- . . . . . . . . . . . . . . . 72

Helfer, Ralph 1937- . . . . . . . . . . . . . . . . . . . . . . . 74

Hepler, Heather . . . . . . . . . . . . . . . . . . . . . . . . . . 76

Hobbs, Will 1947- . . . . . . . . . . . . . . . . . . . . . . . . 77

Hobbs, William Carl
    *See* Hobbs, Will . . . . . . . . . . . . . . . . . . . . . . 77

Hopman, Philip 1961- . . . . . . . . . . . . . . . . . . . . . 83

**J**

Jacobsen, Laura . . . . . . . . . . . . . . . . . . . . . . . . . 85

Jessell, Tim . . . . . . . . . . . . . . . . . . . . . . . . . . . . 86

Johnson, Steve 1960- . . . . . . . . . . . . . . . . . . . . . 88

Juhasz, Victor 1954- . . . . . . . . . . . . . . . . . . . . . . 89

**K**

Kellogg, Steven 1941- . . . . . . . . . . . . . . . . . . . . . 91

Kellogg, Steven Castle
    *See* Kellogg, Steven . . . . . . . . . . . . . . . . . . . 91

Kenny, Jude
    *See* Daly, Jude . . . . . . . . . . . . . . . . . . . . . . . 42

Kono, Erin Eitter 1973- . . . . . . . . . . . . . . . . . . . . 98

Kornprobst, Jacques 1937- . . . . . . . . . . . . . . . . 100

Kuyper, Sjoerd 1952- . . . . . . . . . . . . . . . . . . . . 100

**L**

Lang, T. T.
    *See* Taylor, Theodore . . . . . . . . . . . . . . . . . 187

Langrish, Katherine . . . . . . . . . . . . . . . . . . . . . 102

Lansky, Vicki 1942- . . . . . . . . . . . . . . . . . . . . . 103

Lewison, Wendy Cheyette . . . . . . . . . . . . . . . . . 106

Low, William . . . . . . . . . . . . . . . . . . . . . . . . . . . 109

Lowry, Lois 1937- . . . . . . . . . . . . . . . . . . . . . . . 110

Lowry, Lois Hammersberg
    *See* Lowry, Lois . . . . . . . . . . . . . . . . . . . . . 110

Lupica, Michael Thomas
    *See* Lupica, Mike . . . . . . . . . . . . . . . . . . . . 118

Lupica, Mike 1952- . . . . . . . . . . . . . . . . . . . . . 118

**M**

Mackall, Dandi Daley 1949- . . . . . . . . . . . . . . . 123

MacLean, Christine Kole . . . . . . . . . . . . . . . . . 129

Mannion, Diane
    *See* Paterson, Diane . . . . . . . . . . . . . . . . . . 155

McCue, Lisa 1959- . . . . . . . . . . . . . . . . . . . . . . 131

McCue, Lisa Emiline
    *See* McCue, Lisa . . . . . . . . . . . . . . . . . . . . 131

Montecalvo, Janet . . . . . . . . . . . . . . . . . . . . . . 136

Moray Williams, Ursula 1911-2006
    *Obituary Notice* . . . . . . . . . . . . . . . . . . . . . 136

Munsinger, Lynn 1951- . . . . . . . . . . . . . . . . . . 137

**N**

Nelson, Blake 1960- . . . . . . . . . . . . . . . . . . . . . 144

**O**

Ogilvy, Ian 1943- . . . . . . . . . . . . . . . . . . . . . . . 147

Ogilvy, Ian Raymond
    *See* Ogilvy, Ian . . . . . . . . . . . . . . . . . . . . . 147

Oppenheim, Shulamith Levey 1928- . . . . . . . . . 148

**P**

Paschkis, Julie 1957- . . . . . . . . . . . . . . . . . . . . 152

Paterson, Diane 1946- . . . . . . . . . . . . . . . . . . . 155

Pendziwol, Jean E. 1965- . . . . . . . . . . . . . . . . . 158

Points, Larry G. 1945- . . . . . . . . . . . . . . . . . . . 160

Points, Larry Gene
    *See* Points, Larry G. . . . . . . . . . . . . . . . . . . 160

Pomerantz, Charlotte 1930- . . . . . . . . . . . . . . . 161

Prap, Lila 1955- . . . . . . . . . . . . . . . . . . . . . . . . 164

**Q**

Qualls, Sean . . . . . . . . . . . . . . . . . . . . . . . . . . 167

**R**

Radunsky, Vladimir . . . . . . . . . . . . . . . . . . . . . 168

Rodriguez, Christina 1981- . . . . . . . . . . . . . . . . 171

Rosenthal, Amy Krouse 1965- . . . . . . . . . . . . . 172

**S**

Schoenherr, Ian . . . . . . . . . . . . . . . . . . . . . . . . 175

Scotton, Rob 1960- . . . . . . . . . . . . . . . . . . . . . 176

Smith, Linda 1949- . . . . . . . . . . . . . . . . . . . . . 177

Sorrells, Walter . . . . . . . . . . . . . . . . . . . . . . . . 179

Spowart, Robin 1947- . . . . . . . . . . . . . . . . . . . 182

**T**

Tadgell, Nicole 1969- . . . . . . . . . . . . . . . . . . . . 186

Taylor, Theodore 1921-2006
    *Obituary Notice* . . . . . . . . . . . . . . . . . . . . . 187

Tchana, Katrin Hyman 1963- . . . . . . . . . . . . . . 188

Townley, Rod
    *See* Townley, Roderick . . . . . . . . . . . . . . . . 191

Townley, Roderick 1942- . . . . . . . . . . . . . . . . . 191

# Authors in Forthcoming Volumes

Below are some of the authors and illustrators that will be featured in upcoming volumes of *SATA*. These include new entries on the swiftly rising stars of the field, as well as completely revised and updated entries (indicated with *) on some of the most notable and best-loved creators of books for children.

**\*José Aruego ▌** Aruego, an author and illustrator, brings an optimistic outlook and an interest in human nature to each of his books for children. Working in collaboration with writer/artist Ariane Dewey, Aruego has won acclaim for the pen-and-ink drawings of funny animal characters that have become his trademark. Credited with a long list of engaging picture books, among them award-winning titles such as *Look What I Can Do!* and *We Hide, You Seek*, Aruego is consistently acclaimed for his inventiveness, colorful approach, and sense of whimsy.

**\*Ashley Bryan ▌** A folklorist, award-winning painter, and author, Bryan shares with young readers the many traditions rooted in black culture. His unique versions of time-honored African- and West-Indian folk tales and spirituals, published as *Lion and the Ostrich Chicks, and Other African Folk Tales* and *The Story of Lightning and Thunder,* feature original paintings and drawings, while *Beautiful Blackbird* is enhanced by intricate collage art. In *Ashley Bryan's ABC of African-American Poetry* he pairs a poem with each letter of the alphabet, and draws from the vast tradition of American spirituals in the anthology *Let It Shine.*

**Saxton Freymann ▌** Hailed for his originality in the *New York Times* and elsewhere, sculpture artist and photographer Freymann is the talent behind a number of highly original and imaginative picture books, among them the award-winning *How Are You Peeling?: Foods with Moods* and *Dr. Pompo's Nose.* Armed with an Exacto knife and a bag full of garden-fresh produce, Freymann deftly sizes up each tomato, pear, orange, and yam then gives them new life in his magical world, where creatures look out with eyes of peppercorns or black-eyed peas and smile through corn-kernel teeth.

**Holly Hobbie ▌** Hobbie was phenomenally popular during the late 1960s and 1970s when her country-themed paintings of a little girl in a homespun, prairie-style dress, tidy white pinafore, and large blue bonnet appeared on cards and household products, and eventually inspired the doll that bears her name. While the flesh-and-blood Holly Hobbie was somewhat upstaged by her rag-doll alter-ego, she has gained new fans with the help of the two roly-poly pigs that star in her "Toot and Puddle" picture-book series.

**\*Pat Hutchins ▌** Known for her pared-down texts and vivid artwork, British author/illustrator Hutchins creates books that exude optimism, humor, and a gentle simplicity. Often inspired by the antics of her own siblings, as well as those of her two sons, she creates picture books such as the award-winning *Rosie's Walk* as well as chapter books for older readers. Hutchins is particularly fond of two motifs—a lively family of monsters and a shy boy named Titch—and has patterned several books after each. She is also fond of country motifs, no doubt inspired by her own childhood in rural northern England.

**G. Brian Karas ▌** Determined to be an artist since childhood, Karas has built a successful career as an award-winning illustrator and author of children's books on the strength of his humorous, sketch art. Featuring pencil, gouache, and pastel, his images have appeared in books by Paula Danziger, Kobayashi Issa, and others. His original self-illustrated books, which include *On Earth* and *Skidamarink: A Silly Love Song to Sing Together,* are known for their humor and ability to engage young readers

**Norah McClintock ▌** Canadian editor and novelist McClintock is popular among teen readers, who devour her crime novels and thrillers. A five-time winner of the Crime Writers of Canada award for Best Juvenile Crime Novel, she peoples her compelling storylines with likable teen characters who frequently find themselves involved in unusual and often challenging relationships. In addition to standalone thrillers such as *Jack's Back* and *Password: Murder,* McClintock's fans enjoy her "Mike and Riel," "Chloe and Levesque," and "Robyn Hunter" mystery series, which combine likeable young sleuths and whodunits that keep readers guessing until the very last page.

**Matteo Pericoli ▌** As an architect working in Manhattan, Pericoli gave the city landscape more than a passing glance. His passion—some say obsession—for drawing eventually led him to create two monumental works of art documenting the New York City skyline. Published in book form as *Manhattan Unfurled* and *Manhattan Within,* these works have also sparked Pericoli's career as a children's book author/illustrator. Featuring his detailed pen-and-ink art, his books *See the City: The Journey of Manhattan Unfurled* and *The True Story of Stellina* each paint a lively and loving image of urban life.

**Jeff Stone ▌** In his "Five Ancestors" novels, which include *Tiger, Monkey, Snake,* and *Crane,* Indiana-based writer Stone brings middle-grade readers back to the seventeenth century and introduces them to the art of kung fu, a discipline he practices daily. The five-part series focuses on five orphaned Buddhist monks and was inspired by Stone's own experiences as an adopted child. Drawing from the philosophy underlying his practice of the martial art, Stone created the series to convey a message that is important to him: when each of us embraces our differences and builds on our unique strengths, the world will be a better place for all of us.

**Steve Voake** ▮ A walk in the English countryside near his home, and the annoying horsefly that hounded him on this walk, provided Voake with the inspiration for his first children's book, *The Dreamwalker's Child*. Geared for a pre-teen readership, Voake's fantasy follows a shy boy who is transported to a magical world in a parallel universe ruled by giant insects. Voake's novel, phenomenally popular among middle graders, has spawned a sequel and also attracted the interest of several filmmakers.

# Introduction

*Something about the Author* (*SATA*) is an ongoing reference series that examines the lives and works of authors and illustrators of books for children. *SATA* includes not only well-known writers and artists but also less prominent individuals whose works are just coming to be recognized. This series is often the only readily available information source on emerging authors and illustrators. You'll find *SATA* informative and entertaining, whether you are a student, a librarian, an English teacher, a parent, or simply an adult who enjoys children's literature.

## What's Inside *SATA*

*SATA* provides detailed information about authors and illustrators who span the full time range of children's literature, from early figures like John Newbery and L. Frank Baum to contemporary figures like Judy Blume and Richard Peck. Authors in the series represent primarily English-speaking countries, particularly the United States, Canada, and the United Kingdom. Also included, however, are authors from around the world whose works are available in English translation. The writings represented in *SATA* include those created intentionally for children and young adults as well as those written for a general audience and known to interest younger readers. These writings cover the entire spectrum of children's literature, including picture books, humor, folk and fairy tales, animal stories, mystery and adventure, science fiction and fantasy, historical fiction, poetry and nonsense verse, drama, biography, and nonfiction. Obituaries are also included in *SATA* and are intended not only as death notices but also as concise overviews of people's lives and work. Additionally, each edition features newly revised and updated entries for a selection of *SATA* listees who remain of interest to today's readers and who have been active enough to require extensive revisions of their earlier biographies.

## Autobiography Feature

Beginning with Volume 103, many volumes of *SATA* feature one or more specially commissioned autobiographical essays. These unique essays, averaging about ten thousand words in length and illustrated with an abundance of personal photos, present an entertaining and informative first-person perspective on the lives and careers of prominent authors and illustrators profiled in *SATA*.

## Two Convenient Indexes

In response to suggestions from librarians, *SATA* indexes no longer appear in every volume but are included in alternate (odd-numbered) volumes of the series, beginning with Volume 57.

*SATA* continues to include two indexes that cumulate with each alternate volume: the Illustrations Index, arranged by the name of the illustrator, gives the number of the volume and page where the illustrator's work appears in the current volume as well as all preceding volumes in the series; the Author Index gives the number of the volume in which a person's biographical sketch, autobiographical essay, or obituary appears in the current volume as well as all preceding volumes in the series.

These indexes also include references to authors and illustrators who appear in *Gale's Yesterday's Authors of Books for Children, Children's Literature Review,* and *Something about the Author Autobiography Series.*

## Easy-to-Use Entry Format

Whether you're already familiar with the *SATA* series or just getting acquainted, you will want to be aware of the kind of information that an entry provides. In every *SATA* entry the editors attempt to give as complete a picture of the person's life and work as possible. A typical entry in *SATA* includes the following clearly labeled information sections:

**PERSONAL:** date and place of birth and death, parents' names and occupations, name of spouse, date of marriage, names of children, educational institutions attended, degrees received, religious and political affiliations, hobbies and other interests.

**ADDRESSES:** complete home, office, electronic mail, and agent addresses, whenever available.

**CAREER:** name of employer, position, and dates for each career post; art exhibitions; military service; memberships and offices held in professional and civic organizations.

**MEMBER:** professional, civic, and other association memberships and any official posts held.

**AWARDS, HONORS:** literary and professional awards received.

**WRITINGS:** title-by-title chronological bibliography of books written and/or illustrated, listed by genre when known; lists of other notable publications, such as plays, screenplays, and periodical contributions.

**ADAPTATIONS:** a list of films, television programs, plays, CD-ROMs, recordings, and other media presentations that have been adapted from the author's work.

**WORK IN PROGRESS:** description of projects in progress.

**SIDELIGHTS:** a biographical portrait of the author or illustrator's development, either directly from the biographee—and often written specifically for the *SATA* entry—or gathered from diaries, letters, interviews, or other published sources.

**BIOGRAPHICAL AND CRITICAL SOURCES:** cites sources quoted in "Sidelights" along with references for further reading.

**EXTENSIVE ILLUSTRATIONS:** photographs, movie stills, book illustrations, and other interesting visual materials supplement the text.

## How a *SATA* Entry Is Compiled

*SATA* editors examine a wide variety of published sources to gather information for an entry. Biographical and bibliographic sources are consulted, as are book reviews, feature articles, published interviews, and material sometimes obtained from the biographee's family, publishers, agent, or other associates. Whenever possible, the author or illustrator is sent a copy of the entry to check for accuracy and completeness.

Entries that have not been verified by the biographees or their representatives are marked with an asterisk (*).

## Contact the Editor

We encourage our readers to examine the entire *SATA* series. Please write and tell us if we can make *SATA* even more helpful to you. Give your comments and suggestions to the editor:

Editor
Something about the Author
Thomson Gale
27500 Drake Rd.
Farmington Hills MI 48331-3535

Toll-free: 800-877-GALE
Fax: 248-699-8070

# *Something about the Author* Product Advisory Board

The editors of *Something about the Author* are dedicated to maintaining a high standard of excellence by publishing comprehensive, accurate, and highly readable entries on a wide array of writers for children and young adults. In addition to the quality of the content, the editors take pride in the graphic design of the series, which is intended to be orderly yet inviting, allowing readers to utilize the pages of *SATA* easily and with efficiency. Despite the longevity of the *SATA* print series, and the success of its format, we are mindful that the vitality of a literary reference product is dependent on its ability to serve its users over time. As literature, and attitudes about literature, constantly evolve, so do the reference needs of students, teachers, scholars, journalists, researchers, and book club members. To be certain that we continue to keep pace with the expectations of our customers, the editors of *SATA* listen carefully to their comments regarding the value, utility, and quality of the series. Librarians, who have firsthand knowledge of the needs of library users, are a valuable resource for us. The *Something about the Author* Product Advisory Board, made up of school, public, and academic librarians, is a forum to promote focused feedback about *SATA* on a regular basis. The nine-member advisory board includes the following individuals, whom the editors wish to thank for sharing their expertise:

**Eva M. Davis**
*Youth Department Manager,*
*Ann Arbor District Library,*
*Ann Arbor, Michigan*

**Joan B. Eisenberg**
*Lower School Librarian,*
*Milton Academy,*
*Milton, Massachusetts*

**Francisca Goldsmith**
*Teen Services Librarian,*
*Berkeley Public Library,*
*Berkeley, California*

**Susan Dove Lempke**
*Children's Services Supervisor,*
*Niles Public Library District,*
*Niles, Illinois*

**Robyn Lupa**
*Head of Children's Services,*
*Jefferson County Public Library,*
*Lakewood, Colorado*

**Victor L. Schill**
*Assistant Branch Librarian/Children's Librarian,*
*Harris County Public Library/Fairbanks Branch,*
*Houston, Texas*

**Caryn Sipos**
*Community Librarian,*
*Three Creeks Community Library,*
*Vancouver, Washington*

**Steven Weiner**
*Director,*
*Maynard Public Library,*
*Maynard, Massachusetts*

# SOMETHING ABOUT THE AUTHOR

**ABERCROMBIE, Lynn**
    **See SORRELLS, Walter**

\*    \*    \*

**ABOLAFIA, Yossi**
    **See ABULAFIA, Yossi**

\*    \*    \*

## ABULAFIA, Yossi 1944-
### (Yossi Abolafia)

### Personal

Surname sometimes transliterated "Abolafia"; born Joseph David Abulafia, June 4, 1944, in Tiberias, Israel; son of Jacob (a shopkeeper) and Aliza (a homemaker) Abulafia; married Irit Eliav (a lawyer), July 10, 1972; children: Michal, Tal, Itamar. *Education:* Bezalel Academy of Arts and Design (Jerusalem), graduated, 1965. *Religion:* Jewish.

### Addresses

*Home*—Har Adar, Israel. *Office*—6 Hacarmel St., Jerusalem 94309, Israel.

### Career

Author and illustrator. Israeli Television Authority, Jerusalem, writer, editor, actor, on-camera political cartoonist, and contributor to children's programming, 1968-76, 1978-80; Canadian Broadcasting Corporation (CBC), Toronto, Ontario, animation director, 1976; National Film Board of Canada, Montreal, Quebec, director of animation, 1976-78, 1980-83; freelance animator, New York, NY, 1982-84; freelance writer and illustrator, 1983—. *Military service:* Israel Defense Forces, 1965-68.

### Awards, Honors

Two Ben-Zvi Prizes for illustration, Israel Museum, including 1976; American Israel Cultural Foundation fellowship, 1976; Book of the Year awards, Child Study Association of America, for *Harry's Mom* and *My Parents Think I'm Sleeping,* both 1986, and for *Aviva's Piano,* 1987; American Library Association Notable Book designation, for *Harry's Visit* and *Harry's Dog;* two Hans Christian Andersen citations for illustration; Nahum Gutman Prize for Illustration, 1993.

### Writings

*SELF-ILLUSTRATED*

*My Three Uncles,* Greenwillow (New York, NY), 1985.
*Yanosh's Island,* Greenwillow (New York, NY), 1987.
*A Fish for Mrs. Gardenia,* Greenwillow (New York, NY), 1988.
*Fox Tale,* Greenwillow (New York, NY), 1989.

*ILLUSTRATOR*

Charlotte Pomerantz, *Buffy and Albert,* Greenwillow (New York, NY), 1982.

Jack Prelutsky, *It's Valentine's Day,* Greenwillow (New York, NY), 1983.

Barbara Ann Porte, *Harry's Visit,* Greenwillow (New York, NY), 1983.

Barbara Ann Porte, *Harry's Dog,* Greenwillow (New York, NY), 1984.

Jack Prelutsky, *What I Did Last Summer* (poems), Greenwillow (New York, NY), 1984.

Barbara Ann Porte, *Harry's Mom,* Greenwillow (New York, NY), 1985.

Jack Prelutsky, *My Parents Think I'm Sleeping* (poems), Greenwillow (New York, NY), 1985, reprinted, 2007.

Miriam Chaikin, *Aviva's Piano,* Clarion (New York, NY), 1986.

Susan Love Whitlock, *Donovan Scares the Monsters,* Greenwillow (New York, NY), 1987.

Franz Brandenberg, *Leo and Emily's Zoo,* Greenwillow (New York, NY), 1988.

SuAnn Kiser and Kevin Kiser, *The Birthday Thing,* Greenwillow (New York, NY), 1989.

Barbara Ann Porte, *Harry in Trouble,* Greenwillow (New York, NY), 1989.

Meir Shalev, *Aba 'oseh bushot,* translated by Dagmar Herrmann as *My Father Always Embarrasses Me,* Wellington, 1990.

Barbara Ann Porte, *Harry Gets an Uncle,* Greenwillow (New York, NY), 1991.

Lia Nirgad, *A Kiss for Lily,* [Israel], 1991, McAdam/Cage (San Francisco, CA), 2005.

Barbara Ann Porte, *Taxicab Tales,* Greenwillow (New York, NY), 1992.

Barbara Ann Porte, *A Turkey Drive, and Other Tales,* Greenwillow (New York, NY), 1992.

Else Holmelund Minarik, *Am I Beautiful?,* Greenwillow (New York, NY), 1992.

Nicholas Heller, *Ten Old Pails,* Greenwillow (New York, NY), 1993.

Robert Kalan, *Stop, Thief!,* Greenwillow (New York, NY), 1993.

Jessie Haas, *Busybody Brandy,* Greenwillow (New York, NY), 1994.

Barbara Ann Porte, *Harry's Birthday*, Greenwillow (New York, NY), 1994.

Robert Kalan, *Moving Day,* Greenwillow (New York, NY), 1996.

Robert Kalan, *Clean House,* Greenwillow (New York, NY), 1996.

Barbara Ann Porte, *Harry's Pony*, Greenwillow (New York, NY), 1997.

Hagit Allon and Lena Zehavi, *The Mystery of the Dead Sea Scrolls,* Israel Museum (Jerusalem, Israel), 2003.

Nira Harel, *The Key to My Heart,* Kane-Miller (La Jolla, CA), 2003.

Jack Prelutsky, *It's Snowing! It's Snowing!: Winter Poems,* HarperCollins (New York, NY), 2006.

Also illustrator of Yiddish-language texts for children written by Meir Shalev.

## Sidelights

Israeli artist Yossi Abulafia is an award-winning illustrator who has also worked as a film director, scriptwriter, and animator. Although he has created artwork for his original picture-book texts *My Three Uncles, Yanosh's Island, A Fish for Mrs. Gardenia,* and *Fox Tales,* Abulafia is better known as an illustrator. Since 1982, when his first illustration project, Charlotte Pomerantz's *Buffy and Albert,* was published, he has created art for numerous books, among them Nira Harel's *The Key to My Heart,* Robert Kalan's *Moving Day,* and the "Harry" series of beginning readers featuring stories by Barbara Ann Porte.

Praising the illustrator's work for *Harry's Birthday,* which finds Porte's popular young hero worried about an upcoming birthday, *Horn Book* contributor Ellen Fader wrote that, in addition to incorporating a flip-book cartoon into the bottom corner of each page, "Abulafia's lighthearted watercolor and black line drawings add details that extend the story." Carolyn Phelan had similar praise in her review of another book in the "Harry" series, writing that the illustrator brings to life *Harry's Pony* "with sensitivity and humor." Discussing *The Key to My Heart, Horn Book* contributor Susan P. Bloom praised the illustrator's "good-natured watercolors." Reviewing th same book, a *Kirkus Reviews* writer noted that, in his characteristically "easygoing style," Abulafia draws readers into Harel's story about a father and son's search for lost keys in their "cozy [Israeli] neighborhood." Effectively echoing Harel's "reassuring" theme about "the importance of community" in the opinion of a *Publishers Weekly* contributor, Abulafia also adds a "gentle humor" to *The Key to My Heart* through his "uncomplicated, inviting line drawings."

Growing up near the Sea of Galilee, the artistically inclined Abulafia spent much of his childhood doodling. He became more serious about art when he was sent to a kibbutz high school and assigned the task of illustrating and designing the school's monthly newspaper. After studying graphic design at the Bezalel Art Academy, he worked as an illustrator and cartoonist at the Israeli Army magazine while fulfilling the compulsory military service required of all citizens of his country. In 1968, Abulafia was hired as a news cartoonist for the newly instituted Israeli Television Authority. During the late 1960s and early 1970s he worked as an animator in Israel, then immigrated to Canada and North America for several years where he continued his career in television. In 1974 he was approached by an Israeli publishing house to illustrate some children's picture books, and some years later the chief editor at Greenwillow Books suggested that he try his hand at writing his own stories. In 1985 Abulafia published *My Three Uncles,* the first of his original self-illustrated picture books.

*My Three Uncles* recounts a young girl's efforts to tell her identical triplet uncles apart. Through his simple story, Abulafia suggests to readers that a person's true identity stems from what they do rather than from what

*Artist Yossi Abulafia brings to life* **The Key to My Heart,** *a picture book by fellow Israeli Nira Harel.* (Kane/ Miller Book Publishers, 2003. Reproduced by permission.)

they wear or how they appear. A reviewer in *School Library Journal* wrote that while Abulafia's text consists mainly of dialogue, his story is brought to life by his "breezy line drawings."

Another self-illustrated picture book, *A Fish for Mrs. Gardenia,* finds the lonely Mr. Bennett out fishing for more than just dinner. Catching a fish, the shy, elderly man gathers the courage to invite the middle-aged Mrs. Gardenia to dinner so that she can share in his good luck. When the fish slips from his hands as he is about to put it on the grill, the flummoxed Mr. Bennett is forced to set off on a slapstick chase. Fortunately, the fish finally makes its way back to Mr. Bennett's grill, suitably cooked, allowing the man to host a lovely dinner that marks the beginning of a rewarding friendship. *School Library Journal* contributor Amy Spaulding wrote that Abulafia's story is infused with "gentle amusement," adding that the "cheery" illustrations in *A Fish for Mrs. Gardenia* complement the narrative. *Horn Book* reviewer Margaret A. Bush asserted that while the book's "silliness will appeal to children, . . . adults will enjoy the portrayal of human foibles."

In *Fox Tale,* Abulafia once again draws upon a combination of narrative and illustration to tell his story. *Fox Tale* tells of how Crow, Rabbit, Donkey, and Bear take revenge on Fox, who has previously outsmarted them. *School Library Journal* contributor Starr LaTronica found that "the succinct text is complemented perfectly by the humorously expressive pen-and-watercolor cartoons." Recognizing that the theme of the outsmarted fox is a folklore staple, LaTronica wrote that Abulafia injects "a genuine freshness" into his story. The "creative and nonviolent" scheming performed by the book's cast of animal characters peaks in a moment of "hairy suspense," the critic added.

## Biographical and Critical Sources

*PERIODICALS*

*Booklist,* April 1, 1994, Carolyn Phelan, review of *Ten Old Pails,* p. 1458; April 15, 1996, Carolyn Phelan, review of *Clean House,* p. 1438; August, 1997, Carolyn

Phelan, review of *Harry's Pony,* p. 1910; January 1, 2006, Hazel Rochman, review of *It's Snowing! It's Snowing!: Winter Poems,* p. 106.

*Bulletin of the Center for Children's Books,* October, 1985, review of *My Three Uncles,* p. 21; April, 1991, review of *Fox Tale,* p. 183; April, 2003, review of *The Key to My Heart,* p. 315.

*Horn Book,* November-December, 1988, Margaret A. Bush, review of *A Fish for Mrs. Gardenia,* p. 767; September-October, 1994, Ellen Fader, review of *Harry's Birthday,* p. 583; May-June, 1996, Mary M. Burns, review of *Clean House,* p. 332; September-October, 1997, Maeve Visser Knoth, review of *Harry's Pony,* p. 577; July-August, 2003, Susan P. Bloom, review of *The Key to My Heart,* p. 443.

*Kirkus Reviews,* February 15, 2003, review of *The Key to My Heart,* p. 315; February 15, 2006, review of *It's Snowing! It's Snowing!,* p. 190.

*New York Times Book Review,* October 13, 1985, review of *My Three Uncles,* p. 37.

*Publishers Weekly,* July 10, 1987, Genevieve Stuttaford, review of *Yanosh's Island,* p. 68; May 25, 1992, review of *Fox Tale,* p. 65; May 27, 1996, review of *Moving Day,* p. 79; January 27, 2003, review of *The Key to My Heart,* p. 257; April 24, 2006, review of *A Kiss for Lily,* p. 60.

*School Library Journal,* April, 1985, review of *My Three Uncles,* p. 73; December, 1987, Ellen Loughran, review of *Yanosh's Island,* p. 66; November, 1988, Amy Spaulding, review of *A Fish for Mrs. Gardenia,* p. 83; May, 1991, p. 74; August, 1997, Dina Sherman, review of *Harry's Pony,* p. 138; July, 2004, Susan Scheps, review of *The Mystery of the Dead Sea Scrolls,* p. 90; July, 2006, Lee Bock, review of *It's Snowing! It's Snowing!,* p. 92.*

\*          \*          \*

# AGONITO, Joseph

## Personal

Married Rosemary Giambattista (an author and educator), July 1, 1961; children: Giancarlo, Mae Lee. *Education:* Attended Niagara University; earned Ph.D.

## Addresses

*Home*—NY. *E-mail*—info@agonito.com.

## Career

Historian, educator, and author. Onondaga Community College, Syracuse, NY, professor, now emeritus, of American history.

## Awards, Honors

James L. Sellers Memorial Award, Nebraska State Historical Society, 1999, for article published in *Nebraska History;* (with Rosemary Agonito) Western Heritage Award for Outstanding Western Novel, 2006, for *Buffalo Calf Road Woman.*

## Writings

*The Building of an American Catholic Church: The Episcopacy of John Carroll,* Garland (New York, NY), 1988.

(With wife, Rosemary Agonito) *Buffalo Calf Road Woman: The Story of a Warrior of the Little Bighorn,* Globe Pequot Press (Guilford, CT), 2005.

Contributor of articles to periodicals, including *Nebraska History, True West, Frontiers,* and *Journal of the Order of Indian Wars.*

## Sidelights

For Sidelights, see entry on Rosemary Agonito.

## Biographical and Critical Sources

*PERIODICALS*

*Journal of the West,* summer, 2006, Larry Toll, review of *Buffalo Calf Road Woman: The Story of a Warrior of the Little Bighorn,* p. 109.

*Kliatt,* January, 2006, Edna Boardman, review of *Buffalo Calf Road Woman,* p. 14.

*Post Standard* (Syracuse, NY), September 17, 2006, Laura T. Ryan, "Agonitos Lead Discussion of Their 'Buffalo' Book," p. 6.

*Reference and Research Book News,* May, 2006, review of *Buffalo Calf Road Woman.*

*ONLINE*

*Rosemary and Joseph Agonito Home Page,* http://www.agonito.com (March 15, 2007).*

\*          \*          \*

# AGONITO, Rosemary

## Personal

Born in Syracuse, NY; daughter of Mariangelo and Filomena Giambattista; married Joseph Agonito (a college professor), July 1, 1961; children: Giancarlo, Mae Lee. *Education:* Niagara University, B.A. (literature); M.A. (literature); Syracuse University, Ph.D. (philosophy). *Politics:* "Independent progressive."

## Addresses

*Home*—NY. *E-mail*—info@agonito.com.

## Career

Author and educator. Colgate University, Hamilton, NY, professor, 1973-75; Rochester Institute of Technology, Rochester, NY, senior professor of women's studies and

***Rosemary Agonito*** (Photograph courtesy of Rosemary Agonito.)

director of program, 1976-83; self-employed consultant and trainer, 1983-2004; freelance writer, 2004—. Lecturer; has appeared as a gender-issues expert on television and other media. Member of board of directors, Planned Parenthood of Rochester/Syracuse; served on numerous community boards and task forces, including New York State Task Force on Sex Equity in Education, Elizabeth Cady Stanton Foundation, Matilda Joslyn Gage Foundation, and Syracuse, NY, Task Force on Women Business Enterprises.

## Awards, Honors

Elected Woman Who Makes a Difference, *Minorities and Women in Business* magazine, 1989; Women in Business Advocate of the Year Award for New York State, U.S. Small Business Administration, 1992; (with Joseph Agonito) Western Heritage Award for Outstanding Western Novel, 2006, for *Buffalo Calf Road Woman.*

## Writings

*History of Ideas on Woman,* Putnam's (New York, NY), 1976.
*Promoting Self-Esteem in Young Women,* New York State Education Department (Syracuse, NY), 1987.

*No More "Nice Girl": Power, Sexuality, and Success in the Workplace,* Adams, 1993.
*Your Dream Made Easy: How to Start a Successful Business,* New Futures, 1999.
*Dirty Little Secrets; Sex in the Workplace,* New Futures, 2000.
(With husband, Joseph Agonito) *Buffalo Calf Road Woman: The Story of a Warrior of the Little Bighorn,* Globe Pequot Press (Guilford, CT), 2005.

## Sidelights

A former educator and advocate of women's rights and workplace gender issues, Rosemary Agonito is the author of several books that focus on her area of expertise. In addition, her novel *Buffalo Calf Road Woman: The Story of a Warrior of the Little Bighorn,* a collaboration with husband and fellow educator Joseph Agonito, won the Western Heritage Award for Outstanding Western Novel in 2006.

*Buffalo Calf Road Woman* was the result of over two decades' work; its inspiration lay in the mid-1970s and Joseph Agonito's reading of Dee Brown's *Bury My Heart at Wounded Knee.* Agonito, a professor of American history who specialized in the American West, found Brown's book notable because it approaches history from the perspective of Native Americans. One character who particularly attracted Agonito's notice was a Cheyenne woman named Buffalo Calf. Mentioned only briefly in Brown's book, this woman, in an effort to save her brother's life, joined the fight against U.S. General George Custer and the 7th Cavalry that culminated at the Battle of the Little Bighorn. Fought in June of 1876 in Big Horn County, Montana, the battle—which has become known as Custer's Last Stand—was a victory for the Lakota and northern Cheyenne tribes as they repelled the 7th Cavalry's efforts to encircle them and force them back to a government reservation.

In addition to traveling to libraries, archives, and the same terrain Buffalo Calf traversed in life, Agonito researched original diaries, mined the National Archives, and conducted numerous interviews to piece together the few facts remaining regarding the woman's life. Drawing on several years' worth of her husband's research, Rosemary fashioned a fictional story from this information, staying true to the facts while introducing readers to life as it was lived by the Plains Indians in the years after the U.S. Civil War. Praising the Agonitos' book, Edna Boardman wrote in *Kliatt* that readers of *Buffalo Calf Road Woman* will learn "what life was like for the Indians as their hunting grounds were destroyed, their living area was taken over by white settlers, and their free-roaming way of life was reduced to existence on reservations."

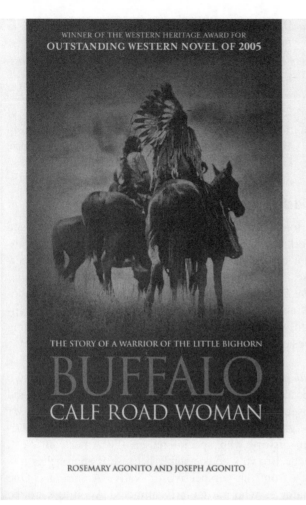

*Cover of* **Buffalo Calf Road Woman,** *a fictionalized account of the life of a Cheyenne woman written by Rosemary and Joseph Agonito.* (Photograph: The Library of Congress.)

## Biographical and Critical Sources

*PERIODICALS*

*Booklist,* June 1, 1993, Virginia Dwyer, review of *No More "Nice Girl": Power, Sexuality, and Success in the Workplace,* p. 1741.

*Journal of the West,* summer, 2006, Larry Toll, review of *Buffalo Calf Road Woman: The Story of a Warrior of the Little Bighorn,* p. 109.

*Kliatt,* January, 2006, Edna Boardman, review of *Buffalo Calf Road Woman,* p. 14.

*Library Journal,* July, 1993, Nancy Magnuson, review of *No More "Nice Girl,"* p. 90.

*Post Standard* (Syracuse, NY), September 17, 2006, Laura T. Ryan, "Agonitos Lead Discussion of Their 'Buffalo' Book," p. 6.

*Reference and Research Book News,* May, 2006, review of *Buffalo Calf Road Woman.*

*ONLINE*

*Rosemary and Joseph Agonito Home Page,* http://www.agonito.com (March 15, 2007).*

## ALLEN, Jonathan 1957-
## (Jonathan Dean Allen)

### Personal

Born February 17, 1957, in Luton, England; two children. *Education:* Attended Impington Village College, and Cambridge College of Arts and Technology; St. Martin's College of Art, B.A. (graphic arts).

### Addresses

*Home and office*—Acorn Cottage, South St., Lillington, NR Royston, Hertfordshire SG8 0QR, England.

### Career

Children's book author and illustrator.

### Awards, Honors

Virginia Young Readers Award, 1989, for illustrations in *The Great White Man-Eating Shark* by Margaret Mahy.

### Writings

*SELF-ILLUSTRATED PICTURE BOOKS*

*A Bad Case of Animal Nonsense* (poems), David Godine (Boston, MA), 1981, reprinted, 1997.

*A Pocketful of Painful Puns and Poems,* Dent (London, England), 1983.

*Guthrie Comes Clean,* Dent (London, England), 1984.

*My Cat,* Dial (New York, NY), 1984.

*My Dog,* Macmillan (London, England), 1987, Gareth Stevens (Milwaukee, WI), 1989.

*Mucky Moose,* Macmillan (New York, NY), 1990.

*Keep Fit Canaries,* Doubleday (New York, NY), 1992.

*Who's at the Door?,* Tambourine Books (New York, NY), 1993.

*Sweetie,* Macmillan (London, England), 1994.

*Two by Two by Two,* Orion Children's Books (London, England), 1994, Dial (New York, NY), 1995.

*Chicken Licken: A Wickedly Funny Lift-the-Flap Book,* Golden (New York, NY), 1996.

*Fowl Play,* Orion Children's Books (London, England), 1996.

*Wake Up, Sleeping Beauty!,* Dial (New York, NY), 1997.

*Wolf Academy,* Orchard Books (London, England), 1997.

*Jonathan Allen Picture Book,* Orchard Books (London, England), 1997.

*Flying Squad,* Yearling (London, England), 1998.

*The Ugly Duckling: A Fiendishly Funny Flap Book,* Corgi (London, England), 1999.

*Don't Wake the Baby!: An Interactive Book with Sounds,* Candlewick Press (Cambridge, MA), 2000.

*Monster Postman,* Orchard Books (London, England), 2000.

*And Pigs Might Fly,* Orchard Books (London, England), 2001.

*The King of the Birds,* Orchard Books (London, England), 2001.

*The Little Red Hen: A Deliciously Funny Flap Book,* Trafalgar (New York, NY), 2003.

*"I'm Not Cute!",* Boxer (St. Albans, England), 2005, Hyperion (New York, NY), 2006.

*Banana!,* Boxer Books (London, England), 2006.

*"WIZARD GRIMWEED" SERIES*

*B.I.G. Trouble,* Orchard Books (London, England), 1993.

*Potion Commotion,* Orchard Books (London, England), 1993.

*The Funniest Man in the World,* Orchard Books (London, England), 1994.

*Nose Grows,* Orchard Books (London, England), 1994.

*The Witch Who Couldn't Spell,* Orchard Books (London, England), 1996.

*Dragon Dramatics,* Orchard Books (London, England), 1996.

*"FRED CAT" BOARD-BOOK SERIES*

*Dressing Up,* Orchard Books (London, England), 1997.

*My Noisy Toys,* Orchard Books (London, England), 1997.

*Weather and Me,* Orchard Books (London, England), 1997.

*What My Friends Say,* Orchard Books (London, England), 1997.

*"JONATHAN ALLEN BOARD BOOKS" SERIES*

*Purple Sock, Pink Sock,* Orchard Books (London, England), Tambourine Books (New York, NY), 1992.

*Big Owl, Little Towel,* Orchard Books (London, England), Tambourine Books (New York, NY), 1992.

*One with a Bun,* Orchard Books (London, England), Tambourine Books (New York, NY), 1992.

*Up the Steps, Down the Slide,* Tambourine Books (New York, NY), 1992.

*ILLUSTRATOR*

Jeremy Strong, *Trouble with Animals,* Thomas Y. Crowell (New York, NY), 1980.

(With John Carter) Gyles Brandreth, *The Big Book of Silly Riddles,* Sterling (New York, NY), 1982.

David Henry Wilson, *There's a Wolf in My Pudding,* Dent (London, England), 1986.

David Henry Wilson, *Yucky Ducky,* Dent (London, England), 1988.

David Henry Wilson, *Gander of the Yard,* Dent (London, England), 1989.

Margaret Mahy, *The Great White Man-Eating Shark,* Dial (New York, NY), 1990.

Gillian Osband, *Boysie's Kitten,* Carolrhoda Books (Minneapolis, MN), 1990.

Gillian Osband, *Boysie's First Birthday,* Carolrhoda Books (Minneapolis, MN), 1990.

David Henry Wilson, *Gideon Gander Solves the World's Greatest Mysteries,* Piper (London, England), 1993.

Margaret Mahy, *The Three-Legged Cat,* Viking (New York, NY), 1993.

Frank O'Rourke, *Burton and Stanley,* David Godine (Boston, MA), 1993.

Edward Lear, *Nonsense Songs,* Henry Holt (New York, NY), 1993.

Stephen Wyllie, *Red Dragon,* Dial (New York, NY), 1993.

Corinne Mellor, *Clark the Toothless Shark,* Western Publishing (New York, NY), 1994.

Rose Impey, *Monster and Frog Get Fit,* Collins (London, England), 1994.

Rose Impey, *Monster's Terrible Toothache,* Collins (London, England), 1994.

Rose Impey, *Monster and Frog,* Collins (London, England), 1994.

Rose Impey, *Monster and Frog Mind the Baby,* Collins (London, England), 1994.

Rose Impey, *Monster and Frog at Sea,* Collins (London, England), 1994.

Stephen Wyllie, *Bear Buys a Car,* Dial (New York, NY), 1995.

Corinne Mellor, *Bruce the Balding Moose,* Dial (New York, NY), 1996.

Bill Grossman, *The Bear Whose Bones Were Jezebel Jones,* Dial (New York, NY), 1997.

Margaret Mahy, *Beaten by a Balloon,* Viking (New York, NY), 1998.

Margaret Mahy, *Simply Delicious!,* Orchard Books (New York, NY), 1999.

Kara May, *Joe Lion's Big Boots,* Kingfisher (New York, NY), 2000.

Alan Brown, *I Am a Dog,* Kane/Miller (La Jolla, CA), 2002.

Pat Thomson, *It's So Unfair!,* Anderson (London, England), 2005.

## Sidelights

British children's book author and illustrator Jonathan Allen is known for creating engaging picture books that feature simple line-and-watercolor art and a child-friendly storyline. In a career that has encompassed dozens of titles, Allen has achieved a reputation for creating the winsome illustrations that appear alongside his own text or with the stories of other authors. Noting that the author/illustrator "specializes in quirky characters" in books such as *Mucky Moose, And Pigs Might Fly,* and *"I'm Not Cute!,"* Dorothy Houlihan added in her *School Library Journal* review that Allen possesses a talent for creating "entertaining [facial] expressions [that] extend and expand the humor of the story." The fact that his storylines are more than slapstick also adds to Allen's appeal; in *"I'm Not Cute!,"* for instance, he pairs a story about an adorable owlet who cringes every time grownup animals coo and cuddle him with entertaining drawings to create what a *Publishers Weekly* critic called a "winning book [that] will resonate with children and grown-ups alike." "Young listeners will recognize themselves without realizing it," a *Kirkus Reviews* writer agreed of the bedtime storybook, adding that "parents will smile knowingly."

*Although a dedicated dad tries hard to be quiet, his efforts prove unsuccessful in Jonathan Allen's self-illustrated—and very noisy—***Don't Wake the Baby!** (Copyright © 2000 by Jonathan Allen. Reproduced by permission of Candlewick Press, Inc.)

Born in 1957, in Luton, England, Allen earned a graphic-arts degree at St. Martin's College of Art, and his first illustrations for a children's book appeared three years later, gracing the pages of Jeremy Strong's *Trouble with Animals.* Shortly thereafter, Allen authored two books of original rhyme. One, *A Bad Case of Animal Nonsense,* brings readers to an imagined Alphabet Game Park in which such animal oddities as a panda taking a bath and a stoat riding a bicycle combine to

help young readers identify sounds and letters. "Allen's sense of humor is uninhibited," noted a *Publishers Weekly* reviewer of this title. Allen continued in the same vein with *A Pocketful of Painful Puns and Poems,* which features enticing word-play images full of child appeal, such as a "hot-air baboon."

In *Mucky Moose* Allen introduces a moose who prefers to wander around in the foulest part of his forest's

swamp and therefore emits a perfectly awful smell. While such a smelly condition has its social drawbacks, it also proves beneficial when the moose's stench discourages a hungry wolf. The determined predator attempts to re-attack, first by pinching its nostrils shut with a clothespin and then by donning a gas mask, among other strategies, but in the end it is always overpowered by Mucky Moose's pungency. Cooper, reviewing the title for *Booklist,* praised *Mucky Moose.* Describing Allen's chronicle as that of a "goofy looking moose," a "razor-toothed wolf," "and accounts of some pretty bad smells," the critic concluded of Allen's book: "What's not to like?"

*Who's at the Door?* is Allen's retelling of the "Three Little Pigs" saga. In the author/illustrator's version, the door separating pig from wolf takes up most of the page spreads; readers see the worried porcine trio on one side and the crafty wolf trying out a number of disguises on the other. Mr. Wolf tries various means to gain entry, including impersonating a police officer and even wearing a pig disguise. In each case, the savvy swine evade the attempted intrusion by various means, including dressing in a wolf costume, which scares their dim-witted tormentor. "The split-page device guarantees a lively pace, while Allen's puckish, cartoon-like pictures heighten the humor still further," wrote a *Publishers Weekly* reviewer. *Five Owls* critic Mary Lou Voigt noted of Allen's interpretation of the popular "Three Little Pigs" tale that, in his whimsical drawings of the creatures, readers "can almost see the ideas forming in their heads as they plan new ways to outwit the wolf."

Allen's zany sense of humor shines through in *The Keep-Fit Canaries,* the story of seven pet-shop birds who leave for a home of their own, only to find that they dislike the boredom of a household as much as they did that of the pet-shop window. The birds—ranging in name from Horace to Doris, Alice to Clarice—discover a stash of aerobics tapes and work hard to become physically fit. They eventually break out of their cage and begin a rampage that culminates in the harassment of their neighbors and the stealing of food. Finally, the muscle-flexing birds find a more constructive way to alleviate their boredom: a steady job as bodyguards to the Lord Mayor's pet parrot. Allen's "up-to-the-minute dialogue sparkles with wit," noted *School Librarian* contributor Elizabeth Finlayson, the critic adding that the story's "minor human characters emerge brilliantly in thumbnail sketches." Allen's fearsome birds return to roost in a sequel, *Flying Squad.*

In *Two by Two by Two* the author/illustrator retells the biblical tale of Noah and his ark. Geared for readers aged four to eight, the story introduces Noah and describes the man's giant vessel, on which he brings two of each species of animal and then waits out a massive flood. Veering slightly from the Bible version, Allen imagines poor bedraggled Noah struggling to keep peace aboard the soggy ship by devised games and even

*A huggable, rolly-polly little owl tries to be taken seriously in Allen's self-illustrated picture book* "I'm Not Cute!" (Copyright © 2005 by Jonathan Allen. Reprinted by permission of Hyperion Books for Children.)

cabaret shows to help relieve his passengers' worry. Allen's "ark is a festive floating jungle, with breezy but accurate gouache-and-ink cartoons of exotic animals," noted a *Publishers Weekly* critic.

Beleaguered farm animals are the subject of several books by Allen. In *Fowl Play* Detective Hubert Hound tracks down the whereabouts of six missing chickens, while *Chicken Licken: A Wickedly Funny Lift-the-Flap Book* presents a reworking of the oft-told story about the creature who announced: "The sky is falling!" In the latter book Allen introduces several new characters to round out the cast, including Funny Bunny and Foxy Loxy. "Beginning readers are sure to enjoy reading this for themselves," predicted *Magpies* critic Annette Dale-Meiklejohn in a review of *Chicken Licken.* Another farmyard farce plays out in *The Little Red Hen: A Deliciously Funny Flap Book.* Beginning with another familiar children's story, Allen creates what a *Kirkus Reviews* writer dubbed a "well-crafted, amusing novelty" in a lift-the-flap book that finds the Little Red Hen shouldering the bulk of the work in baking corn bread while her gadabout farmyard companions dish out naught but excuses until the tasty bread is pulled from the oven.

As he did in *Who's at the Door?,* Allen explores the workings of the lupine mind in his humorous picture book *Wolf Academy.* As the story begins, two wolves adopt an abandoned cub they have found in the forest, believing it to be one of their own. As little Phillip grows, however, he displays increasingly strange behavior that is anything but wolf-like. On a recommen-

dation, Phillip is enrolled at the Wolf Academy, where he performs even more abysmally and even snarls at his classmates. Finally, when the teacher instructs the misfit cub and his classmates to disguise themselves as sheep the problem is revealed: Phillip turns out to be not a wolf at all, but rather a sheepdog skilled in herding sheep and keeping wolves at bay.

Allen has also created board books and stories for younger children who are just beginning to read on their own. Toddler-sized volumes such as *My Cat* and *My Dog* feature simple words as well as appealing images on their stiff, glossy pages. Focusing on a little boy and his tabby, *My Cat* tells the story of how a kitty first came to live with her human family. The book's young narrator also lists his pet's feline quirks and describes how the two play together. "Allen's primitively drawn . . . tabby has a certain endearing charm," noted Ilene Cooper in a *Booklist* review. Allen also uses board books to teach basic skills to very young readers. Part of a series, *Purple Sock, Pink Sock* helps children identify colors by name, while *Big Owl, Little Towel* and *Up the Steps, down the Slide* introduce the concept of

Cover of Kara May's **Joe Lion's Big Boots,** *in which Allen's illustrations reflect a short little boy's desire to be taller.* (Illustration copyright © Jonathan Allen, 2000. All rights reserved. Reprinted by permission of Kingfisher Publications, PLC, an imprint of Houghton Mifflin Company.)

opposites. "Allen's bright watercolors focus attention on the concepts," opined Marge Loch-Wouters in a *School Library Journal* review of the "Jonathan Allen Board Book" series.

Allen's work as an illustrator for other writers continues to earn him kudos from reviewers and readers alike. In his work for Frank O'Rourke's *Burton and Stanley,* he brings to life a story, not about the famed African explorers, but about two marabou storks who are carried by the wind from their native Kenya to a dusty railroad station in Nebraska during the mid-1930s. The town's children love the exotic birds, but the coming Plains winter threatens the creatures' delicate health. Moreover, government wildlife officials are on their way to Nebraska after hearing about the two exotic storks. Fortunately, Burton and Stanley know Morse code and use it to communicate with the local telegraph operator. The man helps the birds plan a speedy exit by directing them to New Orleans, where they stow away aboard a ship bound for Africa and home. A *Publishers Weekly* reviewer commended Allen's feathered main characters, "lugubrious, slightly untidy birds with curiously human features." In *Burton and Stanley,* the critic added, Allen serves up "a thoroughly warmhearted and rather touching entertainment."

Allen's illustrations for Margaret Mahy's *The Three-Legged Cat* also won enthusiastic reviews. Tom, the feline of the title, is missing a leg, and lives quietly with nearsighted Mrs. Gimble, an elderly woman who prides herself on living a respectable and uneventful life. Tom, however, longs for adventure and unseen vistas. One day Mrs. Gimble's brother Danny, whom she calls "a drifter," comes to visit. Danny arrives wearing a molting Russian fur hat and leaves instead with Tom curled up on his head. Mrs. Gimble, mistaking the forgotten hat for Tom, praises the kitty's newly docile demeanor. She is also pleased that he does not seem to eat very much. Meanwhile, the travel-hungry Tom gets to see the world. A *Publishers Weekly* critic wrote that Allen's "cartoony illustrations serve up a deliciously bizarre, out-of-kilter world peopled by flat, pop-eyed characters." Commending Allen and Mahy's collaboration, *Horn Book* reviewer Mary M. Burns noted that the artist's "flair for farce equals [that of the author] . . . , as demonstrated by his agile line and sense for telling detail."

In addition to *The Three-Legged Cat,* Allen and Mahy have worked together to produce a number of other titles, among them *Beaten by a Balloon* and *Simply Delicious!* The latter story features Mr. Minky, who buys his son an ice cream cone while out shopping, then realizes he must speed home on his bicycle before the ice cream melts. Mr. Minky takes a short cut through the jungle where he must evade a series of hungry creatures, including a toucan, a tiger, and a crocodile, some of whom have a hankering for more than just ice cream. "Readers and listeners alike will get into the swing of things, cheering Mr. Minky on over each lumpy bump,

all the way home," predicted a *Horn Book* reviewer, while *Booklist* contributor Michael Cart noted that Allen "captures the rhythm of the text and adds to the fun with droll depictions" of all the jungle animals."

Imaginative young beginning readers have much to enjoy in Allen's interactive work for Stephen Wyllie's *Bear Buys a Car.* Bear is excited about his new vehicle, purchased from Wolf, the somewhat shady owner of Wolf Motors. Bear believes Wolf when he is told that the car runs on potatoes and carrots instead of gasoline. It turns out that Wolf is actually correct: The vegetables are not fuel, however, but rather food for the enslaved pig hidden under the hood, who powers the car with his own hooves. Allen's paper engineering allows readers to move across the pages of scenery with Bear and his unusual car. "Expressive, lighthearted illustrations cheerfully complement this jolly tale," noted a *Publishers Weekly* reviewer, who also praised Allen's depictions of "a gullible Bear and a pleasingly detestable, smirking Wolf" as sure to appeal to children.

Other books featuring Allen's whimsical art include Kara May's *Joe Lion's Big Boots,* in which a diminutive lion cub worries that he's always the smallest, both in his family and at school. To feel larger, Joe takes to wearing a pair of extra-large boots with heels that make him taller. Unfortunately, the boots make it impossible for the cub to play soccer, which he loves. Being larger also has other, more dire drawbacks: now that he can reach the sink, Joe must help washing up the dinner dishes! *School Library Journal* reviewer Maura Bresnahan commended Allen's "colorful, cartoonlike illustrations," noting that they "add to the child-friendly appeal" of May's story.

## Biographical and Critical Sources

*BOOKS*

*St. James Guide to Children's Writers,* 5th edition, St. James Press (Detroit, MI), 1999.

*PERIODICALS*

*Booklist,* March 15, 1986, Ilene Cooper, review of *My Cat,* p. 1078; March 1, 1991, Ilene Cooper, review of *Mucky Moose,* p. 1396; September 1, 1993, Carolyn Phelan, reviews of *Big Owl, Little Towel* and *Up the Steps, down the Slide,* p. 807; July, 1995, Janice Del Negro, review of *Two by Two by Two,* p. 1882; March 15, 1998, Hazel Rochman, review of *Beaten by a Balloon,* p. 1250; September 1, 1999, Michael Cart, review of *Simply Delicious!,* p. 141; December 1, 2000, Ilene Cooper, review of *Don't Wake the Baby!: An Interactive Book with Sounds,* p. 728; April 15, 2006, John Peters, review of *"I'm Not Cute!,"* p. 50.

*Books for Keeps,* May, 1988, Liz Waterland, review of *Guthrie Comes Clean,* p. 9; September, 1988, Moira Small, review of *My Cat,* p. 6; July, 1993, George

Hunt, review of *The Keep-Fit Canaries,* p. 14; September, 1994, Peter Hollindale, review of *A Bad Case of Animal Nonsense,* p. 10; May, 1997, Judith Sharman, review of *Chicken Licken,* p. 20; November, 1997, Jill Bennett, review of *Wolf Academy,* pp. 21-22; March, 1998, George Hunt, review of *Fowl Play,* p. 19.

*Bulletin of the Center for Children's Books,* June, 2006, Deborah Stevenson, review of *"I'm Not Cute!,"* p. 439.

*Five Owls,* May-June, 1993, Mary Lou Voigt, review of *Who's at the Door?,* p. 111.

*Growing Point,* September, 1984, review of *Guthrie Comes Clean,* p. 4319.

*Horn Book,* July-August, 1993, Mary M. Burns, review of *The Three-Legged Cat,* p. 446; September, 1999, review of *Simply Delicious!,* p. 596.

*Junior Bookshelf,* August, 1992, review of *The Keep-Fit Canaries,* p. 145.

*Kirkus Reviews,* June 15, 2003, review of *The Little Red Hen: A Deliciously Funny Flap Book,* p. 855; March 1, 2006, review of *"I'm Not Cute!,"* p. 225.

*Magpies,* November, 1991, Melanie Guile, review of *Mucky Moose,* p. 28; July, 1996, Annette Dale-Meiklejohn, review of *Chicken Licken,* pp. 24-25.

*New Statesman,* December 2, 1983, Michael Rosen, "Rhymeo Nasties," p. 27.

*Publishers Weekly,* October 16, 1981, review of *A Bad Case of Animal Nonsense,* p. 78; October 12, 1992, reviews of *One with a Bun, Big Owl, Little Towel,* and *Purple Sock, Pink Sock,* p. 76; February 1, 1993, review of *Burton and Stanley,* p. 96; April 12, 1993, review of *Who's at the Door?,* p. 61; May 17, 1993, review of *The Three-Legged Cat,* p. 79; April 4, 1994, review of *Clark the Toothless Shark,* p. 77; May 22, 1995, review of *Two by Two by Two,* p. 59; September 25, 1995, review of *Bear Buys a Car,* p. 56; July 21, 1997, review of *The Bear Whose Bones Were Jezebel Jones,* p. 201; February 27, 2006, review of *"I'm Not Cute!,"* p. 59.

*School Librarian,* September, 1983, review of *A Pocketful of Painful Puns and Poems,* p. 231; August, 1992, Elizabeth Finlayson, review of *The Keep-Fit Canaries,* p. 99; August, 1993, Janet Sims, review of *Potion Commotion,* p. 109; May, 1994, Jean Needham, review of *B.I.G. Trouble,* p. 59; May, 1996, Elizabeth J. King, review of *Chicken Licken,* p. 56; February, 1997, Catriona Nicholson, review of *Fowl Play,* p. 17; November, 1997, Julia Marriage, review of *Wolf Academy,* p. 184; summer, 1998, Marie Imeson, review of *Flying Squad,* p. 76; autumn, 2005, Peter Andrews, review of *"I'm Not Cute!,"* p. 129; autumn, 2006, Richard Murphy, review of *It's So Unfair!,* p. 131.

*School Library Journal,* January, 1982, Margaret Bush, review of *A Bad Case of Animal Nonsense;* August, 1986, Lorraine Douglas, review of *My Cat,* p. 78; March, 1990, Nancy A. Gifford, review of *My Dog,* p. 184; August, 1991, Dorothy Houlihan, reviews of *Mucky Moose,* p. 142; March, 1993, Marge Loch-Wouters, reviews of *Pink Sock, Purple Sock, Up the Steps, down the Slide, Big Owl, Little Towel,* and *One with a Bun,* p. 170; June, 1995, Kathy Piehl, review

of *Two by Two by Two,* p. 76; December, 2000, Martha Topol, review of *Don't Wake the Baby!,* p. 94; February, 2001, Maura Bresnahan, review of *Joe Lion's Big Boots,* p. 100; March, 2006, Gay Lynn Van Vleck, review of *"I'm Not Cute!,"* p. 174.*

\* \* \*

## ALLEN, Jonathan Dean
### See ALLEN, Jonathan

# ARZOUMANIAN, Alik

## Personal

Born in Beruit, Lebanon; married. *Education:* Massachusetts College of Art, B.F.A. (illustration).

## Addresses

*Home and office*—Cambridge, MA. *E-mail*—alik@alikart.com.

*Alik Arzoumanian draws on her Middle-Eastern heritage in her illustrations for Margaret Read MacDonald's* **Tunjur! Tunjur! Tunjur!** (Copyright © by Alik Arzoumanian. Reproduced by permission.)

# Career

Children's book illustrator and elementary-school art teacher. Freelance illustrator for advertising and editorial companies.

# Illustrator

Hester Thompson Bass, *So Many Houses,* Children's Press (New York, NY), 2006.

Margaret Read MacDonald, *Tunjur! Tunjur! Tunjur!: A Palestinian Folktale,* Marshall Cavendish (New York, NY), 2006.

# Sidelights

Although Alik Arzoumanian has contributed her illustration talent to a variety of industries, including the advertising and publishing markets, her chief interest is centered on creating art for children's books. Arzoumanian's unique illustrations are created with acrylic paint using a layering technique in which the opaque paint is applied to gessoed hardboard panels. As noted on her home page, the artist's work is inspired by Armenian, Persian, and East Indian illuminated manuscripts. The Near-Eastern influence present in Arzoumanian's work is clearly displayed in her illustrations for *Tunjur! Tunjur! Tunjur!: A Palestinian Folktale,* a children's narrative retold by Margaret Read MacDonald.

The story MacDonald relates in *Tunjur! Tunjur! Tunjur!* commences when a woman prays to Allah and wishes for a child to care for. In her desperate plea, the explains that she will be content even if that child were "nothing more than a cooking pot." Literally granted her wish, the woman is blessed with a red cooking pot that displays human-like characteristics such as emotion and speech. The pot—a "tunjur" in Arabic—at first rattles around its new home, but it quickly becomes restless and begs to be let out to explore the outside world. When its adopted mother reluctantly grants the pot's wish, the tunjur immediately heads to the local market, where its mischievous nature soon reveals itself. At first the pot tricks a merchant into filling it up with honey, then quickly rolls its stolen booty home; on a second outing the pot comes home with a wealth of kingly jewels, obtained through the same trickery. Refusing to make good on its thefts, the pot ultimately finds itself on the receiving end of a particularly dirty trick, and decides to remain at home until it learns the difference between right and wrong.

In reviewing Arzoumanian's illustrations for *Tunjur! Tunjur! Tunjur!,* several critics observed that the artist's work enhances the cultural tone of MacDonald's entertaining text. *Booklist* reviewer Gillian Engberg commented that Arzoumanian's "richly hued, stylized acrylics, bordered with Islamic motifs, add subtle cultural detail," while a *Publishers Weekly* critic praised the illustrator for her ability to "pay homage to Arabic visual traditions—particularly mosaic art" through her jewel-toned, stylized images.

# Biographical and Critical Sources

*PERIODICALS*

*Booklist,* March 1, 2006, Gillian Engberg, review of *Tunjur! Tunjur! Tunjur!: A Palestinian Folktale,* p. 96.

*Kirkus Reviews,* March 15, 2006, review of *Tunjur! Tunjur! Tunjur!,* p. 294.

*Publishers Weekly,* January 30, 2006, review of *Tunjur! Tunjur! Tunjur!,* p. 68.

*School Library Journal,* April, 2006, Miriam Lang Budin, review of *Tunjur! Tunjur! Tunjur!,* p. 128.

*ONLINE*

*Alik Arzoumanian Home Page,* http://www.alikart.com (February 10, 2007).

*Marshall Cavendish Web site,* http://www. marshallcavendish.us/ (February 10, 2007), "Alik Arzoumanian."*

# B

## BAICKER-MCKEE, Carol 1958-

### Personal

Born 1958; children: three. *Education:* Yale University, B.A.; University of Virginia, Ph.D. *Hobbies and other interests:* "Pug lover, procrastinator, chocoholic, and all around silly person."

### Addresses

*Home and office*—Pittsburgh, PA. *E-mail*—baickermckee@adelphia.net.

### Career

Writer, illustrator, and child psychologist.

### Member

Western Pennsylvania Region of Society of Children's Book Writers and Illustrators.

### Writings

*Mapped Out!: The Search for Snookums,* illustrated by Traci O'Very Covey, Gibbs Smith (Salt Lake City, UT), 1997.
*Fussbusters on the Go: Strategies and Games for Stress-Free Outings, Errands, and Vacations with Your Preschooler,* Peachtree (Atlanta, GA), 2002.
*Fussbusters at Home: Around-the-Clock Strategies and Games for Smoothing the Rough Spots in Your Preschooler's Day,* Peachtree (Atlanta, GA), 2002.

Also author and illustrator of *Three Crabby Kids.* Author of monthly column for *Nick Jr. Family* magazine; author of blog, *Doodles and Noodles.*

*ILLUSTRATOR*

Julie Stiegemeyer, *Cheep! Cheep!,* Bloomsbury (New York, NY), 2006.

Julie Stiegemeyer, *Merry Christmas, Cheeps!,* Bloomsbury (New York, NY), 2007.

### Sidelights

Carol Baicker-McKee, a self-taught illustrator and clinical child psychologist, has written books for young readers as well as illustrating titles by herself and by others. A childhood interest in dioramas has inspired

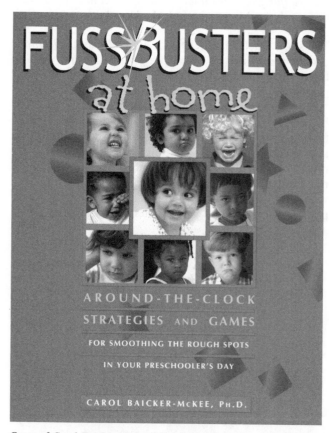

*Cover of Carol Baicker-McKee's* Fussbusters at Home, *which draws on the author's expertise as a child psychologist.* (Cover design by Loraine M. Joyner. Photographs © 2002 by Corbis Images: Asian girl, girl smiling, girl covering ears, pouting baby, angry boy, boy crying, girl showing teeth, boy rubbing eye; EyeWire/ Getty Images Creative: serious girl. Reproduced by permission.)

*Baicker-McKee illustrates a simple tale of farmyard antics in* Cheep! Cheep!, *a board book with a text by Julie Stiegemeyer.* (Copyright © Carol Baicker-McKee, 2006. Reproduced by permission.)

her creative approach as an illustrator, and her use of fabric collage gives her art a three-dimensional look. Baicker-McKee also incorporates found materials such as torn paper, clay, and wood in her illustration work.

As a writer, Baicker-McKee has penned the parent survival guides *Fussbusters on the Go: Strategies and Games for Stress-Free Outings, Errands, and Vacations with Your Preschooler* and *Fussbusters at Home: Around-the-Clock Strategies and Games for Smoothing the Rough Spots in Your Preschooler's Day.* In addition to her other writing projects, she contributes a monthly column to *Nick Jr. Family* magazine, and recommends titles for very young readers through her blog, *Doodles and Noodles.*

When she first began her writing career, Baicker-McKee thought her training in child psychology qualified her to give sensible parenting advice, but this assumption was called into question after she had children of her own. "I didn't have a clue," she confessed to Karen Macpherson of Bergen County, New Jersey's *Record.* Baicker-McKee got the ideas she includes in *FussBusters at Home* while watching other parents struggle to make their children behave while running errands. "I started off very simply, coming up with ideas for activities when parents are out and about with their kids," she explained of the book, which was described by Macpherson as "an idea-packed, lively, and humorous parenting guide." Kay Hogan Smith, writing in *Library Journal,*

noted that *FussBusters on the Go* is "written with an earthy sense of humor" where "fun is the operative word."

As an illustrator, Baicker-McKee has created art to accompany picture-book texts by Julie Stiegemeyer. *Cheep! Cheep!* and *Merry Christmas, Cheeps!* feature three-dimensional chicks constructed by the illustrator using felt, terry cloth, and other household textiles. Despite the minimalist style represented in her collages, Baicker-McKee "comes up with an amazing array of expressions and comic poses," according to a *Publishers Weekly* contributor in a review of *Cheep! Cheep!* "The story comes alive through the almost 3-D collage art," wrote Linda Zeilstra Sawyer in *School Library Journal,* while a *Kirkus Reviews* critic concluded that Stiegemeyer's "chickies are cuteness in action." The Cheeps return to celebrate Christmas in *Merry Christmas, Cheeps!*

## Biographical and Critical Sources

*PERIODICALS*

*Kirkus Reviews,* January 1, 2006, review of *Cheep! Cheep!,* p. 45.
*Library Journal,* October 1, 2002, Kay Hogan Smith, review of *FussBusters on the Go:: Strategies and Games for Stress-Free Outings, Errands, and Vacations with Your Preschooler,* p. 121.
*Publishers Weekly,* February 13, 2006, review of *Cheep! Cheep!,* p. 87.
*Record* (Bergen County, NJ), September 1, 2002, Karen Macpherson, "Whine Coolers for Kids: Author Takes Aim at the Tough Spots," p. F4.
*School Library Journal,* March, 2006, Linda Zeilstra Sawyer, review of *Cheep! Cheep!,* p. 202.

*ONLINE*

*Carol Baicker-McKee's Blog,* http://www.doodlesandnoodles.blogspot.com/ (December 15, 2006).
*Western Pennsylvania Region of the Society of Children's Book Writers and Illustrators Web site,* http://www.wpascbwi.com/ (February 20, 2007), "Carol Baicker-McKee."*

\*       \*       \*

# BARRY, Dan 1958-

## Personal

Born February 11, 1958, in New York, NY; son of Gene (a salesman) and Noreen (a homemaker) Barry; married Mary Trinity; children: Nora, Grace. *Education:* St. Bonaventure University, B.A., 1980; New York University, M.A., 1983.

## Addresses

*Home and office*—Maplewood, NJ.

## Career

Journalist. *Journal Inquirer,* Manchester, CT, reporter, 1983-87; *Providence Journal-Bulletin,* Providence, RI, 1987-95; *New York Times,* reporter and columnist, 1995—.

## Awards, Honors

George Polk Award (with others), 1992; Pulitzer Prize for reporting (with investigative team), 1994; American Society of Newspaper Editors Award for deadline reporting, 2003, for coverage of first anniversary of September 11th terrorist attack; Mike Berger Award, Columbia University Graduate School of Journalism, 2005.

## Writings

(With others) *A Nation Challenged: A Visual History of 9/11 and Its Aftermath,* introduction by Howell Raines, photographs by Nancy Lee and Lonnie Schlein, New York Times/Callway (New York, NY), 2002.
*Pull Me Up: A Memoir,* Norton (New York, NY), 2004.
*City Lights: Stories about New York,* St. Martin's Press (New York, NY), 2007.

## Sidelights

Written for adults but recommended for a high-school audience, *Pull Me Up: A Memoir* is the work of Pulitzer Prize-winning journalist Dan Barry. Rather than reflecting on his lengthy career, Barry—who was only in mid-career when his book was published—focuses on his experiences growing up in a first-generation Irish-American family during the 1960s. Barry grew up Irish and Roman Catholic in a New York suburb, and *Pull Me Up* follows him as he deals with hazing as a student in his Catholic high school as he moves into adulthood. He describes, in detail, his mid-twentieth-century childhood, lingering over such iconographic childhood memories as seasoning a leather baseball mitt. Much of his later narrative is involved with his efforts to deal with not only the loss of his mother, but his own cancer diagnosis received months after his mother's death. Asked why he decided to write a memoir at such a young age, Barry told Chip Scanlan for *Poynter Online:* "The short answer is that I thought I had some stories to share. The long answer is a little messier." While undergoing treatment for his cancer, he began to consider all the stories of his life that would never be told if he should die. "My stories were ordinary," Barry admitted to Scanlan, "but they were mine."

The title of *Pull Me Up* is inspired by a phrase Barry's mother used during the last stages of her cancer when asking her son to help her move from the living-room sofa. Dealing with serious topics such as alcohol, death, illness, and the sexual abuse that existed within the Roman Catholic Church even before it became an international scandal, Barry also ventures into more personal territory, discussing his search for faith in spite of darkness and doubt. Rather than portraying himself as a victim or skirting the problems in his own life, "Barry explores the tragedy of illness, bravely turning his keen journalistic lens on himself to produce a memoir that is riveting, moving, and not the least bit cheap," according to David Gibson in a review of *Pull Me Up* for *Commonweal.* Gibson also noted Barry's devotion to his faith in spite of his own doubt; "Barry himself is an inspiring messenger, whether he intends it or not," Gibson wrote.

Kathy O'Connell, writing for *America,* felt that *Pull Me Up* has "equal measures of grace and guts." Commenting on Barry's forthright prose, O'Connell deemed the book a "gracefully written yet hardheadedly realistic . . . argument for living in the moment" that avoids "the rampant hedonism with which that is usually associated." Janet Julian, writing in *Kliatt,* also praised the author's honesty, writing that "Barry's memoir is hilarious, honest, and poetic. It is a model of writing for mature high school students." A *Publishers Weekly* contributor cited *Pull Me Up* as "a beautiful book," and Wendy Wasserstein concluded in the *New York Times Book Review* that "Barry has managed to find the richness of heart of a now oddly distant America."

## Biographical and Critical Sources

*BOOKS*

Barry, Dan, *Pull Me Up: A Memoir,* Norton (New York, NY), 2004.

*PERIODICALS*

*America,* January 17, 2005, Kathy O'Connell, "Clear-eyed Courage," p. 29.
*Commonweal,* August 13, 2004, David Gibson, "A Reporter's Story," p. 35.
*Kliatt,* May, 2006, Janet Julian, review of *Pull Me Up,* p. 31.
*Providence Business News,* October 15, 2001, "NY Times Reporter to Share Firsthand Experience of Sept. 11," p. 2.
*New York Times Book Review,* May 12, 2004, Wendy Wasserstein, review of *Pull Me Up.*
*Publishers Weekly,* April 5, 2004, review of *Pull Me Up,* p. 55.

*ONLINE*

*New York Times Online,* http://www.nytimes.com/ (February 20, 2007), "Dan Barry."

*Poynter Online,* http://www.poynter.org/ (July 7, 2004), Chip Scanlan, "Stories to Share: A Reporter's Memoir."*

\*    \*    \*

## BELL, Siobhán

### Personal
Born in Somerset, England; children: one son.

### Addresses
*Home and office*—Somerset, England. *E-mail*—info@ siobhanbell.com.

### Career
Illustrator and textile artist. Handbag designer.

### Illustrator
Sheena Roberts, *We All Go Traveling By,* Barefoot Books (Cambridge, MA), 2003.
Stella Blackstone, *Ship Shapes,* Barefoot Books (Cambridge, MA), 2006.

### Biographical and Critical Sources

*ONLINE*

*Siobhán Bell Home Page,* http://www.siobhanbell.com (February 18, 2007).
*Barefoot Books Web site,* http://www.barefoot-books.com.uk/ (February 18, 2007), "Siobhán Bell."

\*    \*    \*

## BERTRAND, Diane Gonzales 1956-

### Personal
Born March 12, 1956, in San Antonio, TX; married Nick C. Bertrand (a self-employed businessman); children: two. *Ethnicity:* "Latina." *Education:* University of Texas, San Antonio, B.A., 1979; Our Lady of the Lake University, M.A., 1992. *Religion:* Roman Catholic.

### Addresses
*Office*—Department of English, St. Mary's University, One Camino Santa Maria, San Antonio, TX 78228.

### Career
St. Mary's University, San Antonio, TX, visiting lecturer in creative writing and English composition and faculty adviser for *Pecan Grove Review* (literary maga-

**Diane Gonzales Bertrand** (Photograph courtesy of Diane Gonzales Bertrand.)

zine), became writer-in-residence. Presents workshops on creative writing for children, young adults, and adult audiences throughout Texas.

### Member
National Council of Teachers of English, Society of Children's Book Writers and Illustrators, Texas Council of Creative Writing Teachers, Austin Writers League, San Antonio Writers Guild.

### Awards, Honors
Named National Hispanic Scholar, 1991; Book of the Year Award, *ForeWord* magazine, 1999, Teddy Award, Austin Writers League, 2000, Best Young-Adult Book (English) designation, National Latino Literary Hall of Fame, 2000, and Lone Star Reading List citation, Texas Library Association, 2000-01, all for *Trino's Choice;* Best Bilingual Children's Book Award, National Latino Literary Hall of Fame, 2000, for *Family/Familia;* Books for the Teen Age citation, New York Public Library, 2000, for *Lessons of the Game;* "Reading with Energy" Hispanic Children's Award, El Paso Energy Corporation, 2001, and Best Bilingual Children's Book Award, National Latino Literary Hall of Fame, 2002, both for *Uncle Chente's Picnic/El picnic de tio Chente;* Best

Young-Adult Book (English) designation, National Latino Literary Hall of Fame, 2002, for *Trino's Time;* Best Bilingual Children's Book Award, National Latino Literary Hall of Fame, 2003, for *The Empanadas That Abuela Made/Las empanadas que hacía la abuela;* Schneider Family Book Award, American Library Association, 2005, for *My Pal, Victor/Mi amigo, Victor.*

## Writings

### ADULT NOVELS

*Touchdown for Love,* Avalon Books (New York, NY), 1990.

*Close to the Heart,* Avalon Books (New York, NY), 1991.

*Carousel of Dreams,* Avalon Books (New York, NY), 1992.

### FICTION; FOR CHILDREN AND YOUNG ADULTS

*Sweet Fifteen* (novel), Arte Público Press (Houston, TX), 1995.

*Alicia's Treasure* (novel), Arte Público Press (Houston, TX), 1996.

*Lessons of the Game* (novel), Arte Público Press (Houston, TX), 1998.

*Trino's Choice* (novel), Piñata Books (Houston, TX), 1999.

*Trino's Time* (novel), Piñata Books (Houston, TX), 2001.

*Upside down and Backwards/De cabeza y al revés* (short stories), Spanish translation by Karina Hernéndez, Piñata Books (Houston, TX), 2004.

*The Ruiz Street Kids/Los muchachos de la calle Ruiz* (novel), Piñata Books (Houston, TX), 2006.

### PICTURE BOOKS

*Sip, Slurp, Soup, Soup/Caldo, caldo, caldo,* illustrated by Alex De Lange, Arte Público Press (Houston, TX), 1997.

*Family/Familia,* illustrated by Pauline Rodriguez Howard, translated by Julia Mercedes Castilla, Piñata Books (Houston, TX), 1999.

*The Last Doll/La ultima muneca,* Piñata Books (Houston, TX), 2000.

*Uncle Chente's Picnic/El picnic de tio Chente,* illustrations by Pauline Rodriguez Howard, Spanish translation by Julia Mercedes Castilla, Piñata Books (Houston, TX), 2001.

*The Empanadas That Abuela Made/Las empanadas que hacía la abuela,* illustrated by Alex Pardo DeLange, Spanish translation by Gabriela Baeza Ventura, Piñata Books (Houston, TX), 2003.

*My Pal, Victor/Mi amigo, Victor,* illustrated by Robert L. Sweetland, Spanish translation by Eida de la Vega, Raven Tree Press (Green Bay, WI), 2004.

*We Are Cousins/Somos primos,* illustrated by Christina Rodriguez, Piñata Books (Houston, TX), 2007.

Poetry has been published in *Palo Alto Review, Concho River Review, English in Texas,* and *Chile Verde Review.*

## Sidelights

Diane Gonzales Bertrand is noted for writing wholesome stories featuring Mexican-American characters and celebrating family life. Her books for middle graders, such as the story collection *Upside down and Backwards/De cabeza y al revés,* introduce likeable Latino characters in humorous tales that feature storylines all children can relate to, while she addresses the concerns of teens in novels such as *Sweet Fifteen* and *Trino's Time* Her bilingual picture books include *My Pal, Victor/Mi amigo, Victor,* about two boys who see past one's disability to share a close friendship. *Uncle Chente's Picnic/El picnic de tio Chente* introduces the Cardenas family as members learn that their truck-driving uncle Chente will be in town to help celebrate the Fourth of July. "This quiet book shows a real delight in family," commented *School Library Journal* contributor Ann Welton in praise of Bertrand's story.

In the picture book *Sip, Slurp, Soup, Soup/Caldo, caldo, caldo,* Bertrand tells the story of the delicious soup Mama cooks up with the help of the whole family, transforming a rainy Sunday into a celebration. Featuring a

*Bertrand's* **Upside down and Backwards** *contains lighthearted short fiction featuring a bilingual text and illustrations by Pauline Rodriguez-Howard.* (Arté Publico Press, 2004. Reproduced by permission.)

bilingual text and the repeated refrain "caldo, caldo, caldo" ("hot, hot, hot!"), *Sip, Slurp, Soup, Soup* relies on repetition to bring rhythm to the story of a warm-hearted family ritual. Ann Welton, reviewing the book for *School Library Journal,* maintained that Bertrand's repetitive text is both "brisk" and "rhythmic." Cooking brings another Latino family together in *The Empanadas That Abuela Made/Las empanadas que hacía abuela.* Bertrand frames this tale as a "rhythmic cumulative rhyme," Welton noted in *School Library Journal,* the critic adding that, as in *Sip, Slurp, Soup, Soup,* "the repetition in the text reinforces vocabulary and recognition skills."

*Alicia's Treasure,* Bertrand's middle-grade novel, introduces ten-year-old Alicia. The girl's dreams come true when she is allowed to accompany her older brother to the seashore during his weekend visit with his girlfriend and her family. At the beach, Alicia swims, surfs, picnics, squabbles with her brother, gets beach tar on her swimsuit, and generally has a great time. "Bertrand keeps the story moving as quickly as the weekend passes for Alicia," remarked Cheryl Cufari in a review of the novel for *School Library Journal.*

Other novels for young readers include the award-winning *Trino's Choice* and its sequel, *Trino's Time.* In *Trino's Choice* Bertrand introduces a seventh grader living in Texas who dislikes his family, including three young stepbrothers and an alcoholic uncle. Trino is also not very fond of school, although he is intrigued when some eighth-grade toughs invite him to join their criminal enterprises. "Overall, this is a dramatic and realistic contemporary novel . . . about a Latino boy struggling to grow into manhood," Annie Ayres concluded in *Booklist.* When readers rejoin Trino in *Trino's Time* he is attempting to deal with the aftermath of the botched robbery that led to the death of one of his friends. When his mother loses her job, Trino realizes that he needs to step up and take care of the family. Taking a part-time job at a grocery store, the teen also falls in with a better group of friends at school, and even finds inspiration in writing a report for history class. "The drama is seldom intense in the story," Roger Leslie wrote in *Booklist,* "but the emotions are sincere, and selfless Trino is an appealing protagonist." "Those readers who were frustrated with the open-ended conclusion of the earlier title will find satisfaction in this well-written sequel," concluded *School Library Journal* reviewer Diane P. Tuccillo.

Bertrand turns to older readers—particularly fans of romance—in books such as *Lessons of the Game* and *Sweet Fifteen.* In *Lessons of the Game,* which a *Publishers Weekly* reviewer deemed "reminiscent of 1950s career-girl romances," overwhelmed student teacher Kaylene Morales struggles to reach her reluctant students while daydreaming about a romance with the school's football coach. A realist as well as a romantic, Kaylene tempers her infatuation with the handsome Alex Garrison by acknowledging her worries whether

*Cover of Bertrand's novel* **Sweet Fifteen,** *featuring an illustration by Gladys Ramirez.* (Arté Publico Press, 1995. Reproduced by permission.)

she could tolerate sharing the man with his other love: football. "The Hispanic setting and characters help fill a void in YA romance," noted *Booklist* reviewer Anne O'Malley.

*Sweet Fifteen* depicts the modern version of the traditional Spanish coming-of-age ritual known as *quinceañera.* Bertrand's story centers on a seamstress who has been hired to make the dress for Stefanie Bonillo's birthday celebration. Stefanie has been resisting her family's efforts to get her to participate in this traditional celebration because she is still grieving over the recent death of her father. "Ethnic values are honestly portrayed in this sincere novel," noted Jana R. Fine in a review of *Sweet Fifteen* for *School Library Journal.* Chris Sherman, reviewing the story in *Booklist,* cited in particular Bertrand's focus on the evolving character of Rita, who finds love with Stefanie's uncle, friendship with Stefanie's mother, and a greater sense of her own identity through her involvement with the grieving family. "The story will engage readers . . . from its beginning to its satisfying end," Sherman concluded.

The *quinceañera.* tradition also figures in the plot of *The Last Doll/La ultima muneca,* a bilingual picture

book about a doll named Sarita who fears being left behind as all of the dolls surrounding her in a toyshop are purchased. Finally Sarita is purchased by a man as a gift for his goddaughter, Teresa. As a *quinceañera* present, Sarita will be the last doll ever given to the now-grown-up girl. "This frothy confection will . . . make non-Latinas long for their own *quinceañera* coming-out parties," Annie Ayres predicted in *Booklist.*

"I call myself a Mexican-American writer," Bertrand told *SATA.* "For me, this is a tribute to the bicultural home my parents gave their seven Gonzales children. Even though my parents made the decision to make English the language of our home so that we could succeed in school, it doesn't mean the culture was put aside. The customs of birth party *piñatas, cascarones* at Easter, making *caldo* or *empanadas* during winter months, and meeting up with *la familia* every Sunday at Abuelita's house gave me a positive childhood that I continue to value as an adult and as a parent myself.

"I always loved to create imaginary playmates as a child," the writer once commented, "and eventually transferred that creativity to the written page. My first 'novel' was written into a spiral notebook when I was in fifth grade. I kept adding to the story for the next fifteen years until I had filled almost seventy notebooks with two main characters, a host of minor characters, and a variety of plots and subplots. When I reviewed those notebooks about ten years ago, I was surprised that I had such a sense of dramatic action. I knew how to write with one viewpoint character, and I instinctively knew how to create a multidimensional story that could sustain the length of a novel.

"I came from a family of seven children, and the least expensive form of entertainment for us was a weekly trip to the library. I have many memories of my mother or father loading us into the family station wagon and heading for a library. To this day, all seven of us still love to read novels in our spare time.

"At Ursuline Academy, my junior English teacher allowed her students to turn in any kind of writing for extra points. So I wrote poetry and paragraphs about my teen life—whatever I was feeling at the time—and she would read it and encourage me to keep writing, no matter what. Her strong push for writing beyond the academic essays allowed me to explore new topics and find more creative ways to express myself. The other teacher who inspired me to take risks with my writing was Dr. Ann Semel at St. Mary's University. She encouraged me to write for children and young adults, something I hadn't considered before I enrolled in her fiction writing class.

"I enrolled in graduate school with a desire to become a better writing teacher. I wanted to learn new theories or modern teaching methods so that when I went back to teaching I'd be able to help students more. On the first day of class, I was told, 'A good writing teacher is a writer herself.' That philosophy completely changed my life.

"I never thought about being a role model until I began to create strong Mexican-American characters for my novels. I wanted women like myself—clever, funny, and educated—and men like my father and brothers—charismatic, sensitive, and loving—to be the essence of the world I created in my fiction. Those first three novels broke new grounds in romantic fiction since my editor had never published books with Mexican-American lead characters.

"I am very proud of the fact that my books give readers a sense of pride in their own customs and simple traditions. When I work with students in their classrooms, I like to remind them that their lives are wonderful sources for writing. I have learned to pay attention to the people and places around me and to capture those experiences in my own words, sometimes using the Spanish language that is part of who I am too."

## Biographical and Critical Sources

*PERIODICALS*

*Booklist,* June 1, 1995, Chris Sherman, review of *Sweet Fifteen,* p. 1750; May 1, 1996, Annie Ayres, review of *Alicia's Treasure,* p. 1505; January 1, 1999, Anne O'Malley, review of *Lessons of the Game,* p. 854; June 1, 1999, Annie Ayres, review of *Trino's Choice,* p. 1812; October 1, 2001, Annie Ayres, review of *The Last Doll/La ultima muneca,* p. 323; November 1, 2001, Roger Leslie, review of *Trino's Time,* p. 466; November 1, 2002, review of *Trino's Time,* p. 485.
*Children's Books Review Service,* spring, 1995, review of *Sweet Fifteen,* p. 140.
*Hispanic,* May, 2004, review of *My Pal, Victor/Mi amigo, Victor,* p. 70.
*Horn Book,* March-April, 2005, "Schneider Family Book Award," p. 236.
*Journal of Adolescent and Adult Literacy,* May, 1996, review of *Sweet Fifteen,* p. 693; October, 2002, Lori Atkins Goodson, review of *Trino's Time,* p. 180.
*Publishers Weekly,* December 21, 1998, review of *Lesson of the Game,* p. 68; June 18, 2001, review of *Trino's Time,* p. 83.
*School Library Journal,* September, 1995, Jana R. Fine, review of *Sweet Fifteen,* p. 218; July, 1996, Cheryl Cufari, review of *Alicia's Treasure,* p. 82; August, 1997, Ann Welton, review of *Sip, Slurp, Soup, Soup/ Caldo, caldo, caldo,* p. 128; April, 2001, Ann Welton, review of *The Last Doll/La ultima muneca,* p. 98; July, 2001, Diane P. Tuccillo, review of *Trino's Time,* p. 102; January, 2002, Ann Welton, review of *Uncle Chente's Picnic/El picnic de tio Chente,* p. 129; December, 2003, Ann Welton, review of *The Empanadas That Abuela Made/Las empanadas que hacía la*

*abuela,* p. 142; September, 2004, Ann Welton, review of *My Pal, Victor/Mi amigo, Victor,* p. 195; January, 2005, Ann Welton, review of *Upside down and Backwards/De cabeza al y revés,* p. 120; October, 2006, Maria Otero-Boisvert, review of *The Ruiz Street Kids/Los muchachos de la calle Ruiz,* p. 144.

*ONLINE*

*Children's Literature,* http://www.childrenslit.com/ (March 20, 2003), "Meet Authors and Illustrators: Diane Gonzales Bertrand."
*Cynthia Leitich Smith Web site,* http://www.cynthialeitichsmith.com/ (October 24, 2005), interview with Bertrand.

\* \* \*

## BIRMINGHAM, Ruth
## See SORRELLS, Walter

\* \* \*

## BOND, Higgins 1951-

### Personal

Born December 14, 1951, in Little Rock, AR; daughter of Henry Higgins and Edna Washington North; married Benny Bond (a recreation therapist), January 20, 1973; children: Benjamin Garnett. *Education:* Attended Phillips University, 1969-70; Memphis College of Arts, B.F.A. (advertising design), 1973.

### Addresses

*Home*—Nashville, TN. *Agent*—Anita Grien Agency, 155 E. 28th St., New York, NY 10016. *E-mail*—bhiggins-bond@netscape.net.

### Career

Illustrator, fine artist, and designer. Freelance illustrator, 1974—. Russ Berrie Company, Oakland, NJ, designer/illustrator, 1982-83; illustrator of periodicals, calendars, ceramics, and commemorative stamps; guest lecturer at colleges and universities. *Exhibitions:* Work exhibited at Metropolitan Museum of Art, New York, NY, 1974; DuSable Museum of African-American History, Chicago, IL, 1977; Children's Museum, Indianapolis, IN, 1981; Memphis College of Art, Memphis, TN, 1988; Tennessee State University, 1992; and Talladega College, 2002.

### Member

Society of Illustrators.

### Awards, Honors

21st Annual National Exhibition Certificate of Merit, Society of Illustrators, 1979; Communications Excellence to Black Audiences Award of Merit, 1979, for

work in *Black Enterprise Magazine;* presented key to the city of Indianapolis, IN, 1981; Medal of Honor, Arkansas Sesquicentennial Committee, 1986; Parents' Choice designation, 1998, for *Song of La Selva* by Joan Banks; inducted into Arkansas Black Hall of Fame, 1997; Green Earth Award for nonfiction, Society of School Librarians International, 1997, for *A Place for Butterflies.*

### Illustrator

Raymond M. Corbin, *1999 Facts about Blacks,* Beckham House Publishers, 1986.
Toyomi Igus, *When I Was Little,* Just Us Books (Orange, NJ), 1992.
Daniel Cohen, *Ancient Rome,* Doubleday (New York, NY), 1992.
Claire Chapelle, *Time for Sleep,* Macmillan (New York, NY), 1993.
Walter Dean Myers, *Young Martin's Promise,* Steck-Vaughn (Austin, TX), 1993.
Denise Jordan, *Suzie King Taylor: Destined to Be Free,* Just Us Books (Orange, NJ), 1994.
Garnet Nelson Jackson, *Thurgood Marshall, Supreme Court Justice,* Modern Curriculum Press (Cleveland, OH), 1994.
Garnet Nelson Jackson, *Toni Morrison, Author,* Modern Curriculum Press (Cleveland, OH), 1995.
Sheri Tan, *Handshake in Space,* Soundprints (Norwalk, CT), 1998.
Joan Banks, *Song of La Selva: A Story of a Costa Rican Rain Forest,* Soundprints (Norwalk, CT), 1998.
Melvin and Gilda Berger, *Why Do Volcanoes Blow Their Tops?: Questions and Answers about Volcanoes and Earthquakes,* Scholastic Reference (New York, NY), 1999.
Melvin and Gilda Berger, *Do Whales Have Belly Buttons?: Questions and Answers about Whales and Dolphins,* Scholastic Reference (New York, NY), 1999.
Melvin and Gilda Berger, *Do Tornadoes Really Twist?: Questions and Answers about Tornadoes and Hurricanes,* Scholastic Reference (New York, NY), 2000.
Melvin and Gilda Berger, *Do Penguins Get Frostbite?: Questions and Answers about Polar Bears,* Scholastic Reference (New York, NY), 2000.
Willa Cather, *Death Comes for the Archbishop,* Easton Press, 2001.
Suzette Haden Elgin, adaptor, *Jesus Is Born* (based on Luke 2.1-21), American Bible Society, 2002.
Suzette Haden Elgin, adaptor, *Jesus Prays to His Father* (based on Matthew 26.36-45), American Bible Society, 2002.
Melvin and Gilda Berger, *Where Did the Butterfly Get Its Name?: Questions and Answers about Butterflies and Moths,* Scholastic Reference (New York, NY), 2002.
Audrey FragEalosch, *Trails above the Tree Line: A Story of a Rocky Mountain Meadow,* Soundprints (Norwalk, CT), 2002.
Mary Batten, *Hey, Daddy! Animal Fathers and Their Babies,* Peachtree (Atlanta, GA), 2002.
Linda Viero, *The Seven Seas: Exploring the World Ocean,* Walker (New York, NY), 2003.

Susan Korman, *Groundhog at Evergreen Road,* Soundprints (Norwalk, CT), 2003.

Martha Whitmore Hickman, *Then I Think of God,* Albert Whitman (Morton Grove, IL), 2003.

Mary Batten, *Who Has a Belly Button?,* Peachtree (Atlanta, GA), 2004.

Richard H. Schneider, *The Christmas Pea Coat,* Ideals (Nashville, TN), 2004.

Michael Rose Ramirez, *Pen Pals,* Mondo (New York, NY), 2004.

Claire Rudolf Murphy, *I Am Sacajawea, I Am York: Our Journey West with Lewis and Clark,* Walker (New York, NY), 2005.

Linda Viera, *The Mighty Mississippi: The Life and Times of America's Greatest River,* Walker (New York, NY), 2005.

Melissa Stewart, *A Place for Butterflies,* Peachtree (Atlanta, GA), 2006.

Laura Gates Galvin, *Alphabet of Space,* Soundprints/ Smithsonian Institution (Washington, DC), 2007.

Contributor of illustrations to periodicals, including *Black Enterprise* and *Essence.*

## Sidelights

Higgins Bond is a prolific artist whose detailed paintings have appeared in magazines and on posters as well as being adapted for reproduction on commemorative U.S. postage stamps, collector plates, and other items. She is also well known to generations of children due to her work as an illustrator of nonfiction books for young people. A versatile artist who often depicts chil-

*Higgins Bond's detailed images, inspired by her love of nature, are featured in books such as Mary Batten's* **Who Has a Belly Button?** (Illustration © 2004 by Higgins Bond. All rights reserved. Reproduced by permission.)

*Melissa Stewart's* A Place for Butterflies, *a picture book for young naturalists, is enhanced by Bond's lush paintings.* (Illustrations © 2006 by Higgins Bond. Reproduced courtesy of Peachtree Publishers.)

dren and wildlife in her paintings, Bond has dozens of books to her credit, among them *The Seven Seas: Exploring the World Ocean* by Laura Viero, *Who Has a Belly Button?* by Mary Batten, and *Young Martin's Promise,* a biography of civil-rights leader Martin Luther King, Jr. with a text by Walter Dean Myers.

Born in Little Rock, Arkansas, Bond developed an interest in art as a young child. After high school, she enrolled at Phillips University, then transferred to the Memphis College of Art where she earned her B.F.A. in advertising design in 1973. Her first illustration project, Raymond M. Corbin's *1999 Facts about Blacks,* was published in 1986; her second, Toyomi Igus's picture book *When I Was Little,* appeared six years later, in 1992. The years since have found Bon producing the bulk of her illustration work for children's books.

Reviewers have consistently praised Bond's work. According to a *Publishers Weekly* reviewer, in her illustrations for Igus's nostalgic *When I Was Little,* Bond's

"strikingly naturalistic, richly hued paintings" are juxtaposed against "black-and-white drawings," a technique "that effectively evoke the lifestyle" of Igus's rural African-American family during the early years of the twentieth century. Discussing Bond's work for Linda Viera's *The Mighty Mississippi: The Life and Times of America's Greatest River, Booklist* contributor John Peters wrote that Bond brings to life the history of this major U.S. waterway in "a patchwork of richly colored paintings" in which life along the Mississippi is "inset into grand, sweeping river vistas." The characteristically detailed acrylic paintings she contributes to Batten's *Hey Daddy! Animal Fathers and Their Babies* were praised by *Booklist* reviewer Kay Weisman for "exhibit[ing] a rich color palate and almost photographic detail." Calling the work "a lovely book to look at," Cathie Bashaw Morton wrote in her *School Library Journal* appraisal that Bond's illustrations "nicely reflect the text" and accurately depict the wildlife habitat of the story's various "characters."

During her long career, Bond has amassed a number of prestigious honors, among them a medal of honor from the Arkansas Sesquicentennial Committee, delivered in 1986 from then-Governor Bill Clinton. Her paintings have been included in exhibitions staged at the Metropolitan Museum of Art in New York City, Chicago's DuSable Museum of African-American Art, and galleries at her alma matter and several other colleges. In addition to appearing on three stamps created for the U.S. Postal Service, Bond's art has appeared on four stamps for the U.N. Postal Administration. In 2006 she participated as one of five judges for the annual Federal Duck Stamp Contest sponsored by the U.S. Fish and Wildlife Service.

## Biographical and Critical Sources

*PERIODICALS*

*Art Direction,* April, 1976.
*Artist Market* (annual), 1983, p. 146.
*Booklist,* March 1, 1993, Ilene Cooper, review of *When I Was Little,* p. 1236; October 1, 2002, Kay Weisman, review of *Hey, Daddy! Animal Fathers and Their Babies,* p. 328; November 15, 2003, John Peters, review of *Groundhog at Evergreen Road,* p. 601; October 1, 2005, John Peters, review of *The Mighty Mississippi: The Life and Times of America's Greatest River,* p. 54; March 15, 2006, Carolyn Phelan, review of *A Place for Butterflies,* p. 52.
*Kirkus Reviews,* April 1, 2003, review of *The Seven Seas,* p. 542; March 1, 2004, review of *Who Has a Belly Button?,* p. 219; October 15, 2005, review of *The Mighty Mississippi,* p. 1147; March 1, 2006, review of *A Place for Butterflies,* p. 241.
*Publishers Weekly,* January 4, 1993, review of *When I Was Little,* p. 73.
*School Library Journal,* August, 1993, Anna DeWind, review of *When I Was Little,* p. 146; July, 1995, Anna DeWind, review of *Suzie King Taylor: Destined to Be Free,* p. 87; February, 2001, Eunice Weech, review of *Do Tornadoes Really Twist?: Questions and Answers about Tornadoes and Hurricanes,* p. 138; December, 2002, Cathie Bashaw Morton, review of *Hey, Daddy!,* p. 116; July, 2003, Helen Foster James, review of *The Seven Seas,* p. 120; September, 2003, Suzanne Crowder, review of *When I Think of God,* p. 180, and Susannah Price, review of *Trails above the Tree Line: A Story of a Rocky Mountain Meadow,* p. 190; May, 2004, Doris Losey, review of *Who Has a Belly Button?,* p. 128; October, 2005, Renee Steinberg, review of *I Am Sacajawea, I Am York: Our Journey West with Lewis and Clark,* p. 123; November, 2005, Lucinda Snyder, Whitehurst, review of *The Mighty Mississippi,* p. 172; June, 2006, Patricia Manning, review of *A Place for Butterflies,* p. 141.

*ONLINE*

*Higgins Bond Home Page,* http://www.higginsbond.com (March 15, 2007).

# BRISSON, Pat 1951-

## Personal

Born February 23, 1951, in Rahway, NJ; daughter of Thomas Francis (a plumber and foreman) and Jane Margaret McDonough; married Emil Girard Brisson (an administrator), May 29, 1971; children: Gabriel, Noah, Benjamin, Zachary. *Education:* Rutgers University, B.A. 1973, M.L.S., 1990. *Politics:* Democrat. *Religion:* Roman Catholic. *Hobbies and other interests:* Butterfly gardening, baking, reading.

## Addresses

*Home*—Phillipsburg, NJ. *Agent*—Tracey Adams, McIntosh & Otis Inc., 353 Lexington Ave., New York, NY 10016. *E-mail*—brisson@enter.net.

## Career

Teacher, librarian, and author. St. Anthony of Padua School, Camden, NJ, elementary school teacher, 1973-75; Phillipsburg Free Public Library, Phillipsburg, NJ, library clerk, 1978-81, reference librarian, 1990-2001; Easton Area Public Library, Easton, PA, library clerk, 1981-88.

## Member

American Library Association, Society of Children's Book Writers and Illustrators.

## Awards, Honors

American Booksellers Pick of the Lists selection, 1990, for *Kate Heads West;* American Booksellers Association Pick-of-the-Liest designation, 1994, for *Wanda's Roses;* New York Public Library 100 Titles for Reading and Sharing inclusion, and Parents' Choice Honor Book designation, both 1997, both for *Hot Fudge Hero,* and both 1999, both for *Little Sister, Big Sister;* Christopher Award, Paterson Prize for Children's Literature, Hodge Podger Award, American Booksellers Pick-of-the-Lists selection, International Reading Association/Children's Book Council Teachers' Choice Award, and National Parenting Publications Awards Honor Book designation, all 1998, all for *The Summer My Father Was Ten;* New York Public Library's 100 Titles for Reading and Sharing, 1999.

## Writings

*FOR CHILDREN*

*Your Best Friend, Kate,* illustrated by Rick Brown, Bradbury Press (New York, NY), 1989.
*Kate Heads West,* illustrated by Rick Brown, Bradbury Press (New York, NY), 1990.

*Magic Carpet,* illustrated by Amy Schwartz, Bradbury Press (New York, NY), 1991.

*Kate on the Coast,* Bradbury Press (New York, NY), 1992.

*Benny's Pennies,* illustrated by Bob Barner, Doubleday (New York, NY), 1993.

*Wanda's Roses,* illustrated by Maryann Cocca-Leffler, Boyds Mills Press (Honesdale, PA), 1994.

*Hot Fudge Hero,* illustrated by Diana Cain Bluthenthal, Holt (New York, NY), 1997.

*The Summer My Father Was Ten,* illustrated by Andrea Shine, Boyds Mills Press (Honesdale, PA), 1998.

*Little Sister, Big Sister,* illustrated by Diana Cain Bluthenthal, Holt (New York, NY), 1999.

*Sky Memories,* illustrated by Wendell Minor, Delacorte Press (New York, NY), 1999.

*Bertie's Picture Day,* illustrated by Diana Cain Bluthenthal, Holt (New York, NY), 2000.

*Star Blanket,* illustrated by Erica Magnus, Boyds Mills Press (Honesdale, PA), 2003.

*Hobbledy-Clop,* illustrated by Maxie Chambliss, Boyds Mills Press (Honesdale, PA), 2003.

*Mama Loves Me from Away,* illustrated by Laurie Caple, Boyds Mills Press (Honesdale, PA), 2004.

*Beach Is to Fun: A Book of Relationships,* illustrated by Sachiko Yoshikawa, Henry Holt (New York, NY), 2004.

*Tap-Dance Fever,* illustrated by Nancy Coté, Boyds Mills Press (Honesdale, PA), 2005.

*Melissa Parkington's Beautiful, Beautiful Hair,* illustrated by Suzanne Bloom, Boyds Mills Press (Honesdale, PA), 2006.

*I Remember Miss Perry,* illustrated by Stéphane Jorisch, Dial (New York, NY), 2006.

Fiction anthologized in books, including *Don't Cramp My Style: Stories about That Time of the Month,* edited by Lisa Rowe Fraustino, Simon & Schuster (New York, NY), 2004.

## Sidelights

Through her experiences as an elementary-school teacher as well as a librarian, not to mention as the mother of four boys, Pat Brisson has finely honed her instinct for what goes into a successful children's book. Beginning her second career as a children's-book author by creating works that combine geography with a young protagonist curious about other places—from the exotic-sounding Orient to regions of the United States not yet visited—Brisson has since expanded her focus, gaining a loyal following in the process. In chapter books like *Bertie's Picture Day* and *Hot Fudge Hero,* as well as in the picture books *Hobbledy-Clop, Beach Is to Fun: A Book of Relationships, Tap-Dance Fever,* and *I Remember Miss Perry,* she introduces likeable protagonists who deal with everyday obstacles—and sometimes life's tragedies—with good humor, resilience, imagination, and a dash of chutzpa.

Brisson was born in Rahway, New Jersey, in 1951, the fourth of five children. Growing up to become a writer was not a childhood ambition, but when her father brought home a typewriter the year she entered the fifth grade, she created her first unsolicited manuscript: an essay on strawberries. During high school Brisson took a course that combined journalism with creative writing, and it was there that she first had the notion that fiction-writing might be in her future. Enrolling at Rutgers University, she took only one course in writing—a poetry class—late in her senior year. "My teacher, Frank McQuilkan, told me if he had known earlier I could write so well he would have nominated me for the writing prize at graduation," Brisson recalled. "This meant a great deal to me. Even though I didn't consider myself a writer, it was there for encouragement later on when I decided to write for publication."

Married in 1971, Brisson soon could be seen frequenting the children's section of her local library in search of picture books for her growing children. In 1982 she decided to try her hand at writing a book of her own. Scouring writers' magazines and books on the craft, she began to learn the ropes, and her newly minted articles soon began appearing in magazines. After five years of work, Brisson's first book for children, *Your Best Friend, Kate,* was accepted by Bradbury Press, setting her on a new career path.

Focusing on stories that help introduce young children to geography, Brisson's "Kate" books begin with *Your Best Friend, Kate.* Documenting a girl's vacation trip along the East Coast of the United States in the form of postcards addressed to best friend Lucy, Kate expresses her excitement about her family's four-week round excursion from New Jersey to Florida, a trip peppered with the hijinks of her annoying little brother Brian. Praising the letters as "convincingly childlike," *School Library Journal* contributor Louise L. Sherman added that Brisson includes in her book "those things that would impress" children of the same age as the reader.

*Kate Heads West* takes readers on a trip through Arizona, Texas, Oklahoma, and New Mexico, this time in the company of Lucy and Lucy's family. Kate's notes home to family, friends, and even her teacher are "entertaining and educational," according to Lois Ringquist in *Five Owls.* Noting the book's value in social studies classes, *School Library Journal* contributor Jeanette Larson added that *Kate Heads West* "will be enjoyed by armchair travelers and families planning a similar trip" of their own. In *Kate on the Coast* the young traveler and her family have moved across the country and now make their home in Seattle, Washington. During their first year on the West Coast, they take numerous vacations, each one chronicled by Kate in correspondence with Lucy. Trips to Hollywood, Alaska, and even as far west as Hawaii inspire letters that "effortlessly impart information" and even serve as what *School Library Journal* reviewer Carla Kozak deemed "an exercise in the art of letter writing."

Many of Brisson's books are geared for beginning readers, and their engaging storylines capture and hold the interest of even those children whose idea of fun is nor-

*Pat Brisson first introduces her likeable second-grade hero, Bertie, in* **Hot Fudge Hero,** *featuring illustrations by Diana Cain Bluthenthal.* (Illustration copyright © 1997 by Diana Cain Bluthenthal. Reproduced by permission of Henry Holt and Company, LLC.)

mally anything but curling up with a good book. In the three short chapters of *Hot Fudge Hero,* a young boy named Bertie manages to get a mis-hit baseball back from his grouchy old neighbor Mr. Muckleberg (and gets a hot fudge sundae); becomes amazed when his feeble efforts at learning to play the saxophone are rewarded by the appearance of his fairy godfather (and a hot fudge sundae); and overcomes the clumsiness of using a new bowling ball (and winds up with a strike and yet another hot fudge sundae). Praising the book's large typeface and Brisson's use of short sentences, Christina Dorr noted in *School Library Journal* that *Hot Fudge Hero* captures "Bertie's determination and good nature." *Booklist* contributor Lauren Peterson added her praise, citing Brisson's "clever tales" as "excellent for beginning readers," while in *Horn Book* Martha A. Parravano noted the story's "nice messages" about "not making assumptions" and "the power of perseverance."

The equally humorous *Bertie's Picture Day* also focuses on second-grader Bertie, revealing his dismay at losing a front tooth just before school pictures are taken in one of its four chapters. "The funny situations" combine with the "short, pithy text" to "make this a very readable story," Carolyn Phelan wrote in *Booklist,* and *School Library Journal* contributor Kay Bowes had special praise for Brisson's young hero and his "unique

irrepressible personality." *Bertie's Picture Day,* Bowes concluded, "is a surefire hit."

Another easy-to-read chapter book, *Little Sister, Big Sister,* describes the relationship between young Edna and her older sister Hester. While Hester uses her age and experience to trick Edna into undertaking horrible tasks like cleaning her room, she also serves as a friend, particularly during thunder storms and when she has a candy bar that needs sharing. According to a *Kirkus Reviews* critic, "Brisson deftly captures the nuances of the relationship between siblings," while in *School Library Journal* Amy Lilien praised the characters as "real" and "the language . . . accessible." Brisson's "clear sentences . . . will draw beginning readers to daily dramas they will recognize," added Hazel Rochman in a *Booklist* review of *Little Sister, Big Sister.*

Expanding her range beyond chapter books, Brisson moved into picture books with *Magic Carpet* and *Benny's Pennies,* both of which combine an introduction to useful skills with an entertaining story. In *Benny's Pennies* a boy is introduced to the role of money as a means of exchange, while *Magic Carpet* finds an imaginative girl named Elizabeth going on a trip as an armchair traveler. While visiting with her aunt, Elizabeth learns to view the things around her with new eyes after she imagines the trip taken by several exotic objects that now have a place in her parents' home. *Magic Carpet* was praised for its ability to encourage creativity while also helping young children become "acquainted with an atlas," in the opinion of *School Library Journal* contributor Jane Saliers.

The engaging *Wanda's Roses* finds a young optimist determined to brighten up the vacant lot next to her inner-city home. The discovery of a scrubby bush with thorns causes Wanda to believe that, with enough care, the empty property can become full of roses. Although her more horticulturally astute neighbors are at first skeptical, they are soon won over by Wanda's enthusiasm and work together to make the girl's vision come true. Praising Brisson's protagonist as "loveable," a *Publishers Weekly* contributor dubbed *Wanda's Roses* an "upbeat urban tale" enhanced by watercolors that "genially depict . . . the city's great variety." In *School Library Journal* reviewer Carolyn Jenks hailed the book for its "story of one person's faith against all odds and a caring community," while also praising Brisson for telling the story "simply and with good humor."

Another upbeat young protagonist stars in *Tap-Dance Fever,* a "deliciously tall tale" in Phelan's opinion. In Brisson's entertaining story, Annabelle Applegate is tap-happy, and her love of tap dancing outlasts tap shoes, her mother's kitchen floor, and even the road she walks to school on, even as it wears away the patience of family, friends, and neighbors. Ultimately, the resourceful girl finds a way to keep tapping, and when she attracts an unusual dance partner her love of dance bring good luck to her neighbors. Phelan praised *Tap-

*Brisson teaches the basics of personal finance in the picture book* **Benny's Pennies,** *featuring torn-paper collage illustrations by Bob Barner.* (Illustration copyright © 1993 by Bob Barner. Used by permission of Random House Children's Books, a division of Random House, Inc.)

*Dance Fever* for inspiring "children who feel driven to do what they love," and in *School Library Journal* Be Astengo wrote that the "appealing watercolor-and-gouache cartoon illustrations" by Nancy Coté "are lively and expressive" and people Brisson's story with a multicultural cast. "This silly fun will have kids dancing in the aisles," predicted a *Kirkus Reviews* writer.

Designed for younger readers, *Beach Is to Fun* helps young children understand the concept of analogies, the rhyming comparisons brought to life in brightly colored illustrations by Sachiko Yoshikawa. According to *Booklist* reviewer Carolyn Phelan, Brisson's "playful picture book . . . makes a game of connecting words in meaningful ways" and introduces beginning wordsmiths with "a different way of thinking." Dubbing most of Brisson's rhyming analogies "clever," Linda L. Walkins praised *Beach Is to Fun* as a "cheery lesson on word relationships." Rhythm is used in a more musical sense in *Hobbledy-Clop,* as Brisson tells a folktale-like story about a boy is joined by a succession of critters on his

way to surprise his Granny with a spot of tea. Brisson's humorous, repetitive text is enhanced by Maxie Chambliss's "clear, watercolor cartoons," resulting in a book *School Library Journal* reviewer Marlene Gawron deemed "good for storytime."

*The Summer My Father Was Ten* takes a different approach, as Brisson pens "a profoundly moving cross-generational story," according to *Booklist* contributor Hazel Rochman. Illustrated with vivid watercolor renderings by Andrea Shine, the story focuses on a ten-year-old boy whose act of inadvertent vandalism results in the destruction of elderly Mr. Bellavista's vegetable garden. When the boy realizes what he has done, he apologizes; the following year he helps till the soil and plant the next crop of vegetables, and remains a friend of Mr. Bellavista until his death. Calling the work "a fine story of intergenerational friendship," a *Kirkus Reviews* contributor praised Brisson for imbuing her characters with "plainspoken, unsentimental, distinct voices."

Also focusing on a serious topic, *I Remember Miss Perry* finds a class of young children confronted with death when a favorite teacher is killed in a traffic accident. By detailing one boy's loving memories of Miss Perry's many kindnesses and her joy in life, and the efforts of grief counselors to help students deal with the tragedy, Brisson "clearly makes the point that memory is an antidote for sadness," noted Ilene Cooper in *Booklist. School Library Journal* reviewer Mary Elam maintained that *I Remember Miss Perry* "fills a need for books that encourage healthy emotional expression." Elam also praised Stepháne Jorisch's illustrations, which "reflect the varied emotions" created through both Miss Perry's optimistic spirit and the void left by her absence. Brisson tackles another serious subject in *Mama Loves Me from Away,* although in this case the absence of a loved one is less final than death: Sugar is sepa-

rated from her mother due to Mama's stay in prison. Again, memory plays a healing role, as Mama creates a homemade book for Sugar that contains the bedtime stories her daughter has missed so much in a story a *Kirkus Reviews* writer deemed "a non-judgmental look at life rocked by unfortunate events."

Supplementing her continued success as a children's book author, Brisson went back to college and earned her master's degree in library science, then worked as a reference librarian in her hometown of Phillipsburg, New Jersey, for ten years. One of her ongoing writing projects, a novel in poems for teens, Brisson described as "a challenge in both audience and format." She continues to find great satisfaction writing stories that help fuel the interest and excitement of children just beginning a lifetime of reading. "I hope to continue writing for a long, long time," Brisson once stated.

*With a simple text and colorful art by Sachiko Yoshikawa, Brisson takes readers on a sun-filled excursion in* **Beach Is to Fun.** (Illustrations copyright © 2004 by Sachiko Yoshikawa. Reprinted by permission of Henry Holt and Company, LLC.)

*Aided by Stéphane Jorisch's illustrations, Brisson tells the poignant story of the bond between a boy and his favorite teacher in* **I Remember Miss Perry.** (Illustrations copyright © 2006 by Stéphane Jorisch. Reproduced by permission of Dial Books for Young Readers, a division of Penguin Young Readers Group.)

## Biographical and Critical Sources

*PERIODICALS*

*Booklist,* March 15, 1992, Carolyn Phelan, review of *Kate on the Coast,* p. 1386; December 15, 1993, Ellen Mandel, review of *Benny's Pennies,* p. 762; April 1, 1997, Lauren Peterson, review of *Hot Fudge Hero,* p. 1333; February 1, 1998, Hazel Rochman, review of *The Summer My Father Was Ten,* p. 913; April 15, 1999, Hazel Rochman, review of *Little Sister, Big Sister,* p. 1528; May 15, 1999, Karen Hutt, review of *Sky Memories,* p. 1695; December 1, 2000, Carolyn Phelan, review of *Bertie's Picture Day,* p. 703; August, 2004, Carolyn Phelan, review of *Beach Is to Fun: A Book of Relationships,* p. 1940; December 15, 2004, Hazel Rochman, review of *Mama Loves Me from Away,* p. 746; March 1, 2005, Carolyn Phelan, review of *Tap-Dance Fever,* p. 1201; February 1, 2006, Ilene Cooper, review of *I Remember Miss Perry,* p. 53.

*Bulletin of the Center of Children's Books,* July-August, 2006, Karen Coats, review of *I Remember Miss Perry,* p. 489.

*Five Owls,* March, 1991, Mary Ann Saurino, review of *Your Best Friend, Kate,* p. 69; September, 1994, Lois Ringquist, "Reading across America," pp. 1-3.

*Horn Book,* November-December, 1991, Elizabeth S. Watson, review of *Magic Carpet,* p. 733; July-August, 1997, Martha A. Parravano, review of *Hot Fudge Hero,* p. 450.

*Kirkus Reviews,* May 15, 1994, review of *Wanda's Roses,* p. 696; February 1, 1998, review of *The Summer My Father Was Ten,* p. 193; April 15, 1999, review of *Little Sister, Big Sister,* p. 628; March 15, 2003, review of *Hobbledy-Clop,* p. 459; October 1, 2003, review of *Star Blanket,* p. 1221; May 15, 2004, review of *Beach Is to Fun,* p. 488; October 15, 2004, review of *Mama Loves Me from Away,* p. 1002; February 1, 2005, review of *Tap-Dance Fever,* p. 174; March 1, 2006, review of *I Remember Miss Perry,* p. 226; September 15, 2006, review of *Melissa Parkington's Beautiful, Beautiful Hair,* p. 947.

*New York Times Book Review,* October 17, 1999, Perry Nodelman, review of *Sky Memories,* p. 31.

*Publishers Weekly,* June 21, 1991, review of *Magic Carpet,* p. 62; February 17, 1992, review of *Your Best Friend, Kate,* p. 64; July 19, 1993, review of *Benny's Pennies,* p. 251; May 16, 1994, review of *Wanda's Roses,* p. 64; June 14, 1999, review of *Sky Memories,* p. 71; December 15, 2003, review of *The Star Blanket,* p. 72; December 6, 2004, review of *Mama Loves Me from Away,* p. 60; June 19, 2006, review of *I Remember Miss Perry,* p. 62.

*School Library Journal,* July, 1989, p. 61, Louise L. Sherman, review of *Your Best Friend, Kate,* pp. 61-62; November, 1990, Jeanette Larson, review of *Kate Heads West,* p. 86; January, 1992, Jane Saliers, review of *Magic Carpet,* p. 88; July, 1992, Carla Kozak, review of *Kate on the Coast,* p. 56; January, 1994, Linda Wicher, review of *Benny's Pennies,* pp. 82-83; December, 1994, Carolyn Jenks, review of *Wanda's Roses,* p. 71; July, 1997, Christina Dorr, review of *Hot Fudge Hero,* p. 60; April, 1998, Susan Pine, review of *The Summer My Father Was Ten,* p. 91; July, 1999, Amy Lilien, review of *Little Sister, Big Sister,* p. 61; August, 1999, Marilyn Payne Phillips, review of *Sky Memories,* p. 125; September, 2000, Kay Bowes, review of *Bertie's Picture Day,* p. 184; February, 2003, Marlene Gawron, review of *Hobbledy-Clop,* p. 102; December, 2003, Sally R. Dow, review of *Star Blanket,* p. 104; July, 2004, Linda L. Walkins, review of *Beach Is to Fun,* p. 68; February, 2005, Holly T. Sneeringer, review of *Mama Loves Me from Away,* p. 94; March, 2005, Be Astengo, review of *Tap-Dance Fever,* p. 168; March, 2006, Mary Elam, review of *I Remember Miss Perry,* p. 175; November, 2006, Rebecca Sheridan, review of *Melissa Parkington's Beautiful, Beautiful Hair,* p. 84.

*ONLINE*

*Pat Brisson Web site,* http://www.patbrisson.com (March 15, 2007).

# BUCKLEY, Michael

## Personal

Born in Akron, OH; married; wife's name Alison. *Education:* Ohio University, B.A. (with honors).

## Addresses

*Home*—New York, NY.

## Career

Children's book author. Worked variously as a stand-up comedian, lead singer of a punk-rock band, and pasta maker; children's programming developer at companies including Discovery Channel, Learning Channel, Music Television, Music Television Animation, and Klasky Csupo, beginning 1996.

## Writings

*"SISTERS GRIMM" NOVEL SERIES*

*The Fairy-Tale Detectives,* illustrated by Peter Ferguson, Amulet (New York, NY), 2005.

*The Unusual Suspects,* illustrated by Peter Ferguson, Amulet (New York, NY), 2005.

*The Problem Child,* illustrated by Peter Ferguson, Amulet (New York, NY), 2006.

*Once upon a Crime,* illustrated by Peter Ferguson, Amulet (New York, NY), 2007.

*Sisters Grimm Books 1, 2, 3* (omnibus), Abrams (New York, NY), 2007.

Contributor to *Storyworks* magazine.

## Sidelights

Michael Buckley started writing in junior high, tinkered with poetry and short fiction in high school, and wrote gags as a stand-up comic after graduating from college. His "Sisters Grimm" novels for young readers, which include *The Fairy-Tale Detectives, The Unusual Suspects, The Problem Child,* and *Once upon a Crime,* were inspired by his love of the stories collected by German scholars Jacob and Wilhelm Grimm during the eighteenth century. As he began researching other fairy tales to flesh out the world he was creating, Buckley realized how much these original folk stories differed from the Disney film versions he had been raised with.

Buckley's "Sisters Grimm" series begins with *The Fairy-Tale Detectives,* which introduces eleven-year-old Sabrina and her seven-year-old sister Daphne. The sisters find themselves shuffling off to another in the series of foster families they have lived with since the disappearance of their parents. This foster home is different

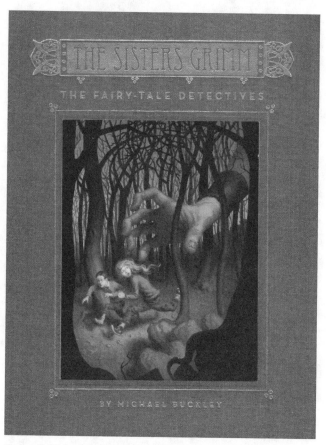

*Cover of Michael Buckley's* **The Sisters Grimm: The Fairy-Tale Detectives,** *featuring an illustration by Peter Ferguson.* (Illustrations © 2005 by Peter Ferguson. Reproduced by permission of Harry N. Abrams, Inc.)

than others, however, and the sisters' new guardian, Granny Relda, actually claims to be the real-life grandmother they thought was dead. As if that was not strange enough, Granny's home town, Fairyport Landing, is not what it seems: it is actually the home of fairy-tale characters and creatures, called "Everafters," who live among the unknowing human population. When Granny and her companion, Mr. Canis, are captured by a giant, Sabrina and Daphne have to decide who to trust in order to save the one person who may know the fate of their missing parents. "Fans of Lemony Snicket will adore this new series," wrote Annette Wells in a *Kliatt* review of *The Fairy-Tale Detectives.* While citing some lags in the novel's plotline, along with Buckley's focus on world building, *Booklist* contributor Gillian Engberg praised the author's "gleefully fractured fairytales," and a *Kirkus Reviews* contributor dubbed *The Fairy-Tale Detectives* a "tongue-in-cheek frolic" featuring "a pair of memorable young sleuths and a madcap plot."

In *The Unusual Suspects* Sabrina and Daphne begin school in Fairyport Landing when mystery once again surfaces. After one of their teachers is murdered, the girls learn that their whole school may be in danger. Sabrina would rather solve the mystery of her missing parents, however, and the girl's anger and frustration lead her to discover dangerous clues that may help her

solve both mysteries, or may get her into even deeper trouble. In *The Problem Child,* Sabrina and Daphne face down one of their scariest opponents: Little Red Riding Hood. This familiar storybook character faced a terrible trauma after the traditional tale ended; she was so traumatized by the Big Bad Wolf's brutal murder of her family that Red went insane. Together with her "pet" Jabberwock, the orphaned girl now terrorizes the Grimm sisters. She even tries to kidnap Granny Relda so that she can complete her replacement family, a group that involves Sabrina and Daphne's unconscious parents.

A *Kirkus Reviews* contributor considered Buckley's second novel "every bit as hilarious and scary" as *The Fairy-Tale Detectives,* and Kathleen Meulen wrote in *School Library Journal* that "free-spirited Daphne is a perfect foil for her older, grumpier sister, Sabrina." In *Kliatt,* Annette Wells ranked *The Problem Child* "highly recommended," and Tina Zubak recommended the title to readers who enjoy "a bit of dark humor rolled up with whimsy and adventure" in her *School Library Journal* review. "Buckley has a grand time adapting fairy, folk, and fictional characters to the modern day," wrote B. Allison Gray in another *School Library Journal* interview.

*Buckley's "Sisters Grimm" saga continues with* **The Problem Child,** *featuring artwork by Peter Ferguson.* (Illustrations © 2006 by Peter Ferguson. Reproduced by permission of Harry N. Abrams, Inc.)

On the *Sisters Grimm* Web site, Buckley explained that a childhood surrounded by books greatly influenced his success as a writer. "My parents were not wealthy people but they managed to find a way to get me books even when the checking account was empty," the novelist recalled. "I had more books than the library at my kindergarten school. To be a good writer is to be a good reader, and I had a great foundation to start from." Buckley hopes that his novel series will encourage young readers to explore the stories collected by the Brothers Grimm and Hans Christian Anderson as well as books by fantasy writers such as L. Frank Baum and Lewis Carroll. "Hopefully," he concluded, "the reader will go back to the library or bookstore after reading my book and ask for the classic stories they've discovered in the Sisters Grimm."

## Biographical and Critical Sources

*PERIODICALS*

*Booklist,* November 15, 2005, Gillian Engberg, review of *The Fairy-Tale Detectives,* p. 58.

*Bulletin of the Center for Children's Books,* December, 2005, review of *The Fairy-Tale Detectives,* p. 172.

*Children's Bookwatch,* December, 2005, review of *The Fairy-Tale Detectives.*

*Kirkus Reviews,* October 1, 2005, review of *The Fairy-Tale Detectives,* p. 1077; November 1, 2005, review of *The Unusual Suspects,* p. 1182; March 15, 2006, review of *The Problem Child,* p. 286.

*Kliatt,* September, 2005, Annette Wells, review of *The Fairy-Tale Detectives,* p. 26; May, 2006, Annette Wells, review of *The Problem Child,* p. 6.

*Library Media Connection,* February, 2006, Suzanne Libra, review of *The Fairy-Tale Detectives,* p. 56.

*Magazine of Fantasy and Science Fiction,* September, 2006, Charles De Lint, review of *The Fairy-Tale Detectives* and *The Unusual Suspects,* p. 35.

*Publishers Weekly,* December 19, 2005, review of *The Fairy-Tale Detectives,* p. 65.

*School Library Journal,* January, 2006, Sharon Grover, review of *The Fairy-Tale Detectives,* and Kathleeen Meulen, review of *The Unusual Suspects,* both p. 128; June, 2006, Tina Zubak, review of *The Problem Child,* p. 97.

*Teacher Librarian,* April, 2006, Betty Winslow, "Can You Keep a Secret?," p. 9; June, 2006, Betty Winslow, "More Fantastic Adventures," p. 44.

*ONLINE*

*Powells Online,* http://www.powells.com/ (February 20, 2007), interview with Buckley.

*Sisters Grimm Web site,* http://www.sistersgrimm.com/ (February 20, 2007).*

# BUTTS, Ed 1951-
## (Edward P. Butts)

## Personal

Born September 16, 1951, in Toronto, Ontario, Canada; son of Edward J. (a businessman) and Patricia M. (a businesswoman) Butts; children: Melanie Lynne. *Education:* University of Waterloo, B.A. (independent studies; with honors), 1981.

## Addresses

*Home*—Guelph, Ontario, Canada. *E-mail*—edpbutts@ yahoo.com.

## Career

Author, editor, and researcher. Researcher for Ontario educational Communication Authority (TV Ontario), c. 1980; substitute teacher in Ontario, Canada; Learning Center of Sosua, Dominican Republic, teacher of English and social studies, 1994-2002.

## Awards, Honors

Canadian Children's Book Centre Our Choice listee, for *She Dared.*

## Writings

*FOR CHILDREN*

*Buffalo: A Fable of the West* (fiction), Colombo & Co. (Toronto, Ontario, Canada), 1998.
*Idioms for Aliens: A Grammar Revue of Plays and Verse,* illustrated by Michael Tonn, Maupin House (Gainesville, FL), 2004.

*Ed Butts* (Photograph courtesy of Ed Butts.)

*She Dared: True Stories of Heroines, Scoundrels, and Renegades* (nonfiction), illustrated by Heather Collins, Tundra Books (Plattsburgh, NY), 2005.
*SOS: Stories of Survival* (nonfiction), Tundra Books (Toronto, Ontario, Canada), 2007.
*Canadian Treasure Tales* (nonfiction), Tundra Books (Toronto, Ontario, Canada), 2008.

*OTHER*

(With Harold Horwood) *Pirates and Outlaws of Canada, 1610-1932* Doubleday (Garden City, NY), 1984, 2nd edition, Lynx Images (Toronto, Ontario, Canada), 2003.
(With Harold Horwood) *Bandits and Privateers: Canada in the Age of Gunpowder,* Doubleday Canada (Toronto, Ontario, Canada), 1987.
*Outlaws of the Lakes: Bootlegging and Smuggling from Colonial Times to Prohibition,* Lynx Images (Toronto, Ontario, Canada), 2004.
*Guiding Lights, Tragic Shadows: Tales of Great Lakes Lighthouses,* Lynx Images (Toronto, Ontario, Canada), 2005.
*True Canadian Disaster Stories,* Key Porter Books (Toronto, Ontario, Canada), 2005.
*The Desperate Ones: Forgotten Canadian Outlaws,* Dundurn Books (Toronto, Ontario, Canada), 2006.
*True Unsolved Canadian Mysteries* (nonfiction), Key Porter (Toronto, Ontario, Canada), 2006.
*The Desperate Ones II: More Stories of Forgotten Canadian Outlaws,* Dundurn Books (Toronto, Ontario, Canada), 2008.
*Underground Canada* (stories), Lynx Images (Toronto, Ontario, Canada), in press.
*Tortured Souls: True Stories behind Twenty Ontario Hauntings* (stories), Lynx Images (Toronto, Ontario, Canada), in press.

Author of educational materials. Contributor of short fiction to *New Quarterly,* and of articles to *Reader's Digest, Touring, Toronto Star, Globe & Mail, Horizon Canada, Old West, Legion, Sailing Canada, Education Forum,* and *Premiere.* Columnist for *La Costa* (monthly magazine). Contributor to *Canadian Encyclopedia.* Editor for documentary film *Vanished in the Mist: Lost Newfoundland,* produced by Lynx Images.

## Sidelights

Ed Butts has channeled his long-time interest in Canadian history into books for both children and adults, many of them focusing on interesting men and women who would otherwise have fallen through the cracks in the historical record. His books include *The Desperate Ones: Forgotten Canadian Outlaws* and *Bandits and Privateers: Canada in the Age of Gunpowder,* the latter one of two books Butts has coauthored with Harold Horwood. Turning his focus to younger readers, Butts collects true stories about young people confronting disasters of all sorts in *SOS: Stories of Survival,* and introduces an interesting pantheon of Canadian women in

*She Dared: True Stories of Heroines, Scoundrels, and Renegades. Idioms for Aliens: A Grammar Revue of Plays and Verse,* which includes twenty-five short plays designed to help introduce the quirks and inconsistencies of English grammar, was inspired by Butts's work teaching his native language at a school in the Dominican Republic. In *Professionally Speaking* online, a reviewer praised the book for "bring[ing] humour to typically mundane grammar lessons" to students across a broad age range, from youngsters to adults.

Butts began his writing career in the early 1980s, after graduating with honors from the University of Waterloo. In the years since, he has alternated writing and researching history-related projects with teaching and journalism. Honored by the Canadian Children's Centre and one of several books to make its way over the border to U.S. readers, *She Dared* was Butts's way to help balance the male-centered historical record. The book includes profiles of fifteen Canadian women who helped expand the opportunities of future generations by breaking with traditions of all sorts. In addition to Molly Brant—a native Iroquois well known for her alliance with the British during the American Revolution and as an early resident of Kingston, Ontario—Butts introduces readers to Sarah Emma Edmonds, who disguised herself as a man in order to join the Union Army; Dr. James Miranda Barry, who was actually a woman in disguise; stagecoach robber Pearl Hart; and groundbreaking journalist Mary Ann Shadd. In *Canadian Review of Materials Online,* Grace Sheppard praised Butts's prose as "crisp," adding that the author "has clearly done a lot of research to support these stories, and he manages to find a good balance between the necessary details and the more naturally exciting parts of each story." "Written in an engaging, conversational style, the entries are well organized and informative," noted Linda Perkins in her *Booklist* review of *She Dared,* while in *School Library Journal* Robyn Walker concluded that the book "provides an objective view of many facets of the Canadian past" that readers should find both "interesting" and "informative."

Butts told *SATA:* "I suppose my writing career began when, as a boy, I wrote little stories for the simple reason that I loved to hear and tell stories.

"I hope to entertain people and to tweak their interest in history, English, or whatever I write on.

"I do some writing in the morning. In the middle of the day I go to the library to do some research. I write again in the afternoon. I often write at night.

"My purpose in writing *She Dared* was twofold. I wanted to tell young people a few of the many fascinat-

ing stories from Canadian history. I also wanted the stories to be about women because they have frequently been overlooked in history books.

"I think my work has been influenced, to varying degrees, by almost every author I've read: Mark Twain, Charles Dickens, Lewis Carroll, Jack London, Louis L'Amour, Colleen McCullough, and the great Canadian historian Pierre Berton, to name just a few. Of my contemporaries who write for young people, I am particularly fond of the works of fellow Canadians Robert Munsch and Dennis Lee.

"My advice to aspiring young writers is to be curious about everything and read all you can. Learn good grammar, because that is the foundation that enables you to make words weave magic. It's important, and not really as difficult as you might think."

## Biographical and Critical Sources

*PERIODICALS*

*Booklist,* December 1, 2005, Linda Perkins, review of *She Dared: True Stories of Heroines, Scoundrels, and Renegades,* p. 34.
*Canadian Book Review Annual,* 2005, Marie St. Onge-Davidson, review of *She Dared,* p. 539.
*Canadian Historical Review,* December, 1985, R.C. MacLeod, review of *Pirates and Outlaws of Canada, 1610-1932,* p. 597.
*Resource Links,* June, 2005, Victoria Pennell, review of *She Dared,* p. 36.
*School Library Journal,* December, 2005, Robyn Walker, review of *She Dared,* p. 162.
*Voice of Youth Advocates,* June, 2005, review of *She Dared,* p. 159.

*ONLINE*

*Canadian Review of Materials Online,* http://www.umanitoba.ca/outreach/cm/ (September 30, 2005), Grace Sheppard, review of *She Dared.*
*Professionally Speaking Web site,* http://www.oct.ca.publications/professionally_speaking/ (June 1, 2005), review of *Idioms for Aliens: A Grammar Revue of Plays and Verse.*

\*        \*        \*

# BUTTS, Edward P.
## See BUTTS, Ed

# C

## CABRERA, Cozbi A. 1963-

### Personal

Born 1963. *Education:* Parsons School of Design, B.F.A.

### Addresses

*Home and office*—New York, NY. *Office*—Cozbi, Inc., 530 Court St., Brooklyn, NY 11231. *E-mail*—cozbi-cab@aol.com.

### Career

Dollmaker and illustrator. Former graphic designer and record album packager for Atlantic Records, Sony Music, and Lop Records; Cozbi, Inc. (retailer), Brooklyn, NY, founder and doll maker, 1997—.

### Illustrator

*PICTURE BOOKS*

Laura Pegram, *Rainbow Is Our Face,* Black Butterfly (New York, NY), 1994.

Laura Pegram, *A Windy Day,* Black Butterfly (New York, NY), 1994.

Sandra Belton, *Beauty, Her Basket,* Amistad (New York, NY), 2004.

Nikki Grimes, *Thanks a Million: Poems,* Amistad (New York, NY), 2006.

### Sidelights

Although she developed a successful career as an art designer for several record labels, Cozbi A. Cabrera "felt that she was not fulfilled and that her voice was not being expressed," according to a contributor to *Oprah.com.* Following her passion, Cabrera turned to sewing, a hobby she had enjoyed since childhood, and transformed it into a new career. Her handmade dolls,

works of art that feature tea-dyed or vintage textiles and dressmaker detailing, are retailed through a store that bears her name; they have gained a strong following and even attracted the attention and promotion of talk-show host Oprah Winfrey. "I've always been drawn to things that are done very well and with integrity," Cabrera told Sonia Alleyne in *Black Enterprise,* adding that she finds great integrity in creating the ethnic dolls she would have enjoyed as a child of color.

Cabrera's creativity extends from dollmaking to her work as an illustrator of picture-book texts such as Sandra Belton's *Beauty, Her Basket.* Set in the Sea Islands off the coast of Georgia, Belton's story introduces a young girl as she learns to appreciate her grandmother's traditional craft: making sea grass baskets. Spending a summer with her grandmother, the girl learns how the weaving of each basket represents her family's heritage. Cabrera's illustrations "immerse readers in the locale's earthy exoticism," noted a *Publishers Weekly* critic, while Terry Glover wrote in *Booklist* that her "dark, sometime dreamy pastels evoke the island setting." A *Kirkus Reviews* contributor commented that "Cabrera displays rare sensitivity to color and light," while Erica Dolland dubbed the book's artwork "breathtaking" in her *Black Issues Book Review* appraisal.

Another book featuring Cabrera's illustrations, *Thanks a Million: Poems,* collects verse by Nikki Grimes that expresses gratitude for life's everyday wonders. The illustrations show simple scenes of thanks and feature a multicultural cast of characters. A *Kirkus Reviews* contributor felt that Cabrera's "vibrant acrylic paintings . . . add pop and personality" to the collection, while Mary N. Oluonye wrote in *School Library Journal* that the images are "distinctive, folksy, and effective."

"In our fast paced world, the items we cherish most and are excited about enjoying for generations are those that are made well, created in love and from heart," Cabrera wrote on her store's Web site. Her artwork, whether in her dollmaking or her illustrations, are done out of love, as she told Lawrence Bilotti for *Country Living.* "I

wanted to feel that if something were to survive as an artifact—25, 50, or 100 years from now—it would be beautifully crafted and a reflection of its maker's skill and pride," she explained.

## Biographical and Critical Sources

*PERIODICALS*

*Booklist,* March 1, 2004, Terry Glover, review of *Beauty, Her Basket,* p. 1192; March 15, 2006, Jennifer Mattson, review of *Thanks a Million: Poems,* p. 48.
*Black Enterprise,* October, 2004, Sonia Alleyne, "The Doll Maker: Cozbi Cabrera Breaks the Mold," p. 203.
*Black Issues Book Review,* March-April, 2004, Erica Dolland, review of *Beauty, Her Basket,* p. 67.
*Bulletin of the Center for Children's Books,* March, 2004, Karen Coats, review of *Beauty, Her Basket,* p. 260.
*Country Living,* October, 2004, Lawrence Bilotti, "Making Muñcas," pp. 75-79.
*Kirkus Reviews,* December 15, 2003, review of *Beauty, Her Basket,* p. 1446; February 15, 2006, review of *Thanks a Million,* p. 183.
*Publishers Weekly,* January 12, 2004, review of *Beauty, Her Basket,* p. 54.
*School Library Journal,* June, 2004, Anna DeWind Walls, review of *Beauty, Her Basket,* p. 96; March, 2006, Mary N. Oluonye, review of *Thanks a Million,* p. 208.

*ONLINE*

*Cozbi, Inc., Web site,* http://www.cozbi.com (February 21, 2007).
*Oprah.com,* http://www.oprah.com/ (February 21, 2007), "Cozbi A. Cabrera."*

\*      \*      \*

## CAREY, Ernestine Gilbreth 1908-2006

*OBITUARY NOTICE—* See index for *SATA* sketch: Born April 5, 1908, in New York, NY; died November 4, 2006, in Fresno, CA. Businessperson and author. Carey was best known for collaborating with her brother Frank Carey on the lightly humorous novel *Cheaper by the Dozen.* One of twelve children, she was the third oldest child of engineer parents who were experts in "motion study": they advised companies on improving worker efficiency. This fascination with efficiency also applied to the home, and Carey's parents made their six sons and six daughters fill out charts to indicate their progress in homework, chores, and other tasks. The scientists also observed their offspring, in one case making note of how each child washed and dried dishes to determine whether or not any movements were being wasted. De-

spite such surveillance, Carey and her siblings enjoyed a loving home, and her parents' quirks are gently spoofed in *Cheaper by the Dozen* (1949; revised edition, 1963) and its sequel, *Belles on Their Toes* (1950). Coauthored with Frank Carey, both were best-selling Book-of-the-Month Club selections. The first volume was adapted for film twice, once in 1950 and a second time in 2003, while the sequel was made into a movie in 1952. Carey went on to graduate from Smith College in 1929, and she pursued a career as a buyer, working for R.H. Macy & Co. from 1930 to 1944 and for James McCrerry and Co. from 1947 to 1949. When her book met with sucess, Carey left her office job and became a professional writer and lecturer. She also published three solo works: *Jumping Jupiter* (1952), *Rings around Us* (1956), and *Giddy Moment* (1958).

*OBITUARIES AND OTHER SOURCES:*

*PERIODICALS*

*Chicago Tribune,* November 7, 2006, Section 2, p. 9.
*Los Angeles Times,* November 7, 2006, p. B10.
*New York Times,* November 6, 2006, p. A21.
*Washington Post,* November 10, 2006, p. B6.

\*      \*      \*

## CHAMBERLIN, Mary 1960-

### Personal
Born 1960; married Rich Chamberlin (an engineer).

### Addresses
*Home and office*—Naperville, IL. *E-mail*—richnmary@prodigy.net.

### Career
Children's author and freelance television producer and director.

### Member
Society of Children's Book Writers and Illustrators.

### Awards, Honors
Gold Award, Oppenheim Toy Portfolio, 2006, for *Mama Panya's Pancakes.*

### Writings

(With husband, Rich Chamberlin) *Mama Panya's Pancakes: A Village Tale from Kenya,* illustrated by Julia Cairns, Barefoot Books (Cambridge, MA), 2005.

Contributor, with Mary Chamberlin, of short fiction and articles to periodicals; author of educational materials.

## Sidelights

An avid traveler, Mary Chamberlin wanted to share with readers the many cultures and adventures she encountered during her trips throughout the world. Together with her husband and co-traveler, Rich Chamberlin, she produced the children's book *Mama Panya's Pancakes: A Village Tale from Kenya,* a story centering on a Kenyan family. As the Chamberlins noted on their home page, they "love to share international stories, play games, and show people that 'We Are All One.'" The couple's travels have taken them to Africa, Australia, China, England, Indonesia, and New Zealand.

A *Kirkus Reviews* critic designated *Mama Panya's Pancakes* as a "contemporary story" that gains a "timeless quality" due to its classic folktale theme of generosity.

The story begins after a young Kenyan boy, Adika, learns that his mother plans to make pancakes for dinner. In a flurry of excitement Adika rashly invites all his family's friends and neighbors to dinner so that all can share in his mother's wonderful meal. Adika's generous invitation puts the boy's mother in a bind: she does not have sufficient ingredients or work space to make enough pancakes for all of her son's invited guests. Fortunately, all those who have received Adika's invitation are worthy: each of the dinner guests arrives with a different dish, stretching the modest pancake dinner into a lavish community feast. The Chamberlins' use of repetition in *Mama Panya's Pancakes* makes the book "a strong selection for a read-aloud," according to *School Library Journal* reviewer Genevieve Gallagher. The authors also add to their archetypical story by including an appendix featuring traditional Kenyan recipes as well as maps and general facts about the African country.

*The writing team of Rich and Mary Chamberlin.* (Photograph courtesy of Mary and Rich Chamberlin.)

**Mama Panya's Pancakes,** *the Chamberlins' adaptation of a Kenyan folk story, is brought to life through Julia Cairns' art.* (Illustrations copyright © 2005 by Julia Cairns. Reproduced by permission.)

## Biographical and Critical Sources

*PERIODICALS*

*Kirkus Reviews,* March 1, 2005, review of *Mama Panya's Pancakes: A Village Tale from Kenya,* p. 285.
*School Library Journal,* May, 2005, Genevieve Gallagher, review of *Mama Panya's Pancakes,* p. 78.

*ONLINE*

*Barefoot Books Web site,* http://www.barefootbooks.com/ (February 12, 2007), "Mary and Rich Chamberlin."
*Mary and Rich Chamberlin Home Page,* http://www.rich-nmarywriters.com (February 12, 2007).
*Society of Children's Book Writers and Illustrators—Illinois Chapter Web site,* http://www.scbwi-illinois.org/ (February 12, 2007), "Mary and Rich Chamberlin."

# CHAMBERLIN, Rich
## (Richard Chamberlin)

## Personal

Married; wife's name Mary (a writer). *Education:* Attended college. *Hobbies and other interests:* Travel, shadow puppets.

## Addresses

*Home*—Naperville, IL. *E-mail*—richnmary@prodigy.net.

## Career

Engineer and author.

## Member

Society of Children's Book Writers and Illustrators.

## Awards, Honors

Gold Award, Oppenheim Toy Portfolio, 2006, for *Mama Panya's Pancakes.*

## Writings

(With wife, Mary Chamberlin) *Mama Panya's Pancakes: A Village Tale from Kenya,* illustrated by Julia Cairns, Barefoot Books (Cambridge, MA), 2005.

Contributor, with Mary Chamberlin, of short fiction and articles to periodicals; author of educational materials.

## Sidelights

For Sidelights, see entry on Mary Chamberlin.

## Biographical and Critical Sources

*PERIODICALS*

*Kirkus Reviews,* March 1, 2005, review of *Mama Panya's Pancakes: A Village Tale from Kenya,* p. 285.
*School Library Journal,* May, 2005, Genevieve Gallagher, review of *Mama Panya's Pancakes,* p. 78.

*ONLINE*

*Barefoot Books Web site,* http://www.barefootbooks.com/ (February 12, 2007), "Mary and Rich Chamberlin."
*Mary and Rich Chamberlin Home Page,* http://www.richnmarywriters.com (February 12, 2007).
*Society of Children's Book Writers and Illustrators—Illinois Chapter Web site,* http://www.scbwi-illinois.org/ (February 12, 2007), "Mary and Rich Chamberlin."

# CHAMBERLIN, Richard
## See CHAMBERLIN, Rich

\*   \*   \*

# COOLEY, Regina Françoise 1940-

## Personal

Born 1940, in Flanders, Belgium; married Leland Frederick Cooley (deceased); children: Michael, Elizabeth Dunn. *Education:* H. Heart College, degree (teaching).

## Addresses

*Home and office*—St. Helena, CA. *E-mail*—reginafcooley@yahoo.com.

## Career

Children's book author. Worked variously as an educator, actress, model, and arts reviewer.

## Member

Authors Guild, Authors League.

## Awards, Honors

Children's Book Award, Northwest Center for the Arts, 1991, for *The Magic Christmas Pony.*

## Writings

*The Magic Christmas Pony,* illustrated by Hans Henrik Hansen, Capstone Publishing (Bellingham, WA), 1991.

## Sidelights

In *The Magic Christmas Pony* Regina Françoise Cooley uses a time-travel tale to introduce young readers to the history and traditions of the Far East. One Christmas Eve, Frederick and his sister Valentina discover that a magical carousel has the ability to take them through time and space. The enchanted carousel transports the siblings back to the nineteenth century and deposits them on the Great Wall of China, where they meet the Dragon of Fantasy. The Dragon guides Frederick and Valentina to the Forbidden City—known today as the Imperial Palace of Beijing—where they meet the Imperial Dragon, as well as China's emperor and empress. Frederick and Valentina's adventures are drawn to an exciting close when they are invited to an elaborate banquet that includes exotic fruits and appetizers and entertainments by cymbal-playing musicians, acrobats, and imperial dancers. When the children finally return home, it is Christmas Day and an assortment of unique Chinese gifts await them under the family Christmas tree.

The illustrations Hans Henrik Hansen creates for *The Magic Christmas Pony* incorporate the deep red tones that, in addition to being symbolic of Chinese culture, "lend regal splendor to the text" in the opinion of *Small Press* reviewer Molly Gill. The critic also commented on Cooley's decision to incorporate advanced vocabulary throughout her text, and deemed *The Magic Christmas Pony* a "wonderful book" containing "a truly magical story."

## Biographical and Critical Sources

*PERIODICALS*

*Small Press,* summer, 1992, Molly Gill, review of *The Magic Christmas Pony.*

*ONLINE*

*Regina Françoise Cooley Home Page,* http://www.themagicchristmaspony.net (February 12, 2007).

\*     \*     \*

## COOPER, Dutch
### See KUYPER, Sjoerd

\*     \*     \*

## CRAWLEY, Dave

### Personal

Born in Frankfurt, Germany. *Education:* Washington and Lee University, B.A. (history); Emerson College, M.A. (mass communication). *Hobbies and other interests:* Writing children's poetry.

### Addresses

*Home*—Pittsburgh, PA.

### Career

Television reporter. WMTV-TV, Madison, WI, news anchor and reporter; KDKA-TV2, Pittsburgh, PA, reporter, 1988—. Writer and producer of documentary, *Celebrating Fifty Years in Our Hometowns.*

### Awards, Honors

Nine Emmy awards for television work.

### Writings

*Cat Poems,* illustrated by Tamara Petrosino, Wordsong/ Boyds Mills Press (Honesdale, PA), 2005.

***Dave Crawley*** (Photograph courtesy of Dave Crawley.)

*Dog Poems,* illustrated by Tamara Petrosino, Wordsong/ Boyds Mills Press (Honesdale, PA), 2007.

Also author of *Sidelights on Wisconsin.* Contributor of poems to anthologies, including *Miles of Smiles, I Invited a Dragon to Dinner, My Teacher's in Detention, Rolling in the Aisles, If Kids Ruled the School,* and *Peter, Peter Pizza Eater.* Contributor of poems to periodicals, including *Jack and Jill, Cricket, Ranger Rick,* and *Spider.*

### Sidelights

Dave Crawley, an Emmy award-winning television journalist, published his first picture book, *Cat Poems,* in 2005. Crawley, who has garnered acclaim for his rhyming television features, also publishes his poetry in periodicals such as *Jack and Jill* and *Cricket,* and his poems have also been collected in anthologies.

In *Cat Poems* Crawley pays tribute to felines of all shapes, sizes, and colors. In the words of a *Kirkus Reviews* contributor, "this collection pairs two dozen rollicking rhymed tributes to the behavior and vagaries of cats with simple, vivacious cartoon portraits." Angoras, Persians, and numerous other breeds all star, courtesy of illustrator Tamara Petrosino. In "Sleeper," Crawley describes a cat in various states of repose—"She slouched on the couch./ She sprawled in the hall./ She curled in a ball on the stool by the wall."—while in "Mind Reader," he introduces a frisky feline that is pleased to learn that its owner would rather play than study. "Crawley utilizes line-ending rhyme schemes in the poems, and the familiar pattern will engage beginning or reluctant readers," observed Shawn Brommer, reviewing *Cat Poems* for *School Library Journal.* According to a critic in *Publishers Weekly,* "cat lovers will likely embrace Crawley's rhyming verse, which ad-

dresses feline types and idiosyncrasies with unapologetic adoration."

Crawley told *SATA:* "I was in the fifth grade when I wrote my first poem, a silly little rhyme called 'Lemon and Lime.' I was so surprised at the result that I tried another, and another—and found that I could keep doing it! Since my parents wouldn't let me buy ice cream sandwiches (the only dessert then offered at my school), I began writing rhyming couplets for fellow students in return for bites of their ice cream sandwiches. Four lines, two bites. This was the first payment I ever received for my work.

"At the age of thirteen I wrote 'An Ode to the Bucs,' a rhyming play-by-play of the Pittsburgh Pirates' World-Series triumph over the powerful Yankees in 1960. It was printed in the Newport News *Daily Press,* the daily paper we received at our home in Hampton, Virginia. It was my first published work, some twenty-eight years before I would actually set foot in my current city of Pittsburgh, Pennsylvania.

"At age fourteen, I wrote a parody of Jimmy Dean's song 'Big Bad John.' My record, 'Big Nik,' was a spoof on Soviet Premiere Nikita Khruschev ('Every morning at the Kremlin you could see him arrive,/ He stood five-foot-three, weighed 385 . . .' etc.). It created a local sensation at my then-home of Anchorage, Alaska (I was an Air Force brat), but missed a million seller by 999,900 records . . . give or take.

"Many stops later, I became 'KD Country' feature reporter at KDKA-TV, the CBS affiliate in Pittsburgh. I produce and report four stories a week, including an occasional story in rhyme. (To see a sampling, please log onto www.davecrawley.com and click on the 'KDKA' link.)

"About ten years ago, I began writing children's poems. When I had early success with magazines and anthologies, I thought 'this is going to be easy.' After my book ideas were rejected more than fifty times, humility set in. I owe thanks to Boyds Mills Press for trusting the work of a new author and publishing *Cat Poems. Dog Poems* naturally followed.

"Writing children's books has opened up a new world of school and library visits. Whereas my TV reports are performed for an unresponsive video camera, school visits give me the opportunity to interact with my audience. It has been a very rewarding experience. And nobody can erase me with a channel zapper!"

*Crawley's rhyming riff on feline behavior,* **Cat Poems,** *features Tamara Petrosino's suitably stylish illustrations.* (Illustrations copyright © 2005 by Tamara Petrosino. Reproduced by permission.)

## Biographical and Critical Sources

*BOOKS*

Crawley, Dave, *Cat Poems,* Wordsong (Honesdale, PA), 2005.

*PERIODICALS*

*Kirkus Reviews,* March 15, 2005, review of *Cat Poems,* p. 349.

*Publishers Weekly,* March 14, 2005, review of *Cat Poems,* p. 67.

*School Library Journal,* Shawn Brommer, June, 2005, review of *Cat Poems,* p. 136.

*ONLINE*

*Dave Crawley Home Page,* http://www.davecrawley.com (March 25, 2007);

*KDKA Television Web site,* http://kdka.com/bios/ (January 25, 2007), "Dave Crawley."

# D

## DALY, Jude 1951-
### (Jude Kenny)

### Personal

Born August 24, 1951, in London, England; married Niki Daly (a writer and illustrator); children: Joseph, Leo. *Education:* Attended Cape Technical College. *Hobbies and other interests:* Music, art, "the quirkiness of people."

### Addresses

*Home and office*—Cape Town, South Africa.

### Career

Illustrator.

### Awards, Honors

Children's Book of Distinction selection, *Hungry Mind Review,* 1994, for *The Dove,* by Dianne Stewart; *Smithsonian* magazine Notable Book designation, and International Board on Books for Young People Honor listee, both 1996, Notable Children's Trade Book designation, and Katrine Harris Award for illustration, both 1997, all for *Gift of the Sun,* by Stewart; Katrine Harris Award, 2003, for *The Stone,* by Dianne Hofmeyr.

### Writings

*SELF-ILLUSTRATED*

*Fair, Brown, and Trembling: An Irish Cinderella Story,* Farrar, Straus & Giroux (New York, NY), 2000.

*ILLUSTRATOR*

Dianne Stewart, *The Dove,* Greenwillow (New York, NY), 1993.

Dianne Hofmeyr, *Do the Whales Still Sing?,* Dial (New York, NY), 1995.

Dianne Stewart, *Gift of the Sun: A Tale from South Africa,* Farrar, Straus & Giroux (New York, NY), 1996.

Rachelle Greef, *Enebene en die ander,* Juta (Cape Town, South Africa), 1996.

Dianne Hofmeyr, *The Stone: A Persian Legend of the Magi,* Farrar, Straus & Giroux (New York, NY), 1998.

Dianne Hofmeyr, *The Star-Bearer: A Creation Myth from Ancient Egypt,* Farrar, Straus & Giroux (New York, NY), 2001.

Sheron Williams, *Imani's Music,* Atheneum (New York, NY), 2002.

Diana Reynolds Roome, *The Elephant's Pillow,* Farrar, Straus & Giroux (New York, NY), 2003.

Nancy Willard, *The Tale of Paradise Lost,* Atheneum (New York, NY), 2004.

*To Every Thing There Is a Season,* Eerdmans (Grand Rapids, MI), 2006.

### Sidelights

Born in England, Jude Daly moved with her family to Cape Town, South Africa, as a child. With an interest in art, she attended college to study graphic design, but left before she finished her degree. "In retrospect it was a good thing as it meant I never mastered being slick and I hope my work reflects this," the illustrator noted on *South African Children's Literature News* online. Often employing stylized, folk-art motifs, Daly has found success creating illustrations for children's book authors such as Dianne Hofmeyr, Diana Reynolds Roome, and Nancy Willard. Many of the picture books that feature her work—including her first title, *The Dove,* by South African writer Dianne Stewart—are set in South Africa. Daly has also worked on Stewart's *Gift of the Sun: A Tale from South Africa,* an original folk tale about a lazy farmer, creating "wonderfully detailed domestic scenes" situated "on the curve of the rolling earth," according to Hazel Rochman, writing in *Booklist.* While a *Publishers Weekly* reviewer cited Daly's "comically detailed" images as echoing "the same playfulness" as Stewart's narrative, in *Horn Book* Martha V.

Parravano maintained that the artist's "expansive, extra-wide horizontal illustrations take in the whole sweep of the rather austere [South African] landscape."

In *Do the Whales Still Sing,* which Daly illustrated for Hofmeyr, a tale of environmentalism and peace is complemented by gouache paintings that "match the text's elements of boldness and restraint," according to a *Publishers Weekly* critic. Daly and Hofmeyr team up again for *The Stone: A Persian Legend of the Magi* and *The Star-Bearer: A Creation Myth from Ancient Egypt.* In reviewing *The Stone, Booklist* critic Helen Rosenberg maintained that Daly's "detailed, mystical illustrations" effectively bring to life the story's exotic Persian setting. Of the illustrations for *The Star-Bearer,* Ilene Cooper wrote in *Booklist* that "Daly's characters look as if they've stepped from hieroglyphics." According to a *Publishers Weekly* contributor, the illustrator's "stylized, willowy figures shine against elegant backgrounds."

In another of Daly's illustration projects, Sheron Williams's *Imani's Music,* she brings to life an original folktale about an African grasshopper named Imani who is given the gift of music. The grasshopper takes music from Africa onto a slave ship, and thence to the New World. According to Natasha K. Woods, writing in the *Black Issues Book Review,* "Daly's illustrations are painterly in their use of color, with broad vivid land and seascapes depicting the world as seen through Imani's eyes on both sides of the Atlantic." *The Elephant's Pillow,* another folktale-like original story, is set in Peking, China, and features a young boy who helps to charm the Imperial elephant to sleep. "The illustrations are the very best part of this tale," exclaimed a *Kirkus Reviews* contributor.

Moving from folktales to more classical works, Daly's "small, occasional, delicately detailed paintings" appear alongside Nancy Willard's text in *The Tale of Paradise Lost,* a simplified version of John Milton's classic poem, "adding a sort of distant elegance," according to a *Kirkus Reviews* contributor. The artist "creates a visual feast in her landscapes of Eden," commented a *Publishers Weekly* critic. Daly's art is also paired with scripture from the King James version of the biblical Book of Ecclesiastes and published as *To Everything There Is a Season.* Daly's choice of a "rural South African setting . . . skillfully illuminates each pair of contrasting concepts," wrote a *Kirkus Reviews* contributor. Although the setting is specific, the words retain their resonance; as John Stewig noted in *Booklist,* the book's "opening spread, stretching to the edge of the pages, suggests a global view of the world."

Moving from artist to author, Daly is also the illustrator of an original retelling of a familiar tale in *Fair, Brown, and Trembling: An Irish Cinderella Story.* Hoping to avoid continued mistreatment at the hands of her older sisters, Fair and Brown, Trembling turns to an elderly henwife to help her find a suitable husband at Sunday Mass. The beautiful young woman finally catches the eye of Prince Emania, and he willingly competes against many other suitors in order to win Trembling's hand in marriage. Daly's "lush, pastoral paintings add depth and charm to a Cinderella variant folktale from the Emerald Isle," wrote a *Publishers Weekly* contributor, while Hazel Rochman concluded in *Booklist* that *Fair, Brown, and Trembling* "has the enduring appeal of the neglected child who's really the best."

## Biographical and Critical Sources

*PERIODICALS*

*Black Issues Book Review,* January-February, 2002, Natasha K. Woods, review of *Imani's Music,* p. 78.
*Booklist,* May 15, 1995, Hazel Rochman, review of *Do the Whales Still Sing?,* p. 1652; September 1, 1996, Hazel Rochman, review of *Gift of the Sun: A Tale from South Africa,* p. 145; October 1, 1998, Helen Rosenberg, review of *The Stone: A Persian Legend of the Magi,* p. 332; September 1, 2000, Hazel Rochman, review of *Fair, Brown, and Trembling: An Irish Cinderella Story,* p. 120; February 15, 2001, Ilene Cooper, review of *The Star-Bearer: A Creation Myth from Ancient Egypt,* p. 1134; February 15, 2002, Hazel Rochman, review of *Imani's Music,* p. 1036; January 1, 2004, Carolyn Phelan, review of *The Elephant's Pillow,* p. 882; October 1, 2004, John Green, review of *The Tale of Paradise Lost,* p. 340; April 15, 2006, John Stewig, review of *To Everything There Is a Season,* p. 50.
*Bulletin of the Center for Children's Books,* December, 1996, review of *Gift of the Sun,* p. 153; July, 2000, review of *Fair, Brown, and Trembling,* p. 395; March, 2001, review of *The Star-Bearer,* p. 262; February, 2006, Elizabeth Bush, review of *To Everything There Is a Season,* p. 260.
*Christian Science Monitor,* November 19, 1998, review of *The Stone,* p. 17.
*Five Owls,* September, 1993, review of *The Dove,* p. 12.
*Horn Book,* November-December, 1996, Martha V. Parravano, review of *Gift of the Sun,* p. 730; March, 2001, review of *The Star-Bearer,* p. 219; November-December, 2004, Deirdre F. Baker, review of *The Tale of Paradise Lost,* p. 719.
*Kirkus Reviews,* November 15, 2001, review of *Imani's Music,* p. 1616; October 1, 2003, review of *The Elephant's Pillow,* p. 1230; October 1, 2004, review of *The Tale of Paradise Lost,* p. 971; February 1, 2006, review of *To Everything There Is a Season,* p. 129.
*Publishers Weekly,* May 15, 1995, review of *Do the Whales Still Sing?,* p. 72; September 16, 1996, review of *Gift of the Sun,* p. 83; September 28, 1998, review of *The Stone,* p. 59; August 21, 2000, review of *Fair, Brown, and Trembling,* p. 71; February 26, 2001, review of *The Star-Bearer,* p. 86; December 10, 2001, review of *Imani's Music,* p. 70; December 8, 2003, review of *The Elephant's Pillow,* p. 60; October 25, 2004, review of *The Tale of Paradise Lost,* p. 48; January 30, 2006, review of *To Everything There Is a Season,* p. 72.

*School Librarian,* November, 1996, review of *Gift of the Sun,* p. 148; autumn, 2000, review of *Fair, Brown, and Trembling,* p. 135; autumn, 2001, review of *The Star-Bearer,* p. 136.

*School Library Journal,* September 16, 1996, Barbara Kiefer, review of *Gift of the Sun,* p. 192; October, 1998, Anne Connor, review of *The Stone,* p. 41; September, 2000, Miriam Lang Budin, review of *Fair, Brown, and Trembling,* p. 214; April, 2001, Nancy Call, review of *The Star-Bearer,* p. 131; January, 2002, Marianne Saccardi, review of *Imani's Music,* p. 114; November, 2003, Liza Graybill, review of *The Elephant's Pillow,* p. 114; January, 2005, Patricia D. Lothrop, review of *The Tale of Paradise Lost,* p. 138; March, 2006, Linda L. Walkins, review of *To Everything There Is a Season,* p. 216.

*Smithsonian,* November, 1996, review of *Gift of the Sun,* p. 169.

ONLINE

*South African Children's Literature News online,* http://www.childlit.org.za/ (February 21, 2007), "Jude Daly."\*

\*　　\*　　\*

# DANDI
## See MACKALL, Dandi Daley

\*　　\*　　\*

# DEMERS, Dominique 1956-

## Personal

Born November 23, 1956, in Montreal, Quebec, Canada; married; children: three. *Education:* McGill University, B.A.; University of Montreal, teaching certificate; University of Sherbrooke, Ph.D.

## Addresses

*Home*—Montreal, Quebec, Canada.

## Career

Writer for children and adults. Former teacher at Charles Lemoyne College, Ste-Catherine, Quebec, Canada; worked as a journalist for twelve years. Has worked as an actress in film adaptations of her novels.

## Member

Union des Écrivaines, Éscrivains Québécois.

## Awards, Honors

Prix Jackman, 1986, for journalism; Prix Judith-Jasmine, 1987, for best article in a magazine; Mr. Christie Prize, 1993, for *Un hiver de tourmente,* 1994, for *Les grands sapins ne meurent pas,* 1998, for *La mystérieuse bibliothécaire,* and 2001, for *Vieux Thomas et la petite fée;* Prix du Signet d'Or de Plaisir, and Prix Québec/Wallonie-Bruxelles, both 1995, both for *Ils dansent dans le tempête;* Honor Book designation, International Board on Books for Young People, for both *Les grands sapins ne neurent pas* and *La mystérieuse bibliothécaires;* Prix de la Livromagie, 1996, for *La nouvelle maîesse;* Governor General's Award (Canada) finalist, Prix Brive/Montréal, and Prix Coup de Coeur Honor designation, all 1997, all for *Maïna;* three other Governor General's award nominations; Grand Prix in children's books category, Montérégiev, 1999, for *La mystérieuse bibliothécaire;* named member, Order of Canada, 2006.

# Writings

*Valentine picotée,* illustrated by Phillippe Béha, Courte Échelle (Montreal, Quebec, Canada), 1991.

*Toto la brute,* illustrated by Phillippe Béha, Courte Échelle (Montreal, Quebec, Canada), 1992.

*Un hiver de tourmente* (novel), Courte Échelle (Montreal, Quebec, Canada), 1992.

*Les grands sapins ne meurent pas* (novel), Amérique (Montreal, Quebec, Canada), 1993.

(With Paul Bleton) *Du petit poucet au dernier des raisins,* illustrated by Anne Villeneuve, Amérique (Boucherville, Quebec, Canada), 1994.

*Ils dansent dans la tempête* (novel), Amérique (Boucherville, Quebec, Canada), 1994.

*La nouvelle maîtresse* (novel), Amérique (Boucherville, Quebec, Canada), 1994.

*Marie-Tempête* (novel; includes *Un hiver de tourmente, Grands sapins ne meurent pas,* and *Ils dansent dans la tempêe*), Amérique (Montreal, Quebec, Canada), 1997.

*Maïna,* Amérique (Montreal, Quebec, Canada), 1997, English translation by Leonard W. Sugden, Ekstasis (Victoria, British Columbia, Canada), 2001.

*Marie la chipie,* illustrated by Phillippe Béha, Amérique (Montreal, Quebec, Canada), 1997.

*La mystérieuse bibliothécaire,* Amérique (Montreal, Quebec, Canada), 1997.

*La chien secret de poucet,* illustrated by Steve Beshwaty, Dominique et Compagnie (Saint-Lambert, Quebec, Canada), 1999.

*Perline Pompette,* illustrated by Marie-Claude Favreau, Dominique et Compagnie (Saint-Lambert, Quebec, Canada), 1999, translation by David Homel published as *Pearl Pennyworth,* 1999.

*Le pari* (novel), Amérique (Montreal, Quebec, Canada), 1999.

*Romé Lebeau,* illustrated by Philippe Béha, Amérique (Montreal, Quebec, Canada), 1999.

*Une bien curieuse Factrice,* Amérique (Montreal, Quebec, Canada), 1999.

*Poucet, le coeur en Miettes,* illustrated by Steve Beshwaty, Dominique et Compagnie (Saint-Lambert, Quebec, Canada), 2000.

*Vieux Thomas et la petite fée,* illustrated by Stéphane Poulin, Dominique et Compagnie (Saint-Lambert, Quebec, Canada), 2000, translation by Sheila Fischman published as *Old Thomas and the Little Fairy,* 2001.

*Léon Maigrichon,* illustrated by Philippe Béha, Amérique (Montreal, Quebec, Canada), 2000.

*Là où la mer commence* (novel), Laffont (Paris, France), 2001.

*Une drôle de ministre,* Amérique (Montreal, Quebec, Canada), 2001.

*Ta voix dans la nuit,* Amérique (Montreal, Quebec, Canada, 2001.

*Annabel et la bête,* illustrated by Stéphane Poulin, Dominique et Compagnie (Saint-Lambert, Quebec, Canada), 2002, translation by Sheila Fischman published as *Annabel and the Beast,* 2002.

*Géant, tu ne me fais pas peur!,* illustrated by Marisol Sarrazin, Éditions du Renouveau Pédagogique (Saint-Laurent, Quebec, Canada), 2002.

*La pire journée de Papi,* illustrated by Daniel Dumont, Dominique et Compagnie (Saint-Lambert, Quebec, Canada), 2002, translated as *Grampy's Bad Day,* Picture Window Books (Minneapolis, MN), 2005.

*Le clip de Cendrillon,* Éditions du Renouveaus Pédagogique (Saint-Laurent, Quebec, Canada), 2002.

*Le monde des grands,* illustrated Philippe Germain, Éditions du Renouveau Pédagogique (Saint-Laurent, Quebec, Canada), 2002.

*Pour noël, Damien veut un chien,* illustrated by Hélène Desputeaux, Dimédia (Saint-Laurent, Quebec, Canada), 2002.

*L'oiseau des sables,* illustrated by Stéphane Poulin, Dominique et Compagnie (Saint-Lambert, Quebec, Canada), 2003.

*Le Zloukch,* illustrated by Fanny, 400 Coups (Montreal, Quebec, Canada), 2003.

*Zachary et son Zloukch,* illustrated by Fanny, 400 Coups (Montreal, Quebec, Canada), 2004.

*L'étonnante concierge,* Amérique (Montreal, Quebec, Canada), 2005.

*Tous les soirs du monde,* illustrated by Nicholas Debon, Imagine (Montreal, Quebec, Canada), 2005, translated by Sarah Quin as *Every Single Night,* Groundwood Books (Toronto, Ontario, Canada), 2005.

*Alexa Gougougaga,* Amérique (Montreal, Quebec, Canada), 2005.

*Pétunia, princesse des pets,* illustrated by Catherine Lepage, Dominique et Compagnie (Saint-Lambert, Quebec, Canada), 2005.

*Boucle d'or et les trois ours: un conte classique,* illustrated by Joanne Ouellet, Imagine (Montreal, Quebec, Canada), 2005.

*La plus belle histoire d'amour,* Imagine (Montreal, Quebec, Canada), 2006.

*Pour Rallumer les étoiles,* Amérique (Montreal, Quebec, Canada), 2006.

Author's works have been translated into several languages, including Spanish.

*OTHER*

*Les nouveaux héros des albums Québécois pour la jeunesse de 1970 à 1985* (master's thesis), Université du Québec (Sainte-Foy, Quebec, Canada),1989.

*La bibliothèque des enfants,* Le Jour (Montreal, Quebec, Canada), 1990.

## Adaptations

Several of Demers' "Mademoiselle Charlotte" novels have been adapted for film, including *La nouvelle maîtresse* and *La mystérieuse bibliothècaire*; *Bien curieuse Factrice* and *Une drôle de ministre* were adapted as the film *L'incomparable Mademoiselle C.*

## Sidelights

Canadian journalist and educator Dominique Demers has an academic interest in children's literature; her master's thesis focuses on the representation and mythification of childhood in children's literature. While her education channeled her intellectual interest, her work as a fiction writer has allowed her to share her creative side in novels and stories for children and young adults. Though Demers writes in French—some of her most popular works among Quebec readers include her "Mademoiselle Charlotte" novels—translations of her books have gained her a following among an English-language readership as well. Calling Demers "one of our leading authors of literature for young people," a writer for the Governor General of Canada's Web site listed the many accomplishments leading to Demers being named a member of the prestigious Order of Canada in 2006.

Demers' first novel for children, *Valentine picotée,* is the story of eight-year-old Alexis, who becomes infatuated with Katarina, the new girl in his class. Although his plans to get Katarina to choose him as her Valentine misfire, when Katarina gets the measles and has to stay home from school on Valentine's Day, Alexis finds a way to prove his devotion to his new friend. Doris Lemoine, writing in the *Canadian Review of Materials,* deemed *Valentine picotée* "a light, humorous story that deals with real human emotions—love, friendship, hate and jealousy."

In *Old Thomas and the Little Fairy* Demers relates a dark tale of a down-on-his-luck fisherman who is unhappy with the world. Fortunately, after the man rescues a little fairy, his good luck allows him to once again find joy in life. When the fisherman is attacked and killed by a wild dog while protecting his miniature friend, the man dies happy, knowing that he has kept the tiny fairy safe. Judith Constantinides, reviewing the book for *School Library Journal,* dubbed *Old Thomas and the Little Fairy* a "strange, haunting story."

*Nicholas Debon provides illustrations for Dominique Demers' poetic bedtime tale* **Every Single Night.** (Originally published by Gallimard/Editions Imagine. Reproduced by permission of Groundwood Books.)

Geared for older readers, the novel *Un hiver de tourmente* is narrated by a fifteen-year-old girl whose mother is dying of cancer. While Nancy Senior cited concerns over Demers' narrative style and the way the author deals with mature themes, she added in her *Canadian Review of Materials* appraisal that "the mother's pain at leaving her daughter and the daughter's shock and confusion are quite moving."

Demers' many works for younger readers include the picture book *Every Single Night,* a translation of *Tous les soirs du monde.* Described as a "unique tale" by a *Kirkus Reviews* contributor, *Every Single Night* describes a father and son's bedtime ritual in which the pair say goodnight to the entire world. Carolyn Phelan, writing in *Booklist,* commented on the "poetic cadences" woven into Demers' text. "The dreamy, poetic language works nicely with the scenes of the natural world slipping into nighttime," wrote Shelley B. Sutherland in her *School Library Journal* review, and *Horn Book* critic Joanna Rudge Long praised *Every Single Night* as "dreamy, lyrical, and as cozy as a familiar lullaby."

## Biographical and Critical Sources

### PERIODICALS

*Bookbird,* summer, 1994, review of *Les grands sapins ne meurent pas,* p. 53.

*Booklist,* March 15, 2006, Carolyn Phelan, review of *Every Single Night,* p. 53.

*Canadian Book Review Annual,* 2001, review of *Maïna,* p. 153.

*Canadian Children's Literature,* spring, 2000, review of *Marie-Tempête* and *Maïna,* pp. 27-30.

*Canadian Review of Materials,* March, 1992, Doris Lemoine, review of *Valentine picotée,* p. 65; September, 1992, Nancy Senior, review of *Un hiver de tourmente,* p. 212.

*Horn Book,* May-June, 2006, Joanna Rudge Long, review of *Every Single Night,* p. 293.

*Kirkus Reviews,* March 1, 2006, review of *Every Single Night,* p. 228.

*Macleans,* December 11, 2000, review of *Old Thomas and the Little Fairy,* p. 58.

*Publishers Weekly,* April 10, 2006, review of *Every Single Night,* p. 71.

*School Library Journal,* April, 2002, Judith Constantinides, review of *Old Thomas and the Little Fairy,* p. 103; May, 2006, Shelley B. Sutherland, review of *Every Single Night,* p. 86.

### ONLINE

*Anansi Press Web site,* http://www.anansi.ca/ (February 23, 2007), "Dominique Demers."

*Governor General of Canada Web site,* http://www.gg.ca/ (February 15, 2006), "Governor General to Invest Thirty-three Recipients into the Order of Canada."

*Littéraire des Éscrivains Québécois Web site,* http://www.litterature.org/ (February 23, 2007), "Dominique Demers."

*Québec Amérique Web site,* http://www.quebec-amerique.com/ (February 23, 2007).*

\*    \*    \*

# DRAY, Matt 1967-
## (Matthew Frederick Dray)

## Personal

Born April 2, 1967, in Proserpine, Queensland, Australia; son of Frederick William (a sugarcane farmer) and Genevieve Amy (a homemaker) Dray. *Education:* St. Joseph's College, graduated, 1984. *Religion:* Roman Catholic.

## Addresses

*Home*—Queensland, Australia. *E-mail*—matt.dray@hotmail.com.

## Career

Children's book writer. Has worked variously as a milkman, farm hand, construction worker, truck driver, fruit picker, security guard, plant operator, and laborer.

*Matt Dray* (Photograph courtesy of Matt Dray.)

## Writings

*FOR CHILDREN*

*Dougal the Garbage Dump Bear,* Penguin Australia (Camberwell, Victoria, Australia), 2004, Kane/Miller (La Jolla, CA), 2005.
*Dougal and Bumble and the Long Walk Home,* Penguin Australia (Camberwell, Victoria, Australia), 2006.
*Dougal and Bumble and the Big Race,* Penguin Australia (Camberwell, Victoria, Australia), 2008.

*FOR ADULTS*

*A Day at the Races* (novel), Penguin Australia (Camberwell, Victoria, Australia), 2000.

## Sidelights

Australian children's book writer Matt Dray told *SATA:* "My career in children's books kicked off one morning at a garbage dump in 2002. I was bulldozing rubbish when a small, brown, furry leg sticking out the top of a pile of white paper caught my eye. It belonged to a little bear who'd seen better days but was still in one

piece. He (he looked like a he) became the dump mascot. One of my workmates, Bryce, found a bench for him to sit on and we called him Dougal.

"Dougal sat on his own for a week or so, them more toys began turning up in the rubbish. Bears, dogs, rabbits, elephants, a bee; the list goes on. In six weeks we had over fifty orphans, all sitting together on couches and chairs and rugs. One Saturday morning I brought two disposable cameras to work and started taking photos of them. A vague idea for a story began to evolve, with Dougal as the main character and Bumble the bee as his sidekick. The photos became the illustrations.

"Comic strips like 'Peanuts,' 'Hagar the Horrible,' 'The Wizard of Id,' and 'Garfield' have definitely had some influence on me, as have my two favourite *Sesame Street* characters: Ernie and Bert. Some of their scenes back in the Seventies were brilliant, and I think Jim Henson and his buddies were simply amusing themselves rather than their audience, which I guess is the key to writing quality books, scripts, or anything. The blokes I've worked with over the years have given me heaps of ideas too.

*Cover of Matt Dray's* **Dougal the Garbage Dump Bear,** *featuring the Aussie author's own illustrations.* (Kane/Miller Book Publishers, 2004. Reproduced by permission.)

"My two favorite comic strips now are 'Dilbert' and 'Calvin and Hobbes.' They're the main reason I buy newspapers. I even skip the sports section."

## Biographical and Critical Sources

*PERIODICALS*

*Kirkus Reviews,* September, 2005, review of *Dougal the Garbage Dump Bear,* p. 971.
*School Library Journal,* November, 2005, Sally R. Dow, review of *Dougal the Garbage Dump Bear,* p. 89.*

\*    \*    \*

# DRAY, Matthew Frederick
## See DRAY, Matt

\*    \*    \*

# DREYER, Ellen

## Personal

Married Jim Yanda (a musician and business owner); children: Aaron. *Education:* University of Michigan, B.A. (literature and writing); University of London, M.A. (English), 1990.

## Addresses

*Home and office*—Maplewood, NJ. *E-mail*—ellen@ellendreyer.com.

## Career

Young-adult and children's author. Worked variously as a doctor's receptionist, children's book editor, freelance writer, and teacher.

## Member

Authors Guild, Authors League.

## Writings

*Speechless in New York,* Four Corners (New York, NY), 2000.
*Grow, Tree, Grow!,* illustrated by Maggie Swanson, Scholastic (New York, NY), 2003.
*The Glow Stone* (young adult novel), Peachtree (Atlanta, GA), 2006.

Also author of dozens of books for educational publishers.

***Ellen Dreyer*** (Photograph courtesy of Ellen Dreyer.)

## Sidelights

Ellen Dreyer began her publishing career as a children's book editor, working on children's educational titles for a variety of trade publishing houses. Her shift to freelance editing eventually expanded to freelance writing and the authorship of numorous books for children as well as the young-adult novel *The Glow Stone.* As Dreyer explained to an interviewer for the *New Jersey Jewish News* online, she is a "fan of books where girls do unusual, empowering things." She creates a character after her own heart in Phoebe, the protagonist of *The Glow Stone.*

According to *School Library Journal* reviewer Laurie Slagenwhite, *The Glow Stone* presents a "realistic portrait of a family's grief" that readers will easily identify with. Phoebe is a fifteen year old who is struggling with both the recent death of her favorite uncle and her mother's depression. She finds her strength and faith put to the test when she goes spelunking—cave exploring—with her aunt and becomes lost within the cave's dark labyrinth. As *Kliatt* reviewer Claire Rosser noted, Dreyer's novel is "filled with thoughtful details and surprising depths." The author commented in an interviewer for the Newark, New Jersey *Star-Ledger* that she hopes

her readers will "take away a sense of their own inner strength, that they can handle whatever challenges . . . they may face."

A dedicated writer, Dreyer noted on her home page that she views her works in progress as a "writer's garden," adding that she"will keep tending and growing these and new 'sprouts' till they are ready for the harvest." The process of writing continues to be important to her because, as she explained, it "has always been a means of knowing myself, of discovering what really matters to me."

## Biographical and Critical Sources

*PERIODICALS*

*Atlanta Parent,* November, 2006, "Fifty Must-Read Books for Kids."

*ForeWord,* July-August, 2006, KaaVonia Houghton, review of *The Glow Stone.*
*Kliatt,* May, 2006, Claire Rosser, review of *The Glow Stone,* p. 8.
*School Library Journal,* March, 2000, Piper L. Nyman, review of *Speechless in New York,* p. 233; July, 2006, Laurie Slagenwhite, review of *The Glow Stone,* p. 100.
*Star-Ledger* (Newark, NJ), May 18, 2006, "Lost in Cave, Girl Finds Herself," p. 3.

*ONLINE*

*Bookslut Online,* http://www.bookslut.com/ (August, 2006), Coleen Mondor, review of *The Glow Stone.*
*Ellen Dreyer Home Page,* http://www.ellendreyer.com (February 14, 2007).
*New Jersey Jewish News Web site,* http://www. njjewishnews.com/ (February 14, 2007), "A 'Gem' of a Novel: A NJ Author Draws on Her Upbringing to Write 'Cathartic' Book for Teens."

# F

## FANCHER, Lou 1960-

### Personal

Born 1960, in MI; married Steve Johnson (a commercial artist and illustrator. *Education:* University of Cincinnati, B.F.A. (dance).

### Addresses

*Home*—Moraga, CA. *E-mail*—fancher@dancingpeople. com.

### Career

Writer, illustrator, children's book designer, ballet mistress, and choreographer. Freelance illustrator with husband, Steve Johnson, c. 1979—; co-creator of pre-production set and character designs for animated films, including *Toy Story,* 1995, and *A Bug's Life,* 1998. Alberta Ballet, former ballet mistress; New Dance Ensemble, former associate artistic director; James Sewell Ballet, Minneapolis, MN, ballet mistress; Company C Contemporary Ballet, Walnut Creek, CA, ballet mistress; choreographer, coach, and instructor to dancers and companies throughout the United States.

### Awards, Honors

(With Steve Johnson) International Reading Association Childrens Book Award 1989 for *No Star Nights* by Anna Smucker; Minnesota Book Award for Children's Books, 1992, for *The Salamander Room,* by Anne Mazer; gold medal, Society of Illustrators, 1993, for *Up North at the Cabin* by Marsha Wilson Chall; Minnesota Book Award for Children's Books finalist, 1993, for *Up North at the Cabin,* 1996, for *Cat You'd Better Come Home* by Garrison Keillor, 1997, for *My Many Colored Days* by Dr. Seuss, 1998, for *The Lost and Found House* by Michael Cadnum, 1999, for *Coppélia* by Margot Fonteyn, 2002, for both *The Day Ocean Came to Visit* by Diane Wolkstein and *Silver Seeds* by Paul Paolilli and Dan Brewer; Nestlé Children's Book Prize shortlist, 2005, for *The*

*Dancing Tiger* by Malachy Doyle. Solo awards include Minnesota State Arts Board artist fellowship for choreography, 2002.

## Writings

*AND ILLUSTRATOR, WITH HUSBAND STEVE JOHNSON*

*The Quest for the One Big Thing* (based on the animated film *A Bug's Life*), Disney Press (New York, NY), 1998.

(Adapter) Margery Williams, *The Velveteen Rabbit; or, How Toys Become Real,* Atheneum (New York, NY), 2002.

*Star Climbing,* Laura Geringer Books (New York, NY), 2006.

*ILLUSTRATOR, WITH STEVE JOHNSON*

Anna Smucker, *No Star Nights,* Knopf (New York, NY), 1989.

Douglas Hill, *Penelope's Pendant,* Doubleday (New York, NY), 1990.

Anne Mazer, *The Salamander Room,* Knopf (New York, NY), 1991.

Jon Scieszka, *The Frog Prince Continued,* Viking (New York, NY), 1991.

Marsha Wilson Chall, *Up North at the Cabin,* Lothrop, Lee & Shephard (New York, NY), 1992.

B.G. Hennessy, *The First Night,* Viking (New York, NY), 1993.

Sarah S. Kilborne, *Peach and Blue,* Knopf (New York, NY), 1994.

Garrison Keillor, *Cat, You Better Come Home,* Viking (New York, NY), 1995.

Dr. Seuss (pseudonym of Theodore Geisel), *My Many Colored Days,* Knopf (New York, NY), 1996.

Michael Cadnum, *The Lost and Found House,* Viking (New York, NY), 1997.

Margot Fonteyn, *Coppélia,* Harcourt Brace (San Francisco, CA), 1998.

Craig Kee Strete, *The Lost Boy and the Monster,* Putnam's (New York, NY), 1999.

Janet Schulman, adaptor, *Felix Salten's Bambi,* Atheneum (New York, NY), 1999.

Lois Duncan, *I Walk at Night,* Viking (New York, NY), 2000.

Alice Hoffman, *Horsefly,* Hyperion (New York, NY), 2000.

Paul Paolilli and Dan Brewer, *Silver Seeds: A Book of Nature Poems,* Viking (New York, NY), 2001.

Diane Wolkstein, *The Day Ocean Came to Visit,* Harcourt (San Diego, CA), 2001.

Margaret Wise Brown, *Robin's Room,* Hyperion (New York, NY), 2002.

Louise Erdrich, *The Range Eternal,* Hyperion (New York, NY), 2002.

Mary Pope Osborne, *New York's Bravest,* Knopf (New York, NY), 2002.

Mavis Jukes, *You're a Bear,* Knopf (New York, NY), 2003.

Kathleen Krull, *The Boy on Fairfield Street: How Ted Geisel Grew up to Become Dr. Seuss,* Random House (New York, NY), 2004.

Dori Chaconas, *Momma, Will You?,* Penguin (New York, NY), 2004.

H.L. Panahi, *Bebop Express,* Laura Geringer Books (New York, NY), 2005.

Malachy Doyle, *The Dancing Tiger,* Simon & Schuster (New York, NY), 2005.

Karen Hill, *All God's Creatures,* Little Simon (New York, NY), 2005.

Dan Gutman, *Casey Back at Bat,* HarperCollins (New York, NY), 2007.

Margie Palatini, *The Cheese,* Katherine Tegen Books (New York, NY), 2007.

Diane Wright Landolf, *What a Good Big Brother!,* Random House (New York, NY), 2008.

Warren Hanson, *Bugtown Boogie,* Laura Geringer Books (New York, NY), 2008.

Stephen Mitchell, reteller, *The Ugly Duckling,* Candlewick Press (New York, NY), 2008.

Maya Angelo, *Amazing Peace,* Random House (New York, NY), 2008.

Diane Wright Landolf, *What a Good Big Brother!,* Random House (New York, NY), 2009.

## Sidelights

Trained in ballet, Lou Fancher has gone on to work on two very different yet equally creative stages. A choreographer and dance teacher, she has served as both artistic director and ballet mistress at many ballet companies in her home state of Minnesota. In addition, Fancher is also one half of the respected artistic collaboration that, with her husband, commercial artist Steve Johnson, produces evocative, vibrantly colored illustrations for dozens of children's books. As well as creating art for text by popular writers such as Mavis Jukes, Dr. Seuss, Margie Palatini, and Maya Angelo, Fancher has also created and co-illustrated the original picture book *Star Climbing.* Praising the book's "rhythmic, lyrical" verses, which follow a child's make-

believe journey up among the constellations on the way to dreamland, a *Publishers Weekly* reviewer predicted that Fancher's "dreamy bedtime poem with its magical, moon-dappled illustrations may well dazzle star-struck young readers." According to a *Kirkus Reviews* contributor, the couple's "lush, rich illustrations highlight [Fancher's] . . . fanciful nighttime adventure," making *Star Climbing* a "peaceful, vivid visual treat" for young listeners.

In their collaborations, Fancher and Johnson work together on all facets of each illustration project: initial conception, drawing, designing, and painting. As a testament to their skill, they were the first illustrators selected by the estate of Theodore Geisel (the man known as Dr. Seuss) to illustrate *My Many-Colored Days,* a manuscript that remained unillustrated and unpublished at Geisel's death. Their work here, which *Booklist* contributor Hazel Rochman dubbed "glowing and lively," is mirrored in a related work, Kathleen Krull's picture-book biography *The Boy on Fairfield Street: How Ted Geisel Grew up to Become Dr. Seuss.* An exploration of Geisel's experiences as a German immigrant in the early twentieth century, Krull's book was deemed a "winner" by Anne Chapman Callaghan, the critic adding in her *School Library Journal* review that Fancher and Johnson's "lovely, full-page illustrations" successfully

*Lou Fancher breathes new life into a classic by co-illustrating a new edition of Margery Williams'* **The Velveteen Rabbit** *with husband and collaborator Steve Johnson* (Copyright © 2002 by Steve Johnson and Lou Fancher. Reproduced by permission of Atheneum Books for Young Readers, an imprint of Simon & Schuster Children's Publishing Division.)

integrate Seuss's own art. The couple has also created art for posters, business publications, commercial advertising, and periodicals and served as part of the creative team that produced the animated films *Toy Story* and *A Bug's Life*. Fancher's book *The Quest for the One Big Thing*, a counting book, is based on *A Bug's Life*.

Born in Michigan, Fancher took classes in art history at the University of Cincinnati while working toward her B.F.A. in dance. After she met and married Minnesota native Johnson, she relocated to the Minneapolis area, where the couple lived until moving to Moraga, California. Among the many collaborations for which Fancher and Johnson share credit are new versions of some childhood classics. One, Margery Williams' *The Velveteen Rabbit; or, How Toys Become Real*, features a text Fancher adapted for younger readers, while another is Janet Schulman's adaptation of Felix Salten's classic *Bambi*. Commenting on the latter book, Elizabeth Spires wrote in the *New York Times Book Review* that the couple's "luminous paintings" in this "richly illustrated" work "capture, by turns, the radiance of Bambi's forest world, its beauty, terror and stillness." Working again with Johnson, Fancher combines her passions for dance and art in illustrating Margot Fonteyn's picture-book adaptation of the ballet based on E.T.A. Hoffman's *Coppélia*. Reviewing this work, Carolyn Phelan dubbed it "a rich, visual interpretation and a wonderful introduction to a performance of the ballet" in her *Booklist* review.

Fancher and Johnson's other collaborations include creating illustrations for *I Walk at Night* by Lois Duncan; *New York's Bravest*, Mary Pope Osborne's tribute to heroic firefighters everywhere; *Horsefly* by Alice Hoffman; and Dan Gutman's retelling of a well-known American fable in *Casey Back at Bat*. The unusual media used in illustrating Duncan's story about the world as seen through the eyes of a nocturnal cat—string and oil paint—prompted a *Publishers Weekly* critic to note that the couple's use of "twilight tones" and a textured surface produce an "overall effect [that] is dreamy and atmospheric, and makes for grand bedtime fare." While framed as the story of Moses Humphreys, a volunteer firefighter who, in nineteenth-century New York, heroically saved countless lives before losing his own, *New York's Bravest* is also a timely tribute to the firefighters who lost their lives on September 11, 2001. As a *Publishers Weekly* contributor noted, Fancher and Johnson's oil paintings combine with Osborne's text to "carefully and respectfully balance" the historic and mythic elements of Humphreys' life, resulting in "a loving tribute . . . that may well help youngsters cope with the loss of these brave leaders." In their illustrations for *Horsefly* the couple "chart the emotional movement" of Hoffman's story about a girl who loses her fear of horses during a magical flight, using what *Booklist* reviewer Connie Fletcher described as "rich artwork" that ranges from "dark and angular. . . . to brightly glowing." Working with author Dan Gutman to revision the

American saga of Casey at the Bat, Fancher and Johnson also received critical praise. In *Booklist*, GraceAnne A. DeCandido wrote of the illustrators that "the fab team . . . makes wonderful, nineteenth-century-inspired paintings" that reflect the mood of Gutman's nostalgic tale through "their amber glow, Victorian colors, and newsprint shadows."

## Biographical and Critical Sources

### PERIODICALS

*Booklist*, November 1, 1996, Hazel Rochman, review of *My Many Colored Days*, p. 510; October 15, 1998, Carolyn Phelan, review of *Coppélia*, p. 416; December 1, 2000, Connie Fletcher, review of *Horsefly*, p. 721; April 15, 2002, Kay Weisman, review of *Robin's Room*, p. 1406; July, 2002, Ilene Cooper, review of *New York's Finest*, p. 1847; December 1, 2003, Louise Brueggemann, review of *You're a Bear*, p. 684; February 15, 2006, Carolyn Phelan, review of *Star Climbing*, p. 101; January 1, 2007, GraceAnne A. DeCandido, review of *Casey Back at Bat*, p. 114.

*Bulletin of the Center for Children's Books*, March, 2004, Krista Hutley, review of *The Boy on Fairfield Street: How Ted Geisel Grew up to Become Dr. Seuss*, p. 284.

*Horn Book*, November-December, 1993, Mary M. Burns, review of *The First Night*, p. 724; November-December, 2002, Roger Sutton, review of *New York's Bravest*, p. 737.

*Kirkus Reviews*, July 1, 2002, review of *New York's Bravest*, p. 951; August 15, 2002, review of *The Range Eternal*, p. 1222; September 15, 2002, review of *The Velveteen Rabbit*, p. 1389; December 15, 2003, review of *The Boy on Fairfield Street*, p. 1451; April 15, 2005, review of *The Dancing Tiger*, p. 472; June 1, 2005, review of *Bebop Express*, p. 642; February 15, 2006, review of *Star Climbing*, p. 182.

*New York Times Book Review*, November 21, 1999, Elizabeth Spires, review of *Bambi*.

*Publishers Weekly*, September 20, 1993, review of *The First Night*, p. 37; November 7, 1994, review of *Peach and Blue*, p. 77; May 8, 1995, review of *Cat, You Better Come Home*, p. 294; October 13, 1997, review of *The Lost and Found House*, p. 74; November 16, 1998, review of *The Quest for the One Big Thing*, p. 77; January 10, 2000, review of *I Walk at Night*, p. 67; August 13, 2001, review of *The Day Ocean Came to Visit*, p. 311; May 20, 2002, review of *Robin's Room*, p. 65; June 24, 2002, review of *New York's Bravest*, p. 56; September 9, 2002, review of *The Range Eternal*, p. 67; January 23, 2006, review of *Star Climbing*, p. 206.

*School Library Journal*, April, 1999, review of *The Quest for the One Big Thing*, p. 94; August, 2001, Margaret A. Chang, review of *The Day Ocean Came to Visit*, p. 174; October, 2002, Susan Oliver, review of *The Range Eternal*, p. 104; December, 2003, Laura Scott, review of *You're a Bear*, p. 118; January, 2004, Anne Chapman Callaghan, review of *The Boy on Fairfield

*Street,* p. 119; November, 2004, Rebecca Sheridan, review of *Momma, Will You?,* p. 94; July, 2005, Grace Oliff, review of *The Dancing Tiger,* p. 88; April, 2006, Susan Weitz, review of *Star Climbing,* p. 105; January, 2007, Marilyn Taniguchi, review of *Casey Back at Bat,* p. 94.

*ONLINE*

*Lou Fancher and Steve Johnson Home Page,* http://www.johnsonandfancher.com (March 15, 2007).

\*      \*      \*

# FELLOWS, Stan 1957-
## (Stanley Fellows)

## Personal

Born 1957; married; children: one daughter. *Education:* Minneapolis College of Art and Design, degree; attended Art Center College of Design (Pasadena, CA). *Hobbies and other interests:* Birding.

## Addresses

*Home*—Iowa City, IA. *Agent*—Joanie Bernstein, 756 8th Ave. S., Naples, FL 34102. *E-mail*—stan@stanfellows.com.

## Career

Illustrator and commercial artist.

## Illustrator

*FOR CHILDREN*

Michael J. Rosen, *The Dog Who Walked with God,* Candlewick Press (Cambridge, MA), 1998.

Jason Root, *Parables That Jesus Told,* Simon & Schuster (New York, NY), 1999.

Carole Lexa Schaefer, *The Copper Tin Cup,* Candlewick Press (Cambridge, MA), 2000.

Kathryn Lasky, *John Muir: America's First Environmentalist,* Candlewick Press (Cambridge, MA), 2006.

Illustrator for "Johnny Appleseed" videos produced by Rabbit Ears.

*OTHER*

Lou Seibert Pappas, *Jams and Jellies* ("Artful Kitchen" series), Chronicle Books (New York, NY), 1996.

Michael J. Rosen, editor, *Horse People: Writers and Artists on Their Love of Horses,* Artisan, 1998.

Contributor of illustrations to periodicals, including *Audubon, Chicago Tribune, Atlantic Monthly, Harper's, Sports Illustrated, Smithsonian,* and *Wall Street Journal.*

## Sidelights

A teacher and commercial artist, Stan Fellows creates an average of three paintings or drawings a day; by his own calculations, he produced approximately 30,000 pieces of art during the first three decades of his career. The prolific Fellows moved into book illustration in the mid-1990s. While many of his illustration projects, which include *The Dog Who Walked with God* by Michael J. Rosen, find him working in water color, Fellows also paints in oils and acrylics.

Born in 1957, Fellows studied at the Minneapolis College of Art and Design, continuing his education at the prestigious Art Center College of Design in Pasadena, California before returning to Minnesota to teach illustration and watercolor painting at his first alma mater. Numerous corporate assignments followed, and Fellows' art also found its way onto the pages of national periodicals such as *Smithsonian,* the *Atlantic Monthly, Harper's, Sports Illustrated,* and *Audubon,* the last which reflects his interest in birding. An assignment creating artwork for a children's video introduced Fellows to a whole new outlet for his art, and his colorful, light-filled paintings have proved to be a perfect fit. His first children's-book assignment involved creating artwork for *The Dog Who Walked with God,* a creation story by Rosen that was adapted from northern California's native Kato culture. In *Publishers Weekly* a contributor commented that Fellows' approach, which involves "pencil drawings with a judicious use of brown watercolor wash," supports Rosen's tale by evoking "shadows of things to come, ideas of beings not yet materialized." Reviewing these same "delicately realistic watercolors," *Booklist* contributor Susan Dove Lempke wrote that Fellows' "lovely, carefully detailed scenes of natural beauty" inspire a comparison to the work of noted illustrator Jim Arnosky.

Other books that feature Fellows' images include Carole Lexa Schaefer's *The Copper Tin Cup* and *John Muir: America's First Environmentalist* by Kathryn Lasky. Citing the "realistic watercolors" used in Schaefer's family-centered story, Hazel Rochman wrote in her *Booklist* review of *The Copper Tin Cup* that Fellows' impressionistic paintings, crafted in tones of blue and green, provide an opportunity "for children to imagine their own family folklore" amid the story's pages. Calling the work a "tender" story that focuses on "the strength of family ties," a *Publishers Weekly* reviewer concluded that Fellows' "portraits exude an earnestness and warmth that have cross-generation appeal."

Praising Lasky's biography of the noted nineteenth-century American naturalist in her review for *School Library Journal,* Margaret Bush wrote that Fellows' paintings in *John Muir* "provide pleasant impressions of the man and the impressive landscape" Muir dedicated his life to preserving. *Horn Book* reviewer Betty Carter

noted that the illustrator's insertion of small paintings of plants and animals, inset into the text itself, helps the picture book "simulate the intimacy of a personal travel diary."

## Biographical and Critical Sources

*PERIODICALS*

*Booklist,* March 15, 1998, Susan Dove Lempke, review of *The Dog Who Walked with God,* p. 1246; May 15, 2000, Hazel Rochman, review of *The Copper Tin Cup,* p. 1749.

*Canadian Review of Materials,* February 19, 1999, review of *The Dog Who Walked with God.*

*Horn Book,* May-June, 2006, Betty Carter, review of *John Muir: America's First Environmentalist,* p. 346.

*Publishers Weekly,* April 6, 1998, review of *The Dog Who Walked with God,* p. 78; June 5, 2000, review of *The Copper Tin Cup,* p. 93.

*School Library Journal,* February, 2000, Kirsten Martindale, review of *Parables That Jesus Told,* p. 70; May, 2000, Tali Balas, review of *The Copper Tin Cup,* p. 154; April, 2006, Margaret Bush, review of *John Muir,* p. 127.

*ONLINE*

*Stan Fellows Home Page,* http://www.stanfellows.com (March 15, 2007).*

\* \* \*

## FELLOWS, Stanley
## See FELLOWS, Stan

\* \* \*

## FISHER, Valorie

## Personal

Married; children: two.

## Addresses

*Home and office*—Cornwall Bridge, CT.

## Career

Children's book author and illustrator and photographer. *Exhibitions:* Photography exhibited at Brooklyn Museum, Brooklyn, NY; Victoria and Albert Museum, London, England; and Bibliothèque Nationale, Paris, France.

## Awards, Honors

Platinum Award, Oppenheim Toy Portfolio, 2003, for *My Big Brother,* and 2004, for *My Big Sister.*

## Writings

*SELF-ILLUSTRATED*

*My Big Brother,* Atheneum Books for Young Readers (New York, NY), 2002.

*Ellsworth's Extraordinary Electric Ears, and Other Amazing Alphabet Anecdotes,* Atheneum Books for Young Readers (New York, NY), 2003.

*My Big Sister,* Atheneum Books for Young Readers (New York, NY), 2003.

*How High Can a Dinosaur Count?, and Other Math Mysteries,* Schwartz & Wade (New York, NY), 2006.

*ILLUSTRATOR*

Edward Lear, *Nonsense!,* Atheneum Books for Young Readers (New York, NY), 2004.

Peggy Gifford, *Moxy Maxwell Does Not Love Stuart Little,* Schwartz & Wade (New York, NY), 2007.

## Sidelights

A print artist, photographer, and author, Valorie Fisher combines her multiple talents to create unique children's books that include *Ellsworth's Extraordinary Electric Ears, and Other Amazing Alphabet Anecdotes* and a newly illustrated edition of Edward Lear's classic *Nonesense!* An established photographer, Fisher has exhibited her work in such well-known institutions as the Victoria and Albert Museum of London and Paris's Bibliothèque Nationale. She has also incorporated her photographs in the children's books *My Big Brother* and *My Big Sister,* both of which received an Oppenheim Toy Portfolio Platinum award. The two companion titles are written from the perspective of a young child who admires the feats of an older sibling. In *My Big Brother* a little girl describes all the wonderful talents of her older brother, such as his ability to make music and balance a ball on his feet. The large boldfaced text is enhanced by Fisher's bright and uniquely angled photographs, which Susan Dove Lempke described in *Booklist* as "creatively composed."

Fisher also uses her artistic talent in *How High Can a Dinosaur Count?, and Other Math Mysteries,* which includes fifteen humorous dioramas. Regarded by *School Library Journal* reviewer Grace Oliff as a "creative combination of text and art," the book matches Fisher's illustrations with a text that encourages young readers to solve simple problems involving general math techniques. Fisher's mixed-media collages also provide hints

*Valorie Fisher's eccentric world view is shared with readers in her self-illustrated* Ellsworth's Extraordinary Electric Ears, and Other Amazing Alphabet Anecdotes. (Copyright © 2003 by Valorie Fisher. Reproduced by permission of Atheneum Books for Young Readers, an imprint of Simon & Schuster Children's Publishing Division.)

to problem solutions and advanced mathematicians are given the opportunity to decipher more complex puzzles in the last pages of the book. Jennifer Mattson, reviewing *How High Can a Dinosaur Count?, and Other Math Mysteries* for *Booklist,* deemed Fisher's mix of dioramas with math problems "confidence-boosting" for young readers, and a *Publishers Weekly* writer concluded that the author/illustrator's "collage-like medium . . . beckons readers to explore these pages on many levels."

## Biographical and Critical Sources

### PERIODICALS

*Booklist,* September 15, 2002, Susan Dove Lempke, review of *My Big Brother,* p. 239; August, 2003, Ilene Cooper, review of *Ellsworth's Extraordinary Electric Ears, and Other Amazing Alphabet Anecdotes,* p. 1988; January 1, 2006, Jennifer Mattson, review of *How High Can a Dinosaur Count?, and Other Math Mysteries,* p. 111.

*Kirkus Reviews,* June 15, 2002, review of *My Big Brother,* p. 880; May 15, 2003, review of *Ellsworth's Extraordinary Electric Ears, and Other Amazing Alphabet Anecdotes,* p. 749; August 1, 2003, review of *My Big Sister,* p. 1016; August 15, 2004, review of *Nonsense!,* p. 808; January 15, 2006, review of *How High Can a Dinosaur Count?, and Other Math Mysteries,* p. 83.

*Publishers Weekly,* May 20, 2002, review of *My Big Brother,* p. 64; November 1, 2004, review of *Nonsense!,* p. 61; February 6, 2006, review of *How High Can a Dinosaur Count?, and Other Math Mysteries,* p. 69.

*School Library Journal,* July, 2002, Marianne Saccardi, review of *My Big Brother,* p. 90; November, 2003, review of *My Big Sister,* p. 92; November, 2004, Lauralyn Persson, review of *Nonsense!,* p. 127; February, 2006, Grace Oliff, review of *How High Can a Dinosaur Count?, and Other Math Mysteries,* p. 118.

ONLINE

*BookLoons,* http://www.bookloons.com/ (February 17, 2007), Hillary Willamson, review of *How High Can a Dinosaur Count?, and Other Math Mysteries.*

*New York Times Online,* http://query.nytimes.com/ (July 14, 2002), Dwight Garner, review of *My Big Brother.*

*Simon & Schuster Web site,* http://www.simonsays.com/ (February 17, 2007), "Valorie Fisher."*

\* \* \*

# FLORIAN, Douglas 1950-

## Personal

Born March 18, 1950, in New York, NY; son of Harold (an artist) and Edith Florian; married November 3, 1985; wife's name Marie; children: five. *Education:* Queens College of the City University of New York, B.A., 1973; attended School of Visual Arts, 1976.

## Addresses

*Home*—New York, NY. *Office*—500 W. 52nd St., New York, NY 10019. *E-mail*—laugheteria@aol.com.

## Career

Author and illustrator, 1971—. Lecturer at elementary schools. *Exhibitions:* Work exhibited at Society of Illustrators show, 1993.

## Awards, Honors

Outstanding Science Trade Book for Children designation, National Science Teachers Association/Children's Book Council, 1987, for *A Winter Day,* and 1992, for *Vegetable Garden;* Parents' Choice Award for story book, 1991, for *An Auto Mechanic;* Gold Medal for poetry, National Parenting Publications Awards, 1994, Lee Bennett Hopkins Award for poetry, 1995, and American Library Association Notable Book citation, all for *Beast Feast;* Reading Magic Award, *Parenting,* 1994, for *Bing Bang Boing;* International Board on Books for Young People honor list inclusion, for *Discovering Seashells;* Gryphon Award, Center for Children's Books, 2004, for *Bow Wow Meow Meow;* Claudia Lewis Award for Poetry, 2001, for *Mammalabilia;* named Children's Book Council Young People's Poetry Poet, 2006.

## Writings

*FOR CHILDREN; SELF-ILLUSTRATED*

*A Bird Can Fly,* Greenwillow (New York, NY), 1980.
*The City,* Crowell (New York, NY), 1982.
*People Working,* Crowell (New York, NY), 1983.
*Airplane Ride,* Crowell (New York, NY), 1984.
*Discovering Butterflies,* Scribner (New York, NY), 1986.
*Discovering Trees,* Scribner (New York, NY), 1986.
*Discovering Frogs,* Scribner (New York, NY), 1986.
*Discovering Seashells,* Scribner (New York, NY), 1986.
*A Winter Day,* Greenwillow (New York, NY), 1987.
*A Summer Day,* Greenwillow (New York, NY), 1988.
*Nature Walk,* Greenwillow (New York, NY), 1989.
*Turtle Day,* Crowell (New York, NY), 1989.
*A Year in the Country,* Greenwillow (New York, NY), 1989.
*A Beach Day,* Greenwillow (New York, NY), 1990.
*City Street,* Greenwillow (New York, NY), 1990.
*Vegetable Garden,* Harcourt (San Diego, CA), 1991.
*At the Zoo,* Greenwillow (New York, NY), 1992.
*Monster Motel: Poems and Paintings,* Harcourt (San Diego, CA), 1993.
*Bing Bang Boing: Poems and Drawings,* Harcourt (San Diego, CA), 1994.
*Beast Feast,* Harcourt (San Diego, CA), 1994.
*On the Wing: Bird Poems and Paintings,* Harcourt (San Diego, CA), 1996.
*In the Swim: Poems and Paintings,* Harcourt (San Diego, CA), 1997.
*Insectlopedia: Poems and Paintings,* Harcourt (San Diego, CA), 1998.
*Laugh-eteria: Poems and Drawings,* Harcourt (San Diego, CA), 1999.
*Winter Eyes: Poems and Paintings,* Greenwillow (New York, NY), 1999.
*Lizards, Frogs, and Polliwogs: Poems and Paintings,* Harcourt (San Diego, CA), 2000.
*Mammalabilia: Poems and Paintings,* Harcourt (San Diego, CA), 2000.
*A Pig Is Big,* Greenwillow (New York, NY), 2000.
*Summersaults: Poems and Paintings,* Greenwillow (New York, NY), 2002.
*Autumnblings: Poems and Paintings,* Greenwillow (New York, NY), 2003.
*Bow Wow Meow Meow: It's Rhyming Cats and Dogs: Poems and Paintings,* Harcourt (San Diego, CA), 2003.
*Omnibeasts: Animal Poems and Paintings,* Harcourt (Orlando, FL), 2004.

*Zoo's Who: Poems and Paintings,* Harcourt (Orlando, FL), 2005.

*Handsprings: Poems and Paintings,* Greenwillow (New York, NY), 2006.

*Comets, Stars, the Moon, and Mars: Space Poems and Paintings,* Harcourt (Orlando, FL), 2007.

*"HOW WE WORK" SERIES*

*An Auto Mechanic,* Greenwillow (New York, NY), 1991.
*A Carpenter,* Greenwillow (New York, NY), 1991.
*A Potter,* Greenwillow (New York, NY), 1991.
*A Chef,* Greenwillow (New York, NY), 1992.
*A Painter,* Greenwillow (New York, NY), 1993.
*A Fisher,* Greenwillow (New York, NY), 1994.

*ILLUSTRATOR*

(With Kristin Linklater) *Freeing the Natural Voice,* Drama Books, 1976.

Dorothy O. Van Woerkom, *Tit for Tat,* Greenwillow (New York, NY), 1977.

Thomas M. Cook and Robert A. Russell, *Introduction to Management Science,* Prentice-Hall (Englewood Cliffs, NJ), 1979.

Mirra Ginsburg, adaptor, *The Night It Rained Pancakes,* Greenwillow (New York, NY), 1980.

Bill Adler, *What Is a Cat?: For Everyone Who Has Ever Loved a Cat,* Morrow (New York, NY), 1987.

Mary Lyn Ray, *A Rumbly Tumbly Glittery Gritty Place,* Harcourt (San Diego, CA), 1993.

Tony Johnston, *Very Scary,* Harcourt (San Diego, CA), 1995.

Contributor of illustrations to periodicals, including *New Yorker, New York Times, Nation, Travel & Leisure,* and *Across the Board.*

*OTHER*

*See for Your Self* ("Meet the Author" series), Richard C. Owen (Katonah, NY), 2005.

## Sidelights

Although he has been writing and illustrating children's books for many years, Douglas Florian did not receive special attention until he moved from writing nonfiction to creating self-illustrated collections of nonsense verse. The silly poems and imaginative artwork in books such as *Beast Feast, Mammalabilia: Poems and Paintings, Insectlopedia: Poems and Paintings,* and the seasonal self-illustrated *Autumnblings* and *Summersaults,* have prompted some reviewers to compare Florian to Ogden Nash, a famous writer of free verse. Other well-known poet/illustrators that have been compared to Florian include Jack Prelutsky, Shel Silverstein, and John Ciardi.

The son of artist Hal Florian, Douglas Florian decided to follow in his father's footsteps at age ten. As Florian later recalled on *Embracing the Child* online, "I studied

drawing with many teachers, but my first was my father. He taught me to love nature in all of its forms." At age fifteen, Florian attended a summer painting course at New York's School of Visual Arts and he enjoyed the experience so much that he decided to make art his career. "When I walked into the school's large studio filled with paint-encrusted easels, vivid palettes, and the smell of linseed oil," Florian explained in a Harcourt Brace publicity release, "I knew then and there I was going to be an artist." He later attended Queens College, studying under the Caldecott award-winning illustrator Marvin Bileck. "He taught me to treat a drawing like a person: with love and affection," Florian noted in *Embracing the Child.*

Florian soon discovered that desire alone was not enough to make it as an artist. The hard work of honing his skills did not pay off until he was twenty-one years old and saw his first drawings published in the *New York Times.* He continued to produce work for a variety of magazines, but eventually grew tired of working to meet deadlines. When his illustrations for Mirra Ginsburg's *The Night It Rained Pancakes* earned praise from critics, Florian turned his focus to children's books. He began working on a series of nonfiction titles, teaching children about nature in one volume of his "Discovering" series and introducing them to adult occupations such chef and auto mechanic in another.

Despite these first efforts, it would ultimately be Florian's self-illustrated poetry collections that earned the author/artist the most praise. When asked how he made the transition to verse, he explained on *Embracing the Child:* "One day at a flea market, I bought a book of poems called *Oh, That's Ridiculous,* edited by William Cole. The poems in that book were so funny that I was inspired to write some of my own. A few early poems wound up in my book *Monster Motel: Poems and Paintings,* and others in *Bing Bang Boing: Poems and Drawings.*"

Florian received praise for both these early nonsense verse collections. With *Monster Motel* the author created fourteen poems about remarkable creatures, including the "Gazzygoo" and the "Fabled Feerz," accompanying each with pen-and-ink and watercolor illustrations. "Similar in style to the works of Jack Prelutsky," Kay Weisman remarked in *Booklist,* "this will make an excellent choice for youngsters." *School Library Journal* contributor Lauralyn Persson concluded in her review of *Monster Motel* that "Florian's seemingly simple watercolors grow more intriguing with each new book." In a *School Library Journal* review of *Bing Bang Boing,* Kathleen Whalin complimented Florian's "control of the medium," comparing his work to that of Ciardi.

Discussing his initial attraction to verse forms with *Booklist* interviewer Gillian Engberg, Florian noted: "I didn't want to be tied down to the literal." "I just felt that I wanted to be able to flex my imagination a little

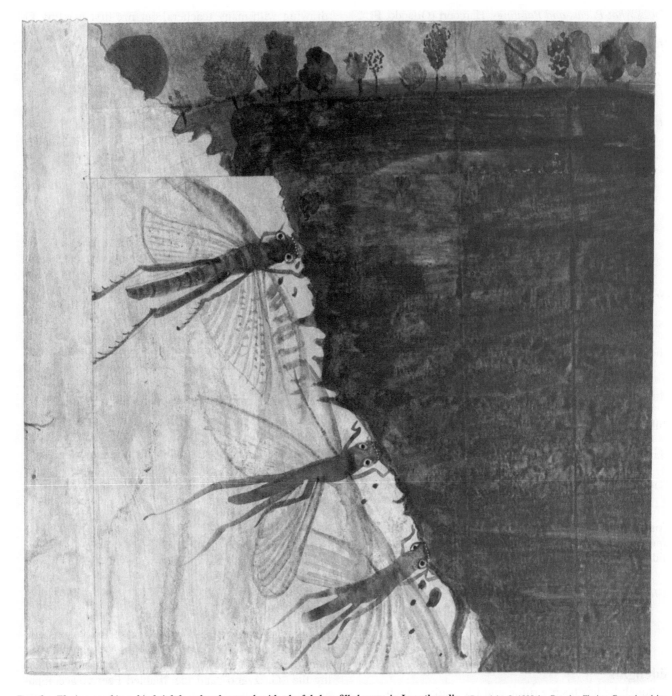

*Douglas Florian combines his brightly colored artwork with playful, bug-filled verse in* **Insectlopedia.** (Copyright © 1998 by Douglas Florian. Reproduced by permission of Harcourt, Inc.)

bit more—," the poet added, "to use my so called poetic license (I get it renewed every six months by the way)." Asked how he handles children's questions about breaking the rules of grammar, spelling, and writing, Florian replied: "I tell them that they should do whatever they have to do to make their poems better, even if it means putting words upside down, or backwards, or spelling words wrong, or using bad grammar. . . . The only rule in poetry is that it has to work."

Following his own instructions for writing children's verse, Florian has produce an award-winning series of books about creatures big and small in *Beast Feast.* A collection of lighthearted poems that feature animals of all types, *Beast Feast* took a great deal of effort on Florian's part to complete. "I actually wrote eighty poems and painted more than fifty watercolors for the book," the author/illustrator said in his publicity release, "and then my editor and I picked the ones we like the best. We wanted *Beast Feast* to be absolutely first-rate."

Earning its author the National Parenting Publications Gold Medal award for poetry along with the Lee Bennett Hopkins Award for poetry in 1995, *Beast Feast* in-

cludes twenty-one carefully selected poems and illustrations. A *Kirkus Reviews* contributor described the work as "subtle, sophisticated, and quite charming." The poems in the collection rely on alliteration and puns based on animal names that invite the verses to be read aloud to children. "Florian's distinctive, full-page watercolors are as playful as his verse," a *Publishers Weekly* reviewer noted, calling the book an "ideal read-aloud." Also remarking on the useful factual information about animals that Florian incorporates into his poems, Lee Bock commented in *School Library Journal* that Florian "knows what children find funny" and deemed *Beast Feast* "a wonderful book."

Florian followed *Beast Feast* with *On the Wing, In the Swim, Insectlopedia, Mammalabilia,* and *Lizards, Frogs, and Polliwogs. On the Wing: Bird Poems and Paintings* offers readers twenty-one poems that focus on a variety of birds, while *In the Swim* presents the same number of poems about water-loving creatures. Writing in *Booklist,* Carolyn Phelan claimed that the appeal of *On the Wing* "lies in its fluent wordplay and generous use of humor in both the poetry and the paintings." Commenting on *In the Swim, Horn Book* contributor Roger Sutton reported that "these clipped verses splash with mischief and wit." In a review of the same book, *School Library Journal* critic Ellen D. Warwick observed: "What's unusual here is the sheer, unforced playfulness, the ease and fluidity informing both verse and pictures."

Continuing his nature theme in *Insectlopedia,* Florian again collects twenty-one short poems, this time entertaining young readers with the uniqueness of different types of bugs. Covering everything from worms and beetles to termites and mayflies, Florian's poems received high praise from reviewers, particularly with regard to his efforts to capture the spirit of the verse in his accompanying watercolor illustrations. "Readers may not be able to stop looking at the inventive watercolor-and-collage illustrations," predicted a *Publishers Weekly* reviewer, the critic going on to add that Florian's "silly, imaginative verses . . . (almost) match the exquisite pictures in playfulness and wit." Phelan, writing in *Booklist,* stated that "the clever artwork, deftly constructed, and the entertaining collection of insect and arachnid verse it illustrates will delight readers." "There are other books of poetry about insects and lots of collections of humorous verses about animals," concluded *School Library Journal* critic Carolyn Angus, "but none match *Insectlopedia.*

Similar high marks were awarded to both *Mammalabilia* and *Lizards, Frogs, and Polliwogs.* Through the twenty-one poems in *Mammalabilia,* Florian covers a wide-range of animals, both familiar and exotic, among them an aardvark, a fox, and a tapir. Citing in particular the author/illustrator's unique gouache artwork, *New York Times* reviewer Cynthia Zarin remarked that Florian's "combination of . . . winsome pictures and often

inspired text transforms the animals he scrutinizes into boarders at his own personal bestiary: they're Florianized." Describing the book as an "irresistible homage to mammal memorabilia," a *Publishers Weekly* critic noticed that the poet's "humor is eccentric, but just right for his target audience." Comparing *Mammalabilia* to its creator's earlier successes *Insectlopedia* and *On the Wing, Booklist* contributor John Peters found the book "ideal for reading aloud, to one listener or to a crowd."

Taking up the cause of reptiles and amphibians, Florian combines short, playful verse with watercolor illustrations to produce *Lizards, Frogs, and Polliwogs.* Constructing poems and pictures that feature such unlikely creatures as geckoes, Gila monsters, and skinks, the author/illustrator again reaped warm words from critics. "This one stands up to the rest," remarked *School Library Journal* reviewer Nina Lindsay, the critic going on to say that, "beautifully designed, this title is as irresistible as Florian's others." A contributor to *Publishers Weekly* pointed out that, in addition to the "mischievous reptile lore that will make young readers laugh," Florian has added a new dimension to his artwork. "These frogs and friends don't necessarily jump out at readers," according to the critic, "but continually take them by surprise."

Animals, animals, and more animals—from slugs to lizards, to sharp-toothed sharks—make an appearance in *Zoo's Who,* while creatures more familiar to young readers take a bow in *Bow Wow Meow Meow: It's Raining Cats and Dogs.* As expected, Florian's fans can continue to indulge in the "simple joys of playing with language and imagery," as a *Kirkus Reviews* writer assured readers of the twenty-one verses in *Zoo's Who,* and *Christian Science Monitor* reviewer Jenny Sawyer praised the poet for his "laugh-out-loud linguistic cleverness." While household pets prove endearing in *Bow Wow Meow Meow,* their wildhearted cousins—wolves and predatory big cats—illustrate the species' more exaggerated characteristics in several of the twenty-one poems included. Noting that the collection is typical of Florian's high standards, Joanna Rudge Long made particular note of the illustrations in the book. "Luscious with offbeat color, [and] composed with wit and grace, Florian's art not only illustrates his verse, it's a pleasure as pure design," Long noted in *Horn Book,* praising *Bow Wow Meow Meow* as a celebration of pets and their people. Some of the most popular animal verses from Florian's books—including *Bow Wow Meow Meow*—are also collected in *Omnibeasts: Animal Poems and Paintings,* which gives children new to Florian's art a healthy dose of whimsical wordplay topped by his colorful art.

Florian moves from the earth's residents to its four seasons in the poetry collections *Winter Eyes, Handsprings, Summersaults,* and *Autumnblings,* all which pair humorous verse and engaging art. In *Winter Eyes* he treats

**Mammalabilia, *one of Florian's most popular self-illustrated poetry collections, was published in 2000.*** (Copyright © 2000 by Douglas Florian. Reproduced by permission of Harcourt, Inc.)

readers to forty-eight short poems that explore the bright and dark sides of the last season of the year. Some verses focus on the joys of cold-weather activities such as sledding, skating, and ice fishing, the poet nonetheless echoing the complaints of some that winter is just too cold and lasts too long. Noting the volume's "appealing" artwork, *New York Times* contributor Tiana Norgren added in her review of *Winter Eyes* that "the beautiful washes of watercolor that make the snow, ice, thawed earth, and pink sunset sky so convincing are punctuated by cheerful penciled patches of bright orange, blue, and hot pink." In a *School Library Journal*

review, Shawn Brommer predicted that "this book will be as welcome as a warm cup of cocoa after a long day of making snowmen and turning figure eights." *Horn Book* reviewer Roger Sutton found "the rhymes are just predictable enough—without being boring—to make [*Winter Eyes*] . . . a good choice for newly independent readers."

Florian allows readers to enjoy warmer weather in both *Handsprings,* which a *Kirkus Reviews* writer described as a "thoughtful but humorous look at the joys of spring," and *Summersaults.* In twenty-eight poems that a *Publishers Weekly* contributor described as "overflow-

ing] . . . with inventive verses celebrating the delights and discontents of summer," *Summersaults* brims with images of those lazy, crazy days: from flies and fleas and grasshoppers to a refreshing bite of watermelon to a day spent at the beach or skateboarding with friends. "Each poem distills one aspect of summer life into a small, polished shell full of rich vocabulary," noted a *Kirkus Reviews* writer, the critic adding that *Summersaults* "is children's poetry at its best." Scrolling further through the seasons, *Autumnblings* begins the move to fall, as patchwork words and engaging rhymes are as animated as windblown autumn leaves. In *School Library Journal* Susan Scheps noted the "childlike style of the various-sized watercolor and colored-pencil paintings" Florian pairs with his playful verse, while GraceAnne A. DeCandido cited the use of varied typefaces as well as the author/illustrator's talent for "Using rhyme, meter, and . . . puns to good effect," in her *Booklist* review of *Autumnblings.*

Children attracted to the rhymes of "Shel Silverstein and Jack Prelutsky and other purveyors of nonsense" are bound to enjoy *Laugh-eteria,* according to *School Library Reviewer* Barbara Chatton. In this collection of short verse, Florian takes on topics familiar to children, including school, dinosaurs, and eating strange foods. "Kids won't have to force their laughter while reading Florian's . . . pithy verses," observed a *Publishers Weekly* critic. Writing in *Booklist,* Phelan remarked that, "Often clever, occasionally gross, the short rhymes appeal to an elementary-school child's sense of humor."

In *A Pig Is Big,* a picture book designed for younger readers, Florian explores the concept of size as a pig is compared to larger and larger objects. On each page, a pig shows his relative size next to other things, beginning with a hat before moving on to other animals and concluding with the entire universe. While admitting that the later pages feature vocabulary that might be out of a preschooler's grasp, a *Publishers Weekly* contributor nonetheless felt the book's "presentation is clever and humorous, well suited for elementary school children prepared to grasp the size of [the] universe." "Florian's illustrations, watercolors with colored pencils, expand the text to make this a satisfying book," claimed Phelan.

Called "one of the most remarkable contemporary versers for young readers" by *Bulletin of the Center for Children's Books* contributor Deborah Stevenson, Florian continues to build upon his well-established reputation as a poet who understands how to delight children and present poetry in an way that appeals to them. Appreciated for his illustrations as well as his verse, he persists, according to critics, in taking both his art work and poetry to new levels. "While it's never possible to have too much good poetry, children's literature is particularly blessed with a fullness in this area," continued Stevenson, adding: "Florian is one of those blessings."

## Biographical and Critical Sources

*PERIODICALS*

*Booklist,* March 15, 1993, Kay Weisman, review of *Monster Motel: Poems and Paintings,* p. 1351; September 15, 1993, Carolyn Phelan, review of *A Painter;* February 15, 1994; August, 1994; March 15, 1996, Carolyn Phelan, review of *On the Wing: Bird Poems and Paintings,* p. 1258; March 15, 1998, Carolyn Phelan, review of *Insectlopedia: Poems and Paintings,* p. 1240; March 15, 1999, Carolyn Phelan, review of *Laugh-eteria,* p. 1340; March 15, 2000, Gillian Engberg, interview with Florian, p. 1382; March 15, 2000, John Peters, review of *Mammalabilia: Poems and Paintings,* p. 1380; September 15, 2000, Carolyn Phelan, review of *A Pig Is Big,* p. 247; April 1, 2002, Gillian Engberg, review of *Summersaults: Poems and Paintings,* p. 1330; February 1, 2003, Gillian Engberg, review of *Bow Wow Meow Meow: It's Raining Cats and Dogs,* p. 994; August, 2003, GraceAnne A. DeCandido, review of *Autumnblings: Poems and Paintings,* p. 1985; October 15, 2004, Diane Foote, review of *Omnibeasts: Animal Poems and Paintings,* p. 407; March 15, 2005, Ilene Cooper, review of *Zoo's Who: Poems and Paintings,* p. 1290; March 15, 2006, Hazel Rochman, review of *Handsprings: Poems and Paintings,* p. 48.

*Bulletin of the Center for Children's Books,* December, 1992, p. 110; July-August, 1994, p. 355; November, 1994, p. 77; May, 2002, review of *Summersaults,* p. 322; May, 2005, review of *Zoo's Who,* p. 381; April, 2003, review of *Bob Wow Meow Meow,* p. 312; September, 2003, Deborah Stevenson, review of *Autumnblings,* p. 13; March, 2006, April Spisak, review of *Handsprings,* p. 311.

*Christian Science Monitor,* November 15, 2005, Jenny Sawyer, review of *Zoo's Who,* p. 16.

*Horn Book,* December, 1980, p. 632; July, 1997, Roger Sutton, review of *In the Swim,* p. 470; November, 1999, Roger Sutton, review of *Winter Eyes: Poems and Paintings,* p. 752; March, 2000, review of *Mammalabilia,* p. 204; May, 2001, Martha V. Parravano, review of *Lizards, Frogs, and Polliwogs,* p. 342; July-August, 2002, Joanna Rudge Long, review of *Summersaults,* p. 478; May-June, 2003, review of *Bow Wow Meow Meow,* p. 363; November-December, 2003, Joanna Rudge Long, review of *Autumnblings,* p. 759; May-June, 2005, Martha V. Parravano, review of *Zoo's Who,* p. 336; March-April, 2006, Joanna Rudge Long, review of *Handsprings,* p. 201.

*Kirkus Reviews,* March 1, 1983, review of *People Working;* April 15, 1994, review of *Beast Feast;* March 1, 2002, review of *Summersaults,* p. 333; March 15, 2003, review of *Bow Wow Meow Meow,* p. 466; July 15, 2003, review of *Autumnblings,* p. 963; April 1, 2005, review of *Zoo's Who,* p. 416; February 15, 2006, review of *Handsprings,* p. 182.

*New York Times,* November 21, 1999, Tiana Norgren, review of *Winter Eyes,* p. 41; November 19, 2000, Cynthia Zarin, review of *Mammalabilia,* p. 46; December 3, 2000, Allison Steele, review of *A Pig Is Big,* p. 85.

*Publishers Weekly,* April 1, 1983, review of *People Working,* p. 60; March 7, 1994, review of *Beast Feast;* March 9, 1998, review of *Insectlopedia,* pp. 69-70; April 19, 1999, review of *Laugh-eteria,* p. 73; March 13, 2000, review of *Mammalabilia,* p. 84; October 9, 2000, review of *A Pig Is Big,* p. 87; March 12, 2001, review of *Lizards, Frogs, and Polliwogs,* p. 90; April 29, 2002, review of *Summersaults,* p. 70; February 10, 2003, review of *Bow Wow Meow Meow,* p. 187; June 30, 2003, review of *Autumnblings,* p. 77.

*School Library Journal,* August, 1982, Mary B. Nickerson, review of *The City,* p. 96; June, 1993, Lauralyn Persson, review of *Monster Motel;* May, 1994; Lee Bock, review of *Beast Feast;* September, 1994, Tom S. Hurlburt, review of *A Fisher,* p. 207; November, 1994, Kathleen Whalin, review of *Bing Bang Boing;* May, 1997, Ellen D. Warwick, review of *In the Swim,* p. 119; April, 1998, Carolyn Angus, review of *Insectlopedia,* pp. 115-116; June, 1999, Barbara Chatton, review of *Laugh-eteria,* p. 114; September, 1999, Shawn Brommer, review of *Winter Eyes,* p. 212; April, 2000, Barbara Chatton, review of *Mammalabilia,* p. 119; April, 2001, Nina Lindsay, review of *Lizards, Frogs, and Polliwogs,* p. 129; May, 2003, Susannah Price, review of *Bow Wow Meow Meow,* p. 136; October, 2003, Susan Scheps, review of *Autumnblings,* p. 149; October, 2004, Lee Bock, review of *Omnibeasts,* p. 140; April, 2005, Margaret Bush, review of *Zoo's Who,* p. 122; April, 2006, Kirsten Cutler, review of *Handsprings,* p. 124.

*ONLINE*

*Bulletin of the Center for Children's Books Online,* http://alexia.lis.uiuc.edu/puboff/bccb/ (July 7, 2001), Deborah Stevenson, "True Blue: Douglas Florian."

*Children's Book Council Web site,* http://www.cbcbooks.org/ (March 8, 2007), interview with Florian.

*Douglas Florian Home Page,* http://www.douglasflorian.com (March 8, 2006).

*Embracing the Child,* http://www.eyeontomorrow.com/ (June 30, 2001), "Meet Douglas Florian."

*Storybook Art,* http://storybookart.com/ (July 7, 2001), "Douglas Florian."

*OTHER*

Florian, Douglas, "Artist/Author at a Glance" (publicity release), Harcourt, c. 1994.

\*      \*      \*

# FRAZIER, Craig 1955-

## Personal

Born 1955; married; children: two children. *Education:* Degree (communication design).

## Addresses

*Home and office*—Mill Valley, CA. *E-mail*—studio@craigfrazier.com; Stanley@stanleybooks.com.

## Career

Author, illustrator, and graphic designer. Frazier Design, Inc., San Francisco, CA, president and owner, 1978-96; Craig Frazier Studio (illustration), president and owner, 1996—. Designer of trademarks for companies, including LucasArts, of postage stamps for U.S. Postal Service, and of "Critter" font for Adobe. Instructor at California College of Arts and Kent State University summer graduate program. Member of board of advisors, The Portfolio Center, Atlanta, GA, and 2005 Illustrators Conference. *Exhibitions:* Works included in permanent collection at San Francisco Museum of Modern Art.

## Awards, Honors

Numerous awards for design.

## Writings

*PICTURE BOOKS*

(Self-illustrated) *Stanley Goes for a Drive,* Chronicle Books (San Francisco, CA), 2004.
(Self-illustrated) *Stanley Mows the Lawn,* Chronicle Books (San Francisco, CA), 2005.
(Self-illustrated) *Stanley Goes Fishing,* Chronicle Books (San Francisco, CA), 2006.
(Illustrator) George Ella Lyon, *Trucks Roll!,* Atheneum (New York, NY), 2007.

*OTHER*

Contributor of illustrations to periodicals, including *Time, Fortune, Forbes, Business Week, Fast Company, Harvard Business Review, Boston Globe, Reader's Digest, Newsweek, Wall Street Journal, Los Angeles Times, Utne Reader,* and *Atlantic Monthly.*

## Sidelights

Craig Frazier is an award-winning graphic designer and illustrator who has also ventured into the world of children's literature. Frazier brings a sense of play and wonder to his surrealistic, self-illustrated works that he believes is best appreciated by youngsters. As he told Kirk Citron in *Graphis,* children "haven't closed down the aperture on the way they see things. They don't know yet that you can't walk on the ceiling, so they just draw it. And they draw it without worrying about how to draw it, yet it communicates."

Frazier published his first self-illustrated children's book, *Stanley Goes for a Drive,* in 2004. The work opens as Stanley goes for a drive in his pickup truck on a hot and cloudless summer day. According to a critic in *Publishers Weekly,* the work "soon sheds its initial pragmatism for a dreamlike flight of fancy." While cruising past a herd of cows, Stanley gets an idea: he

*Illustrator and designer Craig Frazier's unique stylized art is paired with his engaging story in* **Stanley Goes Fishing.** (Used with permission of Chronicle Books, LLC, San Francisco, CA. Visit ChronicleBooks.com.)

grabs a bucket, approaches the only black-and-white spotted cow, and begins milking it. As he does, the white spots magically drain off the animal. When Stanley tosses the contents of the bucket into the sky, the milk floats up and forms fluffy clouds that darken and pour rain on the parched landscape. *Stanley Goes for a Drive* received strong praise from reviewers, who paid special attention to the book's hand-drawn, digitally colored illustrations. Frazier's "masterful use of composition surprises readers with large shapes in the foreground that contrast with small, multiple figures in the background to create asymmetric balance and depth," noted Carolyn Janssen in *School Library Journal*. In the words of a *Kirkus Reviews* contributor, "reading this unusual, visually intriguing story is like examining a surrealist painting where something shifts inexplicably as one watches."

In *Stanley Mows the Lawn,* "what begins as a routine chore literally takes a turn, with a satisfying and visually creative result," observed a *Kirkus Reviews* critic. When the grass in Stanley's yard grows long enough to cover his feet, he brings out his push mower and begins cutting back and forth in straight, precise rows. A rustling in the grass causes Stanley to halt his work, and he spies Hank the snake slithering through the yard.

Abandoning his repetitive pattern of mowing, Stanley begins zig-zagging his way through the lawn, making sure to leave patches of tall grass for Hank. In *School Library Journal,* Suzanne Myers Harold remarked that *Stanley Mows the Lawn* "uses subtle humor to convey its theme of seeing the world from another's point of view and finding a mutually agreeable solution."

*Stanley Goes Fishing* is Frazier's third work featuring the kindly gentleman with a creative bent. Planning to spend a relaxing day with his fishing rod and reel, Stanley launches his boat into a stream and trolls all his favorite spots. Despite his best efforts, however, the only thing he pulls from the water is a soggy old boot. Hoping to change his luck, Stanley casts his line into the sky and starts hauling in one golden fish after another. After catching his fill, a satisfied Stanley returns the fish to the stream. "The crisp, clean illustrations in bright golds, verdant greens, and brilliant blues are a pleasure to behold," wrote *School Library Journal* contributor Maryann H. Owen. Also complimenting Frazier's imaginative artwork, a critic for *Kirkus Reviews* deemed *Stanley Goes Fishing* "a visual conundrum that accentuates the "art" of looking at the world in different ways."

## Biographical and Critical Sources

*PERIODICALS*

*Communication Arts,* January-February, 1991, Marty Neumeier, "Craig Frazier," p. 32.

*Graphis,* July-August, 2002, Kirk Citron, "Craig Frazier: Things Are Not What They Seem," pp. 100-111; November-December, 2002, Petual Vrontikis, interview with Frazier.

*Kirkus Reviews,* July 1, 2004, review of *Stanley Goes for a Drive,* p. 629; April 1, 2005, review of *Stanley Mows the Lawn,* p. 416; April 15, 2006, review of *Stanley Goes Fishing,* p. 405.

*Publishers Weekly,* September 13, 2004, review of *Stanley Goes for a Drive,* p. 77.

*School Library Journal,* September, 2004, Carolyn Janssen, review of *Stanley Goes for a Drive,* p. 160; May, 2005, Suzanne Myers Harold, review of *Stanley Mows the Lawn,* p. 82; June, 2006, Maryann H. Owen, review of *Stanley Goes Fishing,* p. 112.


*ONLINE*

*Craig Frazier Home Page,* http://www.craigfrazier.com (January 21, 2007).

*Stanley Books Web site,* http://www.stanleybooks.com/ (January 21, 2007).

# G

## GARDNER, Sally

### Personal
Born in England; children: twin daughters, one son. *Education:* Degree from London art college (with highest honors); attended theatre school.

### Addresses
*Home*—North London, England.

### Career
Children's book author and illustrator. Theatre designer for the London stage, specializing in costume design, for fifteen years.

### Awards, Honors
Smarties Book Prize Bronze Award, 2003, for *The Countess's Calamity;* Nestlé Children's Book Prize, 2006, for *I, Coriander;* various awards for costume design.

### Writings

*FOR CHILDREN; SELF-ILLUSTRATED*

*The Little Nut Tree,* Tambourine Books (New York, NY), 1993.
*My Little Princess,* Orion (London, England), 1994.
*A Book of Princesses,* Orion (London, England), 1997.
*The Fairy Catalogue: All You Need to Make a Fairy Tale,* Orion (London, England), 2000, published as *The Fairy Tale Catalog: Everything You Need to Make a Fairy Tale,* Chronicle Books (San Francisco, CA), 2001.
(Adaptor) *The Glass Heart: A Tale of Three Princesses* (based on "Die drie Schwestern mit den gläsernen Herzen" by Richard Volkmann-Leander), Orion (London, England), 2001.

(And illustrator) *Mama, Don't Go out Tonight,* Bloomsbury Children's Books (New York, NY), 2002, published as *Mummy, Don't Go out Tonight,* Bloomsbury (London, England), 2002.
*Fairy Shopping,* Orion (London, England), 2003.
*Lucy Willow,* Orion (London, England), 2006.

*"MAGICAL CHILDREN" SERIES; SELF-ILLUSTRATED*

*The Strongest Girl in the World* (also see below), Dolphin (London, England), 1999.
*The Smallest Girl Ever,* Dolphin (London, England), 2000.
*The Boy Who Could Fly* (also see below), Dolphin (London, England), 2001.
*The Invisible Boy* (also see below), Dolphin (London, England), 2002.
*The Boy with the Magic Numbers,* Dolphin (London, England), 2003.
*Magical Children* (includes *The Strongest Girl in the World, The Invisible Boy,* and *The Boy Who Could Fly*), Dolphin (London, England), 2004 published as *Magical Kids: The Strongest Girl in the World and the Invisible Boy,* Dial (New York, NY), 2007.
*The Boy with the Lightning Feet,* Dolphin (London, England), 2006.

*"TALES FROM THE BOX" SERIES; SELF-ILLUSTRATED*

*The Countess's Calamity,* Bloomsbury Children's Books (New York, NY), 2003.
*Boolar's Big Day Out,* Bloomsbury Children's Books (New York, NY), 2003.

*ILLUSTRATOR*

Marjorie Newman, *Robert and the Giant,* Hamish Hamilton (London, England), 1990.
Beverley Birch, *Suzi, Sam, George, and Alice,* Bodley Head (London, England), 1993.
*Playtime Rhymes,* Orion (London, England), 1995.
Adrian Mitchell, *Gynormous: The Ultimate Book of Giants,* Orion (London England), 1996.

Jostein Gaarder, *Hello? Is Anybody There?*, translated by James Anderson, Farrar, Straus & Giroux (New York, NY), 1998.

Georgie Adams, *The Real Fairy Storybook,* Orion (London, England), 1998.

Frances Thomas, *Polly's Running Away Book,* Bloomsbury (London, England), 2000, published as *Polly's Really Secret Diary,* Delacorte Press (New York, NY), 2002.

Frances Thomas, *Polly's Absolutely Worst Birthday Ever,* Bloomsbury (London, England), 2001, Delacorte Press (New York, NY), 2003.

*OTHER*

*I, Coriander* (young-adult novel), Dial (New York, NY), 2005.

## Adaptations

*I, Coriander* was adapted as an audiobook, read by Juliet Stevenson, Listening Library, 2006; Orion adapted several other books by Gardner as book-and-CD packs.

## Sidelights

During Sally Gardner's school-aged years, where poor reading skills found the British schoolgirl struggling to pass class after class, no one—least of all Gardner herself—would have guessed that she would eventually become a successful children's book author. Her difficulty with reading was eventually dealt with through the eye-opening diagnosis of dyslexia, however, and Gardner's whimsical imagination and unique viewpoints have found an outlet in both self-illustrated picture books such as *The Little Nut Tree* and *Mama, Don't Go out Tonight.* Her chapter books for older readers include *The Countess's Calamity* and the multi-volume "Magical Children" series, which includes *The Invisible Boy* and *The Strongest Girl in the World.* Having more recently moved her attention to even older readers, Gardner's debut young-adult novel, *I, Coriander,* earned its author the coveted 2006 Nestlé Children's Book Prize in her native England.

Born and raised in London, Gardner found her success in school hampered by the fact that, due to her dyslexia, she could neither read nor write until her early teens. In fact, she even changed her first name from Sarah to Sally so she would be able to spell it correctly. Dismissed from several schools after being deemed uneducable, Gardner was eventually enrolled at a school for maladjusted children. Fortunately, by the time she reached age fourteen, advances in learning allowed her to deal with her condition, and the first book she read was Charlotte Brontë's *Wuthering Heights.* Writers that soon became favorites included Charles Dickens, E. Nesbit, Rachel Compton, and Jane Austen; in fact, Gardner still ranks Dickens' *Great Expectations* as her favorite book of all time.

Although reading was not Gardner's strong suit, she showed a talent for dealing with three-dimensional form as well as a strong artistic sense that fueled her success

at art college and earned her a scholarship to study theatre design. For the next fifteen years, she worked on the London stage as a designer, and her costume design won her several awards. She moved to book illustration following the births of twin daughters and a son, and from there to writing. Her first self-illustrated picture book, *The Little Nut Tree,* which was published in 1994, has also been translated into Spanish.

Gardner's picture books and chapter books often feature fairytale themes and magical elements. *Mama, Don't Go out Tonight,* a picture book praised for its "gentle humor" by *Booklist* contributor Ellen Mandel, finds a young girl conjuring up a series of fantastical catastrophes that might befall her mother on a night out: from being captured by pirates to becoming a monster's appetizer. Her "Tales from the Box" chapter-book series brings to life the world of five abandoned dolls as they struggle to survive in a hostile world. Helped by a nearby mouse family in *The Countess's Calamity,* Boolar, Stitch, the Chinese doll Ting Tang, the sailor

*Part of Sally Gardner's "Tales from the Box" series,* **The Countess's Calamity** *finds a mouse family befriending a group of lost dolls.* (Bloomsbury Publishing, PLC, 2003. Reproduced by permission.)

doll Quilt, and the Countess are appreciative of their new home, although the fashionably dressed Countess demands a more luxurious abode. Ultimately, when her life is threatened by the sinister Mr. Cuddles, a local cat, the now-tattered doll learns to appreciate the charity of others with the help of a new heart. In *School Library Journal* Susan Helper praised *The Countess's Calamity* for its "fresh and lively" plot, while a *Publishers Weekly* writer deemed it a "diverting and clever fantasy."

Gardner's diminutive doll saga continues in *Boolar's Big Day Out,* as the resourceful Boolar leaves the group to join a puppet troupe as the lead in a production of *The Adventures of Tom Thumb.* While his time away is supposed to be brief, he quickly falls in love with the performing life as well as with his captivating marionette costar. With cold weather coming, the dolls he has left are forced to seek much-needed supplies for themselves, forgotten by their stage-struck friend. Ultimately, however, Boolar learns about the theatre's fickle side and, when his leading role is given to another, he returns to the toy box where all is forgiven. Reviewing *Boolar's Big Day Out,* a *Kirkus Reviews* writer praised Gardner's "charming pencil drawings," while JoAnn Jonas deemed the tale a "satisfying read" in her review for *School Library Journal.* Jonas further praised *Boolar's Big Day Out,* noting that it boasts "engaging writing, an entertaining story line, plus a lesson in friendship and loyalty."

Set in London during the 1600s, *I, Coriander* weaves together fantasy and history in its story of the unhappy daughter of a silk merchant. Following the death of England's King Charles I and the rise to power of Oliver Cromwell, Coriander Hobie's widowed father is forced to flee due to his loyalty to the English crown. Left in the care of an unloving stepmother, the imaginative nine year old is now an obstacle for the grasping woman and her friend, a coldhearted Puritan minister. Locked in a trunk and left to die, the girl instead finds herself in a dream world where she learns that her real mother, a fairy princess, has left her with a quest: to locate a secret object and save fairyland from the control of a destructive queen. The story's use of time shifts—Coriander ages six years during the retrospective tale—and Gardner's juxtaposition of "turbulent seventeenth-century London and the shimmering mysteries of fairyland" reflect the history of England's tumultuous Restoration period, as Jennifer Mattson noted in *Booklist,* the critic adding that *I, Coriander* presents readers with a rewarding challenge. In *Kliatt* Janis Flint-Ferguson characterized the novel as "one of good triumphing over evil and of true love saving the lives of honest people," while Beth Wright deemed *I, Coriander* an "absorbing, picturesque tale." Also commenting on Gardner's use of time travel and dual worlds, Wright added that the novel would have appeal for both fantasy fans and those who enjoy historical fiction, while "readers who love romantic fairy tales will delight" in Coriander's discovery of true love and "the way her dual heritage allows her to

honor her human father and still have her fairy prince." "Deft and dulcet language . . . and the tie to a grim historical season will hold readers fast," predicted a *Kirkus Reviews* writer of Gardner's award-winning novel.

As an illustrator, Gardner has created art for Frances Thomas's amusing diaries of a nine year old named Polly, whose antic life is recounted in *Polly's Running Away Book*—published as *Polly's Really Secret Diary* in the United States—and *Polly's Absolutely Worst Birthday Ever.* She has also served as illustrator for Jostein Gaarder's novel *Hello? Is Anybody There?,* a story about a boy's encounter with a young space traveler. Through what a *Kirkus Reviews* writer characterized as a "combination of childlike pencil illustrations, magazine cut-outs, clip-art, and family photos," Gardner effectively brings to life the "frenetic, yet completely believable" account of Thomas's spunky and single-minded narrator in *Polly's Absolutely Worst Birthday Ever.*

"Fairy tales are the soul of the world," Gardner explained to Orion Web site contributor Danuta Kean

*Cover of Gardner's award-winning young-adult novel* **I, Coriander,** *featuring an illustration by Dan Craig.* (Illustration © 2005 by Dan Craig. Reproduced by permission of Dial Books, a division of Penguin Putnam Books for Young Readers.)

*Before becoming a writer, Gardner illustrated books such as* **Polly's Really Secret Diary,** *part of a series by Frances Thomas.* (Illustrations copyright © 2000 by Sally Gardner. Used by permission of Dell Publishing, a division of Random House, Inc. In the United Kingdom and Canada by permission of Bloomsbury Publishing.)

while discussing her motivation for writing for children. "They talk of great universal truths in a way that is accessible. When you write about a child living in a tower block with a crackhead mother, it is too close to her reality for her to see what else is in the story." However, "place her in a fairy tower with a horrible witch whom she is trying to escape," the author added, "and she can take inspiration from the message that good can triumph over evil."

## Biographical and Critical Sources

*PERIODICALS*

*Booklist,* June 1, 2002, Kelly Milner Halls, review of *Polly's Really Secret Diary,* p. 1726; January 1, 2003, Ellen Mandel, review of *Mama, Don't Go out Tonight,* p. 906; July, 2003, Kay Weisman, review of *Polly's Absolutely Worst Birthday Ever,* p. 1892; August, 2005, Jennifer Mattson, review of *I, Coriander,* p. 2015.

*Horn Book,* November-December, 2005, Jennifer M. Brabander, review of *I, Coriander,* p. 719.
*Kirkus Reviews,* June 1, 2003, review of *Polly's Absolutely Worst Birthday Ever,* p. 812; November 1, 2003, review of *Boolar's Big Day Out,* p. 1310; July 15, 2005, review of *I, Coriander,* p. 789.
*Kliatt,* September, 2005, Janis Flint-Ferguson, review of *I, Coriander,* p. 8.
*Publishers Weekly,* May, 23, 1994, review of *The Little Nut Tree,* p. 87; August 10, 1998, review of *Hello? Is Anybody There?,* p. 388; June 3, 2002, review of *Polly's Really Secret Diary,* p. 88; October 28, 2002, review of *Mama, Don't Go out Tonight,* p. 71; March 24, 2003, review of *The Countess's Calamity,* p. 76; July 18, 2005, review of *I, Coriander,* p. 206.
*School Librarian,* spring, 1998, reviews of *Hello? Is Anybody out There?* and *A Book of Princesses,* p. 24; spring, 2001, review of *The Fairy Catalogue: All You Need to Make a Fairy Tale,* p. 33; spring, 2002, reviews of *The Glass Heart* and *The Boy Who Could Fly,* p. 24; winter, 2002, review of *The Invisible Boy,* p. 186; autumn, 2003, review of *The Countess's Calamity,* p. 136; autumn, 2005, Barbara Sherrard-Smith, review of *I, Coriander,* p. 155; autumn, 2006, Rosemary Woodman, review of *The Boy with the Lightning Feet,* p. 141.
*School Library Journal,* July, 1994, Cyrisse Jaffee, review of *The Little Nut Tree,* p. 76; August, 2002, Marietta Barral Zacker, review of *The Fairy Catalog,* p. 55, and Amy Stultz, review of *Polly's Really Secret Diary,* p. 171; December, 2002, Steven Engelfried, review of *Mama, Don't Go out Tonight,* p. 96; August, 2003, Susan Hepler, review of *The Countess's Calamity,* p. 128; November, 2003, Carolyn Janssen, review of *Polly's Absolutely Worst Birthday Ever,* p. 116; January, 2004, JoAnn Jonas, review of *Boolar's Big Day Out,* p. 98; September, 2005, Beth Wright, review of *I, Coriander,* p. 203.
*Times Educational Supplement,* November 16, 2001, review of *The Boy Who Could Fly,* p. 20; September 5, 2003, review of *The Countess's Calamity,* p. 14; July 29, 2005, Linda Newbery, review of *I, Coriander,* p. 26.

*ONLINE*

*BookBrowse,* http://www.bookbrowse.com/ (August 15, 2005), interview with Gardner.
*Guardian Unlimited,* http://books.guardian.co.uk/ (December 14, 2005), Michelle Pauli, "Dyslexic Writer Savours Nestle Victory."
*Orion Web site,* http://www.orionbooks.co.uk/ (March 7, 2007), Danuta Kean, profile of Gardner.

\*    \*    \*

## GERRITSEN, Paula 1956-

### Personal

Born 1956, in the Netherlands; married; children: three.

## Addresses

*Home and office*—Megen, Netherlands. *E-mail*—paula.gerritsen@planet.nl.

## Career

Author and illustrator. Psychology assistant, beginning 1988.

## Writings

*SELF-ILLUSTRATED*

*Noten,* Lemniscaat (Amsterdam, Netherlands), 2005, translated as *Nuts,* Front Street Books (Asheville, NC), 2006.

*ILLUSTRATOR*

Erik van Os and Elle van Lieshout, *Fijn feestje,* Lemniscaat (Amsterdam, Netherlands), 2002 translated as *A Nice Party,* Boyds Mills Press (Honesdale, PA), 2002.

Erik van Os and Elle van Lieshout, *Nooit meer een luier!,* Mercis (Amsterdam, Netherlands), 2002.

Petra Cremers, *Detectivebureau K & K,* 2003.

Elle van Lieshout and Erik van Os, *Een koning van niks,* Lemniscaat (Amsterdam, Netherlands), 2004, translated as *The Nothing King,* Boyds Mills Press (Honesdale, PA), 2004.

Petra Cremers, *Lella en de bodyguards,* Holland (Amsterdam, Netherlands), 2005.

Erik van Os and Elle van Lieshout, *De wens,* Lemniscaat (Amsterdam, Netherlands), 2006, translated as *The Wish,* Boyds Mills Press (Honesdale, PA), 2007.

Also illustrator of books by Petra Cremers, including *Mickey Magnus, Razende reporters,* and *Oranje boven.*

## Sidelights

Dutch illustrator Paula Gerritsen has created art for stories by authors such as Paula Cremers and popular writing team Elle van Lieshout and Eric van Os. She made her debut as both author and illustrator with *Noten,* a self-illustrated picture book that was published in translation as *Nuts* in 2006.

As readers of *Nuts* discover, Mouse lives atop a hill overlooking a farm with its expansive fields. In the distance, she can see a nut tree that promises food for the coming winter. As the air grows colder and fall approaches, the tiny creature sets out for the tree wearing a coat with large pockets to carry the fallen nuts she intends to gather. As Mouse makes her way across the

*Dutch illustrator Paula Gerritsen pairs her art with an original story in her picture book* Nuts. (Illustration © 2005. Reproduced by permission of Front Street, an imprint of Boyds Mills Press.)

field, friends Gull, Sheep, and Hare warn of a storm that is quickly approaching, but the determined Mouse does not hear them. By the time Mouse reaches the tree, the sky has grown dark. She nestles between the tree's roots and naps until the storm passes, but when she awakens, she finds that all the nuts have blown away. While Mouse is disheartened, after trudging back home she is pleased to discover that the winds have actually worked in her favor; they have blown the nuts up to her home on top of the hill.

Praising Gerritsen's simple tale, Julie Cummins added in *Booklist* that the author's illustrations "make use of the overhead perspective to convey diminutive Mouse's size, while visual aids . . . add wry touches of humor." Mary Hazelton, critiquing the Dutch import for *School Library Journal*, wrote that Gerritsen's self-illustrated picture book features "small details tucked away for curious eyes to discover," and a *Kirkus Reviews* critic dubbed *Nuts* a "triumphant" picture-book debut.

## Biographical and Critical Sources

*PERIODICALS*

*Booklist,* December 15, 2004, Hazel Rochman, review of *The Nothing King,* p. 747; March 1, 2006, Julie Cummins, review of *Nuts,* p. 99.
*Children's Bookwatch,* February, 2005, review of *The Nothing King;* April, 2006, review of *Nuts.*
*Kirkus Reviews,* April 15, 2003, review of *A Nice Party,* p. 612; November 15, 2004, review of *The Nothing King,* p. 1094; January 1, 2006, review of *Nuts,* p. 41.
*Publishers Weekly,* January 10, 2005, review of *The Nothing King,* p. 54; January 8, 2007, review of *The Wish,* p. 50.
*School Library Journal,* August, 2003, Melinda Piehler, review of *A Nice Party,* p. 145; January, 2005, Rachel G. Payne, review of *The Nothing King,* p. 98; March, 2006, Mary Hazelton, review of *Nuts,* p. 187.

*ONLINE*

*Boyds Mills Press Web site,* http://www.boydsmillspress. com/ (March 3, 2007), "Paula Gerritsen."
*Lemniscaat Web site,* http://www.lemniscaat.nl/ (March 20, 2007), "Paula Gerritsen."*

\*    \*    \*

# GILPIN, Stephen

## Personal

Married; wife's name Krista; children: four. *Education:* New York School of Visual Arts, B.F.A. (with honors). *Hobbies and other interests:* Walks on the beach, gardening, bag piping.

## Addresses

*Home and office*—Tulsa, OK. *E-mail*—mail@billythesquid.com.

## Career

Artist and children's book illustrator.

## Illustrator

John Hall, *Mickey McGuffin's Ear,* White Stone Books (Lakeland, FL), 2005.
William Boniface, *The Extraordinary Adventures of Ordinary Boy, Book One: The Hero Revealed,* HarperCollins (New York, NY), 2006.
Deborah Underwood, *Pirate Mom,* Random House (New York, NY), 2006.
John Hall, *How to Get a Gorilla out of Your Bathtub,* Harrison House (Tulsa, OK), 2006.
John Hall, *What If I Pulled This Thread?,* Harrison House (Tulsa, OK), 2006.
Eric A. Kimmel, adaptor, *The Three Cabritos,* Marshall Cavendish (New York, NY), 2007.
Wendi Silvano, *Magnetic Mixables: A Princess Mess,* Innovative Kids (Norwalk, CT), 2007.
William Boniface, *The Extraordinary Adventures of Ordinary Boy, Book Two: The Return of Meteor Boy?,* HarperCollins (New York, NY), 2007.

## Sidelights

Stephen Gilpin was raised in small-town Kansas, but moved to the East Coast to attend the New York School of Visual Arts. While as an artist, he developed an interest in abstract expressionism, Gilpin has also cultivated a career as a children's book illustrator, creating cartoon-like images for a variety of children's titles that often incorporate a humorous tone. For example, Gilpin's illustrations for Deborah Underwood's *Pirate Mom* wittily detail the misadventures of a little boy and his piratical mother. Pete is a fanatic of pirates and always wants to mimic the rogue adventurers, but his mother never wants to play along. In an attempt to distract her son from his pirate games, Pete's mother takes him to see a magician's performance. When she is chosen by the performing magician to be part of his onstage hypnosis act, Pete is thrilled when his mom is hypnotized to think that she is a pirate. When a family emergency causes the magician to suddenly abandon his act before returning Pete's mom to normal, a series of amusing mishaps ensue. According to a *Kirkus Reviews* critic, Gilpin's "appealingly cartoony illustrations suit the silly fun" of Underwood's text, while Carolyn Phelan wrote in *Booklist* that the illustrator's use of "clean lines, muted colors, and comic-style exaggeration of the characters' features," effectively bring *Pirate Mom* to life.

## Biographical and Critical Sources

*PERIODICALS*

*Booklist,* May 1, 2006, Carolyn Phelan, review of *Pirate Mom,* p. 94; June 1, 2006, Ed Sullivan, review of *The Extraordinary Adventures of Ordinary Boy: Book One, The Hero Revealed,* p. 67.

*Kirkus Reviews,* April 15, 2006, review of *Pirate Mom,* p. 418; June 1, 2006, review of *The Extraordinary Adventures of Ordinary Boy: Book One, The Hero Revealed,* p. 568.

*School Library Journal,* June, 2006, Walter Minkel, review of *The Extraordinary Adventures of Ordinary Boy: Book One, The Hero Revealed,* p. 146; September, 2006, Susan Lissim, review of *Pirate Mom,* p. 186.

*ONLINE*

*Flyingman Workshop Web site,* http://www.river3.com/ (February 17, 2007).

*Stephen Gilpin Home Page,* http://www.sgilpin.com (February 17, 2007).*

# H

## HAMILTON, Emma Walton 1962-

### Personal

Born November 27, 1962, in London, England; daughter of Julie Andrews Edwards (an actor and author) and Tony Walton (an illustrator); married Steve Hamilton; children: Sam, Hope.

### Addresses

*Office*—Bay Street Theatre, P.O. Box 810, Sag Harbor, NY 11963.

### Career

HarperCollins Publishers, New York, NY, editorial director of Julie Andrews Collection (imprint). Bay Street Theatre, Sag Harbor, NY, co-founder and director of education and programs for young audiences. Ensemble Studio Theatre Institute, New York, NY, member of faculty.

### Member

International Reading Association, Author's Guild, Society of Children's Book Writers and Illustrators, Dramatists Guild, Association of Songwriters, Composers, and Publishers.

### Writings

*WITH MOTHER, JULIE ANDREWS EDWARDS*

*Dumpy the Dump Truck,* illustrated by father, Tony Walton, Hyperion (New York, NY), 2000.
*Dumpy at School,* illustrated by Tony Walton, Hyperion (New York, NY), 2000.
*Dumpy and His Pals,* illustrated by Tony Walton, Hyperion (New York, NY), 2001.
*Dumpy Saves Christmas,* illustrated by Tony Walton, Hyperion (New York, NY), 2001.

*Dumpy's Friends on the Farm,* illustrated by Tony Walton, Hyperion (New York, NY), 2001.
*Dumpy and the Big Storm,* illustrated by Tony Walton, Hyperion (New York, NY), 2002.
*Dumpy and the Firefighters,* illustrated by Tony Walton, HarperCollins (New York, NY), 2003.
*Simeon's Gift,* illustrated by Gennady Spirin, HarperCollins (New York, NY), 2003.
*Dumpy's Happy Holiday,* illustrated by Tony Walton, HarperCollins (New York, NY), 2004.
*Dumpy's Apple Shop,* illustrated by Tony Walton and Cassandra Boyd, HarperCollins (New York, NY), 2004.
*Dumpy to the Rescue!,* illustrated by Tony Walton and Cassandra Boyd, HarperCollins (New York, NY), 2004.
*Dragon: Hound of Honor,* HarperCollins (New York, NY), 2004.
*Dumpy's Extra-Busy Day,* illustrated by Tony Walton, HarperCollins (New York, NY), 2006.
*Dumpy's Valentine,* illustrated by Tony Walton, HarperCollins (New York, NY), 2006.
*The Great American Mousical,* illustrated by Tony Walton, HarperCollins (New York, NY), 2006.
*Thanks to You: Wisdom from Mother and Child,* HarperCollins (New York, NY), 2007.

### Sidelights

Emma Walton Hamilton is the coauthor, with her mother, Julie Andrews Edwards, of children's books such as *Dumpy the Dump Truck, Simeon's Gift,* and *The Great American Mousical.* Ranging from pre-school picture-books to middle-grade readers, these titles are published through HarperCollins publishers' Julie Andrews Collection, an imprint for which Hamilton is editorial director. Discussing the mother-daughter collaboration with Sally Lodge in *Publishers Weekly,* Hamilton explained: "We want our books to embrace themes of integrity, creativity and the gifts of nature." Hamilton lives in Sag Harbor, New York, with her family.

The mother-daughter team of Hamilton and Edwards began writing picture books after being inspired by Hamilton's truck-crazy young son, Sam. When Ed-

*Emma Walton Hamilton collaborates with her mother, actress Julie Andrews Edwards, on* **Dumpy the Dump Truck,** *and the illustrations by her father, Tony Walton, make it a family affair.* (Illustration copyright © 2000 by Tony Walton. Reprinted by permission of Hyperion Books for Children.)

wards' publishers asked her if she had any story ideas that would appeal to young children, she and Hamilton came up with the idea of a story starring a dump truck, and the "Dumpy" series was born. The first title in the "Dumpy" series, *Dumpy the Dump Truck,* describes how young Charlie and his grandfather decide to fix up the old farm dump truck rather than getting rid of it. After they give Dumpy new seat coverings and a new coat of paint, the truck becomes one of the most reliable vehicles on the farm. The story "may well leave readers with the idea that some things are meant to last," wrote a *Publishers Weekly* contributor. The series continues in *Dumpy Goes to School,* as the helpful ve-

hicle contributes to the construction of a playground and also helps Charlie deal with school anxiety. In *Dumpy and the Big Storm,* after Charlie's seaside village loses power in a storm, it is up to Dumpy and other local trucks to shine their headlights out on the ocean to assist boats at sea while the lighthouse is dark. Kathy Broderick, writing in *Booklist,* noted that the traits Dumpy models include "cooperation, assisting those in need, remaining calm in an urgent situation, [and] friendship."

Along with the "Dumpy" series, Edwards and Hamilton have also written several stand-alone picture books and

middle-grade readers. *Simeon's Gift* is the tale of the minstrel Simeon who decides to prove his love to a noblewoman by traveling and learning the music of the world. Their middle-grade novel *Dragon: Hound of Honor* also uses a medieval setting, this time to retell the legend of the dog of Montargis, an heroic canine that helps to solve the murder of its master. "Readers who like their costume dramas heavily embroidered with high sentiment . . . will enjoy this fare," predicted a contributor to *Publishers Weekly*. Writing in *School Library Journal*, Anna M. Nelson deemed the tale "a well-done historical novel with an exciting mystery," while GraceAnne A. DeCandido maintained in *Booklist* that the coauthors' use of "lavish details" in *Dragon* provides readers with "a good sense of the times."

A miniature Broadway theater is the setting for *The Great American Mousical*, which finds a group of mice struggling to keep their model theater from being destroyed. Hamilton and Edwards, both veterans of the theater, infuse their text with theatrical terms and Broadway settings, while Edwards' former husband, Tony Walton, creates engaging illustrations. Kay Weisman, writing in *Booklist*, dubbed the book "an affectionate spoof of New York theater life" and predicted that the coauthors' "hilarious tale will appeal to would-be thespians everywhere." A *Publishers Weekly* critic concluded of *The Great American Mousical* that, although "the players here may be small in stature, . . . the story is big of heart."

## Biographical and Critical Sources

### PERIODICALS

*Booklist*, December 1, 2002, Kathy Broderick, review of *Dumpy and the Big Storm*, p. 673; September 1, 2004, GraceAnne A. DeCandido, review of *Dragon: Hound of Honor*, p. 120; January 1, 2006, Kay Weisman, review of *The Great American Mousical*, p. 99.
*Kirkus Reviews*, November 1, 2003, review of *Simeon's Gift*, p. 1310; February 1, 2006, review of *The Great American Mousical*, p. 130.
*Publishers Weekly*, September 25, 2000, review of *Dumpy the Dump Truck*, p. 115; July 21, 2003, Sally Lodge, "New Hats in the Ring," p. 85; October 27, 2003, review of *Simeon's Gift*, p. 68; May 31, 2004, review of *Dragon*, p. 75; January 9, 2006, review of *The Great American Mousical*, p. 54.
*School Library Journal*, April, 2001, Martha Link, review of *Dumpy the Dump Truck* and *Dumpy at School*, p. 106; November, 2003, Rosalyn Pierini, review of *Simeon's Gift*, p. 91; June, 2004, Gloria Koster, review of *Dumpy to the Rescue* and *Dumpy's Apple Shop*, p. 108; September, 2004, Anna M. Nelson, review of *Dragon*, p. 204; February, 2006, Eva Mitnick, review of *The Great American Mousical*, p. 96.

### ONLINE

*Julie Andrews Collection Web site*, http://www.julieandrewscollection.com/ (February 23, 2007).*

## HELFER, Ralph 1937-

### Personal

Born 1937, in Chicago, IL; married Toni Ringo (deceased); married Suzzi Matua (a safari guide); children: (first marriage) Tana.

### Addresses

*Home*—Newport Beach, CA; Kenya. *Office*—Eden International, P.O. Box 25971, Los Angeles, CA 90025; Eden International Safaris & Treks, P.O. Box 7101, City Square 00200, Nairobi, Kenya. *E-mail*—ralphhelfersafaris@hotmail.com.

### Career

Animal behaviorist, safari leader, and writer. Motion picture and television stuntman, 1950s; Africa USA (wild animal ranch), Soledad Canyon, CA, owner, c. 1960s-70s; Marine World Africa USA, Vallejo, CA, owner; Enchanted Village (theme park), Buena Park, CA, owner, c. 1970s; Gentle Jungle (wild animal training company), founder and director, 1980s; Eden International (safari company), Los Angeles, CA, founder and director. Supplied wild animals for motion pictures, including *The Island of Dr. Moreau*, *Quest for Fire*, and *Clarence, the Cross-eyed Lion*, and for television shows, including *Gentle Ben*, *Daktari*, and *Star Trek*.

### Awards, Honors

Eighteen PATSY Awards for work with animals.

### Writings

#### NONFICTION

*The Beauty of the Beasts: Tales of Hollywood's Wild Animal Stars*, J.P. Tarcher (Los Angeles, CA), 1990.
*Modoc: The True Story of the Greatest Elephant That Ever Lived*, HarperCollins (New York, NY), 1997.
*Mosey: The Remarkable Friendship of a Boy and His Elephant*, Orchard (New York, NY), 2002.
*Zamba: The True Story of the Greatest Lion That Ever Lived*, HarperCollins (New York, NY), 2005.
*The World's Greatest Elephant* (picture book), illustrated by Ted Lewin, Philomel (New York, NY), 2006.

### Adaptations

*Savage Harvest*, based on a story by Ralph Helfer and Ken Noyle, was produced as a film, 1981; *Modoc: The True Story of the Greatest Elephant That Ever Lived* was optioned for film by Tig Productions.

### Sidelights

Ralph Helfer is a legendary Hollywood animal trainer and behaviorist who developed "affection training," a method that uses respect and kindness to develop strong

bonds between humans and wild animals. During his career, Helfer worked with numerous animal celebrities, including Clarence the Cross-eyed Lion and Judy the Chimp.

Helfer published his first book, *The Beauty of the Beasts: Tales of Hollywood's Wild Animal Stars,* in 1990. In the work, he recounts his experiences working with a variety of animals, including C.J., an orangutan, and Gentle Ben, a black bear. Genevieve Stuttaford, writing in *Publishers Weekly,* stated that "animal lovers will be charmed and entertained by Helfer's menagerie."

*Modoc: The True Story of the Greatest Elephant That Ever Lived* is actually two biographies in one, as Helfer tells the story of a circus elephant as well as her inseparable human companion. Bram Gunterstein, whose father was an animal trainer for a German circus, was born in 1896, the same night that Modoc was born on the Guntersteins' farm. The pair grew up together, and when the circus was sold to an American circus owner, Bram stowed away aboard the ship that would carry the elephant to the United States. A typhoon sank the ship in the Bay of Bengal, and Bram and Modoc were among the only survivors. The duo traveled through India until they were eventually found by the circus owner, who assigned Bram to act as Modoc's trainer in America. After a period of great success with the Ringling Brothers circus, Modoc was sold without Bram's knowledge and vanished for nearly two decades. A production company owned by Helfer eventually found the elephant living on a farm in the Ozarks and reunited her with Bram. According to a reviewer in *Publishers Weekly,* "sentimentalists and animal lovers should flock to this story," and *Booklist* contributor Nancy Bent deemed *Modoc* "a truly fascinating book."

Helfer revisits the tale of Modoc in two more-recent works, *Mosey: The Remarkable Friendship of a Boy and His Elephant* and the picture book *The World's Greatest Elephant.* Written for a young-adult audience, *Mosey* was described as "an unusual but engaging combination of adventure-survival story and boy-and-his-pet tale" by *Booklist* contributor Chris Sherman. In *The World's Greatest Elephant,* Helfer recounts the remarkable story of Bram and Modoc for young readers. "Helfer's impeccable pacing keeps the suspense high as he builds the emotional connection between his two heroes—one human, one animal," noted a critic in *Publishers Weekly.* Several reviewers, including *Booklist* critic Hazel Rochman, offered particular praise for the dramatic illustrations by Ted Lewin. "His gorgeous, watercolor double-page spreads show the . . . rescue drama, but even more stunning are the depictions of the bond between the lifelong friends," Rochman stated. According to *School Library Journal* contributor Margaret Bush, Helfer's "bold and heartwarming adventure tale should have wide appeal."

Helfer chronicles his eighteen-year relationship with a gentle giant in *Zamba: The True Story of the Greatest*

*Animal behaviorist Ralph Helfer shares his experiences with younger readers through* **The World's Greatest Elephant,** *a picture book illustrated by Ted Lewin.* (Illustration copyright © 2006 by Ted Lewin. Reproduced by permission of Philomel Books, a division of Penguin Putnam Books for Young Readers.)

*Lion That Ever Lived.* In the work, the animal behaviorist describes his efforts to turn an orphaned lion cub into a top Hollywood attraction using the revolutionary principles of "affection training." According to Judy McAloon, writing in *School Library Journal,* "the many stories, both humorous and touching, make this a fascinating book." Helfer "beautifully expresses a simple philosophy so many have trouble following: respect for all living creatures, given and returned," noted an appreciative critic in *Kirkus Reviews.*

## Biographical and Critical Sources

*BOOKS*

Helfer, Toni Ringo, *The Gentle Jungle,* Brigham Young University Press (Provo, UT), 1980.

*PERIODICALS*

*Booklist,* September 15, 1997, Nancy Bent, review of *Modoc: The True Story of the Greatest Elephant That Ever Lived,* p. 196; July, 2002, Chris Sherman, review of *Mosey: The Remarkable Friendship of a Boy and His Elephant,* p. 1840; July, 2005, Nancy Bent, re-

view of *Zamba: The True Story of the Greatest Lion That Ever Lived,* p. 1884; February 1, 2006, Hazel Rochman, review of *The World's Greatest Elephant,* p. 48.

*Bulletin of the Center for Children's Books,* April, 2006, Elizabeth Bush, review of *The World's Greatest Elephant,* p. 356.

*Childhood Education,* fall, 2002, Irene A. Allen, review of *Mosey,* p. 50.

*Kirkus Reviews,* May 15, 2005, review of *Zamba,* p. 575; February 1, 2006, review of *The World's Greatest Elephant,* p. 1323.

*Library Journal,* July 1, 2005, Ann Forister, review of *Zamba,* p. 117.

*People,* August 8, 2005, Lisa Kay Greissinger, review of *Zamba,* p. 46.

*Publishers Weekly,* March 9, 1990, review of *The Beauty of the Beasts: Tales of Hollywood's Wild Animal Stars,* p. 56; August 4, 1997, Paul Nathan, "If You Like Androcles," p. 36; September 1, 1997, review of *Modoc,* p. 90; June 13, 2005, review of *Zamba,* p. 46; April 10, 2006, review of *The World's Greatest Elephant,* p. 71.

*School Library Journal,* July, 2002, Vicki Reutter, review of *Mosey,* p. 136; January, 2006, Judy McAloon, review of *Zamba,* p. 174; February, 2006, Margaret Bush, review of *The World's Greatest Elephant,* p. 120.

*Voice of Youth Advocates,* December, 1998, review of *Modoc,* p. 380; August, 2002, review of *Mosey,* p. 192.

ONLINE

*Eden International Safaris & Treks Web site,* http://www.edeninternationalsafaris.net/ (January 25, 2007).

*Talking Animals Web site,* http://www.talkinganimals.net/ (January 20, 2007), Duncan Strauss, "African Safari: Kenya Imagine Seeing So Many Animals—and So Close?"*

\*          \*          \*

# HEPLER, Heather

## Personal

Children: one son. *Education:* University of North Texas (M.L.I.S.).

## Addresses

*Home*—TX. *E-mail*—brad-heather@hotmail.com.

## Career

Novelist, reviewer, and other of short fiction. Instructor in writing on the college level; yoga teacher.

## Awards, Honors

(With Brad Barkley) Teddy Award for middle-grade/young-adult fiction, Writers' League of Texas, 2006, for *Scrambled Eggs at Midnight.*

## Writings

YOUNG-ADULT NOVELS

(With Brad Barkley) *Scrambled Eggs at Midnight,* Dutton (New York, NY), 2006.

(With Brad Barkley) *Dream Factory,* Dutton Children's Books (New York, NY), 2007.

Contributor of reviews to periodicals, including *Voice of Youth Advocates, Kirkus Reviews, Publishers Weekly, Booklist,* and *New York Times Book Review.* Contributor of short fiction to *Southwest Review.*

## Sidelights

Heather Hepler shares the literary limelight with fellow author Brad Barkley as coauthor of the young-adult novels *Scrambled Eggs at Midnight* and *Dream Factory.* In addition to fiction-writing, the Texas-based writer also works as a book reviewer for several major periodicals, including the *New York Times Book Review,* and she teaches writing courses on the college level.

Hepler met Barkley, a fellow writer and writing instructor, while attending a writing workshop Barkley was teaching. As Barkley recalled to Cynthia Leitich Smith on *Cynsations* online, "Mostly it started as a kind of game . . . novel ping-pong, I guess, just bouncing the chapters back and forth." The novel started in Hepler's court, inspired by a road trip to her sister's home in Austin, Texas. "After writing about half of the first chapter . . . I called Brad and asked if he would help me a bit," she explained in the same interview. "I mean, a novel is a lot to take in. We started talking, and somehow the idea of co-writing was brought up. It started out as an experiment of sorts . . . just a game to keep both of us writing. It wasn't until we got about halfway in that we realized that we might just have a book. We actually finished writing it in six weeks. We ended up selling it to Dutton about a month after that."

In *Scrambled Eggs at Midnight* Hepler and Barkley introduce readers to fifteen-year-old Calliope—nicknamed Cal—who is frustrated by the peripatetic life dictated by her hippy mom's passion for Renaissance faires. Currently living in a tent pitched in Asheville, North Carolina, while her mom sells handmade jewelry and performs a costumed role at a faire, Cal meets up with Elliot, a local Ashville teen, at a local bookstore. Elliot has had a similarly unconventional upbringing due to his born-again Christian father's evangelical tendencies and his decision to open a summer camp for overweight Christian children. Although his day-to-day life is more stable, Elliot realizes that the romance that quickly develops between him and Cal will either grow or be quashed based on his father's unpredictable dictum. As the relationship grows stronger, Cal's mother grows restless and Elliot's dad waxes disapproving. Fortunately, other forces at work may help grant Cal her

*Cover of* Scrambled Eggs at Midnight, *a collaborative work of fiction by Brad Barkley and Heather Hepler.* (Clock image © George Diebold/Solus Images/Veer; Egg image © Minorku Kida/Photonica/Getty Images. Reproduced by permission of Dutton Books, a division of Penguin Putnam Books for Young Readers.)

wish: to stay near Elliot and also remain in Asheville where she can enjoy the day-to-day sameness of a typical American life.

Dubbing *Scrambled Eggs at Midnight* a "tender, quirky romance," a *Publishers Weekly* contributor went on to note that, despite the somewhat idealized storyline, "the intensity of the . . . emotions" of both Cal and Elliot seem "authentic." In *Booklist* Gillian Engberg praised Hepler and Barkley's use of alternating chapters, writing that, as "narrated in Cal and Elliot's hilarious, heart-tugging voices," their "potentially routine summer romance" is transformed "into a refreshing, poetic, memorable" tale. "YAs who enjoy love stories that are more than entertaining fluff will appreciate" *Scrambled Eggs at Midnight,* noted Claire Rosser in *Kliatt,* the critic adding that the coauthors imbue their fiction with a "sense of place in the mountains of North Carolina" that makes the region "vividly real." In *Kirkus Reviews,* a critic concluded that *Scrambled Eggs at Midnight* rewards teens with "better writing than that offered in most teen romances."

Discussing the inspiration for *Scrambled Eggs at Midnight,* Hepler noted on her home page: "I wanted to write a smart book about falling in love and by smart I don't mean 'thinky.' I mean a book that explores what love can be like when you just let yourself fall. When you just forget about getting hurt or being cool or acting aloof. When you stop trying to figure it all out in your head and you just let your heart take over and lead you. I wanted to write the book that I wanted to read when I was in junior high and high school."

## Biographical and Critical Sources

*PERIODICALS*

*Booklist,* June 1, 2006, Gillian Engberg, review of *Scrambled Eggs at Midnight,* p. 56.
*Bulletin of the Center for Children's Books,* June, 2006, review of *Scrambled Eggs at Midnight,* p. 439.
*Kirkus Reviews,* May 1, 2006, review of *Scrambled Eggs at Midnight,* p. 453.
*Kliatt,* May, 2006, Claire Rosser, review of *Scrambled Eggs at Midnight,* p. 347.
*Publishers Weekly,* June 19, 2006, review of *Scrambled Eggs at Midnight,* p. 64.

*ONLINE*

*Cynsations Web site,* http://cynthialeitichsmith.blogspot.com. (April 26, 2006), Cynthia Leitich Smith, interview with Hepler and Brad Barkley.
*Heather Hepler and Brad Barkley Home Page,* http://www.bradheather.com (March 15, 2007).*

\*            \*            \*

## HOBBS, Will 1947-
## (William Carl Hobbs)

### Personal

Born August 22, 1947, in Pittsburgh, PA; son of Gregory J. and Mary Hobbs; married Jean Loftus (a former teacher and literary agent), December 20, 1972. *Education:* Stanford University, B.A., 1969, M.A., 1971. *Hobbies and other interests:* Hiking in the mountains and canyons, white water rafting, archaeology, natural history.

### Addresses

*Home*—Durango, CO.

### Career

Educator and author of children's books. Pagosa Springs, CO, and Durango, CO, public schools, taught middle school and high school reading and English, 1973-89; writer, 1990—.

***Will Hobbs, hiking in the San Juan Mountains.*** (Reproduced by permission.)

## Member

Authors Guild, Phi Beta Kappa.

## Awards, Honors

Notable Trade Book in the Field of Social Studies designation, National Council for the Social Studies/Children's Book Council (NCSS/CBC), 1988, and Colorado Blue Spruce Young Adult Book Award, 1992, both for *Changes in Latitudes;* NCSS/CBC Notable Trade Book in the Field of Social Studies designation, 1989, Best Books for Young Adults designation, American Library Association (ALA), 1989, and Teachers' Choice citation, International Reading Association (IRA), and Regional Book Award, Mountains and Plains Booksellers Association, both 1990, all for *Bearstone;* Pick of the Lists choice, American Booksellers Association (ABA), 1991, ALA Best Books for Young Adults and Best Books for Reluctant Young-Adult Readers citations, 1992, included among ALA 100 Best Young-Adult Books of the Past Twenty-five Years, 1994, and California Young Readers Medal, 1995, all for *Downriver;* ALA Best Books for Young Adults designation, 1993, for *The Big Wander;* ABA Pick of the Lists choice and ALA Best Books for Young Adults designation, both 1993, and Spur Award, Western Writers of America, and Colorado Book Award, all for *Beardance;* NCSS/CBC Notable Trade Book in the Field of Social Studies designation, 1995, for *Kokopelli's Flute;* ALA Top-Ten Best Books for Young Adults choice and Quick Picks for Reluctant Young-Adult Readers choice, and NCSS/CBC Notable Trade Book in the Field of Social Studies designation, all 1996, Spur Award, and Colorado Book Award, all for *Far North;* ABA Pick of the Lists choice, 1997, and Edgar Allan Poe Award, Mystery Writers of America, 1998, both for *Ghost Canoe;* ABA Pick of the Lists designation, 1997, and Colorado Center for the Book Award, 1998, both for *Beardream;* IRA Young-Adult Choice selection, 1998, for *River Thunder;* ALA Best Books for Young Adults and Quick Picks for Reluctant Young Adult Readers designations, ABA Pick of the Lists choice, and IRA Teachers' Choice selection, all 1998, all for *The Maze;* ALA Best Books for Young Adults and Quick Picks for Reluctant

Young Adult Readers selections, ABA Pick of the Lists choice, and NCSS/CBC Notable Children's Trade Book in the Field of Social Studies designation, all 1999, all for *Jason's Gold;* National Science Teachers Association (NSTA) Outstanding Science Trade Book for Students designation and Children's Literature Young-Adult Choice designation, both 2003, both for *Wild Man Island;* NSTA Outstanding Science Trade Book for Students designation, 2004, for *Jackie's Wild Seattle;* IRA Notable Books for a Global Society designation and Southwest Book Award, both 2007, both for *Crossing the Wire;* nominations for numerous state readers' choice awards.

## Writings

*YOUNG-ADULT NOVELS*

*Changes in Latitudes,* Atheneum (New York, NY), 1988.
*Bearstone,* Atheneum (New York, NY), 1989.
*Downriver,* Atheneum (New York, NY), 1991.
*The Big Wander,* Atheneum (New York, NY), 1992.
*Beardance,* Atheneum (New York, NY), 1993.
*Kokopelli's Flute,* Simon & Schuster (New York, NY), 1995.
*Far North,* Morrow (New York, NY), 1996.
*Ghost Canoe,* Morrow (New York, NY), 1997.
*River Thunder,* Delacorte (New York, NY), 1997.
*The Maze,* Morrow (New York, NY), 1998.
*Jason's Gold,* Morrow (New York, NY), 1999.
*Down the Yukon,* HarperCollins (New York, NY), 2001.
*Wild Man Island,* HarperCollins (New York, NY), 2002.
*Jackie's Wild Seattle,* HarperCollins (New York, NY), 2003.
*Leaving Protection,* HarperCollins (New York, NY), 2004.
*Crossing the Wire,* HarperCollins (New York, NY), 2006.
*Go Big or Go Home,* HarperCollins (New York, NY), 2008.

Contributor of articles to periodicals, including *Horn Book, ALAN Review, Journal of Youth Services in Libraries, Journal of Adolescent and Adult Literacy, Book Links, Signal, Voices from the Middle, Voice of Youth Advocates,* and numerous state journals.

*PICTURE BOOKS*

*Beardream,* illustrated by Jill Kastner, Simon & Schuster (New York, NY), 1997.
*Howling Hill,* illustrated by Jill Kastner, Morrow (New York, NY), 1998.

## Adaptations

Hobbs's novels have been adapted for audiocassette by Recorded Books, Bantam Doubleday Dell Audio, and Listening Library. *Bearstone* was adapted as a play by

Karen Glenn, published in *Scholastic Scope,* January 14, 1994. *Jason's Gold* and *Down the Yukon* were adapted as plays published in *READ* magazine.

## Sidelights

The wilderness-based novels of author Will Hobbs, which include *Bearstone, Kokopelli's Flute, Far North,* and *Down the Yukon* have been well received by both his young-adult fans and reviewers. A large part of Hobbs's success as a writer is due to the fact that he knows what his audience—predominately middle-school and high school boys—likes. A former English teacher, Hobbs noted in the *Colorado Reading Council Journal* that "if kids come to care about and identify with the characters in stories, they will also learn more about and ultimately care more about preserving the treasures of our natural world." Since his first novel appeared in 1988, Hobbs has seen his readership grow, with the result that almost all of his books have remained in print due to the demands of each new generation of fans.

Born in Pittsburgh, Pennsylvania, Hobbs and his family moved to the Panama Canal Zone when the future author was less than a year old. His father's Air Force career was behind several family moves, including stints in Virginia, Alaska, California, and Texas. Having siblings made the moves easier because all four of the Hobbs children were involved in scouting and had a love of the out-of-doors inspired by their parents.

Although Hobbs hiked and backpacked in many regions, it was the Southwest that most captured his imagination, and he spent several summers during high school and college as a guide and camp director at New Mexico's Philmont Scout Ranch. In 1973, after graduating from Stanford University, he and his wife Jean moved to a remote area of southwestern Colorado, near the San Juan Mountains and the Weminuche Wilderness, and now looks out from his writing desk at snow-capped mountain peaks.

In beginning his writing career in his early thirties, Hobbs was inspired by his local surroundings, and his first novel, *Bearstone,* is set in the Weminuche Wilderness near the Hobbs family's Colorado home. Published after eight years' worth of work, *Bearstone* focuses on Cloyd, a Ute Indian boy who has been sent by his tribe in Utah to spend the summer with an old rancher named Walter. Angry and hostile, Cloyd distrusts the old man's affection. While exploring the mountains near Walter's ranch, Cloyd discovers a Native American burial site and a small bearstone. Inspired by his discovery, the boy renames himself Lone Bear and learns how to "live in a good way," as his grandmother has taught him. An incident concerning a hunter who illegally kills a grizzly bear forces Cloyd to decide between revealing the truth and getting revenge or keeping silent. Cloyd's story continues in *Beardance,* as he rides into the mountains with Walter in search of a lost gold mine. Then they hear that a mother grizzly has been sighted with her three cubs. While searching for the cubs, Cloyd meets a wildlife biologist with the same goal; after the mother bear is reported killed, the boy risks his life in an effort to save the orphaned grizzly cubs and remains alone in the mountains despite winter's approach.

In praising *Bearstone,* *School Library Journal* contributor George Gleason described Hobbs's first novel as "far above other coming-of-age stories." Hobbs's young protagonist's "first experiences with spirit dreams are particularly well done," wrote *Horn Book* critic Elizabeth S. Watson in a review of *Beardance,* while Merlyn Miller observed in the *Voice of Youth Advocates* that the novel "weaves Native American legends with real adventure. Not only is Cloyd connected with his ancestry," Miller added, "but he's focused with courage, determination, and strength."

The main characters in *Beardance* and *Bearstone* return in Hobbs's first picture book, *Beardream.* Illustrated by Jill Kastner, *Beardream* describes how a boy called Short Tail awakens an oversleeping grizzly bear from hibernation, and how, in ancient times, the Ute people learned the bear dance from the bears. In an author's note at the end of *Beardream,* Hobbs stated: "It is my belief that future generations of the human family will have greater and greater need for the inspiration of native wisdom, which sees humankind not apart from nature, but as a part of nature." In the *Journal of Adolescent and Adult Literacy,* a critic recommended that the picture book be read aloud in order that the listener may "experience the beautiful . . . language that is a hallmark of Hobbs's work."

Hobbs's second novel—and the first of his books to see print—*Changes in Latitudes* was inspired by a photograph Hobbs saw in *National Geographic* that depicted a sea turtle swimming underwater. Curious as to what it would be like to swim with the turtles, Hobbs developed a story in which imaginative readers can take that swim with the turtles while also gaining compassion for endangered species. In the novel, sixteen-year-old Travis is the oldest of three siblings. Cynical and self-absorbed, he tries to hide from his problems by withdrawing into his own "cool" world. Vacationing in Mexico with their mother, the teen and his younger brother, Teddy, learn about the plight of the region's sea turtles. When Teddy dies attempting to rescue some turtles, Travis learns to deal with adversity and discovers that strength is gained by overcoming, rather than running away, from setbacks. Nancy Vasilakis, writing in *Horn Book,* wrote that, in *Changes in Latitudes,* Hobbs "neatly balances the perilous situation of these ancient lumbering sea creatures against the breakdown of [Travis's] . . . family." The critic also commended the author for his "sensitive ear for the language of the young."

Having rowed his own whitewater raft through the rapids of the Grand Canyon ten times, Hobbs is familiar with the dangers and the beauty of the journey, and he shares this with readers in *Downriver.* Narrated by

*Cover of Hobbs's novel* **Downriver,** *featuring a cover illustration by Robert McGinnis.* (Cover art copyright © 1992 by Robert McGinnis. Used by permission of Random House Children's Books, a division of Random House, Inc.)

Jessie, a fifteen-year-old girl who has been sent away from home, the novel follows seven teens on a raft trip down the Grand Canyon. Jessie and the rest of the group—known as the "Hoods in the Woods"—leave their leader behind and take off on their own, making their own decisions and coping with the consequences. *Downriver* "is exquisitely plotted, with nail-biting suspense and excitement," wrote George Gleason in a review for *School Library Journal,* while in *Booklist* Candace Smith commended the book's rafting scenes. "The scenery description is beautiful and the kids are believable," concluded Mary Ojibway in her enthusiastic review of *Downriver* for *Voice of Youth Advocates.*

Returning in *River Thunder,* Jessie gets the chance to row through the Grand Canyon by herself. Unexpectedly high water on the Colorado forces Jessie and the rest of the Hoods in the Woods gang to confront their fears when raging rapids threaten. Deborah Stevenson, reviewing *River Thunder* for the *Bulletin of the Center for Children's Books,* described the novel's adventure

sequences as "terrific and involving," while in *School Library Journal* Joel Shoemaker wrote that Hobbs's "descriptions deliver high-volume excitement sure to entice many readers."

Although he has experienced first-hand many of the adventures he writes about in his young-adult novels, Hobbs's descriptions of hang gliding in *The Maze* are based on time spent with friends who fly, watching them jump off cliffs and soar. Hobbs sets his story in the Maze, a remote region of Canyonlands National Park in Utah, an area noted for its beauty. Like Icarus, young protagonist Rick Walker attempts to fly out of his own personal labyrinth, a life of foster homes and dead ends. "Rick is a richly-textured character," noted Sarah K. Herz in her *Voice of Youth Advocates* review of the novel. Todd Morning, writing in *School Library Journal,* asserted that "what sets this book apart is the inclusion of fascinating details about the condors and hang gliding, especially the action-packed description of Rick's first solo flight above the canyons." "Hobbs spins an engrossing yarn, blending adventure with a strong theme," wrote *Horn Book* writer Mary M. Burns, and Morning deemed *The Maze* "an adventure story [readers] . . . can't put down."

A sea-kayaking trip in southeast Alaska with his wife inspired the setting for Hobbs's novel *Wild Man Island.* As readers meet fourteen-year-old Andy Galloway, the book's narrator, Andy has come to the end of an enjoyable guided sea-kayaking vacation. Now, while preparing to return home, he takes his kayak and decides to make a quick, two-mile trip to Hidden Falls, the place where his archaeologist dad accidentally met his death years before. When a freak storm arises, Andy and his craft are washed ashore on a wild, remote island. Hunger, cold, and roaming grizzly bears threaten the teen's life until a Newfoundland dog befriends him and leads Andy to a cave that turns out to be the home of a strange, man that seems to be a Neolithic holdover but ultimately reveals his true history. "Hobbs resolves the story's complexities in ways that protect the characters' integrity," commented Joel Shoemaker in *School Library Journal,* while in the *Journal of Adolescent and Adult Literacy* James Blasingame wrote that the novel's "conflicts are resolved in a satisfying conclusion." *Wild Man Island* features the "short, pithy chapters" guaranteed to "attract readers, reluctant and otherwise," according to Burns, and in *Kirkus Reviews* a critic commended the novel as "a rugged, satisfying episode for outdoorsy readers."

*Jackie's Wild Seattle* takes its name from a wildlife rehabilitation center in Seattle, Washington, where fourteen-year-old Shannon and little brother Cody come to spend their summer vacation. During their stay, the siblings become involved in their Uncle Neal's work with animals, and after Neil is injured, quickly learn how to work with the injured and orphaned coyotes, bear cubs, raccoons, and birds of prey they find in the city. Commenting on Hobbs's back story—Cody is still

haunted by the fall of Manhattan's Twin Towers, which he witnessed from a cliff near his New Jersey home, a *Kirkus Reviews* writer deemed the novel an "absorbing story about animal rehabilitation, the state of the world, fear, achievement, and trust." Writing that "this exciting, poignant, and beautifully developed story covers a crucial few weeks for several people whose lives intertwine to change and benefit all," Mary R. Hoffman added in her *School Library Journal* review that *Jackie's Wild Seattle* "will reach deep into the hearts of young readers."

A meeting with a teacher from Craig a town on Prince of Wales Island, Alaska, inspired Hobbs's novel *Leaving Protection.* The teacher, who had earned her way through college working on her father's fishing boat, now invited the popular novelist to work on her family's boat, and write a novel about life on a salmon trawler. In the novel, when sixteen-year-old Robbie Daniels leaves his home in Port Protection for the nearby fishing town of Craig, he hopes to find work as a deck hand on a commercial fishing boat during king salmon season. Therefore, the teen can hardly believe his good fortune when legendary fisherman Tor Torsen hires him on. Out on the open ocean, alone with Tor, Robbie discovers the reason for his seeming good luck: his mysterious captain is not only fishing, he is searching along the coastline for the historic metal plaques that were buried by early Russian explorers laying claim to Alaska. After Robbie learns how valuable these possession plaques are, Tor's wrath and a violent storm at sea put his courage and wit to the ultimate test. *Leaving Protection* is a "nautical thriller [that] brims with detail about the fishing life," wrote a *Publishers Weekly* contributor, adding that the novel's "climactic finale involving a dramatic and fateful storm at sea [is] grippingly rendered." Reviewing Hobbs's book for *School Library Journal,* Jeffrey Hastings praised *Leaving Protection* as "straightforward outdoor fiction laced with bracing action and heady suspense."

A timely novel that focuses on the problem of illegal immigration in America, *Crossing the Wire* introduces readers to fifteen-year-old Victor Flores, a Mexican teen who, since his father's tragic death, has become the main breadwinner to his mother and four younger siblings. Unable to support his family through farming, Victor attempts the dangerous trip north across the border, encountering fast-moving trains, mountain and desert crossings, drug smugglers, border guards, and unscrupulous men hoping to take advantage of the teen's desperation. In *Kirkus Reviews* a critic wrote that "Hobbs has created a pageturning adventure set squarely in the real world," adding that the novelist "offers no easy answers." In an author's note, Hobbs wrote that he wrote *Crossing the Wire* to "put a human face" to the quandary of the Mexicans risking all to find a better life in America. Noting that the novel is "gritty and realistic," Paula Rohrlick concluded in her *Kliatt* review that, whatever their personal opinions regarding the immi-

gration question, readers "will . . . appreciate Victor's desperation, determination, and courage."

Hobbs weaves elements of fantasy into his characteristic Western setting in *Kokopelli's Flute.* Thirteen-year-old Tepary Jones and his dog, Dusty, journey to the ruins of an ancient Anasazi cliff house overlooking the canyons near the boy's home on a seed farm in New Mexico. Hoping to see a total eclipse of the full moon from this remote location, Tep soon realizes that he is not alone when he surprises looters searching for Anasazi artifacts. Picking up an ancient Anasazi flute made of eagle bone that the looters had dropped in their hurry to escape, the teen is pulled into the grip of an ancient magic which transforms him each night into a bushy-tailed woodrat. With the help of Dusty, Tep is able to track down the looters and also obtains the medicinal herbs needed to save his mother from a deadly sickness. Hobbs "blends fantasy with fact so smoothly that the resulting mix can be consumed without question," wrote Darcy Schild in a *School Library Journal* review of the popular novel, while in *Voice of Youth Advocates* Nancy Zachary called *Kokopelli's Flute* "an engaging and delightful tale."

In *Far North* Hobbs leads readers up into the rugged wilderness of Canada's Northwest Territories. Gabe Rogers, almost sixteen years old and fresh from Texas, enrolls in a boarding school in Yellowknife in order to be closer to his father, who works on nearby diamond exploration rigs. Gabe's roommate, Raymond Providence, a native teen from a remote Dene village, decides to quit school after only a few months, and on a flight home in a small bush plane both Raymond and Gabe end up stranded on the banks of the Nahanni River. The boys' winter survival story was described by *Horn Book* contributor Mary M. Burns as "a thrill-a-minute account" of a battle "against seemingly impossible odds." According to Burns, *Far North* "is not just another page-turner; there are deeper issues addressed," such as the differences between the two boys' cultures. Calling the novel a "classic Hobbs adventure," Diane Tuccillo wrote in *Voice of Youth Advocates* that in *Far North* "characters are well-drawn, and excitement and energy penetrate their entire trek."

Hobbs ventures into mystery with *Ghost Canoe,* winner of an Edgar Allan Poe award for best young-adult mystery. Set in 1874, along the storm-tossed coast of Washington's Olympic Peninsula, this story follows fourteen-year-old Nathan MacAllister, the son of a lighthouse keeper. When a mysterious shipwreck leaves behind a set of unexplained footprints on the shore, Nathan suspects something is amiss. Writing in *School Library Journal,* Gerry Larson called *Ghost Canoe* "a winning tale that artfully combines history, nature, and suspense." In the *Bulletin of the Center for Children's Books,* Elizabeth Bush noted that although the book's mystery is predictable, there is enough action "to keep the pages flipping."

Also set in the past—this time amid the Klondike gold rush of 1897-98—*Jason's Gold* follows Jason Hawthorn as he races to catch up to his older brothers who have taken off for the gold fields in Canada's Yukon. Along the way he meets a not-yet-famous Jack London, the author of *White Fang,* and develops a romantic relationship with traveling performer Jamie Dunavant. Mostly he travels alone, with King, a husky he rescues from a madman. In *Jason's Gold* Hobbs creates an action-packed adventure story filled with vivid descriptions of bone-chilling cold, personal courage, and friendship, and he continues Jason's saga in *Down the Yukon.* As the book begins, Jason's brother Ethan loses the family sawmill business to Cornelius Donner in a poker game. Now sixteen years old, Jason is determined to regain the sawmill. Together with Ethan and girlfriend Jamie, he decides to compete in a canoe race to Nome in which the winner will receive 20,000 dollars in prize money. Unfortunately, ne'er-do-well Donner, who swindled the business from Ethan, has also entered the race; now he and his henchmen manage to sabotage the brothers' canoe. "The ending, though predictable, features an appropriate twist," remarked *Booklist* critic Catherine Andronik in her review of *Down the Yukon,* while *School Library Journal* reviewer Vicki Reutter deemed the novel "more exciting than its predecessor."

Commenting on his decision to write for a teen audience, Hobbs noted on his home page: "My first hope for my novels is that they tell a good story, that the reader will keep turning the pages and will hate to see the story end. Beyond that, I hope to be inspiring a love for the natural world. I'd like my readers to appreciate and to care more about what's happening to wild creatures, wild places, and the diversity of life."

## Biographical and Critical Sources

### BOOKS

*Encyclopedia of Children's Literature,* Continuum (New York, NY), 2001.

Gallo, Donald R., editor, *Speaking for Ourselves Too,* National Council of Teachers of English, 1993.

Hobbs, Will, *Beardream,* Simon & Schuster (New York, NY), 1997.

Hobbs, Will, *Ghost Canoe,* Morrow (New York, NY), 1997.

*Writers for Young Adults,* edited by Ted Hipple, Scribner (New York, NY), 1997, pp. 121-129.

### PERIODICALS

*ALAN Review,* fall, 1994.

*Booklist,* March 1, 1991, Candace Smith, review of *Downriver,* p. 1377; October 15, 1992, p. 424; May 1, 1997; September 1, 1997, p. 106; September 1, 1998, p.

126; February 15, 2000, Jeanette Larson, review of *Ghost Canoe* (audiobook), p. 1128; March 15, 2000, review of *Jason's Gold,* p. 1340; April 1, 2001, Catherine Andronik, review of *Down the Yukon,* p. 1482; November 15, 2001, Anna Rich, review of *Down the Yukon,* p. 589; April 15, 2002, review of *Wild Man Island,* p. 1395; June 1, 2003, Traci Todd, review of *Jackie's Wild Seattle,* p. 1776; May 1, 2006, Jennifer Mattson, review of *Crossing the Wire,* p. 83.

*Bulletin of the Center for Children's Books,* April, 1997, Elizabeth Bush, review of *Ghost Canoe,* p. 285; July, 1997, Deborah Stevenson, review of *River Thunder,* pp. 397-398; May, 2003, review of *Jackie's Wild Seattle,* p. 363; July-August, 2006, Maggie Hommel, review of *Crossing the Wire,* p. 500.

*California Reader,* winter, 1992, pp. 15-16.

*Colorado Reading Council Journal,* spring, 1993, pp. 7-9.

*Five Owls,* fall, 2001, review of *Kokopelli's Flute, The Maze, Downriver,* and *Beardance,* p. 2.

*Horn Book,* May-June, 1988, p. 358; January-February, 1993, p. 91; January-February, 1994, Elizabeth S. Watson, review of *Beardance,* p. 70; March-April, 1996; November-December, 1996, p. 745; September-October, 1998, Mary M. Burns, review of *The Maze,* p. 609; July-August, 2002, Mary M. Burns, review of *Wild Man Island,* p. 462.

*Journal of Adolescent and Adult Literacy,* September, 1997, review of *Beardream,* p. 83; May, 2000, Joel Taxel, review of *The Maze,* pp. 780-781; February, 2003, James Blasingame, review of *Wild Man Island,* pp. 442-443.

*Journal of Youth Services in Libraries,* spring, 1995.

*Kirkus Reviews,* March 15, 1997, p. 462; March 15, 2002, review of *Wild Man Island,* p. 413; March 15, 2003, review of *Jackie's Wild Seattle,* p. 468; March 15, 2004, review of *Leaving Protection,* p. 270; March 1, 2006, review of *Crossing the Wire,* p. 154.

*Kliatt,* September, 1999, p. 8; March, 2002, Claire Rosser, review of *Wild Man Island,* p. 11; July, 2002, Michele Winship, review of *Down the Yukon,* p. 20; March, 2003, Claire Rosser, review of *Jackie's Wild Seattle,* p. 12; May, 2003, Claire Rosser, review of *Wild Man Island,* p. 235; March, 2004, Paula Rohrlick review of *Leaving Protection,* p. 25; July, 2004, Myrna Marler, review of *Far North,* p. 192; March, 2006, Paula Rohrlick, review of *Crossing the Wire,* p. 12.

*Publishers Weekly,* February 12, 1988, p. 88; February 1, 1991, pp. 80-81; November 2, 1992, p. 72; October 12, 1998, review of *Howling Hill,* p. 77; April 12, 2004, review of *Leaving Protection,* p. 67.

*School Library Journal,* March, 1988, pp. 212, 214; September, 1989, p. 272; March, 1991, George Gleason, review of *Downriver,* p. 212; November, 1992, p. 92; December, 1993, p. 134; October, 1995, p. 134; April, 1997, Leda Schubert, review of *Beardream,* p. 104; September, 1997, Joel Shoemaker, review of *River Thunder,* p. 217; October 1998, Virginia Golodetz, review of *Howling Hill,* p. 102; May, 2001, Vicki Reutter, review of *Down the Yukon,* p. 150; May, 2002, Joel Shoemaker, review of *Wild Man Island,* p. 154; May, 2003, Mary R. Hofmann, review of *Jackie's Wild Seattle,* p. 153; April, 2004, Jeffrey Hastings, re-

view of *Leaving Protection*, p. 156; December, 2006, Larry Cooperman, review of *Crossing the Wire*, p. 70.
*Voice of Youth Advocates*, August, 1991, Mary Ojibway, review of *Downriver*, pp. 171-172; December, 1992, p. 279; December, 1993, p. 292; February, 1996, p. 372; February, 1997, p. 328; October, 1997, Cindy Lombardo, review of *River Thunder*, p. 244; February, 1999, Sarah K. Herz, review of *The Maze*, p.434; June, 2001, review of *Down the Yukon*, p. 122; June, 2002, review of *Wild Man Island*, p. 118; August, 2003, review of *Jackie's Wild Seattle*, p. 224; October, 2004, Tim Brennan, review of *Leaving Protection*, p. 202; April 2006, Walter Hogan, review of *Crossing the Wire*, p. 46.

## ONLINE

*Will Hobbs Home Page,* http://www.willhobbsauthor.com (January 15, 2007).

\*    \*    \*

# HOBBS, William Carl
## See HOBBS, Will

\*    \*    \*

# HOPMAN, Philip 1961-

## Personal

Born July 16, 1961, in Egmond, Netherlands; son of a tulip farmer. *Education:* College degree, 1980; Rietveld Academy of Arts (Amsterdam, Netherlands), degree.

## Addresses

*Home*—Netherlands. *E-mail*—philiphopman@hotmail. com.

## Career

Illustrator, muralist, and author.

## Awards, Honors

Ezra Jack Keats Award nomination and Dutch Silver Brush nomination, both for *Een reuze heksentoer;* Silver Brush Award, 1999, for *22 wezen.*

## Writings

(Self-illustrated) *Een reuze heksentoer,* 1988.
(Self-illustrated) *Altijd als ik aan je denk,* Unieboek (Houten, Netherlands), 2006.

### ILLUSTRATOR

Jacques Vriens, *Ik ben ook op jou,* Van Goor (Amsterdam, Netherlands), 1992.

Tjibbe Veldkamp, *Een ober van Niks,* Ploegsma (Amsterdam, Netherlands), 1992.
Tjibbe Veldkamp, *Temmer Tom,* Ploegsma (Amsterdam, Netherlands), 1994.
Diana Lebacs, *Wak—lus Riba Klein Bonaire,* Stichting Culturele (Netherland Antilles), 1997.
Hans Hagen, *De kat en de adelaar,* [Netherlands] 1997.
Tjibbe Veldkamp, *22 wezen,* Lemniscaat (Rotterdam, Netherlands), 1998, translated as *22 Orphans,* Kane/Miller (La Jolla, CA), 1998.
Hans Hagen, *Ledereen min één,* VanGoor (Amsterdam, Netherlands), 1998.
Tjibbe Veldkamp, *Het schoolreisje,* Lemniscaat (Rotterdam, Netherlands), 2000, translated as *The School Trip,* Front Street (Asheville, NC), 2001.
Tony Mitton, *Fluff and Other Stuff,* Orchard (Faversham, England), 2001.
Miles Bouwman, *Rambamboelie,* Ploegsma (Amsterdam, Netherlands), 2002.
Carry Slee, *Hebbes,* Prometheus (Amsterdam, Netherlands), 2002.
*Hans Hagen, De dans van de drummers,* [Netherlands] 2003.
Hans Hagen, *Zwaantje en Lolly Londen,* Van Goor (Amsterdam, Netherlands), 2003.
Carry Slee, *Vals,* Prometheus (Amsterdam, Netherlands), 2003.
Carry Slee, *Botsing met zwarte piet,* Blue in Green (Netherlands), 2004.
Hans Hagen, *Wilde beesten: de avonturen van Maliff en Djit,* Querido (Amsterdam, Netherlands), 2004.
Ted van Lieshout, *Goochelaar!,* VanGoor (Amsterdam, Netherlands), 2004, translated as *Uncle Gus's Magic Box,* Annick Press (Toronto, Ontario, Canada), 2005.
Hans and Monique Hagen, *Het paardenboek,* Querido (Amsterdam, Netherlands), 2005.
*Er woont een liedje in mijn hoofd* (poetry collection), DiVers (Amsterdam, Netherlands), 2005.
Driek van Wissen, *Dierendokter Dik,* Unieboek (Houten, Netherlands), 2005.
Daan Remmertsw de Vries, *Over het uitkomen van Wensen (en hoe je dit kunt laten gebeuren),* Kinderboekenmarkt ('s-Gravenhage, Netherlands), 2005.
Simon Puttock, *Earth to Stella!* Clarion (New York, NY), 2006.
Bette Westera, *De schilderijententoonstelling,* Gottmer (Haarlem, Netherlands), 2006.
Hans Hagen, *Jubelientje wordt wild,* Querido (Amsterdam, Netherlands), 2006.
Bibi Dumon Tak, *Laika Tussen de Sterren,* Stitching Collectieve (Amsterdam, Netherlands), 2006.
Tjibbe Veldkamp, *Het Papegaaienplan,* Lannoo (Arnhem, Netherlands), 2006.
Marjet Huiberts, *Ridder Florian,* Gottmer (Haarlem, Netherlands), 2006.
Sjoerd Kuyper, *Robin is Verliefd,* Nieuw Amsterdam (Amsterdam, Netherlands), 2006.

Also illustrator of Dutch translations of texts by Kate DiCamillo, J.M. Barrie, Astrid Lindgren, and others, and of more than 150 Dutch-language books, including "Computer-Heks" series by Francine Oomen.

## Sidelights

Born into a family of tulip farmers in the Netherlands, Philip Hopman suspected that he was destined to become a tulip farmer as well; although he did not enjoy farming, he was not much better at the academic studies that might have signaled a different sort of career. However, there was one subject at which he excelled, and that was drawing. Ultimately pursuing a career in illustration, Hopman has become a prolific artist whose work appears in over 150 books. His collaboration with writer Tjibbe Veldkamp has produced several books, including *Een ober van Niks, Het schoolreisje,* and *22 wezen,* some of which have been translated into English. His popularity in his native Netherlands prompted Hopman's choice as the illustrator assigned to create art for the Dutch-language edition of Kate DiCamillo's Newbery Award-winning *The Tale of Despereaux* as well as of J.M. Barrie's classic "Peter Pan" novels.

Hopman and Veldkamp's collaboration on *22 wezen*—translated into English as *22 Orphans*—has been translated into six other languages. The picture book has some similarities to Ludwig Bemelman's time-honored "Madeline" picture-book series because the twenty-two orphans in Veldkamp's tale sleep in beds arranged in straight rows and walk in straight-line formation. Breaking with Madeline's tradition, however, the orphans of Veldkamp's story enjoy creating chaos and disarray, and revel in messiness. "Hopman conveys all the energy of imaginative children creating havoc left and right," wrote a *Publishers Weekly* critic of the title.

Hopman and Veldkamp also teamed up for *The School Trip,* in which young Davy decides he would rather build his own school than attend class at the regular schoolhouse. A series of misadventures sets the village school off its foundation, and the building sails off with its delighted students on board while their teacher paddles furiously in an effort to catch up. "Irrepressible Davy is a colorful character," wrote Shawn Brommer in *School Library Journal,* the critic going on to note that Hopman contrasts Davy's bright colors with a dull surrounding world. Hopman's "illustrations have natural fluidity and movement." Brommer also noted. Keely Milner Halls, writing in *Booklist,* described the illustrator's contribution to *The School Trip* as "freewheeling cartoons" that are "as quirky as [Veldkamp's] . . . story."

In addition to his work for Dutch authors, Hopman has also created illustrations for the English-language novel *Earth to Stella* by Simon Puttock. The picture book shows Stella as she gets ready for bed, and every part of her bedtime routine has its parallel in the space journey playing out in her imagination. "Hopman illustrates the voyage with softly colored cartoon views of the helmeted young pilot," wrote a contributor to *Kirkus Reviews.* Wanda Meyers-Hines, writing in *School Library Journal,* noted that the book features "pages bursting with color" and "innovative illustrations."

## Biographical and Critical Sources

*PERIODICALS*

*Booklist,* August, 2001, Keely Milner Halls, review of *The School Trip,* p. 2133.

*Kirkus Reviews,* April 1, 2006, review of *Earth to Stella!,* p. 355.

*Magpies,* March, 2002, review of *Fluff and Other Stuff,* p. 18.

*Publishers Weekly,* October 19, 1998, review of *22 Orphans,* p. 79.

*Reading Teacher,* September, 2002, review of *The School Trip,* p. 89.

*Resource Links,* February, 2006, Elaine Rospad, review of *Uncle Gus's Magic Box,* p. 30.

*School Librarian,* summer, 2002, review of *Fluff and Other Stuff,* p. 97.

*School Library Journal,* July, 2001, Shawn Brommer, review of *The School Trip,* p. 90.

*ONLINE*

*Annick Press Web site,* http://www.annickpress.com/ (February 24, 2007), "Philip Hopman."

*Philip Hopman Home Page,* http://www.philiphopman.nl (February 24, 2007).*

# J

## JACOBSEN, Laura

### Personal
Born in Columbus, OH; married. *Education:* Columbus College of Art and Design, B.F.A. (illustration); Marywood University, M.F.A. (illustration).

### Addresses
*Home and office*—Gilbert, AZ. *E-mail*—laura@laurajacobsen.com.

### Career
Children's book illustrator.

### Member
Society of Children's Book Writers and Illustrators (AZ chapter).

### Awards, Honors
First place in Stylized Category, 2000, Society of Children's Book Writers and Illustrators National Conference Portfolio Show.

### Illustrator
Mary Bahr, *My Brother Loved Snowflakes: The Story of Wilson A. Bentley, the Snowflake Man,* Boyds Mills Press (Honesdale, PA), 2002.

Melinda Lilly, *The Dutch in New Amsterdam,* Rourke Publishing (Vero Beach, FL), 2003.

Rob Jackson, *Animal Mischief: Poems,* Boyds Mills Press (Honesdale, PA), 2006.

Donna Jean Kemmetmueller, *My Muslim Friend: A Young Catholic Learns about Islam,* Pauline Books & Media (Boston, MA), 2006.

Contributor of illustrations to periodicals, including *Highlights for Children* and *Spider.*

### Sidelights
As a children's book illustrator, Arizona-based artist Laura Jacobsen has worked with a variety of educational publishers, including Boyds Mills Press and Scholastic, as well as with children's magazines *Highlights for Children* and *Spider.* Jacobsen has also illustrated an assortment of children's books, among them Mary Bahr's *My Brother Loved Snowflakes: The Story of Wilson A. Bentley, the Snowflake Man, The Dutch in New Amsterdam,* written by Melinda Lilly, and *My Muslim Friend: A Young Catholic Learns about Islam,* by Donna Jean Kemmetmueller. The artist often employs pastel pencil, watercolor, and computer technology in her illustrations for children's books; for instance, she

*Laura Jacobsen's art helps author Mary Bahr illuminate the life of snowflake photographer Wilson Bentley in* **My Brother Loved Snowflakes.** (Illustrations copyright © 2002 by Laura Jacobsen. Reproduced by permission.)

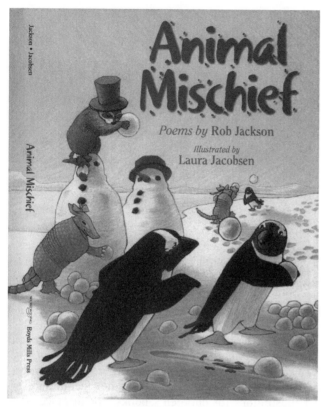

*Cover of Rob Jackson's* **Animal Mischief,** *a poetry collection given added appeal through Jacobsen's engaging art.* (Jacket illustration © 2006 by Laura Jacobsen. Reproduced by permission.)

used pastel pencils to capture the colorful tones of the assortment of animals featured in Rob Jackson's *Animal Mischief: Poems.*

In assessing Jacobsen's illustrations, critics often note her ability to create light, delicate works of art. A critic for *Kirkus Reviews* also described Jacobsen's images for *Animal Mischief* as "whimsical," adding that her illustrations "add to the charm" of Jackson's text. Likewise, *Booklist* reviewer Carolyn Phelan commented that Jacobsen's contribution "reflects the light tone of the verse." Carol L. McKay in her review of *Animal Mischief* for *School Library Journal,* praised Jacobsen's artistic approach, writing that the book's "whimsical creatures cavorting in bright single-and double-page pictures" are "appropriately fun."

## Biographical and Critical Sources

*PERIODICALS*

*Booklist,* April 2, 2006, Carolyn Phelan, review of *Animal Mischief: Poems,* p. 45.
*Kirkus Reviews,* March 1, 2006, review of *Animal Mischief,* p. 232.
*School Library Journal,* September, 2002, Kathleen Kelly MacMillan, review of *My Brother Loved Snowflakes: The Story of Wilson A. Bentley, the Snowflake Man,* p.

209; January, 2003, Marlene Gawron, review of *The Dutch in New Amsterdam,* p. 126; May, 2006, Carol L. MacKay, review of *Animal Mischief,* p. 112.

*ONLINE*

*Children's Literature Web site,* http://childrenslit.com/ (February 19, 2007), Marilyn Courtot, review of *Animal Mischief.*
*Laura Jacobsen Home Page,* http://www.laurajacobsen. com (February 19, 2007).
*Society of Children's Book Writers & Illustrators, Arizona Chapter, Web site,* http://www.scbwi-az.org/ (February 17, 2007).*

\*        \*        \*

## JESSELL, Tim

### Personal

Married; wife's name Ragan; children: Abby, Ben, Molly. *Education:* University of Tulsa, B.F.A. (commercial design; cum laude). *Hobbies and other interests:* Falconry, coaching his children's sports teams.

### Addresses

*Home*—Stillwater, OK. *E-mail*—tim@timjessell.com.

### Career

Commercial artist and illustrator. Freelance illustrator, beginning 1992.

### Awards, Honors

Society of Illustrators Gold Medal Award, Addy, *Print,* Graphex, and other illustration awards; *AdWeek* magazine illustrator-of-the-year designation.

## Writings

*SELF-ILLUSTRATED*

*Amorak,* Creative Education (Mankato, MN), 1994.
*Paper Tiger,* Harcourt (San Diego, CA), 1997.

*ILLUSTRATOR*

Stan Lee, *Stan Lee's Superhero Christmas,* Katherine Tegan Books (New York, NY), 2004.
Paul Haven, *Two Hot Dogs with Everything,* Random House (New York, NY), 2006.
Alan Armstrong, *Raleigh's Page,* Random House (New York, NY), 2007.

Contributor of illustrations to periodicals, including *Boy's Life, Time,* and *Texas Monthly.*

*ILLUSTRATOR; "SECRETS OF DROON" SERIES*

Tony Abbott, *The Hidden Stairs and the Magic Carpet,* Scholastic (New York, NY), 1999.

Tony Abbott, *Journey to the Volcano Palace,* Scholastic (New York, NY), 1999.

Tony Abbott, *The Mysterious Island,* Scholastic (New York, NY), 1999.

Tony Abbott, *City in the Clouds,* Scholastic (New York, NY), 1999.

Tony Abbott, *The Great Ice Battle,* Scholastic (New York, NY), 2000.

Tony Abbott, *The Sleeping Giant of Goll,* Scholastic (New York, NY), 2000.

Tony Abbott, *Into the Land of the Lost Secrets,* Scholastic (New York, NY), 2000.

Tony Abbott, *The Golden Wasp,* Scholastic (New York, NY), 2000.

Tony Abbott, *Tower of the Elf King,* Scholastic (New York, NY), 2000.

Tony Abbott, *Quest for the Queen,* Scholastic (New York, NY), 2000.

Tony Abbott, *The Hawk Bandits of Tarkoom,* Scholastic (New York, NY), 2001.

Tony Abbott, *Under the Serpent Sea,* Scholastic (New York, NY), 2001.

Tony Abbott, *The Mask of Maliban,* Scholastic (New York, NY), 2001.

Tony Abbott, *Voyage of the Jaffa Wind,* Scholastic (New York, NY), 2002.

Tony Abbott, *The Moon Scroll,* Scholastic (New York, NY), 2002.

Tony Abbott, *The Knights of Silversnow,* Scholastic (New York, NY), 2002.

Tony Abbott, *Search for the Dragon Ship,* Scholastic (New York, NY), 2003.

Tony Abbott, *The Coiled Viper,* Scholastic (New York, NY), 2003.

Also illustrator of other books in the "Secrets of Droon" series.

## Sidelights

Award-winning commercial artist Tim Jessell has worked for a wide variety of clients, from Texaco and Nike to Seattle's Best Coffee and Dr. Pepper. However appreciative those clients may be of Jessell's versatile yet realistic style, his biggest fans are likely the countless children who have enjoyed his original self-illustrated picture books *Amorak* and *Paper Tiger* as well as the artwork he has contributed to books by writers such as Paul Haven, Tony Abbott, and Stan Lee.

In addition to creating illustrations for Abbott's multi-volume "Secrets of Droon" middle-grade novel series, Jessell joined Marvel Comics writer Stan Lee to create *Stan Lee's Superhero Christmas.* Lee's first book for children, *Stan Lee's Superhero Christmas* features the yuletide adventures of the Protector, as the musclebound hero attempts to rescue Santa from the evil trolls who have trapped him in an icy kingdom. Calling the project "one of those cases where a book's text is completely overshadowed by the illustrations," Dave Jenkinson wrote in the *Canadian Review of Materials* that in *Stan*

*Cover of* **The Coiled Viper,** *a novel by Tony Abbott that features cover art by Tim Jessell.* (Scholastic Inc., 2003. Jacket art copyright © 2003 by Tim Jessell. Reproduced by permission of Scholastic, Inc.)

*Lee's Superhero Christmas* Jessell's dramatic, high-energy "pastel and mixed media illustrations are visually engrossing."

Raised in Indiana, Jessell studied art in high school, where his teacher gave him a strong grounding in the basics. He earned a football scholarship to the University of Tulsa, and there he earned a B.F.A., cum laude, in commercial design. Jessell's realistic style was a perfect match with the needs of advertisers, and he was able to build a successful career as a commercial artist after going freelance in 1992. He has more recently moved from sketching and working with pastel and other artistic media to creating his images digitally, retaining the traditional approach that has caused his work to be dubbed "tradigital." Jessell's work for Haven's *Two Hot Dogs with Everything,* a novel about an eleven-year-old baseball fan who hopes that superstition can prop up the score of his favorite team, inspired a *Kirkus Reviews* contributor to call the work "magical and delightful."

In 1994 Jessell created his first original picture book, *Amorak.* Featuring compelling and detailed art, the book transports readers to the far north, where a wolf's distant howl is heard as an elderly man tucks his grandson

into bed. To reassure the boy, the man tells an Inuit Creation story in which the Great Being brings all manner of creature forth to inhabit an empty world. When sick and weak creatures begin to gain prominence, taking an increasing share of scarce resources, the Great Being creates Amorak. Father of all wolves, Amorak performs an important service by culling the herds and allowing healthy creatures to thrive. Praising Jessell's picture-book debut, a *Publishers Weekly* contributor wrote that the author/illustrator's "suggestively lit paintings, rich with nocturnal blues and golden firelight, sustain the intensity and wonder of his tale."

## Biographical and Critical Sources

*PERIODICALS*

*Booklist*, April 1, 2006, John Peters, review of *Two Hot Dogs with Everything*, p. 193.

*Bulletin of the Center for Children's Books*, November, 2004, Krista Hutley, review of *Stan Lee's Superhero Christmas*, p. 131; May, 2006, Elizabeth Bush, review of *Two Hot Dogs with Everything*, p. 403.

*Canadian Review of Materials*, February 15, 2005, Dave Jenkinson, review of *Stan Lee's Superhero Christmas*.

*Kirkus Reviews*, April 1, 2006, review of *Two Hot Dogs with Everything*, p. 348.

*Publishers Weekly*, June 27, 1994, review of *Amorak*, p. 76; April 17, 2006, review of *Two Hot Dogs with Everything*, p. 188.

*School Library Journal*, May, 2006, Marilyn Taniguchi, review of *Two Hot Dogs with Everything*, p. 348.

*Texas Monthly*, January, 1991, "Texas Desperado: Award-winning Western Illustrator Tim Jessell," p. 74.

*ONLINE*

*Tim Jessell Home Page*, http://www.timjessell.com (March 15, 2007).*

\* \* \*

# JOHNSON, Steve 1960-

## Personal

Born 1960, in MN; married Lou Fancher (a writer and illustrator). *Education:* School of Associated Arts (St. Paul, MN), B.F.A.

## Addresses

*Home*—Moraga, CA. *E-mail*—fancher@dancingpeople.com.

## Career

Commercial artist and illustrator. Freelance illustrator, with wife, Lou Fancher, beginning 1986; pre-production set and character designer for animated films, including *Toy Story*, 1995, and *A Bug's Life*, 1998.

## Awards, Honors

(With Lou Fancher) International Reading Association Childrens Book Award 1989 for *No Star Nights* by Anna Smucker; Minnesota Book Award for Children's Books, 1992, for *The Salamander Room*, by Anne Mazer; gold medal, Society of Illustrators, 1993, for *Up North at the Cabin* by Marsha Wilson Chall; Minnesota Book Award for Children's Books finalist, 1993, for *Up North at the Cabin* 1996, for *Cat You'd Better Come Home* by Garrison Keillor, 1997, for *My Many Colored Days* by Dr. Seuss, 1998, for *The Lost and Found House* by Michael Cadnum, 1999, for *Coppelia* by Margot Fonteyn, 2002, for both *The Day Ocean Came to Visit* by Diane Wolkstein and *Silver Seeds* by Paul Paolilli and Dan Brewer; Nestlé Children's Book Prize shortlist, 2005, for *The Dancing Tiger* by Malachy Doyle.

## Illustrator

*WITH WIFE, LOU FANCHER*

Anna Smucker, *No Star Nights*, Knopf (New York, NY), 1989.

Douglas Hill, *Penelope's Pendant*, Doubleday (New York, NY), 1990.

Anne Mazer, *The Salamander Room*, Knopf (New York, NY), 1991.

Jon Scieszka, *The Frog Prince Continued*, Viking (New York, NY), 1991.

Marsha Wilson Chall, *Up North at the Cabin*, Lothrop, Lee & Shephard (New York, NY), 1992.

B.G. Hennessy, *The First Night*, Viking (New York, NY), 1993.

Sarah S. Kilborne, *Peach and Blue*, Knopf (New York, NY), 1994.

Garrison Keillor, *Cat, You Better Come Home*, Viking (New York, NY), 1995.

Dr. Seuss (pseudonym of Theodore Geisel), *My Many Colored Days*, Knopf (New York, NY), 1996.

Michael Cadnum, *The Lost and Found House*, Viking (New York, NY), 1997.

Margot Fonteyn, *Coppélia*, Harcourt Brace (San Francisco, CA), 1998.

Lou Fancher, *The Quest for the One Big Thing*, Disney Press (New York, NY), 1998.

Craig Kee Strete, *The Lost Boy and the Monster*, Putnam's (New York, NY), 1999.

Janet Schulman, adaptor, *Felix Salten's Bambi*, Atheneum (New York, NY), 1999.

Lois Duncan, *I Walk at Night*, Viking (New York, NY), 2000.

Alice Hoffman, *Horsefly*, Hyperion (New York, NY), 2000.

Paul Paolilli and Dan Brewer, *Silver Seeds: A Book of Nature Poems*, Viking (New York, NY), 2001.

Diane Wolkstein, *The Day Ocean Came to Visit*, Harcourt (San Diego, CA), 2001.

Margaret Wise Brown, *Robin's Room*, Hyperion (New York, NY), 2002.

Louise Erdrich, *The Range Eternal*, Hyperion (New York, NY), 2002.

Mary Pope Osborne, *New York's Bravest,* Knopf (New York, NY), 2002.

Lou Fancher, adapter, *The Velveteen Rabbit; or, How Toys Become Real* (based on the story by Margery Williams), Atheneum (New York, NY), 2002.

Mavis Jukes, *You're a Bear,* Knopf (New York, NY), 2003.

Kathleen Krull, *The Boy on Fairfield Street: How Ted Geisel Grew up to Become Dr. Seuss,* Random House (New York, NY), 2004.

Dori Chaconas, *Momma, Will You?,* Penguin (New York, NY), 2004.

H.L. Panahi, *Bebop Express,* Laura Geringer Books (New York, NY), 2005.

Malachy Doyle, *The Dancing Tiger,* Simon & Schuster (New York, NY), 2005.

Karen Hill, *All God's Creatures,* Little Simon (New York, NY), 2005.

Lou Fancher, *Star Climbing,* Laura Geringer Books (New York, NY), 2006.

Dan Gutman, *Casey Back at Bat,* HarperCollins (New York, NY), 2007.

Margie Palatini, *The Cheese,* Katherine Tegen Books (New York, NY), 2007.

Diane Wright Landolf, *What a Good Big Brother!,* Random House (New York, NY), 2008.

Warren Hanson, *Bugtown Boogie,* Laura Geringer Books (New York, NY), 2008.

Stephen Mitchell, reteller, *The Ugly Duckling,* Candlewick Press (New York, NY), 2008.

Maya Angelou, *Amazing Peace,* Random House (New York, NY), 2008.

Diane Wright Landolf, *What a Good Big Brother!,* Random House (New York, NY), 2009.

## Sidelights

For Sidelights, see entry on Lou Fancher.

## Biographical and Critical Sources

### PERIODICALS

*Booklist,* November 1, 1996, Hazel Rochman, review of *My Many Colored Days,* p. 510; October 15, 1998, Carolyn Phelan, review of *Copélia,* p. 416; December 1, 2000, Connie Fletcher, review of *Horsefly,* p. 721; April 15, 2002, Kay Weisman, review of *Robin's Room,* p. 1406; July, 2002, Ilene Cooper, review of *New York's Finest,* p. 1847; December 1, 2003, Louise Brueggemann, review of *You're a Bear,* p. 684; February 15, 2006, Carolyn Phelan, review of *Star Climbing,* p. 101; January 1, 2007, GraceAnne A. DeCandido, review of *Casey Back at Bat,* p. 114.

*Bulletin of the Center for Children's Books,* March, 2004, Krista Hutley, review of *The Boy on Fairfield Street: How Ted Geisel Grew up to Become Dr. Seuss,* p. 284.

*Horn Book,* November-December, 1993, Mary M. Burns, review of *The First Night,* p. 724; November-December, 2002, Roger Sutton, review of *New York's Bravest,* p. 737.

*Kirkus Reviews,* July 1, 2002, review of *New York's Bravest,* p. 951; August 15, 2002, review of *The Range Eternal,* p. 1222; September 15, 2002, review of *The Velveteen Rabbit,* p. 1389; December 15, 2003, review of *The Boy on Fairfield Street,* p. 1451; April 15, 2005, review of *The Dancing Tiger,* p. 472; June 1, 2005, review of *Bebop Express,* p. 642; February 15, 2006, review of *Star Climbing,* p. 182.

*New York Times Book Review,* November 21, 1999, Elizabeth Spires, review of *Bambi.*

*Publishers Weekly,* September 20, 1993, review of *The First Night,* p. 37; November 7, 1994, review of *Peach and Blue,* p. 77; May 8, 1995, review of *Cat, You Better Come Home,* p. 294; October 13, 1997, review of *The Lost and Found House,* p. 74; November 16, 1998, review of *The Quest for the One Big Thing,* p. 77; January 10, 2000, review of *I Walk at Night,* p. 67; August 13, 2001, review of *The Day Ocean Came to Visit,* p. 311; May 20, 2002, review of *Robin's Room,* p. 65; June 24, 2002, review of *New York's Bravest,* p. 56; September 9, 2002, review of *The Range Eternal,* p. 67; January 23, 2006, review of *Star Climbing,* p. 206.

*School Library Journal,* April, 1999, review of *The Quest for the One Big Thing,* p. 94; August, 2001, Margaret A. Chang, review of *The Day Ocean Came to Visit,* p. 174; October, 2002, Susan Oliver, review of *The Range Eternal,* p. 104; December, 2003, Laura Scott, review of *You're a Bear,* p. 118; January, 2004, Anne Chapman Callaghan, review of *The Boy on Fairfield Street,* p. 119; November, 2004, Rebecca Sheridan, review of *Momma, Will You?,* p. 94; July, 2005, Grace Oliff, review of *The Dancing Tiger,* p. 88; April, 2006, Susan Weitz, review of *Star Climbing,* p. 105; January, 2007, Marilyn Taniguchi, review of *Casey Back at Bat,* p. 94.

*ONLINE*

*Lou Fancher and Steve Johnson Home Page,* http://www.johnsonandfancher.com (March 15, 2007).

\* \* \*

# JUHASZ, Victor 1954-

## Personal

Born 1954. *Education:* Parsons School of Design, degree.

## Addresses

*Home and office*—Averill Park, NY. *E-mail*—juhasz@taconic.net; vic@victorjuhasz.com.

## Career

Illustrator, beginning 1974.

## Illustrator

William H. Hooks, *Maria's Cave,* Coward, McCann & Geoghegan (New York, NY), 1977.

Nancy Veglahn, *They Mysterious Rays: Marie Curie's World,* Coward, McCann & Geoghegan (New York, NY), 1977.

Sam Epstein, *She Never Looked Back: Margaret Mean in Samoa,* Coward, McCann & Geoghegan (New York, NY), 1980.

Elissa Grodin, *D Is for Democracy: A Citizen's Alphabet,* Sleeping Bear Press (Chelsea, MI), 2004.

Elissa Grodin, *Everyone Counts: A Citizen's Number Book,* Sleeping Bear Press (Chelsea, MI), 2006.

Devin Scillian, *H Is for Honor: A Military Family Alphabet,* Sleeping Bear Press (Chelsea, MI), 2006.

Judy Young, *R Is for Rhyme: A Poetry Alphabet,* Sleeping Bear Press (Chelsea, MI), 2006.

Contributor of illustrations to numerous publications, including *Time, Newsweek, New Yorker, Rolling Stone, New York Times, Washington Post,* and *Gentleman's Quarterly.*

## Biographical and Critical Sources

*PERIODICALS*

*Booklist,* January 1, 2005, Carolyn Phelan, review of *D Is for Democracy: A Citizen's Alphabet,* p. 848.
*Children's Bookwatch,* October, 2004, review of *D Is for Democracy.*
*Library Media Connection,* March, 2005, Jennifer Hartshow, review of *D Is for Democracy,* p. 62.
*Publishers Weekly,* August 23, 2004, "High Concepts," p. 56.
*School Library Journal,* October, 2004, Lynda Ritterman, review of *D Is for Democracy,* p. 140.

*ONLINE*

*Victor Juhasz Home Page,* http://www.victorjuhasz.com/ (February 18, 2007).
*Sleeping Bear Press Web site,* http://www.sleepingbearpress.com/ (February 18, 2007), "Victor Juhasz."*

# K

## KELLOGG, Steven 1941-
### (Steven Castle Kellogg)

### Personal

Born October 26, 1941, in Norwalk, CT; son of Robert E. and Hilma Marie Kellogg; married Helen Hill, 1967; children: (stepchildren) Pamela, Melanie, Kimberly, Laurie, Kevin, Colin. *Education:* Rhode Island School of Design, B.F.A., 1963; graduate study at American University.

### Addresses

*Home*—P.O. Box 280, Essex, NY 12936.

### Career

Author and illustrator of children's books; artist. American University, Washington, DC, instructor in etching, 1966; has also taught printmaking and painting. *Exhibitions:* Works exhibited at American Institute of Graphic Arts Book Show, Children's Book Showcase, and at Bologna International Children's Book Fair.

### Awards, Honors

Dutch Zilveren Griffel, 1974, for *Can I Keep Him?;* Christopher Award, 1976, for *How the Witch Got Alf;* Irma Simonton Black Award, Bank Street College of Education, 1978, for *The Mysterious Tadpole;* American Book Award finalist, 1980, and Georgia Children's Picture Storybook Award, University of Georgia College of Education, and Little Archer Award, University of Wisconsin-Oshkosh Department of Library Services, both 1982, all for *Pinkerton, Behave!;* Parents' Choice Award, Parents' Choice Foundation, 1982, for *Tallyho, Pinkerton!,* and 1986, for *Best Friends;* Michigan Young Reader's Award, Michigan Council of Teachers of English, 1983, for *The Island of the Skog; Boston Globe/ Horn Book* Illustration Award Honor Book, 1985, and Utah Children's Informational, and Young Adult's Book Award, 1988, both for *How Much Is a Million?* by

***Steven Kellogg*** (Reproduced by permission.)

David M. Schwartz; David McCord Children's Literature citation, Framingham (MA) State College/ International Reading Association (IRA), 1987, for significant contribution to excellence in books for children; Regina Medal, Catholic Library Association, 1989; *Horn Book* Honor Book designation, 1994, for *If You Made a Million* by Schwartz; IRA Children's Choice designation, ALA Notable Book designation, and Utah Children's Book Award list, all 1997, all for *Rattlebang Picnic* by Margaret Mahy; New England Booksellers Award, 1996; Bank Street College of Education Best Children's Books of the Year designation, 1996, and IRA Children's Choice designation, 1997, both for *Frogs Jump!* by Alan Brooks; Jo Osborn Medal, 1997; ALA Notable Children's Book designation, for *Jack and the Beanstalk;* Capitol Choice designation, 1997, for *The Three Pigs;* Children's Literature Choice listee, 1998, and Buckeye Children's Book Award listee (OH), 2001, both for *Library Lil* by Suzanne Williams; designations for American Library Association Notable Books for Children, Child Study Association of America

Children's Book of the Year, *New York Times* Outstanding Book of the Year, and *School Library Journal* Best Book of the Year; Notable Children's Book in the Language Arts designation, National Council of Teachers of English, 2000, for *The Three Sillies;* Capitol Choices honor, 2000, Bank Street College of Education Best Children's Books of the Year designation and Children's Literature Choice designation, both 2001, Michigan Reader's Choice Award, 2003, and Volunteer State Book Award, 2004, all for *The Baby BeeBee Bird* by Diane Redfield Massie; Delaware Diamonds Reading list, 2001-02, for *The Missing Mitten Mystery;* Rhode Island School of Design Professional Achievement Award, 2003; *Boston Globe/Horn Book* Nonfiction Award, 2006, for *If You Decide to Go to the Moon* by Faith McNulty.

# Writings

*FOR CHILDREN; SELF-ILLUSTRATED*

*The Wicked Kings of Bloon,* Prentice-Hall (Englewood Cliffs, NJ), 1970.

*Can I Keep Him?,* Dial (New York, NY), 1971.

*The Mystery Beast of Ostergeest,* Dial (New York, NY), 1971.

*The Orchard Cat,* Dial (New York, NY), 1972.

*Won't Somebody Play with Me?,* Dial (New York, NY), 1972.

*The Island of the Skog,* Dial (New York, NY), 1973.

(Reteller) *There Was an Old Woman,* Parents' Magazine Press (New York, NY), 1974.

*Much Bigger than Martin,* Dial (New York, NY), 1976.

*The Mysterious Tadpole,* Dial (New York, NY), 1977, twenty-fifth anniversary edition revised with new illustrations, 2002.

*Pinkerton, Behave!,* Dial (New York, NY), 1979.

*A Rose for Pinkerton,* Dial (New York, NY), 1981.

*Tallyho, Pinkerton!,* Dial (New York, NY), 1982.

*Ralph's Secret Weapon,* Dial (New York, NY), 1983.

(Reteller) *Paul Bunyan: A Tall Tale,* Morrow (New York, NY), 1984.

(Reteller) *Chicken Little,* Morrow (New York, NY), 1985.

(Reteller) *Pecos Bill,* Morrow (New York, NY), 1986.

*Best Friends,* Dial (New York, NY), 1986.

*Aster Aardvark's Alphabet Adventures,* Morrow (New York, NY), 1987.

*Prehistoric Pinkerton,* Dial (New York, NY), 1987.

(Reteller) *Johnny Appleseed,* Morrow (New York, NY), 1988.

(Reteller) *Jack and the Beanstalk,* Morrow (New York, NY), 1991.

(Reteller) *Mike Fink,* Morrow (New York, NY), 1992.

*The Christmas Witch,* Dial (New York, NY), 1992.

(Reteller) *Yankee Doodle,* Aladdin Books (New York, NY), 1994.

(Reteller) *Sally Ann Thunder Ann Whirlwind Crockett: A Tall Tale,* Morrow (New York, NY), 1995.

(Reteller) *I Was Born About 10,000 Years Ago: A Tall Tale,* Morrow (New York, NY), 1996.

(Reteller) *The Three Little Pigs,* Morrow (New York, NY), 1997.

(Reteller) *A-Hunting We Will Go!,* Morrow (New York, NY), 1998.

(Reteller) *The Three Sillies,* Candlewick Press (Cambridge, MA), 1999.

(Reteller) *Give the Dog a Bone,* SeaStar Books (New York, NY), 2000.

*A Penguin Pup for Pinkerton,* Dial (New York, NY), 2001.

*Pinkerton and Friends: A Steven Kellogg Treasury* (omnibus), Dial (New York, NY), 2004.

*"COLOR" STORIES*

*The Mystery of the Missing Red Mitten,* Dial (New York, NY), 1974, revised edition published as *The Missing Mitten Mystery,* 2000.

*The Mystery of the Magic Green Ball,* Dial (New York, NY), 1978.

*The Mystery of the Flying Orange Pumpkin,* Dial (New York, NY), 1980.

*The Mystery of the Stolen Blue Paint,* Dial (New York, NY), 1982.

*ILLUSTRATOR*

George Mendoza, *Gwot! Horribly Funny Hairticklers,* Harper (New York, NY), 1967.

James Copp, *Martha Matilda O'Toole,* Bradbury Press (Englewood Cliffs, NJ), 1969.

Eleanor B. Heady, *Brave Johnny O'Hare,* Parents' Magazine Press (New York, NY), 1969.

Mary Rodgers, *The Rotten Book,* Harper (New York, NY), 1969.

Miriam Young, *Can't You Pretend?,* Putnam (New York, NY), 1970.

Hilaire Belloc, *Matilda Who Told Lies and Was Burned to Death,* Dial (New York, NY), 1970.

Ruth Loomis, *Mrs. Purdy's Children,* Dial (New York, NY), 1970.

Fred Rogers, *Mister Rogers' Songbook,* Random House (New York, NY), 1970.

Peggy Parish, *Granny and the Desperadoes,* Macmillan (New York, NY), 1970.

Anne Mallett, *Here Comes Tagalong,* Parents' Magazine Press (New York, NY), 1971.

Jan Wahl, *Crabapple Night,* Holt (New York, NY), 1971.

Aileen Friedman, *The Castles of the Two Brothers,* Holt (New York, NY), 1972.

Jan Wahl, *The Very Peculiar Tunnel,* Putnam (New York, NY), 1972.

Jeanette Franklin Caines, *Abby,* Harper (New York, NY), 1973.

Joan Lexau Nodset, *Come Here, Cat,* Harper (New York, NY), 1973.

Doris Herold Lund, *You Ought to See Herbert's House,* F. Watts (New York, NY), 1973.

Liesel Moak Skorpen, *Kisses and Fishes,* Harper (New York, NY), 1974.

Jean Van Leeuwen, *The Great Christmas Kidnapping Caper,* Dial (New York, NY), 1975.

Margaret Mahy, *The Boy Who Was Followed Home,* F. Watts (New York, NY), 1975.

Cora Annett, *How the Witch Got Alf,* F. Watts (New York, NY), 1975.

Alice Bach, *The Smartest Bear and His Brother Oliver,* Harper (New York, NY), 1975.

Hilaire Belloc, *The Yak, the Python, the Frog,* Parents' Magazine Press (New York, NY), 1975.

Judith Choate, *Awful Alexander,* Doubleday (New York, NY), 1976.

Lou Ann Bigge Gaeddert, *Gustav the Gourmet Giant,* Dial (New York, NY), 1976.

Edward Bangs, *Steven Kellogg's Yankee Doodle,* Parents' Magazine Press (New York, NY), 1976.

Alice Bach, *The Most Delicious Camping Trip Ever,* Harper (New York, NY), 1976.

Alice Bach, *Grouchy Uncle Otto,* Harper (New York, NY), 1977.

Carol Chapman, *Barney Bipple's Magic Dandelions,* Dutton (New York, NY), 1977, new edition, 1988.

Alice Bach, *Millicent the Magnificent,* Harper (New York, NY), 1978.

Marilyn Singer, *The Pickle Plan,* Dutton (New York, NY), 1978.

Mercer Mayer, *Appelard and Liverwurst,* Four Winds Press (New York, NY), 1978.

Douglas F. Davis, *There's an Elephant in the Garage,* Dutton (New York, NY), 1979.

William Sleator, *Once, Said Darlene,* Dutton (New York, NY), 1979.

Susan Pearson, *Molly Moves Out,* Dial (New York, NY), 1979.

Julia Castiglia, *Jill the Pill,* Atheneum (New York, NY), 1979.

Jean Marzollo, *Uproar on Hollercat Hill,* Dial (New York, NY), 1980.

Trinka Hakes Noble, *The Day Jimmy's Boa Ate the Wash,* Dial (New York, NY), 1980.

Amy Ehrlich, *Leo, Zack and Emmie,* Dial (New York, NY), 1981.

Mercer Mayer, *Liverwurst Is Missing,* Four Winds Press (New York, NY), 1981.

Alan Benjamin, *A Change of Plans,* Four Winds Press (New York, NY), 1982.

Cathy Warren, *The Ten-Alarm Camp-Out,* Lothrop (New York, NY), 1983.

Jane Bayer, *A, My Name Is Alice,* Dial (New York, NY), 1984.

Trinka Hakes Noble, *Jimmy's Boa Bounces Back,* Dial (New York, NY), 1984.

David M. Schwartz, *How Much Is a Million?,* Lothrop (New York, NY), 1985.

Carol Purdy, *Iva Dunnit and the Big Wind,* Dial (New York, NY), 1985.

Amy Ehrlich, *Leo, Zack, and Emmie Together Again,* Dial (New York, NY), 1987.

Trinka Hakes Noble, *Jimmy's Boa and the Big Splash Birthday Bash,* Dial (New York, NY), 1989.

David M. Schwartz, *If You Made a Million,* Lothrop (New York, NY), 1989.

Deborah Guarino, *Is Your Mama a Llama?,* Scholastic (New York, NY), 1989.

Reeve Lindbergh, *The Day the Goose Got Loose,* Dial (New York, NY), 1990.

Tom Paxton, *Engelbert the Elephant,* Morrow (New York, NY), 1990.

Amy Ehrlich, *Parents in the Pigpen, Pigs in the Tub,* Dial (New York, NY), 1993.

Peter Glassman, *The Wizard Next Door,* Morrow (New York, NY), 1993.

James Thurber, *The Great Quillow,* Harcourt (San Diego, CA), 1994.

Mark Twain, *The Adventures of Huckleberry Finn,* Morrow (New York, NY), 1994.

Margaret Mahy, *The Rattlebang Picnic,* Dial (New York, NY), 1994.

Laura Robb, editor, *Snuffles and Snouts,* Dial (New York, NY), 1995.

Alan Brooks, *Frogs Jump!: A Counting Book,* Scholastic (New York, NY), 1996.

Suzanne Williams, *Library Lil,* Dial (New York, NY), 1997.

Bill Martin, Jr., *A Beasty Story,* Silver Whistle/Harcourt (San Diego, CA), 1999.

Diane Redfield Massie, *The Baby Beebee Bird,* HarperCollins (New York, NY), 2000.

Joanne Ryder, *Big Bear Ball,* HarperCollins (New York, NY), 2002.

David M. Schwartz, *Millions to Measure,* HarperCollins (New York, NY), 2003.

Trinka Hakes Noble, *Jimmy's Boa and the Bungee Jump Slam Dunk,* Dial (New York, NY), 2003.

Robert Kinerk, *Clorinda,* Silver Whistle/Harcourt (San Diego, CA), 2003.

J. Fred Coots and Haven Gillespie, *Santa Claus Is Comin' to Town,* HarperCollins (New York, NY), 2004.

Faith McNulty, *If You Decide to Go to the Moon,* Scholastic (New York, NY), 2005.

Dennis Haseley, *The Invisible Moose,* Dial (New York, NY), 2006.

Robert Kinerk, *Clorinda Takes Flight,* Simon & Schuster (New York, NY), 2007.

## Adaptations

Author's works have been adapted into other media by Weston Woods, including: *Chicken Little* (video, film), *The Day Jimmy's Boa Ate the Wash* (video, film, filmstrip/cassette), *How Much Is a Million?* (video, film), *Is Your Mama a Llama?* (video, film), *Island of the Skog* (video, film, filmstrip/cassette), *The Mysterious Tadpole* (video, film, filmstrip/cassette), *Pinkerton, Behave!* (filmstrip/cassette), *Yankee Doodle* (video, film, filmstrip/cassette), and *If You Made a Million* (video).

## Sidelights

While award-winning author and illustrator Steven Kellogg is perhaps best known as the author of the beloved picture book *The Mysterious Tadpole,* he has also created popular children's picture books about Pinkerton the Great Dane, a series of "color" mysteries for

***Kellogg's talent as an artist is paired with his storytelling skills in books such as* The Missing Mitten Mystery.** (Illustration © 2000 by Steven Kellogg. Reproduced by permission of Dial Books for Young Readers, a division of Penguin Putnam Books for Young Readers.)

younger readers, and adaptations of American legends featuring Paul Bunyan, Pecos Bill, Johnny Appleseed and Mike Fink. As a *Publishers Weekly* reviewer pointed out, "one reason for the popularity Kellogg enjoys is that children sense he's laughing with them when they explore his tenderly comic, always surprising stories and pictures."

Noted for his humorous texts and his detailed, action-filled drawings, Kellogg has also illustrated works for many other children's authors, among them Hilaire Belloc, Mercer Mayer, Trinka Hakes Noble, Tom Paxton, David M. Schwartz, James Thurber, Joanne Ryder, Faith McNulty, and Margaret Mahy. His collaborations with Schwartz, which include *How Much Is a Million?, If You Made a Million,* and *Millions to Measure,* showcase his ability to synthesize abstract elements in what

*School Library Journal* reviewer Kathleen Kelly Macmillan described as "trademark whimsical illustrations." Praising Kellogg's artwork for another nonfiction picture book, McNulty's award-winning *If You Decide to Go to the Moon,* as "impressive," a *Publishers Weekly* reviewer added that the illustrator's "sweeping spreads of realistic space-and-moonscapes strike just the right balance of beauty and eeriness" in bringing to life McNulty's environmental "call to action." In his art for Robert Kinerk's *Clorinda,* a picture book that finds a Rubenesque bovine pursuing her dream of becoming a ballet dancer, "Kellogg's costumed dancers, human and livestock both, likewise cavort across the pages with characteristic verve," according to a *Kirkus Reviews* writer. In similar fashion, the title character in Dennis Hasley's *The Invisible Moose* is portrayed in a similarly ludicrous situation—wandering the streets of Manhat-

tan—providing Kellogg's young fans with a picture book that a *Publishers Weekly* reviewer dubbed "a winsome and witty collaboration."

Born in Connecticut in 1941, Kellogg was combining his artistic and storytelling talents from an early age, drawing pictures for his younger sisters while telling them tales to accompany his artwork. He especially enjoyed drawing animals, and he papered his room with many such pieces; one of his favorite growing-up fantasies was to be hired by *National Geographic* magazine to draw animals on location in Africa. Kellogg was encouraged in his childhood ambitions by his grandmother, who taught the boy about the animal inhabitants of the wooded areas near his home.

Kellogg continued to draw and paint throughout his high-school years, and after graduation he won a scholarship to study at the Rhode Island School of Design. One of the highlights of his time there was a semester spent in Florence, Italy, where he was able to study the original drawings of the great artists of the Italian Renaissance. After graduating, he enrolled in graduate

*A well-respected illustrator, Kellogg joins author Robert Kinerk to bring to life the quirky picture book* Clorinda. (Illustrations copyright © 2003 by Steven Kellogg. Reproduced by permission of Simon & Schuster Books for Young Readers, an imprint of Simon & Schuster Children's Publishing Division.)

courses at the American University in Washington, DC, and by 1966, he was teaching an etching class there.

While in graduate school, Kellogg married Helen Hill and gained the six stepchildren who have since served as inspiration for many of his drawings. At about the same time, Kellogg began work on his original picture books *The Orchard Cat* and *The Island of the Skog.* He also illustrated George Mendoza's *Gwot! Horribly Funny Hairticklers.* Several other illustration projects followed, including James Copp's *Martha Matilda O'Toole* and Eleanor B. Heady's *Brave Johnny O'Hare,* before Kellogg's first solo effort, *The Wicked Kings of Bloon,* was published in 1970. In between his self-authored projects, Kellogg has continued to collaborate with other writers, creating art for books such as the award-winning *The BeeBee Bird* by Diane Redfield Massie and *A Beasty Story* by Bill Martin, Jr.

When it was released in 1971, *Can I Keep Him?* gained its author/illustrator an even wider audience and also attracted critical praise. As Kellogg later admitted to Pamela Lloyd in *How Writers Write,* this story about a little boy who begs his mother to allow him to keep the stray animals he finds is "a little bit autobiographical." Animals also figure in *The Orchard Cat,* about a cat who discovers he would rather make friends than follow his mother's cynical, power-hungry advice. *Won't Somebody Play with Me?* is another early work, this time focusing on a little girl who must find a way to fill the time until she is allowed to open her birthday presents.

*The Mystery of the Missing Red Mitten* follows Annie through the many scenarios she imagines for her lost mitten: including serving as the heart for a snowman, or the hat for a hawk. As Kellogg's illustrations consist of black-and-white line drawings, the mitten adds a splash of red as it appears in all the young girl's imaginative incarnations. The success of *The Mystery of the Missing Red Mitten* prompted Kellogg to create several other color-related titles, such as *The Mystery of the Magic Green Ball, The Mystery of the Flying Orange Pumpkin,* and *The Mystery of the Stolen Blue Paint.*

First published in 1977, Kellogg's *The Mysterious Tadpole* quickly won over a generation of young children, and it would do the same thing twenty-five years later when, in 2002, Kellogg re-released the story with a revised plot and new illustrations. Cited by several reviewers as a modern classic, the story begins when a boy receives a tadpole his uncle has brought home from Scotland. Named Alphonse, the tiny amphibian quickly outgrows his original container, and within a short time the creature is large enough to take over the swimming pool and even overwhelms Louis's school. Alphonse's metamorphosis becomes clear to all when it is learned that he was caught along the shore of Scotland's famous Loch Ness. Praising the new edition of the book in *Booklist,* Carolyn Phelan wrote that Kellogg brings to life Louis's humorous efforts to deal with his ungainly pet in "new illustrations [that] are bigger, bolder, brighter, and brimming with lively details."

***Kellogg re-illustrated his award-winning picture book*** **The Mysterious Tadpole** ***in 2002.*** (Reproduced by permission of Puffin Books, a division of Penguin Putnam Books for Young Readers.)

Kellogg's popular Pinkerton character was introduced in 1979 in the pages of *Pinkerton, Behave!* Inspired by the author/illustrator's family's Great Dane of the same name, *Pinkerton, Behave!* chronicles the dog's misadventures in obedience class. Barbara Elleman declared in her *Booklist* review of the book that "Kellogg wittily captures expressions and movements of animal and human," while his "bright, lively colors and spare use of narrative blend to help make this a splendid comedic success." In *A Rose for Pinkerton* the Great Dane meets Rose the cat, a critter based on another of the Kellogg family's pets. *Tallyho, Pinkerton!* finds Pinkerton and Rose entangled in a humorous fox hunt, while the Great Dane is tempted by dinosaur bones during a chaotic visit to a natural history museum in *Prehistoric Pinkerton.* After dreaming that he is the father of a penguin egg in *A Penguin Pup for Pinkerton,* the hapless Great

Dane creates chaos all over town when he mistakes toy balls for real eggs. In the words of *School Library Journal* reviewer Lisa Dennis in a review of the last-named book, "Pinkerton's back—and his new adventures are as outrageous and entertaining as ever."

While much of Kellogg's inspiration has come from his own family, the author/illustrator has also been inspired by larger-than-life characters recalled from his childhood. In *Paul Bunyan: A Tall Tale,* for example, he retells the story of the famed woodsman and his blue ox named Babe, bringing all to life in illustrations that Millicent Lenz described in the *Dictionary of Literary Biography* as "splendidly fitting." Critics were equally appreciative of *Pecos Bill,* in which Kellogg chronicles several of the Texas hero's adventures, including his marriage to cowgirl Slewfoot Sue. Kellogg expands his

collection of tall tales with *Johnny Appleseed, Mike Fink, Sally Ann Thunder Ann Whirlwind Crockett,* and *I Was Born About 10,000 Years Ago: A Tall Tale.* In the last-named book, in which five narrators relate the special—and unlikely—roles they played in events dating back to Adam and Eve's departure from Eden, Kellogg "has pulled out all the stops," according to *Horn Book* contributor Mary M. Burns. Praising Kellogg's art for "lighting up every page," *Booklist* contributor Carolyn Phelan noted that his "expansive, effervescent illustrations interpret the boastful stories with zest, imagination, and wit."

Traditional folktales have also provided the author/illustrator with inspiration, leading to picture books such as *There Was an Old Woman, Chicken Little, The Three Little Pigs, Jack and the Beanstalk,* and *A-Hunting We Will Go!* Another traditional tale, *The Three Sillies,* introduces an exasperated young man who believes that his sweetheart and her family are the three silliest people in the entire world . . . that is, until he meets three other individuals who are even sillier. Calling the picture book "a rollicking farce," a *Publishers Weekly* critic added that Kellogg's "riotous ink-and-watercolor illustrations spill over with preposterous particulars." The author/illustrator's "bizarre use of language and grammar makes [*The Three Sillies*] . . . feel like oral storytelling at its best," added Marta Segal in a *Booklist* review.

*Kellogg's popular and loveable Great Dane shares the spotlight with an unusual new friend in the self-illustrated* **A Penguin Pup for Pinkerton.** (Copyright © 2000 by Steven Kellogg. Reproduced by permission of Dial Books for Young Readers, a division of Penguin Putnam Books for Young Readers.)

"I try to blend illustrations and the words so that each book is a feast for the eye and ear," Kellogg noted on his home page. "I want the time that the reader shares with me and my work to be an enjoyable experience—one that will encourage a lifetime of association with pictures, words, and books."

## Biographical and Critical Sources

### BOOKS

*Children's Literature Review,* Volume 6, Thomson Gale (Detroit, MI), 1984.

Cummings, Pat, editor and compiler, *Talking with Artists,* Bradbury Press (New York, NY), 1992.

*Dictionary of Literary Biography,* Volume 61: *American Writers for Children since 1960: Poets, Illustrators, and Nonfiction Authors,* Thomson Gale (Detroit, MI), 1987.

Lloyd, Pamela, *How Writers Write,* Methuen (London, England), 1987.

*St. James Guide to Children's Writers,* 5th edition, St. James Press (Detroit, MI), 1999.

Silvey, Anita, editor, *Children's Books and Their Creators,* Houghton Mifflin (Boston, MA), 1995.

### PERIODICALS

*Booklist,* November 15, 1979, p. 506; May 15, 1989, Barbara Elleman, interview with Kellogg, pp. 1640-1641; October 15, 1996, Carolyn Phelan, review of *I Was Born About 10,000 Years Ago: A Tall Tale,* p. 422; August, 1998, Shelle Rosenfeld, review of *A-Hunting We Will Go!,* p. 2011; October 1, 1998, Irene Wood, review of *Chicken Little,* p. 348; September 15, 1999, Linda Perkins, review of *A Beasty Story,* p. 268; November 1, 1999, Marta Segal, review of *The Three Sillies,* p. 535; October 15, 2000, Ilene Cooper, review of *The Missing Mitten Mystery,* p. 435; December 1, 2000, Michael Cart, review of *Give the Dog a Bone,* p. 715; December 15, 2000, Amy Brandt, review of *The Baby BeeBee Bird,* p. 827; September 1, 2001, Kay Weisman, review of *A Penguin Pup for Pinkerton,* p. 116; November 1, 2002, Carolyn Phelan, review of *The Mysterious Tadpole,* p. 508; February 1, 2003, Carolyn Phelan, review of *Millions to Measure,* p. 994; November 1, 2003, Ilene Cooper, review of *Clorinda,* p. 513; February 1, 2006, Gillian Engberg, review of *The Invisible Moose,* p. 44.

*Bulletin of the Center for Children's Books,* November, 2005, Elizabeth Bush, review of *If You Decide to Go to the Moon,* p. 148.

*Connecticut,* December, 1989.

*Early Years,* January, 1986, "Steven Kellogg . . . Teachers' Co-Conspirator."

*Horn Book,* November-December, 1990; January-February, 1994, Maeve Visser Knoth, review of *Parents in the Pigpen, Pigs in the Tub,* p. 62; November-December, 1994, Ann A. Flowers, review of *The Great Quillow,*

p. 727; January, 2000, review of *The Three Sillies,* p. 87; September, 2001, Robin Smith, review of *A Penguin Pup for Pinkerton,* p. 574; March-April, 2003, Danielle J. Ford, review of *Millions to Measure,* p. 227; November-December, 2004, review of *Santa Claus Is Comin' to Town,* p. 657; September-October, 2005, Vicky Smith, review of *If You Decide to Go to the Moon,* p. 605; January-February, 2007, Steven Kellogg, transcript of *Boston Globe/Horn Book* Award acceptance speech, p. 25.

*Kirkus Reviews,* February 1, 2003, review of *Millions to Measure,* p. 238; August, 15, 2003, review of *Jimmy's Boa and the Bungee Jump Slam Dunk,* p. 1077; September 15, 2003, review of *Clorinda,* p. 1176; September 1, 2005, review of *If You Decide to Go to the Moon,* p. 979; February 15, 2006, review of *The Invisible Moose,* p. 183.

*Publishers Weekly,* April 16, 1982, p. 71; December 13, 1999, review of *The Three Sillies,* p. 82; April 29, 2002, review of *Big Bear Ball,* p. 68; October 13, 2003, review of *Clorinda,* p. 77; November 14, 2005, review of *If You Decide to Go to the Moon,* p. 67; March 27, 2006, review of *The Invisible Moose,* p. 78.

*School Library Journal,* November 1, 1998, Nancy A. Gifford, review of *A-Hunting We Will Go!,* p. 107; September, 1999, Pat Leach, review of *A Beasty Story,* p. 195; September, 2000, Julie Cummins, *The Baby Bee-Bee Bird,* p. 205; November, 2000, Joy Fleishhacker, review of *Give the Dog a Bone,* p. 144; August, 2001, Lisa Dennis, review of *A Penguin Pup for Pinkerton,* p. 155; April, 2002, Sylvia Veicht, review of *Is Your Mama a Llama?,* p. 76; March, 2003, Kathleen Kelly Macmillan, review of *Millions to Measure,* p. 224; November, 2003, Kristin de Lacoste, review of *Clorinda,* p. 102; October, 2005, DeAnn Tabuchi, review of *If You Decide to Go to the Moon,* p. 141; March, 2006, Wendy Woodfill, review of *The Invisible Moose,* p. 192.

*Times Literary Supplement,* July 18, 1980.

ONLINE

*Children's Literature: Meet Authors and Illustrators Web site,* http://www.childrenslit.com/ (March 8, 2007), "Steven Kellogg."

*Steven Kellogg Home Page,* http://www.stevenkellogg.com (March 8, 2007).

\*    \*    \*

# KELLOGG, Steven Castle
## See KELLOGG, Steven

\*    \*    \*

# KENNY, Jude
## See DALY, Jude

# KONO, Erin Eitter 1973-

## Personal

Born February 26, 1973, in Oshkosh, WI; daughter of Thomas (a university professor and coach) and Geraldine (an administrator) Eitter; married Kirk Isamu Kono (an aerospace engineer) September 29, 2001; children: Caitlyn Akiko. *Education:* University of Iowa, B.A.; study at University of Hull (England) and University of Southern California Los Angeles Extension.

## Addresses

*Home and office*—Redondo Beach, CA. *E-mail*—kikono@aol.com.

## Career

Children's book author and illustrator. Worked as an international flight attendant, 1995-2002; freelance writer and illustrator, 2002—.

## Awards, Honors

Excellence in a Picture Book honor, Children's Literary Council of Southern California, and Best Lullaby and Good-Night Book designation, *Nickelodeon Jr.* maga-

*Erin Eitter Kono* (Photograph courtesy of Erin Eitter Kono.)

zine, both 2005, both for *Hula Lullaby;* Best Books for Children designation, Association of Booksellers for Children, 2005, for *Star Baby* by Margaret O'Hair.

## Writings

*SELF-ILLUSTRATED*

*Hula Lullaby,* Little, Brown (New York, NY), 2005.
*The Twelve Days of Christmas in Wisconsin,* 2007.

*ILLUSTRATOR*

Margaret O'Hair, *Star Baby,* Clarion Books (New York, NY), 2005.
Eileen Ross, *Nellie and the Bandit,* Farrar, Strauss & Giroux (New York, NY), 2005.
Roni Schotter, *Passover!,* Little, Brown (New York, NY), 2006.
Larry Dane Brimner, *A Bit Is a Bite,* Children's Press (New York, NY), 2007.

## Sidelights

Erin Eitter Kono worked for several years as an international airline stewardess before turning to writing and illustrating children's books. In addition to creating artwork for texts by authors Roni Schotter, Lary Dane Brimner, and others, Kono introduces readers to Hawaiian culture in her self-illustrated picture book *Hula Lullaby.* In this story, Kono depicts a firelit evening of music and dance, and a little girl who slowly drifts off to sleep beneath a starlit sky, safe in the lap of her mother. Praising the author-illustrator's rhythmic rhyming text as "an affectionate, even musical bedtime book," Carolyn Phelan wrote in *Booklist* that Kono's "gouache-and-pencil illustrations create an idyllic vision of Hawaiian culture." Comparing Kono's "lovely, lush paintings" to the Tahitian work of noted artist Paul Gauguin, *School Library Journal* contributor Rosalyn Pierini added that the "flowing movement" conveyed in the illustrations is "consistent with the motion and music portrayed" in Kono's bedtime tale.

Among the books Kono has illustrated is Schotter's *Passover!,* published in 2006. In a rhyming text, the book shares with young readers the Passover tradition: a time when Jewish family members come together, both young and old, to celebrate their heritage. Kono's large-scale, colorful illustrations, which feature her signature gouache-and-acrylic technique, depict such Passover traditions as the reading of the Passover story, eating the customary fare of matzoh ball soup and gefilte fish, and the custom of welcoming the prophet Elijah into the family home. Complimenting Kono's upbeat illustrations, Rachel Kamin wrote in *School Library Journal* that the "large, cheerful cartoon illustrations" featured in *Passover!* "colorfully depict a contemporary

*Erin Eitter Kono shares her love of Hawai'i in her self-illustrated picture book* Hula Lullaby. *(Little, Brown and Company, 2005. Reproduced by permission of Hachette Book Group USA.)*

family." In *Booklist,* Ilene Cooper cited the book's "cheerful ink-and-watercolor artwork, mostly in blues, greens, and yellows and highlighted by brighter spring colors," while a *Kirkus Reviews* critic commented that Kono's illustrations lend "a warm familial atmosphere" to Schotter's text.

## Biographical and Critical Sources

*PERIODICALS*

*Booklist,* April 1, 2005, John Peters, review of *Nellie and the Bandit,* p. 1370; May 1, 2005, Carolyn Phelan, review of *Hula Lullaby,* p. 1591; October 15, 2005, Ilene Cooper, review of *Star Baby,* p. 58; February 15, 2006, Ilene Cooper, review of *Passover!,* p. 104.
*Bulletin of the Center for Children's Books,* November, 2005, Loretta Gaffney, review of *Star Baby,* p. 149.
*Kirkus Reviews,* April 1, 2005, review of *Nellie and the Bandit,* p. 423; May 1, 2005, review of *Hula Lullaby,* p. 540; October 15, 2005, review of *Star Baby,* p. 1143; February 15, 2006, review of *Passover!,* p. 190.
*School Library Journal,* July, 2005, Rosalyn Pierini, review of *Hula Lullaby,* p. 76; October, 2005, Amelia Jenkins, review of *Star Baby,* p. 124; April, 2006, Rachel Kamin, review of *Passover!,* p. 117.

*ONLINE*

*Erin Eitter Kono Home Page,* http://www.eekono.com (February 17, 2007).
*Tugeau2 Artist Representatives Web site,* http://www.tugeau2.com/ (February 17, 2007), "Erin Etter Kono."

## KORNPROBST, Jacques 1937-

### Personal

Born 1937, in Strasbourg, France. *Education:* Sorbonne, University of Paris, graduate.

### Addresses

*Office*—1 Laboratoire de Geologie, CNRS, UMR 6524, 5 rue Kessler, 63038, Clermont-Ferrand Cedex, France. *E-mail*—jk@opgc.univ-bpclermont.fr.

### Career

Author. Sorbonne, University of Paris, professor until 1972. Centre national de la recherche scientifique, Clermont-Ferrand, France, professor emeritus and honorary director of geology. Vulcania (volcanological park), Clermont-Ferrand, chairman of scientific committee.

### Member

French Society of Mineralogy and Crstallography (former chairman), Geological Society of France (former chairman).

### Awards, Honors

Awarded Distinguished Cross, French Legion of Honor, 1999.

### Writings

*Métamorphisme et roches métamorphorphiques,* Dunod (Paris France), 1981, translated as *Metamorphic Rocks and Their Geodynamic Significance: A Petrological Handbook,* Kluwer Academic (Boston, MA), 2002.

(Editor) *Kimberlites and Related Rocks: Proceedings of the Third International Kimberlite Conference,* Elseviser (New York, NY), 1984.

(With Christine Laverne) *Living Mountains: How and Why Volcanoes Erupt,* Mountain Press Pub. Co. (Missoula, MT), 2006.

Author of numerous scientific papers.

### Sidelights

French vulcanologist Jacques Kornprobst worked for many years as a professor of geology at France's leading universities. Now, in addition to being professor emeritus of geology at the prestigious Centre national de la recherche scientifique, he is also chairman of the scientific committee of Vulcania, a volcanological park near Clermont-Ferrand, France. As a researcher and academic, Kornprobst has published numerous scientific papers on the science of volcanos. He also shares his expertise with younger readers in *Living Mountains:*

*How and Why Volcanoes Erupt,* a book coauthored with Christine Laverne that introduces the fascinating study of volcanoes around the world. Enhanced with a number of vividly colored watercolor illustrations, *Living Mountains* focuses on the variety of elements that contribute to a volcanic eruption, such as changes in terrain due to new geological formations, crystallization, and the viscosity of lava, among other factors. The coauthors' text includes intriguing examples of volcano lore, such as the history of Santorini, a large volcanic crater in Zaire that is currently collapsing. Starting at Earth's surface and descending deep into its core, the discussion in *Living Mountains* is factual and thorough without becoming to technical. Reviewing the book for *Kliatt,* Mary Ellen Snodgrass praised Kornprobst and Laverne's work as "an attractive introduction to volcanology," and a *California Bookwatch* reviewer cited the coauthors' for their "coverage of the latest volcanology findings."

### Biographical and Critical Sources

*PERIODICALS*

*California Bookwatch,* April, 2006, review of *Living Mountains: How and Why Volcanoes Erupt.*

*Kliatt,* May, 2006, Mary Ellen Snodgrass, review of *Living Mountains,* p. 36.

*Science Books & Films,* July-August, 2006, Jayne R. Koester, review of *Living Mountains,* p. 166.

*ONLINE*

*Mountain Press Web site,* http://mountain-press.com/ (March 3, 2007), "Jacques Kornprobst."*

\*     \*     \*

## KUYPER, Sjoerd 1952-
## (Dutch Cooper)

### Personal

Born March 6, 1952, in Amsterdam, Netherlands; married; wife's name Marjie; children: Joost (son), Marianne. *Education:* University of Amsterdam, B.S. *Hobbies and other interests:* Music.

### Addresses

*Home*—Amsterdam, Netherlands.

### Career

Children's book author, beginning 1974.

### Awards, Honors

Vlag en Wimpel, 1989, for *Majesteit;* Silver Medal, 1994, for *Robin en Suze,* and 1995, for *Het eiland Klaasje;* Gold Medal, 1997, for *Robin en God;* Glimworm prize, 1995, for *Het eiland Klassje.*

# Writings

*Mooie Gedichten,* 1974, translated by Peter Nijmeijer as *Aesthetic Poems,* C.J. Aarts (Amsterdam, Netherlands), 1974.

*Ik herinner mij Klaas Kristiaan* (poems), De Bezige Bij (Amsterdam, Netherlands), 1974.

*Handboek voor overleden knaagdieren,* De Bezige Bij (Amsterdam, Netherlands), 1975.

*Dagen uit het leven,* De Bezige Bij (Amsterdam, Netherlands), 1977.

(Editor) *Ontmoet de dichters,* De Bezige Bij (Amsterdam, Netherlands), 1977.

(With Johan J. Diepstraten) *Het nieuwe proza: interviews met jonge nederlandse schrijvers,* illustrated by Siegfried Woldhek, Athenaeum/Loeb (Amsterdam, Netherlands), 1978.

*Een kleine jongen en z'n beer,* De Bezige Bij (Amsterdam, Netherlands), 1978.

*De glazen kamer: verhalen,* De Bezige Bij (Amsterdam, Netherlands), 1979.

(With Johan J. Diepstraten) *Dichters: interviews,* illustrated by Siegfried Woldhek, De Bezige Bij (Amsterdam, Netherlands), 1980.

*Ratten en flamingo's,* De Bezige Bij (Amsterdam, Netherlands), 1982.

*Een reisgenoot,* De Bezige Bij (Amsterdam, Netherlands), 1985.

(With Johan J. Diepstraten) *De verborgen steeg,* illustrated by Gert Dooreman, B. Bakker (Amsterdam, Netherlands), 1986.

*De ogen van het paard,* B. Bakker (Amsterdam, Netherlands), 1987.

*Het zand: verhalen,* De Bezige Bij (Amsterdam, Netherlands), 1987.

*Majesteit, uw ontbijt* (young-adult novel), illustrated by Gitte Spee, Leopold (Amsterdam, Netherlands), 1988.

*Josje* (also see below), illustrated by Jan Jutte, 1989.

*Het zakmes* (picture book; title means "The Penknife"), International Theatre & Film Books (Amsterdam, Netherlands), 1991.

*Josje's droom* (also see below), illustrated by Jan Jutte, 1992.

*Nachtkind,* Veen (Amsterdam, Netherlands), 1992.

*Zeepziederij de adelaar,* L.J. Veen (Amsterdam, Netherlands), 1994.

*Het eiland Klaasje* (for children), illustrated by Jan Jutte, Leopold (Amsterdam, Netherlands), 1995.

*De rode zwaan* (young-adult novel), Leopold (Amsterdam, Netherlands, 1996.

*Alleen mijn verhalen nam ik mee* (young-adult novel), Leopold (Amsterdam, Netherland), 1998.

*Het boek van Josje* (includes *Josjie, Josje's droom,* and *Josje's lied*), illustrated by Jan Jutte, 1999, translation by Patricia Crampton published under pseudonym Dutch Cooper as *Josie,* Mammoth (London, England), 2000, translation published under name Sjoerd Kuyper, Holiday House (New York, NY), 2005.

(With Annemarie van Häringen) *Malmok,* Leopold (Amsterdam, Netherlands), 1999.

*Josje's lied* (also see below), illustrated by Jan Jutte, 1999.

*Eiber* (picture book), CPNB (Amsterdam, Netherlands), 2000.

*De leukste jongen van de school* (chapter book), Leopold (Amsterdam, Netherlands), 2002.

*Fanfare* (picture book; with CD), Leopold (Amsterdam, Netherlands), 2002.

*Een muts voor de maan,* illustrated by Jan Jutte, Leopold (Amsterdam, Netherlands), 2003.

*Hoofden uit de mist: over de moderne jeugdliteratuur* (nonfiction), L.J. Veen (Amsterdam, Netherlands), 2004.

*"ROBIN" SERIES; PICTURE BOOKS*

*Robins zomer,* Leopold (Amsterdam, Netherlands), 1990.

*Robin en Suze,* Leopold (Amsterdam, Netherlands), 1993.

*Robin en Sinterklaas,* Leopold (Amsterdam, Netherlands), 1993.

*Robin op school,* Leopold (Amsterdam, Netherlands), 1994.

*Robin en God,* illustrated by Sandra Klaassen, Leopold (Amsterdam, Netherlands), 1997.

*Robin en Knor,* Leopold (Amsterdam, Netherlands), 1997.

*Robin en opa,* Leopold (Amsterdam, Netherlands), 1998.

*Robin en de zon,* illustrated by Sandra Kaassen, Leopold (Amsterdam, Netherlands), 2001.

*Robin is jarig,* Leopold (Amsterdam, Netherlands), 2001.

*Robin op het ijs,* illustrated by Sandra Klaassen, Leopold (Amsterdam, Netherlands), 2003.

# Adaptations

Characters based on Kuyper's books have been adapted for award-winning television series. *Het zakmes* was adapted for video by Filmwest Associates Ltd. (Carson City, NE), 1991. *De rode zwaan* was adapted for film, 1999.

# Biographical and Critical Sources

*PERIODICALS*

*Bookbird* (annual), 1999, review of *Malmok,* p. 64.

*Kirkus Reviews,* February 15, 2006, review of *The Swan's Child,* p. 185.

*School Library Journal,* March, 2006, Elizabeth Bird, review of *The Swan's Child,* p. 195.

*ONLINE*

*Sjoerd Kuyper Home Page,* http://home.planet.nl/~kuyper450 (March 19, 2007).*

# L

LANG, T.T.
See TAYLOR, Theodore

\* \* \*

## LANGRISH, Katherine

### Personal

Married; children: two daughters. *Education:* University of London, B.A. (first-class honors), 1979.

### Addresses

*Home*—England.

### Career

Writer. Worked as a riding instructor and waitress; International School, Fontainebleau, France, instructor; Lloyd's Register of Ships, London, England, member of staff; literacy worker in Corning, NY.

### Writings

*JUVENILE FICTION*

*Troll Fell,* HarperCollins (New York, NY), 2004.
*Troll Mill,* HarperCollins (London, England), 2005, Eos (New York, NY), 2006.

### Sidelights

The author of the young-adult fantasy novels *Troll Fell* and *Troll Mill,* Katherine Langrish has been interested in fantasy worlds since childhood. She has taught storytelling at the International School in Fontainebleau, France, and also at schools and festivals in New York state. As Langrish told Caroline Horn in *Bookseller,* "I love fairy stories. People call them escapist but they deal with severities, with death, and with whether or not a child can be successful in this world. So many start with someone who is disadvantaged but they still succeed."

In writing *Troll Fell* and *Troll Mill* Langrish was inspired by the folklore and legends of Scandinavia. In *Troll Fell* readers meet young Peer Ulfsson, has recently lost his father. A stranger soon comes to Peer's village, a gigantic, frightening figure who turns out to be Baldur, Peer's uncle by marriage. Uncle Baldur is also part troll. After claiming all Peer's belongings, Baldur takes the boy back to his home in an old mill at the foot of a trolls' mountain. There, Peer becomes a servant to Baldur and his hideous twin brother, Grim. Despite his miserable predicament, Peer finds companionship with Nis, the spirit who lives in the mill's barn, and a neighbor girl named Hilde. After a time, Peer learns that his troll-uncles intend to present him as a wedding gift to the son of the troll-king, an act that will make Peer a slave to the newlyweds. While bribing the king, Baldur and Grim also scheme to confiscate property rightfully owned by Hilde's family. Peer and Hilde now team up, hopeful that they can thwart the plans of the hideous twins; the adventures they encounter in doing so take them straight into the center of the troll kingdom.

Reviewing *Troll Fell* for the *Magazine of Fantasy and Science Fiction,* Elizabeth Hand called it an "utterly charming, captivating debut." Elements of traditional Scandinavian storytelling and myth blend with a stirring adventure story that Langrish recounts "at breakneck speed," according to Hand. The critic compared *Troll Fell* favorably to the "Harry Potter" series by J.K. Rowling, stating that "in tone and warmth of characterization," the series is also reminiscent of Lloyd Alexander's classic "Prydain Chronicles." A *Kirkus Reviews* contributor noted that, although *Troll Fell* employs many familiar elements, Langrish's "clearly delineated, memorable characters transcend stereotype." Writing in *School Library Journal,* Bruce Anne Shook also praised the novel, predicting that readers will not only "love to

hate" the horrible twin uncles, but will also enjoy the "great fun" of Langrish's story, especially the "nice twist at the conclusion."

Peer's adventures continue in *Troll Mill,* which takes place three years after *Troll Fell* and finds Peer now living as part of Hilde's family. The family grows even larger when Hilde's compassionate parents Ralf and Gudrun take in the web-footed half-selkie child of a local man whose wife was destined to return to the sea. This adoption, as well as Peer's concerns over strange goings-on at his uncles' mill, soon stirs up some otherworldly activity. Peer's worries over the return of Grim and Baldur are ultimately realized in a novel that Farida S. Dowler deemed "tightly woven" in her *Booklist* review. Viewing *Troll Mill* as a coming-of-age novel, a *Kirkus Reviews* writer noted that Langrish weaves into her plot the "struggles with identity, disillusionment and unrequited love" endured by the fifteen-year-old Peer, whose feelings toward Hilde have moved from friendship to romantic love. In her *Kliatt* review, Michele Winship wrote that "Langrish's description of the mill and its various inhabitants is especially chilling," while Dowler maintained that *Troll Mill*'s "conclusion is poignant and true, with enough open-endedness for another sequel."

## Biographical and Critical Sources

*PERIODICALS*

*Booklist,* April 15, 2004, John Peters, review of *Troll Fell,* p. 1457; February 1, 2006, Jennifer Mattson, review of *Troll Mill,* p. 49.

*Bookseller,* April 16, 2004, Caroline Horn, review of *Troll Fell,* p. 30.

*Bulletin of the Center for Children's Books,* March, 2006, Elizabeth Bush, review of *Troll Mill,* p. 317.

*Kirkus Reviews,* June 1, 2004, review of *Troll Fell,* p. 538; February 1, 2006, review of *Troll Mill,* p. 133.

*Kliatt,* January, 2006, Michele Winship, review of *Troll Mill,* p. 10.

*Magazine of Fantasy and Science Fiction,* August, 2004, Elizabeth Hand, review of *Troll Fell,* p. 35.

*School Library Journal,* July, 2004, Bruce Anne Shook, review of *Troll Fell,* p. 106; March, 2006, Farinda S. Dowler, review of *Troll Mill,* p. 226.

*Voice of Youth Advocates,* February, 2006, Leslie McCoombs, review of *Troll Mill,* p. 500.

*ONLINE*

*AllSciFi.com,* http://www.allscifi.com/ (October 15, 2005), Harriet Klausner, review of *Troll Fell.* \*

\*     \*     \*

# LANSKY, Vicki 1942-

## Personal

Born January 6, 1942, in Louisville, KY; daughter of Arthur (a men's clothing industry executive) and Mary

*Vicky Lansky* (Photograph courtesy of Book Peddlers.)

(a homemaker) Rogosin; married S. Bruce Lansky (a publisher and literary agent), June 13, 1967 (divorced, 1983); children: Douglas, Dana. *Education:* Connecticut College, B.A. (art history), 1963. *Hobbies and other interests:* Tending plants, swimming, travel.

## Addresses

*Office*—Book Peddlers, 2828 Hedberg Dr., Minnetonka, MN 55305. *E-mail*—Vickilee@aol.com.

## Career

Writer and publisher. Sportswear buyer for Lord & Taylor and Mercantile Stores, New York, NY, 1965-69; freelance photographer, 1968-72; Childbirth Education Association, Minneapolis, MN, teaching assistant, 1971-74; Meadowbrook Press, Wayzata, MN, founder, treasurer, and executive vice president in charge of operations, 1974-83; Book Peddlers (publisher), Minnetonka, MN, founder and owner, 1983—. *Practical Parenting* (newsletter), editor and publisher, 1979-88. Associated Press Broadcast Features, daily radio commentator, 1981-82; appeared on television programs, including *Donahue, Oprah, Live with Regis and . . .,* and *Today.* Pillsbury/Green Giant Consumer Advisory Panel, past member; spokesperson for American Plastics Council,

1993, 3M Company, 2005, and others. Member of advisory board, Catholic Charities Office for Divorced and Separated, Parenthood Cable TV, National Parenting Center, and Children's Rights Council.

## Awards, Honors

Parents Choice Award, 1990, for *Vicki Lansky's Divorce Book for Parents;* Best New Product Introduction selection, Juvenile Products Manufacturers Association, 1993, for *Games Babies Play.*

## Writings

(With others) *Feed Me! I'm Yours,* Meadowbrook Press (Deephaven, MN), 1974, revised edition, illustrated by Kathy Rogers, 1994, 4th edition, 2004.

*The Taming of the C.A.N.D.Y. (Continuously Advertised, Nutritionally Deficient Yummies!) Monster: A Cookbook,* Meadowbrook Press (Deephaven, MN), 1978, published with illustrations by Lynn Johnston, Book Peddlers (Deephaven, MN), 1988, 3rd edition, 1999.

*Dear Babysitter,* edited by Kathryn Ring, Meadowbrook Press (Deephaven, MN), 1982, published as *Dear Babysitter Handbook,* Bantam Books (New York, NY), 2001.

*Vicki Lansky's Practical Parenting Tips,* illustrated by Kathryn Ring, Meadowbrook Press (Deephaven, MN), 1982, revised edition published as *Practical Parenting Tips: Over 1,500 Helpful Hints for the First Five Years,* Fine Communications (New York, NY), 2003.

*Toilet Training,* Bantam Books (New York, NY), 1984, revised edition published as *Toilet Training: A Practical Guide to Daytime and Nighttime Training,* 1993, 3rd edition, Book Peddlers (Minnetonka, MN), 2002.

*Welcoming Your Second Baby,* Bantam Books (New York, NY), 1984, revised edition, Book Peddlers (Deephaven, MN), 2005.

*Vicki Lansky's Practical Parenting Tips for the School-Age Years,* Bantam Books (New York, NY), 1985.

*Traveling with Your Baby,* Bantam Books (New York, NY), 1985.

*Getting Your Baby to Sleep (and Back to Sleep),* Bantam Books (New York, NY), 1985, published with audiocassette and compact disc as *Getting Your Child to Sleep—and Back to Sleep,* Book Peddlers (Deephaven, MN), 2004.

*Birthday Parties,* Bantam Books (New York, NY), 1986, published as *Vicky Lansky's Birthday Parties,* Book Peddlers (Deephaven, MN), 1989, published as *Birthday Parties: Best Party Tips and Ideas for Ages 1-8,* 1995.

*The Best of Vicki Lansky's Practical Parenting,* Book Peddlers (Deephaven, MN), 1987.

*Fat-Proofing Your Kids,* Bantam Books (New York, NY), 1987, published as *Fat-Proofing Your Children . . . So That They Never Become Diet-Addicted Adults,* 1988.

*101 Ways to Tell Your Child "I Love You,"* illustrated by Kaye Pomeranc White, Contemporary Books (Chicago, IL), 1988.

*Vicki Lansky's Divorce Book for Parents: Helping Your Children Cope with Divorce and Its Aftermath,* New American Library (New York, NY), 1989, 3rd edition, Book Peddlers (Deephaven, MN), 1996.

*Baby-Proofing Basics: How to Keep Your Child Safe,* 1991, 2nd edition, Book Peddlers (Minnetonka, MN), 2002.

*101 Ways to Make Your Child Feel Special,* illustrated by Kaye Pomeranc White, Contemporary Books (Chicago, IL), 1991.

*Another Use for . . . 101 Common Household Items,* illustrated by Martha Campbell, Book Peddlers (Deephaven, MN), 1991.

*101 Ways to Say "I Love You,"* Simon & Schuster (New York, NY), 1991.

*Games Babies Play: From Birth to Twelve Months,* Book Peddlers (Deephaven, MN), 1993.

*Don't Throw That Out!: A Pennywise Parent's Guide to Creative Uses for over 200 Household Items,* Book Peddlers (Deephaven, MN), 1994.

*101 Ways to Be a Special Mom,* illustrated by Kaye Pomeranc White, Contemporary Books (Chicago, IL), 1995.

*101 Ways to Be a Special Dad,* illustrated by Kaye Pomeranc White, Contemporary Books (Chicago, IL), 1995.

*Baking Soda: Over 500 Fabulous, Fun, and Frugal Uses You've Probably Never Thought Of,* illustrated by Martha Campbell, Book Peddlers (Deephaven, MN), 1995, 2nd edition, 2004.

*Transparent Tape: Over 350 Super, Simple, and Surprising Uses You've Probably Never Thought Of,* illustrated by Martha Campbell, Book Peddlers (Deephaven, MN), 1995, 2nd edition, 2005.

(Coauthor) *Healthy Pregnancy, Healthy Babies: A Guide to Prenatal and Baby Care,* Publications International (Lincolnwood, IL), 1995.

*Trouble-Free Travel with Children: Helpful Hints for Parents on the Go,* 1995.

(Coauthor) *Complete Pregnancy and Baby Book: A Guide to Prenatal, Infant, and Toddler Care,* Publications International (Lincolnwood, IL), 1996.

*101 Ways to Spoil Your Grandchild,* illustrated by Rondi Collette, Contemporary Books (Chicago, IL), 1996.

*The Bag Book: Over 500 Great Uses—and Reuses—for Paper, Plastic, and Other Bags to Organize and Enhance Your Life,* illustrated by Martha Campbell, Book Peddlers (Minnetonka, MN), 2000.

*Best New Baby Tips,* Book Peddlers (Minnetonka, MN), 2001.

*Vinegar: Over 400 Various, Versatile, and Very Good Uses You've Probably Never Thought Of,* illustrated by Martha Campbell, Book Peddlers (Minnetonka, MN), 2004.

Sunday newspaper columnist, Minneapolis *Star and Tribune,* 1985-86; columnist, *Sesame Street Parents,* c. 1987-97. Contributing editor, *Family Circle,* 1988—.

*FOR CHILDREN*

*Koko Bear's New Potty,* illustrated by Jane Prince, Bantam Books (New York, NY), 1986.

*Koko Bear's New Babysitter,* illustrated by Jane Prince, Bantam Books (New York, NY), 1987.

*A New Baby at Koko Bear's House,* Bantam Books (New York, NY), 1987.

*Vicki Lansky's Kids Cooking,* Scholastic, Inc. (New York, NY), 1987.

*Koko Bear's Big Earache,* illustrated by Jane Prince, Bantam Books (New York, NY), 1988.

*Sing Along as You Ride Along* (with audiocassette), Scholastic, Inc. (New York, NY), 1988.

*Sing Along Birthday Fun* (with audiocassette), Scholastic, Inc. (New York, NY), 1988.

*Vicki Lansky's Microwave Cooking for Kids,* Scholastic, Inc. (New York, NY), 1991.

*It's Not Your Fault, Koko Bear: A Read-Together Book for Parents and Young Children during Divorce,* illustrated by Jane Prince, Book Peddlers (Minnetonka, MN), 1998.

## Sidelights

In 1974 Vicki Lansky and several other mothers from a local Childbirth Education Association chapter wrote a baby food cookbook for new mothers. Although she believed the book to have commercial appeal, no publisher was interested in it. Undaunted, Lansky and her husband turned their back porch into their own publishing company, Meadowbrook Press, and began producing *Feed Me! I'm Yours* for distribution. Their creative promotional efforts and numerous appearances on television talk shows eventually propelled the book to bestseller status as America's best-selling baby and toddler cookbook.

As her children grew older, Lansky found the struggle to maintain good nutritional habits intensifying. Saturday-morning television commercials for junk food fueled her children's desire for processed foods during favorite cartoon programs, and Lansky realized that one way to counter this offensive was with tasty alternative recipes with child appeal. In *The Taming of the C.A.N. D.Y. (Continuously Advertised, Nutritionally Deficient Yummies!) Monster: A Cookbook* she provides parents with practical ways to improve their children's eating habits. The book rose quickly to the number-one spot on the *New York Times* trade paperback bestseller list.

Drawing on her growing reputation as a savvy parent, in 1979 Lansky began publishing *Practical Parenting,* a bimonthly newsletter consisting of articles and tips on childrearing issues. Remaining in publication until the late 1980s, the newsletter grew into a nationally syndicated radio feature and sparked a series of practical parenting books. Lansky designed each book to cover a single topic, providing a quick and easy source of information for inexperienced parents. Lansky explained to Sue MacDonald in the *Cincinnati Enquirer* that "a lot of these books [are] a replacement for the support group" because new parents often lack parents in close proximity and mothers frequently avoid asking friends of family for child-rearing advice.

*Cover of Vicky Lansky's bestselling kid-centered cook book* **Feed Me! I'm Yours.** (Cover © 2004 by Meadowbrook Press. Reprinted with permission from Meadowbrook Press.)

In the books she has published during her long career—first with Meadowbrook Press and more recently with Book Peddlers—Lansky sometimes pairs a book for parents with a children's book on the same topic. For example, *Welcoming Your Second Baby* is intended to prepare parents for the issues that arise when a new baby arrives in a single-child household. The book's chapter headings take the form of questions that commonly trouble expectant parents, such as caring for a new infant without neglecting an older sibling or handling special issues like adoption, blended families, and even newborn death. For children, her related picture book *A New Baby at Koko's House* is designed to appeal to the older sibling via an entertaining story, while also supporting the adult reader by including parent-focused tips on each page.

As Lansky once noted: "I continue to be fascinated by the world of household trivia, the challenges of book

publishing, . . . the changing world of divorce social services, computer online services as well as desktop publishing and, of course, the ever evolving nature of the human condition and relationships.

"I feel very lucky to be around at this point in time. I doubt that I could have made a living with this type of material seventy-five years ago and I am not sure of the need for it seventy-five years hence. Despite the fact that my titles have probably sold over six million copies, I have no illusions about the literary value of my work. There is none. But I have touched many people's lives and hopefully made it a little better or easier for them."

## Biographical and Critical Sources

*PERIODICALS*

*Booklist,* September 1, 1978, review of *The Taming of the C.A.N.D.Y. (Continuously Advertised, Nutritionally Deficient Yummies!) Monster: A Cookbook,* p. 11; July, 1983, review of *Toilet Training* and *Welcoming Your Second Baby,* p. 1503; March 1, 1985, review of *Vicki Lansky's Practical Parenting Tips for the School-Age Years,* p. 915; September 1, 1985, review of *Getting Your Baby to Sleep (and Back to Sleep),* p. 13; December 15, 1985, review of *Vicki Lansky's Practical Parenting Tips,* p. 635; April 1, 1988, review of *The Taming of the C.A.N.D.Y. (Continuously Advertised, Nutritionally Deficient Yummies!) Monster,* p. 1298; September 15, 1990, review of *Welcoming Your Second Baby,* p. 126; June 1, 1991, review of *Baby-Proofing Basics: How to Keep Your Child Safe,* p. 1846; June 1, 1991, review of *Getting Your Child to Sleep—and Back to Sleep,* p. 1850; February 15, 1994, Jo Peer-Haas, review of *Don't Throw That Out!: A Pennywise Parent's Guide to Creative Uses for Over 200 Household Items,* p. 1045; February 15, 1995, Mike Tribby, review of *Baking Soda: Over 500 Fabulous, Fun, and Frugal Uses You've Probably Never Thought Of,* p. 1046; February 15, 1999, Barbara Jacobs, review of *The Taming of the C.A.N.D.Y. (Continuously Advertised, Nutritionally Deficient Yummies!) Monster,* p. 1022.

*Bookwatch,* January, 1993, review of *Practical Parenting Tips: Over 1,500 Helpful Hints for the First Five Years,* p. 12; April, 1993, review of *Games Babies Play: From Birth to Twelve Months,* p. 12.

*Children's Bookwatch,* June, 1993, review of *101 Ways to Be a Special Dad,* p. 8; January, 1998, review of *It's Not Your Fault, Koko Bear,* p. 1.

*Cincinnati Enquirer,* August 3, 1984, Sue MacDonald, interview with Lansky.

*Library Journal,* July, 1978, review of *The Taming of the C.A.N.D.Y. (Continuously Advertised, Nutritionally Deficient Yummies!) Monster,* p. 1408; March 15, 1985, Kari D. Anderson, review of *Vicki Lansky's Practical Parenting Tips for the School-Age Years,* p. 58; May 15, 1989, Marcia G. Fuchs, review of *Vicki*

*Lansky's Divorce Book for Parents: Helping Your Children Cope with Divorce and Its Aftermath,* p. 80; May 15, 1991, Linda Beck, review of *Baby-Proofing Basics,* p. 103.

*Los Angeles Times,* July 25, 1982, review of *Dear Babysitter,* p. 12.

*New York Times,* November 12, 1995, Laurel Graeber, review of *Trouble-Free Travel with Children: Helpful Hints for Parents on the Go.*

*New York Times Book Review,* April 2, 1978, review of *Feed Me! I'm Yours,* p. 41; November 26, 1989, review of *Vicki Lansky's Divorce Book for Parents,* p. 26.

*Parents,* May, 1990, reviews of *Toilet Training,* p. 226, and *Koko Bear's New Potty,* p. 228.

*Party and Paper Retailer,* February, 1996, "Birthday Parties: Best Party Tips and Ideas," p. 44.

*Publishers Weekly,* January 16, 1978, review of *The Taming of the C.A.N.D.Y. (Continuously Advertised, Nutritionally Deficient Yummies!) Monster,* p. 98; October 10, 1980, Sally A. Lodge, review of *Best Practical Parenting Tips,* p. 72; June 29, 1984, review of *Welcoming Your Second Baby,* p. 103; April 2, 2001, Sally A. Lodge, "Growing-Up Books Come of Age," p. 23.

*Reading Teacher,* February, 1981, review of *The Taming of the C.A.N.D.Y. (Continuously Advertised, Nutritionally Deficient Yummies!) Monster,* p. 585.

*School Library Journal,* June, 1998, Kathy Piehl, review of *It's Not Your Fault, Koko Bear,* p. 130.

*Small Press,* summer, 1991, review of *A New Baby at Koko Bear's House,* p. 57.

*Special Delivery,* fall, 1999, Kamal Bridge, reviews of *A New Baby at Koko Bear's House* and *Welcoming Your Second Baby,* p. 25.

*Us,* June 27, 1978.

*Washington Post Book World,* March 5, 1978, review of *Feed Me! I'm Yours* and *The Taming of the C.A.N.D.Y. (Continuously Advertised, Nutritionally Deficient Yummies!) Monster,* p. F4.

*Whole Earth,* spring, 1995, review of *Trouble-Free Travel with Children,* p. 111.

*ONLINE*

*Book Peddlers Web site,* http://www.bookpeddlers.com/ (March 10, 1007).

*Practical Parenting Home Page,* http://www.practicalparenting.com/ (January 27, 2006).

\* \* \*

## LEWISON, Wendy Cheyette

### Personal

Female.

### Addresses

*Home and office*—Larchmont, NY.

## Career

Children's book author.

## Writings

*Raccoon's Messy Birthday Party,* illustrated by Vickie Learner, Marvel Entertainment Group (New York, NY), 1988.

*Where Is Sammy's Smile?,* illustrated by Katy Bratun, Grosset & Dunlap (New York, NY), 1989.

*My Baby Brother,* illustrated by Stephen Cartwright, Warner Books (New York, NY), 1990.

*My Favorite Doll,* illustrated by Stephen Cartwright, Warner Books (New York, NY), 1990.

*My New Puppy,* illustrated by Stephen Cartwright, Warner Books (New York, NY), 1990.

*Where's My Teddy?,* illustrated by Stephen Cartwright, Warner Books (New York, NY), 1990.

*Mud,* illustrated by Maryann Cocca-Leffler, Random House (New York, NY), 1990, illustrated by Bill Basso, Scholastic (New York, NY), 2002.

*Where's Baby?,* illustrated by True Kelley, Scholastic (New York, NY), 1992.

*"Buzz," Said the Bee,* illustrated by Hans Wilhelm, Scholastic (New York, NY), 1992.

*Bye-bye, Baby,* illustrated by True Kelley, Scholastic (New York, NY), 1992.

*Going to Sleep on the Farm,* illustrated by Juan Wijngaard, Dial Books for Young Readers (New York, NY), 1992.

*Nighty-night,* illustrations by Giulia Orecchia, Grosset & Dunlap (New York, NY), 1992.

*Say Thank You, Theodore: A Book about Manners,* illustrated by Juli Kangas, Platt & Munk (New York, NY), 1992.

*Uh oh, Baby,* illustrated by True Kelley, Scholastic (New York, NY), 1992.

*Baby's First Mother Goose,* illustrated by Mary Morgan, Western Publishing (Racine, WI), 1993.

*Christmas Cookies,* illustrated by Mary Morgan, Grosset & Dunlap (New York, NY), 1993.

*Happy Thanksgiving!,* illustrated by Mary Morgan, Grosset & Dunlap (New York, NY), 1993.

*Shy Vi,* illustrated by Stephen John Smith, Simon & Schuster (New York, NY), 1993.

*Baby Has a Boo-boo,* illustrated by Bettina Paterson, Grosset & Dunlap (New York, NY), 1994.

*Hello, Snow!,* illustrated by Maryann Cocca-Leffler, Grosset & Dunlap (New York, NY), 1994.

*Happy Babies,* illustrated by Jan Palmer, Western Publishing (Racine, WI), 1994.

*The Princess and the Potty,* illustrated by Rick Brown, Simon & Schuster (New York, NY), 1994, 2nd edition, Aladdin (New York, NY), 2005.

*The Rooster Who Lost His Crow,* illustrated by Thor Wickstrom, Dial Books for Young Readers (New York, NY), 1995.

*Don't Wake the Baby!,* illustrated by Jerry Smath, Grosset & Dunlap (New York, NY), 1996.

*I Wear My Tutu Everywhere!,* illustrated by Mary Morgan, Grosset & Dunlap (New York, NY), 1996.

*Our New Baby,* photographs by Nancy Sheehan, Grosset & Dunlap (New York, NY), 1996.

*Ten Little Ballerinas,* illustrated by Joan Holub, Grosset & Dunlap (New York, NY), 1996.

*A Trip to the Firehouse,* photographs by Elizabeth Hathon, Grosset & Dunlap (New York, NY), 1998.

*Buzz, the Little Seaplane,* illustrated by Anthony Lewis, Grosset & Dunlap (New York, NY), 1999.

*I Am a Flower Girl,* photographs by Elizabeth Hathon, Grosset & Dunlap (New York, NY), 1999.

*The Big Snowball,* illustrated by Maryann Cocca-Leffler, Grossett & Dunlap (New York, NY), 2000.

*Eleanor's Enormous Ears,* illustrated by Duendes Del Sur, Scholastic (New York, NY), 2000.

*One Little Butterfly,* illustrated by Jane Conteh-Morgan, Grosset & Dunlap (New York, NY), 2000.

*One Little Dragonfly,* illustrated by Jane Conteh-Morgan, Grosset & Dunlap (New York, NY), 2000.

*So Many Boots,* illustrated by Tony Griego, Scholastic (New York, NY), 2000.

*What Will I Be?,* photographs by James Levin, Scholastic (New York, NY), 2001.

*Princess Buttercup: A Flower Princess Story,* illustrated by Jerry Smath, Grosset & Dunlap (New York, NY), 2001.

*F Is for Flag,* illustrated by Barbara Duke, Grosset & Dunlap (New York, NY), 2002.

*Little Chick's Happy Easter,* illustrated by Debra Ziss, Scholastic (New York, NY), 2002.

*Peekaboo! I See You!,* illustrated by Christopher Moroney, Random House (New York, NY), 2002.

*Wiggly Worm,* illustrated by Judith Moffatt, Scholastic (New York, NY), 2002.

*Baby Faces,* illustrated by Christopher Moroney, Random House (New York, NY), 2002.

*Billy the Bug's New Jug,* illustrated by Maxie Chambliss, Scholastic (New York, NY), 2002.

*Clifford's Loose Tooth,* illustrated by John and Sandrina Kurtz, Scholastic (New York, NY), 2002.

*Easter Bunny's Amazing Egg Machine,* illustrated by Normand Chartier, Random House (New York, NY), 2002.

*Cling-clang! Bang-bang!,* illustrated by Christopher Moroney, Random House (New York, NY), 2003.

*L Is for Liberty,* illustrated by Laura Freeman Hines, Grosset & Dunlap (New York, NY), 2003.

*Raindrop, Plop!,* illustrated by Pam Paparone, Viking (New York, NY), 2004.

*The Prince and the Potty,* illustrated by Keiko Motoyama, Simon & Schuster (New York, NY), 2006.

*Two Is for Twins,* illustrated by Hiroe Nakata, Viking (New York, NY), 2006.

## Sidelights

Wendy Cheyette Lewison's love of writing is rooted in her passion for words, a passion that developed in childhood when she discovered that writing provided her a creative outlet despite her shyness. Lewison touches on the topic of shyness in her novel *Shy Vi.* The book centers on a young girl named Violet who is so incredibly

***Illustration by Normand Chartier of Wendy Cheyette Lewison's holiday-themed picture book* Easter Bunny's Amazing Egg Machine.** (Copyright © 2002 by Normand Chartier. Used by permission of Random House Children's Books, a division of Random House, Inc.)

shy and soft-spoken that she is often drowned out by her more vocal siblings. Violet's parents constantly urge the bashful girl to assert herself and devise techniques to boost their daughter's self-esteem. As Violet ultimately overcomes her shyness, Lewison creates what a *Publishers Weekly* critic deemed "a welcome conclusion to this sensitive, humorously told tale."

Lewison presents another perceptive tale in *Two Is for Twins*, which explores the special relationship between twin brothers. Lewison begins her lighthearted story by listing a series of items that come in twos—two eyes, two ears, two bicycle wheels, two bluebird wings—and ultimately ends with two identical twin brothers. Her depiction of this "twoness" continues as the author describes the twin brothers playing, going to school, and suffering through the chicken pox in her "well-cadenced, rhyming text," in the opinion of *Booklist* reviewer Carolyn Phelan. A critic for *Kirkus Reviews* regarded *Two Is for Twins* as a "worthy selection for young readers," and *School Library Journal* contributor Joy Fleishhacker noted that Lewison's "rhythmic text reads aloud smoothly."

## Biographical and Critical Sources

### PERIODICALS

*Booklist,* June 1, 1992, review of *Going to Sleep on the Farm,* p. 60; April 15, 1994, Mary Harris Veeder, review of *The Princess and the Potty,* p. 1541; March 15, 2004, Terry Glover, review of *Raindrop, Plop!,* p. 1309; May 15, 2006, Carolyn Phelan, review of *Two Is for Twins,* p. 50.

*Kirkus Reviews,* March 1, 2004, review of *Raindrop, Plop!,* p. 225; April 15, 2006, review of *Two Is for Twins,* p. 409; June 1, 2006, review of *The Prince and the Potty,* p. 576.

*Publishers Weekly,* April 19, 1993, review of *Shy Vi,* p. 59; September 20, 1993, review of *Happy Thanksgiving!,* p. 31; January 17, 1994, review of *The Princess and the Potty,* p. 430.

*School Library Journal,* August, 2001, Maura Bresnahan, review of *Princess Buttercup: A Flower Princess Story,* p. 156; August, 2002, Maria Otero-Boisvert, review of *The Big Leaf Pile,* p. S57; February, 2004, Wendy

Woodfill, review of *Raindrop, Plop!,* p. 116; April, 2006, Joy Fleishhacker, review of *Two Is for Twins,* p. 111; July, 2006, Kathleen Kelly, MacMillan, review of *The Prince and the Potty,* p. 82.

*ONLINE*

*Houghton Mifflin Education Place Web site,* http://www. eduplace.com/ (February 19, 2007), "Wendy Cheyette Lewison."

*Penguin Group Web site,* http://us.penguingroup.com/ (February 19, 2007), "Wendy Cheyette Lewison."*

\* \* \*

# LOW, William

## Personal

Born in New York, NY. *Education:* Parson's School of Design, B.F.A.

## Addresses

*Home and office*—New York, NY. *E-mail*—info@williamlow.com.

## Career

Artist and illustrator. Cobalt Illustration Studios, New York, NY, principal artist.

## Awards, Honors

Four-time Silver Medal winner, Society of Illustrators.

## Writings

*SELF-ILLUSTRATED*

*Chinatown,* Holt (New York, NY), 1997.
*Old Penn Station,* Holt (New York, NY), 2007.

*ILLUSTRATOR*

Wallace Earle Stegner, *Crossing to Safety,* Franklin Library (Franklin Center, PA), 1987.
Nola Thacker, *Summer Stories,* Lippincott (Philadelphia, PA), 1988.
Ellen Kindt McKenzie, *Stargone John,* Holt (New York, NY), 1990.
Ellen Kindt McKenzie, *The King, the Princess, and the Tinker,* Holt (New York, NY), 1992.
Abigail Thomas, *Wake up, Wilson Street,* Holt (New York, NY), 1993.
Abigail Thomas, *Lily,* Holt (New York, NY), 1994.
Elaine Moore, *Good Morning, City,* Bridgewater (Mahwah, NJ), 1995.

Eve Bunting, *The Days of Summer,* Harcourt (San Diego, CA), 2001.
Bruce Edward Hall, *Henry and the Kite Dragon,* Philomel (New York, NY), 2004.
Amy Littlesugar, *Willy and Max: A Holocaust Story,* Philomel (New York, NY), 2005.
Elizabeth Foreman Lewis, *Young Fu of the Upper Yangtze,* Holt (New York, NY), 2007.
T.A. Barron, *The Day the Stones Walked,* Philomel (New York, NY), 2007.

## Sidelights

Painter and illustrator William Low has "a reputation for exploiting light, color, visual perspective, and emotion," according to a writer for *FolioPlanet.com.* In addition to working as a fine artist, Low is the author and illustrator of *Chinatown* and *Old Penn Station,* and has created artwork to accompany the texts of such notable authors as Eve Bunting and T.A. Barron. A native New Yorker—Low was actually born in the back seat of a taxicab in the Bronx—he is often mistaken for a tourist in his cosmopolitan home town because he can often be sighted snapping photographs. Rather than gathering souvenirs, Low is collecting evocative images that he will later incorporate into his illustrations.

Discussing Low's work as an illustrator, a *Publishers Weekly* critic wrote of his contributions to Abigail Thomas's *Lily* that the book's chalk drawings feature "softer edges and more emotion, ingeniously convey[ing]" the emotions of the main character. Stephanie Zvirin, writing in *Booklist,* credited Low with giving the picture book "a solid, homey feel through vibrantly colored illustrations." Of his work for *Good Morning, City* by Elaine Moore, a *Publishers Weekly* critic noted that "Low's velvety paintings assume dramatic perspectives." A *Publishers Weekly* critic deemed his illustrations for Bunting's *The Days of Summer* "as carefully and effectively lit as a stage setting," while in his artwork for Bruce Edward Hall's *Henry and the Kite Dragon* "Low fills his pages with vibrant, glowing color . . . that allow the reader to feel the passion, fear, and finally acceptance of the characters," according to a *Kirkus Reviews* contributor. *School Library Journal* contributor Rita Soltan wrote that his artwork for Amy Littlesugar's *Willy and Max: A Holocaust Story* features "a textured, rugged look" that enhances the contrast between a peaceful neighborhood with the environment of intense fear that war ultimately brings.

Low's first self-illustrated title, *Chinatown,* is less a narrative story than a picture book that brings an actual place to life. Turning the page, readers move throughout New York's famed Chinatown, exploring the bustling streets, colorful restaurants, exotic herbal shops, and tai chi classes that make this part of the city unique. "Kids will enjoy the physical evocation of an exciting city place," wrote Hazel Rochman in her *Booklist* review of the picture book.

*In his self-illustrated* Chinatown, *artist William Low shares his cultural heritage with young readers.* (Copyright © 1997 by William Low. Reprinted by permission of Henry Holt and Company, LLC. )

Like *Chinatown, Old Penn Station* provides Low with another opportunity to share his love of New York City. In this book he details one of Manhattan's most notable landmarks, built during the early twentieth century. In his text he describes the history of Pennsylvania Station, from the train terminal's construction to the efforts to preserve the location as an historic site. His accompanying artwork showcases the architectural beauty that has given rise to empassioned preservation efforts made in the face of the cosmopolitan city's continuing growth.

## Biographical and Critical Sources

### PERIODICALS

*Booklist,* April 15, 1994, Stephanie Zvirin, review of *Lily,* p. 1542; September 15, 1997, Hazel Rochman, review of *Chinatown,* p. 242; April 1, 2001, Hazel Rochman, review of *The Days of Summer,* p. 1476; May 15, 2004, Gillian Engberg, review of *Henry and the Kite Dragon,* p. 1625; January 1, 2006, Hazel Rochman, review of *Willy and Max: A Holocaust Story,* p. 117.

*Kirkus Reviews,* May 15, 2004, review of *Henry and the Kite Dragon,* p. 492; February 15, 2006, review of *Willy and Max,* p. 186.

*Publishers Weekly,* January 13, 1992, review of *The King, the Princess, and the Tinker;* February 28, 1994, review of *Lily,* p. 86; July 31, 1995, review of *Good Morning, City,* p. 81; February 5, 2001, review of *The Days of Summer,* p. 88.

*School Library Journal,* September, 1997, Susan Pine, review of *Chinatown,* p. 186; May, 2001, Marilyn Ackerman, review of *The Days of Summer,* p. 112; August, 2004, Grace Oliff, review of *Henry and the Kite Dragon,* p. 87; April, 2005, review of *Henry and the Kite Dragon,* p. S28; March, 2006, Rita Soltan, review of *Willy and Max,* p. 196.

### ONLINE

*FolioPlanet.com,* http://folioplanet.com/ (February 23, 2007), "William Low."

*Houghton Mifflin Web site,* http://www.eduplace.com/ (February 24, 2007), "William Low."

*William Low Home Page,* http://www.williamlow.com (February 24, 2007).*

\*　　\*　　\*

## LOWRY, Lois 1937-
## (Lois Hammersberg Lowry)

### Personal

Born March 20, 1937, in Honolulu, HI; daughter of Robert E. (a dentist) and Katharine Hammersberg; married Donald Grey Lowry (an attorney), June 11, 1956

(divorced, 1977); married Martin Small; children: Alix, Grey (deceased), Kristin, Benjamin. *Education:* Attended Brown University, 1954-56; University of Southern Maine, B.A., 1972; graduate study. *Religion:* Episcopalian.

## Addresses

*Home*—Cambridge, MA. *Agent*—Phyllis Westberg, Harold Ober Associates, 425 Madison Ave., New York, NY 10017.

## Career

Children's book author and photographer, 1972—.

## Member

Society of Children's Book Writers and Illustrators, PEN New England, PEN American Center, Authors Guild, Authors League of America, MacDowell Colony (fellow).

## Awards, Honors

Children's Literature Award, International Reading Association (IRA), Notable Book designation, American Library Association (ALA), and MA and CA state children's choice awards, all 1978, all for *A Summer to Die;* Children's Book of the Year citation, Child Study Association of America, and ALA Notable Book designation, both 1979, both for *Anastasia Krupnik;* ALA Notable Book designation, 1980, and International Board on Books for Young People Honor List citation,

*Lois Lowry* (Reproduced by permission.)

1982, both for *Autumn Street;* ALA Notable Book designation, 1981, and American Book Award nomination in juvenile paperback category, 1983, both for *Anastasia Again!;* ALA Notable Book designation, 1983, for *The One-Hundredth Thing about Caroline;* Children's Book of the Year designation, Child Study Association of America, 1986, for *Us and Uncle Fraud;* NJ state children's choice award, 1986, for *Anastasia, Ask Your Analyst; Boston Globe/Horn Book* Award, Golden Kite Award, Society of Children's Book Writers and Illustrators, and Child Study Award, Children's Book Committee of Bank Street College, all 1987, all for *Rabble Starkey;* Christopher Award, 1988; Newbery Medal, ALA, National Jewish Book Award, and Sidney Taylor Award, National Jewish Libraries, all 1990, all for *Number the Stars;* Newbery Medal, 1994, for *The Giver;* Children's Choice citation, IRA/Children's Book Council, 1997, for *See You Around, Sam!;* Hope S. Dean Memorial Award, 2003.

## Writings

*JUVENILE NOVELS*

*A Summer to Die,* illustrated by Jenni Oliver, Houghton Mifflin (Boston, MA), 1977.

*Find a Stranger, Say Goodbye,* Houghton Mifflin (Boston, MA) 1978.

*Anastasia Krupnik,* Houghton Mifflin (Boston, MA), 1979.

*Autumn Street,* Houghton Mifflin (Boston, MA), 1979.

*Anastasia Again!,* illustrated by Diane deGroat, Houghton Mifflin (Boston, MA), 1981.

*Anastasia at Your Service,* illustrated by Diane deGroat, Houghton Mifflin (Boston, MA), 1982.

*Taking Care of Terrific,* Houghton Mifflin (Boston, MA), 1983.

*Anastasia, Ask Your Analyst,* Houghton Mifflin (Boston, MA), 1984.

*Us and Uncle Fraud,* Houghton Mifflin (Boston, MA), 1984.

*The One Hundredth Thing about Caroline,* Houghton Mifflin (Boston, MA), 1985.

*Anastasia on Her Own,* Houghton Mifflin (Boston, MA), 1985.

*Switcharound,* Houghton Mifflin (Boston, MA), 1985.

*Anastasia Has the Answers,* Houghton Mifflin (Boston, MA), 1986.

*Rabble Starkey,* Houghton Mifflin (Boston, MA), 1987.

*Anastasia's Chosen Career,* Houghton Mifflin (Boston, MA), 1987.

*All about Sam,* illustrated by Diane deGroat, Houghton Mifflin (Boston, MA), 1988.

*Number the Stars,* Houghton Mifflin (Boston, MA), 1989, reprinted, Yearling (New York, NY), 2005.

*Your Move, J.P.!,* Houghton Mifflin (Boston, MA), 1990.

*Anastasia at This Address,* Houghton Mifflin (Boston, MA), 1991.

*Attaboy, Sam!,* illustrated by Diane deGroat, Houghton Mifflin (Boston, MA), 1992.

*The Giver,* Houghton Mifflin (Boston, MA), 1993.

*Anastasia, Absolutely,* Houghton Mifflin (Boston, MA), 1995.

*See You Around, Sam!,* Houghton Mifflin (Boston, MA), 1996.

*Stay!: Keeper's Story,* illustrated by True Kelley, Houghton Mifflin (Boston, MA), 1997.

*Looking Back: A Book of Memories,* Houghton Mifflin (Boston, MA), 1998.

*Zooman Sam,* Houghton Mifflin (Boston, MA), 1999.

*Gathering Blue,* Houghton Mifflin (Boston, MA), 2000.

*Gooney Bird Greene,* illustrated by Middy Thomas, Houghton Mifflin (Boston, MA), 2002.

*The Silent Boy,* Houghton Mifflin (Boston, MA), 2003.

*The Messenger,* Houghton Mifflin (Boston, MA), 2004.

*Gooney Bird and the Room Mother,* illustrated by Middy Thomas, Houghton Mifflin (Boston, MA), 2005.

*Gossamer,* Houghton Mifflin (Boston, MA), 2006.

*Gooney the Fabulous,* illustrated by Middy Thomas, Houghton Mifflin (Boston, MA), 2007.

*OTHER*

*Black American Literature* (textbook), J. Weston Walsh (Portland, ME), 1973.

*Literature of the American Revolution* (textbook), J. Weston Walsh (Portland, ME), 1974.

(Photographer) Frederick H. Lewis, *Here in Kennebunkport,* Durrell (Kennebunkport, ME), 1978.

(Author of introduction) *Dear Author: Students Write about the Books That Changed Their Lives,* Conari Press, 1998.

(And photographer) *Looking Back: A Photographic Memoir* (autobiography), Houghton Mifflin (Boston, MA), 1998.

Contributor of stories, articles, and photographs to periodicals, including *Redbook, Yankee,* and *Down East.*

## Adaptations

*Find a Stranger, Say Goodbye* was adapted as the *Afterschool Special* television film "I Don't Know Who I Am," produced 1980. *Taking Care of Terrific* was adapted as a segment of the television series *Wonderworks,* 1988. *Anastasia at Your Service* was adapted as an audiobook for Learning Library, 1984. *Anastasia Krupnik* was adapted as a filmstrip, Cheshire, 1987. *Gooney Bird Greene and Her True-Life Adventures,* a dramatization by Kent R. Brown, was adapted from *Gooney Bird Greene* and published by Dramatic Publishing, 2005. *The Giver* was adapted as a film by Todd Alcott and directed by Vadim Perelman for Twentieth Century-Fox, c. 2007. Several of Lowry's novels have been adapted as audiobooks by Listening Library.

## Sidelights

Lois Lowry, an award-winning author of young-adult novels, is perhaps best known for the Newbery Award-winning novel *Number the Stars* and her futuristic trilogy consisting of *The Giver, Gathering Blue,* and *Mes-*

*Cover of Lowry's award-winning novel* The Giver, *featuring an illustration by Cliff Neilsen* (Used by permission of Bantam Books, a division of Random House, Inc.)

*senger.* Never one to shy from controversy, her novels deal with topics ranging from the death of a sibling and the Nazi occupation of Denmark to the humorous antics of a rebellious teen named Anastasia Krupnik, to futuristic dystopian societies. Although Lowry's books explore a variety of settings and characters, she distills from her work a single unifying theme: "the importance of human connections," as she wrote on her home page.

In 1937, when Lowry was born, her father, a military dentist and career army officer, was stationed at Schofield Barracks near Pearl Harbor in Honolulu, Hawaii. The family separated with the onset of World War II, Lowry's father serving out his tour of duty while Lowry and her mother stayed with her mother's family in the Amish country of Pennsylvania. "I remember all these relatively normal Christmases with trees, presents, turkeys, and carols, except that they had this enormous hole in them because there was never any father figure," the author recalled in an interview for *Authors and Artists for Young Adults.* This deep sense of loss is

"probably why I've written a terrific father figure into all of my books—sort of a fantasy of mine while growing up." Her grandmother was not especially fond of children, but her grandfather adored her, and Lowry escaped the absolute trauma of war under the shelter of his affection. Much later, Lowry's wartime experience inspired her fourth novel, *Autumn Street.*

In her first novel, *A Summer to Die,* Lowry portrays an adolescent's effort to deal with her older sister's illness and eventual death. When the Chalmers family moves to the country for the summer, thirteen-year-old Meg and fifteen-year-old Molly are forced to share a room. Already jealous of her older sister, Meg becomes increasingly argumentative and resentful when Molly's recurring nosebleeds demand much of her parents' attention. As her sister's condition deteriorates, Meg realizes that Molly is slowly dying of leukemia. For friendship, she turns to Will Banks, an elderly neighbor who encourages the teen's interest in photography, and Ben and Maria, a hippie couple who invites Meg to photograph the birth of their child.

*A Summer to Die* was well received by critics. Lowry's "story captures the mysteries of living and dying without manipulating the reader's emotions, providing understanding and a comforting sense of completion," observed Linda R. Silver in *School Library Journal.* In fact, Lowry's tale of Meg and Molly was drawn from life; her older sister, Helen, died of cancer when Lowry was twenty-five years old. Despite its inspiration, the author has maintained that "very little of [*A Summer to Die*] was factual, except the emotions." Even so, "when my mother read the book she recognized the characters as my sister and me," Lowry added. "She knew that the circumstances in the book were very different, but the characters had great veracity for her."

"Until I was about twelve I thought my parents were terrific, wise, wonderful, beautiful, loving, and well-dressed," Lowry once confessed. "By age twelve and a half they turned into stupid, boring people with whom I did not want to be seen in public. . . . That happens to all kids, and to the kids in my books as well." These same childhood memories, combined with Lowry's experiences as a parent, inspire her most popular character: Anastasia Krupnik, the spunky, rebellious, and irreverent star of books such as *Anastasia, Ask Your Analyst!, Anastasia on Her Own,* and *Anastasia at Your Service.* In the first book of the series, *Anastasia Krupnik,* the ten-year-old heroine faces numerous comic crises, including a crush on a boy who is continually dribbling an imaginary basketball, and the coming arrival of a new sibling. With the passing of each crisis Anastasia gains new insight into herself, and by the book's close she is prepared to move on to a new level of maturity. "Anastasia's feelings and discoveries should be familiar to anyone who has ever been ten," noted Brad Owens in the *Christian Science Monitor,* "and . . . Lowry has a sensitive way of taking problems seriously without ever being shallow or leaning too far over into despair."

The broad audience appeal sparked by the first "Anastasia" book has prompted Lowry to write several other novels that follow the coming of age of her diminutive heroine. In *Anastasia at Your Service* Anastasia is now twelve years old and tackling a summer job serving as maid to a rich, elderly woman. When the woman turns out to be a classmate's grandmother, the girl must deal with the embarrassment of working for the family of a well-to-do peer. "Despite differences the girls become friends; and with the help of Anastasia's precocious brother Sam, they generate a plot that is rich, inviting, and very funny," noted Barbara Elleman in a *Booklist* review of *Anastasia at Your Service.*

The popular Anastasia has gone on to appear in over a dozen more titles, among them *Anastasia Has the Answers, Anastasia's Chosen Career,* and *Anastasia Again!* As a lovestruck thirteen year old plying the personal ads, she generates confusion in *Anastasia at This Address,* showcasing what a *Publishers Weekly* reviewer described as her "headstrong, inventive, endearing in irrepressible" self, while her unwitting tampering of the U.S. mail in *Anastasia Absolutely* prompts a "moral crisis" that results in what *Horn Book* reviewer Maeve Visser Knoth predicted would be "light, satisfying reading" for Anastasia's many fans.

"I have the feeling she's going to go on forever—or until I get sick of her," Lowry once remarked of the fictional Anastasia. While the final book in the series, *Anastasia Absolutely,* was published in 1995, the popular heroine's family has been introduced to younger readers via her little brother in the books *Attaboy Sam!, See You around, Sam!* and *Zooman Sam.* In *Zooman Sam* Sam is on the cusp of learning to read. Acquiring the skill will allow him to be someone special, he believes: specifically, the Chief of Wonderfulness. To help him along, his mother makes Sam a special "Zooman Sam" jumpsuit for him to dress up in during Future Job Day at his nursery school (there was not enough room on the garment to fit the word "zookeeper"). With dreams of being a zookeeper, a special job indeed in a room full of children dreaming of more mundane occupations, Sam feels honored when his teacher tells him that she will let him stand at the head of the circle and tell about a different zoo animal each day for six weeks. With his budding reading skills, Sam is delighted to take on the task and enjoys the attention that comes with it. "Lowry gets everything about Sam just right," wrote Stephanie Zvirin in *Booklist,* while *Horn Book* reviewer Roger Sutton observed that the author "spins interesting variations on her theme," and wraps the book up with "a swell . . . surprise."

Again directed for younger readers, the title character in Lowry's chapter book *Gooney Bird Greene* is the newest arrival to the second grade and the most eccentric person the other students have ever seen. Leaning toward flamboyant dress (a pair of cowboy boots and pajamas one day, a polka-dot shirt and tutu the next), Gooney Bird is also a master storyteller in a small pack-

*Cover of Lowry's middle-grade novel* Gooney Bird Greene, *featuring an illustration by Middy Thomas.* (Cover art © 2002 by Middy Thomas. Used by permission of Random House Children's Books, a division of Random House, Inc.)

age. She delights in relating tales such as her "absolutely true" adventures of how she flew in from China on a flying carpet, how she got her "diamond earrings" (actually gumball machine trinkets) from a noble prince, and how she earned her oddball name. Encouraged in these tall tales by her teacher, Mrs. Pidgeon, Gooney Bird spins out her imaginative saga, prompting her fellow students to create and tell their own stories. In the process, the entire class—and the book's reader—learns important lessons in storytelling and constructing a compelling and believable narrative. GraceAnne A. DeCandido, writing in *Booklist,* called *Gooney Bird Greene* a "laugh-out-loud" story that serves as "quite a debut" for its young heroine. The book's message and the "cleverly titled stories could spark children's interest in writing their own stories," wrote Janet B. Bair in *School Library Journal.* Peter D. Sieruta, reviewing Lowry's story for *Horn Book,* observed that Gooney Bird is "not always convincing as a character, but she's a fine storyteller, and her message to her classmates—that they, too, have stories to share—is a good one."

Like Anastasia before her, Gooney Bird reappears in several other titles. Still impressing members of Mrs. Pidgeon's second-grade class with her storytelling, she

also rises to the challenge of improving her vocabulary in *Gooney Bird and the Room Mother,* arranging a special treat for the school's Thanksgiving celebration as well. Gooney morphs from raconteur to moralist in *Gooney the Fabulous* when her teacher asks each student to write a story inspired by a reading of Aesop's fables. Reviewing *Gooney Bird and the Room Mother,* Kristine M. Casper dubbed the book "a fast-paced read" in her *School Library Journal* review, the critic adding that Lowry's efforts to encourage vocabulary-building is effectively integrated into the story. Hazel Rochman wrote in *Booklist* that Mrs. Pidgeon's Thanksgiving Day lessons "are fun" and that Lowry's story "builds to a tense, beautiful climax." Once more "Gooney takes the lead," announced Ilene Cooper in a *Booklist* review of *Gooney the Fabulous,* the critic adding that the author "nicely individualizes her characters and gets readers interested" in Gooney and her second-grade world.

Although her "Anastasia" and "Gooney Bird Greene" stories have been popular lighthearted fare, much of Lowry's success as a novelist has come through her willingness to explore challenging and sometimes controversial teen-oriented topics. For example, she documents an adopted child's search for her biological mother in *Find a Stranger, Say Goodbye.* Although neither Lowry nor any of her children are adopted, she recognized that the subject was an important one that, at the time, was the subject of little focus. "Maybe it's because of having watched my own kids go through the torture of becoming adults . . . that I think those kinds of issues are important and it's important to deal with them in a sensitive and compassionate way," the author once noted.

Based on a factual account, *Number the Stars* is an historical novel set against the backdrop of Nazi-occupied Denmark. In this 1990 novel—the first of Lowry's books to receive the Newbery honor—ten-year-old Annemarie Johansen and her family are drawn into the resistance movement. As narrated by Annemarie, the book follows the family's efforts to shuttle Jews from Denmark into neutral Sweden during World War II, an activity that helped ensure the survival of nearly all of Denmark's Jewish population. The book "avoids explicit description of the horrors of war, yet manages to convey without oversimplification the sorrow felt by so many people who were forced to flee their homeland," wrote a *Children's Literature Review* critic. As quoted in *School Library Journal,* Newbery Awards Committee chair Caroline Ward commented that in *Number the Stars* "Lowry creates suspense and tension without wavering from the viewpoint of Annemarie, a child who shows the true meaning of courage."

Lowry received a second Newbery Medal for her 1993 novel *The Giver.* A radical departure from her previous works, the novel introduces readers to a futuristic utopian world wherein every aspect of life—birth, death, families, career choices, emotions, even the weather—is strictly controlled in order to create a safe and comfort-

*Cover of Lowry's Holocaust novel* Number the Stars, *featuring a photograph by the author.* (Bantam Doubleday Dell Books for Young Readers, 1998. Used by permission of Random House Children's Books, a division of Random House, Inc.)

able community where humans can live with no fear of violence. Living in this community, twelve-year-old Jonas is looking forward to an important rite of passage: the ceremony in which he, along with all children his age, is to be assigned a life's vocation. Skipped during the ceremony, Jonas is ultimately selected for a unique position when he is assigned to become the new Receiver, a prestigious and powerful person charged with holding all the memories of the community. During his apprenticeship to the current Receiver, an elderly man whom Jonas calls The Giver, the boy begins learning about the things—memories, emotions, and knowledge—that the community has given up in favor of peace. At first, these memories are pleasant: images of snow, colors, feelings of love. But Jonas soon encounters the darker aspects of human experience—war, death, and pain—and discovers that elderly or infirm community members who are "Released" are actually being euthanized. This discovery leads the boy to escape from the community with his young foster brother Gabriel.

Lowry ends *The Giver* with an interestingly ambiguous ending in which readers are left unsure of the boys' fate. In a companion novel, *Gathering Blue,* she describes a technologically primitive world in which, as she states in her author's note, "disorder, savagery, and self-interest" rule. As in *The Giver,* a child is chosen to play a special role in this society. In this world, the child is Kira. Born with a twisted leg—a condition that would normally have resulted in her being put to death as a baby—Kira was somehow allowed to live. Now a talented seamstress, she is chosen to be The Threader, a person whose duty it is to create the robe of The Singer. This garment depicts the history of the world and is used in the society's annual ritual of the Gathering. As The Threader, Kira begins to learn the dark secrets prompting her society's rules and must ultimately make a life-altering choice.

Many reviewers praised both *The Giver* and *Gathering Blue* for their sensitive handling of serious themes, a *Publishers Weekly* reviewer hailing *Gathering Blue* as a "dark, prophetic tale with a strong medieval flavor." Kay Bowes, writing in *Book Report,* called that same novel "thought-provoking" and "challenging," while a *Horn Book* writer wrote that *Gathering Blue* "shares the thematic concerns of *The Giver* . . . [but] adds a layer of questions about the importance of art in creating and, more ominously, controlling community." Ellen Fader, writing in *School Library Journal,* concluded that with *Gathering Blue* "Lowry has once again created a fully-realized world," adding that "readers won't forget these memorable characters or their struggles in an inhospitable world."

*Messenger* continue the story begun in *The Giver* and *Gathering Blue.* Entering the forest sanctuary of "The Village" as a young refugee, Matty has come to love his new home and respect the community's shared values. Now a teen, he has been guided toward adulthood by a blind man named Seer. Increasingly politically aware as he matures, Matty senses that a change has come over those in The Village whom he once respected; rather than welcoming newcomers, most in the community have become greedy and jealous. Unwilling to share their good fortune, they are now determined to wall themselves off from the rest of the world. A young man named Leader, guide of The Village (in fact, Jonas from *The Giver*), is also concerned about this change. When Village members vote to prohibit the influx of more outsiders, Matty is sent by Leader to find Seer's daughter Kira (from *Gathering Blue*). Making his way through the harsh forest environment outside the Village, the teen hopes to reunite Kira with her father before the opportunity is lost forever. Although Kira is lame and the journey to Seer is arduous, she selflessly refuses to take advantage of Matty's skill as a healer because use of this power seems to cause Matty harm.

Calling *Messenger* "simply and beautifully written" in her review for the *New York Times Book Review,* Hazel Rochman noted the book's position as the third volume

in Lowry's loosely knit trilogy. Rereading both *The Giver* and *Gathering Blue,* she noted that these two volumes contain "unresolved endings." While Lowry's unwillingness to create a strong resolution in her futuristic novels might be problematic for some reviewers, "others [have] applauded." "While *Messenger* may tie the three stories together just a little too neatly," Rochman added, "it is still far from a sweet resolution. Up to the last anguished page, Lois Lowry shows how hard it is to build community," leaving readers with the same frustration that her main characters experience. "Lowry's many fans will welcome this return to the fascinating world she has created," wrote Paula Rohrlick in a *Kliatt* review of *Messenger,* the critic also citing "the provocative issues she raises" in the suspenseful novel. "Lowry's skillful writing imbues the story with a strong sense of foreboding," concluded Marie Orlando in a review of the novel for *School Library Journal,* while in *Kirkus Reviews* a critic predicted that "readers will be absorbed in thought and wonder long after" the final page of *Messenger* is turned.

In *The Silent Boy* Lowry again takes up a solemn theme, introducing Katy Thatcher, Kate's physician father, and their life in a small New England town during the early part of the twentieth century. Peggy Stoltz, a local girl who helps on the Thatcher farm, is Katy's best friend. Peggy has a brother named Jacob, as well as a sister named Nell who works on the farm next to the Thatchers' place. Jacob, considered an "imbecile," or "touched in the head," is a gentle thirteen year old who never speaks but has a profound ability to handle and communicate with animals. After Katy knits together a tenuous friensship with Jacob, she begins to sense the wonder in his affinity with animals. Meanwhile, the girl has trouble dealing with the realities of country life, with her upcoming tenth birthday, and with the arrival of a new baby in her family. Nell also expects a baby, the result of a relationship with her employers' son. Ultimately, things come to a head after Jacob disappears with Nell's unwanted and unnamed infant and the baby then turns up dead. Katy cannot believe that the sensitive and gentle Jacob could commit an act of murder, even one that, in his mind, may have been completely acceptable or even desirable. Jacob is eventually incarcerated in an asylum, leaving Katy haunted by the tragedy of his life. "Lowry's graceful, lively prose is dense with historical details," remarked Gillian Engberg in a *Booklist* review of *The Silent Boy.* Ellen Fader, writing in *School Library Journal,* noted of the novel that "Lowry excels in developing strong and unique characters and in showing Katy's life in a small town that changes around her as the first telephones and automobiles arrive." The novel's storyline "balances humor and generosity with the obstacles and injustice of Katy's world," a *Publishers Weekly* reviewer wrote, while a *Kirkus Reviews* writer deemed the novel "a tragedy deftly foreshadowed."

While *The Giver* and its sequels was classified by several reviewers as science fiction, in her novel *Gossamer*

Lowry steps clearly into the realm of fantasy. Dubbed "spellbinding" by a *Publishers Weekly* contributor, the story introduces Littlest One, a young creature who, as a member of a race of dream givers, is learning to practice her ancestral art. In touching the objects that make up a certain human's day, dream givers collect threads of memories, sounds, and images, using these to weave together the dreams that fill the minds of the sleeping. Working with experienced teacher Thin Elderly, Littlest is assigned to practice her art in the home of an elderly foster mother, where she comes in contact with John, the woman's troubled young charge. As her skills develop, the dream giver creates images that reflect the healthy relationship developing between John and his foster mother, but as part of her work she must also fight off the efforts of the Sinisteeds, who find in John the perfect vehicle for their horrific nightmares. Reviewing *Gossamer,* the *Publishers Weekly* contributor cited Lowry for her "exquisite, at times mesmerizing writing," while Lauralyn Persson wrote in *School Library Journal* that the author's "carefully plotted fantasy has inner logic and conviction." Noting that *Gossamer* is "written with Lowry's characteristic elegance and economy, and with her usual attentiveness to the internal consistency of her imaginary world," James Hynes concluded in his *New York Times Book Review* appraisal that the novel is "enormously entertaining and . . . very moving."

While many of Lowry's children's books draw on pleasant memories and experiences from their author's past, as her career has stretched through the years from parenthood to grandparenthood, she has continued to collect experiences, both tragic and joyful. She sifts through this lifetime of remembrances and attempts and in *Looking Back: A Book of Memories.* locates threads of stories and patterns in these experience. More like a visit from a favorite friend than an autobiography, *Looking Back* is "much more intimate and personal than many traditional memoirs," according to *School Library Journal* contributor Barbara Scotto, while a *Publishers Weekly* reviewer observed of the book that "a compelling and inspirational portrait of the author emerges from these vivid snapshots of life's joyful, sad, and surprising moments."

## Biographical and Critical Sources

*BOOKS*

*American Women Writers,* 2nd edition, St. James Press (Detroit, MI), 2000.

*Authors and Artists for Young Adults,* Volume 32, Thomson Gale (Detroit, MI), 2000.

*Beacham's Guide to Literature for Young Adults,* Beacham Publishing (Osprey, FL), 1990, Volume 4, 1990, Volume 6, 1994.

Chaston, Joel D., *Lois Lowry,* Twayne (New York, NY), 1997.

*Children's Literature Review,* Thomson Gale (Detroit, MI), Volume 6, 1984, Volume 46, 1997, Volume 72, pp. 192-206.

*Dictionary of Literary Biography,* Volume 52: *American Writers for Children since 1960: Fiction,* Thomson Gale (Detroit, MI), 1987, pp. 249-261.

Green, Carol Hurd, and Mary Grimley Mason, editors, *American Women Writers,* Volume 5, Continuum Publishing (New York, NY), 1994.

Lowry, Lois, *Looking Back: A Book of Memories,* Houghton Mifflin (Boston, MA), 1998.

*St. James Guide to Young-Adult Writers,* 2nd edition, St. James Press (Detroit, MI), 1999.

Silvey, Anita, editor, *Children's Books and Their Creators,* Houghton Mifflin (Boston, MA), 1995.

*Something about the Author Autobiography Series,* Volume 3, Thomson Gale (Detroit, MI), 1986, pp. 131-146.

*PERIODICALS*

*Book,* May-June, 2003, review of *Gooney Bird Greene,* p. 31.

*Booklist,* October 15, 1979, Barbara Elleman, review of *Anastasia Krupnik,* p. 354; September 1, 1982, Barbara Elleman, review of *Anastasia at Your Service,* p. 46; September 1, 1987, review of *Anastasia's Chosen Career,* pp. 66-67; March 1, 1990, Ilene Cooper, review of *Your Move, J.P.!,* p. 1345; April 1, 1991, Stephanie Zvirin, review of *Anastasia at This Address,* p. 1564; October 1, 1995, Carolyn Phelan, review of *Anastasia, Absolutely,* p. 761; November 1, 1997, Ellen Mandel, review of *Stay!: Keeper's Story,* p. 472; November 1, 1998, Carolyn Phelan, review of *Looking Back,* p. 490; July, 1, 1999, Stephanie Zvirin, review of *Zooman Sam,* p. 1947; September 15, 1999, review of *Looking Back,* p. 254; June 1, 2000, Ilene Cooper, review of *Gathering Blue,* p. 1896; September 1, 2002, GraceAnne A. DeCandido, review of *Gooney Bird Greene,* p. 125; April 15, 2003, Gillian Engberg, review of *The Silent Boy,* p. 1462; February 15, 2004, Hazel Rochman, review of *Messenger,* p. 1056; March 1, 2005, Hazel Rochman, review of *Gooney Bird and the Room Mother,* p. 1197; February 15, 2006, Hazel Rochman, review of *Gossamer,* p. 99; January 1, 2007, Ilene Cooper, review of *Gooney the Fabulous,* p. 81.

*Book Report,* May, 1999, review of *Looking Back,* p. 73; January 2001, Kay Bowes, review of *Gathering Blue,* p. 58.

*Books for Keeps,* January, 2002, review of *Gathering Blue,* p. 26.

*Bulletin of the Center for Children's Books,* January, 1980, Zena Sutherland, review of *Anastasia Krupnik,* p. 99; May, 1984, Zena Sutherland, review of *Anastasia, Ask Your Analyst,* p. 169; March, 1990, Ruth Ann Smith, review of *Your Move, J.P.!,* p. 169; April, 1993, p. 257; September, 1995, Deborah Stevenson, review of *Anastasia, Absolutely,* pp. 20-21; November, 1996, p. 105; January, 1998, Janice Del Negro, review of *Stay!,* p. 165; January, 1999, Janice Del Negro, review of *Looking Back,* p. 174; September, 1999, review of

*Zooman Sam,* p. 21; June, 2004, Krista Hutley, review of *Messenger,* p. 427; July-August, 2006, April Spisak, review of *Gossamer,* p. 507.

*Catholic Library World,* September, 1999, review of *See You Around, Sam,* p. 33.

*Children's Bookwatch,* March, 1999, review of *Looking Back,* p. 6; December, 1999, review of *Zooman Sam,* p. 4; March, 2001, review of *Looking Back,* p. 8.

*Children's Literature* (annual), 2004, Don Latham, "Discipline and Its Discontents: A Foucauldian Reading of 'The Giver,'" pp. 134-151.

*Christian Science Monitor,* January 14, 1980, Brad Owens, review of *Anastasia Krupnik,* p. B6; March 1, 1985, Lyn Littlfield Hoopes, review of *Us and Uncle Fraud,* p. 65; May 1, 1987, Betsy Hearne, "Families Shaped by Love, Not Convention," pp. B3-B4.

*Five Owls,* April, 1989, pp. 59-60; September-October, 1993, Gary D. Schmidt, review of *The Giver,* pp. 14-15; March, 2001, review of *Gathering Blue,* p. 92.

*Horn Book,* August, 1977, Mary M. Burns, review of *A Summer to Die,* p. 451; December, 1979, Ann A. Flowers, review of *Anastasia Krupnik,* p. 663; October, 1981, Mary M. Burns, review of *Anastasia Again!,* pp. 535-536; September-October, 1985, Ann A. Flowers, review of *Anastasia on Her Own,* pp. 556-557; May-June, 1986, Mary M. Burns, review of *Anastasia Has the Answers,* pp. 327-328; July-August, 1987, Ann A. Flowers, review of *Rabble Starkey,* pp. 463-465; May-June, 1989, Mary M. Burns, review of *Number the Stars,* p. 371; March-April, 1990, Ethel R. Twitchell, review of *Your Move, J.P.!,* pp. 201-202; July-August, 1990, Shirley Haley-James, "Lois Lowry"; November-December, 1993, Patty Campbell, "The Sand in the Oyster," pp. 717-721; July-August, 1994, Lois Lowry, "Newbery Medal Acceptance," pp. 414-422, Walter Lorraine, "Lois Lowry," pp. 423-426; November-December, 1995, Maeve Visser Knoth, review of *Anastasia, Absolutely,* p. 761; September-October, 1996, Roger Sutton, review of *See You Around, Sam!,* p. 597; January-February, 1998, Roger Sutton, review of *Stay!,* pp. 76-77; January, 1999, Peter D. Sieruta, review of *Looking Back,* p. 87; September, 1999, Roger Sutton, review of *Zooman Sam,* p. 613; September, 2000, Roger Sutton, review of *Gathering Blue,* p. 573; September-October, 2002, Peter D. Sieruta, review of *Gooney Bird Greene,* pp. 575-577; May-June, 2004, Betty Carter, review of *Messenger,* p. 332; July-August, 2006, review of *Gossamer,* p. 446.

*Instructor,* May, 1999, review of *The Giver,* p. 16; May, 1999, review of *See You Around, Sam,* p. 16; May, 2001, review of *The Giver,* p. 37.

*Journal of Adolescent and Adult Literacy,* September, 2004, Lori Atkins Goodson, review of *The Silent Boy,* p. 75, and Jo Ann Yazzie, review of *Messenger,* p. 80.

*Journal of Youth Services in Libraries,* fall, 1996, pp. 39-40, 49.

*Junior Bookshelf,* August, 1979, Mary Hobbs, review of *A Summer to Die,* pp. 224-225; August, 1980, p. 194.

*Kirkus Reviews,* April 1, 1986, review of *Anastasia Has the Answers,* pp. 546-547; March 1, 1987, review of *Rabble Starkey,* p. 374; March 15, 1991, review of

*Anastasia at This Address,* p. 396; March 1, 1993, review of *The Giver,* p. 301; October 15, 1997, review of *Stay!,* p. 1584; July 15, 1999, review of *Zooman Sam,* p. 1135; March 15, 2003, review of *The Silent Boy,* p. 472; April 1, 2004, review of *Messenger,* p. 333; April 1, 2005, review of *Gooney Bird and the Room Mother,* p. 420; March 1, 2006, review of *Gossamer,* p. 235.

*Kliatt,* March, 2004, Paula Rohrlick, review of *Messenger,* p. 12.

*New York Times Book Review,* May 21, 1989, Edith Milton, "Escape from Copenhagen," p. 32; October 31, 1993, Karen Ray, review of *The Giver,* p. 26; January 14, 1996, Michael Cart, review of *Anastasia, Absolutely,* p. 23; October 15, 1998, review of *Looking Back,* p. 1534; February 14, 1999, review of *Looking Back,* p. 27; November 19, 2003, Elizabeth Spires, review of *Gathering Blue,* p. 57; May 16, 2004, Hazel Rochman, "Something's Rotten in Utopia," p. 17; May 14, 2006, James Hynes, review of *Gossamer,* p. 21.

*Observer* (London, England), October 21, 2001, review of *Gathering Blue,* p. 16.

*Publishers Weekly,* February 21, 1986, interview with Lowry, pp. 152-153; March 13, 1987, p. 86; November 8, 1985, review of *Switcharound,* p. 60; March 15, 1991, review of *Anastasia at This Address,* p. 58; July 28, 1997, review of *Stay!,* p. 75; August 24, 1998, review of *Looking Back,* p. 58; April 5, 1999, review of *Stay!,* p. 243; September 13, 1999, review of *Zooman Sam,* p. 85; July 31, 2000, review of *Gathering Blue,* p. 96; March 24, 2003, review of *The Silent Boy,* p. 76, and Ingrid Roper, interview with Lowry, p. 77; March 6, 2006, review of *Gossamer,* p. 74.

*Reading Teacher,* March, 2001, review of *Gathering Blue,* p. 638.

*School Librarian,* February, 1995, pp. 31-32.

*School Library Journal,* May, 1977, Linda R. Silver, review of *A Summer to Die,* pp. 62-63; April, 1980, Marilyn Singer, review of *Autumn Street,* pp. 125-126; March, 1981, p. 109; October, 1981, Marilyn Kaye, review of *Anastasia Again!,* p. 144; October, 1983, Kathleen Brachmann, review of *The One Hundredth Thing about Caroline,* p. 160; February, 1986, Maria B. Salvadore, review of *Switcharound,* p. 87; September, 1987, Dudley B. Carlson, review of *Anastasia's Chosen Career,* p. 180; August, 1988, Trev Jones, review of *All about Sam,* p. 96; March, 1989, Louise L. Sherman, review of *Number the Stars,* p. 177; May, 1992, Marcia Hupp, review of *Attaboy, Sam!,* p. 114; October, 1996, Starr LaTronica, review of *See You Around, Sam!,* p. 102; October, 1997, Eva Mitnick, review of *Stay!,* p. 134; September, 1998, Barbara Scotto, review of *Looking Back,* p. 221; September, 1999, review of *Zooman Sam,* p. 193; August 2000, Ellen Fader, review of *Gathering Blue,* p. 186; November, 2002, Janet B. Bair, review of *Gooney Bird Greene,* pp. 129-130; April, 2003, Ellen Fader, review of *The Silent Boy,* pp. 164-165; April, 2004, Marie Orlando, review of *Messenger,* p. 50; May, 2005, Kristine M. Casper, review of *Gooney Bird and the Room Mother,* p. 90; May, 2006, Lauralyn Persson, review of *Gossamer,* p. 132.

*Signal,* May, 1980, pp. 119-122.

*Voice of Youth Advocates,* August, 1985, p. 186; April, 1988, p. 26; August, 1993, p. 167; December, 1995, p. 304; April, 1999, review of *Looking Back,* p. 76; August, 1999, review of *Looking Back,* p. 164; April, 2001, review of *Gathering Blue,* p. 12; February, 2005, review of *Messenger,* p. 443.

*Washington Post Book World,* May 9, 1993, p. 15.

ONLINE

*Books 'n' Bytes,* http://www.booksnbytes.com/ (May 28, 2003), Harriet Klausner, review of *Gathering Blue.*

*Lois Lowry Home Page,* http://www.loislowry.com (March 17, 2007).

*Rambles Online,* http://www.rambles.net/ (May 28, 2003), Donna Scanlon, review of *Gathering Blue.*

OTHER

*Good Conversation!: A Talk with Lois Lowry* (video), Tim Podell Productions, 2002.

\*      \*      \*

# LOWRY, Lois Hammersberg
## See LOWRY, Lois

\*      \*      \*

# LUPICA, Michael Thomas
## See LUPICA, Mike

\*      \*      \*

# LUPICA, Mike 1952-
## (Michael Thomas Lupica)

## Personal

Born May 11, 1952, in Oneida, NY; son of Benedict (a personal manager) and Lee Lupica; married; children: three sons. *Education:* Boston College, B.A., 1974.

## Addresses

*Office*—c/o New York Daily News, 220 E. 42nd St., New York, NY 10017. *Agent*—Esther Newberg, International Creative Management, 40 W. 57th St., New York, NY 10019. *E-mail*—mike@lupica.com.

## Career

Journalist and novelist. *Boston Globe,* Boston, MA, correspondent, 1970-74; *Boston Phoenix,* Boston, columnist, 1971-75; *Boston* magazine, Boston, columnist, 1974-75; *Washington Star,* Washington, DC, feature

writer, 1974-75; *New York Post*, New York, NY, basketball writer and columnist, 1975-76; *New York News*, New York, NY, columnist, 1977-81; *New York Daily News*, New York, NY, columnist, 1980—. Writer for *World Tennis*, 1974-81, and columnist for *Esquire*. Broadcast sports journalist for Columbia Broadcasting System (CBS) *Morning News*, 1982-84; WCBS-TV, 1983; and WNBC Radio; Entertainment and Sports Programming Network (ESPN), sports journalist, 1982-83, and panelist for *The Sports Reporters*.

## Member

Newspaper Guild of America.

## Writings

*NONFICTION*

(With Reggie Jackson) *Reggie: The Autobiography*, Villard Books (New York, NY), 1984.
(With Bill Parcells) *Parcells: Autobiography of the Biggest Giant of Them All*, Bonus Books (Chicago, IL), 1987.
*Shooting from the Lip: Essays, Columns, Quips, and Gripes in the Grand Tradition of Dyspeptic Sports Writing* (nonfiction), Bonus Books, 1988.
(With William Goldman) *Wait Till Next Year: The Story of a Season When What Should've Happened Didn't and What Could've Gone Wrong Did*, Bantam (New York, NY), 1988.
*Mad as Hell: How Sports Got away from the Fans—and How We Get It Back*, Putnam (New York, NY), 1996.
(With Fred Imus) *The Fred Book*, Doubleday (New York, NY), 1998.
*Summer of '98: When Homers Flew, Records Fell, and Baseball Reclaimed America*, Putnam (New York, NY), 1999.

*ADULT NOVELS*

*Jump*, Villard Books (New York, NY), 1995.
*Bump and Run*, Putnam (New York, NY), 2000.
*Full Court Press*, Putnam (New York, NY), 2001.
*Wild Pitch*, Putnam (New York, NY), 2002.
*Red Zone*, Putnam (New York, NY), 2003.

*"PETER FINLEY" MYSTERY SERIES*

*Dead Air*, Villard Books (New York, NY), 1986.
*Extra Credits*, Villard Books (New York, NY), 1988.
*Limited Partner*, Villard Books (New York, NY), 1990.

*YOUNG-ADULT NOVELS*

*Travel Team*, Philomel (New York, NY), 2004.
*Too Far*, Putnam (New York, NY), 2004.
*Heat*, Philomel (New York, NY), 2006.

*Miracle on 49th Street*, Philomel (New York, NY), 2006.
*Shooting Guard*, Philomel (New York, NY), 2007.
*Summer Ball*, Philomel (New York, NY), 2007.

## Adaptations

Several of Lupica's books have been adapted as audiobooks by Listening Library, among them *Heat*, 2006.

## Sidelights

"I grew up reading such writers as Dan Jenkins, Jimmy Breslin, and Pete Hamill," sports journalist Mike Lupica once noted, "and always wanted to go the 'Breslin route'—that is, to write a sports column for a major newspaper and then to write books." By any standard, Lupica has fulfilled that ambition; in addition to being a nationally syndicated sports columnist based at the *New York Daily News*, he has written not only sports-related autobiographies and other works of nonfiction, but also fiction for both teens and adults. In novels such as *Bump and Run* and *Wild Pitch* Lupica shares with readers his insider's view of the cutthroat world of professional sports, often centering his stories in and around his own home plate, New York City. Boston serves as the setting for Lupica's young-adult novels *Travel Team* and *Miracle on 49th Street*, while *Too Far* provides an entre into the world of a Long Island high school basketball player who, aided by a disillusioned sportswriter, attempts to solve the murder of a young teammate. "Real-life news reports . . . give Lupica's tale a ripped-from-the-headlines thrill," wrote a *Publishers Weekly* contributor in a review of *Too Far*, while another contributor noted in the same periodical that in *Travel Team* the journalist-turned novelist "clearly shoots from the heart."

After graduating from Boston College in 1974, Lupica stayed in that city while beginning his sports writing career. With a move south to the Big Apple in 1980, he assumed national prominence as part of the staff of the *New York Daily News*. Lupica's reputation as a straight-talking columnist was enhanced by his presence on television shows such as *The Sports Reporters* on ESPN and *The MacNeil-Lehrer NewsHour* on the Public Broadcasting System. His first two book-length works, "as-told-to" autobiographies of baseball legend Reggie Jackson and former New York Giants head coach Bill Parcells, were published in 1984 and 1987 respectively. Inevitably, reviewers' attention focused less on the books themselves than on the personalities of their high-profile subjects: Jackson was often seen as arrogant and boastful and Parcells was known for his single-minded dedication to the sport. In Chicago's *Tribune Books*, however, Robert Cromie described *Reggie: The Autobiography* as "highly readable," while Michael Wilbon, writing in the *Washington Post Book World*, called *Parcells: Autobiography of the Biggest Giant of Them All* "deftly crafted, as one expects from Lupica."

In the mid-1980s Lupica tried his hand at fiction, turning out three genre thrillers featuring a journalist as protagonist. Readers first meet the fictional Peter Fin-

*Cover of Mike Lupica's young-adult basketball novel* **Travel Team.**
(Jacket design by Monica Benalcazar. Jacket photograph courtesy of PM Images/ Getty
Images. Reproduced by permission of Philomel Books, a division of Penguin Putnam
Books for Young Readers.)

ley, an investigative reporter for a New York City cable
television station, in *Dead Air.* The book's plot is set in
motion when a former Miss America, now the host of a
late-night television talk show, disappears and is pre-
sumed dead. When Finley is asked by the victim's husband to look into her disappearance, corpses start turning up, all of them connected with the show's network,
which is about to be taken over by a Christian broadcasting network. In *Extra Credits,* the next book in the
series, Finley is approached by a college student who
persuades the reporter to investigate the mysterious sui-
cide of her wealthy and attractive friend. *Limited Partner* finds Finley probing the death by drug overdose of
a friend, a recovering addict who is also part owner of
a trendy Manhattan night spot. When the victim's girlfriend dies just a few days later, also of an overdose,
Finley is convinced of foul play.

At the center of each of Lupica's "Peter Finley" novels
is the island of Manhattan: its bars and bistros, and its
dark side of drug-dealing and amoral wealth. Jean M.
White, writing in the *Washington Post Book World,*
criticized *Extra Credits* for overemphasizing the details
of its setting, complaining that the book reads like a

"what's-in list for *New York* magazine." In Chicago's
*Tribune Books,* however, Alice Cromie found similar
details in *Dead Air* "amusingly depicted." Reviewers
were similarly divided over Finley, the novels' wise-
cracking, fast-talking hero. In the *New York Times Book
Review,* Michael Lichtenstein wrote that *Limited Partner* is marred by Finley's flip "one-liners." Yet Newgate
Callendar, also in the *New York Times Book Review,* ad-
mired the "street-smart" hero and concluded of *Extra
Credits:* "The writing is sophisticated, the dialogue
bright." In 1988, television star Kevin Dobson took an
option on the Finley character with the goal of developing it into a television series.

The adult novels *Jump, Bump and Run, Too Far, Wild
Pitch, Full Court Press,* and *Red Zone* all draw upon
Lupica's insider's knowledge of high-profile athletics.
In *Jump,* two pro basketball teammates stand accused
of rape by a New York City actress. The players call
upon investigative attorney Mike DiMaggio to piece together the truth about the assault and explore the actress's motivations for waiting a year before she lodged
the charges. Moving to baseball in *Wild Pitch,* Lupica
introduces forty-something Charlie Stoddard, a
washed-up former-pro pitcher who decides to make another go of his athletic career after an old sports injury
clears up. A *Publishers Weekly* reviewer wrote that *Jump*
"crackles with tension, excitement and hip authenticity," and concluded that Lupica's "amalgam of tightly
written sports story and crime fiction sinks a winning
basket." Noting the redemptive theme in *Wild Pitch,*
Wes Lukowsky added in a *Booklist* review of the novel
that Lupica "captures both the insanity" prevalent in the
world of professional sports "and the appeal that baseball still has for the eternal child who lives within every
fan."

*Bump and Run* takes a more comic tone, as Jock Molloy, a Las Vegas casino concierge, inherits his billion-
aire father's pro football team and applies his casino
expertise to the task of constructing a winning fran-
chise. Similar in tone, *Red Zone* finds Molloy still president of the New York Hawks football team. When his
decision to enter into a lucrative partnership threatens
his ability to actively manage the team, Jack draws on
his Vegas-style strong-arming skills to battle his new
partner, a greedy financier willing to clip the Hawks'
wings in exchange for a healthy return on investment.
A *Publishers Weekly* contributor found *Bump and Run*
"hilarious but slightly disturbing," styling the novel "a
deliciously wicked tale of contemporary professional
sports and the people who . . . run the game." In
*Booklist,* Lukowsky likewise praised Lupica for "getting fresh laughs from a classic premise—the streetwise
kid beating a bunch of snotty rich guys at their own
game." Calling Lupica's adult novels "soap-opera fantasies for men,"Lukowsky also noted in his subsequent
review of *Red Zone* that the novelist "propels the plot
at breakneck speed with sitcom-like zingers . . . and an
insider's knowledge of professional sports.

Lupica turns to a younger readership in *Travel Team*, his first novel for teens. Here he draws on his experiences as a youth basketball coach in telling the story of a twelve-year-old player who deals with the advantages and disadvantages of being on a team coached by his dad. Danny Walker's father, Richie, a former basketball pro, is highly competitive, and he wants his son to succeed. Possessing a natural talent but too short to qualify for the middle-school basketball team, Danny has the drive needed to succeed. When Richie starts a new team to give boys like his son another chance at the title, Danny must decide if he really wants basketball to consume his life, the way it did his dad's. Calling *Travel Team* "an excellent sports story," Claire Rosser noted in her *Kliatt* review that the book demonstrates the author's "great respect for the boys struggling to deal with their own skills, their fathers, their teammates, and their coaches." In *School Library Journal,* Joel Shoemaker called *Travel Team* "a fun book for sports fans" that draws comparisons to *Sparkplug of the Hornets,* a YA sports classic penned by Stephen W. Meader.

In *Heat,* another young-adult novel by Lupica, readers meet Michael and Carlos Arroyo, two Cuban-American brothers. Orphaned by their beloved father's recent death, the boys pretend that their dad is still among the living. They claim that he is visiting a relative in Miami so that they can avoid foster care and remain together in the family's Bronx apartment. While Michael is only twelve years old, Carlos is almost eighteen and a legal adult; with the help of a few close friends, the teen is optimistic that the brothers' ruse may actually work. For Michael, however, there are more pressing concerns: when questions about Michael's age surface due to his strength as an ace Little League pitcher, team officials demand to see the boy's birth certificate; but where did Papi keep it? A growing friendship with a girl whose dad once pitched for the New York Yankees provides a bright spot in the young boy's tumultuous world. Citing "dialogue [that] crackles, and the rich cast of supporting characters," Bill Ott wrote in *Booklist* that the author "wrings plenty of genuine emotion" from the boys' predicament. While noting that the plot sometimes "veers toward melodrama," Marilyn Taniguchi praised the novel in her *School Library Journal* review, writing that the "sports scenes are especially well written" and paired with "humor [and] crisp dialogue." In *Publishers Weekly* a reviewer dubbed *Heat* "a baseball story with heart" that features "convincing characterization and exciting on-field action," while *Kliatt* contributor Paula Rohrlick concluded that in *Heat* "sports journalist Lupica . . . pitches another winner."

Another twelve year old takes center field—or, in this case, center court—in *Miracle on 49th Street*. For preteen Molly Parker, basketball is the game of choice, because her dad is Josh Cameron, a star player for the Boston Celtics. For Josh, the fact that he even has a daughter came as something of a shock; Molly had been raised in England by a mom who had moved away and never told her college sweetheart about her preg-

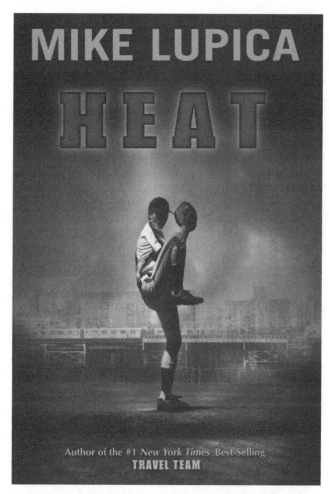

Cover of Lupica's **Heat**, *featuring an illustration by Cliff Neilsen.* (Reproduced by permission of Philomel Books, a division of Penguin Putnam Books for Young Readers.)

nancy. Fortunately father and daughter find a place for each other in their lives, in a "winning novel" that Todd Morning noted in *Booklist* allows readers "a look inside Josh's pampered sports-superstar world." Noting that "friendship is a key element" in *Miracle on 49th Street, Kliatt* reviewer Janice Flint-Ferguson added that through Lupica's novel, readers can gain "a deeper understanding of the complexity of relationships." For *School Library Journal* reviewer Jeffrey A. French, the story contains "enough twists and cliff-hangers to keep the pages turning," while Molly is notable as a "strong female character."

Although he has made a name for himself as a novelist, Lupica is known to many readers due to his journalism, which has been reprinted in several collections. *Shooting from the Lip: Essays, Columns, Quips, and Gripes in the Grand Tradition of Dyspeptic Sports Writing,* for example, collects several of Lupica's essays and newspaper columns. Diane Cole, writing in the *New York Times Book Review,* found the pieces "engaging and often exhilarating" in their reliance on a single mood or moment to capture the essence of a season or an athlete's career. *Mad as Hell: How Sports Got away from the Fans—and How We Get It Back* summarizes the

complaints of many sports enthusiasts: namely, that players are overpaid, owners too greedy, and ordinary fans are priced out of the country's major-league ballparks. In *Booklist*, Lukowsky maintained that those who share Lupica's concerns "will enjoy sputtering angrily as they read this litany of wrongdoing." The columnist strikes a much more optimistic tone in *Summer of '98: When Homers Flew, Records Fell, and Baseball Reclaimed America*. Taking as its subject the eventful 1998 professional baseball season, Lupica weaves together tales of Mark McGwire and Sammy Sosa battling for the home run record with poignant asides on the ability of baseball to unite fathers and sons. A *Publishers Weekly* reviewer deemed *Summer of '98* a "feel-great book" in which Lupica "gives himself completely over to the beauty of baseball as . . . a game."

## Biographical and Critical Sources

*PERIODICALS*

*Booklist*, December 15, 1994, Wes Lukowsky, review of *Jump*, p. 715; October 15, 1996, Wes Lukowsky, review of *Mad as Hell: How Sports Got away from the Fans—and How We Get It Back*, p. 397; September 1, 2000, Wes Lukowsky, review of *Bump and Run*, p. 71; September 1, 2002, Wes Lukowsky, review of *Wild Pitch*, p. 46; October 15, 2003, Wes Lukowsky, review of *Red Zone*, p. 357; November 15, 2004, Alan Moores, review of *Too Far*, p. 532; April 1, 2006, Bill Ott, review of *Heat*, p. 43; May 1, 2006, Karen Cruze, review of *Travel Team*, p. 98; September 1, 2006, Todd Morning, review of *Miracle on 49th Street*, p. 116.

*Bulletin of the Center for Children's Books*, May, 2006, Elizabeth Bush, review of *Heat*, p. 412; November, 2006, Elizabeth Bush, review of *Miracle on 49th Street*, p. 134.

*Kirkus Reviews*, August 15, 2000, review of *Bump and Run*, p. 1136; July 15, 2002, review of *Wild Pitch*, p. 983; October 1, 2003, review of *Red Zone*, p. 1194; October 1, 2004, review of *Travel Team*, p. 964; November 15, 2004, review of *Too Far*, p. 1063; March 1, 2006, review of *Heat*, p. 235; October 1, 2006, review of *Miracle on 49th Street*, p. 1018.

*Kliatt*, January, 2003, review of *Full Court Press*, p. 16; November, 2003, Janet Julian, review of *Wild Pitch*, p. 17; September, 2004, Claire Rosser, review of *Travel Team*, p. 13; March, 2006, Paula Rohrlick, review of *Heat*, p. 14; November, 2006, Janis Flint-Ferguson, review of *Miracle on 49th Street*, p. 14, and Miles Klein, review of *Travel Team*, p. 50.

*Library Journal*, November 1, 2003, David Wright, review of *Red Zone*, p. 124.

*Los Angeles Times*, July 17, 1987.

*New York Times Book Review*, August 19, 1984, p. 19; May 26, 1986, p. 14; May 29, 1988, p. 15; July 31, 1988, p. 25; October 14, 1990, p. 48; May 30, 1999, George Robinson, "Big Mac, Sammy and the Yanks," p. 16.

*Publishers Weekly*, February 6, 1995, review of *Jump*, p. 76; August 26, 1996, review of *Mad as Hell*, p. 85; February 8, 1999, review of *Summer of '98: When Homers Flew, Records Fell, and Baseball Reclaimed America*, p. 202; October 9, 2000, review of *Bump and Run*, p. 70; July 22, 2002, review of *Wild Pitch*, p. 157; October 20, 2003, review of *Red Zone*, p. 33; November 15, 2004, review of *Too Far*, p. 40; January 3, 2005, review of *Travel Team*, p. 56; February 20, 2006, review of *Heat*, p. 157; November 6, 2006, review of *Miracle on 49th Street*, p. 62.

*School Library Journal*, November, 2004, Joel Shoemaker, review of *Travel Team*, p. 149; April, 2006, Marilyn Taniguchi, review of *Heat*, p. 144; November, 2006, Jeffrey A. French, review of *Miracle on 49th Street*, p. 141.

*Tribune Books* (Chicago, IL), July 1, 1984, p. 28; August 10, 1986, p. 47.

*Voice of Youth Advocates*, February, 2007, review of *Heat*, p. 488.

*Washington Post Book World*, October 2, 1987; June 19, 1988, p. 8.

*ONLINE*

*New York Daily News Online*, http://www.nydailynews.com/sports/co/lupica/ (March 20, 2007), "Mike Lupica."*

# M

## MACKALL, Dandi Daley 1949-
### (Dandi)

### Personal

Born Dorothy Ann Daley, March 24, 1949, in Kansas City, MO; daughter of F.R. (a physician) and Helen (a nurse) Daley; married Joseph S. Mackall (a professor and writer); children: Jennifer, Katy, Dan. *Education:* University of Missouri—Columbia, B.A., 1971; University of Central Oklahoma, M.A., 1989; also attended Institute of Biblical Studies (Arrowhead, CA) and Trinity Evangelical Divinity School. *Politics:* "Independent." *Religion:* Christian. *Hobbies and other interests:* Horseback riding, tennis, walking, painting.

### Addresses

*Home and office*—1254 Tupelo Lane, West Salem, OH 44287. *E-mail*—dandi@dandibooks.com.

### Career

Author, educator, and lecturer. Freelance manuscript reviewer and editor, 1978-86; University of Central Oklahoma, Edmond, lecturer in writing for children, 1986-89; freelance writer and public speaker, 1989—. Southwest Community College, Creston, IA, instructor, 1984-86; Southern Nazarene University, instructor, 1986-89; Ashland University, instructor, 1990-94; Institute of Children's Literature, instructor. Speaker at conferences; guest on television and radio programs.

### Member

Society of Children's Book Writers and Illustrators (religious coordinator, 1990-94), PEN International, Phi Beta Kappa.

### Awards, Honors

Silver Medallion Award, for *Degrees of Guilt* and *God Made Me; Romantic Times* Pick of the Month designation, for *Love Rules;* American Library Association Best Books for Young Readers nomination, 2006, and Ohioana Award finalist, 2007, both for *Eva Underground;* Distinguished Alumna Award, University of Missouri, 2006.

***Dandi Daley Mackall*** (Photograph courtesy of Dandi Daley Mackall.)

### Writings

*FOR CHILDREN*

*The Best Christmas Ever,* Standard Publishing (Cincinnati, OH), 1986.

*A Secret Birthday Gift,* Standard Publishing (Cincinnati, OH), 1987.

*A Super Friend,* Standard Publishing (Cincinnati, OH), 1987.

*Me First,* Standard Publishing (Cincinnati, OH), 1987.

*Allyson J. Cat,* Standard Publishing (Cincinnati, OH), 1989.

*Allyson J. Cat Coloring Book,* with cassette, Standard Publishing (Cincinnati, OH), 1989.

*The Christmas Gifts That Didn't Need Wrapping,* illustrated by Dawn Mathers, Augsburg-Fortress (Minneapolis, MN), 1990.

*It's Only Ali Cat,* Standard Publishing (Cincinnati, OH), 1990.

*An Ali Cat Christmas,* illustrated by Kathryn Hutton, Standard Publishing (Cincinnati, OH), 1991.

*Kay's Birthday Surprise,* illustrated by Dawn Mathers, Augsburg-Fortress (Minneapolis, MN), 1992.

*A Gaggle of Galloping Ghosts,* Hanna Barbera, 1995.

*No Biz like Show Biz,* Hanna Barbera, 1995.

*Millionaire Astro,* Hanna Barbera, 1995.

*Home Sweet Jellystone,* Hanna Barbera, 1995.

*Seasons,* Landoll's, 1995.

*Baby Animals,* Landoll's, 1995.

*Secret Night,* Landoll's, 1995.

*Who's a Goblin?,* Landoll's, 1995.

*The Halloween Secret,* Landoll's, 1995.

*Circus Counting,* Landoll's, 1995.

*ABC's of Lunch,* Landoll's, 1995.

*Things That Go,* Landoll's, 1995.

*Bugs and Butterflies,* Landoll's, 1995.

*Under the Water,* Landoll's, 1995.

*Santa's Toy Shop,* Landoll's, 1995.

*Scooby Doo and Scrappy in 1.2.3,* Hanna Barbera, 1996.

*Pebbles and Bamm Bamm in a Colorful Game,* Hanna Barbera, 1996.

*Jetsons in Shapes,* Hanna Barbera, 1996.

*Yogi and Boo Boo ABC's,* Hanna Barbera, 1996.

*Picture Me at Walt Disney World's 25th Anniversary,* Disney (New York, NY), 1997.

*Christmas Buttons,* illustrated by Bryan Fyffe, Playhouse Publishing, 1997.

*Halloween Buttons,* illustrated by Bryan Fyffe, Playhouse Publishing, 1997.

*Chicken Soup for the Kid's Soul,* Batgirl, 1998.

*Joseph, King of Dreams* (movie adaptation), Dreamworks, 1998.

*Easter Adventure,* Concordia (St. Louis, MO), 1998.

(Compiler) *Why I Believe in God: And Other Reflections by Children,* Prima Publishing (Rocklin, CA), 1999.

*Portrait of Lies,* created by Terry Brown, Tommy Nelson (Nashville, TN), 2000.

*Off to Bethlehem!,* HarperCollins (New York, NY), 2000.

*No, No Noah!,* Tommy Nelson (Nashville, TN), 2000.

*The Don't Cry, Lion,* Tommy Nelson (Nashville, TN), 2000.

*Little Lost Donkey,* Tommy Nelson (Nashville, TN), 2000.

*Go, Go Fish!,* Tommy Nelson (Nashville, TN), 2000.

*Moses, Pharaoh, and the Snake,* Broadman (Nashville, TN), 2000.

*Silent Dreams,* illustrated by Karen A. Jerome, Eerdmans (Grand Rapids, MI), 2001.

(Compiler) *What Children Know about Angels,* Sourcebooks (Naperville, IL), 2001.

(Compiler) *101 Things Kids Wonder,* Sourcebooks (Naperville, IL), 2001.

(Compiler) *Kids' Rules for Life: A Guide to Life's Journey from Those Just Starting Out,* Sourcebooks (Naperville, IL), 2001.

*Until the Christ Child Came,* illustrated by Sally Wern Comport, Concordia (St. Louis, MO), 2002.

*Off to Bethlehem!,* illustrated by R.W. Alley, HarperFestival (New York, NY), 2002.

*Off to Plymouth Rock!,* illustrated by Gene Barretta, Tommy Nelson (Nashville, TN), 2002, issued with CD, 2005.

*It Must Be Halloween,* illustrated by Barry Gott, Little Simon (New York, NY), 2002.

*Love and Kisses, Bunny* (board book), illustrated by Hala Wittwer, Little Simon (New York, NY), 2003.

*First Day,* illustrated by Tiphanie Beeke, Harcourt (San Diego, CA), 2003.

*Who'll Light the Chanukah Candles?,* illustrated by Keiko Motoyama, Little Simon (New York, NY), 2003.

*Are We There Yet?,* illustrated by Shannon McNeill, Dutton (New York, NY), 2004.

*A Tree for Christmas,* illustrated by Dominic Catalano, Concordia (St. Louis, MO), 2004.

*Merry Creature Christmas!,* illustrated by Gene Barretta, Tommy Nelson (Nashville, TN), 2004, issued with CD, 2005.

*Journey, Journey, Jesus,* illustrated by Gene Barretta, Tommy Nelson (Nashville, TN), 2004.

*A Friend from Galilee,* illustrated by Jan Spivey Gilchrist, Augsburg Fortress (Minneapolis, MN), 2004.

*Made for a Purpose,* illustrated by Glin Dibley, Zonderkidz (Grand Rapids, MI), 2004.

*My Happy Easter Morning,* illustrated by Rachel O'Neill, Zonderkidz (Grand Rapids, MI), 2005.

*My Christmas Gift to Jesus* (board book), illustrated by Rachel O'Neill, Zonderkidz (Grand Rapids, MI), 2005.

*My Big Birthday* (board book), illustrated by Rachel O'Neill, Zonderkidz (Grand Rapids, MI), 2005.

*My Secret Valentine* (board book), illustrated by Rachel O'Neill, Zonderkidz (Grand Rapids, MI), 2005.

*Jesus in Me,* illustrated by Jenny B. Harris, Standard Publishing (Cincinnati, OH), 2005.

*In the Beginning,* illustrated by James Kandt, Tommy Nelson (Nashville, TN), 2005.

*I'm His Lamb,* illustrated by Jane Dippold, Standard Publishing (Cincinnati, OH), 2005.

*Jesus Said, "Go Tell the World," so I've Got a Job to Do,* illustrated by Jane Dippold, Standard Publishing (Cincinnati, OH), 2005.

*The Legend of Ohio,* illustrated by Greg LaFever, Sleeping Bear Press (Chelsea, MI), 2005.

*God Blesses Me,* illustrated by Jane Dippold, Standard Publishing (Cincinnati, OH), 2005.

*The Best Thing Is Love,* illustrated by Claudine Gèvry, Standard Publishing (Cincinnati, OH), 2005.

*Praying Jesus' Way,* illustrated by Claudine Gèvry, Standard Publishing (Cincinnati, OH), 2005.

*This Is the Lunch That Jesus Served,* illustrated by Benrei Huang, Augsburg Fortress (Minneapolis, MN), 2005.

*The Shepherd's Christmas Story,* illustrated by Dominic Catalano, Concordia (St. Louis, MO), 2005.

*The Golden Rule,* illustrated by Jane Dippold, Standard Publishing (Cincinnati, OH), 2005.

*Three Wise Women of Christmas,* illustrated by Diana Magnuson, Concordia (St. Louis, MO), 2006.

*God Shows the Way,* illustrated by Claudine Gèvry, Standard Publishing (Cincinnati, OH), 2006.

*The Armor of God,* illustrated by Jenny B. Harris, Standard Publishing (Cincinnati, OH), 2006.

*Seeing Stars,* illustrated by Claudien Gevry, Simon & Schuster (New York, NY), 2006.

*I Love You, Mommy,* illustrated by Karen Lee Schmidt, Standard Publishing (Cincinnati, OH), 2006.

*I Love You, Daddy,* illustrated by Karen Lee Schmidt, Standard Publishing (Cincinnati, OH), 2006.

*God Made Me,* illustrated by Hiroe Nakata, Simon & Schuster (New York, NY), 2006.

*A Glorious Angel Show,* illustrated by Susan Mitchell, Integrity Publishers 2006.

*Treetops Are Whispering,* illustrated by Vincent Nguyen, Simon & Schuster (New York, NY), 2007.

*Rudy Rides the Rails: A Depression-Era Story,* illustrated by Chris Ellison, Sleeping Bear Press (Chelsea, MI), 2007.

*Easter Is for Me,* illustrated by Anton Petrov, Concordia (St. Louis, MO), 2007.

*For God So Loved the World: My First John 3:16 Book,* illustrated by Elena Selivanova, Thomas Nelson (Nashville, TN), 2007.

*Make Me a Blessing,* Simon & Schuster (New York, NY), 2007.

*The Blanket Show!,* illustrated by David Hohn, WaterBrook/Random House (New York, NY), 2007.

*A Gaggle of Geese and a Clutter of Cats,* WaterBrook/Random House (New York, NY), 2007.

*The Legend of Saint Nicholas: A Story of Christmas Giving,* illustrated by Guy Porfirio, Zonderkids (Grand Rapids, MI), 2007.

*Christmas Light,* Concordia (St. Louis, MO), 2007.

*The Wonder of Christmas,* Concordia (St. Louis, MO), 2008.

*The Legend of the Christmas Cookie: An Inspirational Story of Sharing,* illustrated by Deborah Chabrian Zonderkids (Grand Rapids, MI), 2008.

*The Legend of the Easter Robin,* Zonderkids (Grand Rapids, MI), 2008.

*It Was Not Such a Silent Night,* Dutton (New York, NY), 2008.

*A Girl Named Dan,* Sleeping Bear Press (Chelsea, MI), 2008.

*The Legend of the Valentine: An Inspirational Story of Love,* illustrated by Edward Gazsi, Zonderkids (Grand Rapids, MI), 2009.

*The Legend of Christmas Holly,* Zonderkids (Grand Rapids, MI), 2009.

Also author of pop-up books *Daniel and the Lion's Den, Noah's Ark,* and *Jonah and the Whale,* all 1995; author of *The Princess and the Pea, Town and Country Mouse,* and "My First Book" series. Author of coloring books, under pseudonym Dandi. Contributor to books, including *Christmas Programs for Organizations,* Standard Publishing (Cincinnati, OH), 1986. Contributor to periodicals, including *Guidepost, Moody Monthly, Christianity Today, Power for Living, Christian Parenting,* and *Today's Christian Woman.* Author of humor column in an Iowa newspaper, 1984-86.

Author's works have been translated into over a dozen languages.

*"LITTLE BLESSINGS" PICTURE BOOKS*

*Blessings Everywhere,* illustrated by Elena Kucharik, Tyndale House (Wheaton, IL), 2000.

*God Makes Nighttime Too!,* illustrated by Elena Kucharik, Tyndale House (Wheaton, IL), 2000.

*Rain or Shine,* illustrated by Elena Kucharik, Tyndale House (Wheaton, IL), 2000.

*Birthday Blessings,* illustrated by Elena Kucharik, Tyndale House (Wheaton, IL), 2001.

*Count Your Blessings,* illustrated by Elena Kucharik, Tyndale House (Wheaton, IL), 2002.

*ABC's,* illustrated by Elena Kucharik, Tyndale House (Wheaton, IL), 2002.

*Many-Colored Blessings,* illustrated by Elena Kucharik, Tyndale House (Wheaton, IL), 2005.

*Blessings Come in Shapes,* illustrated by Elena Kucharik, Tyndale House (Wheaton, IL), 2005.

*"FIRST THINGS FIRST" BOARD-BOOK SERIES*

*Things I Do,* illustrated by Megan Halsey, Augsburg Fortress (Minneapolis, MN), 2002.

*Rainbow Party,* illustrated by Megan Halsey, Augsburg Fortress (Minneapolis, MN), 2002.

*The Lost Sheep,* illustrated by Megan Halsey, Augsburg Fortress (Minneapolis, MN), 2002.

*Made by God,* illustrated by Megan Halsey, Augsburg Fortress (Minneapolis, MN), 2002.

*"IMAGINATION" PICTURE-BOOK SERIES*

*The Shape of Things,* illustrated by Jill Newton, Augsburg Fortress (Minneapolis, MN), 2003.

*Color My World,* illustrated by Jill Newton, Augsburg Fortress (Minneapolis, MN), 2003.

*Cloud Counting,* illustrated by Jill Newton, Augsburg Fortress (Minneapolis, MN), 2003.

*Animal Babies,* illustrated by Jill Newton, Augsburg Fortress (Minneapolis, MN), 2003.

*"READY, SET, READ!" BEGINNING-READER SERIES*

*God Made Me,* illustrated by Michelle Neavill, Augsburg-Fortress (Minneapolis, MN), 1992.

*Jesus Loves Me,* illustrated by Kathy Rogers, Augsburg-Fortress (Minneapolis, MN), 1994.

*So I Can Read,* illustrated by Deborah A. Kirkeeide, Augsburg-Fortress (Minneapolis, MN), 1994.

*COMPILER; "KIDS SAY" SERIES*

*Kids Say the Cutest Things about Mom!,* Trade Life Books (Tulsa, OK), 1996.

*Kids Say the Cutest Things about Dad!,* Trade Life Books (Tulsa, OK), 1997.

*Kids Say the Cutest Things about Love,* Trade Life Books (Tulsa, OK), 1998.

*"PICTURE ME" SERIES; UNDER PSEUDONYM DANDI*

*Picture Me as Goldilocks,* illustrated by Wendy Rasmussen, Picture Me Books (Akron, OH), 1997.

*Picture Me as Jack and the Beanstalk,* illustrated by Wendy Rasmussen, Picture Me Books (Akron, OH), 1997.

*Picture Me as Little Red Riding Hood,* illustrated by Wendy Rasmussen, Picture Me Books (Akron, OH), 1997.

*Picture Me with Jonah,* Picture Me Books (Akron, OH), 1997.

*Picture Me with Noah,* Picture Me Books (Akron, OH), 1997.

*Picture Me with Moses,* Picture Me Books (Akron, OH), 1997.

*Picture Me with Jesus,* Picture Me Books (Akron, OH), 1997.

*"PUZZLE CLUB" MYSTERY SERIES*

*The Puzzle Club Christmas Mystery,* illustrated by Mike Young Productions, Concordia (St. Louis, MO), 1997.

*The Puzzle Club Activity Book,* Concordia (St. Louis, MO), 1997.

*The Puzzle Club Picture Book,* Concordia (St. Louis, MO), 1997.

*The Mystery of Great Price,* Concordia (St. Louis, MO), 1997.

*The Puzzle Club Case of the Kidnapped Kid,* Concordia (St. Louis, MO), 1998.

*The Puzzle Club Poison-Pen Mystery,* Concordia (St. Louis, MO), 1998.

*The Puzzle Club Musical Mystery,* Concordia (St. Louis, MO), 1998.

*The Puzzle Club Meets the Jigsaw Kids,* Concordia (St. Louis, MO), 1999.

Also author of *The Counterfeit Caper, The Case of the Missing Memory,* and *The Petnapping Mystery,* 1997-2000.

*MIDDLE-GRADE AND YOUNG-ADULT NOVELS*

*Kyra's Story: Degrees of Guilt,* Tyndale House (Wheaton, IL), 2003.

*Sierra's Story: Degrees of Betrayal,* Tyndale House (Wheaton, IL), 2004.

*Love Rules,* Tyndale House (Wheaton, IL), 2005.

*Eva Underground,* Harcourt (Orlando, FL), 2006.

*Maggie's Story,* Tyndale House (Carol Stream, IL), 2006.

*Larger-than-Life Lara,* Dutton (New York, NY), 2006.

*Crazy in Love,* Dutton (New York, NY), 2007.

*"CINNAMON LAKE" MYSTERY SERIES*

*The Secret Society of the Left Hand,* illustrated by Kay Salem, Concordia (St. Louis, MO), 1996.

*The Case of the Disappearing Dirt,* illustrated by Kay Salem, Concordia (St. Louis, MO), 1996.

*The Cinnamon Lake Meow Mystery,* illustrated by Kay Salem, Concordia (St. Louis, MO), 1997.

*Don't Bug Me Molly!,* illustrated by Kay Salem, Concordia (St. Louis, MO), 1997.

*Of Spies and Spider Webs,* illustrated by Kay Salem, Concordia (St. Louis, MO), 1997.

*The Cinnamon Lake-ness Monster,* illustrated by Kay Salem, Concordia (St. Louis, MO), 1997.

*Soup Kitchen Suspicion,* illustrated by Kay Salem, Concordia (St. Louis, MO), 1998.

*The Presidential Mystery,* illustrated by Kay Salem, Concordia (St. Louis, MO), 1999.

*"HORSEFEATHERS!" SERIES; YOUNG-ADULT NOVELS*

*Horsefeathers!,* Concordia (St. Louis, MO), 2000.

*Horse Cents,* Concordia (St. Louis, MO), 2000.

*A Horse of a Different Color,* Concordia (St. Louis, MO), 2000.

*Horse Whispers in the Air,* Concordia (St. Louis, MO), 2000.

*Horse Angels,* Concordia (St. Louis, MO), 2000.

*Home Is Where Your Horse Is,* Concordia (St. Louis, MO), 2000.

*"WINNIE THE HORSE GENTLER" NOVEL SERIES*

*Bold Beauty,* Tyndale House (Wheaton, IL), 2002.

*Midnight Mystery,* Tyndale House (Wheaton, IL), 2002.

*Unhappy Appy,* Tyndale House (Wheaton, IL), 2002.

*Wild Thing,* Tyndale House (Wheaton, IL), 2002.

*Eager Star,* Tyndale House (Wheaton, IL), 2002.

*Gift Horse,* Tyndale House (Wheaton, IL), 2003.

*Friendly Foal,* Tyndale House (Wheaton, IL), 2004.

*Buckshot Bandit,* Tyndale House (Wheaton, IL), 2004.

*"BLOG ON" YOUNG-ADULT NOVEL SERIES*

*Grace Notes,* Zonderkidz (Grand Rapids, MI), 2006.

*Love, Annie,* Zonderkidz (Grand Rapids, MI), 2006.

*Just Jazz,* Zonderkidz (Grand Rapids, MI), 2006.

*Storm Rising,* Zonderkidz (Grand Rapids, MI), 2006.

*Grace under Pressure,* Zonderkidz (Grand Rapids, MI), 2007.

*Jazz Off Key,* Zonderkidz (Grand Rapids, MI), 2007.

*Storm Warning,* Zonderkidz (Grand Rapids, MI), 2007.

*"STARLIGHT ANIMAL RESCUE" NOVEL SERIES*

*Runaway,* Tyndale House (Wheaton, IL), 2008.

*Mad Dog,* Tyndale House (Wheaton, IL), 2008.

*Kat Shrink,* Tyndale House (Wheaton, IL), 2008.

*Fur Ball,* Tyndale House (Wheaton, IL), 2008.

FOR ADULTS

*The Blessing Is in the Doing,* Broadman (Nashville, TN), 1983.

*A Spiritual Handbook for Women,* Prentice-Hall (Englewood Cliffs, NJ), 1984.

*Remembering . . . ,* Tyndale House (Wheaton, IL), 1985.

*When the Answer Is No,* Broadman (Nashville, TN), 1985.

*Splitting Up: When Your Friend Gets a Divorce,* Harold Shaw (Wheaton, IL), 1988.

*Just One of Me,* Harold Shaw (Wheaton, IL), 1989.

*Kindred Sisters: New Testament Women Speak to Us Today; A Book of Meditation and Reflection,* Augsburg Fortress (Minneapolis, MN), 1996.

*101 Ways to Talk to God,* Sourcebooks (Naperville, IL), 2000.

OTHER

(Compiler) *Kids Are Still Saying the Darndest Things,* Prima Publishing (Rocklin, CA), 1993.

(Compiler) *Kids Say the Greatest Things about God: A Kid's-Eye View of Life's Biggest Subject,* Tyndale House (Wheaton, IL), 1995.

*Problem Solving* (nonfiction), Ferguson (Chicago, IL), 1998, 2nd edition, 2004.

*Teamwork Skills* (nonfiction), Ferguson (New York, NY), 1998, 2nd edition, 2004.

*Self-Development* (nonfiction), Ferguson (Chicago, IL), 1998, 2nd edition published as *Professional Ethics and Etiquette,* 2004.

*Portrait of Lies,* Tommy Nelson (Nashville, TN), 2001.

*Please Reply!,* Tommy Nelson (Nashville, TN), 2002.

*Kids Say the Best Things about Life: Devotions and Conversations for Families on the Go,* Jossey-Bass (San Francisco, CA), 2004.

*Kids Say the Best Things about God: Devotions and Conversations for Families on the Go,* Jossey-Bass (San Francisco, CA), 2004.

## Adaptations

Three titles in the "Puzzle Club" mystery series were adapted as animated television programs. *Kindred Sisters* has been adapted as an audiobook.

## Sidelights

A prolific writer whose work has been published in over twenty countries, Dandi Daley Mackall has hundreds of books to her credit, the majority of which reflect her Christian faith. Mackall's works range from picture books and novels for children and young adults to historical fiction and nonfiction for a variety of ages. Mackall finds the seeds of stories everywhere, especially in her own life and her experiences raising her three children. For example, the writer's lifelong love of horses is reflected in her "Winnie the Horse Gentler" novel series, about a twelve year old who is able to communicate with horses. The time-honored mantra of the American family road trip inspired her picture book

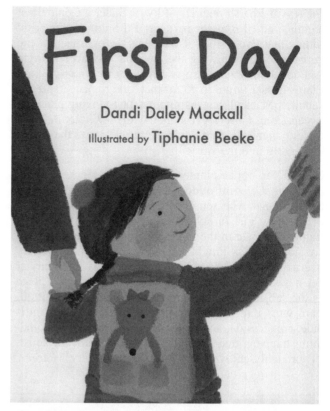

*Cover of Mackall's picture book* First Day, *featuring illustrations by Tiphanie Beeke.* (Copyright © 2003 by Tiphanie Beeke. Reproduced by permission of Harcourt, Inc.)

*Are We There Yet?,* while another picture book, *First Day,* reflects universally shared worries as the first day of school approaches. Mackall's young-adult novel *Eva Underground* is based on memories of her eighteen-month venture into Poland in the 1970s, where she experienced life behind the iron curtain prior to the end of the cold war. Readers of *Eva Underground* are treated to a "distinctive human portrayal of a troubling time and place," according to *School Library Journal* reviewer Suzanne Gordon, while a *Kirkus Reviews* contributor stated that "modern Communism is rarely depicted in children's literature, and never before this well." In *Booklist* Stephanie Zvirin dubbed *First Day* "cheerful" and "encouraging." *Are We There Yet?,* featuring what a *Publishers Weekly* contributor described as a "cleverly rhymed" text, also benefits from illustrations by Shannon McNeill that the reviewer praised as "chock full of detail."

Taking place in 1978, *Eva Underground* introduces Eva Lott, a Chicago high school senior. While still grieving her mother's death, Eva finds her secure suburban world further disrupted when her father, a college teacher, decides to put his energy into fighting as part of the Polish anti-communist underground. Making the dangerous border crossing, Eva begins to understand the plight of the Polish people. While her father helps organize an underground press, the American teen becomes involved with one of the underground's young radicals, and ultimately learns the cost of freedom. "Mackall effectively

conveys the harsh realities of living under a Communist regime," noted *Booklist* reviewer Ed Sullivan, the critic adding that Eve's story also reflects the optimism of the Polish people following the election of Karol Wojtyla as Pope John Paul. Also reviewing *Eva Underground,* Claire Rosser wrote in *Kliatt* that "the romance and adventure" Mackall weaves into her fast-moving plot will sweep along most YA readers," while a *Kirkus Reviews* writer commented that Eva's narration "draws the reader inexorably into the story."

Geared for upper elementary-grade readers, *Larger-than-Life Lara* introduces Laney Grafton, a friendly fourth grader who sets down on paper the experiences of the new girl in school, carefully and consciously framing her tale in the multi-part structure her language arts teacher has taught her. Laney's subject, grossly overweight, ten-year-old Lara Phelps, has problems at her new school, where she quickly takes Laney's place as the subject of many schoolyard jokes. Through it all, Lara wins Laney's admiration due to her upbeat attitude, compassion, and ready smile, but ultimately something happens that breaks even Lara's buoyant spirit. "Thoroughly enjoyable and unexpectedly wry," *Larger-*

*Cover of Mackall's* **Larger-than-Life Lara,** *featuring an illustration by* **Linda McCarthy.** (Penguin Group, 2006. Reproduced by permission of Dutton Children's Books, a division of Penguin Putnam Books for Young Readers.)

*than-Life Lara* ". . . is as intelligent as it is succinct," noted *School Library Journal* contributor Elizabeth Bird, while in *Booklist* Carolyn Phelan commented that Mackall's story includes "touching moments and offers food for thought" for younger readers.

Mackall once told *SATA:* "I love to write! I even love to rewrite and revise. When I was a ten-year-old tomboy, I won my first contest with fifty words on 'why I want to be bat boy for the Kansas City A's.' But the team wouldn't let a girl be bat boy—my first taste of rejection! I've amassed drawerfuls of rejections since, but along the way I've hung in there and have seen hundreds of my books into print.

"Although I began writing books for grownups—humor, how-to's, inspirationals—when my children were born, I added children's books to the mix. Beginning with board books and baby books when my children were infants, I progressed through picture books and chapter books, middle-grade fiction and nonfiction, never dropping an age group, but simply adding another one. With our teens all in high school, I started a new series of young-adult fiction, 'Horsefeathers!' I grew up with horses, backyard horses: the kind you keep as friends in your own backyard. It's been great to draw on my earlier horse-loving days to build my main character in the series, a teenaged, female horse whisperer.

"I'm blessed with a husband who is also a writer and understands why the beds aren't made and there's nothing on the table at dinner time, and I'm blessed with children who offer encouragement and a never-ending supply of stories. I believe that God has stories already created for us if we're listening and looking and willing to work like crazy to make those stories the best they can be. I suppose that's really why I write."

## Biographical and Critical Sources

*PERIODICALS*

*Booklist,* November 1, 1993, Denise Perry Donavin, review of *Kids Are Still Saying the Darndest Things,* p. p. 500; August, 2003, Stephanie Zvirin, review of *First Day,* p. 1994; March 1, 2006, Ed Sullivan, review of *Eva Underground,* p. 81; May 1, 2006, Carolyn Phelan, review of *Seeing Stars,* p. 86; August 1, 2006, Carolyn Phelan, review of *Larger-than-Life Lara,* p. 78.

*Bulletin of the Center for Children's Books,* October, 2002, review of *Off to Bethlehem!,* p. 67; May, 2006, Loretta Gaffney, review of *Eva Underground,* p. 413; October, 2006, Deborah Stevenson, review of *Larger-than-Life Lara,* p. 82.

*Christian Parenting Today,* summer, 2002, review of "Winnie the Horse Gentler" series, p. 62.

*Kirkus Reviews,* November 1, 2002, review of *Off to Bethlehem!,* p. 1621; February 15, 2006, review of *Eva Underground,* p. 186.

*Kliatt,* March, 2006, Claire Rosser, review of *Eva Underground,* p. 15.

*Publishers Weekly,* September 23, 2002, review of *Until the Christ Child Came . . . ,* p. 36; May 5, 2003, review of *Are We There Yet?,* p. 209; August 25, 2003, review of *First Day,* p. 62; September 22, 2003, review of *Who'll Light the Chanukah Candles?,* p. 68; December 15, 2003, review of *Love and Kisses, Bunny,* p. 76; March 22, 2004, review of *Kids Say the Best Things about Life: Devotions and Conversations for Families on the Go,* p. 16.

*School Library Journal,* October, 1997, Jane Marino, review of *The Puzzle Club Christmas Mystery,* p. 44; October, 2002, Eva Mitnick, review of *Off to Bethlehem!,* p. 61; January, 2003, review of *Rainbow Party,* p. 106; April, 2003, Laurie von Mehren, review of *Silent Dreams,* p. 134; September, 2003, Lisa Gangemi Kropp, review of *First Day,* p. 184; January, 2004, Olga R. Kuharets, review of *Cloud Counting,* p. 102; January, 2005, Cass Kvenild, review of *Professional Ethics,* p. 144; June, 2006, Suzanne Gordon, review of *Eva Underground,* p. 161; September, 2006, Elizabeth Bird, review of *Larger-than-Life Lara,* p. 212.

*Voice of Youth Advocates,* August, 1998, pp. 223-224; December, 2000, review of "Horsefeathers!" series, p. 343; February, 2007, Vikki Terrile, review of *Crazy in Love,* p. 528.

ONLINE

*Dandi E. Mackall Home Page,* http://www.dandibooks. com (March 18, 2007).

\*    \*    \*

# MacLEAN, Christine Kole

## Personal

Born in MI; married; children: one son, one daughter. *Education:* B.A. (English literature).

## Addresses

*Home*—Holland, MI. *E-mail*—christinemaclean@contentstudio.com.

## Career

Freelance writer.

## Member

Society of Children's Book Writers and Illustrators.

## Writings

*Even Firefighters Hug Their Moms,* illustrated by Mike Reed, Dutton (New York, NY), 2002.

*Mary Margaret and the Perfect Pet Plan,* illustrated by Vicki Lowe, Dutton (New York, NY), 2004.

***Christine Kole MacLean*** (Photograph by BKB Studio. Courtesy of Christine Kole MacLean.)

*Everybody Makes Mistakes,* illustrated by C.B. Decker, Dutton (New York, NY), 2005.

*How It's Done* (young-adult novel), Flux (Woodbury, MN), 2006.

*Mary Margaret, Center Stage,* illustrated by Vicki Lowe, Dutton (New York, NY), 2006.

*Mary Margaret Meets Her Match,* illustrated by Vicki Lowe, Dutton (New York, NY), 2007.

*Mary Margaret Christmas,* illustrated by Vicki Low, Dutton (New York, NY), 2008.

## Sidelights

Christine Kole MacLean is the author of a number of children's books, including *Everybody Makes Mistakes* and *Mary Margaret and the Perfect Pet Plan,* as well as of the young-adult novel *How It's Done.*

*How It's Done* examines the complex relationship between a younger woman and an older man. Raised in a conservative home by a fundamentalist Christian father and a timid mother, eighteen-year-old Grace Passedge longs for independence and excitement. When she meets Michael Irving, a worldly college professor, Grace falls head-over-heels in love and agrees to marry the man, only to discover that their differences are greater than she imagined. Discussing the theme of her novel in an interview for the *Young Adult (& Kids) Books Central* Web site, MacLean stated: "There are no shortcuts to finding yourself. It's messy, complex, difficult work— and you are the only person who can do it."

MacLean published her first work for young readers, *Even Firefighters Hug Their Moms,* in 2002. In this story, a lively toddler becomes so involved in creating imaginary spaceships to launch and fires to douse that he ignores his mom's pleas for a hug. "MacLean really captures how single-minded children can sometimes be," remarked *Booklist* critic Ilene Cooper, and Joy Fleishhacker, writing in *School Library Journal,* observed that the mother's "recurrent request makes a familiar refrain that adds a bit of humor to the story and helps to connect the child's flights of fancy to the everyday world."

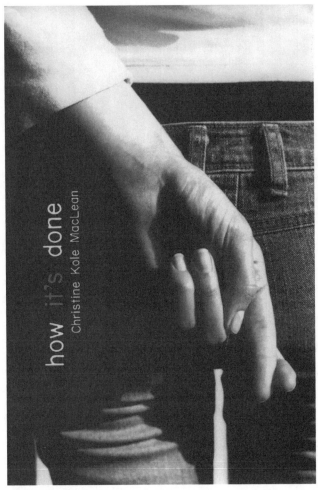

*Cover of MacLean's young-adult novel* **How It's Done,** *about a teen's efforts to integrate her fundamentalist faith with her future.* (Flux, 2006. Cover design by Gavin Dayton Duffy. Cover image © Picture Quest. Reproduced by permission of Llewellyn Publications and Picture Quest.)

In *Everybody Makes Mistakes* young Jack tries to explain his way out of trouble by noting that even adults make errors, such as the time Jack's teacher sat on his snack. Jack's mom is unwilling to listen, however, especially after Jack performs an unsightly makeover on his little sister on the day of a family wedding. A contributor to *Kirkus Reviews* deemed *Everybody Makes Mistakes* "entertaining and clever," and *Booklist* critic Hazel Rochman predicted that readers "will laugh about Jack and about their own embarrassing moments."

In MacLean's chapter book *Mary Margaret and the Perfect Pet Plan,* the author introduces an irrepressible nine year old with a seemingly limitless supply of energy. When Mary Margaret spots her neighbor's new puppy, she decides she must have a pet for herself. Although she concocts what seems to be a foolproof, three-step plan to raise the money needed for purchase, Mary Margaret's scheme has a couple of flaws: her father is allergic to pet dander and her frazzled and pregnant mother does not need another distraction. Calling the story's young heroine "lively, spirited, and full of energy," Terrie Dorio added in *School Library Journal*

that "all of the characters are well drawn and the narrative sparkles with humor."

Readers reunite with Mary Margaret in *Mary Margaret, Center Stage,* which follows the fourth grader's efforts to land the lead role in the school play. When a fellow classmate is chosen to play Cinderella, however, Mary Margaret becomes even more determined to get her time in the spotlight. According to *Booklist* reviewer Ilene Cooper, "the action is nonstop and the embellishments are fun, especially the relationship between Mary Margaret and her brother." In another book in the series, *Mary Margaret Meets Her Match,* the youngster learns a valuable lesson when she is paired with an uncooperative horse while vacationing at a dude ranch, resulting in a story that a *Kirkus Reviews* writer predicted "is sure to make cowgirls cheer."

On her home page, MacLean noted that perseverance and stamina are the keys to her success as an author, even when her work seems less than satisfactory. "I have to remember that losing faith and flailing and mucking about are all part of my writing process," the

*Cover of MacLean's* **Mary Margaret, Center Stage,** *featuring an illustration by Vicky Lowe.* (Copyright © 2006 by Vicky Lowe. Reproduced by permission of Dutton Children's Books, a division of Penguin Putnam Books for Young Readers.)

author remarked, "and I have to believe that it will all lead somewhere."

## Biographical and Critical Sources

*PERIODICALS*

*Bulletin of the Center for Children's Books,* June, 2004, Timnah Card, review of *Mary Margaret and the Perfect Pet Plan,* p. 428; April, 2006, Deborah Stevenson, review of *Mary Margaret, Center Stage,* p. 365.

*Booklist,* November 15, 2002, Ilene Cooper, review of *Even Firefighters Hug Their Moms,* p. 611; May 15, 2005, Hazel Rochman, review of *Everybody Makes Mistakes,* p. 1666; February 1, 2006, Ilene Cooper, review of *Mary Margaret, Center Stage,* p. 50.

*Kirkus Reviews,* September 1, 2002, review of *Even Firefighters Hug Their Moms,* p. 1314; May 1, 2004, review of *Mary Margaret and the Perfect Pet Plan,* p. 444; May 15, 2005, review of *Everybody Makes Mistakes,* p. 592; March 1, 2006, review of *Mary Margaret, Center Stage,* p. 236; February 1, 2007, review of *Mary Margaret Meets Her Match.*

*School Library Journal,* October, 2002, Joy Fleishhacker, review of *Even Firefighters Hug Their Moms,* p. 120; July, 2004, Terrie Dorio, review of *Mary Margaret and the Perfect Pet Plan,* p. 109; July, 2005, Roxanne Burg, review of *Everybody Makes Mistakes,* p. 78; June, 2006, Tina Zubak, review of *Mary Margaret, Center Stage,* p. 122.

*Tribune Books* (Chicago, IL), September 8, 2002, review of *Even Firefighters Hug Their Moms,* p. 4.

*ONLINE*

*Christine Kole MacLean Home Page,* http://www.christinekolemaclean.com (January 21, 2007).

*Not Your Mother's Book Club Online,* http://community.livejournal.com/notyourmothers/ (September 5, 2006), interview with MacLean.

*Young Adult (& Kids) Books Central Web site,* http://www.yabookscentral.com/ (January 21, 2007), "Christine Kole MacLean Talks to Marla Arbach about *How It's Done.*"

*       *       *

# MANNION, Diane
## See PATERSON, Diane

*       *       *

# McCUE, Lisa 1959-
## (Lisa Emiline McCue)

## Personal

Born February 16, 1959, in New York, NY; daughter of Richard (a television director and producer) and Emiline (an artist) McCue; married Kenneth Stephen Karsten, Jr. (an electrical engineer), 1986. *Education:* Attended University of Hartford, 1978-79; University of Southeastern Massachusetts, B.A., 1981.

## Addresses

*Home*—Annapolis, MD. *Agent*—Publisher's Graphics, 251 Greenwood Ave., Bethel, CT 06801.

## Career

Illustrator and author. Designer and creator of Fuzzytail Greetings (card line).

## Writings

*SELF-ILLUSTRATED*

*Fun and Games in Fraggle Rock,* Holt (New York, NY), 1984.

*The Little Chick,* Random House (New York, NY), 1986.

*Ten Little Puppy Dogs,* Random House (New York, NY), 1987.

*Puppy Peek-a-Boo,* Random House (New York, NY), 1989.

*Kittens Love,* Random House (New York, NY), 1990.

*Puppies Love,* Random House (New York, NY), 1990.

*Whose Little Baby Says . . . ?,* Random House (New York, NY), 1990.

*Bunnies Love,* Random House (New York, NY), 1991.

*Ducklings Love,* Random House (New York, NY), 1991.

*Christmas Stories and Poems,* Whistlestop (Mahwah, NJ), 1994.

*Kitty's Carrier,* Random House (New York, NY), 1995.

*Little Fuzzytail,* Random House (New York, NY), 1995.

*Fuzzytail Farm,* Random House (New York, NY), 1996.

*Quick, Quack, Quick,* Random House (New York, NY), 1996.

*Fuzzytail Friends: Lift-and-Look Animal Book,* Random House (New York, NY), 1997.

*Jingle Bell Mice,* Whistlestop (Mahwah, NJ), 1997.

*WITH FATHER, DICK McCUE; SELF-ILLUSTRATED*

*Ducky's Seasons,* Simon & Schuster (New York, NY), 1983.

*Froggie's Treasure,* Simon & Schuster (New York, NY), 1983.

*Teddy Dresses,* Simon & Schuster (New York, NY), 1983.

*Kitty's Colors,* Simon & Schuster (New York, NY), 1983.

*Puppy's Day School,* Simon & Schuster (New York, NY), 1984.

*Bunny's Numbers,* Simon & Schuster (New York, NY), 1984.

*Kitten's Christmas,* Simon & Schuster (New York, NY), 1985.

*Baby Elephant's Bedtime,* Simon & Schuster (New York, NY), 1985.

*Panda's Playtime,* Simon & Schuster (New York, NY), 1985.

*Raccoon's Hide and Seek,* Simon & Schuster (New York, NY), 1985.

*ILLUSTRATOR*

Marguerite Muntean Corsello, *Who Said That,* Western Publications, 1982.

Carol North, reteller, *The Three Bears,* Western Publications, 1983.

Michaela Muntean, *They Call Me Boober Fraggle,* Holt (New York, NY), 1983.

Michaela Muntean, *The Tale of the Traveling Matt,* Holt (New York, NY), 1984.

Louise Gikow, *Sprocket's Christmas Tale,* Holt (New York, NY), 1984.

M.C. Delaney, *Henry's Special Delivery,* Dutton (New York, NY), 1984.

Marilyn Elson, *Duffy on the Farm,* Western Publications, 1984.

Louise Gikow, *Wembley and the Soggy Map,* Holt (New York, NY), 1986.

Katharine Ross, *The Baby's Animal Party,* Random House (New York, NY), 1986.

Ben Cruise, reteller, *The Ugly Duckling,* Western Publications, 1987.

Katharine Ross, *Bear Island,* Random House (New York, NY), 1987.

Katharine Ross, *My Little Library of Fuzzy Tales: A Fuzzy Fussy Tale, A Fuzzy Sleepy Tale, A Fuzzy Wake-up Tale, A Fuzzy Friendly Tale,* Random House (New York, NY), 1987.

Katharine Ross, *Farm Fun,* Random House (New York, NY), 1987.

Stephanie Calmenson, *Spaghetti Manners,* Western Publications, 1987.

Stephanie Calmenson, *One Red Shoe,* Western Publications, 1987.

Jane Thayer, *The Puppy Who Wanted a Boy,* Morrow (New York, NY), 1988.

Katharine Ross, *Nighty-night, Little One,* Random House (New York, NY), 1988.

Jan Wahl, *Timothy Tiger's Terrible Toothache,* Western Publications, 1988.

Katharine Ross, *Animal Babies Book and Puzzle Set,* Random House (New York, NY), 1988.

Katharine Ross, *Sweetie and Petie,* Random House (New York, NY), 1988.

Judy Delton, *Hired Help for Rabbit,* Macmillan (New York, NY), 1988.

Katharine Ross, *The Fuzzytail Friends' Great Egg Hunt,* Random House (New York, NY), 1988.

Bill Wallace, *Snot Steb,* Holiday House (New York, NY), 1989.

Diane Namm, *Little Bear,* Grolier, 1989.

Ann Turner, *Hedgehog for Breakfast,* Macmillan (New York, NY), 1989.

Jane Thayer, *The Popcorn Dragon,* new edition, Morrow (New York, NY), 1989.

Judy Delton, *My Mom Made Me Go to Camp,* Dell (New York, NY), 1990.

Ted Bailey, *Skunks! Go to Bed!,* Western Publications, 1990.

Judy Delton, *My Mom Made Me Go to School,* Dell (New York, NY), 1991.

Jim Latimer, *Fox under First Base,* Macmillan (New York, NY), 1991.

Judy Delton, *My Mom Made Me Take Piano Lessons,* Dell (New York, NY), 1994.

Ben Cruise, adaptor, *The Ugly Duckling* (based on the story by Hans Christian Andersen), Western Publishing (Racine, WI), 1995.

Marsha Arnold, *Quick, Quack, Quick!,* Random House (New York, NY), 1996.

Cynthia Alvarez, *Professor Pipsqueak's Guide to Birds,* Random House (New York, NY), 1997.

Cynthia Alvarez, *Professor Pipsqueak's Guide to Bugs,* Random House (New York, NY), 1997.

Herman Gall, *The Lion and the Mouse,* Random House (New York, NY), 1998.

Margaret Wise Brown, *Bunny's Noisy Book,* Hyperion (New York, NY), 2000.

Susan Ring, *Polar Babies,* Random House (New York, NY), 2001.

Annie Ingle, *Lift the Lid, Use the Potty!,* Random House (New York, NY), 2001.

Jane Thayer, *The Puppy Who Wanted a Boy,* HarperCollins (New York, NY), 2003.

Irving Berlin, *Easter Parade,* HarperCollins (New York, NY), 2003.

Gail Herman, *The Lion and the Mouse,* Random House (New York, NY), 2003.

Jane Thayer, *Part-Time Dog,* HarperCollins (New York, NY), 2004.

Eileen Spinelli, *Feathers: Poems about Birds,* Henry Holt (New York, NY), 2004.

Dori Chaconas, *Cork and Fuzz,* Viking (New York, NY), 2005.

Rick Walton, *The Remarkable Friendship of Mr. Cat and Mr. Rat,* Putnam (New York, NY), 2006.

Leslie Kimmelman, *How Do I Love You?,* HarperCollins (New York, NY), 2006.

Dori Chaconas, *Cork and Fuzz: Short and Tall,* Viking (New York, NY), 2006.

Dori Chaconas, *Cork and Fuzz: Good Sports,* Viking (New York, NY), 2007.

*ILLUSTRATOR; "SEBASTIAN (SUPER SLEUTH)" SERIES*

Mary Blount Christian, *Sebastian (Super Sleuth) and the Hair of the Dog Mystery,* Macmillan (New York, NY), 1982.

Mary Blount Christian, *Sebastian (Super Sleuth) and the Crummy Yummies Caper,* Macmillan (New York, NY), 1983.

Mary Blount Christian, *Sebastian (Super Sleuth) and the Bone to Pick Mystery,* Macmillan (New York, NY), 1983.

Mary Blount Christian, *Sebastian (Super Sleuth) and the Santa Claus Caper,* Macmillan (New York, NY), 1984.

Mary Blount Christian, *Sebastian (Super Sleuth) and the Secret of the Skewered Skier,* Macmillan (New York, NY), 1984.

Mary Blount Christian, *Sebastian (Super Sleuth) and the Clumsy Cowboy,* Macmillan (New York, NY), 1985.

Mary Blount Christian, *Sebastian (Super Sleuth) and the Purloined Sirloin,* Macmillan (New York, NY), 1986.

Mary Blount Christian, *Sebastian (Super Sleuth) and the Stars-in-His-Eyes Mystery,* Macmillan (New York, NY), 1987.

Mary Blount Christian, *Sebastian (Super Sleuth) and the Egyptian Connection,* Macmillan (New York, NY), 1988.

Mary Blount Christian, *Sebastian (Super Sleuth) and the Time Capsule Caper,* Macmillan (New York, NY), 1989.

Mary Blount Christian, *Sebastian (Super Sleuth) and the Baffling Bigfoot,* Macmillan (New York, NY), 1990.

Mary Blount Christian, *Sebastian (Super Sleuth) and the Mystery Patient,* Macmillan (New York, NY), 1991.

Mary Blount Christian, *Sebastian (Super Sleuth) and the Impossible Crime,* Macmillan (New York, NY), 1992.

Mary Blount Christian, *Sebastian (Super Sleuth) and the Flying Elephant,* Macmillan (New York, NY), 1994.

*ILLUSTRATOR; "CORDUROY" SERIES; BASED ON THE CHARACTER BY DON FREEMAN*

B.G. Hennessy, *Corduroy's Day,* Penguin (New York, NY), 1985.

B.G. Hennessy, *Corduroy's Party,* Penguin (New York, NY), 1985.

B.G. Hennessy, *Corduroy's Toys,* Penguin (New York, NY), 1985.

B.G. Hennessy, *Corduroy Goes to the Doctor,* Viking (New York, NY), 1987.

B.G. Hennessy, *Corduroy on the Go,* Viking (New York, NY), 1987.

B.G. Hennessy, *Corduroy's Busy Street,* Penguin (New York, NY), 1987.

*Corduroy's Christmas Surprise* (board-book adaptation), Grosset & Dunlap (New York, NY), 2000.

*Corduroy's Easter Party* (board-book adaptation), Grosset & Dunlap (New York, NY), 2000.

*Corduroy* (board-book adaptation), Viking Penguin (New York, NY), 2002.

*Rhymes and Riddles with Corduroy* (board-book adaptation), Viking Penguin (New York, NY), 2002.

*Happy Easter, Corduroy* (board-book adaptation), Viking Penguin (New York, NY), 2004.

*Corduroy's Snow Day* (board-book adaptation), Viking Penguin (New York, NY), 2005.

*Corduroy's Thanksgiving* (board-book adaptation), Viking Penguin (New York, NY), 2006.

## Adaptations

McCue's illustrated version of *The Ugly Duckling* was adapted as both audio-and videocassettes, Western Publications, 1987.

## Sidelights

Lisa McCue has illustrated dozens upon dozens of children's books, including the canine detective series "Sebastian (Super Sleuth)" and several adaptations of Don Freeman's popular "Corduroy" series about a lovable

*Lisa McCue works with Dori Chaconas on the easy-reader series that begins with 2005's* **Meet Cork and Fuzz.** (Copyright © Lisa McCue, 2005. Reproduced by permission of Viking, a division of Penguin Putnam Books for Young Readers.)

bear, and has also written self-illustrated stories for very young children. Other authors whose texts have been brought to life through McCue's endearing art include Leslie Kimmelman, Judy Delton, and Dori Chaconas. In a review of Chaconas's beginning reader *Cork and Fuzz,* Kathleen Meulen wrote in *School Library Journal* that "McCue's endearing drawings add personality and humor to the animals' faces," while a *Kirkus Reviews* contributor noted that in *How Do I Love You?,* Kimmelman's poetic paean to the love between a crocodile mother and child, the "illustrations positively sing with the love and the joy the two bring to each other's lives." The focus is on a more slow-growing camaraderie in Rick Walton's *The Remarkable Friendship of Mr. Cat and Mr. Rat,* brought to humorous life by McCue in what *School Library Journal* contributor Catherine Callegari dubbed "detailed watercolor illustrations." The critic added that the illustrator's effective use of "simple backgrounds keep the focus on the action."

Because fuzzy and fluffy animal characters are among the artist's favorite subjects, McCue's own story books not surprisingly feature titles such as *Jinglebell Mice, Little Fuzzytail,* and *Ten Little Puppy Dogs.* In her work for others, if there is a way to work animals into the

plot, McCue will find it. Describing the artist's unique illustrated version of Irving Berlin's classic popular song for *Easter Parade,* Ilene Cooper wrote in *Booklist* that the illustrator's "stuffed animal-like characters are instantly appealing, and children will have fun singing the familiar refrain."

Despite McCue's love of animals, she did not enjoy a rural upbringing; in fact, she experienced quite the opposite. Born in Brooklyn, New York, McCue was raised in a nearby suburb. "My mother was a big influence on me," she once recalled of her budding artistic career. "She is an artist. Ever since I can remember, she was painting and drawing and doing every kind of craft. I was always involved in crafts. In elementary school, every time there was a classroom party or art involved, everybody would turn and say, 'Oh, Lisa could do it.' So I was always zeroed in on as the artist of the class. The more you're told you're good at something, the more you head toward that area."

McCue enjoyed the benefits of a happy childhood spent near a major city. "My parents liked to go to museums, so I ended up going with them. I would always go to the Metropolitan Museum and go to their costume exhibit, that was my favorite place. I loved all the costumes and stepping back in history and seeing how the people dressed, just trying to imagine lifestyles."

Art was not her only interest, however; as McCue explained, "Music and dance were big interests of mine. I played a lot of sports. In school, I ran track and I played soccer, but my main sport is skiing."

Despite her competing hobbies, drawing and painting eventually won out, and after high school McCue studied art at Southeastern Massachusetts University. There she met Dutch author Loek Kessels, and it was at Kessels' suggestion that she sent a portfolio of her work to the editors of a children's book Kessels was then producing. The editors liked her work, and before she even graduated from college McCue had illustrated her first published book. "It was the best thing I ever did," the artist/author recalled: "I got right into children's books the summer after I graduated. I haven't had much time for anything else."

Most of McCue's illustration projects feature animal characters, and her style has sometimes been compared to that of Garth Williams, the illustrator of E.B. White's beloved *Charlotte's Web* and the "Little House" series by Laura Ingalls Wilder. "When I started I was much more comfortable doing animals, and my portfolio had a lot of animal drawings," McCue explained. "As my agent showed my portfolio around, clients tended to give me a lot of animal books, and it snowballed from there." When asked to describe her drawing style, she explained that she concentrates on accuracy and finds that her everyday experiences are helpful sources, as are animal picture books. "I have an extensive library of animal encyclopedias, but if you go through my

books, you'll see all the neighborhood animals and children. My own cat and dog have . . . starred in many books, and bits and pieces of my home and places around my neighborhood and places I travel to show up in all the books. I try and make everything very happy. I try to give as much life and personality as I can. And since I have so much fun when I'm drawing, I think that comes through in the art work.

When choosing an illustrating project, McCue sidesteps the tedious whenever possible. "I think in terms of what type of pictures I would enjoy doing," she once explained. "Sometimes I've gotten stories where I thought the story was just wonderful but it took place in the same room. The characters were doing something different but it all took place in the same background. I like books where there's a lot going on. The characters will be outdoors one time, indoors one time. On every page there's something new going on so that it doesn't all start to look alike. You just get tired of drawing if you're drawing an animal in a kitchen and the kitchen is the background for every page. You get tired of drawing that stove and all the little doo-dahs on top of that stove over a hundred times. So I look for books that I think I can make interesting pictures from. I like upbeat stories, funny, silly stories."

Discussing her approach to illustrating a text by another writer, McCue noted: "I start with a sketch just like any other illustrator. You get your story, you do sketches, and you send it to the publisher for an 'okay.' As I'm reading a story for the first time, I visualize. I see things in my mind and I don't really go too far from what my initial reaction to the story is—everything down to what I think characters should be wearing, what type of setting they should be in, and, if it's a rabbit, what kind of rabbit?

"I'll start with a very, very rough, scribbly sketch, put a piece of tracing paper over it, and start neatening it up—maybe changing action and motion a little bit to get more of the feeling that I want, or enlarge or make things smaller to fit in better. I think when I'm figuring out a book and I'm working at a very steady pace, I can average a page a day. But this average varies with the size of the book and the amount of background and characters on each page.

"I use acrylics a lot in a background because they won't bleed later. When I'm doing my animals, I like colored inks because I can get a nice fine line with them, and they're waterproof to an extent. If I'm doing a background with watercolors, a lot of times I get brighter colors. Luma dyes also get nice bright colors, and I'll use those for clothing or things that need to be brighter, more colorful than I might be able to get with some of the acrylics or colored inks."

To gauge the success of her work, McCue relies on the reactions of children who encounter her books. "I have good friends and relatives . . . and they'll always call

*In addition to her other illustration projects, McCue creates art for ongoing series titles by Don Freeman, such as* **Corduroy Goes to the Beach.**
(Copyright © Lisa McCue, 2006. Reproduced by permission of Viking, a division of Penguin Putnam Books for Young Readers.)

and say, 'Oh, so and so loves this page and every time we open the book up she only wants to skip right to that because she loves the kitty popping his head out of the bag.' And they tell me what pictures and what books tend to go over big with their children and why. I keep that in mind for the next stories. It's funny. My favorite pictures are the ones that compositionally work perfectly, but those are not necessarily the ones the kids go for. They tend to like the ones where there's a character that's being a little naughty or hiding or searching for something where the child can get involved."

## Biographical and Critical Sources

### PERIODICALS

*Booklist,* June 1, 1993, Kay Weisman, review of *My Mom Made Me Take Piano Lessons,* p. 1836; December 1, 1994, Kay Weisman, review of *Sebastian (Super Sleuth) and the Flying Elephant,* p. 680; March 15, 2003, Ilene Cooper, review of *Easter Parade,* p. 1328; March 15, 2004, Carolyn Phelan, review of *Feathers: Poems about Birds,* p. 1308; August, 2004, Karen

Hutt, review of *Part-Time Dog,* p. 1946; January 1, 2006, Hazel Rochman, review of *Cork and Fuzz: Short and Tall,* p. 109; January 1, 2007, Ilene Cooper, review of *The Remarkable Friendship of Mr. Cat and Mr. Rat,* p. 118.

*Horn Book,* May-June, 2006, Betty Carter, review of *Cork and Fuzz: Short and Tall,* p. 311.

*Kirkus Reviews,* February 15, 2004, review of *Feathers,* p. 185; March 1, 2005, review of *Cork and Fuzz,* p. 284; February 14, 2006, review of *Cork and Fuzz: Short and Tall,* p. 179.

*Publishers Weekly,* December 5, 2005, review of *How Do I Love You?,* p. 54.

*School Library Journal,* April, 2004, Susan Scheps, review of *Feathers,* p. 114; September, 2004, Andrea Tarr, review of *Part-Time Dog,* p. 182; May, 2005, Kathleen Meulen, review of *Cork and Fuzz,* p. 78; February, 2005, Kathy Piehl, review of *How Do I Love You?,* p. 104; April, 2006, Laura Scott, review of *Cork and Fuzz: Short and Tall,* p. 98; December, 2006, Catherine Callegari, review of *The Remarkable Friendship of Mr. Cat and Mr. Rat,* p. 118.*

\*    \*    \*

## McCUE, Lisa Emiline
## See McCUE, Lisa

\*    \*    \*

## MONTECALVO, Janet

### Personal

Born in Quincy, MA; married, 1981; children: Jamie, Mattie. *Education:* Emmanuel College (Boston, MA), B.A. (art).

### Addresses

*Home and office*—10 Cavatorta Dr., Framingham, MA 01701. *E-mail*—janetmontecalvo@hotmail.com.

### Career

Illustrator, graphic designer, and educator. Formerly worked as a sign painter; freelance illustrator and graphic designer for feature films, including *Mermaids, Second Sight, I'll Be Home for Christmas,* and *Stanley and Iris,* beginning 1981. Framingham Public Schools, Framingham, MA, art teacher, beginning 2001; teaches art for community organizations. *Exhibitions:* Work exhibited at Danforth Museum of Art, Framingham, MA.

### Awards, Honors

Emmy Award for graphic design, 1989, for contributions to *I'll be Home for Christmas.*

### Illustrator

David Neufeld, *Finding Animal Tracks,* Houghton Mifflin (Boston, MA), 1996.

Sarah Weeks, *The Perfect Garden,* Addison-Wesley, 1998.

Yartria Cooetti, *Un lugar para la mariposa,* Harcourt (New York, NY), 2001.

Polly Peterson, *Salt and Sand,* Harcourt (New York, NY), 2002.

Karima Grant, *Sofie and the City,* Boyds Mills Press (Honesdale, PA), 2006.

## Biographical and Critical Sources

*PERIODICALS*

*Kirkus Reviews,* March 1, 2006, review of *Sofie and the City,* p. 230.

*Library Media Connection,* November-December, 2006, Brenda Rogers, review of *Sofie and the City,* p. 68.

*MetroWest Daily News Online* (Framingham, MA), August 31, 2006, Jennifer Lord, "Signs of Success."

*Publishers Weekly,* March 13, 2006, review of *Sofie and the City,* p. 66.

*School Library Journal,* May, 2006, Julie R. Ranelli, review of *Sofie and the City,* p. 88.

*ONLINE*

*Janet Montecalvo Home Page,* http://www.janetmontecalvo.com (March 2, 2007).*

\*    \*    \*

## MORAY WILLIAMS, Ursula 1911-2006

*OBITUARY NOTICE*— See index for *SATA* sketch: Born April 19, 1911, in Petersfield, Hampshire, England; died October 17, 2006. Illustrator and author. Moray Williams was a prolific author and illustrator of children's books such as 1938's *Adventures of the Little Wooden Horse.* Benefiting from an idyllic childhood spent in a mansion near Southampton, she lived comfortably with her twin sister, Barbara; her memories of her early life would greatly influence her later writings. After attending the Winchester School of Art from 1928 to 1929, she decided she was more interested in writing than art and left to pursue her career. Initially illustrating her own books, such as *Jean-Pierre* (1931), *The Three Toymakers* (1945), *The Binklebys at Home* (1951), and *Golden Horse with a Silver Tail* (1957), Moray Williams later worked closely with other artists, such as Edward Ardizzone, Faith Jacques, Shirley Hughes, and Glenys Ambrus, and published actively through the late 1980s. Among her other titles are *Gobbolino the Witch's Cat* (1942), *A Picnic with the Aunts* (1972), and *Grandma and the Ghowlies* (1986). Refusing to follow popular literary trends in children's literature, Moray Williams indulged in a style that some critics described as quaint and old fashioned, though in a flattering way. She remained faithful to creating simple tales that re-

flected back on her happy memories, whether she was writing fantasy, history, humor, or in any other genre. Also the author of a number of plays for children, Moray Williams was active in promoting education and literacy. She organized children's writing competitions, was a leader in local schools, and was a former president of the Women's Royal British Legion.

*OBITUARIES AND OTHER SOURCES:*

PERIODICALS

*Times* (London, England), December 27, 2006, p. 58.

\*     \*     \*

# MUNSINGER, Lynn 1951-

## Personal

Born December 24, 1951, in Greenfield, MA; daughter of Robert William and Jeanne Munsinger; married Dan Lace (a sales manager), November 27, 1981. *Education:* Tufts University, B.A., 1974; Rhode Island School of Design, B.F.A. (illustration), 1977; additional study in London, England.

## Addresses

*Home*—CT and VT.

## Career

Freelance illustrator, 1977—. Has created designs for greeting cards.

## Awards, Honors

Volunteer State Award, 1984, for *Howliday Inn* by James Howe; *New York Times* Notable Book selection, 1986, for *Hugh Pine and the Good Place* by Janwillem Van de Wetering; Emphasis on Reading Award (Grades 2-3), 1987-88, for *My Mother Never Listens to Me* by Marjorie Weinman Sharmat; Little Archer Award, 1989, for *Underwear!* by Mary Monsell; Colorado Children's Book Award, 1990, California Young Reader Award (Primary), 1991, and Golden Sower Award (K-3), 1991, all for *Tacky the Penguin* by Helen Lester; Washington Children's Choices Picture Book Award, 2001, for *Hooway for Wodney Wat* by Lester.

## Illustrator

Margret Elbow, *The Rootomom Tree,* Houghton Mifflin (Boston, MA), 1978.

William Cole, editor, *An Arkful of Animals: Poems for the Very Young,* Houghton Mifflin (Boston, MA), 1978.

Jane Sutton, *What Should a Hippo Wear,* Houghton Mifflin (Boston, MA), 1979.

Nancy Robison, *The Lizard Hunt,* Lothrop (New York, NY), 1979.

Gloria Skurzynski, *Martin by Himself,* Houghton Mifflin (Boston, MA), 1979.

Elaine M. Willoughby, *Boris and the Monsters,* Houghton Mifflin (Boston, MA), 1980.

Janwillem van de Wetering, *Hugh Pine,* Houghton Mifflin (Boston, MA), 1980.

Karen J. Gounaud, *A Very Mice Joke Book,* Houghton Mifflin (Boston, MA), 1981.

Sandol Stoddard, *Bedtime Mouse,* Houghton Mifflin (Boston, MA), 1981.

James Howe, *Howliday Inn,* Atheneum (New York, NY), 1982.

Judy Delton, *A Pet for Duck and Bear,* edited by Ann Fay, Albert Whitman (Morton Grove, IL), 1982.

Galway Kinnell, *How the Alligator Missed Breakfast,* Houghton Mifflin (Boston, MA), 1982.

Phyllis Rose Eisenberg, *Don't Tell Me a Ghost Story,* Harcourt (New York, NY), 1982.

Helen Lester, *The Wizard, the Fairy, and the Magic Chicken,* Houghton Mifflin (Boston, MA), 1983.

Judy Delton, *Duck Goes Fishing,* Albert Whitman (Morton Grove, IL), 1983.

Joseph Slate, *The Mean, Clean, Giant Canoe Machine,* Crowell, 1983.

Caroline Levine, *Silly School Riddles and Other Classroom Crack-Ups,* Albert Whitman (Morton Grove, IL), 1984.

Judy Delton, *Bear and Duck on the Run,* Albert Whitman (Morton Grove, IL), 1984.

Richard Latta, *This Little Pig Had a Riddle,* Albert Whitman (Morton Grove, IL), 1984.

Ann Tompert, *Nothing Sticks like a Shadow,* Houghton Mifflin (Boston, MA), 1984.

Eve Bunting, *Monkey in the Middle,* Harcourt (New York, NY), 1984.

Marjorie Weinman Sharmat, *My Mother Never Listens to Me,* Albert Whitman (Morton Grove, IL), 1984.

Virginia Mueller, *A Playhouse for Monster,* Albert Whitman (Morton Grove, IL), 1985.

Virginia Mueller, *Monster and the Baby,* Albert Whitman (Morton Grove, IL), 1985.

Seymour Reit and others, *When Small Is Tall, and Other Read-Together Tales,* Random House (New York, NY), 1985.

Helen Lester, *It Wasn't My Fault,* Houghton Mifflin (Boston, MA), 1985.

Judy Delton, *The Elephant in Duck's Garden,* Albert Whitman (Morton Grove, IL), 1985.

Helen Lester, *A Porcupine Named Fluffy,* Houghton Mifflin (Boston, MA), 1986.

Joan Phillips, *My New Boy,* Random House (New York, NY), 1986.

Virginia Mueller, *Monster Can't Sleep,* Albert Whitman (Morton Grove, IL), 1986.

Judy Delton, *Rabbit Goes to Night School,* Albert Whitman (Morton Grove, IL), 1986.

Janwillem van de Wetering, *Hugh Pine and the Good Place,* Houghton Mifflin (Boston, MA), 1986.

William H. Hooks and others, *Read-a-Rebus: Tales and Rhymes in Words and Pictures,* Random House (New York, NY), 1986.

Virginia Mueller, *A Halloween Mask for Monster,* Albert Whitman (Morton Grove, IL), 1986.

Helen Lester, *Pookins Gets Her Way,* Houghton Mifflin (Boston, MA), 1987.

Barbara Bottner, *Zoo Song,* Scholastic (New York, NY), 1987.

Joanna Cole, *Norma Jean, Jumping Bean,* Random House (New York, NY), 1987.

Helen Lester, *Tacky the Penguin,* Houghton Mifflin (Boston, MA), 1988.

Gloria Whelan, *A Week of Raccoons,* Knopf (New York, NY), 1988.

Linda Hayward, *Hello, House!,* Random House (New York, NY), 1988.

Mary Ada Schwartz, *Spiffen, a Tale of a Tidy Pig,* Albert Whitman (Morton Grove, IL), 1988.

Sandol Stoddard, *Bedtime for Bear,* Houghton Mifflin (Boston, MA), 1988.

Mary Elise Monsell, *Underwear!,* Albert Whitman (Morton Grove, IL), 1988.

Susan Heyboer O'Keefe, *One Hungry Monster: A Counting Book in Rhyme,* Little, Brown (Boston, MA), 1989.

Janwillem van de Wetering, *Hugh Pine and Something Else,* Houghton Mifflin (Boston, MA), 1989.

William J. Smith, *Ho for a Hat!,* Little, Brown (Boston, MA), 1989.

Pat Lowery Collins, *Tomorrow, Up and Away,* Houghton Mifflin (Boston, MA), 1990.

Maryann Macdonald, *Hedgehog Bakes a Cake,* Gareth Stevens (Milwaukee, WI), 1990.

Joanna Cole, *Don't Call Me Names,* Random House (New York, NY), 1990.

Helen Lester, *The Revenge of the Magic Chicken,* Houghton Mifflin (Boston, MA), 1990.

Virginia Mueller, *Monster's Birthday Hiccups,* Albert Whitman (Morton Grove, IL), 1991.

Virginia Mueller, *Monster Goes to School,* Albert Whitman (Morton Grove, IL), 1991.

Maryann Macdonald, *Rabbit's Birthday Kite,* Bantam (New York, NY), 1991.

Joanne Oppenheim, *Rooter Remembers: A Bank Street Book about Values,* Viking (New York, NY), 1991.

William Cole, selector, *A Zooful of Animals,* Houghton Mifflin (Boston, MA), 1992.

Helen Lester, *Me First,* Houghton Mifflin (Boston, MA), 1992.

William H. Hooks, *Rough, Tough, Rowdy: A Bank Street Book about Values,* Viking (New York, NY), 1992.

Barbara Brenner, *Group Soup: A Bank Street Book about Values,* Viking (New York, NY), 1992.

Ann Tompert, *Just a Little Bit,* Houghton Mifflin (Boston, MA), 1993.

Valiska Gregory, *Babysitting for Benjamin,* Little, Brown (Boston, MA), 1993.

Helen Lester, *Three Cheers for Tacky,* Houghton Mifflin (Boston, MA), 1994.

William H. Hooks and Betty Boegehold, *The Rainbow Ribbon: A Bank Street Book about Values,* Puffin (New York, NY), 1994.

Abby Levine, *Ollie Knows Everything,* Albert Whitman (Morton Grove, IL), 1994.

Helen Lester, *Lin's Backpack,* Addison-Wesley (New York, NY), 1994.

Sandol Stoddard, *Turtle Time: A Bedtime Story,* Houghton Mifflin (Boston, MA), 1995.

Stephen Krensky, *The Three Blind Mice Mystery,* Dell (New York, NY), 1995.

Ogden Nash, *The Tale of Custard the Dragon,* Little, Brown (Boston, MA), 1995.

Helen Lester, *Listen, Buddy,* Houghton Mifflin (Boston, MA), 1995.

Joanna Cole and Stephanie Calmenson, *Gator Girls,* Morrow (New York, NY), 1995.

Helen Lester, *Princess Penelope's Parrot,* Houghton Mifflin (Boston, MA), 1996.

Ogden Nash, *Custard the Dragon and the Wicked Knight,* Little, Brown (Boston, MA), 1996.

A.M. Monson, *Wanted—Best Friend,* Dial (New York, NY), 1997.

Stephanie Calmenson and Joanna Cole, *Rockin' Reptiles,* Morrow Junior Books (New York, NY), 1997.

Kay Winters, *The Teeny Tiny Ghost,* HarperCollins (New York, NY), 1998.

Helen Lester, *Tacky in Trouble,* Houghton Mifflin (Boston, MA), 1998.

Stephanie Calmenson and Joanna Cole, *Get Well, Gators!,* Morrow Junior Books (New York, NY), 1998.

Jackie French Koller, *One Monkey Too Many,* Harcourt Brace (San Diego, CA), 1999.

Helen Lester, *Hooway for Wodney Wat,* Houghton Mifflin (New York, NY), 1999.

Maryann Macdonald, *Rabbit's Birthday Kite,* Gareth Stevens (Milwaukee, WI), 1999.

Kay Winters, *Whooo's Haunting the Teeny Tiny Ghost?,* HarperCollins (New York, NY), 1999.

Stephanie Calmenson and Joanna Cole, *Gator Halloween,* Morrow Junior Books (New York, NY), 1999.

Carolyn Crimi, *Don't Need Friends,* Doubleday (New York, NY), 1999.

William Wise, *Dinosaurs Forever,* Dial (New York, NY), 2000.

Helen Lester, *Tacky and the Emperor,* Houghton, Mifflin (New York, NY), 2000.

Laura Joffe Numeroff, *What Grandmas Do Best/What Grandpas Do Best,* Little Simon (New York, NY), 2000, published separately, 2001.

Laura Joffe Numeroff, *What Daddies Do Best,* Little Simon (New York, NY), 2001.

Helen Lester, *Score One for the Sloths,* Houghton Mifflin (Boston, MA), 2001.

Patricia Hooper, *A Stormy Ride on Noah's Ark,* Putnam (New York, NY), 2001.

David T. Greenberg, *Skunks!,* Little, Brown (Boston, MA), 2001.

Deborah Lee Rose, *Birthday Zoo,* Albert Whitman (Morton Grove, IL), 2002.

Laura Joffe Numeroff, *What Mommies Do Best,* Little Simon (New York, NY), 2002.

Helen Lester, *Tackylocks and the Three Bears,* Houghton Mifflin (New York, NY), 2002.

Irving Berlin, *God Bless America,* HarperCollins (New York, NY), 2002.

Laura Malone Elliott, *Hunter's Best Friend at School,* HarperCollins (New York, NY), 2002.

*My New Boy,* Random House (New York, NY), 2003.

Laura Joffe Numeroff, *What Sisters Do Best; What Brothers Do Best,* Little Simon (New York, NY), 2003.

Helen Lester, *Something Might Happen,* Houghton Mifflin (Boston, MA), 2003.

Joanna Cole, *Norma Jean, Jumping Bean,* Random House (New York, NY), 2003.

Kay Winters, *The Teeny Tiny Ghost and the Monster,* HarperCollins (New York, NY), 2004.

Laura Joffe Numeroff, *What Aunts Do Best/What Uncles Do Best,* Simon & Schuster (New York, NY), 2004.

Laura Joffe Numeroff, *Beatrice Doesn't Want To,* Candlewick Press (Cambridge, MA), 2004.

Helen Lester, *Hurty Feelings,* Houghton Mifflin (Boston, MA), 2004.

David T. Greenberg, *Snakes!,* Little, Brown (New York, NY), 2004.

Helen Lester, *Tacky and the Winter Games,* Houghton Mifflin (Boston, MA), 2005.

Jackie French Killer, *Seven Spunky Monkeys,* Harcourt (Orlando, FL), 2005.

Barbara Brenner, William H. Hooks, and Betty Boegehold, *Bunny Tails,* Milk and Cookies Press, 2005.

Laura Malone Elliott, *Hunter and Stripe and the Soccer Showdown,* Katherine Tegen Books (New York, NY), 2005.

William Wise, *Zany Zoo,* Houghton Mifflin (Boston, MA), 2006.

Helen Lester, *Batter up Wombat,* Houghton Mifflin (Boston, MA), 2006.

James Howe, *Howliday Inn,* Aladdin (New York, NY), 2006.

David J. Olson, *The Thunderstruck Stork,* Albert Whitman (Morton Grove, IL), 2007.

Susan Heyboer O'Keefe, *Hungry Monster ABC,* Little, Brown (New York, NY), 2007.

Helen Lester, *The Sheep in Wolf's Clothing,* Houghton Mifflin (Boston, MA), 2007.

David Greenberg, *Crocs!,* Little, Brown (New York, NY), 2008.

Laura Malone Elliott, *Hunter's Annoying Big Sister,* Katherine Tegen Books (New York, NY), 2008.

Illustrator of textbooks. Contributor of illustrations to *Cricket.*

## Sidelights

The whimsical animal characters created by illustrator Lynn Munsinger, familiar to several generations of young readers, decorate the pages of children's books by a wide variety of authors. From Ogden Nash's early-twentieth-century classic *The Tale of Custard the Dragon* to works by such contemporary writers as Joanna Cole, Laura Malone Elliott, Helen Lester, William Wise, Laura Joffe Numeroff, and Virginia Mueller, the illustrator has brought her creative talent and imagination to bear. "It is easy to recognize Munsinger's personable animal characters," wrote Stephanie Zvirin in a *Booklist* review of Elliott's *Hunter's Best Friend at*

*School,* adding that these characters "always seem to sparkle with mischief and good humor." "I . . . feel very fortunate to be an illustrator," the prolific artist once told *SATA.* "I really enjoy my work and cannot conceive of doing anything else."

Born in Greenfield, Massachusetts, in 1951, Munsinger knew she wanted to be an artist from the time she was a young girl. After graduating from high school, she attended Tufts University, moving on to Rhode Island School of Design (RISDI) after earning her B.A. in 1974, and obtained her B.F.A. degree three yeas later. She began looking for freelance assignments immediately after graduation, and her first illustration job, Margret Elbow's *The Rootomom Tree,* was published a year later. Many more book illustration projects have followed in the years since, earning Munsinger not only legions of young fans but critical praise as well. Of her work for Mary Elise Monsell's *Underwear!,* for instance, a *Booklist* reviewer called the "zany," "perky-colored" illustrations "a perfect foil for the text," while Lori A. Janick maintained in *School Library Journal* that "what could have been an unbelievable moralistic tale . . . is saved by Munsinger's delightful illustrations." Reviewing Judy Delton's *Rabbit Goes to Night School, Booklist* contributor Denise M. Wilms stated that "Munsinger's deft pen-and-ink drawings . . . lend a good deal of personality to the story," while the illustrator's work for *A Stormy Ride on Noah's Ark,* "featuring expressive animal characters and shifting perspectives, capture the balance between the comic and the contemplative achieved in the lilting text" by Patricia Hooper.

While Munsinger has illustrated books for numerous authors, including Delton, Marjorie Weinman Sharmat, Galway Kinnell, and Ann Tompert, she has developed multi-book working relationships with several popular children's book writers. Dutch-immigrant author Janwillem van de Wetering's three-book series featuring a large, elderly porcupine named Hugh Pine was the first collaboration to benefit from Munsinger's pen-and-ink renderings. In series opener *Hugh Pine,* the wise porcupine learns to walk upright and mimic a small human being in order to avoid being hit by passing cars, and eventually helps his younger, more inexperienced friends learn to cross busy roads in safety. In *Hugh Pine and the Good Place,* the elderly porcupine longs to move out to the deserted island he can see from his home in a tree growing on the Maine coast. However, following the adage "be careful what you wish for," Pine ultimately changes his mind after a few days of loneliness. "Munsinger provides sprightly line drawings with just the right elan to give this porcupine person believability," commented Barbara Elleman in a *Booklist* review. In *Hugh Pine and Something Else* Munsinger captures the wise old porcupine as he accompanies his friend, Postman McTosh, to New York City, meeting a host of sophisticated city-dwelling animals before returning to his comfortable woodland home in Maine.

*A prolific illustrator, Lynn Munsinger has worked with Helen Lester on the popular 1996 picture book* **Princess Penelope's Parrot.** (Illustrations copyright © 1996 by Lynn Munsinger. All rights reserved. Reproduced by permission of Houghton Mifflin Company.)

The humorous "Monster" stories by Virginia Mueller have also been enhanced by Munsinger's artwork. In full-color illustrations, the illustrator portrays green-furred, toothsome young Monster in a variety of child-like situations and makes the setting particularly monster-like: the Monster family has carnivorous Venus fly-traps instead of regular houseplants, and their anti-macassars are made of spider webs! In *Monster and the Baby* Monster tries to quiet his baby sister with a game of building blocks, but discovers that she is only happy when the buildings crash to the ground. In *A Playhouse for Monster,* which also features Munsinger's art, the young creature thrills to having a place all his own, until he realizes that sharing his new playhouse with friends is far more fun. *A Halloween Mask for Monster* finds the furry green creature donning fearsome masks that look like human children—and scaring everyone in his family—until he decides that the masks are truly *too* scary and his own face will do just fine. A *Publishers Weekly* reviewer praised Mueller's story, noting that it is "made more agreeable because of Munsinger's good-natured pictures." Other "Monster" stories featuring Munsinger art include *Monster Can't Sleep, Monster's Birthday Hiccups,* and *Monster Goes to School.*

Munsinger's most prolific working relationship has been with author Helen Lester. Beginning with Lester's 1983 picture book *The Wizard, the Fairy, and the Magic Chicken,* the two have joined forces on numerous stories filled with a whimsical humor that often borders on zany. Beginning their collaboration with the story of a competition between three sorcerers, Lester and Munsinger produced a sequel, *The Revenge of the Magic Chicken,* which reunites Chicken with his magical friends, a wizard and a fairy. "The text's humor gets the full treatment in Munsinger's raucous art," noted Ilene Cooper, reviewing the appealing picture book for *Booklist.*

Several books featuring a penguin named Tacky have also hatched from the creative collaboration between Munsinger and Lester. While most penguins try hard to fit in with their formally attired fellows, in *Tacky the Penguin* readers meet a free spirit. Unlike the properly bow-tied Angel, Goodly, Lovely, and friends, Tacky wears gaudy, rumpled Hawaiian-print shirts, making him a bit of a stand-out around the Arctic Circle. However, when Tacky encounters a band of penguin-

snatching hunters, his crazy antics and outrageous garb confound the men so much that they question whether these birds are penguins after all. *Three Cheers for Tacky* finds the nonconformist penguin making a muddle of his team's cheer routine for the Penguin Cheering Contest, although ultimately the out-of-step penguin becomes the highlight of what would otherwise have been a forgettable competition. Athletic training takes a backseat to doughnuts, late-night television, and other lazy habits in *Tacky and the Winter Games,* which finds the penguin taking a less-than-stellar role in the annual penguin games. *Booklist* reviewer Kathryn Broderick praised Munsinger's "slyly humorous watercolors" and called *Three Cheers for Tacky* "a funny, funny picture book," while Carolyn Phelan wrote in the same periodical that with *Tacky and the Winter Games* "Lester and Munsinger create a winning combination of action, detail, and understated wit."

Lester and Munsinger have also worked together on several other picture books for young children, many of which feature animal characters. In *A Porcupine Named Fluffy* a prickly young porcupine earns the nickname "Fluffy," despite the fact that his "fluff" consists of sharp, barbed quills. Only after Fluffy meets a young rhinoceros with an equally silly name—Hippo—does he begin to think of his name as a source of fun. In *Me First* portly Pinkerton Pig learn a lesson about being

*Munsinger teams up with William Wise to bring to life an engaging collection of creatures in the picture book* **Z**any Zoo.

pushy via Munsinger's brightly hued watercolor art, and an opposite dilemma—about a young hippopotamus who takes everything too seriously—is profiled in lighthearted fashion in *Hurty Feelings. Listen, Buddy* features a hare whose mind is wandering in the clouds instead of focusing on what people are telling him, while a rodent with a severe speech impediment stars in the popular picture book *Hooway for Wodney Wat.* "Munsinger's expressively drawn pictures . . . wring out every funny nuance," noted Ilene Cooper in a *Booklist* review of *A Porcupine Named Fluffy,* while Julie Roach wrote in *School Library Journal* that the watercolor illustrations for *Hurty Feelings* "bring the tale to life, making Lester's creatures all the more entertaining and enjoyable."

Although animals figure most prominently in Munsinger's drawings, human children take center stage in several books. In Lester's *It Wasn't My Fault,* a young boy is always quick to blame something else for his own actions, while Deborah Lee Rose's *Birthday Zoo* finds a more upbeat fellow enjoying a special party given by the inhabitants of a local zoo. A spoiled girl who utters the foolish wish that she be transformed into a flower is featured in another book by Lester, *Pookins Gets Her Way,* which contains illustrations that are "full of mischief," according to a *Publishers Weekly* critic. *Princess Penelope's Parrot* introduces readers to yet another spoiled child, this time a princess whose nasty words come back to haunt her during her birthday party, when a parrot who refused to speak to her suddenly begins mimicking the girl's mantra—"Gimme, Gimme, Gimme"—in earshot of the wealthy prince Penelope was hoping to impress. The author's "spoiled-brat princess is perfectly embodied in Munsinger's . . . illustration," asserted Janice M. Del Negro in a review of *Princess Penelope's Parrot* for the *Bulletin of the Center for Children's Books.*

While Munsinger concentrates mainly upon illustrating picture books for young children, she has also done artwork for children's textbooks, designed greeting cards, and contributed illustrations to *Cricket* magazine. Her media of choice continue to be Indian ink and crow quill pens, to which she often adds watercolor washes. "The aspect of illustration that most interests me is development of the characters," Munsinger once explained to *SATA*. "I feel humor and expression add to a character's appeal and aid in telling a story." While Munsinger enjoys drawing all sorts of characters, she admits to a special affection for drawing animals. Fortunately for her, that affection has translated itself into talent. As a *Publishers Weekly* contributor noted in discussing her illustrations for William Wise's poetry collection *Zany Zoo:* "When it comes to imagining anthropomorphized animals, [Munsinger] . . . has few peers. No matter what species she puts her pen to, the result is [both] . . . touching and tickling."

## Biographical and Critical Sources

### PERIODICALS

*Booklist,* April 15, 1986, Ilene Cooper, review of *A Porcupine Named Fluffy,* pp. 1223-1224; December 1, 1986,

***Munsinger and Lester have collaborated on several books featuring Tacky the penguin; they follow Tacky's career as an actor in* Tackylocks *and the* Three Bears.** (Illustrations © 2002 by Lynn Munsinger. All rights reserved. Reproduced by permission of Houghton Mifflin Company.)

Barbara Elleman, review of *Hugh Pine and the Good Place,* p. 582; February 1, 1987, Denise M. Wilms, review of *Rabbit Goes to Night School,* p. 842; April 1, 1988, review of *Underwear!,* p. 1352; March 1,

1990, Ilene Cooper, review of *The Revenge of the Magic Chicken,* p. 1344; October 1, 1992, Annie Ayres, review of *Me First,* p. 336; February 15, 1994, Kathryn Broderick, review of *Three Cheers for Tacky,*

pp. 1092-1093; October 15, 1995, Hazel Rochman, review of *Listen, Buddy,* p. 412; September 1, 1999, Stephanie Zvirin, review of *Gator Halloween,* p. 145; November, 15, 1999, Hazel Rochman, review of *Don't Need Friends,* p. 635; March 15, 2000, review of *Hooway for Wodney Wat,* p. 1346; August, 2002, Hazel Rochman, review of *God Bless America,* p. 1966; September 15, 2002, Cynthia Turnquest, review of *Birthday Zoo,* p. 242; October 1, 2002, Stephanie Zvirin, review of *Hunter's Best Friend at School,* p. 334, and Kathy Broderick, review of *Tackyocks and the Three Bears,* p. 337; September 15, 2003, Gillian Engberg, review of *Something Might Happen,* p. 246; December 1, 2004, Jennifer Mattson, review of *Beatrice Doesn't Want To,* p. 661; September 1, 2005, Shelle Rosenfeld, review of *Hunter and Stripe and the Soccer Showdown,* p. 119, and Carolyn Phelan, review of *Tacky and the Winter Games,* p. 120; April 15, 2006, Jennifer Mattson, review of *Zany Zoo,* p. 55; September 15, 2006, Ilene Cooper, review of *Batter up Wombat,* p. 68.

*Bulletin of the Center for Children's Books,* April, 1988, review of *Tacky the Penguin,* p. 159; March, 1990, review of *The Revenge of the Magic Chickens,* pp. 168-169; April, 1996, review of *Custard the Dragon and the Wicked Knight,* p. 273; January, 1997, Janice M. Del Negro, review of *Princess Penelope's Parrot,* p. 179.

*Horn Book,* March-April, 1987, Karen Jameyson, review of *Hugh Pine and the Good Place,* p. 214; May-June, 1987, Hanna B. Zeiger, review of *Rabbit Goes to Night School,* pp. 328-329; November-December, 1992, Carolyn K. Jenks, review of *Me First,* pp. 716-717; July-August, 1995, review of *Listen, Buddy,* p. 485; September, 2001, review of *Score One for the Sloths,* p. 576; November-December, 2001, review of *A Stormy Ride on Noah's Ark,* p. 736; November-December, 2002, Mary M. Burns, review of *Birthday Zoo,* p. 738; May-June, 2004, Roger Sutton, review of *Snakes!,* p. 313.

*Kirkus Reviews,* July 15, 2002, review of *Tackylocks and the Three Bears,* p. 1037; May 1, 2004, review of *Snakes!,* p. 442; July 1, 2004, review of *Hurty Feelings,* p. 632; July 1, 2005, review of *Hunter and Stripe and the Soccer Showdown,* p. 734; August 15, 2005, review of *Seven Spunky Monkeys,* p. 917; October 15, 2005, review of *Tacky and the Winter Games,* p. 1141.

*Publishers Weekly,* September 19, 1980, review of *Hugh Pine,* p. 161; May 27, 1983, review of *Duck Goes Fishing,* p. 68; April 25, 1986, review of *A Porcupine Named Fluffy,* p. 73; August 22, 1986, review of *A Halloween Mask for Monster,* p. 93; February 27, 1987, review of *Pookins Gets Her Way,* p. 163; May 8, 1995, review of *The Tale of Custard the Dragon,* p. 295; February 13, 2005, review of *Bunny Tails,* p. 76; February 27, 2006, review of *Zany Zoo,* p. 60.

*School Library Journal,* December, 1985, review of *A Playhouse for Monster,* pp. 109-110; August, 1987, review of *Pookins Gets Her Way,* p. 70; March, 1988, Lori A. Janick, review of *Underwear!,* p. 172; April, 1988, Bonnie Wheatley, review of *Tacky the Penguin,* p. 82; October, 1992, George Delalis, review of *Me First,* p. 91; May, 1994, Donna L. Scanlon, review of *Three Cheers for Tacky,* p. 98; November, 2000, Martha Link, review of *Tacky and the Emperor,* p. 126; October, 2001, Robin L. Gibson, review of *Score One for the Sloths,* p. 123; December, 2001, Kathy Piehl, review of *A Stormy Ride on Noah's Ark,* p. 104; September, 2002, Melinda Piehler, review of *Hunter's Best Friend at School,* p. 190; September, 2003, Be Astengo, review of *Something Might Happen,* p. 183; August, 2004, Linda Staskus, review of *The Teeny Tiny Ghost and the Monster,* p. 104; September, 2004, Blair Christolon, review of *Hunter and Stripe and the Soccer Showdown,* p. 169; October, 2004, Julie Roach, review of *Hurty Feelings,* p. 12; November, 2004, Wanda Meyers-Hines, review of *Beatrice Doesn't Want To,* p. 113; September, 2005, Linda Staskus, review of *Seven Spunky Monkeys,* p. 176; August, 2006, Piper L. Nyman, review of *Zany Zoo,* p. 100; October, 2006, Lynn K. Vanca, review of *Batter up Wombat,* p. 116.*

# N-O

## NELSON, Blake 1960-

### Personal
Born 1960, in Portland, OR; married. *Education:* Bachelor's degree.

### Addresses
*Home*—Brooklyn, NY. *Agent*—Jodi Reamer, Writers House, LLC, 21 W. 26th St., New York, NY 10010. *E-mail*—blake@blakenelsonbooks.com.

### Career
Fiction writer and columnist. Humor columnist for *Details* magazine.

### Writings

*YOUNG-ADULT NOVELS*

*The New Rules of High School,* Viking (New York, NY), 2003.
*Rock Star Superstar,* Viking (New York, NY), 2004.
*Gender Blender,* Delacorte (New York, NY), 2006.
*Paranoid Park,* Viking (New York, NY), 2006.
*Prom Anonymous,* Viking (New York, NY), 2006.

*ADULT NOVELS*

*Girl,* Simon & Schuster (New York, NY), 1994.
*Exile,* Scribner (New York, NY), 1997.
*User,* Versus Press (San Francisco, CA), 2001.

### Adaptations
*Girl* was adapted as a motion picture, 1998; *Paranoid Park* was adapted as a motion picture, directed by Gus Van Sant; *Gender Blender* was optioned for film by Nickelodeon.

**Blake Nelson** (Photograph courtesy of Blake Nelson.)

### Sidelights
Blake Nelson is the author of a number of critically acclaimed novels for young adults, including *The New Rules of High School* and *Paranoid Park.* Born in Portland, Oregon, Nelson developed an early interest in literature and music. After graduating from college, he played in a series of alternative bands before landing a job writing humor pieces for *Details* magazine. Nelson's fiction began generating interest among publishers

*Cover of Nelson's young-adult novel* The New Rules of High School, *featuring an illustration by Hadley Hooper.* (Cover illustration copyright © Hadley Hooper, 2003. Reproduced by permission of Speak, a division of Penguin Putnam Books for Young Readers.)

after excerpts from his first novel, *Girl,* appeared in the popular teen magazine *Sassy.*

Published in book form in 1994, *Girl* was actually promoted as a novel for adults. In the book, Nelson focuses on Andrea Marr, a high school student living in Portland who is struggling to find her identity. "I *am* the Andrea type . . . ," Nelson commented to an interviewer for *Teenreads.com.* "I tried at the beginning to make Andrea a clueless mall chick, but she quickly became more of an observer (like me!) and she did what I did in high school, which is become friends with a lot of different people from different cliques and especially befriend the weirdest, most creative people." Although several critics noted Nelson's ability to accurately capture the rhythms of teen speech in the novel, the author admitted that he did not go to great lengths to research *Girl.* "I just remembered what high school was like," he explained. "And I guess in some part of my brain I have always been younger than I really am. I love high school. I think it is a great time in a person's life, an epic time, when love seems absolute and infinite and there's still room for heroism and bravery and romance. After that, everyone just gets jobs and watches TV."

Although he wrote two more works for adult readers following *Girl,* Nelson has since focused his attention on young-adult literature. *The New Rules of High School,* his first work specifically geared for a teen readership, introduces Max Caldwell, an overachieving high school senior. At first glance, Max appears to have it all: he serves as editor-in-chief of the school newspaper and captain of the debate team, earns straight A's in class, and dates a beautiful girl. When the pressure to live up to his own high standards becomes too much for him, Max begins to self-destruct, dumping his girlfriend and then jeopardizing his other close relationships. "Thus begins an intense journey of self-discovery, told in an achingly honest narrative," observed a critic in *Publishers Weekly.* "Nelson skillfully reveals Max's character and problems in 'show-don't-tell' style," noted a *Kirkus Reviews* contributor, and Gillian Engberg noted of Max in her *Booklist* review that "there's a refreshing honesty in his 'averageness" and in his bewildered disconnection." "Whether Max is grieving over his breakup or testing the waters of singledom," wrote *School Library Journal* critic Vicki Reutter, "readers are empathetic to his emotional vulnerability."

A teenager takes his shot at fame and fortune in *Rock Star Superstar,* "a brilliant, tender, funny, and utterly believable novel about music and relationships," according to *School Library Journal* contributor Miranda Doyle. In Nelson's story, Pete, a talented bass player whose parents were also musicians, is asked to join the Tiny Masters of Today, a rock band on the verge of hitting it big. Despite reservations about his bandmates' devotion to their craft, Pete agrees to tour with the group, learning some hard lessons about the music industry along the way. He also enters an intense, complicated relationship with Margaret, his first true love. "Nelson paints Pete as endearingly clueless," remarked a critic in *Publishers Weekly,* "yet the teen proves his loyalty throughout the book—to his girlfriend, to his dad and ultimately to his music."

Two sixth graders learn firsthand what it is like to be a member of the opposite sex in Nelson's humorous novel *Gender Blender.* Colliding mid-air during a jump on a trampoline, Tom Witherspoon and Emma Baker magically swap bodies. While forced to impersonate each other, Tom must learn the intricacies of fastening a bra while Emma copes with her counterpart's goofy male friends and their childish pranks. "Speaking in alternating chapters, the shell-shocked pre-teens hilariously navigate (and gain insights from) their differing hobbies, social situations, [and] academic reputations," noted *Booklist* reviewer Jennifer Mattson in a review of the novel, while a *Publishers Weekly* critic remarked that in *Gender Blender* "Nelson demonstrates his keen understanding of peer pressure and gender stereotyping."

A skateboarder's journey to a rough-and-tumble neighborhood goes terribly wrong in *Paranoid Park,* a "deeply disturbing cautionary tale," in the words of a *Kirkus Reviews* critic. When the unnamed sixteen-year-old narrator decides one night to visit Paranoid Park, an area of town with a reputation as a sketchy, dangerous place, he meets Scratch, a street kid who convinces him to hop a train. Confronted by a vicious security guard, the narrator lashes out with his skateboard and watches in horror as the guard falls beneath a moving train. "Written in the form of a confessional letter," a *Publishers Weekly* contributor noted, "the book details the narrator's moral dilemma after the incident." "Gritty and aching, the narrative will have readers pondering what they might do under the circumstances," concluded *Kliatt* reviewer Paula Rohrlick.

In *Prom Anonymous* a high-school junior hopes to reunite with two old friends for the night of the big dance. Though Laura has drifted apart from Chloe and Jace, she is determined to play matchmaker for them, although she begins to ignore her own boyfriend in the process. "As might be expected, prom night is filled with crises, but creative resolutions make for a gratify-

*Cover illustration of Nelson's 2006 novel* **Paranoid Park,** *featuring artwork by Emilian Gregory.* (Jacket illustration copyright © Emilian Gregory, 2006. Reproduced by permission of Viking, a division of Penguin Putnam Books for Young Readers.)

ing all's-well-that-ends-well conclusion," noted a critic in *Publishers Weekly.*

Discussing his motivation for becoming a writer, Nelson remarked on his home page: "You have one life. What are you gonna do with it? If you go into the arts, that's a big risk. There's no certain reward. You are really sort of throwing yourself at the mercy of the fates. But if that's really what you feel called to do, then you do it."

## Biographical and Critical Sources

*PERIODICALS*

*Booklist,* August, 2003, Gillian Engberg, review of *The New Rules of High School,* p. 1972; November 1, 2004, Todd Morning, review of *Rock Star, Superstar,* p. 476; March 1, 2006, Jennifer Mattson, review of *Gender Blender,* p. 88; April 1, 2006, Anne O'Malley, review of *Prom Anonymous,* p. 37; September 1, 2006, Ilene Cooper, review of *Paranoid Park,* p. 115.

*Cover of Nelson's humorous middle-grade novel* **Gender Blender,** *featuring artwork by Molly Zakrajsek.* (Jacket illustration copyright © 2006 by Molly Zakrajsek. Used by permission of Dell Publishing, a division of Random House, Inc.)

*Kirkus Reviews,* June 1, 2003, review of *The New Rules of High School,* p. 809; August 1, 2004, review of *Rock Star, Superstar,* p. 746; February 15, 2006, review of *Gender Blender,* p. 188, and review of *Prom Anonymous,* p. 189; August 1, 2006, review of *Paranoid Park,* p. 793.

*Kliatt,* September, 2006, Paula Rohrlick, review of *Paranoid Park,* p. 16.

*Publishers Weekly,* June 23, 2003, review of *The New Rules of High School,* p. 68; September 20, 2004, review of *Rock Star, Superstar,* p. 63; February 6, 2006, reviews of *Gender Blender* and *Prom Anonymous,* p. 70; August 21, 2006, review of *Paranoid Park,* p. 69.

*School Library Journal,* June, 2003, Vicki Reutter, review of *The New Rules of High School,* p. 148; October, 2004, Miranda Doyle, review of *Rock Star, Superstar,* p. 173; March, 2006, Morgan Johnson-Doyle, review of *Prom Anonymous,* p. 228; April, 2006, Laurie Slagenwhite, review of *Gender Blender,* p. 145.

*Voice of Youth Advocates,* October, 2004, Patrick Jones, review of *Rock Star, Superstar,* p. 306.

ONLINE

*Blake Nelson Home Page,* http://www.blakenelsonbooks. com (January 21, 2007).

*Teenreads.com,* http://www.teenreads.com/ (February 26, 2002), "Author Profile: Blake Nelson."

\*       \*       \*

# OGILVY, Ian 1943-
## (Ian Raymond Ogilvy)

## Personal

Born September 30, 1943, in Woking, Surrey, England; son of Francis Ogilvy (an advertising executive) and Aileen Raymond (an actress); married (divorced); first wife's name Diane; married Kathryn Holcomb (an actress), 1992; children: (first marriage) Emma, Titus; two stepsons. *Hobbies and other interests:* Playing computer games, gardening, building things out of wood, riding his motorcycle, SCUBA diving.

## Addresses

*Home and office*—Southern CA.

## Career

Actor and author. Actor on stage and in films, including (as Desmond Flower) *Stranger in the House,* 1967; (as Mike Roscoe) *The Sorcerers,* 1967; (as Ronald) *The Invincible Six,* 1967; (as Edgar Linton) *Wuthering Heights,* 1970; (as William De Lancy) *Waterloo,* 1970; (as William Seaton) *From beyond the Grave,* 1973; and (as Captain Starch) *Eddie Presley,* 1992. Actor in television films and series, including *The Liars,* 1966; *The Avengers,* 1968; (as Lawrence Kirbridge) *Upstairs, Down-*stairs, 1972; (as Edward VIII) *The Gathering Storm,* 1974; (as Humphrey Oliver) *Moll Flanders,* 1975; *Ripping Yarns,* 1976; (as Drusus) *I, Claudius,* 1976; (as Simon Templar) *Return of the Saint,* 1978-79; (as Lord Edgar) *Robin of Sherwood,* 1986; (as Reginald Hewitt) *Generations,* 1990; *Walker, Texas Ranger,* 1994; (as Harold Baines) *Murder, She Wrote,* 1989-94; (as Jerry Lane) *Diagnosis: Murder,* 1995-99; *The Faculty,* 1996; (as Marc Delacourt) *Malibu Shores,* 1996; *Murphy Brown,* 1997; (as Lional Spencer) *Caroline in the City,* 1997; *JAG,* 1997; (as Leo Turnlow) *Melrose Place,* 1999; *Fugitive Mind,* 1999; *Dharma and Greg,* 2000; *The Parkers,* 2002; and *After Midnight,* 2007. Has appeared in television specials, and worked as a voice-over actor.

## Writings

*"MEASLE" NOVEL SERIES; FOR CHILDREN*

*Measle and the Wrathmonk,* illustrated by Chris Mould, HarperCollins (New York, NY), 2004.

*Measle and the Dragodon,* illustrated by Chris Mould, Oxford University Press (Oxford, England), 2004, HarperCollins (New York, NY), 2005.

*Measle and the Mallockee,* HarperCollins (New York, NY), 2006.

*Measle and the Slitherghoul,* Oxford University Press (Oxford, England), 2006.

*Measle and the Doompit,* Oxford University Press (Oxford, England), 2007.

The "Measle" series has been translated into over fifteen languages.

*OTHER*

*The Stud Farm* (screenplay), produced, 1969.

*Loose Chippings* (adult novel), Headline (London, England), 1996.

*The Polkerton Giant* (adult novel), Headline (London, England), 1997.

*A Slight Hangover: A Comedy* (stage play), Samuel French (New York, NY), 2002.

## Sidelights

Though Ian Ogilvy is perhaps best known as a television and film actor, he has also built a loyal audience as a writer. Beginning his authorial career penning novels, Ogilvy has more recently turned his attention to a younger audience. With each installment in his "Measle" novel series he has earned an increasing readership, both in his native England and among readers of the fifteen other languages his novels have been translated into. Beginning with *Measle and the Wrathmonk,* Ogilvy's series draws readers into a fantasy world and the adventures of an orphaned boy as he battles the legion

of evil wizards known as wrathmonks, defending those who are threatened by the wizards' evil plans. "I still can't shake the idea that I'm a bit of a fraud," the author admitted to an interviewer for the London *Times Online.* "I keep thinking I'm an actor who has merely dabbled in books and got lucky."

Readers first meet Ogilvy's stalwart young hero in *Measle and the Wrathmonk.* After his parents mysteriously disappear, Measle Stubbs goes to live with his uncle, Basil Tramplebone, A totally unpleasant man, Uncle Basil is, as the boy soon discovers, also a wrathmonk. This discovery comes with consequences: the boy is shrunk to the size of a thimble and exiled to a toy train set in his uncle's attic. There Measle soon meets up with Prudence, a wrathmonk-ologist who has suffered a similar fate, and sets about forcing his uncle to return him to his proper size. "Ogilvy's storytelling will remind readers a little of Lemony Snicket, with a dash of Harry Potter tossed in," wrote Michele Winship in her *Kliatt* review of *Measle and the Wrathmonk.* Ed Sullivan, writing in *Booklist,* concluded that Ogilvy's "entertaining, fast-paced novel has moments of humor and suspense," while a *Publishers Weekly* critic compared the book to Jonathan Swift's *Gulliver's Travels,* writing that the story's "Lilliputian scenes offer some keen suspense."

In *Measle and the Dragodon* Measle's mother becomes the target of an army of wrathmonks led by a wicked dragodon, or dragon rider. After Mom is kidnapped, Measle tracks down clues as to her fate in an abandoned amusement park, and must rely on such whimsically inspired talismans as magic jellybeans in order to extract himself from the quandary that results. *Measle and the Mallockee* finds our hero confronted by his nemesis, supposed friend Toby Jugg, as he protects his little sister so that she can fulfill her destiny as a mallockee, or powerful wizard. Although Measle himself possesses no magical powers, he uses brainpower to get himself and his spell-wielding sibling out of trouble. Walter Minkel, reviewing *Measle and the Dragodon* for *School Library Journal,* felt that, while Ogilvy's villains are too inept to be truly threatening, characters such as Tinker, Measle's canine sidekick, add plot dimensions that "are often pretty funny." A *Kirkus Reviews* contributor dubbed *Measle and the Mallockee* the best entry in the series to date, and Shelle Rosenfeld, reviewing the same book for *Booklist,* described Ogilvy's novel as "a fast-reading, occasionally humorous tale of magic and mayhem."

Ogilvy continues the adventures of Measle in *Measle and the Slitherghoul,* in which the slimy creature that has eaten the wrathmonks now desires Measle as desert. Readers of *Measle and the Doompit* follow the boy on a journey to Dystopia, an aptly named land of horrors wherein Measle must once again confront arch enemy Jugg.

## Biographical and Critical Sources

*PERIODICALS*

*Booklist,* October 1, 2004, Ed Sullivan, review of *Measle and the Wrathmonk,* p. 329; January 1, 2006, Shelle Rosenfeld, review of *Measle and the Mallockee,* p. 88.

*Kirkus Reviews,* March 1, 2005, review of *Measle and the Dragodon,* p. 293; November 15, 2005, review of *Measle and the Mallockee,* p. 1235.

*Kliatt,* July, 2004, Michele Winship, review of *Measle and the Wrathmonk,* p. 11.

*Publishers Weekly,* November 8, 2004, review of *Measle and the Wrathmonk,* p. 56.

*School Librarian,* winter, 2004, Tim Saunders, "Spotlight on Ian Ogilvy," p. 174; spring, 2005, Cherie Gladstone, review of *Measle and the Dragodon,* p. 36; summer, 2006, Lesley Martin, review of *Measle and the Mallockee,* p. 90.

*School Library Journal,* September, 2004, Eva Mitnick, review of *Measle and the Wrathmonk,* p. 214; August, 2005, Walter Minkel, review of *Measle and the Dragodon,* p. 132; February, 2006, Carly B. Wiskoff, review of *Measle and the Mallockee,* p. 134.

*Voice of Youth Advocates,* April, 2005, Christina Fairman, review of *Measle and the Wrathmonk,* p. 60; February, 2006, Christina Fairman, review of *Measle and the Mallockee,* p. 502.

*ONLINE*

*HarperCollins Web site,* http://www.harpercollins.com/ (February 24, 2007), "Ian Ogilvy."

*Ian Ogilvy Home Page,* http://www.ianogilvy.com (February 24, 2004).*

\*    \*    \*

# OGILVY, Ian Raymond
## See OGILVY, Ian

\*    \*    \*

# OPPENHEIM, Shulamith Levey 1928-

## Personal

Born September 2, 1928, in Shaker Heights, OH; daughter of Irving M. (a rabbi and professor) and Sarah (a teacher) Levey; married Felix Errera Oppenheim (a professor of political science), May 29, 1949; children: Daniel, Claire, Paul. *Education:* Attended Radcliffe College, 1947-49; University of Delaware, B.A., 1953. *Hobbies and other interests:* Classical music, travel, gardening, playing the piano, swimming, power walking.

## Addresses

*Home*—Amherst, MA. *Agent*—Marilyn Marlow, Curtis Brown Ltd., 575 Madison Ave., New York, NY 10022. *E-mail*—Shulamith@comcast.net.

## Career

Writer. Presented freelance literary programs on public radio, 1961-70; freelance writer, beginning 1970. Volunteer nurses' aide.

## Member

Society of Children's Book Writers, Jane Austen Society, Folklore Society of England.

## Awards, Honors

American Library Association Notable Book designation, 1994, for *Iblis*.

## Writings

*FOR CHILDREN*

*A Trio for Grandpapa,* illustrated by Gioia Fiammenghi, Thomas Crowell (New York, NY), 1974.

*The Selchie's Seed,* illustrated by Dianne Goode, Bradbury (Scarsdale, NY), 1975.

*Waiting for Noah,* illustrated by Lillian Hoban, Harper & Row (New York, NY), 1990.

*Appleblossom,* illustrated by Joanna Yardley, Harcourt (San Diego, CA), 1991.

*The Lily Cupboard: A Story of the Holocaust,* illustrated by Ronald Himler, HarperCollins (New York, NY), 1992.

*Fireflies for Nathan,* illustrated by John Ward, Tambourine Books (New York, NY), 1994.

*Iblis,* illustrated by Ed Young, Harcourt Brace (San Diego, CA), 1994.

*The Hundredth Time,* illustrated by Michael Hays, Boyds Mills Press (Honesdale, PA), 1995.

*I Love You, Bunny Rabbit,* illustrated by Cyd Moore, Boyds Mills Press (Honesdale, PA), 1995.

*And the Earth Trembled: The Creation of Adam and Eve,* illustrated by Neil Waldman, Harcourt (San Diego, CA), 1996.

*What Is the Full Moon Full Of?,* illustrated by Cyd Moore, Boyds Mills Press (Honesdale, PA), 1997.

*Yanni Rubbish,* illustrated by Doug Chayka, Boyds Mills Press (Honesdale, PA), 1999.

*The Fish Prince, and Other Stories: Mermen Folk Tales,* illustrated by Paul Hoffman, Interlink Books (New York, NY), 2001.

*Ali and the Magic Stew,* illustrated by Winslow Pels, Boyds Mills Press (Honesdale, PA), 2002.

(With Jane Yolen) *The Sea King,* illustrated by Stefan Czernecki, Crocodile Books (Brooklyn, NY), 2003.

*Rescuing Einstein's Compass,* illustrated by George Juhasz, Crocodile Books (Brooklyn, NY), 2003.

Work anthologized in *Scribner Anthology for Young People,* Scribner, 1976. Contributor of short fiction to periodicals, including *Cricket.* Children's book reviewer for *New York Times Book Review,* 1960-70.

## Sidelights

Inspired by her travels to many parts of the world, Shulamith Levey Oppenheim introduces young readers to the colorful patchwork that makes up human culture in her folktale-inspired picture books: from Russian folklore in *The Sea King* to tales from Iran in *Ali and the Magic Stew,* Egypt in *The Hundredth Name,* and Scotland in *The Selchie's Seed.* Oppenheim's books range in subject; in *The Fish Prince, and Other Stories: Mermen Folk Tales* she collects stories about supernatural creatures from many corners of the globe, while in *Einstein's Compass* her focus narrows to a personal recollection of a family encounter with noted twentieth-century physicist Albert Einstein. In the picture book *Fireflies for Nathan,* Oppenheim shares a story about a close-knit family living in a simpler place and time, recounting six-year-old Nathan's efforts to carry on his father's childhood sport of capturing fireflies in a jar. Praising the international approach Oppenheim and co-author Jane Yolen adopt in *The Fish Prince, and Other Stories, Booklist* contributor Todd Morning cited the book's text as "graceful, fast moving, and entertaining throughout," while her ability to create "particularly childlike dialogue" in *Fireflies for Nathan* "infuses the proceedings with believable enthusiasm," according to a *Publishers Weekly* reviewer.

Raised by highly educated and cultured parents, Oppenheim inherited her professor father's love of books. As she recalled on her home page, her family's library was a diverse one, containing "rare books, especially Judaica and languages—obscure and otherwise. But not only eclectic books. Books on myth, myths themselves, legend, folklore, books on the Bible and from the Bible, books on animal, vegetable, and mineral." For the inquisitive young Oppenheim, these books "held worlds I couldn't wait to enter." As a teen, she moved into novels, as well as literary classics by Jane Austen, T.S. Eliot, William Shakespeare, and the classics of nineteenth-century poetry. Her love of books moved to writing in later years, on the suggestion of a friend who was also a children's book writer, and her first published book, *A Trio for Grandpapa,* in 1974.

Oppenheim's interest in world cultures has been long standing, and in *Iblis* and *As the Earth Trembled: The Creation of Adam and Eve* she retells two creation stories drawn from the works of a ninth-century Islamic text. Featuring illustrations by award-winning artist Ed Young, *Iblis* follows the story of Adam and Eve and their departure from Paradise as it is represented in the Muslim tradition. In the creation myth *As the Earth Trembled* God's loneliness prompts the deity to bring to life the first human. Problems arise, however, when the angels argue that giving the human a high measure of

intelligence will spark tendencies toward jealousy, greed, and hatred and result in destructive behavior. Ultimately, God is assisted only by the angel of death, and through this collaboration mankind is ultimately rendered mortal. The ending of *As the Earth Trembled* shares with *Iblis* the actions of Soul, who is unwilling to participate in God's creation and must therefore enter and leave the body only at God's whim. When the angel Iblis refuses to worship the resulting creation, Adam, he is cast from Heaven; in revenge, Iblis (a.k.a. Satan) uses his ability as a shapeshifter to eventually seduce the newly made man and his consort, Eve, from their home in Paradise. In a *Booklist* review of *Iblis* Elizabeth Bush praised Oppenheim for her "fluid retelling" of the ancient tale, calling the book "an outstanding aid to understanding the continuity between Islamic and Western culture."

Underlying the picture book *Yanni Rubbish* is Oppenheim's love of Greece, which she has visited repeatedly since the early 1950s. In the picture book, Yanni Stavros works hard to fill his father's shoes as the trash collector for his small village. Helped by his donkey Lamia, the eight year old rises early each day to steer the family's rickety wagon through the streets, earning the money to support his family, but also earning a taunting from a group of young bullies. Dubbed "Yanni Rubbish," the boy is even more frustrated by the insults hurled at the hard-working Lamia, and ultimately he finds a way to end the bullies' hurtful words. In *Booklist* Hazel Rochman called *Yanni Rubbish* a "touching story," and a *Publishers Weekly* contributor gave special note to Doug Chayka's illustrations due to their ability to "capture the feel of Yanni's town and the tender relationship between mother and son."

Focusing on the history of modern Europe, Oppenheim turns her attention to World War II and German Chancellor Adolf Hitler's efforts to exterminate the Jews then living in Europe in *The Lily Cupboard: A Story of the Holocaust.* Framing her subject in a manner meaningful to young children, Oppenheim relates the tale of Miriam, a young Dutch Jew whose worried parents send her to live with a gentile farm family. In her new home, the girl is assigned a secret hiding place designed to hide her should German soldiers discover her whereabouts. For Miriam, however, the fear of discovery is eclipsed by her feelings of sadness over being separated from her loving parents and her worry over their safety. "Miriam's ordeal is sure to provoke further discussion and may serve to introduce the themes of war and racism," noted a *Publishers Weekly,* while Rochman dubbed *The Lily Cupboard* a "powerful" tale in her *Booklist* review.

As Oppenheim once explained, she believes deeply in the idea of "true magic in art, and that it is closely tied with metaphor, in that art itself is a metaphor for life, and this is a kind of magic. Folklore, legend, myth, all are the most rewarding repositories of such metaphors, they are themselves metaphors. I draw my material

*Shulamith Levey Oppenheim tells a story inspired by her love of Greek culture in* **Yanni Rubbish,** *a picture book illustrated by Doug Chayka.* (Boyd Mills Press, 1999. Illustrations copyright © 1999 by Doug Chayka. Reproduced by permission.)

from these sources, hoping to transmute them into fresh tales, with a new inference, a surprise, which to me is the essential hallmark of genuine originality in any art . . . the putting together of two hitherto unconnected elements.

"Too much material straight from the therapist's couch passes today for art," Oppenheim continued. "Too much self-indulgence is allowed in publishing. It is difficult, it often requires hard labor to turn something into another thing. With facility, many writers, painters, etc., get away with mediocre creations. Flaubert often spent months on one paragraph, until it sang out as he wanted it to sing. I find this exhilarating and a more than useful fact to keep before me." Regarding her decision to write for younger readers, Oppenheim noted on her home page: "I write for children because I love and admire their honesty. You can't fool them. And so, I hope, we who do write for them must be honest with ourselves, not fool ourselves."

## Biographical and Critical Sources

### PERIODICALS

*Booklist,* March 15, 1994, Elizabeth Bush, review of *Iblis,* p. 1368; January 1, 1995, April Judge, review of *I Love You, Bunny Rabbit,* p. 826; September 15, 1995,

Hazel Rochman, review of *The Hundredth Name,* p. 176; October 1, 1996, Susan Dove Lempke, review of *And the Earth Trembled: The Creation of Adam and Eve,* p. 337; December 1, 1997, Stephanie Zvirin, review of *What Is the Full Moon Made Of?,* p. 643; March 1, 1999, Hazel Rochman, review of *Yanni Rubbish,* p. 1222; July, 2000, Hazel Rochman, review of *The Lily Cupboard: A Story of the Holocaust,* p. 2027; November 15, 2001, Todd Morning, review of *The Fish Prince, and Other Stories,* p. 562; April 15, 2002, Hazel Rochman, review of *Ali and the Magic Stew,* p. 1408.

*Bulletin of the Center for Children's Books,* February, 1995, review of *I Love You, Bunny Rabbit,* p. 211; February, 1997, review of *And the Earth Trembled,* p. 218; May, 2002, review of *Ali and the Magic Stew,* p. 336.

*Horn Book,* May-June, 1990, Hanna B. Zeiger, review of *Waiting for Noah,* p. 328; January-February, 1996, Hanna B. Zeiger, review of *The Hundredth Name,* p. 68.

*Kirkus Reviews,* March 1, 2002, review of *Ali and the Magic Stew,* p. 342; December 1, 2002, review of *The Sea King,* p. 1776.

*New York Times Book Review,* March 31, 1991, review of *Appleblossom,* p. 29.

*Publishers Weekly,* January 1, 1992, review of *The Lily Cupboard,* p. 55; February 14, 1994, review of *Iblis,* p. 87; June 27, 1994, review of *Fireflies for Nathan,* p. 78; December 12, 1994, review of *I Love You, Bunny Rabbit,* p. 61; March 13, 1995, review of *The Lily Cupboard,* p. 70; March 8, 1999, review of *Yanni Rubbish,* p. 68; February 18, 2002, review of *Ali and the Magic Stew,* p. 96.

*Resource Links,* June, 2003, Deb Nielsen, review of *The Sea King,* p. 9; December, 2003, Carroll Chapman, review of *Rescuing Einstein's Compass,* p. 7.

*School Library Journal,* July, 1990, Anna Biagioni Hart, review of *Waiting for Noah,* p. 63; February, 1995, Lynn Cockett, review of *I Love You, Bunny Rabbit,* p. 78; September, 1996, Patricia Lothrop Green, review of *And the Earth Trembled,* p. 219; December, 1997, Peggy Morgan, review of *What Is the Full Moon Full Of?,* p. 99; April, 2002, Ann Welton, review of *Ali and the Magic Stew,* p. 118; February, 2004, Jean Lowery, review of *Rescuing Einstein's Compass,* p. 120.

*ONLINE*

*Shulamith Levey Oppenheim Home Page,* http://www.ShulamithOppenheim.com (March 18, 2007).

# P

## PASCHKIS, Julie 1957-

### Personal
Born 1957. *Education:* Attended Cornell University; Rochester Institute of Technology, B.F.A.

### Addresses
*Home and office*—Seattle, WA. *E-mail*—julie@juliepaschkis.com.

### Career
Children's book illustrator and artist. Art teacher, 1983-91. *Exhibitions:* Work included in solo exhibitions at Grover/Thurston Gallery, Seattle, WA, 2003, 2006; Alysia Duckler Gallery, Portland, OR, 1999, 2001-02; Davidson Gallery, Seattle, 1998, 2000-01; Mia Gallery, Seattle, 1991, 1993, 1996; and Portland Community College Gallery, 1994.

### Member
Society of Children's Book Writers and Illustrators (Western Washington chapter).

### Awards, Honors
*New York Times* Ten Best Illustrated Books inclusion, 2000, for *Night Garden* by Janet Wong; *Boston Globe/Horn Book* Honor Book designation, 2006, for *Yellow Elephant* by Julie Larios.

### Writings

#### SELF-ILLUSTRATED

*So Sleepy; Wide Awake,* Henry Holt (New York, NY), 1994.
*Play All Day,* Little, Brown (Boston, MA), 1998.

*Julie Paschkis* (Photograph courtesy of Julie Paschkis.)

#### ILLUSTRATOR

Dennis Fairchild, *Palm Reading: A Little Guide to Life's Secrets,* Running Press (Philadelphia, PA), 1995.
*So Happy; So Sad,* Henry Holt (New York, NY), 1995.
Henry and Melissa Billings, *Young People's Stories of Sharing,* Young People's Press (San Diego, CA), 1995.
John McCutcheon, *Happy Adoption Day!,* Little, Brown (Boston, MA), 1996.
Dennis Fairchild, *Fortune Telling: Palmistry and Tarot,* Running Press (Philadelphia, PA), 1996.

Joe Famularo, *Italian Soup Cookbook,* Workman (New York, NY), 1998.

Dennis Fairchild, *Tarot,* Running Press (Philadelphia, PA), 1999.

Lee Wardlaw, *First Steps,* HarperFestival (New York, NY), 1999.

Janet S. Wong, *Night Garden: Poems from the World of Dreams,* Margaret K. McElderry Books (New York, NY), 2000.

Margaret Read MacDonald, reteller, *Fat Cat: A Danish Folktale,* August House (Little Rock, AR), 2001.

*The Nutcracker,* Chronicle Books (San Francisco, CA), 2001.

Won-Ldy Paye and Margaret H. Lippert, retellers, *Head, Body, Legs: A Story from Liberia,* Henry Holt (New York, NY), 2002.

Dennis Fairchild, *The Fortune Telling Handbook: The Interactive Guide to Tarot, Palm Reading, and More,* Running Press (Philadelphia, PA), 2003.

Won-Ldy Paye and Margaret H. Lippert, *Mrs. Chicken and the Hungry Crocodile,* Henry Holt (New York, NY), 2003.

Janet S. Wong, *Knock on Wood: Poems about Superstitions,* Margaret K. McElderry Books (New York, NY), 2003.

Melissa Eskridge Slaymaker, *Bottle Houses: The Creative World of Grandma Prisbrey,* Henry Holt (New York, NY), 2004.

Janet Lord, *Here Comes Grandma!,* Henry Holt (New York, NY), 2005.

Maxie Baum, *I Have a Little Dreidel,* Scholastic (New York, NY), 2006.

Won-Ldy Paye and Margaret H. Lippert, retellers, *The Talking Vegetables,* Henry Holt (New York, NY), 2006.

Rachel Rodriguez, *Through Georgia's Eyes,* Henry Holt (New York, NY), 2006.

*Paschkis reveals her love of color and design in her illustrations for Julie Larios's animal-filled picture book* **Yellow Elephant.** (Copyright © 2006 by Julie Paschkis. Reproduced by permission of Harcourt, Inc.)

Julie Larios, *Yellow Elephant: A Bright Bestiary,* Harcourt (Orlando, FL), 2006.

Janet W. Wong, *Twist: Yoga Poems,* Margaret K. McElderry Books (New York, NY), 2007.

## Sidelights

Julie Paschkis has illustrated works of children's fiction as well as nonfiction books for adults. Regardless of theme, Paschkis consistently pairs vibrant colors and intricate patterns in the majority of her artwork. Called a "creative exploration of color" by *School Library Journal* contributor Carol L. MacKay, Paschkis's illustrations for *Yellow Elephant: A Bright Bestiary* feature vibrant, stylized animal images within a "visually stimulating" folk-art-inspired design as the setting for Julia Larios's poetry. Her collaboration with Melissa Eskridge Slaymaker, *Bottle Houses: The Creative World of Grandma Prisbrey,* showcases the creative life's work of a creative artist in vibrant colors that reflect the colored glass used as the artist's unusual medium. Beyond the pages of books, her art has also appeared on greeting cards and in solo exhibitions staged in and around her home in the Pacific Northwest. As Paschkis noted on her home page, illustrating children's books is akin to storytelling; she views each illustration project as creating "a 32-page painting in service to the story and characters of the book."

Paschkis's work for Rachel Rodriguez's *Through Georgia's Eyes* reveals her versatility as an artist because it required her to recreate paintings by noted twentieth-century painter Georgia O'Keeffe. The picture book recounts O'Keeffe's early influences, including her upbringing on a Wisconsin farm and her metamorphosis into an artist. A *Publishers Weekly* reviewer acknowledged Paschkis's ability to interpret O'Keeffe's recognizable images, noting that the illustrator "recreates the feel of O'Keeffe's work but with her own style." In her illustrations for *Through Georgia's Eyes* Paschkis incorporated cut-paper collages into her paintings, done in blues and reds, and this method was praised by a *Kirkus Reviews* critic because it "perfectly evoke O'Keeffe's vision without ever seeming like mere imitation." *School Library Journal* contributor Carolyn Janssen cited the illustrator's incorporation of "bold shapes of flowers, skulls, and mountains" as a way of revealing the images emblematic of O'Keeffe's own work. Lolly Robinson, reviewing *Through Georgia's Eyes* for *Horn Book,* lauded Paschkis for her ability to capture the shapes typical of the artist's work and cited the illustrator for using "sweeping arcs" to conveyed O'Keeffe's unique "way of seeing the world around us."

## Biographical and Critical Sources

*PERIODICALS*

*Booklist,* December 1, 1996, Julie Corsaro, review of *Happy Adoption Day!,* p. 667; May 15, 1998, Kay Weisman, review of *Play All Day,* p. 1633; November 15, 2001, Helen Rosenberg, review of *Fat Cat: A Danish Folktale,* p. 577; August, 2002, Gillian Engberg, review of *Head, Body, Legs: A Story from Liberia,* p. 1968; November 15, 2003, Gillian Engberg, review of *Knock on Wood: Poems about Superstitions,* p. 596; March 1, 2004, Jennifer Mattson, review of *Bottlehouses: The Creative World of Grandma Prisbrey,* p. 1206; October 1, 2005, Jennifer Mattson, review of *Here Comes Grandma,* p. 64; February 15, 2006, Carolyn Phelan, review of *Through Georgia's Eyes,* p. 109; March 15, 2006, Gillian Engberg, review of *Yellow Elephant: A Bright Bestiary,* p. 49; September 15, 2006, Ilene Cooper, review of *I Have a Little Dreidel,* p. 60.

*Horn Book,* May-June, 2002, Lauren Adams, review of *Head, Body, Legs,* p. 340; September-October, 2003, Susan Dove Lempke, review of *Knock on Wood,* p. 624; July-August, 2004, Lolly Robinson, review of *Bottle Houses,* p. 470; May-June, 2006, Lolly Robinson, review of *Through Georgia's Eyes,* p. 347.

*Kirkus Reviews,* October 15, 2001, review of *The Nutcracker,* p. 1484; August 15, 2003, review of *Knock on Wood,* p. 1081; March 1, 2004, review of *Bottle Houses,* p. 229; February 1, 2006, review of *Yellow Elephant,* p. 294; March 15, 2006, review of *Here Comes Grandma,* p. September 15, 2006, review of *The Talking Vegetables,* p. 963.

*Publishers Weekly,* August 5, 1996, review of *Poems from the World of Dreams,* p. 84; March 13, 2000, review

*Paschkis collaborated with writer Melissa Eskridge Slaymaker in profiling an unusual California artist in* Bottle Houses. (Copyright © 2004 by Julie Paschkis. Reprinted by permission of Henry Holt and Company, LLC. )

of *Here Comes Grandma,* p. April 1, 2002, review of
*Head, Body, Legs,* p. 82; April 10, 2006, review of
*Yellow Elephant,* p. 71; April 26, 2004, review of
*Bottle Houses,* p. 65; February 20, 2006, review of
*Through Georgia's Eyes,* p. 156; September 25, 2006,
review of *Through Georgia's Eyes,* p. 68.

*School Library Journal,* July, 1998, Judith Gloyer, review
of *Play All Day,* p. 81; March, 2000, Barbara Chatton,
review of *Night Garden: Poems from the World of
Dreams,* p. 232; April, 2002, Susan Helper, review of
*Head, Body, Legs,* p. 140; July, 2003, Susan Oliver,
review of *Mrs. Chicken and the Hungry Crocodile,* p.
116; December, 2003, Margaret Bush, review of *Knock
on Wood,* p. 140; June, 2005, Steven Englefried, review of *Head, Body, Legs,* p. 56; September, 2005,
DeAnn Tabuchi, review of *Here Comes Grandma!,* p.
177; March, 2006, Carolyn Janssen, review of *Through
Georgia's Eyes,* p. 212; March, 2006, John Peters, review of *Bottle Houses,* p. 89; April, 2006, Carol L.
McKay, review of *Yellow Elephant,* p. 127.

*ONLINE*

*Art for All of Us Web site,* http://www.artforallofus.com/
(February 20, 2007), "Julie Paschkis."

*Julie Paschkis Home Page,* http://www.juliepaschkis.com
(February 20, 2007).

*KUOW Web site,* http://www.kuow.org/ (February 20,
2007), "One Artist Works for Civil Rights."

*Sculpin Web site,* http://www.sculpin.com/ (February 20,
2007), "Julie Paschkis Liberty Notes."

\*        \*        \*

## PATERSON, Diane 1946-
## (Diane Mannion)

### Personal

Born July 23, 1946, in Brooklyn, NY; daughter of A.R.
and T.E. Cole; married (divorced, 1978); married John
Mannion (a craftsman and gallery owner); children:
(first marriage) Elizabeth, Jana. *Education:* Attended
Pratt Institute, 1966-68; State University of New York,
B.A. (English). *Hobbies and other interests:* Gardening,
yoga, painting, sailing, kayaking.

### Addresses

*Home*—Southwest FL. *Office*—Mannion Gallery, 3502
N. Access Rd., Englewood, FL 34224. *E-mail*—diane@
dianepaterson.com.

### Career

Writer, illustrator, and fine artist under name Diane
Mannion. State University of New York, former instructor in English; lecturer at Vassar College.

### Member

Authors Guild, Society of Children's Book Writers and
Illustrator.

*Diane Paterson* (Photograph courtesy of Diane Paterson.)

## Writings

*SELF-ILLUSTRATED*

*The Biggest Snowstorm Ever,* Dial (New York, NY), 1974.

*Eat!,* Dial (New York, NY), 1975.

*Smile for Auntie,* Dial (New York, NY), 1976, published
as *I'll Give You Kisses,* 2003.

*If I Were a Toad,* Dial (New York, NY), 1977.

*Wretched Rachel,* Dial (New York, NY), 1978.

*The Bathtub Ocean,* Dial (New York, NY), 1979.

*Hey Cowboy,* Knopf (New York, NY), 1983.

*Soap and Suds,* Knopf (New York, NY), 1984.

*Someday,* Bradbury Press (New York, NY), 1993.

*Hurricane Wolf,* Albert Whitman (Morton Grove, IL),
2006.

*ILLUSTRATOR*

Beverly Keller, *Fiona's Bee,* Coward, McCann & Geoghegan (New York, NY), 1975.

Roger Caras, *Skunk for a Day,* Windmill Books (New
York, NY), 1975.

Robert Kraus, *Kittens for Nothing,* Windmill Books (New
York, NY), 1976.

Barbara Greenberg, *The Bravest Babysitter,* Dial Press
(New York, NY), 1977.

Roger Caras, *Coyote for a Day,* Windmill Books (New
York, NY), 1977.

Jacob and Wilhelm Grimm, *The Golden Goose,* Troll Communications (Mahwah, NJ), 1981.

*Diane Paterson illustrates the variety of jobs a parent can do in her artwork for Norma Simon's* **All Kinds of Children.** (Albert Whitman & Company, 1999. Illustrations © 1999 by Diane Paterson. Reproduced by permission.)

Beverly Keller, *Fiona's Flea,* Coward, McCann & Geoghegan (New York, NY), 1981.

Robie H. Harris, *I Hate Kisses,* Knopf (New York, NY), 1981.

*Stone Soup,* Troll Communications (Mahwah, NJ), 1981.

David Cutts, *Pinocchio and the Great Whale*, Troll Communications (Mahwah, NJ), 1982.

David Cutts, *Pinocchio and the Puppet Show*, Troll Communications (Mahwah, NJ), 1982.

David Cutts, *Pinocchio Goes to School*, Troll Communications (Mahwah, NJ), 1982.

David Cutts, *Pinocchio Meets the Cat and Fox*, Troll Communications (Mahwah, NJ), 1982.

Beverly Keller, *The Bee Sneeze,* Coward, McCann & Geoghegan (New York, NY), 1982.

Judith Graham Collins, *Josh's Scary Dad*, Abingdon (Nashville, TN), 1983.

Maureen Brett Hooper, *The Christmas Drum,* Boyds Mills Press (Honesdale, PA), 1984.

Caroline Feller Bauer, *Too Many Books!*, F. Arne (New York, NY), 1984.

Ski Michaels, *The Big Surprise,* Troll Communications (Mahwah, NJ), 1986.

Michael J. Pellowski, *The Duck Who Loved Puddles,* Troll Communications (Mahwah, NJ), 1986.

Robyn Supraner, *Kitty: A Cat's Diary,* Troll Communications (Mahwah, NJ), 1986.

Michael J. Pellowski, *Fun in the Sun,* Troll Communications (Mahwah, NJ), 1986.

Michael J. Pellowski, *The Messy Monster,* Troll Communications (Mahwah, NJ), 1986.

Erica Frost, *The Littlest Pig*, Troll Communications (Mahwah, NJ), 1986.

Laura Damon, *Fun in the Snow*, Troll Communications (Mahwah, NJ), 1988.

Kira Daniel, *Teacher*, Troll Communications (Mahwah, NJ), 1989.

Gale Clifford, *Night Animals,* Celebration Press, 1989.

David A. Adler, *You Breathe In, You Breathe Out: All about Your Lungs*, F. Watts (New York, NY), 1991.

Deborah Gould, *Camping in the Temple of the Sun*, Bradbury Press (New York, NY), 1992.

Carmen Santiago Nodar, *Abuelita's Paradise,* Albert Whtiman (Morton Grove, IL), 1992.

Carolina Ortega, *Keep the Beat,* Scott Foresman (Glenview, IL), 1993.

Janice Gibala-Broxholm, *Let Me Do It!*, Bradbury Press (New York, NY), 1993.

Maria Testa, *Thumbs up, Rico!*, Albert Whitman (Morton Grove, IL), 1994.

Joan Hoffman, *The Last Game,* School Zone Publishing (Grand Haven, MI), 1994.

Lila McGinnis, *If Daddy Only Knew,* Albert Whitman (Morton Grove, IL), 1995.

Michelle Markel, *Gracias, Rosa,* Albert Whitman (Morton Grove, IL), 1995.

Fay Robinson, *Sara's Lovely Songs,* Modern Curriculum Press (Parsippany, NJ), 1996.

Bobbi Katz, *The Story of Passover,* Random House (New York, NY), 1996.

Dorothy Corey, *You Go Away*, new edition, Albert Whitman (Morton Grove, IL), 1999.

Norma Simon, *All Kinds of Children,* Albert Whitman (Morton Grove, IL), 1999.

Kelli Kyle Dominguez, *The Perfect Piñata/La piñata perfecta,* Spanish translation by Teresa Mlawer, Albert Whitman (Morton Grove, IL), 2002.

Lisa Tucker McElroy, *Love Lizzie: Letters to a Military Mom,* Albert Whitman (Morton Grove, IL), 2005.

Illustrations have appeared in periodicals, including *Babybug* and *Ladybug.*

## Sidelights

An author and illustrator of books for younger readers, Diane Paterson is primarily noted for the pen-and-ink and watercolor illustrations she creates for books by other authors. Noting the "bright and busy" illustrations Paterson contributes to Kelli Kyle Dominguez's bilingual picture book *The Perfect Piñata/La piñata perfecta School Library Journal* reviewer Ann Welton added that the book's "signature" images of a five-year-old girl celebrating a traditional Latin-American birthday "enhance the story nicely." Similarly, her vibrantly colored illustrations for Janice Gibala-Broxholm's *Let Me Do It!* add energy to the story of an independent-minded toddler by using vibrant tones of yellow, orange, and

*A child's fear of hurricanes turns to understanding in Paterson's* **Hurricane Wolf,** *which follows one family as they wisely prepare their home for an approaching storm.* (Albert Whitman & Company, 2006. Copyright © 2006 by Diane Paterson. Reproduced by permission.)

pink to "extend the glorious confusion" created by a small child determined to go it alone. Among her many illustration projects has been a new edition of *You Go Away*, a story by Dorothy Corey that *Booklist* contributor Carolyn Phelan cited as the "picture book of choice for helping children deal with separation anxiety." Phelan credited Paterson's "bright, clearly defined" illustrations with enhancing the reissued story, while a *Horn Book* writer commended the artist for providing children with a reassuring and inclusive reading experience by contributing "cozy" images featuring a "multiethnic cast."

*Hurricane Wolf*, Paterson's original self-illustrated story, is her response to the trauma caused by a hurricane that devastated parts her native Florida in 2004. In the story, she introduces readers to Noah and his family as they wisely prepare for an approaching storm by storing food and water, shuttering windows, and finding a safe location from which to monitor the storm's progress overhead. For Noah, the howling storm sounds like the big bad wolf of Three Little Pigs fame, and reminding himself of the story's upbeat ending gives him reassurance. In framing her story, Paterson also draws on the metaphor of a wild animal as a way to help young children visualize the relative strength of gale-force winds and other meteorological manifestations of hurricanes. In her review for *Booklist*, Shelle Rosenfeld noted that *Hurricane Wolf* will "help children get through a scary experience," and *School Library Journal* contributor Angela J. Reynolds concluded that Paterson's story "presents the facts and the how and why of preparedness" in a way that avoids "being too scary."

Paterson once noted: "Sometimes I draw a character and then another and they carry on their own story which hopefully leads to a humorous situation. I illustrate all of my books and feel a close relationship between image and words. I draw words into the pictures so they are one, trying to get as close to animation as possible. I hope to keep my material humorous and imaginative to appeal to all ages."

## Biographical and Critical Sources

### PERIODICALS

*Booklist*, January 15, 1994, Hazel Rochman, review of *Let Me Do It!*, p. 936; April 15, 1994, Carolyn Phelan, review of *Thumbs up, Rico!*, p. 1536; October 1, 1994, Carolyn Phelan, review of *The Christmas Drum*, p. 333; September 1, 1999, Carolyn Phelan, review of *You Go Away*, p. 139; April 15, 2002, Linda Perkins, review of *The Perfect Piñata/La piñata perfecta*, p. 1407; September 1, 2005, GraceAnne A. DeCandido, review of *Love, Lizzie: Letters to a Military Mom*, p 145; March 1, 2006, Shelle Rosenfeld, review of *Hurricane Wolf*, p. 101.

*Bulletin of the Center for Children's Books*, April, 2006, Deborah Stevenson, review of *Hurricane Wolf*, p. 368.

*Horn Book*, January, 2000, review of *You Go Away*, p. 60.

*Kirkus Reviews*, February 15, 2002, review of *The Perfect Piñata*, p. 254; September 1, 2005, review of *Love, Lizzie*, p. 978; February 15, 2006, review of *Hurricane Wolf*, p. 189.

*Publishers Weekly*, September 7, 1992, review of *Abuelita's Paradise*, p. 96; September 19, 1994, review of *The Christmas Drum*, p. 30.

*School Library Journal*, June, 2002, Ann Welton, review of *The Perfect Piñata*, p. 128; October, 2005, Pamela K. Bomboy, review of *Love, Lizzie*, p. 120; March, 2006, Angela J. Reynolds, review of *Hurricane Wolf*, p. 200.

*ONLINE*

*Diane Paterson Home Page*, http://www.dianepaterson.com (March 8, 2007).

\*    \*    \*

# PENDZIWOL, Jean E. 1965-

## Personal

Born 1965, in Thunder Bay, Ontario, Canada; married; husband's name Richard; children: Erin, Colin, Ryan.

## Addresses

*Home*—Thunder Bay, Ontario, Canada. *E-mail*—pendzi5@hotmail.com.

## Career

Author and storyteller. Worked for a printing company and an advertising agency; freelance writer and photographer.

## Writings

*No Dragons for Tea: Fire Safety for Kids (and Dragons)*, illustrated by Martine Gourbault, Kids Can Press (Toronto, Ontario, Canada), 1999.

*Dawn Watch*, illustrated by Nicolas Debon, Douglas & McIntyre/Groundwood Books (Toronto, Ontario, Canada), 2004.

*The Red Sash*, illustrated by Nicolas Debon, Anansi/Groundwood Books (Toronto, Ontario, Canada), 2005.

*A Treasure at Sea for Dragon and Me: Water Safety for Kids (and Dragons)*, illustrated by Martine Gourbault, Kids Can Press (Toronto, Ontario, Canada), 2005.

*Once upon a Dragon: Stranger Safety for Kids (and Dragons)*, illustrated by Martine Gourbault, Kids Can Press (Toronto, Ontario, Canada), 2006.

*The Tale of Sir Dragon: Bullying Strategies for Kids (and Dragons)*, illustrated by Martine Gourbault, Kids Can Press (Toronto, Ontario, Canada), 2007.

## Sidelights

Canadian author and storyteller Jean E. Pendziwol has published a number of books for young readers, including *Dawn Watch* and *The Red Sash*. Pendziwol made her literary debut in 1999 with *No Dragons for Tea: Fire Safety for Kids (and Dragons),* "a fine non-didactic and 'non-frightening' book to use in teaching fire safety to young children," according to Dave Jenkinson in *Canadian Review of Materials*. After a young girl meets a friendly dragon at the beach, she invites her new fire-breathing friend back to her home for tea. All is well until the dragon sneezes, causing him to spew flames from his nostrils that set the girl's house ablaze. While the dragon panics and tries to hide from the fire, the little girl, who has been trained to handle emergencies, takes the necessary steps to get them both safely outdoors. *Booklist* contributor Lauren Peterson complimented Pendziwol's "lively rhyming text, which ends with a catchy fire safety poem that kids can easily memorize." Racquel Holladay, writing in *Childhood Education,* noted that the entertaining book "will definitely heighten children's awareness of fire safety."

The little girl and her amiable companion make a return appearance in *A Treasure at Sea for Dragon and Me: Water Safety for Kids (and Dragons)*. During an outing to the beach, the friends pretend to be pirates searching for buried treasure. When the dragon recklessly dives into shallow water and swims beyond the designated safety zone, the girl, her father, and a lifeguard work together to teach the creature some valuable lessons. According to *School Library Journal* reviewer Judith Constantinides, Penzivol's book addresses "an important topic for which there is a scarcity of easy material." In *Once upon a Dragon: Stranger Safety for Kids (and Dragons)* the two friends enter a fairy-tale world where they are tempted by such characters as the Big Bad Wolf and the witch from "Hansel and Gretel." Though the dragon is all too willing to accept the strangers' offerings, the little girl manages to steer him out of harm's way. "In rhyming text, this book introduces important messages about personal safety without being alarmist," noted Linda Berezowski in a review of *Once upon a Dragon* for *Resource Links*.

A girl and her father take a sailing trip across Lake Superior in *Dawn Watch,* "an evocative view of an elemental experience," according to *Booklist* contributor Gillian Engberg. As they cross the water, the pair basks in the beauty of the night sky. Just before daybreak, the father heads briefly to the cabin, leaving his daughter to keep watch for ships and lights. The youngster imagines all sorts of dangers, including pirates and sea monsters, but her fears vanish once she spies land. "The lyrical, first-person narrative quietly captures the wonder of the universe during a late-night journey," Shawn Brommer observed in *School Library Journal*.

Set in the early nineteenth century, *The Red Sash* provides a glimpse into the lives of Canadian fur traders, known as voyageurs, through the eyes of a young Metis

*A lesson on water safety is given a humorous slant in Jean E. Pendziwol's* **A Treasure at Sea for Dragon and Me,** *a picture book illustrated by Martine Gourbault.* (Illustration © 2005 Martine Gourbault. Used by permission of Kids Can Press Ltd., Toronto, Ontario, Canada.)

boy. Living near Fort William, a major British trading post, the boy longs to be just like his father, who, like all voyageurs, is a skilled and respected canoeist who can be identified by the red sash he wears. When another trader damages his canoe in a squall, the boy gets an opportunity to prove his worth. "Historically accurate, this story is full of interesting details that add to its authenticity," *School Library Journal* reviewer Robyn Walker commented. Writing in *Horn Book,* Joanna Rudge Long similarly noted that in *The Red Sash* "Pendziwol gives just enough detail for a real sense of this long-ago way of life."

## Biographical and Critical Sources

*PERIODICALS*

*Booklist,* February 1, 1999, Lauren Peterson, review of *No Dragons for Tea: Fire Safety for Kids (and Dragons),* p. 982; November 1, 2004, Gillian Engberg, review of *Dawn Watch,* p. 493; April 15, 2005, Carolyn Phelan, review of *A Treasure at Sea for Dragon and Me: Water Safety for Kids (and Dragons),* p. 1458; December 1, 2005, Hazel Rochman, review of *The Red Sash,* p. 55; May 15, 2006, Carolyn Phelan, review of *Once upon a Dragon,* p. 52.
*Canadian Review of Materials,* October 29, 1999, Dave Jenkinson, review of *No Dragons for Tea.*

*Childhood Education,* fall, 1999, Racquel Holladay, review of *No Dragons for Tea,* p. 45.

*Horn Book,* January-February, 2006, Joanna Rudge Long, review of *The Red Sash,* p. 69.

*Kirkus Reviews,* October 1, 2004, review of *Dawn Watch,* p. 966; September 1, 2005, review of *The Red Sash,* p. 980.

*Resource Links,* June, 1999, Shirley Lewis, review of *A Treasure at Sea for Dragon and Me,* p. 6; June, 2005, Linda Ludke, review of *No Dragons for Tea,* p. 8; December, 2005, Victoria Pennell, review of *The Red Sash,* p. 7; April, 2006, Linda Berezowski, review of *Once upon a Dragon,* p. 9.

*School Library Journal,* December, 2004, Shawn Brommer, review of *Dawn Watch,* p. 117; July, 2005, Judith Constantinides, review of *A Treasure at Sea for Dragon and Me,* p. 91; January, 2006, Robyn Walker, review of *The Red Sash,* p. 111; June, 2006, Lisa Gangemi Kropp, review of *Once upon a Dragon,* p. 124.

*ONLINE*

*Groundwood Books Web site,* http://www.groundwoodbooks.com/ (January 21, 2007), "Jean E. Pendziwol."

\*　　\*　　\*

# POINTS, Larry G. 1945-
## (Larry Gene Points)

## Personal

Born January 14, 1945, in Dodge City, KS; son of Gene Earl and Helen Louise Points; married Beverly Ann Watts (a school teacher and administrator) December 23, 1981; children: Kristy, Kara. *Education:* Southeast Missouri State University, B.S. (biology), 1966.

## Addresses

*Home and office*—Delmar, MD. *E-mail*—larry@seacritters.com.

## Career

Mt. Ranier National Park, Longmire, WA, park ranger, 1969-70; Hopewell Furnace National Historic Site, Elverson, PA, supervisory park ranger, 1970-74; Assateague Island National Seashore, Berlin, MD, chief of park interpretation, 1974-2001. Deputy mayor of Delman, MD. Speaker at schools. *Military service:* U.S. Army, 1967-69; served in Thailand.

## Member

Assateague Costal Trust, Mid-Atlantic Marine Education Association, Maryland Reading Association.

*Larry Points* (Photograph courtesy of Larry G. Points.)

## Awards, Honors

Conservation Award, Isaac Walton League, 1973; several agency awards from National Park Service.

## Writings

(With Andrea Jauck) *Assateague: Island of the Wild Ponies,* Macmillan (New York, NY), 1993, revised and updated edition, Sierra Press (Mariposa, CA), 1997.

(With Andrea Jauck) *Ribbons of Sand: Exploring Atlantic Beaches,* Panorama International Publications (Mariposa, CA), 1997.

(With Andrea Jauck) *Barrier Islands Are for the Birds,* Sierra Press (Mariposa, CA), 2000.

## Sidelights

In addition to his career serving as a park ranger in several prominent U.S. national parks, Larry G. Points has also published children's nature books in collaboration with fellow naturalist Andrea Jauck. In *Assateague: Island of the Wild Ponies* Points introduces readers to the beaches, marshes, forests, and coastal regions of the barrier island located off the coast of Maryland and Virginia. Based on knowledge gained while Points served as chief of Park Interpretation on the National Park Service site, the book provides an intimate view of the remote region, and features photographs—many taken by Points himself—that capture the overwhelming beauty to be seen throughout the park.

Points told *SATA:* "I grew up in Cape Girardeau, Missouri, on the Mississippi River and at the edge of the Ozarks. This afforded me the opportunity to experience the outdoors and develop interests that would lead to a career in that realm. Following graduation from my hometown college in 1966, I joined the National Park

Service and received training to be a park ranger at the Grand Canyon. Following a two-year interlude with the military, I rejoined the park service for a year of additional training at Mt. Rainier National Park in Washington state. Then I transferred east to Hopewell Furnace National Historic Site in Pennsylvania, where I served as the park's chief of interpretation and resource management. In 1974 I transferred to Assateague Island National Seashore where I spent the next twenty-seven years of my career, retiring in early 2001.

"At Assateague Island I served as the chief of park interpretation and directed the development of a wide variety of educational services. These included ranger-guided programs, children's activities, visitor centers, nature trails, audio-visual resources, and exhibits of all kinds. My professional writing began with a variety of publications intended for visitors to help them achieve understanding of park resources. In the late 1980s I embarked with a fellow park naturalist, Andrea Jauck, on the creation of an extensive series of wayside (outdoor) exhibits for Assateague Island. This work involved researching images and graphics, and writing text.

"Andrea and I worked so well together on the exhibits that we decided to privately coauthor a series of nonfiction children's books on subjects of the Atlantic seashore. We knew what interested children and their families and attempted to answer the most common questions they had. We were particularly interested in presenting photographs to support the text and are pleased to say that, in the current era of digital images and computer manipulation, the images in our books are "the real stuff": i.e., un-retouched 35mm photos actually taken by a variety of nature photographers in the field."

*Cover of* **Assateague: Island of the Wild Ponies,** *coauthored by Points and Andrea Jauck and featuring a photograph by Padraic Hughes.* (Sierra Press, 1997. Reproduced by permission.)

## Biographical and Critical Sources

*PERIODICALS*

*Booklist,* March 15, 1993, Deborah Abbott, review of *Assateague: Island of the Wild Ponies,* p. 1353.
*Childhood Education,* fall, 2000, review of *Barrier Islands Are for the Birds,* p. 45.
*School Library Journal,* June, 1993, Charlene Strickland, review of *Assateague,* p. 98.

*ONLINE*

*Larry Points Home Page,* http://www.seacritters.com (February 18, 2007).*

\*      \*      \*

## POINTS, Larry Gene
## See POINTS, Larry G.

\*      \*      \*

## POMERANTZ, Charlotte 1930-

### Personal

Born July 24, 1930, in Brooklyn, NY; daughter of Abraham L. (an attorney) and Phyllis Pomerantz; married Carl Marzani (a writer and publisher), November 12, 1966 (died December 11, 1994); children: Gabrielle Rose, David Avram. *Education:* Sarah Lawrence College, B.A., 1953.

### Addresses

*Home and office*—260 W. 21st St., New York, NY 10011.

### Career

Writer. Has worked as a salesperson, waitress, researcher, copy editor, and editor.

### Awards, Honors

Jane Addams Peace Association, Children's Book Award, 1975, for *The Princess and the Admiral,* and Honor Award, 1983, for *If I Had a Paka;* Outstanding Picture Book of the Year designation, *New York Times,* 1977, for *The Piggy in the Puddle;* International Year of the Child selection, International Board on Books for Young People, 1978, for *The Day They Parachuted Cats on Borneo;* Notable Book designation, American Library Association, for *The Tamarindo Puppy, and Other Poems;* Christopher Award, 1984, for *Posy,* and 2000, for *Thunderboom!;* Top-Ten Picture Book of the Year selection, *Boston Globe,* 1989, and Parent's Choice

***Charlotte Pomerantz*** (Photograph by Daniel Pomerantz courtesy of Charlotte Pomerantz.)

Award, 1990, both for *The Chalk Doll;* Children's Book of the Year selection, Library of Congress, 1991, for *How Many Trucks Can a Tow Truck Tow?*

## Writings

### JUVENILE FICTION

*The Bear Who Couldn't Sleep,* illustrated by Meg Wohlberg, Morrow (New York, NY), 1965.

*The Moon Pony,* illustrated by Loretta Trezzo, Young Scott Books, 1967.

*Ask the Windy Sea,* illustrated by Nancy Grossman and Anita Siegel, Young Scott Books, 1968.

*Why You Look like You Whereas I Tend to Look like Me,* illustrated by Rosemary Wells and Susan Jeffers, Young Scott Books, 1969.

*The Piggy in the Puddle,* illustrated by James Marshall, Macmillan (New York, NY), 1974, reprinted, Aladdin (New York, NY), 1989.

(Adaptor) *The Princess and the Admiral,* illustrated by Tony Chen, Addison-Wesley, 1974, reprinted, Feminist Press at the City University of New York (New York, NY), 1992.

*The Ballad of the Long-Tailed Rat* (rhyme), illustrated by Marian Parry, Macmillan (New York, NY), 1975.

*Detective Poufy's First Case; or, The Missing Battery-operated Pepper Grinder,* illustrated by Marty Norman, Addison-Wesley (Reading, MA), 1976.

*The Mango Tooth,* illustrated by Marylin Hafner, Greenwillow (New York, NY), 1977.

*The Downtown Fairy Godmother,* illustrated by Susanna Natti, Addison-Wesley (Reading, MA), 1978.

*The Tamarindo Puppy, and Other Poems* (bilingual English-Spanish), Greenwillow (New York, NY), 1979.

*Noah and Namah's Ark,* illustrated by Kelly Carson, Holt (New York, NY), 1980.

*If I Had a Paka: Poems in Eleven Languages,* illustrated by Nancy Tafuri, Greenwillow (New York, NY), 1982.

*Buffy and Albert,* illustrated by Yossi Abolafia, Greenwillow (New York, NY), 1983.

*Posy,* illustrated by Catherine Stock, Greenwillow (New York, NY), 1983.

*Whiff, Sniff, Nibble, and Chew: The Gingerbread Boy Retold* (also see below), illustrated by Monica Incisa, Greenwillow (New York, NY), 1984.

*Where's the Bear?,* illustrated by Byron Barton, Greenwillow (New York, NY), 1984, published as a board book, HarperFestival (New York, NY), 2003.

*The Half-Birthday Party,* illustrated by DyAnne Di Salvo-Ryan, Clarion (New York, NY), 1984.

*All Asleep* (lullabies), illustrated by Nancy Tafuri, Greenwillow (New York, NY), 1984.

*One Duck, Another Duck,* illustrated by José Aruego and Ariane Dewey, Greenwillow (New York, NY), 1984.

*How Many Trucks Can a Tow Truck Tow?,* illustrated by R.W. Alley, Random House (New York, NY), 1987.

*Timothy Tall Feather,* illustrated by Catherine Stock, Greenwillow (New York, NY), 1987.

*The Chalk Doll,* illustrated by Frane Lessac, HarperCollins (New York, NY), 1989.

*Flap Your Wings and Try* (rhyming verse), illustrated by Nancy Tafuri, Greenwillow (New York, NY), 1989.

*The Outside Dog,* illustrated by Jennifer Plecas, HarperCollins (New York, NY), 1992.

*You're Not My Friend,* Dial Books for Young Readers (New York, NY), 1992.

*Serena Katz,* illustrated by R.W. Alley, Macmillan (New York, NY), 1992.

*Halfway to Your House,* illustrated by Gabrielle Vincent, Greenwillow (New York, NY), 1993.

*Here Comes Henny,* illustrated by Nancy Winslow Parker, Greenwillow (New York, NY), 1994.

*Mangaboom,* illustrated by Anita Lobel, Greenwillow (New York, NY), 1997.

*You're Not My Best Friend Anymore,* illustrated by David Soman, Dial Books for Young Readers (New York, NY), 1998.

*The Mousery,* illustrated by Kurt Cyrus, Harcourt (New York, NY), 2000.

*The Birthday Letters,* illustrated by JoAnn Adinolfi, Greenwillow (New York, NY), 2000.

*Thunderboom!: Poems for Everyone,* illustrated by Rob Shepperson, Front Street Books (Asheville, NC), 2005.

*JUVENILE PLAYS*

*The Day They Parachuted Cats on Borneo: A Drama of Ecology* (play in rhyme), illustrated by José Aruego, Young Scott Books, 1971.

(Co-author and lyricist) *Eureka!*, produced in New York, NY, 1979.

*Rap, Snap: The Electric Gingerbread Boy* (adapted from *Whiff, Sniff, Nibble and Chew: The Gingerbread Boy Retold*), produced by Children's Dance Theater, 1984.

*OTHER*

(Editor) *A Quarter-Century of Un-Americana, 1938-1963: A Tragicomical Memorabilia of HUAC, House Un-American Activities Committee*, foreword by H.H. Wilson, Marzani & Munsell, 1963.

Work included in anthologies, including *Sounds of a Distant Drum*, Holt, 1967; *Read-Aloud Rhymes for the Very Young*, edited by Jack Prelutsky, Knopf, 1986; and *To the Moon and Back*, compiled by Nancy Larrick, Delacorte, 1991. Contributor to periodicals, including *Ladybug, Humpty Dumpty, New York Times Book Review, Publishers Weekly, Horn Book*, and *Ms*.

Author's work has been published in French, Japanese, and Afrikaans.

## Adaptations

*The Princess and the Admiral* was adapted for the stage and produced at public schools throughout the United States.

## Sidelights

Beginning her writing career in the mid-1960s, Charlotte Pomerantz has achieved critical and popular success in her work for children. With a number of prestigious awards to her credit, including the 1975 Jane Addams' Children's Book Award for *The Princess and the Admiral* and Christopher Awards for both *Posy* and *Thunderboom!: Poems for Everyone*, Pomerantz is known for her ability to crystallize familiar moments in evocative verse, as well as create entertaining read-alouds for young children that incorporate a multicultural perspective. Praising her poetry collection *Halfway to Your House*, Hazel Rochman noted in a *Booklist* review that Pomerantz expresses "quiet, intimate moments with a physical immediacy" in her "informal" verse. The picture book *The Birthday Letters*—in which a dog's birthday celebration is disrupted by a young guest who strays from proper pet-party decorum when she asks to bring her two gerbils—showcases its author's talent for capturing language; as Tina Hudak noted in a *School Library Journal* review, the correspondence that makes up the text of the book "reflect[s] the language structure and sentiments of children," and also provides a good jumping-off point for "discussing the topic of parties, guests, and feelings."

Born in Brooklyn, New York, Pomerantz attended Sarah Lawrence College and graduated in 1953. She worked as a salesperson, waitress, researcher, and editor before moving into writing. Although her first book, *The Bear Who Couldn't Sleep*, was published before she married and began her family, Pomerantz gained a great deal of inspiration by watching and listening to her own two children during their growing-up years. "I found increasingly that the children provide rich raw material, with the emphasis on *raw*," the author once told *SATA*. "Many years back my son, then age four, was heard to mumble, 'Fee fi fo fum, I smell the blood of an English muffin.' That started me thinking about writing a detective story. It finally became *Detective Poufy's First Case; or, The Missing Battery-operated Pepper Grinder*, published in 1976." Another book, 1977's *The Mango Tooth*, "would not have been written had my little girl not been at the age where the tooth fairy was making frequent visits," the author explained, hastening to add, however, that "the story is fiction."

Pomerantz's lighthearted approach to poetry is clearly apparent to readers of *Here Comes Henny*. In repetitive, rhyming dialogue, the author follows a dapper mother hen whose three chicks go hungry after turning up their beaks at the healthy snack provided during a family picnic. Inspired, the author told *SATA*, by the wordplay and characters in James Joyce's novel *Finnegan's Wake*,

*Pomerantz sounds out in the playful parade of noise-making poems included in* **Thunderboom!,** *a collection featuring illustrations by Rob Shepperson.* (Illustrations copyright © 2005 by Rob Shepperson. Reproduced by permission.)

Pomerantz's "appealingly silly, tonguetwisting rhyme makes [*Here Comes Henny*] . . . a rollicking read-aloud," asserted a *Publishers Weekly* contributor. Another high-energy offering that features a combined English/Spanish text, *Mangaboom* features what another *Publishers Weekly* reviewer characterized as "strong flashes of humor" along with "a clear message about self-acceptance." At nineteen feet tall and weighing in at 682 pounds, Pomerantz's beautiful, energetic protagonist is determined to make the most of her time on earth, despite the admonishment of three disapproving suitors who believe a young woman's place is at home. Praising the "gorgeous" illustrations Anita Lobel created to pair with Pomerantz's text, Rochman predicted in her *Booklist* review that "kids will enjoy the parody of fairy tale traditions" presented in *Mangaboom*.

Writing that the author's "skill in bringing language to life has never been more evident" than in the verses collected as *Thunderboom!*, *School Library Journal* reviewer Lee Bock praised Pomerantz for creating "unpredictable, joyful rhymes" that can be enjoyed by both children and adults. Featuring pen-and-ink and watercolor art by Rob Shepperson, the volume contains limericks, parodies, and longer poems among its many selections, sharing with *Here Comes Henny* a playfulness drawn from *Finnegan's Wake*. The book's themes range from formal holiday celebrations to quiet moments when one can savor the simple joys of everyday life. While Pomerantz's decision to create a poetry patchwork was questioned by a *Kirkus Reviews* writer due to its somewhat scattershot cultural references, the critic nonetheless noted the "appeal" of individual poems in *Thunderboom!*, as well as "the undeniable quality of the writing." Dubbing the book a "superb collection of clever poems," a *Midwest Book Review Online* critic predicted that *Thunderboom!* will "engage and entertain" young listeners "from first page to last."

## Biographical and Critical Sources

*PERIODICALS*

*Booklist,* October 15, 1993, Hazel Rochman, review of *Halfway to Your House,* p. 447; October 15, 1994, Ilene Cooper, review of *Here Comes Henny,* p. 438; April 1, 1997, Hazel Rochman, review of *Mangaboom,* p. 1339; April 15, 1998, Hazel Rochman, review of *You're Not My Best Friend Anymore,* p. 1450; April 1, 2006, Hazel Rochman, review of *Thunderboom!: Poems for Everyone,* p. 45.

*Chicago Tribune Book World,* November 9, 1980, review of *The Tamarindo Puppy, and Other Poems*; September 5, 1982, review of *If I Had a Parka.*

*Horn Book,* January-February, 1994, Maeve Visser Knoth, review of *The Outside Dog,* p. 68.

*Kirkus Reviews,* March 1, 2006, review of *Thunderboom!,* p. 237.

*Language Arts,* March 15, 1974, review of *The Princess and the Admiral;* February 2, 1976; February 1, 1977; September, 1977, review of *The Mango Tooth;* November 1, 1978, review of *The Downtown Fairy Godmother.*

*New York Times Book Review,* August 27, 1980, X.J. Kennedy, review of *The Tamarindo Puppy, and Other Poems,* p. 47; April 25, 1982, Ardis Kimzey, review of *If I Had a Parka,* p. 37; May 5, 1984; June 18, 1989, Kathleen Krull, review of *The Chalk Doll,* p. 35; April 10, 1994, Cynthia Zarin, review of *Halfway to Your House,* p. 35.

*Publishers Weekly,* January 25, 1993, review of *The Tamarindo Puppy, and Other Poems,* p. 88; June 20, 1994, review of *Here Comes Henny,* p. 104; October 11, 1993, review of *Halfway to Your House,* p. 87; March 31, 1997, review of *Mangaboom,* p. 74; July 31, 2000, review of *The Mousery,* p. 94.

*Saturday Review,* May 10, 1969, review of *Why You Look like You Whereas I Tend to Look like Me.*

*School Library Journal,* June, 2000, Tina Hudak, review of *The Birthday Letters,* p. 124; November, 2000, Marlene Gawron, review of *The Mousery,* p. 130; May, 2006, Lee Bock, review of *Thunderboom!,* p. 116.

*ONLINE*

*Midwest Book Review Online,* http://www.midwestbookreview.com/cbw/ (July 1, 2006), review of *Thunderboom!*

\* \* \*

# PRAP, Lila 1955-
## (Lilijana Praprotnik Zupancic)

## Personal

Born September 28, 1955, in Celje, Slovenia; married; husband's name Bori (an art therapist); children: Izidor (son). *Education:* University of Ljubljana, graduate (architecture). *Hobbies and other interests:* Reading, tennis, gardening, films, skiing.

## Addresses

*Home and office*—Smarjeta, Slovenia.

## Career

Author and illustrator. Also worked as an architect, teacher, and graphic designer.

## Awards, Honors

International Board on Books for Young People Certificate of Honor for illustration, 2002; Hans Christian Andersen Award nominee, 2006.

## Writings

### SELF-ILLUSTRATED

*Male Zivali* (title means "Little Creatures"), Mladinska Knijiga (Ljubljana, Slovania), 1999.

*Zivalske uspavanke,* Mladinska Knijiga (Ljubljana, Slovania), 2000, translation published as *Animal Lullabies,* North-South Books (New York, NY), 2006.

*Zivalska abeceda* (title means "Animal ABC"), Mladinska Knijiga (Ljubljana, Slovania), 2002.

*Zakaj?,* Mladinska Knijiga (Ljubljana, Slovania), 2003, translation published as *Why?,* Kane/Miller (La Jolla, CA), 2005.

*Animals Speak,* Mladinska Knijiga (Ljubljana, Slovania), 2004, North-South Books (New York, NY), 2006.

*1001 Stories,* Kane/Miller (La Jolla, CA), 2006.

### ILLUSTRATOR

Barbara Jean Hicks, *I Like Black and White,* Hutchinson (London, England), 2005, Tiger Tales (Wilton, CT), 2006.

Barbara Jean Hicks, *I Like Colours,* Hutchinson (London, England), 2005, published as *I Like Colors,* Tiger Tales (Wilton, CT), 2006.

## Sidelights

Slovenian children's book author and illustrator Lila Prap has illustrated numerous books for distribution in both the United States and in her Eastern European homeland. Trained as an architect, Prap's graphic style—she favors the look of brightly colored chalk on dark paper—is shown to good effect in many of her book project, among them *Animal Lullabies* and *Animals Speak.* In the latter book, first published in Slovakian, Prap pairs each animal image with the respective animal's sound as it is interpreted in over forty languages, from English to German to Chinese. While an English sheep may say "baaah," for example, as Prap shows, the same creature would be heard to say "mäh" by a German child. In *Booklist* Carolyn Phelan deemed the book "an accessible introduction to world languages," while Alexa Sandmann called Prap's illustrations "colorful and charming" in her review of *Animals Speak* for *School Library Journal.*

In *1001 Stories* Prap again creates images featuring her signature graphic art, this time pairing it with an "ingenious amalgamation of fairy tales [that] will have readers opening [the book] . . . over and over," according to a *Kirkus Reviews* critic. The work allows readers the opportunity to mix and match their wildest fairy-tale dreams; on each illustrated page there is a choice to be made that will directly alter the story's outcome. Elements of well-known fairy tales are featured throughout *1001 Stories,* as well as characters such as Little Red Riding Hood, Goldilocks and the Three Bears, and the savvy siblings Hansel and Gretel. Every reading elicits a unique version of the tale, encouraging re-reading. Prap also provides large, colorful illustrations that in-

*Lila Prap's characteristic graphic style is on full display in her multi-hued artwork for Barbara Jean Hick's* I Like Colors. (Tiger Tales, 2006. Illustrations copyright © 2005 Lila Prap. Reproduced by permission.)

corporate strong lines, creating "lively pictures" in the opinion of a reviewer for *Publishers Weekly.*

## Biographical and Critical Sources

*PERIODICALS*

*Booklist,* March 1, 2006, Carolyn Phelan, review of *Animals Speak,* p. 101; May 15, 2006, Carolyn Phelan, review of *I Like Black and White,* p. 50.

*Kirkus Reviews,* March 1, 2006, review of *1001 Stories,* p. 238; September 1, 2006, review of *Animal Lullabies,* p. 911.

*Publishers Weekly,* August 22, 2005, review of *Why?,* p. 64; January 23, 2006, review of *1001 Stories,* p. 207; May 29, 2006, review of *I Like Black and White,* p. 61.

*School Library Journal,* May, 2006, Alexa Sandmann, review of *Animals Speak,* p. 116; November, 2006, Kara Schaff Dean, review of *Animal Lullabies,* p. 108.

*ONLINE*

*Barbara Jean Hicks Web site,* http://www.barbarajeanhicks. com/ (March 4, 2007), "Lila Prap."

# Q-R

## QUALLS, Sean

### Personal

Married Selina Alko (an illustrator); children: Isaiah.

### Addresses

*Home and office*—Brooklyn, NY. *E-mail*—seanqualls@ hotmail.com.

### Career

Artist and children's book illustrator.

### Member

Society of Children's Book Writers and Illustrators.

### Awards, Honors

Silver Award, Parents' Choice, 2004, for *Powerful Words;* Blue Ribbon Award, *Bulletin of the Center for Children's Books,* 2006, for both *Dizzy* by Jonah Winter and *The Poet Slave of Cuba* by Margarita Engle; *Horn Book* Fanfare designation, 2006, and American Library Association (ALA) Notable Children's Book designation, 2007, both for *Dizzy;* Best Book for Young Adults, ALA, 2007, for *The Poet Slave of Cuba;* Christopher Award, for *How We Are Smart* by W. Nikola Lisa.

### Illustrator

Wade Hudson, *Powerful Words: More than 200 Years of Extraordinary Writing by African Americans,* Scholastic (New York, NY), 2004.

Karen English, *The Baby on the Way,* Farrar, Straus & Giroux (New York, NY), 2005.

Margarita Engle, *The Poet Slave of Cuba: A Biography of Juan Francisco Manzano,* Henry Holt (New York, NY), 2006.

W. Nikola-Lisa, *How We Are Smart,* Lee & Low (New York, NY), 2006.

Jonah Winter, *Dizzy,* Arthur A. Levine Books (New York, NY), 2006.

Carole Boston Weatherford, *Before John Was a Jazz Giant,* Henry Holt (New York, NY), 2008.

Catherine Clinton, *Phillis's Big Tets,* Houghton Mifflin (Boston, MA), 2008.

### Sidelights

Sean Qualls had an auspicious start to his career in children's-book illustration, earning several awards with only a few publications to his credit. At the beginning of his career, Qualls garnered two Blue Ribbon citations from the *Bulletin of the Center for Children's Books,* an accomplishment that was cited as "a little un-

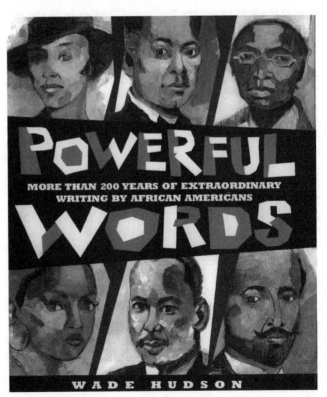

*Cover of Wade Hudson's* Powerful Words, *which features Sean Qualls' equally powerful images.* (Jacket art © 2003 by Sean Qualls. Reprinted by permission of Scholastic, Inc.)

*Cover of Margarita Engle's* **The Poet Slave of Cuba,** *an award-winning picture book featuring Qualls' illustrations.* (Illustration © 2006 by Sean Qualls. Reprinted by permission of Henry Holt and Company, LLC.)

usual" by the periodical's editor, Deborah Stevenson. Stevenson was also quick to add, however, that Qualls was honored as a result of his "serious craftsmanship and original style" that combines acrylic paints with other artistic media. Referencing his work for such books as *Powerful Words: More than 200 Years of Extraordinary Writing by African Americans* by Wade Hudson and *The Baby on the Way* by Karen English, Stevenson summarized Qualls' unique collage artwork as "sometimes crisp and close-cropped . . . and sometimes adding subtle tracery to backgrounds." In a joint online interview with wife and fellow illustrator Selina Alko for *AltPick.com,* Qualls commented that his art work is predominantly "about emotion and atmosphere. . . . I try to capture a feeling and perhaps not tangible things like music and a character's history." In the same interview, the artist and illustrator noted that his inspiration comes from "memories of my childhood and a sense of nostalgia," as well as from the works of well-known artists such as Jacob Lawrence and Romare Bearden.

Among Qualls' award-winning illustration projects is *The Poet Slave of Cuba: A Biography of Juan Francisco Manzano.* Featuring a rhyming text by Margarita Engle and based on the childhood of the noted Cuban

poet, *The Poet Slave of Cuba* contains high-contrast black-and-white illustrations. Hazel Rochman, writing in *Booklist,* noted that Qualls' charcoal drawings "express Juan's suffering and strength," while Carol Jones Collins wrote in her *School Library Journal* review that Qualls' visual works provide readers with a "suitably stark and compelling" counterpoint to Manzano's life story.

## Biographical and Critical Sources

*PERIODICALS*

*Black Issues Book Review,* Suzanne Rust, "Learning as We Climb: Stories about the Civil Rights Movement for Young Readers," p. 58.
*Booklist,* February 15, 2004, Carolyn Phelan, review of *Powerful Words: More than 200 Years of Extraordinary Writing by African Americans,* p. 1068; October 1, 2005, Hazel Rochman, review of *The Baby on the Way,* p. 62; February 15, 2006, Hazel Rochman, review of *The Poet Slave of Cuba: A Biography of Juan Francisco Manzano,* p. 95.
*Horn Book,* July-August, 2006, Lelac Almagor, review of *The Poet Slave of Cuba,* p. 459.
*Kirkus Reviews,* October 1, 2005, review of *The Baby on the Way,* p. 1079; March 15, 2006, review of *The Poet Slave of Cuba,* p. 289.
*New York Times Book Review,* November 13, 2005, review of *The Baby on the Way,* p. L30.
*Publishers Weekly,* October 31, 2005, review of *The Baby on the Way,* p. 55; April 17, 2006, review of *The Poet Slave of Cuba,* p. 190.
*School Library Journal,* February, 2004, Mary N. Oluonye, review of *Powerful Words,* p. 164; November, 2005, Mary N. Oluonye, review of *The Baby on the Way,* p. 89; April, 2006, Carol Jones Collins, review of *The Poet Slave of Cuba,* p. 154; Joy Fleishhacker, June, 2006, review of *How We Are Smart,* p. 182.

*ONLINE*

*AltPick.com,* http://altpick.com/ (February 20, 2007), interview with Qualls and Selina Alko.
*Bulletin of the Center for Children's Books Online,* http://bccb.lis.uiuc.edu/ (February 20, 2007), Maggie Hommel, review of *The Poet Slave of Cuba;* Deborah Stevenson, "Rising Star: Sean Qualls."
*Sean Qualls Home Page,* http://www.seanqualls.com (February 20, 2007).
*ZoomInfo.com,* http://www.zoominfo.com/ (February 20, 2007), "Sean Qualls."

\*     \*     \*

# RADUNSKY, Vladimir

## Personal

Born in USSR (now Russia); immigrated to United States, 1982; married; wife's name Eugenia (an illustrator).

## Addresses

*Home*—New York, NY; Rome, Italy. *E-mail*—ooshik@earthlink.net.

## Career

Author and illustrator. Also worked as a book designer.

## Writings

*SELF-ILLUSTRATED*

(With wife, Eugenia Radunsky) *Square, Triangle, Round, Skinny: Four Books in a Box,* Holt (New York, NY), 1992.

(With Eugenia Radunsky) *Yucka Drucka Droni,* Scholastic (New York, NY), 1998.

(With Chris Raschka) *Table Manners: The Edifying Story of Two Friends Whose Discovery of Good Manners Promises Them a Glorious Future,* Candlewick Press (Cambridge, MA), 2001.

*Manneken Pis: A Simple Story of a Boy Who Peed on a War,* Atheneum (New York, NY), 2002.

*Ten: A Wonderful Story,* Viking (New York, NY), 2002.

*One: A Nice Story about an Awful Braggart,* Viking (New York, NY), 2003.

(With Chris Raschka) *Boy Meets Girl/Girl Meets Boy,* Seuil Chronicle (San Francisco, CA), 2004.

*The Mighty Asparagus,* Harcourt (Orlando, FL), 2004.

*What Does Peace Feel Like?,* Atheneum (New York, NY), 2004.

*I Love You Dude,* translated by Eugenia Radunsky, Gulliver Books (Orlando, FL), 2005.

(With others) *Why Did the Chicken Cross the Road?,* Penguin (New York, NY), 2006.

*ILLUSTRATOR*

(With Robert Rayevsky) Adele Vernon, *The Riddle,* Dodd, Mead (New York, NY), 1987.

Samuel Marshak, *The Pup Grew Up!,* translated from the Russian by Richard Pevear, Holt (New York, NY), 1989.

Samuel Marshak, *Hail to Mail,* translated from the Russian by Richard Pevear, Holt (New York, NY), 1990.

Daniil Kharms, *The Story of a Boy Named Will, Who Went Sledding down a Hill,* translated from the Russian by Jamey Gambrell, North-South Books (New York, NY), 1993.

Bill Martin, Jr., *The Maestro Plays,* Holt (New York, NY), 1994.

Jamey Gambrell, *Telephone,* North-South Books (New York, NY), 1996.

Edward Lear, *An Edward Lear Alphabet,* HarperCollins (New York, NY), 1999.

Joseph Brodsky, *Discovery,* Farrar, Straus (New York, NY), 1999.

Woody Guthrie, *Howdi Do,* Candlewick Press (Cambridge, MA), 2000.

Woody Guthrie, *Bling Blang,* Candlewick Press (Cambridge, MA), 2000.

Woody Guthrie, *My Dolly,* Candlewick Press (Cambridge, MA), 2001.

Bill Martin, Jr., *"Fire! Fire!" Said Mrs. McGuire,* Harcourt (Orlando, FL), 2006.

Mikhail Baryshnikov, *Because . . .,* Atheneum (New York, NY), 2007.

Mem Fox, *Where the Giant Sleeps,* Harcourt (Orlando, FL), 2007.

## Sidelights

Born in the former Soviet Union, Vladimir Radunsky is the author and illustrator of a number of critically acclaimed works for young readers. "Each of Radunsky's picture books is a delightfully off-kilter pastiche that sets off an energetic interplay of vibrant colors, flat perspectives and vaudeville-esque characters," remarked a critic in *Publishers Weekly*. "Skirting the thin line between the whimsical and the absurd," the critic added, "Radunsky's work is almost guaranteed to pique the curiosity of young readers and draw appreciative smiles from adults."

In addition to creating original, self-illustrated texts, Radunsky, a former book designer, has also created art for books by writers as diverse as Edward Lear, Joseph Brodsky, and Woody Guthrie. In *The Story of a Boy Named Will, Who Went Sledding down a Hill,* a cumulative poem by Daniil Kharms, a youngster careens down a snowy slope, picking up an unlikely set of passengers along the way. Radunsky's "oil and acrylic paintings accentuate the hurtling motion," noted a *Publishers Weekly* contributor. A clown-like figure attempts to coax sound from more than a dozen musical instruments in *The Maestro Plays,* a story written by Bill Martin, Jr. Radunsky's "bright collage-style artwork is cleverly executed and deceptively simple," stated *Booklist* reviewer Ilene Cooper in an appraisal of Martin's book.

In 1992, Radunsky published his first self-illustrated work, *Square, Triangle, Round, Skinny: Four Books in a Box,* a book-length collaboration between the illustrator and his wife, Eugenia Radunsky. The pair also combine their talents on *Yucka Drucka Droni,* a tongue-twister about a trio of oddly named brothers who marry a trio of oddly named sisters. "The giddiness of the art speeds the momentum of the rhyme, spinning out its unabashedly silly pleasures," commented a *Publishers Weekly* critic. Radunsky has also teamed with Chris Raschka on *Table Manners: The Edifying Story of Two Friends Whose Discovery of Good Manners Promises Them a Glorious Future.* In the work, serious-minded Chester and his sidekick Dudunya discuss the finer points of etiquette. According to a contributor in *Publishers Weekly,* "Raschka's lissome brush strokes revel in free-spiritedness, and Radunsky's crazy-quilt collages and casual swats of paint lack even a trace of fussiness."

*In* The Mighty Asparagus *author/illustrator Vladimir Radunsky recounts a time when one particular vegetable grew and grew, until it towered as high as an oak tree.* (Copyright © 2004 by Vladimir Radunsky. Reproduced by permission of Harcourt, Inc.)

Inspired by a famous statue located in the city of Brussels, Belgium, *Manneken Pis: A Simple Story of a Boy Who Peed on a War* retells a Belgian legend. After a military battle moves into his town, a youngster becomes separated from his parents. Lonely and frightened, the boy also has to urinate; he climbs atop a wall and accidentally relieves himself on the combatants below; their shock and amazement quickly turn to laughter. "Radunsky tells the tale simply and well, so children will come away understanding the message of peace," noted *Booklist* reviewer Ilene Cooper. "It is hard to imagine anyone being able to pull this very odd offering off," a *Kirkus Reviews* critic stated, "but Radunsky manages to do just that."

Folk tales and tall tales are at the core of several other books by Radunsky. *The Mighty Asparagus* is based on an account of events that took place in sixteenth-century Russia, and, in folktale fashion, an armadillo couple become parents to a host of newborns in *Ten: A Wonderful Story.* Reviewing the author's self-illustrated book, *Booklist* contributor Michael Cart praised "the antic nature of Radunsky's collage art and the energetic, reckless way he places it on the page." In a sequel, titled *One: A Nice Story about an Awful Braggart,* baby armadillo number Six proves to be less than humble. A

critic in *Kirkus Reviews* described the work as "another verbal and visual blast laced with silliness and affection."

In Radunsky's unusual picture book *I Love You Dude,* a blue elephant leaps off a wall of graffiti and embarks on a search for happiness. "This odd story of acceptance and finding one's place is accompanied by Radunsky's quirky artwork, expertly rendered in mixed media and collage," noted *School Library Journal* contributor Angela J. Reynolds in a review of the 2005 work, which features a text translated by Radunsky's wife.

## Biographical and Critical Sources

*PERIODICALS*

*Booklist,* February 1, 1998, John Peters, review of *Yucka Drucka Droni,* p. 923; November 1, 1994, Ilene Cooper, review of *The Maestro Plays,* p. 507; December 15, 1996, Michael Cart, review of *Telephone,* p. 729; June 1, 1997, Sue-Ellen Beauregard, review of *The Maestro Plays,* p. 1728; April 1, 1999, John Peters, review of *An Edward Lear Alphabet,* p. 1417; March 15, 2000, Gillian Engberg, review of *Howdi Do,* p. 1381; January 1, 2002, John Peters, review of *Table Manners: The Edifying Story of Two Friends Whose Discovery of Good Manners Promises Them a Glorious Future,* p. 867; October 15, 2002, Ilene Cooper, review of *Manneken Pis: A Simple Story of a Boy Who Peed on a War,* p. 413; November 15, 2002, Michael Cart, review of *Ten: A Wonderful Story,* p. 612; November 15, 2003, Terry Glover, review of *One: A Nice Story about an Awful Braggart,* p. 602; May 15, 2004, Jennifer Mattson, review of *The Mighty Asparagus,* p. 1620; November 1, 2004, Hazel Rochman, review of *What Does Peace Feel Like?,* p. 487; December 1, 2005, Hazel Rochman, review of *I Love You Dude,* p. 56; May 1, 2006, Michael Cart, review of *"Fire! Fire!" Said Mrs. McGuire,* p. 92.

*Canadian Review of Materials,* November 26, 1999, Janice Foster, review of *Yucka Drucka Droni.*

*Entertainment Weekly,* August 19, 1994, Michele Landsberg, review of *The Maestro Plays,* p. 74.

*Horn Book,* March-April, 1994, Lolly Robinson, review of *The Story of a Boy Named Will, Who Went Sledding down the Hill,* p. 191; March-April, 1995, Lolly Robinson, review of *The Maestro Plays,* p. 186; September-October, 2002, Roger Sutton, review of *Manneken Pis,* p. 557.

*Kirkus Reviews,* October 1, 2002, review of *Table Manners,* p. 1431; July 1, 2002, review of *Manneken Pis,* p. 961; August 15, 2002, review of *Ten,* p. 1232; October 1, 2003, review of *One,* p. 1229; August 1, 2004, review of *Boy Meets Girl/Girl Meets Boy,* p. 748; November 1, 2004, review of *What Does Peace Feel Like?,* p. 1046; October 1, 2005, review of *I Love You Dude,* p. 1087; April 15, 2006, review of *"Fire! Fire!" Said Mrs. McGuire,* p. 410.

*Liverpool Echo* (Liverpool, England), February 22, 2003, Janet Tansley, review of *Manneken Pis,* p. 138.

*Publishers Weekly,* September 28, 1990, review of *Hail to Mail,* p. 100; August 23, 1993, review of *The Story of a Boy Named Will, Who Went Sledding down the Hill,* p. 70; August 8, 1994, review of *The Maestro Plays,* p. 426; November 18, 1996, review of *Telephone,* p. 74; January 19, 1998, review of *Yucka Drucka Droni,* p. 376; February 16, 1998, interview with Radunsky, p. 119; April 26, 1999, review of *An Edward Lear Alphabet,* p. 81; October 18, 1999, review of *Discovery,* p. 80; March 27, 2000, review of *Howdi Do,* p. 79; August 28, 2000, review of *Bling Blang,* p. 82; October 29, 2001, review of *Table Manners,* p. 62; June 24, 2002, review of *Manneken Pis,* p. 55; September 23, 2002, review of *Ten,* p. 72; September 28, 1992, review of *Square, Triangle, Round, Skinny: Four Books in a Box,* p. 78; November 10, 2003, review of *One,* p. 60; May 10, 2004, review of *The Mighty Asparagus,* p. 58; June 14, 2004, Sally Lodge, "All Things Asparagus," p. 32; August 30, 2004, review of *Boy Meets Girl/Girl Meets Boy,* p. 53; December 20, 2004, review of *What Does Peace Feel Like?,* p. 57; August 29, 2005, review of *I Love You Dude,* p. 55; May 15, 2006, review of *"Fire! Fire!" Said Mrs. McGuire,* p. 70.

*School Library Journal,* June, 2000, Barbara Scotto, review of *Howdi Do,* p. 132; June, 2001, Martha Topol, review of *My Dolly,* p. 116; November, 2001, Kathleen Whalin, review of *Table Manners,* p. 134; September, 2002, Linda Ludke, review of *Ten,* p. 204; December, 2002, Melissa Yurechko, review of *Manneken Pis,* p. 106; October, 2003, Kathy Krasniewicz, review of *One,* p. 134; July, 2004, Liza Graybill, review of *The Mighty Asparagus,* p. 86; November, 2004, Marie Orlando, review of *Boy Meets Girl/Girl Meets Boy,* p. 116; January, 2005, Blair Christolon, review of *What Does Peace Feel Like?,* p. 113; October, 2005, Angela J. Reynolds, review of *I Love You Dude,* p. 125; June, 2006, Susan Weitz, review of *"Fire! Fire!" Said Mrs. McGuire,* p. 138.

*New York Times Book Review,* January 17, 1998, review of *The Riddle,* p. 28; December 16, 2001, review of *Table Manners,* p. 20; November 17, 2002, review of *Ten,* p. 45; September 11, 2005, Emily Jenkins, review of *I Love You Dude,* p. 18.

*Sunday Times* (London, England), February 16, 2003, Nicolette Jones, review of *Manneken Pis,* p. 47.

*ONLINE*

*Vladimir Radunsky Home Page* http://www.vladimirradunsky.com (January 25, 2007).*

\*    \*    \*

# RODRIGUEZ, Christina 1981-

## Personal

Born August, 1981, in Lakenheath, England; daughter of Filiverto G. and Vernia Rodriguez; married. *Education:* Rhode Island School of Design, B.F.A. (illustration), 2003.

*Christina Rodriguez* (Photograph by Lower Studio courtesy of Christina Rodriguez.)

## Addresses

*Home and office*—Stillwater, MN. *E-mail*—mail@christinarodriguez.com.

## Career

Freelance illustrator and designer. Art instructor for after-school, summer, and private programs, 2003—.

## Member

Society of Children's Book Writers and Illustrators (illustration coordinator for Minnesota chapter, beginning 2006), Minnesota Society of Children's Book Writers and Illustrators.

## Illustrator

*PICTURE BOOKS*

Bobby Jackson, *Boon the Raccoon and Easel the Weasel,* Multicultural Publications (Akron, OH), 2005.

Anilu Bernardo, *Un dia con mis tias/A Day with My Aunts,* Piñata Books (Houston, TX), 2006.

Ada Gonzalez, *Mayte and the Bogeyman,* Piñata Books (Houston, TX), 2006.

Diane Gonzalez Bertrand, *We Are Cousins/Somos primos,* Piñata Books (Houston, TX), 2007.

Tracy Nelson Maurer, *Storm Codes,* Finney Co. (Lakeville, MN), 2007.

## Sidelights

Born overseas to multicultural parents, Christina Rodriguez grew up as an "Air Force brat," moving from place to place. As she told *SATA,* "As a child I loved to draw and paint, and wherever I lived I excelled in my art classes. Upon graduation from high school, I was awarded a generous scholarship to the Rhode Island School of Design. There I trained in many different art mediums, eventually finding my niche in a mixture of watercolor, watercolor pencils, and gouache. In 2003 I earned a fine-arts degree in illustration.

"Currently I work as a freelance illustrator and designer for many clients nationwide. Reviewers have described my painting style as bold, vibrant, and full of detail, highlighted with an old-fashioned sense of simplified realism and strong outlines. In addition to illustrating children's books, I dabble in graphic design, creating items such as note cards for nature centers and wedding invitation ensembles.

"In my spare time I enjoy cooking authentic Mexican cuisine, volunteering as illustrator coordinator with the Minnesota chapter of the Society of Children's Book Writers and Illustrators, hula-hooping, and hiking along the St. Croix River, near the home I share with my husband and dog in historic Stillwater, Minnesota."

## Biographical and Critical Sources

*PERIODICALS*

*Kirkus Reviews,* March 1, 2006, review of *Mayte and the Bogeyman,* p. 230; October 15, 2006, review of *Un dia con mis tias/A Day with My Aunts,* p. 1065.

*School Library Journal,* June, 2006, Maria Otero-Boisvert, review of *Mayte and the Bogeyman,* p. 144; October, 2006, Maria Otero-Boisvert, review of *Un dia con mis tias/A Day with My Aunts,* p. 144.

*ONLINE*

*Christina Rodriguez Home Page,* http://www.christinarodriguez.com (March 2, 2007).*

\*          \*          \*

## ROSENTHAL, Amy Krouse 1965-

## Personal

Born April 29, 1965, in Chicago, IL; married; children: three. *Education:* Tufts University, graduated; attended Sorbonne, University of Paris.

## Addresses

*Home*—Chicago, IL. *Agent*—Amy Rennert, 98 Main St., No. 302, Tiburon, CA 94920. *E-mail*—missamykr@yahoo.com; amy@encyclopediaofanordinarylife.com.

## Career

Writer, author of books for children and adults, and radio commentator. Freelance writer, beginning 1997; *Writers' Block Party,* Chicago Public Radio, Chicago, IL, host; contributor to radio programs *All Things Considered* and *Morning Edition,* National Public Radio. Creator of "Amy K." note cards. Former copywriter for advertising agencies, including McConnaughy Stein Schmidt Brown, Chicago, IL; Goodby, Berlin & Silverstein, San Francisco, CA; Zechman & Associates, Chicago; Mitchiner Ross & Kahn, Chicago; and Foote, Cone & Belding, Chicago. Founder of Boy & Girl Advertising, Chicago; co-founder of 272 Productions (T-shirt company), Chicago.

## Writings

*PICTURE BOOKS*

*Little Pea,* illustrated by Jen Corace, Chronicle Books (San Francisco, CA), 2005.

*Cookies: Bite-size Life Lessons,* illustrated by Jane Dyer, HarperCollins (New York, NY), 2006.

*One of Those Days,* illustrated by Rebecca Doughty, Putnam (New York, NY), 2006.

(With Tom Lichtenheld) *The OK Book,* HarperCollins (New York, NY), 2007.

*Al Pha's Bet,* illustrated by Delphine Durand, Putnam (New York, NY), 2007.

(With Tom Lichtenheld) *It's Not Fair,* HarperCollins (New York, NY), 2008.

*Little Hoot,* illustrated by Jen Corace, Chronicle Books (San Francisco, CA), 2008.

*Spoon,* illustrated by Scott Magoon, Hyperion (New York, NY), 2008.

*Christmas Cookies,* illustrated by Jane Dyer, HarperCollins (New York, NY), 2008.

*FOR ADULTS*

*The Book of Eleven: An Itemized Collection of Brain Lint,* Andrews McMeel (Kansas City, MO), 1998.

*The Same Phrase Describes My Marriage and My Breasts: Before the Kids, They Used to Be Such a Cute Couple,* Andrews McMeel (Kansas City, MO), 1999.

*The Mother's Guide to the Meaning of Life: What I've Learned in My Never-ending Quest to Become a Dalai Mama,* Rodale Press (Emmaus, PA), 2001.

*Encyclopedia of an Ordinary Life,* illustrated by Jeffrey Middleton, Crown (New York, NY), 2005.

Also author of gift books, including *The Belly Book: A Nine-Month Journal for You and Your Growing Belly,* 2006, and *Karma Checks* and *The Birthday Book,* both 2007. Columnist and contributor to periodicals, including *Might, Newsweek, New York Times, Family Life, Utne Reader, O, the Oprah Magazine, Parenting,* and *Hallmark* magazine.

## Sidelights

Chicago-based freelance writer and commentator Amy Krouse Rosenthal is an author of books for children and adults, a contributor to National Public Radio, and the host of *Writer's Block Party,* her own radio show. A former advertising copywriter, Rosenthal has also co-founded her own T-shirt company, created humorous note cards, and published a fanzine. "My life is sort of a smorgasbord," Rosenthal admitted to Kathy DeSalvo in *Shoot.* "My basic drive to do anything is just a love of making things. There's something about having an idea and watching it turn into something tangible that people connect with—be it a refrigerator magnet, a print ad, a commercial or a T-shirt. I just like that whole

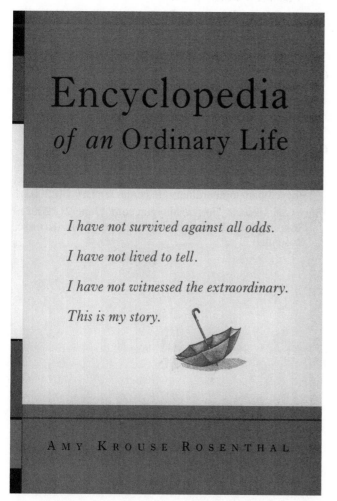

**Cover of Amy Krouse Rosenthal's unusual and unusually revealing memoir** Encyclopedia of an Ordinary Life, *featuring illustrations by Jeffrey Middleton.* (Three Rivers Press, 2005. Reproduced by permission of Crown Publishers, a division of Random House, Inc.)

process." In *Encyclopedia of an Ordinary Life,* Rosenthal gives her creativity full rein by compiling lists, charts, and vignettes in an encyclopedia format. Weaving together her sometimes wry, sometimes poignant, and oftentimes humorous observations and ruminations, Rosenthal creates a work that *Booklist* contributor Leon Wagner described as an "immensely readable" memoir sure to prompt readers to reflect on "how much there is to celebrate in their own ordinary lives."

*Little Pea,* Rosenthal's first children's book, introduces "a decidedly atypical family . . . facing a familiar dinnertime issue" and treats readers to "a delicious final twist" in the process, according to a critic for *Kirkus Reviews.* Little Pea enjoys most everything about his life, especially rolling down hills with his friends and being launched off spoons by Papa Pea. The one thing he hates, though, is candy, which his parents insist he eat every night for supper, as all good peas do. Finally, at one meal Little Pea manages to choke down five sweets and earns a heaping bowl of his favorite dessert—spinach! "Young readers will take glee in Little Pea's absurd yet familiar predicament," noted a *Publishers Weekly* contributor, the critic adding that "parents will surely identify with Mama and Papa Pea's universal struggle." Writing in *School Library Journal,* Wendy Woodfill commented that "picky eaters will enjoy the subtle humor of this topsy-turvy tale."

Rosenthal's first *New York Times* bestselling title, the children's book *Cookies: Bite-size Life Lessons* dishes up a "deliciously charming collection of defined and illustrated vocabulary words that serve as gentle guides to etiquette," according to a *Publishers Weekly* critic. As her cast of children and animal characters busy themselves with making and eating cookies, Rosenthal develops character-building concepts such as patience, pride, modesty and respect. On one spread, for example, a tousled redhead mixes a bowl of batter while his rabbit and dog pals help by pouring in some chocolate chips to illustrate cooperation. According to *School Library Journal* contributor Judith Constantinides, Rosenthal's decision to use "cookies to explain the concepts is a brilliant idea and works well on a child's level." "Cookies provide the framework for this clever book," observed Ilene Cooper in *Booklist,* "but the focus is really on the lessons to be learned about life."

In *One of Those Days* Rosenthal "enumerates ways in which a child's happiness can be squelched by a rotten day," observed *School Library Journal* reviewer Gloria Koster. Rosenthal identifies, in a humorous manner, twenty-two downer scenarios that are familiar to children, such as "Keep Spilling Stuff Day," "Not Big Enough Day," and "Answer to Everything Is No Day." "Reading this picture book aloud is a sure way to get children talking about some of 'those days,'" noted *Booklist* contributor Carolyn Phelan. Reviewing the

*While things may not always go your way, they don't go wrong forever, as Rosenthal reminds readers in* One of Those Days, *a picture book illustrated by Rebecca Doughty.* (Illustrations copyright © 2006 by Rebecca Doughty. Reproduced by permission of G.P. Putnam's Sons, a division of Penguin Putnam Books for Young Readers.)

work in *Horn Book,* Kitty Flynn called *One of Those Days* "a sympathetic reminder that no matter how bad they seem, those days don't last forever."

## Biographical and Critical Sources

### PERIODICALS

*Booklist,* February 15, 2005, Leon Wagner, review of *Encyclopedia of an Ordinary Life,* p. 1057; April 1, 2006, Ilene Cooper, review of *Cookies: Bite-size Life Lessons,* p. 43; June 1, 2006, Carolyn Phelan, review of *One of Those Days,* p. 89.

*Bulletin of the Center for Children's Books,* September, 2006, Karen Coats, review of *Cookies,* p. 31, and *One of Those Days,* p. 32.

*Chicago,* March, 2005, Claire Zulkey, "'A' Is for Amy," p. 23.

*Horn Book,* May-June, 2006, Kitty Flynn, review of *One of Those Days,* p. 302.

*Kirkus Reviews,* May 1, 2005, review of *Little Pea,* p. 545; April 15, 2006, review of *Cookies,* p. 414.

*Publishers Weekly,* October 18, 2004, review of *Encyclopedia of an Ordinary Life,* p. 54; May 9, 2005, review of *Little Pea,* p. 69; June 5, 2006, review of *Cookies,* p. 62.

*School Library Journal,* May, 2005, Wendy Woodfill, review of *Little Pea,* p. 95; May, 2006, Gloria Koster, review of *One of Those Days,* p. 103, and Judith Constantinides, review of *Cookies,* p. 116.

*Shoot,* January 14, 1994, Kathy DeSalvo, "Renaissance Woman," p. 26; September 23, 1994, Michael Clark, "Channel Surfing," p. 52.

*Writer's Digest,* September, 2005, Marnie Engel Hayutin, review of *Encyclopedia of an Ordinary Life,* p. 31.

### ONLINE

*Amy Krouse Rosenthal Home Page,* http://www.mommy-mommy.com (January 21, 2007).

*CNN Online,* http://www.cnn.com/ (March 3, 2005), Kelly Gyenes, "An 'Ordinary Life' Not So Ordinary."

*Encyclopedia of an Ordinary Life Web site,* http://www.encyclopediaofanordinarylife.com/ (January 21, 2007).

*Shiny Gun Web site,* http://shinygun.com/ (June 21, 2002), Samantha Bornemann, "Q&A with Amy Krouse Rosenthal."

# S

## SCHOENHERR, Ian

### Personal

Son of John Schoenherr (a children's book illustrator). *Education:* Cooper Union, B.A. *Hobbies and other interests:* Researching the life and collecting the works of Howard Pyle.

### Addresses

*Home and office*—Woodside, NY. *Agent*—c/o Marcia Wernick, Sheldon Fogelman Agency, Inc., 10 E. 40th St., New York, NY 10016. *E-mail*—ian@ianschoenherr. com.

### Career

Children's book illustrator and author. Creator of maps and artwork for book jackets and editorial projects. *Exhibitions:* Works exhibited in Society of Illustrators annual exhibitions, 1999, 2005.

### Awards, Honors

First prize, Marion Vannett Ridgway Award, 1993, for *Newf.*

### Writings

SELF-ILLUSTRATED

*Pip & Squeak,* Greenwillow Books (New York, NY), 2007.

ILLUSTRATOR; FOR CHILDREN

Marie Killilea, *Newf,* Philomel Books (New York, NY), 1992.

Jean Karl, *America Alive: A History,* Philomel Books (New York, NY), 1994.

Cristina Kessler, *One Night: A Story from the Desert,* Philomel Books (New York, NY), 1995.

Amy Littlesugar, *Marie in Fourth Position: The Story of Degas's "The Little Dancer,"* Philomel Books (New York, NY), 1996.

Amy Littlesugar, *Jonkonnu: A Story from the Sketchbook of Winslow Homer,* Philomel Books (New York, NY), 1997.

Brian Jacques, *Castaways of the Flying Dutchman,* Philomel Books (New York, NY), 2001.

Miriam Schlein, *Little Raccoon's Big Question,* Greenwillow Books (New York, NY), 2004.

Sheldon Harnick, *Sunrise, Sunset,* HarperCollins (New York, NY), 2005.

Lisa Westberg Peters, *Sleepyhead Bear,* Greenwillow Books (New York, NY), 2006.

### Sidelights

An illustrator whose credits include *Newf* by Marie Killilea and *Marie in Fourth Position* by Amy Littlesugar, Ian Schoenherr creates detailed images that have been described as "remarkably lifelike" by a *Kirkus Reviews* critic in an assessment of Schoenherr's artwork for Lisa Westberg Peters' *Sleepyhead Bear,* The same critic also noted that the artist's talent for creating "spot-on facial expressions make Schoenherr's illustrations shine." Schoenherr's realistic images also capture the gentleness that is present in each story he illustrates. For example, a *Publishers Weekly* reviewer observed that Schoenherr's paintings for Miriam Schlein's picture book *Little Raccoon's Big Question* "exude a luxuriant, reassuring feel" and reflect the artist's "wonderful sense of volume and space."

Growing up in New Jersey, Schoenherr was surrounded by an array of animals—including a turtle, birds, cats, and dogs—as well as the never-ending supply of art materials made available by his father, Caldecott award-winning illustrator John Schoenherr. As Ian Schoenherr recalled to *Publishers Weekly* interviewer Diane Patrick, his father "wouldn't get on my back about appropriating his materials. Every now and then I'd get my own

sketchbook, but usually I'd use his, and take it over completely." In addition to following in his father's footsteps, Schoenherr keeps a studio in the same house his great-grandparents bought in 1920. As he mentioned on his home page, his work space "is crowded with books, furniture, costumes, relics, and files"; despite the clutter—or perhaps because of it—he still draws with the same vigor of his childhood days. In 2007 he expanded into writing with the self-illustrated picture book *Pip & Squeak,* which share with readers a mouse-eye-view of winter. Schoenherr's "briskly succinct text" pairs well with "action-packed" illustrations, according to a *Kirkus Reviews* writer, the critic adding that the art in *Pip & Squeak* demonstrates "a nimble handling of color, texture, perspective and momentum."

## Biographical and Critical Sources

*PERIODICALS*

*Booklist,* March 1, 2001, GraceAnne A. DeCandido, review of *Castaways of the Flying Dutchman,* p. 1271; April 15, 2004, Jennifer Mattson, review of *Little Raccoon's Big Question,* p. 1449; July, 1995, Janice Del Negro, review of *One Night: A Story from the Desert,* p. 1882; January 1, 1998, Carolyn Phelan, review of *Jonkonnu,* p. 824; December 1, 2005, Jennifer Mattson, review of *Sunrise, Sunset,* p. 50; May 15, 2006, Hazel Rochman, review of *Sleepyhead Bear,* p. 52.

*Horn Book,* March, 2001, review of *Castaways of the Flying Dutchman,* p. 208.

*Instructor,* April, 1997, Judy Freeman, review of *Marie in Fourth Position: The Story of Degas,* p. 24.

*Kirkus Reviews,* February 15, 2004, review of *Little Raccoon's Big Question,* p. 184; September 15, 2005, review of *Sunrise, Sunset,* p. 1027; April 15, 2006, review of *Sleepyhead Bear,* p. 413; December 15, 2006, review of *Pip & Squeak,* p. 1272.

*Publishers Weekly,* August 17, 1992, review of *Newf,* p. 498; October 17, 1994, review of *America Alive: A History,* p. 83; May 1, 1995, review of *One Night,* p. 58; February 8, 1999, Diane Patrick, "A Living Legacy (Second-Generation Children's Literature Authors and Illustrators)," p. 120; February 23, 2004, review of *Little Raccoon's Big Question,* p. 75.

*School Library Journal,* March, 2001, Eva Mitnick, review of *Castaways of the Flying Dutchman,* p. 250; March, 2004, Grace Oliff, review of *Little Raccoon's Big Question,* p. 181; October, 2005, Rachel Kamin, review of *Sunrise, Sunset,* p. 138; May, 2006, Martha Topol, review of *Sleepyhead Bear,* p. 96.

*ONLINE*

*HarperCollins Web site,* http://www.harpercollins.com/ (February 21, 2007), "Ian Schoenherr."

*Ian Schoenherr Home Page,* http://www. http://ianschoenherr.com (February 21, 2007).

*Marion Vannett Ridgway Web site,* http://www.marionvannettridgwayaward.com/ (February 21, 2007), "Ian Schoenherr."

\*   \*   \*

# SCOTTON, Rob 1960-

## Personal

Born September 26, 1960, in England; married; wife's name Liz (an artist). *Education:* Leicester Polytechnic, graduate (with honors).

## Addresses

*Home and office*—Rutland, England. *E-mail*—rscotton00@mac.com.

## Career

Commercial illustrator and author; graphic designer with work appearing on cards as well as on ceramics, glassware, and other household items produced by Portmeirion Studio.

## Awards, Honors

Border's Original Voice Award, Parents' Choice Highly Commended designation, International Reading Association honor, Kate Greenaway Award shortlist, *Booksense* Best New Illustrator Award shortlist, Sheffield Book-of-the-Year Award shortlist, and Utah Beehive Award shortlist, all 2005, all for *Russell the Sheep;* Coventry Inspiration Book designation shortlist, 2006, for *Russell and the Lost Treasure.*

## Writings

*SELF-ILLUSTRATED PICTURE BOOKS*

*Russell the Sheep,* HarperCollins (New York, NY), 2005.

*Russell and the Lost Treasure,* HarperCollins (New York, NY), 2006.

*Go to Sleep, Russell the Sheep,* HarperFestival (New York, NY), 2007.

*Russell's Christmas Magic,* HarperFestival (New York, NY), 2007.

## Sidelights

A bicycle ride through the rolling British countryside, with its picturesque hillsides dotted with fluffy white sheep, inspired popular commercial illustrator Rob Scotton to create the first of his playful picture books starring a woolly sheep named Russell. As Scotton recalled on his home page, after sorting through some greeting-card designs he had created, "I found the card I was looking for, a simple sheep character on an Easter

Greetings card that I had painted in a previous life. I sat at my computer and began to doodle. Before long a boggle-eyed character was staring back from my screen. He was a simple, uncomplicated soul and so ridiculous." The first name that came to mind was Russell the Sheep, his residence Frogsbottom field. In the years since, Russell's adventures have played out, courtesy of Scotton's whimsical imagination, in the pages of *Russell the Sheep, Russell and the Lost Treasure,* and *Go to Sleep, Russell the Sheep.*

When readers first meet Russell in the award-winning *Russell the Sheep,* the sleepy creature has donned his long blue nightcap in readiness for bed, but finds himself tormented by insomnia. Plumping pillows, changing position, even sleeping in a tree bordering his pasture are each tried in turn, but to no avail. Nothing seems to work for the frustrated creature until the sheep resorts to counting things. Praising *Russell the Sheep* as "a droll bedtime read-aloud," *Booklist* contributor Carolyn Phelan noted that Scotton's "simple, satisfying story [is] told with economy and illustrated with wit."

*Russell and the Lost Treasure* finds Scotton's woolly hero inspired to hunt for buried treasure after spying what appears to be a treasure map dangling from the beak of a crow. The silly sheep, convinced that treasure is in his future, sets about creating a special treasure detector. After "detecting" a buried trunk filled with a variety of obviously cast-off objects, the sheep does stumble upon a treasure of sorts: an old camera that provides him with treasured photographs of his friends in the flock. "Scenes of popeyed livestock mugging for the camera capture the profound flakiness of the entire episode," noted a *Kirkus Reviews* writer, while Phelan commented that young readers will relish Russell's "exaggerated antics and expressions, as well as the final affirmation that his album of family and friends is the 'best treasure ever.'"

## Biographical and Critical Sources

*PERIODICALS*

*Booklist,* August, 2005, Carolyn Phelan, review of *Russell the Sheep,* p. 2036; June 1, 2006, Carolyn Phelan, review of *Russell and the Lost Treasure,* p. 89.

*Bulletin of the Center for Children's Books,* May, 2005, review of *Russell the Sheep,* p. 401.

*Kirkus Reviews,* April 1, 2005, review of *Russell the Sheep,* p. 424; April 1, 2006, review of *Russell and the Lost Treasure,* p. 357.

*Publishers Weekly,* April 25, 2005, review of *Russell the Sheep,* p. 55; April 3, 2006, review of *Russell and the Lost Treasure,* p. 72.

*School Library Journal,* April, 2005, Be Astengo, review of *Russell the Sheep,* p. 110; May, 2006, Marge Loch-Wouters, review of *Russell and the Lost Treasure,* p. 104.

*Times Educational Supplement,* September 22, 2006, Jane Doonan, "Where Beasties Collide," p. 34.

*ONLINE*

*Rob Scotton Home Page,* http://www.robscotton.com (March 4, 2007).

\*       \*       \*

# SMITH, Linda 1949-

## Personal

Born 1949, in Lethbridge, Alberta, Canada. *Education:* University of Calgary, B.A., 1969; University of Alberta, M.L.S.; Simmons College, M.A. (children's literature). *Hobbies and other interests:* Reading, walking, traveling, politics, social-justice work.

## Addresses

*Home*—Grand Prairie, Alberta, Canada. *E-mail*—lindaas@telusplanet.net.

## Career

Writer and librarian. Children's librarian in Truro, Nova Scotia; Saskatoon, Saskatchewan; and Grande Prairie, Alberta, Canada, 1984-2001.

## Member

Writers' Union of Canada, Children's Literature Roundtable, Writers' Guild of Alberta.

## Awards, Honors

R. Ross Annett Award for Children's Literature, 1996, for *Wind Shifter;* Canadian Children's Book Centre Our Choice Book Award, 2001, and Golden Eagle Young Readers' Choice Book Award finalist, 2004, both for *The Turning Time;* second prize, *Storyteller* magazine's Great Canadian Story Contest, 2003; Independent Book Publishers Award shortlist, 2005, Manitoba Young Reader's Choice Award shortlist, Diamond Willow Young Readers' Choice designation, Rocky Mountain Young Readers' Choice designation, and Golden Eagle Young Readers' Choice designation, all 2006, and Red Cedar Young Readers' Choice Award, 2007, all for *The Minstrel's Daughter.*

## Writings

*PICTURE BOOKS*

*Sir Cassie to the Rescue,* illustrated by Karen Patkau, Orca Book Publishers (Victoria, British Columbia, Canada), 2003.

**Linda Smith** (Photograph courtesy of Linda Smith.)

*Kelly's Cabin,* illustrated by Zorica Krasulja, Orca Book Publishers (Victoria, British Columbia, Canada), 2006.

*"FREYAN" TRILOGY*

*Wind Shifter,* Thistledown Press (Saskatoon, Saskatchewan, Canada), 1995.

*Sea Change,* Thistledown Press (Saskatoon, Saskatchewan, Canada), 1999.

*The Turning Time,* Thistledown Press (Saskatoon, Saskatchewan, Canada), 2001.

*"TALES OF THREE LANDS" TRILOGY*

*The Minstrel's Daughter,* Coteau Books (Regina, Saskatchewan, Canada), 2004.

*Talisa's Song,* Coteau Books (Regina, Saskatchewan, Canada), 2005.

*The Weathermage,* Coteau Books (Regina, Saskatchewan, Canada), 2006.

*OTHER*

Also author of mystery plays. Contributor to books, including *Kakwa Rising,* Smoky Peace Press, 2001; *Nose Mountain Moods,* Smoky Peace Press, 2002; and *The*

*Boreal Factor,* Smoky Peace Press, 2003. Contributor of stories to periodicals, including *On Spec* and *Storyteller.* Canadian Broadcasting Corporation (CBC) Radio, contributor to *Alberta Anthology* (radio program).

## Adaptations

Author's short stories have been broadcast on CBC Radio's *Alberta Anthology.*

## Sidelights

A native of Canada and a former librarian, Linda Smith is the author of several fantasy novels for young adults, including the volumes in her "Freyan" and "Tales of Three Lands" trilogies. Geared for younger readers, her picture books for children include *Sir Cassie to the Rescue.* "Part of my love for fantasy comes from the fact that it's a genre that involves characters not only in confronting the problems and issues of their own lives, but in those of the world beyond," Smith noted on her home page.

Smith published her debut title, *Wind Shifter,* in 1995. The first installment in her "Freyan" trilogy of fantasy novels, *Wind Shifter* concerns the relationship between Kerstin Speller, the daughter of a powerful wizard, and Alaric, an orphaned boy. As wizard's apprentices. the two are called into battle when an old enemy, the Uglessians, attack the land of Freya. "Smith continually holds the reader's interest by propelling the story forward through exciting challenges to the credible characters," noted Jo-Anne Mary Benson in an appraisal of *Wind Shifter,* for *Canadian Review of Materials.*

In *Sea Change,* Kerstin and her father journey to the Misty Isles to learn from the Wise Women, a group of nine females who practice the magic and healing arts. Conflicts soon arise between the Freyans and the islanders, however. "Kerstin is a well-rounded character who deals with her own problems and easily bruised teenage emotions in an entirely convincing manner," observed *Canadian Review of Materials* reviewer Betsy Fraser. In *The Turning Time,* which concludes the series, Kerstin returns to her native land, where she must prevent another conflict with the Uglessians. According to *Resource Links* critic Connie Forst, in this novel "Smith has created a world that is at once fantastic and compellingly real, moved forward with great suspense and exhilarating action."

In *The Minstrel's Daughter,* the first work in Smith's "Tales of Three Lands" trilogy, Catrina Ashdale journeys to the city of Freyfall to locate her long-lost father, a wandering minstrel. Once there, she meets Garth, a wizard's apprentice who agrees to help with Catrina's search after he unwittingly turns her into a cat. *Kliatt* reviewer Erin Darr dubbed the book "a well-written magical romp that will have the reader anxiously turn-

ing the pages to see what happens next." *Talisa's Song* focuses on Talisa Thatcher, a talented Uglessian singer who is born into a family of magicians. While studying music in Freya, Talisa becomes attracted to Cory, a young man who is accused of a horrible crime he did not commit. Talisa's "journey from childhood toward maturity is accompanied by a delicately handled love interest," remarked K.V. Johansen in *Resource Links*. In *The Weathermage* Catrina and Talisa join forces with Galia Soradotter, a wizard from the Misty Isles, to save their homelands from disaster.

*Sir Cassie to the Rescue* appeared in 2003. After reading a book about knights in shining armor, Cassie and her brother, Trevor, construct a castle in their living room. When Cassie asks Trevor to pretend to be a damsel in distress in a game of imagination, he understandably balks at the idea; instead, he agrees to portray a fierce dragon guarding a cave filled with treasure. "This sets the tone for an amusing romp into Medieval make-believe," noted Isobel Lang in *Resource Links*. According to *School Library Journal* contributor Wendy Woodfill, *Sir Cassie to the Rescue* "is an appealing look at the resourcefulness of children and the relationship between siblings."

Another of Smith's books for young readers, *Kelly's Cabin* centers on a young girl who transforms a refrigerator box into a comfortable playhouse. In a review of the book for *Canadian Review of Materials,* Deborah Mervold praised the book's "believable dialogue," adding that the story's "content is interesting yet easy to read and follow."

## Biographical and Critical Sources

*PERIODICALS*

*Canadian Book Review Annual,* 2004, Dave Jenkinson, review of *The Minstrel's Daughter,* p. 524.
*Canadian Children's Literature,* fall, 2002, J.R. Wytenbroek, review of *Sea Change,* p. 92.
*Canadian Review of Materials,* March 14, 1997, Jo-Anne Mary Benson, review of *Wind Shifter*; February 18, 2000, Betsy Fraser, review of *Sea Change;* September 5, 2003, Mary Thomas, review of *Sir Cassie to the Rescue;* October 13, 2006, Deborah Mervold, review of *Kelly's Cabin;* November 26, 2006, Mary Thomas, review of *Weathermage.*
*Kliatt,* July, 2005, Erin Darr, review of *The Minstrel's Daughter,* p. 32.
*Resource Links,* December, 1999, review of *Sea Change,* p. 30; October, 2001, Connie Forst, review of *The Turning Time,* p. 42; February, 2004, Isobel Lang, review of *Sir Cassie to the Rescue,* p. 6; February, 2006, K.V. Johansen, review of *Talisa's Song,* p. 50.
*School Library Journal,* December, 2003, Wendy Woodfill, review of *Sir Cassie to the Rescue,* p. 126; June, 2006, Eva Mitnick, review of *Talisa's Song,* p. 166.

*ONLINE*

*Linda Smith Home Page,* http://www.telusplanet.net/public/lindaas/main.html (January 21, 2007).

\*      \*      \*

# SORRELLS, Walter
# (Lynn Abercrombie, Ruth Birmingham)

## Personal

Born in Nashville, TN; married; wife's name Patti; children: Jake. *Education:* Haverford College, degree (history), 1985; earned J.D. *Hobbies and other interests:* Martial arts, sword-smithing, blues guitar, harmonica.

## Addresses

*Home*—Atlanta, GA. *E-mail*—walter@waltersorrells.com.

## Career

Novelist. Formerly worked as a paralegal; *Mystery Zone* (Internet magazine), editor.

## Member

Mystery Writers of America (member, board of directors).

## Awards, Honors

Edgar Allan Poe Award nomination, Mystery Writers of America, for *Atlanta Graves;* Edgar Allan Poe Award and Shamus Award, both for *Fulton County Blues;* Top-Ten Mystery designation, *Booklist,* for *Fake ID.*

## Writings

*NOVELS*

*Power of Attorney,* 1994.
*Cry for Justice,* Avon (New York, NY), 1994.
*Will to Murder,* 1996.
(With William J. Coughlin) *Proof of Intent,* Thomas Dunne Books (New York, NY), 2002.
*The Silent Room* (for young adults), Dutton (New York, NY), 2006.
*First Shot,* 2007.

*"HUNTED" SERIES; YOUNG-ADULT NOVELS*

*Fake ID,* Sleuth (New York, NY), 2005.
*Club Dread,* Sleuth Dutton (New York, NY), 2006.

*YOUNG-ADULT NOVELIZATIONS; BASED ON TELEVISION SERIES "FLIGHT 29 DOWN"*

*Ten Rules,* Grosset & Dunlap (New York, NY), 2006.
*Static,* Grosset & Dunlap (New York, NY), 2006.

(With Robert T. Sorrells) *Scratch,* Grosset & Dunlap (New York, NY), 2006.
*Survival,* Grosset & Dunlap (New York, NY), 2007.
*On Fire,* Grosset & Dunlap (New York, NY), 2007.
(Under pseudonym Lynn Abercrombie) *Blind Fear,* 2008.

*"SUNNY CHILDS" MYSTERY NOVELS; UNDER PSEUDONYM RUTH BIRMINGHAM*

*Atlanta Graves,* Berkley Books (New York, NY), 1998.
*Fulton County Blues,* Berkley Books (New York, NY), 1999.
*Sweet Georgia,* Berkley Books (New York, NY), 2000.
*Blue Plate Special,* Berkley Books (New York, NY), 2001.
*Cold Trail,* Berkley Books (New York, NY), 2002.
*Feet of Clay,* Berkley Books (New York, NY), 2006.

*"COLD CASE THRILLER" MYSTERY NOVELS; UNDER PSEUDONYM LYNN ABERCROMBIE*

*The Body Box,* Pinnacle (New York, NY), 2005.
*Blind Fear,* Pinnacle (New York, NY), 2006.

## Sidelights

Walter Sorrells, the Edgar Award-winning author of legal and crime thrillers, has a name that is not immediately recognizable to fans of his popular "Sunny Childs" mystery series. The reason: the series is published under the pseudonym Ruth Birmingham, one of several pen names employed by the prolific Georgia-based novelist. Under his own name, Sorrells has also gained a large following among teen readers through his "Hunted" series and his novelizations of the *Flight 29 Down* television series. When he is not writing, the author pursues his long-held interests in weaponry and the martial arts. In addition to studying aikido, Tai Chi, and Japanese Iaido and Shinkendo weapon art, Sorrells is a 3rd-degree black belt in Japanese Shito-ryu karate. In his spare time, he creates Japanese-styled knives and long blades in the backyard forge at his Atlanta home.

In 1995, while teaching English in Japan, Sorrells broke into the mystery field with the legal thriller *Power of Attorney.* Interestingly, although the Nashville native had, at this point, never lived in Atlanta, where the novel is set, he and his wife Patty now make the Georgia city their home. Although his first novel did not reach blockbuster status, it encouraged Sorrells to continue writing, and after Patty completed her own professional training, he decided to give himself two years to make a go as a novelist. His first "Sunny Childs" novel, *Atlanta Graves,* was published twenty months later.

In *Atlanta Graves* Childs, an intrepid private-eye, is running the Atlanta-based Peachtree Investigations firm for her seldom-seen boss, Gunnar Brushurd. Sunny's workday is complicated by problems both external—her "perp" is shot while she is investigating a stolen-

*Cover of Walter Sorrells' young-adult novel* Fake ID, *featuring an illustration by Alex Williamson.* (Jacket illustration copyright © 2005 by Alex Williamson. Reproduced by permission of Dutton Children's Books, a division of Penguin Putnam Books.)

painting case—and internal. It seems that Gunnar has left the firm deeply in debt, and Sunny now finds she has four days in which to find a way to avoid bankruptcy. Praising Sunny as "an appealing lead," David Pitt added in *Booklist* that Sorrells's heroine is "tough, funny, likable, insecure, and smart." In *BookBrowser* online, Harriet Klausner cited *Atlanta Graves* for introducing "a terrific series that brings alive the mean streets of Atlanta."

The popular "Sunny Childs" series has continued to expand, and by 2006 it included the Edgar Award-winning *Fulton County Blues* as well as *Blue Plate Special* and *Feet of Clay.* In *Fulton County Blues* Sunny is again on the case, this time investigating the death of her late father's friend, a Vietnam War veteran. As Sunny begins to unearth long-hidden stories of wartime horror, one of the man's former comrades-in-arms is determined to keep these stories untold so they do not compromise his career path in the upper echelons of the Central Intelligence Agency. While the revealed wartime stories are "quite terrible and hard to comprehend," according to *Mystery Reader* online critic Martha Moore, Sorrells "makes his [protagonist's] plight believable and his character is richer when we discover he wasn't perfect. Sunny learns some things about the dark side of human nature, but she also discovers the meaning of family."

*Feet of Clay* finds Childs helping her younger sister, filmmaker Lee-Lee, shoot a documentary profiling a soon-to-be executed death-row inmate. When Lee-Lee is arrested shortly after arriving in the town where the condemned man's crimes took place, the two women realize that the true murderer may still be on the loose. "Solid dialogue, . . . entertaining characters and regional humor make this a fun, fast read," wrote a *Publishers Weekly* contributor.

While fans of the "Sunny Childs" novels include high-school-aged mystery buffs, Sorrells' "Hunted" series, which includes *Fake ID* and *Club Dread,* were his first books specifically geared for teen readers. In *Fake ID* readers meet Chastity, a teen who lives on the run. The chameleon lifestyle Chass has shared with her single mom—they move every few years, and change their names in every new town they temporarily call home—has seemed so normal that the teen has never questioned why they live on the run; she does not even know her true name or the identity of her father. The night she turns sixteen answers to these questions suddenly become paramount: her mom is missing and her car shows blood and other signs of a struggle. Realizing that her own life is also in danger, Chass must now discover her mom's fate, while also keeping one step ahead of the police and social workers who are determined to consign the teen to foster care. "Sorrells masterfully sustains suspense throughout" his story, wrote Connie Fletcher in her *Booklist* review of *Fake ID,* the critic adding that the author's technique of "spiking the drama with some truly frightening scenes" results in "a terrific read." In *Kliatt* Claire Rosser had the same opinion, noting that Sorrells' "suspenseful, tight plot and interesting characters make [*Fake ID*] . . . ideal YA popular literature."

*Cover of Sorrells' 2006 teen thriller* **The Silent Room,** *featuring an illustration by Tony Sahara.* (Jacket art © 2006 and design by Tony Sahara. Reproduced by permission of Dutton Children's Books, a division of Penguin Putnam Books for Young Readers.)

Readers rejoin Chass in *Club Dread,* and take in new surroundings now that the girl has moved from Alabama to San Francisco. Following her interest in music, Chass is busy forming a rock band, but the last thing she really wants is a high profile. When a local pop star is shot down in the street, the dying man passes the teen a clue to his killer. This clue draws Chass into the city's seedy underground-music world as she attempts to out the killer before she becomes his—or her—next victim. Dubbing *Club Dread* "a thoroughly satisfying thriller," Connie Fletcher added in her *Booklist* review that the second novel in the "Hunted" series is "as riveting as the first book," while *School Library Journal* contributor Miranda Doyle concluded: "Readers searching for a quick, suspenseful read will find a winner here."

Also focusing on teens, *The Silent Room* introduces readers to fifteen-year-old Oswald Turner—Oz for short. While most teens look with suspicion on their parent's new spouse, for Oz the man who has married his recently widowed mother is truly out to get him. Implicated in a drug possession charge, Oz is whisked away to a reform school in the middle of a Florida swamp,

where he finds himself living like a prisoner in true Southern style. As he survives the brutal conditions at Briarwood School, he learns that his stepfather had a reason for wanting Oz out of the way: he is somehow involved with the school's nefarious goings on, and Oz's mom may be next on the man's hit list unless the teen can find a way to escape. Noting that *The Silent Room* treats teen readers to adults who are "over-the-top vicious," Stephanie Zvirin added in her *Booklist* review that "it's impossible not to be caught up by Oz's naiveté." Comparing the tension Sorrells builds to that created in the popular television program *24,* Rosser wrote in *Kliatt* that *The Silent Room* shows its author to be "an experienced writer of mysteries." A *Kirkus Reviews* critic concluded: "This one's a thriller that really thrills."

Continuing to alternate between YA and adult novels, Sorrells also writes the "Cold Case Thriller" series under the pseudonym Lynn Abercrombie. Again taking place in Atlanta, series installments *The Body Box* and *Blind Fear* draw readers into the workings of the city's Cold Case unit, where African-American detective Mechelle Deakes sifts through the departments unsolved

crimes, looking for clues. Writing that Deakes provides readers with a likeable central character, a *Publishers Weekly* also cited the "breezy dialogue" in *The Body Box* and noted that Sorrells' story will keep fans riveted to each page by including "challenging procedural details." In a review of *Blind Fear,* a *Publishers Weekly* contributor remarked on the "improbable plot" but nonetheless recommended the novel as a "who-dunit police procedural with a fast pace and action enough to keep readers along for the ride."

## Biographical and Critical Sources

*PERIODICALS*

*Booklist,* February 15, 1998, David Pitt, review of *Atlanta Graves,* p. 987; May 1, 2005, Stephanie Zvirin, "Leave the Blood at the Door: Adult Mystery Writers Try Children's Books," p. 1512, and Connie Fletcher, review of *Fake ID,* p. 1542; January 1, 2006, Connie Fletcher, review of *Club Dread,* p. 85; May 1, 2006, Stephanie Zvirin, review of *The Silent Room,* p. 47.

*Bulletin of the Center for Children's Books,* July-August, 2005, review of *Fake ID,* p. 512; July-August, 2006, Loretta Gaffney, review of *The Silent Room,* p. 518.

*Kirkus Reviews,* September 1, 2002, review of *Proof of Intent,* p. 1249; February 1, 2006, review of *Club Dread,* p. 137; May 1, 2006, review of *The Silent Room,* p. 467.

*Kliatt,* July, 2006, Claire Rosser, review of *Fake ID,* p. 15; March, 2006, Claire Rosser, review of *Club Dread,* p. 17; May, 2006, Claire Rosser, review of *The Silent Room,* p. 15.

*Publishers Weekly,* January 3, 1994, review of *Power of Attorney,* p. 77; June 10, 1996, review of *Cry for Justice,* p. 96; October 28, 2002, review of *Proof of Intent,* p. 51; October 24, 2005, review of *The Body Box,* p. 45; February 20, 2006, review of *Feet of Clay,* p. 138; October 9, 2006, review of *Blind Fear,* p. 42.

*School Library Journal,* June, 2005, Miranda Doyle, review of *Fake ID,* p. 170; March, 2006, Lynn Evarts, reviews of *Static* and *Club Dread,* p. 230; July, 2006, Beth Gallego, review of *The Silent Room,* p. 113.

*Voice of Youth Advocates,* August, 2005, Deborah Fisher, review of *Fake ID,* p. 226.

*ONLINE*

*BookBrowser,* http://www.bookbrowser.com/ (March 20, 2001), Harriet Klausner, review of *Atlanta Graves.*

*Mystery Reader Web site,* http://www.themysteryreader.com/ (March 20, 2001), Martha Moore, review of *Fulton County Blues.*

*Walter Sorrells Home Page,* http://www.waltersorrells.com (March 15, 2007).

\*    \*    \*

## SPOWART, Robin 1947-

## Personal

Born August 14, 1947, in Martinez, CA; son of James Cambell (an oil refinery worker) and Violet Louise (a homemaker and artist) Spowart; married Jeanne Modesitt (a children's book author), September 16, 1978. *Education:* Attended Ventura City College; University of California at Santa Cruz, B.A., 1981. *Politics:* "Independent." *Hobbies and other interests:* "Taking long walks in quiet places."

## Addresses

*Home*—Northern CA.

## Career

Commercial artist, 1975-85; children's book illustrator, 1985—. *Exhibitions:* Work exhibited at galleries, including Elizabeth Stone Gallery of Original Children's Book Art, Birmingham, MI, and VA; Mazza Centennial Collection, University of Findlay, OH; and Dromkeen Collection of Australian Children's Literature. *Military service:* U.S. Army.

## Member

Society of Children's Book Writers and Illustrators.

## Awards, Honors

American Booksellers' Pick of the Lists, for *Latkes and Applesauce* and *Sometimes I Feel like a Mouse.*

## Writings

*SELF-ILLUSTRATED*

*Inside, outside Christmas,* Holiday House (New York, NY), 1998.

*Ten Little Bunnies,* Scholastic (New York, NY), 2001.

*ILLUSTRATOR*

Clement C. Moore, *The Night before Christmas,* Dodd (New York, NY), 1986.

Charlotte Zolotow, *A Rose, a Bridge, and a Wild Black Horse,* HarperCollins (New York, NY), 1987.

*The Three Bears,* Knopf (New York, NY), 1987.

Jeanne Modesitt, *Vegetable Soup,* Macmillan (New York, NY), 1988.

April Halprin Wayland, *To Rabbittown,* Scholastic (New York, NY), 1989.

Christine Barker Widman, *The Star Grazers,* HarperCollins (New York, NY), 1989.

Jeanne Modesitt, *The Night Call,* Viking (New York, NY), 1989.

Nancy Larrick, compiler, *Songs from Mother Goose,* HarperCollins (New York, NY), 1989.

Fran Manushkin, *Latkes and Applesauce,* Scholastic (New York, NY), 1990.

Jeanne Modesitt, compiler, *Songs of Chanukah,* Little, Brown (Boston, MA), 1992.

Jeanne Modesitt, *Sometimes I Feel like a Mouse,* Scholastic (New York, NY), 1992.

Jeanne Modesitt, *Mama, If You Had a Wish,* Green Tiger Press (New York, NY), 1993.

Jeanne Modesitt, *Lunch with Milly,* Bridgewater Books (New York, NY), 1995.

Lynn Manuel, *The Night the Moon Blew Kisses,* Houghton (Boston, MA), 1996.

Jeanne Modesitt, *Little Bunny's Easter Surprise,* Simon & Schuster (New York, NY), 1999.

Jeanne Modesitt, *It's Hanukkah!,* Holiday House (New York, NY), 1999.

Susan Heyboer O'Keefe, *Love Me, Love You,* Boyds Mills Press (Honesdale, PA), 2001.

Jeanne Modesitt, *1 2 3 Valentine's Day,* Boyds Mills Press (Honesdale, PA), 2002.

Jeanne Modesitt, *Little Bunny's Christmas Tree,* Simon & Schuster (New York, NY), 2003.

Jeanne Modesitt, *Mouse's Halloween Party,* Boyds Mills Press (Honesdale, PA), 2004.

Susan Heyboer O'Keefe, *Baby Day,* Boyds Mills Press (Honesdale, PA), 2006.

Jeanne Modesitt, *Little Mouse's Happy Birthday,* Boyds Mills Press (Honesdale, PA), 2007.

## Sidelights

The endearing animals created by illustrator Robin Spowart are beloved by fans of the stories by Jeanne Modesitt, Susan Heyboer O'Keefe, and others. It is no surprise that Modesitt and Spowart have produced such effective picture books; they are, in fact, husband and wife. Their collaborations, which include *Sometimes I Feel like a Mouse, Little Bunny's Easter Surprise,* and *Mouse's Halloween Party,* have great toddler appeal due to Modesitt's gentle texts and Spowart's smudgy pastel-toned illustrations that feature tender, loving relationships. In praising his work for Fran Manushkin's *Latkes and Applesauce: A Hanukkah Story,* a *Publishers Weekly* contributor noted that "Spowart's soft, blurred pastels give the story an added sense of warmth and security." Carolyn Phelan viewed his work for *Little Bunny's Easter Surprise* in a similar way, noting that Spowart's "soft-edged crayon drawings in spring-hued pastels" pair with Modesitt's story to "personify the comfort and joy that children find in loving families."

In addition to his work for other writers, Spowart has also created several original text to pair with his artwork. *Inside, Outside Christmas* uses a rhyming text to describe a mouse family's preparation for the holiday season. Sledding, baking cookies, and collecting toys for young mice in need are among the activities depicted in Spowart's colorful images, in which "strokes of overlapping lines in rich hues create their own rhythm of repeated shapes and graceful movements," according to Phelan. In *Ten Little Bunnies* the author/ illustrator creates a cumulative tale that moves young listeners from one to ten while describing young bunnies engaged in a variety of playful, toddler-type tasks. Reviewing the book for *School Library Journal,* Bina

*Robin Spowart is known for gently toned animal drawings, such as the bunnies he casts in Susan Heyboer O'Keefe's* Love Me, Love You. (Illustration copyright © 2001 by Robin Spowart. Reproduced by permission.)

Williams deemed *Ten Little Bunnies* "a good choice for bedtime reading."

Spowart once told *SATA:* "I enjoyed drawing as a kid (what kid doesn't?), and much preferred it over any other type of school work (I was a pretty normal kid). Did I dream of being an artist when I 'grew up'? Nope. I knew I liked drawing, but the idea of being a professional artist never occurred to me. No one—no adults, as far as I can remember—ever encouraged me to continue to draw. If any kid artists are reading this, please allow me to say something VERY IMPORTANT: If you like drawing, keep at it, no matter what anyone else says (or does not say).

"I first considered the idea of illustrating children's books when I was in the U.S. Army, stationed in Germany. To relieve some of the monotony of army life, I had put together a couple of sketches I had drawn— sketches of imaginary places and people—and shown them to a German couple I had recently met. The couple liked my work and suggested I try my hand at children's book illustration. The seed was planted! After I was discharged from the army, I went to Ventura City College and took some art classes. I really enjoyed those classes, and my art instructors encouraged me to keep on doing my art! I'll never forget them for that.

"After Ventura College, I took on both art-related jobs (illustrating for newspapers, etc.) and non-art related jobs. Neither were satisfactory. I went back to school—

this time the University of California at Santa Cruz (UCSC)—so that I could devote myself full time to art. While at UCSC, I did many 'fine art' paintings, that is, figure drawings, portraits, and landscape paintings. While doing such paintings had certain enjoyable aspects to them, it still wasn't right for me. I graduated from UCSC and began doing art work that was closer to my heart: imaginary images for greeting cards. This work proved to be satisfactory for me, at least for a while. Then it became boring, not challenging enough. And if that wasn't enough of a kick in the pants to get me to start something new, the fact that the greeting card companies stopped commissioning me to do work was! In my eyes, there was only one thing left for me to do: pursue my secret dream of illustrating children's books.

"The first book I illustrated was *The Night before Christmas* by Clement. Moore. (I had to pick a story that was in the public domain as I can't write worth a hill of beans and my wife, Jeanne Modesitt, wasn't writing at the time.) Seeing that it was the 'Year of the Teddy Bear,' Jeanne came up with the idea to illustrate all the characters in the book as teddy bears. We thought we had a sure seller on our hands. Wrong! Thirty publishers turned down the (very amateurish) dummy I had put together, saying that the teddy bear idea was 'cute,' but not right for their list. Boy, was I discouraged. But then, a miracle occurred. An editor from one house, who had seen the dummy, moved to another house, and decided that the second house would be the perfect publisher for the book. The lesson I learned from all this was: DON'T GIVE UP. No matter how many rejections you receive, keep at it until you drop.

"Getting a book to illustrate was never as hard as that first book. Publishers weren't breaking down my doors to get me to illustrate their manuscripts, but there was

*Among Spowart's many collaborations with wife, writer Jeanne Modesitt, is the holiday-themed counting book* **1, 2, 3, Valentine's Day.** (Illustrations copyright © 2002 by Robin Spowart. Reproduced by permission.)

interest on their parts once they saw *The Night before Christmas* and some other individual pieces of art I had put together for my portfolio. I have illustrated several books by my wife. These include *The Night Call, Vegetable Soup, Sometimes I Feel like a Mouse, Songs of Chanukah, Mama, If You Had a Wish,* and *Lunch with Milly.* Jeanne and I work together very well. We're not envious or jealous of each other's work; on the contrary, we honor and respect each other's creative impulses.

"I seem to be drawn primarily to stories that have some sort of magical quality to them. However, I try not to make a rule of this. I'm open to illustrating all types of manuscripts. The only thing that matters is whether a particular story interests me. If it doesn't (no matter how good the story is), then it's best for me to turn the story down because it's agonizing (and boring and tedious) for me to work on something that my heart is not into.

"When I first started illustrating books, I had a lot of self-doubt. 'Can I really do this?,' I kept asking myself. I would rush through each one of my paintings just to see that, yes, I CAN do it! What an exhausting process that was! Today, I still have feelings of self-doubt when faced with a new story to illustrate, but I don't act on these feelings like I used to. As a result, the process of illustrating books is much more enjoyable to me (and much slower too!).

"Each story calls for its own medium. In illustrating books, I have used watercolor, acrylic, pastel pencil, and colored pencil. Sometimes it takes me a while to figure out which medium would be best suited for a particular story. For example, with *Lunch with Milly*, I tried acrylic, watercolor, and pastel pencil, but none of them seemed to fit the book just right. At last, I settled on colored pencil, which seem to be the perfect medium for this story (and my response to the story).

"The most important piece of advice I can give to aspiring artists is to follow your own inner guidance. This can be difficult at times, at least it is for me. Sometimes, when following my inner guidance on how to illustrate a particular story, I run into people who think the story should be illustrated altogether differently. Such disapproval can be a hard thing to face, but in the end, it hurts more to disobey one's own inner guidance than to receive disapproval. Surrender to the story— that's what I keep telling others, including myself."

## Biographical and Critical Sources

*PERIODICALS*

*Booklist,* July 15, 1993, Kay Weisman, review of *Mama, If You Had a Wish,* p. 1975; September 1, 1998, Carolyn Phelan, review of *Inside, Outside Christmas,* p. 134; February 1, 1999, Carolyn Phelan, review of *Little Bunny's Easter Surprise,* p. 982; April 15, 2001, Lauren Peterson, review of *Love Me, Love You,* p. 1566; January 1, 2003, Diane Foote, review of *1 2 3 Valentine's Day,* p. 908; August, 2004, Ilene Cooper, review of *Mouse's Halloween Party,* p. 1943; March, 2006, Carolyn Phelan, review of *Baby Day,* p. 100.

*Kirkus Reviews,* November 15, 2002, review of *1 2 3 Valentine's Day,* p. 1699; March 1, 2006, review of *Baby Day,* p. 237.

*Publishers Weekly,* October 30, 1987, p. 67; January 29, 1988; September 14, 1990, review of *Latkes and Applesauce: A Hanukkah Story,* p. 123; May 31, 1993, review of *Mama, If You Had a Wish,* p. 52; January 2, 1995, review of *Lunch with Milly,* p. 76; July 15, 1996, review of *The Night the Moon Blew Kisses,* p. 73; September 28, 1998, review of *Inside, Outside Christmas,* p. 45; January 22, 1999, review of *Little Bunny's Easter Surprise,* p. 70; September 27, 1999, review of *It's Hanukkah!,* p. 52; February 5, 2001, review of *Love Me, Love You,* p. 87.

*School Library Journal,* October, 1987, p. 120; January, 1990; October, 1998, Lisa Falk, review of *Inside, Outside Christmas,* p. 45; April, 2001, Lisa Dennis, review of *Love Me, Love You,* p. 119; August, 2001, Bina Williams, review of *Ten Little Bunnies* p. 162; January, 2003, Liza Graybill, review of *1 2 3 Valentine's Day,* p. 106; October, 2003, Lisa Israelson, review of *Little Bunny's Christmas Tree,* p. 66; August, 2004, Linda Staskus, review of *Mouse's Halloween Party,* p. 90; March, 2006, Gary Lynn Van Vleck, review of *Baby Day,* p. 200.*

# T-U

## TADGELL, Nicole 1969-

### Personal

Born 1969, in Highland Park, MI; married. *Education:* Wheaton College, degree.

### Addresses

*Home and office*—14 Sampson St., Spencer, MA 01562. *E-mail*—nic.art@verizon.net.

### Career

Illustrator.

### Member

Society of Children's Book Writers and Illustrators.

### Illustrator

*PICTURE BOOKS*

Jean Alicia Elster, *Just Call Me Joe Joe,* Judson Press (Valley Forge, PA), 2001.
Jean Alicia Elster, *I Have a Dream, Too!,* Judson Press (Valley Forge, PA), 2002.
Jean Alicia Elster, *I'll Fly My Own Plane,* Judson Press (Valley Forge, PA), 2002.
Leslie Bulion, *Fatuma's New Cloth,* Moon Mountain (North Kingston, RI), 2002.
Jean Alicia Elster, *I'll Do the Right Thing,* Judson Press (Valley Forge, PA), 2003.
Nikki Grimes, *A Day with Daddy,* Scholastic (New York, NY), 2004.
Angela Shelf Medearis, *Lights Out!,* Scholastic (New York, NY), 2004.
Jennifer Riesmeyer Elvgren, *Josias, Hold the Book,* Boyds Mills Press (Honesdale, PA), 2005.

### Sidelights

Michigan-born artist and illustrator Nicole Tadgell admits to a long-time love affair with children's books. While growing up she also loved to draw, and now, in her work as an illustrator, she frequently works watercolor into her pencil renderings. Since the publication of her first illustration project, Jean Alicia Elster's 2001 picture book *Just Call Me Joe Joe,* Tadgell has created art for several other writers, including Leslie Bulion, Nikki Grimes, Jennifer Riesmeyer Elvgren, and Angela Shelf Medearis.

Praising the use of "luminescent watercolors" in Tadgell's art for Bulion's *Fatuma's New Cloth,* a *Pub-*

*Nicole Tadgell creates illustrations for Leslie Bulion's folklore-inspired picture book* Fatuma's New Cloth, *which introduces readers to African culture.* (Illustrations copyright © 2002 Nicole Tadgell. Reproduced by permission.)

*lishers Weekly* contributor wrote that the illustrator0 "highlights the glorious colors" of the story's East African setting "and demonstrates the warmth of a closely knit community in which tradition is paramount." In *Booklist,* Hazel Rochman cited the art in Grimes' beginning reader *A Day with Daddy,* noting that "Tadgell's exuberant watercolors show the family bonds, the longing, and the love" that are central to Grimes' story.

In her work for Elvgren's *Josias, Hold the Book,* Tadgell takes readers to Haiti, where Josias lives in an impoverished neighborhood. While the boy longs to attend school, the family garden requires constant attention in order to keep everyone fed. However, when a blight that strikes the garden is diagnosed by Josias with the help of books at the school's library, the boy's father learns to appreciate the importance of education. He decides to send his son to school, and allow Josias to "hold the book." In her review of *Josias, Hold the Book* for *School Library Journal,* Catherine Callegari commented that through Tadgell's "muted watercolor" images the feelings of Josias and his family "are clearly depicted, giving [these] characters added dimension and believability." A *Kirkus Reviews* critic had a similar reaction, writing that the Haitian boy's "well-meaning, earnest behavior comes through" in Tadgell's "expressive facial portrayals as he thinks about solutions to his problem."

## Biographical and Critical Sources

### PERIODICALS

*Booklist,* October 15, 2004, Hazel Rochman, review of *A Day with Daddy,* p. 409; February 15, 2006, Ilene Cooper, review of *Josias, Hold the Book,* p. 101.

*Kirkus Reviews,* March 1, 2006, review of *Josias, Hold the Book,* p. 229.

*Library Media Connection,* November-December, 2006, Karen Sebesta, review of *Josias, Hold the Book,* p. 67.

*Publishers Weekly,* February 25, 2002, review of *Just Call Me Joe Joe,* p. 63; May 20, 2002, review of *Fatuma's New Cloth,* p. 65.

*School Library Journal,* January, 2002, Kathleen Simonetta, review of *Just Call Me Joe Joe,* p. 98; December, 2002, Anna DeWind Walls, review of *Fatuma's New Cloth,* p. 85; January, 2005, Corrina Austin, review of *Lights Out!,* p. 85; February, 2005, Catherine Callegari, review of *The Girls in the Circle,* p. 97; March, 2006, Catherine Callegari, review of *Josias, Hold the Book,* p. 187.

*Tribune Books* (Chicago, IL), August 4, 2002, review of *Fatuma's New Cloth,* p. 5.

### ONLINE

*Nicole Tadgell Home Page,* http://www.nicoletadgell.com (March 4, 2007).

*Illustrator Source Web site,* http://www.author-illustr-source.com/ (March 4, 2007), "Nicole Tadgell."

\* \* \*

## TAYLOR, Theodore 1921-2006
## (T.T. Lang)

*OBITUARY NOTICE*— See index for *SATA* sketch: Born June 23, 1921, in Statesville, NC; died of complications from a heart attack, October 26, 2006, in Laguna Beach, CA. Journalist and author. Taylor was an award-winning writer best known for his young-adult novel *The Cay.* He enjoyed writing from an early age, with his first interest being journalism. The young Taylor got his start when he was just thirteen years old, contributing sports stories to the *Portsmouth Star.* He dropped out of high school, because he was unable to complete the math requirements for graduation, and was a cub reporter for the *Washington Daily News* and a radio sports writer for the National Broadcasting Company. In 1942 he joined the Merchant Marine, and two years later, he was commissioned an ensign in the U.S. Navy. Taylor served in the U.S. military until 1946, and enlisted again in the early 1950s during the Korean War. Between his military assignments, he was briefly a sports editor for *Sunset News* and was in public relations for New York University and YMCA schools. From 1949 to 1950 he also was a reporter for Florida's *Orlando Sentinel Star.* After his war duties in Korea, Taylor returned to publicity, working in Hollywood for Paramount Pictures and then as a story editor, writer, and associate producer for Perlberg-Seaton Productions. From 1961 to 1968 he was a freelance press agent, and from 1965 to 1968 he was a screenwriter for Twentieth Century-Fox. Taylor's Hollywood employment was due to a need for income while he pursued a writing career in his spare time. His early books were nonfiction, and he was researching one such title, *Fire on the Beaches* (1997), when he stumbled on the story that would inspire *The Cay* (1969). He read about an incident in which a young boy, one of many victims of a German U-boat attack during World War II, was lost at sea. Taylor imagined what might have happened had the boy survived, filling out the characterizations with people he knew from life. The story of the marooned, prejudiced white boy Phillip and the wise black man Timothy who helps Phillip outgrow his racism drew criticism from some who felt Timothy was portrayed stereotypically. Many more critics and readers, however, praised the novel, which went on to win a Lewis Carroll Shelf Award and other honors. It was also adapted as a television movie in 1974. At first resisting the demand for a sequel, in 1993 Taylor published *Timothy of the Cay,* which was also critically acclaimed. *The Cay* would prove to be Taylor's greatest success, however. He went on to publish numerous other young-adult novels, including *The Children's War* (1971), *Sweet Friday Island* (1984), *The Weirdo* (1991), and *Ice Drift* (2004). While these often

earned Taylor praise and literary honors, readers always remembered him best for *The Cay*. Taylor was also the author of novels and nonfiction for adults. His numerous other honors include a Young Reader's Medal for *The Trouble with Tuck* (1981) and the Scott O'Dell Historical Fiction Award for *The Bomb* (1995).

*OBITUARIES AND OTHER SOURCES:*

*PERIODICALS*

*Los Angeles Times,* October 28, 2006, p. B10.
*Washington Post,* October 30, 2006, p. B4.

\*    \*    \*

## TCHANA, Katrin Hyman 1963-

### Personal

Born May 2, 1963, in Malden, MA; daughter of Harris (an engineer) and Trina Schart (an illustrator) Hyman; married Eugene Y. Tchana (a computer systems administrator), 1988 (divorced, 2003); partner of Mary Helen Bentley (a human and animal resource manager); children: Michou Tchana Hyman, Xavier Tchana Tchatchoua. *Education:* Attended Bennington College, 1979-81; College of the Atlantic, B.A. (human ecology), 1983; Columbia University, M.A. (teaching), 1991. *Politics:* "Progressive." *Hobbies and other interests:* Tai chi, gardening.

### Addresses

*Home*—Norwich, VT. *E-mail*—katrint@adelphia.net.

### Career

U.S. Peace Corps, Washington, DC, volunteer teacher in Cameroon, 1985-88; teacher of English as a second language, 1988-98; Headrest (substance abuse treatment center), Lebanon, NH, hotline counselor, 1998-2000; Clara Martin Center (community mental-health center), Randolph, VT, community mental health clinician, 2000-04; West Central Services, NH, community mental health clinician, 2004—. Open Fields School, member of board of directors; volunteer for domestic violence hotline.

### Awards, Honors

*Booklist* Top Ten Religion Books for Youth designation, 2007, for *Changing Woman and Her Sisters.*

### Writings

*FOR CHILDREN*

*Anastasia Reading,* Golden Books (New York, NY), 1997.
(With sister-in-law Louise Tchana Pami) *Oh No, Toto!,* illustrated by Colin Bootman, Scholastic (New York, NY), 1998.

*Katrin Hyman Tchana* (Photograph courtesy of Katrin Hyman Tchana.)

(Reteller) *The Serpent Slayer, and Other Stories of Strong Women,* illustrated by mother, Trina Schart Hyman, Little, Brown (Boston, MA), 2000.
(Reteller) *Sense Pass King: A Story from Cameroon,* illustrated by Trina Schart Hyman, Holiday House (New York, NY), 2001.
(Reteller) *Changing Woman and Her Sisters: Stories of Goddesses from around the World,* illustrated by Trina Schart Hyman, Holiday House (New York, NY), 2006.

### Sidelights

The daughter of noted children's book illustrator Trina Schart Hyman, Katrin Hyman Tchana expands upon the family tradition by retelling stories for young children that introduce new cultures in traditional tales. Featuring artwork by noted illustrator Colin Bootman and a text that features colorful pidgin English, *Oh No, Toto!* is a collaboration with Tchana's then-sister-in-law Louise Tchana Pami that was inspired by the author's experiences working in Cameroon as a teacher for the Peace Corps during the 1980s. Another picture book—one of several collaborations between mother and daughter that features what a *Publishers Weekly* reviewer praised as Hyman's "gleaming, realistic oil paintings"—*Sense Pass King: A Story from Cameroon* again draws on Tchana's love of central African culture.

Focusing on a wise and kind-hearted young girl named Ma'antah whose ability to speak the language of animals allows her to ultimately triumph over a jealous monarch, *Sense Pass King* contains what *Horn Book* reviewer Margaret A. Bush dubbed "an entertaining story of youthful heroics" that ends with "the triumph of wisdom and goodness." In *Black Issues Book Review*, Lynda Jones praised Tchana's retelling as "wonderfully rich," adding that Ma'antah "is a brave child who is not only sure of herself but is a quick thinker." Noting that Hyman's "riveting acrylic paintings shine with clarity, humanity, and beauty," a *Kirkus Reviews* writer praised the book as "gorgeously illustrated," while a *Publishers Weekly* contributor concluded that Tchana's story includes "lots of action and smart thinking," making it "a welcome alternative to trickster tales, where intelligence is often associated with deviousness."

Two other highly praised collaborations between Tchana and Hyman, the anthologies *The Serpent Slayer, and Other Stories of Strong Women* and *Changing Woman and Her Sisters: Stories of Goddesses from around the World,* are notable not only for their contents, but also because they are among the last volumes to be illustrated by Hyman before the award-winning illustrator tragically passed away in 2004. Containing eighteen traditional tales drawn from a wide variety of cultures, *The Serpent Slayer, and Other Stories of Strong Women* introduces strong-willed, resourceful heroines that juggle "swords, needles and stew pots with equal skill, marry whom they please and even outwit the devil," according to an enthusiastic *Publishers Weekly* writer. In a similar fashion, *Changing Woman and Her Sisters* mines the mythology of ancient Sumer and Egypt, Mayan, Fong, and Navajo cultures, and even Ireland to present a pantheon of "vain, assertive, abused, and lavishly fer-

***Katrin Hyman Tchana collaborates with her mother, illustrator Trina Schart Hyman, on*** Sense Pass King, *a story that takes place in Cameroon.* (Copyright © 2002 by Trina Schart Hyman. Reproduced by permission of Holiday House, Inc.)

*Mother and daughter again team up for* **The Serpent Slayer, and Other Stories of Strong Women,** *an award-winning collection by Tchana that features Hyman's award-winning images.* (Copyright © 2000 by Trina Schart Hyman. All rights reserved. Reproduced by permission of Hachette Book Group USA.)

tile" deities, according to *Horn Book* critic Deirdre F. Baker. In her review of *The Serpent Slayer, and Other Stories of Strong Women* for the *Bulletin of the Center for Children's Books online,* Janice M. Del Negro praised the mother-daughter collaboration, citing Tchana's "solid retellings" of the tales. "Tchana's fresh and unpretentious storytelling voice is reinforced by the earthy glory of Hyman's illustrations," the critic added, "and the result is an elegantly conceived and executed volume." While Baker commended Tchana's choice of stories in *Changing Woman and Her Sisters* for helping "readers . . . notice the imagery and symbolism associated with female deities," a *Kirkus Reviews* writer cited the author's "spare, yet richly detailed retellings" as a central component of "a transcendent collaboration that will reward repeated study."

"Writing for children's books is hard!!," Tchana exclaimed in an interview for the *Peace Corps Global Teachnet Online.* "You have to say a lot with a very few words. Every word has to count." The Vermont-based writer added that she strives to create books that "celebrate diversity and increase tolerance by introducing children to different cultures in an interesting and amusing way. It's also important to me," Tchana added

"that we have stories available for our children that portray girls and women as people of strength and power."

## Biographical and Critical Sources

*PERIODICALS*

*Black Issues Book Review,* March-April, 2003, Lynda Jones, review of *Sense Pass King: A Story from Cameroon,* p. 64.

*Booklist,* March 1, 1997, Julie Corsaro, review of *Oh, No, Toto!,* p. 1174; December 15, 2000, Linda Perkins, review of *The Serpent Slayer, and Other Stories of Strong Women,* p. 502; November 1, 2002, Hazel Rochman, review of *Sense Pass King,* p. 502; June 1, 2006, Carolyn Phelan, review of *Changing Woman and Her Sisters: Stories of Goddesses from around the World,* p. 75.

*Bulletin of the Center for Children's Books,* March, 1997, review of *Oh, No, Toto!,* p. 259; November, 2000, review of *The Serpent Slayer, and Other Stories of Strong Women,* p. 95; January, 2003, review of *Sense Pass King,* p. 213; September, 2006, Maggie Hommel, review of *Changing Woman and Her Sisters,* p. 37.

*Horn Book,* November, 2000, Jennifer M. Brabander, review of *The Serpent Slayer, and Other Stories of Strong Women,* p. 765; November-December, 2002, Margaret A. Bush, review of *Sense Pass King,* p. 770; July-August, 2006, Deirdre F. Baker, review of *Changing Woman and Her Sister,* p. 458.

*Kirkus Reviews,* September 15, 2002, review of *Sense Pass King,* p. 1402; May 1, 2006, review of *Changing Woman and Her Sisters,* p. 468.

*New York Times Book Review,* December 8, 2002, review of *Sense Pass King,* p. 76.

*Publishers Weekly,* February 10, 1997, review of *Oh, No, Toto!,* p. 82; August 7,2000, review of *The Serpent Slayer, and Other Stories of Strong Women,* p. 95; July 22, 2002, review of *Sense Pass King,* p. 176.

*School Library Journal,* March, 1997, Judith Gloyer, review of *Oh, No, Toto!,* p. 168; November, 2000, Anne Chapman Callaghan, review of *The Serpent Slayer, and Other Stories of Strong Women,* p. 148; September, 2002, Ajoke' T.I. Kokodoko, review of *Sense Pass King,* p. 218; August, 2006, Miriam Lang Budin, review of *Changing Woman and Her Sisters,* p. 143.

*Tribune Books* (Chicago, IL), January 7, 2001, review of *The Serpent Slayer, and Other Stories of Strong Women,* p. 4; November 10, 2002, review of *Sense Pass King,* p. 5.

*ONLINE*

*Peace Corps Global Teachnet,* http://www.rpcv.org/ (March-April, 2006), "Meet the Author: Katrin Hyman Tchana."

*Bulletin of the Center of Children's Book Online,* http://bccb.lis.uiuc.edu/ (November 1, 2000), Janice M. Del Negro, review of *The Serpent Slayer, and Other Stories of Strong Women.**

## TOWNLEY, Rod
### See TOWNLEY, Roderick

\*     \*     \*

## TOWNLEY, Roderick 1942-
### (Rod Townley)

### Personal

Born June 7, 1942, in Orange, NJ; son of William Richard (a businessman) and Elise Townley; married Libby Blackman, April 4, 1970 (divorced, 1980); married Wyatt Baker (a poet and yoga instructor), February 15, 1986; children: (first marriage) Jesse Blackman; (second marriage) Grace Whitman. *Education:* Attended Hamilton College, 1960-61, and University of Chicago, 1961-62; Bard College, A.B., 1965; Rutgers University, M.A., 1970, Ph.D., 1972.

### Addresses

*Home*—Kansas City, MO. *Agent*—c/o Writers House, 21 W. 26th St., New York, NY 10010. *E-mail*—rodericktownley@everestkc.net.

### Career

Writer. Passaic County Community College, Paterson, NJ, associate professor of world literature, 1972-73; *TV Guide,* New York, NY, former editorial writer, beginning 1980. Visiting professor, University of Concepcion, Chile, 1978-79.

### Awards, Honors

Fulbright fellowship, 1978-79.

### Writings

#### FOR CHILDREN

(Translator) Rene Escudie, *Paul and Sebastian,* Kane/Miller (La Jolla, CA), 1988.

*The Great Good Thing* (novel), Atheneum Books for Young Readers (New York, NY), 2001.

*Into the Labyrinth* (novel; sequel to *The Great Good Thing*), Atheneum Books for Young Readers (New York, NY), 2002.

*Sky: A Novel in Three Sets and an Encore,* Atheneum Books for Young Readers (New York, NY), 2004.

*The Constellation of Sylvie* (novel; sequel to *Into the Labyrinth*), Atheneum Books for Young Readers (New York, NY), 2005.

*The Red Thread: A Novel in Three Incarnations,* Atheneum Books for Young Readers (New York, NY), 2007.

#### POETRY; FOR ADULTS

(Under name Rod Townley) *Blue Angels Black Angels,* privately printed, 1972.

(Under name Rod Townley) *Summer Street* (chapbook), The Smith (New York, NY), 1975.

(Under name Rod Townley) *Three Musicians,* The Smith (New York, NY), 1978.

*Final Approach,* Countryman Press (Woodstock, VT), 1986.

#### OTHER

(Under name Rod Townley) *The Early Poetry of William Carlos Williams* (criticism), Cornell University Press (Ithaca, NY), 1975.

(Under name Rod Townley) *Minor Gods* (novel), St. Martin's Press (New York, NY), 1976.

(Under name Rod Townley) *The Year in Soaps: 1983,* Crown (New York, NY), 1984.

*Safe and Sound: A Parent's Guide to Child Protection,* Simon & Schuster (New York, NY), 1985.

(Editor) *Night Errands: How Poets Use Dreams,* University of Pittsburgh Press (Pittsburgh, PA), 1998.

Contributor to books, including *University and College Poetry Prizes: 1967-1972,* edited by Daniel Hoffman, Academy of American Poets (New York, NY), 1974; *Eleven Young Poets: The Smith Seventeen,* edited by Ray Boxer, The Smith (New York, NY), 1975; *William Carlos Williams: Man and Poet,* edited by Carroll F. Terrell, National Poetry Foundation (Orono, ME), 1983; *Conversations with Ralph Ellison,* edited by Maryemma Graham and Amritjit Singh, University Press of Mississippi (Jackson, MS), 1995; and *Ravishing Disunities,* edited by Agha Shahid Ali, Wesleyan University Press (Hanover, NH), 2000. Contributor, sometimes under name Rod Townley, to periodicals, including *Studies in Short Fiction, Philadelphia, New York Times, Washington Post, TV Guide, Village Voice,* and *Detroit Free Press.*

### Sidelights

Roderick Townley began his writing career as a poet, and produced several works of literary criticism, before making a name for himself as the author of children's novels. In addition to *The Great Good Thing* and its sequels *Into the Labyrinth* and *The Constellation of Sylvie,* Townley has also authored stand-alone young-adult novels such as *Sky: A Novel in Three Sets and an Encore,* and *The Red Thread: A Novel in Three Incarnations.* In addition to his poetry and fiction, Townley has also worked as an entertainment journalist.

In *The Great Good Thing* Townley introduces Princess Sylvie and the many friends who live with her within the pages of an old, almost forgotten book titled *The Great Good Thing.* To perform her role in the story, the twelve-year-old princess yearns to do "one great good thing" before she submits to marriage, and Townley's novel follows her swashbuckling adventures in pursuit of that goal, however it is ultimately defined. When young Claire reads the book—the same copy her grandmother had once read and loved—the characters return

to life, acting out each part of the story anew. When the volume is destroyed by Claire's vile brother, the characters have nowhere else to go and cross into Claire's mind, where they live on in the young reader's dreams. Without the printed page to preserve them, the passage of time now threatens Sylvie and her friends, for Claire may one day forget them. Therefore, the resourceful Sylvie rescues herself and her friends by crossing into the mind of Lily, Claire's daughter. Inspired to retell and republish the story, Lily gives the storybook characters a renewed life. In *School Library Journal* Debbie Whitbeck deemed Townley's approach "an extremely clever and multilayered concept," but questioned whether younger readers would be able to grasp its multiple levels. A *Publishers Weekly* reviewer called *The Great Good Thing* a "clever, deftly written" novel for younger readers.

*Into the Labyrinth* finds Princess Sylvie and her cohorts busily reenacting their story in the wake of a fresh printing, repeating her search for the "one great good thing" she needs to do before marriage. When their story is published on the Internet, however, the pace of this quest becomes exhausting; their story must be reenacted again and again as each new reader discovers the tale. Not only must the characters get used to a frenzied pace, they also have to come to terms with new threats and phenomena unique to the online world, including wordpools, unexpected changes to their individual stories, the loss of sections of text, and deliberate changes by readers with access to electronic versions of the story. When a dragonlike "bot" appears, created by a descendent of the original author, its mission appears to be simply to destroy the tale as it rips out chunks of text and brings in characters from other stories. Determined not to passively watch while their fictional world is corrupted, Sylvie and her friends mount an expedition to confront and delete the dangerous dragon-bot. Their adventures continue in *The Constellation of Sylvie* as a copy of *The Great Good Thing* finds its way aboard a spaceship bound for Jupiter. During a reading by the ship-bound crew, the princess is confronted by the romantic advances of a blackmailing jester named Pingree. Once again, survival becomes an issue for the fictional cast when the space ship misses its window of reentry to Earth, providing Sylvie and company with yet another challenge.

Reviewing *Into the Labyrinth*, a *Kirkus Reviews* critic dubbed the book a "brilliantly imagined sequel" that continues to explore the concepts of how fiction affects individual readers that Townley first introduced in *The Great Good Thing*. *Booklist* contributor John Peters called the first sequel a "grand, tongue-in-cheek adventure," and Beth L. Meister commented in *School Library Journal* that "Sylvie is an appealing, thoughtful, and involving heroine, pulling the fast-paced plot to its satisfying conclusion." Praising the princess for her "plucky, resourceful nature," Krista Hurley added in her appraisal of *The Constellation of Sylvie* that Townley's "metafictional premise is deftly realized," while *Kliatt*

reviewer Lesley Farmer predicted that because of its focus on "strong females" and its mix of fantasy and science-fiction, Townley's series "should capture the attention of a special reading niche."

Directed to slightly older readers, Townley's young-adult novel *Sky* centers on fifteen-year-old jazz pianist Alex "Sky" Schuyler. Though his private-school classmates think little of him, Sky is a driving force in his jazz band, which includes drummer Max, bass player Larry, and manager Suze. Unfortunately for Sky, his conservative, workaday father views jazz as a waste of time and encourages his son to quit the band and devote his time to something more practical. As punishment for sneaking out to attend a Count Basie concert, Sky's father takes away the teen's piano, an instrument that had belonged to Sky's mother. Pushed beyond endurance, Sky runs away to make a life on the street. When he meets a blind jazz pianist in rapidly declining health, Sky bonds instantly with the weathered musician and ultimately learns important lessons about music and about life. *Sky* "brings the beatnik era to life while expressing timeless, universal themes about the generation gap," observed a *Publishers Weekly* reviewer. Paula Rohrlick, writing in *Kliatt*, called the novel an "appealing coming-of-age tale about finding yourself and finding your calling."

Townley profiles another troubled teen in *The Red Thread*. Plagued with horribly realistic nightmares and feelings of claustrophobia, Dana Landgrave hopes therapy can provide her with some relief. However, the belligerent sixteen year old may have misplaced her trust in Dr. Sprague when her therapy sessions cause more problems. When Sprague hypnotizes her, he unlocks a series of past lives that include a ten-year-old William, a boy who is murdered in the late 1500s, and Hannah, the niece of an ill-tempered artist who lives in eighteenth-century London. Soon Dana is drawn into an age-old mystery that not only threatens family relationships and her current romance; it also forces her to question the person she has assumed herself to be. According to a *Publishers Weekly* contributor, in *The Red Thread* Townley "raises an intriguing question about the nature of the soul" and its ability to reincarnate itself from generation to generation. Viewing the novel as a time-travel mystery, Claire Rosser praised its "highly intelligent" teen protagonist, adding in her *Kliatt* review that Townley "makes the places and people seem real, and he is able to keep the tension high throughout" his imaginative tale. In *Booklist*, Stephanie Zvirin found less to like about the petulant Dana, but nonetheless praised *The Red Thread*, citing the book's "deliciously scary premise and the melodramatic outcome" that is guaranteed to captivate teen readers. Describing the story as "captivating and shivery," a *Kirkus Reviews* writer noted that the twin themes of "revenge and devotion" infuse Townley's tale with "first-rate suspense and emotion."

## Biographical and Critical Sources

*PERIODICALS*

*Booklist,* November 1, 2002, John Peters, review of *Into the Labyrinth,* p. 499; June 1, 2006, Krista Hutley, review of *The Constellation of Sylvie,* p. 76; February 15, 2007, Stephanie Zvirin, review of *The Red Thread: A Novel in Three Incarnations,* p. 73.

*Bulletin of the Center for Children's Books,* September, 2004, Elizabeth Bush, review of *Sky: A Novel in Three Sets and an Encore,* p. 42.

*Guardian* (London, England), April 26, 2003, Jan Mark, "The Never-Ending Story," review of *The Great Good Thing.*

*Kirkus Reviews,* September 15, 2002, review of *Into the Labyrinth,* p. 1402; July 1, 2004, review of *Sky,* p. 638; February 1, 2006, review of *The Constellation of Sylvie,* p. 137; January 15, 2007, review of *The Red Thread,* p. 82.

*Kliatt,* July, 2004, Paula Rohrlick, review of *Sky,* p. 13; March, 2006, Lesley Farmer, review of *The Constellation of Sylvie,* p. 18; March, 2007, Claire Rosser, review of *The Red Thread,* p. 19.

*Library Journal,* September 1, 1998, Kim Woodbridge, review of *Night Errands: How Poets Use Dreams,* p. 181.

*Publishers Weekly,* May 21, 2001, review of *The Great Good Thing,* p. 108; August 30, 2004, review of *Sky,* p. 56; March 19, 2007, review of *The Red Thread,* p. 64.

*School Library Journal,* July, 2001, Debbie Whitbeck, review of *The Great Good Thing,* p. 114; October, 2001, Louise T. Sherman, review of *The Great Good Thing,* p. 89; October, 2002, Beth L. Meister, review of *Into the Labyrinth,* p. 174; July, 2004, Susan Riley, review of *Sky,* p. 113; August, 2006, Robyn Gioia, review of *The Constellation of Sylvie,* p. 130.

*ONLINE*

*Books for Sleepless Nights,* http://www.sleephomepage.org/ (November 5, 2005), review of *Night Errands.*

*Kidsreads.com,* http://www.kidsreads.com/ (November 5, 2005), Lisa Marx, review of *The Great Good Thing.**

\*     \*     \*

# URSU, Anne

## Personal

Born in Minneapolis, MN; married. *Education:* Brown University, graduated.

## Addresses

*E-mail*—anne@cronuschronicles.com.

## Career

Writer. Worked in a bookstore; *City Pages,* Minneapolis, MN, theater critic; *Phoenix,* Portland, ME, arts writer.

## Awards, Honors

Minnesota Book Award, and Bay Area Book Reviewers Award, both for *Spilling Clarence.*

## Writings

*NOVELS; FOR ADULTS*

*Spilling Clarence,* Theia (New York, NY), 2002.
*The Disapparation of James,* Theia (New York, NY), 2003.

*"CRONUS CHRONICLES"; YOUNG-ADULT NOVELS*

*The Shadow Thieves* illustrated by Eric Fortune, Atheneum (New York, NY), 2006.
*The Siren Song,* illustrated by Eric Fortune, Atheneum (New York, NY), 2007.
*The Promethean Flame,* illustrated by Eric Fortune, Atheneum (New York, NY), 2008.

Contributor of reviews and articles to periodicals, including various newspapers and *Glamour* magazine.

## Sidelights

Anne Ursu began her career writing for adults before turning her attention to a younger reading audience with the "Cronus Chronicles" novels. In the series, Ursu draws readers into a world peopled by characters from Greek myth and legend. There, modern-day characters find themselves embarking on a challenging and sometimes frightening quest that leads them from the depths of Hades' underworld to the heights of Mount Olympus, home of the gods. In addition to several works of adult fiction, she has penned theatre and arts reviews for regional newspapers, and also seen her articles published in national periodicals such as *Glamour* magazine. Discussing her decision to write for younger readers, Ursu noted in an interview for *Powells.com* that, in addition to her own love of reading children's books, younger readers "give you a chance to really be a storyteller. And there are no limits; a kid never tells you what you can and can't do in a book—they just want good stories, no matter where those stories take them."

Ursu begins her "Cronus Chronicles" with *The Shadow Thieves,* which finds thirteen-year-old Charlotte teaming up with her visiting cousin Zee and her English teacher Mr. Metos, to discover the origin of the strange illness that has rendered most of Zee's schoolmates comatose. A trip to the underworld leads the trio to the source of the plague: Philonecron, an immortal demi-demon who has tapped into the students' spirits as a means of animating the shadow army with which he hopes to overthrow Hades, god of the underworld. Battles with animated skeletons, vampires, and harpies provide high points in Ursu's humorous, Greek-inspired story, which *Horn Book* contributor Anita L. Burkam deemed a "fast-

paced action adventure." Charlotte's "irreverently casual" narration contains "a ridiculous exaggeration that pleasantly leavens the danger," Burkam added, while in *Booklist* Holly Koelling noted that the teen's narrative tone contains "such unabashed cheerfulness and gusto that readers will find much to enjoy." "With a wit and cynicism that will enchant most readers, Ursu weaves an extraordinary tale," concluded *School Library Journal* reviewer Lisa Marie Williams in a review of *The Shadow Thieves,* while a *Kirkus Reviews* writer dubbed the book "a fun and funny tale of youthful heroism." The "Cronus Chronicles," which features illustrations by Eric Fortune, continues with *The Siren Song.*

The first of Ursu's adult novels, *Spilling Clarence,* is set in Clarence, Minnesota, a fictional college town that also boasts a psychopharmaceutical plant. When a fire breaks out in the plant and a chemical cloud is released into the air, town residents are told to stay indoors while men in hazmat suits enter the area. Although an assurance of safety is made, the mind-altering drug deletrium begins to cause the townspeople's forgotten memories to return. In Ursu's story, the focus rests on the experiences of a small group of people stranded at a local bookstore café as a result of this drug. Christine Perkins commented in her *Library Journal* review of *Spilling Clarence* that "Ursu is a writer who cares deeply about her characters." "With compelling, scarred characters and a cleverly rendered setting, Ursu's debut is both thought-provoking and enjoyable," concluded *Booklist* critic Kristine Huntley.

Ursu followed *Spilling Clarence* with *The Disapparation of James.* In this haunting novel, a Midwestern family's outing to a traveling circus results in tragedy when the five-year-old son participates in a clown's disappearing act and consequently vanishes, leaving his parents distraught and his pragmatic older sister determined to solve the mystery. Ursu's story focuses on "the worry and longing, guilt and rage, protectiveness and resentment that characterize parental love," noted a *Publishers Weekly* contributor, and in *Kliatt* Nola Theiss concluded that the novelist "writes with great feeling and empathy for the family members." While noting that the boy's disappearance is never explained, *Booklist* contributor Elsa Gaztamide nonetheless praised *The*

*Disapparation of James* as "a very innovative work of fiction" that focuses on the evolution of a family loss "in a credible and insightful fashion."

## Biographical and Critical Sources

### PERIODICALS

*Booklist,* December 1, 2001, Kristine Huntley, review of *Spilling Clarence,* p. 631; March 1, 2006, Holly Koelling, review of *The Shadow Thieves,* p. 94.

*Horn Book,* March-April, 2006, Anita L. Burkam, review of *The Shadow Thieves,* p. 197.

*Kirkus Reviews,* November 15, 2001, review of *Spilling Clarence,* p. 1578; October 15, 2002, review of *The Disapparation of James,* p. 1502; March 1, 2006, review of *The Shadow Thieves,* p. 241.

*Kliatt,* May, 2004, Nola Theiss, review of *The Disapparation of James,* p. 24.

*Library Journal,* November 15, 2001, Christine Perkins, review of *Spilling Clarence,* p. 99.

*New York Times Book Review,* July 28, 2002, Jeff Waggoner, review of *Spilling Clarence,* p. 17.

*Philadelphia Inquirer,* January 6, 2002, Carlin Romano, review of *Spilling Clarence.*

*Publishers Weekly,* November 12, 2001, review of *Spilling Clarence,* p. 34; October 28, 2002, review of *The Disapparation of James,* p. 46.

*School Library Journal,* April, 2006, Lisa Marie Williams, review of *The Shadow Thieves,* p. 149.

*Times-Picayune* (New Orleans, LA), June 17, 2002, Susan Larson, review of *Spilling Clarence.*

*USA Today,* January 30, 2001, Jackie Pray, review of *Spilling Clarence.*

*US Weekly,* January 7, 2002, Janet Steen, review of *Spilling Clarence,* p. 64.

### ONLINE

*Anne Ursu Home Page,* http://www.anneursu.com (March 15, 2007).

*Bookreporter.com,* http://www.bookreporter.com/ (January 2, 2002), Kate Ayers, review of *Spilling Clarence* and interview with Ursu.

*Powells.com,* http://www.powells.com/kidsqa/ (March 15, 2007), "Anne Ursu."

# W-Z

## WHATLEY, Bruce 1954-

### Personal

Born 1954, in Wales; married Rosie Smith (an author); children: Ben, Ellyn. *Education:* Manchester Polytechnic, B.A. (illustration), 1975; study toward Ph.D.

### Addresses

*Home and office*—New South Wales, Australia.

### Career

Author and illustrator. Worked in advertising as an art director in London, England, 1775-80, and Sydney, New South Wales, Australia.

### Awards, Honors

Children's Book Council of Australia (CBCA) Notable Picture Book designation, 1993, for *The Ugliest Dog in the World;* CBCA Picture Book of the Year award short-list, 1993, for *Looking for Crabs,* and 2003, for *The Diary of a Wombat;* CBCA Picture Book of the Year Honor designation, 1998, for *Detective Donut and the Wild Goose Chase.*

### Writings

*SELF-ILLUSTRATED*

*Looking for Crabs,* Angus & Robertson (North Ryde, New South Wales, Australia), 1992.

*The Ugliest Dog in the World,* Angus & Robertson (Pymble, New South Wales, Australia), 1992.

*I Wanna Be Famous,* Angus & Robertson (Pymble, New South Wales, Australia), 1993.

*The Magic Dictionary,* Angus & Robertson (Pymble, New South Wales, Australia), 1993.

*The Magnetic Dog,* Angus & Robertson (Pymble, New South Wales, Australia), 1994.

**Bruce Whatley** (Photograph courtesy of Bruce Whatley.)

(With Rosie Smith) *Whatley's Quest,* Angus & Robertson (Pymble, New South Wales, Australia), 1994.

(With Rosie Smith) *Tails from Grandad's Attic,* Angus & Robertson (Pymble, New South Wales, Australia), 1996.

(And adaptor) Betty MacDonald, *Mrs. Piggle-Wiggle's Won't-Take-a-Bath Cure,* HarperCollins (New York, NY), 1997.

(And adaptor) Betty MacDonald, *The Won't-Pick-up-Toys Cure,* HarperCollins (New York, NY), 1997.

(With Rosie Smith) *Detective Donut and the Wild Goose Chase,* HarperCollins (New York, NY), 1997.

*My First Nursery Rhymes,* HarperFestival (New York, NY), 1999.

*The Flying Emu,* Koala Books (Mascot, New South Wales, Australia), 1999.

*The Boing Boing Races,* Koala Books (Mascot, New South Wales, Australia), 1999.

*Elvis Presley's The First Noel,* HarperCollins (New York, NY), 1999.

(With Rosie Smith) *Captain Pajamas,* HarperCollins (New York, NY), 1999.

(With Rosie Smith) *Little White Dogs Can't Jump,* Angus & Robertson (Pymble, New South Wales, Australia), 2001.

*Wait! No Paint!,* HarperCollins (New York, NY), 2001.

*Cowboy Pirate,* HarperCollins (Pymble, New South Wales, Australia), 2001.

(With Gary Crew) *Quetta,* Lothian (South Melbourne, Victoria, Australia), 2002.

*Dragons of Galapagos,* Lothian (South Melbourne, Victoria, Australia), 2003.

(With Gary Crew) *Lantern,* Hatchette (Sydney, New South Wales, Australia), 2005.

*The Watchmaker Who Saved Christmas,* Random House Australia (Milsons Point, New South Wales, Australia), 2006.

(With Rosie Smith) *The Adventures of Danny da Vinci and the Giant Horse of Milan,* ABC Books (Sydney, New South Wales, Australia), 2007.

*ILLUSTRATOR*

Jerry Garcia and David Grisman, arrangers, *The Teddy Bears' Picnic,* HarperCollins (New York, NY), 1996.

Clement C. Moore, *The Night before Christmas,* HarperCollins (New York, NY), 1999.

Jerry Garcia, *There Ain't No Bugs on Me,* HarperCollins (New York, NY), 1999.

Jerry Garcia, *What Will You Wear, Jenny Jenkins?,* HarperCollins (New York, NY), 2000.

Rolf Harris and John D. Brown, *Six White Boomers* (with recording), Margaret Hamilton Books (Hunters Hill, New South Wales, Australia), 2001.

Cecil Frances Alexander, *All Things Bright and Beautiful,* HarperCollins (New York, NY), 2001.

Jackie French, *Diary of a Wombat,* Clarion (New York, NY), 2002.

Gene Autry, *Here Comes Santa Claus,* HarperCollins (New York, NY), 2002.

Maribeth Boelts, *Lullaby Lullabook,* HarperFestival (New York, NY), 2002.

Jackie French, *Too Many Pears!,* Star Bright Books (New York, NY), 2003.

Margie Palatini, *The Perfect Pet,* HarperCollins (New York, NY), 2003.

Emily Brenner, *On the First Day of Grade School,* HarperCollins (New York, NY), 2004.

Jackie French, *Pete the Sheep-Sheep,* HarperCollins (Pymble, New South Wales, Australia), 2004, Clarion (New York, NY), 2005.

John Rox, *I Want a Hippopotamus for Christmas,* HarperCollins (New York, NY), 2005.

Beth Raisner Glass and Susan Lubner, *Noises at Night,* Harry N. Abrams (New York, NY), 2005.

Jackie French, *The Secret World of Wombats,* Angus & Robertson (Pymble, New South Wales, Australia), 2005.

Gary Crew, *Pig on the Titanic: A True Story!,* HarperCollins (New York, NY), 2005.

A.B. Banjo Paterson, *Mulga Bill's Bicycle, and Other Classics,* ABC Books (Sydney, New South Wales, Australia), 2005.

Jackie French, *Josephine Wants to Dance,* HarperCollins (Pymble, New South Wales, Australia), 2006.

Nette Hilton, *The Smallest Bilby and the Midnight Star,* Working Title Press (Kingswood, South Australia, Australia), 2006.

Susan Lubner, *Ruthie Bon Bair,* Abrams (New York, NY), 2006.

Nette Hilton, *The Smallest Bilby and the Easter Games,* Working Title Press (Kingswood, South Australia, Australia), 2007.

## Sidelights

Although artist Bruce Whatley could not read until he was ten years old, that did not stop him from building a successful career as an author of children's books such as *Whatley's Quest, Wait! No Paint!,* and *The Watchmaker Who Saved Christmas.* Immigrating to Australia with his family when he was a young boy, Whatley spent time working in the United Kingdom and the United States before settling in New South Wales, Australia, with his wife and coauthor, Rosie Smith. While he still struggles with reading, he has developed a passion for telling stories. "I mainly like to make people laugh," he explained on the HarperCollins Web site. "I like to entertain but subtly take the reader somewhere unexpected. You can't beat a good twist at the end, and I strive to make those last few pages a total surprise."

A collaboration with Smith, *Whatley's Quest* features hidden pictures that go with each letter of the alphabet. The book contains no text; instead, "readers" are encouraged to create their own stories using the images found on each page. Whatley and Smith include a sample story on the book's dust jacket that serves as a guide for readers inexperienced at mining story ideas. *Whatley's Quest* "is a treat for the eye and a most satisfactory launching pad for literacy," concluded a *Publishers Weekly* contributor, and Stephanie Zvirin wrote in *Booklist* that the coauthors' "oversized picture book certainly isn't a traditional ABC." Noting that the book is among his own favorites, Whatley added on the HarperCollins Web site that *Whatley's Quest* "is a journey through the alphabet in search of a hidden treasure: the ability to read." "It was the hardest story to write, and yet it has no words," he added.

For *Detective Donut and the Wild Goose Chase* Whatley and Smith draw on such well-known classic detective films as *The Maltese Falcon,* creating an entertaining mystery for young readers. "Artfully strewn with inventive details," Whatley's illustrations "evoke a bygone film era," according to a contributor for *Publishers Weekly.* In *Captain Pajamas,* another Whatley-Smith collaboration, Brian is convinced that aliens are invading his home town. To stop the advancing menace, the

rambunctious boy assumes the persona of Captain Pajamas, Defender of the Universe. "Lots of sly details make this a book kids can look at more than once—and giggle at each time," wrote Irene Cooper in her *Booklist* review.

One of Whatley's solo efforts, *Wait! No Paint!*, is a fractured-fairytale version of the Three Little Pigs saga. While some elements will be familiar, the real story is that the illustrator, known as the Voice, has run out of red paint. He attempts to use several different colors to paint the poor pigs before deciding they should be characters in a different story all together. "The book will be of great help in starting discussions on what an illustrator does," commented Debbie Stewart in *School Library Journal*. Discussing another of Whatley's solo efforts, the nonfiction *Dragons of Galapagos*, Kathryn Kosiorek noted in *School Library Journal* that his "representational style is bold," and serves up an effective match for the "spare, descriptive text" used to describe the journey of a Galapagos dragon to safe hatching grounds.

Along with his self-illustrated and coauthored works, Whatley has provided illustrations for a number of texts by other writers using his characteristic variety of mediums: gouache, pen and ink, and watercolor. He teamed up with fellow Australian Jackie French on a number of books, among them *Diary of a Wombat* and *Too Many Pears!* The former is told through the voice of a wombat as he explains his daily routine. Noting that the wombat diarist is captured in many distinct poses, a *Publishers Weekly* critic praised Whatley for his ability to "give . . . the star expressive eyes without anthropomorphizing her." A *Kirkus Reviews* contributor felt that the illustrations "provide the perfect counterpoint to French's deadpan narration." In *Too Many Pears!*, Pamela the cow eats so much of the sweet fruit that her owners worry that there will be no pears left for them to eat. Young Amy comes up with a solution: give Pamela all the pears she wants and hope she will become bored with them. According to Maryann H. Owen, writing in *School Library Journal*, the "facial expressions on humans and cow are priceless." Another collaboration between French and Whatley, *Pete the Sheep-Sheep*, is a story about learning to accept others' differences . . . including their haircuts. "Most of the fun in the ink-and-watercolor drawings comes from the expressions on the sheeps' faces," Ilene Cooper noted in *Booklist*, echoing the opinion of several other critics.

Whatley worked with well-known Australian writer Gary Crew in producing *Pig on the Titanic: A True Story*. A passenger named Edith Rosenbaum carries her musical toy pig onto the doomed *Titanic* ocean liner, and through Edith readers learn the story of those who survived that ship's tragic fate. "Whatley's realistic watercolors showcase the grandeur and opulence of the doomed ship," wrote Grace Oliff in her *School Library Journal* review. A *Kirkus Reviews* contributor commented on "Whatley's crisply detailed constructions," and a *Publishers Weekly* reviewer noted that the illustrator "lavishes attention on every inch of the scenes."

## Biographical and Critical Sources

*PERIODICALS*

*Booklist*, September 15, 1995, Stephanie Zvirin, review of *Whatley's Quest*, p. 158; February 1, 1999, Hazel Rochman, review of *My First Nursery Rhymes*, p. 997; August, 1999, Ilene Cooper, review of *There Ain't No Bugs on Me*, p. 2060; September 1, 1999, Susan Dove Lempke, review of *The Night before Christmas*, p. 148; May 15, 2000, Irene Cooper, review of *Captain Pajamas*, p. 1750; August, 2001, Helen Rosenberg, review of *Wait! No Paint!*, p. 2133; October 1, 2002, Carolyn Phelan, review of *Here Comes Santa Claus*, p. 328; July, 2003, Helen Rosenbert, review of *The Perfect Pet*, p. 1898; August, 2004, Jennifer Mattson, review of *On the First Day of Grade School*, p. 1947; June 1, 2005, Julie Cummins, review of *Pig on the Titanic: A True Story!*, p. 1820; January 1, 2006, Ilene Cooper, review of *Pete the Sheep-Sheep*, p. 112.

*Horn Book*, September, 2001, review of *Wait! No Paint!* p. 580; January-February, 2006, Kitty Flynn, review of *Pete the Sheep-Sheep*, p. 68.

*Kirkus Reviews*, November 1, 2002, review of *Here Comes Santa Claus*, p. 1615; March 15, 2003, review of *The Perfect Pet*, p. 475; July 15, 2003, review of *Diary of a Wombat*, p. 963; June 1, 2004, review of *On the First Day of Grade School*, p. 534; March 1, 2005, review of *Pig on the Titanic*, p. 285; October 1, 2005, review of *Noises at Night*, p. 1080; November 1, 2005, review of *I Want a Hippopotamus for Christmas*, p. 1196; September 15, 2006, review of *Ruthie Bon Bair*, p. 960.

*New Yorker*, November 27, 1995, review of *Whatley's Quest*, p. 98.

*Publishers Weekly*, September 4, 1995, review of *Whatley's Quest*, p. 68; July 29, 1996, review of *The Teddy Bears' Picnic*, p. 41; April 14, 1997, review of *Detective Donut and the Wild Goose Chase*, p. 74; May 10, 1999, review of *There Ain't No Bugs on Me*, p. 67; May 17, 1999, review of *Detective Donut and the Wild Goose Chase*, p. 81; September 27, 1999, reviews of *The Night before Christmas*, p. 53, and *Elvis Presley's The First Noel*, p. 54; June 19, 2000, review of *Captain Pajamas*, p. 78; July 21, 2003, review of *Diary of a Wombat*, p. 193; April 11, 2005, review of *Pig on the Titanic*, p. 55; August 1, 2005, review of *Noises at Night*, p. 64.

*School Library Journal*, January, 1996, JoAnn Rees, review of *Whatley's Quest*, p. 98; July, 2001, Debbie Stewart, review of *Wait! No Paint!*, p. 91; October, 2002, Maureen Wade, review of *Here Comes Santa Claus*, p. 56; May, 2003, review of *The Perfect Pet*, p. 128; August, 2003, Gay Lynn Van Vleck, review of *Diary of a Wombat*, p. 128; November, 2003, Mary-

ann H. Owen, review of *Too Many Pears!*, p. 93; January, 2004, Kathryn Kosiorek, review of *Dragons of Galapagos*, p. 107; July, 2004, Lisa Gangemi Kropp, review of *On the First Day of Grade School*, p. 68; May, 2005, Grace Oliff, review of *Pig on the Titanic*, p. 80; November, 2005, Grace Oliff, review of *Pete the Sheep-Sheep*, p. 90.

*ONLINE*

*AustList*, http://www.austlist.edu.au/ (February 23, 2007), "Bruce Whatley."

*Department of Education and Training of the Government of Western Australia Web site*, http://www.det.wa.edu.au/ (February 23, 2007), "Bruce Whatley."

*HarperCollins Web site*, http://www.harpercollins.com/ (February 23, 2007),"Bruce Whatley."

*Lateral Learning Speaker's Agency Web site*, http://www.laterallearning.com/ (February 27, 2007), "Bruce Whatley."

\* \* \*

# WHYTOCK, Cherry

## Personal

Married; children: two daughters. *Education:* Studied art and textile design. *Hobbies and other interests:* Painting, gardening, dog walking.

## Addresses

*Home*—Tunbridge Wells, Kent, England.

## Career

Novelist and illustrator.

## Writings

*"ANGEL" SERIES; YOUNG-ADULT NOVELS*

*Disasters, Diets, and D-Cups*, Picadilly Press (London, England), 2003, published as *My Cup Runneth Over: The Life of Angelica Cookson Potts*, Simon & Schuster (New York, NY), 2003.

*Haggis Horrors and Heavenly Bodies*, Picadilly Press (London, England), 2003, published as *My Scrumptious Scottish Dumplings: The Life of Angelica Cookson Potts*, Simon & Schuster (New York, NY), 2004.

*Secrets, Suspicions, and Sun-kissed Beaches*, Picadilly Press (London, England), 2004, published as *My Saucy Stuffed Ravioli: The Life of Angelica Cookson Potts*, Simon & Schuster (New York, NY), 2006.

*Loving, Loathing, and Luscious Lunches*, Picadilly Press (London, England), 2004.

*Deli Dramas and Dreamy Doormen*, Picadilly Press (London, England), 2005.

*YOUNG-ADULT NOVELS*

(With Caroline Plaisted) *Cringe!: The Top Secret Diary of Amaryllis Flowerdew; or, How a Star Is Born*, Macmillan (London, England), 2003.

(With Caroline Plaisted) *Do I Look Like I Care?: What Amaryllis Did Next* (sequel to *Cringe!*), Macmillan (London, England), 2003.

*Fizzy Pink*, Puffin (London, England), 2005.

*Fabberoony Fizzy Pink*, Puffin (London, England), 2006.

*Honeysuckle Lovelace: The Dogwalkers' Club*, Piccadilly (London, England), 2006.

*Honeysuckle Lovelace: Ghosthunters*, Piccadilly (London, England), 2007.

## Sidelights

In the "Angel" novels, her first foray into teen fiction, author and illustrator Cherry Whytock created a popular and likeable protagonist who shared one of the most vexing worries facing many girls her age: her weight. Published in the author's native Great Britain as well as in the United States (although under different titles), the series earned Whytock a devoted readership. Continuing her focus on teen life, Whytock has also created several more multi-volume storylines, among them *Cringe!: The Top Secret Diary of Amaryllis Flowerdew; or, How a Star Is Born* and *Do I Look like I Care?: What Amaryllis Did Next*. Co-authored with popular teen novelist Caroline Plaisted and featuring Whytock's cartoon art, the two books contain the animated diary entries of Amaryllis Flowerdew and her efforts to live the life of a normal materialistic teen despite her strange name and the fact that she lives under the sway of her counterculture, hippie parents.

In *My Cup Runneth Over: The Life of Angelica Cookson Potts*—published in England as *Disasters, Diets, and D-Cups*—Whytock introduces a full-figured fourteen year old who loves food but struggles with the inevitable conflict between being herself and living up to society's model-thin severe expectations. It does not help that Angel's friends—as well as her mom, a former model—are all rail thin. Although they insist that they love her just the way she is, as *School Library Journal* reviewer Linda L. Plevak put it, Angel "knows she needs to make life changes and pokes fun at all that is wrong in her life." She gives an all-cabbage diet a try until the object of her desire invites one her friends, rather than her, to the school dance. An attempt at kickboxing comes next, but that proves equally unsuccessfully. Eventually "help arrives in the form of a new brassiere, which provides the emotional and literal boost she needs to model in a school fashion show," as Jennifer Mattson explained in *Booklist*. In addition to noting the uplifting message in *My Cup Runneth Over*, *Kliatt* reviewer Paula Rohrlick predicted that readers "will enjoy the bubbly sense of humor and the chatter about friends, clothes, and boys" in Whytock's pun-filled text, as well as the bonus of eight recipes salted with Angel's witty comments on cooking and enjoying food.

*Cover of Cherry Whytock's young-adult novel* My Cup Runneth Over, *featuring a photograph by Michael Frost.* (Cover photograph copyright © 2004 by Michael Frost. Reproduced by permission of Michael Frost, Inc.)

In *My Scrumptious Scottish Dumplings: The Life of Angelica Cookson Potts* (titled *Haggis Horrors and Heavenly Bodies* for British publication), Angel's problems "stem not from her physique . . . but from her Scottish father's eccentricity," according to Mattson. All seems well when the Potts family takes a trip north to Scotland to revisit their ancestral roots, but after their return to London, a bit of upheaval occurs. Stirred up with national pride, Angel's dad, nicknamed "Potty," starts a protest against the famed Harrod's department store, which he accuses of stocking an inferior type of haggis. After Potty is arrested, Angel finds herself banned from the store, and thus from access to many of the prized recipe ingredients she can find nowhere else in London. Realizing that she will have to prove her father justified in his charge if she is ever to shop at her beloved Harrod's again, Angel enlists her friends—and even an old foe—in the cause. The teen's life is further complicated by the presence of two appealing boys, one who lives with her family and the other a schoolmate who is starting to show an interest in her. "Angel's obsessions with

fatness, fashion, and food are funny and fast," concluded a *Kirkus Reviews* contributor. As with *My Cup Runneth Over,* recipes for Angel's favorite foods— which do not include haggis—are sprinkled throughout *My Scrumptious Scottish Dumplings.*

Angel's adventures, as well as her battle with her naturally ample waistline, continue in *My Saucy Stuffed Ravioli: The Life of Angelica Cookson Potts.* Vacationing in Italy with her family and friends, Angel braves the beach but pines for potential boyfriend Sydney, especially when her friends find romance in the Mediterranean sun. The teen is forced back down to earth, however, when her mom begins to act love-struck and the possibility of an extramarital affair casts a cloud on the holiday. In *School Library Journal,* Tracy Karbel described Angel as "a wonderful, lovable character," and noted that the secondary characters in *My Saucy Stuffed Ravioli* are "kind to one another and value friendship." Fine cuisine and the adventures of the likeable Angel continue in *Loving, Loathing, and Luscious Lunches* and *Deli Dramas and Dreamy Doormen.*

In her "Angel" books, as well as her other novels for teens, Whytock begins each story with a sketch. "I always begin with drawings of the characters as I like to be able to 'see' them before I begin to write about them," she once noted. Recalling the experience of writing her first "Angel" novel, the author added: "Initially I found writing terrifying. But the more I wrote the more I loved it! After really careful planning and outlines I write fast and furiously on my laptop. I find writing increasingly addictive—I can see all the characters in my head and miss them dreadfully when a book is finished!"

## Biographical and Critical Sources

*PERIODICALS*

*Booklist,* November 15, 2003, Jennifer Mattson, review of *My Cup Runneth Over: The Life of Angelica Cookson Potts,* p. 607; January 1, 2005, Jennifer Mattson, review of *My Scrumptious Scottish Dumplings: The Life of Angelica Cookson Potts,* p. 847; December 1, 2005, Jennifer Mattson, review of *My Saucy Stuffed Ravioli: The Life of Angelica Cookson Potts,* p. 47.

*Bulletin of the Center for Children's Books,* November, 2003, Karen Coats, review of *My Cup Runneth Over,* p. 129.

*Children's Book Review,* February, 2005, review of *My Scrumptious Scottish Dumplings.*

*Kirkus Reviews,* August 15, 2003, review of *My Cup Runneth Over,* p. 1081; September 15, 2004, review of *My Scrumptious Scottish Dumplings,* p. 923; December 1, 2005, review of *My Saucy Stuffed Ravioli,* p. 1281.

*Kliatt,* September, 2003, Paula Rohrlick, review of *My Cup Runneth Over,* p. 14; September, 2004, Paula Rohrlick, review of *My Scrumptious Scottish Dumplings,* p. 17.

*Publishers Weekly,* September 1, 2003, review of *My Cup Runneth Over,* p. 90; October 18, 2004, reviews of *My Cup Runneth Over* and *My Scrumptious Scottish Dumplings,* p. 66.

*School Library Journal,* September, 2003, Linda L. Plevak, review of *My Cup Runneth Over,* p. 222; January, 2005, Karen Hoth, review of *My Scrumptious Scottish Dumplings,* p. 138; January, 2006, Tracy Karbel, review of *My Saucy Stuffed Ravioli,* p. 145.

*Voice of Youth Advocates,* February, 2006, Walter Hogan, review of *My Saucy Stuffed Ravioli,* p. 495.

\* \* \*

# WILLIAMS, Sam 1955-

## Personal

Born 1955, in London, England; married; three children. *Education:* Essex Art and Design College, studied graphic design.

## Addresses

*Home*—Hertfordshire, England. *E-mail*—samwill@schmeen.demon.co.uk.

## Career

Illustrator and author.

## Awards, Honors

Children's Choice selection, International Reading Association/Children's Book Council, 2001, for *Cold Little Duck, Duck, Duck* by Lisa Westberg Peters.

## Writings

### FOR CHILDREN

*Santa's Toys,* illustrated by Tim Gill, David Bennett (St. Albans, England), 1998.

*The Teddy Bears' Christmas Tree,* illustrated by Jacqueline McQuade, David Bennett (St. Albans, England), 2000, published as *The Teddy Bears Trim the Tree: A Christmas Pull-the-Tab Book,* Scholastic (New York, NY), 2000.

*Spots and Slots: A Slide-the-Spot Book of Colors,* illustrated by Manya Stojic, Scholastic (New York, NY), 2001.

*The Teddy Bears' Trick or Treat,* Cartwheel (New York, NY), 2001.

*Long Train: 101 Cars on the Track,* Cartwheel (New York, NY), 2001.

*Talk Peace,* illustrated by Mique Moriuchi, Holiday House (New York, NY), 2005.

*That's Love,* illustrated by Mique Moriuchi, Holiday House (New York, NY), 2006.

### SELF-ILLUSTRATED

*The Baby's Word Book,* David Bennett (St. Albans, England), 1993, Greenwillow (New York, NY), 1999.

*Who Goes Moo?,* Books for Children, 1996.

*Whose Baby?,* Books for Children, 1996.

*Whose Home?,* Books for Children, 1996.

*Beach Baby,* Campbell (London, England), 2001.

*Wiggly Toes,* Campbell (London, England), 2001.

*Yum Yum,* Campbell (London, England), 2001.2001.

*Giggle Giggle,* Campbell (London, England), 2001.

*Wakey Wakey, Night Night,* Cartwheel (New York, NY), 2001.

*Christmas Bear,* Gullane Children's Books (London, England), 2002.

*Snowy Magic,* HarperCollins (New York, NY), 2002.

*Angel's Christmas Cookies,* HarperFestival (New York, NY), 2002.

*Bunny and Bee's Noisy Night,* Orchard (London, England), 2003.

*Bunny and Bee's Playful Day,* Orchard (London, England), 2003.

*Bunny and Bee's Forest Friend,* Orchard (London, England), 2004.

*Bunny and Bee's Rainbow Colors,* Orchard (London, England), 2004.

### ILLUSTRATOR

*Rock-a-Bye Baby* (board-book series), ten volumes, Dutton (New York, NY), 1992.

*Toddler Playtime,* Collins (London, England), 1998.

*Toddler Bedtime,* Collins (London, England), 1998.

Ros Asquith, *Ball!,* DK Publishing (New York, NY), 1998.

Nanette Newman, *Up to the Skies,* Hodder Children's (London, England), 1999.

Ros Asquith, *My Do It!,* Dorling Kindersley (London, England and New York, NY), 2000.

Lisa Westberg Peters, *Cold Little Duck, Duck, Duck,* Greenwillow (New York, NY), 2000.

Grace Maccarone, *A Child Was Born: A First Nativity Book,* Scholastic (New York, NY), 2000.

Isabel Wilner, *The Baby's Game Book,* Greenwillow (New York, NY), 2000.

Marni McGee, *Sleepy Me,* Simon & Schuster (New York, NY), 2000.

Grace Maccarone, *A Child's Good Night Prayer,* Scholastic (New York, NY), 2001.

Hiawyn Oram, *Shall We Do That Again?,* Orchard (London, England), 2001, published as *Let Us Do That Again!,* Dutton (New York, NY), 2003.

Mathew Price, *Who Loves You, Baby Bear?,* Mathew Price (Sherborne, England), 2001.

Laura E. Richards, *Jiggle Joggle Jee!,* Greenwillow (New York, NY), 2001.

Marni McGee, *Wake up, Me!,* Simon & Schuster (New York, NY), 2001.

Grace MacCarone, *A Child's Goodnight Prayer,* Scholastic (New York, NY), 2001.

Ros Asquith, *Babies,* Macmillan (London, England), 2002, Simon & Schuster (New York, NY), 2003.

Karen Baicker, *Tumble Me Tumbily,* Handprint Books (Brooklyn, NY), 2002, board-book adaptation published as *Yum Tummy Tickly!,* 2004.

Sarah Ferguson, *Little Red,* Simon & Schuster (New York, NY), 2003.

Karen Baicker, *Pea Pod Babies,* Handprint Books (Brooklyn, NY), 2003.

Ellen Weiss, *Twins in the Park,* Aladdin (New York, NY), 2003.

Ellen Weiss, *Twins Take a Bath,* Aladdin (New York, NY), 2003.

Ellen Weiss, *Twins Go to Bed,* Aladdin (New York, NY), 2004.

Ellen Weiss, *Twins Have a Fight,* Aladdin (New York, NY), 2004.

Sarah Ferguson, *Little Red's Christmas Story,* Simon & Schuster (New York, NY), 2004.

Karen Baicker, *Wake-ity Wake!,* Handprint Books (Brooklyn, NY), 2004.

Sarah Ferguson, *Little Red's Summer Adventure,* Simon & Schuster (New York, NY), 2006.

Bernette Ford, *No More Diapers for Ducky!,* Sterling Publishing (New York, NY), 2006.

Jane Kemp and Clare Walters, *My Favorite Toys!,* Tiger Tales (Wilton, CT), 2006, published as *My First Toy Catalogue,* Oxford University Press (Oxford, England), 2006.

George Shannon, *Busy in the Garden,* Greenwillow Books (New York, NY), 2006.

Sarah Weeks, *Overboard!,* Harcourt (Orlando, FL), 2006.

Roseanne Thong, *Tummy Girl,* Henry Holt (New York, NY), 2007.

Sarah Weeks, *Bunny Fun,* Harcourt (Orlando, FL), 2007.

## Sidelights

Sam Williams, a British illustrator and author, is perhaps best known for his drawings of babies and tod-

*Sam Williams has done many illustration projects for other authors, among them* **A Child Was Born,** *Grace Maccarone's retelling of the nativity story.* (Illustrations copyright © 2000 by Sam Williams. Reproduced by permission of Scholastic, Inc.)

dlers. These simple drawings are the highlight of his earliest solo efforts, such as the *Rock-a-Bye Baby* series of ten miniature board books. Nesting inside a cradle-shaped box with a rounded bottom, the books feature texts consisting of a string of words, one to a page, which relate to bedtime, playtime, bath time, home, and other familiar elements of a young child's life. Each word is coupled with one of Williams' signature illustrations, in which a chubby little person beams cherubically out at the reader. *The Baby's Word Book* is an oversized version of the same concept; in this case, each page is mapped out in a grid of nine pictures, each accompanied by the word and phrase for the object, feeling, or activity depicted. The result was described as "great fun for toddlers" by *School Library Journal* reviewer Lisa Falk. According to *Horn Book* reviewer Lauren Adams, Williams's characteristic "gentle pencil and watercolor illustrations" also accompany Isabel Wilner's *The Baby's Game Book*, a collection of thirty-five games that are suitable for adult and toddler sharing. Appraising Williams' illustration output, a *Publishers Weekly* contributor described his Williams's contributions to children's literature as "warm, attractive art."

Williams teamed up with author Lisa Westberg Peters for the picture book *Cold Little Duck, Duck, Duck,* which Catherine Andronik dubbed "a wonderful read-aloud pick-me-up for those blah, between-season March days" in her *Booklist* review. In the book, Peters tells the story of a little duck who returns to her pond too early one spring and finds the water still frozen over. By closing her eyes and imagining the sights, sounds, and smells of spring, the duck brings the warm season back. Peters' simple rhyming text repeats each end-of-the-phrase word three times, making the book a perfect choice for reading aloud, reviewers noted. Best of all, "story, art, and design work together well, and there's plenty here to engage duck-loving preschoolers preparing to dive into words and reading," observed *Horn Book* reviewer Kitty Flynn. In contrasting the muted colors of winter with the brighter colors of spring, Williams helps create "a beautiful book for sharing with toddlers," asserted Judith Constantinides in *School Library Journal*, while a *Publishers Weekly* critic called *Cold Little Duck, Duck, Duck* a "visually sumptuous testimony to patience and the power of positive thinking."

In his contribution to *A Child Was Born: A First Nativity Book*, Grace Maccarone's rhyming rendition of the Christian nativity story, Williams creates "softly muted, double-page watercolor spreads," according to a reviewer in *School Library Journal*. His "simple, uncluttered" illustrations also grace several books by Ros Asquith. As its title makes plain, *My Do It!* is a lift-the-flap book about an independent-minded toddler who insists on doing everything for himself. Young readers can help by lifting the flaps, according to Olga R. Barnes in *School Library Journal*. *Babies,* also featuring a rhyming text by Asquith that skips along a list of tod-

dler differences, including likes and dislikes. In *Booklist,* Carolyn Phelan commented in particular on the book's "consistently light, sunny tone," and citing Williams' artistic contribution of "well-drawn," multiracial infants. In *School Library Journal,* Blair Christolon praised the illustrator for casting toddlers as "well-rounded figures with expressive, yet gentle features" in *Babies,* while a *Kirkus Reviews* writer noted that the illustrator's "soft, subtly shaded watercolors perfectly render the many babies and toys" that star in Asquith's "poetic celebration" of infanthood.

In his illustrations for Laura E. Richards' *Jiggle Joggle Jee!,* Williams brings to life the imaginary adventures of a child as he drifts off to sleep and dreams of riding a toy train through an imaginary landscape. Williams trades his simple, lucid style for what a *Publishers Weekly* critic dubbed "an impressionistic approach," effectively conveying Richards's fantasy. As in several of his other collaborative efforts *Jiggle Joggle Jee!* features a playful rhyme scheme designed to engage small children. Paired with this text, "Williams' watercolors are stunners, densely colored yet shimmering with light," according to a reviewer in *Publishers Weekly.* Praised by *School Library Journal* reviewer Rosalyn Pierini as "an absolute delight from start to finish," Karen Baicker's *Pea Pod Babies* is also enhanced by Williams's "inviting, wispy-lined artwork," his portraits of round-faced infants cited by *Booklist* reviewer Jenni-

*Sam Williams' best-known collaborations include* **Little Red's Summer Adventure,** *a picture book penned by Sarah Ferguson, Duchess of York.* (Illustrations copyright © 2003 by Sam Williams. Reproduced by permission of Simon & Schuster Books for Young Readers, an imprint of Simon & Schuster Children's Publishing Division.)

*Mique Moriuchi takes over illustration duties as Williams turns storyteller in* **Talk Peace,** *a picture book that celebrates global harmony.* (Illustrations copyright © Mique Moriuchi, 2005. Reproduced by permission of Holiday House, Inc.)

fer Mattson as "excellent" for laptime readings. Other writers whose works have been brought to life in Williams's art include Sarah Weeks, Hiawyn Oram, George Shannon, and Ellen Weiss.

Among the many writers who have seen their text paired with Williams's art, perhaps the most high profile has been British author Sarah Ferguson, duchess of York. Published in 2003, *Little Red* introduces readers to a red-haired, gingham-clad girl who lives in an idyllic forest cottage, surrounded by animal friends Gino the spotted dog, Roany the pink pony, and the simply named Squirrel, as well as human neighbor Little Blue. During a picnic, the friends come to the rescue of a waterbound bunny, with Williams's "detailed watercolor illustrations add[ing] considerable, genuine charm to the effort," according to a *Kirkus Reviews* writer. Ferguson's writing efforts have also produced *Little Red's Summer Adventure,* which finds the friends competing in a local boat-building contest by transforming Red's turquoise wagon into a watercraft. In *School Library Journal,* Kirsten Cutler wrote that Williams' pencil drawings "do a nice job of conveying" Ferguson's simple storyline, and a *Kirkus Reviews* writer concluded that his "detailed paintings neatly capture the fey, otherworldliness" of the child-friendly world brought to life in *Little Red's Summer Adventure.*

Although Williams is best known for the illustrations he provides for texts written by other authors, he has also written several original children's books, among them *The Teddy Bears Trim the Tree: A Christmas Pull-the-Tab Book, The Teddy Bears' Trick or Treat,* and *Angel's Christmas Cookies.* In *Talk Peace* he hands over illustration duties to artist Mique Moriuchi, and concen-

trates his efforts on the rhyming text of a book that a *Publishers Weekly* contributor described as "bouncy and effervescent" as well as "colorful and inclusive." The book, inspired by Williams' reaction to world events at the turn of the twenty-first century, encourages young readers to, as it's title states, "On the street,/ when you meet,/ . . . talk Peace." A companion volume, *That's Love,* also features Moriuchi's artwork, described by a *Kirkus Reviews* writer as "simple, soft-edged scenes of children and animals at play."

## Biographical and Critical Sources

### BOOKS

William, Sam, *Talk Peace,* illustrated by Mique Moriuchi, Hodder Childrens (London, England), 2005.

### PERIODICALS

*Booklist,* May 15, 2000, Catherine Andronik, review of *Cold Little Duck, Duck, Duck,* p. 1749; December 1, 2000, Ilene Cooper, review of *Teddy Bears Trim the Tree: A Christmas Pull-the-Tab Book,* p. 728; January 1, 2003, Karin Snelson, review of *Let's Do That Again!,* p. 909; February 1, 2003, Carolyn Phelan, review of *Babies,* p. 999; November 15, 2003, Jennifer Mattson, review of *Pea Pod Babies,* p. 103; January 1, 2006, Gillian Engberg, review of *Busy in the Garden,* p. 106; February 15, 2006, Carolyn Phelan, review of *Overboard!,* p. 106; June 1, 2006, Jennifer Mattson, review of *No More Diapers for Ducky!,* p. 82.

*Children's Book Review Annual,* 1998, review of *Santa's Toys,* p. 492.

*Horn Book,* spring, 1993, review of *Rock-a-Bye Baby,* p. 17; July, 2000, Kitty Flynn, review of *Cold Little Duck, Duck, Duck,* p. 443, and Lauren Adams, review of *The Baby's Game Book,* p. 449; March-April, 2006, Susan Dove Lempke, review of *Busy in the Garden,* p. 202.

*Kirkus Reviews,* September 15, 2002, review of *Tumble Me Tumbily,* p. 1383; December 15, 2002, review of *Babies,* p. 1845; September 1, 2003, review of *Little Red,* p. 1122; February 15, 2006, review of *Overboard!,* p. 191; March 1, 2006, review of *Busy in the Garden,* p. 239; June 15, 2006, review of *Little Red's Summer Adventure,* p. 632; September 1, 2006, review of *That's Love,* p. 915.

*Publishers Weekly,* October 26, 1992, review of *Rock-a-Bye Baby,* p. 68; September 6, 1999, review of *The Baby's Word Book,* p. 106; March 20, 2000, review of *Cold Little Duck, Duck, Duck,* p. 92; April 2, 2001, review of *Jiggle Joggle Jee!,* p. 62; April 17, 2000, "Rhymes in Action," p. 82; September 25, 2000, review of *A Child Was Born: A First Nativity Book,* p. 68; September 23, 2002, review of *Angel's Christmas Cookies,* p. 36; November 11, 2002, review of *Tumble Me Tumbily,* p. 62; December 15, 2002, review of *Babies,* p. 65; July 21, 2003, review of *Little Red,* p. 193; January 5, 2004, review of *Pea Pod Babies,* p. 59; February 28, 2005, review of *Talk Peace,* p. 65; March 27, 2006, review of *Overboard!* and *No More Diapers for Ducky!,* p. 77.

*School Library Journal,* January, 2000, Lisa Falk, review of *The Baby's Word Book,* p. 127; May, 2000, Judith Constantinides, review of *Cold Little Duck, Duck, Duck,* p. 151; October, 2000, review of *a Child Was Born,* p. 61, and Olga R. Barnes, review of *My Do It!,* p. 110; June, 2001, Martha Topol, review of *Sleepy Me,* p. 126; October, 2002, Eva Mitnick, review of *Angel's Christmas Cookies,* p. 65; March, 2003, Blair Christolon, review of *Babies,* p. 176, and Lisa Dennis, review of *Let's Do That Again!,* p. 200; April, 2003, Steven Engelfried, review of *Tumble Me Tumbily,* p. 114; September, 2003, Nancy A. Gifford, review of *Little Red,* p. 177; November, 2003, Joy Fleishhacker, review of *Twins in the Park,* p. 200; December, 2003, Rosalyn Pierini, review of *Pea Pod Babies,* p. 103; August, 2004, Anne Knickerbocker, review of *Twins Go to Bed,* p. 103; April, 2005, Blair Christolon, review of *Talk Peace,* p. 116; February, 2006, Carolyn Janssen, review of *Busy in the Garden,* p. 124; April, 2006, Martha Topol, review of *Overboard!,* p. 120; July, 2006, Kirsten Cutler, review of *Little Red's Summer Adventure,* p. 77; August, 2006, Martha Topol, review of *No More Diapers for Ducky!,* p. 87; September, 2006, Tamara E. Richman, review of *That's Love,* p. 187.

ONLINE

*Sam Williams Web site,* http://www.schmeem.demon.co.uk/ (March 19, 2007).*

# WYATT, Melissa 1963-

## Personal

Born 1963, in York, PA; married Andy Wyatt; children: Ned, Will.

## Addresses

*Home and office*—York, PA. *E-mail*—Melissa@melissawyatt.com.

## Career

Children's book author.

## Awards, Honors

Best of the Best designation, Missouri Library Association, 2004, Thumbs Up! Award nomination, Michigan Library Association, and Best Books for the Teen Age designation, New York Public Library Books, both 2005; and Tayshas List, 2005-06, all for *Raising the Griffin.*

## Writings

*YOUNG-ADULT NOVELS*

*Raising the Griffin,* Wendy Lamb Books (New York, NY), 2004.
*Almost Heaven,* Farrar, Straus (New York, NY), 2009.

## Sidelights

After working on her manuscript for four years—one year on the initial story and three years on revisions—Melissa Wyatt made her publishing debut in 2004 with the young-adult novel *Raising the Griffin.* The story introduces readers to sixteen-year-old Alex Varenhoff, a British teen who has just discovered that he is heir to the throne of the small communist country of Rovenia. While the young man's father decides to move to Rovenia to take his place as the newly restored king of the impoverished eastern European country, Alex would rather continue leading a low-profile life at his English boarding school. His princely destiny ultimately wins out, however, and Alex must learn to shoulder the responsibility not only for himself but also for his family and the vulnerable young nation. Noting that "there are no easy answers" for Wyatt's teen protagonist, *School Library Journal* reviewer Sharon Rawlins called *Raising the Griffin* a "powerfully affecting novel that avoids cliché and the expected fairy-tale ending." In *Kliatt* Heather Rader also enjoyed Wyatt's debut. Comparing the novel to the popular "Princess Diaries" books by Meg Cabot, Rader commented that "the characters ring true . . . and the pace is nonstop." Todd Morning, writing in *Booklist,* predicted that Wyatt's "serious, realistic" tale "will draw plenty of young readers with Alex's taut, first-person narration of his predicaments."

*Cover of Melissa Wyatt's novel* Raising the Griffin, *featuring an illustration by Cynthia von Buhler.* (Dell Laurel-Leaf, 2004. Used by permission of Wendy Lamb Books, an imprint of Random House Children's Books, a division of Random House, Inc.)

Discussing her writing career on her home page, Wyatt explained that she decided to write for a young-adult audience because "it's the age group that excites me the most. Think about what's going on in your life between the ages of twelve and eighteen. It's all about change inside and out. I'm not talking about your body. I'm talking about how you begin to see yourself fitting into the world. And it's about making choices; New, exciting, and sometimes scary ones. And since change and choice are conflict and conflict is the basis of great stories, what could be better to write about?"

## Biographical and Critical Sources

*PERIODICALS*

*Booklist,* January 1, 2004, Todd Morning, review of *Raising the Griffin,* p. 848.
*Bookwatch,* February, 2004, James A. Cox and Diane C. Donovan, review of *Raising the Griffin,* p. 2.
*Bulletin of the Center for Children's Books,* February, 2004, Deborah Stevenson, review of *Raising the Griffin,* p. 250.
*Kirkus Reviews,* November 15, 2003, review of *Raising the Griffin,* p. 1365.
*Kliatt,* January, 2006, Heather Rader, review of *Raising the Griffin,* p. 20.
*Publishers Weekly,* January 12, 2004, review of *Raising the Griffin,* p. 54.
*School Library Journal,* February, 2004, Sharon Rawlins, review of *Raising the Griffin,* p. 153.

*ONLINE*

*Debbi Michiko Florence Web site,* http://www.debbimichikoflorence.com/ (March 5, 2007), interview with Wyatt.
*Melissa Wyatt Home Page,* http://www.melissawyatt.com (March 5, 2007).

\*     \*     \*

# ZUPANCIC, Lilijana Praprotnik
# See PRAP, Lila

# Illustrations Index

(In the following index, the number of the *volume* in which an illustrator's work appears is given *before* the colon, and the *page number* on which it appears is given *after* the colon. For example, a drawing by Adams, Adrienne appears in Volume 2 on page 6, another drawing by her appears in Volume 3 on page 80, another drawing in Volume 8 on page 1, and so on and so on. . . .)

## YABC

Index references to *YABC* refer to listings appearing in the two-volume *Yesterday's Authors of Books for Children,* also published by Thomson Gale. *YABC* covers prominent authors and illustrators who died prior to 1960.

## A

Aas, Ulf *5:* 174
Abbe, S. van
   *See* van Abbe, S.
Abel, Raymond *6:* 122; *7:* 195; *12:* 3; *21:* 86; *25:* 119
Abelliera, Aldo *71:* 120
Abolafia, Yossi *60:* 2; *93:* 163; *152:* 202
Abrahams, Hilary *26:* 205; *29:* 24, 25; *53:* 61
Abrams, Kathie *36:* 170
Abrams, Lester *49:* 26
Abulafia, Yossi *154:* 67; *177:* 3
Accorsi, William *11:* 198
Acs, Laszlo *14:* 156; *42:* 22
Adams, Adrienne *2:* 6; *3:* 80; *8:* 1; *15:* 107; *16:* 180; *20:* 65; *22:* 134, 135; *33:* 75; *36:* 103, 112; *39:* 74; *86:* 54; *90:* 2, 3
Adams, Connie J. *129:* 68
Adams, John Wolcott *17:* 162
Adams, Lynn *96:* 44
Adams, Norman *55:* 82
Adams, Pam *112:* 1, 2
Adams, Sarah *98:* 126; *164:* 180
Adamson, George *30:* 23, 24; *69:* 64
Addams, Charles *55:* 5
Ade, Rene *76:* 198
Adinolfi, JoAnn *115:* 42; *176:* 2
Adkins, Alta *22:* 250
Adkins, Jan *8:* 3; *69:* 4; *144:* 2, 3, 4
Adler, Peggy *22:* 6; *29:* 31
Adler, Ruth *29:* 29
Adlerman, Daniel *163:* 2
Adragna, Robert *47:* 145
Agard, Nadema *18:* 1
Agee, Jon *116:* 8, 9, 10; *157:* 4
Agre, Patricia *47:* 195
Aguirre, Alfredo *152:* 218
Ahl, Anna Maria *32:* 24
Ahlberg, Allan *68:* 6, 7, 9; *165:* 5
Ahlberg, Janet *68:* 6, 7, 9
Aicher-Scholl, Inge *63:* 127
Aichinger, Helga *4:* 5, 45
Aitken, Amy *31:* 34
Akaba, Suekichi *46:* 23; *53:* 127
Akasaka, Miyoshi *YABC 2:* 261
Akino, Fuku *6:* 144
Alain *40:* 41
Alajalov *2:* 226
Alborough, Jez *86:* 1, 2, 3; *149:* 3

Albrecht, Jan *37:* 176
Albright, Donn *1:* 91
Alcala, Alfredo *91:* 128
Alcantará, Felipe Ugalde *171:* 186
Alcorn, John *3:* 159; *7:* 165; *31:* 22; *44:* 127; *46:* 23, 170
Alcorn, Stephen *110:* 4; *125:* 106; *128:* 172; *150:* 97; *160:* 188; *165:* 48
Alcott, May *100:* 3
Alda, Arlene *44:* 24; *158:* 2
Alden, Albert *11:* 103
Aldridge, Andy *27:* 131
Aldridge, George *105:* 125
Alejandro, Cliff *176:* 75
Alex, Ben *45:* 25, 26
Alexander, Ellen *91:* 3
Alexander, Lloyd *49:* 34
Alexander, Martha *3:* 206; *11:* 103; *13:* 109; *25:* 100; *36:* 131; *70:* 6, 7; *136:* 3, 4, 5; *169:* 120
Alexander, Paul *85:* 57; *90:* 9
Alexeieff, Alexander *14:* 6; *26:* 199
Alfano, Wayne *80:* 69
Aliki
   *See* Brandenberg, Aliki
Allamand, Pascale *12:* 9
Allan, Judith *38:* 166
Alland, Alexandra *16:* 255
Allen, Gertrude *9:* 6
Allen, Graham *31:* 145
Allen, Jonathan *131:* 3, 4; *177:* 8, 9, 10
Allen, Joy *168:* 185
Allen, Pamela *50:* 25, 26, 27, 28; *81:* 9, 10; *123:* 4, 5
Allen, Rowena *47:* 75
Allen, Thomas B. *81:* 101; *82:* 248; *89:* 37; *104:* 9
Allen, Tom *85:* 176
Allender, David *73:* 223
Alley, R.W. *80:* 183; *95:* 187; *156:* 100, 153; *169:* 4, 5
Allison, Linda *43:* 27
Allon, Jeffrey *119:* 174
Allport, Mike *71:* 55
Almquist, Don *11:* 8; *12:* 128; *17:* 46; *22:* 110
Aloise, Frank *5:* 38; *10:* 133; *30:* 92
Althea
   *See* Braithwaite, Althea
Altschuler, Franz *11:* 185; *23:* 141; *40:* 48; *45:* 29; *57:* 181
Alvin, John *117:* 5

Ambrus, Victor G. *1:* 6, 7, 194; *3:* 69; *5:* 15; *6:* 44; *7:* 36; *8:* 210; *12:* 227; *14:* 213; *15:* 213; *22:* 209; *24:* 36; *28:* 179; *30:* 178; *32:* 44, 46; *38:* 143; *41:* 25, 26, 27, 28, 29, 30, 31, 32; *42:* 87; *44:* 190; *55:* 172; *62:* 30, 144, 145, 148; *86:* 99, 100, 101; *87:* 66, 137; *89:* 162; *134:* 160
Ames, Lee J. *3:* 12; *9:* 130; *10:* 69; *17:* 214; *22:* 124; *151:* 13
Amon, Aline *9:* 9
Amoss, Berthe *5:* 5
Amstutz, Andre *152:* 102
Amundsen, Dick *7:* 77
Amundsen, Richard E. *5:* 10; *24:* 122
Ancona, George *12:* 11; *55:* 144; *145:* 7
Anderson, Alasdair *18:* 122
Andersen, Bethanne *116:* 167; *162:* 189; *175:* 17
Anderson, Bob *139:* 16
Anderson, Brad *33:* 28
Anderson, C.W. *11:* 10
Anderson, Carl *7:* 4
Anderson, Catherine Corley *72:* 2
Anderson, Cecil *127:* 152
Anderson, David Lee *118:* 176
Anderson, Derek *169:* 9; *174:* 180
Anderson, Doug *40:* 111
Anderson, Erica *23:* 65
Anderson, Laurie *12:* 153, 155
Anderson, Lena *99:* 26
Anderson, Sara *173:* 3
Anderson, Scoular *138:* 13
Anderson, Susan *90:* 12
Anderson, Wayne *23:* 119; *41:* 239; *56:* 7; *62:* 26; *147:* 6
Andreasen, Daniel *86:* 157; *87:* 104; *103:* 201, 202; *159:* 75; *167:* 106, 107; *168:* 184
Andrew, Ian *111:* 37; *116:* 12; *166:* 2
Andrew, John *22:* 4
Andrews, Benny *14:* 251; *31:* 24; *57:* 6, 7
Andrews, Vaughn *166:* 28
Anelay, Henry *57:* 173
Angel, Marie *47:* 22
Angelo, Valenti *14:* 8; *18:* 100; *20:* 232; *32:* 70
Anglund, Joan Walsh *2:* 7, 250, 251; *37:* 198, 199, 200
Anholt, Catherine *74:* 8; *131:* 7; *141:* 5
Anholt, Laurence *141:* 4
Anno, Mitsumasa *5:* 7; *38:* 25, 26, 27, 28, 29, 30, 31, 32; *77:* 3, 4; *157:* 10, 11

Antal, Andrew *1:* 124; *30:* 145
Antram, David *152:* 133
Apostolou, Christy Hale
  *See* Hale, Christy
Apple, Margot *33:* 25; *35:* 206; *46:* 81; *53:* 8;
  *61:* 109; *64:* 21, 22, 24, 25, 27; *71:* 176; *77:*
  53; *82:* 245; *92:* 39; *94:* 180; *96:* 107; *152:*
  4, 5; *162:* 192, 194; *173:* 44
Appleyard, Dev *2:* 192
Aragones, Sergio *48:* 23, 24, 25, 26, 27
Araneus *40:* 29
Arbo, Cris *103:* 4
Archambault, Matthew *85:* 173; *138:* 19, 20;
  *143:* 33; *145:* 144
Archer, Janet *16:* 69
Ardizzone, Edward *1:* 11, 12; *2:* 105; *3:* 258;
  *4:* 78; *7:* 79; *10:* 100; *15:* 232; *20:* 69, 178;
  *23:* 223; *24:* 125; *28:* 25, 26, 27, 28, 29, 30,
  31, 33, 34, 35, 36, 37; *31:* 192, 193; *34:*
  215, 217; *60:* 173; *64:* 145; *87:* 176; *YABC*
  *2:* 25
Arena, Jill *176:* 49
Arenella, Roy *14:* 9
Argent, Kerry *103:* 56; *138:* 17; *158:* 134
Arisman, Marshall *162:* 50
Armer, Austin *13:* 3
Armer, Laura Adams *13:* 3
Armer, Sidney *13:* 3
Armitage, David *47:* 23; *99:* 5; *155:* 4
Armitage, Eileen *4:* 16
Armstrong, George *10:* 6; *21:* 72
Armstrong, Shelagh *102:* 114
Arno, Enrico *1:* 217; *2:* 22, 210; *4:* 9; *5:* 43;
  *6:* 52; *29:* 217, 219; *33:* 152; *35:* 99; *43:* 31,
  32, 33; *45:* 212, 213, 214; *72:* 72; *74:* 166;
  *100:* 169
Arnold, Caroline *174:* 5
Arnold, Emily *76:* 7, 9, 10
Arnold, Katya *115:* 11; *168:* 2, 3
Arnold, Tedd *116:* 14; *133:* 152; *160:* 5
Arnosky, James Edward *22:* 20; *70:* 9, 10, 11;
  *118:* 3, 5; *160:* 8, 10
Arnsteen, Katy Keck *105:* 97; *116:* 145
Arrowood, Clinton *12:* 193; *19:* 11; *65:* 210
Artell, Mike *89:* 8
Arting, Fred J. *41:* 63
Artzybasheff, Boris *13:* 143; *14:* 15; *40:* 152,
  155
Aruego, Ariane *6:* 4
Aruego, Jose *4:* 140; *6:* 4; *7:* 64; *33:* 195; *35:*
  208; *68:* 16, 17; *75:* 46; *93:* 91, 92; *94:* 197;
  *109:* 65, 67; *125:* 2, 3, 4, 5; *127:* 188; *143:*
  25
Arzoumanian, Alik *177:* 12
Asare, Meshack *86:* 9; *139:* 19
Ascensios, Natalie *105:* 139
Asch, Frank *5:* 9; *66:* 2, 4, 6, 7, 9, 10; *102:*
  18, 19, 21; *154:* 12
Ashby, Gail *11:* 135
Ashby, Gil *146:* 4
Ashby, Gwynneth *44:* 26
Ashley, C.W. *19:* 197
Ashmead, Hal *8:* 70
Aska, Warabe *56:* 10
Assel, Steven *44:* 153; *77:* 22, 97
Astrop, John *32:* 56
Atene, Ann *12:* 18
Atherton, Lisa *38:* 198
Atkinson, Allen *60:* 5
Atkinson, J. Priestman *17:* 275
Atkinson, Janet *86:* 147; *103:* 138
Atkinson, Mike *127:* 74
Atkinson, Wayne *40:* 46
Attebery, Charles *38:* 170
Atwell, Debby *150:* 6
Atwood, Ann *7:* 9
Aubrey, Meg Kelleher *77:* 159
Auch, Herm *173:* 7, 8
Auch, Mary Jane *173:* 7
Augarde, Steve *25:* 22; *159:* 7
Austerman, Miriam *23:* 107

Austin, Margot *11:* 16
Austin, Robert *3:* 44
Austin, Virginia *81:* 205; *127:* 221
Auth, Tony *51:* 5
Avendano, Dolores *158:* 74
Avedon, Richard *57:* 140
Averill, Esther *1:* 17; *28:* 39, 40, 41
Axeman, Lois *2:* 32; *11:* 84; *13:* 165; *22:* 8;
  *23:* 49; *61:* 116; *101:* 124
Axtel, David *155:* 110
Ayer, Jacqueline *13:* 7
Ayer, Margaret *15:* 12; *50:* 120
Ayers, Alan *91:* 58; *107:* 169
Ayliffe, Alex *95:* 164
Ayto, Russell *111:* 5; *112:* 54
Azarian, Mary *112:* 9, 10; *114:* 129; *117:* 171;
  *137:* 163; *171:* 4, 5

**B**

B.T.B.
  *See* Blackwell, Basil T.
Babbitt, Bradford *33:* 158
Babbitt, Natalie *6:* 6; *8:* 220; *68:* 20; *70:* 242,
  243
Baca, Maria *104:* 5
Bacchus, Andy *94:* 87
Bacha, Andy *109:* 169
Bachem, Paul *48:* 180; *67:* 65; *144:* 206
Back, Adam *63:* 125
Back, George *31:* 161
Backhouse, Colin *78:* 142
Bacon, Bruce *4:* 74
Bacon, Paul *7:* 155; *8:* 121; *31:* 55; *50:* 42;
  *56:* 175; *62:* 82, 84
Bacon, Peggy *2:* 11, 228; *46:* 44
Baek, Matthew J. *169:* 95
Baer, Julie *161:* 2
Baicker-McKee, Carol *177:* 15
Bailey, Peter *58:* 174; *87:* 221
Bailey, Sheila *155:* 11
Baker, Alan *22:* 22; *61:* 134; *93:* 11, 12; *146:*
  6, 7, 10
Baker, Charlotte *2:* 12
vBaker, Garin *89:* 65
Baker, Jeannie *23:* 4; *88:* 18, 19, 20
Baker, Jim *22:* 24
Baker, Joe *82:* 188; *111:* 55; *124:* 70
Baker, Leslie *112:* 214; *132:* 103, 246
Baldridge, Cyrus LeRoy *19:* 69; *44:* 50
Baldus, Zachary *152:* 231
Balet, Jan *11:* 22
Balian, Lorna *9:* 16; *91:* 16
Balit, Christina *102:* 24; *159:* 9; *162:* 118, 119
Ballantyne, R.M. *24:* 34
Ballis, George *14:* 199
Balouch, Kristen *176:* 11
Baltzer, Hans *40:* 30
Banbery, Fred *58:* 15
Banfill, A. Scott *98:* 7; *112:* 59
Bang, Molly Garrett *24:* 37, 38; *69:* 8, 9, 10;
  *111:* 7, 9, 10, 11; *140:* 11; *158:* 37, 38, 39
Banik, Yvette Santiago *21:* 136
Banner, Angela
  *See* Maddison, Angela Mary
Bannerman, Helen *19:* 13, 14
Bannon, Laura *6:* 10; *23:* 8
Bantock, Nick *74:* 229; *95:* 6
Baptist, Michael *37:* 208
Baracca, Sal *135:* 206
Barasch, Lynne *126:* 16
Barbarin, Lucien C., Jr. *89:* 88
Barbour, Karen *96:* 5; *74:* 209; *170:* 16
Bare, Arnold Edwin *16:* 31
Bare, Colleen Stanley *32:* 33
Barger, Jan *147:* 11
Bargery, Geoffrey *14:* 258
Barkat, Jonathan *149:* 177; *164:* 254
Barker, Carol *31:* 27

Barker, Cicely Mary *49:* 50, 51
Barkley, James *4:* 13; *6:* 11; *13:* 112
Barks, Carl *37:* 27, 28, 29, 30, 31, 32, 33, 34
Barling, Joy *62:* 148
Barling, Tom *9:* 23
Barlow, Gillian *62:* 20
Barlow, Perry *35:* 28
Barlowe, Dot *30:* 223
Barlowe, Wayne *37:* 72; *84:* 43; *105:* 5
Barnard, Bryn *88:* 53; *13:* 55; *169:* 13
Barner, Bob *29:* 37; *128:* 33; *136:* 19, 20;
  *177:* 27
Barnes, Hiram P. *20:* 28
Barnes, Tim *137:* 28
Barnes-Murphy, Rowan *88:* 22
Barnett, Charles II *175:* 150
Barnett, Ivan *70:* 14
Barnett, Moneta *16:* 89; *19:* 142; *31:* 102; *33:*
  30, 31, 32; *41:* 153; *61:* 94, 97
Barney, Maginel Wright *39:* 32, 33, 34; *YABC*
  *2:* 306
Barnum, Jay Hyde *11:* 224; *20:* 5; *37:* 189,
  190
Baron, Alan *80:* 3; *89:* 123
Barr, George *60:* 74; *69:* 64
Barragan, Paula S. *134:* 116
Barrall, Tim *115:* 152
Barrauds *33:* 114
Barrer-Russell, Gertrude *9:* 65; *27:* 31
Barret, Robert *85:* 134
Barrett, Angela *40:* 136, 137; *62:* 74; *75:* 10;
  *76:* 142; *144:* 137; *145:* 14
Barrett, Jennifer *58:* 149
Barrett, John E. *43:* 119
Barrett, Moneta *74:* 10
Barrett, Peter *55:* 169; *86:* 111
Barrett, Robert *62:* 145; *77:* 146; *82:* 35
Barrett, Ron *14:* 24; *26:* 35
Barron, John N. *3:* 261; *5:* 101; *14:* 220
Barrow, Ann *136:* 27
Barrows, Walter *14:* 268
Barry, Ethelred B. *37:* 79; *YABC 1:* 229
Barry, James *14:* 25
Barry, Katharina *2:* 159; *4:* 22
Barry, Robert E. *6:* 12
Barry, Scott *32:* 35
Bartenbach, Jean *40:* 31
Barth, Ernest Kurt *2:* 172; *3:* 160; *8:* 26; *10:*
  31
Bartlett, Alison *101:* 88; *165:* 93
Barton, Byron *8:* 207; *9:* 18; *23:* 66; *80:* 181;
  *90:* 18, 19, 20, 21; *126:* 29, 30
Barton, Harriett *30:* 71
Barton, Jill *129:* 108; *135:* 120; *145:* 185, 189
Bartram, Robert *10:* 42
Bartsch, Jochen *8:* 105; *39:* 38
Bascove, Barbara *45:* 73
Base, Graeme *101:* 15, 16, 17, 18; *162:* 8, 10,
  12
Baseman, Gary *174:* 12
Bash, Barbara *132:* 9
Baskin, Leonard *30:* 42, 43, 46, 47; *49:* 125,
  126, 128, 129, 133; *173:* 120
Bass, Saul *49:* 192
Bassett, Jeni *40:* 99; *64:* 30
Basso, Bill *99:* 139
Batchelor, Joy *29:* 41, 47, 48
Bate, Norman *5:* 16
Bates, Leo *24:* 35
Batet, Carmen *39:* 134
Batherman, Muriel *31:* 79; *45:* 185
Battaglia, Aurelius *50:* 44
Batten, John D. *25:* 161, 162
Batten, Mary *162:* 14, 15
Battles, Asa *32:* 94, 95
Bauer, Jutta *150:* 32
Bauernschmidt, Marjorie *15:* 15
Baum, Allyn *20:* 10
Baum, Willi *4:* 24, 25; *7:* 173
Bauman, Leslie *61:* 121
Baumann, Jill *34:* 170

Baumhauer, Hans *11:* 218; *15:* 163, 165, 167
Baxter, Glen *57:* 100
Baxter, Leon *59:* 102
Baxter, Robert *87:* 129
Bayley, Dorothy *37:* 195
Bayley, Nicola *40:* 104; *41:* 34, 35; *69:* 15; *129:* 33, 34, 35
Baylin, Mark *158:* 233
Baynes, Pauline *2:* 244; *3:* 149; *13:* 133, 135, 137, 141; *19:* 18, 19, 20; *32:* 208, 213, 214; *36:* 105, 108; *59:* 12, 13, 14, 16, 17, 18, 20; *100:* 158, 159, 243; *133:* 3, 4
Beach, Lou *150:* 150
Beame, Rona *12:* 40
Bear's Heart *73:* 215
Beard, Dan *22:* 31, 32
Beard, J.H. *YABC 1:* 158
Bearden, Romare *9:* 7; *22:* 35
Beardshaw, Rosalind *169:* 22
Beardsley, Aubrey *17:* 14; *23:* 181; *59:* 130, 131
Bearman, Jane *29:* 38
Beaton, Cecil *24:* 208
Beaton, Clare *125:* 28
Beauce, J.A. *18:* 103
Beaujard, Sophie *81:* 54
Beck, Charles *11:* 169; *51:* 173
Beck, Ian *138:* 27
Beck, Ruth *13:* 11
Becker, Harriet *12:* 211
Beckett, Sheilah *25:* 5; *33:* 37, 38
Beckhoff, Harry *1:* 78; *5:* 163
Beckman, Kaj *45:* 38, 39, 40, 41
Beckman, Per *45:* 42, 43
Beddows, Eric *72:* 70
Bedford, F.D. *20:* 118, 122; *33:* 170; *41:* 220, 221, 230, 233
Bee, Joyce *19:* 62
Beeby, Betty *25:* 36
Beech, Carol *9:* 149
Beek *25:* 51, 55, 59
Beeke, Tiphanie *177:* 127
Beekman, Doug *125:* 146, 148
Beerbohm, Max *24:* 208
Beeson, Bob *108:* 57
Begin, Maryjane *82:* 13
Beha, Philippe *172:* 85
Behr, Joyce *15:* 15; *21:* 132; *23:* 161
Behrens, Hans *5:* 97
Beier, Ellen *135:* 170; *139:* 47
Beinicke, Steve *69:* 18
Beisner, Monika *46:* 128, 131; *112:* 127
Belden, Charles J. *12:* 182
Belina, Renate *39:* 132
Bell, Corydon *3:* 20
Bell, Graham *54:* 48
Bell, Julia *151:* 214
Bell, Julie *159:* 172; *165:* 18
Bell, Thomas P. *76:* 182
Bellamy, Glen *127:* 15
Beltran, Alberto *43:* 37
Bemelmans, Ludwig *15:* 19, 21; *100:* 27
Ben-Ami, Doron *75:* 96; *84:* 107; *108:* 132; *110:* 63; *159:* 157
Bendall-Brunello, John *150:* 4; *157:* 163
Benda, Wladyslaw T. *15:* 256; *30:* 76, 77; *44:* 182
Bender, Robert *77:* 162; *79:* 13; *160:* 23
Bendick, Jeanne *2:* 24; *68:* 27, 28
Benioff, Carol *121:* 42; *175:* 23
Benner, Cheryl *80:* 11
Bennett, Charles H. *64:* 6
Bennett, Erin Susanne *165:* 216
Bennett, F.I. *YABC 1:* 134
Bennett, James *146:* 240
Bennett, Jill *26:* 61; *41:* 38, 39; *45:* 54
Bennett, Rainey *15:* 26; *23:* 53
Bennett, Richard *15:* 45; *21:* 11, 12, 13; *25:* 175
Bennett, Susan *5:* 55
Benny, Mike *142:* 78

Benoit, Elise *77:* 74
Benson, Linda *60:* 130; *62:* 91; *75:* 101; *79:* 156; *134:* 129
Benson, Patrick *68:* 162; *147:* 17, 18, 19, 20
Bentley, Carolyn *46:* 153
Bentley, James *149:* 30
Bentley, Roy *30:* 162
Benton, Jim *172:* 22
Benton, Thomas Hart *2:* 99
Berelson, Howard *5:* 20; *16:* 58; *31:* 50
Berenstain, Jan *12:* 47; *64:* 33, 34, 36, 37, 38, 40, 42, 44; *135:* 25, 28, 31, 35
Berenstain, Stan *12:* 47; *64:* 33, 34, 36, 37, 38, 40, 42, 44; *135:* 25, 28, 31, 35
Berenzy, Alix *65:* 13; *73:* 6; *78:* 115
Berg, Joan *1:* 115; *3:* 156; *6:* 26, 58
Berg, Ron *36:* 48, 49; *48:* 37, 38; *67:* 72
Bergen, David *115:* 44
Berger, Barbara *77:* 14
Berger, William M. *14:* 143; *YABC 1:* 204
Bergherr, Mary *74:* 170; *151:* 123
Bergin, Mark *114:* 8, 9; *143:* 95; *160:* 26, 27
Bergstreser, Douglas *69:* 76
Bergum, Constance R. *121:* 14, 15
Bering, Claus *13:* 14
Berkeley, Jon *139:* 218
Berkowitz, Jeanette *3:* 249
Berman, Paul *66:* 14
Bernal, Richard *154:* 176
Bernadette
    *See* Watts, Bernadette
Bernardin, James *112:* 24; *167:* 94
Bernath, Stefen *32:* 76
Bernhard, Durga *80:* 13
Bernhard, Durga *80:* 13
Bernstein, Michel J. *51:* 71
Bernstein, Ted *38:* 183; *50:* 131
Bernstein, Zena *23:* 46
Berridge, Celia *86:* 63
Berrill, Jacquelyn *12:* 50
Berry, Erick
    *See* Best, Allena
Berry, William D. *14:* 29; *19:* 48
Berry, William A. *6:* 219
Berson, Harold *2:* 17, 18; *4:* 28, 29, 220; *9:* 10; *12:* 19; *17:* 45; *18:* 193; *22:* 85; *34:* 172; *44:* 120; *46:* 42; *80:* 240
Berton, Patsy *99:* 16
Bertschmann, Harry *16:* 1
Besco, Don *70:* 99
Beskow, Elsa *20:* 13, 14, 15
Bess, Clayton *63:* 94
Best, Allena *2:* 26; *34:* 76
Betera, Carol *74:* 68
Bethell, Thomas N. *61:* 169
Bethers, Ray *6:* 22
Bettina
    *See* Ehrlich, Bettina
Betts, Ethel Franklin *17:* 161, 164, 165; *YABC 2:* 47
Betz, Rudolf *59:* 161
Bewick, Thomas *16:* 40, 41, 43, 44, 45, 47; *54:* 150; *YABC 1:* 107
Beyer, Paul J. III *74:* 24
Bezencon, Jacqueline *48:* 40
Biamonte, Daniel *40:* 90
Bianchi, John *91:* 19
Bianco, Pamela *15:* 31; *28:* 44, 45, 46
Bible, Charles *13:* 15
Bice, Clare *22:* 40
Bierman, Don *57:* 184
Biggers, John *2:* 123
Bileck, Marvin *3:* 102; *40:* 36, 37
Bilibin, Ivan *61:* 8, 9, 12, 13, 14, 15, 151, 152, 154, 162
Billington, Patrick *98:* 71
Billout, Guy *144:* 38, 39
Bimen, Levent *5:* 179
Binch, Caroline *81:* 18; *140:* 15, 16; *144:* 115
Binder, Hannes *169:* 163
Bing, Christopher *126:* 34
Binger, Bill *121:* 46

Binks, Robert *25:* 150
Binzen, Bill *24:* 47
Birch, Reginald *15:* 150; *19:* 33, 34, 35, 36; *37:* 196, 197; *44:* 182; *46:* 176; *YABC 1:* 84; *2:* 34, 39
Birchall, Mark *123:* 188
Bird, Esther Brock *1:* 36; *25:* 66
Birdsong, Keith *167:* 85
Birkett, Rachel *78:* 206
Birling, Paul *109:* 30
Birmingham, Christian *132:* 243; *143:* 114
Birmingham, Lloyd P. *12:* 51; *83:* 13
Biro, Val *1:* 26; *41:* 42; *60:* 178; *67:* 23, 24; *84:* 242, 243
Bischoff, Ilse *44:* 51
Bishop, Gavin *97:* 17, 18; *144:* 42, 44
Bishop, Kathleen Wong *115:* 67
Bishop, Rich *56:* 43
Bite, I. *60:* 14
Bittinger, Ned *93:* 117
Bjorklund, Lorence *3:* 188, 252; *7:* 100; *9:* 113; *10:* 66; *19:* 178; *33:* 122, 123; *35:* 36, 37, 38, 39, 41, 42, 43; *36:* 185; *38:* 93; *47:* 106; *66:* 194; *YABC 1:* 242
Bjorkman, Steve *91:* 199; *160:* 110
Black Sheep *164:* 100
Blackburn, Loren H. *63:* 10
Blackford, John *137:* 105
Blackwell, Basil T. *YABC 1:* 68, 69
Blackwood, Gary L. *118:* 17
Blades, Ann *16:* 52; *37:* 213; *50:* 41; *69:* 21; *99:* 215
Blair, Jay *45:* 46; *46:* 155
Blaisdell, Elinore *1:* 121; *3:* 134; *35:* 63
Blake, Robert J. *160:* 28, 29
Blake, Quentin *3:* 170; *10:* 48; *13:* 38; *21:* 180; *26:* 60; *28:* 228; *30:* 29, 31; *40:* 108; *45:* 219; *46:* 165, 168; *48:* 196; *52:* 10, 11, 12, 13, 14, 15, 16, 17; *73:* 41, 43; *78:* 84, 86; *80:* 250, 251; *84:* 210, 211, 212; *87:* 177; *96:* 24, 26, 28; *124:* 79; *125:* 32, 34
Blake, Robert J. *37:* 90; *53:* 67; *54:* 23
Blake, William *30:* 54, 56, 57, 58, 59, 60
Blanchard, N. Taylor *82:* 140
Blass, Jacqueline *8:* 215
Blazek, Scott R. *91:* 71
Bleck, Cathie *118:* 116
Blegvad, Erik *2:* 59; *3:* 98; *5:* 117; *7:* 131; *11:* 149; *14:* 34, 35; *18:* 237; *32:* 219; *60:* 106; *66:* 16, 17, 18, 19; *70:* 233; *76:* 18; *82:* 106; *87:* 45; *100:* 188; *129:* 125; *132:* 17, 18, 19, 20; *176:* 14; *YABC 1:* 201
Blessen, Karen *93:* 126
Bliss, Corinne Demas *37:* 38
Bloch, Lucienne *10:* 12
Blondon, Herve *129:* 48
Bloom, Lloyd *35:* 180; *36:* 149; *47:* 99; *62:* 117; *68:* 231; *72:* 136; *75:* 185; *83:* 99; *108:* 19
Bloom, Suzanne *172:* 23, 24
Blossom, Dave *34:* 29
Blumenschein, E.L. *YABC 1:* 113, 115
Blumer, Patt *29:* 214
Blundell, Kim *29:* 36
Bluthenthal, Diana Cain *93:* 32; *104:* 106; *177:* 26
Blythe, Benjamin *128:* 7
Blythe, Gary *112:* 52
Boake, Kathy *176:* 185
Board, Perry *171:* 99
Boardman, Gwenn *12:* 60
Bober, Richard *125:* 145; *132:* 40
Bobri *30:* 138; *47:* 27
Bock, Vera *1:* 187; *21:* 41
Bock, William Sauts *8:* 7; *14:* 37; *16:* 120; *21:* 141; *36:* 177; *62:* 203
Bodecker, N(iels) M(ogens) *8:* 13; *14:* 2; *17:* 55, 56, 57; *73:* 22, 23, 24
Boehm, Linda *40:* 31
Bogacki, Tomek *138:* 31, 32; *144:* 123
Bogdan, Florentina *107:* 43

Bohdal, Susi 22: 44; *101:* 20
Bohlen, Nina *58:* 13
Boies, Alex *96:* 53
Bolam, Emily *101:* 216; *159:* 12
Bolian, Polly *3:* 270; *4:* 30; *13:* 77; *29:* 197
Bolle, Frank *87:* 100
Bollen, Roger *79:* 186; *83:* 16
Bolling, Vickey *114:* 44
Bollinger, Peter *101:* 7; *128:* 198; *172:* 26
Bolognese, Don *2:* 147, 231; *4:* 176; *7:* 146; *17:* 43; *23:* 192; *24:* 50; *34:* 108; *36:* 133; *71:* 24, 25; *103:* 131; *129:* 39, 40
Bolton, A.T. *57:* 158
Bond, Arnold *18:* 116
Bond, Barbara Higgins *21:* 102
Bond, Bruce *52:* 97
Bond, Felicia *38:* 197; *49:* 55, 56; *89:* 170; *90:* 171; *126:* 37
Bond, Higgins *177:* 22, 23
Bonn, Pat *43:* 40
Bonners, Susan *41:* 40; *85:* 36; *94:* 99, 100; *151:* 105, 106
Bonsall, Crosby *23:* 6
Boon, Debbie *103:* 6; *144:* 188
Boon, Emilie *86:* 23, 24
Boone, Debbie *165:* 77
Boore, Sara *60:* 73
Bootman, Colin *155:* 13; *159:* 35; *174:* 192
Booth, Franklin *YABC 2:* 76
Booth, Graham *32:* 193; *37:* 41, 42
Borda, Juliette *102:* 188
Bordier, Georgette *16:* 54
Boren, Tinka *27:* 128
Borges, Jose Francisco *119:* 62
Borja, Robert *22:* 48
Born, Adolf *49:* 63
Bornstein, Ruth *14:* 44; *88:* 45, 46; *107:* 30
Borten, Helen *3:* 54; *5:* 24
Bosin, Blackbear *69:* 104
Bossom, Naomi *35:* 48
Bostock, Mike *83:* 221; *114:* 14
Boston, Peter *19:* 42
Bosustow, Stephen *34:* 202
Boszko, Ron *75:* 47
Bottner, Barbara *14:* 46
Boucher, Joelle *41:* 138
Boulat, Pierre *44:* 40
Boulet, Susan Seddon *50:* 47
Bouma, Paddy *118:* 25; *128:* 16
Bour, Daniele *66:* 145
Bourke-White, Margaret *15:* 286, 287; *57:* 102
Boutet de Monvel, M. *30:* 61, 62, 63, 65
Bowen, Betsy *105:* 222
Bowen, Richard *42:* 134
Bowen, Ruth *31:* 188
Bower, Ron *29:* 33
Bowers, David *95:* 38; *115:* 20; *127:* 169, 170; *165:* 57
Bowman, Claire *174:* 177
Bowman, Eric *151:* 23
Bowman, Leslie *85:* 203; *105:* 108; *116:* 76; *128:* 234
Bowman, Peter *146:* 214, 215; *150:* 115
Bowser, Carolyn Ewing *22:* 253
Boyd, Aaron *158:* 242
Boyd, Patti *45:* 31
Boyle, Eleanor Vere *28:* 50, 51
Boynton, Sandra *57:* 13, 14, 15; *107:* 36, 37; *152:* 12, 13, 14
Bozzo, Frank *4:* 154
Brabbs, Derry *55:* 170
Brace, Eric *132:* 193, 194; *152:* 71
Brackers de Hugo, Pierre *115:* 21
Bradford, June *158:* 138
Bradford, Ron *7:* 157
Bradley, David P. *69:* 105
Bradley, Richard D. *26:* 182
Bradley, William *5:* 164
Brady, Irene *4:* 31; *42:* 37; *68:* 191
Bragg, Michael *32:* 78; *46:* 31
Bragg, Ruth Gembicki *77:* 18

Brainerd, John W. *65:* 19
Braithwaite, Althea *23:* 12, 13; *119:* 16
Brak, Syd *146:* 187
Bralds, Braldt *90:* 28; *91:* 151
Bram, Elizabeth *30:* 67
Bramley, Peter *4:* 3
Brandenberg, Aliki *2:* 36, 37; *24:* 222; *35:* 49, 50, 51, 52, 53, 54, 56, 57; *75:* 15, 17; *92:* 205; *113:* 18, 19, 20; *157:* 28; *156:* 111
Brandenburg, Alexa *75:* 19
Brandenburg, Jim *47:* 58; *150:* 212
Brandi, Lillian *31:* 158
Brandon, Brumsic, Jr. *9:* 25
Bransom, Paul *17:* 121; *43:* 44
Braren, Loretta Trezzo *87:* 193
Braun, Wendy *80:* 17, 18
Brautigam, Don *115:* 175, 176
Brazell, Derek *75:* 105; *79:* 9
Breathed, Berkeley *86:* 27, 28, 29; *161:* 13, 14
Brennan, Steve *83:* 230; *101:* 184
Brenner, Fred *22:* 85; *36:* 34; *42:* 34
Brett, Bernard *22:* 54
Brett, Harold M. *26:* 98, 99, 100
Brett, Jan *30:* 135; *42:* 39; *71:* 31, 32; *130:* 23, 24, 25, 26, 27; *171:* 15, 16
Brewer, Paul *106:* 115; *145:* 202
Brewer, Sally King *33:* 44
Brewster, Patience *40:* 68; *45:* 22, 183; *51:* 20; *66:* 144; *89:* 4; *97:* 30, 31
Brick, John *10:* 15
Brickman, Robin D. *131:* 88; *142:* 150; *155:* 18
Bridge, David R. *45:* 28
Bridgman, L.J. *37:* 77
Bridwell, Norman *4:* 37; *138:* 36, 37, 40
Brierley, Louise *91:* 22; *96:* 165
Briggs, Harry *172:* 187
Briggs, Raymond *10:* 168; *23:* 20, 21; *66:* 29, 31, 32; *131:* 28, 29
Brigham, Grace A. *37:* 148
Bright, Robert *24:* 55
Brighton, Catherine *107:* 39
Brinckloe, Julie *13:* 18; *24:* 79, 115; *29:* 35; *63:* 140; *81:* 131
Brion *47:* 116
Brisley, Joyce L. *22:* 57
Brisson, James F. *110:* 60
Brittingham, Geoffrey *88:* 37
Brix-Henker, Silke *81:* 194
Brock, Charles E. *15:* 97; *19:* 247, 249; *23:* 224, 225; *36:* 88; *42:* 41, 42, 43, 44, 45; *100:* 189; *YABC 1:* 194, 196, 203
Brock, Emma *7:* 21
Brock, Henry Matthew *15:* 81; *16:* 141; *19:* 71; *34:* 115; *40:* 164; *42:* 47, 48, 49; *49:* 66
Brocksopp, Arthur *57:* 157
Broda, Ron *136:* 180; *174:* 123
Brodkin, Gwen *34:* 135
Brodovitch, Alexi *52:* 22
Bromhall, Winifred *5:* 11; *26:* 38
Bromley, Lizzy *159:* 179
Bronson, Linda *150:* 210; *174:* 133
Brooke, L. Leslie *16:* 181, 182, 183, 186; *17:* 15, 16, 17; *18:* 194
Brooker, Christopher *15:* 251
Brooker, Krysten *111:* 94; *140:* 28; *162:* 111; *175:* 108
Brooks, Erik *166:* 52
Brooks, Maya Itzna *92:* 153
Brooks, Ron *94:* 15
Broomfield, Maurice *40:* 141
Brotman, Adolph E. *5:* 21
Brown, Buck *45:* 48
Brown, Christopher *62:* 124, 125, 127, 128
Brown, Craig McFarland *73:* 28; *84:* 65
Brown, Dan *61:* 167; *115:* 183, 184; *116:* 28, 29
Brown, David *7:* 47; *48:* 52
Brown, Denise *11:* 213
Brown, Don *172:* 29
Brown, Ford Madox *48:* 74

Brown, Judith Gwyn *1:* 45; *7:* 5; *8:* 167; *9:* 182, 190; *20:* 16, 17, 18; *23:* 142; *29:* 117; *33:* 97; *36:* 23, 26; *43:* 184; *48:* 201, 223; *49:* 69; *86:* 227; *110:* 188; *153:* 7
Brown, Kathryn *98:* 26
Brown, Laurie Krasny *99:* 30
Brown, Marc (Tolon) *10:* 17, 197; *14:* 263; *51:* 18; *53:* 11, 12, 13, 15, 16, 17; *75:* 58; *80:* 24, 25, 26; *82:* 261; *99:* 29; *145:* 22, 23, 25, 27; *162:* 198
Brown, Marcia *7:* 30; *25:* 203; *47:* 31, 32, 33, 34, 35, 36, 37, 38, 39, 40, 42, 43, 44; *YABC 1:* 27
Brown, Margery W. *5:* 32, 33; *10:* 3
Brown, Martin *101:* 43
Brown, Mary Barrett *97:* 74
Brown, Palmer *36:* 40
Brown, Paul *25:* 26; *26:* 107
Brown, Richard *61:* 18; *67:* 30
Brown, Rick *78:* 71; *150:* 154
Brown, Robert S. *85:* 33
Brown, Rod *157:* 142
Brown, Ruth *55:* 165; *86:* 112, 113; *105:* 16, 17, 18; *171:* 178
Brown, Trevor *99:* 160; *139:* 247
Browne, Anthony *45:* 50, 51, 52; *61:* 21, 22, 23, 24, 25; *105:* 21, 22, 23, 25
Browne, Dik *8:* 212; *67:* 32, 33, 35, 37, 39
Browne, Gordon *16:* 97; *64:* 114, 116, 117, 119, 121
Browne, Hablot K. *15:* 65, 80; *21:* 14, 15, 16, 17, 18, 19, 20; *24:* 25
Browne, Jane *165:* 222
Browning, Coleen *4:* 132
Browning, Mary Eleanor *24:* 84
Bruce, Robert *23:* 23
Brude, Dick *48:* 215
Bruel, Nick *166:* 41
Brule, Al *3:* 135
Brumbeau, Jeff *157:* 29
Bruna, Dick *43:* 48, 49, 50; *76:* 27, 28
Brundage, Frances *19:* 244
Brunhoff, Jean de *24:* 57, 58
Brunhoff, Laurent de *24:* 60; *71:* 35, 36, 37
Brunkus, Denise *84:* 50; *123:* 117
Brunson, Bob *43:* 135
Bryan, Ashley F. *31:* 44; *72:* 27, 28, 29; *107:* 92; *116:* 192; *132:* 24
Bryant, Laura J. *176:* 36
Bryant, Michael *93:* 74
Brychta, Alex *21:* 21
Bryer, Diana *107:* 121
Bryson, Bernarda *3:* 88, 146; *39:* 26; *44:* 185; *131:* 40
Buba, Joy *12:* 83; *30:* 226; *44:* 56
Buchanan, George *166:* 198
Buchanan, Lilian *13:* 16
Buchanan, Rachel *171:* 71
Bucholtz-Ross, Linda *44:* 137
Buchs, Thomas *40:* 38
Buck, Margaret Waring *3:* 30
Buckhardt, Marc *172:* 59
Buckley, Mike *166:* 180
Budwine, Greg *175:* 172
Buehner, Mark *104:* 12, 15; *105:* 160; *119:* 98; *157:* 188; *159:* 39, 40, 43
Buehr, Walter *3:* 31
Buff, Conrad *19:* 52, 53, 54
Buff, Mary *19:* 52, 53
Bull, Charles Livingston *18:* 207; *88:* 175, 176
Bullen, Anne *3:* 166, 167
Bullock, Kathleen *77:* 24
Bumgarner-Kirby, Claudia *77:* 194
Burbank, Addison *37:* 43
Burchard, Peter Duncan *3:* 197; *5:* 35; *6:* 158, 218; *143:* 17
Burckhardt, Marc *94:* 48; *110:* 89
Burger, Carl *3:* 33; *45:* 160, 162
Burgeson, Marjorie *19:* 31
Burgess, Anne *76:* 252
Burgess, Gelett *32:* 39, 42

Burgess, Mark *157:* 31
Burke, Phillip *95:* 117
Burkert, Nancy Ekholm *18:* 186; *22:* 140; *24:* 62, 63, 64, 65; *26:* 53; *29:* 60, 61; *46:* 171; *YABC 1:* 46
Burkhardt, Bruce *142:* 86
Burkhardt, Melissa A. *142:* 86
Burleson, Joe *104:* 35; *172:* 139
Burn, Doris *6:* 172
Burn, Jeffrey *89:* 125; *152:* 132
Burn, Ted
    *See* Burn, Thomas E.
Burn, Thomas E. *151:* 41
Burnard, Damon *115:* 23
Burnett, Virgil *44:* 42
Burningham, John *9:* 68; *16:* 60, 61; *59:* 28, 29, 30, 31, 32, 33, 35; *111:* 18, 19, 21; *160:* 37
Burns, Howard M. *12:* 173
Burns, Jim *47:* 70; *86:* 32; *91:* 197; *123:* 16
Burns, M.F. *26:* 69
Burns, Raymond *9:* 29
Burns, Robert *24:* 106
Burr, Dan *65:* 28; *108:* 134; *164:* 203
Burr, Dane *12:* 2
Burra, Edward *YABC 2:* 68
Burrell, Galen *56:* 76
Burri, Rene *41:* 143; *54:* 166
Burridge, Marge Opitz *14:* 42
Burris, Burmah *4:* 81
Burroughs, John Coleman *41:* 64
Burroughs, Studley O. *41:* 65
Burton, Marilee Robin *46:* 33
Burton, Virginia Lee *2:* 43; *44:* 49, 51; *100:* 46, 47; *YABC 1:* 24; *147:* 56
Busoni, Rafaello *1:* 186; *3:* 224; *6:* 126; *14:* 5; *16:* 62, 63
Butchkes, Sidney *50:* 58
Butler, Geoff *94:* 20
Butler, Ralph *116:* 212
Butterfield, Ned *1:* 153; *27:* 128; *79:* 63
Butterworth, Nick *106:* 43, 44; *149:* 34
Buxton, John *123:* 12
Buzelli, Christopher *105:* 149
Buzonas, Gail *29:* 88
Buzzell, Russ W. *12:* 177
Byard, Carole *39:* 44; *57:* 18, 19, 20; *60:* 60; *61:* 93, 96; *69:* 210; *78:* 246; *79:* 227
Byars, Betsy *46:* 35
Byfield, Barbara Ninde *8:* 18
Byfield, Graham *32:* 29
Bynum, Janie *176:* 50
Byrd, Robert *13:* 218; *33:* 46; *158:* 70
Byrd, Samuel *123:* 104

### C

Cabat, Erni *74:* 38
Cabban, Vanessa *138:* 73; *176:* 39
Cabrera, Jane *103:* 24; *152:* 27
Caddy, Alice *6:* 41
Cady, Harrison *17:* 21, 23; *19:* 57, 58
Caffrey, Aileen *72:* 223; *141:* 154
Cairns, Julia *177:* 37
Caldecott, Randolph *16:* 98, 103; *17:* 32, 33, 36, 38, 39; *26:* 90; *100:* 49, 50; *YABC 2:* 172
Calder, Alexander *18:* 168
Calderon, W. Frank *25:* 160
Caldwell, Ben *105:* 75; *149:* 60
Caldwell, Clyde *98:* 100; *116:* 39
Caldwell, Doreen *23:* 77; *71:* 41
Caldwell, John *46:* 225
Call, Greg *126:* 135; *165:* 49
Callahan, Kevin *22:* 42
Callahan, Philip S. *25:* 77
Callan, Jamie *59:* 37
Calvin, James *61:* 92
Camburn-Bracalente, Carol A. *118:* 22

Cameron, Julia Margaret *19:* 203
Cameron, Scott *99:* 18
Camm, Martin *140:* 208, 209, 210
Campbell, Ann *11:* 43; *123:* 182
Campbell, Bill *89:* 39
Campbell, Ken *126:* 143
Campbell, Robert *55:* 120
Campbell, Rod *51:* 27; *98:* 34
Campbell, Walter M. *YABC 2:* 158
Camps, Luis *28:* 120, 121; *66:* 35
Cann, Helen *124:* 50; *141:* 78; *170:* 138
Cannon, Janell *78:* 25; *128:* 40
Canright, David *36:* 162
Canty, Thomas *85:* 161; *92:* 47; *113:* 192; *134:* 60
Canyon, Christopher *150:* 44; *151:* 112
Caporale, Wende *70:* 42
Capp, Al *61:* 28, 30, 31, 40, 41, 43, 44
Cappon, Manuela *154:* 64
Caras, Peter *36:* 64
Caraway, Caren *57:* 22
Caraway, James *3:* 200, 201
Carbe, Nino *29:* 183
Cares, Linda *67:* 176
Carigiet, Alois *24:* 67
Carle, Eric *4:* 42; *11:* 121; *12:* 29; *65:* 32, 33, 34, 36; *73:* 63, 65; *163:* 55, 56
Carling, Amelia Lau *164:* 46
Carlino, Angela *168:* 43
Carlson, Nancy L. *41:* 116; *56:* 25; *90:* 45; *144:* 48, 50
Carlluccio, Maria *175:* 129
Carmi, Giora *79:* 35; *149:* 40
Carpenter, Nancy *76:* 128; *86:* 173; *89:* 171; *131:* 186; *134:* 8; *138:* 215; *153:* 204; *159:* 93; *165:* 232
Carr, Archie *37:* 225
Carrick, Donald *5:* 194; *39:* 97; *49:* 70; *53:* 156; *63:* 15, 16, 17, 18, 19, 21; *80:* 131; *86:* 151; *118:* 24
Carrick, Malcolm *28:* 59, 60
Carrick, Paul *118:* 26
Carrick, Valery *21:* 47
Carrier, Lark *71:* 43
Carroll, Jim *88:* 211; *140:* 177; *153:* 99
Carroll, Lewis
    *See* Dodgson, Charles L.
Carroll, Michael *72:* 5
Carroll, Pamela *84:* 68; *128:* 214
Carroll, Ruth *7:* 41; *10:* 68
Carter, Abby *81:* 32; *97:* 121; *102:* 61; *163:* 139; *164:* 125
Carter, Barbara *47:* 167, 169
Carter, David A. *114:* 24, 25; *170:* 42, 43
Carter, Don *124:* 54
Carter, Harry *22:* 179
Carter, Helene *15:* 38; *22:* 202, 203; *YABC 2:* 220, 221
Carter, Penny *173:* 91
Cartlidge, Michelle *49:* 65; *96:* 50, 51
Cartwright, Reg *63:* 61, 62; *78:* 26; *143:* 4
Cartwright, Shannon *176:* 81
Carty, Leo *4:* 196; *7:* 163; *58:* 131
Cary *4:* 133; *9:* 32; *20:* 2; *21:* 143
Cary, Page *12:* 41
Casale, Paul *71:* 63; *109:* 122; *136:* 28
Case, Sandra E. *16:* 2
Caseley, Judith *87:* 36; *159:* 47, 48, 49
Casilla, Robert *78:* 7; *167:* 124
Casino, Steve *85:* 193
Cassel, Lili
    *See* Wronker, Lili Cassel
Cassel-Wronker, Lili
    *See* Wronker, Lili Cassel
Cassels, Jean *8:* 50; *150:* 119; *173:* 37
Cassen, Melody *140:* 51
Cassity, Don *104:* 24
Cassler, Carl *75:* 137, 138; *82:* 162
Casson, Hugh *65:* 38, 40, 42, 43
Castellon, Federico *48:* 45, 46, 47, 48
Castle, Jane *4:* 80

Castro, Antonio *84:* 71
Catalano, Dominic *94:* 79; *163:* 60, 61; *162:* 54
Catalanotto, Peter *63:* 170; *70:* 23; *71:* 182; *72:* 96; *74:* 114; *76:* 194, 195; *77:* 7; *79:* 157; *80:* 28, 67; *83:* 157; *85:* 27; *108:* 11; *113:* 30, 31, 33, 34, 36; *114:* 27, 28, 29; *117:* 53; *124:* 168; *159:* 54, 55
Catania, Tom *68:* 82
Cather, Carolyn *3:* 83; *15:* 203; *34:* 216
Catrow, David *117:* 179; *152:* 31, 33; *173:* 24
Cauley, Lorinda Bryan *44:* 135; *46:* 49
Cayard, Bruce *38:* 67
Cazet, Denys *52:* 27; *99:* 39, 40; *163:* 65, 66
Cecil, Randy *127:* 132, 133
Cellini, Joseph *2:* 73; *3:* 35; *16:* 116; *47:* 103
Cepeda, Joe *90:* 62; *109:* 91; *134:* 172; *159:* 57, 58, 164
Chabrian, Debbi *45:* 55
Chabrian, Deborah *51:* 182; *53:* 124; *63:* 107; *75:* 84; *79:* 85; *82:* 247; *89:* 93; *101:* 197
Chagnon, Mary *37:* 158
Chalmers, Mary *3:* 145; *13:* 148; *33:* 125; *66:* 214
Chamberlain, Christopher *45:* 57
Chamberlain, Margaret *46:* 51; *106:* 89
Chamberlain, Nigel *78:* 140
Chambers, C.E. *17:* 230
Chambers, Dave *12:* 151
Chambers, Jill *134:* 110
Chambers, Mary *4:* 188
Chambliss, Maxie *42:* 186; *56:* 159; *93:* 163, 164; *103:* 178
Champlin, Dale *136:* 124
Chan, Harvey *96:* 236; *99:* 153; *143:* 218
Chandler, David P. *28:* 62
Chaney, Howard *139:* 27
Chang, Warren *101:* 209
Chapel, Jody *68:* 20
Chapman, C.H. *13:* 83, 85, 87
Chapman, Frederick T. *6:* 27; *44:* 28
Chapman, Gaynor *32:* 52, 53
Chapman, Jane *145:* 186; *150:* 56; *166:* 220; *174:* 202; *176:* 43, 44
Chapman, Lynne *175:* 31
Chappell, Warren *3:* 172; *21:* 56; *27:* 125
Charles, Donald *30:* 154, 155
Charlip, Remy *4:* 48; *34:* 138; *68:* 53, 54; *119:* 29, 30
Charlot, Jean *1:* 137, 138; *8:* 23; *14:* 31; *48:* 151; *56:* 21
Charlot, Martin *64:* 72
Charlton, Michael *34:* 50; *37:* 39
Charmatz, Bill *7:* 45
Chartier, Normand *9:* 36; *52:* 49; *66:* 40; *74:* 220; *145:* 169; *168:* 91; *177:* 108
Chase, Lynwood M. *14:* 4
Chast, Roz *97:* 39, 40
Chastain, Madye Lee *4:* 50
Chateron, Ann *152:* 19
Chatterton, Martin *68:* 102; *152:* 19
Chau, Tungwai *140:* 35
Chauncy, Francis *24:* 158
Chayka, Doug *145:* 97; *177:* 150
Chee, Cheng-Khee *79:* 42; *81:* 224
Chen, Chih-sien *90:* 226
Chen, Tony *6:* 45; *19:* 131; *29:* 126; *34:* 160
Cheney, T.A. *11:* 47
Cheng, Judith *36:* 45; *51:* 16
Chermayeff, Ivan *47:* 53
Cherry, David *93:* 40
Cherry, Lynne *34:* 52; *65:* 184; *87:* 111; *99:* 46, 47
Chesak, Lina *135:* 118
Chess, Victoria *12:* 6; *33:* 42, 48, 49; *40:* 194; *41:* 145; *69:* 80; *72:* 100; *92:* 33, 34; *104:* 167
Chessare, Michele *41:* 50; *56:* 48; *69:* 145
Chesterton, G.K. *27:* 43, 44, 45, 47
Chestnutt, David *47:* 217

Chesworth, Michael 75: 24, 152; 88: 136; 94: 25; 98: 155; 160: 42
Chetham, Celia 134: 34
Chetwin, Grace 86: 40
Cheung, Irving 158: 96
Chevalier, Christa 35: 66
Chew, Ruth 7: 46; 132: 147
Chewning, Randy 92: 206
Chichester Clark, Emma 72: 121; 77: 212; 78: 209; 87: 143; 117: 37, 39, 40; 144: 138; 156: 24, 25
Chifflart 47: 113, 127
Child, Lauren 119: 32
Chin, Alex 28: 54
Chitwood, Susan Tanner 163: 16
Cho, Shinta 8: 126
Chodos-Irvine, Margaret 52: 102, 103, 107; 152: 44
Choi, Yangsook 171: 134; 173: 135
Chollat, Emilie 170: 203
Chollick, Jay 25: 175
Choma, Christina 99: 169
Chorao, Kay 7: 200, 201; 8: 25; 11: 234; 33: 187; 35: 239; 69: 35; 70: 235; 123: 174
Chowdhury, Subrata 62: 130; 162: 22, 23
Christelow, Eileen 38: 44; 83: 198, 199; 90: 57, 58
Christensen, Bonnie 93: 100; 153: 67
Christensen, Gardell Dano 1: 57
Christensen, James C. 140: 226
Christiana, David 90: 64; 135: 13; 171: 7
Christiansen, Per 40: 24
Christie, R. Gregory 116: 107; 127: 20, 21; 162: 179; 164: 114; 165: 137; 174: 157
Christy, Howard Chandler 17: 163, 164, 165, 168, 169; 19: 186, 187; 21: 22, 23, 24, 25
Chronister, Robert 23: 138; 63: 27; 69: 167
Church, Frederick YABC 1: 155
Chute, Marchette 1: 59
Chwast, Jacqueline 1: 63; 2: 275; 6: 46, 47; 11: 125; 12: 202; 14: 235
Chwast, Seymour 3: 128, 129; 18: 43; 27: 152; 92: 79; 96: 56, 57, 58; 146: 32, 33
Cieslawksi, Steve 101: 142; 127: 116; 158: 169, 171
Cinelli, Lisa 146: 253
Cirlin, Edgard 2: 168
Clairin, Georges 53: 109
Clapp, John 105: 66; 109: 58; 126: 7; 129: 148; 130: 165
Clark, Brenda 119: 85; 153: 55
Clark, David 77: 164; 134: 144, 145
Clark, Emma Chichester
    See Chichester Clark, Emma
Clark, Victoria 35: 159
Clarke, Greg 169: 134
Clarke, Gus 72: 226; 134: 31
Clarke, Harry 23: 172, 173
Clarke, Peter 75: 102
Claverie, Jean 38: 46; 88: 29
Clayton, Elaine 159: 60
Clayton, Robert 9: 181
Cleaver, Elizabeth 8: 204; 23: 36
Cleland, T.M. 26: 92
Clemens, Peter 61: 125
Clement, Charles 20: 38
Clement, Rod 97: 42
Clement, Stephen 88: 3
Clementson, John 84: 213
Clevin, Jorgen 7: 50
Clifford, Judy 34: 163; 45: 198
Clokey, Art 59: 44
Clouse, James 84: 15
Clouse, Nancy L. 78: 31; 114: 90
Clover, Peter 152: 45
Cneut, Carll 156: 166; 165: 67
Coalson, Glo 9: 72, 85; 25: 155; 26: 42; 35: 212; 53: 31; 56: 154; 94: 37, 38, 193
Cober, Alan E. 17: 158; 32: 77; 49: 127
Cober-Gentry, Leslie 92: 111

Cocca-Leffler, Maryann 80: 46; 136: 60; 139: 193
Cochran, Bobbye 11: 52
CoConis, Ted 4: 41; 46: 41; 51: 104
Cocozza, Chris 87: 18; 110: 173; 111: 149
Cockroft, Jason 152: 20
Coerr, Eleanor 1: 64; 67: 52
Coes, Peter 35: 172
Cogancherry, Helen 52: 143; 69: 131; 77: 93; 78: 220; 109: 204; 110: 129
Coggins, Jack 2: 69
Cohen, Alix 7: 53
Cohen, Miriam 155: 23, 24
Cohen, Nancy R. 165: 35
Cohen, Santiago 164: 26
Cohen, Sheldon 105: 33, 34; 166: 46, 47
Cohen, Vincent O. 19: 243
Cohen, Vivien 11: 112
Coker, Paul 51: 172
Colbert, Anthony 15: 41; 20: 193
Colby, C.B. 3: 47
Cole, Babette 58: 172; 96: 63, 64; 155: 29
Cole, Brock 68: 223; 72: 36, 37, 38, 192; 127: 23; 136: 64, 65
Cole, Gwen 87: 185
Cole, Herbert 28: 104
Cole, Michael 59: 46
Cole, Olivia H.H. 1: 134; 3: 223; 9: 111; 38: 104
Colin, Paul 102: 59; 123: 118; 126: 152
Collicott, Sharleen 98: 39; 143: 29, 30
Collier, Bryan 126: 54; 151: 166; 174: 16, 17, 18
Collier, David 13: 127
Collier, John 27: 179
Collier, Steven 50: 52
Collier-Morales, Roberta 168: 61
Collins, Heather 66: 84; 67: 68; 81: 40; 98: 192, 193; 129: 95, 96, 98
Collins, Matt 167: 90
Collins, Ross 140: 23, 24
Colman, Audrey 146: 161
Colon, Raul 108: 112; 113: 5; 117: 167; 134: 112; 146: 23; 159: 92; 166: 73
Colonna, Bernard 21: 50; 28: 103; 34: 140; 43: 180; 78: 150
Comport, Sally Wern 117: 169; 169: 104
Conde, J.M. 100: 120
Condon, Grattan 54: 85 Condon, Ken 161: 44
Cone, Ferne Geller 39: 49
Cone, J. Morton 39: 49
Conklin, Paul 43: 62
Connolly, Howard 67: 88
Connolly, Jerome P. 4: 128; 28: 52
Connolly, Peter 47: 60
Conoly, Walle 110: 224
Conover, Chris 31: 52; 40: 184; 41: 51; 44: 79
Contreras, Gerry 72: 9
Converse, James 38: 70
Conway 62: 62
Conway, Michael 69: 12; 81: 3; 92: 108
Cook, G.R. 29: 165
Cook, Joel 108: 160
Cookburn, W.V. 29: 204
Cooke, Donald E. 2: 77
Cooke, Tom 52: 118
Coomaraswamy, A.K. 50: 100
Coombs, Charles 43: 65
Coombs, Deborah 139: 175
Coombs, Patricia 2: 82; 3: 52; 22: 119; 51: 32, 33, 34, 35, 36, 37, 38, 39, 40, 42, 43
Cooney, Barbara 6: 16, 17, 50; 12: 42; 13: 92; 15: 145; 16: 74, 111; 18: 189; 23: 38, 89, 93; 32: 138; 38: 105; 59: 48, 49, 51, 52, 53; 74: 222; 81: 100; 91: 25; 96: 71, 72, 74; 100: 149; YABC 2: 10
Cooper, Elisha 157: 38, 39
Cooper, Floyd 79: 95; 81: 45; 84: 82; 85: 74; 91: 118; 96: 77, 78; 103: 149; 144: 54; 145: 151; 159: 198; 176: 133, 134
Cooper, Heather 50: 39

Cooper, Helen 102: 42, 43, 44
Cooper, Mario 24: 107
Cooper, Marjorie 7: 112
Cope, Jane 61: 201; 108 52
Copelman, Evelyn 8: 61; 18: 25
Copley, Heather 30: 86; 45: 57
Corbett, Grahame 30: 114; 43: 67
Corbino, John 19: 248
Corcos, Lucille 2: 223; 10: 27; 34: 66
Corey, Robert 9: 34
Corlass, Heather 10: 7
Cornell, James 27: 60
Cornell, Jeff 11: 58
Cornell, Laura 94: 179; 95: 25
Corrigan, Barbara 8: 37
Corrigan, Patrick 145: 149
Corwin, Judith Hoffman 10: 28
Cory, Fanny Y. 20: 113; 48: 29
Cosentino, Ralph 169: 32
Cosgrove, Margaret 3: 100; 47: 63; 82: 133
Costabel, Eva Deutsch 45: 66, 67
Costanza, John 58: 7, 8, 9
Costello, Chris 86: 78
Costello, David F. 23: 55
Cote, Nancy 126: 139; 156: 101; 174: 101
Couch, Greg 94: 124; 110: 13; 162: 31; 168: 149
Councell, Ruth Tietjen 79: 29
Courtney, Cathy 58: 69, 144; 59: 15; 61: 20, 87
Courtney, R. 35: 110
Counihan, Claire 133: 106
Cousineau, Normand 89: 180; 112: 76
Cousins, Lucy 172: 53, 54
Couture, Christin 41: 209
Covarrubias, Miguel 35: 118, 119, 123, 124, 125
Coville, Katherine 32: 57; 36: 167; 92: 38
Covington, Neverne 113: 87
Cowdrey, Richard 169: 170
Cowell, Cressida 140: 39
Cowell, Lucinda 77: 54
Cox 43: 93
Cox, Charles 8: 20
Cox, David 56: 37; 90: 63; 119: 38
Cox, Palmer 24: 76, 77
Cox, Steve 140: 96
Coxe, Molly 69: 44
Coxon, Michele 158: 80
Crabb, Gordon 70: 39
Crabtree, Judith 98: 42
Craft, Kinuko 22: 182; 36: 220; 53: 122, 123, 148, 149; 74: 12; 81: 129; 86: 31; 89: 139; 127: 27, 28, 29; 132: 142; 139: 38
Craig, Dan 177: 67
Craig, David 136: 198
Craig, Helen 49: 76; 62: 70, 71, 72; 69: 141; 94: 42, 43, 44; 112: 53; 135: 101, 102
Crane, Alan H. 1: 217
Crane, H.M. 13: 111
Crane, Jack 43: 183
Crane, Jordan 174: 21
Crane, Walter 18: 46, 47, 48, 49, 53, 54, 56, 57, 59, 60, 61; 22: 128; 24: 210, 217; 100: 70, 71
Cravath, Lynne W. 98: 45
Crawford, Denise 137: 213
Crawford, Will 43: 77
Credle, Ellis 1: 69
Czernecki, Stefan 154: 104
Crespi, Francesca 87: 90
Cressy, Michael 124: 55
Crews, Donald 32: 59, 60; 76: 42, 43, 44
Crews, Nina 97: 49
Crichlow, Ernest 74: 88; 83: 203
Croft, James 150: 57
Crofut, Bob 80: 87; 81: 47
Crofut, Susan 23: 61
Croll, Carolyn 80: 137; 102: 52
Cross, Peter 56: 78; 63: 60, 65
Crowe, Elizabeth 88: 144

Crowell, Pers *3:* 125
Cruikshank, George *15:* 76, 83; *22:* 74, 75, 76, 77, 78, 79, 80, 81, 82, 84, 137; *24:* 22, 23
Crump, Fred H. *11:* 62
Cruz, Ray *6:* 55; *70:* 234; *123:* 173; *172:* 192
Csatari, Joe *44:* 82; *55:* 152; *63:* 25, 28; *102:* 58
Cuetara, Mittie *158:* 85
Cuffari, Richard *4:* 75; *5:* 98; *6:* 56; *7:* 13, 84, 153; *8:* 148, 155; *9:* 89; *11:* 19; *12:* 55, 96, 114; *15:* 51, 202; *18:* 5; *20:* 139; *21:* 197; *22:* 14, 192; *23:* 15, 106; *25:* 97; *27:* 133; *28:* 196; *29:* 54; *30:* 85; *31:* 35; *36:* 101; *38:* 171; *42:* 97; *44:* 92, 192; *45:* 212, 213; *46:* 36, 198; *50:* 164; *54:* 80, 136, 137, 145; *56:* 17; *60:* 63; *66:* 49, 50; *70:* 41; *71:* 132; *77:* 157; *78:* 58, 149; *79:* 120; *85:* 2, 152
Cugat, Xavier *19:* 120
Cumings, Art *35:* 160
Cummings, Chris *29:* 167
Cummings, Michael *159:* 142
Cummings, Pat *42:* 61; *61:* 99; *69:* 205; *71:* 57, 58; *78:* 24, 25; *93:* 75; *107:* 49, 50; *164:* 259
Cummings, Richard *24:* 119
Cunette, Lou *20:* 93; *22:* 125
Cunningham, Aline *25:* 180
Cunningham, David *11:* 13
Cunningham, Imogene *16:* 122, 127
Cunningham, Kelley *176:* 159
Cupples, Pat *107:* 12; *126:* 109
Curlee, Lynn *98:* 48; *141:* 39
Curry, John Steuart *2:* 5; *19:* 84; *34:* 36; *144:* 126
Curry, Tom *127:* 131
Curtis, Bruce *23:* 96; *30:* 88; *36:* 22
Curtis, Neil *167:* 30
Cusack, Margaret *58:* 49, 50, 51
Cushman, Doug *65:* 57; *101:* 39, 40; *133:* 179; *157:* 45
Cyrus, Kurt *132:* 39
Czechowski, Alicia *95:* 21; *171:* 37
Czernecki, Stefan *117:* 173

**D**

Dabcovich, Lydia *25:* 105; *40:* 114; *99:* 75, 76
Dacey, Bob *82:* 175; *152:* 65
d'Achille, Gino *127:* 175, 176
Dailey, Don *78:* 197
Dain, Martin J. *35:* 75
Dale, Penny *127:* 224; *151:* 57; *160:* 89
Dale, Rae *72:* 197
Daley, Joann *50:* 22
Dalton, Anne *40:* 62; *63:* 119
Daly, Deborah M. *74:* 213
Daly, Jim *103:* 60; *150:* 48
Daly, Jude *138:* 118, 119
Daly, Nicholas *37:* 53; *76:* 48, 49
Daly, Niki *107:* 15; *114:* 38, 39, 40; *164:* 86
Daly, Paul *97:* 205
Dalziel, Brothers *33:* 113
D'Amato, Alex *9:* 48; *20:* 25
D'Amato, Janet *9:* 48; *20:* 25; *26:* 118
D'Amico, Steve *170:* 52
Danalis, Johnny *167:* 27
Daniel, Alan *23:* 59; *29:* 110; *76:* 50, 53, 55, 56; *153:* 76 *115:* 74; *134:* 70
Daniel, Lea *76:* 53, 55; *153:* 76
Daniel, Lewis C. *20:* 216
Daniels, Beau *73:* 4
Daniels, Steve *22:* 16
Daniels, Stewart *56:* 12
Dann, Bonnie *31:* 83
Dann, Penny *82:* 128
Danska, Herbert *24:* 219
Danyell, Alice *20:* 27

Darley, F.O.C. *16:* 145; *19:* 79, 86, 88, 185; *21:* 28, 36; *35:* 76, 77, 78, 79, 80, 81; *YABC 2:* 175
Darling, Lois *3:* 59; *23:* 30, 31
Darling, Louis *1:* 40, 41; *2:* 63; *3:* 59; *23:* 30, 31; *43:* 54, 57, 59; *121:* 53
Darrow, David R. *84:* 101
Darrow, Whitney, Jr. *13:* 25; *38:* 220, 221
Darwin, Beatrice *43:* 54
Darwin, Len *24:* 82
Dastolfo, Frank *33:* 179
Dauber, Liz *1:* 22; *3:* 266; *30:* 49
Daugherty, James *3:* 66; *8:* 178; *13:* 27, 28, 161; *18:* 101; *19:* 72; *29:* 108; *32:* 156; *42:* 84; *YABC 1:* 256; *2:* 174
d'Aulaire, Edgar Parin *5:* 51; *66:* 53
d'Aulaire, Ingri Parin *5:* 51; *66:* 53
Davalos, Felipe *99:* 197; *159:* 66; *174:* 163
Davenier, Christine *125:* 88; *127:* 32; *128:* 152
Davick, Linda *151:* 124
David, Jonathan *19:* 37
Davidson, Kevin *28:* 154
Davidson, Raymond *32:* 61
Davie, Helen K. *77:* 48, 49
Davis, Allen *20:* 11; *22:* 45; *27:* 222; *29:* 157; *41:* 99; *47:* 99; *50:* 84; *52:* 105
Davis, Bette J. *15:* 53; *23:* 95
Davis, Dimitris *45:* 95
Davis, Hendon *151:* 122
Davis, Jack E. *145:* 139; *175:* 84, 85
Davis, Jim *32:* 63, 64
Davis, Katie *152:* 52, 53, 54
Davis, Lambert *110:* 23, 24; *176:* 58
Davis, Marguerite *31:* 38; *34:* 69, 70; *100:* 34; *YABC 1:* 126, 230
Davis, Nelle *69:* 191
Davis, Paul *78:* 214
Davis, Yvonne LeBrun *94:* 144
Davisson, Virginia H. *44:* 178
DaVolls, Andy *85:* 53
Dawson, Diane *24:* 127; *42:* 126; *52:* 130; *68:* 104
Day, Alexandra *67:* 59; *97:* 54; *166:* 65; *169:* 40
Day, Larry *169:* 88
Day, Rob *94:* 110; *127:* 24
Dean, Bob *19:* 211
de Angeli, Marguerite *1:* 77; *27:* 62, 65, 66, 67, 69, 70, 72; *100:* 75, 76; *YABC 1:* 166
DeArmond, Dale *70:* 47
Deas, Michael *27:* 219, 221; *30:* 156; *67:* 134; *72:* 24; *75:* 155; *84:* 206; *88:* 124
Debon, Nicolas *151:* 60; *177:* 46
de Bosschere, Jean *19:* 252; *21:* 4
De Bruyn, M(onica) G. *13:* 30, 31
Decker, C.B. *172:* 120
De Cuir, John F. *1:* 28, 29
Deeter, Catherine *74:* 110; *103:* 150; *137:* 50
Degen, Bruce *40:* 227, 229; *57:* 28, 29; *56:* 156; *75:* 229; *76:* 19; *81:* 36, 37; *92:* 26; *93:* 199; *97:* 56, 58, 59; *124:* 40; *147:* 39, 40, 41; *168:* 23
De Grazia *14:* 59; *39:* 56, 57
DeGrazio, George *88:* 40
deGroat, Diane *9:* 39; *18:* 7; *23:* 123; *28:* 200, 201; *31:* 58, 59; *34:* 151; *41:* 152; *43:* 88; *46:* 40, 200; *49:* 163; *50:* 89; *52:* 30, 34; *54:* 43; *63:* 5; *70:* 136; *71:* 99; *73:* 117, 156; *77:* 34; *85:* 48; *86:* 201; *87:* 142; *90:* 72, 73, 143; *95:* 182; *111:* 123; *118:* 160; *126:* 8; *130:* 130; *138:* 93, 94; *169:* 46, 47
de Groot, Lee *6:* 21
Deines, Brian *110:* 139
DeJohn, Marie *89:* 78
Dekhteryov, B. *61:* 158
de Kiefte, Kees *94:* 107
Delacre, Lulu *36:* 66; *156:* 35
Delaney, A. *21:* 78
Delaney, Molly *80:* 43
Delaney, Ned *28:* 68; *56:* 80; *102:* 11
DeLapine, Jim *79:* 21

De La Roche Saint Andre, Anne *75:* 37
de Larrea, Victoria *6:* 119, 204; *29:* 103; *72:* 203; *87:* 199
Delessert, Etienne *7:* 140; *46:* 61, 62, 63, 65, 67, 68; *130:* 38, 39, 40, 41, 42; *YABC 2:* 209
DeLorenzo, Christopher *154:* 149
Delulio, John *15:* 54
DeLuna, Tony *88:* 95
Demarest, Chris L. *45:* 68, 69, 70; *73:* 172, 173, 176; *78:* 106; *82:* 48, 49; *89:* 212; *92:* 86; *128:* 57, 58; *175:* 46, 48
De Mejo, Oscar *40:* 67
Demi *11:* 135; *15:* 245; *66:* 129, 130; *89:* 216; *102:* 66, 67, 68
Denetsosie, Hoke *13:* 126; *82:* 34
Denise, Christopher *147:* 43, 44; *176:* 101
Dennis, Morgan *18:* 68, 69; *64:* 89
Dennis, Wesley *2:* 87; *3:* 111; *11:* 132; *18:* 71, 72, 73, 74; *22:* 9; *24:* 196, 200; *46:* 178; *69:* 94, 96; *129:* 62
Denslow, W.W. *16:* 84, 85, 86, 87; *18:* 19, 20, 24; *29:* 211; *100:* 21
Denton, Kady MacDonald *110:* 82; *130:* 70
Denton, Terry *72:* 163; *174:* 26
DePalma, Mary Newell *132:* 114; *139:* 75
de Paola, Tomie *8:* 95; *9:* 93; *11:* 69; *25:* 103; *28:* 157; *29:* 80; *39:* 52, 53; *40:* 226; *46:* 187; *59:* 61, 62, 63, 64, 65, 66, 67, 68, 69, 71, 72, 74; *62:* 19; *108:* 63, 67, 68, 70; *155:* 62, 64, 66
Deraney, Michael J. *77:* 35; *78:* 148
deRosa, Dee *70:* 48; *71:* 210; *91:* 78
Dervaux, Isabelle *111:* 117
De Saulles, Tony *119:* 39
de Seve, Peter *146:* 261
Deshaprabhu, Meera Dayal *86:* 192
Desimini, Lisa *86:* 68; *94:* 47; *96:* 7; *104:* 107; *125:* 194; *131:* 180; *172:* 56
de St. Menin, Charles *70:* 17
Detmold, Edward J. *22:* 104, 105, 106, 107; *35:* 120; *64:* 5; *YABC 2:* 203
Detrich, Susan *20:* 133
Deutermann, Diana *77:* 175
DeVelasco, Joseph E. *21:* 51
de Veyrac, Robert *YABC 2:* 19
DeVille, Edward A. *4:* 235
de Visser, John *55:* 119
Devito, Bert *12:* 164
Devlin, Harry *11:* 74; *74:* 63, 65; *136:* 77, 78
Dewan, Ted *108:* 73; *157:* 55; *165:* 129
Dewar, Nick *133:* 122
Dewey, Ariane *7:* 64; *33:* 195; *35:* 208; *68:* 16, 17; *75:* 46; *93:* 91; *94:* 197; *109:* 65, 66, 67; *125:* 2, 3, 4, 5; *127:* 188; *143:* 25
Dewey, Jennifer (Owings) *58:* 54; *64:* 214; *65:* 207; *88:* 169; *103:* 45
Dewey, Kenneth *39:* 62; *51:* 23; *56:* 163
de Zanger, Arie *30:* 40
Diakité, Baba Wagué *174:* 28
Diamond, Donna *21:* 200; *23:* 63; *26:* 142; *35:* 83, 84, 85, 86, 87, 88, 89; *38:* 78; *40:* 147; *44:* 152; *50:* 144; *53:* 126; *69:* 46, 47, 48, 201; *71:* 133; *123:* 19
Dias, Ron *71:* 67
Diaz, David *80:* 213; *96:* 83, 84; *108:* 228; *110:* 29; *149:* 106; *150:* 63
Dibley, Glin *138:* 83; *141:* 128
DiCesare, Joe *70:* 38; *71:* 63, 106; *79:* 214; *93:* 147; *116:* 217; *143:* 111; *166:* 57
Dick, John Henry *8:* 181
Dickens, Frank *34:* 131
Dickey, Robert L. *15:* 279
Dickson, Mora *84:* 21
Didier, Sam *166:* 114
Dietz, James *128:* 223
di Fate, Vincent *37:* 70; *90:* 11; *93:* 60; *109:* 219, 220
Di Fiori, Lawrence *10:* 51; *12:* 190; *27:* 97; *40:* 219; *93:* 57; *130:* 45
Digby, Desmond *97:* 180
Di Grazia, Thomas *32:* 66; *35:* 241

Dillard, Annie *10:* 32
Dillard, Sarah *136:* 186
Dillon, Corinne B. *1:* 139
Dillon, Diane *4:* 104, 167; *6:* 23; *13:* 29; *15:* 99; *26:* 148; *27:* 136, 201; *51:* 29, 48, 51, 52, 53, 54, 55, 56, 57, 58, 59, 60, 61, 62; *54:* 155; *56:* 69; *58:* 127, 128; *61:* 95; *62:* 27; *64:* 46; *68:* 3; *69:* 209; *74:* 89; *79:* 92; *86:* 89; *92:* 28, 177; *93:* 7, 210; *94:* 239, 240; *97:* 167; *106:* 58, 59, 61, 64; *107:* 3; *139:* 246; *167:* 77
Dillon, Leo *4:* 104, 167; *6:* 23; *13:* 29; *15:* 99; *26:* 148; *27:* 136, 201; *51:* 29, 48, 51, 52, 53, 54, 55, 56, 57, 58, 59, 60, 61, 62; *54:* 155; *56:* 69; *58:* 127, 128; *61:* 95; *62:* 27; *64:* 46; *68:* 3; *69:* 209; *74:* 89; *79:* 92; *86:* 89; *92:* 28, 177; *93:* 7, 210; *94:* 239, 240; *97:* 167; *106:* 58, 59, 61, 64; *107:* 3; *139:* 246; *167:* 77
Dillon, Sharon Saseen *59:* 179, 188
DiMaccio, Gerald *121:* 80
DiMaggio, Joe *36:* 22
DiMassi, Gina *169:* 17
Dinan, Carol *25:* 169; *59:* 75
Dines, Glen *7:* 66, 67
Dinesen, Thomas *44:* 37
Dinh, Pham Viet *167:* 184
Dinnerstein, Harvey *42:* 63, 64, 65, 66, 67, 68; *50:* 146
Dinsdale, Mary *10:* 65; *11:* 171
Dinyer, Eric *86:* 148; *109:* 163; *110:* 239; *124:* 11; *150:* 69; *170:* 4; *171:* 30
Dion, Nathalie *170:* 124
DiSalvo-Ryan, DyAnne *59:* 77; *62:* 185; *117:* 46; *144:* 64; *150:* 153
Disney, Walt *28:* 71, 72, 73, 76, 77, 78, 79, 80, 81, 87, 88, 89, 90, 91, 94
DiTerlizzi, Tony *105:* 7; *147:* 22; *154:* 31, 32, 33
Divito, Anna *83:* 159
Dixon, Don *74:* 17; *109:* 196
Dixon, Larry *127:* 125
Dixon, Maynard *20:* 165
Doares, Robert G. *20:* 39
Dobias, Frank *22:* 162
Dobrin, Arnold *4:* 68
Dobson, Steven Gaston *102:* 103
Dockray, Tracy *139:* 77
Docktor, Irv *43:* 70
Dodd, Ed *4:* 69
Dodd, Julie *74:* 73
Dodd, Lynley *35:* 92; *86:* 71; *132:* 45, 46, 47
Dodge, Bill *96:* 36; *118:* 7, 8, 9; *133:* 135
Dodgson, Charles L. *20:* 148; *33:* 146; *YABC 2:* 98
Dodson, Bert *9:* 138; *14:* 195; *42:* 55; *54:* 8; *60:* 49; *101:* 125
Dodson, Liz Brenner *105:* 117; *111:* 15
Dohanos, Stevan *16:* 10
Dolce, J. Ellen *74:* 147; *75:* 41
Dolch, Marguerite P. *50:* 64
Dolesch, Susanne *34:* 49
Dollar, Diane *57:* 32
Dolobowsky, Mena *81:* 54
Dolson, Hildegarde *5:* 57
Domanska, Janina *6:* 66, 67; *YABC 1:* 166
Domi *134:* 113
Dominguez, El *53:* 94
Domjan, Joseph *25:* 93
Domm, Jeffrey C. *84:* 69; *135:* 70
Donahey, William *68:* 209
Donahue, Dorothy *76:* 170
Donahue, Vic *2:* 93; *3:* 190; *9:* 44
Donald, Elizabeth *4:* 18
Donalty, Alison *149:* 195, 196, 197
Donato *85:* 59; *149:* 204
Doney, Todd L.W. *87:* 12; *93:* 112; *98:* 135; *101:* 57; *104:* 40; *118:* 163; *135:* 162, 163; *151:* 18
Donna, Natalie *9:* 52
Donohue, Dorothy *95:* 2; *132:* 30; *176:* 54, 55

Dooling, Michael *82:* 19; *105:* 55; *106:* 224; *125:* 135; *171:* 46; *172:* 12; *176:* 120
Doran, Ben-Ami *128:* 189
Dore, Gustave *18:* 169, 172, 175; *19:* 93, 94, 95, 96, 97, 98, 99, 100, 101, 102, 103, 104, 105; *23:* 188; *25:* 197, 199
Doremus, Robert *6:* 62; *13:* 90; *30:* 95, 96, 97; *38:* 97
Dorfman, Ronald *11:* 128
Doriau *86:* 59; *91:* 152
Dorros, Arthur *78:* 42, 43; *91:* 28
Doruyter, Karel *165:* 105
dos Santos, Joyce Audy *57:* 187, 189
Doty, Roy *28:* 98; *31:* 32; *32:* 224; *46:* 157; *82:* 71; *142:* 7
Doucet, Bob *132:* 238; *169:* 159
Dougherty, Charles *16:* 204; *18:* 74
Doughty, Rebecca *177:* 174
Doughty, Thomas *118:* 31; *140:* 60
Douglas, Aaron *31:* 103
Douglas, Carole Nelson *73:* 48
Douglas, Goray *13:* 151
Dow, Brian *150:* 92
Dowd, Jason *52:* 51, 52; *164:* 244
Dowd, Vic *3:* 244; *10:* 97
Dowden, Anne Ophelia *7:* 70, 71; *13:* 120
Dowdy, Mrs. Regera *29:* 100
Downing, Julie *60:* 140; *81:* 50; *86:* 200; *99:* 129
Doyle, Janet *56:* 31
Doyle, Richard *21:* 31, 32, 33; *23:* 231; *24:* 177; *31:* 87
Draper, Angie *43:* 84
Drath, Bill *26:* 34
Drawson, Blair *17:* 53; *126:* 65
Dray, Matt *177:* 47
Drescher, Henrik *105:* 60, 62, 63; *172:* 72
Drescher, Joan *30:* 100, 101; *35:* 245; *52:* 168; *137:* 52
Drew, Patricia *15:* 100
Drummond, V.H. *6:* 70
Drury, Christian Potter *105:* 97
Dubanevich, Arlene *56:* 44
Ducak, Danilo *99:* 130; *108:* 214
Duchesne, Janet *6:* 162; *79:* 8
Duda, Jana *102:* 155
Dudash, Michael *32:* 122; *77:* 134; *82:* 149
Duer, Douglas *34:* 177
Duffy, Daniel Mark *76:* 37; *101:* 196; *108:* 147, 148
Duffy, Joseph *38:* 203
Duffy, Pat *28:* 153
Dugin, Andrej *77:* 60
Dugina, Olga *77:* 60
Duke, Chris *8:* 195; *139:* 164
Duke, Kate *87:* 186; *90:* 78, 79, 80, 81
Duke, Marion *165:* 87
Dulac, Edmund *19:* 108, 109, 110, 111, 112, 113, 114, 115, 117; *23:* 187; *25:* 152; *YABC 1:* 37; *2:* 147
Dulac, Jean *13:* 64
Dumas, Philippe *52:* 36, 37, 38, 39, 40, 41, 42, 43, 45; *119:* 40, 41, 42
Dunaway, Nancy *108:* 161
Dunbar, James *76:* 63
Duncan, Beverly *72:* 92
Duncan, John *116:* 94
Dunn, H.T. *62:* 196
Dunn, Harvey *34:* 78, 79, 80, 81
Dunn, Iris *5:* 175
Dunn, Phoebe *5:* 175
Dunne, Jeanette *72:* 57, 173, 222
Dunnick, Regan *176:* 51
Dunnington, Tom *3:* 36; *18:* 281; *25:* 61; *31:* 159; *35:* 168; *48:* 195; *79:* 144; *82:* 230
Dunn-Ramsey, Marcy *117:* 131
Dunrea, Olivier *59:* 81; *118:* 53, 54; *124:* 43
Duntze, Dorothee *88:* 28; *160:* 76
Dupasquier, Philippe *86:* 75; *104:* 76; *151:* 63
DuQuette, Keith *90:* 83; *155:* 73, 74
Duroussy, Nathalie *146:* 150

Durrell, Julie *82:* 62; *94:* 62
Dutz *6:* 59
Duvoisin, Roger *2:* 95; *6:* 76, 77; *7:* 197; *28:* 125; *30:* 101, 102, 103, 104, 105, 107; *47:* 205; *84:* 254
Dyer, Dale *141:* 71
Dyer, Jane *75:* 219; *129:* 28; *147:* 49, 50, 51; *168:* 121
Dypold, Pat *15:* 37

**E**

E.V.B.
    *See* Boyle, Eleanor Vere (Gordon)
Eachus, Jennifer *29:* 74; *82:* 201; *164:* 153
Eadie, Bob *63:* 36
Eagle, Bruce *95:* 119
Eagle, Ellen *82:* 121; *89:* 3
Eagle, Jeremy *141:* 71
Eagle, Michael *11:* 86; *20:* 9; *23:* 18; *27:* 122; *28:* 57; *34:* 201; *44:* 189; *73:* 9; *78:* 235; *85:* 43
Earl-Bridges, Michele *159:* 128
Earle, Edwin *56:* 27
Earle, Olive L. *7:* 75
Earle, Vana *27:* 99
Early, Lori *132:* 2
Early, Margaret *72:* 59
East, Stella *131:* 223
Eastman, P.D. *33:* 57
Easton, Reginald *29:* 181
Eaton, Tom *4:* 62; *6:* 64; *22:* 99; *24:* 124
Ebel, Alex *11:* 89
Ebert, Len *9:* 191; *44:* 47
Echevarria, Abe *37:* 69
Eckersley, Maureen *48:* 62
Eckert, Horst *72:* 62
Ede, Janina *33:* 59
Edens, Cooper *49:* 81, 82, 83, 84, 85; *112:* 58
Edens, John *109:* 115
Edgar, Sarah E. *41:* 97
Edliq, Emily S. *131:* 107
Edrien *11:* 53
Edwards, Freya *45:* 102
Edwards, George Wharton *31:* 155
Edwards, Gunvor *2:* 71; *25:* 47; *32:* 71; *54:* 106
Edwards, Jeanne *29:* 257
Edwards, Linda Strauss *21:* 134; *39:* 123; *49:* 88, 89
Edwards, Michelle *152:* 62, 63
Edwards, Wallace *170:* 55
Egan, Tim *155:* 76, 77, 78
Egge, David *102:* 71
Eggenhofer, Nicholas *2:* 81
Eggleton, Bob *74:* 40; *81:* 190, 191; *105:* 6; *121:* 183; *149:* 203; *166:* 215
Egielski, Richard *11:* 90; *16:* 208; *33:* 236; *38:* 35; *49:* 91, 92, 93, 95, 212, 213, 214, 216; *79:* 122; *106:* 67, 68, 69; *134:* 135; *144:* 244; *163:* 82, 84
Ehlert, Lois *35:* 97; *69:* 51; *112:* 7; *113:* 208; *128:* 63, 64, 65; *172:* 77, 79, 80
Ehrlich, Bettina *1:* 83
Eitan, Ora *160:* 165
Eichenberg, Fritz *1:* 79; *9:* 54; *19:* 248; *23:* 170; *24:* 200; *26:* 208; *50:* 67, 68, 69, 70, 71, 72, 73, 74, 75, 77, 79, 80, 81; *60:* 165; *100:* 137; *YABC 1:* 104, 105; *2:* 213
Einsel, Naiad *10:* 35; *29:* 136
Einsel, Walter *10:* 37
Einzig, Susan *3:* 77; *43:* 78; *67:* 155; *129:* 154
Eisner, Will *165:* 82, 83
Eitzen, Allan *9:* 56; *12:* 212; *14:* 226; *21:* 194; *38:* 162; *76:* 218
Eldridge, H. *54:* 109
Eldridge, Harold *43:* 83
Elgaard, Greta *19:* 241
Elgin, Kathleen *9:* 188; *39:* 69

Ellacott, S.E. *19:* 118
Elliott, Mark *93:* 69; *105:* 108; *107:* 123; *140:* 53; *165:* 189; *173:* 67
Elliott, Sarah M. *14:* 58
Ellis, Dianne *130:* 208
Ellis, Jan Davey *88:* 50; *115:* 80
Ellis, Richard *130:* 47, 48
Ellison, Pauline *55:* 21
Elmer, Richard *78:* 5
Elmore, Larry *90:* 8
Elwell, Tristan *110:* 39; *121:* 182; *127:* 46; *137:* 144; *141:* 173; *151:* 236; *158:* 264; *167:* 119, 120, 121; *169:* 20
Elzbieta *88:* 80, 81
Emberley, Ed *8:* 53; *70:* 53, 54; *146:* 65, 69, 70
Emberley, Michael *34:* 83; *80:* 72; *119:* 47, 48; *147:* 100; *158:* 115
Emerling, Dorothy *104:* 27
Emery, Leslie *49:* 187
Emmett, Bruce *49:* 147; *80:* 175; *101:* 206
Emry-Perrott, Jennifer *61:* 57
Emshwiller, Ed *174:* 45
Engel, Diana *70:* 57
Engle, Mort *38:* 64
Englebert, Victor *8:* 54
English, Mark *101:* 207
Enik, Ted *142:* 39
Enos, Randall *20:* 183
Enright, Maginel Wright *19:* 240, 243; *39:* 31, 35, 36
Enrique, Romeo *34:* 135
Epstein, Stephen *50:* 142, 148
Erdogan, Buket *174:* 179
Erdrich, Louise *141:* 62
Erhard, Walter *1:* 152
Erickson, Phoebe *11:* 83; *59:* 85
Erikson, Mel *31:* 69
Eriksson, Eva *63:* 88, 90, 92, 93
Ering, Timothy Basil *131:* 100; *176:* 63, 64
Ernst, Lisa Campbell *47:* 147; *95:* 47; *154:* 46, 47, 48; *164:* 88
Esco, Jo *61:* 103
Escourido, Joseph *4:* 81
Escriva, Vivi *119:* 51
Este, Kirk *33:* 111
Estep, David *73:* 57
Estes, Eleanor *91:* 66
Estoril, Jean *32:* 27
Estrada, Pau *74:* 76
Estrada, Ric *5:* 52, 146; *13:* 174
Etchemendy, Teje *38:* 68
Etheredges, the *73:* 12
Etienne, Kirk-Albert *145:* 184
Ets, Marie Hall *2:* 102
Ettlinger, Doris *171:* 98
Eulalie *YABC 2:* 315
Evans, Greg *73:* 54, 55, 56; *143:* 40, 41
Evans, Katherine *5:* 64
Evans, Leslie *144:* 227
Evans, Shane W. *159:* 142; *160:* 190; *168:* 39
Everitt, Betsy *151:* 110
Ewart, Claire *76:* 69; *145:* 59, 60
Ewing, Carolyn *66:* 143; *79:* 52
Ewing, Juliana Horatia *16:* 92
Eyolfson, Norman *98:* 154

**F**

Fabian, Limbert *136:* 114
Facklam, Paul *132:* 62
Falconer, Ian *125:* 66
Falconer, Pearl *34:* 23
Falkenstern, Lisa *70:* 34; *76:* 133; *78:* 171; *127:* 16
Falls, C.B. *1:* 19; *38:* 71, 72, 73, 74
Falter, John *40:* 169, 170
Falwell, Cathryn *118:* 77; *137:* 185

Fancher, Lou *138:* 219; *141:* 64; *144:* 199; *177:* 51
Fanelli, Sara *89:* 63; *126:* 69
Faria, Rosana *150:* 143
Farmer, Andrew *49:* 102
Farmer, Peter *24:* 108; *38:* 75
Farnsworth, Bill *93:* 189; *116:* 147; *124:* 8; *135:* 52; *146:* 242, 243, 244
Farquharson, Alexander *46:* 75
Farrell, David *40:* 135
Farris, David *74:* 42
Fasolino, Teresa *118:* 145
Fatigati, Evelyn *24:* 112
Faul-Jansen, Regina *22:* 117
Faulkner, Jack *6:* 169
Faulkner, Matt *161:* 174; *167:* 75
Fava, Rita *2:* 29
Fax, Elton C. *1:* 101; *4:* 2; *12:* 77; *25:* 107
Fay *43:* 93
Fearnley, Jan *153:* 82, 83
Fearrington, Ann *146:* 80
Federspiel, Marian *33:* 51
Fedorov, Nickolai Ivanovich *110:* 102
Feelings, Tom *5:* 22; *8:* 56; *12:* 153; *16:* 105; *30:* 196; *49:* 37; *61:* 101; *69:* 56, 57; *93:* 74; *105:* 88
Fehr, Terrence *21:* 87
Feiffer, Jules *3:* 91; *8:* 58; *61:* 66, 67, 70, 74, 76, 77, 78; *111:* 47, 48, 49, 50; *132:* 122; *157:* 62
Feigeles, Neil *41:* 242
Feldman, Elyse *86:* 7
Feller, Gene *33:* 130
Fellows, Muriel H. *10:* 42
Felstead, Cathie *116:* 85
Felts, Shirley *33:* 71; *48:* 59
Fennell, Tracy *171:* 69
Fennelli, Maureen *38:* 181
Fenton, Carroll Lane *5:* 66; *21:* 39
Fenton, Mildred Adams *5:* 66; *21:* 39
Ferguson, Peter *177:* 30, 31
Ferguson, Walter W. *34:* 86
Fernandes, Eugenie *77:* 67
Fernandes, Stanislaw *70:* 28
Fernandez, Fernando *77:* 57
Fernandez, Laura *77:* 153; *101:* 117; *131:* 222; *170:* 119; *175:* 182
Ferrington, Susan *172:* 22
Fetz, Ingrid *11:* 67; *12:* 52; *16:* 205; *17:* 59; *29:* 105; *30:* 108, 109; *32:* 149; *43:* 142; *56:* 29; *60:* 34; *85:* 48; *87:* 146
Fiammenghi, Gioia *9:* 66; *11:* 44; *12:* 206; *13:* 57, 59; *52:* 126, 129; *66:* 64; *85:* 83; *91:* 161; *166:* 169
Fiedler, Joseph Daniel *96:* 42; *113:* 173; *129:* 164; *146:* 17; *159:* 68; *162:* 104
Field, Rachel *15:* 113
Fielding, David *70:* 124
Fieser, Stephen *152:* 36
Fine, Howard *145:* 159; *159:* 64; *165:* 134; *174:* 129
Fine, Peter K. *43:* 210
Finger, Helen *42:* 81
Fink, Sam *18:* 119
Finlay, Winifred *23:* 72
Finney, Pat *79:* 215
Fiore, Peter *99:* 196; *125:* 139; *144:* 225; *160:* 169
Fiorentino, Al *3:* 240
Firehammer, Karla *174:* 202
Firmin, Charlotte *29:* 75; *48:* 70
Firmin, Peter *58:* 63, 64, 65, 67, 68, 70, 71
Firth, Barbara *81:* 208; *127:* 218
Fischel, Lillian *40:* 204
Fischer, Hans *25:* 202
Fischer-Nagel, Andreas *56:* 50
Fischer-Nagel, Heiderose *56:* 50
Fisher, Carolyn *154:* 50
Fisher, Chris *79:* 62; *158:* 248
Fisher, Cynthia *117:* 45; *137:* 118
Fisher, Jeffrey *142:* 80

Fisher, Leonard Everett *3:* 6; *4:* 72, 86; *6:* 197; *9:* 59; *16:* 151, 153; *23:* 44; *27:* 134; *29:* 26; *34:* 87, 89, 90, 91, 93, 94, 95, 96; *40:* 206; *50:* 150; *60:* 158; *73:* 68, 70, 71, 72, 73; *176:* 71, 72, 73; *YABC 2:* 169
Fisher, Lois *20:* 62; *21:* 7
Fisher, Valorie *177:* 55
Fisk, Nicholas *25:* 112
Fitschen, Marilyn *2:* 20, 21; *20:* 48
Fitz-Maurice, Jeff *175:* 2
Fitzgerald, F.A. *15:* 116; *25:* 86, 87
Fitzhugh, Louise *1:* 94; *9:* 163; *45:* 75, 78
Fitzgerald, Joanne *157:* 153, 154
Fitzhugh, Susie *11:* 117
Fitzpatrick, Jim *109:* 130
Fitzpatrick, Marie-Louise *125:* 69, 70
Fitzsimmons, Arthur *14:* 128
Fix, Philippe *26:* 102
Flack, Marjorie *21:* 67; *100:* 93; *YABC 2:* 122
Flagg, James Montgomery *17:* 227
Flavin, Teresa *132:* 115
Flax, Zeona *2:* 245
Fleetwood, Tony *171:* 51
Fleishman, Seymour *14:* 232; *24:* 87
Fleming, Denise *71:* 179; *81:* 58; *126:* 71, 72, 73; *173:* 52, 53
Fleming, Guy *18:* 41
Flesher, Vivienne *85:* 55
Fletcher, Claire *80:* 106; *157:* 159
Flint, Russ *74:* 80
Floate, Helen *111:* 163
Floca, Brian *155:* 88, 89
Floethe, Richard *3:* 131; *4:* 90
Floherty, John J., Jr. *5:* 68
Flook, Helen *160:* 81
Flora, James *1:* 96; *30:* 111, 112
Florczak, Robert *166:* 51
Florian, Douglas *19:* 122; *83:* 64, 65; *125:* 71, 72, 74, 76; *128:* 130; *177:* 58, 60
Flory, Jane *22:* 111
Flower, Renee *125:* 109
Floyd, Gareth *1:* 74; *17:* 245; *48:* 63; *62:* 35, 36, 37, 39, 40, 41; *74:* 245; *79:* 56
Fluchere, Henri A. *40:* 79
Flynn, Barbara *7:* 31; *9:* 70
Fogarty, Thomas *15:* 89
Folger, Joseph *9:* 100
Folkard, Charles *22:* 132; *29:* 128, 257, 258
Foott, Jeff *42:* 202
Forberg, Ati *12:* 71, 205; *14:* 1; *22:* 113; *26:* 22; *48:* 64, 65
Ford, George *24:* 120; *31:* 70, 177; *58:* 126; *81:* 103; *107:* 91; *136:* 100
Ford, H.J. *16:* 185, 186
Ford, Jason *174:* 119
Ford, Pamela Baldwin *27:* 104
Fordham, John *168:* 160, 161
Foreman, Michael *2:* 110, 111; *67:* 99; *73:* 78, 79, 80, 81, 82; *93:* 146; *135:* 55, 56, 57
Forrester, Victoria *40:* 83
Forsey, Chris *140:* 210
Fortnum, Peggy *6:* 29; *20:* 179; *24:* 211; *26:* 76, 77, 78; *39:* 78; *58:* 19, 21, 23, 27; *YABC 1:* 148
Foster, Brad W. *34:* 99
Foster, Genevieve *2:* 112
Foster, Gerald *7:* 78
Foster, Jon *146:* 18
Foster, Laura Louise *6:* 79
Foster, Marian Curtis *23:* 74; *40:* 42
Foster, Sally *58:* 73, 74
Foucher, Adele *47:* 118
Foust, Mitch *168:* 50
Fowler, Mel *36:* 127
Fowler, Richard *87:* 219
Fowles, Selley *165:* 127
Fox, Charles Phillip *12:* 84
Fox, Jim *6:* 187
Fox-Davies, Sarah *76:* 150
Frace, Charles *15:* 118
Frailey, Joy *72:* 108

Frame, Paul 2: 45, 145; 9: 153; 10: 124; 21: 71; 23: 62; 24: 123; 27: 106; 31: 48; 32: 159; 34: 195; 38: 136; 42: 55; 44: 139; 60: 39, 40, 41, 42, 43, 44, 46; 73: 183
Frampton, David 85: 72; 102: 33; 139: 182; 152: 37
Francois, Andre 25: 117
Francoise
  *See* Seignobosc, Francoise
Frank, Lola Edick 2: 199
Frank, Mary 4: 54; 34: 100
Franke, Phil 45: 91
Frankel, Alona 66: 70
Frankel, Julie 40: 84, 85, 202
Frankenberg, Robert 22: 116; 30: 50; 38: 92, 94, 95; 68: 111
Frankfeldt, Gwen 84: 223; 110: 92
Frankland, David 169: 137
Franklin, Ashton 165: 144
Franklin, John 24: 22
Franson, Leanne R. 111: 57, 58; 151: 7
Frascino, Edward 9: 133; 29: 229; 33: 190; 48: 80, 81, 82, 83, 84, 85, 86
Frasconi, Antonio 6: 80; 27: 208; 53: 41, 43, 45, 47, 48; 68: 145; 73: 226; 131: 68
Fraser, Betty 2: 212; 6: 185; 8: 103; 31: 72, 73; 43: 136; 111: 76
Fraser, Eric 38: 78; 41: 149, 151
Fraser, F.A. 22: 234
Fraser, James 171: 68
Fraser, Mary Ann 137: 63
Frasier, Debra 69: 60; 112: 67
Fraustino, Lisa Rowe 146: 87
Frazee, Marla 72: 98; 105: 79, 80; 151: 67, 68; 164: 165; 171: 190, 191
Frazetta, Frank 41: 72; 58: 77, 78, 79, 80, 81, 82, 83
Frazier, Craig 177: 63
Freas, John 25: 207
Fredrickson, Mark 103: 33
Freeland, Michael J. 118: 115
Freeman, Don 2: 15; 13: 249; 17: 62, 63, 65, 67, 68; 18: 243; 20: 195; 23: 213, 217; 32: 155; 55: 129
Freeman, Irving 67: 150
Freeman, Laura 144: 111
Freeman, Pietri 140: 223
Freeman, Tom 167: 118
Freeman, Tor 164: 93
Fregosi, Claudia 24: 117
Fremaux, Charlotte Murray 138: 29; 141: 95
French, Fiona 6: 82, 83; 75: 61; 109: 170; 132: 79, 80, 81, 82
French, Martin 163: 4
Frendak, Rodney 126: 97, 98
Freschet, Gina 175: 73
Freynet, Gilbert 72: 221
Friedman, Judith 43: 197; 131: 221
Friedman, Marvin 19: 59; 42: 86
Frinta, Dagmar 36: 42
Frith, Michael K. 15: 138; 18: 120
Fritz, Ronald 46: 73; 82: 124
Fromm, Lilo 29: 85; 40: 197
Frost, A.B. 17: 6, 7; 19: 123, 124, 125, 126, 127, 128, 129, 130; 100: 119; YABC 1: 156, 157, 160; 2: 107
Frost, Kristi 118: 113
Frost, Michael 151: 209
Froud, Brian 150: 82, 83
Froud, Wendy 151: 237
Fry, Guy 2: 224
Fry, Rosalie 3: 72; YABC 2: 180, 181
Fry, Rosalind 21: 153, 168
Fryer, Elmer 34: 115
Fuchs, Bernie 110: 10; 162: 46
Fuchs, Erich 6: 84
Fuchsuber, Annegert 43: 96
Fufuka, Mahiri 32: 146
Fuge, Charles 144: 91, 93
Fujikawa, Gyo 39: 75, 76; 76: 72, 73, 74
Fulford, Deborah 23: 159

Fuller, Margaret 25: 189
Fulweiler, John 93: 99
Funai, Mamoru 38: 105
Funk, Tom 7: 17, 99
Furchgott, Terry 29: 86
Furness, William Henry, Jr. 94: 18
Furukawa, Mel 25: 42
Fusari, Erika 164: 227

G

Gaadt, David 78: 212; 121: 166
Gaadt, George 71: 9
Gaber, Susan 99: 33; 115: 57, 58; 164: 195; 169: 61, 62, 63
Gaberell, J. 19: 236
Gabler, Mirko 99: 71
Gackenbach, Dick 19: 168; 41: 81; 48: 89, 90, 91, 92, 93, 94; 54: 105; 79: 75, 76, 77
Gad, Victor 87: 161
Gaetano, Nicholas 23: 209
Gaffney-Kessell, Walter 94: 219; 174: 188
Gag, Flavia 17: 49, 52
Gag, Wanda 100: 101, 102; YABC 1: 135, 137, 138, 141, 143
Gagnon, Cecile 11: 77; 58: 87
Gal, Laszlo 14: 127; 52: 54, 55, 56; 65: 142; 68: 150; 81: 185; 96: 104, 105
Galazinski, Tom 55: 13
Galdone, Paul 1: 156, 181, 206; 2: 40, 241; 3: 42, 144; 4: 141; 10: 109, 158; 11: 21; 12: 118, 210; 14: 12; 16: 36, 37; 17: 70, 71, 72, 73, 74; 18: 111, 230; 19: 183; 21: 154; 22: 150, 245; 33: 126; 39: 136, 137; 42: 57; 51: 169; 55: 110; 66: 80, 82, 139; 72: 73; 100: 84
Gale, Cathy 140: 22; 143: 52
Gall, Chris 176: 79, 80
Gallagher, S. Saelig 105: 154
Gallagher, Sears 20: 112
Galloway, Ewing 51: 154
Galouchko, Annouchka Gravel 95: 55
Galster, Robert 1: 66
Galsworthy, Gay John 35: 232
Galvez, Daniel 125: 182
Gamble, Kim 112: 64, 65; 124: 77
Gammell, Stephen 7: 48; 13: 149; 29: 82; 33: 209; 41: 88; 50: 185, 186, 187; 53: 51, 52, 53, 54, 55, 56, 57, 58; 54: 24, 25; 56: 147, 148, 150; 57: 27, 66; 81: 62, 63; 87: 88; 89: 10; 106: 223; 126: 2; 128: 71, 73, 74, 77; 154: 34
Gamper, Ruth 84: 198
Gampert, John 58: 94
Ganly, Helen 56: 56
Gannett, Ruth Chrisman 3: 74; 18: 254; 33: 77, 78
Gantschev, Ivan 45: 32
Garafano, Marie 73: 33
Garbot, Dave 131: 106
Garbutt, Bernard 23: 68
Garcia 37: 71
Garcia, Manuel 74: 145
Garcia-Franco, Rebecca 173: 46
Gardner, Earle 45: 167
Gardner, Joan 40: 87
Gardner, Joel 40: 87, 92
Gardner, John 40: 87
Gardner, Lucy 40: 87
Gardner, Richard
  *See* Cummings, Richard
Gardner, Sally 171: 177; 177: 66, 68
Gargiulo, Frank 84: 158
Garland, Michael 36: 29; 38: 83; 44: 168; 48: 78, 221, 222; 49: 161; 60: 139; 71: 6, 11; 72: 229; 74: 142; 89: 187; 93: 183; 104: 110; 131: 55; 139: 209; 168: 56
Garland, Peggy 60: 139
Garland, Sarah 62: 45; 135: 67, 68; 171: 118

Garn, Aimee 75: 47
Garner, Joan 128: 170
Garneray, Ambroise Louis 59: 140
Garnett, Gary 39: 184
Garns, Allen 80: 125; 84: 39; 165: 231
Garraty, Gail 4: 142; 52: 106
Garrett, Agnes 46: 110; 47: 157
Garrett, Edmund H. 20: 29
Garrett, Tom 107: 194
Garrick, Jacqueline 67: 42, 43; 77: 94
Garrison, Barbara 19: 133; 104: 146; 109: 87
Garro, Mark 108: 131; 128: 210
Garvey, Robert 98: 222
Garza, Carmen Lomas 80: 211
Gates, Frieda 26: 80
Gaughan, Jack 26: 79; 43: 185
Gaver, Becky 20: 61
Gawing, Toby 72: 52
Gay, Marie-Louise 68: 76, 77, 78; 102: 136; 126: 76, 78, 81, 83; 127: 55, 56
Gay, Zhenya 19: 135, 136
Gaydos, Tim 62: 201
Gazsi, Ed 80: 48
Gazso, Gabriel 73: 85
Geary, Clifford N. 1: 122; 9: 104; 51: 74
Geary, Rick 142: 44, 46
Gee, Frank 33: 26
Geehan, Wayne 157: 181
Geer, Charles 1: 91; 3: 179; 4: 201; 6: 168; 7: 96; 9: 58; 10: 72; 12: 127; 39: 156, 157, 158, 159, 160; 42: 88, 89, 90, 91; 55: 111, 116
Geerinck, Manuel 173: 128
Gehm, Charlie 36: 65; 57: 117; 62: 60, 138
Geisel, Theodor Seuss 1: 104, 105, 106; 28: 108, 109, 110, 111, 112, 113; 75: 67, 68, 69, 70, 71; 89: 127, 128; 100: 106, 107, 108
Geisert, Arthur 92: 67, 68; 133: 72, 73, 74; 165: 97, 98; 171: 64, 65
Geldart, William 15: 121; 21: 202
Genia 4: 84
Gentry, Cyrille R. 12: 66
Genzo, John Paul 136: 74
George, Jean 2: 113
George, Lindsay Barrett 95: 57; 155: 97, 98
Geraghty, Paul 130: 60, 61
Gerard, Jean Ignace 45: 80
Gerard, Rolf 27: 147, 150
Gerber, Mark 61: 105
Gerber, Mary Jane 112: 124; 171: 56
Gerber, Stephanie 71: 195
Gerdstein, Mordecai 169: 105
Gergely, Tibor 54: 15, 16
Geritz, Franz 17: 135
Gerlach, Geff 42: 58
Gerrard, Roy 47: 78; 90: 96, 97, 98, 99
Gerritsen, Paula 177: 69
Gershinowitz, George 36: 27
Gerstein, Mordicai 31: 117; 47: 80, 81, 82, 83, 84, 85, 86; 51: 173; 69: 134; 107: 122; 142: 49, 52; 165: 209; 176: 119
Gervase 12: 27
Geter, Tyrone 146: 249; 150: 86
Getz, Arthur 32: 148
Gewirtz, Bina 61: 81
Giancola, Donato 95: 146; 164: 226
Gibbons, Gail 23: 78; 72: 77, 78, 79; 82: 182; 104: 65; 160: 99, 100
Gibbs, Tony 40: 95
Gibran, Kahlil 32: 116
Gider, Iskender 81: 193
Giebfried, Rosemary 170: 135
Giesen, Rosemary 34: 192, 193
Giffard, Hannah 83: 70
Giguere, George 20: 111
Gilbert, John 19: 184; 54: 115; YABC 2: 287
Gilbert, W.S. 36: 83, 85, 96
Gilbert, Yvonne 116: 70; 128: 84; 149: 119

Gilchrist, Jan Spivey *72:* 82, 83, 84, 85, 87; *77:* 90; *105:* 89, 91; *130:* 63, 64; *155:* 105, 107
Giles, Will *41:* 218
Gili, Phillida *70:* 73
Gill, Margery *4:* 57; *7:* 7; *22:* 122; *25:* 166; *26:* 146, 147
Gillen, Denver *28:* 216
Gillette, Henry J. *23:* 237
Gilliam, Stan *39:* 64, 81
Gillies, Chuck *62:* 31
Gilliland, Jillian *87:* 58
Gillman, Alec *98:* 105
Gilman, Esther *15:* 124
Gilman, Phoebe *104:* 70, 71
Ginsberg, Sari *111:* 184
Ginsburg, Max *62:* 59; *68:* 194 *Girard, Roge 161:* 30
Girouard, Patrick *155:* 100
Giovanopoulos, Paul *7:* 104; *60:* 36
Giovine, Sergio *79:* 12; *93:* 118; *139:* 118
Githens, Elizabeth M. *5:* 47
Gladden, Scott *99:* 108; *103:* 160
Gladstone, Gary *12:* 89; *13:* 190
Gladstone, Lise *15:* 273
Glanzman, Louis S. *2:* 177; *3:* 182; *36:* 97, 98; *38:* 120, 122; *52:* 141, 144; *71:* 191; *91:* 54, 56
Glaser, Byron *154:* 59, 60
Glaser, Milton *3:* 5; *5:* 156; *11:* 107; *30:* 26; *36:* 112; *54:* 141; *151:* 70
Glass, Andrew *36:* 38; *44:* 133; *48:* 205; *65:* 3; *68:* 43, 45; *90:* 104, 105; *150:* 89
Glass, Marvin *9:* 174
Glasser, Judy *41:* 156; *56:* 140; *69:* 79; *72:* 101
Glattauer, Ned *5:* 84; *13:* 224; *14:* 26
Glauber, Uta *17:* 76
Gleeson, J.M. *YABC 2:* 207
Glegg, Creina *36:* 100
Glienke, Amelie *63:* 150
Gliewe, Unada *3:* 78, 79; *21:* 73; *30:* 220
Gliori, Debi *72:* 91; *138:* 82; *162:* 37
Glovach, Linda *7:* 105
Gobbato, Imero *3:* 180, 181; *6:* 213; *7:* 58; *9:* 150; *18:* 39; *21:* 167; *39:* 82, 83; *41:* 137, 251; *59:* 177
Goble, Paul *25:* 121; *26:* 86; *33:* 65; *69:* 68, 69; *131:* 79, 80
Goble, Warwick *46:* 78, 79
Godal, Eric *36:* 93
Godkin, Celia *145:* 84, 86
Godfrey, Michael *17:* 279
Godon, Ingrid *166:* 163
Goembel, Ponder *42:* 124
Goffe, Toni *61:* 83, 84, 85; *89:* 11; *90:* 124
Goffstein, M.B. *8:* 71; *70:* 75, 76, 77
Golbin, Andre *15:* 125
Gold, Robert *166:* 151, 152
Goldfeder, Cheryl *11:* 191
Goldsborough, June *5:* 154, 155; *8:* 92, *14:* 226; *19:* 139; *54:* 165
Goldsmith, Robert *110:* 77
Goldstein, Leslie *5:* 8; *6:* 60; *10:* 106
Goldstein, Nathan *1:* 175; *2:* 79; *11:* 41, 232; *16:* 55
Goldstrom, Robert *98:* 36; *145:* 51, 52
Golembe, Carla *79:* 80, 81; *136:* 91; *144:* 113
Golin, Carlo *74:* 112
Gomez, Elizabeth *127:* 70; *133:* 76
Gomi, Taro *64:* 102; *103:* 74, 76
Gon, Adriano *101:* 112
Gonzalez, Maya Christina *104:* 3; *136:* 92
Goodall, John S. *4:* 92, 93; *10:* 132; *66:* 92, 93; *YABC 1:* 198
Goode, Diane *15:* 126; *50:* 183; *52:* 114, 115; *76:* 195; *84:* 94; *99:* 141; *114:* 76, 77, 78; *170:* 99, 101
Goodelman, Aaron *40:* 203
Goodenow, Earle *40:* 97
Goodfellow, Peter *62:* 95; *94:* 202

Goodman, Joan Elizabeth *50:* 86
Goodman, Vivienne *82:* 251; *146:* 181, 182
Goodnow, Patti *117:* 33
Goodwin, Harold *13:* 74
Goodwin, Philip R. *18:* 206
Goor, Nancy *39:* 85, 86
Goor, Ron *39:* 85, 86
Gorbachev, Valeri *89:* 96; *112:* 97; *143:* 63, 64
Gordon, Gwen *12:* 151
Gordon, Margaret *4:* 147; *5:* 48, 49; *9:* 79
Gordon, Mike *101:* 62, 63, 64
Gordon, Russell *136:* 204; *137:* 214
Gordon, Walter *138:* 9
Gore, Leonid *89:* 51; *94:* 74; *136:* 8; *158:* 117; *166:* 136; *168:* 36; *170:* 107
Gorecka-Egan, Erica *18:* 35
Gorey, Edward *1:* 60, 61; *13:* 169; *18:* 192; *20:* 201; *29:* 90, 91, 92, 93, 94, 95, 96, 97, 98, 99, 100; *30:* 129; *32:* 90; *34:* 200, *65:* 48; *68:* 24, 25; *69:* 79; *70:* 80, 82, 83, 84, 85; *136:* 136; *127:* 62
Gorsline, Douglas *1:* 98; *6:* 13; *11:* 113; *13:* 104; *15:* 14; *28:* 117, 118; *YABC 1:* 15
Gorton, Julia *108:* 94
Gosfield, Josh *118:* 165, 166; *149:* 67
Gosner, Kenneth *5:* 135
Gosney, Joy *167:* 142
Gotlieb, Jules *6:* 127
Goto, Scott *115:* 86; *136:* 69
Gottlieb, Dale *67:* 162; *107:* 16; *149:* 6
Goudey, Ray *97:* 86
Gough, Alan *91:* 57
Gough, Philip *23:* 47; *45:* 90
Gould, Chester *49:* 112, 113, 114, 116, 117, 118
Gould, Jason *151:* 232
Gourbault, Martine *177:* 159
Govern, Elaine R. *26:* 94
Gower, Teri *102:* 184
Gowing, Toby *60:* 25; *63:* 33; *78:* 70, 252; *83:* 228; *86:* 187; *93:* 145; *108:* 133; *110:* 217
Grabianski *20:* 144
Grabianski, Janusz *39:* 92, 93, 94, 95
Graboff, Abner *35:* 103, 104
Graef, Renee *61:* 188; *72:* 207
Grafe, Max *156:* 173
Graham, A.B. *11:* 61
Graham, Bob *101:* 66, 67, 68; *151:* 74, 75
Graham, L. *7:* 108
Graham, Margaret Bloy *11:* 120; *18:* 305, 307
Graham, Mark *88:* 208; *159:* 153
Grahame-Johnstone, Janet *13:* 61
Grahame-Johnstone, Anne *13:* 61
Grainger, Sam *42:* 95
Gralley, Jean *166:* 86
Gramatky, Hardie *1:* 107; *30:* 116, 119, 120, 122, 123
Gran, Julie *168:* 118
Granahan, Julie *84:* 84
GrandPre, Mary *84:* 131; *109:* 199; *118:* 76
Grandström, Brita *176:* 139
Grandville, J.J. *45:* 81, 82, 83, 84, 85, 86, 87, 88; *47:* 125; *64:* 10
Granger, Paul *39:* 153
Granström, Brita *162:* 35; *167:* 46
Grant, (Alice) Leigh *10:* 52; *15:* 131; *20:* 20; *26:* 119; *48:* 202
Grant, Gordon *17:* 230, 234; *25:* 123, 124, 125, 126; *52:* 69; *YABC 1:* 164
Grant, Melvyn *159:* 186, 187; *170:* 48, 49
Grant, Renee *77:* 40
Grant, Shirley *109:* 45
Graves, Elizabeth *45:* 101
Graves, Keith *167:* 89
Gray, Harold *33:* 87, 88
Gray, Les *82:* 76; *83:* 232
Gray, Reginald *6:* 69
Greder, Armin *76:* 235
Green, Ann Canevari *62:* 48
Green, Eileen *6:* 97
Green, Elizabeth Shippen *139:* 109

Green, Jonathan *86:* 135; *105:* 109
Green, Ken *111:* 68
Green, Michael *32:* 216
Green, Robina *87:* 138
Green, Jonathan *157:* 105
Greene, Jeffrey *117:* 93
Greenaway, Kate *17:* 275; *24:* 180; *26:* 107; *41:* 222, 232; *100:* 115, 116; *YABC 1:* 88, 89; *2:* 131, 133, 136, 138, 139, 141
Greenberg, Melanie Hope *72:* 93; *80:* 125; *101:* 174; *133:* 180
Greenstein, Elaine *150:* 100
Greenwald, Sheila *1:* 34; *3:* 99; *8:* 72
Greger, Carol *76:* 86
Gregorian, Joyce Ballou *30:* 125
Gregory, Emilian *177:* 146
Gregory, Fran *130:* 4; *140:* 93
Gregory, Frank M. *29:* 107
Greiffenhagen, Maurice *16:* 137; *27:* 57; *YABC 2:* 288
Greiner, Robert *6:* 86
Gretter, J. Clemens *31:* 134
Gretz, Susanna *7:* 114
Gretzer, John *1:* 54; *3:* 26; *4:* 162; *7:* 125; *16:* 247; *18:* 117; *28:* 66; *30:* 85, 211; *33:* 235; *56:* 16
Grey, Mini *166:* 90
Grey Owl *24:* 41
Gri *25:* 90
Grieder, Walter *9:* 84
Griesbach/Martucci *59:* 3
Grifalconi, Ann *2:* 126; *3:* 248; *11:* 18; *13:* 182; *46:* 38; *50:* 145; *66:* 99, 100, 101, 104, 106; *69:* 38; *70:* 64; *87:* 128; *90:* 53; *93:* 49; *128:* 48; *133:* 79, 81
Griffin, Gillett Good *26:* 96
Griffin, James *30:* 166
Griffin, John Howard *59:* 186
Griffin, Rachel *131:* 23
Griffith, Gershom *94:* 214
Griffiths, Dave *29:* 76
Griffiths, Dean *168:* 180; *169:* 182
Grimsdell, Jeremy *83:* 75
Grimwood, Brian *82:* 89
Gringhuis, Dirk *6:* 98; *9:* 196
Gripe, Harald *2:* 127; *74:* 98
Grisha *3:* 71
Grohmann, Susan *84:* 97
Gropper, William *27:* 93; *37:* 193
Gros *60:* 199
Grose, Helen Mason *YABC 1:* 260; *2:* 150
Grossman, Nancy *24:* 130; *29:* 101
Grossman, Robert *11:* 124; *46:* 39
Groth, John *15:* 79; *21:* 53, 54; *83:* 230
Grover, Lorie Ann *168:* 59
Grubb, Lisa *160:* 116
Gruelle, Johnny *35:* 107
Gschwind, William *11:* 72
Guay, Rebecca *110:* 95, 96; *135:* 240
Guback, Georgia *88:* 102
Guerguerion, Claudine *105:* 73
Guevara, Susan *97:* 87; *167:* 49
Guggenheim, Hans *2:* 10; *3:* 37; *8:* 136
Guida, Lisa Chauncy *172:* 188
Guilbeau, Honore *22:* 69
Guillette, Joseph *137:* 37
Guisewite, Cathy *57:* 52, 53, 54, 56, 57
Gukova, Julia *95:* 104; *154:* 103; *168:* 195
Gundersheimer, Karen *35:* 240; *82:* 100
Gunderson, Nick *57:* 120
Gurney, James *76:* 97; *86:* 32
Gurney, John Steven *75:* 39, 82; *110:* 175; *143:* 67, 68; *169:* 172
Gusman, Annie *38:* 62
Gustafson, Scott *34:* 111; *43:* 40
Gustavson, Adam *104:* 10; *171:* 183; *176:* 87
Guthridge, Bettina *108:* 79
Guthrie, R. Dale *64:* 143
Guthrie, Robin *20:* 122
Gutierrez, Akemi *172:* 87
Gutierrez, Alan *136:* 31, 32

Gutierrez, Rudy *97:* 162
Gutmann, Bessie Pease *73:* 93, 94
Gwynne, Fred *41:* 94, 95
Gyberg, Bo-Erik *38:* 131

**H**

Haas, Irene *17:* 77; *87:* 46; *96:* 117
Hack, Konrad *51:* 127
Hader, Berta H. *16:* 126
Hader, Elmer S. *16:* 126
Haeffele, Deborah *76:* 99
Haemer, Alan *62:* 109
Hafner, Marylin *22:* 196, 216; *24:* 44; *30:* 51; *35:* 95; *51:* 25, 160, 164; *86:* 16; *105:* 196; *121:* 93, 94; *149:* 208, 209
Hagerty, Sean *62:* 181
Hague, Michael *32:* 128; *48:* 98, 99, 100, 101, 103, 105, 106, 107, 108, 109, 110; *49:* 121; *51:* 105; *64:* 14, 15; *79:* 134; *80:* 91, 92; *83:* 135; *100:* 241; *102:* 29; *129:* 101, 103, 104
Hair, Jonathan *115:* 135
Halas, John *29:* 41, 47, 48
Haldane, Roger *13:* 76; *14:* 202
Hale, Christy *79:* 124; *84:* 200; *114:* 201; *128:* 2, 3; *146:* 203; *158:* 243; *167:* 99
Hale, Irina *26:* 97
Hale, James Graham *88:* 207
Hale, Kathleen *17:* 79; *66:* 114, 116, 118
Haley, Gail E. *43:* 102, 103, 104, 105; *78:* 65, 67; *136:* 106, 107
Hall, Amanda *96:* 110
Hall, Chuck *30:* 189
Hall, Douglas *15:* 184; *43:* 106, 107; *86:* 100; *87:* 82; *129:* 72
Hall, H. Tom *1:* 227; *30:* 210
Hall, Melanie *116:* 48, 49; *169:* 77, 78
Hall, Sydney P. *31:* 89
Hall, Tim *164:* 196
Hall, Vicki *20:* 24
Hallinan, P.K. *39:* 98
Hallman, Tom *98:* 166
Hally, Greg *101:* 200; *151:* 224
Halperin, Wendy Anderson *96:* 151; *125:* 96, 97, 98, 99; *139:* 22; *140:* 84
Halpern, Joan *10:* 25
Halpern, Shari *174:* 172
Halsey, Megan *96:* 172; *114:* 185
Halstead, Virginia *125:* 105
Halverson, Janet *49:* 38, 42, 44
Hallensleben, Georg *134:* 5, 6; *172:* 17
Hamanaka, Sheila *71:* 100
Hamann, Brad *78:* 151
Hamann, Sigune *104:* 115
Hamberger, John *6:* 8; *8:* 32; *14:* 79; *34:* 136; *88:* 78
Hamil, Tom *14:* 80; *43:* 163
Hamilton, Bill and Associates *26:* 215
Hamilton, Helen S. *2:* 238
Hamilton, J. *19:* 83, 85, 87
Hamilton, Laurie *116:* 210
Hamilton, Todd Cameron *84:* 15
Hamlin, Janet *97:* 136; *124:* 90; *137:* 157
Hamlin, Louise *71:* 135
Hammond, Chris *21:* 37
Hammond, Elizabeth *5:* 36, 203
Hampshire, Michael *5:* 187; *7:* 110, 111; *48:* 150; *51:* 129
Hampson, Denman *10:* 155; *15:* 130
Hampton, Blake *41:* 244
Handford, Martin *64:* 105, 106, 107, 109
Handforth, Thomas *42:* 100, 101, 102, 103, 104, 105, 107
Handville, Robert *1:* 89; *38:* 76; *45:* 108, 109
Hane, Roger *17:* 239; *44:* 54
Haney, Elizabeth Mathieu *34:* 84
Hanke, Ted *71:* 10
Hanley, Catherine *8:* 161
Hann, Jacquie *19:* 144

Hanna, Cheryl *91:* 133
Hanna, Wayne A. *67:* 145
Hannon, Mark *38:* 37
Hansen, Gabby *159:* 11
Hansen, Mia *149:* 76
Hanson, Joan *8:* 76; *11:* 139
Hanson, Peter E. *52:* 47; *54:* 99, 100; *73:* 21; *84:* 79; *116:* 144
Hansson, Gunilla *64:* 111, 112
Hardcastle, Nick *121:* 82; *175:* 185
Hardy, David A. *9:* 96; *119:* 74
Hardy, Paul *YABC 2:* 245 *Haring, Keith 145:* 65
Harlan, Jerry *3:* 96
Harlin, Greg *89:* 194; *103:* 82; *118:* 161; *121:* 167
Harness, Cheryl *106:* 80; *131:* 87
Harnischfeger *18:* 121
Harper, Arthur *YABC 2:* 121
Harper, Betty *126:* 90
Harper, Jamie *174:* 71
Harper, Piers *79:* 27; *105:* 102; *161:* 67
Harrington, Glenn *82:* 18; *94:* 66, 68
Harrington, Jack *83:* 162
Harrington, Richard *5:* 81
Harris, Jim *127:* 130
Harris, John *83:* 25
Harris, Nick *86:* 177
Harris, Susan Yard *42:* 121
Harrison, Florence *20:* 150, 152
Harrison, Harry *4:* 103
Harrison, Jack *28:* 149
Harrison, Mark *105:* 157; *165:* 190
Harrison, Ted *56:* 73
Harsh, Fred *72:* 107
Harston, Jerry *105:* 143
Hart, Lewis *98:* 115
Hart, William *13:* 72
Hartland, Jessie *171:* 80, 81
Hartung, Susan Kathleen *150:* 107, 108; *173:* 106; *175:* 106
Hartelius, Margaret *10:* 24
Hartshorn, Ruth *5:* 115; *11:* 129
Harvey, Amanda *145:* 44
Harvey, Bob *48:* 219
Harvey, Gerry *7:* 180
Harvey, Lisa *97:* 21
Harvey, Paul *88:* 74
Harvey, Roland *71:* 88; *123:* 63
Hassall, Joan *43:* 108, 109
Hassell, Hilton *YABC 1:* 187
Hassett, John *162:* 59
Hasselriis, Else *18:* 87; *YABC 1:* 96
Hastings, Glenn *89:* 183
Hastings, Ian *62:* 67
Hauman, Doris *2:* 184; *29:* 58, 59; *32:* 85, 86, 87
Hauman, George *2:* 184; *29:* 58, 59; *32:* 85, 86, 87
Hausherr, Rosmarie *15:* 29
Hawkes, Kevin *78:* 72; *104:* 198; *105:* 197; *112:* 109; *126:* 87; *144:* 88; *149:* 210; *150:* 110, 135; *156:* 94; *164:* 35
Hawkins, Jacqui *112:* 86; *162:* 64
Hawkinson, John *4:* 109; *7:* 83; *21:* 64
Hawkinson, Lucy *21:* 64
Hawthorne, Mike *140:* 228
Haxton, Elaine *28:* 131
Haydock, Robert *4:* 95
Hayes, Geoffrey *26:* 111; *44:* 133; *91:* 85
Haynes, Max *72:* 107
Hays, Michael *73:* 207; *83:* 93; *139:* 197; *146:* 202, 250
Haywood, Carolyn *1:* 112; *29:* 104
Heale, Jonathan *104:* 117
Healy, Daty *12:* 143
Healy, Deborah *58:* 181, 182; *101:* 111
Heap, Sue *102:* 207; *150:* 113, 114
Hearn, Diane Dawson *79:* 99; *113:* 13
Hearon, Dorothy *34:* 69
Heaslip, William *57:* 24, 25

Hechtkopf, H. *11:* 110
Heck, Ed *173:* 81
Hedderwick, Mairi *30:* 127; *32:* 47; *36:* 104; *77:* 86; *145:* 91, 93, 95
Hefferman, Phil *146:* 197
Hefter, Richard *28:* 170; *31:* 81, 82; *33:* 183
Hehenberger, Shelly *126:* 91
Heigh, James *22:* 98
Heighway, Richard *25:* 160; *64:* 4
Heighway-Bury, Robin *159:* 89
Heine, Helme *67:* 86; *135:* 91, 92
Heinly, John *45:* 113
Hellard, Susan *81:* 21
Hellebrand, Nancy *26:* 57
Heller, Linda *46:* 86
Heller, Ruth M. *66:* 125; *77:* 30, 32
Hellmuth, Jim *38:* 164
Helms, Georgeann *33:* 62
Helquist, Brett *142:* 203; *146:* 133, 134; *156:* 10; *173:* 25
Helweg, Hans *41:* 118; *50:* 93; *58:* 22, 26
Henba, Bobbie *90:* 195
Henderson, Dave *73:* 76; *75:* 191, 192, 193, 194; *82:* 4
Henderson, Douglas *103:* 68
Henderson, Kathy *55:* 32; *155:* 118
Henderson, Keith *35:* 122
Henderson, Meryl *127:* 58, 60; *169:* 81
Hendry, Linda *80:* 104; *83:* 83; *164:* 216
Hengeveld, Dennis *142:* 86
Henkes, Kevin *43:* 111; *108:* 106, 107, 108
Henneberger, Robert *1:* 42; *2:* 237; *25:* 83
Henriksen, Harold *35:* 26; *48:* 68
Henriquez, Celeste *103:* 137
Henriquez, Elsa *82:* 260
Henriquez, Emile F. *89:* 88
Henry, Everett *29:* 191
Henry, Matthew *117:* 58
Henry, Paul *93:* 121
Henry, Thomas *5:* 102
Hensel *27:* 119
Henshaw, Jacqui *141:* 127
Henstra, Friso *8:* 80; *36:* 70; *40:* 222; *41:* 250; *73:* 100, 101
Henterly, Jamichael *93:* 4
Heo, Yumi *89:* 85, 86; *94:* 89, 90; *146:* 40, 137, 138; *163:* 227
Hepple, Norman *28:* 198
Herbert, Helen *57:* 70
Herbert, Wally *23:* 101
Herbster, Mary Lee *9:* 33
Herge
   See Remi, Georges
Hermansen, Pal *133:* 113
Hermanson, Dennis *10:* 55
Hermes, Gertrude *54:* 161
Herr, Margo *57:* 191
Herr, Susan *83:* 163
Herriman, George *140:* 74, 75, 76, 77, 78
Herriman, Lisa *87:* 190
Herring, Michael *121:* 76
Herrington, Roger *3:* 161
Herscovici, C. *165:* 240
Hescox, Richard *85:* 86; *90:* 30; *139:* 35
Heslop, Mike *38:* 60; *40:* 130
Hess, Lydia J. *85:* 17
Hess, Mark *111:* 146; *113:* 207
Hess, Paul *134:* 47; *166:* 133
Hess, Richard *42:* 31
Hester, Ronnie *37:* 85
Heuser, Olga J. *121:* 116
Heusser, Sibylle *168:* 195
Heustis, Louise L. *20:* 28
Hewitson, Jennifer *74:* 119; *124:* 167
Hewitt, Kathryn *80:* 126; *149:* 105
Hewitt, Margaret *84:* 112
Heyduck-Huth, Hilde *8:* 82
Heyer, Carol *74:* 122; *130:* 72, 73
Heyer, Hermann *20:* 114, 115
Heyer, Marilee *102:* 108
Heyman, Ken *8:* 33; *34:* 113

Heyne, Ulrike *146:* 151
Heywood, Karen *48:* 114
Hickling, P.B. *40:* 165
Hickman, Stephen *85:* 58; *136:* 33; *171:* 128
Hierstein, Judy *56:* 40; *162:* 168
Higashi, Sandra *154:* 59, 60
Higginbottom, J. Winslow *8:* 170; *29:* 105, 106
Higgins, Chester *101:* 79
Higham, David *50:* 104
Hilb, Nora *176:* 8
Hildebrandt, Greg *8:* 191; *55:* 35, 36, 38, 39, 40, 42, 46; *172:* 110
Hildebrandt, Tim *8:* 191; *55:* 44, 45, 46
Hilder, Rowland *19:* 207
Hill, Eric *66:* 127, 128; *133:* 91
Hill, Gregory *35:* 190
Hill, Pat *49:* 120
Hillenbrand, Will *84:* 115; *92:* 76, 80; *93:* 131; *104:* 168; *128:* 137; *145:* 187; *146:* 184; *147:* 105, 106, 107; *152:* 59
Hillier, Matthew *45:* 205
Hillman, Priscilla *48:* 115
Hills, Tad *113:* 4; *137:* 147; *173:* 83
Himler, Ronald *6:* 114; *7:* 162; *8:* 17, 84, 125; *14:* 76; *19:* 145; *26:* 160; *31:* 43; *38:* 116; *41:* 44, 79; *43:* 52; *45:* 120; *46:* 43; *54:* 44, 83; *58:* 180; *68:* 146; *69:* 231; *70:* 98; *71:* 177, 178; *77:* 219; *79:* 212; *83:* 62; *89:* 5; *91:* 160; *92:* 91, 92, 93; *94:* 93; *95:* 69, 174, 194; *99:* 99, 112; *113:* 92; *118:* 114; *137:* 73, 74, 77, 167; *163:* 99; *165:* 138
Himmelman, John *47:* 109; *65:* 87; *94:* 96, 97; *159:* 85
Hinds, Bill *37:* 127, 130
Hines, Anna Grossnickle *51:* 90; *74:* 124; *95:* 78, 79, 80, 81
Hines, Bob *135:* 149, 150
Hiroko *99:* 61
Hiroshige *25:* 71
Hirsh, Marilyn *7:* 126
Hiscock, Bruce *137:* 80, 81
Hissey, Jane *103:* 90; *130:* 81
Hitch, Jeff *99:* 206; *128:* 86
Hitz, Demi *11:* 135; *15:* 245; *66:* 129, 130; *152:* 94, 95
Hnizdovsky, Jacques *32:* 96; *76:* 187
Ho, Kwoncjan *15:* 132
Hoban, Lillian *1:* 114; *22:* 157; *26:* 72; *29:* 53; *40:* 105, 107, 195; *41:* 80; *69:* 107, 108; *71:* 98; *77:* 168; *106:* 50; *113:* 86; *136:* 118
Hoban, Tana *22:* 159; *104:* 82, 83, 85
Hobbs, Leigh *166:* 95
Hoberman, Norman *5:* 82
Hobson, Sally *77:* 185
Hockerman, Dennis *39:* 22; *56:* 23
Hodgell, P.C. *42:* 114
Hodges, C. Walter *2:* 139; *11:* 15; *12:* 25; *23:* 34; *25:* 96; *33:* 165; *44:* 197; *45:* 95; *100:* 57; *YABC 2:* 62, 63
Hodges, David *9:* 98
Hodgetts, Victoria *43:* 132
Hofbauer, Imre *2:* 162
Hoff, Syd *9:* 107; *10:* 128; *33:* 94; *72:* 115, 116, 117, 118; *138:* 114, 115
Hoffman, Rosekrans *15:* 133; *50:* 219; *63:* 97
Hoffman, Sanford *38:* 208; *76:* 174; *88:* 160, 161; *151:* 156
Hoffmann, Felix *9:* 109
Hoffnung, Gerard *66:* 76, 77
Hofsinde, Robert *21:* 70
Hogan, Inez *2:* 141
Hogarth, Burne *41:* 58; *63:* 46, 48, 49, 50, 52, 53, 54, 55, 56
Hogarth, Paul *41:* 102, 103, 104; *YABC 1:* 16
Hogarth, William *42:* 33
Hogenbyl, Jan *1:* 35
Hogner, Nils *4:* 122; *25:* 144

Hogrogian, Nonny *3:* 221; *4:* 106, 107; *5:* 166; *7:* 129; *15:* 2; *16:* 176; *20:* 154; *22:* 146; *25:* 217; *27:* 206; *74:* 127, 128, 129, 149, 152; *127:* 99; *YABC 2:* 84, 94
Hokanson, Lars *93:* 111; *172:* 137
Hokusai *25:* 71
Hol, Colby *126:* 96
Holberg, Richard *2:* 51
Holbrook, Kathy *107:* 114
Holdcroft, Tina *38:* 109
Holden, Caroline *55:* 159
Holder, Heidi *36:* 99; *64:* 9
Holder, Jimmy *151:* 224
Holiday, Henry *YABC 2:* 107
Holl, F. *36:* 91
Holland, Brad *45:* 59, 159
Holland, Gay W. *128:* 105
Holland, Janice *18:* 118
Holland, Marion *6:* 116
Holldobler, Turid *26:* 120
Holliday, Keaf *144:* 236
Holling, Holling C. *15:* 136, 137
Hollinger, Deanne *12:* 116
Holm, Sharon Lane *114:* 84; *115:* 52
Holmes, B. *3:* 82
Holmes, Bea *7:* 74; *24:* 156; *31:* 93
Holmes, Dave *54:* 22
Holmes, Lesley *135:* 96
Holmgren, George Ellen *45:* 112
Holmlund, Heather D. *150:* 140
Holt, Norma *44:* 106
Holt, Pater *151:* 188
Holtan, Gene *32:* 192
Holub, Joan *149:* 72
Holyfield, John *149:* 231
Holz, Loretta *17:* 81
Hom, Nancy *79:* 195
Homar, Lorenzo *6:* 2
Homer, Winslow *128:* 8; *YABC 2:* 87
Honey, Elizabeth *112:* 95, 96; *137:* 93, 94
Honeywood, Varnette P. *110:* 68, 70
Hong, Lily Toy *76:* 104
Honigman, Marian *3:* 2
Honore, Paul *42:* 77, 79, 81, 82
Hood, Alun *69:* 145, 218; *72:* 41; *80:* 226; *87:* 4; *95:* 139
Hood, Susan *12:* 43
Hook, Christian *104:* 103
Hook, Frances *26:* 188; *27:* 127
Hook, Jeff *14:* 137; *103:* 105
Hook, Richard *26:* 188
Hooks *63:* 30
Hooper, Hadley *177:* 145
Hoover, Carol A. *21:* 77
Hoover, Russell *12:* 95; *17:* 2; *34:* 156
Hope, James *141:* 116
Hopkins, Chris *99:* 127
Hoppin, Augustus *34:* 66
Horacek, Petr *163:* 117
Horder, Margaret *2:* 108; *73:* 75
Horen, Michael *45:* 121
Horne, Daniel *73:* 106; *91:* 153; *109:* 127; *110:* 232; *164:* 176
Horne, Richard *111:* 80
Horse, Harry *128:* 195; *169:* 86
Horvat, Laurel *12:* 201
Horvath, Ferdinand Kusati *24:* 176
Horvath, Maria *57:* 171
Horwitz, Richard *57:* 174
Hotchkiss, De Wolfe *20:* 49
Hough, Charlotte *9:* 112; *13:* 98; *17:* 83; *24:* 195
Houlihan, Ray *11:* 214
Housman, Laurence *25:* 146, 147
Houston, James *13:* 107; *74:* 132, 134, 135
Hovland, Gary *88:* 172; *171:* 148
Hoyt, Eleanor *158:* 231
How, W.E. *20:* 47
Howard, Alan *16:* 80; *34:* 58; *45:* 114
Howard, Arthur *165:* 111, 112
Howard, J.N. *15:* 234

Howard, John *33:* 179
Howard, Kim *116:* 71
Howard, Paul *142:* 126, 129; *144:* 187
Howard, Rob *40:* 161
Howarth, Daniel *170:* 34
Howe, John *115:* 47; *176:* 106
Howe, John F. *79:* 101; *80:* 150
Howe, Phillip *79:* 117; *175:* 115
Howe, Stephen *1:* 232
Howell, Karen *119:* 123
Howell, Pat *15:* 139
Howell, Troy *23:* 24; *31:* 61; *36:* 158; *37:* 184; *41:* 76, 235; *48:* 112; *56:* 13; *57:* 3; *59:* 174; *63:* 5; *74:* 46; *89:* 188; *90:* 231; *95:* 97; *98:* 130; *99:* 189; *153:* 156, 157, 158; *176:* 104
Howes, Charles *22:* 17
Hoyt, Ard *145:* 141
Hranilovich, Barbara *127:* 51
Hu, Ying-Hwa *116:* 107; *152:* 236; *173:* 171
Huang, Benrei *137:* 55
Huang, Zhong-Yang *117:* 30, 32
Hubbard, Woodleigh Marx *98:* 67; *115:* 79; *160:* 138
Hubley, Faith *48:* 120, 121, 125, 130, 131, 132, 134
Hubley, John *48:* 125, 130, 131, 132, 134
Hudak, Michal *143:* 74
Hudnut, Robin *14:* 62
Huerta, Catherine *76:* 178; *77:* 44, 45; *90:* 182
Huffaker, Sandy *10:* 56
Huffman, Joan *13:* 33
Huffman, Tom *13:* 180; *17:* 212; *21:* 116; *24:* 132; *33:* 154; *38:* 59; *42:* 147
Hughes, Arthur *20:* 148, 149, 150; *33:* 114, 148, 149
Hughes, Darren *95:* 44
Hughes, David *36:* 197
Hughes, Shirley *1:* 20, 21; *7:* 3; *12:* 217; *16:* 163; *29:* 154; *63:* 118; *70:* 102, 103, 104; *73:* 169; *88:* 70; *110:* 118, 119; *159:* 103
Hugo, Victor *47:* 112
Hull, Cathy *78:* 29
Hull, Richard *95:* 120; *123:* 175; *172:* 195
Hulsmann, Eva *16:* 166
Hummel, Berta *43:* 137, 138, 139
Hummel, Lisl *29:* 109; *YABC 2:* 333, 334
Humphrey, Henry *16:* 167
Humphreys, Graham *25:* 168
Humphries, Tudor *76:* 66; *80:* 4; *124:* 4, 5
Hunt, James *2:* 143
Hunt, Jonathan *84:* 120
Hunt, Paul *119:* 104; *129:* 135; *139:* 160; *173:* 112
Hunt, Robert *110:* 206, 235; *147:* 136, 137; *170:* 3
Hunter, Anne *133:* 190
Hurd, Clement *2:* 148, 149; *64:* 127, 128, 129, 131, 133, 134, 135, 136; *100:* 37, 38
Hurd, Peter *24:* 30, 31,; *YABC 2:* 56
Hurd, Thacher *46:* 88, 89; *94:* 114, 115, 116; *123:* 81, 82, 84
Hurlimann, Ruth *32:* 99
Hussar, Michael *114:* 113; *117:* 159
Hustler, Tom *6:* 105
Hutchins, Laurence *55:* 22
Hutchins, Pat *15:* 142; *70:* 106, 107, 108
Hutchinson, Sascha *95:* 211
Hutchinson, William M. *6:* 3, 138; *46:* 70
Hutchison, Paula *23:* 10
Hutton, Clarke *YABC 2:* 335
Hutton, Kathryn *35:* 155; *89:* 91
Hutton, Warwick *20:* 91
Huyette, Marcia *29:* 188
Hyatt, John *54:* 7
Hyde, Maureen *82:* 17; *121:* 145, 146
Hyman, David *117:* 64
Hyman, Trina Schart *1:* 204; *2:* 194; *5:* 153; *6:* 106; *7:* 138, 145; *8:* 22; *10:* 196; *13:* 96; *14:* 114; *15:* 204; *16:* 234; *20:* 82; *22:* 133; *24:* 151; *25:* 79, 82; *26:* 82; *29:* 83; *31:* 37,

39; *34:* 104; *38:* 84, 100, 128; *41:* 49; *43:* 146; *46:* 91, 92, 93, 95, 96, 97, 98, 99, 100, 101, 102, 103, 104, 105, 108, 109, 111, 197; *48:* 60, 61; *52:* 32; *60:* 168; *66:* 38; *67:* 214; *72:* 74; *75:* 92; *79:* 57; *82:* 95, 238; *89:* 46; *95:* 91, 92, 93; *100:* 33, 199; *132:* 12; *147:* 33, 35, 36; *167:* 58, 60; *177:* 189, 190

## I

Ibarra, Rosa *147:* 91
Ibatoulline, Bagram *156:* 48; *174:* 33, 82
Ichikawa, Satomi *29:* 152; *41:* 52; *47:* 133, 134, 135, 136; *78:* 93, 94; *80:* 81; *146:* 143, 145, 146
Ide, Jacqueline *YABC 1:* 39
Ilsley, Velma *3:* 1; *7:* 55; *12:* 109; *37:* 62; *38:* 184
in den Bosch, Nicole *150:* 204
Inga *1:* 142
Ingman, Bruce *134:* 50
Ingpen, Robert *109:* 103, 104; *132:* 138; *137:* 177; *166:* 103
Ingraham, Erick *21:* 177; *84:* 256; *103:* 66
Inkpen, Mick *99:* 104, 105; *106:* 44
Innerst, Stacy *149:* 104
Innocenti, Roberto *21:* 123; *96:* 122; *159:* 111, 197
Inoue, Yosuke *24:* 118
Iofin, Michael *97:* 157
Iosa, Ann *63:* 189
Ipcar, Dahlov *1:* 124, 125; *49:* 137, 138, 139, 140, 141, 142, 143, 144, 145; *147:* 122, 124, 126
Irvin, Fred *13:* 166; *15:* 143, 144; *27:* 175
Irving, Jay *45:* 72
Irving, Laurence *27:* 50
Isaac, Joanne *21:* 76
Isaacs, Gary *170:* 188
Isadora, Rachel *43:* 159, 160; *54:* 31; *79:* 106, 107, 108; *121:* 100, 102; *165:* 116, 117
Ishmael, Woodi *24:* 111; *31:* 99
Ives, Ruth *15:* 257
Iwai, Melissa *149:* 233

## J

Jabar, Cynthia *101:* 201
Jackness, Andrew *94:* 237
Jackson, Julian *91:* 104, 106
Jackson, Michael *43:* 42
Jackson, Shelley *79:* 71; *99:* 109
Jacob, Murv *89:* 30
Jacobi, Kathy *62:* 118
Jacobs, Barbara *9:* 136
Jacobs, Lou, Jr. *9:* 136; *15:* 128
Jacobsen, Laura *176:* 98; *177:* 85, 86
Jacobson, Rick *131:* 222; *170:* 119
Jacobus, Tim *79:* 140; *109:* 126; *129:* 180
Jacques, Robin *1:* 70; *2:* 1; *8:* 46; *9:* 20; *15:* 187; *19:* 253; *32:* 102, 103, 104; *43:* 184; *73:* 135; *YABC 1:* 42
Jaffee, Al *66:* 131, 132
Jagr, Miloslav *13:* 197
Jahn-Clough, Lisa *88:* 114; *152:* 104
Jahnke, Robert *84:* 24
Jainschigg, Nicholas *80:* 64; *91:* 138; *95:* 63; *99:* 25; *108:* 50; *171:* 41
Jakesavic, Nenad *85:* 102
Jakobsen, Kathy *116:* 83
Jakubowski, Charles *14:* 192
Jambor, Louis *YABC 1:* 11
James, Ann *73:* 50; *82:* 113; *158:* 61
James, Brian *140:* 91
James, Derek *35:* 187; *44:* 91; *61:* 133; *74:* 2; *80:* 57; *86:* 88; *130:* 30

James, Gilbert *YABC 1:* 43
James, Harold *2:* 151; *3:* 62; *8:* 79; *29:* 113; *51:* 195; *74:* 90
James, Kennon *126:* 211
James, Robin *50:* 106; *53:* 32, 34, 35
James, Will *19:* 150, 152, 153, 155, 163
Janosch
  *See* Eckert, Horst
Janovitch, Marilyn *68:* 168
Janovitz, Marilyn *87:* 187; *130:* 198
Jansons, Inese *48:* 117
Jansson, Tove *3:* 90; *41:* 106, 108, 109, 110, 111, 113, 114
Jaques, Faith *7:* 11, 132, 133; *21:* 83, 84; *69:* 114, 116; *73:* 170
Jaques, Frances Lee *29:* 224
Jauss, Anne Marie *1:* 139; *3:* 34; *10:* 57, 119; *11:* 205; *23:* 194
Jay, Alison *158:* 97, 98
Jeffers, Oliver *175:* 111
Jeffers, Susan *17:* 86, 87; *25:* 164, 165; *26:* 112; *50:* 132, 134, 135; *70:* 111, 112, 113; *137:* 107, 108, 109, 110, 111
Jefferson, Louise E. *4:* 160
Jenkin-Pearce, Susie *78:* 16
Jenkins, Debra Reid *85:* 202; *114:* 89; *173:* 134
Jenkins, Jean *98:* 79, 102
Jenkins, Leonard *157:* 169; *167:* 128
Jenkins, Patrick *72:* 126
Jenkins, Steve *124:* 177; *154:* 90, 91, 92, 93
Jenks, Aleta *73:* 117; *124:* 225
Jenkyns, Chris *51:* 97
Jensen, Bruce *95:* 39
Jensinius, Kirsten *56:* 58
Jeram, Anita *89:* 135; *102:* 122, 123; *129:* 112; *154:* 96, 97, 98; *164:* 154
Jernigan, E. Wesley *85:* 92
Jerome, Karen A. *72:* 194
Jeruchim, Simon *6:* 173; *15:* 250
Jeschke, Susan *20:* 89; *39:* 161; *41:* 84; *42:* 120
Jessel, Camilla *29:* 115
Jessell, Tim *159:* 3; *177:* 87
Jiang, Cheng An *109:* 108
Jiang, Wei *109:* 108
Jimenez, Maria *77:* 158; *93:* 127
Jobling, Curtis *138:* 74
Jocelyn, Marthe *118:* 83; *137:* 219; *163:* 119, 120
Joerns, Consuelo *38:* 36; *44:* 94
John, Diana *12:* 209
John, Helen *1:* 215; *28:* 204
Johns, Elizabeth *127:* 33
Johns, Jasper *61:* 172
Johns, Jeanne *24:* 114
Johnson, Adrian *143:* 50
Johnson, Bruce *9:* 47
Johnson, Cathy *92:* 136
Johnson, Crockett
  *See* Leisk, David
Johnson, D. William *23:* 104
Johnson, David *175:* 18
Johnson, Gillian *119:* 175; *164:* 217
Johnson, Harper *1:* 27; *2:* 33; *18:* 302; *19:* 61; *31:* 181; *44:* 46, 50, 95
Johnson, Ingrid *37:* 118
Johnson, James Ralph *1:* 23, 127
Johnson, James David *12:* 195
Johnson, Jane *48:* 136
Johnson, Joel Peter *98:* 18; *128:* 111
Johnson, John E. *34:* 133
Johnson, Kevin *72:* 44
Johnson, Kevin Eugene *109:* 215
Johnson, Larry *47:* 56; *123:* 107; *159:* 203
Johnson, Margaret S. *35:* 131
Johnson, Meredith Merrell *71:* 181; *83:* 158; *89:* 103; *104:* 88
Johnson, Milton *1:* 67; *2:* 71; *26:* 45; *31:* 107; *60:* 112; *68:* 96

Johnson, Pamela *16:* 174; *52:* 145; *62:* 140; *73:* 116; *85:* 64
Johnson, Paul Brett *83:* 95; *132:* 119
Johnson, Stephen T. *80:* 15; *131:* 35; *141:* 96; *145:* 40; *164:* 187; *175:* 32
Johnson, Steve *138:* 219; *141:* 64; *144:* 199; *177:* 51
Johnson, William R. *38:* 91
Johnson-Petrov, Arden *115:* 206
Johnston, David McCall *50:* 131, 133
Johnston, Lynne *118:* 85, 87, 89
Johnstone, Anne *8:* 120; *36:* 89
Johnstone, Janet Grahame *8:* 120; *36:* 89
Jonas, Ann *50:* 107, 108, 109; *135:* 113
Jones, Bob *71:* 5; *77:* 199
Jones, Carol *5:* 131; *72:* 185, 186; *153:* 111, 112
Jones, Chuck *53:* 70, 71
Jones, Davy *89:* 176
Jones, Elizabeth Orton *18:* 124, 126, 128, 129
Jones, Harold *14:* 88; *52:* 50
Jones, Holly *127:* 3
Jones, Jeff *41:* 64
Jones, Laurian *25:* 24, 27
Jones, Margaret *74:* 57
Jones, Randy *131:* 104
Jones, Richard *127:* 222
Jones, Robert *25:* 67
Jones, Wilfred *35:* 115; *YABC 1:* 163
Jordan, Charles *89:* 58
Jordan, Jess *158:* 136
Jordan, Martin George *84:* 127
Jordan, Richard *84:* 36
Jorgenson, Andrea *91:* 111
Jorisch, Stephane *153:* 56, 193; *177:* 29
Joseph, James *53:* 88
Joudrey, Ken *64:* 145; *78:* 6
Joyce, William *72:* 131, 132, 133, 134; *73:* 227; *145:* 37
Joyner, Jerry *34:* 138
Juan, Ana *175:* 38
Jucker, Sita *5:* 93
Judkis, Jim *37:* 38
Juhasz, Victor *31:* 67
Jullian, Philippe *24:* 206; *25:* 203
Jung, Tom *91:* 217
Junge, Walter *67:* 150
Jupo, Frank *7:* 148, 149
Jurisch, Stephane *154:* 105
Justice, Martin *34:* 72

## K

Kabatova-Taborska, Zdenka *107:* 153
Kachik, John *165:* 230
Kaczman, James *156:* 98
Kahl, David *74:* 95; *97:* 35; *109:* 174; *110:* 213
Kahl, M.P. *37:* 83
Kahl, Virginia *48:* 138
Kahn, Katherine Janus *90:* 135
Kakimoo, Kozo *11:* 148
Kalett, Jim *48:* 159, 160, 161
Kalin, Victor *39:* 186
Kalman, Maira *96:* 131, 132; *137:* 115
Kalmenoff, Matthew *22:* 191
Kalow, Gisela *32:* 105
Kamen, Gloria *1:* 41; *9:* 119; *10:* 178; *35:* 157; *78:* 236; *98:* 82
Kaminsky, Jef *102:* 153
Kandell, Alice *35:* 133
Kane, Henry B. *14:* 90; *18:* 219, 220
Kane, Robert *18:* 131
Kanfer, Larry *66:* 141
Kappes, Alfred *28:* 104
Karalus, Bob *41:* 157
Karas, G. Brian *80:* 60; *99:* 179; *115:* 41; *118:* 50; *136:* 168; *145:* 166; *149:* 245; *159:* 65; *171:* 192

Karasz, Ilonka *128:* 163
Karlin, Eugene *10:* 63; *20:* 131
Karlin, Nurit *63:* 78; *103:* 110
Karpinski, Tony *134:* 160
Kasamatsu, Shiro *139:* 155
Kasparavicius, Kestutis *139:* 210
Kassian, Olena *64:* 94
Kastner, Jill *79:* 135; *117:* 84, 85
Kasuya, Masahiro *41:* 206, 207; *51:* 100
Katona, Robert *21:* 85; *24:* 126
Katz, Karen *158:* 123
Kauffer, E. McKnight *33:* 103; *35:* 127; *63:* 67
Kaufman, Angelika *15:* 156
Kaufman, Joe *33:* 119
Kaufman, John *13:* 158
Kaufman, Stuart *62:* 64; *68:* 226; *137:* 44
Kaufmann, John *1:* 174; *4:* 159; *8:* 43, 1; *10:* 102; *18:* 133, 134; *22:* 251
Kaye, Graham *1:* 9; *67:* 7, 8
Kaye, M.M. *62:* 95
Kazalovski, Nata *40:* 205
Keane, Bil *4:* 135
Kearney, David *72:* 47; *121:* 83
Keating, Pamel T. *77:* 37
Keats, Ezra Jack *3:* 18, 105, 257; *14:* 101, 102; *33:* 129; *57:* 79, 80, 82, 83, 84, 87
Keegan, Charles *166:* 211
Keegan, Marcia *9:* 122; *32:* 93
Keeler, Patricia A. *81:* 56
Keely, Jack *119:* 95
Keely, John *26:* 104; *48:* 214
Keen, Eliot *25:* 213
Keep, Richard C. *170:* 122
Keeping, Charles *9:* 124, 185; *15:* 28, 134; *18:* 115; *44:* 194, 196; *47:* 25; *52:* 3; *54:* 156; *69:* 123, 124; *74:* 56; *155:* 9
Keeter, Susan *168:* 46
Keith, Eros *4:* 98; *5:* 138; *31:* 29; *43:* 220; *52:* 91, 92, 93, 94; *56:* 64, 66; *60:* 37; *79:* 93
Keleinikov, Andrei *65:* 101, 102
Kelen, Emery *13:* 115
Keller, A.J. *62:* 198
Keller, Arthur I. *2:* 106
Keller, Dick *36:* 123, 125
Keller, Holly *45:* 79; *76:* 118, 119, 120, 121; *108:* 137, 138, 140; *157:* 117, 118, 119
Keller, Katie *79:* 222; *93:* 108
Keller, Ronald *45:* 208
Kelley, True *41:* 114, 115; *42:* 137; *75:* 35; *92:* 104, 105; *124:* 62; *130:* 100, 101
Kellogg, Steven *8:* 96; *11:* 207; *14:* 130; *20:* 58; *29:* 140, 141; *30:* 35; *41:* 141; *57:* 89, 90, 92, 93, 94, 96; *59:* 182; *73:* 141; *77:* 129; *130:* 105, 106; *177:* 94, 95, 96, 97; *YABC 1:* 65, 73
Kelly, Billy *158:* 143
Kelly, Geoff *97:* 196; *112:* 25
Kelly, Irene *147:* 134
Kelly, Joseph *174:* 94
Kelly, Kathleen M. *71:* 109
Kelly, Laura *89:* 217
Kelly, True *163:* 87
Kelly, Walt *18:* 136, 137, 138, 139, 140, 141, 144, 145, 146, 148, 149
Kemble, E.W. *34:* 75; *44:* 178; *YABC 2:* 54, 59
Kemp-Welsh, Lucy *24:* 197; *100:* 214
Kendall, Jane *150:* 105
Kendall, Peter *152:* 85
Kendrick, Dennis *79:* 213
Kennaway, Adrienne *60:* 55, 56; *171:* 88, 89
Kennedy, Paul Edward *6:* 190; *8:* 132; *33:* 120
Kennedy, Richard *3:* 93; *12:* 179; *44:* 193; *100:* 15; *YABC 1:* 57
Kent, Jack *24:* 136; *37:* 37; *40:* 81; *84:* 89; *86:* 150; *88:* 77
Kent, Rockwell *5:* 166; *6:* 129; *20:* 225, 226, 227, 229; *59:* 144
Kenyon, Tony *81:* 201; *127:* 74
Kepes, Juliet *13:* 119
Kerins, Anthony *76:* 84

Kerr, Judity *24:* 137
Kerr, Phyllis Forbes *72:* 141
Kessler, Leonard *1:* 108; *7:* 139; *14:* 107, 227; *22:* 101; *44:* 96; *67:* 79; *82:* 123
Kest, Kristin *168:* 99; *173:* 23
Kesteven, Peter *35:* 189
Ketcham, Hank *28:* 140, 141, 142
Kettelkamp, Larry *2:* 164
Key, Alexander *8:* 99
Khalsa, Dayal Kaur *62:* 99
Kiakshuk *8:* 59
Kidd, Chip *94:* 23
Kidd, Richard *152:* 110
Kidd, Tom *64:* 199; *81:* 189
Kiddell-Monroe, Joan *19:* 201; *55:* 59, 60; *87:* 174; *121:* 112
Kidder, Harvey *9:* 105; *80:* 41
Kidwell, Carl *43:* 145
Kieffer, Christa *41:* 89
Kiesler, Kate *110:* 105; *136:* 142
Kiff, Ken *40:* 45
Kilbride, Robert *37:* 100
Kilby, Don *141:* 144
Kim, Glenn *99:* 82
Kimball, Anton *78:* 114; *119:* 105
Kimball, Yeffe *23:* 116; *37:* 88
Kimber, Murray *171:* 91
Kimmel, Warren *176:* 112
Kincade, Orin *34:* 116
Kindersley, Barnabas *96:* 110
Kindred, Wendy *7:* 151
King, Colin *53:* 3
King, Robin *10:* 164, 165
King, Stephen Michael *141:* 31
King, Tara Calahan *139:* 172
King, Tony *39:* 121
Kingman, Dong *16:* 287; *44:* 100, 102, 104
Kingsley, Charles *YABC 2:* 182
Kingston, Julie *147:* 14
Kingston, Maxine Hong *53:* 92
Kipling, John Lockwood *YABC 2:* 198
Kipling, Rudyard *YABC 2:* 196
Kipniss, Robert *29:* 59
Kirchherr, Astrid *55:* 23
Kirchhoff, Art *28:* 136
Kirk, Daniel *153:* 115, 116, 117; *173:* 101
Kirk, David *117:* 88, 89; *161:* 97, 98
Kirk, Ruth *5:* 96
Kirk, Steve *170:* 37
Kirk, Tim *32:* 209, 211; *72:* 89; *83:* 49
Kirmse, Marguerite *15:* 283; *18:* 153
Kirsch, Vincent X. *124:* 207
Kirschner, Ruth *22:* 154
Kish, Ely *73:* 119; *79:* 2
Kitamura, Satoshi *62:* 102; *98:* 91; *101:* 147; *138:* 2; *143:* 83, 85, 86
Kiss, Andrew *168:* 115
Kitchel, JoAnn E. *133:* 32
Kitchen, Herbert Thomas *70:* 126
Kittelsen, Theodor *62:* 14
Kiuchi, Tatsuro *114:* 71
Kiwak, Barbara *172:* 135
Klahr, Susan *176:* 196
Klapholz, Mel *13:* 35
Klein, Bill *89:* 105
Klein, Robert *55:* 77
Klein, Suzanna *63:* 104
Kleinman, Zalman *28:* 143
Kleven, Elisa *173:* 96, 97
Kliban, B. *35:* 137, 138
Kline, Michael *127:* 66
Knabel, Lonnie *73:* 103; *75:* 187, 228
Kneen, Maggie *140:* 139
Knight, Ann *34:* 143
Knight, Christopher *13:* 125
Knight, Hilary *1:* 233; *3:* 21; *15:* 92, 158, 159; *16:* 258, 259, 260; *18:* 235; *19:* 169; *35:* 242; *46:* 167; *52:* 116; *69:* 126, 127; *132:* 129; *YABC 1:* 168, 169, 172
Knorr, Peter *126:* 92, 93
Knotts, Howard *20:* 4; *25:* 170; *36:* 163

Knutson, Barbara *112:* 134
Knutson, Kimberley *115:* 90
Kobayashi, Ann *39:* 58
Kocsis, J.C.
    *See* Paul, James
Koehler, Hanne Lore *176:* 203
Koehn, Ilse *34:* 198; *79:* 123
Koelsch, Michael *99:* 182; *107:* 164; *109:* 239; *138:* 142; *150:* 94; *176:* 105
Koering, Ursula *3:* 28; *4:* 14; *44:* 5; *64:* 140, 141; *85:* 46
Koerner, Henry
    *See* Koerner, W.H.D.
Koerner, W.H.D. *14:* 216; *21:* 88, 89, 90, 91; *23:* 211
Koetsch, Mike *166:* 68
Koffler, Camilla *36:* 113
Kogan, Deborah Ray *161:* 101, 102
Koide, Yasuko *50:* 114
Kolado, Karen *102:* 228
Komoda, Kiyo *9:* 128; *13:* 214
Kompaneyets, Marc *169:* 92
Konashevich, Vladimir *61:* 160
Konashevicha, V. *YABC 1:* 26
Konigsburg, E.L. *4:* 138; *48:* 141, 142, 144, 145; *94:* 129, 130; *126:* 129, 130, 131
Kono, Erin Eitter *177:* 99
Kooiker, Leonie *48:* 148
Koonook, Simon *65:* 157
Koontz, Robin Michal *136:* 155
Koopmans, Loek *101:* 121
Kopelke, Lisa *154:* 107
Kopper, Lisa *72:* 152, 153; *105:* 135, 136
Korach, Mimi *1:* 128, 129; *2:* 52; *4:* 39; *5:* 159; *9:* 129; *10:* 21; *24:* 69
Koren, Edward *5:* 100; *65:* 65, 67
Kosaka, Fumi *164:* 130
Koscielniak, Bruce *99:* 122; *153:* 120, 121, 122
Koshkin, Alexander *92:* 180
Kossin, Sandy *10:* 71; *23:* 105
Kostin, Andrej *26:* 204
Kosturko, Bob *164:* 56
Kotzky, Brian *68:* 184
Kovacevic, Zivojin *13:* 247
Kovalski, Maryann *58:* 120; *84:* 88; *97:* 124, 125, 126, *158:* 3
Krahn, Fernando *2:* 257; *34:* 206; *49:* 152
Kramer, Anthony *33:* 81
Kramer, David *96:* 162; *109:* 132; *150:* 220
Kramer, Frank *6:* 121
Krantz, Kathy *35:* 83
Kratter, Paul *139:* 65
Kraus, Robert *13:* 217; *65:* 113; *93:* 93, 94
Krause, Jon *176:* 62
Krauss, Trisha *174:* 10
Kredel, Fritz *6:* 35; *17:* 93, 94, 95, 96; *22:* 147; *24:* 175; *29:* 130; *35:* 77; *YABC 2:* 166, 300
Krementz, Jill *17:* 98; *49:* 41
Krenina, Katya *117:* 106; *125:* 133; *176:* 117
Kresin, Robert *23:* 19
Krieger, Salem *54:* 164
Kriegler, Lyn *73:* 29
Krommes, Beth *128:* 141; *149:* 136
Krone, Mike *101:* 71
Kronheimer, Ann *135:* 119
Krosoczka, Jarrett J. *155:* 142
Kruck, Gerald *88:* 181
Krupinski, Loretta *67:* 104; *102:* 131; *161:* 105, 106
Krupp, Robin Rector *53:* 96, 98
Krush, Beth *1:* 51, 85; *2:* 233; *4:* 115; *9:* 61; *10:* 191; *11:* 196; *18:* 164, 165; *32:* 72; *37:* 203; *43:* 57; *60:* 102, 103, 107, 108, 109
Krush, Joe *2:* 233; *4:* 115; *9:* 61; *10:* 191; *11:* 196; *18:* 164, 165; *32:* 72, 91; *37:* 203; *43:* 57; *60:* 102, 103, 107, 108, 109
Krych, Duane *91:* 43
Krykorka, Vladyana *96:* 147; *143:* 90, 91; *168:* 14

Kubick, Dana *165:* 91
Kubinyi, Laszlo *4:* 116; *6:* 113; *16:* 118; *17:* 100; *28:* 227; *30:* 172; *49:* 24, 28; *54:* 23; *167:* 149
Kubricht, Mary *73:* 118
Kucharik, Elena *139:* 31
Kuchera, Kathleen *84:* 5
Kuhn, Bob *17:* 91; *35:* 235
Kulikov, Boris *163:* 185
Kukalis, Romas *90:* 27; *139:* 37
Kuklin, Susan *63:* 82, 83, 84
Kunhardt, Dorothy *53:* 101
Kunhardt, Edith *67:* 105, 106
Kunstler, Mort *10:* 73; *32:* 143
Kurchevsky, V. *34:* 61
Kurczok, Belinda *121:* 118
Kurelek, William *8:* 107
Kuriloff, Ron *13:* 19
Kurisu, Jane *160:* 120
Kuskin, Karla *2:* 170; *68:* 115, 116; *111:* 116
Kutzer, Ernst *19:* 249
Kuzma, Steve *57:* 8; *62:* 93
Kuznetsova, Berta *74:* 45
Kvasnosky, Laura McGee *93:* 103; *142:* 83
Kyong, Yunmee *165:* 139

**L**

LaBlanc, Andre *24:* 146
Laboccetta, Mario *27:* 120
LaBrose, Darcie *157:* 134
Labrosse, Darcia *58:* 88; *108:* 77
LaCava, Vince *95:* 118
Laceky, Adam *32:* 121
Lacis, Astra *85:* 117
Lacome, Julie *174:* 96, 97
La Croix *YABC 2:* 4
Ladwig, Tim *98:* 212; *117:* 76
La Farge, Margaret *47:* 141
LaFave, Kim *64:* 177; *72:* 39; *97:* 146; *99:* 172; *106:* 123; *149:* 126
Lafontaine, Roger *167:* 158
Lagarrigue, Jerome *136:* 102
Laimgruber, Monika *11:* 153
Laite, Gordon *1:* 130, 131; *8:* 209; *31:* 113; *40:* 63; *46:* 117
Laliberté, Louise-Andrée *169:* 98
LaMarche, Jim *46:* 204; *61:* 56; *94:* 69; *114:* 22; *129:* 163; *162:* 78, 80
Lamb, Jim *10:* 117
Lambase, Barbara *101:* 185; *150:* 221; *166:* 234
Lambert, J.K. *38:* 129; *39:* 24
Lambert, Sally Anne *133:* 191
Lambert, Saul *23:* 112; *33:* 107; *54:* 136
Lambert, Stephen *109:* 33; *174:* 99
Lambo, Don *6:* 156; *35:* 115; *36:* 146
Lamontagne, Jacques *166:* 227
Lamut, Sonja *57:* 193
Lamut, Sonya *85:* 102
Landa, Peter *11:* 95; *13:* 177; *53:* 119
Landau, Jacob *38:* 111
Landis, Joan *104:* 23
Landon, Lucinda *79:* 31
Landshoff, Ursula *13:* 124
Landström, Lena *146:* 165, 166
Landström, Olof *146:* 166, 168; *170:* 22
Lane, Daniel *112:* 60
Lane, John R. *8:* 145
Lane, John *15:* 176, 177; *30:* 146
Lane, Nancy *166:* 74
Lang, G.D. *48:* 56
Lang, Gary *73:* 75
Lang, Jerry *18:* 295
Lange, Dorothea *50:* 141
Langley, Jonathan *162:* 128
Langner, Nola *8:* 110; *42:* 36
Lanino, Deborah *105:* 148

Lantz, Paul *1:* 82, 102; *27:* 88; *34:* 102; *45:* 123
Larkin, Bob *84:* 225
Laroche, Giles *126:* 140; *146:* 81
LaRochelle, David *171:* 97
Larrecq, John *44:* 108; *68:* 56
Larsen, Suzanne *1:* 13
Larson, Gary *57:* 121, 122, 123, 124, 125, 126, 127
Larsson, Carl *35:* 144, 145, 146, 147, 148, 149, 150, 152, 153, 154
Larsson, Karl *19:* 177
Lartitegui, Ana G. *105:* 167
LaRue, Jenna *167:* 20
La Rue, Michael D. *13:* 215
Lasker, Joe *7:* 186, 187; *14:* 55; *38:* 115; *39:* 47; *83:* 113, 114, 115
Latham, Barbara *16:* 188, 189; *43:* 71
Lathrop, Dorothy *14:* 117, 118, 119; *15:* 109; *16:* 78, 79, 81; *32:* 201, 203; *33:* 112; *YABC 2:* 301
Lattimore, Eleanor Frances *7:* 156
Lauden, Claire *16:* 173
Lauden, George, Jr. *16:* 173
Laune, Paul *2:* 235; *34:* 31
Laure, Jason *49:* 53; *50:* 122
Lauter, Richard *63:* 29; *67:* 111; *77:* 198
Lavallee, Barbara *74:* 157; *92:* 154; *96:* 126; *145:* 193; *166:* 125, 126
Lave, Fitz Hugh *59:* 139
Lavis, Stephen *43:* 143; *87:* 137, 164, 165
Layton, Neal *152:* 120, 121
Lawrason, June *168:* 30
Lawrence, John *25:* 131; *30:* 141; *44:* 198, 200
Lawrence, Stephen *20:* 195
Lawson, Carol *6:* 38; *42:* 93, 131; *174:* 56
Lawson, George *17:* 280
Lawson, Robert *5:* 26; *6:* 94; *13:* 39; *16:* 11; *20:* 100, 102, 103; *54:* 3; *66:* 12; *100:* 144, 145; *YABC 2:* 222, 224, 225, 227, 228, 229, 230, 231, 232, 233, 234, 235, 237, 238, 239, 240, 241
Layfield, Kathie *60:* 194
Lazare, Jerry *44:* 109; *74:* 28
Lazarevich, Mila *17:* 118
Lazarus, Claire *103:* 30
Lazarus, Keo Felker *21:* 94
Lazzaro, Victor *11:* 126
Lea, Bob *166:* 208
Lea, Tom *43:* 72, 74
Leacroft, Richard *6:* 140
Leaf, Munro *20:* 99
Leake, Donald *70:* 41
Leander, Patricia *23:* 27
Lear, Edward *18:* 183, 184, 185
Lear, Rebecca *149:* 46
Lebenson, Richard *6:* 209; *7:* 76; *23:* 145; *44:* 191; *87:* 153
Le Cain, Errol *6:* 141; *9:* 3; *22:* 142; *25:* 198; *28:* 173; *68:* 128, 129; *86:* 49
Lechon, Daniel *113:* 211
Leder, Dora *129:* 172
Leduc, Bernard *102:* 36
Lee, Alan *62:* 25, 28
Lee, Bryce *99:* 60; *101:* 195
Lee, Dom *83:* 118, 120; *93:* 123; *121:* 121, 126; *146:* 174, 175, 206, 207; *174:* 204
Lee, Doris *13:* 246; *32:* 183; *44:* 111
Lee, Hector Viveros *115:* 96
Lee, Jeanne M. *158:* 56
Lee, Jared *93:* 200; *157:* 229
Lee, Jody *81:* 121; *82:* 225; *91:* 155; *100:* 182
Lee, Jody A. *127:* 124, 126, 127
*See also* Lee, Jody
Lee, Manning de V. *2:* 200; *17:* 12; *27:* 87; *37:* 102, 103, 104; *YABC 2:* 304
Lee, Marie G. *138:* 157
Lee, Paul *97:* 100; *105:* 72, 209; *109:* 177; *128:* 113
Lee, Robert J. *3:* 97; *67:* 124

Lee, Victor *96:* 228; *105:* 182; *140:* 196
Leech, Dorothy *98:* 76
Leech, John *15:* 59
Leedy, Loreen *84:* 142; *128:* 144, 145, 146; *175:* 125, 126, 127
Leeman, Michael *44:* 157
Leeming, Catherine *87:* 39
Lees, Harry *6:* 112
LeFever, Bill *88:* 220, 221
Legenisel *47:* 111
Legrand, Edy *18:* 89, 93
Lehman, Barbara *73:* 123; *170:* 130
Lehrman, Rosalie *2:* 180
Leichman, Seymour *5:* 107
Leighton, Clare *25:* 130; *33:* 168; *37:* 105, 106, 108, 109
Leisk, David *1:* 140, 141; *11:* 54; *30:* 137, 142, 143, 144
Leister, Brian *89:* 45; *106:* 37; *114:* 67; *149:* 236
Leloir, Maurice *18:* 77, 80, 83, 99
Lematire, Pascal *144:* 175; *176:* 130
Lemieux, Michele *100:* 148; *139:* 153
Lemke, Horst *14:* 98; *38:* 117, 118, 119
Lemke, R.W. *42:* 162
Lemon, David Gwynne *9:* 1
LeMoult, Adolph *82:* 116
Lenn, Michael *136:* 89
Lennon, John *114:* 100
Lennox, Elsie *95:* 163; *143:* 160
Lenski, Lois *1:* 144; *26:* 135, 137, 139, 141; *100:* 153, 154
Lent, Blair *1:* 116, 117; *2:* 174; *3:* 206, 207; *7:* 168, 169; *34:* 62; *68:* 217; *133:* 101
Leonard, Richard *91:* 128
Leone, Leonard *49:* 190
Lerner, Carol *86:* 140, 141, 142
Lerner, Judith *116:* 138
Lerner, Sharon *11:* 157; *22:* 56
Leroux-Hugon, Helene *132:* 139
Leslie, Cecil *19:* 244
Lessac, Frane *80:* 182, 207; *96:* 182
Lessing, Erich *167:* 52; *173:* 60
Lester, Alison *50:* 124; *90:* 147, 148; *129:* 130
Le Tord, Bijou *49:* 156; *95:* 112
Leutz, Emanuel *165:* 27
Levai, Blaise *39:* 130
Levin, Ted *12:* 148
Levine, David *43:* 147, 149, 150, 151, 152; *64:* 11
Levine, Joe *71:* 88
Levine, Marge *81:* 127
Levit, Herschel *24:* 223
Levstek, Ljuba *131:* 192; *134:* 216; *149:* 65; *168:* 180
Levy, Jessica Ann *19:* 225; *39:* 191
Levy, Lina *117:* 126
Lewin, Betsy *32:* 114; *48:* 177; *90:* 151; *91:* 125; *92:* 85; *115:* 105; *169:* 110, 111
Lewin, Ted *4:* 77; *8:* 168; *20:* 110; *21:* 99, 100; *27:* 110; *28:* 96, 97; *31:* 49; *45:* 55; *48:* 223; *60:* 20, 119, 120; *62:* 139; *66:* 108; *71:* 12; *72:* 21; *74:* 226; *76:* 139, 140; *77:* 82; *79:* 87; *85:* 49, 177; *86:* 55; *88:* 182; *93:* 28, 29; *94:* 34, 182, 194; *99:* 156; *104:* 8; *115:* 123; *118:* 74; *119:* 114, 116; *131:* 54; *145:* 99; *165:* 151; *177:* 75
Lewis, Allen *15:* 112
Lewis, E.B. *88:* 143; *93:* 109; *119:* 79; *124:* 113; *128:* 49; *151:* 167; *168:* 110; *173:* 121; *174:* 66; *176:* 7
Lewis, H.B. *170:* 124
Lewis, J. Patrick *162:* 83
Lewis, Jan *81:* 22
Lewis, Kim *136:* 165
Lewis, Richard W. *52:* 25
Lewis, Robin Baird *98:* 193
Leydon, Rita Floden *21:* 101
Lichtenheld, Tom *152:* 125, 126
Lieblich, Irene *22:* 173; *27:* 209, 214
Lieder, Rick *108:* 197

Lies, Brian *92:* 40; *141:* 101; *150:* 138
Liese, Charles *4:* 222
Life, Kay *79:* 49
Lifton, Robert Jay *66:* 154
Lightburn, Ron *86:* 153; *91:* 122
Lightfoot, Norman R. *45:* 47
Lignell, Lois *37:* 114
Lill, Debra *121:* 70
Lilly, Charles *8:* 73; *20:* 127; *48:* 53; *72:* 9, 16; *77:* 98; *102:* 94
Lilly, Ken *37:* 224
Lim, John *43:* 153
Limona, Mercedes *51:* 183
Lin, Grace *143:* 217; *162:* 86, 87; *174:* 185
Lincoln, Patricia Henderson *27:* 27; *78:* 127
Lindahn, Ron *84:* 17
Lindahn, Val *84:* 17
Lindberg, Howard *10:* 123; *16:* 190
Lindberg, Jeffrey *64:* 77; *77:* 71; *79:* 54; *80:* 149; *174:* 109
Linden, Seymour *18:* 200, 201; *43:* 140
Lindenbaum, Pija *144:* 143
Linder, Richard *27:* 119
Lindman, Maj *43:* 154
Lindsay, Norman *67:* 114
Lindsay, Vachel *40:* 118
Lindstrom, Jack *145:* 118
Line, Les *27:* 143
Linell
    *See* Smith, Linell
Lionni, Leo *8:* 115; *72:* 159, 160, 161
Lipinsky, Lino *2:* 156; *22:* 175
Lippincott, Gary A. *70:* 35; *119:* 118
Lippman, Peter *8:* 31; *31:* 119, 120, 160
Lisi, Victoria *89:* 145
Lisker, Emily *169:* 114
Lisker, Sonia O. *16:* 274; *31:* 31; *44:* 113, 114
Lisowski, Gabriel *47:* 144; *49:* 157
Lissim, Simon *17:* 138
Little, Ed *89:* 145; *151:* 53
Little, Harold *16:* 72
Little, Mary E. *28:* 146
Littlewood, Karen *165:* 126
Litty, Julie *111:* 63
Litzinger, Rosanne *151:* 101; *176:* 118
Liu, Lesley *143:* 72
Lively, Lorna *19:* 216
Livingston, Susan *95:* 22
Liwska, Renata *164:* 113
Llerena, Carlos Antonio *19:* 181
Lloyd, Errol *11:* 39; *22:* 178
Lloyd, Megan *77:* 118; *80:* 113; *97:* 75; *117:* 94, 95
Lo, Beth *165:* 154
Lo, Koon-chiu *7:* 134
Loates, Glen *63:* 76
Lobel, Anita *6:* 87; *9:* 141; *18:* 248; *55:* 85, 86, 87, 88, 93, 104; *60:* 67; *78:* 263; *82:* 110; *96:* 157, 159; *101:* 84; *132:* 35; *162:* 93, 94
Lobel, Arnold *1:* 188, 189; *5:* 12; *6:* 147; *7:* 167, 209; *18:* 190, 191; *25:* 39, 43; *27:* 40; *29:* 174; *52:* 127; *55:* 89, 91, 94, 95, 97, 98, 99, 100, 101, 102, 103, 105, 106; *60:* 18, 31; *66:* 181, 183; *75:* 57; *82:* 246; *136:* 146
Locker, Thomas *109:* 134
Lodge, Bernard *107:* 125, 126; *153:* 93
Loeb, Jeph *153:* 177
Lodge, Jo *112:* 119
Loefgren, Ulf *3:* 108
Loescher, Ann *20:* 108
Loescher, Gil *20:* 108
Loew, David *93:* 184; *171:* 120
Lofting, Hugh *15:* 182, 183; *100:* 161, 162
Lofts, Pamela *60:* 188
Loh, George *38:* 88
Lomberg, Jon *58:* 160
Lonette, Reisie *11:* 211; *12:* 168; *13:* 56; *36:* 122; *43:* 155
Long, Ethan *168:* 146
Long, Laurel *162:* 135

Long, Loren *99:* 176; *172:* 65
Long, Melinda *152:* 128
Long, Miles *115:* 174
Long, Sally *42:* 184
Long, Sylvia *74:* 168; *132:* 63
Longoni, Eduardo *73:* 85
Longtemps, Ken *17:* 123; *29:* 221; *69:* 82
Looser, Heinz *YABC 2:* 208
Lopshire, Robert *6:* 149; *21:* 117; *34:* 166; *73:* 13
Lord, John Vernon *21:* 104; *23:* 25; *51:* 22
Lorenz, Albert *40:* 146; *115:* 127
Loretta, Sister Mary *33:* 73
Lorraine, Walter H. *3:* 110; *4:* 123; *16:* 192; *103:* 119
Los, Marek *146:* 22
Loss, Joan *11:* 163
Louderback, Walt *YABC 1:* 164
Lousada, Sandra *40:* 138
Louth, Jack *149:* 252; *151:* 191, 192
Love, Judy *173:* 43
Low, Joseph *14:* 124, 125; *18:* 68; *19:* 194; *31:* 166; *80:* 239
Low, William *62:* 175; *80:* 147; *112:* 194; *150:* 202; *169:* 175; *177:* 110
Lowe, Vicky *177:* 130
Lowenheim, Alfred *13:* 65, 66
Lowenstein, Sallie *116:* 90, 91
Lowitz, Anson *17:* 124; *18:* 215
Lowrey, Jo *8:* 133
Lubach, Vanessa *142:* 152
Lubell, Winifred *1:* 207; *3:* 15; *6:* 151
Lubin, Leonard B. *19:* 224; *36:* 79, 80; *45:* 128, 129, 131, 132, 133, 134, 135, 136, 137, 139, 140, 141; *70:* 95; *YABC 2:* 96
Lucht, Irmgard *82:* 145
Ludwig, Helen *33:* 144, 145
Lufkin, Raymond *38:* 138; *44:* 48
Luhrs, Henry *7:* 123; *11:* 120
Lujan, Tonita *82:* 33
Lupo, Dom *4:* 204
Lustig, Loretta *30:* 186; *46:* 134, 135, 136, 137
Luthardt, Kevin *172:* 125, 126
Luxbacher, Irene *153:* 145
Luzak, Dennis *52:* 121; *99:* 142
Lydbury, Jane *82:* 98
Lydecker, Laura *21:* 113; *42:* 53
Lynch, Charles *16:* 33
Lynch, Marietta *29:* 137; *30:* 171
Lynch, P.J. *126:* 228; *129:* 110; *132:* 247
Lyon, Carol *102:* 26
Lyon, Elinor *6:* 154
Lyon, Fred *14:* 16
Lyon, Tammie *175:* 170
Lyons, Oren *8:* 193
Lyster, Michael *26:* 41

**M**

Maas, Dorothy *6:* 175
Maas, Julie *47:* 61
Macaulay, David *46:* 139, 140, 141, 142, 143, 144, 145, 147, 149, 150; *72:* 167, 168, 169; *137:* 129, 130, 131, 132
MacCarthy, Patricia *69:* 141
Macdonald, Alister *21:* 55
Macdonald, Roberta *19:* 237; *52:* 164
MacDonald, Norman *13:* 99
MacDonald, Suse *54:* 41; *109* 138; *130:* 156
Mace, Varian *49:* 159
Macguire, Robert Reid *18:* 67
Machetanz, Fredrick *34:* 147, 148
MacInnes, Ian *35:* 59
MacIntyre, Elisabeth *17:* 127, 128
Mack, Jeff *161:* 128
Mack, Stan *17:* 129; *96:* 33
Mackay, Donald *17:* 60
MacKaye, Arvia *32:* 119

Mackenzie, Stuart *73:* 213
MacKenzie, Garry *33:* 159
Mackie, Clare *87:* 134
Mackinlay, Miguel *27:* 22
MacKinstry, Elizabeth *15:* 110; *42:* 139, 140, 141, 142, 143, 144, 145
MacLeod, Lee *91:* 167
Maclise, Daniel *YABC 2:* 257
Madden, Don *3:* 112, 113; *4:* 33, 108, 155; *7:* 193; *78:* 12; *YABC 2:* 211
Maddison, Angela Mary *10:* 83
Madsen, Jim *146:* 259; *152:* 237
Maestro, Giulio *8:* 124; *12:* 17; *13:* 108; *25:* 182; *54:* 147; *59:* 114, 115, 116, 117, 118, 121, 123, 124, 125, 126, 127; *68:* 37, 38; *106:* 129, 130, 131, 136, 137, 138
Maffia, Daniel *60:* 200
Maggio, Viqui *58:* 136, 181; *74:* 150; *75:* 90; *85:* 159; *90:* 158; *109:* 184
Magnus, Erica *77:* 123
Magnuson, Diana *28:* 102; *34:* 190; *41:* 175
Magovern, Peg *103:* 123
Maguire, Sheila *41:* 100
Magurn, Susan *91:* 30
Mahony, Will *37:* 120
Mahony, Will *85:* 116
Mahood, Kenneth *24:* 141
Mahurin, Matt *164:* 225; *175:* 95
Maik, Henri *9:* 102
Maione, Heather Harms *106:* 5
Maisto, Carol *29:* 87
Maitland, Antony *1:* 100, 176; *8:* 41; *17:* 246; *24:* 46; *25:* 177, 178; *32:* 74; *60:* 65, 195; *67:* 156; *87:* 131; *101:* 110
Majewski, Dawn W. *169:* 95
Mak, Kam *72:* 25; *75:* 43; *87:* 186; *97:* 24; *102:* 154; *149:* 195
Makie, Pam *37:* 117
Maktima, Joe *116:* 191
Maland, Nick *99:* 77
Male, Alan *132:* 64
Malone, James Hiram *84:* 161
Malone, Nola Langner *82:* 239
Malsberg, Edward *51:* 175
Malvern, Corinne *2:* 13; *34:* 148, 149
Manchess, Gregory *165:* 241
Mancusi, Stephen *63:* 198, 199
Mandelbaum, Ira *31:* 115
Manders, John *138:* 152, 155
Manet, Edouard *23:* 170
Mangiat, Jeff *173:* 127
Mangurian, David *14:* 133
Manham, Allan *42:* 109; *77:* 180; *80:* 227
Manley, Matt *103:* 167; *117:* 98; *172:* 49
Manniche, Lise *31:* 121
Manning, Jane *96:* 203
Manning, Jo *63:* 154
Manning, Mick *176:* 139
Manning, Samuel F. *5:* 75
Mantel, Richard *57:* 73; *63:* 106; *82:* 255
Maraja *15:* 86; *YABC 1:* 28; *2:* 115
Marcellino, Fred *20:* 125; *34:* 222; *53:* 125; *58:* 205; *61:* 64, 121, 122; *68:* 154, 156, 157, 158, 159; *72:* 25; *86:* 184; *98:* 181; *118:* 129, 130, 131; *149:* 218
Marchesi, Stephen *34:* 140; *46:* 72; *50:* 147; *66:* 239; *70:* 33; *73:* 18, 114, 163; *77:* 47, 76, 147; *78:* 79; *80:* 30; *81:* 6; *89:* 66; *93:* 21, 130; *94:* 94; *97:* 66; *98:* 96; *114:* 115, 116
Marchiori, Carlos *14:* 60
Marciano, John Bemelmans *118:* 133; *167:* 110, 111, 112
Marcus, Barry David *139:* 248; *145:* 18
Margules, Gabriele *21:* 120
Mariana
    *See* Foster, Marian Curtis
Mariano, Michael *52:* 108
Marino, Dorothy *6:* 37; *14:* 135
Mario, Heide Stetson *101:* 202
Maris, Ron *71:* 123

Maritz, Nicolaas *85:* 123
Mark, Mona *65:* 105; *68:* 205; *116:* 213
Markham, R.L. *17:* 240
Marks, Alan *104:* 104; *109:* 182; *164:* 92
Marks, Cara *54:* 9
Marokvia, Artur *31:* 122
Marquez, Susan *108:* 121
Marrella, Maria Pia *62:* 116
Marriott, Pat *30:* 30; *34:* 39; *35:* 164, 165, 166; *44:* 170; *48:* 186, 187, 188, 189, 191, 192, 193; *91:* 92
Mars, W.T. *1:* 161; *3:* 115; *4:* 208, 225; *5:* 92, 105, 186; *8:* 214; *9:* 12; *13:* 121; *27:* 151; *31:* 180; *38:* 102; *48:* 66; *62:* 164, 165; *64:* 62; *68:* 229; *79:* 55
Marschall, Ken *85:* 29
Marsh, Christine *3:* 164
Marsh, James *73:* 137
Marsh, Reginald *17:* 5; *19:* 89; *22:* 90, 96
Marshall, Anthony D. *18:* 216
Marshall, Felicia *170:* 190
Marshall, James *6:* 160; *40:* 221; *42:* 24, 25, 29; *51:* 111, 112, 113, 114, 115, 116, 117, 118, 119, 120, 121; *64:* 13; *75:* 126, 127, 128, 129; *102:* 10, 12
Marshall, Janet *97:* 154
Marstall, Bob *55:* 145; *84:* 153, 170; *104:* 145; *154:* 166, 167, 168
Martchenko, Michael *50:* 129, 153, 155, 156, 157; *83:* 144, 145; *154:* 137, 138, 139
Marten, Ruth *129:* 52
Martin, Charles E. *70:* 144
Martin, David Stone *24:* 232; *62:* 4
Martin, Fletcher *18:* 213; *23:* 151
Martin, Rene *7:* 144; *42:* 148, 149, 150
Martin, Richard E. *51:* 157; *131:* 203
Martin, Ron *32:* 81
Martin, Stefan *8:* 68; *32:* 124, 126; *56:* 33
Martin, Whitney *166:* 137
Martinez, Ed *58:* 192; *72:* 231; *77:* 33; *80:* 214; *167:* 123
Martinez, John *6:* 113; *118:* 13; *139:* 143
Martinez, Sergio *158:* 190
Martiniere, Stephan *171:* 130
Marton, Jirina *95:* 127, 128; *144:* 145
Martorell, Antonio *84:* 6; *97:* 161
Martucci, Griesbach *52:* 106
Marvin, Frederic *83:* 86
Marx, Robert F. *24:* 143
Masefield, Judith *19:* 208, 209
Masheris, Robert *78:* 51
Mason, George F. *14:* 139
Mason, Robert *84:* 96
Massey, Barbara *68:* 142
Massie, Diane Redfield *16:* 194
Massie, Kim *31:* 43
Mataya, David *121:* 66
Mathers, Petra *119:* 135; *163:* 104; *176:* 143, 144
Mathewuse, James *51:* 143
Mathieu, Joseph *14:* 33; *39:* 206; *43:* 167; *56:* 180; *79:* 126; *94:* 147
Matje, Martin *169:* 177, 178; *172:* 180
Matsubara, Naoko *12:* 121
Matsuda, Shizu *13:* 167
Matte, L'Enc *22:* 183
Mattelson, Marvin *36:* 50, 51
Matthews, F. Leslie *4:* 216
Mattingly, David *71:* 76, 77; *82:* 64; *91:* 216, 217; *109:* 25
Matulay, Laszlo *5:* 18; *43:* 168
Matus, Greta *12:* 142
Mauldin, Bill *27:* 23
Mauterer, Erin Marie *119:* 5
Mawicke, Tran *9:* 137; *15:* 191; *47:* 100
Mawson, Matt *74:* 115
Max, Peter *45:* 146, 147, 148, 149, 150
Maxie, Betty *40:* 135
Maxwell, John Alan *1:* 148
Mayan, Earl *7:* 193
Mayer, Danuta *117:* 103

Mayer, Marianna *32:* 132
Mayer, Mercer *11:* 192; *16:* 195, 196; *20:* 55, 57; *32:* 129, 130, 132, 133, 134; *41:* 144, 248, 252; *58:* 186; *73:* 140, 142, 143; *137:* 137, 138
Mayforth, Hal *166:* 77
Mayhew, James *85:* 121; *138:* 187; *149:* 140
Mayhew, Richard *3:* 106
Mayo, Gretchen Will *38:* 81; *84:* 166
Mays, Victor *5:* 127; *8:* 45, 153; *14:* 245; *23:* 50; *34:* 155; *40:* 79; *45:* 158; *54:* 91; *66:* 240
Mazal, Chanan *49:* 104
Maze, Deborah *71:* 83
Mazellan, Ron *75:* 97, 98
Mazetti, Alan *112:* 72
Mazille, Capucine *96:* 168
Mazza, Adriana Saviozzi *19:* 215
Mazzella, Mary Jo *82:* 165
Mazzetti, Alan *45:* 210
McAfee, Steve *135:* 146; *167:* 176
McAlinden, Paul *112:* 128
McBride, Angus *28:* 49; *103:* 40
McBride, Will *30:* 110
McCaffery, Janet *38:* 145
McCallum, Graham *78:* 78
McCallum, Stephen *141:* 143; *156:* 5; *166:* 228
McCann, Gerald *3:* 50; *4:* 94; *7:* 54; *41:* 121
McCarthy, Dan *174:* 74
McCarthy, Linda *177:* 128
McCarthy, Meghan *168:* 134
McCauley, Adam *157:* 36
McCay, Winsor *41:* 124, 126, 128, 129, 130, 131; *134:* 77, 79
McClary, Nelson *1:* 111
McClintock, Barbara *57:* 135; *95:* 130; *146:* 190
McClintock, Theodore *14:* 141
McCloskey, Robert *1:* 184, 185; *2:* 186, 187; *17:* 209; *39:* 139, 140, 141, 142, 143, 146, 147, 148; *85:* 150, 151; *100:* 172, 173, 174
McClung, Robert *2:* 189; *68:* 166, 167
McClure, Gillian *31:* 132; *150:* 53
McConnel, Jerry *31:* 75, 187
McConnell, Mary *102:* 49
McCord, Kathleen Garry *78:* 236
McCormack, John *66:* 193
McCormick, A.D. *35:* 119
McCormick, Dell J. *19:* 216
McCrady, Lady *16:* 198; *39:* 127
McCrea, James *3:* 122; *33:* 216
McCrea, Ruth *3:* 122; *27:* 102; *33:* 216
McCue, Lisa *65:* 148, 149; *77:* 54; *80:* 132; *175:* 33; *177:* 133, 135
McCully, Emily Arnold *2:* 89; *4:* 120, 121, 146, 197; *5:* 2, 129; *7:* 191; *11:* 122; *15:* 210; *33:* 23; *35:* 244; *37:* 122; *39:* 88; *40:* 103; *50:* 30, 31, 32, 33, 34, 35, 36, 37; *52:* 89, 90; *57:* 6; *62:* 3; *70:* 195; *86:* 82; *96:* 192; *97:* 93; *110:* 143, 144; *117:* 47; *167:* 96
McCurdy, Michael *13:* 153; *24:* 85; *81:* 160; *82:* 157, 158; *86:* 125; *97:* 92; *117:* 178; *132:* 6; *147:* 159, 160
McCusker, Paul *99:* 19
McDaniel, Jerry *132:* 135
McDaniel, Preston *160:* 206; *170:* 139
McDermott, Beverly Brodsky *11:* 180
McDermott, Gerald *16:* 201; *74:* 174, 175; *163:* 150, 151
McDermott, Mike *96:* 187
McDonald, Jill *13:* 155; *26:* 128
McDonald, Mercedes *169:* 118
McDonald, Ralph J. *5:* 123, 195
McDonnell, Flora *119:* 199, 200
McDonough, Don *10:* 163
McElmurry, Jill *137:* 148; *163:* 141
McElrath-Eslick, Lori *129:* 145; *142:* 21; *173:* 123
McEntee, Dorothy *37:* 124
McEwan, Keith *88:* 116; *165:* 122, 123

McEwen, Katharine *169:* 34
McFall, Christie *12:* 144
McFeely, Daniel *160:* 213
McGaw, Laurie *109:* 243; *143:* 216
McGee, Barbara *6:* 165
McGee, Marni *163:* 153
McGillvray, Kim *158:* 171; *165:* 213
McGinley-Nally, Sharon *131:* 19
McGinnis, Robert *110:* 113; *177:* 80
McGovern, Tara *98:* 171
McGraw, Sheila *83:* 146
McGregor, Malcolm *23:* 27
McGuirk, Leslie *152:* 159
McHale, John *138:* 190
McHugh, Tom *23:* 64
McIntosh, Jon *42:* 56
McKay, Donald *2:* 118; *32:* 157; *45:* 151, 152
McKean, Dave *150:* 71; *174:* 156
McKeating, Eileen *44:* 58
McKee, David *10:* 48; *21:* 9; *70:* 154, 155; *107:* 139, 140, 141; *134:* 218; *158:* 148, 149, 150, 151
McKee, Diana *109:* 185
McKelvey, Patrick *164:* 141
McKendry, Joe *170:* 136
McKeveny, Tom *164:* 60; *173:* 79
McKie, Roy *7:* 44
McKillip, Kathy *30:* 153
McKinney, Ena *26:* 39
McKinnon, James *136:* 75
McKowen, Scott *172:* 63
McLachlan, Edward *5:* 89
McLaren, Chesley *133:* 53
McLaren, Kirsty *123:* 99; *124:* 226
Mclean, Andrew *113:* 117, 118, 120, 121; *172:* 130, 131
Mclean, Janet *172:* 130
McLean, Meg *94:* 196
McLean, Sammis *32:* 197
McLean, Wilson *90:* 29; *113:* 195
McLoughlin, John C. *47:* 149
McLoughlin, Wayne *102:* 230; *134:* 178
McMahon, Robert *36:* 155; *69:* 169
McManus, Shawn *85:* 71
McMenemy, Sarah *156:* 139
McMillan, Bruce *22:* 184
McMullan, James *40:* 33; *67:* 172; *87:* 142; *99:* 63, 64
McMullen, Nigel *146:* 177
McNeely, Tom *162:* 55
McNaught, Harry *12:* 80; *32:* 136
McNaughton, Colin *39:* 149; *40:* 108; *92:* 144, 145, 146; *134:* 104, 106
McNicholas, Maureen *38:* 148
McNicholas, Shelagh *173:* 61
McPhail, David *14:* 105; *23:* 135; *37:* 217, 218, 220, 221; *47:* 151, 152, 153, 154, 155, 156, 158, 159, 160, 162, 163, 164; *71:* 211; *81:* 139, 140, 142; *86:* 123; *132:* 150; *140:* 129, 131, 132
McPhee, Richard B. *41:* 133
McPheeters, Neal *78:* 132; *86:* 90; *99:* 162; *111:* 141; *142:* 162
McQuade, Jacqueline *124:* 223
McQueen, Lucinda *28:* 149; *41:* 249; *46:* 206; *53:* 103
McQuillan, Mary *153:* 97
McVay, Tracy *11:* 68
McVicker, Charles *39:* 150
Mead, Ben Carlton *43:* 75
Meade, Holly *90:* 102; *94:* 101; *149:* 8; *151:* 107
Mecray, John *33:* 62
Meddaugh, Susan *20:* 42; *29:* 143; *41:* 241; *77:* 50; *84:* 173, 174, 175, 176, 177, 178; *125:* 160, 161, 162; *176:* 148, 149, 150, 151
Meehan, Dennis B. *56:* 144
Meents, Len W. *73:* 147, 150
Meers, Tony *99:* 113
Meisel, Paul *98:* 137; *124:* 18; *162:* 180
Melanson, Luc *149:* 229

Melendez, Francisco *72:* 180
Melnychuk, Monika *153:* 65
Melo, John *16:* 285; *58:* 203
Meloni, Maria Teresa *98:* 62
Meltzer, Ericka
  *See* O'Rourke, Ericka
Menasco, Milton *43:* 85
Mendelson, Steven T. *86:* 154
Mendelssohn, Felix *19:* 170
Mendola, Christopher *88:* 223
Meng, Heinz *13:* 158
Merian, Maria Sibylla *140:* 88
Mero, Lee *34:* 68
Merrill, Frank T. *16:* 147; *19:* 71; *YABC 1:*
  226, 229, 273
Merriman, Rachel *98:* 108; *114:* 122; *149:* 142
Meryman, Hope *27:* 41
Meryweather, Jack *10:* 179
Meseldzija, Petar *168:* 97
Messick, Dale *64:* 150, 151, 152
Meth, Harold *24:* 203
Meyer, Herbert *19:* 189
Meyer, Renate *6:* 170
Meyers, Bob *11:* 136
Meyers, Nancy *172:* 124
Meynell, Louis *37:* 76
Micale, Albert *2:* 65; *22:* 185
Miccuci, Charles *82:* 163; *144:* 150
Micich, Paul *164:* 163
Middleton, Jeffrey *177:* 173
Middleton-Sandford, Betty *2:* 125
Mieke, Anne *45:* 74
Mighell, Patricia *43:* 134
Miglio, Paige *101:* 203; *151:* 223
Mikolaycak, Charles *9:* 144; *12:* 101; *13:* 212;
  *21:* 121; *22:* 168; *30:* 187; *34:* 103, 150; *37:*
  183; *43:* 179; *44:* 90; *46:* 115, 118, 119; *49:*
  25; *78:* 121, 122, 205, 207; *81:* 4
Milelli, Pascal *129:* 66; *135:* 153
Miles, Elizabeth *117:* 77
Miles, Jennifer *17:* 278
Milgrim, David *158:* 157
Milhous, Katherine *15:* 193; *17:* 51
Millais, John E. *22:* 230, 231
Millar, H.R. *YABC 1:* 194, 195, 203
Millard, C.E. *28:* 186
Millard, Kerry *105:* 124
Miller, Don *15:* 195; *16:* 71; *20:* 106; *31:* 178
Miller, Edna *29:* 148
Miller, Edward *115:* 64
Miller, Frank J. *25:* 94
Miller, Grambs *18:* 38; *23:* 16
Miller, Ian *99:* 128
Miller, Jane *15:* 196
Miller, Marcia *13:* 233
Miller, Marilyn *1:* 87; *31:* 69; *33:* 157
Miller, Mitchell *28:* 183; *34:* 207
Miller, Phil *175:* 150
Miller, Shane *5:* 140
Miller, Virginia *81:* 206
Millman, Isaac *172:* 18
Mills, Elaine *72:* 181
Mills, Judith Christine *130:* 168, 169
Mills, Lauren *92:* 170
Mills, Yaroslava Surmach *35:* 169, 170; *46:*
  114
Millsap, Darrel *51:* 102
Milone, Karen *89:* 169
Milord, Susan *147:* 163, 164
Milton, Debbie *162:* 161
Mims, Ashley *170:* 51
Miner, Julia *98:* 69
Minor, Wendell *39:* 188; *52:* 87; *56:* 171; *58:*
  116; *62:* 56; *66:* 109; *74:* 93; *78:* 129; *94:*
  67; *117:* 12, 13; *124:* 84, 86; *136:* 121; *164:*
  168, 169; *170:* 71
Minter, Daniel *176:* 154
Mirocha, Paul *81:* 133
Mitchell, Judith *109:* 117
Mitchell, Mark *91:* 208
Mitgutsch, Ali *76:* 161

Mitsuhashi, Yoko *45:* 153
Miyake, Yoshi *38:* 141
Mizumura, Kazue *10:* 143; *18:* 223; *36:* 159
Mochi, Ugo *8:* 122; *38:* 150
Mock, Paul *55:* 83; *123:* 32
Modarressi, Mitra *90:* 236; *126:* 168; *173:*
  165, 166
Modell, Frank *39:* 152
Mogenson, Jan *74:* 183
Mohn, Susan *89:* 224
Mohr, Mark *133:* 201
Mohr, Nicholasa *8:* 139; *113:* 127
Molan, Christine *60:* 177; *84:* 183
Moldon, Peter L. *49:* 168
Molk, Laurel *92:* 150
Momaday, N. Scott *48:* 159
Mombourquette, Paul *112:* 91; *126:* 142
Monks, Julie *165:* 231
Montgomery, Lucy *150:* 126
Montgomery-Higham, Amanda *169:* 131
Montiel, David *69:* 106; *84:* 145
Montresor, Beni *2:* 91; *3:* 138; *38:* 152, 153,
  154, 155, 156, 157, 158, 159, 160; *68:* 63
Montserrat, Pep *128:* 135
Moon, Carl *25:* 183, 184, 185
Moon, Eliza *14:* 40
Moon, Ivan *22:* 39; *38:* 140
Moore, Adrienne *67:* 147
Moore, Agnes Kay Randall *43:* 187
Moore, Cyd *117:* 107, 108; *159:* 137, 138
Moore, Gustav *127:* 181, 182; *170:* 162, 163
Moore, Jackie *128:* 79
Moore, Janet *63:* 153
Moore, Margie *176:* 156
Moore, Mary *29:* 160
Moore, Yvette *101:* 11, 12; *154:* 141
Mora, Raul Mina *20:* 41
Moraes, Odilon *102:* 144
Morales, Yuyi *154:* 144
Moran, Rosslyn *111:* 26
Moran, Tom *60:* 100
Mordvinoff, Nicolas *15:* 179
Moreno, René King *169:* 59
Morgan, Barbara *169:* 116
Morgan, Jacqui *58:* 57
Morgan, Mary *114:* 133, 134, 135; *123:* 11
Morgan, Tom *42:* 157
Morgan, Pierr *173:* 148
Morgenstern, Michael *158:* 7, 57; *171:* 103;
  *174:* 60
Morice, Dave *93:* 142
Morin, Paul *73:* 132; *79:* 130; *88:* 140; *137:*
  143
Moriuchi, Mique *177:* 203
Morozumi, Atsuko *110:* 155
Morrill, Leslie *18:* 218; *29:* 177; *33:* 84; *38:*
  147; *42:* 127; *44:* 93; *48:* 164, 165, 167,
  168, 169, 170, 171; *49:* 162; *63:* 136, 180;
  *70:* 72; *71:* 70, 91, 92; *72:* 228; *80:* 163,
  164, 165; *90:* 121; *121:* 88
Morrill, Rowena A. *84:* 16; *98:* 163
Morris *47:* 91
Morris, Frank *55:* 133; *60:* 28; *76:* 2
Morris, Harry O. *119:* 138
Morris, Jackie *128:* 194; *144:* 119; *151:* 146
Morris, Oradel Nolen *128:* 180
Morris, Tony *62:* 146; *70:* 97
Morrison, Bill *42:* 116; *66:* 170; *69:* 40
Morrison, Gordon *87:* 150; *113:* 93; *128:* 181,
  182
Morrison, Frank *169:* 162
Morrison, Taylor *159:* 144, 145
Morrow, Gray *2:* 64; *5:* 200; *10:* 103, 114; *14:*
  175
Morton, Lee Jack *32:* 140
Morton, Marian *3:* 185
Mosberg, Hilary *117:* 195; *118:* 164; *149:* 55

Moser, Barry *56:* 68, 117, 118, 119, 120, 121,
  122, 123, 124; *59:* 141; *60:* 160; *79:* 91,
  147, 149, 151, 152; *82:* 81; *90:* 118; *91:* 35;
  *95:* 210; *97:* 91, 93; *102:* 152; *126:* 4; *128:*
  175; *133:* 141; *138:* 167, 171, 174; *153:*
  205; *174:* 130
Moser, Cara *90:* 118; *138:* 167
Moses, Grandma *18:* 228
Moskof, Martin Stephen *27:* 152
Mosley, Francis *57:* 144
Moss, Donald *11:* 184
Moss, Geoffrey *32:* 198
Moss, Marissa *71:* 130; *104:* 127; *163:* 156
Most, Bernard *48:* 173; *91:* 142, 143; *134:* 120
Mowry, Carmen *50:* 62
Moxley, Sheila *96:* 174; *169:* 26
Moyers, William *21:* 65
Moyler, Alan *36:* 142
Mozley, Charles *9:* 87; *20:* 176, 192, 193; *22:*
  228; *25:* 205; *33:* 150; *43:* 170, 171, 172,
  173, 174; *YABC 2:* 89
Mueller, Hans Alexander *26:* 64; *27:* 52, 53
Mugnaini, Joseph *11:* 35; *27:* 52, 53; *35:* 62
Mujica, Rick *72:* 67; *88:* 95; *111:* 53
Muller, Robin *86:* 161
Muller, Steven *32:* 167
Muller, Jorg *35:* 215; *67:* 138, 139
Mulock, Julie *163:* 112
Mullins, Edward S. *10:* 101
Mullins, Patricia *51:* 68
Multer, Scott *80:* 108
Munari, Bruno *15:* 200
Munch, Edvard *140:* 143
Munowitz, Ken *14:* 148; *72:* 178, 179
Munro, Roxie *58:* 134; *136:* 177; *137:* 218
Munsinger, Lynn *33:* 161; *46:* 126; *71:* 92; *82:*
  80; *89:* 218; *92:* 125; *94:* 157, 158, 159,
  160; *98:* 196; *103:* 198; *142:* 143; *145:* 133,
  134, 136; *153:* 203; *176:* 162; *177:* 140, 141,
  142
Munson, Russell *13:* 9
Munster, Sebastian *166:* 107
Munoz, William *42:* 160
Munzar, Barbara *149:* 75
Murdocca, Salvatore *73:* 212; *98:* 132; *111:*
  168; *157:* 228; *164:* 257
Murphy, Bill *5:* 138; *130:* 170
Murphy, Jill *37:* 142; *70:* 166; *142:* 132, 134
Murphy, Kelly *130:* 212; *143:* 119; *176:* 158
Murr, Karl *20:* 62
Murray, Joe *175:* 37
Murray, Ossie *43:* 176
Mussino, Attilio *29:* 131; *100:* 164
Mutchler, Dwight *1:* 25
Myers, Bernice *9:* 147; *36:* 75; *81:* 146, 147,
  148
Muth, Jon J. *165:* 169; *167:* 109
Myers, Duane O. *99:* 145
Myers, Tim *147:* 168
Myers, V.G. *142:* 41
Myers, Lou *11:* 2

**N**

Nachreiner, Tom *29:* 182
Nacht, Merle *65:* 49
Nadler, Ellis *88:* 91
Najaka, Marlies *62:* 101
Nakai, Michael *30:* 217; *54:* 29
Nakata, Hiroe *157:* 156; *162:* 30
Nakatani, Chiyoko *12:* 124
Narahashi, Keiko *77:* 188; *82:* 213; *115:* 142,
  143, 144
Nascimbene, Yan *133:* 128; *173:* 132, 133
Nash, Lesa *87:* 135
Nash, Linell *46:* 175
Nash, Scott *130:* 36
Naso, John *33:* 183
Nason, Thomas W. *14:* 68

Nasser, Muriel 48: 74
Nast, Thomas 21: 29; 28: 23; 51: 132, 133, 134, 135, 136, 137, 138, 139, 141
Nasta, Vincent 78: 185
Natale, Vincent 76: 3; 78: 125; 112: 47; 166: 81; 174: 189
Natchev, Alexi 96: 177
Nathan, Charlott 125: 151
Nathan, Cheryl 150: 104
Natti, Susanna 20: 146; 32: 141, 142; 35: 178; 37: 143; 71: 49; 93: 98; 125: 166, 168; 126: 228; 151: 6
Navarra, Celeste Scala 8: 142
Naylor, Penelope 10: 104
Nazz, James 72: 8
Nebel, M. 45: 154
Neebe, William 7: 93
Needler, Jerry 12: 93
Neel, Alice 31: 23
Neely, Beth 119: 184
Neely, Keith R. 46: 124
Neff, Leland 78: 74
Negri, Rocco 3: 213; 5: 67; 6: 91, 108; 12: 159
Negrin, Fabian 174: 125; 175: 15
Neidigh, Sherry 128: 53
Neill, John R. 18: 8, 10, 11, 21, 30; 100: 22
Neilsen, Cliff 158: 131; 177: 112, 121
Neilsen, Terese 116: 74
Nelson, Craig 62: 151; 153
Nelson, Gail White 68: 140
Nelson, Jennifer 129: 152
Nelson, Kadir 151: 185; 154: 146, 147; 157: 189, 222
Nelson, S.D. 131: 34
Ness, Evaline 1: 164, 165; 2: 39; 3: 8; 10: 147; 12: 53; 26: 150, 151, 152, 153; 49: 30, 31, 32; 56: 30; 60: 113
Neubecker, Robert 170: 143
Neville, Vera 2: 182
Nevwirth, Allan 79: 168
Newberry, Clare Turlay 1: 170
Newbold, Greg 108: 125; 145: 199; 151: 23
Newfeld, Frank 14: 121; 26: 154
Newman, Andy 149: 61
Newman, Ann 43: 90
Newsham, Ian 143: 162
Newsom, Carol 40: 159; 44: 60; 47: 189; 65: 29; 70: 192; 80: 36; 85: 137, 138; 92: 167
Newsom, Tom 49: 149; 71: 13, 62; 75: 156; 91: 113
Newton, Jill 83: 105
Ng, Michael 29: 171
Ng, Simon 167: 7
Nicholson, William 15: 33, 34; 16: 48
Nickens, Bessie 104: 153
Nicklaus, Carol 45: 194; 62: 132, 133
Nickless, Will 16: 139
Nicholas, Corasue 154: 20
Nicolas 17: 130, 132, 133; YABC 2: 215
Niebrugge, Jane 6: 118
Nielsen, Jon 6: 100; 24: 202
Nielsen, Kay 15: 7; 16: 211, 212, 213, 215, 217; 22: 143; YABC 1: 32, 33
Nielsen, Cliff 95: 207, 208; 105: 58; 114: 112; 124: 12; 125: 91, 92; 132: 124; 135: 187; 136: 40; 137: 168; 145: 54; 149: 28; 158: 129; 165: 64, 158; 168: 169; 170: 6; 175: 114, 116
Niland, Deborah 25: 191; 27: 156; 135: 50; 172: 143
Niland, Kilmeny 25: 191; 75: 143
Nino, Alex 59: 145
Ninon 1: 5; 38: 101, 103, 108
Nissen, Rie 44: 35
Nithael, Mark 158: 237
Nivola, Claire A. 78: 126; 140: 147
Nixon, K. 14: 152
Noble, Louise 61: 170
Noble, Marty 97: 168; 125: 171
Noble, Trinka Hakes 39: 162; 84: 157

Noda, Takayo 168: 143
Noguchi, Yoshie 30: 99
Nolan, Dennis 42: 163; 67: 163; 78: 189; 82: 225; 83: 26; 92: 169, 170; 103: 166; 111: 35; 112: 213; 127: 171; 166: 161
Noll, Sally 82: 171
Nolte, Larry 121: 63, 65
Nones, Eric Jon 61: 111; 76: 38; 77: 177
Noonan, Daniel 100: 224
Noonan, Julia 4: 163; 7: 207; 25: 151; 91: 29; 95: 149
Norcia, Ernie 108: 155; 140: 47
Nordenskjold, Birgitta 2: 208
Noreika, Robert 173: 20
Norling, Beth 149: 153, 154
Norman, Elaine 77: 72, 176; 94: 35; 136: 63
Norman, Mary 36: 138, 147
Norman, Michael 12: 117; 27: 168
Northway, Jennifer 85: 96
Nostlinger, Christiana 162: 131
Novak, Linda 166: 205
Novak, Matt 104: 132, 133; 165: 173, 174
Novelli, Luca 61: 137
Nugent, Cynthia 106: 189
Numeroff, Laura Joffe 28: 161; 30: 177
Nurse, Chris 164: 91
Nussbaumer, Paul 16: 219; 39: 117
Nutt, Ken 72: 69; 97: 170
Nyce, Helene 19: 219
Nygren, Tord 30: 148; 127: 164

## O

Oakley, Graham 8: 112; 30: 164, 165; 84: 188, 189, 190, 191, 192
Oakley, Thornton YABC 2: 189
Oberheide, Heide 118: 37
Obligado, Lilian 2: 28, 66, 67; 6: 30; 14: 179; 15: 103; 25: 84; 61: 138, 139, 140, 141, 143
Obrant, Susan 11: 186
O'Brien, Anne Sibley 53: 116, 117; 155: 115
O'Brien, John 41: 253; 72: 12; 89: 59, 60; 98: 16; 161: 185; 169: 16
O'Brien, Teresa 87: 89
O'Brien, Tim 93: 25; 136: 94; 164: 57; 169: 57; 173: 55; 175: 86
O'Clair, Dennis 127: 25
Odell, Carole 35: 47
Odem, Mel 99: 164; 167: 84, 87
O'Donohue, Thomas 40: 89
Oechsli, Kelly 5: 144, 145; 7: 115; 8: 83, 183; 13: 117; 20: 94; 81: 199
Offen, Hilda 42: 207
Ogden, Bill 42: 59; 47: 55
Ogg, Oscar 33: 34
Ogle, Nancy Gray 163: 144
Ohi, Ruth 90: 175, 177; 131: 63; 135: 106; 175: 107
Ohlsson, Ib 4: 152; 7: 57; 10: 20; 11: 90; 19: 217; 41: 246; 82: 106; 92: 213
Ohtomo, Yasuo 37: 146; 39: 212, 213
O'Keefe, Jennifer 136: 184
O'Kelley, Mattie Lou 36: 150
Olbinski, Rafal 149: 27; 158: 77
Oliver, Isaac 171: 182
Oliver, Jenni 23: 121; 35: 112
Oliver, Narelle 152: 192
Oller, Erika 128: 186; 134: 126
Olschewski, Alfred 7: 172
Olsen, Ib Spang 6: 178, 179; 81: 164
Olson, Alan 77: 229
Olugebefola, Ademola 15: 205
O'Malley, Kevin 94: 180; 106: 8; 113: 108; 136: 70; 157: 193
O'Neil, Dan IV 7: 176
O'Neill, Catharine 72: 113; 84: 78; 134: 153
O'Neill, Jean 22: 146
O'Neill, Michael J. 54: 172
O'Neill, Rose 48: 30, 31

O'Neill, Steve 21: 118
Ono, Chiyo 7: 97
Orbaan, Albert 2: 31; 5: 65, 171; 9: 8; 14: 241; 20: 109
Orbach, Ruth 21: 112
Orfe, Joan 20: 81
Org, Ed 119: 93
Ormai, Stella 72: 129
Ormerod, Jan 55: 124; 70: 170, 171; 90: 39; 132: 172, 173, 174; 147: 98
Ormsby, Virginia H. 11: 187
O'Rourke, Ericka 108: 216; 117: 194; 111: 142; 119: 194; 137: 152; 150: 134; 167: 64; 172: 164
O'Rourke, Ericka Meltzer
   See O'Rourke, Ericka
Orozco, Jose Clemente 9: 177
Orr, Forrest W. 23: 9
Orr, N. 19: 70
Ortiz, Vilma 88: 158
Osborn, Cathy 152: 232
Osborn, Robert 65: 49
Osborne, Billie Jean 35: 209
Osmond, Edward 10: 111
O'Sullivan, Tom 3: 176; 4: 55; 78: 195
Otani, June 124: 42; 156: 53
Ottley, Matt 147: 221; 171: 133
Otto, Svend 22: 130, 141; 67: 188, 189
Oudry, J.B. 18: 167
Oughton, Taylor 5: 23; 104: 136
Overeng, Johannes 44: 36
Overlie, George 11: 156
Owens, Carl 2: 35; 23: 521
Owens, Gail 10: 170; 12: 157; 19: 16; 22: 70; 25: 81; 28: 203, 205; 32: 221, 222; 36: 132; 46: 40; 47: 57; 54: 66, 67, 68, 69, 70, 71, 72, 73; 71: 100; 73: 64; 77: 157; 80: 32; 82: 3; 99: 226
Owens, Mary Beth 113: 202, 203
Owens, Nubia 84: 74
Oxenbury, Helen 3: 150, 151; 24: 81; 68: 174, 175, 176; 81: 209; 84: 213, 245; 129: 56; 149: 159
Oz, Robin 88: 167

## P

Padgett, Jim 12: 165
Page, Homer 14: 145
Page, Mark 162: 70
Paget, Sidney 24: 90, 91, 93, 95, 97
Paget, Walter 64: 122
Paillot, Jim 173: 89
Pajouhesh, Noushin 160: 121
Pak 12: 76
Pak, Yu Cha 86: 174
Paladino, Lance 134: 30
Palazzo, Tony 3: 152, 153
Palecek, Josef 56: 136; 89: 158
Palen, Debbie 135: 88
Palencar, John Jude 84: 12, 45; 85: 87; 92: 187; 99: 128; 110: 204; 150: 122; 171: 86
Palin, Nicki 81: 201; 89: 161
Palladini, David 4: 113; 40: 176, 177, 178, 179, 181, 224, 225; 50: 138; 78: 186
Pallarito, Don 43: 36
Palmer, Carol 158: 230
Palmer, Heidi 15: 207; 29: 102
Palmer, Jan 42: 153; 82: 161
Palmer, Judd 153: 160, 161
Palmer, Juliette 6: 89; 15: 208
Palmer, Kate Salley 104: 143; 154: 169
Palmer, Lemuel 17: 25, 29
Palmisciano, Diane 110: 62; 162: 26
Palmquist, Eric 38: 133
Panesis, Nicholas 3: 127
Panton, Doug 52: 99
Paparone, Pamela 129: 174
Papas, William 11: 223; 50: 160

Papin, Joseph *26:* 113
Papish, Robin Lloyd *10:* 80
Paradis, Susan *40:* 216
Paraquin, Charles H. *18:* 166
Paris, Peter *31:* 127
Parisi, Elizabeth B. *141:* 82; *164:* 57
Park, Nick *113:* 143
Park, Seho *39:* 110
Park, W.B. *22:* 189
Parker, Ant *82:* 87, 88; *104:* 121
Parker, Lewis *2:* 179
Parker, Nancy Winslow *10:* 113; *22:* 164; *28:* 47, 144; *52:* 7; *69:* 153; *91:* 171, 174; *132:* 175
Parker, Robert *4:* 161; *5:* 74; *9:* 136; *29:* 39
Parker, Robert Andrew *11:* 81; *29:* 186; *39:* 165; *40:* 25; *41:* 78; *42:* 123; *43:* 144; *48:* 182; *54:* 140; *74:* 141; *91:* 24; *111:* 115; *151:* 201; *154:* 156
Parker-Rees, Guy *149:* 145
Parkin, Trevor *140:* 151
Parkins, David *114:* 123; *146:* 176; *176:* 168
Parkinson, Kathy *71:* 143; *144:* 234
Parkinson, Keith *70:* 66
Parks, Gordon, Jr. *33:* 228
Parnall, Peter *5:* 137; *16:* 221; *24:* 70; *40:* 78; *51:* 130; *69:* 17, 155; *136:* 22, 23, 24
Parnall, Virginia *40:* 78
Parow, Lorraine *158:* 127
Parr, Todd *134:* 139, 140
Parrish, Anne *27:* 159, 160
Parrish, Dillwyn *27:* 159
Parrish, Maxfield *14:* 160, 161, 164, 165; *16:* 109; *18:* 12, 13; *YABC 1:* 149, 152, 267; *2:* 146, 149
Parry, David *26:* 156
Parry, Marian *13:* 176; *19:* 179
Partch, Virgil *45:* 163, 165
Pascal, David *14:* 174
Paschkis, Julie *177:* 153, 154
Pasquier, J.A. *16:* 91
Pasternak, Robert *119:* 53
Paterson, Diane *13:* 116; *39:* 163; *59:* 164, 165, 166, 167; *72:* 51, 53; *129:* 175; *177:* 156, 157
Paterson, Helen *16:* 93
Patkau, Karen *112:* 123
Paton, Jane *15:* 271; *35:* 176
Patrick, John *139:* 190
Patrick, Pamela *90:* 160; *93:* 211; *105:* 12
Patterson, Geoffrey *54:* 75
Patterson, Robert *25:* 118
Patz, Nancy *111:* 40; *154:* 161
Paul, James *4:* 130; *23:* 161
Paul, Korky *102:* 85
Paull, Grace *24:* 157; *87:* 127
Paulsen, Ruth Wright *79:* 160, 164
Pavlov, Elena *80:* 49
Payne, Adam S. *135:* 166
Payne, C.F. *145:* 138, 140
Payne, Joan Balfour *1:* 118
Payne, Tom *170:* 27
Payson, Dale *7:* 34; *9:* 151; *20:* 140; *37:* 22
Payzant, Charles *21:* 147
Peacock, Ralph *64:* 118
Peake, Mervyn *22:* 136, 149; *23:* 162, 163, 164; *YABC 2:* 307
Pearson, Larry *38:* 225
Pearson, Tracey Campbell *64:* 163, 164, 167, 168, 169; *118:* 51; *156:* 169, 171, 172; *163:* 140
Peat, Fern B. *16:* 115
Peck, Anne Merriman *18:* 241; *24:* 155
Peck, Beth *66:* 242; *79:* 166; *80:* 136; *91:* 34; *95:* 9; *101:* 77; *164:* 197
Pedersen, Judy *66:* 217; *121:* 36; *172:* 67
Pedersen, Vilhelm *YABC 1:* 40
Pederson, Sharleen *12:* 92
Pedlar, Elaine *161:* 45
Peek, Merle *39:* 168

Peet, Bill *2:* 203; *41:* 159, 160, 161, 162, 163; *78:* 158, 159, 160, 161
Peguero, Adrian *116:* 133
Peguero, Gerard *116:* 133
Pels, Winslow Pinney *55:* 126
Peltier, Leslie C. *13:* 178
Penberthy, Mark *171:* 78
Pendle, Alexy *7:* 159; *13:* 34; *29:* 161; *33:* 215; *86:* 62
Pendola, Joanne *76:* 203; *81:* 125; *105:* 181
Pene du Bois, William *4:* 70; *10:* 122; *26:* 61; *27:* 145, 211; *35:* 243; *41:* 216; *68:* 180, 181; *73:* 45
Penfound, David *102:* 185
Pennington, Eunice *27:* 162
Peppe, Mark *28:* 142
Peppe, Rodney *4:* 164, 165; *74:* 187, 188, 189
Pepper, Hubert *64:* 143
Percy, Graham *63:* 2
Perini, Ben *173:* 77
Perkins, David *60:* 68
Perkins, Lucy Fitch *72:* 199
Perkins, Lynne Rae *172:* 146
Perl, Susan *2:* 98; *4:* 231; *5:* 44, 45, 118; *6:* 199; *8:* 137; *12:* 88; *22:* 193; *34:* 54, 55; *52:* 128; *YABC 1:* 176
Perrone, Donna *78:* 166
Perry, Marie Fritz *165:* 180
Perry, Patricia *29:* 137; *30:* 171
Perry, Roger *27:* 163
Perske, Martha *46:* 83; *51:* 108, 147
Persson, Stina *175:* 166
Pesek, Ludek *15:* 237
Petach, Heidi *149:* 166
Peters, David *72:* 205
Petersham, Maud *17:* 108, 147, 148, 149, 150, 151, 152, 153
Petersham, Miska *17:* 108, 147, 148, 149, 150, 151, 152, 153
Peterson, Eric *109:* 125
Peterson, Nisse *99:* 27
Peterson, R.F. *7:* 101
Peterson, Russell *7:* 130
Petie, Haris *2:* 3; *10:* 41, 118; *11:* 227; *12:* 70
Petricic, Dusan *153:* 75, 76, 77; *170:* 12; *172:* 13; *176:* 170
Petrides, Heidrun *19:* 223
Petrone, Valeria *159:* 160; *171:* 92
Petrosino, Tamara *177:* 40
Petruccio, Steven James *67:* 159; *127:* 5
Pettingill, Ondre *64:* 181; *70:* 64
Peyo *40:* 56, 57
Peyton, K.M. *15:* 212
Pfeifer, Herman *15:* 262
Pfister, Marcus *83:* 165, 166, 167; *146:* 152; *150:* 160
Pfloog, Jan *124:* 60
Pham, LeUyen *160:* 48; *175:* 154, 156
Phillips, Craig *70:* 151
Phillips, Douglas *1:* 19
Phillips, F.D. *6:* 202
Phillips, Louise *133:* 67
Phillips, Thomas *30:* 55
Philpot, Glyn *54:* 46
Phiz
　　*See* Browne, Hablot K.
Piatti, Celestino *16:* 223
Pica, Steve *115:* 181
Picarella, Joseph *13:* 147
Picart, Gabriel *121:* 165
Pichon, Liz *174:* 139
Pickard, Charles *12:* 38; *18:* 203; *36:* 152
Picken, George A. *23:* 150
Pickens, David *22:* 156
Pienkowski, Jan *6:* 183; *30:* 32; *58:* 140, 141, 142, 143, 146, 147; *73:* 3; *87:* 156, 157; *131:* 189
Pignataro, Anna *163:* 220 Pileggi, Steve *145:* 122
Pilkey, Dav *68:* 186; *115:* 164, 166; *166:* 173, 174, 175

Pimlott, John *10:* 205
Pincus, Harriet *4:* 186; *8:* 179; *22:* 148; *27:* 164, 165; *66:* 202
Pini, Wendy *89:* 166
Pinkett, Neil *60:* 8
Pinkney, Brian *81:* 184, 185; *94:* 107; *113:* 146, 147; *117:* 121, 166; *132:* 145; *158:* 108, 191; *160:* 189
Pinkney, Jerry *8:* 218; *10:* 40; *15:* 276; *20:* 66; *24:* 121; *33:* 109; *36:* 222; *38:* 200; *41:* 165, 166, 167, 168, 169, 170, 171, 173, 174; *44:* 198; *48:* 51; *53:* 20; *56:* 61, 68; *58:* 184; *60:* 59; *61:* 91; *71:* 146, 148, 149; *72:* 17; *73:* 149; *74:* 159, 192; *75:* 45; *80:* 206; *81:* 44; *85:* 144; *95:* 50; *107:* 158, 159, 160; *108:* 164; *112:* 114, 115; *133:* 58
Pinkwater, Daniel Manus *46:* 180, 181, 182, 185, 188, 189, 190; *151:* 161 76: 178, 179, 180
Pinkwater, Manus *8:* 156; *46:* 180
　　*See also* Pinkwater, Daniel Manus
Pinkwater, Jill *114:* 160, 161; *158:* 179
Pinto, Ralph *10:* 131; *45:* 93
Pinon, Mark *74:* 22
Piven, Hanoch *173:* 142
Pistolesi *73:* 211
Pittman, Helena Clare *71:* 151
Pitz, Henry C. *4:* 168; *19:* 165; *35:* 128; *42:* 80; *YABC 2:* 95, 176
Pitzenberger, Lawrence J. *26:* 94
Player, Stephen *82:* 190
Plecas, Jennifer *84:* 201; *106:* 124; *149:* 168
Plowden, David *52:* 135, 136
Plume, Ilse *170:* 149
Plummer, William *32:* 31
Podwal, Mark *56:* 170, 173; *101:* 154, 155, 157; *149:* 176; *160:* 194
Pogany, Willy *15:* 46, 49; *19:* 222, 256; *25:* 214; *44:* 142, 143, 144, 145, 146, 147, 148
Pohrt, Tom *67:* 116; *104:* 80; *152:* 199
Poirson, V.A. *26:* 89
Polacco, Patricia *74:* 195, 196, 197, 198; *123:* 121, 122, 123
Polgreen, John *21:* 44
Politi, Leo *1:* 178; *4:* 53; *21:* 48; *47:* 173, 174, 176, 178, 179, 180, 181
Pollema-Cahill, Phyllis *123:* 126
Pollen, Samson *64:* 80
Polonsky, Arthur *34:* 168
Polseno, Jo *1:* 53; *3:* 117; *5:* 114; *17:* 154; *20:* 87; *32:* 49; *41:* 245
Pomaska, Anna *117:* 148
Ponter, James *5:* 204
Poole, Colin *111:* 27
Poortvliet, Rien *6:* 212; *65:* 165, 166, 167
Popp, Wendy *72:* 122; *158:* 68
Poppel, Hans *71:* 154, 155
Porfirio, Guy *76:* 134
Portal, Colette *6:* 186; *11:* 203
Porter, George *7:* 181
Porter, Janice Lee *136:* 175; *164:* 37
Porter, John *113:* 47
Porter, Pat Grant *84:* 112; *125:* 101
Porter, Sue *146:* 246, 247
Porter, Walter *124:* 175
Posen, Michael *175:* 82
Posthuma, Sieb *150:* 163
Postma, Lidia *79:* 17
Potter, Beatrix *100:* 194, 195; *132:* 179, 180, 181, 182; *YABC 1:* 208, 209, 210, 212, 213
Potter, Giselle *117:* 123; *143:* 44; *144:* 170, 197; *149:* 7; *150:* 165
Potter, Katherine *104:* 147; *171:* 135; *173:* 136
Potter, Miriam Clark *3:* 162
Poulin, Stephane *98:* 140, 141
Poullis, Nick *146:* 210
Powell, Constance Buffington *174:* 141
Powell, Gary *151:* 208
Powell, Ivan *67:* 219
Power, Margaret *105:* 122
Powers, Daniel *161:* 173

Powers, Richard M. *1:* 230; *3:* 218; *7:* 194; *26:* 186
Powledge, Fred *37:* 154
Powzyk, Joyce *74:* 214
Poydar, Nancy *96:* 149
Pracher, Richard *91:* 166
Prachaticka, Marketa *126:* 126
Prap, Lila *177:* 165
Prater, John *103:* 142, 143, 144; *149:* 172
Pratt, Charles *23:* 29
Pratt, George *116:* 208
Pratt, Pierre *150:* 73; *166:* 183; *168:* 172
Prebenna, David *73:* 174
Preiss-Glasser, Robin *123:* 176; *152* 40; *172:* 194
Press, Jenny *116:* 95
Preston, Mark *152:* 162
Pretro, Korinna *91:* 126
Price, Christine *2:* 247; *3:* 163, 253; *8:* 166
Price, Cynthia *118:* 156
Price, Edward *33:* 34
Price, Garrett *1:* 76; *2:* 42
Price, Hattie Longstreet *17:* 13
Price, Norman *YABC 1:* 129
Price, Willard *48:* 184
Priceman, Marjorie *81:* 171; *136:* 169; *156:* 200; *168:* 153, 154
Priestley, Alice *168:* 33
Primavera, Elise *26:* 95; *58:* 151; *73:* 37; *80:* 79; *86:* 156; *105:* 161
Primrose, Jean *36:* 109
Prince, Alison *86:* 188, 189
Prince, Leonora E. *7:* 170
Pritchett, Shelley *116:* 148
Prittie, Edwin J. *YABC 1:* 120
Proimos, James *176:* 4
Proimos, John *173:* 144
Prosmitsky, Jenya *132:* 33
Provensen, Alice *37:* 204, 215, 222; *70:* 176, 177, 178, 180; *71:* 213; *147:* 184
Provensen, Martin *37:* 204, 215, 222; *70:* 176, 177, 178, 180; *71:* 213
Pucci, Albert John *44:* 154
Pudlo *8:* 59
Pulver, Harry, Jr. *129:* 159
Pulver, Robin *160:* 4
Punchatz, Don *99:* 57
Purdy, Susan *8:* 162
Pursell, Weimer *55:* 18
Purtscher, Alfons *97:* 6
Puskas, James *5:* 141
Pyk, Jan *7:* 26; *38:* 123
Pyle, Chuck *99:* 149
Pyle, Howard *16:* 225, 226, 227, 228, 230, 231, 232, 235; *24:* 27; *34:* 124, 125, 127, 128; *59:* 132; *100:* 198

**Q**

Quackenbush, Robert *4:* 190; *6:* 166; *7:* 175, 178; *9:* 86; *11:* 65, 221; *41:* 154; *43:* 157; *70:* 185, 186; *71:* 137; *85:* 47; *92:* 148; *133:* 154, 164, 169
Qualls, Sean *177:* 167, 168
Quennell, Marjorie (Courtney) *29:* 163, 164
Quidor, John *19:* 82
Quirk, John *62:* 170
Quirk, Thomas *12:* 81

**R**

Rackham, Arthur *15:* 32, 78, 214-227; *17:* 105, 115; *18:* 233; *19:* 254; *20:* 151; *22:* 129, 131, 132, 133; *23:* 175; *24:* 161, 181; *26:* 91; *32:* 118; *64:* 18; *100:* 9, 16, 203, 204; *YABC 1:* 25, 45, 55, 147; *2:* 103, 142, 173, 210

Racz, Michael *56:* 134
Radcliffe, Andrew *82:* 215
Rader, Laura *101:* 219
Radunsky, Vladimir *177:* 170
Rafilson, Sidney *11:* 172
Raglin, Tim *125:* 24
Raible, Alton *1:* 202, 203; *28:* 193; *35:* 181; *110:* 207
Raine, Patricia *82:* 74; *88:* 154
Rama, Sue *173:* 45
Ramhorst, John *117:* 11
Ramirez, Gladys *177:* 19
Ramsey, James *16:* 41
Ramsey, Marcy Dunn *82:* 11
Ramus, Michael *51:* 171
Rand, Paul *6:* 188
Rand, Ted *67:* 9, 10, 121, 123; *74:* 190; *84:* 170; *103:* 170; *112:* 6; *114:* 73; *139:* 168; *143:* 194; *156:* 154; *161:* 9, 10
Randazzo, Tony *81:* 98
Randell, William *55:* 54
Rane, Walter *93:* 144; *143:* 109
Rankin, Joan *163:* 40
Rankin, Laura *176:* 173, 174
Ransome, Arthur *22:* 201
Ransome, James E. *74:* 137; *75:* 80; *84:* 181; *94:* 108; *117:* 115; *123:* 128, 129, 130; *158:* 101, 102; *159:* 205
Rantz, Don *119:* 184
Rao, Anthony *28:* 126
Raphael, Elaine *23:* 192; *71:* 24, 25
Rappaport, Eva *6:* 190
Raschka, Chris *80:* 187, 189, 190; *97:* 211; *115:* 210; *117:* 151, 152, 153, 154; *143:* 195; *145:* 153; *166:* 190, 191; *170:* 114
Rash, Andy *158:* 178; *162:* 172
Raskin, Ellen *2:* 208, 209; *4:* 142; *13:* 183; *22:* 68; *29:* 139; *36:* 134; *38:* 173, 174, 175, 176, 177, 178, 179, 180, 181; *60:* 163; *86:* 81
Rathmann, Peggy *93:* 32; *94:* 168; *157:* 212, 214
Ratkus, Tony *77:* 133
Ratzkin, Lawrence *40:* 143
Rau, Margaret *9:* 157
Raverat, Gwen *YABC 1:* 152
Ravid, Joyce *61:* 73
Ravielli, Anthony *1:* 198; *3:* 168; *11:* 143
Ravilious, Robin *77:* 169
Rawlins, Donna *72:* 198; *73:* 15, 129
Rawlins, Janet *76:* 79
Rawlings, Steve *143:* 139; *151:* 54
Rawlinson, Debbie *75:* 132
Ray, Deborah Kogan *8:* 164; *29:* 238; *50:* 112, 113; *62:* 119; *78:* 191
Ray, Jane *96:* 166; *97:* 104; *152:* 208
Ray, Ralph *2:* 239; *5:* 73
Rayann, Omar *162:* 205
Rayevsky, Robert *64:* 17; *70:* 173; *80:* 204; *117:* 79
Raymond, Larry *31:* 108; *97:* 109
Rayner, Hugh *151:* 170
Rayner, Mary *22:* 207; *47:* 140; *72:* 191; *87:* 171, 172
Rayner, Shoo
    *See* Rayner, Hugh
Raynes, John *71:* 19
Raynor, Dorka *28:* 168
Raynor, Paul *24:* 73
Rayyan, Omar *110:* 222; *112:* 17; *125:* 131
Razzi, James *10:* 127
Read, Alexander D. *20:* 45
Reader, Dennis *71:* 157
Reasoner, Charles *53:* 33, 36, 37
Reczuch, Karen *115:* 132; *145:* 131
Redlich, Ben *163:* 221
Reed, Joseph *116:* 139
Reed, Lynn Rowe *115:* 173; *171:* 146
Reed, Tom *34:* 171
Reeder, Colin *74:* 202; *77:* 113
Rees, Mary *134:* 219

Reese, Bob *60:* 135
Reeve, Philip *171:* 50
Reeves, Eira B. *130:* 173, 174; *141:* 151
Regan, Dana *117:* 116
Regan, Laura *103:* 198; *153:* 206
Reichert, Renée *169:* 127
Reid, Barbara *82:* 178; *92:* 17; *93:* 169, 170
Reid, Stephen *19:* 213; *22:* 89
Reim, Melanie *104:* 151; *150:* 98
Reinert, Kirk *89:* 138
Reinertson, Barbara *44:* 150; *62:* 103
Reiniger, Lotte *40:* 185
Reisberg, Mira *119:* 2
Reisch, Jesse *158:* 130
Reiser, Lynn *81:* 175; *138:* 184
Reiss, John J. *23:* 193
Relf, Douglas *3:* 63
Relyea, C.M. *16:* 29; *31:* 153
Remi, Georges *13:* 184
Remington, Frederic *19:* 188; *41:* 178, 179, 180, 181, 183, 184, 185, 186, 187, 188; *62:* 197
Remkiewicz, Frank *67:* 102; *77:* 171; *80:* 130; *113:* 107; *152:* 116; *152:* 211, 212; *157:* 148
Rendon, Maria *116:* 141; 192; *134:* 152
Renfro, Ed *79:* 176
Renlie, Frank *11:* 200
Reschofsky, Jean *7:* 118
Rethi *60:* 181
Rethi, Lili *2:* 153; *36:* 156
Reusswig, William *3:* 267
Rex, Adam *156:* 172; *169:* 91
Rex, Michael *157:* 147
Rey, H.A. *1:* 182; *26:* 163, 164, 166, 167, 169; *69:* 172, 173, 174, 175; *86:* 195, 196, 197; *100:* 211; *YABC 2:* 17
Reynolds, Doris *5:* 71; *31:* 77
Reynolds, Peter *142:* 12
Rhead, Louis *31:* 91; *100:* 228
Rhodes, Andrew *38:* 204; *50:* 163; *54:* 76; *61:* 123, 124; *87:* 200
Ribbons, Ian *3:* 10; *37:* 161; *40:* 76
Ricci, Regolo *93:* 22; *164:* 148
Rice, Elizabeth *2:* 53, 214
Rice, Eve *34:* 174, 175; *91:* 172
Rice, James *22:* 210; *93:* 173
Richards, Chuck *170:* 154
Richards, George *40:* 116, 119, 121; *44:* 179
Richards, Henry *YABC 1:* 228, 231
Richardson, Ernest *2:* 144
Richardson, Frederick *18:* 27, 31
Richardson, John *110:* 88
Richman, Hilda *26:* 132
Richmond, George *24:* 179
Riddell, Chris *114:* 170, 195; *166:* 179
Riddle, Tohby *74:* 204; *151:* 179
Riding, Peter *63:* 195
Rieniets, Judy King *14:* 28
Riger, Bob *2:* 166
Riggio, Anita *73:* 191; *85:* 63; *137:* 184; *172:* 165
Riley, Jon *74:* 70
Riley, Kenneth *22:* 230
Riley-Webb, Charlotte *153:* 143
Rinaldi, Angelo *165:* 60, 69
Ringgold, Faith *71:* 162; *114:* 173, 174, 176
Ringi, Kjell *12:* 171
Rios, Tere
    *See* Versace, Marie
Ripper, Charles L. *3:* 175
Ripplinger, Henry *117:* 31
Ritchie, William *74:* 183
Ritter, John *175:* 14
Ritz, Karen *41:* 117; *72:* 239; *87:* 125; *102:* 7; *106:* 6
Rivkin, Jay *15:* 230
Rivoche, Paul *45:* 125
Roach, Marilynne *9:* 158
Robbin, Jodi *44:* 156, 159
Robbins, Frank *42:* 167
Robbins, Ken *147:* 191, 192

Robbins, Ruth *52:* 102
Roberts, Cliff *4:* 126
Roberts, David *154:* 4, 6
Roberts, Doreen *4:* 230; *28:* 105
Roberts, Jim *22:* 166; *23:* 69; *31:* 110
Roberts, Tony *109:* 195, 214
Roberts, W. *22:* 2, 3
Robins, Arthur *137:* 172; *151:* 225
Robinson, Aminah Brenda Lynn *86:* 205; *103:* 55; *159:* 175
Robinson, Charles [1870-1937] *17:* 157, 171, 172, 173, 175, 176; *24:* 207; *25:* 204; *YABC 2:* 308, 309, 310, 331
Robinson, Charles *3:* 53; *5:* 14; *6:* 193; *7:* 150; *7:* 183; *8:* 38; *9:* 81; *13:* 188; *14:* 248, 249; *23:* 149; *26:* 115; *27:* 48; *28:* 191; *32:* 28; *35:* 210; *36:* 37; *48:* 96; *52:* 33; *53:* 157; *56:* 15; *62:* 142; *77:* 41; *111:* 148
Robinson, Jerry *3:* 262
Robinson, Joan G. *7:* 184
Robinson, Lolly *90:* 227
Robinson, T.H. *17:* 179, 181, 182, 183; *29:* 254
Robinson, W. Heath *17:* 185, 187, 189, 191, 193, 195, 197, 199, 202; *23:* 167; *25:* 194; *29:* 150; *YABC 1:* 44; *2:* 183
Roche, Christine *41:* 98
Roche, Denis *99:* 184
Roche, P.K. *57:* 151, 152
Rocker, Fermin *7:* 34; *13:* 21; *31:* 40; *40:* 190, 191
Rocklen, Margot *101:* 181
Rockwell, Anne *5:* 147; *33:* 171, 173; *71:* 166, 167, 168; *114:* 183, 184
Rockwell, Gail *7:* 186
Rockwell, Harlow *33:* 171, 173, 175
Rockwell, Lizzy *114:* 182; *162:* 182
Rockwell, Norman *23:* 39, 196, 197, 199, 200, 203, 204, 207; *41:* 140, 143; *123:* 47; *YABC 2:* 60
Rockwood, Richard *119:* 75
Rodanas, Kristina *156:* 183, 184
Rodegast, Roland *43:* 100
Rodgers, Frank *69:* 177
Rodriguez, Joel *16:* 65
Rodriguez, Robert *145:* 145
Rodriguez-Howard, Pauline *177:* 18
Roeckelein, Katrina *134:* 223
Roennfeldt, Robert *66:* 243
Roever, J.M. *4:* 119; *26:* 170
Roffey, Maureen *33:* 142, 176, 177
Rogasky, Barbara *46:* 90
Rogé *173:* 160
Rogers, Carol *2:* 262; *6:* 164; *26:* 129
Rogers, Chris M. *150:* 59
Rogers, Forest *87:* 160; *101:* 76
Rogers, Frances *10:* 130
Rogers, Gregory *104:* 76; *126:* 57; *171:* 26
Rogers, Jacqueline *78:* 249; *80:* 34; *86:* 54 *103:* 70; *115:* 72; *129:* 173; *131:* 57, 225; *143:* 211; *153:* 100
Rogers, Walter S. *31:* 135, 138; *67:* 65, 168; *100:* 81
Rogers, William A. *15:* 151, 153, 154; *33:* 35
Rogoff, Barbara *95:* 20
Rohmann, Eric *103:* 152
Rojankovsky, Feodor *6:* 134, 136; *10:* 183; *21:* 128, 129, 130; *25:* 110; *28:* 42; *68:* 120
Rolfsen, Alf *62:* 15
Romain, Trevor *134:* 157
Roman, Barbara J. *103:* 171
Romas *114:* 111; *165:* 63
Romano, Robert *64:* 68
Roos, Maryn *168:* 198
Root, Barry *80:* 212; *90:* 196; *146:* 78; *156:* 165; *159:* 161
Root, Kimberly Bulcken *86:* 72; *98:* 21; *108:* 111; *127:* 114; *159:* 162; *176:* 134
Roper, Bob *65:* 153
Roraback, Robin *111:* 156
Rorer, Abigail *43:* 222; *85:* 155

Rosales, Melodye *80:* 35
Rosamilia, Patricia *36:* 120
Rose, Carl *5:* 62
Rose, David S. *29:* 109; *70:* 120
Rose, Gerald *68:* 200, 201; *86:* 48
Rose, Ted *93:* 178
Rosenbaum, Jonathan *50:* 46
Rosenberg, Amye *74:* 207, 208
Rosenberry, Vera *87:* 22, 26; *144:* 212, 213; *158:* 120
Rosenblum, Richard *11:* 202; *18:* 18
Rosier, Lydia *16:* 236; *20:* 104; *21:* 109; *22:* 125; *30:* 151, 158; *42:* 128; *45:* 214; *77:* 227, 228
Rosing, Jens *85:* 142
Ross
    *See* Thomson, Ross
Ross, Christine *83:* 172, 173
Ross, Clare Romano *3:* 123; *21:* 45; *48:* 199
Ross, Dave *32:* 152; *57:* 108
Ross, Herbert *37:* 78
Ross, John *3:* 123; *21:* 45
Ross, Johnny *32:* 190
Ross, Larry *47:* 168; *60:* 62
Ross, Ruth *109:* 233
Ross, Tony *17:* 204; *56:* 132; *65:* 176, 177, 179; *90:* 123; *123:* 186, 187, 190; *130:* 188, 190, 191, 192; *132:* 242; *174:* 159; *176:* 181, 182, 183
Rossetti, Dante Gabriel *20:* 151, 153
Roth, Arnold *4:* 238; *21:* 133
Roth, Marci *135:* 223
Roth, Rob *105:* 98; *146:* 41
Roth, Robert *176:* 159
Roth, Roger *61:* 128
Roth, Stephanie *136:* 171, 172
Roth, Susan L. *80:* 38; *93:* 78; *134:* 165, 166
Rothenberg, Joani Keller *162:* 190, 191
Rothman, Michael *139:* 62 Rotman, Jeffrey L. *145:* 30
Rotondo, Pat *32:* 158
Roughsey, Dick *35:* 186
Rouille, M. *11:* 96
Rounds, Glen *8:* 173; *9:* 171; *12:* 56; *32:* 194; *40:* 230; *51:* 161, 162, 166; *56:* 149; *70:* 198, 199; *YABC 1:* 1, 2, 3; *112:* 163
Roundtree, Katherine *114:* 88; *168:* 102
Rowan, Evadne *52:* 51
Rowe, Eric *111:* 161
Rowe, Gavin *27:* 144; *72:* 47; *88:* 201
Rowe, John *132:* 70, 71
Rowell, Kenneth *40:* 72
Rowen, Amy *52:* 143
Rowena *116:* 101
Rowland, Andrew *164:* 136
Rowland, Jada *83:* 73
Rowles, Daphne *58:* 24
Roy, Jeroo *27:* 229; *36:* 110
Royo *118:* 32; *144:* 105, 106, 108; *165:* 19; *166:* 166
Rubel, Nicole *18:* 255; *20:* 59; *81:* 66, 67; *95:* 169, 170; *119:* 60; *135:* 177, 179, 180; *169:* 68
Rubel, Reina *33:* 217
Rud, Borghild *6:* 15
Ruddell, Gary *110:* 238; *116:* 207
Rudolph, Norman Guthrie *17:* 13
Rue, Leonard Lee III *37:* 164
Ruelle, Karen Gray *126:* 193
Ruff, Donna *50:* 173; *72:* 203; *78:* 49; *80:* 120, 121; *93:* 162; *164:* 121
Ruffins, Reynold *10:* 134, 135; *41:* 191, 192, 193, 194, 195, 196; *125:* 187, 188, 189; *162:* 197
Ruhlin, Roger *34:* 44
Ruiz, Art *95:* 154; *110:* 91
Runnerstroem, Bengt Arne *75:* 161
Ruse, Margaret *24:* 155
Rush, Ken *98:* 74
Rush, Peter *42:* 75
Russell, Charles M. *167:* 171

Russell, E.B. *18:* 177, 182
Russell, Jim *53:* 134
Russell, P. Craig *80:* 196; *146:* 102; *162:* 186
Russo, Marisabina *84:* 51; *106:* 164; *151:* 183
Russo, Susan *30:* 182; *36:* 144
Russon, Mary *87:* 145
Ruth, Rod *9:* 161
Rutherford, Alexa *110:* 108
Rutherford, Jenny *78:* 5
Rutherford, Meg *25:* 174; *34:* 178, 179; *69:* 73; *72:* 31
Rutland, Jonathan *31:* 126
Ruurs, Margriet *147:* 195
Ruzzier, Sergio *159:* 176, 177; *163:* 184
Ryan, Will *86:* 134
Ryden, Hope *8:* 176
Rylant, Cynthia *112:* 170, 172
Rymer, Alta M. *34:* 181
Rystedt, Rex *49:* 80

S

Saaf, Chuck *49:* 179
Saaf, Donald *101:* 220; *124:* 180
Sabaka, Donna R. *21:* 172
Sabin, Robert *45:* 35; *60:* 30; *99:* 161
Sabuda, Robert *170:* 166, 167, 168
Sacker, Amy *16:* 100
Saelig, S.M. *129:* 73; *173:* 59
Saffioti, Lino *36:* 176; *48:* 60
Saflund, Birgitta *94:* 2
Sagsoorian, Paul *12:* 183; *22:* 154; *33:* 106; *87:* 152
Sahara, Tony *168:* 106; *177:* 181
Sahlberg, Myron *57:* 165
Saidens, Amy *145:* 162
Saint Exupery, Antoine de *20:* 157
Saint James, Synthia *152:* 220
Saldutti, Denise *39:* 186; *57:* 178
Sale, Morton *YABC 2:* 31
Sale, Tim *153:* 177
Salerno, Steven *150:* 79; *176:* 188
Salter, George *72:* 128, 130
Saltzberg, Barney *135:* 184, 185
Saltzman, David *86:* 209
Salwowski, Mark *71:* 54
Salzman, Yuri *86:* 12
Sambourne, Linley *YABC 2:* 181
Sampson, Katherine *9:* 197
Samson, Anne S. *2:* 216
San Souci, Daniel *40:* 200; *96:* 199, 200; *113:* 171; *157:* 149; *170:* 69
Sancha, Sheila *38:* 185
Sanchez, Enrique O. *155:* 84
Sand, George X. *45:* 182
Sandberg, Lasse *15:* 239, 241
Sanders, Beryl *39:* 173
Sanderson, Ruth *21:* 126; *24:* 53; *28:* 63; *33:* 67; *41:* 48, 198, 199, 200, 201, 202, 203; *43:* 79; *46:* 36, 44; *47:* 102; *49:* 58; *62:* 121, 122; *85:* 3; *109:* 207, 208, 209, 210; *172:* 157, 158
Sandia *119:* 74
Sandin, Joan *4:* 36; *6:* 194; *7:* 177; *12:* 145, 185; *20:* 43; *21:* 74; *26:* 144; *27:* 142; *28:* 224, 225; *38:* 86; *41:* 46; *42:* 35; *59:* 6; *80:* 136; *94:* 188; *140:* 116; *153:* 179, 180
Sandland, Reg *39:* 215
Sandoz, Edouard *26:* 45, 47
Sanford, John *66:* 96, 97
Sankey, Tom *72:* 103
sano, Kazuhiko *153:* 208
Santore, Charles *54:* 139
Santoro, Christopher *74:* 215
Santos, Jesse J. *99:* 24
Sapieha, Christine *1:* 180
Saport, Linda *123:* 137, 138
Sara
    *See* De La Roche Saint Andre, Anne

Sardinha, Rick *175:* 151
Sarg, Tony *YABC 2:* 236
Sargent, Claudia *64:* 181
Sargent, Robert *2:* 217
Saris *1:* 33
Sarony *YABC 2:* 170
Sasaki, Goro *170:* 46
Sasek, Miroslav *16:* 239, 240, 241, 242
Sassman, David *9:* 79
Satty *29:* 203, 205
Sauber, Robert *40:* 183; *76:* 256; *78:* 154; *87:* 92
Saunders, Dave *85:* 163, 164, 165
Savadier, Elivia *84:* 50; *145:* 45; *164:* 206
Savage, Naomi *56:* 172
Savage, Steele *10:* 203; *20:* 77; *35:* 28
Savage, Stephen *174:* 182
Savio *76:* 4
Savitt, Sam *8:* 66, 182; *15:* 278; *20:* 96; *24:* 192; *28:* 98
Sawyer, Kem Knapp *84:* 228, 229
Say, Allen *28:* 178; *69:* 182, 183, 232; *110:* 194, 195, 196; *161:* 154, 155
Sayles, Elizabeth *82:* 93; *105:* 155; *109:* 116
Scabrini, Janet *13:* 191; *44:* 128
Scanlan, Peter *83:* 27; *153:* 165
Scanlon, Paul *83:* 87
Scannell, Reece *105:* 105
Scarry, Huck *35:* 204, 205
Scarry, Richard *2:* 220, 221; *18:* 20; *35:* 193, 194, 195, 196, 197, 198, 199, 200, 201, 202; *75:* 165, 167, 168
Schachner, Judith Byron *88:* 180; *92:* 163; *93:* 102; *142:* 82
Schaeffer, Mead *18:* 81, 94; *21:* 137, 138, 139; *47:* 128
Schaffer, Amanda *90:* 206
Schanzer, Rosalyn *138:* 192, 193
Scharl, Josef *20:* 132; *22:* 128
Scheel, Lita *11:* 230
Scheib, Ida *29:* 28
Schermer, Judith *30:* 184
Schick, Eleanor *82:* 210, 211; *144:* 222
Schick, Joel *16:* 160; *17:* 167; *22:* 12; *27:* 176; *31:* 147, 148; *36:* 23; *38:* 64; *45:* 116, 117; *52:* 5, 85; *104:* 159
Schields, Gretchen *75:* 171, 203
Schindelman, Joseph *1:* 74; *4:* 101; *12:* 49; *26:* 51; *40:* 146; *56:* 158; *73:* 40
Schindler, Edith *7:* 22
Schindler, S.D. *38:* 107; *46:* 196; *74:* 162; *75:* 172, 173; *99:* 133; *112:* 177; *118:* 185, 186; *121:* 71; *136:* 159; *143:* 45; *149:* 120; *156:* 30; *169:* 135; *171:* 161, 162, 163; *172:* 9
Schlesinger, Bret *7:* 77
Schmid, Eleanore *12:* 188; *126:* 196, 197
Schmiderer, Dorothy *19:* 224
Schmidt, Bill *73:* 34; *76:* 220, 222, 224
Schmidt, Elizabeth *15:* 242
Schmidt, George Paul *132:* 122
Schmidt, Karen Lee *54:* 12; *71:* 174; *92:* 56; *94:* 190, 191; *127:* 103
Schmidt, Lynette *76:* 205
Schneider, Christine M. *171:* 165
Schneider, Rex *29:* 64; *44:* 171
Schnurr, Edward *170:* 62
Schoberle, Cecile *80:* 200; *92:* 134
Schoenherr, Ian *32:* 83; *173:* 41
Schoenherr, John *1:* 146, 147, 173; *3:* 39, 139; *17:* 75; *29:* 72; *32:* 83; *37:* 168, 169, 170; *43:* 164, 165; *45:* 160, 162; *51:* 127; *66:* 196, 197, 198; *68:* 83; *72:* 240; *75:* 225; *88:* 176
Scholder, Fritz *69:* 103
Schomburg, Alex *13:* 23
Schongut, Emanuel *4:* 102; *15:* 186; *47:* 218, 219; *52:* 147, 148, 149, 150
Schoonover, Frank *17:* 107; *19:* 81, 190, 233; *22:* 88, 129; *24:* 189; *31:* 88; *41:* 69; *YABC 2:* 282, 316
Schories, Pat *164:* 210

Schottland, Miriam *22:* 172
Schramm, Ulrik *2:* 16; *14:* 112
Schreiber, Elizabeth Anne *13:* 193
Schreiber, Ralph W. *13:* 193
Schreiter, Rick *14:* 97; *23:* 171; *41:* 247; *49:* 131
Schroeder, Binette *56:* 128, 129
Schroeder, E. Peter *12:* 112
Schroeder, Ted *11:* 160; *15:* 189; *30:* 91; *34:* 43
Schrotter, Gustav *22:* 212; *30:* 225
Schubert, Dieter *101:* 167, 168
Schubert-Gabrys, Ingrid *101:* 167, 168
Schucker, James *31:* 163
Schuett, Stacey *72:* 137
Schulder, Lili *146:* 29
Schulke, Debra *57:* 167
Schulke, Flip *57:* 167
Schulz, Barbara *167:* 24
Schulz, Charles M. *10:* 137, 138, 139, 140, 141, 142; *118:* 192, 193, 194, 196, 199
Schutzer, Dena *109:* 32
Schwark, Mary Beth *51:* 155; *72:* 175
Schwartz, Amy *47:* 191; *82:* 100; *83:* 178, 179, 180, 181; *129:* 107; *131:* 197, 198
Schwartz, Carol *124:* 41; *130:* 199
Schwartz, Charles *8:* 184
Schwartz, Daniel *46:* 37
Schwartz, Joanie *124:* 170
Schwartzberg, Joan *3:* 208
Schweitzer, Iris *2:* 137; *6:* 207
Schweninger, Ann *29:* 172; *82:* 246; *159:* 202, 168: 166
Schwinger, Laurence *84:* 44; *91:* 61
Scofield, Penrod *61:* 107; *62:* 160
Scott, Anita Walker *7:* 38
Scott, Art *39:* 41
Scott, Frances Gruse *38:* 43
Scott, Julian *34:* 126
Scott, Roszel *33:* 238
Scott, Sally *87:* 27
Scott, Steve *166:* 230, 231; *171:* 93
Scott, Trudy *27:* 172
Scrace, Carolyn *143:* 95, 96
Scribner, Joanne *14:* 236; *29:* 78; *33:* 185; *34:* 208; *78:* 75; *164:* 237
Scrofani, Joseph *31:* 65; *74:* 225
Seaman, Mary Lott *34:* 64
Searle, Ronald *24:* 98; *42:* 172, 173, 174, 176, 177, 179; *66:* 73, 74; *70:* 205, 206, 207
Searle, Townley *36:* 85
Sebree, Charles *18:* 65
Sedacca, Joseph M. *11:* 25; *22:* 36
Seder, Jason *108:* 102
Seeger, Laura Vaccaro *172:* 162
Seegmiller, Don *174:* 57
Seely, David *164:* 173
Seeley, Laura L. *97:* 105
Segar, E.C. *61:* 179, 181
Segur, Adrienne *27:* 121
Seibold, J. Otto *83:* 188, 190, 191; *149:* 212, 214, 215, 216
Seignobosc, Francoise *21:* 145, 146
Sejima, Yoshimasa *8:* 187
Selig, Sylvie *13:* 199
Seltzer, Isadore *6:* 18; *133:* 59
Seltzer, Meyer *17:* 214
Selven, Maniam *144:* 133
Selway, Martina *169:* 157
Selznick, Brian *79:* 192; *104:* 25; *117:* 175; *126:* 156; *134:* 171; *158:* 76, 78; *169:* 70; *171:* 172, 173
Sempe, Jean-Jacques *47:* 92; *YABC 2:* 109
Sendak, Maurice *1:* 135, 190; *3:* 204; *7:* 142; *15:* 199; *17:* 210; *27:* 181, 182, 183, 185, 186, 187, 189, 190, 191, 192, 193, 194, 195, 197, 198, 199, 203; *28:* 181, 182; *32:* 108; *33:* 148, 149; *35:* 238; *44:* 180, 181; *45:* 97, 99; *46:* 174; *73:* 225; *91:* 10, 11 *YABC 1:* 167; *113:* 163, 165, 167, 168; *118:* 153; *127:* 161

Sengler, Johanna *18:* 256
Senn, Steve *60:* 145
Seredy, Kate *1:* 192; *14:* 20, 21; *17:* 210
Sergeant, John *6:* 74
Servello, Joe *10:* 144; *24:* 139; *40:* 91; *70:* 130, 131; *146:* 159
Seton, Ernest Thompson *18:* 260-269, 271
Seuss, Dr.
    *See* Geisel, Theodor
Severin, John Powers *7:* 62
Sewall, Marcia *15:* 8; *22:* 170; *37:* 171, 172, 173; *39:* 73; *45:* 209; *62:* 117; *69:* 185, 186; *71:* 212; *90:* 232; *96:* 127; *102:* 101; *107:* 129; *119:* 176, 177, 178, 180
Seward, James *70:* 35
Seward, Prudence *16:* 243
Sewell, Helen *3:* 186; *15:* 308; *33:* 102; *38:* 189, 190, 191, 192
Seymour, Stephen *54:* 21
Shachat, Andrew *82:* 179
Shahn, Ben *39:* 178; *46:* 193
Shalansky, Len *38:* 167
Shanks, Anne Zane *10:* 149
Shannon, David *57:* 137; *107:* 184; *112:* 216; *135:* 12; *152:* 223, 224, 225; *158:* 192
Sharp, Paul *52:* 60
Sharp, William *6:* 131; *19:* 241; *20:* 112; *25:* 141
Sharratt, Nick *102:* 207, 208; *104:* 163; *153:* 198; *175:* 176
Shaw, Barclay *74:* 14, 16; *118:* 138
Shaw, Charles *21:* 135; *38:* 187; *47:* 124; *126:* 219
Shaw, Charles G. *13:* 200
Shaw-Smith, Emma *144:* 117
Shea, Edmund *56:* 19
Shearer, Ted *43:* 193, 194, 195, 196
Shecter, Ben *16:* 244; *25:* 109; *33:* 188, 191; *41:* 77
Shed, Greg *74:* 94; *84:* 204; *129:* 149, *167:* 91
Sheeban, Chris *144:* 190; *158:* 163
Shefcik, James *48:* 221, 222; *60:* 141
Shefelman, Karl *58:* 168
Shefts, Joelle *48:* 210
Shein, Bob *139:* 189
Shekerjian, Haig *16:* 245
Shekerjian, Regina *16:* 245; *25:* 73
Shemie, Bonnie *96:* 207
Shenton, Edward *45:* 187, 188, 189; *YABC 1:* 218, 219, 221
Shepard, Ernest H. *3:* 193; *4:* 74; *16:* 101; *17:* 109; *25:* 148; *33:* 152, 199, 200, 201, 202, 203, 204, 205, 206, 207; *46:* 194; *98:* 114; *100:* 111, 178, 179, 217, 219, 220, 221; *YABC 1:* 148, 153, 174, 176, 180, 181
Shepard, Mary *4:* 210; *22:* 205; *30:* 132, 133; *54:* 150, 152, 153, 157, 158; *59:* 108, 109, 111; *100:* 246
Shepherd, Irana *171:* 112
Shepperson, Rob *96:* 153; *177:* 163
Sherman, Theresa *27:* 167
Sherwan, Earl *3:* 196
Shields, Charles *10:* 150; *36:* 63
Shields, Leonard *13:* 83, 85, 87
Shiffman, Lena *139:* 167; *168:* 136
Shigley, Neil K. *66:* 219
Shillabeer, Mary *35:* 74
Shilston, Arthur *49:* 61; *62:* 58
Shimin, Symeon *1:* 93; *2:* 128, 129; *3:* 202; *7:* 85; *11:* 177; *12:* 139; *13:* 202, 203; *27:* 138; *28:* 65; *35:* 129; *36:* 130; *48:* 151; *49:* 59; *56:* 63, 65, 153
Shine, Andrea *104:* 165; *128:* 34
Shinn, Everett *16:* 148; *18:* 229; *21:* 149, 150, 151; *24:* 218
Shinn, Florence Scovel *63:* 133, 135
Shore, Robert *27:* 54; *39:* 192, 193; *YABC 2:* 200
Shortall, Leonard *4:* 144; *8:* 196; *10:* 166; *19:* 227, 228, 229, 230; *25:* 78; *28:* 66, 167; *33:* 127; *52:* 125; *73:* 12, 212

Shortt, T.M. *27:* 36
Shpitalnik, Vladimir *83:* 194
Shropshire, Sandy *170:* 191
Shtainments, Leon *32:* 161
Shulevitz, Uri *3:* 198, 199; *17:* 85; *22:* 204; *27:* 212; *28:* 184; *50:* 190, 191, 192, 193, 194, 195, 196, 197, 198, 199, 201; *106:* 181, 182, 183; *165:* 203, 205; *166:* 138
Shupe, Bobbi *139:* 80, 81
Shute, A.B. *67:* 196
Shute, Linda *46:* 59; *74:* 118
Siberell, Anne *29:* 193
Sibley, Don *1:* 39; *12:* 196; *31:* 47
Sibthorp, Fletcher *94:* 111, 112
Sidjakov, Nicolas *18:* 274
Siebel, Fritz *3:* 120; *17:* 145
Siebold, J. Otto *158:* 227
Siegel, Hal *74:* 246
Siegl, Helen *12:* 166; *23:* 216; *34:* 185, 186
Sill, John *140:* 194; *141:* 157
Sills, Joyce *5:* 199
Silva, Simon *108:* 122
Silver, Maggie *85:* 210
Silveria, Gordon *96:* 44
Silverstein, Alvin *8:* 189
Silverstein, Shel *33:* 211; *92:* 209, 210
Silverstein, Virginia *8:* 189
Silvey, Joe *135:* 203
Simard, Remy *95:* 156
Simmons, Elly *110:* 2; *127:* 69; *134:* 181
Simon, Eric M. *7:* 82
Simon, Hilda *28:* 189
Simon, Howard *2:* 175; *5:* 132; *19:* 199; *32:* 163, 164, 165
Simont, Marc *2:* 119; *4:* 213; *9:* 168; *13:* 238, 240; *14:* 262; *16:* 179; *18:* 221; *26:* 210; *33:* 189, 194; *44:* 132; *58:* 122; *68:* 117; *73:* 204, 205, 206; *74:* 221; *126:* 199, 200; *133:* 195; *164:* 128
Sims, Agnes *54:* 152
Sims, Blanche *44:* 116; *57:* 129; *75:* 179, 180; *77:* 92; *104:* 192; *152:* 117; *156:* 160; *160:* 70; *168:* 174, 175
Singer, Edith G. *2:* 30
Singer, Gloria *34:* 56; *36:* 43
Singer, Julia *28:* 190
Siomades, Lorianne *134:* 45
Simont, Marc *163:* 40
Siracusa, Catherine *68:* 135; *82:* 218
Sis, Peter *67:* 179, 181, 183, 184, 185; *96:* 96, 98; *106:* 193, 194, 195; *149:* 224, 226
Sivard, Robert *26:* 124
Sivertson, Liz *116:* 84
Skardinski, Stanley *23:* 144; *32:* 84; *66:* 122; *84:* 108
Slackman, Charles B. *12:* 201
Slade, Paul *61:* 170
Slark, Albert *99:* 212
Slater, Rod *25:* 167
Sloan, Joseph *16:* 68
Sloane, Eric *21:* 3; *52:* 153, 154, 155, 156, 157, 158, 160
Sloat, Teri *164:* 231
Slobodkin, Louis *1:* 200; *3:* 232; *5:* 168; *13:* 251; *15:* 13, 88; *26:* 173, 174, 175, 176, 178, 179; *60:* 180
Slobodkina, Esphyr *1:* 201
Slonim, David *166:* 167, 168
Small, David *50:* 204, 205; *79:* 44; *95:* 189, 190, 191; *126:* 203, 204; *136:* 119; *143:* 201, 202, 203; *144:* 246; *150:* 5; *161:* 176
Small, W. *33:* 113
Smalley, Janet *1:* 154
Smedley, William T. *34:* 129
Smee, David *14:* 78; *62:* 30
Smee, Nicola *167:* 156
Smith, A.G., Jr. *35:* 182
Smith, Alvin *1:* 31, 229; *13:* 187; *27:* 216; *28:* 226; *48:* 149; *49:* 60
Smith, Anne Warren *41:* 212
Smith, Barry *75:* 183

Smith, Carl *36:* 41
Smith, Cat Bowman *146:* 39; *164:* 219
Smith, Craig *97:* 197; *172:* 175
Smith, Doris Susan *41:* 139
Smith, Duane *171:* 152
Smith, E. Boyd *19:* 70; *22:* 89; *26:* 63; *YABC 1:* 4, 5, 240, 248, 249
Smith, Edward J. *4:* 224
Smith, Elwood H. *157:* 231
Smith, Eunice Young *5:* 170
Smith, Gary *113:* 216
Smith, George *102:* 169
Smith, Howard *19:* 196
Smith, J. Gerard *95:* 42
Smith, Jacqueline Bardner *27:* 108; *39:* 197
Smith, Jay J. *61:* 119
Smith, Jeff *93:* 191
Smith, Jessie Willcox *15:* 91; *16:* 95; *18:* 231; *19:* 57, 242; *21:* 29, 156, 157, 158, 159, 160, 161; *34:* 65; *100:* 223; *YABC 1:* 6; *2:* 180, 185, 191, 311, 325
Smith, Jos. A. *52:* 131; *72:* 120; *74:* 151; *84:* 147, 148; *85:* 146; *87:* 96; *94:* 219; *96:* 97; *104:* 33; *108:* 126, 127, 128; *111:* 140; *136:* 145
Smith, Kenneth R. *47:* 182
Smith, Kevin Warren *89:* 112
Smith, L.H. *35:* 174
Smith, Lane *76:* 211, 213; *88:* 115; *105:* 202, 203, 204, 205; *131:* 207; *160:* 217, 221
Smith, Lee *29:* 32
Smith, Linell Nash *2:* 195
Smith, Maggie Kaufman *13:* 205; *35:* 191; *110:* 158
Smith, Mavis *101:* 219
Smith, Moishe *33:* 155
Smith, Philip *44:* 134; *46:* 203
Smith, Ralph Crosby *2:* 267; *49:* 203
Smith, Robert D. *5:* 63
Smith, Sally J. *84:* 55
Smith, Susan Carlton *12:* 208
Smith, Terry *12:* 106; *33:* 158
Smith, Virginia *3:* 157; *33:* 72
Smith, William A. *1:* 36; *10:* 154; *25:* 65
Smith-Moore, J.J. *98:* 147
Smolinski, Dick *84:* 217
Smoljan, Joe *112:* 201
Smollin, Mike *39:* 203
Smyth, Iain *105:* 207
Smyth, M. Jane *12:* 15
Smythe, Fiona *151:* 213
Smythe, Theresa *141:* 37
Snair, Andy *176:* 4
Sneed, Brad *125:* 25
Snyder, Andrew A. *30:* 212
Snyder, Jerome *13:* 207; *30:* 173
Snyder, Joel *28:* 163
So, Meilo *162:* 201
Soentpiet, Chris K. *97:* 208; *110:* 33; *159:* 184; *161:* 10; *163:* 130
Sofia *1:* 62; *5:* 90; *32:* 166; *86:* 43
Sofilas, Mark *93:* 157
Sokol, Bill *37:* 178; *49:* 23
Sokolov, Kirill *34:* 188
Solbert, Ronni *1:* 159; *2:* 232; *5:* 121; *6:* 34; *17:* 249
Solomon, Michael *174:* 115
Solonevich, George *15:* 246; *17:* 47
Soma, Liana *81:* 118
Soman, David *90:* 122; *102:* 126; *140:* 120; 93
Sommer, Robert *12:* 211
Sorel, Edward *4:* 61; *36:* 82; *65:* 191, 193; *126:* 214
Sorensen, Henrik *62:* 16
Sorensen, Svend Otto *22:* 130, 141; *67:* 188, 189
Sorra, Kristin *155:* 80
Sotomayor, Antonio *11:* 215
Souhami, Jessica *112:* 128; *176:* 193
Souza, Diana *71:* 139
Sovak, Jan *115:* 190

Soyer, Moses *20:* 177
Spaenkuch, August *16:* 28
Spafford, Suzy *160:* 228
Spain, Valerie *105:* 76
Spain, Sunday Sahara *133:* 204
Spalenka, Greg *149:* 69; *151:* 228
Spanfeller, James *1:* 72, 149; *2:* 183; *19:* 230, 231, 232; *22:* 66; *36:* 160, 161; *40:* 75; *52:* 166; *76:* 37
Sparks, Mary Walker *15:* 247
Speidel, Sandra *78:* 233; *94:* 178; *134:* 180
Speirs, John *67:* 178
Spence, Geraldine *21:* 163; *47:* 196
Spence, Jim *38:* 89; *50:* 102
Spencer, Laurie *113:* 12
Spencer, Mark *57:* 170
Spengler, Kenneth J. *146:* 256
Sperling, Andrea *133:* 182
Spiegel, Doris *29:* 111
Spiegelman, Art *109:* 227
Spier, Jo *10:* 30
Spier, Peter *3:* 155; *4:* 200; *7:* 61; *11:* 78; *38:* 106; *54:* 120, 121, 122, 123, 124, 125, 126, 127, 128, 129, 130, 131, 132, 133, 134
Spilka, Arnold *5:* 120; *6:* 204; *8:* 131
Spirin, Gennady *95:* 196, 197; *113:* 172; *128:* 9; *129:* 49; *134:* 210; *153:* 9
Spivak, I. Howard *8:* 10; *13:* 172
Spohn, David *72:* 233
Spohn, Kate *87:* 195; *147:* 201, 202
Spollen, Christopher J. *12:* 214
Spooner, Malcolm *40:* 142
Spowart, Robin *82:* 228; *92:* 149; *133:* 131; *176:* 163; *177:* 183, 184
Sprague, Kevin *150:* 60
Sprattler, Rob *12:* 176
Spring, Bob *5:* 60
Spring, Ira *5:* 60
Springer, Harriet *31:* 92
Spudvilas, Anne *110:* 74
Spurll, Barbara *78:* 199; *88:* 141, 142; *99:* 215
Spurrier, Steven *28:* 198
Spuvilas, Anne *85:* 114
Spy
  *See* Ward, Leslie
Squires, Stuart *127:* 74
St. John, J. Allen *41:* 62
Stabin, Victor *101:* 131; *164:* 158
Stadler, John *62:* 33
Staffan, Alvin E. *11:* 56; *12:* 187
Stahl, Ben *5:* 181; *12:* 91; *49:* 122; *71:* 128; *87:* 206; *112:* 107
Stair, Gobin *35:* 214
Stallwood, Karen *73:* 126
Stamaty, Mark Alan *12:* 215
Stammen, JoEllen McAllister *113:* 14
Stampnick, Ken *51:* 142
Stanbridge, Joanne *150:* 91
Stanley, Diane *3:* 45; *37:* 180; *80:* 217, 219
Stanley, Sanna *145:* 228
Starcke, Helmut *86:* 217
Starr, Branka *73:* 25
Stasiak, Krystyna *49:* 181; *64:* 194
Staub, Leslie *103:* 54
Staunton, Ted *112:* 192
Stawicki, Matt *164:* 250
Stead, L. *55:* 51, 56
Steadman, Broeck *97:* 185, 186; *99:* 56; *121:* 48
Steadman, Ralph *32:* 180; *123:* 143, 145
Steckler, June *90:* 178
Steele, Robert Gantt *169:* 174
Steichen, Edward *30:* 79
Steig, William *18:* 275, 276; *70:* 215, 216, 217, 218; *111:* 173, 174, 175, 176, 177
Stein, Harve *1:* 109
Steinberg, Saul *47:* 193
Steinel, William *23:* 146
Steiner, Charlotte *45:* 196
Steiner, Joan *110:* 219
Steirnagel, Michael *80:* 56

Stemp, Eric *60:* 184
Stephens, Alice Barber *66:* 208, 209
Stephens, Charles H. *YABC 2:* 279
Stephens, Pat *126:* 110; *128:* 101
Stephens, William M. *21:* 165
Steptoe, Javaka *151:* 203, 204
Steptoe, John *8:* 197; *57:* 9; *63:* 158, 159, 160, 161, 163, 164, 165, 166, 167; *96:* 4; *105:* 87
Stern, Simon *15:* 249, 250; *17:* 58; *34:* 192, 193
Sterret, Jane *53:* 27
Stetsios, Debbie *165:* 108, 109
Steven, Kat *158:* 237
Stevens, David *62:* 44
Stevens, Janet *40:* 126; *57:* 10, 11; *80:* 112; *90:* 221, 222; *109:* 156; *130:* 34; *166:* 202; *176:* 53, 116
Stevens, Mary *11:* 193; *13:* 129; *43:* 95
Stevenson, Harvey *66:* 143; *80:* 201, 221; *153:* 60
Stevenson, James *42:* 182, 183; *51:* 163; *66:* 184; *71:* 185, 187, 188; *78:* 262; *87:* 97; *113:* 182, 183, 184, 185; *161:* 182, 183
Stevenson, Sucie *92:* 27; *104:* 194, 195; *112:* 168; *160:* 202
Stewart, April Blair *75:* 210
Stewart, Arvis *33:* 98; *36:* 69; *60:* 118; *75:* 91; *127:* 4
Stewart, Charles *2:* 205
Stewart, Joel *151:* 205
Stieg, William *172:* 58
Stiles, Fran *26:* 85; *78:* 56; *82:* 150
Stillman, Susan *44:* 130; *76:* 83
Stimpson, Tom *49:* 171
Stinemetz, Morgan *40:* 151
Stinson, Paul *110:* 86
Stirnweis, Shannon *10:* 164
Stites, Joe *86:* 96
Stobbs, William *1:* 48, 49; *3:* 68; *6:* 20; *17:* 117, 217; *24:* 150; *29:* 250; *60:* 179; *87:* 204, 205, 206
Stock, Catherine *37:* 55; *65:* 198; *72:* 7; *99:* 225; *114:* 197, 198, 199; *126:* 3; *145:* 161; *161:* 82; *173:* 149
Stockman, Jack *113:* 24
Stoeke, Janet Morgan *90:* 225; *136:* 196
Stoerrle, Tom *55:* 147
Stolp, Jaap *49:* 98
Stolp, Todd *89:* 195
Stone, David L. *87:* 154
Stone, David *9:* 173
Stone, David K. *4:* 38; *6:* 124; *9:* 180; *43:* 182; *60:* 70
Stone, Helen V. *6:* 209
Stone, Helen *44:* 121, 122, 126
Stone, Kazuko G. *134:* 43
Stone, Phoebe *86:* 212; *134:* 213; *162:* 188
Stone, Steve *166:* 213
Stone, Tony *150:* 34, 35
Stoud, Virginia A. *89:* 31
Stover, Jill *82:* 234
Stratton, Helen *33:* 151
Stratton-Porter, Gene *15:* 254, 259, 263, 264, 268, 269
Streano, Vince *20:* 173
Street, Janet Travell *84:* 235
Streeter, Clive *121:* 2
Stringer, Lauren *129:* 187; *154:* 172, 173; *161:* 127
Strodl, Daniel *47:* 95
Strogart, Alexander *63:* 139
Stromoski, Rick *111:* 179; *124:* 161, 190
Strong, Joseph D., Jr. *YABC 2:* 330
Stroyer, Poul *13:* 221
Strugnell, Ann *27:* 38
Struzan, Drew *117:* 6
Stubbs, William *73:* 196
Stubis, Talivaldis *5:* 182, 183; *10:* 45; *11:* 9; *18:* 304; *20:* 127
Stubley, Trevor *14:* 43; *22:* 219; *23:* 37; *28:* 61; *87:* 26

Stuck, Marion *104:* 44
Stuecklen, Karl W. *8:* 34, 65; *23:* 103
Stull, Betty *11:* 46
Stutzman, Mark *119:* 99
Stutzmann, Laura *73:* 185
Suarez, Maribel *162:* 208
Suba, Susanne *4:* 202, 203; *14:* 261; *23:* 134; *29:* 222; *32:* 30
Sueling, Barbara *98:* 185
Sueling, Gwenn *98:* 186
Sugarman, Tracy *3:* 76; *8:* 199; *37:* 181, 182
Sugimoto, Yugo *170:* 144
Sugita, Yutaka *36:* 180, 181
Suh, John *80:* 157
Sullivan, Dorothy *89:* 113
Sullivan, Edmund J. *31:* 86
Sullivan, James F. *19:* 280; *20:* 192
Sully, Tom *104:* 199, 200
Sumichrast, Jozef *14:* 253; *29:* 168, 213
Sumiko *46:* 57
Summers, Leo *1:* 177; *2:* 273; *13:* 22
Summers, Mark *118:* 144
Sutton, Judith *94:* 164
Svarez, Juan *56:* 113
Svolinsky, Karel *17:* 104
Swain, Carol *172:* 182
Swain, Su Zan Noguchi *21:* 170
Swan, Susan *22:* 220, 221; *37:* 66; *60:* 146; *145:* 205
Swann, Susan *86:* 55
Swanson, Karl *79:* 65; *89:* 186
Swayne, Sam *53:* 143, 145
Swayne, Zoa *53:* 143, 145
Swearingen, Greg *152:* 56; *165:* 135; *173:* 2
Sweat, Lynn *25:* 206; *57:* 176; *73:* 184; *168:* 178
Sweet, Darrell K. *60:* 9; *69:* 86; *74:* 15; *75:* 215; *76:* 130, 131; *81:* 96, 122; *82:* 253; *83:* 11; *84:* 14; *85:* 37; *89:* 140; *90:* 6; *91:* 137, 139; *95:* 160, 161; *126:* 25
Sweet, Darrell K. *1:* 163; *4:* 136; *164:* 175
Sweet, Melissa *71:* 94; *72:* 172; *111:* 82; *139:* 53, 58; *141:* 88; *142:* 231; *155:* 121; *159:* 121, 122; *172:* 185
Sweet, Ozzie *31:* 149, 151, 152
Sweetland, Robert *12:* 194
Swiatkowska, Gabi *132:* 43; *175:* 139
Swope, Martha *43:* 160; *56:* 86, 87, 89
Sylvada, Peter *154:* 174
Sylvester, Natalie G. *22:* 222
Szafran, Gene *24:* 144
Szasz, Susanne *13:* 55, 226; *14:* 48
Szekeres, Cyndy *2:* 218; *5:* 185; *8:* 85; *11:* 166; *14:* 19; *16:* 57, 159; *26:* 49, 214; *34:* 205; *60:* 150, 151, 152, 153, 154; *73:* 224; *74:* 218; *131:* 213, 215
Szpura, Beata *81:* 68; *119:* 65; *168:* 201

**T**

Taback, Simms *40:* 207; *52:* 120; *57:* 34; *80:* 241; *104:* 202, 203; *170:* 176, 177
Taber, Patricia *75:* 124
Tabor, Nancy Maria Grande *89:* 210; *161:* 188
Taddei, Richard *112:* 13, 14
Tadgell, Nicole *150:* 77; *161:* 20; *177:* 186
Tadiello, Ed *133:* 200
Tafuri, Nancy *39:* 210; *75:* 199, 200; *92:* 75; *130:* 215, 216, 217
Tailfeathers, Gerald *86:* 85
Tait, Douglas *12:* 220; *74:* 105, 106
Takabayashi, Mari *113:* 112; *130:* 22; *156:* 169
Takahashi, Hideko *136:* 160
Takakjian, Portia *15:* 274
Takashima, Shizuye *13:* 228
Talarczyk, June *4:* 173
Talbott, Hudson *84:* 240; *163:* 100
Tallarico, Tony *116:* 197

Tallon, Robert *2:* 228; *43:* 200, 201, 202, 203, 204, 205, 206, 207, 209
Tamas, Szecsko *29:* 135
Tamburine, Jean *12:* 222
Tandy, H.R. *13:* 69
Tandy, Russell H. *65:* 9; *100:* 30, 131
Tang, Charles *81:* 202; *90:* 192
Tang, Susan *80:* 174; *108:* 158
Tang, You-shan *63:* 100
Tankersley, Paul *69:* 206; *133:* 219
Tannenbaum, Robert *48:* 181
Tanner, Jane *87:* 13; *97:* 37
Tanner, Tim *72:* 192; *84:* 35
Tanobe, Miyuki *23:* 221
Tarabay, Sharif *110:* 149; *113:* 123; *169:* 83
Tarkington, Booth *17:* 224, 225
Tarlow, Phyllis *61:* 198
Tate, Don *159:* 141, 191
Tauss, Herbert *95:* 179
Tauss, Marc *117:* 160; *126:* 155
Tavares, Matt *159:* 192, 193
Taylor, Ann *41:* 226
Taylor, Dahl *129:* 157
Taylor, Geoff *93:* 156
Taylor, Isaac *41:* 228
Taylor, Mike *143:* 99, 100
Teague, Mark *83:* 6; *139:* 241; *170:* 180, 181
Teale, Edwin Way *7:* 196
Teason, James *1:* 14
Teeple, Lyn *33:* 147
Tee-Van, Helen Damrosch *10:* 176; *11:* 182
Teicher, Dick *50:* 211
Teichman, Mary *77:* 220; *124:* 208; *127:* 22
Temertey, Ludmilla *96:* 232; *104:* 43, 45; *109:* 244
Tempest, Margaret *3:* 237, 238; *88:* 200
Temple, Frances *85:* 185, 186, 187
Temple, Herbert *45:* 201
Templeton, Owen *11:* 77
Tenggren, Gustaf *18:* 277, 278, 279; *19:* 15; *28:* 86; *YABC 2:* 145
Tennent, Julie *81:* 105
Tenneson, Joyce *153:* 166
Tenney, Gordon *24:* 204
Tenniel, John *74:* 234, 235; *100:* 89; *YABC 2:* 99; *153:* 63
Tepper, Matt *116:* 80
Terkel, Ari *103:* 162
Terry, Will *131:* 73
Teskey, Donald *71:* 51
Thacher, Mary M. *30:* 72
Thackeray, William Makepeace *23:* 224, 228
Thamer, Katie *42:* 187
Tharlet, Eve *146:* 149
Thelwell, Norman *14:* 201
Theobalds, Prue *40:* 23
Theurer, Marilyn Churchill *39:* 195
Thiesing, Lisa *89:* 134; *95:* 202; *156:* 190; *159:* 195
Thiewes, Sam *133:* 114
Thistlethwaite, Miles *12:* 224
Thollander, Earl *11:* 47; *18:* 112; *22:* 224
Thomas, Allan *22:* 13
Thomas, Art *48:* 217
Thomas, Eric *28:* 49
Thomas, Harold *20:* 98
Thomas, Jacqui *125:* 95
Thomas, Mark *42:* 136
Thomas, Martin *14:* 255
Thomas, Middy *177:* 114
Thompson, Arthur *34:* 107
Thompson, Carol *85:* 189; *95:* 75; *102:* 86; *147:* 166
Thompson, Colin *95:* 204
Thompson, Ellen *51:* 88, 151; *60:* 33; *67:* 42; *77:* 148; *78:* 75, 219; *79:* 122, 170; *84:* 219; *85:* 97; *87:* 37; *88:* 192, 194; *89:* 80; *93:* 37; *98:* 59; *132:* 14
Thompson, George W. *22:* 18; *28:* 150; *33:* 135

Thompson, John *58:* 201; *102:* 226; *124:* 154; *128:* 228; *129:* 157; *150:* 49
Thompson, Julie *44:* 158
Thompson, Katherine *132:* 146
Thompson, K. Dyble *84:* 6
Thompson, Miles *152:* 77
Thompson, Sharon *74:* 113; *158:* 60; *165:* 87
Thomson, Arline K. *3:* 264
Thomson, Hugh *26:* 88
Thomson, Ross *36:* 179
Thorkelson, Gregg *95:* 183, 184; *98:* 58; *165:* 30, 31
Thornberg, Dan *104:* 125
Thornburgh, Rebecca McKillip *143:* 37
Thorne, Diana *25:* 212
Thornhill, Jan *77:* 213
Thorpe, Peter *58:* 109
Thorvall, Kerstin *13:* 235
Threadgall, Colin *77:* 215
Thurber, James *13:* 239, 242, 243, 245, 248, 249
Thurman, Mark *63:* 173; *168:* 116
Tibbles, Jean-Paul *115:* 200
Tibbles, Paul *45:* 23
Tibo, Gilles *67:* 207; *107:* 199, 201
Tichenor, Tom *14:* 207
Tichnor, Richard *90:* 218
Tiegreen, Alan *36:* 143; *43:* 55, 56, 58; *77:* 200; *94:* 216, 217; *121:* 54, 59
Tierney, Tom *113:* 198, 200, 201
Tilley, Debbie *102:* 134; *133:* 226; *137:* 101; *159:* 96
Tilney, F.C. *22:* 231
Timbs, Gloria *36:* 90
Timmins, Harry *2:* 171
Tinkelman, Murray *12:* 225; *35:* 44
Titherington, Jeanne *39:* 90; *58:* 138; *75:* 79; *135:* 161
Tobin, Nancy *145:* 197
Toddy, Irving *172:* 144
Tolbert, Jeff *128:* 69
Tolford, Joshua *1:* 221
Tolkien, J.R.R. *2:* 243; *32:* 215
Tolmie, Ken *15:* 292
Tomei, Lorna *47:* 168, 171
Tomes, Jacqueline *2:* 117; *12:* 139
Tomes, Margot *1:* 224; *2:* 120, 121; *16:* 207; *18:* 250; *20:* 7; *25:* 62; *27:* 78, 79; *29:* 81, 199; *33:* 82; *36:* 186, 187, 188, 189, 190; *46:* 129; *56:* 71; *58:* 183; *70:* 228; *75:* 73, 75; *80:* 80; *83:* 97; *90:* 205
Toner, Raymond John *10:* 179
Tong, Gary *66:* 215
Tongier, Stephen *82:* 32
Tooke, Susan *173:* 162
Toothill, Harry *6:* 54; *7:* 49; *25:* 219; *42:* 192
Toothill, Ilse *6:* 54
Topolski, Feliks *44:* 48
Torbert, Floyd James *22:* 226
Torgersen, Don *55:* 157
Torline, Kevin *169:* 171
Torrecilla, Pablo *176:* 207
Torres, Leyla *156:* 199, 201
Torrey, Helen *87:* 41
Torrey, Marjorie *34:* 105
Toschik, Larry *6:* 102
Totten, Bob *13:* 93
Toy, Julie *128:* 112
Trachok, Cathy *131:* 16
Tracy, Libba *82:* 24
Trago, Keith *158:* 253
Trail, Lee *55:* 157
Trang, To Ngoc *167:* 180
Trang, Winson *89:* 151
Trapani, Iza *116:* 202
Travers, Bob *49:* 100; *63:* 145
Treatner, Meryl *95:* 180
Tremain, Ruthven *17:* 238
Tresilian, Stuart *25:* 53; *40:* 212
Trez, Alain *17:* 236

Trezzo, Loretta *86:* 45
Trier, Walter *14:* 96
Trimby, Elisa *47:* 199
Trinkle, Sally *53:* 27
Tripp, F.J. *24:* 167
Tripp, Wallace *2:* 48; *7:* 28; *8:* 94; *10:* 54, 76; *11:* 92; *31:* 170, 171; *34:* 203; *42:* 57; *60:* 157; *73:* 182
Trivas, Irene *53:* 4; *54:* 168; *82:* 46, 101
Trnka, Jiri *22:* 151; *43:* 212, 213, 214, 215; *YABC 1:* 30, 31
Troughton, Joanna *37:* 186; *48:* 72
Troyer, Johannes *3:* 16; *7:* 18
Trudeau, G.B. *35:* 220, 221, 222; *48:* 119, 123, 126, 127, 128, 129, 133; *168:* 189
Trueman, Matthew *165:* 208
Truesdell, Sue *55:* 142; *108:* 219, 220
Tryon, Leslie *84:* 7; *139:* 214; *143:* 10
Tseng, Jean *72:* 195; *94:* 102; *119:* 126; *151:* 106; *173:* 138, 139
Tseng, Mou-sien *72:* 195; *94:* 102; *119:* 126; *151:* 106; *173:* 138, 139
Tsinajinie, Andy *2:* 62
Tsugami, Kyuzo *18:* 198, 199
Tucker, Ezra *156:* 31
Tuckwell, Jennifer *17:* 205
Tudor, Bethany *7:* 103
Tudor, Tasha *18:* 227; *20:* 185, 186, 187; *36:* 111; *69:* 196, 198; *100:* 44; *YABC 2:* 46, 314; *160:* 234
Tuerk, Hanne *71:* 201
Tulloch, Maurice *24:* 79
Tunis, Edwin *1:* 218, 219; *28:* 209, 210, 211, 212
Tunnicliffe, C.F. *62:* 176; *177:* 178, 179; *181*
Turkle, Brinton *1:* 211, 213; *2:* 249; *3:* 226; *11:* 3; *16:* 209; *20:* 22; *50:* 23; *67:* 50; *68:* 65; *79:* 205, 206, 207; *128:* 47; *YABC 1:* 79
Turnbull, Christopher J. *143:* 99, 100
Turner, Gwenda *59:* 195
Turska, Krystyna *12:* 103; *31:* 173, 174, 175; *56:* 32, 34; *100:* 66
Tusa, Tricia *72:* 242; *111:* 180, 181; *157:* 165; *164:* 186
Tusan, Stan *6:* 58; *22:* 236, 237
Tworkov, Jack *47:* 207
Tyers, Jenny *89:* 220
Tylden-Wright, Jenny *114:* 119
Tyrol, Adelaide Murphy *103:* 27
Tyrrell, Frances *107:* 204
Tzimoulis, Paul *12:* 104

**U**

Uchida, Yoshiko *1:* 220
Uderzo *47:* 88
Ueno, Noriko *59:* 155
Ulm, Robert *17:* 238
Ulrich, George *73:* 15; *75:* 136, 139; *99:* 150
Ulriksen, Mark *101:* 58
Unada *84:* 67
*See* Gliewe, Unada
Underhill, Liz *53:* 159
Underwood, Clarence *40:* 166
Unger, Jim *67:* 208
Ungerer, Tomi *5:* 188; *9:* 40; *18:* 188; *29:* 175; *33:* 221, 222, 223, 225; *71:* 48; *106:* 209, 210, 211, 212
Unwin, Nora S. *3:* 65, 234, 235; *4:* 237; *44:* 173, 174; *YABC 1:* 59; *2:* 301
Upitis, Alvis *145:* 179
Urban, Helle *149:* 243
Urbanovic, Jackie *86:* 86
Uris, Jill *49:* 188, 197
Ursell, Martin *50:* 51
Utpatel, Frank *18:* 114
Utz, Lois *5:* 190

**V**

Vagin, Vladimir *66:* 10; *142:* 215
Vaillancourt, Francois *107:* 199
Vainio, Pirkko *123:* 157, 158
Vallejo, Boris *62:* 130; *72:* 212; *91:* 38; *93:* 61
Van Abbe, S. *16:* 142; *18:* 282; *31:* 90; *YABC 2:* 157, 161
Van Allsburg, Chris *37:* 205, 206; *53:* 161, 162, 163, 165, 166, 167, 168, 169, 170, 171; *105:* 215, 216, 217, 218; *156:* 176, 177, 178
Vance, James *65:* 28
Van Der Linde, Henry *99:* 17
van der Meer, Ron *98:* 204, 205
van der Meer, Atie *98:* 204, 205
Vandivert, William *21:* 175
Van Dongen, H.R. *81:* 97
Van Dusen, Chris W. *173:* 169
Van Everen, Jay *13:* 160; *YABC 1:* 121
Van Fleet, John *165:* 12, 13
Van Frankenhuyzen, Gijsbert *145:* 230; *149:* 164
van Genechten, Guido *165:* 226
Van Horn, William *43:* 218
van Lawick, Hugo *62:* 76, 79
Van Loon, Hendrik Willem *18:* 285, 289, 291
Van Munching, Paul *83:* 85
Van Rynbach, Iris *102:* 192
Van Sciver, Ruth *37:* 162
VanSeveren, Joe *63:* 182
Van Stockum, Hilda *5:* 193
Van Wely, Babs *16:* 50; *79:* 16
Van Wright, Cornelius *72:* 18; *102:* 208; *116:* 107; *152:* 236; *173:* 170, 171
Van Zyle, Jon *103:* 125; *160:* 181, 182; *176:* 199, 200
Vardzigulyants, Ruben *90:* 54
Varga, Judy *29:* 196
Vargo, Kurt *79:* 224
Varley, Susan *61:* 199; *63:* 176, 177; *101:* 148; *134:* 220
Vasconcellos, Daniel *80:* 42
Vasiliu, Mircea *2:* 166, 253; *9:* 166; *13:* 58; *68:* 42
Vaughn, Frank *34:* 157
Vavra, Robert *8:* 206
Vawter, Will *17:* 163
Vayas, Diana *71:* 61
Vazquez, Carlos *125:* 184
Veeder, Larry *18:* 4
Velasquez, Eric *45:* 217; *61:* 45; *63:* 110, 111; *88:* 162; *90:* 34, 144; *94:* 213; *107:* 147; *132:* 192; *138:* 213; *159:* 126
Velasquez, Jose A. *63:* 73
Velez, Walter *71:* 75; *91:* 154; *121:* 181; *168:* 49
Velthuijs, Max *110:* 228, 229
Vendrell, Carme Sole *42:* 205
Venezia, Mike *54:* 17
Venti, Anthony Bacon *124:* 103; *126:* 26
Venturo, Piero *61:* 194, 195
Ver Beck, Frank *18:* 16, 17
Verkaaik, Ben *110:* 209
Verling, John *71:* 27
Verney, John *14:* 225; *75:* 8
Verrier, Suzanne *5:* 20; *23:* 212
Versace, Marie *2:* 255
Verstraete, Randy *108:* 193
Vestal, H.B. *9:* 134; *11:* 101; *27:* 25; *34:* 158
Vicatan *59:* 146
Vickrey, Robert *45:* 59, 64
Victor, Joan Berg *30:* 193
Viereck, Ellen *3:* 242; *14:* 229
Vigna, Judith *15:* 293; *102:* 194, 195, 196, 197
Vilato, Gaspar E. *5:* 41
Villiard, Paul *51:* 178
Vimnera, A. *23:* 154
Vincent, Eric *34:* 98
Vincent, Felix *41:* 237
Vincent, Gabrielle *121:* 175

Vip *45:* 164
Viskupic, Gary *83:* 48
Vitale, Stefano *109:* 71, 107; *114:* 219, 220;
    *123:* 106; *138:* 232
Vivas, Julie *51:* 67, 69; *96:* 225
Voake, Charlotte *114:* 221, 222
Vo-Dinh, Mai *16:* 272; *60:* 191
Vogel, Ilse-Margret *14:* 230
Voigt, Erna *35:* 228
Vojnar, Kamil *95:* 31; *114:* 4; *115:* 62; *121:*
    90; *124:* 72; *130:* 31; *141:* 81; *146:* 196;
    *150:* 123; *158:* 5, 6; *158:* 154; *171:* 119, 188
Vojtech, Anna *42:* 190; *108:* 222, 223; *150:*
    203; *174:* 173
von Buhler, Cynthia *149:* 237; *162:* 177; *177:*
    205
von Roehl, Angela *126:* 191
von Schmidt, Eric *8:* 62; *50:* 209, 210
von Schmidt, Harold *30:* 80
Vosburgh, Leonard *1:* 161; *7:* 32; *15:* 295,
    296; *23:* 110; *30:* 214; *43:* 181
Voss, Tom *127:* 104
Voter, Thomas W. *19:* 3, 9
Vroman, Tom *10:* 29
Vulliamy, Clara *72:* 65

### W

Waber, Bernard *47:* 209, 210, 211, 212, 213,
    214; *95:* 215, 216, 217; *156:* 203, 205, 206,
    207
Wack, Jeff *95:* 140; *110:* 90
Wagner, John *8:* 200; *52:* 104
Wagner, Ken *2:* 59
Waide, Jan *29:* 225; *36:* 139
Wainwright, Jerry *14:* 85
Waites, Joan C. *171:* 2
Wakeen, Sandra *47:* 97
Wakiyama, Hanako *171:* 96
Waldherr, Kris *81:* 186
Waldman, Bruce *15:* 297; *43:* 178
Waldman, Neil *35:* 141; *50:* 163; *51:* 180; *54:*
    78; *77:* 112; *79:* 162; *82:* 174; *84:* 5, 56,
    106; *94:* 232, 233, 234; *96:* 41; *111:* 139;
    *113:* 9; *118:* 30; *142:* 220, 223
Waldrep, Richard *111:* 147
Walker, Brian *144:* 128
Walker, Charles *1:* 46; *4:* 59; *5:* 177; *11:* 115;
    *19:* 45; *34:* 74; *62:* 168; *72:* 218
Walker, Dugald Stewart *15:* 47; *32:* 202; *33:*
    112
Walker, Gil *8:* 49; *23:* 132; *34:* 42
Walker, Jeff *55:* 154; *123:* 116
Walker, Jim *10:* 94
Walker, Mort *8:* 213
Walker, Norman *41:* 37; *45:* 58
Walker, Stephen *12:* 229; *21:* 174
Wallace, Beverly Dobrin *19:* 259
Wallace, Cly *87:* 93
Wallace, Ian *53:* 176, 177; *56:* 165, 166; *58:*
    4; *98:* 4; *101:* 191; *112:* 124; *141:* 197, 198,
    199, 200; *151:* 212
Wallace, John *105:* 228
Wallace, Nancy Elizabeth *141:* 204
Wallenta, Adam *123:* 180
Waller, S.E. *24:* 36
Wallner, Alexandra *15:* 120; *156:* 183
Wallner, John C. *9:* 77; *10:* 188; *11:* 28; *14:*
    209; *31:* 56, 118; *37:* 64; *51:* 186, 187, 188,
    189, 190, 191, 192, 193, 194, 195; *52:* 96;
    *53:* 23, 26; *71:* 99; *73:* 158; *89:* 215; *141:* 9
Wallner, John *162:* 17
Wallower, Lucille *11:* 226
Walotsky, Ron *93:* 87
Walsh, Ellen Stoll *99:* 209; *147:* 219
Walsh, Rebecca *158:* 193
Walsh, Vivian *149:* 215; *158:* 227
Walters, Audrey *18:* 294
Walther, Tom *31:* 179

Walton, Garry *69:* 149
Walton, Tony *11:* 164; *24:* 209; *153:* 8; *177:*
    73
Waltrip, Lela *9:* 195
Waltrip, Mildred *3:* 209; *37:* 211
Waltrip, Rufus *9:* 195
Wan *12:* 76
Warburton, Sarah *154:* 187
Wappers, G. *121:* 40
Ward, Fred *52:* 19
Ward, Helen *72:* 244; *144:* 240, 242
Ward, John *42:* 191; *96:* 54; *97:* 110; *123:*
    105; *124:* 71; *173:* 66
Ward, Keith *2:* 107; *132:* 69
Ward, Leslie *34:* 126; *36:* 87
Ward, Lynd *1:* 99, 132, 133, 150; *2:* 108, 158,
    196, 259; *18:* 86; *27:* 56; *29:* 79, 187, 253,
    255; *36:* 199, 200, 201, 202, 203, 204, 205,
    206, 207, 209; *43:* 34; *56:* 28; *60:* 116; *100:*
    65
Ward, Peter *37:* 116
Waring, Geoff *172:* 84
Warhola, James *92:* 5; *115:* 85, 87; *118:* 174,
    175, 177; *176:* 84
Warner, Ben *159:* 171
Warner, Peter *14:* 87
Warnes, Tim *175:* 159
Warnick, Elsa *113:* 223
Warren, Betsy *2:* 101
Warren, Jim *85:* 81
Warren, Marion Cray *14:* 215
Warshaw, Jerry *30:* 197, 198; *42:* 165
Wasden, Kevin *102:* 162
Washington, Nevin *20:* 123
Washington, Phyllis *20:* 123
Wasserman, Amy L. *92:* 110
Waterman, Stan *11:* 76
Watkins-Pitchford, D.J. *6:* 215, 217
Watling, James *67:* 210; *78:* 112; *101:* 81;
    *117:* 189, 190; *127:* 119, 120
Watson, Aldren A. *2:* 267; *5:* 94; *13:* 71; *19:*
    253; *32:* 220; *42:* 193, 194, 195, 196, 197,
    198, 199, 200, 201; *YABC 2:* 202
Watson, G. *83:* 162
Watson, Gary *19:* 147; *36:* 68; *41:* 122; *47:*
    139
Watson, J.D. *22:* 86
Watson, Karen *11:* 26
Watson, Mary *117:* 193
Watson, Richard Jesse *62:* 188, 189
Watson, Wendy *5:* 197; *13:* 101; *33:* 116; *46:*
    163; *64:* 12; *74:* 242, 243; *91:* 21; *142:* 228
Watt, Melanie *136:* 206
Wattenberg, Jane *174:* 200
Watterson, Bill *66:* 223, 225, 226
Watts, Bernadette *4:* 227; *103:* 182, 183
Watts, James *59:* 197; *74:* 145; *86:* 124
Watts, John *37:* 149
Watts, Leslie Elizabeth *150:* 207; *165:* 106
Watts, Stan *116:* 205
Weatherby, Mark Alan *77:* 141
Webb, Jennifer *110:* 79
Webb, Lanny *142:* 175
Webb, Sophie *135:* 214
Webber, Helen *3:* 141
Webber, Irma E. *14:* 238
Weber, Erik *56:* 19, 20
Weber, Florence *40:* 153
Weber, Jill *127:* 227, 228
Weber, Roland *61:* 204
Weber, William J. *14:* 239
Webster, Jean *17:* 241
Weeks, Sarah *162:* 39
Wegman, William *78:* 243
Wegner, Fritz *14:* 250; *20:* 189; *44:* 165; *86:*
    62
Weidenear, Reynold H. *21:* 122
Weigel, Jeff *170:* 193
Weihs, Erika *4:* 21; *15:* 299; *72:* 201; *107:*
    207, 208

Weil, Lisl *7:* 203; *10:* 58; *21:* 95; *22:* 188,
    217; *33:* 193
Weiman, Jon *50:* 162, 165; *52:* 103; *54:* 78,
    79, 81; *78:* 80; *82:* 107; *93:* 82; *97:* 69; *105:*
    179
Weiner, Sandra *14:* 240
Weiner, Scott *55:* 27
Weinhaus, Karen Ann *53:* 90; *71:* 50; *86:* 124
Weisgard, Leonard *1:* 65; *2:* 191, 197, 204,
    264, 265; *5:* 108; *21:* 42; *30:* 200, 201, 203,
    204; *41:* 47; *44:* 125; *53:* 25; *85:* 196, 198,
    200, 201; *100:* 139, 207; *YABC 2:* 13
Weisman, David *173:* 47
Weiss, Ellen *44:* 202
Weiss, Emil *1:* 168; *7:* 60
Weiss, Harvey *1:* 145, 223; *27:* 224, 227; *68:*
    214; *76:* 245, 246, 247
Weiss, Nicki *33:* 229
Weissman, Bari *49:* 72; *90:* 125; *139:* 142
Weitzman, David L. *172:* 199
Welch, Sheila Kelly *130:* 221
Welkes, Allen *68:* 218
Wellington, Monica *99:* 223; *157:* 259, 260,
    261
Welliver, Norma *76:* 94
Wellner, Fred *127:* 53
Wells, Frances *1:* 183
Wells, H.G. *20:* 194, 200
Wells, Haru *53:* 120, 121
Wells, Rosemary *6:* 49; *18:* 297; *60:* 32; *66:*
    203; *69:* 215, 216; *114:* 227; *118:* 149, 150;
    *156:* 188, 189, 190, 191
Wells, Rufus III *56:* 111, 113
Wells, Susan *22:* 43
Wendelin, Rudolph *23:* 234
Wengenroth, Stow *37:* 47
Werenskiold, Erik *15:* 6; *62:* 17
Werner, Honi *24:* 110; *33:* 41; *88:* 122
Werth, Kurt *7:* 122; *14:* 157; *20:* 214; *39:* 128
West, Harry A. *124:* 38
Westcott, Nadine Bernard *68:* 46; *84:* 49; *86:*
    133; *106:* 199; *111:* 78; *113:* 111; *130:* 224;
    *139:* 54; *158:* 256
Westerberg, Christine *29:* 226
Westerduin, Anne *105:* 229
Westerman, Johanna *162:* 206
Weston, Martha *29:* 116; *30:* 213; *33:* 85, 100;
    *53:* 181, 182, 183, 184; *77:* 95; *80:* 152;
    *119:* 196, 197, 198, 199; *127:* 189; *133:* 196
Wetherbee, Margaret *5:* 3
Wexler, Jerome *49:* 73; *150:* 129
Whalley, Peter *50:* 49
Wheatley, Arabelle *11:* 231; *16:* 276
Wheeler, Cindy *49:* 205
Wheeler, Dora *44:* 179
Wheelright, Rowland *15:* 81; *YABC 2:* 286
Whelan, Michael *56:* 108; *70:* 27, 29, 67, 68,
    148; *74:* 18; *84:* 14; *91:* 195, 196; *95:* 147;
    *98:* 150, 151; *106:* 157; *113:* 218, 220; *116:*
    99, 100
Whelan, Patrick *135:* 145
Whistler, Rex *16:* 75; *30:* 207, 208
White, Craig *110:* 130; *119:* 193; *130:* 33
White, David Omar *5:* 56; *18:* 6
White, Joan *83:* 225
White, Martin *51:* 197; *85:* 127
Whitear *32:* 26
Whitehead, Beck *86:* 171
Whitehead, S.B. *154:* 132
Whithorne, H.S. *7:* 49
Whitney, George Gillett *3:* 24
Whitney, Jean *99:* 53
Whitson, Paul *102:* 161
Whittam, Geoffrey *30:* 191
Whyte, Mary *96:* 127
Wiberg, Harald *38:* 127; *93:* 215
Wick, Walter *77:* 128
Wickstrom, Sylvie *106:* 87; *169:* 180
Widener, Terry *105:* 230; *106:* 7; *163:* 23

Wiese, Kurt *3:* 255; *4:* 206; *14:* 17; *17:* 18, 19, 19; *19:* 47; *24:* 152; *25:* 212; *32:* 184; *36:* 211, 213, 214, 215, 216, 217, 218; *45:* 161; *100:* 92
Wiesner, David *33:* 47; *51:* 106; *57:* 67; *58:* 55; *64:* 78, 79, 81; *69:* 233; *72:* 247, 248, 249, 251, 252, 253, 254; *83:* 134; *104:* 31; *117:* 197, 199, 200, 202; *139:* 223, 224; *151:* 51
Wiesner, William *4:* 100; *5:* 200, 201; *14:* 262
Wiggins, George *6:* 133
Wijngaard, Juan *111:* 36; *114:* 124
Wikkelsoe, Otto *45:* 25, 26
Wikland, Ilon *5:* 113; *8:* 150; *38:* 124, 125, 130; *127:* 162
Wikler, Madeline *114:* 233
Wilbur, C. Keith, M.D. *27:* 228
Wilburn, Kathy *53:* 102; *68:* 234
Wilcox, Cathy *105:* 123
Wilcox, J.A.J. *34:* 122
Wilcox, R. Turner *36:* 219
Wild, Jocelyn *46:* 220, 221, 222; *80:* 117
Wilde, George *7:* 139
Wildsmith, Brian *16:* 281, 282; *18:* 170, 171; *66:* 25; *69:* 224, 225, 227; *77:* 103; *83:* 218; *124:* 214, 217, 219
Wildsmith, Mike *140:* 229
Wilhelm, Hans *58:* 189, 191; *73:* 157; *77:* 127; *135:* 229, 230, 233, 234
Wilkin, Eloise *36:* 173; *49:* 208, 209, 210
Wilkinson, Barry *50:* 213
Wilkinson, Gerald *3:* 40
Wilkon, Jozef *31:* 183, 184; *71:* 206, 207, 209; *133:* 222
Wilks, Mike *34:* 24; *44:* 203
Willems, Mo *154:* 245, 246, 247
Willey, Bee *103:* 129; *139:* 159; *173:* 115
Willhoite, Michael A. *71:* 214
William, Maria *168:* 51
Williams, Berkeley, Jr. *64:* 75
Williams, Ferelith Eccles *22:* 238
Williams, Garth *1:* 197; *2:* 49, 270; *4:* 205; *15:* 198, 302, 304, 307; *16:* 34; *18:* 283, 298, 299, 300, 301; *29:* 177, 178, 179, 232, 233, 241, 242, 243, 244, 245, 248; *40:* 106; *66:* 229, 230, 231, 233, 234; *71:* 192; *73:* 218, 219, 220; *78:* 261; *100:* 251, 252, 255; *136:* 117; *YABC 2:* 15, 16, 19
Williams, J. Scott *48:* 28
Williams, Jennifer *102:* 201
Williams, Jenny *60:* 202; *81:* 21; *88:* 71
Williams, Kit *44:* 206, 207, 208, 209, 211, 212
Williams, Marcia *97:* 214; *159:* 208, 209
Williams, Maureen *12:* 238
Williams, Patrick *14:* 218
Williams, Richard *44:* 93; *72:* 229; *74:* 133; *78:* 155, 237; *91:* 178; *110:* 212; *136:* 201, 202, 203; *152:* 115
Williams, Sam *124:* 222; *153:* 11; *177:* 201, 202
Williams, Sophy *135:* 236
Williams, Vera B. *53:* 186, 187, 188, 189; *102:* 201, 202, 203
Williamson, Alex *177:* 180
Williamson, Mel *60:* 9
Willingham, Fred *104:* 206; *154:* 157
Willmore, J.T. *54:* 113, 114
Wilson, Anne *160:* 114
Wilson, Charles Banks *17:* 92; *43:* 73
Wilson, Connie *113:* 179
Wilson, Dagmar *10:* 47
Wilson, Dawn *67:* 161; *81:* 120; *113:* 158
Wilson, Edward A. *6:* 24; *16:* 149; *20:* 220, 221; *22:* 87; *26:* 67; *38:* 212, 214, 215, 216, 217
Wilson, Forrest *27:* 231
Wilson, Gahan *35:* 234; *41:* 136
Wilson, George *76:* 87
Wilson, Helen Miranda *140:* 61
Wilson, Jack *17:* 139

Wilson, Janet *77:* 154; *96:* 114; *99:* 219, 220; *153:* 64 *106:* 122; *130:* 210; *145:* 178; *173:* 64
Wilson, John *22:* 240
Wilson, Maurice *46:* 224
Wilson, Patten *35:* 61
Wilson, Peggy *15:* 4; *84:* 20
Wilson, Rowland B. *30:* 170
Wilson, Sarah *50:* 215
Wilson, Tom *33:* 232
Wilson, W.N. *22:* 26
Wilson-Max, Ken *170:* 196
Wilton, Nicholas *103:* 52
Wilwerding, Walter J. *9:* 202
Wimmer, Mike *63:* 6; *70:* 121; *75:* 186; *76:* 21, 22, 23; *91:* 114; *97:* 45, 68; *98:* 28; *107:* 130; *146:* 21; *149:* 47; *173:* 126
Winborn, Marsha *78:* 34; *99:* 70
Winch, John *165:* 233
Winchester, Linda *13:* 231
Wind, Betty *28:* 158
Windham, Kathryn Tucker *14:* 260
Winfield, Alison *115:* 78
Winfield, Wayne *72:* 23
Wing, Gary *64:* 147
Wing, Ron *50:* 85
Wingerter, Linda S. *132:* 199; *174:* 181
Winick, Judd *124:* 227, 228, 229
Winslow, Will *21:* 124
Winsten, Melanie Willa *41:* 41
Winter, Jeanette *151:* 240, 241, 242
Winter, Milo *15:* 97; *19:* 221; *21:* 181, 203, 204, 205; *64:* 19; *YABC 2:* 144
Winter, Paula *48:* 227
Winter, Susan *163:* 177
Winters, Greg *70:* 117
Winters, Nina *62:* 194
Wise, Louis *13:* 68
Wiseman, Ann *31:* 187
Wiseman, B. *4:* 233
Wishnefsky, Phillip *3:* 14
Wiskur, Darrell *5:* 72; *10:* 50; *18:* 246
Wisniewski, David *95:* 220, 221
Wisniewski, Robert *95:* 10; *119:* 192
Witschonke, Alan *153:* 149, 150
Witt, Dick *80:* 244
Wittmann, Patrick *162:* 204
Wittman, Sally *30:* 219
Wittner, Dale *99:* 43
Wittwer, Hala *158:* 267
Woehr, Lois *12:* 5
Wohlberg, Meg *12:* 100; *14:* 197; *41:* 255
Wohnoutka, Mike *137:* 68
Wojtowycz, David *167:* 168
Woldin, Beth Weiner *34:* 211
Wolf, Elizabeth *133:* 151
Wolf, J. *16:* 91
Wolf, Janet *78:* 254
Wolf, Linda *33:* 163
Wolfe, Corey *72:* 213
Wolff, Ashley *50:* 217; *81:* 216; *156:* 216, 217; *170:* 57; *174:* 174
Wolfsgruber, Linda *166:* 61
Wondriska, William *6:* 220
Wong, Janet S. *98:* 225; *152:* 43
Wong, Nicole *174:* 13
Wonsetler, John C. *5:* 168
Wood, Audrey *50:* 221, 222, 223; *81:* 219, 221
Wood, Don *50:* 220, 225, 226, 228, 229; *81:* 218, 220; *139:* 239, 240
Wood, Grant *19:* 198
Wood, Heather *133:* 108
Wood, Ivor *58:* 17
Wood, Muriel *36:* 119; *77:* 167; *171:* 55
Wood, Myron *6:* 220
Wood, Owen *18:* 187; *64:* 202, 204, 205, 206, 208, 210
Wood, Ruth *8:* 11
Woodbridge, Curtis *133:* 138
Wooding, Sharon L. *66:* 237
Woodruff, Liza *132:* 239

Woodruff, Thomas *171:* 73
Woods, John, Jr. *109:* 142
Woodson, Jack *10:* 201
Woodson, Jacqueline *94:* 242
Woodward, Alice *26:* 89; *36:* 81
Wool, David *26:* 27
Woolley, Janet *112:* 75
Woolman, Steven *106:* 47; *163:* 73
Wooten, Vernon *23:* 70; *51:* 170
Worboys, Evelyn *1:* 166, 167
Word, Reagan *103:* 204
Wormell, Christopher *154:* 251
Worth, Jo *34:* 143
Worth, Wendy *4:* 133
Wosmek, Frances *29:* 251
Wrenn, Charles L. *38:* 96; *YABC 1:* 20, 21
Wright, Barbara Mullarney *98:* 161
Wright, Cliff *168:* 203
Wright, Dare *21:* 206
Wright-Frierson, Virginia *58:* 194; *110:* 246
Wright, George *YABC 1:* 268
Wright, Joseph *30:* 160
Wronker, Lili Cassel *3:* 247; *10:* 204; *21:* 10
Wummer, Amy *154:* 181; *168:* 150; *176:* 85
Wyant, Alexander Helwig *110:* 19
Wyatt, David *97:* 9; *101:* 44; *114:* 194; *140:* 20; *167:* 13
Wyatt, Stanley *46:* 210
Wyeth, Andrew *13:* 40; *YABC 1:* 133, 134
Wyeth, Jamie *41:* 257
Wyeth, N.C. *13:* 41; *17:* 252, 253, 254, 255, 256, 257, 258, 259, 264, 265, 266, 267, 268; *18:* 181; *19:* 80, 191, 200; *21:* 57, 183; *22:* 91; *23:* 152; *24:* 28, 99; *35:* 61; *41:* 65; *100:* 206; *YABC 1:* 133, 223; *2:* 53, 75, 171, 187, 317
Wyman, Cherie R. *91:* 42

**X**

Xuan, YongSheng *119:* 202, 207, 208; *140:* 36

**Y**

Yaccarino, Dan *141:* 208, 209; *147:* 171
Yakovetic, Joe *59:* 202; *75:* 85
Yalowitz, Paul *93:* 33
Yamaguchi, Marianne *85:* 118
Yamasaki, James *167:* 93
Yang, Belle *170:* 198
Yang, Jay *1:* 8; *12:* 239
Yap, Weda *6:* 176
Yaroslava
    See Mills, Yaroslava Surmach
Yashima, Taro *14:* 84
Yates, John *74:* 249, 250
Yee, Cora *166:* 233
Yee, Wong Herbert *115:* 216, 217; *172:* 204, 205
Yeo, Brad *135:* 121
Yezerski, Thomas F. *162:* 29
Ylla
    See Koffler, Camilla
Yohn, F.C. *23:* 128; *YABC 1:* 269
Yorinks, Adrienne *144:* 248
Yorke, David *80:* 178
Yoshida, Toshi *77:* 231
Yoshikawa, Sachiko *168:* 104; *177:* 28
Youll, Paul *91:* 218
Youll, Stephen *92:* 227; *118:* 136, 137; *164:* 248
Young, Cybéle *167:* 9
Young, Ed *7:* 205; *10:* 206; *40:* 124; *63:* 142; *74:* 250, 251, 252, 253; *75:* 227; *81:* 159; *83:* 98; *94:* 154; *115:* 160; *137:* 162; *YABC 2:* 242; *173:* 174, 175, 176

Young, Mary O'Keefe *77:* 95; *80:* 247; *134:* 214; *140:* 213
Young, Noela *8:* 221; *89:* 231; *97:* 195
Young, Selina *153:* 12
Yun, Cheng Mung *60:* 143

### Z

Zacharow, Christopher *88:* 98
Zacks, Lewis *10:* 161
Zadig *50:* 58
Zaffo, George *42:* 208
Zagwyn, Deborah Turney *138:* 227
Zaid, Barry *50:* 127; *51:* 201
Zaidenberg, Arthur *34:* 218, 219, 220
Zalben, Jane Breskin *7:* 211; *79:* 230, 231, 233; *170:* 202
Zallinger, Jean *4:* 192; *8:* 8, 129; *14:* 273; *68:* 36; *80:* 254; *115:* 219, 220, 222
Zallinger, Rudolph F. *3:* 245

Zakrajsek, Molly *177:* 146
Zebot, George *83:* 214
Zeck, Gerry *40:* 232
Zeifert, Harriet *154:* 265, 267
Zeiring, Bob *42:* 130
Zeldich, Arieh *49:* 124; *62:* 120
Zeldis, Malcah *86:* 239; *94:* 198; *146:* 265, 266
Zelinsky, Paul O. *14:* 269; *43:* 56; *49:* 218-223; *53:* 111; *68:* 195; *102:* 219, 222, 221, 222; *154:* 255, 256, 257; *171:* 141
Zelvin, Diana *72:* 190; *76:* 101; *93:* 207
Zemach, Kaethe *149:* 250
Zemach, Margot *3:* 270; *8:* 201; *21:* 210, 211; *27:* 204, 205, 210; *28:* 185; *49:* 22, 183, 224; *53:* 151; *56:* 146; *70:* 245, 246; *92:* 74
Zeman, Ludmila *153* 212
Zemsky, Jessica *10:* 62
Zepelinsky, Paul *35:* 93
Zerbetz, Evon *127:* 34; *158:* 109
Zhang, Ange *101:* 190; *172:* 41
Zhang, Son Nang *163:* 113; *170:* 206
Ziegler, Jack *84:* 134

Zimdars, Berta *129:* 155
Zimet, Jay *147:* 94; *152:* 74
Zimic, Tricia *72:* 95
Zimmer, Dirk *38:* 195; *49:* 71; *56:* 151; *65:* 214; *84:* 159; *89:* 26; *147:* 224
Zimmer, Tracie Vaughn *169:* 183
Zimmermann, H. Werner *101:* 223; *112:* 197
Zimnik, Reiner *36:* 224
Zinkeisen, Anna *13:* 106
Zinn, David *97:* 97
Zoellick, Scott *33:* 231
Zonia, Dhimitri *20:* 234, 235
Zorn, Peter A., Jr. *142:* 157
Zudeck, Darryl *58:* 129; *63:* 98; *80:* 52
Zug, Mark *88:* 131
Zulewski, Tim *164:* 95
Zuma *99:* 36
Zvorykin, Boris *61:* 155
Zweifel, Francis *14:* 274; *28:* 187
Zwerger, Lisbeth *54:* 176, 178; *66:* 246, 247, 248; *130:* 230, 231, 232, 233
Zwinger, Herman H. *46:* 227
Zwolak, Paul *67:* 69, 71, 73, 74

# Author Index

The following index gives the number of the volume in which an author's biographical sketch, Autobiography Feature, Brief Entry, or Obituary appears.

This index includes references to all entries in the following series, which are also published by The Gale Group.

**YABC**—*Yesterday's Authors of Books for Children: Facts and Pictures about Authors and Illustrators of Books for Young People from Early Times to 1960*

**CLR**—*Children's Literature Review: Excerpts from Reviews, Criticism, and Commentary on Books for Children*

**SAAS**—*Something about the Author Autobiography Series*

## A

Aaron, Chester 1923- ..................................... 74
  Earlier sketch in SATA 9
  *See also* SAAS 12
Aaseng, Nate
  *See* Aaseng, Nathan
Aaseng, Nathan 1953- .................................. 172
  Brief entry ............................................... 38
  Earlier sketches in SATA 51, 88
  *See also* CLR 54
  *See also* SAAS 12
Abbas, Jailan 1952- ...................................... 91
Abbey, Lynn
  *See* Abbey, Marilyn Lorraine
Abbey, Marilyn Lorraine 1948- ................. 156
Abbott, Alice
  *See* Borland, Kathryn Kilby
  and Speicher, Helen Ross S(mith)
Abbott, Jacob 1803-1879 ........................... 22
Abbott, Manager Henry
  *See* Stratemeyer, Edward L.
Abbott, R(obert) Tucker 1919-1995 ........... 61
  Obituary .................................................... 87
Abbott, Sarah
  *See* Zolotow, Charlotte (Gertrude) S(hapiro)
Abbott, Tony 1952- ..................................... 159
Abdelsayed, Cindy 1962- .......................... 123
Abdul, Raoul 1929- .................................... 12
Abel, Raymond 1911- ................................. 12
Abell, Kathleen 1938- ................................... 9
Abelove, Joan ............................................. 110
Abels, Harriette S(heffer) 1926- ................ 50
Abercrombie, Barbara (Mattes) 1939- ........ 16
Abercrombie, Lynn
  *See* Sorrells, Walter
Abernethy, Robert G(ordon) 1927- .............. 5
Abisch, Roslyn Kroop 1927- ........................ 9
Abisch, Roz
  *See* Abisch, Roslyn Kroop
Abodaher, David J. (Naiph) 1919- ............. 17
Abolafia, Yossi 1944-
  *See* Abulafia, Yossi
Abouzeid, Chris ......................................... 175
Abrahall, Clare Hoskyns
  *See* Hoskyns-Abrahall, Clare (Constance Drury)
Abrahams, Hilary (Ruth) 1938- .................. 29
Abrahams, Robert David 1905-1998 ............ 4

Abrams, Joy 1941- ...................................... 16
Abrams, Lawrence F. ................................... 58
  Brief entry ............................................... 47
Abrashkin, Raymond 1911-1960 ................. 50
Abulafia, Yossi 1944- ................................ 177
  Brief entry ............................................... 46
  Earlier sketch in SATA 60
Acampora, Paul .......................................... 175
Achebe, Albert Chinualumogu
  *See* Achebe, Chinua
Achebe, Chinua 1930- ................................ 40
  Brief entry ............................................... 38
  Earlier sketch in SATA 38
  *See also* CLR 20
Ackerman, Diane 1948- ............................. 102
Ackerman, Eugene (Francis) 1888-1974 ..... 10
Ackerman, Karen 1951- ............................. 126
Ackerman, Susan Yoder 1945- .................... 92
Ackison, Wendy Wassink 1956- ................. 103
Ackley, Peggy Jo 1955- ............................... 58
Ackroyd, Peter 1949- ................................ 153
Acorn, John (Harrison) 1958- ..................... 79
Acredolo, Linda (Potter) 1947- ................. 159
Acs, Laszlo (Bela) 1931- ............................. 42
  Brief entry ............................................... 32
Acuff, Selma Boyd 1924- ............................ 45
Ada, Alma Flor 1938- ............................... 143
  Earlier sketches in SATA 43, 84
  *See also* CLR 62
Adair, Gilbert 1944- .................................... 98
Adair, Ian 1942- .......................................... 53
Adair, Margaret Weeks (?)-1971 ................. 10
Adam, Cornel
  *See* Lengyel, Cornel Adam
Adam, Mark
  *See* Alexander, Marc
Adam, Robert 1948- .................................... 93
Adams, Adrienne 1906- ............................... 90
  Earlier sketch in SATA 8
  *See also* CLR 73
Adams, Andy 1859-1935
  *See* YABC 1
Adams, Barbara Johnston 1943- .................. 60
Adams, Bruin
  *See* Ellis, Edward S(ylvester)
Adams, Captain Bruin
  *See* Ellis, Edward S(ylvester)
Adams, Captain J. F. C.
  *See* Ellis, Edward S(ylvester)

Adams, Dale
  *See* Quinn, Elisabeth
Adams, Daniel
  *See* Nicole, Christopher (Robin)
Adams, Debra
  *See* Speregen, Devra Newberger
Adams, Douglas 1952-2001 ....................... 116
  Obituary .................................................. 128
Adams, Douglas Noel
  *See* Adams, Douglas
Adams, Edith
  *See* Shine, Deborah
Adams, Florence 1932- ............................... 61
Adams, Harriet S(tratemeyer) 1892(?)-1982 . 1
  Obituary .................................................... 29
Adams, Harrison
  *See* Rathborne, St. George (Henry)
  and Stratemeyer, Edward L.
Adams, Hazard 1926- .................................... 6
Adams, Hazard Simeon
  *See* Adams, Hazard
Adams, John Anthony 1944- ........................ 67
Adams, Laurie 1941- .................................... 33
Adams, Lowell
  *See* Joseph, James (Herz)
Adams, Nicholas
  *See* Pine, Nicholas
Adams, Nicholas
  *See* Smith, Sherwood
Adams, Nicholas
  *See* Doyle, Debra
  and Macdonald, James D.
Adams, Pam 1919- .................................... 112
Adams, Pamela
  *See* Adams, Pam
Adams, Richard (George) 1920- ................. 69
  Earlier sketch in SATA 7
  *See also* CLR 121
Adams, Ruth Joyce ...................................... 14
Adams, William Taylor 1822-1897 ............. 28
Adam Smith, Janet (Buchanan) 1905-1999
  ................................................................. 63
Adamson, Gareth 1925-1982(?) ................. 46
  Obituary .................................................... 30
Adamson, George (Worsley) 1913-2005 ..... 30
Adamson, Graham
  *See* Groom, Arthur William

Adamson, Joy(-Friederike Victoria) 1910-1980
........................................... *11*
Obituary ......................................... *22*
Adamson, Wendy Writson 1942- ................ *22*
Addona, Angelo F. 1925- ........................ *14*
Addy, Sharon Hart 1943- ....................... *108*
Addy, Ted
*See* Winterbotham, R(ussell) R(obert)
Adelberg, Doris
*See* Orgel, Doris
Adelson, Leone 1908- .............................. *11*
Adinolfi, JoAnn ................................... *176*
Adkins, Jan 1944- ................................. *144*
Earlier sketches in SATA *8, 69*
*See also* CLR *77*
*See also* SAAS *19*
Adler, C(arole) S(chwerdtfeger) 1932- ...... *126*
Earlier sketches in SATA *26, 63, 102*
*See also* CLR *78*
*See also* SAAS *15*
Adler, David A. 1947- ............................ *151*
Earlier sketches in SATA *14, 70, 106*
*See also* CLR *108*
Adler, Irene
*See* Penzler, Otto
and Storr, Catherine (Cole)
Adler, Irving 1913- .............................. *29*
Autobiography Feature ......................... *164*
Earlier sketch in SATA *1*
*See also* CLR *27*
*See also* SAAS *15*
Adler, Larry 1939- ................................ *36*
Adler, Peggy ...................................... *22*
Adler, Ruth 1915-1968 ............................ *1*
Adlerman, Daniel (Ezra) 1963- ................. *163*
Earlier sketch in SATA *96*
Adlerman, Kim
*See* Adlerman, Kimberly M(arie)
Adlerman, Kimberly M(arie) 1964- .......... *163*
Earlier sketch in SATA *96*
Adoff, Arnold 1935- .............................. *96*
Earlier sketches in SATA *5, 57*
*See also* CLR *7*
*See also* SAAS *15*
Adoff, Jaime (Levi) ............................... *163*
Adorjan, Carol (Madden) 1934- ................ *71*
Earlier sketch in SATA *10*
Adrian, Frances
*See* Polland, Madeleine A(ngela Cahill)
Adrian, Mary
*See* Jorgensen, Mary Venn
Adshead, Gladys L(ucy) 1896-1985 ............. *3*
Aesop 620(?)B.C.-560(?)B.C. ...................... *64*
*See also* CLR *14*
Aesop, Abraham
*See* Newbery, John
Affabee, Eric
*See* Stine, R.L.
Agapida, Fray Antonio
*See* Irving, Washington
Agard, John 1949- ................................ *138*
Agard, Nadema 1948- ............................. *18*
Agarwal, Deepa 1947- ............................ *141*
Agee, Jon 1960- ................................... *157*
Earlier sketch in SATA *116*
Agell, Charlotte 1959- ........................... *150*
Earlier sketch in SATA *99*
Agent Orange
*See* Moseley, James W(illett)
Aghill, Gordon
*See* Garrett, (Gordon) Randall (Phillip)
and Silverberg, Robert
Agle, Nan Hayden 1905- ........................... *3*
*See also* SAAS *10*
Agnew, Edith J(osephine) 1897-1988 .......... *11*
Agonito, Joseph ................................... *177*
Agonito, Rosemary 1937- ........................ *177*
Ahern, Margaret McCrohan 1921- ............. *10*
Ahl, Anna Maria 1926- ........................... *32*

Ahlberg, Allan 1938- ............................. *165*
Brief entry ...................................... *35*
Earlier sketches in SATA *68, 120*
*See also* CLR *18*
Ahlberg, Janet 1944-1994 ....................... *120*
Brief entry ...................................... *32*
Obituary ......................................... *83*
Earlier sketch in SATA *68*
*See also* CLR *18*
Aichinger, Helga 1937- ............................ *4*
Aiken, Clarissa (M.) Lorenz 1899-1992 ..... *12*
Obituary ......................................... *109*
Aiken, Conrad (Potter) 1889-1973 ............. *30*
Earlier sketch in SATA *3*
Aiken, Joan (Delano) 1924-2004 ............... *73*
Autobiography Feature .......................... *109*
Obituary ......................................... *152*
Earlier sketches in SATA *2, 30*
*See also* CLR *90*
*See also* SAAS *1*
Ainsley, Alix
*See* Steiner, Barbara A(nnette)
Ainsworth, Catherine Harris 1910- ............. *56*
Ainsworth, Norma 1911-1987 ..................... *9*
Ainsworth, Ruth (Gallard) 1908- ............... *73*
Earlier sketch in SATA *7*
Ainsworth, William Harrison 1805-1882 ..... *24*
Aistrop, Jack 1916- .............................. *14*
Aitken, Amy 1952- ................................ *54*
Brief entry ...................................... *40*
Aitken, Dorothy 1916- ........................... *10*
Aitmatov, Chingiz (Torekulovich) 1928- ..... *56*
*See* Aytmatov, Chingiz
Akaba, Suekichi 1910- ............................ *46*
Akers, Floyd
*See* Baum, L(yman) Frank
Aks, Patricia 1926-1994 .......................... *68*
Alagoa, Ebiegberi Joe 1933- .................... *108*
Alain
*See* Brustlein, Daniel
Alan, David
*See* Horsfield, Alan
Alan, Robert
*See* Silverstein, Robert Alan
Alarcon, Francisco X(avier) 1954- ............ *104*
Albert, Burton 1936- ............................. *22*
Albert, Louise 1928- ............................. *157*
Albert, Richard E. 1909-1999 ................... *82*
Albert, Susan Wittig 1940- ..................... *107*
Alberts, Frances Jacobs 1907-1989 ............ *14*
Albertson, Susan
*See* Wojciechowski, Susan
Albion, Lee Smith ................................ *29*
Alborough, Jez 1959- ............................ *149*
Earlier sketch in SATA *86*
Albrecht, Lillie (Vanderveer H.) 1894-1985
........................................... *12*
Albyn, Carole Lisa 1955- ........................ *83*
Alcock, Gudrun 1908- ............................ *56*
Brief entry ...................................... *33*
Alcock, Vivien (Dolores) 1924-2003 .......... *76*
Brief entry ...................................... *38*
Obituary ......................................... *148*
Earlier sketch in SATA *45*
*See also* CLR *26*
Alcorn, John 1935- ............................... *31*
Brief entry ...................................... *30*
Alcorn, Stephen 1958- ........................... *110*
Alcott, Louisa May 1832-1888 ................. *100*
*See also* YABC *1*
*See also* CLR *109*
Alda, Arlene 1933- ............................... *158*
Brief entry ...................................... *36*
Earlier sketches in SATA *44, 106*
*See also* CLR *93*
Alden, Isabella (Macdonald) 1841-1930 ... *115*
*See also* YABC *2*
Alden, Sue
*See* Francis, Dorothy Brenner
Alderman, Clifford Lindsey 1902-1988 ........ *3*

Alderson, Sue Ann 1940- .......................... *59*
Brief entry ...................................... *48*
Alding, Peter
*See* Jeffries, Roderic
Aldis, Dorothy (Keeley) 1896-1966 .............. *2*
Aldiss, Brian W. 1925- ............................ *34*
Aldiss, Brian Wilson
*See* Aldiss, Brian W.
Aldon, Adair
*See* Meigs, Cornelia Lynde
Aldous, Allan (Charles) 1911- ................... *27*
Aldrich, Ann
*See* Meaker, Marijane
Aldrich, Bess Streeter 1881-1954
*See* CLR *70*
Aldrich, Thomas (Bailey) 1836-1907 ........ *114*
Earlier sketch in SATA *17*
Aldridge, (Harold Edward) James 1918- .... *87*
Aldridge, Josephine Haskell ..................... *14*
Alegria, Ricardo E(nrique) 1921- ................ *6*
Aleksin, Anatolii Georgievich 1924- .......... *36*
Alenov, Lydia 1948- ............................... *61*
Alex, Ben (a pseudonym) 1946- ................. *45*
Alex, Marlee (a pseudonym) 1948- ............. *45*
Alexander, Anna B(arbara Cooke) 1913- ...... *1*
Alexander, Anne
*See* Alexander, Anna B(arbara Cooke)
Alexander, Ellen 1938- ........................... *91*
Alexander, Frances (Laura) 1888-1979 ......... *4*
Alexander, Jocelyn Anne Arundel 1930- .... *22*
Alexander, Linda 1935- ............................ *2*
Alexander, Lloyd (Chudley) 1924- ........... *135*
Earlier sketches in SATA *3, 49, 81, 129*
*See also* CLR *48*
*See also* SAAS *19*
Alexander, Marc 1929- ........................... *117*
Alexander, Martha 1920- ......................... *136*
Earlier sketches in SATA *11, 70*
Alexander, Rae Pace
*See* Alexander, Raymond Pace
Alexander, Raymond Pace 1898-1974 ........ *22*
Alexander, Rod
*See* Pellowski, Michael (Joseph)
Alexander, Sally Hobart 1943- ................... *84*
Alexander, Sue 1933- ............................. *136*
Earlier sketches in SATA *12, 89*
*See also* SAAS *15*
Alexeieff, Alexandre A. 1901-1979 ............. *14*
Alger, Horatio, Jr.
*See* Stratemeyer, Edward L.
Alger, Horatio, Jr. 1832-1899 ................... *16*
*See also* CLR *87*
Alger, Leclaire (Gowans) 1898-1969 .......... *15*
Aliki
*See* CLR *71*
*See* Brandenberg, Aliki (Liacouras)
Alkema, Chester Jay 1932- ...................... *12*
Al-Khalili, Jim 1962- ............................ *124*
Alkiviades, Alkis 1953- .......................... *105*
Allaby, John Michael
*See* Allaby, Michael
Allaby, Michael 1933- ............................ *167*
Allamand, Pascale 1942- ......................... *12*
Allan, Mabel Esther 1915-1998 ................. *75*
Earlier sketches in SATA *5, 32*
*See also* CLR *43*
*See also* SAAS *11*
Allan, Nicholas 1956- ............................ *123*
Earlier sketch in SATA *79*
Allan-Meyer, Kathleen 1918- .................... *51*
Brief entry ...................................... *46*
Allard, Harry
*See* Allard, Harry G(rover), Jr.
Allard, Harry G(rover), Jr. 1928- ............. *102*
Earlier sketch in SATA *42*
*See also* CLR *85*
Allee, Marjorie Hill 1890-1945 ................. *17*
Allen, Adam
*See* Epstein, Beryl (M. Williams)
and Epstein, Samuel

Allen, Alex B.
  *See* Heide, Florence Parry
Allen, Allyn
  *See* Eberle, Irmengarde
Allen, Betsy
  *See* Harrison, Elizabeth (Allen) Cavanna
Allen, Bob 1961- ............................................ 76
Allen, Gertrude E(lizabeth) 1888-1984 ......... 9
Allen, Grace
  *See* Hogarth, Grace (Weston Allen)
Allen, Jeffrey (Yale) 1948- ......................... 42
Allen, John
  *See* Perry, Ritchie (John Allen)
Allen, Jonathan 1957- ................................ 177
  Earlier sketch in SATA *131*
Allen, Jonathan Dean
  *See* Allen, Jonathan
Allen, Judy (Christina) 1941- ..................... 124
  Earlier sketch in SATA *80*
Allen, Kenneth S. 1913-1981 ....................... 56
Allen, Leroy 1912- ....................................... 11
Allen, Linda 1925- ....................................... 33
Allen, Marjorie 1931- .................................. 22
Allen, Maury 1932- ...................................... 26
Allen, Merritt Parmelee 1892-1954 ............. 22
Allen, Nancy Kelly 1949- ........................... 171
  Earlier sketch in SATA *127*
Allen, Nina (Stroemgren) 1935- .................. 22
Allen, Pamela (Kay) 1934- ......................... 123
  Earlier sketches in SATA *50, 81*
  *See also* CLR *44*
Allen, Rodney F. 1938-1999 ......................... 27
Allen, Roger MacBride 1957- ..................... 105
Allen, Ruth
  *See* Peterson, Esther (Allen)
Allen, Samuel W(ashington) 1917- .............. 9
Allen, T. D.
  *See* Allen, Terril Diener
Allen, Terril Diener 1908- ........................... 35
  *See* Allen, T. D.
Allen, Terry D.
  *See* Allen, Terril Diener
Allen, Thomas B(enton) 1929- .................... 140
  Earlier sketch in SATA *45*
Allen, Tom
  *See* Allen, Thomas B(enton)
Allende, Isabel 1942- ................................ 163
  *See also* CLR *99*
Allerton, Mary
  *See* Govan, (Mary) Christine Noble
Alley, Robert W.
  *See* Alley, R.W.
Alley, R.W. ................................................. 169
Alleyn, Ellen
  *See* Rossetti, Christina
Allington, Richard L(loyd) 1947- ................ 39
  Brief entry ................................................ 35
Allison, Amy 1956- .................................... 138
Allison, Bob ............................................... 14
Allison, Diane Worfolk ............................... 78
Allison, Jennifer ....................................... 173
Allison, Linda 1948- ................................... 43
Allman, Barbara 1950- .............................. 137
Allmendinger, David F(rederick), Jr. 1938-
  ................................................................. 35
Allred, Alexandra Powe 1965- ................... 144
Allred, Gordon T(hatcher) 1930- ................ 10
Allsop, Kenneth 1920-1973 ......................... 17
Almedingen, E. M. ....................................... 3
  *See* Almedingen, Martha Edith von
Almon, Russell
  *See* Clevenger, William R.
  and Downing, David A(lmon)
Almond, David 1951- ................................ 158
  Earlier sketch in SATA *114*
  *See also* CLR *85*
Almquist, Don 1929- ................................... 11
Alphin, Elaine Marie 1955- ........................ 139
  Autobiography Feature ............................ 139
  Earlier sketches in SATA *80, 130*

Alsop, Mary O'Hara 1885-1980 ................... 34
  Obituary .................................................. 24
  Earlier sketch in SATA *2*
  *See* O'Hara, Mary
Alter, Anna 1974- ...................................... 135
Alter, Judith (MacBain) 1938- ................... 101
  Earlier sketch in SATA *52*
Alter, Judy
  *See* Alter, Judith (MacBain)
Alter, Robert Edmond 1925-1965 ................. 9
Althea
  *See* Braithwaite, Althea
Altman, Linda Jacobs 1943- ....................... 21
Altman, Suzanne
  *See* Orgel, Doris
  and Schecter, Ellen
Alton, Steve .............................................. 169
Altschuler, Franz 1923- ............................. 45
Altsheler, Joseph A(lexander) 1862-1919
  *See* YABC *1*
Alvarez, John
  *See* del Rey, Lester
Alvarez, Joseph A. 1930- ............................ 18
Alvarez, Julia 1950- .................................. 129
al-Windawi, Thura
  *See* Windawi, Thura al-
Alyer, Philip A.
  *See* Stratemeyer, Edward L.
Amann, Janet 1951- .................................... 79
Amato, Carol A. 1942- ................................ 92
Amato, Mary 1961- ................................... 140
Ambrose, Stephen E. 1936-2002 ............... 138
  Earlier sketch in SATA *40*
Ambrose, Stephen Edward
  *See* Ambrose, Stephen E.
Ambrus, Gyozo Laszlo 1935- ...................... 41
  *See* Ambrus, Victor G.
Ambrus, Victor G. ........................................ 1
  *See also* SAAS *4*
  *See* Ambrus, Gyozo Laszlo
Amend, Bill 1962- ...................................... 147
Amerman, Lockhart 1911-1969 ..................... 3
Ames, Evelyn 1908-1990 ............................. 13
  Obituary .................................................. 64
Ames, Gerald 1906-1993 ............................. 11
  Obituary .................................................. 74
Ames, Lee J(udah) 1921- ........................... 151
  Earlier sketch in SATA *3*
Ames, Mildred 1919-1994 ............................ 85
  Earlier sketches in SATA *22, 81*
Amico, Tom 1960(?)- ................................ 176
Ammon, Richard 1942- .............................. 124
Amon, Aline 1928- ....................................... 9
Amoss, Berthe 1925- ................................ 112
  Earlier sketch in SATA *5*
Anastasio, Dina 1941- ................................ 94
  Brief entry ................................................ 30
  Earlier sketch in SATA *37*
Anckarsvard, Karin Inez Maria 1915-1969 ... 6
Ancona, George 1929- .............................. 145
  Earlier sketches in SATA *12, 85*
  *See also* SAAS *18*
Anders, C. J.
  *See* Bennett, Cherie
Anders, Isabel 1946- ................................ 101
Anders, Lou ............................................. 176
Andersdatter, Karla M(argaret) 1938- ......... 34
Andersen, Hans Christian 1805-1875 ........ 100
  *See also* YABC *1*
  *See also* CLR *113*
Andersen, Ted
  *See* Boyd, Waldo T.
Andersen, Yvonne 1932- ............................. 27
Anderson, Bernice G(oudy) 1894-1997 ...... 33
Anderson, Bob 1944- ................................ 139
  Earlier sketch in SATA *136*
Anderson, Brad(ley Jay) 1924- ................... 33
  Brief entry ................................................ 31
Anderson, C. C.
  *See* Anderson, Catherine Corley

Anderson, C(larence) W(illiam) 1891-1971
  ................................................................. 11
Anderson, Catherine C.
  *See* Anderson, Catherine Corley
Anderson, Catherine Corley 1909-2001 ...... 72
Anderson, Clifford
  *See* Gardner, Richard (M.)
Anderson, Daryl Shon 1963- ....................... 93
Anderson, Dave
  *See* Anderson, David (Poole)
Anderson, David (Poole) 1929- ................... 60
Anderson, Derek 1969- ............................. 169
Anderson, Eloise Adell 1927- ....................... 9
Anderson, George
  *See* Groom, Arthur William
Anderson, Grace Fox 1932- ........................ 43
Anderson, J(ohn) R(ichard) L(ane) 1911-1981
  ................................................................. 15
  Obituary .................................................. 27
Anderson, Joy 1928- ..................................... 1
Anderson, Kevin J. 1962- ......................... 117
  Earlier sketch in SATA *74*
Anderson, Kevin James
  *See* Anderson, Kevin J.
Anderson, Kirsty 1978- ............................. 108
Anderson, Laurie Halse 1961- ................... 132
  Earlier sketch in SATA *95*
Anderson, LaVere Francis Shoenfelt 1907-1998
  ................................................................. 27
Anderson, Leone Castell 1923- ................... 53
  Brief entry ................................................ 49
Anderson, Lisa G. 1963- ........................... 108
Anderson, Lonzo ......................................... 2
  *See* Anderson, John L(onzo)
Anderson, Lucia (Lewis) 1922- .................... 10
Anderson, Madelyn Klein 1926-2005 .......... 28
Anderson, Margaret J(ean) 1931- ................ 27
  *See also* SAAS *8*
Anderson, Marilyn D. 1943- ....................... 144
Anderson, Mary 1939- ................................ 82
  Earlier sketch in SATA *7*
  *See also* SAAS *23*
Anderson, Matthew Tobin
  *See* Anderson, M.T.
Anderson, Mona 1910-2004 ........................ 40
Anderson, Mrs. Melvin
  *See* Anderson, Catherine Corley
Anderson, M.T. 1968- ............................... 146
  Earlier sketch in SATA *97*
Anderson, Norman Dean 1928- .................... 22
Anderson, Peggy Perry 1953- ..................... 84
Anderson, Poul 1926-2001 ......................... 90
  Autobiography Feature ............................ 106
  Brief entry ................................................ 39
  *See also* CLR *58*
Anderson, Poul William
  *See* Anderson, Poul
Anderson, Rachel 1943- .............................. 86
  Earlier sketch in SATA *34*
  *See also* SAAS *18*
Anderson, Richard
  *See* Anderson, J(ohn) R(ichard) L(ane)
Anderson, Sara ......................................... 173
Anderson, (Tom) Scoular ........................... 138
Anderson, Susan 1952- .............................. 90
Anderson, W. B.
  *See* Schultz, James Willard
Anderson, Wayne 1946- ............................ 147
  Earlier sketch in SATA *56*
Andre, Evelyn M(arie) 1924- ....................... 27
Andreassen, Karl
  *See* Boyd, Waldo T.
Andreassi, K. Robert
  *See* DeCandido, Keith R.A.
Andrew, Ian 1962- .................................... 166
  Earlier sketch in SATA *116*
Andrew, Ian Peter
  *See* Andrew, Ian
Andrew, Prudence (Hastings) 1924- ............ 87
Andrews, Benny 1930-2006 ........................ 31

Andrews, Eleanor Lattimore
   See Lattimore, Eleanor Frances
Andrews, Elton V.
   See Pohl, Frederik
Andrews, F(rank) Emerson 1902-1978 ....... 22
Andrews, J(ames) S(ydney) 1934- ............... 4
Andrews, Jan 1942- ................................... 167
   Brief entry ............................................ 49
   Earlier sketches in SATA 58, 98
Andrews, Julie 1935- ................................ 153
   Earlier sketch in SATA 7
   See also CLR 85
Andrews, Roy Chapman 1884-1960 .......... 19
Andrews, Tamra 1959- ............................. 129
Andrews, Wendy
   See Sharmat, Marjorie Weinman
Andrews, William G(eorge) 1930- ............. 74
Andrezel, Pierre
   See Blixen, Karen (Christentze Dinesen)
Andriani, Renee
   See Williams-Andriani, Renee
Andrist, Ralph K. 1914-2004 ................... 45
Andryszewski, Tricia 1956- ...................... 148
   Earlier sketch in SATA 88
Angel, Marie 1923- .................................... 47
Angeles, Peter A. 1931- ............................ 40
Angeletti, Roberta 1964- .......................... 124
Angeli, Marguerite (Lofft) de
   See de Angeli, Marguerite (Lofft)
Angell, Madeline 1919- .............................. 18
Angelo, Valenti 1897- ................................ 14
Angelou, Maya 1928- ............................... 136
   Earlier sketch in SATA 49
   See also CLR 53
Angier, Bradford -1997 ............................. 12
Anglund, Joan Walsh 1926- ........................ 2
   See also CLR 94
Ango, Fan D.
   See Longyear, Barry B(rookes)
Angrist, Stanley W(olff) 1933- ..................... 4
Anholt, Catherine 1958- ............................ 131
   Earlier sketch in SATA 74
Anholt, Laurence 1959- ............................ 141
   Earlier sketch in SATA 74
Anita
   See Daniel, Anita
Anmar, Frank
   See Nolan, William F(rancis)
Annett, Cora
   See Scott, Cora Annett (Pipitone)
Annie-Jo
   See Blanchard, Patricia
   and Suhr, Joanne
Annixter, Jane
   See Sturtzel, Jane Levington
Annixter, Paul
   See Sturtzel, Howard A(llison)
Anno, Mitsumasa 1926- ............................ 157
   Earlier sketches in SATA 5, 38, 77
   See also CLR 122
Anrooy, Francine Van
   See Van Anrooy, Francine
Ansary, Mir Tamim 1948- ........................ 140
Anstey, Caroline 1958- .............................. 81
Antell, Will D. 1935- ................................. 31
Anthony, Barbara
   See Barber, Antonia
Anthony, C. L.
   See Smith, Dorothy Gladys
Anthony, Edward 1895-1971 ..................... 21
Anthony, John
   See Beckett, Ronald Brymer
   and Ciardi, John (Anthony)
   and Sabini, John Anthony
Anthony, Joseph Patrick 1964- ................. 103
Anthony, Patricia 1947- ............................ 109
Anthony, Piers 1934- ................................ 129
   Autobiography Feature ........................... 129
   Earlier sketch in SATA 84
   See also CLR 118
   See also SAAS 22

Anthony, Susan C(arol) 1953- ..................... 87
Anticaglia, Elizabeth 1939- ........................ 12
Antle, Nancy 1955- ................................. 102
Anton, Michael J(ames) 1940- ................... 12
Antonacci, Robert J(oseph) 1916- ............... 45
   Brief entry ............................................ 37
Anvil, Christopher
   See Crosby, Harry C., Jr.
Aoki, Hisako 1942- .................................... 45
Apfel, Necia H(alpern) 1930- ..................... 51
   Brief entry ............................................ 41
Aphrodite, J.
   See Livingston, Carole
Apikuni
   See Schultz, James Willard
Apostolou, Christine Hale 1955- ............... 128
   Earlier sketch in SATA 82
Appel, Allen (R.) 1945- ............................ 115
Appel, Benjamin 1907-1977 ...................... 39
   Obituary ............................................... 21
Appel, Martin E(liot) 1948- ....................... 45
Appel, Marty
   See Appel, Martin E(liot)
Appelbaum, Diana Muir Karter 1953- ...... 132
Appelt, Kathi 1954- ................................. 129
   Earlier sketch in SATA 83
Apperley, Dawn 1969- ............................. 135
Appiah, Peggy 1921-2006 .......................... 84
   Earlier sketch in SATA 15
   See also SAAS 19
Apple, Margot ........................................ 152
   Brief entry ............................................ 42
   Earlier sketch in SATA 64
Applebaum, Stan 1922- ............................. 45
Applegate, K. A.
   See CLR 90
   See Applegate, Katherine (Alice)
Applegate, Katherine (Alice) 1956- .......... 162
   Earlier sketch in SATA 109
   See Applegate, K. A.
Appleton, Victor ........................................ 67
   Earlier sketch in SATA 1
   See Barrett, Neal, Jr.
   and Doyle, Debra
   and Macdonald, James D.
   and Stratemeyer, Edward L.
   and Vardeman, Robert E(dward)
Appleton, Victor II .................................... 67
   Earlier sketch in SATA 1
   See Goulart, Ron(ald Joseph)
Apsler, Alfred 1907-1982 ........................... 10
Aragones, Sergio 1937- .............................. 48
   Brief entry ............................................ 39
Araujo, Frank P. 1937- .............................. 86
Arbo, Cris 1950- .................................... 103
Arbuthnot, May Hill 1884-1969 .................. 2
Archambault, John .................................. 163
   Earlier sketches in SATA 67, 112
Archbold, Rick 1950- ................................ 97
Archer, Colleen Rutherford 1949- ............. 164
Archer, Jules 1915- ................................... 85
   Earlier sketch in SATA 4
   See also SAAS 5
Archer, Marion Fuller 1917- ...................... 11
Archibald, Joe
   See Archibald, Joseph S(topford)
Archibald, Joseph S(topford) 1898-1986 ...... 3
   Obituary ............................................... 47
Ardagh, Philip 1961- ............................... 154
Ardai, Charles 1969- ................................. 85
Arden, Barbi
   See Stoutenburg, Adrien (Pearl)
Arden, William
   See Lynds, Dennis
Ardizzone, Edward (Jeffrey Irving) 1900-1979
   .......................................................... 28
   Obituary ............................................... 21
   Earlier sketch in SATA 1
   See also CLR 3
Ardley, Neil (Richard) 1937- ..................... 121
   Earlier sketch in SATA 43

Arehart-Treichel, Joan 1942- ..................... 22
Arena, Felice 1968- ................................ 151
Arenella, Roy 1939- .................................. 14
Argent, Kerry 1960- ................................ 138
Arkin, Alan 1934- ..................................... 59
   Brief entry ............................................ 32
Arkin, Alan Wolf
   See Arkin, Alan
Arksey, Neil ........................................... 158
Arlen, Leslie
   See Nicole, Christopher (Robin)
Arley, Robert
   See Jackson, Mike
Armer, Alberta (Roller) 1904-1986 .............. 9
Armer, Laura Adams 1874-1963 ................ 13
Armistead, John 1941- ............................. 130
Armitage, David 1943- ............................. 155
   Brief entry ............................................ 38
   Earlier sketch in SATA 99
Armitage, Frank
   See Carpenter, John (Howard)
Armitage, Ronda (Jacqueline) 1943- ........ 155
   Brief entry ............................................ 38
   Earlier sketches in SATA 47, 99
Armour, Richard (Willard) 1906-1989 ........ 14
   Obituary ............................................... 61
Armstrong, Alan 1939- ............................. 172
Armstrong, Alan W.
   See Armstrong, Alan
Armstrong, George D. 1927- ...................... 10
Armstrong, Gerry (Breen) 1929- ................ 10
Armstrong, Jeannette (C.) 1948- ............... 102
Armstrong, Jennifer 1961- ....................... 165
   Autobiography Feature ........................... 120
   Earlier sketches in SATA 77, 111
   See also CLR 66
   See also SAAS 24
Armstrong, Louise ..................................... 43
   Brief entry ............................................ 33
Armstrong, Martin Donisthorpe 1882-1974
   .......................................................... 115
Armstrong, Ralph Richard
   See Armstrong, Richard
Armstrong, Richard 1903-1986 ................... 11
Armstrong, William H(oward) 1914-1999 .... 4
   Obituary ............................................... 111
   See also CLR 117
   See also SAAS 7
Armstrong-Ellis, Carey (Fraser) 1956- ...... 145
Arndt, Ursula (Martha H.) .......................... 56
   Brief entry ............................................ 39
Arneson, D(on) J(on) 1935- ....................... 37
Arnett, Caroline
   See Cole, Lois Dwight
Arnett, Jack
   See Goulart, Ron(ald Joseph)
Arnette, Robert
   See Silverberg, Robert
Arno, Enrico 1913-1981 ............................. 43
   Obituary ............................................... 28
Arnold, Caroline 1944- ............................ 174
   Brief entry ............................................ 34
   Earlier sketches in SATA 36, 85, 131
   See also CLR 61
   See also SAAS 23
Arnold, Elizabeth 1944- ........................... 164
Arnold, Elliott 1912-1980 ............................ 5
   Obituary ............................................... 22
Arnold, Emily 1939- .................................. 76
   Earlier sketch in SATA 50
   See McCully, Emily Arnold
Arnold, Katya 1947- ............................... 168
   Earlier sketches in SATA 82, 115
Arnold, Louise ....................................... 175
Arnold, Marsha Diane 1948- ..................... 147
   Earlier sketch in SATA 93
Arnold, Nick 1961- .................................. 113
Arnold, Oren 1900-1980 ............................. 4
Arnold, Susan (Riser) 1951- ....................... 58
Arnold, Tedd 1949- ................................. 160
   Earlier sketches in SATA 69, 116

Arnoldy, Julie
   *See* Bischoff, Julia Bristol
Arnosky, James Edward 1946- .................. *160*
   Earlier sketch in SATA *22*
   *See also* CLR *93*
   *See* Arnosky, Jim
Arnosky, Jim ................................... *118*
   Earlier sketch in SATA *70*
   *See also* CLR *93*
   *See* Arnosky, James Edward
Arnott, Kathleen 1914- .............................. *20*
Arnov, Boris, Jr. 1926- ............................ *12*
Arnow, Harriette (Louisa) Simpson 1908-1986
   ........................................................... *42*
   Obituary ............................................ *47*
Arnsteen, Katy Keck 1934- ....................... *68*
Arnstein, Helene S(olomon) 1915- ............ *12*
Arntson, Herbert E(dward) 1911-1982 ....... *12*
Aroner, Miriam ........................................ *82*
Aronson, Marc 1950- .............................. *175*
   Earlier sketch in SATA *126*
Aronson, Virginia 1954- .......................... *122*
Arora, Shirley (Lease) 1930- ...................... *2*
Arrasmith, Patrick .................................. *176*
Arrigan, Mary 1943- ............................... *142*
Arrington, Stephen L. 1948- ...................... *97*
Arrington, Stephen Lee
   *See* Arrington, Stephen L.
Arrley, Richmond
   *See* Delany, Samuel R., Jr.
Arrowood, (McKendrick Lee) Clinton 1939-
   ........................................................... *19*
Artell, Mike 1948- .................................. *134*
   Earlier sketch in SATA *89*
Arthur, Robert, (Jr.) 1909-1969 ................ *118*
   *See* Arthur, Robert (Andrew)
Arthur, Robert (Andrew) 1909-1969
   *See* Arthur, Robert, (Jr.)
Arthur, Ruth M(abel) 1905-1979 ................ *26*
   Earlier sketch in SATA *7*
Artis, Vicki Kimmel 1945- ........................ *12*
Artzybasheff, Boris (Miklailovich) 1899-1965
   ........................................................... *14*
Aruego, Ariane
   *See* Dewey, Ariane
Aruego, Jose (Espiritu) 1932- ................... *125*
   Earlier sketches in SATA *6, 68*
   *See also* CLR *5*
Arundel, Honor (Morfydd) 1919-1973 .......... *4*
   Obituary ............................................ *24*
   *See also* CLR *35*
Arundel, Jocelyn
   *See* Alexander, Jocelyn Anne Arundel
Arvey, Michael 1948- ............................... *79*
Arzoumanian, Alik .................................. *177*
Asare, Meshack (Yaw) 1945- .................... *139*
   Earlier sketch in SATA *86*
Asaro, Catherine 1955- ........................... *165*
   Earlier sketch in SATA *101*
   *See* Asaro, Catherine Ann
Asaro, Catherine Ann 1955-
   *See* Asaro, Catherine
Asay, Donna Day 1945- ........................... *127*
Asbjornsen, Peter Christen 1812-1885 ........ *15*
   *See also* CLR *104*
   *See* Asbjornsen and Moe
Asch, Frank 1946- .................................. *154*
   Earlier sketches in SATA *5, 66, 102*
Ash, Jutta 1942- ...................................... *38*
Ashabranner, Brent 1921- ........................ *166*
   Earlier sketches in SATA *1, 67, 130*
   *See also* CLR *28*
   *See also* SAAS *14*
Ashabranner, Brent Kenneth
   *See* Ashabranner, Brent
Ashbless, William
   *See* Powers, Tim
Ashby, Gil 1958- .................................... *146*
Ashby, Gwynneth 1922- ............................ *44*
Ashby, Ruth ........................................... *170*
Ashby, Yvonne 1955- .............................. *121*

Ashe, Arthur (Robert, Jr.) 1943-1993 .......... *65*
   Obituary ............................................ *87*
Ashe, Geoffrey (Thomas) 1923- .................. *17*
   Autobiography Feature ......................... *125*
Ashe, Mary Ann
   *See* Lewis, Mary (Christianna)
Asher, Sandra Fenichel .............................. *71*
   Brief entry .......................................... *34*
   Earlier sketch in SATA *36*
   *See also* SAAS *13*
   *See* Asher, Sandy
Asher, Sandy 1942- ................................. *158*
   Autobiography Feature ......................... *158*
   Earlier sketch in SATA *118*
   *See* Asher, Sandra Fenichel
Asheron, Sara
   *See* Moore, Lilian
Ashey, Bella
   *See* Breinburg, Petronella
Ashford, Daisy
   *See* Ashford, Margaret Mary
Ashford, Jeffrey
   *See* Jeffries, Roderic
Ashford, Margaret Mary 1881-1972 .......... *10*
Ashley, Bernard (John) 1935- .................... *155*
   Brief entry .......................................... *39*
   Earlier sketches in SATA *47, 79*
   *See also* CLR *4*
Ashley, Elizabeth
   *See* Salmon, Annie Elizabeth
Ashley, Ray
   *See* Abrashkin, Raymond
Ashman, Linda 1960- .............................. *150*
Ashton, Lorayne
   *See* Gottfried, Theodore Mark
Ashton, Warren T.
   *See* Adams, William Taylor
Asimov, Isaac 1920-1992 .......................... *74*
   Earlier sketches in SATA *1, 26*
   *See also* CLR *79*
Asinof, Eliot 1919- .................................... *6*
Aska, Warabe ......................................... *56*
   *See* Masuda, Takeshi
Asprin, Robert L(ynn) 1946- ...................... *92*
Asquith, Cynthia Mary Evelyn (Charteris)
   1887-1960 ........................................ *107*
Asquith, Ros ......................................... *153*
Astley, Juliet
   *See* Lofts, Norah (Robinson)
Aston, Dianna Hutts 1964- ...................... *176*
Aston, James
   *See* White, T(erence) H(anbury)
Ata, Te 1895-1995 .................................. *119*
Atene, Ann
   *See* Atene, (Rita) Anna
Atene, (Rita) Anna 1922- .......................... *12*
Atheling, William, Jr.
   *See* Blish, James (Benjamin)
Atkins, Catherine .................................. *160*
Atkins, Jeannine 1953- ............................ *172*
   Earlier sketch in SATA *113*
Atkinson, Allen G. 1953(?)-1987 ................ *60*
   Brief entry .......................................... *46*
   Obituary ............................................ *55*
Atkinson, M. E.
   *See* Frankau, Mary Evelyn Atkinson
Atkinson, Margaret Fleming ...................... *14*
Attema, Martha 1949- ............................. *156*
   Earlier sketch in SATA *94*
Atticus
   *See* Davies, Hunter
   and Fleming, Ian
   and Pawle, Gerald Strachan
   and Wilson, (Thomas) Woodrow
Atwater, Florence (Hasseltine Carroll)
   1896-1979 ........................................ *66*
   Earlier sketch in SATA *16*
   *See also* CLR *19*
Atwater, Montgomery Meigs 1904-1976 .... *15*

Atwater, Richard (Tupper) 1892-1948 ........ *66*
   Brief entry .......................................... *27*
   Earlier sketch in SATA *54*
   *See also* CLR *19*
Atwater-Rhodes, Amelia 1984- .................. *170*
   Earlier sketch in SATA *124*
Atwell, Debby 1953- ................................ *150*
   Earlier sketch in SATA *87*
Atwood, Ann (Margaret) 1913-1992 ............. *7*
Atwood, Margaret 1939- .......................... *170*
   Earlier sketch in SATA *50*
Atwood, Margaret Eleanor
   *See* Atwood, Margaret
Aubrey, Meg Kelleher 1963- ....................... *83*
Aubry, Claude B. 1914-1984 ...................... *29*
   Obituary ............................................ *40*
Auch, Herm .......................................... *173*
Auch, Mary Jane ................................... *173*
   Earlier sketch in SATA *138*
Auch, M.J.
   *See* Auch, Mary Jane
Auch, M.J.
   *See* Auch, Mary Jane
Auclair, Joan 1960- .................................. *68*
Auel, Jean M(arie) 1936- .......................... *91*
Auer, Martin 1951- .................................. *77*
Augarde, Steve 1950- ............................. *159*
   Earlier sketch in SATA *25*
Augelli, John P(at) 1921- ........................... *46*
Augustine, Mildred
   *See* Benson, Mildred (Augustine Wirt)
Ault, Phil
   *See* Ault, Phillip H(alliday)
Ault, Phillip H(alliday) 1914- ..................... *23*
Ault, Rosalie Sain 1942- ........................... *38*
Ault, Roz
   *See* Ault, Rosalie Sain
Aung, (Maung) Htin 1909- ......................... *21*
Aunt Weedy
   *See* Alcott, Louisa May
Auseon, Andrew 1976- ........................... *166*
Austen, Carrie
   *See* Bennett, Cherie
Austin, Carrie
   *See* Seuling, Barbara
Austin, Elizabeth S. 1907-1977 .................... *5*
Austin, Harry
   *See* McInerny, Ralph
Austin, Margot 1909(?)-1990 ...................... *11*
   Obituary ............................................ *66*
Austin, Oliver L(uther), Jr. 1903-1988 .......... *7*
   Obituary ............................................ *59*
Austin, Patricia 1950- ............................. *137*
Austin, R. G.
   *See* Gelman, Rita Golden
   and Lamb, Nancy
Austin, Virginia 1951- ............................. *152*
   Earlier sketch in SATA *80*
Auteur, Hillary
   *See* Gottfried, Theodore Mark
Auth, Tony
   *See* Auth, William Anthony, Jr.
Auth, William Anthony, Jr. 1942- ............... *51*
Autry, Gloria Diener
   *See* Allen, Terril Diener
Auvil, Peggy A 1954- .............................. *122*
Auvil, Peggy Appleby
   *See* Auvil, Peggy A
Averill, Esther (Holden) 1902-1992 ............. *28*
   Obituary ............................................ *72*
   Earlier sketch in SATA *1*
Avery, A. A.
   *See* Montgomery, Rutherford George
Avery, Al
   *See* Montgomery, Rutherford George
Avery, Gillian (Elise) 1926- ...................... *137*
   Autobiography Feature ......................... *137*
   Earlier sketches in SATA *7, 75*
   *See also* SAAS *6*
Avery, Kay 1908- ...................................... *5*

Avery, Lorraine
    See Older, Effin
    and Older, Jules
Avery, Lynn
    See Cole, Lois Dwight
Avi ........................................................ 108
    Earlier sketch in SATA 71
    See also CLR 68
    See Wortis, Avi
Avishai, Susan 1949- ............................ 82
Awdry, Christopher Vere 1940- ............ 67
Awdry, Wilbert Vere 1911-1997 .......... 94
    See also CLR 23
Axelrod, Amy ........................................ 131
Axelsen, Stephen 1953- ........................ 165
Axton, David
    See Koontz, Dean R.
Ayars, James S(terling) 1898-1986 ........ 4
Aye, A. K.
    See Edwards, Hazel (Eileen)
Ayer, Eleanor H. 1947-1998 ................ 121
    Earlier sketch in SATA 78
Ayer, Jacqueline 1930- .......................... 13
Ayer, Margaret (?)-1981 ........................ 15
Aylesworth, Jim 1943- .......................... 139
    Earlier sketches in SATA 38, 89
    See also CLR 89
Aylesworth, Thomas G(ibbons) 1927-1995 . 88
    Earlier sketch in SATA 4
    See also CLR 6
    See also SAAS 17
Aylward, Marcus
    See Alexander, Marc
Aymar, Brandt 1911- .............................. 22
Ayme, Marcel (Andre) 1902-1967 .......... 91
    See also CLR 25
Ayres, Becky
    See Hickox, Rebecca (Ayres)
Ayres, Pam 1947- .................................. 90
Aytmatov, Chingiz
    See Aitmatov, Chingiz (Torekulovich)
Ayto, Russell 1960- .............................. 166
    Earlier sketch in SATA 111
Azaid
    See Zaidenberg, Arthur
Azar, Penny 1952- ................................ 121
Azarian, Mary 1940- ............................ 171
    Earlier sketch in SATA 112

B

Baastad, Babbis Friis
    See Friis-Baastad, Babbis Ellinor
Bab
    See Gilbert, W(illiam) S(chwenck)
Babbis, Eleanor
    See Friis-Baastad, Babbis Ellinor
Babbitt, Lucy Cullyford 1960- .............. 85
Babbitt, Natalie (Zane Moore) 1932- .... 106
    Earlier sketches in SATA 6, 68
    See also CLR 53
    See also SAAS 5
Babcock, Chris 1963- ............................ 83
Babcock, Dennis Arthur 1948- .............. 22
Baber, Carolyn Stonnell 1936- .............. 96
Baca, Maria 1951- ................................ 104
Bach, Alice (Hendricks) 1942- .............. 93
    Brief entry ...................................... 27
    Earlier sketch in SATA 30
Bach, Bellamy
    See Windling, Terri
Bach, Mary 1960- ................................ 125
Bach, Richard 1936- .............................. 13
Bach, Richard David
    See Bach, Richard
Bache, Ellyn 1942- ................................ 124
Bachel, Beverly K. 1957- ...................... 142
Bachman, Fred 1949- ............................ 12

Bachman, Richard
    See King, Stephen
Bachrach, Deborah ................................ 80
Bacmeister, Rhoda W(arner) 1893-1991 ..... 11
Bacon, Betty
    See Bacon, Elizabeth
Bacon, Elizabeth 1914-2001 .................... 3
    Obituary ........................................ 131
Bacon, Joan Chase
    See Bowden, Joan Chase
Bacon, Josephine Dodge (Daskam) 1876-1961
    ........................................................ 48
Bacon, Margaret Frances
    Obituary .......................................... 50
    See Bacon, Peggy
Bacon, Margaret Hope 1921- .................. 6
Bacon, Martha Sherman 1917-1981 ........ 18
    Obituary .......................................... 27
    See also CLR 3
Bacon, Melvin 1950- ............................ 93
Bacon, Melvin L.
    See Bacon, Melvin
Bacon, Peggy 1895-1987 ........................ 2
    See Bacon, Margaret Frances
Bacon, R(onald) L(eonard) 1924- ............ 84
    Earlier sketch in SATA 26
Baden, Robert 1936- ............................ 70
Baden-Powell, Robert (Stephenson Smyth)
    1857-1941 ........................................ 16
Badt, Karin L(uisa) 1963- ...................... 91
Baehr, Kingsley M. 1937- ...................... 89
Baehr, Patricia 1952- ............................ 65
Baehr, Patricia Goehner
    See Baehr, Patricia
Baer, Jill
    See Gilbert, (Agnes) Joan (Sewell)
Baer, Judy 1951- .................................... 71
Baer, Julie 1960- .................................. 161
Baer-Block, Roxanna ............................ 172
Baerg, Harry J(ohn) 1909-1996 ............ 12
Baeten, Lieve 1954- .............................. 83
Bagert, Brod 1947- ................................ 80
Baggette, Susan K. 1942- ...................... 126
Bagnold, Enid 1889-1981 ...................... 25
    Earlier sketch in SATA 1
Bahlke, Valerie Worth 1933-1994 .......... 81
    See Worth, Valerie
Bahous, Sally 1939- .............................. 86
Bahr, Mary (Madelyn) 1946- .................. 95
Bahr, Robert 1940- ................................ 38
Bahti, Tom 1926-1972 .......................... 57
    Brief entry ...................................... 31
Baicker-McKee, Carol 1958- ................ 177
Bailey, Alice Cooper 1890-1978 ............ 12
Bailey, Anne 1958- ................................ 71
Bailey, Bernadine (Freeman) 1901-1995 ..... 14
Bailey, Carolyn Sherwin 1875-1961 ...... 14
Bailey, Debbie 1954- ............................ 123
Bailey, Donna (Veronica Anne) 1938- ...... 68
Bailey, Jane H(orton) 1916- .................... 12
Bailey, John (Robert) 1940- .................... 52
Bailey, Linda 1948- .............................. 107
Bailey, Maralyn Collins (Harrison) 1941- ... 12
Bailey, Matilda
    See Radford, Ruby L(orraine)
Bailey, Maurice Charles 1932- ................ 12
Bailey, Pearl (Mae) 1918-1990 .............. 81
Bailey, Ralph Edgar 1893-1982 .............. 11
Bailey, Sheila (Lucas) 1960- .................. 155
Baillie, Allan 1943- .............................. 151
    Earlier sketch in SATA 87
    See also CLR 49
    See also SAAS 21
Baillie, Allan Stuart
    See Baillie, Allan
Baines, John (David) 1943- .................... 71
Bains, Larry
    See Sabin, Louis
Baird, Alison 1963- .............................. 138
Baird, Bil 1904-1987 ............................ 30
    Obituary .......................................... 52

Baird, Thomas (P.) 1923-1990 .............. 45
    Brief entry ...................................... 39
    Obituary .......................................... 64
Baird, William Britton
    See Baird, Bil
Baity, Elizabeth Chesley 1907-1989 ........ 1
Baiul, Oksana 1977- ............................ 108
Bakeless, John (Edwin) 1894-1978 .......... 9
Bakeless, Katherine Little 1895-1992 ...... 9
Baker, Alan 1951- ................................ 146
    Earlier sketches in SATA 22, 93
Baker, Augusta 1911-1998 ...................... 3
Baker, Betty Lou 1928-1987 .................. 73
    Obituary .......................................... 54
    Earlier sketch in SATA 5
Baker, Carin Greenberg 1959- ................ 79
Baker, Charlotte 1910- ............................ 2
Baker, Christopher W. 1952- ................ 144
Baker, (Mary) Elizabeth (Gillette) 1923- ...... 7
Baker, Gayle Cunningham 1950- ............ 39
Baker, James W. 1924- .......................... 65
    Earlier sketch in SATA 22
Baker, James W. 1926- .......................... 122
Baker, Janice E(dla) 1941- .................... 22
Baker, Jeannie 1950- ............................ 156
    Earlier sketches in SATA 23, 88
    See also CLR 28
Baker, Jeffrey J(ohn) W(heeler) 1931- ...... 5
Baker, Jim
    See Baker, James W.
Baker, Ken 1962- ................................ 133
Baker, Laura Nelson 1911- ...................... 3
Baker, Margaret 1890-1965 ...................... 4
Baker, Margaret J(oyce) 1918- ................ 12
    See also SAAS 8
Baker, Mary Gladys Steel 1892-1974 ...... 12
Baker, (Robert) Michael (Graham) 1938- ..... 4
Baker, Nina (Brown) 1888-1957 ............ 15
Baker, Pamela J. 1947- .......................... 66
Baker, Rachel 1904-1978 ........................ 2
    Obituary .......................................... 26
Baker, Rosalie F. 1945- ........................ 166
Baker, Samm Sinclair 1909-1997 ............ 12
    Obituary .......................................... 96
Baker, Susan (Catherine) 1942-1991 ...... 29
Balaam
    See Lamb, G(eoffrey) F(rederick)
Balan, Bruce 1959- .............................. 113
Balcavage, Dynise 1965- ...................... 137
Balch, Glenn 1902-1989 .......................... 3
    Obituary .......................................... 83
    See also SAAS 11
Balderose, Nancy Ward 1952- ................ 93
Balderson, Margaret 1935- .................... 151
Baldry, Cherith 1947- .......................... 167
    Earlier sketch in SATA 72
Balducci, Carolyn (Feleppa) 1946- .......... 5
Baldwin, Alex
    See Griffin, W.E.B.
Baldwin, Anne Norris 1938- .................... 5
Baldwin, Clara ...................................... 11
Baldwin, Gordo
    See Baldwin, Gordon C(ortis)
Baldwin, Gordon C(ortis) 1908-1983 ........ 12
Baldwin, James 1841-1925 .................... 24
Baldwin, James 1924-1987 ...................... 9
    Obituary .......................................... 54
Baldwin, Louis 1919- .......................... 110
Baldwin, Margaret
    See Weis, Margaret
Baldwin, Stan(ley C.) 1929- .................. 62
    Brief entry ...................................... 28
Bales, Carol Ann 1940- ........................ 57
    Brief entry ...................................... 29
Balet, Jan (Bernard) 1913- .................... 11
Balgassi, Haemi 1971- .......................... 131
Balian, Lorna 1929- .............................. 91
    Earlier sketch in SATA 9
Balit, Christina 1961- .......................... 159
    Earlier sketch in SATA 102
Ball, Duncan 1941- .............................. 73

Ball, Zachary
  *See* Janas, Frankie-Lee
  and Masters, Kelly R(ay)
Ballantine, Lesley Frost
  *See* Frost, Lesley
Ballantyne, R(obert) M(ichael) 1825-1894 . *24*
Ballard, James Graham
  *See* Ballard, J.G.
Ballard, Jane
  *See* Gorman, Carol
Ballard, J.G. 1930- ..................................... *93*
Ballard, John 1945- ................................... *110*
Ballard, Lowell C(lyne) 1904-1986 ............ *12*
  Obituary ............................................... *49*
Ballard, (Charles) Martin 1929- ................... *1*
Ballard, Mignon F(ranklin) 1934- .............. *64*
  Brief entry ............................................. *49*
Ballard, Robert D(uane) 1942- ................... *85*
  *See also* CLR *60*
Ballard, Robin 1965- ................................ *126*
Balliett, Blue 1955- ................................. *156*
Ballinger, Bryan 1968- .............................. *161*
Ballouhey, Pierre 1944- ............................. *90*
Balogh, Penelope 1916-1975 ....................... *1*
  Obituary ............................................... *34*
Balouch, Kristen ..................................... *176*
Balow, Tom 1931- .................................... *12*
Baltazzi, Evan S(erge) 1921- ....................... *90*
Baltimore, J.
  *See* Catherall, Arthur
Baltzer, Hans (Adolf) 1900- ....................... *40*
Bambara, Toni Cade 1939-1995 .............. *112*
Bamfylde, Walter
  *See* Bevan, Tom
Bamman, Henry A. 1918- ........................... *12*
Banat, D. R.
  *See* Bradbury, Ray
Bancroft, Griffing 1907-1999 ....................... *6*
Bancroft, Laura
  *See* Baum, L(yman) Frank
Bandel, Betty 1912- .................................. *47*
Baner, Skulda Vanadis 1897-1964 .............. *10*
Banerjee, Anjali ..................................... *174*
Banfill, A. Scott 1956- .............................. *98*
Bang, Betsy 1912- .................................... *48*
  Brief entry ............................................. *37*
Bang, Garrett
  *See* Bang, Molly
Bang, Molly 1943- ................................... *158*
  Earlier sketches in SATA *24, 69, 111*
  *See also* CLR *8*
Bang, Molly Garrett
  *See* Bang, Molly
Bang-Campbell, Monika ........................... *140*
Banjo, The
  *See* Paterson, A(ndrew) B(arton)
Banke, Cecile de
  *See* de Banke, Cecile
Banks, Kate 1960- .................................... *172*
  Earlier sketch in SATA *134*
Banks, Lynne Reid
  *See* CLR *86*
  *See* Reid Banks, Lynne
Banks, Michael A. 1951- ........................... *101*
Banks, Paul 1952- ................................... *174*
Banks, Sara (Jeanne Gordon Harrell) .......... *26*
  *See* Harrell, Sara (Jeanne) Gordon
Bannatyne-Cugnet, Elizabeth Jo-Anne
  *See* Bannatyne-Cugnet, Jo
Bannatyne-Cugnet, Jo 1951- ..................... *101*
Banner, Angela
  *See* CLR *24*
  *See* Maddison, Angela Mary
Bannerman, Helen (Brodie Cowan Watson)
  1862(?)-1946 ........................................ *19*
  *See also* CLR *21*
Banning, Evelyn I. 1903-1993 ..................... *36*
Bannon, Laura (?)-1963 .............................. *6*
Bannor, Brett 1959- ................................. *143*
Bantock, Nick 1950(?)- .............................. *95*

Barasch, Lynne 1939- ............................. *126*
  Earlier sketch in SATA *74*
Barbalet, Margaret 1949- ........................... *77*
Barbary, James
  *See* Beeching, Jack
Barbash, Shepard 1957- ............................. *84*
Barbe, Walter Burke 1926- ......................... *45*
Barber, Antonia 1932- .............................. *163*
  Earlier sketch in SATA *29*
Barber, Lynda
  *See* Graham-Barber, Lynda
Barber, Lynda Graham
  *See* Graham-Barber, Lynda
Barber, Richard (William) 1941- ................. *35*
Barbera, Joe 1911-2006 ............................. *51*
Barbera, Joseph
  *See* Barbera, Joe
Barbera, Joseph Roland
  *See* Barbera, Joe
Barberis, Juan C(arlos) 1920- ..................... *61*
Barbour, Karen 1956- .............................. *170*
  Earlier sketches in SATA *63, 121*
Barbour, Ralph Henry 1870-1944 .............. *16*
Barclay, Bill
  *See* Moorcock, Michael
Barclay, Isabel
  *See* Dobell, I(sabel) M(arian) B(arclay)
Barclay, William Ewert
  *See* Moorcock, Michael
Bardhan-Quallen, Sudipta ......................... *168*
Bare, Arnold Edwin 1920- ......................... *16*
Bare, Colleen Stanley ............................... *32*
Bargar, Gary W. 1947-1985 ....................... *63*
Barger, Jan 1948- ................................... *147*
Barish, Matthew 1907-2000 ....................... *12*
Barkan, Joanne ..................................... *127*
  Earlier sketch in SATA *77*
Barker, Albert W. 1900- .............................. *8*
Barker, Carol (Minturn) 1938- ..................... *31*
Barker, Cicely Mary 1895-1973 ................... *49*
  Brief entry ............................................. *39*
  *See also* CLR *88*
Barker, Melvern 1907-1989 ......................... *11*
Barker, S(quire) Omar 1894-1985 ................ *10*
Barker, Will 1913-1983 ................................ *8*
Barkin, Carol 1944- .................................. *52*
  Earlier sketch in SATA *42*
Barklem, Jill 1951- .................................. *96*
  *See also* CLR *31*
Barkley, James Edward 1941- ....................... *6*
Barks, Carl 1901-2000 ............................... *37*
Barley, Janet Crane 1934- ........................... *95*
Barnaby, Ralph S(tanton) 1893-1986 ............ *9*
Barnard, A. M.
  *See* Alcott, Louisa May
Barnard, Bryn 1956- ................................ *169*
  Earlier sketch in SATA *115*
Barne, Kitty
  *See* Barne, Marion Catherine
Barne, Marion Catherine 1883-1957 .......... *97*
  *See* Barne, Kitty
Barner, Bob 1947- ................................... *136*
  Earlier sketch in SATA *29*
Barnes, Dawn 1957- ................................ *175*
Barnes, (Frank) Eric Wollencott 1907-1962
  ........................................................... *22*
Barnes, Joyce Annette 1958- ....................... *85*
Barnes, Laura T. 1958- ............................. *119*
Barnes, Loutricia
  *See* Barnes-Svarney, Patricia L(ou)
Barnes, Michael 1934- ............................... *55*
Barnes-Murphy, Frances 1951- ................... *88*
Barnes-Murphy, Rowan 1952- ..................... *88*
Barnes-Svarney, Patricia L(ou) 1953- ......... *67*
Barnet, Nancy 1954- ................................. *84*
Barnett, Ivan 1947- .................................. *70*
Barnett, Lincoln (Kinnear) 1909-1979 ......... *36*
Barnett, Moneta 1922-1976 ......................... *33*
Barnett, Naomi 1927- ............................... *40*
Barney, Maginel Wright 1881(?)-1966 ........ *39*
  Brief entry ............................................. *32*

Barnhart, Clarence L(ewis) 1900-1993 ....... *48*
  Obituary ............................................... *78*
Barnouw, Victor 1915-1989 ....................... *43*
  Brief entry ............................................. *28*
Barnstone, Willis 1927- ............................. *20*
Barnum, Jay Hyde 1888(?)-1962 ................ *20*
Barnum, P. T., Jr.
  *See* Stratemeyer, Edward L.
Barnum, Richard ..................................... *67*
  Earlier sketch in SATA *1*
Barnum, Theodore
  *See* Stratemeyer, Edward L.
Baron, Kathy 1954- .................................. *90*
Baron, Virginia Olsen 1931- ....................... *46*
  Brief entry ............................................. *28*
Barr, Donald 1921-2004 ............................. *20*
  Obituary ............................................... *152*
Barr, George 1907-1992 .............................. *2*
Barr, Jene 1922-1985 ................................ *16*
  Obituary ............................................... *42*
  *See* Cohen, Jene Barr
Barr, Nevada 1952- .................................. *126*
  Earlier sketch in SATA *115*
Barrer, Gertrude
  *See* Barrer-Russell, Gertrude
Barrer-Russell, Gertrude 1921- ................... *27*
Barrett, Angela (Jane) 1955- ..................... *145*
  Earlier sketch in SATA *75*
Barrett, Ethel ....................................... *87*
  Brief entry ............................................. *44*
Barrett, Joyce Durham 1943- ..................... *138*
Barrett, Judi
  *See* Barrett, Judith
Barrett, Judith 1941- ................................ *26*
  *See also* CLR *98*
Barrett, Robert T(heodore) 1949- ................ *92*
Barrett, Ron 1937- ................................... *14*
Barrett, Susan (Mary) 1938- ....................... *113*
Barrett, Tracy 1955- ................................ *156*
  Earlier sketches in SATA *84, 115*
Barretta, Gene ..................................... *176*
Barrie, J(ames) M(atthew) 1860-1937 ....... *100*
  *See also* YABC *1*
  *See also* CLR *16*
Barringer, William 1940-1996 ................... *153*
Barrington, Michael
  *See* Moorcock, Michael
Barris, George 1925- ................................ *47*
Barrol, Grady
  *See* Bograd, Larry
Barron, Rex 1951- ................................... *84*
Barron, T(homas) A(rchibald) 1952- ......... *126*
  Earlier sketch in SATA *83*
  *See also* CLR *86*
Barron, Tom
  *See* Barron, T(homas) A(rchibald)
Barrow, Lloyd H. 1942- ............................. *73*
Barry, Dan 1958- ................................... *177*
Barry, Dana (Marie Malloy) 1949- ............. *139*
Barry, James P(otvin) 1918- ....................... *14*
Barry, Katharina Watjen 1936- ..................... *4*
Barry, Robert (Everett) 1931- ...................... *6*
Barry, Scott 1952- ................................... *32*
Barry, Sheila Anne -2003 ........................... *91*
Bartell, Susan S. ................................... *175*
Bartenbach, Jean 1918- ............................. *40*
Barth, Edna 1914-1980 ............................... *7*
  Obituary ............................................... *24*
Barth, Kelly L. 1964- ............................... *152*
Barthelme, Donald 1931-1989 ....................... *7*
  Obituary ............................................... *62*
Bartholomew, Barbara 1941- ....................... *86*
  Brief entry ............................................. *42*
Bartholomew, Jean
  *See* Beatty, Patricia (Robbins)
Bartlett, Alison ..................................... *153*
Bartlett, Philip A. ...................................... *1*
Bartlett, Robert Merrill 1899-1995 ............ *12*
Bartoletti, Susan Campbell 1958- ............. *173*
  Earlier sketches in SATA *88, 129, 135*

Barton, Byron 1930- .................................. 126
Earlier sketches in SATA 9, 90
Barton, Jill(ian) 1940- ............................... 75
Barton, May Hollis ................................... 67
Earlier sketch in SATA 1
Barton, Pat ........................................... 59
See Arrowsmith, Pat
Bartos-Hoeppner, Barbara 1923- .................. 5
Bartram, Simon ...................................... 156
Bartsch, Jochen 1906- ................................ 39
Baruch, Dorothy W(alter) 1899-1962 ......... 21
Barunga, Albert 1912(?)-1977 ................... 120
Bas, Rutger
See Rutgers van der Loeff-Basenau, An(na)
Maria Margaretha
Base, Graeme (Rowland) 1958- ................. 162
Earlier sketches in SATA 67, 101
See also CLR 22
Baseman, Gary 1960- ............................... 174
Bash, Barbara 1948- ................................ 132
Bashevis, Isaac
See Singer, Isaac Bashevis
Bashevis, Yitskhok
See Singer, Isaac Bashevis
Baskin, Leonard 1922-2000 ..................... 120
Brief entry ........................................... 27
Earlier sketch in SATA 30
Baskin, Nora Raleigh 1961- ..................... 129
Bason, Lillian 1913- ................................. 20
Bass, L. G.
See Geringer, Laura
Bassett, Jeni 1959- .................................. 64
Brief entry ........................................... 43
Bassett, John Keith
See Keating, Lawrence A.
Bassett, Lisa 1958- .................................. 61
Bassil, Andrea
See Nilsen, Anna
Bastyra, Judy ........................................ 108
Bat-Ami, Miriam 1950- ............................ 150
Autobiography Feature ........................... 150
Earlier sketches in SATA 82, 122
Bate, Lucy 1939-1993 .............................. 18
Bate, Norman (Arthur) 1916- ...................... 5
Bateman, Colin 1962- .............................. 172
Bateman, Teresa 1957- ............................. 168
Earlier sketch in SATA 112
Bates, Barbara S(nedeker) 1919- ................ 12
Bates, Betty .......................................... 19
See Bates, Elizabeth
Bates, Dianne 1948- ................................ 147
Bates, Ivan ........................................... 175
Bates, Katharine Lee 1859-1929 ................ 113
See Lincoln, James
Bates, Martine
See Leavitt, Martine
Bateson, Catherine 1960- .......................... 157
Batey, Tom 1946- ................................... 52
Brief entry ........................................... 41
Bath, Kevin P.
See Bath, K.P.
Bath, K.P. .............................................. 171
Batherman, Muriel
See Sheldon, Muriel
Batson, Larry 1930- ................................ 35
Batt, Tanya Robyn 1970- ......................... 131
Battaglia, Aurelius 1910- ......................... 50
Brief entry ........................................... 33
Batten, H(arry) Mortimer 1888-1958 ......... 25
Batten, Mary 1937- ................................ 162
Earlier sketches in SATA 5, 102
Batterberry, Ariane Ruskin 1935- ............... 13
Batterberry, Michael Carver 1932- .............. 32
Battle-Lavert, Gwendolyn 1951- ................ 155
Earlier sketch in SATA 85
See Lavert, Gwendolyn Battle
Battles, (Roxy) Edith 1921- ........................ 7
Baudouy, Michel-Aime 1909- ...................... 7

Bauer, Caroline Feller 1935- ...................... 98
Brief entry ........................................... 46
Earlier sketch in SATA 52
See also SAAS 24
Bauer, Fred 1934- ................................... 36
Bauer, Helen 1900-1988 ............................. 2
Bauer, Joan 1951- ................................... 160
Earlier sketch in SATA 117
Bauer, Jutta 1955- .................................. 150
Bauer, Marion Dane 1938- ....................... 144
Autobiography Feature ........................... 144
Earlier sketches in SATA 20, 69, 113
See also SAAS 9
Bauer, Michael Gerard 1955(?)- ................ 167
Bauer, Steven 1948- ................................ 125
Bauerschmidt, Marjorie 1926- ..................... 15
Baughman, Dorothy 1940- ......................... 61
Baum, Allyn Z(elton) 1924-1997 ................ 98
Earlier sketch in SATA 20
Baum, L. Frank
See Thompson, Ruth Plumly
Baum, L(yman) Frank 1856-1919 .............. 100
Earlier sketch in SATA 18
See also CLR 107
Baum, Louis 1948- ................................... 64
Brief entry ........................................... 52
Baum, Louis F.
See Baum, L(yman) Frank
Baum, Willi 1931- ..................................... 4
Baumann, Amy (Brown) Beeching 1922- ... 10
Baumann, Hans 1914- ................................. 2
See also CLR 35
Baumann, Kurt 1935- ................................ 21
Baumgartner, Barbara 1939- ...................... 86
Baurys, Flo(rence) 1938- ......................... 122
Bausum, Ann ......................................... 173
Bawden, Nina (Mary Mabey) 1925- ........... 72
Earlier sketch in SATA 4
See also CLR 51
See also SAAS 16
See Kark, Nina Mary
Bay, Jeanette Graham 1928- ........................ 88
Bayer, Harold
See Gregg, Andrew K.
Bayley, Nicola 1949- ............................... 129
Earlier sketches in SATA 41, 69
Baylor, Byrd 1924- .................................. 136
Earlier sketches in SATA 16, 69
See also CLR 3
Baynes, Pauline (Diana) 1922- ................... 133
Earlier sketches in SATA 19, 59
BB
See Watkins-Pitchford, Denys James
Beach, Charles
See Reid, (Thomas) Mayne
Beach, Charles Amory ................................. 1
Beach, Edward L. 1918-2002 ...................... 12
Obituary .............................................. 140
Beach, Edward Latimer
See Beach, Edward L.
Beach, Lisa 1957- ................................... 111
Beach, Lynn
See Lance, Kathryn
Beach, Stewart T(aft) 1899-1979 ................ 23
Beachcroft, Nina 1931- .............................. 18
Beagle, Peter S. 1939- ............................. 130
Earlier sketch in SATA 60
Beagle, Peter Soyer
See Beagle, Peter S.
Beaglehole, Helen 1946- ........................... 117
Beale, Fleur .......................................... 107
Bealer, Alex W(inkler III) 1921-1980 ............ 8
Obituary .............................................. 22
Beales, Valerie 1915- ................................ 74
Beals, Carleton 1893-1979 .......................... 12
Beame, Rona 1934- ................................... 12
Beamer, (George) Charles (Jr.) 1942- ......... 43
Bean, Normal
See Burroughs, Edgar Rice
Beaney, Jan
See Udall, Jan Beaney

Beaney, Jane
See Udall, Jan Beaney
Bear, Carolyn
See Rayban, Chloe
Bear, Greg(ory Dale) 1951- ...................... 105
Earlier sketch in SATA 65
Bearanger, Marie
See Messier, Claire
Beard, Charles A(ustin) 1874-1948 ............. 18
Beard, Dan(iel Carter) 1850-1941 .............. 22
Beard, Darleen Bailey 1961- ...................... 96
Bearden, Romare (Howard) 1914(?)-1988 .. 22
Obituary .............................................. 56
Beardmore, Cedric
See Beardmore, George
Beardmore, George 1908-1979 .................... 20
Beardsley, Martyn R. 1957- ...................... 150
Bearman, Jane (Ruth) 1917- ....................... 29
Beaton, Clare 1947- ................................ 125
Beatty, Elizabeth
See Holloway, Teresa (Bragunier)
Beatty, Hetty Burlingame 1907-1971 ............. 5
Beatty, Jerome, Jr. 1918- ........................... 5
Beatty, John (Louis) 1922-1975 .................... 6
Obituary .............................................. 25
Beatty, Patricia (Robbins) 1922-1991 ......... 73
Obituary .............................................. 68
Earlier sketches in SATA 1, 30
See also SAAS 4
Beaty, Mary (T.) 1947- ............................ 146
Bechard, Margaret 1953- .......................... 164
Earlier sketch in SATA 85
Bechtel, Louise Seaman 1894-1985 ............... 4
Obituary .............................................. 43
Beck, Barbara L. 1927- ............................. 12
Beck, Ian (Archibald) 1947- ...................... 138
Beck, Peggy 1949- .................................. 171
Becker, Beril 1901-1999 ............................ 11
Becker, Deborah Zimmett 1955- ................ 138
Becker, Helaine 1961- .............................. 142
Becker, John (Leonard) 1901- ...................... 12
Becker, John E(mil) 1942- ........................ 148
Becker, Joyce 1936- ................................. 39
Becker, May Lamberton 1873-1958 .............. 33
Becker, Neesa 1951- ................................ 123
Becker, Shari ......................................... 174
Beckett, Sheilah 1913- .............................. 33
Beckman, Delores 1914-1994 ....................... 51
Beckman, Gunnel 1910- .............................. 6
See also CLR 25
See also SAAS 9
Beckman, Kaj
See Beckman, Karin
Beckman, Karin 1913- ............................... 45
Beckman, Per (Frithiof) 1913- .................... 45
Bedard, Michael 1949- ............................. 154
Earlier sketch in SATA 93
See also CLR 35
Beddows, Eric
See Nutt, Ken
Bedford, A. N.
See Watson, Jane Werner
Bedford, Annie North
See Watson, Jane Werner
Bedford, David ....................................... 159
Bedoukian, Kerop 1907-1981 ...................... 53
Bee, Jay
See Brainerd, John W(hiting)
Beebe, B(urdetta) F(aye) ............................. 1
See Johnson, B(urdetta) F(aye)
Beebe, (Charles) William 1877-1962 ........... 19
Beeby, Betty 1923- .................................. 25
Beech, Webb
See Griffin, W.E.B.
Beecham, Jahnna ................................... 161
Beechcroft, William
See Hallstead, William F(inn III)
Beeching, Jack 1922- ................................ 14
Beeke, Tiphanie ..................................... 163
Beeler, Janet
See Shaw, Janet

Beeler, Nelson F(rederick) 1910-1978 ........ 13
Beere, Peter 1951- ............................................. 97
Beers, Dorothy Sands 1917- ................................ 9
Beers, Lorna 1897-1989 ....................................... 14
Beers, V(ictor) Gilbert 1928- ................... 130
  Earlier sketch in SATA 9
Beeton, Max
  See Redding, Robert Hull
Begay, Shonto 1954- ....................................... 137
Begaye, Lisa Shook
  See Beach, Lisa
Begin, Maryjane 1963- .................................. 82
Begin-Callanan, Maryjane
  See Begin, Maryjane
Begley, Kathleen A(nne) 1948- ................... 21
Behan, Leslie
  See Gottfried, Theodore Mark
Behler, Deborah A. 1947- ......................... 145
Behler, John L. 1943-2006 ........................ 145
  Obituary ............................................... 173
Behler, John Luther
  See Behler, John L.
Behn, Harry 1898-1973 ................................ 2
  Obituary ................................................. 34
Behnke, Frances L. ........................................ 8
Behr, Joyce 1929- ........................................ 15
Behrens, June York 1925- ........................... 19
Behrman, Carol H(elen) 1925- ................... 144
  Earlier sketch in SATA 14
Beifuss, John, (Jr.) 1959- .......................... 92
Beil, Karen Magnuson 1950- ..................... 124
Beiler, Edna 1923- ...................................... 61
Beinicke, Steve 1956- .................................. 69
Beirne, Barbara 1933- ................................. 71
Beiser, Arthur 1931- ..................................... 22
Beiser, Germaine 1931- ................................. 11
Belair, Richard L. 1934- ............................. 45
Belaney, Archibald Stansfeld 1888-1938 .... 24
  See Grey Owl
Belbin, David 1958- ................................... 164
  Earlier sketch in SATA 106
Belden, Wilanne Schneider 1925- .............. 56
Belfrage, Sally 1936-1994 ........................... 65
  Obituary ................................................. 79
Belknap, B. H.
  See Ellis, Edward S(ylvester)
Belknap, Boynton
  See Ellis, Edward S(ylvester)
Belknap, Boynton M.D.
  See Ellis, Edward S(ylvester)
Bell, Anthea 1936- ..................................... 148
  Earlier sketch in SATA 88
Bell, Clare (Louise) 1952- ........................... 99
Bell, Corydon Whitten 1894-1980 ............... 3
Bell, David Owen 1949- ............................... 99
Bell, Emerson
  See Stratemeyer, Edward L.
Bell, Emily Mary
  See Cason, Mabel Earp
Bell, Frank
  See Benson, Mildred (Augustine Wirt)
Bell, Gertrude (Wood) 1911-1987 .............. 12
Bell, Hilari 1958- ....................................... 151
Bell, Jadrien
  See Golden, Christie
Bell, Janet
  See Clymer, Eleanor
Bell, Janet Cheatham 1937- ........................ 127
Bell, Krista (Anne Blakeney) 1950- ........... 126
Bell, Margaret E(lizabeth) 1898-1990 .......... 2
Bell, Mary Reeves 1946- ............................. 88
Bell, Norman (Edward) 1899- ..................... 11
Bell, Raymond Martin 1907-1999 ............... 13
Bell, Siobhan ........................................... 177
Bell, Thelma Harrington 1896-1985 ............. 3
Bell, William 1945- ...................................... 90
  See also CLR 91
Bellairs, John (Anthony) 1938-1991 .......... 160
  Obituary ................................................. 66
  Earlier sketches in SATA 2, 68
  See also CLR 37

Beller, Susan Provost 1949- .................. 128
  Earlier sketch in SATA 84
  See also CLR 106
Bellingham, Brenda 1931- ....................... 99
  Brief entry .............................................. 51
Bello, Rosario de
  See De Bello, Rosario
Belloc, (Joseph) Hilaire (Pierre Sebastien Rene
  Swanton) 1870-1953 ........................... 112
  See also YABC 1
  See also CLR 102
Belloc, Joseph Peter Rene Hilaire
  See Belloc, (Joseph) Hilaire (Pierre Sebastien
  Rene Swanton)
Belloc, Joseph Pierre Hilaire
  See Belloc, (Joseph) Hilaire (Pierre Sebastien
  Rene Swanton)
Belloli, Andrea P. A. 1947- ..................... 86
Bellville, Cheryl Walsh 1944- ................. 54
  Brief entry .............................................. 49
Belpre, Pura 1899-1982 .......................... 16
  Obituary ................................................. 30
Belting, Natalia Maree 1915-1997 ............ 6
Belton, John Raynor 1931- ..................... 22
Belton, Sandra (Yvonne) 1939- .............. 134
  Earlier sketch in SATA 85
Beltran, Alberto 1923- ............................ 43
Beltran-Hernandez, Irene 1945- ............. 74
Belvedere, Lee
  See Grayland, Valerie (Merle Spanner)
Bemelmans, Ludwig 1898-1962 .............. 100
  Earlier sketch in SATA 15
  See also CLR 93
Benander, Carl D. 1941- ......................... 74
Benary, Margot
  See Benary-Isbert, Margot
Benary-Isbert, Margot 1889-1979 ............ 2
  Obituary ................................................. 21
  See also CLR 12
Benasutti, Marion 1908-1992 .................... 6
Benatar, Raquel 1955- ............................ 167
Benchley, Nathaniel (Goddard) 1915-1981 . 25
  Obituary ................................................. 28
  Earlier sketch in SATA 3
Benchley, Peter 1940-2006 ..................... 164
  Earlier sketches in SATA 3, 89
Benchley, Peter Bradford
  See Benchley, Peter
Bender, Edna 1941- ................................. 92
Bender, Esther 1942- ............................... 88
Bender, Lucy Ellen 1942- ........................ 22
Bender, Robert 1962- .............................. 160
  Earlier sketch in SATA 79
Bendick, Jeanne 1919- ............................ 135
  Earlier sketches in SATA 2, 68
  See also CLR 5
  See also SAAS 4
Bendick, Robert L(ouis) 1917- ................. 11
Benedict, Andrew
  See Arthur, Robert, (Jr.)
Benedict, Dorothy Potter 1889-1979 ......... 11
  Obituary ................................................. 23
Benedict, Lois Trimble 1902-1967 ............ 12
Benedict, Rex 1920-1995 ........................... 8
Benedict, Stewart H(urd) 1924- ............... 26
Beneduce, Ann Keay ............................... 128
Benet, Laura 1884-1979 ............................ 3
  Obituary ................................................. 23
Benet, Stephen Vincent 1898-1943
  See YABC 1
Benet, Sula 1906-1982 ............................ 21
  Obituary ................................................. 33
Ben-Ezer, Ehud 1936- ............................ 122
Benezra, Barbara (Beardsley) 1921- ........ 10
Benham, Leslie 1922- .............................. 48
Benham, Lois (Dakin) 1924- .................... 48
Benham, Mary Lile 1914-1991 ................. 55
Benjamin, E. M. J.
  See Bache, Ellyn
Benjamin, Nora
  See Kubie, Nora Gottheil Benjamin

Benjamin, Saragail Katzman 1953- .......... 86
Benner, Cheryl 1962- .............................. 80
Benner, Judith Ann 1942- ........................ 94
Bennett, Alice
  See Ziner, Florence
Bennett, Cherie 1960- ............................. 158
  Earlier sketch in SATA 97
Bennett, Dorothea
  See Young, Dorothea Bennett
Bennett, James (W.) 1942- ..................... 153
  Autobiography Feature ........................... 153
  Earlier sketches in SATA 93, 148
Bennett, Jay 1912- .................................. 87
  Brief entry .............................................. 27
  Earlier sketch in SATA 41
  See also SAAS 4
Bennett, Jill (Crawford) 1934- ................. 41
Bennett, John 1865-1956
  See YABC 1
Bennett, Penelope (Agnes) 1938- ............ 94
Bennett, Rachel
  See Hill, Margaret (Ohler)
Bennett, Rainey 1907-1998 ..................... 15
  Obituary ................................................. 111
Bennett, Richard 1899- ........................... 21
Bennett, Russell H(oradley) 1896- .......... 25
Bennett, William (John) 1943- ................. 102
Benning, Elizabeth
  See Rice, Bebe Faas
Benson, Elizabeth P(olk) 1924- ............... 65
Benson, Kathleen 1947- .......................... 111
  Earlier sketch in SATA 62
Benson, Linda M(aria) 1959- ................... 84
Benson, Mildred (Augustine Wirt) 1905-2002
  ........................................................... 100
  Obituary ................................................. 135
  Earlier sketch in SATA 65
  See Keene, Carolyn
Benson, Mildred Wirt
  See Benson, Mildred (Augustine Wirt)
Benson, Millie
  See Benson, Mildred (Augustine Wirt)
Benson, Patrick 1956- ............................. 147
Benson, Sally 1900-1972 ........................ 35
  Obituary ................................................. 27
  Earlier sketch in SATA 1
Bentley, Judith (McBride) 1945- .............. 89
  Earlier sketch in SATA 40
Bentley, Nancy (L.) 1946- ........................ 78
Bentley, Phyllis Eleanor 1894-1977 .......... 6
  Obituary ................................................. 25
Bentley, Roy 1947- .................................. 46
Bentley, William (George) 1916- ............. 84
Benton, Jim 1963- .................................... 172
ben Uzair, Salem
  See Horne, Richard Henry Hengist
Bercaw, Edna Coe 1961- ......................... 124
Berck, Judith 1960- ................................. 75
Berelson, Howard 1940- ........................... 5
Berends, Polly Berrien 1939- ................... 50
  Brief entry .............................................. 38
Berenstain, Jan 1923- ............................. 135
  Earlier sketches in SATA 12, 64, 129
  See also CLR 19
  See also SAAS 20
Berenstain, Janice
  See Berenstain, Jan
Berenstain, Michael 1951- ....................... 45
Berenstain, Stan 1923-2005 .................... 135
  Obituary ................................................. 169
  Earlier sketches in SATA 12, 64, 129
  See also CLR 19
  See also SAAS 20
Berenstain, Stanley
  See Berenstain, Stan
Berenzy, Alix 1957- ................................. 168
  Earlier sketch in SATA 65
Beresford, Elisabeth 1928- ...................... 141
  Earlier sketches in SATA 25, 86
  See also SAAS 20
Berg, Adriane G(ilda) 1948- .................... 152

Berg, Dave
  *See* Berg, David
Berg, David 1920-2002 ........................... 27
  Obituary ................................................ 137
Berg, Elizabeth 1948- ............................. 104
Berg, Jean Horton 1913-1995 ................... 6
Berg, Joan
  *See* Victor, Joan Berg
Berg, Ron 1952- ........................................ 48
Bergaust, Erik 1925-1978 ....................... 20
Bergel, Colin J. 1963- ............................. 137
Bergen, Joyce 1949- ................................. 95
Berger, Barbara (Helen) 1945- ............... 77
Berger, Gilda 1935- ................................. 88
  Brief entry ............................................. 42
Berger, Josef 1903-1971 ......................... 36
Berger, Melvin H. 1927- ......................... 158
  Autobiography Feature ........................ 124
  Earlier sketches in SATA 5, 88
  *See also* CLR 32
  *See also* SAAS 2
Berger, Phil 1942-2001 ........................... 62
Berger, Samantha (Allison) 1969- ......... 140
Berger, Terry 1933- .................................... 8
Bergey, Alyce (Mae) 1934- ..................... 45
Bergin, Mark 1961- ................................. 160
  Earlier sketch in SATA 114
Bergman, Donna 1934- ............................. 73
Bergman, Tamar 1939- ............................. 95
Bergsma, Jody Lynn ............................... 163
Bergum, Constance R. 1952- ................. 121
Berkes, Marianne ................................... 173
Berkey, Barry Robert 1935- ..................... 24
Berkowitz, Freda Pastor 1908-1994 ....... 12
Berkus, Clara Widess 1909- ..................... 78
Berlan, Kathryn Hook 1946- ..................... 78
Berlfein, Judy Reiss 1958- ....................... 79
Berliner, Don 1930- .................................. 33
Berliner, Franz 1930- ............................... 13
Berlitz, Charles (L. Frambach) 1914-2003 . 32
  Obituary ................................................ 151
Berman, Linda 1948- ............................... 38
Berman, Paul (Lawrence) 1949- ............. 66
Berna, Paul 1910-1994 ............................. 15
  Obituary ................................................ 78
  *See also* CLR 19
Bernadette
  *See* Watts, (Anna) Bernadette
Bernard, Bruce 1928-2000 ....................... 78
  Obituary ................................................ 124
Bernard, George I. 1949- ......................... 39
Bernard, Jacqueline (de Sieyes) 1921-1983 .. 8
  Obituary ................................................ 45
Bernard, Patricia 1942- ........................... 106
Bernardin, James (B.) 1966- ................... 112
Bernards, Neal 1963- ............................... 71
Bernays, Anne 1930- ............................... 32
Bernhard, Durga T. 1961- ....................... 80
Bernhard, Emery 1950- ........................... 80
Bernstein, Daryl (Evan) 1976- ............... 81
Bernstein, Joanne E(ckstein) 1943- ....... 15
Bernstein, Margery 1933- ....................... 114
Bernstein, Theodore M(enline) 1904-1979 . 12
  Obituary ................................................ 27
Berrien, Edith Heal
  *See* Heal, Edith
Berrill, Jacquelyn (Batsel) 1905- ........... 12
Berrington, John
  *See* Brownjohn, Alan
Berry, B. J.
  *See* Berry, Barbara J.
Berry, Barbara J. 1937- ............................. 7
Berry, Erick
  *See* Best, (Evangel) Allena Champlin
Berry, James 1925- ................................. 110
  Earlier sketch in SATA 67
  *See also* CLR 22
Berry, Joy
  *See* Berry, Joy Wilt
Berry, Joy Wilt 1944- ............................... 58
  Brief entry ............................................. 46

Berry, William D(avid) 1926- ................... 14
Bersani, Shennen 1961- ........................... 164
Berson, Harold 1926- ................................. 4
Bertagna, Julie 1962- ............................... 151
Bertin, Charles-Francois
  *See* Berlitz, Charles (L. Frambach)
Bertolet, Paul
  *See* McLaughlin, Frank
Berton, Pierre (Francis de Marigny) 1920-2004
  ............................................................. 99
  Obituary ................................................ 158
Bertrand, Cecile 1953- ............................. 76
Bertrand, Diane Gonzales 1956- ............. 177
  Earlier sketch in SATA 106
Bertrand, Lynne 1963- ............................. 164
  Earlier sketch in SATA 81
Beskow, Elsa (Maartman) 1874-1953 ....... 20
  *See also* CLR 17
Bess, Clayton
  *See* CLR 39
  *See* Locke, Robert
Best, (Evangel) Allena Champlin 1892-1974
  ................................................................. 2
  Obituary ................................................ 25
Best, Cari 1951- ....................................... 149
  Earlier sketch in SATA 107
Best, (Oswald) Herbert 1894-1980 ........... 2
Bestall, A(lfred) E(dmeades) 1892-1986 ..... 97
  Obituary ................................................ 48
Betancourt, Jeanne 1941- ....................... 148
  Brief entry ............................................. 43
  Earlier sketches in SATA 55, 96
Beth, Mary
  *See* Miller, Mary Beth
Bethancourt, T. Ernesto ........................... 11
  *See also* CLR 3
  *See* Paisley, Tom
Bethel, Dell 1929- ..................................... 52
Bethell, Jean (Frankenberry) 1922- ........... 8
Bethers, Ray 1902-1973 ............................. 6
Bethke, Bruce Raymond 1955- ............... 114
Bethlen, T. D.
  *See* Silverberg, Robert
Bethune, J. G.
  *See* Ellis, Edward S(ylvester)
Bethune, J. H.
  *See* Ellis, Edward S(ylvester)
Betteridge, Anne
  *See* Potter, Margaret (Newman)
Bettina
  *See* Ehrlich, Bettina Bauer
Bettmann, Otto Ludwig 1903-1998 ......... 46
Betts, James
  *See* Haynes, Betsy
Betz, Eva Kelly 1897-1968 ....................... 10
Bevan, Tom 1868-1930(?)
  *See* YABC 2
Bewick, Thomas 1753-1828 ..................... 16
Beyer, Audrey White 1916- ........................ 9
Beyer, Paul J. III 1950- ........................... 74
Beynon, John
  *See* Harris, John (Wyndham Parkes Lucas)
  Beynon
Bezencon, Jacqueline (Buxcel) 1924- ....... 48
Bial, Morrison David 1917- ..................... 62
Bial, Raymond 1948- ............................... 165
  Earlier sketches in SATA 76, 116
Biala
  *See* Brustlein, Janice Tworkov
Biale, Rachel 1952- ................................... 99
Bialk, Elisa
  *See* Krautter, Elisa (Bialk)
Bianchi, John 1947- ................................... 91
Bianchi, Robert S(teven) 1943- ............... 92
Bianco, Margery
  *See* Bianco, Margery Williams
Bianco, Margery Williams 1881-1944 ....... 15
  *See also* CLR 19
Bianco, Pamela 1906- ............................... 28
Bibby, Violet 1908- ................................... 24
Bible, Charles 1937- ................................. 13

Bibo, Bobette
  *See* Gugliotta, Bobette
Bice, Clare 1909-1976 ............................... 22
Bickerstaff, Isaac
  *See* Swift, Jonathan
Biegel, Paul 1925- ..................................... 79
  Earlier sketch in SATA 16
  *See also* CLR 27
  *See also* SAAS 18
Biemiller, Carl L(udwig), Jr.) 1912-1979 .... 40
  Obituary ................................................ 21
Bienenfeld, Florence L(ucille) 1929- ....... 39
Bierhorst, John (William) 1936- ............. 149
  Autobiography Feature ........................ 149
  Earlier sketches in SATA 6, 91
  *See also* SAAS 10
Biggar, Joan R(awlins) 1936- ................. 120
Biggle, Lloyd, Jr. 1923-2002 ..................... 65
Bilal, Abdel W(ahab) 1970- ....................... 92
Bilbrough, Norman 1941- ....................... 111
Bildner, Phil ........................................... 173
Bileck, Marvin 1920- ............................... 40
Bilibin, Ivan (Iakolevich) 1876-1942 ....... 61
Bill, Alfred Hoyt 1879-1964 ..................... 44
Billam, Rosemary 1952- ........................... 61
Billings, Charlene W(interer) 1941- ......... 41
Billingsley, Franny 1954- ....................... 132
Billington, Elizabeth T(hain) ................... 50
  Brief entry ............................................. 43
Billout, Guy (Rene) 1941- ....................... 144
  Earlier sketch in SATA 10
  *See also* CLR 33
Bilson, Geoffrey 1938-1987 ..................... 99
Binch, Caroline (Lesley) 1947- ............... 140
  Earlier sketch in SATA 81
Bing, Christopher (H.) ............................. 126
Bingham, Caroline 1962- ......................... 158
Bingham, Jane M. 1941- ......................... 163
Bingham, Jane Marie
  *See* Bingham, Jane M.
Bingham, Sam(uel A.) 1944- ..................... 96
Bingley, Margaret (Jane Kirby) 1947- ....... 72
Binkley, Anne
  *See* Rand, Ann (Binkley)
Binzen, Bill ............................................... 24
  *See* Binzen, William
Birch, David (W.) 1913-1996 ................... 89
Birch, Reginald B(athurst) 1856-1943 ....... 19
Birchman, David 1949- ............................. 72
Birchmore, Daniel A. 1951- ..................... 92
Bird, Carmel 1940- ................................. 124
Bird, E(lzy) J(ay) 1911- ........................... 58
Birdsall, Jeanne 1952(?)- ....................... 170
Birdseye, Tom 1951- ............................... 148
  Earlier sketches in SATA 66, 98
Birenbaum, Barbara 1941- ....................... 65
Birmingham, Lloyd P(aul) 1924- ............. 83
  Earlier sketch in SATA 12
Birmingham, Ruth
  *See* Sorrells, Walter
Birney, Betty G. 1947- ............................. 169
  Earlier sketch in SATA 98
Biro, B.
  *See* Biro, B(alint) S(tephen)
Biro, B(alint) S(tephen) 1921- ................... 67
  *See* Biro, Val
Biro, Val ....................................................... 1
  *See also* CLR 28
  *See also* SAAS 13
  *See* Biro, B(alint) S(tephen)
Bischoff, Julia Bristol 1899-1970 ........... 12
Bishop, Bonnie 1943- ............................... 37
Bishop, Claire Huchet 1899(?)-1993 ....... 14
  Obituary ................................................ 74
  *See also* CLR 80
Bishop, Courtney
  *See* Ruemmler, John D(avid)
Bishop, Curtis (Kent) 1912-1967 ............... 6
Bishop, Gavin 1946- ............................... 144
  Earlier sketch in SATA 97
Bishop, Kathleen Wong 1954- ............... 120

Bishop, Kathy
  *See* Bishop, Kathleen Wong
Bishop, Nic 1955- .................................... *161*
  Earlier sketch in SATA *107*
Bisset, Donald 1910-1995 ........................ 86
  Earlier sketch in SATA *7*
Bisson, Terry 1942- ................................. 99
Bisson, Terry Ballantine
  *See* Bisson, Terry
Bitter, Gary G(len) 1940- ....................... 22
Bixby, William (Courtney) 1920-1986 ......... 6
  Obituary ............................................ 47
Bjoerk, Christina 1938- ........................... 99
  Earlier sketch in SATA *67*
  *See also* CLR *22*
Bjork, Christina
  *See* Bjoerk, Christina
Bjorklund, Lorence F. 1913-1978 .............. 35
  Brief entry ......................................... 32
Bjorkman, Steve ................................... *163*
Black, Algernon David 1900-1993 ............. 12
  Obituary ............................................ 76
Black, Holly 1971- ................................ *147*
Black, Irma Simonton 1906-1972 ............... 2
  Obituary ............................................ 25
Black, Mansell
  *See* Trevor, Elleston
Black, MaryAnn
  *See* Easley, MaryAnn
Black, Susan Adams 1953- ....................... 40
Blackall, Bernie 1956- .......................... *126*
Blackburn, Claire
  *See* Altman, Linda Jacobs
Blackburn, John(ny) Brewton 1952- .......... 15
Blackburn, Joyce Knight 1920- ................. 29
Blackett, Veronica Heath 1927- ................ 12
Blackie, Jean Cutler 1943- ...................... 79
Blacklin, Malcolm
  *See* Chambers, Aidan
Blacklock, Dyan 1951- .......................... *112*
Blackman, Malorie 1962- ........................ *128*
  Earlier sketch in SATA *83*
Blackton, Peter
  *See* Wilson, Lionel
Blackwood, Alan 1932- ........................... 70
Blackwood, Gary L. 1945- ...................... *169*
  Earlier sketches in SATA *72, 118*
Blade, Alexander
  *See* Garrett, (Gordon) Randall (Phillip)
    and Hamilton, Edmond
    and Silverberg, Robert
Blades, Ann (Sager) 1947- ....................... 69
  Earlier sketch in SATA *16*
  *See also* CLR *15*
Bladow, Suzanne Wilson 1937- ................ 14
Blaine, John
  *See* Goodwin, Harold L(eland)
Blaine, Marge
  *See* Blaine, Margery Kay
Blaine, Margery Kay 1937- ...................... *11*
Blair, Alison
  *See* Lerangis, Peter
Blair, Anne Denton 1914-1993 .................. 46
Blair, David Nelson 1954- ....................... 80
Blair, Eric (Arthur) 1903-1950 ................. 29
  *See* Orwell, George
Blair, Jay 1953- ..................................... 45
Blair, Lucile
  *See* Yeakley, Marjory Hall
Blair, Margaret Whitman 1951- ............... *124*
Blair, Pauline Hunter
  *See* Clarke, Pauline
Blair, Ruth Van Ness 1912-1999 ............... 12
Blair, Shannon
  *See* Kaye, Marilyn
Blair, Walter 1900-1992 .......................... 12
  Obituary ............................................ 72
Blaisdell, Bob
  *See* Blaisdell, Robert
Blaisdell, Robert 1959- .......................... *105*
Blake, Bronwyn 1940- ........................... *149*

Blake, Jon 1954- .................................... *171*
  Earlier sketch in SATA *78*
Blake, Olive
  *See* Supraner, Robyn
Blake, Quentin (Saxby) 1932- ................. *125*
  Earlier sketches in SATA *9, 52, 96*
  *See also* CLR *31*
Blake, Robert 1949- ............................... 42
Blake, Robert J. ................................... *160*
Blake, Walker E.
  *See* Griffin, W.E.B.
Blake, William 1757-1827 ....................... 30
  *See also* CLR *52*
Blakely, Gloria 1950- ............................ *139*
Blakely, Roger K. 1922- ......................... 82
Blakeney, Jay D.
  *See* Chester, Deborah
Blakey, Nancy 1955- .............................. 94
Blanc, Esther S. 1913-1997 ...................... 66
Blanchard, Patricia ............................... *125*
Blanchet, M(uriel) Wylie 1891-1961 ........ *106*
Blanco, Richard L(idio) 1926- .................. 63
Bland, E.
  *See* Nesbit, E(dith)
Bland, Edith Nesbit
  *See* Nesbit, E(dith)
Bland, Fabian
  *See* Nesbit, E(dith)
Blank, Clarissa Mabel 1915-1965 .............. 62
Blassingame, Wyatt Rainey 1909-1985 ....... 34
  Obituary ............................................ 41
  Earlier sketch in SATA *1*
Blatchford, Claire H. 1944- ...................... 94
Blauer, Ettagale 1940- ........................... 49
Bledsoe, Glen L. 1951- ......................... *108*
Bledsoe, Glen Leonard
  *See* Bledsoe, Glen L.
Bledsoe, Karen E. 1962- ........................ *167*
  Earlier sketch in SATA *108*
Bledsoe, Karen Elizabeth
  *See* Bledsoe, Karen E.
Bledsoe, Lucy Jane 1957- ...................... *162*
  Earlier sketch in SATA *97*
Bleeker, Sonia ...................................... 2
  Obituary ............................................ 26
  *See* Zim, Sonia Bleeker
Blegen, Daniel M. 1950- .......................... 92
Blegvad, Erik 1923- ............................. *132*
  Earlier sketches in SATA *14, 66*
Blegvad, Lenore 1926- .......................... *176*
  Earlier sketches in SATA *14, 66*
Blish, James (Benjamin) 1921-1975 ........... 66
Blishen, Edward (William) 1920-1996 ........ 66
  Obituary ............................................ 93
  Earlier sketch in SATA *8*
Bliss, Corinne Demas 1947- ..................... 37
  *See* Demas, Corinne
Bliss, Frederick
  *See* Card, Orson Scott
Bliss, Gillian
  *See* Paton Walsh, Jill
Bliss, Harry 1964- ............................... *156*
Bliss, Reginald
  *See* Wells, H(erbert) G(eorge)
Bliss, Ronald G(ene) 1942- ...................... 12
Bliven, Bruce, Jr. 1916-2002 .................... 2
Blixen, Karen (Christentze Dinesen)
  1885-1962 .......................................... 44
  *See* Dinesen, Isak
Blizzard, Gladys S. (?)-1992 .................... 79
Blobaum, Cindy 1966- .......................... *123*
Bloch, Lucienne 1909-1999 ...................... 10
Bloch, Marie Halun 1910-1998 .................. 6
  *See also* SAAS *9*
Bloch, Robert (Albert) 1917-1994 ............. 12
  Obituary ............................................ 82
Blochman, Lawrence G(oldtree) 1900-1975
  ....................................................... 22

Block, Francesca Lia 1962- ..................... *158*
  Earlier sketches in SATA *80, 116*
  *See also* CLR *116*
  *See also* SAAS *21*
Block, Irvin 1917- ................................. 12
Blomgren, Jennifer (Alice) 1954- ............ *136*
Blood, Charles Lewis 1929- ..................... 28
Bloom, Barbara Lee 1943- ...................... *146*
Bloom, Freddy 1914-2000 ....................... 37
  Obituary ........................................... *121*
Bloom, Lloyd 1947- .............................. *108*
  Brief entry ......................................... 43
Bloom, Suzanne 1950- .......................... *172*
Bloomfield, Michaela 1966- ..................... 70
Bloor, Edward (William) 1950- ................ *155*
  Earlier sketch in SATA *98*
Blos, Joan W(insor) 1928- ...................... *153*
  Autobiography Feature ........................ *153*
  Brief entry ......................................... 27
  Earlier sketches in SATA *33, 69, 109*
  *See also* CLR *18*
  *See also* SAAS *11*
Blough, Glenn O(rlando) 1907-1995 ........... *1*
Blue, Rose 1931- ................................. *166*
  Autobiography Feature ........................ *117*
  Earlier sketches in SATA *5, 91, 93*
  *See also* SAAS *24*
Blue, Zachary
  *See* Stine, R.L.
Bluggage, Oranthy
  *See* Alcott, Louisa May
Blumberg, Leda 1956- ............................ 59
Blumberg, Rhoda 1917- ......................... *123*
  Earlier sketches in SATA *35, 70*
  *See also* CLR *21*
Blume, Judy (Sussman) 1938- .................. *142*
  Earlier sketches in SATA *2, 31, 79*
  *See also* CLR *69*
Blumenthal, Deborah ........................... *161*
Blumenthal, Shirley 1943- ....................... 46
Blutig, Eduard
  *See* Gorey, Edward (St. John)
Bly, Janet (Chester) 1945- ....................... 43
Bly, Stephen A(rthur) 1944- ................... *116*
  Earlier sketch in SATA *43*
Blyler, Allison Lee 1966- ........................ 74
Blyton, Carey 1932-2002 ........................ 9
  Obituary ........................................... *138*
Blyton, Enid (Mary) 1897-1968 ................. 25
  *See also* CLR *31*
Boardman, Fon Wyman, Jr. 1911-2000 ........ 6
Boardman, Gwenn R. ............................ 12
  *See* Petersen, Gwenn Boardman
Boase, Wendy 1944-1999 ........................ 28
  Obituary ........................................... *110*
Boatner, Mark Mayo III 1921- .................. 29
Bobbe, Dorothie de Bear 1905-1975 ........... *1*
  Obituary ............................................ 25
Bober, Natalie S. 1930- ......................... *134*
  Earlier sketch in SATA *87*
  *See also* SAAS *23*
Bobette, Bibo
  *See* Gugliotta, Bobette
Bobritsky, Vladimir ............................... 47
  Brief entry ......................................... 32
  *See* Bobri, Vladimir V.
Bochak, Grayce 1956- ............................ 76
Bock, Hal
  *See* Bock, Harold I.
Bock, Harold I. 1939- ............................ 10
Bock, William Sauts Netamux'we 1939- .... 14
Bode, Janet 1943-1999 ........................... 96
  Obituary ........................................... *118*
  Earlier sketch in SATA *60*
Bodecker, N(iels) M(ogens) 1922-1988 ...... 73
  Obituary ............................................ 54
  Earlier sketch in SATA *8*
Boden, Hilda
  *See* Bodenham, Hilda Morris
Bodenham, Hilda Morris 1901- ................. 13

Bodett, Tom ............................................. *70*
See Bodett, Thomas Edward
Bodie, Idella F(allaw) 1925- ..................... *89*
Earlier sketch in SATA *12*
Bodker, Cecil 1927- ............................... *133*
Earlier sketch in SATA *14*
See also CLR 23
Bodker, Cecil 1927-
See Bodker, Cecil
Bodsworth, (Charles) Fred(erick) 1918- ..... *27*
Boeckman, Charles 1920- ......................... *12*
Boelts, Maribeth 1964- ........................... *163*
Earlier sketch in SATA *78*
Boerst, William J. 1939- ........................ *170*
Earlier sketch in SATA *121*
Boesch, Mark J(oseph) 1917- .................... *12*
Boesen, Victor 1908- .............................. *16*
Bogacki, Tomek 1950- ............................. *138*
Bogaerts, Gert 1965- .............................. *80*
Bogan, Paulette 1960- ............................ *129*
Bogart, Jo Ellen 1945- ............................ *92*
See also CLR 59
Boggs, Ralph Steele 1901-1994 .................. *7*
Bograd, Larry 1953- ............................... *89*
Earlier sketch in SATA *33*
See also SAAS 21
Bohdal, Susi 1951- ................................ *101*
Earlier sketch in SATA *22*
Bohlen, Nina 1931- ................................ *58*
Bohlmeijer, Arno 1956- ........................... *94*
Bohner, Charles (Henry) 1927- ................... *62*
Bohnhoff, Maya Kaathryn 1954- ................ *88*
Boissard, Janine 1932- ............................ *59*
Bojunga, Lygia
See Nunes, Lygia Bojunga
Bojunga-Nunes, Lygia
See Nunes, Lygia Bojunga
Boland, Janice ..................................... *98*
Bolden, Tonya 1959- .............................. *138*
Earlier sketch in SATA *79*
Bolden, Tonya Wilyce
See Bolden, Tonya
Boles, Paul Darcy 1916-1984 ..................... *9*
Obituary .......................................... *38*
Bolian, Polly 1925- ................................. *4*
Bollen, Roger 1941(?)- ............................ *83*
Brief entry ....................................... *29*
Bolliger, Max 1929- ................................. *7*
Bollinger, Max 1929- ............................. *167*
Bollinger, Peter .................................... *172*
Bolognese, Don(ald Alan) 1934- ................. *129*
Earlier sketches in SATA *24, 71*
Bolotin, Norman (Phillip) 1951- ................. *93*
Bolton, Carole 1926- ............................... *6*
Bolton, Elizabeth
See St. John, Nicole
Bolton, Evelyn
See Bunting, (Anne) Eve(lyn)
Bonar, Veronica
See Bailey, Donna (Veronica Anne)
Bond, B. J.
See Heneghan, James
Bond, Bruce 1939- .................................. *61*
Bond, Felicia 1954- ................................ *126*
Earlier sketch in SATA *49*
Bond, Gladys Baker 1912- ........................ *14*
Bond, Higgins 1951- ............................... *177*
Earlier sketch in SATA *83*
Bond, J. Harvey
See Winterbotham, R(ussell) R(obert)
Bond, (Thomas) Michael 1926- .................. *157*
Earlier sketches in SATA *6, 58*
See also CLR 95
See also SAAS 3
Bond, Nancy 1945- ................................ *159*
Autobiography Feature ......................... *159*
Earlier sketches in SATA *22, 82*
See also CLR 11
See also SAAS 13
Bond, Nancy Barbara
See Bond, Nancy

Bond, Rebecca 1972- ............................. *130*
Bond, Ruskin 1934- ................................ *87*
Earlier sketch in SATA *14*
Bondie, J. D.
See Cunningham, Chet
Bondoux, Anne-Laure 1971- ..................... *175*
Bone, Ian 1956- ................................... *158*
Earlier sketch in SATA *117*
Bonehill, Captain Ralph
See Stratemeyer, Edward L.
Bonham, Barbara Thomas 1926- .................. *7*
Bonham, Frank 1914-1989 ......................... *49*
Obituary .......................................... *62*
Earlier sketch in SATA *1*
See also SAAS 3
Boniface, William 1963- .......................... *102*
Bonn, Pat
See Bonn, Patricia Carolyn
Bonn, Patricia Carolyn 1948- .................... *43*
Bonner, Mary Graham 1890-1974 ............... *19*
Bonner, Mike 1951- ............................... *121*
Bonners, Susan 1947- ............................. *85*
Brief entry ....................................... *48*
Bonnett-Rampersaud, Louise .................... *173*
Bonning, Tony 1948- .............................. *169*
Bonsall, Crosby Barbara (Newell) 1921-1995
.................................................... *23*
Obituary .......................................... *84*
Bonsall, Joseph S. 1948- ......................... *119*
Bonsignore, Joan 1959- ........................... *140*
Bontemps, Arna(ud Wendell) 1902-1973 .... *44*
Obituary .......................................... *24*
Earlier sketch in SATA *2*
See also CLR 6
Bonzon, Paul-Jacques 1908-1978 ................ *22*
Boock, Paula 1964- ............................... *134*
Booher, Dianna Daniels 1948- ................... *33*
Book, Rick 1949- .................................. *119*
Book, Rita
See Holub, Joan
Bookman, Charlotte
See Zolotow, Charlotte (Gertrude) S(hapiro)
Boon, Debbie 1960- ............................... *103*
Boon, Emilie (Laetitia) 1958- .................... *86*
Boone, Charles Eugene
See Boone, Pat
Boone, Pat 1934- ................................... *7*
Boorman, Linda (Kay) 1940- ..................... *46*
Boorstin, Daniel J(oseph) 1914-2004 .......... *52*
Booth, Ernest Sheldon 1915-1984 ............... *43*
Booth, Graham (Charles) 1935- .................. *37*
Bootman, Colin .................................... *159*
Borden, Louise (Walker) 1949- ................. *141*
Autobiography Feature ......................... *141*
Earlier sketches in SATA *68, 104*
Bordier, Georgette 1924- ......................... *16*
Borgman, James
See Borgman, Jim
Borgman, James Mark
See Borgman, Jim
Borgman, Jim 1954- ............................... *122*
See Borgman, James Mark
Boring, Mel 1939- ................................. *168*
Earlier sketch in SATA *35*
Borja, Corinne 1929- .............................. *22*
Borja, Robert 1923- ............................... *22*
Borland, Hal ........................................ *5*
Obituary .......................................... *24*
See Borland, Harold Glen
Borland, Kathryn Kilby 1916- .................... *16*
Borlenghi, Patricia 1951- ......................... *79*
Born, Adolf 1930- ................................. *49*
Bornstein, Ruth Lercher
Autobiography Feature ......................... *107*
See Bornstein-Lercher, Ruth
Bornstein-Lercher, Ruth 1927- ................... *88*
Earlier sketch in SATA *14*
See Bornstein, Ruth Lercher
Borski, Lucia Merecka .............................. *18*
Borten, Helen Jacobson 1930- ..................... *5*
Bortolotti, Dan 1969- ............................. *157*

Borton, Elizabeth
See Trevino, Elizabeth B(orton) de
Borton, Lady 1942- ................................ *98*
Borton de Trevino, Elizabeth
See Trevino, Elizabeth B(orton) de
Bortstein, Larry 1942- ............................ *16*
Bortz, Alfred B(enjamin) 1944- ................. *139*
Earlier sketch in SATA *74*
Bortz, Fred
See Bortz, Alfred B(enjamin)
Bosco, Jack
See Holliday, Joseph
Boshell, Gordon 1908- ............................ *15*
Boshinski, Blanche 1922- ......................... *10*
Bosman, Paul 1929- ............................... *107*
Bosse, Malcolm (Joseph, Jr.) 1926-2002 .. *136*
Earlier sketch in SATA *35*
Bosserman, (Charles) Phillip 1931- ............. *84*
Bossom, Naomi 1933- ............................. *35*
Bostock, Mike 1962- ............................. *114*
Boston, L(ucy) M(aria Wood) 1892-1990 ... *19*
Obituary .......................................... *64*
See also CLR 3
Bostrom, Kathleen (Susan) Long 1954- .... *139*
Bostrom, Kathy
See Bostrom, Kathleen (Susan) Long
Bosworth, J. Allan 1925- ......................... *19*
Bothwell, Jean (?)-1977 ............................ *2*
Botkin, B(enjamin) A(lbert) 1901-1975 ...... *40*
Botsford, Ward 1927-2004 ........................ *66*
Botting, Douglas (Scott) 1934- .................. *43*
Bottner, Barbara 1943- ........................... *170*
Autobiography Feature ......................... *121*
Earlier sketches in SATA *14, 93*
See also SAAS 26
Bottone, Frank G., Jr. 1969- .................... *141*
Bouchard, David 1952- ........................... *117*
Boucher, (Clarence) Carter 1954- .............. *129*
Boudelang, Bob
See Pell, Ed(ward)
Boughton, Richard 1954- ......................... *75*
Boulet, Susan Seddon 1941- ..................... *50*
Boulle, Pierre (Francois Marie-Louis)
1912-1994 ...................................... *22*
Obituary .......................................... *78*
Boulton, Jane 1921- ............................... *91*
Bouma, Paddy 1947- .............................. *128*
Bour, Daniele 1939- ............................... *62*
Bourdon, David 1934-1998 ....................... *46*
Bourgeois, Paulette 1951- ....................... *153*
Bourne, Lesley
See Marshall, Evelyn
Bourne, Miriam Anne 1931-1989 ............... *16*
Obituary .......................................... *63*
Boutet de Monvel, (Louis) M(aurice)
1850(?)-1913 .................................. *30*
See also CLR 32
Bova, Ben 1932- .................................. *133*
Earlier sketches in SATA *6, 68*
See also CLR 96
Bova, Benjamin William
See Bova, Ben
Bovaird, Anne E(lizabeth) 1960- ............... *90*
Bow, Patricia 1946- ............................... *168*
Bowden, Joan Chase 1925- ....................... *51*
Brief entry ....................................... *38*
Bowen, Alexandria Russell ....................... *97*
Bowen, Andy Russell
See Bowen, Alexandria Russell
Bowen, Anne 1952- ............................... *170*
Bowen, Betty Morgan
See West, Betty
Bowen, Catherine (Shober) Drinker 1897-1973
.................................................... *7*
Bowen, David
See Bowen, Joshua David
Bowen, Fred 1953- ............................... *136*
Bowen, Joshua David 1930- ...................... *22*
Bowen, Rhys
See Quin-Harkin, Janet

Bowen, Robert Sydney 1900-1977 ............. 52
  Obituary ............................................ 21
Bowermaster, Jon 1954- ......................... 135
  Earlier sketch in SATA 77
Bowers, Terrell L. 1945- ......................... 101
Bowers, Terry
  *See* Bowers, Terrell L.
Bowie, C. W.
  *See* Old, Wendie C(orbin)
  and Wirths, Claudine (Turner) G(ibson)
Bowie, Jim
  *See* Norwood, Victor G(eorge) C(harles)
  and Stratemeyer, Edward L.
Bowkett, Stephen 1953- .............................. 67
Bowler, Jan Brett
  *See* Brett, Jan
Bowler, Tim 1953- ................................. 149
Bowman, Crystal 1951- ............................ 105
Bowman, James Cloyd 1880-1961 ............. 23
Bowman, John S(tewart) 1931- .................. 16
Bowman, Kathleen (Gill) 1942- .................. 52
  Brief entry ........................................ 40
Boyce, George A(rthur) 1898- ................... 19
Boyd, Candy Dawson 1946- ...................... 72
  *See also* CLR 50
Boyd, Pauline
  *See* Schock, Pauline
Boyd, Selma
  *See* Acuff, Selma Boyd
Boyd, Waldo T. 1918- .............................. 18
Boyden, Linda 1948- ............................... 143
Boyer, Allen B. 1963- .............................. 153
Boyer, Robert E(rnst) 1929- ...................... 22
Boyes, Vivien 1952- ............................... 106
Boyes, Vivien Elizabeth
  *See* Boyes, Vivien
Boyle, Ann (Peters) 1916- .......................... 10
Boyle, Eleanor Vere (Gordon) 1825-1916 .. 28
Boyle, Robert H. 1928- ............................. 65
Boylston, Helen Dore 1895-1984 ............... 23
  Obituary ............................................ 39
Boynton, Sandra (Keith) 1953- ................. 152
  Brief entry ........................................ 38
  Earlier sketches in SATA 57, 107
  *See also* CLR 105
Boz
  *See* Dickens, Charles (John Huffam)
Bracken, Charles
  *See* Pellowski, Michael (Joseph)
Brackers de Hugo, Pierre 1960- ................ 115
Brackett, Dolli Tingle 1911-1993 ............. 137
Brackett, Virginia 1950- .......................... 166
  Earlier sketch in SATA 121
Brackett, Virginia Roberts Meredith
  *See* Brackett, Virginia
Bradbury, Bianca (Ryley) 1908-1982 .......... 56
  Earlier sketch in SATA 3
Bradbury, Edward P.
  *See* Moorcock, Michael
Bradbury, Ray 1920- ............................... 123
  Earlier sketches in SATA 11, 64
Bradbury, Ray Douglas
  *See* Bradbury, Ray
Bradby, Marie ............................................ 161
Bradfield, Carl 1942- ................................ 91
Bradford, Ann (Liddell) 1917- ................... 56
  Brief entry ........................................ 38
Bradford, Barbara Taylor 1933- ................. 66
Bradford, Karleen 1936- ............................ 96
  Earlier sketch in SATA 48
Bradford, Lois J(ean) 1936- ....................... 36
Bradford, Richard (Roark) 1932-2002 ........ 59
  Obituary .......................................... 135
Bradley, Duane
  *See* Sanborn, Duane

Bradley, Marion Zimmer 1930-1999 ......... 139
  Obituary .......................................... 116
  Earlier sketch in SATA 90
  *See* Chapman, Lee
  and Dexter, John
  and Gardner, Miriam
  and Ives, Morgan
  and Rivers, Elfrida
Bradley, Virginia 1912- ............................. 23
Bradley, Will
  *See* Strickland, (William) Brad(ley)
Bradman, Tony 1954- .............................. 152
  Earlier sketch in SATA 81
Bradshaw, Gillian (Joan) 1949- ................. 118
Bradshaw, Gillian 1956- .......................... 127
Bradshaw, Gillian Marucha
  *See* Bradshaw, Gillian
Bradstreet, T. J.
  *See* Thesman, Jean
Brady, Esther Wood 1905-1987 .................. 31
  Obituary ............................................ 53
Brady, Irene 1943- ..................................... 4
Brady, Kimberley S. 1953- ....................... 101
Brady, Kimberley Smith
  *See* Brady, Kimberley S.
Brady, Lillian 1902- ................................... 28
Bragdon, Elspeth MacDuffie 1897-1980 ....... 6
Bragdon, Lillian Jacot ................................ 24
Brager, Bruce L. 1949- ............................ 146
Bragg, Mabel Caroline 1870-1945 ............. 24
Bragg, Michael 1948- ................................ 46
Bragg, Ruth Gembicki 1943- ...................... 77
Brahm, Sumishta 1954- ............................. 58
Brailsford, Frances
  *See* Wosmek, Frances
Brainerd, John W(hiting) 1918- .................. 65
Braithwaite, Althea 1940- .......................... 23
  Autobiography Feature ......................... 119
  *See also* SAAS 24
Bram, Elizabeth 1948- ............................... 30
Brancato, Robin F(idler) 1936- ................... 97
  *See also* CLR 32
  *See also* SAAS 9
Branch, Muriel Miller 1943- ..................... 152
  Earlier sketch in SATA 94
Brand, Christianna
  *See* Lewis, Mary (Christianna)
Brand, Rebecca
  *See* Charnas, Suzy McKee
Brandel, Marc 1919- ................................. 71
Brandenberg, Alexa (Demetria) 1966- .......... 97
Brandenberg, Aliki (Liacouras) 1929- ........ 157
  Earlier sketches in SATA 2, 35, 75, 113
  *See* Aliki
Brandenberg, Franz 1932- .......................... 75
  Earlier sketches in SATA 8, 35
Brandenburg, Jim 1945- ............................. 87
Brandhorst, Carl T(heodore) 1898-1988 ..... 23
Brandis, Marianne 1938- .......................... 149
  Earlier sketches in SATA 59, 96
Brandon, Brumsic, Jr. 1927- ......................... 9
Brandon, Curt
  *See* Bishop, Curtis (Kent)
Brandreth, Gyles 1948- .............................. 28
  *See* Brandreth, Gyles Daubeney
Brandreth, Gyles Daubeney 1948-
  *See* Brandreth, Gyles
Brandt, Catharine 1905-1997 ..................... 40
Brandt, Keith
  *See* Sabin, Louis
Brandt, Sue R(eading) 1916- ...................... 59
Branfield, John (Charles) 1931- .................. 11
Branford, Henrietta 1946-1999 ................. 106
Branley, Franklyn M(ansfield) 1915-2002

.................................................................. 136
  Earlier sketches in SATA 4, 68
  *See also* CLR 13
  *See also* SAAS 16

Branscum, Robbie (Tilley) 1937-1997 ........ 72
  Obituary ............................................ 96
  Earlier sketch in SATA 23
  *See also* SAAS 17
Bransom, (John) Paul 1885-1979 ............... 43
Brashares, Ann 1967- ............................... 145
  *See also* CLR 113
Braswell, E.J.
  *See* Lynn, Tracy
Braswell, Elizabeth J.
  *See* Lynn, Tracy
Braswell, Liz
  *See* Lynn, Tracy
Bratton, Helen 1899-1986 ............................ 4
Bratun, Katy 1950- .................................. 160
  Earlier sketch in SATA 83
Braude, Michael 1936- ............................... 23
Braun, Lilian Jackson 1916(?)- .................. 109
Brautigan, Richard (Gary) 1935-1984 ......... 56
Bray, Libba ............................................. 159
Braymer, Marjorie Elizabeth 1911-1988 ....... 6
Breathed, Berke 1957- ............................. 161
  Earlier sketch in SATA 86
Breathed, Guy Berkeley
  *See* Breathed, Berke
Brecht, Edith 1895-1975 .............................. 6
  Obituary ............................................ 25
Breck, Vivian
  *See* Breckenfeld, Vivian Gurney
Breckenfeld, Vivian Gurney 1895-1992 ......... 1
Breda, Tjalmar
  *See* DeJong, David C(ornel)
Bredeson, Carmen 1944- ........................... 163
  Earlier sketch in SATA 98
Breinburg, Petronella 1927- ........................ 11
  *See also* CLR 31
Breisky, William J(ohn) 1928- .................... 22
Brenaman, Miriam ................................... 172
Brennan, Gale (Patrick) 1927- .................... 64
  Brief entry ........................................ 53
Brennan, Herbie
  *See* Brennan, J(ames) H(erbert)
Brennan, J(ames) H(erbert) 1940- ............. 140
Brennan, Jan
  *See* Brennan, J(ames) H(erbert)
Brennan, Joseph Lomas 1903-2000 .............. 6
Brennan, Linda Crotta 1952- ..................... 130
Brenner, Anita 1905-1974 .......................... 56
Brenner, Barbara (Johnes) 1925- ............... 124
  Earlier sketches in SATA 4, 42, 76
  *See also* SAAS 14
Brenner, Fred 1920- .................................. 36
  Brief entry ........................................ 34
Brent, Stuart .......................................... 14
Breslin, Theresa .................................... 128
  Autobiography Feature ......................... 128
  Earlier sketch in SATA 70
Breslow, Maurice 1935- ............................. 72
Breslow, Maurice A
  *See* Breslow, Maurice
Breslow, Susan 1951- ................................ 69
Brett, Bernard 1925- ................................. 22
Brett, Grace N(eff) 1900-1975 .................... 23
Brett, Jan 1949- ...................................... 171
  Earlier sketches in SATA 42, 71, 130
  *See also* CLR 27
Brett, Jan Churchill
  *See* Brett, Jan
Brett Bowler, Jan
  *See* Brett, Jan
Brewer, James D. 1951- ............................ 108
Brewer, Sally King 1947- ............................ 33
Brewster, Benjamin
  *See* Folsom, Franklin (Brewster)
Brewster, Hugh 1950- ................................ 95
Brewster, Patience 1952- ............................ 97
Brewton, John E(dmund) 1898-1982 ............ 5
Brian, Janeen (Paulette) 1948- .................. 141
Brick, John 1922-1973 ............................... 10
Brickman, Robin D. 1954- ......................... 155

Bride, Nadja
　　*See* Nobisso, Josephine
Bridgers, Sue Ellen 1942- ........................... *90*
　　Autobiography Feature ........................... *109*
　　Earlier sketch in SATA *22*
　　*See also* CLR *18*
　　*See also* SAAS *1*
Bridges, Laurie
　　*See* Bruck, Lorraine
Bridges, Ruby (Nell) 1954- ........................ *131*
Bridges, William (Andrew) 1901-1984 ........ *5*
Bridwell, Norman (Ray) 1928- ................. *138*
　　Earlier sketches in SATA *4, 68*
　　*See also* CLR *96*
Brier, Howard M(axwell) 1903-1969 .......... *8*
Brierley, (Louise) 1958- .............................. *59*
Briggs, Katharine Mary 1898-1980 .......... *101*
　　Obituary ....................................................... *25*
Briggs, Peter 1921-1975 .............................. *39*
　　Obituary ....................................................... *31*
Briggs, Raymond 1934- .............................. *131*
　　Earlier sketches in SATA *23, 66*
　　*See also* CLR *10*
Briggs, Raymond Redvers
　　*See* Briggs, Raymond
Bright, Robert (Douglas Sr.) 1902-1988 ..... *63*
　　Obituary ....................................................... *60*
　　Earlier sketch in SATA *24*
Bright, Sarah
　　*See* Shine, Deborah
Brightfield, Richard 1927- .......................... *65*
　　Brief entry .................................................... *53*
Brightfield, Rick
　　*See* Brightfield, Richard
Brighton, Catherine 1943- ........................ *107*
　　Earlier sketch in SATA *65*
Brill, Marlene Targ 1945- .......................... *124*
　　Earlier sketch in SATA *77*
Brimberg, Stanlee 1947- ................................ *9*
Brimner, Larry Dane 1949- ........................ *170*
　　Autobiography Feature ........................... *112*
　　Earlier sketch in SATA *79*
Brin, David 1950- ......................................... *65*
Brin, Ruth Firestone 1921- .......................... *22*
Brinckloe, Julie (Lorraine) 1950- ............... *13*
Brindel, June (Rachuy) 1919- ....................... *7*
Brindle, Max
　　*See* Fleischman, Sid
Brindze, Ruth 1903-1984 ............................. *23*
Brink, Carol Ryrie 1895-1981 ................... *100*
　　Obituary ....................................................... *27*
　　Earlier sketches in SATA *1, 31*
　　*See also* CLR *30*
Brinsmead, H. F(ay)
　　*See* Brinsmead, H(esba) F(ay)
Brinsmead, H. F.
　　*See* Brinsmead, H(esba) F(ay)
Brinsmead, H(esba) F(ay) 1922- ................. *78*
　　Earlier sketch in SATA *18*
　　*See also* CLR *47*
　　*See also* SAAS *5*
Briquebec, John
　　*See* Rowland-Entwistle, (Arthur) Theodore
　　(Henry)
Brisbane, Henry R.
　　*See* Ellis, Edward S(ylvester)
Brisco, P. A.
　　*See* Matthews, Patricia
Brisco, Patty
　　*See* Matthews, Patricia
　　and Matthews, Clayton (Hartley)
Briscoe, Jill (Pauline) 1935- ....................... *56*
　　Brief entry .................................................... *47*
Brisley, Joyce Lankester 1896-1978 ............ *22*
　　Obituary ....................................................... *84*
Brissenden, Connie
　　*See* Brissenden, Constance
Brissenden, Constance 1947- ...................... *150*
Brisson, Pat 1951- ........................................ *177*
　　Autobiography Feature ........................... *133*
　　Earlier sketches in SATA *67, 128, 133*

Britt, Dell 1934- ............................................... *1*
Brittain, Bill
　　*See* SAAS *7*
　　*See* Brittain, William (E.)
Brittain, C. Dale 1948- ................................ *82*
Brittain, William (E.) 1930- ....................... *76*
　　Earlier sketch in SATA *36*
　　*See* Brittain, Bill
Brittingham, Geoffrey (Hugh) 1959- .......... *76*
Britton, Kate ............................................... *49*
　　*See* Stegeman, Janet Allais
Britton, Louisa
　　*See* McGuire, Leslie (Sarah)
Britton, Rick 1952- ....................................... *82*
Bro, Margueritte (Harmon) 1894-1977 ........ *19*
　　Obituary ....................................................... *27*
Broach, Elise 1963- .................................... *173*
Broadhead, Helen Cross 1913- ................... *25*
Brochmann, Elizabeth 1938- ....................... *41*
Brock, Betty (Carter) 1923-2003 .................. *4*
　　Obituary ..................................................... *150*
Brock, C(harles) E(dmund) 1870-1938 ....... *42*
　　Brief entry .................................................... *32*
Brock, Delia
　　*See* Ephron, Delia
Brock, Emma L(illian) 1886-1974 ................. *8*
Brock, H(enry) M(atthew) 1875-1960 ......... *42*
Brockett, Eleanor Hall 1913-1967 .............. *10*
Brockman, C(hristian) Frank 1902-1985 ..... *26*
Brockmeier, Kevin 1972- ............................ *176*
Broderick, Dorothy M. 1929- ....................... *5*
Brodeur, Ruth Wallace
　　*See* Wallace-Brodeur, Ruth
Brodie, Sally
　　*See* Cavin, Ruth (Brodie)
Brodsky, Beverly
　　*See* McDermott, Beverly Brodsky
Brody, Wendy
　　*See* Staub, Wendy Corsi
Broeger, Achim 1944- ................................. *31*
Broekel, Rainer Lothar 1923- ...................... *38*
Broekel, Ray
　　*See* Broekel, Rainer Lothar
Broekstra, Lorette 1964- ............................ *124*
Broger, Achim
　　*See* Broeger, Achim
Broida, Marian ......................................... *154*
Brokamp, Marilyn 1920- ............................. *10*
Broman, Fred
　　*See* Moseley, James W(illett)
Bromhall, Winifred ...................................... *26*
Brommer, Gerald F(rederick) 1927- ............ *28*
Brondfield, Jerome 1913-1998 ..................... *22*
Brondfield, Jerry
　　*See* Brondfield, Jerome
Bronner, Stephen Eric 1949- ...................... *101*
Bronowski, Jacob 1908-1974 ....................... *55*
Bronson, Lynn
　　*See* Lampman, Evelyn Sibley
Brook, Judith (Penelope) 1926- ................... *59*
　　Brief entry .................................................... *51*
Brook, Judy
　　*See* Brook, Judith (Penelope)
Brooke, L(eonard) Leslie 1862-1940 .......... *17*
　　*See also* CLR *20*
Brooke, William J. 1946- ........................... *139*
Brooke-Haven, P.
　　*See* Wodehouse, P(elham) G(renville)
Brookins, Dana 1931- ................................. *28*
Brooks, Anita ................................................. *5*
　　*See* Abramovitz, Anita (Zeltner Brooks)
Brooks, Bill 1939- ......................................... *59*
Brooks, Bruce 1950- ................................... *112*
　　Brief entry .................................................... *53*
　　Earlier sketch in SATA *72*
　　*See also* CLR *25*
Brooks, Caryl 1924- ...................................... *84*
Brooks, Charlotte K(endrick) 1918-1998 .... *24*
　　Obituary ..................................................... *112*
Brooks, Erik 1972- ..................................... *152*

Brooks, George
　　*See* Baum, L(yman) Frank
Brooks, Gwendolyn 1917-2000 ..................... *6*
　　Obituary ..................................................... *123*
　　*See also* CLR *27*
Brooks, Gwendolyn Elizabeth
　　*See* Brooks, Gwendolyn
Brooks, Jerome 1931- .................................. *23*
Brooks, Kevin M. 1959- ............................ *150*
Brooks, Lester 1924- ...................................... *7*
Brooks, Martha 1944- ................................ *134*
　　Autobiography Feature ........................... *134*
　　Earlier sketches in SATA *68, 121*
Brooks, Maurice (Graham) 1900- ................ *45*
Brooks, Polly Schoyer 1912- ....................... *12*
Brooks, Ron(ald George) 1948- ................... *94*
　　Brief entry .................................................... *33*
Brooks, Terry 1944- ...................................... *60*
Brooks, Walter R(ollin) 1886-1958 ............. *17*
Brooks-Hill, Helen (Mason) 1908-1994 ...... *59*
Broome, Errol 1937- ................................... *158*
　　Earlier sketch in SATA *105*
Brophy, Nannette 1963- ............................... *73*
Brosnan, James Patrick 1929- ...................... *14*
Brosnan, Jim
　　*See* Brosnan, James Patrick
Brostoff, Anita 1931- ................................. *132*
Brothers Grimm
　　*See* Grimm, Jacob Ludwig Karl
　　and Grimm, Wilhelm Karl
Brothers Hildebrandt, The
　　*See* Hildebrandt, Greg
　　and Hildebrandt, Tim
Broun, Emily
　　*See* Sterne, Emma Gelders
Brouwer, S. W.
　　*See* Brouwer, Sigmund (W.)
Brouwer, Sigmund (W.) 1959- ................... *109*
Brow, Thea 1934- ......................................... *60*
Brower, Millicent ........................................... *8*
Brower, Pauline 1929- .................................. *22*
Browin, Frances Williams 1898-1986 ........... *5*
Brown, Alexis
　　*See* Baumann, Amy (Brown) Beeching
Brown, Anne Ensign 1937- ........................... *61*
Brown, Beverly Swerdlow ............................. *97*
Brown, Bill
　　*See* Brown, William L(ouis)
Brown, Billye Walker
　　*See* Cutchen, Billye Walker
Brown, Bob
　　*See* Brown, Robert Joseph
Brown, Buck 1936- ....................................... *45*
Brown, Cassie 1919-1986 ............................. *55*
Brown, Conrad 1922- .................................... *31*
Brown, Craig McFarland 1947- ................... *73*
Brown, David
　　*See* Brown, David A(lan)
　　and Myller, Rolf
Brown, Dee 1908-2002 ............................... *110*
　　Obituary ..................................................... *141*
　　Earlier sketch in SATA *5*
Brown, Dee Alexander
　　*See* Brown, Dee
Brown, Don 1949- ....................................... *172*
Brown, Drew T. III 1955- ............................ *83*
Brown, Drollene P. 1939- ............................. *53*
Brown, Eleanor Frances 1908-1987 ............... *3*
Brown, Elizabeth Ferguson 1937- .............. *153*
Brown, Elizabeth M(yers) 1915- ................. *43*
Brown, Fern G. 1918- ................................... *34*
Brown, (Robert) Fletch 1923- ...................... *42*
Brown, Fornan 1901-1996 ............................ *71*
　　Obituary ....................................................... *88*
Brown, George Earl 1883-1964 ................... *11*
Brown, George Mackay 1921-1996 ............. *35*
Brown, Irene Bennett 1932- ........................... *3*
Brown, Irving
　　*See* Adams, William Taylor
Brown, Ivor (John Carnegie) 1891-1974 ...... *5*
　　Obituary ....................................................... *26*

Brown, Jane Clark 1930- ............................. 81
Brown, Janet Mitsui ................................. 87
Brown, Jo 1964- ..................................... 170
Brown, Joanne 1933- ................................ 147
Brown, Joe David 1915-1976 ......................... 44
Brown, Joseph E(dward) 1929- ...................... 59
　Brief entry ....................................... 51
Brown, Judith Gwyn 1933- ........................... 20
Brown, Kathryn 1955- .............................. 168
　Earlier sketch in SATA 98
Brown, Kathy
　See Brown, Kathryn
Brown, Ken (James) ................................. 129
Brown, Kevin 1960- ................................ 101
Brown, Laurene Krasny 1945- ........................ 99
　Earlier sketch in SATA 54
Brown, Laurie Krasny
　See Brown, Laurene Krasny
Brown, Lloyd Arnold 1907-1966 ...................... 36
Brown, Mahlon A.
　See Ellis, Edward S(ylvester)
Brown, Marc (Tolon) 1946- ......................... 145
　Earlier sketches in SATA 10, 53, 80
　See also CLR 29
Brown, Marcia (Joan) 1918- .......................... 47
　Earlier sketch in SATA 7
　See also CLR 12
Brown, Margaret Wise 1910-1952 .................... 100
　See also YABC 2
　See also CLR 107
Brown, Margery (Wheeler) ........................... 78
　Earlier sketch in SATA 5
Brown, Marion Marsh 1908-2001 ....................... 6
Brown, Myra Berry 1918- ............................. 6
Brown, Palmer 1919- ................................ 36
Brown, Pamela (Beatrice) 1924-1989 ................. 5
　Obituary .......................................... 61
Brown, Reeve Lindbergh
　See Lindbergh, Reeve
Brown, Richard E. 1946- ............................ 61
Brown, Robert Joseph 1907-1989 ..................... 14
Brown, Roderick (Langmere) Haig-
　See Haig-Brown, Roderick (Langmere)
Brown, Rosalie .................................... 9
　See Moore, Rosalie (Gertrude)
Brown, Roswell
　See Webb, Jean Francis (III)
Brown, Roy (Frederick) 1921-1982 .................. 51
　Obituary .......................................... 39
Brown, Ruth 1941- ................................ 170
　Earlier sketch in SATA 105
Brown, Scott 1971- ............................... 134
Brown, Sue Ellen 1954- ............................ 81
Brown, Tricia 1954- .............................. 114
Brown, Vinson 1912-1991 ........................... 19
Brown, Walter R(eed) 1929- ........................ 19
Brown, Will
　See Ainsworth, William Harrison
Brown, William L(ouis) 1910-1964 ................... 5
Browne, Anthony (Edward Tudor) 1946- . 163
　Brief entry ....................................... 44
　Earlier sketches in SATA 45, 61, 105
　See also CLR 19
Browne, Dik
　See Browne, Richard Arthur Allen
Browne, Hablot Knight 1815-1882 .............. 21
Browne, Matthew
　See Rands, William Brighty
Browne, Nicky Matthews
　See Browne, N.M.
Browne, N.M. 1960- ............................... 167
Browne, Richard Arthur Allen 1917-1989 .. 67
　Brief entry ....................................... 38
　See Browne, Dik
Browne, Vee F(rances) 1956- ....................... 90
Browning, Robert 1812-1889
　See YABC 1
　See also CLR 97
Brownjohn, Alan 1931- .............................. 6
Brownlee, Walter 1930- ............................ 62
Brownlie, Betty 1946- ............................ 159

Brownlow, Kevin 1938- ............................. 65
Brownridge, William R(oy) 1932- ................... 94
Bruce, (William) Harry 1934- ...................... 77
Bruce, Mary 1927- .................................. 1
Bruchac, Joseph III
　See Bruchac, Joseph
Bruchac, Joseph 1942- ............................ 176
　Autobiography Feature ........................... 176
　Earlier sketches in SATA 42, 89, 131
　See also CLR 46
Bruck, Lorraine 1921- ............................. 55
　Brief entry ....................................... 46
　See Bridges, Laurie
Bruel, Nick ...................................... 166
Bruemmer, Fred 1929- .............................. 47
Brugman, Alyssa (F.) 1974- ....................... 152
Brumbeau, Jeff 1955- ............................. 157
Bruna, Dick 1927- ................................. 76
　Brief entry ....................................... 30
　Earlier sketch in SATA 43
　See also CLR 7
Brunhoff, Jean de 1899-1937 ....................... 24
　See also CLR 116
Brunhoff, Laurent de 1925- ....................... 150
　Earlier sketches in SATA 24, 71
　See also CLR 116
Brunskill, Elizabeth Ann Flatt 1966- ........... 88
Brush, Karen A(lexandra) 1960- .................... 85
Brussel-Smith, Bernard 1914- ...................... 58
Brust, Steven K. 1955- ........................... 121
　Earlier sketch in SATA 86
Brust, Steven K. Zoltan
　See Brust, Steven K.
Brustlein, Daniel 1904- ........................... 40
Brustlein, Janice Tworkov -2000 ................... 40
　Obituary ......................................... 126
Brutschy, Jennifer 1960- ........................... 84
Bryan, Ashley 1923- .............................. 132
　Earlier sketches in SATA 31, 72
　See also CLR 66
Bryan, Ashley F.
　See Bryan, Ashley
Bryant, Bernice (Morgan) 1908-1976 .......... 11
Bryant, Jen 1960- ................................ 175
　Earlier sketch in SATA 94
Bryant, Jennifer Fisher
　See Bryant, Jen
Bryant, Laura J. ................................. 176
Brychta, Alex 1956- ............................... 21
Brynie, Faith H. 1946- ........................... 113
Brynie, Faith Hickman
　See Brynie, Faith H.
Bryson, Bernarda 1903-2004 ......................... 9
　See Shahn, Bernarda Bryson
Buba, Joy Flinsch 1904- ........................... 44
Buchan, Bryan 1945- ............................... 36
Buchan, John 1875-1940
　See YABC 2
Buchanan, Debby 1952- ............................. 82
Buchanan, Deborah Leevonne
　See Buchanan, Debby
Buchanan, Jane 1956- ............................. 160
Buchanan, Paul 1959- ............................. 116
Buchanan, Sue 1939- .............................. 139
Buchheimer, Naomi Barnett
　See Barnett, Naomi
Buchignani, Walter 1965- ........................... 84
Buchwald, Art 1925-2007 ........................... 10
Buchwald, Arthur
　See Buchwald, Art
Buchwald, Emilie 1935- ............................. 7
Buck, Gisela 1941- ............................... 101
Buck, Lewis 1925- ................................. 18
Buck, Margaret Waring 1905-1997 ................... 3
Buck, Pearl S(ydenstricker) 1892-1973 ....... 25
　Earlier sketch in SATA 1
Buck, Siegfried 1941- ............................ 101
Buckeridge, Anthony (Malcolm) 1912-2004
　................................................. 85
　Earlier sketch in SATA 6

Buckholtz, Eileen (Garber) 1949- .............. 54
　Brief entry ....................................... 47
Buckler, Ernest 1908-1984 ......................... 47
Buckless, Andrea K. 1968- ........................ 117
Buckley, Helen E(lizabeth) 1918- .................. 90
　Earlier sketch in SATA 2
Buckley, James, Jr. 1963- ........................ 166
　Earlier sketch in SATA 114
Buckley, Michael ................................. 177
Buckmaster, Henrietta ............................. 6
　See Stephens, Henrietta Henkle
Bucks, Brad
　See Holub, Joan
Budd, E. S.
　See Sirimarco, Elizabeth
Budd, Lillian (Peterson) 1897-1989 ............. 7
Budhos, Marina .................................. 173
Buehler, Stephanie Jona 1956- ..................... 83
Buehner, Caralyn (M.) 1963- ...................... 159
　Earlier sketch in SATA 104
Buehner, Mark 1959- .............................. 159
　Earlier sketch in SATA 104
Buehr, Walter Franklin 1897-1971 .............. 3
Buell, Janet 1952- ............................... 106
Buergel, Paul-Hermann H. 1949- .................... 83
Buettner, Dan 1960- ............................... 95
Buff, Conrad 1886-1975 ............................ 19
Buff, Mary (E. Marsh) 1890-1970 ................... 19
Buffett, Jimmy 1946- ............................. 110
　Earlier sketch in SATA 76
Buffie, Margaret 1945- ........................... 161
　Earlier sketches in SATA 71, 107
　See also CLR 39
Bugni, Alice 1951- ............................... 122
Buhhos, Marina Tamar
　See Budhos, Marina
Buhhos, Marina Tamar
　See Budhos, Marina
Bujold, Lois McMaster 1949- ...................... 136
Bulfinch, Thomas 1796-1867 ........................ 35
Bulion, Leslie 1958- ............................. 161
Bull, Angela (Mary) 1936- ......................... 45
Bull, Emma 1954- ................................. 99
　Autobiography Feature ........................... 103
Bull, Norman John 1916- ........................... 41
Bull, Schuyler M. 1974- .......................... 138
Bulla, Clyde Robert 1914- ........................ 139
　Earlier sketches in SATA 2, 41, 91
　See also SAAS 6
Bullard, Lisa 1961- .............................. 142
Bullock, Kathleen (Mary) 1946- .................... 77
Bullock, Robert (D.) 1947- ........................ 92
Bulpin, (Barbara) Vicki ........................... 92
Bumstead, Kathleen Mary 1918-1987 ........ 53
Bundles, A'Lelia Perry 1952- ...................... 76
Bunin, Catherine 1967- ............................ 30
Bunin, Sherry 1925- ............................... 30
Bunkers, Suzanne L. 1950- ........................ 136
Bunting, A. E.
　See Bunting, (Anne) Eve(lyn)
Bunting, Eve
　See Bunting, (Anne) Eve(lyn)
Bunting, (Anne) Eve(lyn) 1928- ................... 158
　Earlier sketches in SATA 18, 64, 110
　See also CLR 82
　See Bunting, Eve
Bunting, Glenn (Davison) 1957- .................... 22
Burack, Sylvia K. 1916-2003 ....................... 35
　Obituary ......................................... 143
Burbank, Addison (Buswell) 1895-1961 ..... 37
Burch, Joann J(ohansen) ........................... 75
Burch, Robert J(oseph) 1925- ...................... 74
　Earlier sketch in SATA 1
　See also CLR 63
Burchard, Peter Duncan 1921- ..................... 143
　Earlier sketches in SATA 5, 74
　See also SAAS 13
Burchard, S. H.
　See Burchard, Sue
Burchard, Sue 1937- ............................... 22
Burchardt, Nellie 1921- ............................ 7

Burdett, Lois .................................................. *117*
Burdick, Eugene (Leonard) 1918-1965 ....... *22*
Burford, Eleanor
   *See* Hibbert, Eleanor Alice Burford
Burgan, Michael 1960- .................................. *167*
   Earlier sketch in SATA *118*
Burger, Carl 1888-1967 .................................. *9*
Burgess, Ann Marie
   *See* Gerson, Noel Bertram
Burgess, Barbara Hood 1926- ....................... *69*
Burgess, Em
   *See* Burgess, Mary Wyche
Burgess, (Frank) Gelett 1866-1951 ............. *32*
   Brief entry ............................................... *30*
Burgess, Mark ............................................... *157*
Burgess, Mary Wyche 1916- ........................ *18*
Burgess, Melvin 1954- .................................. *146*
   Earlier sketch in SATA *96*
Burgess, Michael
   *See* Gerson, Noel Bertram
Burgess, Robert F(orrest) 1927- ................... *4*
Burgess, Thornton Waldo 1874-1965 .......... *17*
Burgess, Trevor
   *See* Trevor, Elleston
Burgwyn, Mebane Holoman 1914-1992 ....... *7*
Burke, David 1927- ........................................ *46*
Burke, Diana G.
   *See* Gallagher, Diana G.
Burke, Diana Gallagher
   *See* Gallagher, Diana G.
Burke, Dianne O'Quinn 1940- ...................... *89*
Burke, Janine 1952- ...................................... *139*
Burke, Katie 1953- ........................................ *168*
Burke, Patrick 1958- ..................................... *114*
Burke, Ralph
   *See* Garrett, (Gordon) Randall (Phillip)
   and Silverberg, Robert
Burkert, Nancy Ekholm 1933- ....................... *24*
   *See also* SAAS *14*
Burke-Weiner, Kimberly 1962- ..................... *95*
Burks, Brian 1955- ........................................ *95*
Burland, Brian (Berkeley) 1931- ................... *34*
Burland, C. A.
   *See* Burland, Cottie (Arthur)
Burland, Cottie (Arthur) 1905-1983 ............. *5*
Burleigh, Robert 1936- .................................. *146*
   Earlier sketches in SATA *55, 98*
Burlingame, (William) Roger 1889-1967 ...... *2*
Burman, Ben Lucien 1896-1984 ................... *6*
   Obituary ................................................... *40*
Burn, Doris 1923- .......................................... *1*
Burn, Ted
   *See* Burn, Thomas E.
Burn, Thomas E. 1940- .................................. *150*
Burnard, Damon 1963- ................................... *115*
Burnett, Constance Buel 1893-1975 ............. *36*
Burnett, Frances (Eliza) Hodgson 1849-1924
   ................................................................ *100*
   *See also* YABC *2*
   *See also* CLR *122*
Burnford, Sheila (Philip Cochrane Every)
   1918-1984 ................................................ *3*
   Obituary ................................................... *38*
   *See also* CLR *2*
Burnham, Gretchen
   *See* Sprague, Gretchen
Burnham, Nicole 1970- .................................. *161*
Burnham, Niki
   *See* Burnham, Nicole
Burnham, Sophy 1936- .................................. *65*
Burningham, John (Mackintosh) 1936- ..... *160*
   Earlier sketches in SATA *16, 59, 111*
   *See also* CLR *9*
Burns, Diane L. 1950- .................................... *81*
   *See also* SAAS *24*
Burns, Eloise Wilkin
   *See* Wilkin, Eloise
Burns, Florence M. 1905-1988 ..................... *61*
Burns, Khephra 1950- .................................... *92*
Burns, Marilyn 1941- ..................................... *96*
   Brief entry ............................................... *33*

Burns, Olive Ann 1924-1990 ....................... *65*
Burns, Paul C. ............................................... *5*
Burns, Ray
   *See* Burns, Raymond (Howard)
Burns, Raymond (Howard) 1924- ................. *9*
Burns, Theresa 1961- ..................................... *84*
Burns, William A. 1909-1999 ....................... *5*
Burr, Dan 1951- ............................................. *65*
Burr, Lonnie 1943- ........................................ *47*
Burrell, Roy E(ric) C(harles) 1923- ............. *72*
Burroughs, Edgar Rice 1875-1950 ............... *41*
Burroughs, Jean Mitchell 1908- ................... *28*
Burroughs, Polly 1925- .................................. *2*
Burroway, Janet (Gay) 1936- ........................ *23*
Burstein, Chaya M(alamud) 1923- ............... *64*
Burstein, Fred 1950- ...................................... *83*
Burstein, John 1949- ...................................... *54*
   Brief entry ............................................... *40*
Burstein, Stanley M.
   *See* Burstein, Stanley Mayer
Burstein, Stanley Mayer 1941- ..................... *175*
Bursztynski, Sue 1953- .................................. *114*
Burt, Jesse Clifton 1921-1976 ...................... *46*
   Obituary ................................................... *20*
Burt, Olive Woolley 1894-1981 ................... *4*
Burton, Gennett 1945- ................................... *95*
Burton, Hester (Wood-Hill) 1913-2000 ....... *74*
   Earlier sketch in SATA *7*
   *See also* CLR *1*
   *See also* SAAS *8*
Burton, Leslie
   *See* McGuire, Leslie (Sarah)
Burton, Marilee Robin 1950- ........................ *82*
   Earlier sketch in SATA *46*
Burton, Maurice 1898-1992 .......................... *23*
Burton, Robert (Wellesley) 1941- ................. *22*
Burton, Virginia Lee 1909-1968 ................... *100*
   Earlier sketch in SATA *2*
   *See also* CLR *11*
Burton, William H(enry) 1890-1964 ............ *11*
Busby, Cylin 1970- ........................................ *118*
Buscaglia, (Felice) Leo(nardo) 1924-1998 .. *65*
   *See* Buscaglia, Leo F.
Buscaglia, Leo F.
   *See* Buscaglia, (Felice) Leo(nardo)
Busch, Phyllis S. 1909- ................................. *30*
Bush, Anne Kelleher
   *See* Kelleher, Anne
Bush, Catherine 1961- ................................... *128*
Bushnell, Jack 1952- ..................................... *86*
Busoni, Rafaello 1900-1962 ......................... *16*
Buss, Helen M.
   *See* Clarke, Margaret
Busselle, Rebecca 1941- ................................ *80*
Bustard, Anne 1951- ...................................... *173*
Butcher, Kristin 1951- ................................... *140*
Butenko, Bohdan 1931- ................................. *90*
Butler, Beverly Kathleen 1932- .................... *7*
Butler, Bill
   *See* Butler, William (Arthur) Vivian
   and Butler, Ernest Alton
   and Butler, William Huxford
Butler, Charles 1963- .................................... *175*
   Earlier sketch in SATA *121*
Butler, Charles Cadman
   *See* Butler, Charles
Butler, Dori Hillestad 1965- ......................... *164*
Butler, Dorothy 1925- .................................... *73*
Butler, Geoff 1945- ........................................ *94*
Butler, M. Christina 1934- ............................. *170*
   Earlier sketch in SATA *72*
Butler, Octavia E. 1947-2006 ....................... *84*
   *See also* CLR *65*
Butler, Octavia Estelle
   *See* Butler, Octavia E.
Butler, Vivian
   *See* Butler, William (Arthur) Vivian
Butler, William
   *See* Butler, William (Arthur) Vivian

Butler, William (Arthur) Vivian 1927-1987
   ................................................................ *79*
   *See* Marric, J. J.
Butters, Dorothy Gilman .............................. *5*
   *See* Gilman, Dorothy
Butterworth, Emma Macalik 1928- .............. *43*
Butterworth, Nick 1946- ................................ *149*
   Earlier sketch in SATA *106*
Butterworth, Oliver 1915-1990 .................... *1*
   Obituary ................................................... *66*
Butterworth, W.E.
   *See* Griffin, W.E.B.
Butterworth, William E.
   *See* Griffin, W.E.B.
Butterworth, William Edmund III
   *See* Griffin, W.E.B.
Butts, Ed 1951- .............................................. *177*
Butts, Edward P.
   *See* Butts, Ed
Butts, Ellen R(ubinstein) 1942- .................... *93*
Buxton, Ralph
   *See* Silverstein, Alvin
   and Silverstein, Virginia B(arbara Opshelor)
Buzzeo, Toni 1951- ........................................ *135*
Byalick, Marcia 1947- ................................... *141*
   Earlier sketch in SATA *97*
Byard, Carole (Marie) 1941- ......................... *57*
Byars, Betsy 1928- ......................................... *163*
   Autobiography Feature .............................. *108*
   Earlier sketches in SATA *4, 46, 80*
   *See also* CLR *72*
   *See also* SAAS *1*
Byars, Betsy Cromer
   *See* Byars, Betsy
Byfield, Barbara Ninde 1930- ........................ *8*
Byman, Jeremy 1944- ..................................... *129*
Bynum, Janie ............................................... *133*
Byrd, Elizabeth 1912-1989 ........................... *34*
Byrd, Nicole
   *See* Zach, Cheryl (Byrd)
Byrd, Robert (John) 1942- ............................. *158*
   Earlier sketches in SATA *33, 112*
Byrne, Mary Gregg 1951- .............................. *162*

C

C. 3. 3.
   *See* Wilde, Oscar (Fingal O'Flahertie Wills)
Cabaniss, J(ames) Allen 1911-1997 ............. *5*
Cabat, Erni 1914- .......................................... *74*
Cabban, Vanessa 1971- ................................. *176*
Cable, Mary 1920- ......................................... *9*
Cabot, Meg 1967- .......................................... *175*
   Earlier sketch in SATA *127*
   *See also* CLR *85*
Cabot, Meggin
   *See* Cabot, Meg
Cabot, Patricia
   *See* Cabot, Meg
Cabral, O. M.
   *See* Cabral, Olga
Cabral, Olga 1909- ........................................ *46*
Cabrera, Cozbi A. 1963- ................................ *177*
Cabrera, Jane 1968- ....................................... *152*
   Earlier sketch in SATA *103*
Cabrera, Marcela 1966- ................................. *90*
Cade, Toni
   *See* Bambara, Toni Cade
Cadmus and Harmonia
   *See* Buchan, John
Cadnum, Michael 1949- ................................. *165*
   Earlier sketches in SATA *87, 121*
   *See also* CLR *78*
Caduto, Michael J. 1955- .............................. *103*
Cadwallader, Sharon 1936- ........................... *7*
Cady, (Walter) Harrison 1877(?)-1970 ........ *19*
Caffey, Donna (J.) 1954- ............................... *110*
Cagle, Malcolm W(infield) 1918- ................ *32*
Cahn, Rhoda 1922- ........................................ *37*

Cahn, William 1912-1976 .............................. *37*
Cain, Arthur H(omer) 1913-1981 ................. *3*
Caine, Geoffrey
    *See* Walker, Robert W(ayne)
Caines, Jeannette (Franklin) 1938- ............. *78*
    Brief entry ................................................ *43*
    *See also* CLR 24
Cairns, Trevor 1922- .................................... *14*
Calabro, Marian 1954- .................................. *79*
Caldecott, Moyra 1927- ................................ *22*
Caldecott, Randolph (J.) 1846-1886 ......... *100*
    Earlier sketch in SATA *17*
    *See also* CLR 110
Calder, Charlotte 1952- ............................... *125*
Calder, David 1932-1997 ............................. *105*
Calder, Lyn
    *See* Calmenson, Stephanie
Calder, Marie D(onais) 1948- ...................... *96*
Calderone-Stewart, Lisa
    *See* Calderone-Stewart, Lisa-Marie
Calderone-Stewart, Lisa-Marie 1958- ........ *123*
Caldwell, Doreen (Mary) 1942- .................. *71*
Caldwell, John C(ope) 1913-1984 ............... *7*
Caletti, Deb 1963- ...................................... *171*
Calhoun, B. B. 1961- ................................... *98*
Calhoun, Chad
    *See* Barrett, Neal, Jr.
    and Cunningham, Chet
    and Goulart, Ron(ald Joseph)
Calhoun, Dia 1959- ..................................... *129*
Calhoun, Mary ............................................... *2*
    *See also* CLR 42
    *See* Wilkins, Mary Huiskamp
Calhoun, T.B.
    *See* Bisson, Terry
Calif, Ruth 1922- ......................................... *67*
Calkins, Franklin
    *See* Stratemeyer, Edward L.
Call, Hughie Florence 1890-1969 ................. *1*
Callahan, Dorothy M(onahan) 1934- ........... *39*
    Brief entry ................................................ *35*
Callahan, Philip Serna 1923- ...................... *25*
Callan, Jamie 1954- ..................................... *59*
Callaway, Bernice (Anne) 1923- ................. *48*
Callaway, Kathy 1943- ................................. *36*
Callen, Larry
    *See* Callen, Lawrence Willard, Jr.
Callen, Lawrence Willard, Jr. 1927- ........... *19*
Calley, Karin 1965- ..................................... *92*
Calmenson, Stephanie 1952- ...................... *139*
    Brief entry ................................................ *37*
    Earlier sketches in SATA *51, 84*
Calvert, Elinor H.
    *See* Lasell, Elinor H.
Calvert, John
    *See* Leaf, (Wilbur) Munro
Calvert, Patricia 1931- ................................ *132*
    Earlier sketches in SATA *45, 69*
    *See also* SAAS 17
Camburn, Carol A.
    *See* Camburn-Bracalente, Carol A.
Camburn-Bracalente, Carol A. 1962- ......... *118*
Cameron, Ann 1943- .................................... *129*
    Earlier sketches in SATA *27, 89*
    *See also* SAAS 20
Cameron, Edna M. 1905-1999 ..................... *3*
Cameron, Eleanor (Frances) 1912-1996 ...... *25*
    Obituary ................................................... *93*
    Earlier sketch in SATA *1*
    *See also* CLR 72
    *See also* SAAS 10
Cameron, Elizabeth
    *See* Nowell, Elizabeth Cameron
Cameron, Elizabeth Jane 1910-1976 .......... *32*
    Obituary ................................................... *30*
Cameron, Ian
    *See* Payne, Donald Gordon
Cameron, M(alcolm) G(ordon) Graham
    *See* Graham-Cameron, M(alcolm) G(ordon)
Cameron, M. Graham
    *See* Graham-Cameron, M(alcolm) G(ordon)

Cameron, Mike Graham
    *See* Graham-Cameron, M(alcolm) G(ordon)
Cameron, Polly 1928- ................................... *2*
Cameron, Scott 1962- ................................... *84*
Camp, Lindsay 1957- .................................... *133*
Camp, Walter (Chauncey) 1859-1925
    *See* YABC *1*
Campbell, (Elizabeth) Andrea 1963- ........... *50*
Campbell, Ann R. 1925- .............................. *11*
Campbell, Bill 1960- .................................... *89*
Campbell, Bruce
    *See* Epstein, Samuel
Campbell, Camilla 1905-1992 ..................... *26*
Campbell, Carole R. 1939- ........................... *125*
Campbell, Hope 1925- .................................. *20*
Campbell, Hugh 1930- .................................. *90*
Campbell, Jane
    *See* Edwards, Jane Campbell
Campbell, Julie
    *See* Tatham, Julie Campbell
Campbell, Patricia J(ean) 1930- ................. *45*
Campbell, Patty
    *See* Campbell, Patricia J(ean)
Campbell, Peter A. 1948- ............................ *99*
Campbell, R. W.
    *See* Campbell, Rosemae Wells
Campbell, Robin
    *See* Strachan, Ian
Campbell, Rod 1945- .................................... *98*
    Brief entry ................................................ *44*
    Earlier sketch in SATA *51*
Campbell, Rosemae Wells 1909- ................. *1*
Camper, Cathy 1956- .................................... *170*
Campion, Nardi Reeder 1917- ...................... *22*
Campling, Elizabeth 1948- ........................... *53*
Campoy, F. Isabel (Coronado) 1946- ......... *143*
Camps, Luis 1928- ....................................... *66*
Canales, Viola 1957- .................................... *141*
Canfield, Dorothea F.
    *See* Fisher, Dorothy (Frances) Canfield
Canfield, Dorothea Frances
    *See* Fisher, Dorothy (Frances) Canfield
Canfield, Dorothy
    *See* Fisher, Dorothy (Frances) Canfield
Canfield, Jack 1944- .................................... *164*
Canfield, Jane White 1897-1984 ................. *32*
    Obituary ................................................... *38*
Canfield, Muriel 1935- ................................. *94*
Cann, Helen 1969- ....................................... *124*
Cann, Kate 1954- ......................................... *152*
    Earlier sketch in SATA *103*
Cannan, Joanna ............................................. *82*
    *See* Pullein-Thompson, Joanna Maxwell
Cannon, A(nn) E(dwards) ............................ *163*
    Earlier sketch in SATA *93*
Cannon, Bettie (Waddell) 1922- ................. *59*
Cannon, Curt
    *See* Hunter, Evan
Cannon, Eileen E(mily) 1948- .................... *119*
Cannon, Frank
    *See* Mayhar, Ardath
Cannon, Janell 1957- ................................... *128*
    Earlier sketch in SATA *78*
    *See also* CLR 120
Cannon, Marian G. 1923- ............................ *85*
Cannon, Taffy
    *See* Cannon, Eileen E(mily)
Canusi, Jose
    *See* Barker, S(quire) Omar
Canyon, Christopher 1966- .......................... *150*
    Earlier sketch in SATA *104*
Capek, Michael 1947- .................................. *142*
    Earlier sketch in SATA *96*
Capes, Bernard (Edward Joseph) 1854-1918
    .................................................................. *116*
Caponigro, John Paul 1965- ......................... *84*
Capote, Truman 1924-1984 ......................... *91*
Capp, Al ......................................................... *61*
    *See* Caplin, Alfred Gerald
Cappel, Constance 1936- .............................. *22*
Cappetta, Cynthia 1949- .............................. *125*

Cappo, Nan Willard 1955- ........................... *143*
Capps, Benjamin (Franklin) 1922- ............... *9*
Captain Kangaroo
    *See* Keeshan, Robert J.
Captain Wheeler
    *See* Ellis, Edward S(ylvester)
Captain Young of Yale
    *See* Stratemeyer, Edward L.
Capucilli, Alyssa Satin 1957- ..................... *163*
    Earlier sketch in SATA *115*
Capucine
    *See* Mazille, Capucine
Caraher, Kim(berley Elizabeth) 1961- ...... *105*
Caraker, Mary 1929- .................................... *74*
Caras, Roger A(ndrew) 1928-2001 ............. *12*
    Obituary ................................................... *127*
Caravantes, Peggy 1935- ............................. *140*
Caraway, Caren 1939- .................................. *57*
Carbone, Elisa 1954- .................................... *137*
    Earlier sketch in SATA *81*
    *See* Carbone, Elisa Lynn
Carbone, Elisa Lynn ...................................... *173*
    *See* Carbone, Elisa
Carbonnier, Jeanne 1894-1974 ..................... *3*
    Obituary ................................................... *34*
Card, Orson Scott 1951- .............................. *127*
    Earlier sketch in SATA *83*
    *See also* CLR 116
Carew, Jan (Rynveld) 1925- ........................ *51*
    Brief entry ................................................ *40*
Carey, Bonnie
    *See* Marshall, Bonnie C.
Carey, Charles W., Jr. 1951- ...................... *170*
Carey, Ernestine Gilbreth 1908-2006 ......... *2*
    Obituary ................................................... *177*
Carey, Lisa ................................................... *110*
Carey, M. V.
    *See* Carey, Mary V(irginia)
Carey, Mary V(irginia) 1925-1994 .............. *44*
    Brief entry ................................................ *39*
Carey, Peter 1943- ....................................... *94*
Carey, Valerie Scho 1949- ........................... *60*
Carheden, Goorel Kristina
    *See* Naaslund, Goorel Kristina
Carigiet, Alois 1902-1985 ........................... *24*
    Obituary ................................................... *47*
    *See also* CLR 38
Carini, Edward 1923- .................................... *9*
Carkeet, David 1946- .................................... *75*
Carle, Eric 1929- .......................................... *163*
    Earlier sketches in SATA *4, 65, 120*
    *See also* CLR 72
    *See also* SAAS 6
Carleton, Captain L. C.
    *See* Ellis, Edward S(ylvester)
Carleton, Captain Latham C.
    *See* Ellis, Edward S(ylvester)
Carleton, Latham C.
    *See* Ellis, Edward S(ylvester)
Carling, Amelia Lau 1949- .......................... *164*
    Earlier sketch in SATA *119*
Carlisle, Carolyn
    *See* Hawes, Louise
Carlisle, Clark
    *See* Holding, James (Clark Carlisle, Jr.)
Carlisle, Olga Andreyev 1930- .................... *35*
Carlsen, G(eorge) Robert 1917- .................. *30*
Carlsen, Ruth C(hristoffer) 1918- ............... *2*
Carlson, Bernice Wells 1910- ..................... *8*
Carlson, Dale (Bick) 1935- .......................... *1*
Carlson, Daniel (Bick) 1960- ...................... *27*
Carlson, Laurie 1952- ................................... *173*
    Earlier sketch in SATA *101*
Carlson, Laurie Winn
    *See* Carlson, Laurie
Carlson, Melody 1956- ................................. *171*
    Earlier sketch in SATA *113*
Carlson, Nancy L.
    *See* Carlson, Nancy L(ee)

Carlson, Nancy L(ee) 1953- .................... *144*
  Brief entry ........................................ *45*
  Earlier sketches in SATA *56, 90*
Carlson, Natalie Savage 1906-1997 .......... *68*
  Earlier sketch in SATA *2*
  *See also* SAAS *4*
Carlson, Susan Johnston 1953- .................. *88*
Carlson, Vada F. 1897- .............................. *16*
Carlstrom, Nancy White 1948- ................ *156*
  Brief entry ........................................ *48*
  Earlier sketches in SATA *53, 92*
Carlton, Keith
  *See* Robertson, Keith (Carlton)
Carlyon, Richard .................................... *55*
Carman, Patrick .................................... *161*
Carmer, Carl (Lamson) 1893-1976 ............ *37*
  Obituary ............................................ *30*
Carmer, Elizabeth Black 1904- .................. *24*
Carmi, Giora 1944- ................................ *149*
  Earlier sketch in SATA *79*
Carmichael, Carrie ................................ *40*
  *See* Carmichael, Harriet
Carmody, Isobelle 1958- .......................... *161*
Carmody, Isobelle Jane
  *See* Carmody, Isobelle
Carney, Mary Lou 1949- .......................... *170*
Carol, Bill J.
  *See* Knott, William C(ecil, Jr.)
Caron, Romi
  *See* Caron-Kyselkova', Romana
Caron-Kyselkova', Romana 1967- .............. *94*
Caroselli, Remus F(rancis) 1916- .............. *36*
Carpelan, Bo (Gustaf Bertelsson) 1926- ...... *8*
Carpenter, (John) Allan 1917- .................. *81*
  Earlier sketch in SATA *3*
Carpenter, Angelica Shirley 1945- ............ *153*
  Earlier sketch in SATA *71*
Carpenter, Frances 1890-1972 .................... *3*
  Obituary ............................................ *27*
Carpenter, John (Howard) 1948- ................ *58*
Carpenter, Johnny
  *See* Carpenter, John (Howard)
Carpenter, Patricia (Healy Evans) 1920- ..... *11*
Carr, Glyn
  *See* Styles, (Frank) Showell
Carr, Harriett H(elen) 1899-1977 .............. *3*
Carr, Jan 1953- .................................... *132*
  Earlier sketch in SATA *89*
Carr, M. J.
  *See* Carr, Jan
Carr, Mary Jane 1899-1988 ........................ *2*
  Obituary ............................................ *55*
Carr, Philippa
  *See* Hibbert, Eleanor Alice Burford
Carr, Roger Vaughan 1937- ...................... *95*
Carrel, Annette Felder 1929- .................... *90*
Carrick, Carol (Hatfield) 1935- ................ *118*
  Earlier sketches in SATA *7, 63*
  *See also* SAAS *18*
Carrick, Donald (F.) 1929-1989 ................ *63*
  Earlier sketch in SATA *7*
Carrick, Malcolm 1945- .......................... *28*
Carrier, Lark 1947- ................................ *71*
  Brief entry ........................................ *50*
Carrier, Roch 1937- .............................. *166*
  Earlier sketch in SATA *105*
Carrighar, Sally 1898-1985 ...................... *24*
Carrington, G. A.
  *See* Cunningham, Chet
Carrington, Marsha Gray 1954- ................ *168*
  Earlier sketch in SATA *111*
Carris, Joan Davenport 1938- .................... *44*
  Brief entry ........................................ *42*
Carroll, Curt
  *See* Bishop, Curtis (Kent)
Carroll, Elizabeth
  *See* Barkin, Carol
  and James, Elizabeth
Carroll, Jenny
  *See* Cabot, Meg
Carroll, (Archer) Latrobe 1894-1996 .......... *7*

Carroll, Laura
  *See* Parr, Lucy
Carroll, Lewis
  *See* CLR *108*
  *See* Dodgson, Charles L(utwidge)
Carroll, Raymond 1924- .......................... *86*
  Brief entry ........................................ *47*
Carruth, Hayden 1921- .......................... *47*
Carryl, Charles E. 1841-1920 .................. *114*
Carryl, Charles Edward
  *See* Carryl, Charles E.
Carse, Robert 1902-1971 .......................... *5*
Carson, J(ohn) Franklin 1920-1981 ............ *1*
  Obituary .......................................... *107*
Carson, Mary Kay 1964- ........................ *150*
Carson, Rachel
  *See* Carson, Rachel Louise
Carson, Rachel Louise 1907-1964 .............. *23*
  *See* Carson, Rachel
Carson, Rosalind
  *See* Chittenden, Margaret
Carson, S. M.
  *See* Gorsline, (Sally) Marie
Carson, William C. 1928- ...................... *154*
Carter, Alden R 1947- .......................... *137*
  Earlier sketch in SATA *67*
  *See also* CLR *22*
  *See also* SAAS *18*
Carter, Alden Richardson
  *See* Carter, Alden R
Carter, Andy 1948- .............................. *134*
Carter, Angela 1940-1992 ........................ *66*
  Obituary ............................................ *70*
Carter, Angela Olive
  *See* Carter, Angela
Carter, Anne Laurel 1953- ...................... *135*
Carter, Asa Earl
  *See* Carter, Forrest
Carter, Avis Murton
  *See* Allen, Kenneth S.
Carter, Bruce
  *See* Hough, Richard (Alexander)
Carter, Carol S(hadis) 1948- .................... *124*
Carter, David A. 1957- .......................... *170*
  Earlier sketch in SATA *114*
Carter, Don 1958- ................................ *124*
Carter, Dorothy Sharp 1921- ...................... *8*
Carter, Forrest 1927(?)-1979 .................... *32*
Carter, Helene 1887-1960 ........................ *15*
Carter, (William) Hodding, Jr. 1907-1972 .... *2*
  Obituary ............................................ *27*
Carter, James Earl, Jr.
  *See* Carter, Jimmy
Carter, Jimmy 1924- .............................. *79*
Carter, Katharine J(ones) 1905-1984 .......... *2*
Carter, Lin(wood Vrooman) 1930-1988 ...... *91*
Carter, Mike 1936- .............................. *138*
Carter, Nick
  *See* Avallone, Michael (Angelo, Jr.)
  and Ballard, (Willis) Todhunter
  and Crider, Bill
  and Cassiday, Bruce (Bingham)
  and Chastain, Thomas
  and Dey, Frederic (Merrill) Van Rensselaer
  and Garside, (Clifford) Jack
  and Hayes, Ralph E(ugene)
  and Henderson, M(arilyn) R(uth)
  and Lynds, Dennis
  and Lynds, Gayle (Hallenbeck)
  and Randisi, Robert J.
  and Rasof, Henry
  and Stratemeyer, Edward L.
  and Smith, Martin Cruz
  and Swain, Dwight V(reeland)
  and Vardeman, Robert E(dward)
  and Wallmann, Jeffrey M(iner)
  and White, Lionel
Carter, Peter 1929- .............................. *57*
Carter, Phyllis Ann
  *See* Eberle, Irmengarde

Carter, Samuel (Thomson) III 1904-1988 ... *37*
  Obituary ............................................ *60*
Carter, William E. 1926-1983 .................... *1*
  Obituary ............................................ *35*
Cartlidge, Michelle 1950- ........................ *96*
  Brief entry ........................................ *37*
  Earlier sketch in SATA *49*
Cartner, William Carruthers 1910- .............. *11*
Cartwright, Ann 1940- .......................... *78*
Cartwright, Reg(inald Ainsley) 1938- ........ *64*
Cartwright, Sally 1923- ............................ *9*
Carusone, Al 1949- .............................. *89*
Carvell, Marlene .................................. *172*
Carver, John
  *See* Gardner, Richard (M.)
Carwell, L'Ann
  *See* McKissack, Patricia C.
Cary
  *See* Cary, Louis F(avreau)
Cary, Kate 1967(?)- .............................. *174*
Cary, Louis F(avreau) 1915- ...................... *9*
Caryl, Jean
  *See* Kaplan, Jean Caryl Korn
Casanova, Mary 1957- .......................... *136*
  Earlier sketch in SATA *94*
Cascone, A.G.
  *See* Cascone, Annette
  and Cascone, Gina
Cascone, Annette 1960- .......................... *103*
Cascone, Gina 1955- ............................ *103*
Case, Marshal T(aylor) 1941- .................... *9*
Case, Michael
  *See* Howard, Robert West
Caseley, Judith 1951- ............................ *159*
  Brief entry ........................................ *53*
  Earlier sketch in SATA *87*
Casewit, Curtis W(erner) 1922-2002 ............ *4*
Casey, Barbara (Louise) 1944- .................. *147*
  Earlier sketch in SATA *79*
Casey, Brigid 1950- ................................ *9*
Casey, Tina 1959- ................................ *141*
Cash, Megan Montague .......................... *160*
Casilla, Robert 1959- ............................ *146*
  Earlier sketch in SATA *75*
Cason, Mabel Earp 1892-1965 .................. *10*
Cass, Joan E(velyn) .................................. *1*
Cass-Beggs, Barbara 1904- ...................... *62*
Cassedy, Patrice (Rinaldo) 1953- .............. *149*
Cassedy, Sylvia 1930-1989 ...................... *77*
  Obituary ............................................ *61*
  Earlier sketch in SATA *27*
  *See also* CLR *26*
Cassel, Lili
  *See* Wronker, Lili Cassel
Cassels, Jean .................................... *173*
Cassidy, Anne 1952- ............................ *166*
Casson, Hugh Maxwell 1910-1999 ............ *65*
  Obituary .......................................... *115*
Cassutt, Michael 1954- .......................... *78*
Cassutt, Michael Joseph
  *See* Cassutt, Michael
Castaldo, Nancy Fusco 1962- .................... *151*
  Earlier sketch in SATA *93*
Castaneda, Omar S. 1954- ........................ *71*
Castell, Megan
  *See* Williams, Jeanne
Castellanos, Jane Mollie Robinson 1913-2001
  .................................................... *9*
Castellon, Federico 1914-1971 .................. *48*
Castellucci, Cecil 1969- ........................ *176*
Castillo, Edmund L. 1924-2005 .................. *1*
  Obituary .......................................... *167*
Castle, Lee
  *See* Ogan, George F.
  and Ogan, Margaret E. (Nettles)
Castle, Paul
  *See* Howard, Vernon (Linwood)
Castle, Robert
  *See* Hamilton, Edmond
Caswell, Brian 1954- ............................ *171*
  Earlier sketch in SATA *97*

Caswell, Helen (Rayburn) 1923- .................. *12*
Catalano, Dominic 1956- ........................... *163*
   Earlier sketch in SATA *76*
Catalano, Grace (A.) 1961- ......................... *99*
Catalanotto, Peter 1959- ........................... *159*
   Autobiography Feature ........................... *113*
   Earlier sketches in SATA *70, 114*
   See also CLR *68*
   See also SAAS *25*
Cate, Dick
   See Cate, Richard Edward Nelson
Cate, Richard Edward Nelson 1932- ........... *28*
Cather, Willa (Sibert) 1873-1947 ............... *30*
   See also CLR *98*
Catherall, Arthur 1906-1980 ....................... *74*
   Earlier sketch in SATA *3*
   See Ruthin, Margaret
Cathon, Laura E(lizabeth) 1908-1991 ......... *27*
Catlett, Elizabeth 1919(?)- ......................... *82*
Catlin, Wynelle 1930- ................................. *13*
Cato, Heather ............................................ *105*
Cato, Sheila .............................................. *114*
Catrow, David
   See Catrow, David J. III
Catrow, David J. III .................................... *152*
Catt, Louis
   See French, Vivian
Cattell, James 1954- ................................. *123*
Catton, (Charles) Bruce 1899-1978 ............. *2*
   Obituary ................................................. *24*
Catz, Max
   See Glaser, Milton
Caudell, Marian 1930- ................................ *52*
Caudill, Rebecca 1899-1985 ......................... *1*
   Obituary ................................................. *44*
Cauley, Lorinda Bryan 1951- ..................... *46*
   Brief entry ............................................. *43*
Cauman, Samuel 1910-1971 ....................... *48*
Causley, Charles (Stanley) 1917-2003 ........ *66*
   Obituary ............................................... *149*
   Earlier sketch in SATA *3*
   See also CLR *30*
Cavallaro, Ann (Abelson) 1918- ................. *62*
Cavallo, Diana 1931- ................................... *7*
Cavanagh, Helen (Carol) 1939- .................. *98*
   Brief entry ............................................. *37*
   Earlier sketch in SATA *48*
Cavanah, Frances 1899-1982 ...................... *31*
   Earlier sketch in SATA *1*
Cavanna, Betty ........................................... *30*
   Earlier sketch in SATA *1*
   See also SAAS *4*
   See Harrison, Elizabeth (Allen) Cavanna
Cavanna, Elizabeth
   See Harrison, Elizabeth (Allen) Cavanna
Cave, Kathryn 1948- ................................. *123*
   Earlier sketch in SATA *76*
Cavendish, Peter
   See Horler, Sydney
Cavin, Ruth (Brodie) 1918- ........................ *38*
Cavoukian, Raffi 1948- .............................. *68*
Cawley, Winifred 1915- .............................. *13*
Caxton, Pisistratus
   See Lytton, Edward G(eorge) E(arle) L(ytton)
   Bulwer-Lytton Baron
Cazeau, Charles J(ay) 1931- ...................... *65*
Cazet, Denys 1938- ................................... *163*
   Brief entry ............................................. *41*
   Earlier sketches in SATA *52, 99*
Cazzola, Gus 1934- ................................... *73*
Cebulash, Mel 1937- ................................... *91*
   Earlier sketch in SATA *10*
Ceder, Georgiana Dorcas -1985 ................... *10*
Celenza, Anna Harwell .............................. *133*
Celestino, Martha Laing 1951- ................... *39*
Cepeda, Joe .............................................. *159*
Cerf, Bennett (Alfred) 1898-1971 ................ *7*
Cerf, Christopher (Bennett) 1941- ............... *2*
Cerullo, Mary M. 1949- ............................ *145*
   Earlier sketch in SATA *86*

Cervon, Jacqueline
   See Moussard, Jacqueline
Cetin, Frank Stanley 1921- .......................... *2*
Chabon, Michael 1963- .............................. *145*
Chaconas, D.J.
   See Chaconas, Dori
Chaconas, Dori 1938- ................................ *175*
   Earlier sketch in SATA *145*
Chaconas, Doris J.
   See Chaconas, Dori
Chadwick, Lester ........................................ *67*
   Earlier sketch in SATA *1*
Chaffee, Allen .............................................. *3*
Chaffin, Lillie D(orton) 1925- ....................... *4*
Chaikin, Miriam 1924- .............................. *152*
   Earlier sketches in SATA *24, 102*
Chall, Marsha Wilson ................................ *150*
Challand, Helen J(ean) 1921- ...................... *64*
Challans, Mary 1905-1983 .......................... *23*
   Obituary ................................................. *36*
   See Renault, Mary
Chalmers, Mary (Eileen) 1927- ..................... *6*
   See also SAAS *14*
Chamberlain, Margaret 1954- ...................... *46*
Chamberlin, Kate 1945- ............................. *105*
Chamberlin, Mary 1960- ............................ *177*
Chamberlin, Rich ....................................... *177*
Chamberlin, Richard
   See Chamberlin, Rich
Chambers, Aidan 1934- ............................. *171*
   Earlier sketches in SATA *1, 69, 108*
   See also SAAS *12*
Chambers, Catherine E.
   See St. John, Nicole
Chambers, John W. 1933- ............................ *57*
   Brief entry ............................................. *46*
Chambers, Kate
   See St. John, Nicole
Chambers, Margaret Ada Eastwood 1911- .... *2*
Chambers, Peggy
   See Chambers, Margaret Ada Eastwood
Chambers, Robert W(illiam) 1865-1933 ... *107*
Chan, Gillian 1954- ................................... *147*
   Earlier sketch in SATA *102*
Chance, James T.
   See Carpenter, John (Howard)
Chance, John T.
   See Carpenter, John (Howard)
Chance, Stephen
   See Turner, Philip (William)
Chandler, Caroline A(ugusta) 1906-1979 .... *22*
   Obituary ................................................. *24*
Chandler, David P(orter) 1933- ................... *28*
Chandler, Edna Walker 1908-1982 .............. *11*
   Obituary ................................................. *31*
Chandler, Jennifer
   See Westwood, Jennifer
Chandler, Karen 1959- .............................. *122*
Chandler, Linda S(mith) 1929- .................... *39*
Chandler, Pauline ..................................... *175*
Chandler, Robert 1953- .............................. *40*
Chandler, Ruth Forbes 1894-1978 ................ *2*
   Obituary ................................................. *26*
Chandonnet, Ann F. 1943- ......................... *92*
Chaney, Jill 1932- ...................................... *87*
Chang, Chih-Wei 1966- ............................. *111*
Chang, Cindy 1968- ................................... *90*
Chang, Margaret (Scrogin) 1941- ............... *71*
Chang, Raymond 1939- ............................. *142*
   Earlier sketches in SATA *71, 142 PEN*
Chanin, Michael 1952- ................................ *84*
Channel, A. R.
   See Catherall, Arthur
Chapian, Marie 1938- ................................. *29*
Chapin, Tom 1945- ..................................... *83*
Chapman, Allen ........................................... *67*
   Earlier sketch in SATA *1*
Chapman, Cheryl O(rth) 1948- .................... *80*
Chapman, (Constance) Elizabeth (Mann) 1919-
   ............................................................... *10*
Chapman, Gaynor 1935- ............................. *32*

Chapman, Gillian 1955- ............................. *120*
Chapman, Jane 1970- ................................ *176*
   Earlier sketch in SATA *122*
Chapman, Jean ......................................... *104*
   Earlier sketch in SATA *34*
   See also CLR *65*
Chapman, Lee
   See Bradley, Marion Zimmer
Chapman, Lynne F(erguson) 1963- ............. *150*
   Earlier sketch in SATA *94*
Chapman, Vera (Ivy May) 1898-1996 ......... *33*
Chapman, Walker
   See Silverberg, Robert
Chappell, Audrey 1954- .............................. *72*
Chappell, Warren 1904-1991 ....................... *68*
   Obituary ................................................. *67*
   Earlier sketch in SATA *6*
   See also SAAS *10*
Charbonneau, Eileen 1951- ........................ *118*
   Earlier sketch in SATA *84*
Charbonnet, Gabrielle 1961- ....................... *81*
Chardiet, Bernice (Kroll) 1927(?)- ............... *27*
Charles, Donald
   See Meighan, Donald Charles
Charles, Louis
   See Stratemeyer, Edward L.
Charles, Nicholas J.
   See Kuskin, Karla
Charles, Norma ......................................... *153*
Charlip, Remy 1929- ................................. *119*
   Earlier sketches in SATA *4, 68*
   See also CLR *8*
Charlot, Jean 1898-1979 .............................. *8*
   Obituary ................................................. *31*
Charlot, Martin (Day) 1944- ....................... *64*
Charlton, Michael (Alan) 1923- ................... *34*
Charmatz, Bill 1925-2005 ............................. *7*
Charnas, Suzy McKee 1939- ...................... *110*
   Earlier sketch in SATA *61*
Charosh, Mannis 1906- ................................ *5*
Chartier, Normand L. 1945- ........................ *66*
Chase, Alice
   See McHargue, Georgess
Chase, Alyssa 1965- ................................... *92*
Chase, Andra 1942- .................................... *91*
Chase, Emily
   See Aks, Patricia
   and Garwood, Julie
   and Sachs, Judith
   and White, Carol
Chase, Mary (Coyle) 1907-1981 .................. *17*
   Obituary ................................................. *29*
Chase, Mary Ellen 1887-1973 ..................... *10*
Chase, Richard 1904-1988 .......................... *64*
   Obituary ................................................. *56*
Chase, Samantha
   See Glick, Ruth (Burtnick)
Chast, Roz 1954- ....................................... *97*
Chastain, Madye Lee 1908-1989 ................... *4*
Chataway, Carol 1955- .............................. *140*
Chatterjee, Debjani 1952- ............................ *83*
Chauncy, Nan(cen Beryl Masterman)
   1900-1970 .............................................. *6*
   See also CLR *6*
Chaundler, Christine 1887-1972 .................... *1*
   Obituary ................................................. *25*
Chbosky, Stephen 1972- ............................ *164*
Chee, Cheng-Khee 1934- ............................ *79*
Cheese, Chloe 1952- ................................. *118*
Chekhonte, Antosha
   See Chekhov, Anton (Pavlovich)
Chekhov, Anton (Pavlovich) 1860-1904 ..... *90*
Chen, Anthony 1929- .................................... *6*
Chen, Chih-Yuan 1975- ............................. *155*
Chen, Ju-Hong 1941- .................................. *78*
Chen, Sara
   See Odgers, Sally Farrell
Chen, Tony
   See Chen, Anthony
Chen, Yuan-tsung 1932- .............................. *65*

Chenault, Nell
    *See* Smith, Linell Nash
Chenery, Janet (Dai) 1923- ......................... 25
Cheney, Cora 1916-1999 ............................... 3
    Obituary .................................................. *110*
Cheney, Glenn (Alan) 1951- ....................... 99
Cheney, Lynne V. 1941- ............................ 152
Cheney, Ted
    *See* Cheney, Theodore Albert
Cheney, Theodore A. Rees
    *See* Cheney, Theodore Albert
Cheney, Theodore Albert 1928- ................... 11
Cheng, Andrea 1957- ................................. 172
    Earlier sketch in SATA *128*
Cheng, Christopher 1959- ........................... 173
    Earlier sketch in SATA *106*
Cheng, Judith 1955- ................................... 36
Cheng, Shan
    *See* Jiang, Cheng An
Cheripko, Jan 1951- .................................. 155
    Earlier sketch in SATA *83*
Chermayeff, Ivan 1932- ............................. 47
Chernoff, Dorothy A.
    *See* Ernst, (Lyman) John
Chernoff, Goldie Taub 1909- ...................... 10
Cherry, Carolyn Janice ................................ 93
    *See* Cherryh, C.J.
Cherry, Lynne 1952- ................................... 99
    Earlier sketch in SATA *34*
Cherryh, C.J. 1942- .................................. 172
    *See* Cherry, Carolyn Janice
Cherryholmes, Anne
    *See* Price, Olive
Cheshire, Simon ....................................... 172
Chesler, Bernice 1932-2002 ......................... 59
Chess, Victoria (Dickerson) 1939- .............. 92
    Earlier sketch in SATA *33*
Chester, Deborah 1957- ............................... 85
Chester, Kate
    *See* Guccione, Leslie Davis
Chesterton, G(ilbert) K(eith) 1874-1936 ..... 27
Chesworth, Michael ................................... 160
Chetin, Helen 1922- ..................................... 6
Chetwin, Grace ........................................... 86
    Brief entry .................................................. 50
Chevalier, Christa 1937- ............................. 35
Chevalier, Tracy 1962- .............................. 128
Chew, Ruth 1920- ......................................... 7
Chichester Clark, Emma 1955- ................... 156
    Earlier sketch in SATA *117*
    *See* Clark, Emma Chichester
Chidsey, Donald Barr 1902-1981 ................... 3
    Obituary .................................................... 27
Chiefari, Janet D. 1942- .............................. 58
Chien-min, Lin
    *See* Rumford, James
Child, L. Maria
    *See* Child, Lydia Maria
Child, Lauren 1965- ................................... 160
    Earlier sketch in SATA *119*
Child, Lincoln B. 1957- .............................. 113
Child, Lydia Maria 1802-1880 ..................... 67
Child, Mrs.
    *See* Child, Lydia Maria
Child, Philip 1898-1978 .............................. 47
Children's Shepherd, The
    *See* Westphal, Arnold Carl
Childress, Alice 1920-1994 ........................... 81
    Earlier sketches in SATA *7, 48*
    *See also* CLR *14*
Childs, H(alla) Fay (Cochrane) 1890-1971 ... *1*
    Obituary .................................................... 25
Chilton, Charles (Frederick William) 1917-
    ................................................................ *102*
Chimaera
    *See* Farjeon, Eleanor
Chin, Richard (M.) 1946- ............................ 52
Chinery, Michael 1938- ............................... 26
Chin-Lee, Cynthia D. 1958- ....................... 102
Chippendale, Lisa A. .................................. 158

Chipperfield, Joseph Eugene 1912-1980(?) . 87
    Earlier sketch in SATA *2*
Chisholm, P. F.
    *See* Finney, Patricia
Chislett, Gail (Elaine) 1948- ....................... 58
Chittenden, Elizabeth F. 1903-1999 ............... 9
Chittenden, Margaret 1935- ......................... 28
Chittum, Ida 1918- ....................................... 7
Chitwood, Suzanne Tanner 1958- .............. 160
Chmielarz, Sharon Lee 1940- ....................... 72
Choate, Judith (Newkirk) 1940- ................... 30
Chocolate, Debbi 1954- ............................... 96
Chocolate, Deborah M. Newton
    *See* Chocolate, Debbi
Chodos-Irvine, Margaret ........................... 152
Choi, Sook Nyul 1937- ................................ 73
    Autobiography Feature ............................. 126
    *See also* CLR *53*
Choldenko, Gennifer 1957- ......................... 135
Chorao, (Ann Mc)Kay (Sproat) 1936- ...... 162
    Earlier sketches in SATA *8, 69*
Choron, Sandra (Zena Samelson) 1950- ... 146
Chown, Marcus 1959- ................................ 137
Choyce, Lesley 1951- ................................. 165
    Earlier sketch in SATA *94*
Chrisman, Arthur Bowie 1889-1953 ........ *124*
    *See also* YABC *1*
Christelow, Eileen 1943- .............................. 90
    Autobiography Feature ............................. 120
    Brief entry .................................................. 35
    Earlier sketch in SATA *38*
Christensen, Bonnie 1951- .......................... 157
    Earlier sketch in SATA *110*
Christensen, Gardell Dano 1907-1991 .......... *1*
Christensen, Laurie
    *See* Steding, Laurie
Christesen, Barbara 1940- ............................ 40
Christgau, Alice Erickson 1902-1977 ........... 13
Christian, Mary Blount 1933- ......................... 9
Christie, Agatha (Mary Clarissa) 1890-1976
    ................................................................ 36
Christie, Gregory
    *See* Christie, R. Gregory
Christie, Philippa ..................................... *129*
    Earlier sketches in SATA *1, 67*
    *See also* CLR *9*
    *See* Pearce, Philippa
Christie, R. Gregory 1971- ......................... *127*
Christopher, John
    *See* CLR *2*
    *See* Youd, (Christopher) Samuel
Christopher, Louise
    *See* Hale, Arlene
Christopher, Matt(hew Frederick) 1917-1997
    ................................................................ 80
    Obituary .................................................... 99
    Earlier sketches in SATA *2, 47*
    *See also* CLR *119*
    *See also* SAAS *9*
Christopher, Milbourne 1914(?)-1984 ........ 46
Christy, Howard Chandler 1873-1952 ........ 21
Chrustowski, Rick ..................................... *176*
Chrystie, Frances N(icholson) 1904-1986 ... 60
Chu, Daniel 1933- ........................................ 11
Chukovsky, Kornei (Ivanovich) 1882-1969
    ................................................................ 34
    Earlier sketch in SATA *5*
Church, Richard 1893-1972 ........................... 3
Churchill, E(lmer) Richard 1937- ............... 11
Churchill, Elizabeth
    *See* Hough, Richard (Alexander)
Chute, B(eatrice) J(oy) 1913-1987 ................ 2
    Obituary .................................................... 53
Chute, Marchette (Gaylord) 1909-1994 ........ *1*
Chwast, Jacqueline 1932- .............................. 6
Chwast, Seymour 1931- ............................. 146
    Earlier sketches in SATA *18, 96*

Ciardi, John (Anthony) 1916-1986 ............. 65
    Obituary .................................................... 46
    Earlier sketch in SATA *1*
    *See also* CLR *19*
    *See also* SAAS *26*
Ciccone, Madonna Louise Veronica
    *See* Madonna
Ciment, James D. 1958- ............................. 140
Cisneros, Sandra 1954-
    *See* CLR *123*
Citra, Becky 1954- ................................... 137
Clair, Andree ................................................ 19
Clampett, Robert ........................................ 44
    *See* Clampett, Bob
Clapp, John 1968- ..................................... 109
Clapp, Patricia 1912- .................................. 74
    Earlier sketch in SATA *4*
    *See also* SAAS *4*
Clare, Ellen
    *See* Sinclair, Olga
Clare, Helen
    *See* Clarke, Pauline
Claremont, Chris 1950- ................................ 87
Claremont, Christopher Simon
    *See* Claremont, Chris
Clark, Ann Nolan 1896-1995 ....................... 82
    Obituary .................................................... 87
    Earlier sketch in SATA *4*
    *See also* CLR *16*
    *See also* SAAS *16*
Clark, Champ 1923-2002 ............................. 47
Clark, Christopher (Anthony) Stuart
    *See* Stuart-Clark, Christopher (Anthony)
Clark, Clara Gillow 1951- .......................... *154*
    Earlier sketch in SATA *84*
Clark, David
    *See* Hardcastle, Michael
Clark, David Allen
    *See* Ernst, (Lyman) John
Clark, Emma Chichester ............................. 69
    *See* Chichester Clark, Emma
Clark, Frank J(ames) 1922- ......................... 18
Clark, Garel
    *See* Garelick, May
Clark, Halsey
    *See* Deming, Richard
Clark, Joan
    *See* Benson, Mildred (Augustine Wirt)
Clark, Joan 1934- ....................................... 96
    Earlier sketch in SATA *59*
Clark, Leonard 1905-1981 ........................... 30
    Obituary .................................................... 29
Clark, M. R.
    *See* Clark, Mavis Thorpe
Clark, Margaret (D.) 1943- ....................... *126*
Clark, Margaret Goff 1913- ......................... 82
    Earlier sketch in SATA *8*
Clark, Mary Higgins 1929- ......................... 46
Clark, Mavis Thorpe 1909-1999 ................. 74
    Earlier sketch in SATA *8*
    *See also* CLR *30*
    *See also* SAAS *5*
Clark, Merle
    *See* Gessner, Lynne
Clark, Patricia Denise 1921- ..................... *117*
    *See* Lorrimer, Claire
Clark, Patricia Finrow 1929- ........................ *11*
Clark, Ronald William 1916-1987 ................. 2
    Obituary .................................................... 52
Clark, Sherryl 1956- .................................. 149
Clark, Van D(eusen) 1909-1974 .................... 2
Clark, Virginia
    *See* Gray, Patricia (Clark)
Clark, Walter Van Tilburg 1909-1971 .......... 8
Clarke, Arthur C. 1917- ............................. 115
    Earlier sketches in SATA *13, 70*
    *See also* CLR *119*
Clarke, Arthur Charles
    *See* Clarke, Arthur C.
Clarke, Clorinda 1917- ................................. 7
Clarke, Gus 1948- ..................................... 134

Clarke, J.
*See* Clarke, Judith
Clarke, James Hall
*See* Rowland-Entwistle, (Arthur) Theodore
(Henry)
Clarke, Joan B. 1921- .................................. 42
Brief entry ........................................ 27
Clarke, John
*See* Laklan, Carli
and Sontup, Dan(iel)
Clarke, Judith 1943- .................................. 164
Earlier sketches in SATA 75, 110
*See also* CLR 61
Clarke, Julia 1950- .................................. 138
Clarke, Kenneth 1957- .............................. 107
Clarke, Lea
*See* Rowland-Entwistle, (Arthur) Theodore
(Henry)
Clarke, Margaret 1941-
*See* CLR 99
Clarke, Mary Stetson 1911-1994 .................. 5
Clarke, Michael
*See* Newlon, (Frank) Clarke
Clarke, Pauline 1921- .............................. 131
*See also* CLR 28
*See* Clare, Helen
and Hunter Blair, Pauline
Clarke-Rich, Elizabeth L. 1934- ................. 103
Clarkson, E(dith) Margaret 1915- .............. 37
Clarkson, Ewan 1929- .............................. 9
Claudia, Susan
*See* Goulart, Ron(ald Joseph)
and Johnston, William
Claverie, Jean 1946- .............................. 38
Clay, Patrice 1947- .............................. 47
Claypool, Jane .................................. 103
*See* Miner, Jane Claypool
Clayton, Elaine 1961- .............................. 159
Earlier sketch in SATA 94
Clayton, Lawrence (Otto, Jr.) 1945- .......... 75
Clayton, Sandra 1951- .............................. 110
Cleary, Beverly 1916- .............................. 121
Earlier sketches in SATA 2, 43, 79
*See also* CLR 72
*See also* SAAS 20
Cleary, Beverly Atlee Bunn
*See* Cleary, Beverly
Cleary, Brian P. 1959- .............................. 132
Earlier sketch in SATA 93
Cleaver, Bill .................................. 22
Obituary .................................. 27
*See also* CLR 6
*See* Cleaver, William J(oseph)
Cleaver, Carole 1934- .............................. 6
Cleaver, Elizabeth (Ann Mrazik) 1939-1985
.................................. 23
Obituary .................................. 43
*See also* CLR 13
Cleaver, Hylton Reginald 1891-1961 .......... 49
Cleaver, Vera (Allen) 1919-1993 .............. 76
Earlier sketch in SATA 22
*See also* CLR 6
Cleishbotham, Jebediah
*See* Scott, Sir Walter
Cleland, Mabel
*See* Widdemer, Mabel Cleland
Clem, Margaret H(ollingsworth) 1923- ....... 90
Clemens, Samuel Langhorne 1835-1910 ... 100
*See also* YABC 2
*See* Twain, Mark
Clemens, Virginia Phelps 1941- ................. 35
Clement, Priscilla Ferguson 1942- ........... 171
Clement, Rod .................................. 97
Clements, Andrew 1949- .......................... 158
Earlier sketch in SATA 104
Clements, Bruce 1931- .............................. 94
Earlier sketch in SATA 27
Clemons, Elizabeth
*See* Nowell, Elizabeth Cameron
Clerk, N. W.
*See* Lewis, C.S.

Cleveland-Peck, Patricia .......................... 80
Cleven, Cathrine
*See* Cleven, Kathryn Seward
Cleven, Kathryn Seward .......................... 2
Clevenger, William R. 1954- .................... 84
Clevenger, William Russell
*See* Clevenger, William R.
Clevin, Joergen 1920- .............................. 7
Clevin, Jorgen
*See* Clevin, Joergen
Clewes, Dorothy (Mary) 1907-2003 .......... 86
Obituary .................................. 138
Earlier sketch in SATA 1
Clifford, David
*See* Rosenberg, Eth(el) Clifford
Clifford, Eth .................................. 92
*See also* SAAS 22
*See* Rosenberg, Eth(el) Clifford
Clifford, Harold B(urton) 1893-1988 ......... 10
Clifford, Margaret Cort 1929- .................... 1
Clifford, Martin
*See* Hamilton, Charles (Harold St. John)
Clifford, Mary Louise Beneway 1926- ....... 23
Clifford, Peggy
*See* Clifford, Margaret Cort
Clifford, Rachel Mark
*See* Lewis, Brenda Ralph
Clifton, Lucille 1936- .............................. 128
Earlier sketches in SATA 20, 69
*See also* CLR 5
Clifton, Thelma Lucille
*See* Clifton, Lucille
Climo, Shirley 1928- .............................. 166
Autobiography Feature .......................... 110
Brief entry .................................. 35
Earlier sketches in SATA 39, 77
*See also* CLR 69
Clinton, Cathryn 1957- .............................. 136
Clinton, Dirk
*See* Silverberg, Robert
Clinton, Jon
*See* Prince, J(ack) H(arvey)
Clish, (Lee) Marian 1946- .......................... 43
Clive, Clifford
*See* Hamilton, Charles (Harold St. John)
Clokey, Art 1921- .................................. 59
Cloudsley-Thompson, J(ohn) L(eonard) 1921-
.................................. 19
Clouse, Nancy L. 1938- .............................. 78
Clover, Peter 1952- .............................. 152
Clutha, Janet Paterson Frame 1924-2004 .. 119
*See* Frame, Janet
Clymer, Eleanor 1906-2001 .......................... 85
Obituary .................................. 126
Earlier sketch in SATA 9
*See also* SAAS 17
Clyne, Patricia (Edwards) .......................... 31
Coalson, Glo 1946- .............................. 94
Earlier sketch in SATA 26
Coates, Anna 1958- .............................. 73
Coates, Belle 1896-1986 .......................... 2
Coates, Ruth Allison 1915- .......................... 11
Coats, Alice M(argaret) 1905-1976 ............ 11
Coatsworth, Elizabeth (Jane) 1893-1986 ... 100
Obituary .................................. 49
Earlier sketches in SATA 2, 56
*See also* CLR 2
Cobalt, Martin
*See* Mayne, William (James Carter)
Cobb, Mary 1931- .................................. 88
Cobb, Vicki 1938- .................................. 136
Autobiography Feature .......................... 136
Earlier sketches in SATA 8, 69, 131
*See also* CLR 2
*See also* SAAS 6
Cobbett, Richard
*See* Pluckrose, Henry (Arthur)
Cober, Alan E(dwin) 1935-1998 .................. 7
Obituary .................................. 101
Cobham, Sir Alan
*See* Hamilton, Charles (Harold St. John)

Coburn, Jake 1978- .............................. 155
Cocagnac, Augustin Maurice(-Jean) 1924- ... 7
Cocca-Leffler, Maryann 1958- .................. 136
Earlier sketch in SATA 80
Cochran, Bobbye A. 1949- .......................... 11
Cockett, Mary .................................. 3
Coddell, Esme Raji
*See* Codell, Esme Raji
Codell, Esme Raji 1968- .......................... 160
Cody, C. S.
*See* Waller, Leslie
Cody, Jess
*See* Cunningham, Chet
Coe, Anne (E.) 1949- .............................. 95
Coe, Douglas
*See* Epstein, Beryl (M. Williams)
and Epstein, Samuel
Coen, Rena Neumann 1925- .......................... 20
Coerr, Eleanor (Beatrice) 1922- .................. 67
Earlier sketch in SATA 1
Cofer, Judith Ortiz 1952- .......................... 164
Earlier sketch in SATA 110
*See* Ortiz Cofer, Judith
Coffey, Brian
*See* Koontz, Dean R.
Coffin, Geoffrey
*See* Mason, F(rancis) van Wyck
Coffin, M. T.
*See* Stanley, George Edward
Coffman, Ramon Peyton 1896-1989 ............ 4
Cogan, Karen 1954- .............................. 125
Coggins, Jack (Banham) 1911-2006 .............. 2
Cohen, Barbara 1932-1992 .......................... 77
Obituary .................................. 74
Earlier sketch in SATA 10
*See also* SAAS 7
Cohen, Daniel (E.) 1936- .......................... 70
Earlier sketch in SATA 8
*See also* CLR 43
*See also* SAAS 4
Cohen, Jan Barger
*See* Barger, Jan
Cohen, Jene Barr
*See* Barr, Jene
Cohen, Joan Lebold 1932- .......................... 4
Cohen, Judith Love 1933- .......................... 78
Cohen, Miriam 1926-1955 .......................... 155
Earlier sketches in SATA 29, 106
*See also* SAAS 11
Cohen, Nora .................................. 75
Cohen, Paul S. 1945- .............................. 58
Cohen, Peter Zachary 1931- .......................... 150
Earlier sketch in SATA 4
Cohen, Robert Carl 1930- .......................... 8
Cohen, Sholom 1951- .............................. 94
Cohn, Angelo 1914-1997 .......................... 19
Cohn, Rachel 1968- .............................. 161
Coit, Margaret Louise 1922-2003 ................. 2
Obituary .................................. 142
Colato Lainez, Rene 1970- .......................... 176
Colbert, Anthony 1934- .......................... 15
Colbert, Nancy A. 1936- .......................... 139
Colby, C(arroll) B(urleigh) 1904-1977 ........ 35
Earlier sketch in SATA 3
Colby, Jean Poindexter 1909-1993 .............. 23
Cole, Annette
*See* Steiner, Barbara A(nnette)
Cole, Babette 1949- .............................. 155
Earlier sketches in SATA 61, 96
Cole, Betsy 1940- .............................. 83
Cole, Brock 1938- .............................. 136
Earlier sketch in SATA 72
*See also* CLR 18
Cole, Davis
*See* Elting, Mary
Cole, Hannah 1954- .............................. 74
Cole, Jack -1974
*See* Stewart, John (William)

Cole, Jackson
  *See* Curry, Thomas Albert
  and Germano, Peter B.
  and Heckelmann, Charles N(ewman)
  and Newton, D(wight) B(ennett)
  and Schisgall, Oscar
Cole, Jennifer
  *See* Zach, Cheryl (Byrd)
Cole, Joanna 1944- .................................. 168
  Brief entry ........................................ 37
  Earlier sketches in SATA 49, 81, 120
  *See also* CLR 40
Cole, Lois Dwight 1903-1979 .................. 10
  Obituary ............................................ 26
Cole, Michael 1947- .............................. 59
Cole, Sheila R. 1939- ............................ 171
  Earlier sketches in SATA 24, 95
Cole, Sheila Rotenberg
  *See* Cole, Sheila R.
Cole, Stephen 1971- .............................. 161
Cole, William (Rossa) 1919-2000 .......... 71
  Earlier sketch in SATA 9
  *See also* SAAS 9
Coleman, Andrew
  *See* Pine, Nicholas
Coleman, Clare
  *See* Bell, Clare (Louise)
  and Easton, M(alcolm) Coleman
Coleman, Loren 1947- ............................ 164
Coleman, Loren Elwood, Jr.
  *See* Coleman, Loren
Coleman, Mary Ann 1928- ...................... 83
Coleman, Michael (Lee) 1946- .............. 133
  Autobiography Feature .......................... 133
  Earlier sketch in SATA 108
Coleman, William L(eRoy) 1938- .............. 49
  Brief entry ........................................ 34
Coles, Robert (Martin) 1929- .................. 23
Colfer, Eoin 1965- ................................ 148
  *See also* CLR 112
Colin, Ann
  *See* Ure, Jean
Collard, Sneed B. III 1959- .................... 139
  Earlier sketch in SATA 84
Colledge, Anne 1939- ............................ 142
Collicott, Sharleen 1937- ........................ 143
  Earlier sketch in SATA 98
Collier, Bryan ...................................... 174
  Earlier sketch in SATA 126
Collier, Christopher 1930- ...................... 70
  Earlier sketch in SATA 16
Collier, Ethel 1903-1999 ........................ 22
Collier, James Lincoln 1928- .................. 166
  Earlier sketches in SATA 8, 70
  *See also* CLR 3
  *See also* SAAS 21
Collier, Jane
  *See* Collier, Zena
Collier, Steven 1942- ............................ 61
Collier, Zena 1926- .............................. 23
  *See* Collier, Jane
Collings, Gillian 1939- .......................... 102
Collington, Peter 1948- .......................... 99
  Earlier sketch in SATA 59
Collins, Ace 1953- ................................ 82
Collins, Andrew J.
  *See* Collins, Ace
Collins, David R(aymond) 1940-2001 ...... 121
  Earlier sketch in SATA 7
Collins, Heather 1946- .......................... 81
Collins, Hunt
  *See* Hunter, Evan
Collins, Michael
  *See* Lynds, Dennis
Collins, Michael 1930- .......................... 58
Collins, Pat(ricia) Lowery 1932- ............ 151
  Earlier sketch in SATA 31
Collins, Paul 1954- .............................. 126
Collinson, A. S.
  *See* Collinson, Alan S.
Collinson, Alan S. 1934- ........................ 80

Collinson, Roger (Alfred) 1936- .............. 133
Collodi, Carlo
  *See* CLR 120
  *See* Lorenzini, Carlo
Colloms, Brenda 1919- .......................... 40
Colman, Hila .......................................... 53
  Earlier sketch in SATA 1
  *See also* SAAS 14
Colman, Penny (Morgan) 1944- .............. 160
  Autobiography Feature .......................... 160
  Earlier sketches in SATA 77, 114
Colman, Warren (David) 1944- ................ 67
Colombo, John Robert 1936- .................. 50
Colon, Raul ........................................ 156
Colonius, Lillian 1911-1992 .................... 3
Colorado, Antonio J.
  *See* Colorado (Capella), Antonio J(ulio)
Colorado (Capella), Antonio J(ulio) 1903-1994
  ...................................................... 23
  Obituary ............................................ 79
Colquhoun, Glenn 1964- ........................ 165
Colston, Fifi E. 1960- ............................ 150
Colt, Martin
  *See* Epstein, Beryl (M. Williams)
  and Epstein, Samuel
Colum, Padraic 1881-1972 ...................... 15
  *See also* CLR 36
Columbus, Chris 1959- .......................... 97
Columbus, Christopher
  *See* Columbus, Chris
Columella
  *See* Moore, Clement Clarke
Colver, Anne 1908- .............................. 7
Colvin, James
  *See* Moorcock, Michael
Colwell, Eileen (Hilda) 1904-2002 .......... 2
Coman, Carolyn .................................... 127
Combs, Lisa M.
  *See* McCourt, Lisa
Combs, Robert
  *See* Murray, John
Comfort, Jane Levington
  *See* Sturtzel, Jane Levington
Comfort, Mildred Houghton 1886-1976 ...... 3
Comins, Ethel M(ae) .............................. 11
Comins, Jeremy 1933- .......................... 28
Commager, Henry Steele 1902-1998 ...... 23
  Obituary ............................................ 102
Compere, Mickie
  *See* Davidson, Margaret
Compestine, Ying Chang 1963- .............. 140
Compton, Patricia A. 1936- .................... 75
Comte, The Great
  *See* Hawkesworth, Eric
Comus
  *See* Ballantyne, R(obert) M(ichael)
Comyns, Nance
  *See* Comyns-Toohey, Nantz
Comyns-Toohey, Nantz 1956- .................. 86
Conan Doyle, Arthur
  *See* Doyle, Sir Arthur Conan
Condit, Martha Olson 1913- .................... 28
Condon, Bill 1949- .............................. 142
Condon, Judith .................................... 83
Condy, Roy 1942- ................................ 96
Cone, Ferne Geller 1921- ...................... 39
Cone, Molly (Lamken) 1918- .................. 151
  Autobiography Feature .......................... 151
  Earlier sketches in SATA 1, 28, 115
  *See also* SAAS 11
Cone, Patrick 1954- .............................. 89
Coney, Michael G. 1932-2005 ................ 61
  Obituary ............................................ 170
Coney, Michael Greatrex
  *See* Coney, Michael G.
Coney, Mike
  *See* Coney, Michael G.
Conford, Ellen 1942- ............................ 162
  Earlier sketches in SATA 6, 68, 110
  *See also* CLR 71

Conger, Lesley
  *See* Suttles, Shirley (Smith)
Conklin, Gladys Plemon 1903- ................ 2
Conklin, Paul S. 1929(?)-2003 ................ 43
  Brief entry ........................................ 33
  Obituary ............................................ 147
Conkling, Hilda 1910-1986 ...................... 23
Conlan, Kathleen Elizabeth 1950- .......... 145
Conlan, Kathy
  *See* Conlan, Kathleen Elizabeth
Conley-Weaver, Robyn 1963- .................. 125
Conlon-McKenna, Marita 1956- .............. 71
Conly, Jane Leslie 1948- ........................ 164
  Earlier sketches in SATA 80, 112
Conly, Robert Leslie 1918(?)-1973 .......... 23
  *See* O'Brien, Robert C.
Connolly, Jerome P(atrick) 1931- .............. 8
Connolly, Pat 1943- .............................. 74
Connolly, Peter 1935- ............................ 105
  Earlier sketch in SATA 47
Conover, Chris 1950- ............................ 31
Conquest, Owen
  *See* Hamilton, Charles (Harold St. John)
Conrad, Joseph 1857-1924 ...................... 27
Conrad, Pam 1947-1996 ........................ 133
  Brief entry ........................................ 49
  Obituary ............................................ 90
  Earlier sketches in SATA 52, 80
  *See also* CLR 18
  *See also* SAAS 19
Conroy, Jack ........................................ 19
  *See* Conroy, John Wesley
Conroy, Robert
  *See* Goldston, Robert (Conroy)
Constable, Kate 1966- .......................... 172
Constant, Alberta Wilson 1908-1981 ...... 22
  Obituary ............................................ 28
Conway, Diana C(ohen) 1943- ................ 91
Conway, Gordon
  *See* Hamilton, Charles (Harold St. John)
Cook, Bernadine 1924- .......................... 11
Cook, Fred J(ames) 1911-2003 ................ 2
  Obituary ............................................ 145
Cook, Glen 1944- ................................ 171
  Earlier sketch in SATA 108
Cook, Glen Charles
  *See* Cook, Glen
Cook, Hugh 1956- ................................ 85
Cook, Hugh, Walter Gilbert
  *See* Cook, Hugh
Cook, Jean Thor 1930- .......................... 94
Cook, Joel 1934- .................................. 79
Cook, Joseph Jay 1924- .......................... 8
Cook, Lisa Broadie ................................ 157
Cook, Lyn
  *See* Waddell, Evelyn Margaret
Cook, Roy
  *See* Silverberg, Robert
Cook, Trish .......................................... 175
Cooke, Ann
  *See* Cole, Joanna
Cooke, Arthur
  *See* Lowndes, Robert A(ugustine) W(ard)
Cooke, Barbara
  *See* Alexander, Anna B(arbara Cooke)
Cooke, David Coxe 1917- ........................ 2
Cooke, Donald Ewin 1916-1985 ................ 2
  Obituary ............................................ 45
Cooke, Frank E. 1920- .......................... 87
Cooke, Jean (Isobel Esther) 1929- .......... 74
Cooke, John Estes
  *See* Baum, L(yman) Frank
Cooke, Trish 1962- .............................. 129
Cookson, Catherine (McMullen) 1906-1998 . 9
  Obituary ............................................ 116
Cooley, Regina Francoise 1940- .............. 177
Coolidge, Olivia E(nsor) 1908- ................ 26
  Earlier sketch in SATA 1
Cooling, Wendy .................................... 169
  Earlier sketch in SATA 111

Coombs, Charles I(ra) 1914-1994 ............... *43*
  Earlier sketch in SATA *3*
  *See also* SAAS *15*
Coombs, Chick
  *See* Coombs, Charles I(ra)
Coombs, Patricia 1926- ......................... *51*
  Earlier sketch in SATA *3*
  *See also* SAAS *22*
Cooney, Barbara 1917-2000 ...................... *96*
  Obituary ................................ *123*
  Earlier sketches in SATA *6, 59*
  *See also* CLR *23*
Cooney, Caroline B. 1947- ...................... *130*
  Brief entry ................................ *41*
  Earlier sketches in SATA *48, 80, 113*
Cooney, Nancy Evans 1932- ...................... *42*
Coontz, Otto 1946- ............................ *33*
Cooper, Ann (Catharine) 1939- ................ *104*
Cooper, Dutch
  *See* Kuyper, Sjoerd
Cooper, Elisha 1971- ........................... *157*
  Earlier sketch in SATA *99*
Cooper, Elizabeth Keyser -1992 ................. *47*
Cooper, Floyd ................................. *144*
  Earlier sketch in SATA *96*
  *See also* CLR *60*
Cooper, Gordon 1932- ........................... *23*
Cooper, Helen 1963- ............................ *169*
  Earlier sketch in SATA *102*
Cooper, Henry S(potswood) F(enimore), Jr.
  1933- ..................................... *65*
Cooper, Ilene 1948- ............................ *145*
  Earlier sketches in SATA *66, 97*
Cooper, James Fenimore 1789-1851 .......... *19*
  *See also* CLR *105*
Cooper, John R. ................................. *1*
Cooper, Kay 1941- .............................. *11*
Cooper, Lee Pelham 1926- ....................... *5*
Cooper, Lester (Irving) 1919-1985 ............. *32*
  Obituary .................................. *43*
Cooper, Lettice (Ulpha) 1897-1994 ............. *35*
  Obituary .................................. *82*
Cooper, Louise 1952- ........................... *152*
Cooper, M.E.
  *See* Lerangis, Peter
Cooper, M.E.
  *See* Davis, Maggie S.
Cooper, Melrose
  *See* Kroll, Virginia L.
Cooper, Michael L. 1950- ....................... *117*
  Earlier sketch in SATA *79*
Cooper, Patrick 1949- .......................... *134*
Cooper, Susan 1935- ............................ *151*
  Earlier sketches in SATA *4, 64, 104*
  *See also* CLR *67*
  *See also* SAAS *6*
Cooper, Susan Mary
  *See* Cooper, Susan
Cope, Jane U(rsula) 1949- ..................... *108*
Copeland, Helen 1920- .......................... *4*
Copeland, Paul W. ............................. *23*
Coplans, Peta 1951- ............................ *84*
Copley (Diana) Heather Pickering 1918- .... *45*
Coppard, A(lfred) E(dgar) 1878-1957
  *See* YABC *1*
Copper, Melinda 1952- ......................... *172*
Copper, Melinda McConnaughey
  *See* Copper, Melinda
Coralie
  *See* Anderson, Catherine Corley
Corbett, Grahame ............................. *43*
  Brief entry ................................ *36*
Corbett, Scott 1913- ........................... *42*
  Earlier sketch in SATA *2*
  *See also* CLR *1*
  *See also* SAAS *2*
Corbett, Sue ................................. *174*
Corbett, W(illiam) J(esse) 1938- .............. *102*
  Brief entry ................................ *44*
  Earlier sketch in SATA *50*
  *See also* CLR *19*

Corbin, Sabra Lee
  *See* Malvern, Gladys
Corbin, William
  *See* McGraw, William Corbin
Corby, Dan
  *See* Catherall, Arthur
Corcoran, Barbara (Asenath) 1911- ............. *77*
  Autobiography Feature ...................... *125*
  Earlier sketch in SATA *3*
  *See also* CLR *50*
  *See also* SAAS *20*
Corcos, Lucille 1908-1973 ..................... *10*
Cordell, Alexander
  *See* Graber, Alexander
Cordell, Alexander
  *See* Graber, (George) Alexander
Corder, Zizou
  *See* Young, Louisa
Corella, Joseph
  *See* Odgers, Sally Farrell
Coren, Alan 1938- ............................. *32*
Corey, Dorothy ............................... *23*
Corey, Shana 1974- ............................ *133*
Corfe, Thomas Howell 1928- .................... *27*
Corfe, Tom
  *See* Corfe, Thomas Howell
Corfield, Robin Bell 1952- ..................... *74*
Corlett, William 1938-2005 .................... *46*
  Brief entry ................................ *39*
Cormack, M(argaret) Grant 1913- .............. *11*
Cormack, Maribelle B. 1902-1984 ............. *39*
Cormier, Robert 1925-2000 ..................... *83*
  Obituary .................................. *122*
  Earlier sketches in SATA *10, 45*
  *See also* CLR *55*
Cormier, Robert Edmund
  *See* Cormier, Robert
Cornelius, Carol 1942- ......................... *40*
Cornelius, Kay 1933- ........................... *157*
Cornell, J.
  *See* Cornell, Jeffrey
Cornell, James (Clayton, Jr.) 1938- ........... *27*
Cornell, Jean Gay 1920- ........................ *23*
Cornell, Jeffrey 1945- ......................... *11*
Cornish, Sam(uel James) 1935- ................. *23*
Cornwall, Nellie
  *See* Sloggett, Nellie
Correy, Lee
  *See* Stine, G(eorge) Harry
Corrick, James A. 1945- ........................ *76*
Corrigan, (Helen) Adeline 1909- ............... *23*
Corrigan, Barbara 1922- ........................ *8*
Corrigan, Eireann 1977- ....................... *163*
Corrin, Sara 1918- ............................ *86*
  Brief entry ................................ *48*
Corrin, Stephen ............................... *86*
  Brief entry ................................ *48*
Cort, M. C.
  *See* Clifford, Margaret Cort
Cort, Margaret
  *See* Clifford, Margaret Cort
Corwin, Judith H(offman) 1946- ............... *10*
Cory, Rowena
  *See* Lindquist, Rowena Cory
Cosby, Bill
  *See* Cosby, William Henry, Jr.
Cosby, William Henry, Jr. 1937- ............... *110*
  Earlier sketch in SATA *66*
  *See* Cosby, Bill
Cosentino, Ralph .............................. *169*
Cosgrove, Margaret (Leota) 1926- ............. *47*
Cosgrove, Stephen E(dward) 1945- ............. *53*
  Brief entry ................................ *40*
Coskey, Evelyn 1932- .......................... *7*
Cosner, Shaaron 1940- ......................... *43*
Cossi, Olga 1921- ............................. *102*
  Earlier sketch in SATA *67*
Costabel, Eva Deutsch 1924- ................... *45*
Costabel-Deutsch, Eva
  *See* Costabel, Eva Deutsch
Costello, David ............................... *174*

Costello, David F(rancis) 1904-1990 .......... *23*
Cott, Jonathan 1942- .......................... *23*
Cottam, Clarence 1899-1974 .................... *25*
Cottle, Joan 1960- ............................ *135*
Cottler, Joseph 1899-1996 ..................... *22*
Cottonwood, Joe 1947- ......................... *92*
Cottrell, Leonard 1913-1974 ................... *24*
Cottringer, Anne 1952- ........................ *150*
  Earlier sketch in SATA *97*
Coulman, Valerie 1969- ........................ *161*
Couloumbis, Audrey ........................... *173*
Counsel, June 1926- ........................... *70*
Countryman, The
  *See* Whitlock, Ralph
Courlander, Harold 1908-1996 .................. *6*
  Obituary .................................. *88*
Coursen, Valerie 1965(?)- ..................... *102*
Courtney, Dayle
  *See* Goldsmith, Howard
Cousins, Linda 1946- .......................... *90*
Cousins, Lucy 1964- ........................... *172*
Cousins, Margaret 1905-1996 ................... *2*
  Obituary .................................. *92*
Cousteau, Jacques-Yves 1910-1997 ............. *98*
  Earlier sketch in SATA *38*
Couture, Christin 1951- ....................... *73*
Coville, Bruce 1950- .......................... *155*
  Autobiography Feature ...................... *155*
  Earlier sketches in SATA *32, 77, 118*
Covington, Dennis ............................ *109*
Covington, Linda
  *See* Windsor, Linda
Cowan, Catherine ............................. *121*
Cowell, Cressida 1966- ........................ *140*
Cowen, Eve
  *See* Werner, Herma
Cowen, Ida 1898-1993 .......................... *64*
Cowie, Leonard W(allace) 1919- ............... *4*
Cowles, Kathleen
  *See* Krull, Kathleen
Cowley, Cassia Joy
  *See* Cowley, Joy
Cowley, Joy 1936- ............................. *164*
Cowley, (Cassia) Joy 1936- .................... *90*
  Autobiography Feature ...................... *118*
  Earlier sketch in SATA *4*
  *See also* CLR *55*
  *See also* SAAS *26*
Cowley, Marjorie 1925- ........................ *111*
Cox, (Christopher) Barry 1931- ............... *62*
Cox, Clinton 1934- ............................ *108*
  Earlier sketch in SATA *74*
Cox, David (Dundas) 1933- ..................... *56*
Cox, Donald William 1921- ..................... *23*
Cox, Jack
  *See* Cox, John Roberts
Cox, John Roberts 1915-1981 ................... *9*
Cox, Judy 1954- ............................... *160*
  Earlier sketch in SATA *117*
Cox, Palmer 1840-1924 ......................... *24*
  *See also* CLR *24*
Cox, Vic 1942- ................................ *88*
Cox, Vicki 1945- .............................. *158*
Cox, Victoria
  *See* Garretson, Victoria Diane
Cox, Wally ................................... *25*
  *See* Cox, Wallace (Maynard)
Cox, William R(obert) 1901-1988 .............. *46*
  Brief entry ................................ *31*
  Obituary .................................. *57*
  *See* Ward, Jonas
Coxe, Molly 1959- ............................. *101*
  Earlier sketch in SATA *69*
Coxon, Michele 1950- .......................... *158*
  Earlier sketch in SATA *76*
Coy, Harold 1902-1986 ......................... *3*
Coy, John 1958- ............................... *171*
  Earlier sketch in SATA *120*
Craats, Rennay 1973- .......................... *131*
Crabtree, Judith 1928- ........................ *98*
  Earlier sketch in SATA *63*

Cracker, Edward E.B.
*See* Odgers, Sally Farrell
Craft, K. Y.
*See* Craft, Kinuko Y(amabe)
Craft, Kinuko
*See* Craft, Kinuko Y(amabe)
Craft, Kinuko Y(amabe) 1940- ............... *127*
Earlier sketch in SATA *65*
Craft, Ruth 1935- .......................................... *87*
Brief entry .................................................... *31*
Craig, A. A.
*See* Anderson, Poul
Craig, Alisa
*See* MacLeod, Charlotte (Matilda)
Craig, Helen 1934- ...................................... *94*
Earlier sketches in SATA *46, 49*
Craig, John Eland
*See* Chipperfield, Joseph Eugene
Craig, John Ernest 1921- ............................. *23*
Craig, Kit
*See* Reed, Kit
Craig, M. F.
*See* Craig, Mary (Francis) Shura
Craig, M. Jean ........................................... *17*
Craig, M. S.
*See* Craig, Mary (Francis) Shura
Craig, Margaret (Maze) 1911-1964 .............. *9*
Craig, Mary
*See* Craig, Mary (Francis) Shura
Craig, Mary Shura
*See* Craig, Mary (Francis) Shura
Craig, Mary (Francis) Shura 1923-1991 ..... *86*
Obituary .................................................... *65*
Earlier sketch in SATA *6*
*See also* SAAS *7*
Craig, Ruth 1922- ........................................ *95*
Craik, Mrs.
*See* Craik, Dinah Maria (Mulock)
Craik, Dinah Maria (Mulock) 1826-1887 ... *34*
*See* Craik, Mrs.
and Mulock, Dinah Maria
Crandall, Court 1965- ................................. *175*
Crandell, Rachel 1943- ............................... *152*
Crane, Barbara (Joyce) 1934- ...................... *31*
Crane, Caroline 1930- ................................. *11*
Crane, Jordan 1973- .................................... *174*
Crane, M. A.
*See* Wartski, Maureen (Ann Crane)
Crane, Stephen (Townley) 1871-1900
*See* YABC *2*
Crane, Walter 1845-1915 ............................ *100*
Earlier sketch in SATA *18*
*See also* CLR *56*
Crane, William D(wight) 1892-1976 ............. *1*
Cranfield, Ingrid 1945- ................................ *74*
Cranshaw, Stanley
*See* Fisher, Dorothy (Frances) Canfield
Crary, Elizabeth (Ann) 1942- ....................... *99*
Brief entry .................................................... *43*
Crary, Margaret (Coleman) 1906-1986 ......... *9*
Cravath, Lynne W(oodcock) 1951- ........... *148*
Earlier sketch in SATA *98*
Craven, Thomas 1889-1969 .......................... *22*
Crawford, Charles P. 1945- .......................... *28*
Crawford, Deborah 1922- .............................. *6*
Crawford, John E(dmund) 1904-1971 ............. *3*
Crawford, K(aren) Michael 1959- ............. *155*
Crawford, Mel 1925- .................................... *44*
Brief entry .................................................... *33*
Crawford, Phyllis 1899- ................................ *3*
Crawley, Dave .............................................. *177*
Cray, Roberta
*See* Emerson, Ru
Crayder, Dorothy ............................................. *7*
Crayder, Teresa
*See* Colman, Hila
Crayon, Geoffrey
*See* Irving, Washington
Craz, Albert G. 1926- .................................. *24*
Crebbin, June 1938- .................................... *169*
Earlier sketch in SATA *80*

Crecy, Jeanne
*See* Williams, Jeanne
Credle, Ellis 1902-1998 ................................. *1*
Creech, Sharon 1945- ................................. *172*
Earlier sketches in SATA *94, 139*
*See also* CLR *89*
Creeden, Sharon 1938- ................................ *91*
Creighton, Jill 1949- ................................... *96*
Crenson, Victoria 1952- .............................. *159*
Earlier sketch in SATA *88*
Cresp, Gael 1954- ....................................... *119*
Crespo, George 1962- .................................. *82*
Cresswell, Helen 1934-2005 ......................... *79*
Obituary .................................................... *168*
Earlier sketches in SATA *1, 48*
*See also* CLR *18*
*See also* SAAS *20*
Cressy, Michael 1955- ................................ *124*
Cressy, Mike
*See* Cressy, Michael
Cretan, Gladys (Yessayan) 1921- ................... *2*
Cretzmeyer, Stacy (Megan) 1959- ............. *124*
Crew, Gary 1947- ........................................ *163*
Earlier sketches in SATA *75, 110*
*See also* CLR *42*
Crew, Helen (Cecilia) Coale 1866-1941
*See* YABC *2*
Crew, Linda (Jean) 1951- ............................ *137*
Earlier sketch in SATA *71*
Crews, Donald 1938- .................................... *76*
Brief entry .................................................... *30*
Earlier sketch in SATA *32*
*See also* CLR *7*
Crews, Nina 1963- ....................................... *158*
Earlier sketch in SATA *97*
Crichton, John Michael
*See* Crichton, Michael
Crichton, Michael 1942- ............................... *88*
Earlier sketch in SATA *9*
Crider, Allen Billy
*See* Crider, Bill
Crider, Bill 1941- ........................................ *99*
Crilley, Mark 1966- .................................... *148*
Autobiography Feature ............................. *148*
Earlier sketch in SATA *120*
Crimi, Carolyn 1959- ................................. *176*
Cripps, Enid Margaret
*See* Appiah, Peggy
Crisman, Ruth 1914- .................................... *73*
Crisp, Marta Marie 1947- ........................... *128*
Crisp, Marty
*See* Crisp, Marta Marie
Crispin, A(nn) C(arol) 1950- ........................ *86*
Crist, James J. ............................................. *168*
Cristall, Barbara .......................................... *79*
Crist-Evans, Craig 1954- ............................ *153*
Crofford, Emily (Ardell) 1927- ..................... *61*
Crofut, William E. III 1934- ........................ *23*
Croll, Carolyn 1945- ................................... *102*
Brief entry .................................................... *52*
Earlier sketch in SATA *56*
Croman, Dorothy Young
*See* Rosenberg, Dorothy
Cromie, Alice Hamilton 1914-2000 .............. *24*
Cromie, William J(oseph) 1930- .................... *4*
Crompton, Anne Eliot 1930- ........................ *73*
Earlier sketch in SATA *23*
Crompton, Richmal
*See* Lamburn, Richmal Crompton
Cronbach, Abraham 1882-1965 ..................... *11*
Crone, Ruth 1919-2003 .................................. *4*
Cronin, A(rchibald) J(oseph) 1896-1981 ..... *47*
Obituary .................................................... *25*
Cronin, Doreen (A.) .................................... *125*
*See also* CLR *105*
Crook, Beverly Courtney ............................... *38*
Brief entry .................................................... *35*
Crook, Connie Brummel 1930- ................... *168*
Earlier sketch in SATA *98*
Crook, Constance
*See* Crook, Connie Brummel

Crosby, Alexander L. 1906-1980 .................... *2*
Obituary .................................................... *23*
Crosby, Harry C., Jr. ................................... *102*
Crosby, Margaret
*See* CLR *77*
*See* Rathmann, Peggy
Crosher, G. R. ............................................. *14*
Cross, Gilbert B. 1939- ................................ *60*
Brief entry .................................................... *51*
Cross, Gillian 1945- ................................... *165*
Earlier sketches in SATA *38, 71, 110*
*See also* CLR *28*
Cross, Gillian Clare
*See* Cross, Gillian
Cross, Helen Reeder
*See* Broadhead, Helen Cross
Cross, Peter 1951- ....................................... *95*
Cross, Tom 1954- ........................................ *146*
Cross, Verda 1914- ....................................... *75*
Cross, Wilbur Lucius III 1918- ...................... *2*
Crossland, Caroline 1964- ............................ *83*
Crossley-Holland, Kevin 1941- .................... *165*
Earlier sketches in SATA *5, 74, 120*
*See also* CLR *84*
*See also* SAAS *20*
Crossley-Holland, Kevin John William
*See* Crossley-Holland, Kevin
Crouch, Marcus 1913-1996 ............................ *4*
Crout, George C(lement) 1917- ..................... *11*
Crow, Donna Fletcher 1941- ........................ *40*
Crowe, Andrew .......................................... *111*
Crowe, John
*See* Lynds, Dennis
Crowe, (Bettina) Peter Lum 1911- .................. *6*
Crowell, Grace Noll 1877-1969 .................... *34*
Crowell, Pers 1910-1990 ................................ *2*
Crowell, Robert Leland 1909-2001 ............. *63*
Crowfield, Christopher
*See* Stowe, Harriet (Elizabeth) Beecher
Crowley, Arthur McBlair 1945- .................... *38*
Crowley, John 1942- ................................... *140*
Earlier sketch in SATA *65*
Crownfield, Gertrude 1867-1945
*See* YABC *1*
Crowther, James Gerald 1899-1983 ............. *14*
Crowther, Robert 1948- .............................. *163*
Cruikshank, George 1792-1878 ................... *22*
*See also* CLR *63*
Crum, Shutta ............................................. *134*
Crummel, Susan Stevens 1949- ................... *176*
Earlier sketch in SATA *130*
Crump, Fred H., Jr. 1931- ............................ *76*
Earlier sketch in SATA *11*
Crump, J(ames) Irving 1887-1979 ............... *57*
Obituary .................................................... *21*
Crump, William D(rake) 1949- .................... *138*
Crunden, Reginald
*See* Cleaver, Hylton Reginald
Crunk, T.
*See* Crunk, Tony
Crunk, Tony 1956- ...................................... *130*
Crutcher, Chris 1946- ................................. *153*
Earlier sketches in SATA *52, 99*
*See also* CLR *28*
Crutcher, Christopher C.
*See* Crutcher, Chris
Cruz, Ray(mond) 1933- .................................. *6*
Cruz Martinez, Alejandro (?)-1987 ............. *74*
Crystal, Billy 1947- ................................... *154*
Cuetara, Mittie 1957- ................................. *158*
Earlier sketch in SATA *106*
Cuffari, Richard 1925-1978 ......................... *66*
Obituary .................................................... *25*
Earlier sketch in SATA *6*
Cullen, Countee 1903-1946 ......................... *18*
Culliford, Pierre 1928-1992 ......................... *40*
Obituary .................................................... *74*
Cullinan, Bernice E(llinger) 1926- ............. *135*
Culp, Louanna McNary 1901-1965 ............... *2*
Culper, Felix
*See* McCaughrean, Geraldine

Cumbaa, Stephen 1947- ............................. 72
Cumming, Peter 1951- ............................. 168
Cumming, Primrose Amy 1915- ................ 24
Cumming, Robert 1945- ............................ 65
Cummings, Betty Sue 1918- ...................... 15
  See also SAAS 9
Cummings, Parke 1902-1987 ....................... 2
  Obituary ................................................. 53
Cummings, Pat (Marie) 1950- ................. 107
  Earlier sketches in SATA 42, 71
  See also CLR 48
  See also SAAS 13
Cummings, Phil 1957- ............................. 123
  Earlier sketch in SATA 74
Cummings, Priscilla 1951- ....................... 170
  Earlier sketch in SATA 129
Cummings, Richard
  See Gardner, Richard (M.)
Cummins, Maria Susanna 1827-1866
  See YABC 1
Cuneo, Mary Louise -2001 ......................... 85
Cunliffe, John Arthur 1933- ...................... 86
  Earlier sketch in SATA 11
Cunliffe, Marcus (Falkner) 1922-1990 ........ 37
  Obituary ................................................. 66
Cunnane, Kelly ...................................... 175
Cunningham, Bob
  See May, Julian
Cunningham, Captain Frank
  See Glick, Carl (Cannon)
Cunningham, Cathy
  See Cunningham, Chet
Cunningham, Chet 1928- ........................... 23
Cunningham, Dale S(peers) 1932- ............... 11
Cunningham, Dru ..................................... 91
Cunningham, E. V.
  See Fast, Howard
Cunningham, Julia (Woolfolk) 1916- ......... 132
  Earlier sketches in SATA 1, 26
  See also SAAS 2
Cunningham, Lawrence J. 1943- ............... 125
Cunningham, Virginia
  See Holmgren, Virginia C(unningham)
Curiae, Amicus
  See Fuller, Edmund (Maybank)
Curie, Eve 1904- ....................................... 1
Curlee, Lynn 1947- ................................. 141
  Earlier sketch in SATA 98
Curley, Daniel 1918-1988 .......................... 23
  Obituary ................................................. 61
Curley, Marianne 1959- ........................... 175
  Earlier sketch in SATA 131
Currie, Robin 1948- ................................ 120
Currie, Stephen 1960- ............................. 132
  Earlier sketch in SATA 82
Curry, Ann (Gabrielle) 1934- .................... 72
Curry, Jane L(ouise) 1932- ...................... 138
  Autobiography Feature ........................... 138
  Earlier sketches in SATA 1, 52, 90
  See also CLR 31
  See also SAAS 6
Curry, Peggy Simson 1911-1987 .................. 8
  Obituary ................................................. 50
Curtis, Bruce (Richard) 1944- .................... 30
Curtis, Chara M(ahar) 1950- ...................... 78
Curtis, Christopher Paul 1954(?)- ............. 140
  Earlier sketch in SATA 93
  See also CLR 68
Curtis, Gavin 1965- ................................ 107
Curtis, Jamie Lee 1958- .......................... 144
  Earlier sketch in SATA 95
  See also CLR 88
Curtis, Marci ...................................... 160
Curtis, Patricia 1921- ............................ 101
  Earlier sketch in SATA 23
Curtis, Peter
  See Lofts, Norah (Robinson)
Curtis, Philip (Delacourt) 1920- ................ 62
Curtis, Richard (Alan) 1937- ..................... 29

Curtis, Richard Hale
  See Deming, Richard
  and Levinson, Leonard
  and Rothweiler, Paul Roger
Curtis, Wade
  See Pournelle, Jerry (Eugene)
Curtiss, A(rlene) B. 1934- ......................... 90
Cusack, Margaret 1945- ............................ 58
Cushman, Doug 1953- .............................. 157
  Earlier sketches in SATA 65, 101
Cushman, Jerome ...................................... 2
Cushman, Karen 1941- ............................. 147
  Earlier sketch in SATA 89
  See also CLR 55
Cusick, Richie Tankersley 1952- ............... 140
  Earlier sketch in SATA 67
Cutchen, Billye Walker 1930- ..................... 15
Cutchins, Judy 1947- ................................ 59
Cutler, Daniel S(olomon) 1951- .................. 78
Cutler, Ebbitt 1923- .................................. 9
Cutler, Ivor 1923-2006 ............................. 24
  Obituary ............................................... 174
Cutler, Jane 1936- ................................. 162
  Earlier sketches in SATA 75, 118
Cutler, May Ebbitt
  See Cutler, Ebbitt
Cutler, Samuel
  See Folsom, Franklin (Brewster)
Cutlip, Kimbra L(eigh-Ann) 1964- ............ 128
Cutrate, Joe
  See Spiegelman, Art
Cutt, W(illiam) Towrie 1898-1981 ............... 16
  Obituary ................................................. 85
Cuyler, Margery S(tuyvesant) 1948- ......... 156
  Earlier sketches in SATA 39, 99
Cuyler, Stephen
  See Bates, Barbara S(nedeker)
Cyrus, Kurt 1954- ................................... 132

**D**

Dabba Smith, Frank ................................ 174
Dabcovich, Lydia ..................................... 99
  Brief entry ............................................. 47
  Earlier sketch in SATA 58
Dace, Dolores B(oelens) 1929- ................... 89
Dadey, Debbie 1959- ............................... 136
  Earlier sketch in SATA 73
Dahl, Borghild (Margarethe) 1890-1984 ....... 7
  Obituary ................................................. 37
Dahl, Roald 1916-1990 ............................. 73
  Obituary ................................................. 65
  Earlier sketches in SATA 1, 26
  See also CLR 111
Dahlberg, Maurine F. 1951- ...................... 171
Dahlstedt, Marden (Stewart) 1921-1983 ........ 8
  Obituary ............................................... 110
Dain, Martin J. 1924-2000 ......................... 35
Dakos, Kalli 1950- ................................. 115
  Earlier sketch in SATA 80
Dale, Anna 1971- .................................. 170
Dale, Gary
  See Reece, Colleen L.
Dale, George E.
  See Asimov, Isaac
Dale, Jack
  See Holliday, Joseph
Dale, Kim 1957- .................................... 123
Dale, Margaret J(essy) Miller 1911- ............ 39
Dale, Mitzi
  See Gillian
Dale, Norman
  See Denny, Norman (George)
Dale, Penny 1954- .................................. 151
  Earlier sketch in SATA 70
Daley, Michael J. .................................. 170
Dalgliesh, Alice 1893-1979 ........................ 17
  Obituary ................................................. 21
  See also CLR 62

Dalkey, Kara 1953- ................................ 132
Dalkey, Kara Mia
  See Dalkey, Kara
Dallas, Ruth
  See Mumford, Ruth
Dalmas, John
  See Jones, John R(obert)
Dalton, Annie 1948- ............................... 140
  Earlier sketch in SATA 40
Dalton, Kit
  See Cunningham, Chet
Dalton, Pamela
  See Johnson, Pamela
Dalton, Sean
  See Chester, Deborah
Dalton, Sheila 1949- .............................. 108
Daly, Jim
  See Stratemeyer, Edward L.
Daly, Jude 1951- ................................... 177
Daly, Kathleen N(orah) ........................... 124
  Brief entry ............................................. 37
Daly, Maureen 1921-2006 ........................ 129
  Obituary ............................................... 176
  Earlier sketch in SATA 2
  See also CLR 96
  See also SAAS 1
Daly, Nicholas 1946- .............................. 164
  Earlier sketches in SATA 37, 76, 114
  See also CLR 41
  See Daly, Niki
Daly, Niki
  See SAAS 21
  See Daly, Nicholas
D'Amato, Alex 1919- ................................ 20
D'Amato, Janet (Potter) 1925- ..................... 9
Damerow, Gail 1944- ................................ 83
Damerow, Gail Jane
  See Damerow, Gail
D'Amico, Carmela ................................... 170
D'Amico, Steve ..................................... 170
Damrell, Liz 1956- .................................. 77
Damrosch, Helen
  See Tee-Van, Helen Damrosch
Dana, Barbara 1940- ................................ 22
Dana, Richard Henry, Jr. 1815-1882 ............ 26
Danachair, Caoimhin O
  See Danaher, Kevin
Danaher, Kevin 1913-2002 ......................... 22
Danakas, John 1963- ................................ 94
Dandi
  See Mackall, Dandi Daley
D'Andrea, Kate
  See Steiner, Barbara A(nnette)
Dangerfield, Balfour
  See McCloskey, (John) Robert
Daniel, Alan 1939- .................................. 76
  Brief entry ............................................. 53
Daniel, Anita 1893(?)-1978 ........................ 23
  Obituary ................................................. 24
Daniel, Anne
  See Steiner, Barbara A(nnette)
Daniel, Becky 1947- ................................ 56
Daniel, Claire 1949- .............................. 164
Daniel, Colin
  See Windsor, Patricia
Daniel, Hawthorne 1890- ............................ 8
Daniel, (Donna) Lee 1944- ......................... 76
Daniel, Rebecca
  See Daniel, Becky
Daniels, Guy 1919-1989 ............................ 11
  Obituary ................................................. 62
Daniels, Lucy
  See Oldfield, Jenny
Daniels, Max
  See Gellis, Roberta
Daniels, Olga
  See Sinclair, Olga
Daniels, Patricia 1955- ............................. 93
Daniels, Zoe
  See Laux, Constance

Dank, Gloria Rand 1955- .............................. 56
  Brief entry ........................................ 46
Dank, Leonard D(ewey) 1929- ................... 44
Dank, Milton 1920- ................................. 31
Dann, Max 1955- ..................................... 62
Danneberg, Julie 1958- ........................... 173
Dantz, William R.
  *See* Philbrick, Rodman
Danziger, Paula 1944-2004 ....................... 149
  Brief entry ........................................ 30
  Obituary .......................................... 155
  Earlier sketches in SATA *36, 63, 102*
  *See also* CLR *20*
Darby, Gene Kegley
  *See* Darby, Jean (Kegley)
Darby, J. N.
  *See* Govan, (Mary) Christine Noble
Darby, Jean (Kegley) 1921- ....................... 68
Darby, Patricia (Paulsen) ........................... 14
Darby, Ray(mond) 1912-1982 ...................... 7
d'Arcy, Willard
  *See* Cox, William R(obert)
Dare, Geena
  *See* McNicoll, Sylvia (Marilyn)
Darian, Shea 1959- ................................... 97
Daringer, Helen Fern 1892-1986 ................... 1
Darke, Marjorie 1929- ............................... 87
  Earlier sketch in SATA *16*
Darley, F(elix) O(ctavius) C(arr) 1822-1888
  ..................................................... 35
Darling, David J. 1953- ............................. 60
  Brief entry ........................................ 44
Darling, Kathy
  *See* Darling, Mary Kathleen
Darling, Lois (MacIntyre) 1917-1989 ........... 3
  Obituary ........................................... 64
Darling, Louis, (Jr.) 1916-1970 ................... 3
  Obituary ........................................... 23
Darling, Mary Kathleen 1943- ................... 124
  Earlier sketches in SATA *9, 79*
Darling, Sandra Louise Woodward
  *See* Day, Alexandra
Darnell, K(athryn) L(ynne) 1955- ............. 150
Darroll, Sally
  *See* Odgers, Sally Farrell
Darrow, Whitney, (Jr.) 1909-1999 .............. 13
  Obituary .......................................... 115
Darwin, Len
  *See* Darwin, Leonard
Darwin, Leonard 1916- .............................. 24
Dasent, Sir George Webbe 1817-1896 ......... 62
  Brief entry ........................................ 29
Dash, Joan 1925- ................................... 142
Daskam, Josephine Dodge
  *See* Bacon, Josephine Dodge (Daskam)
D'ath, Justin 1953- ................................. 174
  Earlier sketch in SATA *106*
Dauer, Rosamond 1934- ............................ 23
Daugherty, Charles Michael 1914- .............. 16
Daugherty, James (Henry) 1889-1974 ......... 13
  *See also* CLR *78*
Daugherty, Richard D(eo) 1922- ................. 35
d'Aulaire, Edgar Parin 1898-1986 ............... 66
  Obituary ........................................... 47
  Earlier sketch in SATA *5*
  *See also* CLR *21*
d'Aulaire, Ingri (Mortenson Parin) 1904-1980
  ..................................................... 66
  Obituary ........................................... 24
  Earlier sketch in SATA *5*
  *See also* CLR *21*
Dave, Dave
  *See* Berg, David
Daveluy, Paule Cloutier 1919- .................... 11
Davenier, Christine 1961- ......................... 127
Davenport, John 1960- ............................. 156
Daves, Michael 1938- ............................... 40
David, A. R.
  *See* David, A(nn) Rosalie
David, A(nn) Rosalie 1946- ....................... 103

David, Jonathan
  *See* Ames, Lee J(udah)
David, Lawrence 1963- ............................ 165
  Earlier sketch in SATA *111*
David, Rosalie
  *See* David, A(nn) Rosalie
Davidson, Alice Joyce 1932- ....................... 54
  Brief entry ........................................ 45
Davidson, Basil 1914- ............................... 13
Davidson, (Marie) Diane 1924- ................... 91
Davidson, Hugh
  *See* Hamilton, Edmond
Davidson, Jessica 1915-1986 ........................ 5
Davidson, Judith 1953- .............................. 40
Davidson, Lionel 1922- .............................. 87
Davidson, Margaret 1936- ............................ 5
Davidson, Marion
  *See* Garis, Howard R(oger)
Davidson, Mary R. 1885-1973 ....................... 9
Davidson, Mary S. 1940- ............................ 61
Davidson, Mickie
  *See* Davidson, Margaret
Davidson, Nicole
  *See* Jensen, Kathryn
Davidson, R.
  *See* Davidson, Raymond
Davidson, Raymond 1926- ........................... 32
Davidson, Rosalie 1921- ............................. 23
Davie, Helen K(ay) 1952- ......................... 148
  Earlier sketch in SATA *77*
Davies, Andrew (Wynford) 1936- ................. 27
Davies, Bettilu D(onna) 1942- ..................... 33
Davies, Hunter 1936- ................................ 55
  Brief entry ........................................ 45
Davies, Jacqueline 1962- .......................... 155
Davies, Joan 1934- ................................... 50
  Brief entry ........................................ 47
Davies, Nicola 1958- ............................... 150
  Earlier sketch in SATA *99*
Davies, Peter J(oseph) 1937- ....................... 52
Davies, Sumiko 1942- ................................ 46
Davis, (A.) Aubrey 1949- ......................... 153
Davis, Barbara Steincrohn
  *See* Davis, Maggie S.
Davis, Bette J. 1923- ................................ 15
Davis, Burke 1913- .................................... 4
Davis, Christopher 1928- ............................. 6
Davis, D(elbert) Dwight 1908-1965 .............. 33
Davis, Daniel S(heldon) 1936- ..................... 12
Davis, David R. 1948- .............................. 106
Davis, Donald 1944- ................................ 169
  Earlier sketch in SATA *93*
Davis, Donald D.
  *See* Davis, Donald
Davis, Emma
  *See* Davis, Maggie S.
Davis, Gibbs 1953- ................................. 102
  Brief entry ........................................ 41
  Earlier sketch in SATA *46*
Davis, Grania 1943- .................................. 88
  Brief entry ........................................ 50
Davis, H(arold) L(enoir) 1896-1960 ............ 114
Davis, Hubert J(ackson) 1904-1997 .............. 31
Davis, James Robert 1945- .......................... 32
  *See* Davis, Jim
Davis, Jenny 1953- ................................... 74
Davis, Jim
  *See* Davis, James Robert
Davis, Julia 1900(?)-1993 ............................ 6
  Obituary ........................................... 75
Davis, Karen (Elizabeth) 1944- ................... 109
Davis, Katie 1959(?)- .............................. 152
Davis, Lambert ...................................... 176
Davis, Leslie
  *See* Guccione, Leslie Davis
Davis, Louise Littleton 1921- ...................... 25
Davis, Maggie S. 1943- .............................. 57
Davis, Marguerite 1889- ............................. 34
Davis, Mary L(ee) 1935- .............................. 9
Davis, Mary Octavia 1901-1976 ..................... 6
Davis, Nelle 1958- ................................... 73

Davis, Ossie 1917-2005 .............................. 81
  *See also* CLR *56*
Davis, Paxton 1925-1994 ............................ 16
Davis, Robert 1881-1949
  *See* YABC *1*
Davis, Robin W(orks) 1962- ......................... 87
Davis, Russell Gerard 1922- .......................... 3
Davis, Tim(othy N.) 1957- ........................... 94
Davis, Verne Theodore 1889-1973 .................. 6
Davis, Yvonne 1927- ................................ 115
Davol, Marguerite W. 1928- ....................... 146
  Earlier sketch in SATA *82*
DaVolls, Andy (P.) 1967- ............................ 85
DaVolls, Linda 1966- ................................ 85
Davys, Sarah
  *See* Manning, Rosemary (Joy)
Dawes, Claiborne 1935- ............................ 111
Dawson, Elmer A. ..................................... 67
  Earlier sketch in SATA *1*
Dawson, Imogen (Zoe) 1948- ...................... 126
  Earlier sketch in SATA *90*
Dawson, Mary 1919- .................................. 11
Day, A(rthur) Grove 1904-1994 ..................... 59
Day, Alexandra 1941- .............................. 169
  Earlier sketches in SATA *67, 97*
  *See also* CLR *22*
  *See also* SAAS *19*
Day, Beth (Feagles) 1924- ........................... 33
Day, Donna
  *See* Asay, Donna Day
Day, Edward C. 1932- ................................ 72
Day, Jon 1936(?)- .................................... 79
Day, Nancy 1953- ................................... 140
Day, Nancy Raines 1951- .......................... 148
  Earlier sketch in SATA *93*
Day, Shirley 1962- ................................... 94
Day, Thomas 1748-1789
  *See* YABC *1*
Day, Trevor 1955- ................................... 124
Dazey, Agnes J(ohnston) ............................. 2
Dazey, Frank M. ....................................... 2
Deacon, Alexis 1978- .............................. 139
Deacon, Eileen
  *See* Geipel, Eileen
Deacon, Richard
  *See* McCormick, (George) Donald (King)
Deak, Erzsi 1959- ................................... 152
Dean, Anabel 1915- .................................. 12
Dean, Carolee 1962- ................................ 148
Dean, Karen Strickler 1923- ........................ 49
Dean, Ruth (Brigham) 1947- ....................... 145
Dean, Zoey
  *See* Bennett, Cherie
de Angeli, Marguerite (Lofft) 1889-1987 .. 100
  Obituary ........................................... 51
  Earlier sketches in SATA *1, 27*
  *See also* CLR *1*
Deans, Sis Boulos 1955- ........................... 136
  Earlier sketch in SATA *78*
DeArmand, Frances Ullmann 1904(?)-1984
  ..................................................... 10
  Obituary ........................................... 38
DeArmond, Dale 1914- ............................... 70
DeArmond, Dale Burlison
  *See* DeArmond, Dale
Deary, Terry 1946- .................................. 171
  Brief entry ........................................ 41
  Earlier sketches in SATA *51, 101*
Deaver, Julie Reece 1953- ........................... 68
de Banke, Cecile 1889-1965 ......................... 11
De Bello, Rosario 1923- ............................. 89
Debon, Nicolas ..................................... 151
de Bono, Edward 1933- .............................. 66
de Brissac, Malcolm
  *See* Dickinson, Peter (Malcolm de Brissac)
de Brunhoff, Jean
  *See* Brunhoff, Jean de
De Brunhoff, Laurent
  *See* Brunhoff, Laurent de
De Bruyn, Monica G. 1952- ......................... 13

De Bruyn, Monica Jean Grembowicz
  *See* De Bruyn, Monica G.
DeBry, Roger K. 1942- ............................ *91*
de Camp, Catherine Crook 1907-2000 ........ *83*
  Earlier sketch in SATA *12*
de Camp, L(yon) Sprague 1907-2000 ........ *83*
  Earlier sketch in SATA *9*
DeCandido, Keith R.A. ............................ *112*
Dechausay, Sonia E. ................................ *94*
Decker, C.B. ............................................ *172*
Decker, Cynthia B.
  *See* Decker, C.B.
Decker, Duane 1910-1964 ........................ *5*
DeClements, Barthe (Faith) 1920- ............ *131*
  Earlier sketches in SATA *35, 71*
  *See also* CLR *23*
de Conte, Sieur Louis
  *See* Clemens, Samuel Langhorne
Dedman, Stephen ...................................... *108*
Dee, Catherine 1964- ................................ *138*
Dee, Ruby ................................................ *77*
  *See* Wallace, Ruby Ann
Deedy, John 1923- .................................... *24*
Deegan, Paul Joseph 1937- ...................... *48*
  Brief entry .......................................... *38*
Deem, James M. 1950- ............................ *134*
  Earlier sketch in SATA *75*
Deem, James Morgan
  *See* Deem, James M.
Deeter, Catherine 1947- ............................ *137*
DeFelice, Cynthia 1951- .......................... *165*
  Earlier sketches in SATA *79, 121*
DeFelice, Cynthia C.
  *See* DeFelice, Cynthia
Defoe, Daniel 1660(?)-1731 .................... *22*
  *See also* CLR *61*
DeFord, Deborah H. .................................. *123*
deFrance, Anthony
  *See* DiFranco, Anthony (Mario)
Degen, Bruce 1945- .................................. *147*
  Brief entry .......................................... *47*
  Earlier sketches in SATA *57, 97*
DeGering, Etta (Belle) Fowler 1898-1996 .... *7*
De Goldi, Kate
  *See* De Goldi, Kathleen Domenica
De Goldi, Kathleen Domenica 1959- ........ *123*
De Grazia, Ted .......................................... *39*
  *See* De Grazia, Ettore
deGroat, Diane 1947- .............................. *169*
  Earlier sketches in SATA *31, 90*
deGros, J. H.
  *See* Villiard, Paul
de Grummond, Lena Young ........................ *62*
  Earlier sketch in SATA *6*
de Hamel, Joan Littledale 1924- .............. *86*
De Haven, Tom 1949- .............................. *72*
de Hugo, Pierre
  *See* Brackers de Hugo, Pierre
Deiss, Joseph Jay 1915- .......................... *12*
de Jenkins, Lyll Becerra 1925-1997 ........ *102*
DeJong, David C(ornel) 1905-1967 .......... *10*
de Jong, Dola 1911-2003 ........................ *7*
  Obituary .............................................. *149*
  *See* de Jong, Dorothea Rosalie
DeJong, Meindert 1906-1991 .................... *2*
  Obituary .............................................. *68*
  *See also* CLR *73*
DeJonge, Joanne E. 1943- ........................ *56*
Deka, Connie
  *See* Laux, Constance
de Kay, Ormonde (Jr.) 1923-1998 ............ *7*
  Obituary .............................................. *106*
de Kiriline, Louise
  *See* Lawrence, Louise de Kiriline
Dekker, Carl
  *See* Laffin, John (Alfred Charles)
  and Lynds, Dennis
deKruif, Paul (Henry) 1890-1971 ............ *50*
  Earlier sketch in SATA *5*
Delacre, Lulu 1957- ................................ *156*
  Earlier sketch in SATA *36*

DeLaCroix, Alice 1940- ............................ *75*
De la Garza, Phyllis 1942- ...................... *169*
De Lage, Ida 1918- .................................. *11*
de la Mare, Walter (John) 1873-1956 ........ *16*
  *See also* CLR *23*
Delaney, Harry 1932- .............................. *3*
Delaney, Joseph 1945- ............................ *172*
Delaney, Michael 1955- .......................... *96*
Delaney, Ned ............................................ *28*
  *See* Delaney, Thomas Nicholas III
Delano, Hugh 1933- ................................ *20*
Delany, Samuel R., Jr. 1942- .................. *92*
Delany, Samuel Ray
  *See* Delany, Samuel R., Jr.
De La Ramee, Marie Louise 1839-1908 ..... *20*
  *See* Ouida
de la Roche, Mazo 1879-1961 .................. *64*
De La Roche Saint Andre, Anne 1950- ...... *75*
Delaune, (Jewel) Lynn (de Grummond) ........ *7*
DeLaurentis, Louise Budde 1920- ............ *12*
Delderfield, Eric R(aymond) 1909-1995 ..... *14*
Delderfield, Ronald Frederick 1912-1972 ... *20*
DeLeeuw, Adele (Louise) 1899-1988 ........ *30*
  Obituary .............................................. *56*
  Earlier sketch in SATA *1*
De Leon, Nephtali 1945- .......................... *97*
Delessert, Etienne 1941- .......................... *130*
  Brief entry .......................................... *27*
  Earlier sketch in SATA *46*
  *See also* CLR *81*
Delgado, James P. 1958- .......................... *122*
de Lint, Charles 1951- ............................ *157*
  Earlier sketch in SATA *115*
de Lint, Charles Henri Diederick Hofsmit
  *See* de Lint, Charles
Delmar, Roy
  *See* Wexler, Jerome (LeRoy)
Deloria, Vine, Jr. 1933-2005 .................... *21*
  Obituary .............................................. *171*
Deloria, Vine Victor, Jr.
  *See* Deloria, Vine, Jr.
del Rey, Lester 1915-1993 ...................... *22*
  Obituary .............................................. *76*
Delrio, Martin
  *See* Doyle, Debra
  and Macdonald, James D.
Delton, Judy 1931-2001 .......................... *77*
  Obituary .............................................. *130*
  Earlier sketch in SATA *14*
  *See also* SAAS *9*
Delulio, John 1938- ................................ *15*
Delving, Michael
  *See* Williams, Jay
Demarest, Chris L. 1951- ........................ *175*
  Brief entry .......................................... *44*
  Earlier sketches in SATA *45, 82, 128*
Demarest, Christopher Lynn
  *See* Demarest, Chris L.
Demarest, Doug
  *See* Barker, Will
Demas, Corinne ........................................ *131*
  *See* Bliss, Corinne Demas
Demas, Vida 1927- .................................. *9*
De Mejo, Oscar 1911-1992 ...................... *40*
Demers, Dominique 1956- ........................ *177*
de Messieres, Nicole 1930- ...................... *39*
Demi
  *See* Hitz, Demi
Demijohn, Thom
  *See* Disch, Thomas M.
  and Sladek, John
Deming, Richard 1915-1983 .................... *24*
  *See* Queen, Ellery
Demuth, Patricia Brennan 1948- .............. *84*
  Brief entry .......................................... *51*
Dendinger, Roger E. 1952- ...................... *158*
Denenberg, Barry .................................... *175*
Dengler, Marianna (Herron) 1935- .......... *103*
Dengler, Sandy 1939- .............................. *54*
  Brief entry .......................................... *40*

Denim, Sue
  *See* Pilkey, Dav
Denise, Christopher 1968- ........................ *147*
Denmark, Harrison
  *See* Zelazny, Roger
Dennard, Deborah 1953- .......................... *136*
  Earlier sketch in SATA *78*
Denney, Diana 1910-2000 ........................ *25*
  Obituary .............................................. *120*
Dennis, Morgan 1891(?)-1960 .................. *18*
Dennis, Wesley 1903-1966 ...................... *18*
Denny, Norman (George) 1901-1982 .......... *43*
Denslow, Sharon Phillips 1947- .............. *142*
  Earlier sketch in SATA *68*
Denslow, W(illiam) W(allace) 1856-1915 .. *16*
  *See also* CLR *15*
Denton, Kady MacDonald ........................ *110*
  Earlier sketch in SATA *66*
  *See also* CLR *71*
Denver, Walt
  *See* Redding, Robert Hull
  and Sherman, Jory (Tecumseh)
Denzel, Justin F(rancis) 1917-1999 .......... *46*
  Brief entry .......................................... *38*
Denzer, Ann Wiseman
  *See* Wiseman, Ann (Sayre)
DePalma, Mary Newell 1961- .................. *139*
dePaola, Thomas Anthony 1934- .............. *155*
  Earlier sketches in SATA *11, 59, 108*
  *See* dePaola, Tomie
dePaola, Tomie
  *See* CLR *81*
  *See also* SAAS *15*
  *See* dePaola, Thomas Anthony
deParrie, Paul 1949- ................................ *74*
DePauw, Linda Grant 1940- .................... *24*
DeRan, David 1946- ................................ *76*
Derby, Pat 1942- ...................................... *172*
Derby, Sally 1934- .................................. *132*
  Earlier sketch in SATA *89*
de Regniers, Beatrice Schenk (Freedman)
  1914-2000 .......................................... *68*
  Obituary .............................................. *123*
  Earlier sketch in SATA *2*
  *See also* SAAS *6*
Dereske, Jo 1947- .................................... *72*
Derleth, August (William) 1909-1971 ........ *5*
Derman, Martha (Winn) .......................... *74*
Derman, Sarah Audrey 1915- .................. *11*
DeRoberts, Lyndon
  *See* Silverstein, Robert Alan
de Roo, Anne Louise 1931-1997 .............. *84*
  Earlier sketch in SATA *25*
  *See also* CLR *63*
deRosa, Dee ............................................ *70*
Derrick, Lionel
  *See* Cunningham, Chet
Derrickson, Jim 1959- .............................. *141*
Derry Down Derry
  *See* Lear, Edward
Dervaux, Isabelle 1961- .......................... *106*
Derwent, Lavinia ...................................... *14*
Desai, Anita 1937- .................................. *126*
  Earlier sketch in SATA *63*
De Saulles, Tony 1958- .......................... *119*
Desbarats, Peter 1933- ............................ *39*
de Selincourt, Aubrey 1894-1962 ............ *14*
Deshpande, Chris 1950- .......................... *69*
Desimini, Lisa 1964- .............................. *148*
  Earlier sketch in SATA *86*
Desjarlais, John 1953- ............................ *71*
Desjarlais, John J.
  *See* Desjarlais, John
Desmoinaux, Christel 1967- .................... *149*
  Earlier sketch in SATA *103*
Desmond, Adrian J(ohn) 1947- ................ *51*
Desmond, Alice Curtis 1897-1990 ............ *8*
DeSpain, Pleasant 1943- .......................... *87*
Desputeaux, Helene 1959- ........................ *95*
Dessen, Sarah 1970- ................................ *172*
  Earlier sketch in SATA *120*

Detine, Padre
  See Olsen, Ib Spang
de Trevino, Elizabeth B.
  See Trevino, Elizabeth B(orton) de
de Trevino, Elizabeth Borton
  See Trevino, Elizabeth B(orton) de
Detwiler, Susan Dill 1956- ........................ 58
Deuker, Carl 1950- ................................. 150
  Earlier sketch in SATA 82
Deutsch, Babette 1895-1982 ........................ 1
  Obituary ........................................ 33
Deutsch, Eva Costabel
  See Costabel, Eva Deutsch
Deutsch, Helen 1906-1992 .......................... 76
Deutsch, Kurt
  See Singer, Kurt D.
Devaney, John 1926-1994 ........................... 12
de Varennes, Monique 1947- ...................... 168
de Varona, Frank J. 1943- ......................... 83
Devereux, Frederick L(eonard), Jr. 1914-1993
  ................................................ 9
Devi, Nila
  See Woody, Regina Jones
deVinck, Christopher 1951- ........................ 85
DeVito, Cara 1956- ............................... 80
Devlin, Dorothy Wende
  See Devlin, Wende
Devlin, Harry 1918-2001 .......................... 136
  Earlier sketches in SATA 11, 74
Devlin, Wende 1918-2002 ........................... 74
  Earlier sketch in SATA 11
Devon, Paddie 1953- .............................. 92
Devons, Sonia 1974- .............................. 72
Devorah-Leah ..................................... 111
de Vos, Gail 1949- ............................... 122
DeVries, Douglas 1933- ........................... 122
De Waard, E(lliott) John 1935- .................... 7
Dewan, Ted 1961- ................................ 157
  Earlier sketch in SATA 108
Dewdney, Selwyn (Hanington) 1909-1979 . 64
DeWeese, Gene
  See DeWeese, Thomas Eugene
DeWeese, Jean
  See DeWeese, Thomas Eugene
DeWeese, Thomas Eugene 1934- ..................... 46
  Brief entry ..................................... 45
Dewey, Ariane 1937- ............................. 109
  Earlier sketch in SATA 7
Dewey, Jennifer (Owings) 1941- ................... 103
  Brief entry ..................................... 48
  Earlier sketch in SATA 58
Dewey, Kenneth Francis 1940- ..................... 39
deWit, Dorothy (May Knowles) 1916-1980
  ................................................ 39
  Obituary ........................................ 28
Dexter, Alison 1966- ............................. 125
Dexter, John
  See Bradley, Marion Zimmer
Deyneka, Anita 1943- ............................. 24
Deyrup, Astrith Johnson 1923- ..................... 24
Dhami, Narinder 1958- ............................ 152
Dhondy, Farrukh 1944- ............................ 152
  Earlier sketch in SATA 65
  See also CLR 41
Diakite, Baba Wague 1961- ........................ 174
Diakite, Penda 1993(?)- .......................... 174
Diamond, Arthur 1957- ............................ 76
Diamond, Donna 1950- ............................. 69
  Brief entry ..................................... 30
  Earlier sketch in SATA 35
Diamond, Petra
  See Sachs, Judith
Diamond, Rebecca
  See Sachs, Judith
Dias, Earl Joseph 1916- .......................... 41
Dias, Ron 1937- .................................. 71
Diaz, David 1959(?)- ............................. 150
  Earlier sketch in SATA 96
  See also CLR 65

DiCamillo, Kate 1964- ............................ 163
  Earlier sketch in SATA 121
  See also CLR 117
Di Certo, J(oseph) J(ohn) 1933- ................... 60
DiCianni, Ron 1952- .............................. 107
Dick, Trella Lamson 1889-1974 ..................... 9
Dickens, Charles (John Huffam) 1812-1870
  ................................................ 15
  See also CLR 95
Dickens, Frank
  See Huline-Dickens, Frank William
Dickens, Monica (Enid) 1915-1992 .................. 4
  Obituary ........................................ 74
Dickinson, Emily (Elizabeth) 1830-1886 .... 29
Dickinson, Mary 1949- ............................ 48
  Brief entry ..................................... 41
Dickinson, Mary-Anne
  See Rodda, Emily
Dickinson, Peter (Malcolm de Brissac) 1927-
  ................................................ 150
  Earlier sketches in SATA 5, 62, 95
  See also CLR 29
Dickinson, Susan 1931- ............................ 8
Dickinson, Terence 1943- ......................... 102
Dickinson, W(illiam) Croft 1897-1963 .... 13
Dickson, Gordon R(upert) 1923-2001 ......... 77
Dickson, Naida 1916- .............................. 8
Diehn, Gwen 1943- ................................ 80
Dieterich, Michele M. 1962- ...................... 78
Dietz, David H(enry) 1897-1984 ................... 10
  Obituary ........................................ 41
Dietz, Lew 1907-1997 ............................. 11
  Obituary ........................................ 95
Diffily, Deborah ................................. 159
Di Fiori, Larry
  See Di Fiori, Lawrence
Di Fiori, Lawrence 1934- ......................... 130
DiFranco, Anthony (Mario) 1945- .................. 42
Digby, Anne 1935- ................................ 72
Digges, Jeremiah
  See Berger, Josef
Digman, Kristina 1959- ........................... 176
D'Ignazio, Fred(erick) 1949- ..................... 39
  Brief entry ..................................... 35
Di Grazia, Thomas (?)-1983 ....................... 32
Dikty, Julian May
  See May, Julian
Dillard, Annie 1945- ............................. 140
  Earlier sketch in SATA 10
Dillard, Kristine 1964- .......................... 113
Dillard, Polly Hargis 1916- ...................... 24
Diller, Harriett 1953- ........................... 78
Dillon, Barbara 1927- ............................ 44
  Brief entry ..................................... 39
Dillon, Diane (Claire) 1933- ..................... 106
  Earlier sketches in SATA 15, 51
  See also CLR 44
Dillon, Eilis 1920-1994 .......................... 74
  Autobiography Feature ........................... 105
  Obituary ........................................ 83
  Earlier sketch in SATA 2
  See also CLR 26
Dillon, Jana (a pseudonym) 1952- ................. 117
Dillon, Leo 1933- ................................ 106
  Earlier sketches in SATA 15, 51
  See also CLR 44
Dillon, Sharon Saseen
  See Saseen, Sharon (Dillon)
Dils, Tracey E. 1958- ............................ 83
Dilson, Jesse 1914-1988 .......................... 24
Dinan, Carolyn ................................... 59
  Brief entry ..................................... 47
Dines, Carol 1956- ............................... 175
Dines, (Harry) Glen 1925-1996 ..................... 7
Dinesen, Isak
  See Blixen, Karen (Christentze Dinesen)
Dinessi, Alex
  See Schembri, Jim
Dinneen, Betty 1929- ............................. 61
Dinnerstein, Harvey 1928- ........................ 42
Dinsdale, Tim(othy Kay) 1924-1987 .......... 11

Diouf, Sylviane A. 1952- ......................... 168
Diouf, Sylviane Anna
  See Diouf, Sylviane A.
DiPucchio, Kelly ................................. 159
Dirk
  See Gringhuis, Richard H.
Dirks, Wilhelmina 1916- .......................... 59
Dirks, Willy
  See Dirks, Wilhelmina
Dirtmeister
  See Tomecek, Steve
DiSalvo, DyAnne 1960- ............................ 144
  Earlier sketch in SATA 59
DiSalvo-Ryan, DyAnne
  See DiSalvo, DyAnne
Disch, Thomas M. 1940- ........................... 92
  See also CLR 18
  See also SAAS 15
  See Disch, Tom
Disch, Thomas Michael
  See Disch, Thomas M.
Disch, Tom
  See Disch, Thomas M.
Disher, Garry 1949- .............................. 125
  Earlier sketch in SATA 81
Disney, Walt(er Elias) 1901-1966 ................. 28
  Brief entry ..................................... 27
DiTerlizzi, Tony 1969- ........................... 154
Divakaruni, Chitra Banerjee 1956- ........... 160
Di Valentin, Maria (Amelia) Messuri
  1911-1985 ....................................... 7
Dixon, Ann R(enee) 1954- ......................... 127
  Earlier sketch in SATA 77
Dixon, Dougal 1947- .............................. 127
  Earlier sketch in SATA 45
Dixon, Franklin W. ............................... 100
  Earlier sketches in SATA 1, 67
  See also CLR 61
  See Barrett, Neal, Jr.
  and Goulart, Ron(ald Joseph)
  and Lantz, Francess L(in)
  and Lerangis, Peter
  and McFarlane, Leslie (Charles)
  and Stanley, George Edward
  and Stratemeyer, Edward L.
Dixon, Jeanne 1936- .............................. 31
Dixon, Paige
  See Corcoran, Barbara (Asenath)
Dixon, Peter L(ee) 1931- .......................... 6
Dixon, Rachel 1952- .............................. 74
Djoleto, (Solomon Alexander) Amu 1929- . 80
d'Lacey, Chris 1949- ............................. 165
Doak, Annie
  See Dillard, Annie
Doane, Pelagie 1906-1966 .......................... 7
Dobell, I(sabel) M(arian) B(arclay) 1909-1998
  ................................................ 11
Dobie, J(ames) Frank 1888-1964 ................... 43
Dobler, Lavinia G. 1910- .......................... 6
Dobrin, Arnold 1928- .............................. 4
Dobson, Jill 1969- ............................... 140
Dobson, Julia 1941- .............................. 48
Dobson, Mary 1954- ............................... 117
Dockery, Wallene T. 1941- ........................ 27
Dockray, Tracy 1962- ............................. 139
Dockrey, Karen 1955- ............................. 103
Doctor, Bernard
  See Doctor, Bernard Aquina
Doctor, Bernard Aquina 1950- ..................... 81
Doctor X
  See Nourse, Alan E(dward)
Dodd, Ed(ward Benton) 1902-1991 .................. 4
  Obituary ........................................ 68
Dodd, Lynley (Stuart) 1941- ...................... 132
  Earlier sketches in SATA 35, 86
  See also CLR 62
Dodd, Marty 1921- ................................ 142
Dodd, Quentin 1972- .............................. 137
Dodds, Bill 1952- ................................ 78
Dodds, Dayle Ann 1952- ........................... 150
  Earlier sketch in SATA 75

Dodge, Bertha S(anford) 1902-1995 ............ 8
Dodge, Fremont
    *See* Grimes, Lee
Dodge, Gil
    *See* Hano, Arnold
Dodge, Mary (Elizabeth) Mapes 1831(?)-1905
    ................................................ 100
    Earlier sketch in SATA 21
    *See also* CLR 62
Dodgson, Charles L(utwidge) 1832-1898 . 100
    *See also* YABC 2
    *See also* CLR 2
    *See* Carroll, Lewis
Dodson, Kenneth MacKenzie 1907-1999 .... 11
Dodson, Susan 1941- ............................ 50
    Brief entry ...................................... 40
Dogyear, Drew
    *See* Gorey, Edward (St. John)
Doherty, Berlie 1943- .......................... 111
    Earlier sketch in SATA 72
    *See also* CLR 21
    *See also* SAAS 16
Doherty, Charles Hugh 1913- .................. 6
Doherty, Craig A. 1951- ...................... 169
    Earlier sketch in SATA 83
Doherty, Katherine M(ann) 1951- ............ 83
Doherty, Kieran 1945- ........................ 164
Dokey, Cameron 1956- ........................ 97
Dolan, Edward F(rancis), Jr. 1924- ......... 94
    Brief entry ...................................... 31
    Earlier sketch in SATA 45
Dolan, Ellen M(eara) 1929-1998 .............. 88
Dolan, Sean J. 1958- .......................... 74
Dolce, J. Ellen 1948- ......................... 75
Dolch, Edward William 1889-1961 ............ 50
Dolch, Marguerite Pierce 1891-1978 ......... 50
Dollar, Diane (Hills) 1933- ................... 57
Dolson, Hildegarde ............................. 5
    *See* Lockridge, Hildegarde (Dolson)
Domanska, Janina 1913(?)-1995 .............. 68
    Obituary ......................................... 84
    Earlier sketch in SATA 6
    *See also* CLR 40
    *See also* SAAS 18
Dominguez, Angel 1953- ....................... 76
Domino, John
    *See* Averill, Esther (Holden)
Domjan, Joseph (Spiri) 1907-1992 ............ 25
Domm, Jeffrey C. 1958- ....................... 84
Donald, Rhonda Lucas 1962- .................. 147
Donalds, Gordon
    *See* Shirreffs, Gordon D(onald)
Donaldson, Bryna
    *See* Stevens, Bryna
Donaldson, Gordon 1913-1993 ................. 64
    Obituary ......................................... 76
Donaldson, Joan 1953- ........................ 78
Donaldson, Julia 1948- ....................... 132
    Earlier sketch in SATA 82
Donaldson, Stephen R(eeder) 1947- ......... 121
Doner, Kim 1955- ............................... 91
Doney, Todd L. W. 1959- ...................... 104
Donkin, Nance (Clare) 1915- .................. 95
Donna, Natalie 1934-1979 ...................... 9
Donnelly, Elfie 1950-
    *See* CLR 104
Donnelly, Jennifer 1963- ..................... 154
Donnelly, Matt 1972- ......................... 148
Donoghue, Emma 1969- ......................... 101
Donoughue, Carol 1935- ....................... 139
Donovan, John 1928-1992 ...................... 72
    Brief entry ...................................... 29
    *See also* CLR 3
Donovan, Mary Lee 1961- ...................... 86
Donze, Mary Terese 1911- ..................... 89
Doob, Leonard W(illiam) 1909-2000 ........... 8
Dooley, Norah 1953- ........................... 74
Dooling, Michael 1958- ....................... 105
Dor, Ana
    *See* Ceder, Georgiana Dorcas

Dore, (Louis Christophe Paul) Gustave
    1832-1883 ...................................... 19
Doremus, Robert 1913- ......................... 30
Doren, Marion (Walker) 1928- ................. 57
Dorenkamp, Michelle 1957- .................... 89
Dorflinger, Carolyn 1953- ..................... 91
Dorian, Edith M(cEwen) 1900-1983 ............ 5
Dorian, Harry
    *See* Hamilton, Charles (Harold St. John)
Dorian, Marguerite .............................. 7
Dorin, Patrick C(arberry) 1939- .............. 59
    Brief entry ...................................... 52
Dorman, Michael 1932- .......................... 7
Dorman, N. B. 1927- ........................... 39
Dorris, Michael 1945-1997 ..................... 75
    Obituary ......................................... 94
    *See also* CLR 58
Dorris, Michael A.
    *See* Dorris, Michael
Dorris, Michael Anthony
    *See* Dorris, Michael
Dorritt, Susan
    *See* Schlein, Miriam
Dorros, Arthur 1950- ......................... 168
    Earlier sketches in SATA 78, 122
    *See also* CLR 42
    *See also* SAAS 20
Dorros, Arthur M.
    *See* Dorros, Arthur
Dorson, Richard M(ercer) 1916-1981 ......... 30
Doss, Helen (Grigsby) 1918- .................. 20
Doss, Margot Patterson .......................... 6
Dothers, Anne
    *See* Chess, Victoria (Dickerson)
Dottig
    *See* Grider, Dorothy
Dotts, Maryann J. 1933- ....................... 35
Doty, Jean Slaughter 1929- .................... 28
Doty, Roy 1922- ................................ 28
Doubtfire, Dianne (Abrams) 1918- ............ 29
Doucet, Sharon Arms 1951- ................... 144
    Autobiography Feature ........................ 144
    Earlier sketch in SATA 125
Dougherty, Charles 1922- ...................... 18
Dougherty, Terri (L.) 1964- ................. 146
Doughty, Rebecca 1955- ....................... 174
Douglas, Blaise 1960- ........................ 101
Douglas, Carole Nelson 1944- .................. 73
Douglas, Garry
    *See* Kilworth, Garry
Douglas, James McM.
    *See* Griffin, W.E.B.
Douglas, Kathryn
    *See* Ewing, Kathryn
Douglas, Leonard
    *See* Bradbury, Ray
Douglas, Marjory Stoneman 1890-1998 ..... 10
Douglas, Michael
    *See* Crichton, Michael
Douglas, Michael
    *See* Bright, Robert (Douglas Sr.)
Douglass, Barbara 1930- ....................... 40
Douglass, Frederick 1817(?)-1895 ............ 29
Douglass, Keith
    *See* Cunningham, Chet
Douty, Esther M(orris) 1909-1978 ............. 8
    Obituary ......................................... 23
Dow, Emily R. 1904-1987 ...................... 10
Dow, Vicki
    *See* McVey, Vicki
Dowd, John David 1945- ....................... 78
Dowdell, Dorothy (Florence) Karns 1910- . 12
Dowden, Anne Ophelia 1907-2007 ............. 7
    *See also* SAAS 10
Dowdey, Landon Gerald 1923- .................. 11
Dowdy, Mrs. Regera
    *See* Gorey, Edward (St. John)
Dowell, Frances O'Roark ...................... 157
Dowling, Terry 1947- ......................... 101
Downer, Ann 1960- ............................ 155
Downer, Marion 1892(?)-1971 .................. 25

Downey, Fairfax D(avis) 1893-1990 ............ 3
    Obituary ......................................... 66
Downie, John 1931- ............................ 87
Downie, Mary Alice 1934- ..................... 171
    Earlier sketches in SATA 13, 87
Downie, Mary Alice Dawe
    *See* Downie, Mary Alice
Downing, David A(lmon) 1958- ................. 84
Downing, Julie 1956- ......................... 148
    Earlier sketch in SATA 81
Downing, Paula E. 1951- ....................... 80
Downing, Warwick 1931- ....................... 138
Downing, Wick
    *See* Downing, Warwick
Doyle, A. Conan
    *See* Doyle, Sir Arthur Conan
Doyle, Sir Arthur Conan 1859-1930 .......... 24
    *See also* CLR 106
    *See* Conan Doyle, Arthur
Doyle, Brian 1935- ............................ 156
    Earlier sketches in SATA 67, 104
    *See also* CLR 22
    *See also* SAAS 16
Doyle, Charlotte (Lackner) 1937- .............. 94
Doyle, Conan
    *See* Doyle, Sir Arthur Conan
Doyle, Debra 1952- ........................... 165
    Earlier sketch in SATA 105
    *See* Appleton, Victor
Doyle, John
    *See* Graves, Robert
Doyle, Malachy 1954- ......................... 165
    Earlier sketch in SATA 120
    *See also* CLR 83
Doyle, Richard 1824-1883 ...................... 21
Doyle, Sir A. Conan
    *See* Doyle, Sir Arthur Conan
Dr. A
    *See* Asimov, Isaac
    and Silverstein, Alvin
    and Silverstein, Virginia B(arbara Opshelor)
Dr. Alphabet
    *See* Morice, Dave
Dr. Fred
    *See* Bortz, Alfred B(enjamin)
Dr. Laura
    *See* Schlessinger, Laura (Catherine)
Dr. Seuss
    *See* CLR 100
    *See* Geisel, Theodor Seuss
    and LeSieg, Theo.
    and Seuss, Dr.
    and Stone, Rosetta
Dr. Zed
    *See* Penrose, Gordon
Drabble, Margaret 1939- ....................... 48
Drackett, Phil(ip Arthur) 1922- ............... 53
Draco, F.
    *See* Davis, Julia
Dracup, Angela 1943- .......................... 74
Dragisic, Patricia ............................ 116
Dragonwagon, Crescent 1952- ................. 133
    Earlier sketches in SATA 11, 41, 75
    *See also* SAAS 14
Drake, David 1945- ............................ 85
Drake, David Allen
    *See* Drake, David
Drake, Frank
    *See* Hamilton, Charles (Harold St. John)
Drake, Jane 1954- ............................. 82
Drakeford, Dale B 1952- ...................... 113
Drakeford, Dale Benjamin
    *See* Drakeford, Dale B
Draper, Hastings
    *See* Jeffries, Roderic
Draper, Sharon M. ............................. 146
    Autobiography Feature ........................ 146
    Earlier sketch in SATA 98
    *See also* CLR 57
Draper, Sharon Mills
    *See* Draper, Sharon M.

Drapier, M. B.
  *See* Swift, Jonathan
Drawson, Blair 1943- ............................ *126*
  Earlier sketch in SATA *17*
Dray, Matt 1967- ................................... *177*
Dray, Matthew Frederick
  *See* Dray, Matt
Dresang, Eliza (Carolyn Timberlake) 1941-
  ........................................................ *19*
Drescher, Henrik 1955- ......................... *172*
  Earlier sketches in SATA *67, 105*
  *See also* CLR *20*
Drescher, Joan E(lizabeth) 1939- ........... *137*
  Earlier sketch in SATA *30*
Drew, Patricia (Mary) 1938- .................... *15*
Drewery, Mary 1918- .............................. *6*
Drewery, Melanie 1970- ......................... *165*
Drewry, Henry N(athaniel) 1924- ........... *138*
Dreyer, Ellen ....................................... *177*
Drial, J. E.
  *See* Laird, Jean E(louise)
Drimmer, Frederick 1916-2000 ............... *60*
  Obituary ............................................ *124*
Driskill, J. Lawrence 1920- ..................... *90*
Driskill, Larry
  *See* Driskill, J. Lawrence
Driving Hawk, Virginia
  *See* Sneve, Virginia Driving Hawk
Drucker, Malka 1945- ........................... *111*
  Brief entry ......................................... *29*
  Earlier sketch in SATA *39*
Drucker, Olga Levy 1927- ........................ *79*
Drummond, V(iolet) H(ilda) 1911-2000 ....... *6*
Drummond, Walter
  *See* Silverberg, Robert
Drury, Clare Marie
  *See* Hoskyns-Abrahall, Clare (Constance
  Drury)
Drury, Roger W(olcott) 1914-1996 ............ *15*
Druse, Eleanor
  *See* King, Stephen
Dryden, Pamela
  *See* St. John, Nicole
D.T., Hughes
  *See* Hughes, Dean
Duane, Diane (Elizabeth) 1952- ................ *145*
  Brief entry ......................................... *46*
  Earlier sketches in SATA *58, 95*
Dubanevich, Arlene 1950- ........................ *56*
Dubelaar, Thea 1947- ............................. *60*
du Blane, Daphne
  *See* Groom, Arthur William
Duble, Kathleen Benner 1958- ................. *164*
Du Bois, Shirley Graham 1907(?)-1977 ..... *24*
  *See* Graham, Shirley
Du Bois, W(illiam) E(dward) B(urghardt)
  1868-1963 ......................................... *42*
du Bois, William Pene
  *See* Pene du Bois, William (Sherman)
Duboise, Novella 1911-1999 ..................... *88*
Dubosarsky, Ursula (Bridget) 1961- .......... *147*
  Earlier sketch in SATA *107*
DuBose, LaRocque (Russ) 1926- ................ *2*
Dubrovin, Vivian 1931- .......................... *139*
  Earlier sketch in SATA *65*
DuBurke, Randy ..................................... *172*
Ducey, Jean Sparks 1915- ........................ *93*
Du Chaillu, Paul (Belloni) 1835(?)-1903 .... *26*
Ducharme, Dede Fox
  *See* Ducharme, Lilian Fox
Ducharme, Lilian Fox 1950- ..................... *122*
Ducornet, Erica 1943- ............................. *7*
  *See* Ducornet, Rikki
Ducornet, Rikki
  *See* Ducornet, Erica
Duden, Jane 1947- ................................. *136*
Duder, Tessa 1940- ................................ *117*
  Earlier sketch in SATA *80*
  *See also* CLR *43*
  *See also* SAAS *23*

Dudley, Helen
  *See* Hope Simpson, Jacynth
Dudley, Nancy
  *See* Cole, Lois Dwight
Dudley, Robert
  *See* Baldwin, James
Dudley, Ruth H(ubbell) 1905-2001 ............ *11*
Dudley-Smith, T.
  *See* Trevor, Elleston
Due, Linnea A. 1948- ............................. *64*
Dueck, Adele 1955- ................................ *97*
Dueland, Joy V(ivian) ............................ *27*
Duerr, Gisela 1968- ............................... *89*
Duey, Kathleen 1950- ............................. *132*
Dufault, Joseph Ernest Nephtali
  *See* James, Will(iam Roderick)
Duff, Maggie
  *See* Duff, Margaret K(app)
Duff, Margaret K(app) 1916-2003 ............. *37*
  Obituary ............................................ *144*
Duffey, Betsy (Byars) 1953- ..................... *131*
  Earlier sketch in SATA *80*
Duffie, Charles 1960- ............................. *144*
Duffield, Katy S. 1961- .......................... *147*
Duffy, Carol Ann 1955- .......................... *165*
  Earlier sketch in SATA *95*
Dugan, Jack
  *See* Griffin, W.E.B.
Dugan, John Kevin
  *See* Griffin, W.E.B.
Dugan, Michael (Gray) 1947- ................... *15*
Duggan, Alfred Leo 1903-1964 ................. *25*
Duggan, Maurice (Noel) 1922-1974 .......... *40*
  Obituary ............................................ *30*
Duggleby, John 1952- ............................. *94*
Dugin, Andrej 1955- ............................... *77*
Dugina, Olga 1964- ................................ *77*
du Jardin, Rosamond Neal 1902-1963 ........ *2*
Duke, Kate 1956- ................................... *148*
  Earlier sketch in SATA *90*
  *See also* CLR *51*
Duke, Will
  *See* Gault, William Campbell
Dulac, Edmund 1882-1953 ....................... *19*
Dumas, Alexandre (pere) 1802-1870 .......... *18*
Dumas, Jacqueline 1946- ......................... *55*
Dumas, Philippe 1940- ........................... *119*
  Earlier sketch in SATA *52*
du Maurier, Daphne 1907-1989 ................ *27*
  Obituary ............................................ *60*
Dumbleton, Mike 1948- ......................... *124*
  Earlier sketch in SATA *73*
Dunbar, Fiona 1961- .............................. *167*
Dunbar, Joyce 1944- .............................. *162*
  Earlier sketches in SATA *76, 112*
Dunbar, Paul Laurence 1872-1906 ............ *34*
Dunbar, Robert E(verett) 1926- ............... *32*
Duncan, Alexandra
  *See* Moore, Ishbel (Lindsay)
Duncan, Alice Faye 1967- ........................ *168*
  Earlier sketch in SATA *95*
Duncan, Gregory
  *See* McClintock, Marshall
Duncan, Jane
  *See* Cameron, Elizabeth Jane
Duncan, Julia K. ..................................... *1*
  *See* Benson, Mildred (Augustine Wirt)
Duncan, Lois 1934- ................................ *141*
  Autobiography Feature .......................... *141*
  Earlier sketches in SATA *1, 36, 75, 133*
  *See also* CLR *29*
  *See also* SAAS *2*
Duncan, Norman 1871-1916
  *See* YABC *1*
Duncan, Terence
  *See* Nolan, William F(rancis)
Duncombe, Frances (Riker) 1900-1994 ....... *25*
  Obituary ............................................ *82*
Dunham, Montrew 1919- ......................... *162*
Dunham, Montrew Goetz
  *See* Dunham, Montrew

Dunkle, Clare B. 1964- ........................... *155*
Dunlap, Julie 1958- ................................ *84*
Dunleavy, Deborah 1951- ........................ *133*
Dunlop, Agnes M. R. (?)-1982 .................. *87*
  *See* Kyle, Elisabeth
Dunlop, Eileen (Rhona) 1938- .................. *76*
  Earlier sketch in SATA *24*
  *See also* SAAS *12*
Dunn, Anne M. 1940- ............................. *107*
Dunn, Harvey T(homas) 1884-1952 ........... *34*
Dunn, Herb
  *See* Gutman, Dan
Dunn, John M. (III) 1949- ....................... *93*
Dunn, Judy
  *See* Spangenberg, Judith Dunn
Dunn, Mary Lois 1930- ........................... *6*
Dunnahoo, Terry Janson 1927- ................. *7*
Dunne, Jeanette 1952- ............................ *72*
Dunne, Kathleen 1933- ........................... *126*
Dunne, Marie
  *See* Clark, Ann Nolan
Dunne, Mary Collins 1914- ...................... *11*
Dunne, Mary Jo
  *See* Dunne, Mary Collins
Dunnett, Kaitlyn
  *See* Emerson, Kathy Lynn
Dunnett, Margaret (Rosalind) 1909-1977 ... *42*
Dunrea, Olivier 1953- ............................. *160*
  Brief entry ......................................... *46*
  Earlier sketches in SATA *59, 118*
Dunrea, Olivier Jean-Paul Dominique
  *See* Dunrea, Olivier
Dunton, Dorothy 1912- ........................... *92*
Dupasquier, Philippe 1955- ..................... *151*
  Earlier sketch in SATA *86*
DuPrau, Jeanne 1944- ............................. *144*
Dupuy, T(revor) N(evitt) 1916-1995 ........... *4*
  Obituary ............................................ *86*
DuQuette, Keith 1960- ........................... *155*
  Earlier sketch in SATA *90*
Duran, Gloria 1924- ............................... *171*
Duran, Gloria Bradley
  *See* Duran, Gloria
Duranceau, Suzanne 1952- ....................... *162*
Durango, Julia 1967- .............................. *173*
Durant, Alan 1958- ................................ *165*
  Earlier sketch in SATA *121*
Durant, John 1902- ................................ *27*
Durbin, William 1951- ........................... *174*
  Earlier sketch in SATA *143*
Durell, Ann 1930- .................................. *66*
Durkee, Sarah ...................................... *173*
Durrant, Lynda 1954- ............................. *148*
  Earlier sketch in SATA *96*
Durrell, Gerald (Malcolm) 1925-1995 ........ *8*
  Obituary ............................................ *84*
Durrell, Julie 1955- ............................... *94*
Durrett, Deanne 1940- ........................... *144*
  Earlier sketch in SATA *92*
Du Soe, Robert C. 1892-1958
  *See* YABC *2*
Dussling, Jennifer 1970- ......................... *143*
  Earlier sketch in SATA *96*
DuTemple, Lesley A. 1952- ...................... *113*
Dutz
  *See* Davis, Mary Octavia
Duval, Katherine
  *See* James, Elizabeth
Duvall, Aimee
  *See* Thurlo, Aimee
  and Thurlo, David
Duvall, Evelyn Millis 1906- ...................... *9*
Duvall, Jill D(onovan) 1932- .................... *102*
Duvoisin, Roger (Antoine) 1904-1980 ........ *30*
  Obituary ............................................ *23*
  Earlier sketch in SATA *2*
  *See also* CLR *23*
Dwiggins, Don(ald J.) 1913-1988 .............. *4*
  Obituary ............................................ *60*
Dwight, Allan
  *See* Cole, Lois Dwight

Dwyer, Deanna
  *See* Koontz, Dean R.
Dwyer, K. R.
  *See* Koontz, Dean R.
Dyck, Peter J. 1914- ............................ 75
Dyer, James (Frederick) 1934- .................. 37
Dyer, Jane ................................... 147
Dyess, John (Foster) 1939- ..................... 76
Dygard, Thomas J. 1931-1996 ................... 97
  Obituary ................................... 92
  Earlier sketch in SATA 24
  *See also* SAAS 15
Dyke, John 1935- ............................. 35

**E**

E. V. L.
  *See* Lucas, E(dward) V(errall)
Eagar, Frances (Elisabeth Stuart) 1940-1978
  .......................................... 11
  Obituary ................................... 55
Eager, Edward (McMaken) 1911-1964 ........ 17
  *See also* CLR 43
Eager, George 1921- .......................... 56
  *See* Eager, George B.
Eager, George B.
  *See* Eager, George
Eagle, Ellen 1953- ........................... 61
Eagle, Kin
  *See* Adlerman, Daniel (Ezra)
  and Adlerman, Kimberly M(arie)
Eagle, Mike 1942- ............................ 11
Earle, Olive L(ydia) 1888-1982 ................ 7
Earle, William
  *See* Johns, W(illiam) E(arle)
Earls, Nick 1963- ........................... 156
  Earlier sketch in SATA 95
Early, Jack
  *See* Scoppettone, Sandra
Early, Jon
  *See* Johns, W(illiam) E(arle)
Early, Margaret 1951- ........................ 72
Earnshaw, Brian 1929- ........................ 17
Earnshaw, Micky
  *See* Earnshaw, Spencer Wright
Earnshaw, Spencer Wright 1939- .............. 88
Easley, MaryAnn ............................. 94
Eastman, Charles A(lexander) 1858-1939
  *See* YABC 1
Eastman, P(hilip) D(ey) 1909-1986 ........... 33
  Obituary ................................... 46
Easton, Kelly 1960- ......................... 141
Eastwick, Ivy (Ethel) O(live) .................. 3
Eaton, Anne T(haxter) 1881-1971 ............. 32
Eaton, Anthony 1971- ....................... 167
Eaton, George L.
  *See* Verral, Charles Spain
Eaton, Janet
  *See* Givens, Janet E(aton)
Eaton, Jeanette 1886-1968 .................... 24
Eaton, Tom 1940- ............................ 22
Ebel, Alex 1927- ............................. 11
Eber, Dorothy (Margaret) Harley 1930- ....... 27
Eberle, Irmengarde 1898-1979 .................. 2
  Obituary ................................... 23
Eble, Diane 1956- ........................... 74
Eboch, Chris ............................... 113
Echlin, Kim 1955- ........................... 166
Eckblad, Edith Berven 1923- .................. 23
Eckert, Allan W. 1931- ....................... 91
  Brief entry ................................. 27
  Earlier sketch in SATA 29
  *See also* SAAS 21
Eckert, Horst 1931- .......................... 72
  Earlier sketch in SATA 8
  *See* Janosch
Ecklar, Julia (Marie) 1964- .................. 112
Eddings, David (Carroll) 1931- ............... 91
Ede, Janina 1937- ........................... 33

Edell, Celeste ............................... 12
Edelman, Lily (Judith) 1915-1981 ............. 22
Edelson, Edward 1932- ........................ 51
Edens, Cooper 1945- ......................... 166
  Earlier sketches in SATA 49, 112
Edens, (Bishop) David 1926- .................. 39
Edey, Maitland A(rmstrong) 1910-1992 ....... 25
  Obituary ................................... 71
Edgeworth, Maria 1768-1849 ................... 21
Edgy, Wardore
  *See* Gorey, Edward (St. John)
Edison, Theodore
  *See* Stratemeyer, Edward L.
Edler, Tim(othy) 1948- ....................... 56
Edmiston, Jim 1948- .......................... 80
Edmonds, I(vy) G(ordon) 1917- ................. 8
Edmonds, Walter D(umaux) 1903-1998 ....... 27
  Obituary ................................... 99
  Earlier sketch in SATA 1
  *See also* SAAS 4
Edmund, Sean
  *See* Pringle, Laurence P(atrick)
Edsall, Marian (Stickney) 1920- ............... 8
Edwards, Al
  *See* Nourse, Alan E(dward)
Edwards, Anne 1927- .......................... 35
Edwards, Audrey 1947- ........................ 52
  Brief entry ................................. 31
Edwards, Becky (Jane) 1966- ................. 125
Edwards, Bertram
  *See* Edwards, Herbert Charles
Edwards, Bronwen Elizabeth
  *See* Rose, Wendy
Edwards, Cecile Pepin 1916- .................. 25
Edwards, Dorothy 1914-1982 ................... 88
  Obituary ................................... 31
  Earlier sketch in SATA 4
Edwards, F. E.
  *See* Nolan, William F(rancis)
Edwards, Frank B. 1952- ...................... 93
Edwards, Gunvor ............................. 32
Edwards, Harvey 1929- ......................... 5
Edwards, Hazel (Eileen) 1945- ............... 135
Edwards, Herbert Charles 1912- ............... 12
Edwards, Jane Campbell 1932- ................. 10
Edwards, Julia
  *See* Stratemeyer, Edward L.
Edwards, Julie
  *See* Andrews, Julie
Edwards, Julie Andrews
  *See* Andrews, Julie
Edwards, Linda Strauss 1948- ................. 49
  Brief entry ................................. 42
Edwards, Michelle 1955- ..................... 152
  Earlier sketch in SATA 70
Edwards, Monica le Doux Newton 1912-1998
  .......................................... 12
Edwards, Olwen
  *See* Gater, Dilys
Edwards, Page (Lawrence, Jr.) 1941-1999 .. 59
Edwards, R. T.
  *See* Goulart, Ron(ald Joseph)
Edwards, Sally (Cary) 1929- ................... 7
Edwards, Samuel
  *See* Gerson, Noel Bertram
Edwards, Wallace 1957(?)- ................... 170
Egan, E(dward) W(elstead) 1922- .............. 35
Egan, Kerry .................................. 175
Egan, Lorraine Hopping 1960- ................ 134
  Earlier sketch in SATA 91
Egan, Tim 1957- ............................. 155
  Earlier sketch in SATA 89
Egermeier, Elsie E(milie) 1890-1986 .......... 65
Eggenberger, David 1918- ...................... 6
Eggleston, Edward 1837-1902 .................. 27
Egielski, Richard 1952- ..................... 163
  Earlier sketches in SATA 11, 49, 106
Egypt, Ophelia Settle 1903-1984 .............. 16
  Obituary ................................... 38

Ehlert, Lois 1934- .......................... 172
  Earlier sketches in SATA 35, 69, 128
  *See also* CLR 28
Ehlert, Lois Jane
  *See* Ehlert, Lois
Ehling, Katalin Olah 1941- ................... 93
Ehrenfreund, Norbert 1921- ................... 86
Ehrlich, Amy 1942- .......................... 132
  Earlier sketches in SATA 25, 65, 96
Ehrlich, Bettina Bauer 1903-1985 .............. 1
Ehrlich, H. M.
  *See* Ziefert, Harriet
Eichenberg, Fritz 1901-1990 .................. 50
  Earlier sketch in SATA 9
Eichler, Margrit 1942- ....................... 35
Eichner, James A. 1927- ....................... 4
Eidson, Thomas 1944- ........................ 112
Eifert, Virginia (Louise) S(nider) 1911-1966
  ........................................... 2
Eige, (Elizabeth) Lillian 1915- ............... 65
Eiken, J. Melia 1967- ....................... 125
Einsel, Naiad ............................... 10
Einsel, Walter 1926- ......................... 10
Einzig, Susan 1922- .......................... 43
Eiseman, Alberta 1925- ....................... 15
Eisenberg, Azriel (Louis) 1903-1985 .......... 12
Eisenberg, Lisa 1949- ....................... 155
  Brief entry ................................. 50
  Earlier sketch in SATA 57
Eisenberg, Phyllis Rose 1924- ................ 41
Eisner, Vivienne
  *See* Margolis, Vivienne
Eisner, Will 1917-2005 ...................... 165
  Earlier sketch in SATA 31
Eisner, William Erwin
  *See* Eisner, Will
Eitzen, Allan 1928- ........................... 9
Eitzen, Ruth (Carper) 1924- ................... 9
Ekwensi, C. O. D.
  *See* Ekwensi, Cyprian (Odiatu Duaka)
Ekwensi, Cyprian (Odiatu Duaka) 1921- .... 66
Elam, Richard M(ace, Jr.) 1920- ............... 9
Elborn, Andrew
  *See* Clements, Andrew
  and Clements, Andrew
Elboz, Stephen 1956- ........................ 152
Eldin, Peter 1939- .......................... 154
Eldon, Kathy 1946- .......................... 107
Elfman, Blossom 1925- ......................... 8
Elgin, Kathleen 1923- ........................ 39
Elia
  *See* Lamb, Charles
Eliot, A. D.
  *See* Jewett, (Theodora) Sarah Orne
Eliot, Alice
  *See* Jewett, (Theodora) Sarah Orne
Eliot, Anne
  *See* Cole, Lois Dwight
Eliot, Dan
  *See* Silverberg, Robert
Elish, Dan 1960- ............................ 129
  Earlier sketch in SATA 68
Elisha, Ron 1951- ........................... 104
Elkin, Benjamin 1911-1995 ..................... 3
Elkins, Dov Peretz 1937- ...................... 5
Ellacott, S(amuel) E(rnest) 1911- ............ 19
Elleman, Barbara 1934- ...................... 147
Ellen, Jaye
  *See* Nixon, Joan Lowery
Eller, Scott
  *See* Holinger, William (Jacques)
  and Shepard, Jim
Ellestad, Myrvin H. 1921- .................... 120
Elliot, David 1952- ......................... 122
Elliott, Bruce
  *See* Field, Edward
Elliott, David 1952- ........................ 163
Elliott, Don
  *See* Silverberg, Robert
Elliott, Elizabeth Shippen Green
  *See* Green, Elizabeth Shippen

Elliott, Janice 1931-1995 ............................ *119*
Elliott, Joey
  *See* Houk, Randy
Elliott, Louise ..................................... *111*
Elliott, Odette 1939- ................................. *75*
Elliott, Patricia 1946- .............................. *176*
Elliott, Sarah M(cCarn) 1930- .................... *14*
Elliott, (Robert) Scott 1970- .................... *153*
Elliott, William
  *See* Bradbury, Ray
Ellis, (Mary) Amabel (Nassau Strachey)
  Williams
  *See* Williams-Ellis, (Mary) Amabel (Nassau
  Strachey)
Ellis, Anyon
  *See* Rowland-Entwistle, (Arthur) Theodore
  (Henry)
Ellis, Deborah 1960- ................................ *129*
Ellis, E. S.
  *See* Ellis, Edward S(ylvester)
Ellis, Edward S(ylvester) 1840-1916
  *See* YABC *1*
Ellis, Ella Thorp 1928- ........................... *127*
  Earlier sketch in SATA *7*
  *See also* SAAS *9*
Ellis, Harry Bearse 1921-2004 .................... *9*
Ellis, Herbert
  *See* Wilson, Lionel
Ellis, Mel(vin Richard) 1912-1984 ................ *7*
  Obituary ............................................ *39*
Ellis, Richard 1938- ............................... *130*
Ellis, Sarah 1952- ................................. *131*
  Earlier sketch in SATA *68*
  *See also* CLR *42*
Ellison, Emily ................................... *114*
Ellison, Lucile Watkins 1907(?)-1979 ......... *50*
  Obituary ............................................ *22*
Ellison, Virginia H(owell) 1910- ................. *4*
Ellsberg, Edward 1891-1983 ....................... *7*
Ellsworth, Mary Ellen (Tressel) 1940- ...... *146*
Elmer, Robert 1958- .............................. *154*
  Earlier sketch in SATA *99*
Elmore, (Carolyn) Patricia 1933- ............... *38*
  Brief entry ......................................... *35*
El-Moslimany, Ann P(axton) 1937- ............. *90*
Elspeth
  *See* Bragdon, Elspeth MacDuffie
Elster, Jean Alicia 1953- ......................... *150*
Elting, Mary 1906- ................................. *88*
  Earlier sketch in SATA *2*
  *See also* SAAS *20*
Elwart, Joan Potter 1927- .......................... *2*
Elwood, Ann 1931- ................................. *55*
  Brief entry ......................................... *52*
Elwood, Roger 1943- .............................. *58*
Elya, Susan M(iddleton) 1955- ................... *159*
  Earlier sketch in SATA *106*
Elzbieta ............................................. *88*
Emberley, Barbara A(nne) 1932- ................ *146*
  Earlier sketches in SATA *8, 70*
  *See also* CLR *5*
Emberley, Ed(ward Randolph) 1931- ......... *146*
  Earlier sketches in SATA *8, 70*
  *See also* CLR *81*
Emberley, Michael 1960- ......................... *119*
  Earlier sketches in SATA *34, 80*
Embry, Margaret Jacob 1919-1975 ................ *5*
Emecheta, Buchi 1944- ............................. *66*
Emecheta, Florence Onye Buchi
  *See* Emecheta, Buchi
Emerson, Alice B. ................................. *67*
  Earlier sketch in SATA *1*
  *See* Benson, Mildred (Augustine Wirt)
Emerson, Kathy Lynn 1947- ........................ *63*
Emerson, Ru 1944- ................................. *107*
  Earlier sketch in SATA *70*
Emerson, Sally 1952- .............................. *111*
Emerson, William K(eith) 1925- ................. *25*
Emert, Phyllis R(aybin) 1947- .................... *93*
Emery, Anne (McGuigan) 1907- ................... *33*
  Earlier sketch in SATA *1*

Emmens, Carol Ann 1944- ......................... *39*
Emmett, Jonathan 1965- .......................... *138*
Emory, Jerry 1957- ................................. *96*
Emrich, Duncan (Black Macdonald)
  1908-1970(?) ....................................... *11*
Emshwiller, Carol 1921- .......................... *174*
  Autobiography Feature ............................ *174*
Emshwiller, Carol Fries
  *See* Emshwiller, Carol
Emslie, M. L.
  *See* Simpson, Myrtle L(illias)
Ende, Michael (Andreas Helmuth) 1929-1995
  ...................................................... *130*
  Brief entry ......................................... *42*
  Obituary ............................................ *86*
  Earlier sketch in SATA *61*
  *See also* CLR *14*
Enderle, Dotti 1954- .............................. *145*
Enderle, Judith (Ann) Ross 1941- ............... *89*
  Autobiography Feature ............................ *114*
  Earlier sketch in SATA *38*
  *See also* SAAS *26*
Enell, Trinka (Gochenour) 1951- ................ *79*
Enfield, Carrie
  *See* Smith, Susan Vernon
Engdahl, Sylvia Louise 1933- ...................... *4*
  Autobiography Feature ............................ *122*
  *See also* CLR *2*
  *See also* SAAS *5*
Engel, Diana 1947- ................................. *70*
Engelbreit, Mary 1952- ........................... *169*
Engelhart, Margaret S. 1924- ..................... *59*
Engelmann, Kim (V.) 1959- ....................... *87*
England, George Allan 1877-1936 .............. *102*
Englart, Mindi Rose 1965- ....................... *146*
Engle, Eloise ....................................... *9*
  *See* Paananen, Eloise (Katherine)
Englebert, Victor 1933- ............................ *8*
English, James W(ilson) 1915- .................... *37*
Engstrom, Elizabeth 1951- ....................... *110*
Enright, D(ennis) J(oseph) 1920-2002 ......... *25*
  Obituary ........................................... *140*
Enright, Elizabeth (Wright) 1909-1968 .......... *9*
  *See also* CLR *4*
Ensor, Robert (T.) 1922- .......................... *93*
Entwistle, (Arthur) Theodore (Henry) Rowland
  *See* Rowland-Entwistle, (Arthur) Theodore
  (Henry)
Enys, Sarah L.
  *See* Sloggett, Nellie
Epanya, Christian A(rthur Kingue) 1956- ... *91*
Ephraim, Shelly S(chonebaum) 1952- ......... *97*
Ephron, Delia 1944- ............................... *65*
  Brief entry ......................................... *50*
Epler, Doris M. 1928- ............................. *73*
Epp, Margaret A(gnes) 1913- ..................... *20*
Epple, Anne Orth 1927- ........................... *20*
Epstein, Anne Merrick 1931- ..................... *20*
Epstein, Beryl (M. Williams) 1910- ............ *31*
  Earlier sketch in SATA *1*
  *See also* CLR *26*
  *See also* SAAS *17*
Epstein, Perle S(herry) 1938- .................... *27*
Epstein, Rachel S. 1941- ......................... *102*
Epstein, Samuel 1909-2000 ....................... *31*
  Earlier sketch in SATA *1*
  *See also* CLR *26*
  *See also* SAAS *17*
Erdman, Loula Grace 1905(?)-1976 ............... *1*
Erdoes, Richard 1912- ............................. *33*
  Brief entry ......................................... *28*
Erdrich, Karen Louise
  *See* Erdrich, Louise
Erdrich, Louise 1954- ............................ *141*
  Earlier sketch in SATA *94*
Erickson, Betty J. 1923- .......................... *97*
Erickson, Betty Jean
  *See* Erickson, Betty J.
Erickson, John R. 1943- .......................... *136*
  Earlier sketch in SATA *70*
Erickson, Jon 1948- .............................. *141*

Erickson, Phoebe .................................. *59*
Erickson, Russell E(verett) 1932- ............... *27*
Erickson, Sabra Rollins 1912-1995 .............. *35*
Erickson, Walter
  *See* Fast, Howard
Ericson, Walter
  *See* Fast, Howard
Ericsson, Jennifer A. ............................. *170*
Erikson, Mel 1937- ................................. *31*
Ering, Timothy Basil .............................. *176*
Erlanger, Baba
  *See* Trahey, Jane
Erlbach, Arlene 1948- ............................. *160*
  Earlier sketches in SATA *78, 115*
Erlich, Lillian (Feldman) 1910-1983 .......... *10*
Ermatinger, James W. 1959- ..................... *170*
Ernst, (Lyman) John 1940- ........................ *39*
Ernst, Kathleen A. 1959- ......................... *162*
Ernst, Kathryn (Fitzgerald) 1942- .............. *25*
Ernst, Lisa Campbell 1957- ...................... *154*
  Brief entry ......................................... *44*
  Earlier sketches in SATA *55, 95*
Ervin, Janet Halliday 1923- ........................ *4*
Erwin, Will
  *See* Eisner, Will
Esbaum, Jill ....................................... *174*
Esbensen, Barbara J(uster) 1925-1996 ........ *97*
  Brief entry ......................................... *53*
  Earlier sketch in SATA *62*
Eschbacher, Roger ................................. *160*
Eseki, Bruno
  *See* Mphahlele, Ezekiel
Eshmeyer, R. E. .................................... *29*
  *See* Eschmeyer, R(einhart) E(rnst)
Eskridge, Ann E. 1949- ............................ *84*
Espeland, Pamela (Lee) 1951- ................... *128*
  Brief entry ......................................... *38*
  Earlier sketch in SATA *52*
Espriella, Don Manuel Alvarez
  *See* Southey, Robert
Espy, Willard R(ichardson) 1910-1999 ....... *38*
  Obituary ........................................... *113*
Essrig, Harry 1912- ................................ *66*
Estep, Irene Compton ............................... *5*
Esterl, Arnica 1933- ............................... *77*
Estes, Eleanor (Ruth) 1906-1988 ................. *91*
  Obituary ............................................ *56*
  Earlier sketch in SATA *7*
  *See also* CLR *70*
Estoril, Jean
  *See* Allan, Mabel Esther
Estrada, Pau 1961- ................................. *74*
Etchemendy, Nancy 1952- ......................... *166*
  Earlier sketch in SATA *38*
Etchemendy, Nancy Elise Howell
  *See* Etchemendy, Nancy
Etchison, Birdie L(ee) 1937- ..................... *38*
Etchison, Craig 1945- ............................. *133*
Etherington, Frank 1945- .......................... *58*
Ets, Marie Hall 1893-1984 ......................... *2*
  *See also* CLR *33*
Ettlinger, Doris 1950- ............................. *173*
Eunson, (John) Dale 1904-2002 .................... *5*
  Obituary ........................................... *132*
Evan, Frances Y. 1951- ........................... *167*
Evanoff, Vlad 1916- ................................ *59*
Evans, Douglas 1953- ............................. *144*
  Earlier sketch in SATA *93*
Evans, Eva (Knox) 1905-1998 ..................... *27*
Evans, Freddi Williams 1957- ................... *134*
Evans, Greg 1947- ................................. *143*
  Earlier sketch in SATA *73*
Evans, Hubert Reginald 1892-1986 ........... *118*
  Obituary ............................................ *48*
Evans, Katherine (Floyd) 1901-1964 ........... *5*
Evans, Larry
  *See* Evans, Laurence Chubb
Evans, Laurence Chubb 1939- ................... *88*
Evans, Lawrence Watt .............................. *75*
  *See* Watt-Evans, Lawrence
Evans, Mari 1923- .................................. *10*

Evans, Mark ...................................... *19*
Evans, Nancy 1950- ............................. *65*
Evans, Patricia Healy
 *See* Carpenter, Patricia (Healy Evans)
Evans, (Alice) Pearl 1927- ..................... *83*
Evans, Shirlee 1931- ........................... *58*
Evans, Tabor
 *See* Cameron, Lou
 and Knott, William C(ecil, Jr.)
 and Wallmann, Jeffrey M(iner)
 and Whittington, Harry (Benjamin)
Evarts, Esther
 *See* Benson, Sally
Evarts, Hal G., (Jr.) 1915-1989 ............... *6*
Everett, Gail
 *See* Hale, Arlene
Evernden, Margery 1916- ....................... *5*
Eversole, Robyn 1971- ......................... *74*
Eversole, Robyn H.
 *See* Eversole, Robyn
Eversole, Robyn Harbert
 *See* Eversole, Robyn
Evslin, Bernard 1922-1993 ..................... *83*
 Brief entry .................................. *28*
 Obituary .................................... *77*
 Earlier sketch in SATA *45*
Ewart, Claire 1958- ........................... *145*
 Earlier sketch in SATA *76*
Ewen, David 1907-1985 ......................... *4*
 Obituary .................................... *47*
Ewing, Juliana (Horatia Gatty) 1841-1885 . *16*
 *See also* CLR *78*
Ewing, Kathryn 1921- .......................... *20*
Eyerly, Jeannette (Hyde) 1908- ................ *86*
 Earlier sketch in SATA *4*
 *See also* SAAS *10*
Eyre, Dorothy
 *See* McGuire, Leslie (Sarah)
Eyre, Katherine Wigmore 1901-1970 ......... *26*
Ezzell, Marilyn 1937- ......................... *42*
 Brief entry .................................. *38*

      **F**

Fabe, Maxene 1943- ............................ *15*
Faber, Doris (Greenberg) 1924- ................ *78*
 Earlier sketch in SATA *3*
Faber, Harold 1919- ........................... *5*
Fabre, Jean Henri (Casimir) 1823-1915 ...... *22*
Facklam, Margery (Metz) 1927- ................. *132*
 Earlier sketches in SATA *20, 85*
Fadiman, Clifton (Paul) 1904-1999 ............ *11*
 Obituary .................................... *115*
Fahs, Sophia Blanche Lyon 1876-1978 ..... *102*
Fair, David 1952- ............................. *96*
Fair, Sylvia 1933- ............................ *13*
Fairfax-Lucy, Brian (Fulke Cameron-Ramsay)
 1898-1974 ..................................... *6*
 Obituary .................................... *26*
Fairfield, Flora
 *See* Alcott, Louisa May
Fairman, Joan A(lexandra) 1935- ............... *10*
Faithfull, Gail 1936- ......................... *8*
Falcone, L(ucy) M. 1951- ...................... *155*
Falconer, Ian 1959- ........................... *125*
 *See also* CLR *90*
Falconer, James
 *See* Kirkup, James
Falconer, Lee N.
 *See* May, Julian
Falkner, Leonard 1900-1977 .................... *12*
Fall, Andrew
 *See* Arthur, Robert, (Jr.)
Fall, Thomas
 *See* Snow, Donald Clifford
Falls, C(harles) B(uckles) 1874-1960 ......... *38*
 Brief entry .................................. *27*
Falstein, Louis 1909-1995 ..................... *37*
Fancher, Lou 1960- ............................ *177*

Fanelli, Sara 1969- ........................... *126*
 Earlier sketch in SATA *89*
Fanning, Leonard M(ulliken) 1888-1967 ...... *5*
Faralla, Dana 1909- ........................... *9*
Faralla, Dorothy W.
 *See* Faralla, Dana
Farb, Peter 1929-1980 ......................... *12*
 Obituary .................................... *22*
Farber, Norma 1909-1984 ....................... *75*
 Obituary .................................... *38*
 Earlier sketch in SATA *25*
Farish, Terry 1947- ........................... *146*
 Earlier sketch in SATA *82*
Farjeon, (Eve) Annabel 1919-2004 ............. *11*
 Obituary .................................... *153*
Farjeon, Eleanor 1881-1965 .................... *2*
 *See also* CLR *34*
Farley, Carol (J.) 1936- ...................... *137*
 Earlier sketch in SATA *4*
Farley, Terri ................................. *165*
Farley, Walter (Lorimer) 1915-1989 .......... *132*
 Earlier sketches in SATA *2, 43*
Farlow, James O(rville, Jr.) 1951- ........... *75*
Farmer, Nancy 1941- ........................... *161*
 Earlier sketches in SATA *79, 117*
Farmer, Patti 1948- ........................... *79*
Farmer, Penelope (Jane) 1939- ................. *105*
 Brief entry .................................. *39*
 Earlier sketch in SATA *40*
 *See also* CLR *8*
 *See also* SAAS *22*
Farmer, Peter 1950- ........................... *38*
Farmer, Philip Jose 1918- ..................... *93*
Farnham, Burt
 *See* Clifford, Harold B(urton)
Farnsworth, Bill 1958- ........................ *135*
 Earlier sketch in SATA *84*
Farquhar, Margaret C(utting) 1905-1988 .... *13*
Farquharson, Alexander 1944- .................. *46*
Farquharson, Martha
 *See* Finley, Martha
Farr, Diana (Pullein-Thompson) ................ *82*
 *See* Pullein-Thompson, Diana
Farr, Finis (King) 1904-1982 .................. *10*
Farrar, Jill
 *See* Morris, Jill
Farrar, Susan Clement 1917- ................... *33*
Farrell, Ben
 *See* Cebulash, Mel
Farrell, Patrick
 *See* Odgers, Sally Farrell
Farrell, Sally
 *See* Odgers, Sally Farrell
Farrer, Vashti ............................... *167*
Farrington, S(elwyn) Kip, Jr. 1904-1983 .... *20*
Farshtey, Greg(ory T.) 1965- .................. *148*
Farthing, Alison 1936- ........................ *45*
 Brief entry .................................. *36*
Farthing-Knight, Catherine 1933- .............. *92*
Fassler, Joan (Grace) 1931- ................... *11*
Fast, Howard 1914-2003 ........................ *7*
 Autobiography Feature ....................... *107*
Fast, Howard Melvin
 *See* Fast, Howard
Fasulo, Michael 1963- ......................... *83*
Fatchen, Max 1920- ............................ *84*
 Earlier sketch in SATA *20*
 *See also* SAAS *20*
Fate, Marilyn
 *See* Collins, Paul
Father Goose
 *See* Ghigna, Charles
Fatigati, (Frances) Evelyn 1948- .............. *24*
Fatio, Louise 1904-1993 ....................... *6*
Faulhaber, Martha 1926- ....................... *7*
Faulkner, Anne Irvin 1906- .................... *23*
Faulkner, Frank
 *See* Ellis, Edward S(ylvester)
Faulkner, Nancy
 *See* Faulkner, Anne Irvin
Faulknor, Cliff(ord Vernon) 1913- ............. *86*

Favole, Robert J(ames) 1950- .................. *125*
Fax, Elton Clay 1909-1993 ..................... *25*
Faxon, Lavinia
 *See* Russ, Lavinia (Faxon)
Feagles, Anita M(acRae) 1927- ................. *9*
Feagles, Elizabeth
 *See* Day, Beth (Feagles)
Feague, Mildred H. 1915- ...................... *14*
Fearnley, Jan 1965- ........................... *153*
Fearrington, Ann (Peyton) 1945- ............... *146*
Fecher, Constance
 *See* Heaven, Constance (Christina)
Feder, Chris Welles 1938- ..................... *81*
Feder, Harriet K. 1928- ....................... *73*
Feder, Paula (Kurzband) 1935- ................. *26*
Federici, Debbie 1965- ........................ *175*
Federici, Debbie Tanner
 *See* Federici, Debbie
Feelings, Muriel (Lavita Grey) 1938- ......... *16*
 *See also* CLR *5*
 *See also* SAAS *8*
Feelings, Thomas 1933-2003 .................... *8*
 Obituary .................................... *148*
 *See* Feelings, Tom
Feelings, Tom ................................. *69*
 *See also* CLR *58*
 *See also* SAAS *19*
 *See* Feelings, Thomas
Fehler, Gene 1940- ............................ *74*
Fehrenbach, T(heodore) R(eed, Jr.) 1925- .. *33*
Feiffer, Jules 1929- .......................... *157*
 Earlier sketches in SATA *8, 61, 111*
Feiffer, Jules Ralph
 *See* Feiffer, Jules
Feiffer, Kate 1964- ........................... *170*
Feig, Barbara Krane 1937- ..................... *34*
Feikema, Feike
 *See* Manfred, Frederick (Feikema)
Feil, Hila 1942- .............................. *12*
Feilen, John
 *See* May, Julian
Feinberg, Barbara Jane 1938- .................. *58*
 *See* Feinberg, Barbara Silberdick
Feinberg, Barbara Silberdick ................. *123*
 *See* Feinberg, Barbara Jane
Feinstein, John 1956- ......................... *163*
Feldman, Anne (Rodgers) 1939- ................. *19*
Feldman, Elane ............................... *79*
Felix
 *See* Vincent, Felix
Fell, Derek 1939- ............................. *167*
Fell, Derek John
 *See* Fell, Derek
Fellows, Muriel H. ........................... *10*
Fellows, Stan 1957- ........................... *177*
Fellows, Stanley
 *See* Fellows, Stan
Felsen, Henry Gregor 1916-1995 ................ *1*
 *See also* SAAS *2*
Feltenstein, Arlene (H.) 1934- ................ *119*
Felton, Harold William 1902-1991 ............. *1*
Felton, Ronald Oliver 1909- ................... *3*
Felts, Shirley 1934- .......................... *33*
Fenderson, Lewis H., Jr. 1907-1983 .......... *47*
 Obituary .................................... *37*
Fenner, Carol (Elizabeth) 1929-2002 ......... *89*
 Obituary .................................... *132*
 Earlier sketch in SATA *7*
 *See also* SAAS *24*
Fenner, Phyllis R(eid) 1899-1982 ............. *1*
 Obituary .................................... *29*
Fensham, Elizabeth ........................... *169*
Fenten, Barbara D(oris) 1935- ................. *26*
Fenten, D(onald) X. 1932- ..................... *4*
Fenton, Carroll Lane 1900-1969 ............... *5*
Fenton, Edward 1917-1995 ...................... *7*
 Obituary .................................... *89*
Fenton, Mildred Adams 1899-1995 ............. *21*
Fenwick, Patti
 *See* Grider, Dorothy
Feravolo, Rocco Vincent 1922- ................. *10*

Ferber, Edna 1887-1968 .......................... 7
Fergus, Charles .................................. *114*
Ferguson, Alane 1957- ......................... 85
Ferguson, Bob
  *See* Ferguson, Robert Bruce
Ferguson, Cecil 1931- .......................... 45
Ferguson, Robert Bruce 1927-2001 ........... *13*
Ferguson, Sarah 1959- ........................ *110*
  Earlier sketch in SATA 66
Ferguson, Sarah Margaret
  *See* Ferguson, Sarah
Ferguson, Walter (W.) 1930- ................. 34
Fergusson, Erna 1888-1964 .................... 5
Fermi, Laura 1907-1977 ........................ 6
  Obituary .................................... 28
Fern, Eugene A. 1919-1987 ................... *10*
  Obituary .................................... 54
Fernandes, Eugenie 1943- ................... *139*
  Earlier sketch in SATA 77
Fernandez, Laura 1960- ...................... *171*
Ferrari, Maria ................................. *123*
Ferreiro, Carmen 1958- ...................... *158*
Ferrell, Nancy Warren 1932- .................. 70
Ferrier, Lucy
  *See* Penzler, Otto
Ferris, Helen Josephine 1890-1969 ........... 21
Ferris, James Cody .............................. *1*
  *See* McFarlane, Leslie (Charles)
Ferris, Jean 1939- ............................ *149*
  Brief entry ................................. 50
  Earlier sketches in SATA 56, 105
Ferris, Jeri Chase 1937- ....................... 84
Ferry, Charles 1927- ........................... 92
  Earlier sketch in SATA 43
  *See also* CLR 34
  *See also* SAAS 20
Fetz, Ingrid 1915- ............................ 30
Feydy, Anne Lindbergh
  Brief entry ................................. 32
  *See* Sapieyevski, Anne Lindbergh
Fiammenghi, Gioia 1929- ....................... 66
  Earlier sketch in SATA 9
Fiarotta, Noel ................................. *15*
  *See* Ficarotta, Noel
Fiarotta, Phyllis .............................. *15*
  *See* Ficarotta, Phyllis
Fichter, George S. 1922-1993 ................... 7
Fidler, Kathleen (Annie) 1899-1980 ........... 87
  Obituary .................................... 45
  Earlier sketch in SATA 3
Fiedler, Jean(nette Feldman) .................... 4
Fiedler, Joseph Daniel ........................ *159*
Field, Dorothy 1944- .......................... 97
Field, Edward 1924- .......................... *109*
  Earlier sketch in SATA 8
Field, Eugene 1850-1895 ....................... *16*
Field, Gans T.
  *See* Wellman, Manly Wade
Field, James 1959- ........................... *113*
Field, Peter
  *See* Drago, Harry Sinclair
  and Dresser, Davis
  and Mann, E(dward) B(everly)
Field, Rachel (Lyman) 1894-1942 ............. *15*
  *See also* CLR 21
Fielding, Kate
  *See* Oldfield, Jenny
Fienberg, Anna 1956- ......................... *112*
Fife, Dale (Odile Hollerbach) 1901- .......... *18*
Fighter Pilot, A
  *See* Johnston, H(ugh) A(nthony) S(tephen)
Figler, Jeanie 1949- ......................... *123*
Figley, Marty Rhodes 1948- ................... *158*
  Earlier sketch in SATA 88
Figueredo, D(anilo) H. 1951- ................. *155*
Figueroa, Pablo 1938- .......................... *9*
Fijan, Carol 1918- ............................ *12*
Filderman, Diane E(lizabeth) 1959- ........... 87
Files, Meg 1946- ............................. *107*
Fillmore, Parker H(oysted) 1878-1944
  *See* YABC *1*

Filstrup, Chris
  *See* Filstrup, E(dward) Christian
Filstrup, E(dward) Christian 1942- ........... *43*
Finchler, Judy 1943- .......................... 93
Finder, Martin
  *See* Salzmann, Siegmund
Findlay, Jamieson 1958- ...................... *169*
Findon, Joanne 1957- ......................... *161*
Fine, Anne 1947- ............................. *160*
  Earlier sketches in SATA 29, 72, 111
  *See also* CLR 25
  *See also* SAAS 15
Fine, Edith Hope ............................. *169*
Fine, Jane
  *See* Ziefert, Harriet
Finger, Charles J(oseph) 1869(?)-1941 ....... *42*
Fink, William B(ertrand) 1916- ............... 22
Finke, Blythe Foote 1922- ..................... 26
Finkel, George (Irvine) 1909-1975 ............. 8
Finkelstein, Norman H. 1941- ................ *137*
  Earlier sketch in SATA 73
Finlay, Alice Sullivan 1946- .................. 82
Finlay, Winifred Lindsay Crawford
  (McKissack) 1910-1989 ..................... 23
Finlayson, Ann 1925- .......................... 8
Finley, Martha 1828-1909 ...................... *43*
Finley, Mary Peace 1942- ...................... 83
Finney, Jack ................................. *109*
  *See* Finney, Walter Braden
Finney, Patricia 1958- ....................... *163*
Finney, Shan 1944- ............................ 65
Firer, Ben Zion
  *See* Firer, Benzion
Firer, Benzion 1914- .......................... 64
Fireside, Bryna J. 1932- ...................... *73*
Firmin, Charlotte 1954- ....................... 29
Firmin, Peter 1928- ........................... 58
  Earlier sketch in SATA 15
Fischbach, Julius 1894-1988 ................... 10
Fischer, John
  *See* Fluke, Joanne
Fischer, R.J.
  *See* Fluke, Joanne
Fischer-Nagel, Andreas 1951- .................. 56
Fischer-Nagel, Heiderose 1956- ................ 56
Fischler, Shirley (Walton) ..................... 66
Fischler, Stan(ley I.) ......................... 66
  Brief entry ................................. 36
Fisher, Aileen (Lucia) 1906-2002 ............. *73*
  Obituary .................................... *143*
  Earlier sketches in SATA 1, 25
  *See also* CLR 49
Fisher, Barbara 1940- .......................... 44
  Brief entry ................................. 34
Fisher, Carolyn 1968- ........................ *154*
Fisher, Catherine 1957- ...................... *155*
Fisher, Chris 1958- ........................... 80
Fisher, Clavin C(argill) 1912- ................ 24
Fisher, Dorothy (Frances) Canfield 1879-1958
  *See* YABC *1*
  *See also* CLR 71
Fisher, Gary L. 1949- ......................... 86
Fisher, John (Oswald Hamilton) 1909- ........ *15*
Fisher, Laura Harrison 1934- ................... 5
Fisher, Leonard Everett 1924- ................ *176*
  Autobiography Feature ...................... *122*
  Earlier sketches in SATA 4, 34, 73, 120
  *See also* CLR 18
  *See also* SAAS *1*
Fisher, Lois I. 1948- .......................... 38
  Brief entry ................................. 35
Fisher, Margery (Turner) 1913-1992 .......... 20
  Obituary .................................... 74
Fisher, Marshall Jon 1963- ................... *113*
Fisher, Nikki
  *See* Strachan, Ian
Fisher, Robert (Tempest) 1943- ............... 47
Fisher, Suzanne
  *See* Staples, Suzanne Fisher
Fisher, Valorie ............................... *177*
Fishman, Cathy Goldberg 1951- ............... *106*

Fisk, Nicholas ............................... *25*
  *See* Higginbottom, David
Fisk, Pauline 1948- .......................... *160*
  Earlier sketch in SATA 66
Fiske, Tarleton
  *See* Bloch, Robert (Albert)
Fisscher, Catharina G. M. 1958- ............. *142*
Fisscher, Tiny
  *See* Fisscher, Catharina G. M.
Fitch, Clarke
  *See* Sinclair, Upton
Fitch, John IV
  *See* Cormier, Robert
Fitch, Sheree 1956- ......................... *108*
Fitschen, Dale 1937- .......................... 20
Fitzalan, Roger
  *See* Trevor, Elleston
Fitzgerald, Captain Hugh
  *See* Baum, L(yman) Frank
Fitzgerald, Dawn ............................. *175*
Fitzgerald, Edward Earl 1919-2001 ........... 20
Fitzgerald, F(rancis) A(nthony) 1940- ........ *15*
Fitzgerald, John D(ennis) 1907(?)-1988 ....... 20
  Obituary .................................... 56
  *See also* CLR *1*
Fitzgerald, Merni Ingrassia 1955- ............ 53
Fitzgibbon, Terry 1948- ...................... *121*
Fitzhardinge, Joan Margaret 1912- ............ *73*
  Earlier sketch in SATA 2
  *See* Phipson, Joan
Fitzhugh, Louise (Perkins) 1928-1974 ........ 45
  Obituary .................................... 24
  Earlier sketch in SATA *1*
  *See also* CLR 72
Fitzhugh, Percy Keese 1876-1950 ............. 65
Fitzpatrick, Marie-Louise 1962- ............. *125*
FitzRalph, Matthew
  *See* McInerny, Ralph
Fitz-Randolph, Jane (Currens) 1915- ......... 51
Fitzsimons, Cecilia 1952- ..................... 97
Fitzsimons, Cecilia A.L.
  *See* Fitzsimons, Cecilia
Flack, Marjorie 1897-1958 ................... *100*
  *See also* YABC 2
  *See also* CLR 28
Flack, Naomi John White -1999 ............... 40
  Brief entry ................................. 35
Flake, Sharon G. ............................. *166*
Flannery, Kate
  *See* De Goldi, Kathleen Domenica
Flatt, Lizann
  *See* Brunskill, Elizabeth Ann Flatt
Fleagle, Gail S(hatto) 1940- ................. *117*
Fleetwood, Jenni 1947- ........................ 80
Fleischer, Jane
  *See* Oppenheim, Joanne
Fleischhauer-Hardt, Helga 1936- .............. 30
Fleischman, Albert Sidney
  *See* Fleischman, Sid
Fleischman, John 1948- ...................... *145*
Fleischman, Paul 1952- ...................... *156*
  Brief entry ................................. 32
  Earlier sketches in SATA 39, 72, 110
  *See also* CLR 66
  *See also* SAAS 20
Fleischman, Sid 1920- ....................... *148*
  Earlier sketches in SATA 8, 59, 96
  *See also* CLR 15
Fleischner, Jennifer 1956- .................... 93
Fleisher, Paul 1948- ......................... *132*
  Earlier sketch in SATA 81
Fleisher, Robbin 1951-1977 ................... 52
  Brief entry ................................. 49
Fleishman, Seymour 1918- ..................... 66
  Brief entry ................................. 32
Fleming, A. A.
  *See* Arthur, Robert, (Jr.)
Fleming, Alice Mulcahey 1928- ................. 9
Fleming, Candace 1962- ...................... *143*
  Earlier sketch in SATA 94

Fleming, Denise 1950- ............ *173*
  Earlier sketches in SATA *81, 126*
Fleming, Ian 1908-1964 ............ *9*
Fleming, Ian Lancaster
  *See* Fleming, Ian
Fleming, Ronald Lee 1941- ............ *56*
Fleming, Sally
  *See* Walker, Sally M(acArt)
Fleming, Stuart
  *See* Knight, Damon (Francis)
Fleming, Susan 1932- ............ *32*
Fleming, Thomas 1927- ............ *8*
Fleming, Thomas James
  *See* Fleming, Thomas
Fleming, Virginia (Edwards) 1923- ............ *84*
Flesch, Y.
  *See* Flesch, Yolande (Catarina)
Flesch, Yolande (Catarina) 1950- ............ *55*
Fletcher, Charlie May Hogue 1897-1977 ...... *3*
Fletcher, Colin 1922- ............ *28*
Fletcher, Dirk
  *See* Cunningham, Chet
Fletcher, George U.
  *See* Pratt, (Murray) Fletcher
Fletcher, Helen Jill 1910- ............ *13*
Fletcher, Ralph (J.) 1953- ............ *149*
  Earlier sketch in SATA *105*
  *See also* CLR *104*
Fletcher, Susan (Clemens) 1951- ............ *110*
  Earlier sketch in SATA *70*
Fleur, Paul
  *See* Pohl, Frederik
Flexner, James Thomas 1908-2003 ............ *9*
Flinn, Alex 1966- ............ *159*
Flint, Helen 1952- ............ *102*
Flint, Russ 1944- ............ *74*
Flitner, David P(erkins), Jr. 1949- ............ *7*
Floca, Brian ............ *155*
Floethe, Louise Lee 1913-1988 ............ *4*
Floethe, Richard 1901-1998 ............ *4*
Floherty, John Joseph 1882-1964 ............ *25*
Flood, Bo
  *See* Flood, Nancy Bo
Flood, Nancy Bo 1945- ............ *130*
Flood, Pansie Hart 1964- ............ *140*
Flood, William 1942- ............ *129*
Flooglebuckle, Al
  *See* Spiegelman, Art
Flora, James (Royer) 1914-1998 ............ *30*
  Obituary ............ *103*
  Earlier sketch in SATA *1*
  *See also* SAAS *6*
Florian, Douglas 1950- ............ *177*
  Earlier sketches in SATA *19, 83, 125*
Flory, Jane Trescott 1917- ............ *22*
Flournoy, Valerie 1952- ............ *95*
Flournoy, Valerie Rose
  *See* Flournoy, Valerie
Flowerdew, Phyllis -1994 ............ *33*
Flowers, Pam 1946- ............ *136*
Flowers, Sarah 1952- ............ *98*
Floyd, Gareth 1940- ............ *62*
  Brief entry ............ *31*
Fluchere, Henri 1914-1991 ............ *40*
Fluke, Joanne ............ *88*
Flutsztejn-Gruda, Ilona 1930- ............ *170*
Flynn, Barbara 1928- ............ *9*
Flynn, Jackson
  *See* Bensen, Donald R.
  and Shirreffs, Gordon D(onald)
Flynn, Nicholas
  *See* Odgers, Sally Farrell
Flynn, Rachel 1953- ............ *171*
  Earlier sketch in SATA *109*
Flynn, Warren (G.) 1950- ............ *154*
Fodor, R(onald) V(ictor) 1944- ............ *25*
Fogelin, Adrian 1951- ............ *175*
  Earlier sketch in SATA *129*
Foley, (Anna) Bernice Williams 1902-1987
  ............ *28*
Foley, June 1944- ............ *44*

Foley, (Mary) Louise Munro 1933- .......... *106*
  Brief entry ............ *40*
  Earlier sketch in SATA *54*
Folke, Will
  *See* Bloch, Robert (Albert)
Folsom, Franklin (Brewster) 1907-1995 ....... *5*
  Obituary ............ *88*
Folsom, Michael (Brewster) 1938-1990 ...... *40*
  Obituary ............ *88*
Fontenot, Mary Alice 1910- ............ *91*
  Earlier sketch in SATA *34*
Fontes, Justine ............ *172*
Foon, Dennis 1951- ............ *119*
Fooner, Michael ............ *22*
Foote, Timothy (Gilson) 1926- ............ *52*
Forberg, Ati ............ *22*
  *See* Forberg, Beate Gropius
Forbes, Anna 1954- ............ *101*
Forbes, Bryan 1926- ............ *37*
Forbes, Cabot L.
  *See* Hoyt, Edwin P(almer), Jr.
Forbes, Esther 1891-1967 ............ *100*
  Earlier sketch in SATA *2*
  *See also* CLR *27*
Forbes, Graham B. ............ *1*
Forbes, Kathryn
  *See* McLean, Kathryn (Anderson)
Forbes, Robert
  *See* Arthur, Robert, (Jr.)
Ford, Albert Lee
  *See* Stratemeyer, Edward L.
Ford, Barbara ............ *56*
  Brief entry ............ *34*
Ford, Brian J(ohn) 1939- ............ *49*
Ford, Carolyn (Mott) 1938- ............ *98*
Ford, Christine 1953- ............ *176*
Ford, Elbur
  *See* Hibbert, Eleanor Alice Burford
Ford, Ellen 1949- ............ *89*
Ford, George (Jr.) ............ *31*
Ford, Hilary
  *See* Youd, (Christopher) Samuel
Ford, Hildegarde
  *See* Morrison, Velma Ford
Ford, Jerome W. 1949- ............ *78*
Ford, Jerry
  *See* Ford, Jerome W.
Ford, Juwanda G(ertrude) 1967- ............ *102*
Ford, Marcia
  *See* Radford, Ruby L(orraine)
Ford, Peter 1936- ............ *59*
Ford, S. M.
  *See* Uhlig, Susan
Forde, Catherine 1961- ............ *170*
Foreman, Michael 1938- ............ *135*
  Earlier sketches in SATA *2, 73, 129*
  *See also* CLR *32*
  *See also* SAAS *21*
Foreman, Wilmoth 1939- ............ *153*
Forest, Dial
  *See* Gault, William Campbell
Forest, Heather 1948- ............ *120*
Forester, C(ecil) S(cott) 1899-1966 ............ *13*
Forman, Brenda 1936- ............ *4*
Forman, James
  *See* Forman, James D(ouglas)
Forman, James D(ouglas) 1932- ............ *70*
  Earlier sketch in SATA *8*
Forrest, Elizabeth
  *See* Salsitz, Rhondi Vilott
Forrest, Mary
  *See* Pausacker, Jenny
Forrest, Sybil
  *See* Markun, Patricia Maloney
Forrestal, Elaine 1941- ............ *165*
  Earlier sketch in SATA *117*
Forrester, Helen ............ *48*
  *See* Bhatia, Jamunadevi
Forrester, Jade
  *See* Pausacker, Jenny

Forrester, Marian
  *See* Schachtel, Roger
Forrester, Sandra 1949- ............ *166*
  Earlier sketch in SATA *90*
Forrester, Victoria 1940- ............ *40*
  Brief entry ............ *35*
Forsee, (Frances) Aylesa -1986 ............ *1*
Forsey, Chris 1950- ............ *59*
Forshay-Lunsford, Cin 1965- ............ *60*
Forster, E(dward) M(organ) 1879-1970 ...... *57*
Forsyth, Kate 1966- ............ *154*
Fort, Paul
  *See* Stockton, Francis Richard
Forte, Maurizio 1961- ............ *110*
Fortey, Richard (Alan) 1946- ............ *109*
Forth, Melissa D(eal) ............ *96*
Fortnum, Peggy ............ *26*
  *See* Nuttall-Smith, Margaret Emily Noel
Forward, Robert L(ull) 1932-2002 ............ *82*
Foster, Alan Dean 1946- ............ *70*
Foster, Brad W. 1955- ............ *34*
Foster, Doris Van Liew 1899-1993 ............ *10*
Foster, E(lizabeth) C(onnell) 1902- ............ *9*
Foster, Elizabeth 1902- ............ *12*
Foster, Elizabeth 1905-1963 ............ *10*
Foster, F. Blanche 1919- ............ *11*
Foster, G(eorge) Allen 1907-1969 ............ *26*
Foster, Genevieve (Stump) 1893-1979 .......... *2*
  Obituary ............ *23*
  *See also* CLR *7*
Foster, Hal
  *See* Foster, Harold (Rudolf)
Foster, Harold (Rudolf) 1892-1982 ............ *31*
  *See* Foster, Hal
Foster, Jeanne
  *See* Williams, Jeanne
Foster, John
  *See* Foster, John L(ouis)
  and Furcolo, Foster
Foster, John (Thomas) 1925- ............ *8*
Foster, John L(ouis) 1941- ............ *102*
Foster, Laura Louise (James) 1918- ............ *6*
Foster, Leila Merrell 1929- ............ *73*
Foster, Lynne 1937- ............ *74*
Foster, Marian Curtis 1909-1978 ............ *23*
Foster, Sally ............ *58*
Foulds, E. V.
  *See* Foulds, Elfrida Vipont
Foulds, Elfrida Vipont 1902-1992 ............ *52*
  *See* Vipont, Elfrida
Fourie, Corlia 1944- ............ *91*
Fourth Brother, The
  *See* Aung, (Maung) Htin
Fowke, Edith (Margaret) 1913-1996 ............ *14*
Fowles, John 1926-2005 ............ *22*
  Obituary ............ *171*
Fowles, John Robert
  *See* Fowles, John
Fox, Aileen 1907-2005 ............ *58*
  Obituary ............ *170*
Fox, Aileen Mary
  *See* Fox, Aileen
Fox, Annie 1950- ............ *175*
Fox, Charles Philip 1913-2003 ............ *12*
  Obituary ............ *150*
Fox, Eleanor
  *See* St. John, Wylly Folk
Fox, Freeman
  *See* Hamilton, Charles (Harold St. John)
Fox, Geoffrey 1941- ............ *73*
Fox, Grace
  *See* Anderson, Grace Fox
Fox, Larry ............ *30*
Fox, Lorraine 1922-1976 ............ *27*
  Earlier sketch in SATA *11*
Fox, Louisa
  *See* Kroll, Virginia L.
Fox, Mary Virginia 1919- ............ *152*
  Brief entry ............ *39*
  Earlier sketches in SATA *44, 88*

Fox, Mem .................................................... 103
  See also CLR 23
  See Fox, Merrion Frances
Fox, Merrion Frances 1946- ....................... 155
  Earlier sketch in SATA 51
  See also CLR 80
  See Fox, Mem
Fox, Michael W(ilson) 1937- ....................... 15
Fox, Paula 1923- ........................................ 167
  Earlier sketches in SATA 17, 60, 120
  See also CLR 96
Fox, Robert J. 1927- ................................... 33
Fradin, Dennis
  See Fradin, Dennis Brindell
Fradin, Dennis Brindell 1945- .................... 135
  Earlier sketches in SATA 29, 90
Fradin, Judith (Bernette) Bloom 1945- ..... 152
  Earlier sketch in SATA 90
Frailey, Paige (Menefee) 1965- .................. 82
Frame, Janet
  See Clutha, Janet Paterson Frame
Frame, Paul 1913-1994 ................................ 60
  Brief entry ................................................ 33
  Obituary ................................................... 83
Frances, Miss
  See Horwich, Frances R(appaport)
Franchere, Ruth .......................................... 18
Francis, Charles
  See Holme, Bryan
Francis, Dee
  See Haas, Dorothy F.
Francis, Dorothy Brenner 1926- ................. 127
  Earlier sketch in SATA 10
Francis, Jaye
  See Pausacker, Jenny
Francis, Pamela (Mary) 1926- ..................... 11
Franck, Eddie
  See Cooke, Frank E.
Franco, Betsy ........................................... 150
Franco, Eloise (Bauder) 1910- .................... 62
Franco, Johan (Henri Gustave) 1908-1988 . 62
Franco, Marjorie ........................................ 38
Francois, Andre 1915-2005 ........................ 25
Francoise
  See Seignobosc, Francoise
Frank, Anne(lies Marie) 1929-1945 ............ 87
  Brief entry ................................................ 42
  See also CLR 101
Frank, Daniel B. 1956- ................................ 55
Frank, Emily R.
  See Frank, E.R.
Frank, E.R. 1967- ...................................... 157
Frank, Helene
  See Vautier, Ghislaine
Frank, Hillary 1976- ................................. 148
Frank, Josette 1893-1989 ........................... 10
  Obituary ................................................... 63
Frank, Lucy 1947- ..................................... 166
  Earlier sketch in SATA 94
Frank, Mary 1933- ...................................... 34
Frank, R., Jr.
  See Ross, Frank (Xavier), Jr.
Frankau, Mary Evelyn Atkinson 1899-1974 . 4
Frankel, Alona 1937- .................................. 66
Frankel, Bernice ........................................... 9
Frankel, Edward 1910- ................................ 44
Frankel, Ellen 1951- ................................... 78
Frankel, Julie 1947- .................................... 40
  Brief entry ................................................ 34
Frankenberg, Robert 1911- ......................... 22
Franklin, Cheryl J. 1955- ............................ 70
Franklin, Harold 1926- ................................ 13
Franklin, Kristine L. 1958- ........................ 124
  Earlier sketch in SATA 80
Franklin, Lance
  See Lantz, Francess L(in)
Franklin, Max
  See Deming, Richard
Franklin, Steve
  See Stevens, Franklin
Franson, Leanne R. 1963- .......................... 111

Franzen, Nils-Olof 1916- ............................ 10
Frascino, Edward ....................................... 48
  Brief entry ................................................ 33
  See also SAAS 9
Frasconi, Antonio 1919- ............................ 131
  Earlier sketches in SATA 6, 53
  See also SAAS 11
Fraser, Betty
  See Fraser, Elizabeth Marr
Fraser, Elizabeth Marr 1928- ...................... 31
Fraser, Eric (George) 1902-1983 ................. 38
Fraser, Mary Ann 1959- ............................ 137
  Earlier sketch in SATA 76
  See also SAAS 23
Fraser, Wynnette (McFaddin) 1925- ............ 90
Frasier, Debra 1953- .................................. 112
  Earlier sketch in SATA 69
Fraustino, Lisa Rowe 1961- ....................... 146
  Autobiography Feature ............................ 146
  Earlier sketch in SATA 84
Frazee, Marla 1958- ................................... 151
  Earlier sketch in SATA 105
Frazetta, Frank 1928- .................................. 58
Frazier, Craig 1955- .................................. 177
Frazier, Neta (Osborn) Lohnes 1890-1990 .... 7
Frederic, Mike
  See Cox, William R(obert)
Fredericks, Anthony D. 1947- .................... 113
Freed, Alvyn M. 1913-1993 ......................... 22
Freedman, Benedict 1919- ........................... 27
Freedman, Jeff 1953- .................................. 90
Freedman, Nancy 1920- ............................... 27
Freedman, Russell 1929- ........................... 175
  Earlier sketches in SATA 16, 71, 123
  See also CLR 71
Freedman, Russell Bruce
  See Freedman, Russell
Freeman, Barbara C(onstance) 1906- .......... 28
Freeman, Bill
  See Freeman, William Bradford
Freeman, Don 1908-1978 ............................. 17
  See also CLR 90
Freeman, Ira Maximilian 1905-1987 ............ 21
Freeman, Lucy (Greenbaum) 1916-2004 .... 24
Freeman, Mae (Blacker) 1907- ................... 25
Freeman, Marcia S. 1937- .......................... 102
Freeman, Martha 1956- .............................. 152
  Earlier sketch in SATA 101
Freeman, Nancy 1932- ................................ 61
Freeman, Peter J.
  See Calvert, Patricia
Freeman, Sarah (Caroline) 1940- ................ 66
Freeman, Tor 1977- ................................... 164
Freeman, VicToria
  See Freeman, Tor
Freeman, William Bradford 1938- ............... 58
  Brief entry ................................................ 48
Fregosi, Claudia (Anne Marie) 1946- ......... 24
French, Allen 1870-1946
  See YABC 1
French, Dorothy Kayser 1926- ...................... 5
French, Fiona 1944- .................................. 132
  Earlier sketches in SATA 6, 75
  See also CLR 37
  See also SAAS 21
French, Jackie ........................................... 139
  Autobiography Feature ............................ 139
  Earlier sketch in SATA 108
  See French, Jacqueline Anne
French, Kathryn
  See Mosesson, Gloria R(ubin)
French, Martin .......................................... 176
French, Michael 1944- ................................ 49
  Brief entry ................................................ 38
French, Paul
  See Asimov, Isaac
French, Simon 1957- ................................. 147
  Earlier sketch in SATA 86
French, Vivian .......................................... 165
Frenette, Liza .......................................... 126

Freschet, Gina 1960- ................................. 175
  Earlier sketch in SATA 139
Frewer, Glyn (M.) 1931- ............................. 11
Frey, Darcy ................................................ 98
Freymann-Weyr, (Rhoda) Garret (Michaela)
  1965- .................................................... 145
Frick, C. H.
  See Irwin, Constance (H.) Frick
Frick, Constance
  See Irwin, Constance (H.) Frick
Fricke, Aaron 1962- ................................... 89
Fridell, Ron 1943- .................................... 124
Friedlander, Joanne K(ohn) 1930- ................ 9
Friedman, Debra 1955- .............................. 150
Friedman, Estelle (Ehrenwald) 1920- ............ 7
Friedman, Frieda 1905- .............................. 43
Friedman, Ina R(osen) 1926- ..................... 136
  Brief entry ................................................ 41
  Earlier sketch in SATA 49
Friedman, Jerrold David
  See Gerrold, David
Friedman, Judi 1935- .................................. 59
Friedman, Laurie 1964- ............................. 138
Friedman, Marvin 1930- .............................. 42
  Brief entry ................................................ 33
Friedman, Robin 1968- .............................. 162
Friedmann, Stan 1953- ................................ 80
Friedrich, Otto (Alva) 1929-1995 ................ 33
Friedrich, Priscilla 1927- ............................ 39
Friendlich, Dick
  See Friendlich, Richard J.
Friendlich, Richard J. 1909- ........................ 11
Friermood, Elisabeth Hamilton 1903-1992 ... 5
Friesen, Bernice (Sarah Anne) 1966- ........ 105
Friesen, Gayle 1960- ................................. 109
Friesner, Esther M. 1951- .......................... 168
  Earlier sketch in SATA 71
Friis-Baastad, Babbis Ellinor 1921-1970 ...... 7
Frimmer, Steven 1928- ................................ 31
Frischmuth, Barbara 1941- ........................ 114
Friskey, Margaret (Richards) 1901-1995 ....... 5
Fritts, Mary Bahr
  See Bahr, Mary (Madelyn)
Fritz, Jean (Guttery) 1915- ........................ 163
  Autobiography Feature ............................ 122
  Earlier sketches in SATA 1, 29, 72, 119
  See also CLR 96
  See also SAAS 2
Froehlich, Margaret W(alden) 1930- ............ 56
Frois, Jeanne 1953- .................................... 73
Froissart, Jean 1338(?)-1410(?) .................. 28
Froman, Elizabeth Hull 1920-1975 .............. 10
Froman, Robert (Winslow) 1917- .................. 8
Fromm, Lilo 1928- ...................................... 29
Frommer, Harvey 1937- ............................... 41
Frost, A(rthur) B(urdett) 1851-1928 ............ 19
Frost, Erica
  See Supraner, Robyn
Frost, Helen 1949- ..................................... 157
Frost, Lesley 1899-1983 .............................. 14
  Obituary ................................................... 34
Frost, Robert 1874-1963 ............................. 14
  See also CLR 67
Frost, Robert Lee
  See Frost, Robert
Frost, Shelley 1960- ................................... 138
Froud, Brian 1947- ................................... 150
Fry, Annette R(iley) .................................... 89
Fry, Christopher 1907-2005 ......................... 66
Fry, Edward Bernard 1925- .......................... 35
Fry, Rosalie Kingsmill 1911-1992 .................. 3
  See also SAAS 11
Fry, Virginia Lynn 1952- ............................. 95
Frye, Sally
  See Moore, Elaine
Fuchs, Bernie 1932- .................................. 162
  Earlier sketch in SATA 95
Fuchs, Erich 1916- ....................................... 6
Fuchshuber, Annegert 1940- ........................ 43
Fuerst, Jeffrey B. 1956- ............................ 143
Fuertes, Gloria 1918-1998 ......................... 115

Fuge, Charles 1966- .............................................. 144
  Earlier sketch in SATA 74
Fujikawa, Gyo 1908-1998 ......................... 76
  Brief entry ...................................................... 30
  Obituary ...................................................... 110
  Earlier sketch in SATA 39
  See also CLR 25
  See also SAAS 16
Fujita, Tamao 1905-1999 ............................. 7
Fujiwara, Kim 1957- ..................................... 81
Fujiwara, Michiko 1946- ............................. 15
Fuller, Catherine Leuthold 1916- ............... 9
Fuller, Edmund (Maybank) 1914- ............. 21
Fuller, Iola
  See McCoy, Iola Fuller
Fuller, John G(rant, Jr.) 1913-1990 ............ 65
Fuller, Kathleen
  See Gottfried, Theodore Mark
Fuller, Lois Hamilton 1915- ....................... 11
Fuller, Margaret
  See Ossoli, Sarah Margaret (Fuller)
Fuller, Maud
  See Petersham, Maud (Sylvia Fuller)
Fuller, Roy (Broadbent) 1912-1991 ........... 87
Fuller, Sarah Margaret
  See Ossoli, Sarah Margaret (Fuller)
Fuller, Sarah Margaret
  See Ossoli, Sarah Margaret (Fuller)
Fults, John Lee 1932- ................................... 33
Funk, Thompson 1911- .................................. 7
Funk, Tom
  See Funk, Thompson
Funke, Cornelia 1958- ................................. 174
  Earlier sketch in SATA 154
Funke, Cornelia Caroline
  See Funke, Cornelia
Funke, Lewis 1912-1992 ............................. 11
Fuqua, Jonathon Scott 1966- ..................... 141
Furbee, Mary R.
  See Furbee, Mary Rodd
Furbee, Mary Rodd 1954- ......................... 138
Furchgott, Terry 1948- ................................ 29
Furlong, Monica (Mavis) 1930-2003 ......... 86
  Obituary ...................................................... 142
Furman, Gertrude Lerner Kerman 1909- .... 21
Furniss, Tim 1948- ....................................... 49
Furrow, Robert 1985- ................................. 172
Furukawa, Toshi 1924- ................................. 24
Fusillo, Archimede 1962- ......................... 137
Futcher, Jane P. 1947- ................................. 76
Fyleman, Rose (Amy) 1877-1957 .............. 21
Fyson, J(enny) G(race) 1904- ..................... 42

## G

Gaan, Margaret 1914- ................................. 65
Gaber, Susan 1956- ................................... 169
  Earlier sketch in SATA 115
Gaberman, Judie Angell 1937- ................... 78
  Earlier sketch in SATA 22
  See also CLR 33
Gabhart, Ann 1947- ..................................... 75
Gabler, Mirko 1951- ................................... 77
Gabriel, Adriana
  See Rojany, Lisa
Gabrys, Ingrid Schubert
  See Schubert-Gabrys, Ingrid
Gackenbach, Dick 1927- ............................. 79
  Brief entry ...................................................... 30
  Earlier sketch in SATA 48
Gadd, Jeremy 1949- ................................... 116
Gaddis, Vincent H. 1913-1997 ................... 35
Gadler, Steve J. 1905-1985 ......................... 36
Gaeddert, Lou Ann (Bigge) 1931- ............. 103
  Earlier sketch in SATA 20
Gaeddert, Louann
  See Gaeddert, Lou Ann (Bigge)
Gaer, Joseph 1897-1969 ............................. 118

Gaer, Yossef
  See Gaer, Joseph
Gaetz, Dayle Campbell 1947- ................... 138
Gaffney, Timothy R. 1951- ....................... 170
  Earlier sketch in SATA 69
Gaffron, Norma (Bondeson) 1931- ............. 97
Gag, Wanda (Hazel) 1893-1946 ............... 100
  See also YABC 1
  See also CLR 4
Gage, Brian ................................................. 162
Gage, Wilson
  See Steele, Mary Q(uintard Govan)
Gagliano, Eugene M. 1946- ....................... 150
Gagnon, Cecile 1936- ................................. 58
Gaiman, Neil 1960- ................................... 146
  Earlier sketch in SATA 85
  See also CLR 109
Gaiman, Neil Richard
  See Gaiman, Neil
Gainer, Cindy 1962- ..................................... 74
Gaines, Ernest J. 1933- ............................... 86
  See also CLR 62
Gaines, Ernest James
  See Gaines, Ernest J.
Gaither, Gloria 1942- ................................. 127
Gal, Laszlo 1933- ......................................... 96
  Brief entry ...................................................... 32
  Earlier sketch in SATA 52
  See also CLR 61
Galbraith, Kathryn O(sebold) 1945- ........... 85
Galdone, Paul 1907(?)-1986 ....................... 66
  Obituary ...................................................... 49
  Earlier sketch in SATA 17
  See also CLR 16
Galinsky, Ellen 1942- ................................. 23
Gall, Chris 1961- ....................................... 176
Gallagher, Diana G. 1946- ......................... 153
Gallagher, Lurlene Nora
  See McDaniel, Lurlene
Gallant, Roy A(rthur) 1924- ....................... 110
  Earlier sketches in SATA 4, 68
  See also CLR 30
Gallardo, Evelyn 1948- ............................... 78
Gallaz, Christophe 1948- ........................... 162
Gallego Garcia, Laura 1977- ..................... 173
Gallico, Paul (William) 1897-1976 ............. 13
Gallo, Donald R. 1938- ............................. 112
  Autobiography Feature ............................. 104
Gallo, Donald Robert
  See Gallo, Donald R.
Galloway, Owateka (S.) 1981- ................... 121
Galloway, Priscilla 1930- ........................... 112
  Earlier sketch in SATA 66
Gallup, Joan 1957- ..................................... 128
Galouchko, Annouchka Gravel 1960- ......... 95
Galt, Thomas Franklin, Jr. 1908-1989 ......... 5
Galt, Tom
  See Galt, Thomas Franklin, Jr.
Galvin, Matthew R. 1950- ........................... 93
Galvin, Matthew Reppert
  See Galvin, Matthew R.
Gamble, Kim 1952- ..................................... 124
  Earlier sketch in SATA 81
Gambrell, Jamey ........................................ 82
Gamerman, Martha 1941- ........................... 15
Gammell, Stephen 1943- ........................... 128
  Earlier sketches in SATA 53, 81
  See also CLR 83
Ganly, Helen (Mary) 1940- ......................... 56
Gannett, Ruth Chrisman (Arens) 1896-1979
  ...................................................................... 33
Gannett, Ruth Stiles 1923- ........................... 3
Gannon, Robert Haines 1931- ..................... 8
Gano, Lila 1949- ......................................... 76
Gans, Roma 1894-1996 ............................... 45
  Obituary ...................................................... 93
Gant, Matthew
  See Hano, Arnold
Gantner, Susan (Verble) 1939- ................... 63

Gantos, Jack 1951- ................................... 169
  Earlier sketches in SATA 20, 81, 119
  See also CLR 85
Gantos, John Bryan, Jr.
  See Gantos, Jack
Ganz, Yaffa 1938- ....................................... 61
  Brief entry ...................................................... 52
Garafano, Marie 1942- ................................. 84
Garant, Andre J. 1968- ............................. 123
Garbe, Ruth Moore
  See Moore, Ruth (Ellen)
Garcia, Yolanda P. 1952- ........................... 113
Garcia, Yolanda Pacheco
  See Garcia, Yolanda P.
Gard, Janice
  See Latham, Jean Lee
Gard, Joyce
  See Reeves, Joyce
Gard, Robert Edward 1910-1992 ................. 18
  Obituary ...................................................... 74
Gardam, Jane (Mary) 1928- ....................... 130
  Brief entry ...................................................... 28
  Earlier sketches in SATA 39, 76
  See also CLR 12
  See also SAAS 9
Gardella, Tricia 1944- ................................. 96
Garden, Nancy 1938- ................................. 147
  Autobiography Feature ............................. 147
  Earlier sketches in SATA 12, 77, 114
  See also CLR 51
  See also SAAS 8
Gardiner, John Reynolds 1944-2006 ........... 64
  Obituary ...................................................... 174
Gardiner, Lindsey 1971- ............................. 144
Gardner, Craig Shaw 1949- ......................... 99
Gardner, Dic
  See Gardner, Richard (M.)
Gardner, Graham ....................................... 159
Gardner, Jane Mylum 1946- ....................... 83
Gardner, Jeanne LeMonnier 1925- ............... 5
Gardner, John, Jr. 1933-1982 ..................... 40
  Obituary ...................................................... 31
Gardner, John Champlin, Jr.
  See Gardner, John, Jr.
Gardner, Martin 1914- ............................... 142
  Earlier sketch in SATA 16
Gardner, Miriam
  See Bradley, Marion Zimmer
Gardner, Richard (M.) 1931- ....................... 24
Gardner, Richard A(lan) 1931-2003 ........... 13
  Obituary ...................................................... 144
Gardner, Sally .............................................. 177
Gardner, Sandra 1940- ................................. 70
Gardner, Scot 1968- ................................... 143
Gardner, Sheldon 1934- ............................... 33
Gardner, Ted
  See Gardner, Theodore Roosevelt II
Gardner, Theodore Roosevelt II 1934- ........ 84
Garelick, May 1910-1989 ........................... 19
Garfield, James B. 1881-1984 ..................... 6
  Obituary ...................................................... 38
Garfield, Leon 1921-1996 ........................... 76
  Obituary ...................................................... 90
  Earlier sketches in SATA 1, 32
  See also CLR 21
Garis, Howard R(oger) 1873-1962 ............. 13
Garland, Mark 1953- ................................... 79
Garland, Mark A.
  See Garland, Mark
Garland, Michael 1952- ............................. 168
Garland, Sarah 1944- ................................. 135
  Earlier sketch in SATA 62
Garland, Sherry 1948- ............................... 145
  Autobiography Feature ............................. 145
  Earlier sketches in SATA 73, 114
Garner, Alan 1934- ....................................... 69
  Autobiography Feature ............................. 108
  Earlier sketch in SATA 18
  See also CLR 20
Garner, David 1958- ................................... 78
Garner, Eleanor Ramrath 1930- ............... 122

Garner, James Finn 1960(?)- .......... 92
Garnet, A. H.
 *See* Slote, Alfred
Garnett, Eve C. R. 1900-1991 .......... 3
 Obituary .......... 70
Garou, Louis P.
 *See* Bowkett, Stephen
Garraty, John A(rthur) 1920- .......... 23
Garren, Devorah-Leah
 *See* Devorah-Leah
Garret, Maxwell R. 1917- .......... 39
Garretson, Victoria Diane 1945- .......... 44
Garrett, Helen 1895- .......... 21
Garrett, Richard 1920- .......... 82
Garrigue, Sheila 1931- .......... 21
Garrison, Barbara 1931- .......... 163
 Earlier sketch in SATA 19
Garrison, Frederick
 *See* Sinclair, Upton
Garrison, Mary 1952- .......... 146
Garrison, Webb B(lack) 1919-2000 .......... 25
Garrity, Jennifer Johnson 1961- .......... 124
Garrity, Linda K. 1947- .......... 128
Garst, Doris Shannon 1894-1981 .......... 1
Garst, Shannon
 *See* Garst, Doris Shannon
Garth, Will
 *See* Hamilton, Edmond
 and Kuttner, Henry
Garthwaite, Marion H(ook) 1893-1981 .......... 7
Garvie, Maureen 1944- .......... 175
Garvie, Maureen McCallum
 *See* Garvie, Maureen
Gascoigne, Bamber 1935- .......... 62
Gaskins, Pearl Fuyo 1957- .......... 134
Gasperini, Jim 1952- .......... 54
 Brief entry .......... 49
Gater, Dilys 1944- .......... 41
Gates, Doris 1901-1987 .......... 34
 Obituary .......... 54
 Earlier sketch in SATA 1
 *See also* SAAS 1
Gates, Frieda 1933- .......... 26
Gates, Susan 1950- .......... 153
Gates, Viola R. 1931- .......... 101
Gathorne-Hardy, Jonathan G. 1933- .......... 124
 Earlier sketch in SATA 26
Gatti, Anne 1952- .......... 103
Gatty, Juliana Horatia
 *See* Ewing, Juliana (Horatia Gatty)
Gauch, Patricia Lee 1934- .......... 80
 Earlier sketch in SATA 26
 *See also* CLR 56
 *See also* SAAS 21
Gaul, Randy 1959- .......... 63
Gault, Clare 1925- .......... 36
Gault, Frank 1926-1982 .......... 36
 Brief entry .......... 30
Gault, William Campbell 1910-1995 .......... 8
Gauthier, Gail 1953- .......... 160
 Earlier sketch in SATA 118
Gaver, Becky
 *See* Gaver, Rebecca
Gaver, Rebecca 1952- .......... 20
Gavin, Jamila 1941- .......... 125
 Earlier sketch in SATA 96
Gay, Amelia
 *See* Hogarth, Grace (Weston Allen)
Gay, Kathlyn 1930- .......... 144
 Earlier sketch in SATA 9
Gay, Marie-Louise 1952- .......... 126
 Earlier sketch in SATA 68
 *See also* CLR 27
 *See also* SAAS 21
Gay, Michel 1947- .......... 162
Gay, Zhenya 1906-1978 .......... 19
Gaze, Gillian
 *See* Barklem, Jill
Gear, Kathleen M. O'Neal
 *See* Gear, Kathleen O'Neal

Gear, Kathleen O'Neal 1954- .......... 166
 Earlier sketch in SATA 71
Gear, W. Michael 1955- .......... 166
 Earlier sketch in SATA 71
Geary, Rick 1946- .......... 142
Geason, Susan 1946- .......... 122
Gedalof, Robin
 *See* McGrath, Robin
Gedge, Pauline (Alice) 1945- .......... 101
Gee, Maurice 1931- .......... 101
 Earlier sketch in SATA 46
 *See also* CLR 56
Gee, Maurice Gough
 *See* Gee, Maurice
Geehan, Wayne (E.) 1947- .......... 107
Geer, Charles 1922- .......... 42
 Brief entry .......... 32
Geeslin, Campbell 1925- .......... 163
 Earlier sketch in SATA 107
Gehman, Mary W. 1923- .......... 86
Gehr, Mary 1910(?)-1997 .......... 32
 Obituary .......... 99
Geipel, Eileen 1932- .......... 30
Geis, Darlene Stern 1918(?)-1999 .......... 7
 Obituary .......... 111
Geisel, Helen 1898-1967 .......... 26
Geisel, Theodor Seuss 1904-1991 .......... 100
 Obituary .......... 67
 Earlier sketches in SATA 1, 28, 75
 *See also* CLR 100
 *See* Dr. Seuss
Geisert, Arthur 1941- .......... 171
 Brief entry .......... 52
 Earlier sketches in SATA 56, 92, 133
 *See also* CLR 87
 *See also* SAAS 23
Geisert, Arthur Frederick
 *See* Geisert, Arthur
Geisert, Bonnie 1942- .......... 165
 Earlier sketch in SATA 92
Geldart, William 1936- .......... 15
Gelinas, Paul J. 1904-1996 .......... 10
Gellis, Roberta 1927- .......... 128
Gellis, Roberta Leah Jacobs
 *See* Gellis, Roberta
Gellman, Marc .......... 112
Gelman, Amy 1961- .......... 72
Gelman, Jan 1963- .......... 58
Gelman, Rita Golden 1937- .......... 131
 Brief entry .......... 51
 Earlier sketch in SATA 84
Gelman, Steve 1934- .......... 3
Gemming, Elizabeth 1932- .......... 11
Gennaro, Joseph F(rancis), Jr. 1924- .......... 53
Gentile, Petrina 1969- .......... 91
Gentle, Mary 1956- .......... 48
Gentleman, David (William) 1930- .......... 7
Geoghegan, Adrienne 1962- .......... 143
George, Barbara
 *See* Katz, Bobbi
George, Emily
 *See* Katz, Bobbi
George, Gail
 *See* Katz, Bobbi
George, Jean
 *See* George, Jean Craighead
George, Jean Craighead 1919- .......... 170
 Earlier sketches in SATA 2, 68, 124
 *See also* CLR 1, 80
George, John L(othar) 1916- .......... 2
George, Kristine O'Connell 1954- .......... 156
 Earlier sketch in SATA 110
George, Lindsay Barrett 1952- .......... 155
 Earlier sketch in SATA 95
George, S(idney) C(harles) 1898- .......... 11
George, Sally
 *See* Orr, Wendy
George, Twig C. 1950- .......... 114
Georgiou, Constantine 1927- .......... 7
Georgiou, Theo
 *See* Odgers, Sally Farrell

Geraghty, Paul 1959- .......... 130
Gerard, Jean Ignace Isidore 1803-1847 .......... 45
Geras, Adele 1944- .......... 173
 Earlier sketches in SATA 23, 87, 129
 *See also* SAAS 21
 *See* Geras, Adele Daphne Weston
Geras, Adele Daphne Weston 1944-
 *See* Geras, Adele
Gerber, Merrill Joan 1938- .......... 170
 Autobiography Feature .......... 170
 Earlier sketches in SATA 64, 127
Gerber, Perren 1933- .......... 104
Gerberg, Mort 1931- .......... 64
Gergely, Tibor 1900-1978 .......... 54
 Obituary .......... 20
Geringer, Laura 1948- .......... 164
 Earlier sketches in SATA 29, 94
Gerler, William R(obert) 1917-1996 .......... 47
Gerrard, Jean 1933- .......... 51
Gerrard, Roy 1935-1997 .......... 90
 Brief entry .......... 45
 Obituary .......... 99
 Earlier sketch in SATA 47
 *See also* CLR 23
Gerritsen, Paula 1956- .......... 177
Gerrold, David 1944- .......... 144
 Earlier sketch in SATA 66
Gershator, Phillis 1942- .......... 158
 Earlier sketch in SATA 90
Gerson, Corinne 1927- .......... 37
Gerson, Mary-Joan .......... 136
 Earlier sketch in SATA 79
Gerson, Noel Bertram 1914-1988 .......... 22
 Obituary .......... 60
Gerstein, Mordicai 1935- .......... 142
 Brief entry .......... 36
 Earlier sketches in SATA 47, 81
 *See also* CLR 102
Gertridge, Allison 1967- .......... 132
Gervais, Bernadette 1959- .......... 80
Gesner, Clark 1938-2002 .......... 40
 Obituary .......... 143
Gessner, Lynne 1919- .......... 16
Geter, Tyrone .......... 150
Getz, David 1957- .......... 91
Getzinger, Donna 1968- .......... 128
Gevirtz, Eliezer 1950- .......... 49
Gewe, Raddory
 *See* Gorey, Edward (St. John)
Ghan, Linda (R.) 1947- .......... 77
Ghent, Natale 1962- .......... 148
Gherman, Beverly 1934- .......... 123
 Earlier sketch in SATA 68
Ghigna, Charles 1946- .......... 153
 Earlier sketch in SATA 108
Giacobbe, Beppe 1953- .......... 174
Giambastiani, Kurt R. A. 1958- .......... 141
Giannini, Enzo 1946- .......... 68
Gibbons, Alan 1953- .......... 124
Gibbons, Faye 1938- .......... 103
 Earlier sketch in SATA 65
Gibbons, Gail (Gretchen) 1944- .......... 160
 Earlier sketches in SATA 23, 72, 104
 *See also* CLR 8
 *See also* SAAS 12
Gibbons, Kaye 1960- .......... 117
Gibbs, Adrea 1960- .......... 126
Gibbs, Alonzo (Lawrence) 1915-1992 .......... 5
Gibbs, Tony
 *See* Gibbs, Wolcott, Jr.
Gibbs, Wolcott, Jr. 1935- .......... 40
Giblin, James Cross 1933- .......... 122
 Earlier sketches in SATA 33, 75
 *See also* CLR 29
 *See also* SAAS 12
Gibson, Andrew (William) 1949- .......... 72
Gibson, Betty 1911- .......... 75
Gibson, Jo
 *See* Fluke, Joanne
Gibson, William 1914- .......... 66

Gibson, William Ford
  *See* Gibson, William
Gidal, Nachum
  *See* Gidal, Tim Nachum
Gidal, Sonia (Epstein) 1922- ..................... 2
Gidal, Tim Nachum 1909-1996 ................... 2
Gidalewitsch, Nachum
  *See* Gidal, Tim Nachum
Gideon, Melanie 1963- ............................. 175
Giegling, John A(llan) 1935- ..................... 17
Gifaldi, David 1950- .................................. 76
Giff, Patricia Reilly 1935- ....................... 160
  Earlier sketches in SATA 33, 70, 121
Giffard, Hannah 1962- ............................. 83
Gifford, Griselda 1931- ........................... 171
  Earlier sketch in SATA 42
Gifford, Kerri 1961- ................................. 91
Gilbert, Ann
  *See* Taylor, Ann
Gilbert, Anne Yvonne 1951- .................... 128
Gilbert, Barbara Snow 1954- .................... 97
Gilbert, Frances
  *See* Collings, Gillian
Gilbert, Harriett 1948- ............................. 30
Gilbert, (Agnes) Joan (Sewell) 1931- ......... 10
Gilbert, John (Raphael) 1926- ................... 36
Gilbert, Nan
  *See* Gilbertson, Mildred Geiger
Gilbert, Roby Goodale 1966- .................... 90
Gilbert, Ruth Gallard Ainsworth
  *See* Ainsworth, Ruth (Gallard)
Gilbert, Sara (Dulaney) 1943- ................... 82
  Earlier sketch in SATA 11
Gilbert, Sheri L. ...................................... 157
Gilbert, Suzie 1956- ................................. 97
Gilbert, W(illiam) S(chwenck) 1836-1911 .. 36
Gilbert, Yvonne
  *See* Gilbert, Anne Yvonne
Gilbertson, Mildred Geiger 1908-1988 ........ 2
Gilbreath, Alice 1921- .............................. 12
Gilbreth, Frank B(unker), Jr. 1911-2001 ...... 2
Gilchrist, Jan Spivey 1949- ..................... 130
  Earlier sketch in SATA 72
Gilden, Mel 1947- .................................... 97
Giles, Gail ...................................... 152
Gilfond, Henry ......................................... 2
Gilge, Jeanette 1924- ............................... 22
Gili, Phillida 1944- .................................. 70
Gill, Derek (Lewis Theodore) 1919-1997 ..... 9
Gill, Margery Jean 1925- .......................... 22
Gill, Shelley .......................................... 176
Gill, Stephen 1932- .................................. 63
Gillespie, Carol Ann 1951- ...................... 158
Gillett, Mary (Bledsoe) .............................. 7
Gillette, Henry Sampson 1915- .................. 14
Gillette, J(an) Lynett 1946- ..................... 103
Gilley, Jeremy 1969- ............................... 174
Gillham, Bill
  *See* Gillham, W(illiam) E(dwin) C(harles)
Gillham, W(illiam) E(dwin) C(harles) 1936-
  ................................................................ 42
Gilliam, Stan 1946- .................................. 39
  Brief entry ............................................. 35
Gillian 1956- ......................................... 173
Gilliland, Alexis A(rnaldus) 1931- ............. 72
Gilliland, (Cleburne) Hap 1918- ................ 92
Gillmor, Don 1954- ................................ 127
Gilman, Esther 1925- ............................... 15
Gilman, Phoebe 1940-2002 ..................... 104
  Obituary ............................................... 141
  Earlier sketch in SATA 58
Gilmore, Iris 1900-1982 ............................ 22
Gilmore, Kate 1931- ................................. 87
Gilmore, Mary (Jean Cameron) 1865-1962
  ................................................................ 49
Gilmore, Susan 1954- ............................... 59
Gilpin, Stephen ..................................... 177
Gilroy, Beryl (Agatha) 1924- ..................... 80
Gilson, Barbara
  *See* Gilson, Charles James Louis

Gilson, Charles James Louis 1878-1943
  *See* YABC 2
Gilson, Jamie 1933- ............................... 176
  Brief entry ............................................. 34
  Earlier sketches in SATA 37, 91
Ginsburg, Mirra 1909-2000 ....................... 92
  Earlier sketch in SATA 6
  *See also* CLR 45
Giovanni, Nikki 1943- ............................ 107
  Earlier sketch in SATA 24
  *See also* CLR 73
Giovanopoulos, Paul (Arthur) 1939- ........... 7
Gipson, Fred(erick Benjamin) 1908-1973 ..... 2
  Obituary ................................................ 24
Girard, Linda (Walvoord) 1942- ................ 41
Girion, Barbara 1937- .............................. 78
  Earlier sketch in SATA 26
  *See also* SAAS 14
Girouard, Patrick 1957- .......................... 155
Girzone, Joseph F. 1930- .......................... 76
Girzone, Joseph Francis
  *See* Girzone, Joseph F.
Gise, Joanne
  *See* Mattern, Joanne
Gittings, Jo (Grenville) Manton 1919- .......... 3
Gittings, Robert (William Victor) 1911-1992
  ................................................................ 6
  Obituary ................................................ 70
Givens, Janet E(aton) 1932- ...................... 60
Givner, Joan 1936- ................................. 171
Givner, Joan Mary
  *See* Givner, Joan
Gladstone, Eve
  *See* Werner, Herma
Gladstone, Gary 1935- .............................. 12
Gladstone, M(yron) J. 1923- ...................... 37
Glanville, Brian (Lester) 1931- .................. 42
Glanzman, Louis S. 1922- ......................... 36
Glaser, Byron 1954- ............................... 154
Glaser, Dianne E(lizabeth) 1937- ............... 50
  Brief entry ............................................. 31
Glaser, Isabel Joshlin 1929- ...................... 94
Glaser, Milton 1929- .............................. 151
  Earlier sketch in SATA 11
Glaser, Shirley ...................................... 151
Glaspell, Susan 1882(?)-1948
  *See* YABC 2
Glass, Andrew 1949- .............................. 150
  Brief entry ............................................. 46
  Earlier sketch in SATA 90
Glass, Linzi ......................................... 175
Glass, Linzi Alex
  *See* Glass, Linzi
Glasscock, Amnesia
  *See* Steinbeck, John (Ernst)
Glassman, Bruce 1961- ............................. 76
Glauber, Uta (Heil) 1936- ......................... 17
Glazer, Thomas (Zachariah) 1914-2003 ........ 9
Glazer, Tom
  *See* Glazer, Thomas (Zachariah)
Gleasner, Diana (Cottle) 1936- .................. 29
Gleason, Judith 1929- ............................... 24
Gleason, Katherine (A.) 1960- .................. 104
Gleeson, Libby 1950- ............................. 142
  Autobiography Feature ........................... 142
  Earlier sketches in SATA 82, 118
Gleiter, Jan 1947- ................................... 111
Gleitzman, Morris 1953- ......................... 156
  Earlier sketch in SATA 88
  *See also* CLR 88
Glen, Maggie 1944- .................................. 88
Glendinning, Richard 1917-1988 ............... 24
Glendinning, Sally
  *See* Glendinning, Sara W(ilson)
Glendinning, Sara W(ilson) 1913-1993 ........ 24
Glenn, Mel 1943- .................................... 93
  Brief entry ............................................. 45
  Earlier sketch in SATA 51
  *See also* CLR 51
Glenn, Patricia Brown 1953- ..................... 86
Glenn, Sharlee ...................................... 159

Glenn, Sharlee Mullins
  *See* Glenn, Sharlee
Glennon, Karen M. 1946- .......................... 85
Gles, Margaret Breitmaier 1940- ............... 22
Glick, Carl (Cannon) 1890-1971 ................ 14
Glick, Ruth (Burtnick) 1942- ................... 125
Gliewe, Unada (Grace) 1927- ...................... 3
Glimmerveen, Ulco 1958- ......................... 85
Glines, Carroll V(ane), Jr. 1920- ............... 19
Gliori, Debi 1959- ................................. 138
  Earlier sketch in SATA 72
Globe, Leah Ain 1900- ............................. 41
Glori Ann
  *See* Blakely, Gloria
Glovach, Linda 1947- ............................. 105
  Earlier sketch in SATA 7
Glover, Denis (James Matthews) 1912-1980
  ................................................................ 7
Glubok, Shirley (Astor) ......................... 146
  Autobiography Feature ........................... 146
  Earlier sketches in SATA 6, 68
  *See also* CLR 1
  *See also* SAAS 7
Glyman, Caroline A. 1967- ...................... 103
Glynne-Jones, William 1907-1977 ............. 11
Gobbato, Imero 1923- .............................. 39
Gobbletree, Richard
  *See* Quackenbush, Robert M(ead)
Goble, Dorothy ...................................... 26
Goble, Paul 1933- .................................. 131
  Earlier sketches in SATA 25, 69
  *See also* CLR 21
Goble, Warwick (?)-1943 .......................... 46
Godden, (Margaret) Rumer 1907-1998 ........ 36
  Obituary ............................................... 109
  Earlier sketch in SATA 3
  *See also* CLR 20
  *See also* SAAS 12
Gode, Alexander
  *See* Gode von Aesch, Alexander (Gottfried
  Friedrich)
Gode von Aesch, Alexander (Gottfried
  Friedrich) 1906-1970 ............................. 14
Godfrey, Jane
  *See* Bowden, Joan Chase
Godfrey, Martyn
  *See* Godfrey, Martyn N.
  and Godfrey, Martyn N.
Godfrey, Martyn N. 1949-2000 ................... 95
  *See also* CLR 57
  *See* Godfrey, Martyn
Godfrey, William
  *See* Youd, (Christopher) Samuel
Godkin, Celia (Marilyn) 1948- .................. 145
  Earlier sketch in SATA 66
Goedecke, Christopher (John) 1951- ........... 81
Goekler, Susan
  *See* Wooley, Susan Frelick
Goertzen, Glenda .................................. 172
Goettel, Elinor 1930- ............................... 12
Goetz, Delia 1898-1996 ............................ 22
  Obituary ................................................ 91
Goffe, Toni 1936- .................................... 61
Goffstein, Brooke
  *See* Goffstein, M(arilyn) B(rooke)
Goffstein, M(arilyn) B(rooke) 1940- ........... 70
  Earlier sketch in SATA 8
  *See also* CLR 3
Goforth, Ellen
  *See* Francis, Dorothy Brenner
Gogol, Sara 1948-2004 .............................. 80
Goh, Chan Hon 1969- ............................. 145
Going, K(elly) L. ................................... 156
Golann, Cecil Paige 1921-1995 .................. 11
Golbin, Andree 1923- ............................... 15
Gold, Alison Leslie 1945- ....................... 104
Gold, Bernice ...................................... 150
Gold, Phyllis ......................................... 21
  *See* Goldberg, Phyllis
Gold, Robert S(tanley) 1924- ..................... 63
Gold, Sharlya .......................................... 9

Gold, Susan
    See Gold, Susan Dudley
Gold, Susan Dudley 1949- .......................... 147
Goldberg, Grace 1956- .................................. 78
Goldberg, Herbert S. 1926- ......................... 25
Goldberg, Jacob 1943- .................................. 94
Goldberg, Jake
    See Goldberg, Jacob
Goldberg, Jan .............................................. 123
    See Curran, Jan Goldberg
Goldberg, Stan J. 1939- ............................... 26
Goldberg, Susan 1948- .................................. 71
Goldberg, Whoopi 1955- ............................. 119
Golden, Christie 1963- ................................ 167
    Earlier sketch in SATA 116
Goldentyer, Debra 1960- .............................. 84
Goldfeder, Cheryl
    See Pahz, Cheryl Suzanne
Goldfeder, James
    See Pahz, James Alon
Goldfeder, Jim
    See Pahz, James Alon
Goldfrank, Helen Colodny 1912- .................... 6
Goldin, Augusta 1906-1999 .......................... 13
Goldin, Barbara Diamond 1946- ................. 129
    Autobiography Feature .......................... 129
    Earlier sketch in SATA 92
    See also SAAS 26
Goldin, David 1963- .................................... 101
Golding, Theresa Martin 1960- ................... 150
Golding, William 1911-1993
    See CLR 94
Golding, William Gerald
    See Golding, William
Goldman, Alex J. 1917- ................................ 65
Goldman, E(leanor) M(aureen) 1943- ......... 103
Goldman, Elizabeth 1949- ............................ 90
Goldring, Ann 1937- ................................... 149
Goldsborough, June 1923- ............................ 19
Goldsmith, Connie 1945- ............................ 147
Goldsmith, Howard 1943- ........................... 108
    Earlier sketch in SATA 24
Goldsmith, Oliver 1730(?)-1774 .................... 26
Goldsmith, Ruth M. 1919- ............................ 62
Goldstein, Nathan 1927- .............................. 47
Goldstein, Philip 1910-1997 ......................... 23
Goldston, Robert (Conroy) 1927- ................... 6
Goldstone, Lawrence A.
    See Treat, Lawrence
Golembe, Carla 1951- ................................... 79
Golenbock, Peter 1946- ................................ 99
Goll, Reinhold W(eimar) 1897-1993 ............. 26
Gollub, Matthew 1960- ............................... 134
    Earlier sketch in SATA 83
Gomez, Elizabeth ...................................... 133
Gomez-Freer, Elizabeth
    See Gomez, Elizabeth
Gomi, Taro 1945- ....................................... 103
    Earlier sketch in SATA 64
    See also CLR 57
Gondosch, Linda 1944- ................................. 58
Gonzalez, Catherine Troxell 1917-2000 ....... 87
Gonzalez, Christina
    See Gonzalez, Maya Christina
Gonzalez, Gloria 1940- ................................ 23
Gonzalez, Julie 1958- ................................. 174
Gonzalez, Maya
    See Gonzalez, Maya Christina
Gonzalez, Maya Christina 1964- ................. 175
    Earlier sketch in SATA 115
Gonzalez, Rigoberto 1970- .......................... 147
Goobie, Beth 1959- ..................................... 128
Good, Alice 1950- ........................................ 73
Goodall, Daphne Machin
    See Machin Goodall, Daphne (Edith)
Goodall, Jane 1934- .................................... 111
Goodall, John S(trickland) 1908-1996 ........... 66
    Obituary ................................................ 91
    Earlier sketch in SATA 4
    See also CLR 25

Goodbody, Slim
    See Burstein, John
Goode, Diane 1949- .................................... 170
    Earlier sketches in SATA 15, 84, 114
Goode, Diane Capuozzo
    See Goode, Diane
Goode, Stephen Ray 1943- ............................ 55
    Brief entry ............................................. 40
Goodenow, Earle 1913- ................................ 40
Goodhart, Pippa 1958- ................................ 153
Goodhue, Thomas W. 1949- ......................... 143
Goodin, Sallie (Brown) 1953- ....................... 74
Goodman, Alison 1966- ............................... 111
Goodman, Deborah Lerme 1956- ................... 50
    Brief entry ............................................. 49
Goodman, Elaine 1930- .................................. 9
Goodman, Joan Elizabeth 1950- .................. 162
    Earlier sketches in SATA 50, 94
Goodman, Walter 1927-2002 .......................... 9
Goodrich, Samuel Griswold 1793-1860 ........ 23
GoodWeather, Harley
    See King, Thomas
Goodwin, Hal
    See Goodwin, Harold L(eland)
Goodwin, Harold L(eland) 1914-1990 ........... 51
    Obituary ................................................ 65
    Earlier sketch in SATA 13
Goodwin, William 1943- ............................. 117
Goor, Nancy (Ruth Miller) 1944- ................... 39
    Brief entry ............................................. 34
Goor, Ron(ald Stephen) 1940- ....................... 39
    Brief entry ............................................. 34
Goossen, Agnes
    See Epp, Margaret A(gnes)
Gopnik, Adam 1956- .................................... 171
Gorbachev, Valeri 1944- .............................. 143
    Autobiography Feature .......................... 143
    Earlier sketch in SATA 98
Gordion, Mark
    See Turtledove, Harry
Gordon, Ad
    See Hano, Arnold
Gordon, Amy 1949- ..................................... 156
    Earlier sketch in SATA 115
Gordon, Bernard Ludwig 1931- ..................... 27
Gordon, Colonel H. R.
    See Ellis, Edward S(ylvester)
Gordon, Donald
    See Payne, Donald Gordon
Gordon, Dorothy 1893-1970 .......................... 20
Gordon, Esther S(aranga) 1935- ................... 10
Gordon, Frederick ........................................... 1
Gordon, Gaelyn 1939-1997
    See CLR 75
Gordon, Gary
    See Edmonds, I(vy) G(ordon)
Gordon, Hal
    See Goodwin, Harold L(eland)
Gordon, Jeffie Ross
    See Enderle, Judith (Ann) Ross
    and Gordon, Stephanie Jacob
Gordon, John
    See Gesner, Clark
Gordon, John (William) 1925- ....................... 84
Gordon, Lew
    See Baldwin, Gordon C(ortis)
Gordon, Margaret (Anna) 1939- ...................... 9
Gordon, Mike 1948- .................................... 101
Gordon, Selma
    See Lanes, Selma Gordon
Gordon, Sheila 1927- .................................... 88
    See also CLR 27
Gordon, Shirley 1921- ................................... 48
    Brief entry ............................................. 41
Gordon, Sol 1923- ......................................... 11
Gordon, Stephanie Jacob 1940- ..................... 89
    Autobiography Feature .......................... 114
    Earlier sketch in SATA 64
    See also SAAS 26
Gordon, Stewart
    See Shirreffs, Gordon D(onald)

Gorelick, Molly C(hernow) 1920-2003 ............ 9
    Obituary ............................................... 153
Gorey, Edward (St. John) 1925-2000 ............. 70
    Brief entry ............................................. 27
    Obituary ............................................... 118
    Earlier sketch in SATA 29
    See also CLR 36
Gorham, Charles Orson 1868-1936 ................ 36
Gorham, Michael
    See Folsom, Franklin (Brewster)
Gorman, Carol ....................................... 150
Gorman, Jacqueline Laks 1955- .................. 148
Gormley, Beatrice 1942- ............................. 127
    Brief entry ............................................. 35
    Earlier sketch in SATA 39
Gorog, Judith (Katharine Allen) 1938- .......... 75
    Earlier sketch in SATA 39
Gorrell, Gena K. 1946- ............................... 170
Gorrell, Gena Kinton
    See Gorrell, Gena K.
Gorsline, Douglas (Warner) 1913-1985 .......... 11
    Obituary ................................................ 43
Gorsline, (Sally) Marie 1928- ....................... 28
Gorsline, S. M.
    See Gorsline, (Sally) Marie
Gorton, Kaitlyn
    See Emerson, Kathy Lynn
Goryan, Sirak
    See Saroyan, William
Goscinny, Rene 1926-1977 ........................... 47
    Brief entry ............................................. 39
    See also CLR 37
Goss, Clay(ton E.) 1946- .............................. 82
Goss, Gary 1947- ....................................... 124
Gottesman, S. D.
    See Kornbluth, C(yril) M.
    and Lowndes, Robert A(ugustine) W(ard)
    and Pohl, Frederik
Gottfried, Ted
    See Gottfried, Theodore Mark
Gottfried, Theodore Mark 1928- .................. 150
    Earlier sketch in SATA 85
Gottlieb, Gerald 1923- .................................... 7
Gottlieb, William P. 1917-2006 ..................... 24
Gottlieb, William Paul
    See Gottlieb, William P.
Goudey, Alice E(dwards) 1898-1993 .............. 20
Goudge, Eileen 1950- ................................... 88
Goudge, Elizabeth (de Beauchamp) 1900-1984
    .............................................................. 2
    Obituary ................................................ 38
    See also CLR 94
Gough, Catherine ....................................... 24
    See Mulgan, Catherine
Gough, Philip 1908- ..................................... 45
Gough, Sue 1940- ...................................... 106
Goulart, Ron(ald Joseph) 1933- .................. 138
    Earlier sketch in SATA 6
    See Appleton, Victor II
    and Dixon, Franklin W.
    and Hope, Laura Lee
    and Keene, Carolyn
Gould, Alberta 1945- .................................... 96
Gould, Chester 1900-1985 ............................ 49
    Obituary ................................................ 43
Gould, Jean R(osalind) 1909-1993 ................. 11
    Obituary ................................................ 77
Gould, Lilian ............................................... 6
Gould, Marilyn 1928- ................................... 76
    Earlier sketch in SATA 15
Gould, Robert .......................................... 154
Gould, Steven 1955- ..................................... 95
Gould, Steven Charles
    See Gould, Steven
Gourley, Catherine 1950- .............................. 95
Gourse, (Roberta) Leslie 1939-2004 ............. 89
Govan, (Mary) Christine Noble 1898-1985 .... 9
Gove, Doris 1944- ........................................ 72
Govern, Elaine 1939- .................................... 26
Gowen, L. Kris 1968- .................................. 156

Graaf, Peter
  *See* Youd, (Christopher) Samuel
Graber, Alexander 1914-1997 .................... 98
  Earlier sketch in SATA 7
Graber, (George) Alexander 1914-1997 ...... 98
Graber, Janet 1942- ................................. 170
Graber, Richard (Fredrick) 1927- ............. 26
Grabianski, Janusz 1928-1976 ................... 39
  Obituary .............................................. 30
Graboff, Abner 1919-1986 ........................ 35
Grace, Fran(ces Jane) ............................... 45
Grace, Theresa
  *See* Mattern, Joanne
Gracza, Margaret Young 1928- .................. 56
Graduate of Oxford, A
  *See* Ruskin, John
Graeber, Charlotte Towner ....................... 106
  Brief entry ........................................... 44
  Earlier sketch in SATA 56
Graeme, Roderic
  *See* Jeffries, Roderic
Graf, Michael
  *See* Graf, Mike
Graf, Mike 1960- ..................................... 164
Graff, Polly Anne Colver
  *See* Colver, Anne
Graff, (S.) Stewart 1908- ............................ 9
Graham, Ada 1931- .................................... 11
Graham, Alastair 1945- ............................. 74
Graham, Arthur Kennon
  *See* Harrison, David L(ee)
Graham, Bob 1942- ................................. 151
  Earlier sketches in SATA 63, 101
  *See also* CLR 31
Graham, Brenda Knight 1942- .................... 32
Graham, Charlotte
  *See* Bowden, Joan Chase
Graham, Eleanor 1896-1984 ..................... 18
  Obituary .............................................. 38
Graham, Ennis
  *See* Molesworth, Mary Louisa
Graham, Frank, Jr. 1925- ........................... 11
Graham, Ian 1953- .................................. 112
Graham, John 1926- .................................. 11
Graham, Kennon
  *See* Harrison, David L(ee)
Graham, Larry
  *See* Graham, Lawrence (Otis)
Graham, Lawrence (Otis) 1962- .................. 63
Graham, Linda
  *See* Graham-Barber, Lynda
Graham, Lorenz (Bell) 1902-1989 .............. 74
  Obituary .............................................. 63
  Earlier sketch in SATA 2
  *See also* CLR 10
  *See also* SAAS 5
Graham, Margaret Bloy 1920- ................... 11
Graham, Robin Lee 1949- ............................ 7
Graham, Shirley 1896(?)-1977
  *See* Du Bois, Shirley Graham
Graham-Barber, Lynda 1944- .................... 159
  Earlier sketch in SATA 42
Graham-Cameron, M.
  *See* Graham-Cameron, M(alcolm) G(ordon)
Graham-Cameron, M(alcolm) G(ordon) 1931-
  ............................................................ 53
  Brief entry ........................................... 45
Graham-Cameron, Mike
  *See* Graham-Cameron, M(alcolm) G(ordon)
Grahame, Kenneth 1859-1932 ................... 100
  *See also* YABC 1
  *See also* CLR 5
Gralley, Jean ............................................ 166
Gramatky, Hardie 1907-1979 .................... 30
  Obituary .............................................. 23
  Earlier sketch in SATA 1
  *See also* CLR 22
Grambling, Lois G. 1927- ......................... 148
  Earlier sketch in SATA 71
Grambo, Rebecca L(ynn) 1963- ................. 109
Grammer, June Amos 1927- ....................... 58

Grand, Samuel 1912-1988 ......................... 42
Grandville, J. J.
  *See* Gerard, Jean Ignace Isidore
Grandville, Jean Ignace Isidore Gerard
  *See* Gerard, Jean Ignace Isidore
Granfield, Linda 1950- ............................. 160
  Earlier sketch in SATA 96
Grange, Peter
  *See* Nicole, Christopher (Robin)
Granger, Michele 1949- ............................. 88
Granowsky, Alvin 1936- ........................... 101
Granstaff, Bill 1925- ................................. 10
Granstrom, Brita 1969- ............................ 167
  Earlier sketch in SATA 111
Grant, Bruce 1893-1977 .............................. 5
  Obituary .............................................. 25
Grant, Cynthia D. 1950- ........................... 147
  Earlier sketches in SATA 33, 77
Grant, Eva 1907-1996 .................................. 7
Grant, Gordon 1875-1962 .......................... 25
Grant, Gwen(doline Ellen) 1940- ............... 47
Grant, Katie M.
  *See* Grant, K.M.
Grant, K.M. .............................................. 175
Grant, (Alice) Leigh 1947- ......................... 10
Grant, Matthew G.
  *See* May, Julian
Grant, Maxwell
  *See* Gibson, Walter B(rown)
  and Lynds, Dennis
Grant, Myrna (Lois) 1934- ......................... 21
Grant, Neil 1938- .................................... 154
  Earlier sketch in SATA 14
Grant, Nicholas
  *See* Nicole, Christopher (Robin)
Grant, Richard 1948- ................................. 80
Grant, Skeeter
  *See* Spiegelman, Art
Grater, Michael 1923- ............................... 57
Gravel, Fern
  *See* Hall, James Norman
Gravelle, Karen 1942- .............................. 166
  Earlier sketch in SATA 78
Graves, Charles Parlin 1911-1972 ................. 4
Graves, Keith ....................................... 156
Graves, Robert 1895-1985 ........................ 45
Graves, Robert von Ranke
  *See* Graves, Robert
Graves, Valerie
  *See* Bradley, Marion Zimmer
Gray, Betsy
  *See* Poole, Gray Johnson
Gray, Caroline
  *See* Nicole, Christopher (Robin)
Gray, Elizabeth Janet
  *See* Vining, Elizabeth Gray
Gray, Genevieve S(tuck) 1920-1995 ............. 4
Gray, Harold (Lincoln) 1894-1968 ............. 33
  Brief entry ........................................... 32
Gray, Jenny
  *See* Gray, Genevieve S(tuck)
Gray, John Lee
  *See* Jakes, John
Gray, Judith A. 1949- ................................ 93
Gray, Judith Anne
  *See* Gray, Judith A.
Gray, Keith ........................................... 151
Gray, Kes 1960- ...................................... 153
Gray, Les 1929- ....................................... 82
Gray, Libba Moore 1937- .......................... 83
Gray, Luli 1945- ..................................... 149
  Earlier sketch in SATA 90
Gray, Marian
  *See* Pierce, Edith Gray
Gray, Nicholas Stuart 1922-1981 .................. 4
  Obituary .............................................. 27
Gray, Nigel 1941- ................................... 104
  Earlier sketch in SATA 33
Gray, (Lucy) Noel (Clervaux) 1898-1983 ... 47
Gray, Patricia (Clark) ................................. 7

Gray, Patsey
  *See* Gray, Patricia (Clark)
Graydon, Shari 1958- ............................... 158
Grayland, V. Merle
  *See* Grayland, Valerie (Merle Spanner)
Grayland, Valerie (Merle Spanner) ............... 7
Grayson, Devin (Kalile) 1970- .................. 119
Grayson, Kristine
  *See* Rusch, Kristine Kathryn
Grayson, Paul 1946- ................................. 79
Graystone, Lynn
  *See* Brennan, Joseph Lomas
Great Comte, The
  *See* Hawkesworth, Eric
Greaves, Margaret 1914-1995 .................... 87
  Earlier sketch in SATA 7
Greaves, Nick 1955- ................................. 77
Gree, Alain 1936- .................................... 28
Green, Adam
  *See* Weisgard, Leonard (Joseph)
Green, Anne Canevari 1943- ....................... 62
Green, Brian
  *See* Card, Orson Scott
Green, Cliff(ord) 1934- ............................ 126
Green, Connie Jordan 1938- ....................... 80
Green, D.
  *See* Casewit, Curtis W(erner)
Green, Elizabeth Shippen 1871-1954 ......... 139
Green, Hannah
  *See* Greenberg, Joanne (Goldenberg)
Green, Jane 1937- ...................................... 9
Green, John 1978(?)- ............................... 170
Green, Mary Moore 1906- ......................... 11
Green, Morton 1937- .................................. 8
Green, Norma B(erger) 1925- ..................... 11
Green, Phyllis 1932- ................................ 20
Green, Roger (Gilbert) Lancelyn 1918-1987
  .............................................................. 2
  Obituary .............................................. 53
Green, (James Le)Roy 1948- ...................... 89
Green, Sheila Ellen 1934- ......................... 148
  Earlier sketches in SATA 8, 87
Green, Timothy 1953- ............................... 91
Greenaway, Kate 1846-1901 ..................... 100
  *See also* YABC 2
  *See also* CLR 111
Greenbank, Anthony Hunt 1933- ................ 39
Greenberg, David T. 1954- ....................... 171
Greenberg, Harvey R. 1935- ........................ 5
Greenberg, Jan 1942- .............................. 125
  Earlier sketch in SATA 61
Greenberg, Joanne (Goldenberg) 1932- ...... 25
Greenberg, Melanie Hope 1954- ................. 72
Greenberg, Polly 1932- ............................. 52
  Brief entry ........................................... 43
Greenblat, Rodney Alan 1960- .................. 106
Greenburg, Dan 1936- ............................. 175
  Earlier sketch in SATA 102
Greene, Bette 1934- ................................ 161
  Earlier sketches in SATA 8, 102
  *See also* CLR 2
  *See also* SAAS 16
Greene, Carla 1916- ................................. 67
  Earlier sketch in SATA 1
Greene, Carol ....................................... 102
  Brief entry ........................................... 44
  Earlier sketch in SATA 66
Greene, Constance C(larke) 1924- .............. 72
  Earlier sketch in SATA 11
  *See also* CLR 62
  *See also* SAAS 11
Greene, Edgar
  *See* Papademetriou, Lisa
Greene, Ellin 1927- ................................. 23
Greene, Graham 1904-1991 ....................... 20
Greene, Graham Henry
  *See* Greene, Graham
Greene, Jacqueline Dembar 1946- ............. 131
  Earlier sketch in SATA 76
Greene, Laura Offenhartz 1935- ................. 38

Greene, Meg
See Malvasi, Meg Greene
Greene, Rhonda Gowler 1955- ................ *160*
Earlier sketch in SATA *101*
Greene, Stephanie 1953- ........................ *173*
Earlier sketch in SATA *127*
Greene, Wade 1933- ................................. *11*
Greene, Yvonne
See Flesch, Yolande (Catarina)
Greenfeld, Howard (Scheinman) 1928- ..... *140*
Earlier sketch in SATA *19*
Greenfeld, Josh(ua Joseph) 1928- ............. *62*
Greenfield, Eloise 1929- ......................... *155*
Earlier sketches in SATA *19, 61, 105*
See also CLR *38*
See also SAAS *16*
Greening, Hamilton
See Hamilton, Charles (Harold St. John)
Greenlaw, M. Jean 1941- ........................ *107*
Greenleaf, Barbara Kaye 1942- ................... *6*
Greenleaf, Peter 1910-1997 ...................... *33*
Greenlee, Sharon 1935- ........................... *77*
Greeno, Gayle 1949- ............................... *81*
Greenseid, Diane 1948- ........................... *93*
Greenspun, Adele Aron 1938- ................. *142*
Earlier sketch in SATA *76*
Greenstein, Elaine 1959- ......................... *150*
Earlier sketch in SATA *82*
Greenwald, Sheila
See Green, Sheila Ellen
Greenwood, Barbara 1940- ...................... *129*
Earlier sketch in SATA *90*
Greenwood, Pamela D. 1944- ................... *115*
Greer, Richard
See Garrett, (Gordon) Randall (Phillip)
and Silverberg, Robert
Gregg, Andrew K. 1929- .......................... *81*
Gregg, Charles T(hornton) 1927- ............... *65*
Gregg, Walter H(arold) 1919- .................... *20*
Gregor, Arthur 1923- ............................... *36*
Gregor, Lee
See Pohl, Frederik
Gregori, Leon 1919- ................................ *15*
Gregorian, Joyce Ballou 1946-1991 ............ *30*
Obituary ............................................ *83*
Gregorich, Barbara 1943- ......................... *66*
Gregorowski, Christopher 1940- ................. *30*
Gregory, Diana (Jean) 1933- ..................... *49*
Brief entry .......................................... *42*
Gregory, Harry
See Gottfried, Theodore Mark
Gregory, Jean
See Ure, Jean
Gregory, Kristiana 1951- ......................... *136*
Earlier sketch in SATA *74*
Gregory, Nan 1944- ................................ *148*
Gregory, Philippa 1954- ........................... *122*
Gregory, Stephen
See Penzler, Otto
Gregory, Valiska 1940- ............................. *82*
Greisman, Joan Ruth 1937- ........................ *31*
Grendon, Stephen
See Derleth, August (William)
Grenville, Pelham
See Wodehouse, P(elham) G(renville)
Gretz, Susanna 1937- ................................ *7*
Gretzer, John ....................................... *18*
Grewdead, Roy
See Gorey, Edward (St. John)
Grey, Carol
See Lowndes, Robert A(ugustine) W(ard)
Grey, Jerry 1926- ..................................... *11*
Grey, Mini .......................................... *166*
Greybeard the Pirate
See Macintosh, Brownie
Grey Owl
See CLR *32*
See Belaney, Archibald Stansfeld
Gri
See Denney, Diana
Gribbin, John 1946- ............................... *159*

Gribbin, John R.
See Gribbin, John
Grice, Frederick 1910-1983 ......................... *6*
Grider, Dorothy 1915- ............................. *31*
Gridley, Marion E(leanor) 1906-1974 ......... *35*
Obituary ............................................ *26*
Grieco-Tiso, Pina 1954- ........................... *108*
Grieder, Walter 1924- ................................ *9*
Griego, Tony A. 1955- ............................. *77*
Griese, Arnold A(lfred) 1921- ...................... *9*
Griessman, Annette 1962- ........................ *170*
Earlier sketch in SATA *116*
Grieve, James 1934- ................................ *146*
Grifalconi, Ann 1929- ............................. *133*
Earlier sketches in SATA *2, 66*
See also CLR *35*
See also SAAS *16*
Griffin, Adele 1970- ................................ *153*
Earlier sketch in SATA *105*
Griffin, Elizabeth May 1985- ...................... *89*
Griffin, Gillett Good 1928- ......................... *26*
Griffin, Judith Berry ................................ *34*
Griffin, Kitty 1951- ................................. *137*
Griffin, Peni R(ae Robinson) 1961- ............. *99*
Earlier sketch in SATA *67*
Griffin, Steven A. 1953- ............................ *89*
Griffin, Steven Arthur
See Griffin, Steven A.
Griffin, W.E.B. 1929- ................................. *5*
See Butterworth, W.E.
Griffith, Connie 1946- ............................... *89*
Griffith, Gershom 1960- ............................. *85*
Griffith, Helen V(irginia) 1934- .................... *87*
Autobiography Feature ......................... *107*
Earlier sketch in SATA *39*
Griffith, Jeannette
See Eyerly, Jeannette (Hyde)
Griffiths, Andy 1961- ............................... *152*
Griffiths, Helen 1939- ................................ *86*
Earlier sketch in SATA *5*
See also CLR *75*
See also SAAS *5*
Grigson, Jane (McIntire) 1928-1990 ........... *63*
Grimes, Lee 1920- .................................... *68*
Grimes, Nikki 1950- ................................ *174*
Earlier sketches in SATA *93, 136*
See also CLR *42*
Grimm, Jacob Ludwig Karl 1785-1863 ....... *22*
See also CLR *112*
See Grimm Brothers
Grimm, Wilhelm Karl 1786-1859 ............... *22*
See also CLR *112*
See Grimm Brothers
Grimm, William C(arey) 1907-1992 ........... *14*
Grimm and Grim
See Grimm, Jacob Ludwig Karl
and Grimm, Wilhelm Karl
Grimm Brothers
See CLR *112*
See Grimm, Jacob Ludwig Karl
and Grimm, Wilhelm Karl
Grimsdell, Jeremy 1942- ............................ *83*
Grimshaw, Nigel (Gilroy) 1925- .................. *23*
Grimsley, Gordon
See Groom, Arthur William
Grindley, (Jane) Sally 1953- ...................... *148*
Gringhuis, Dirk
See Gringhuis, Richard H.
Gringhuis, Richard H. 1918-1974 ................. *6*
Obituary ............................................ *25*
Grinnell, George Bird 1849-1938 ................ *16*
Grinspoon, David
See Grinspoon, David H.
Grinspoon, David H. 1959- ....................... *156*
Grinspoon, David Harry
See Grinspoon, David H.
Gripe, Maria 1923- ................................... *74*
Earlier sketch in SATA *2*
See also CLR *5*
Gripe, Maria Kristina
See Gripe, Maria

Groch, Judith (Goldstein) 1929- ................ *25*
Grode, Redway
See Gorey, Edward (St. John)
Groener, Carl
See Lowndes, Robert A(ugustine) W(ard)
Groening, Matt 1954- ............................... *116*
Earlier sketch in SATA *81*
Grohmann, Susan 1948- ............................ *84*
Grohskopf, Bernice ................................... *7*
Grol, Lini R(icharda) 1913- ......................... *9*
Grollman, Earl A. 1925- ............................. *22*
Groom, Arthur William 1898-1964 ............. *10*
Grooms, Duffy 1964- ............................... *169*
Gross, Alan 1947- ................................... *54*
Brief entry .......................................... *43*
Gross, Ernie 1913- ................................... *67*
Gross, Philip 1952- ................................. *164*
Earlier sketch in SATA *84*
Gross, Philip John
See Gross, Philip
Gross, Ruth Belov 1929- ............................ *33*
Gross, Sarah Chokla 1906-1976 ................... *9*
Obituary ............................................ *26*
Grosser, Morton 1931- .............................. *74*
Grosser, Vicky 1958- ................................ *83*
Grossman, Bill 1948- ............................... *126*
Earlier sketch in SATA *72*
Grossman, Nancy 1940- ............................ *29*
Grossman, Patricia 1951- ........................... *73*
Grossman, Robert 1940- ............................ *11*
Grote, JoAnn A. 1951- ............................. *113*
Groten, Dallas 1951- ................................ *64*
Groth, John (August) 1908-1988 ................. *21*
Obituary ............................................ *56*
Groth-Fleming, Candace
See Fleming, Candace
Grove, Vicki 1948- ................................. *151*
Autobiography Feature ......................... *151*
Earlier sketch in SATA *122*
Grover, Lorie Ann 1964- ........................... *168*
Grover, Wayne 1934- ................................ *69*
Groves, Georgina
See Symons, (Dorothy) Geraldine
Groves, Maketa 1950- .............................. *107*
Groves, Seli ......................................... *77*
Grubb, Lisa ......................................... *160*
Gruber, Michael 1940- ............................. *173*
Gruber, Terry (deRoy) 1953- ....................... *66*
Gruelle, John (Barton) 1880-1938 ............... *35*
Brief entry .......................................... *32*
See Gruelle, Johnny
Gruelle, Johnny
See CLR *34*
See Gruelle, John (Barton)
Gruenberg, Sidonie Matsner 1881-1974 ....... *2*
Obituary ............................................ *27*
Gruhzit-Hoyt, Olga (Margaret) 1922- ....... *127*
Earlier sketch in SATA *16*
Grummer, Arnold E(dward) 1923- ............. *49*
Grunewalt, Pine
See Kunhardt, Edith
Grunwell, Jeanne Marie 1971- ................. *147*
Grupper, Jonathan .................................. *137*
Gryski, Camilla 1948- .............................. *72*
Guarino, Dagmar
See Guarino, Deborah
Guarino, Deborah 1954- ............................ *68*
Guay, Georgette (Marie Jeanne) 1952- ....... *54*
Guback, Georgia ..................................... *88*
Guccione, Leslie Davis 1946- ................... *111*
Earlier sketch in SATA *72*
Guck, Dorothy 1913-2002 ........................ *27*
Guerny, Gene
See Gurney, Gene
Guest, Elissa Haden 1953- ....................... *125*
Guest, Jacqueline 1952- ........................... *135*
Guevara, Susan ..................................... *167*
Earlier sketch in SATA *97*
Gugler, Laurel Dee ................................ *95*
Gugliotta, Bobette 1918-1994 ...................... *7*
Guianan, Eve 1965- ............................... *102*

Guiberson, Brenda Z. 1946- ...................... *124*
  Earlier sketch in SATA *71*
Guile, Melanie 1949- .................................... *152*
  Earlier sketch in SATA *104*
Guillaume, Jeanette G. Flierl 1899-1990 ...... *8*
Guillot, Rene 1900-1969 ........................... *7*
  *See also* CLR *22*
Guisewite, Cathy (Lee) 1950- ...................... *57*
Gulbis, Stephen 1959- ................................ *142*
Gulley, Judie 1942- ..................................... *58*
Gump, P. Q.
  *See* Card, Orson Scott
Gundrey, Elizabeth 1924- ......................... *23*
Gunn, James E(dwin) 1923- ...................... *35*
Gunn, Robin Jones 1955- ........................... *84*
Gunning, Monica Olwen 1930- ................ *161*
Gunston, Bill
  *See* Gunston, William Tudor
Gunston, William Tudor 1927- ..................... *9*
Gunther, John 1901-1970
Guravich, Dan 1918- .................................. *74*
Gurko, Leo 1914- .......................................... *9*
Gurko, Miriam 1910(?)-1988 ..................... *9*
  Obituary .................................................... *58*
Gurney, Gene 1924- .................................... *65*
Gurney, James 1958- ................................ *120*
  Earlier sketch in SATA *76*
Gurney, John Steven 1962- ....................... *143*
  Earlier sketch in SATA *75*
Gustafson, Sarah R.
  *See* Riedman, Sarah R(egal)
Gustafson, Scott 1956- .............................. *34*
Gustavson, Adam ....................................... *176*
Guthrie, A(lfred) B(ertram), Jr. 1901-1991 .. *62*
  Obituary .................................................... *67*
Guthrie, Anne 1890-1979 ......................... *28*
Guthrie, Donna W. 1946- .......................... *105*
  Earlier sketch in SATA *63*
Gutierrez, Akemi ...................................... *172*
Gutman, Bill ............................................... *128*
  Brief entry ................................................ *43*
  Earlier sketch in SATA *67*
Gutman, Dan 1955- .................................... *139*
  Earlier sketch in SATA *77*
Gutmann, Bessie Pease 1876-1960 ........... *73*
Guy, Geoffrey 1942- ................................. *153*
Guy, Ginger Foglesong 1954- ................... *171*
Guy, Rosa (Cuthbert) 1925- ...................... *122*
  Earlier sketches in SATA *14, 62*
  *See also* CLR *13*
Guy, Susan 1948- ...................................... *149*
Guymer, (Wilhelmina) Mary 1909- ........... *50*
Guzman, Lila 1952- .................................. *168*
Guzman, Rick 1957- .................................. *168*
Gwynne, Fred(erick Hubbard) 1926-1993 .. *41*
  Brief entry ................................................ *27*
  Obituary .................................................... *75*
Gwynne, Oscar A.
  *See* Ellis, Edward S(ylvester)
Gwynne, Oswald A.
  *See* Ellis, Edward S(ylvester)

**H**

Haab, Sherri 1964- .................................... *169*
  Earlier sketch in SATA *91*
Haar, Jaap ter
  *See* CLR *15*
  *See* ter Haar, Jaap
Haas, Carolyn Buhai 1926- ...................... *43*
Haas, Dan 1957- ....................................... *105*
Haas, Dorothy F. .......................................... *46*
  Brief entry ................................................ *43*
  *See also* SAAS *17*
Haas, Irene 1929- ....................................... *96*
  Earlier sketch in SATA *17*
Haas, James E(dward) 1943- ..................... *40*

Haas, (Katherine) Jessie 1959- ................ *135*
  Autobiography Feature ............................. *135*
  Earlier sketch in SATA *98*
Habenstreit, Barbara 1937- ........................ *5*
Haber, Karen 1955- .................................... *78*
Haber, Louis 1910-1988 ........................... *12*
Hackett, John Winthrop 1910-1997 ........... *65*
Haddix, Margaret Peterson 1964- ............. *125*
  Earlier sketch in SATA *94*
Haddon, Mark 1962- ................................. *155*
Hader, Berta (Hoerner) 1891(?)-1976 ......... *16*
Hader, Elmer (Stanley) 1889-1973 ............. *16*
Hadithi, Mwenye
  *See* Hobson, Bruce
Hadley, Franklin
  *See* Winterbotham, R(ussell) R(obert)
Hadley, Lee 1934-1995 ............................... *89*
  Brief entry ................................................ *38*
  Obituary .................................................... *86*
  Earlier sketch in SATA *47*
  *See also* CLR *40*
  *See* Irwin, Hadley
Haeffele, Deborah 1954- ........................... *76*
Haenel, Wolfram 1956- .............................. *89*
  *See also* CLR *64*
Hafner, Marylin 1925- .............................. *121*
  Earlier sketch in SATA *7*
Hager, Alan 1940- .................................... *176*
Hager, Betty 1923- ...................................... *89*
Hager, Sarah ............................................... *171*
Hager, Thomas 1953- ............................... *119*
Hager, Tom
  *See* Hager, Thomas
Haggard, H(enry) Rider 1856-1925 ........... *16*
Haggerty, James J(oseph) 1920- .................. *5*
Hagon, Priscilla
  *See* Allan, Mabel Esther
Hague, (Susan) Kathleen 1949- ................ *49*
  Brief entry ................................................ *45*
Hague, Michael R. 1948- .......................... *129*
  Brief entry ................................................ *32*
  Earlier sketches in SATA *48, 80*
Hahn, Emily 1905-1997 .............................. *3*
  Obituary .................................................... *96*
Hahn, Hannelore ........................................... *8*
Hahn, James (Sage) 1947- ........................... *9*
Hahn, (Mona) Lynn 1949- ........................... *9*
Hahn, Mary Downing 1937- ..................... *157*
  Autobiography Feature ............................. *157*
  Brief entry ................................................ *44*
  Earlier sketches in SATA *50, 81, 138*
  *See also* SAAS *12*
Hahn, Michael T. 1953- ............................. *92*
Haig-Brown, Roderick (Langmere) 1908-1976
  ................................................................ *12*
  *See also* CLR *31*
Haight, Rip
  *See* Carpenter, John (Howard)
Haight, Sandy 1949- ................................... *79*
Haij, Vera
  *See* Jansson, Tove (Marika)
Haines, Gail Kay 1943- ............................. *11*
Haines, Margaret Ann Beck
  *See* Beck, Peggy
Haining, Peter (Alexander) 1940- ............. *14*
Hains, Harriet
  *See* Watson, Carol
Hajdusiewicz, Babs Bell ........................... *163*
Hakim, Joy 1931- ..................................... *173*
  Earlier sketch in SATA *83*
Halacy, D(aniel) S(tephen), Jr. 1919-2002 .. *36*
  *See* Halacy, Dan
Halacy, Dan
  *See* SAAS *8*
  *See* Halacy, D(aniel) S(tephen), Jr.
Halam, Ann
  *See* Jones, Gwyneth A(nn)
Haldane, Roger John 1945- ....................... *13*
Hale, Arlene 1924-1982 ............................. *49*
Hale, Bruce 1957- ...................................... *123*

Hale, Christy
  *See* Apostolou, Christine Hale
Hale, Edward Everett 1822-1909 ............... *16*
Hale, Glenn
  *See* Walker, Robert W(ayne)
Hale, Helen
  *See* Mulcahy, Lucille Burnett
Hale, Irina 1932- ....................................... *26*
Hale, Kathleen 1898-2000 ......................... *66*
  Obituary .................................................... *121*
  Earlier sketch in SATA *17*
Hale, Linda (Howe) 1929- ........................... *6*
Hale, Lucretia P.
  *See* Hale, Lucretia Peabody
Hale, Lucretia Peabody 1820-1900 ........... *26*
  *See also* CLR *105*
Hale, Nancy 1908-1988 ............................. *31*
  Obituary .................................................... *57*
Hale, Shannon .......................................... *158*
Haley, Gail E(inhart) 1939- ...................... *161*
  Autobiography Feature ............................. *161*
  Brief entry ................................................ *28*
  Earlier sketches in SATA *43, 78, 136*
  *See also* CLR *21*
  *See also* SAAS *13*
Haley, Neale .............................................. *52*
Hall, Adam
  *See* Trevor, Elleston
Hall, Adele 1910- .......................................... *7*
Hall, Anna Gertrude 1882-1967 .................. *8*
Hall, Barbara 1960- .................................... *68*
Hall, Beverly B. 1918- ............................... *95*
Hall, Borden
  *See* Yates, Raymond F(rancis)
Hall, Brian P(atrick) 1935- ....................... *31*
Hall, Cameron
  *See* del Rey, Lester
Hall, Caryl
  *See* Hansen, Caryl (Hall)
Hall, Donald 1928- .................................... *97*
  Earlier sketch in SATA *23*
Hall, Donald Andrew, Jr.
  *See* Hall, Donald
Hall, Douglas 1931- ................................... *43*
Hall, Elizabeth 1929- ................................ *77*
Hall, Elvajean 1910-1984 ............................ *6*
Hall, Francie 1940- ................................... *166*
Hall, James Norman 1887-1951 ................ *21*
Hall, Jesse
  *See* Boesen, Victor
Hall, Katy
  *See* McMullan, Kate
Hall, Kirsten Marie 1974- .......................... *67*
Hall, Lynn 1937- ....................................... *79*
  Earlier sketches in SATA *2, 47*
  *See also* SAAS *4*
Hall, Malcolm 1945- .................................... *7*
Hall, Marjory
  *See* Yeakley, Marjory Hall
Hall, Melanie W. 1949- ............................. *169*
  Earlier sketches in SATA *78, 116*
Hall, Patricia 1940- .................................. *136*
Hall, Rosalys Haskell 1914- ........................ *7*
Hall, Willis 1929-2005 ............................... *66*
Hallard, Peter
  *See* Catherall, Arthur
Hallas, Richard
  *See* Knight, Eric
Hall-Clarke, James
  *See* Rowland-Entwistle, (Arthur) Theodore
  (Henry)
Hallensleben, Georg 1958- ....................... *173*
Haller, Dorcas Woodbury 1946- ............... *46*
Hallett, Mark 1947- ................................... *83*
Halliburton, Richard 1900-1939(?) ........... *81*
Halliburton, Warren J. 1924- ..................... *19*
Halliday, Brett
  *See* Dresser, Davis
  and Johnson, (Walter) Ryerson
  and Terrall, Robert
Halliday, William R(oss) 1926- ................ *52*

Hallin, Emily Watson 1916-1995 ................. *6*
Hallinan, P(atrick) K(enneth) 1944- ........... *39*
  Brief entry ........................................ *37*
Hallman, Ruth 1929- ............................... *43*
  Brief entry ........................................ *28*
Hallowell, Tommy
  *See* Hill, Thomas
Hall-Quest, (Edna) Olga W(ilbourne)
  1899-1986 ................................. *11*
  Obituary ........................................ *47*
Halls, Kelly Milner 1957- ...................... *131*
Hallstead, William F(inn III) 1924- ........... *11*
Hallward, Michael 1889-1982 ............... *12*
Halperin, Michael ............................... *156*
Halperin, Wendy Anderson 1952- ........... *125*
  Earlier sketch in SATA *80*
Halpin, Marlene 1927- ......................... *88*
Halsell, Grace (Eleanor) 1923-2000 ........... *13*
Halter, Jon C(harles) 1941- ..................... *22*
Halvorson, Marilyn 1948- ..................... *123*
Hamalian, Leo 1920- ............................. *41*
Hamberger, John 1934- ......................... *14*
Hamblin, Dora Jane 1920- ..................... *36*
Hambly, Barbara 1951- ......................... *108*
Hamer, Martyn
  *See* Eldin, Peter
Hamerstrom, Frances 1907-1998 ............... *24*
Hamil, Thomas Arthur 1928- ..................... *14*
Hamill, Ethel
  *See* Webb, Jean Francis (III)
Hamilton, (John) Alan 1943- ..................... *66*
Hamilton, Alice
  *See* Cromie, Alice Hamilton
Hamilton, Anita 1919- ......................... *92*
Hamilton, Buzz
  *See* Hemming, Roy G.
Hamilton, Carol (Jean Barber) 1935- .......... *94*
Hamilton, Charles (Harold St. John) 1876-1961
  ........................................................ *13*
Hamilton, Charles 1913-1996 ................... *65*
  Obituary ........................................ *93*
Hamilton, Clive
  *See* Lewis, C.S.
Hamilton, Dorothy (Drumm) 1906-1983 .... *12*
  Obituary ........................................ *35*
Hamilton, Edith 1867-1963 ..................... *20*
Hamilton, Edmond 1904-1977 ................. *118*
Hamilton, (Muriel) Elizabeth (Mollie) 1906-
  ........................................................ *23*
Hamilton, Emma Walton 1962- ............... *177*
Hamilton, Franklin
  *See* Silverberg, Robert
Hamilton, Gail
  *See* Corcoran, Barbara (Asenath)
  and Dodge, Mary Abigail
Hamilton, Kersten 1958- ..................... *134*
Hamilton, Martha 1953- ....................... *123*
Hamilton, Mary (E.) 1927- ..................... *55*
Hamilton, Mollie
  *See* Kaye, M.M.
Hamilton, Morse 1943-1998 ................... *101*
  Earlier sketch in SATA *35*
Hamilton, Peter F. 1960- ..................... *109*
Hamilton, Priscilla
  *See* Gellis, Roberta
Hamilton, Ralph
  *See* Stratemeyer, Edward L.
Hamilton, Virginia 1936-2002 ................. *123*
  Obituary ........................................ *132*
  Earlier sketches in SATA *4, 56, 79*
  *See also* CLR *40*
Hamilton, Virginia Esther
  *See* Hamilton, Virginia
Hamilton-Paterson, James 1941- ............. *82*
Hamlet, Ova
  *See* Lupoff, Richard A(llen)
Hamley, Dennis 1935- ......................... *69*
  Earlier sketch in SATA *39*
  *See also* CLR *47*
  *See also* SAAS *22*
Hamlin, Peter J. 1970- ......................... *84*

Hamm, Diane Johnston 1949- ................... *78*
Hammer, Charles 1934- ......................... *58*
Hammer, Richard 1928- ......................... *6*
Hammerman, Gay M(orenus) 1926- ........... *9*
Hammond, Ralph
  *See* Hammond Innes, Ralph
Hammond, Winifred G(raham) 1899-1992 . *29*
  Obituary ........................................ *107*
Hammond Innes, Ralph 1913-1998 ........... *116*
  *See* Innes, (Ralph) Hammond
Hammontree, Marie (Gertrude) 1913- ......... *13*
Hample, Zack 1977- ............................. *161*
Hampshire, Joyce Gregorian
  *See* Gregorian, Joyce Ballou
Hampshire, Susan 1942- ......................... *98*
Hampson, (Richard) Denman 1929- ........... *15*
Hampton, Wilborn ................................. *156*
Hamre, Leif 1914- ................................. *5*
Hamsa, Bobbie 1944- ............................. *52*
  Brief entry ........................................ *38*
Han, Jenny 1981- ................................. *175*
Han, Lu
  *See* Stickler, Soma Han
Han, Soma
  *See* Stickler, Soma Han
Han, Suzanne Crowder 1953- ................... *89*
Hancock, Mary A. 1923- ......................... *31*
Hancock, Sibyl 1940- ............................. *9*
Hand, Elizabeth 1957- ......................... *167*
  Earlier sketch in SATA *118*
Handford, Martin (John) 1956- ................. *64*
  *See also* CLR *22*
Handforth, Thomas (Schofield) 1897-1948 . *42*
Handville, Robert (Tompkins) 1924- ........... *45*
Hanel, Wolfram
  *See* Haenel, Wolfram
Haney, Lynn 1941- ............................... *23*
Hanff, Helene 1916-1997 ....................... *97*
  Earlier sketch in SATA *11*
Hanley, Boniface Francis 1924- ................. *65*
Hanlon, Emily 1945- ............................. *15*
Hann, Jacquie 1951- ............................. *19*
Hann, Judith 1942- ............................... *77*
Hanna, Bill
  *See* Hanna, William (Denby)
Hanna, Cheryl 1951- ............................. *84*
Hanna, Jack (Bushnell) 1947- ................... *74*
Hanna, Nell(ie L.) 1908- ......................... *55*
Hanna, Paul R(obert) 1902-1988 ............... *9*
Hanna, William (Denby) 1910-2001 ........... *51*
  Obituary ........................................ *126*
Hannam, Charles 1925- ......................... *50*
Hannigan, Katherine ............................. *170*
Hannon, Ezra
  *See* Hunter, Evan
Hann-Syme, Marguerite ......................... *127*
Hano, Arnold 1922- ............................... *12*
Hano, Renee Roth
  *See* Roth-Hano, Renee
Hanover, Terri
  *See* Huff, Tanya
Hansen, Ann Larkin 1958- ..................... *96*
Hansen, Brooks 1965- ......................... *104*
Hansen, Caryl (Hall) 1929- ..................... *39*
Hansen, Ian V. 1929- ........................... *113*
Hansen, Jennifer 1972- ......................... *156*
Hansen, Joyce 1942- ........................... *172*
  Autobiography Feature ....................... *172*
  Brief entry ........................................ *39*
  Earlier sketches in SATA *46, 101*
  *See also* CLR *21*
  *See also* SAAS *15*
Hansen, Joyce Viola
  *See* Hansen, Joyce
Hansen, Mark Victor ............................. *112*
Hansen, Ron(ald Thomas) 1947- ............... *56*
Hanser, Richard (Frederick) 1909-1981 ...... *13*
Hanson, Joan 1938- ............................... *8*
Hanson, Warren 1949- ......................... *155*
Hansson, Gunilla 1939- ......................... *64*

Harald, Eric
  *See* Boesen, Victor
Hard, Charlotte (Ann) 1969- ..................... *98*
Hardcastle, Michael 1933- ..................... *47*
  Brief entry ........................................ *38*
Harding, Lee 1937- ............................... *32*
  Brief entry ........................................ *31*
Hardt, Helga Fleischhauer
  *See* Fleischhauer-Hardt, Helga
Hardwick, Richard Holmes, Jr. 1923- ........ *12*
Hardy, Alice Dale ................................. *67*
  Earlier sketch in SATA *1*
Hardy, David A(ndrews) 1936- ................... *9*
Hardy, Jon 1958- ................................. *53*
Hardy, LeAnne 1951- ........................... *154*
Hardy, Stuart
  *See* Schisgall, Oscar
Hare, Norma Q(uarles) 1924- ................... *46*
  Brief entry ........................................ *41*
Harel, Nira 1936- ............................... *154*
Harford, Henry
  *See* Hudson, W(illiam) H(enry)
Hargrave, Leonie
  *See* Disch, Thomas M.
Hargrove, James 1947- ......................... *57*
  Brief entry ........................................ *50*
Hargrove, Jim
  *See* Hargrove, James
Hariton, Anca I. 1955- ......................... *79*
Hark, Mildred
  *See* McQueen, Mildred Hark
Harkaway, Hal
  *See* Stratemeyer, Edward L.
Harkins, Philip 1912-1997 ..................... *6*
  Obituary ........................................ *129*
Harlan, Elizabeth 1945- ....................... *41*
  Brief entry ........................................ *35*
Harlan, Glen
  *See* Cebulash, Mel
Harlan, Judith 1949- ........................... *135*
  Earlier sketch in SATA *74*
  *See also* CLR *81*
Harland, Richard 1947- ......................... *152*
Harlee, J. V.
  *See* Leese, Jennifer L.B.
Harler, Ann
  *See* Van Steenwyk, Elizabeth (Ann)
Harley, Bill 1954- ............................... *87*
Harlow, Joan Hiatt 1932- ..................... *157*
Harmelink, Barbara (Mary) ..................... *9*
Harmer, Mabel 1894-1992 ..................... *45*
Harmon, Dan
  *See* Harmon, Daniel E(lton)
Harmon, Daniel E(lton) 1949- ................. *157*
Harmon, Margaret 1906- ....................... *20*
Harmon, William (Ruth) 1938- ................. *65*
Harnan, Terry 1920- ............................. *12*
Harness, Cheryl 1951- ......................... *131*
Harnett, Cynthia (Mary) 1893-1981 ........... *5*
  Obituary ........................................ *32*
Harper, Anita 1943- ............................. *41*
Harper, Betty 1946- ............................. *126*
Harper, Elaine
  *See* Hallin, Emily Watson
Harper, Ellen
  *See* Noble, Marty
Harper, Jamie ................................. *174*
Harper, Jessica (R.) 1949- ..................... *148*
Harper, Jo 1932- ............................... *169*
  Earlier sketch in SATA *97*
Harper, Mary Wood
  *See* Dixon, Jeanne
Harper, Piers 1966- ............................. *161*
  Earlier sketch in SATA *105*
Harper, Wilhelmina 1884-1973 ................. *4*
  Obituary ........................................ *26*
Harrah, Madge 1931- ........................... *154*
Harrah, Michael 1940- ......................... *41*
Harrah, Monique
  *See* Harrah, Madge
Harrar, George E. 1949- ....................... *124*

Harrell, Beatrice Orcutt 1943- ..................... 93
Harrell, Janice 1945- ................................... 70
Harries, Joan 1922- ..................................... 39
Harrill, Ronald 1950- ................................... 90
Harrington, Denis J(ames) 1932- ............... 88
Harrington, Lyn ............................................. 5
  *See* Harrington, Evelyn Davis
Harris, Alan 1944- ....................................... 71
Harris, Aurand 1915-1996 .......................... 37
  Obituary ................................................... 91
Harris, Carol Flynn 1933- ......................... 135
Harris, Catherine
  *See* Ainsworth, Catherine Harris
Harris, Christie
  *See* Harris, Christie (Lucy) Irwin
Harris, Christie (Lucy) Irwin 1907-2002 .... 74
  Autobiography Feature ........................... 116
  Earlier sketch in SATA 6
  *See also* CLR 47
  *See also* SAAS 10
Harris, Christine 1955- ............................. 105
Harris, Colver
  *See* Colver, Anne
Harris, David (William) 1942- .................. 118
Harris, Dorothy Joan 1931- ...................... 153
  Earlier sketch in SATA 13
Harris, Geraldine (Rachel) 1951- ............... 54
Harris, Jacqueline L. 1929- ........................ 62
Harris, Janet 1932-1979 ............................... 4
  Obituary ................................................... 23
Harris, Jesse
  *See* Standiford, Natalie
Harris, Joan 1946- .................................... 146
Harris, Joel Chandler 1848-1908 .............. 100
  *See also* YABC 1
  *See also* CLR 49
Harris, John (Wyndham Parkes Lucas) Beynon
  1903-1969 ............................................. 118
  *See* Wyndham, John
Harris, Johnson
  *See* Harris, John (Wyndham Parkes Lucas)
  Beynon
Harris, Jonathan 1921-1997 ........................ 52
Harris, Larry Vincent 1939- ....................... 59
Harris, Lavinia
  *See* St. John, Nicole
Harris, Leon A., Jr. 1926-2000 ..................... 4
Harris, Lorle K(empe) 1912-2001 ............... 22
Harris, Marilyn
  *See* Springer, Marilyn Harris
Harris, Mark Jonathan 1941- ....................... 84
  Earlier sketch in SATA 32
Harris, Mary K(athleen) 1905-1966 .......... 119
Harris, Robie H. 1940- ............................. 147
  Brief entry ................................................ 53
  Earlier sketch in SATA 90
Harris, Robin
  *See* Shine, Deborah
Harris, Rosemary (Jeanne) ......................... 82
  Earlier sketch in SATA 4
  *See also* CLR 30
  *See also* SAAS 7
Harris, Ruth Elwin 1935- .......................... 164
Harris, Sherwood 1932- .............................. 25
Harris, Steven Michael 1957- ..................... 55
Harris, Trudy 1949- .................................. 128
Harris-Filderman, Diane
  *See* Filderman, Diane E(lizabeth)
Harrison, C(hester) William 1913-1994 ...... 35
Harrison, Carol
  *See* Harrison, Carol Thompson
Harrison, Carol Thompson ........................ 113
Harrison, David L(ee) 1937- ..................... 150
  Earlier sketches in SATA 26, 92
Harrison, Deloris 1938- ................................ 9
Harrison, Edward Hardy 1926- ................... 56
Harrison, Elizabeth (Allen) Cavanna
  1909-2001 ............................................. 142
  *See* Cavanna, Betty
Harrison, Harry (Max) 1925- ........................ 4
Harrison, Mette Ivie 1970- ....................... 149

Harrison, Michael 1939- ........................... 106
Harrison, Molly (Hodgett) 1909-2002 ......... 41
Harrison, Sarah 1946- ................................. 63
Harrison, Ted
  *See* Harrison, Edward Hardy
Harsh, Fred (T.) 1925- ............................... 72
Harshaw, Ruth H(etzel) 1890-1968 ............. 27
Harshman, Marc 1950- ............................. 109
  Earlier sketch in SATA 71
Hart, Alison
  *See* Leonhardt, Alice
Hart, Bruce 1938-2006 ............................... 57
  Brief entry ................................................ 39
Hart, Carole 1943- ..................................... 57
  Brief entry ................................................ 39
Hart, Carolyn 1936- ................................... 74
Hart, Carolyn G.
  *See* Hart, Carolyn
Hart, Carolyn Gimpel
  *See* Hart, Carolyn
Hart, Jan Siegel 1940- ................................ 79
Hart, Joyce 1954- ..................................... 148
Hart, Lenore ............................................. 171
Hart, Virginia 1949- ................................... 83
Harte, (Francis) Bret(t) 1836(?)-1902 ......... 26
Harter, Debbie 1963- ............................... 107
Hartfield, Claire 1957- ............................. 147
Hartinger, Brent 1964- ............................. 174
  Earlier sketch in SATA 145
Hartland, Jessie ......................................... 171
Hartley, Ellen (Raphael) 1915-1980 ........... 23
Hartley, Fred Allan III 1953- ...................... 41
Hartley, William B(rown) 1913-1980 .......... 23
Hartling, Peter
  *See* CLR 29
  *See* Hartling, Peter
Hartling, Peter 1933- .................................. 66
  *See* Hartling, Peter
Hartman, Evert 1937- ................................. 38
  Brief entry ................................................ 35
Hartman, Jane E(vangeline) 1928- .............. 47
Hartman, Louis F(rancis) 1901-1970 .......... 22
Hartman, Rachel ....................................... 174
Hartman, Victoria 1942- ............................. 91
Hartnett, Sonya 1968- .............................. 176
  Earlier sketches in SATA 93, 130
Hartshorn, Ruth M. 1928- .......................... 11
Hartung, Susan Kathleen ......................... 150
Hartwig, Manfred 1950- ............................. 81
Harvey, Brett 1936- .................................... 61
Harvey, Karen D. 1935- .............................. 88
Harvey, Roland 1945- ............................... 123
  Earlier sketch in SATA 71
Harwick, B. L.
  *See* Keller, Beverly L(ou)
Harwin, Brian
  *See* Henderson, LeGrand
Harwood, Pearl Augusta (Bragdon) 1903-1998
  ................................................................... 9
Haseley, Dennis 1950- ............................. 157
  Brief entry ................................................ 44
  Earlier sketches in SATA 57, 105
Hashmi, Kerri 1955- ................................. 108
Haskell, Arnold L(ionel) 1903-1981(?) ......... 6
Haskins, James
  *See* Haskins, James S.
Haskins, James S. 1941-2005 ................... 132
  Autobiography Feature ........................... 132
  Earlier sketches in SATA 9, 69, 105
  *See also* CLR 39
  *See* Haskins, Jim
Haskins, Jim
  *See* SAAS 4
  *See* Haskins, James S.
Hasler, Joan 1931- ..................................... 28
Hass, Robert 1941- ..................................... 94
Hassall, Joan 1906-1988 ............................. 43
  Obituary ................................................... 56
Hassett, Ann 1958- .................................. 162
Hassett, John ........................................... 162
Hassler, Jon 1933- ...................................... 19

Hassler, Jon Francis
  *See* Hassler, Jon
Hastings, Beverly
  *See* Barkin, Carol
  and James, Elizabeth
Hastings, Graham
  *See* Jeffries, Roderic
Hastings, Ian 1912- .................................... 62
Hatch, Lynda S. 1950- ................................ 90
Hathaway, Barbara ................................... 164
Hathorn, Libby 1943- ............................... 156
  Autobiography Feature ........................... 156
  Earlier sketches in SATA 74, 120
  *See* Hathorn, Elizabeth Helen
Haugaard, Erik Christian 1923- .................. 68
  Earlier sketch in SATA 4
  *See also* CLR 11
  *See also* SAAS 12
Haugaard, Kay ......................................... 117
Haugen, Hayley Mitchell 1968- ................ 172
Haugen, Tormod 1945- ............................... 66
Hauman, Doris 1898-1984 .......................... 32
Hauman, George 1890-1961 ....................... 32
Hauptly, Denis J(ames) 1945- ..................... 57
Hauser, Jill Frankel 1950- ........................ 127
Hauser, Margaret L(ouise) 1909- ................ 10
Hausherr, Rosmarie 1943- ........................... 86
Hausman, Gerald 1945- ............................ 132
  Earlier sketches in SATA 13, 90
  *See also* CLR 89
Hausman, Gerry
  *See* Hausman, Gerald
Hauth, Katherine B. 1940- ......................... 99
Hautman, Pete 1952- ................................ 173
  Earlier sketches in SATA 82, 128
Hautman, Peter Murray
  *See* Hautman, Pete
Hautzig, Deborah 1956- ........................... 106
  Earlier sketch in SATA 31
Hautzig, Esther Rudomin 1930- ................ 148
  Earlier sketches in SATA 4, 68
  *See also* CLR 22
  *See also* SAAS 15
Havel, Geoff 1955- ................................... 152
Havel, Jennifer
  *See* Havill, Juanita
Havelin, Kate 1961- ................................. 143
Havighurst, Walter (Edwin) 1901-1994 ......... 1
  Obituary ................................................... 79
Haviland, Virginia 1911-1988 ....................... 6
  Obituary ................................................... 54
Havill, Juanita 1949- ............................... 155
  Earlier sketch in SATA 74
Hawes, Judy 1913- ....................................... 4
Hawes, Louise 1943- ................................... 60
Hawke, Rosanne 1953- ............................. 165
  Earlier sketch in SATA 124
Hawke, Rosanne Joy
  *See* Hawke, Rosanne
Hawkes, Kevin (Cliff) 1959- ..................... 150
  Earlier sketch in SATA 78
Hawkes, Nigel 1943- ................................ 119
Hawkesworth, Eric 1921- ........................... 13
Hawkins, Arthur 1903-1985 ....................... 19
Hawkins, Colin 1945- .............................. 162
  Earlier sketch in SATA 112
Hawkins, Jacqui ...................................... 162
  Earlier sketch in SATA 112
Hawkins, Laura 1951- ................................ 74
Hawkins, (Helena Ann) Quail 1905-2002 ..... 6
  Obituary ................................................. 141
Hawkinson, John (Samuel) 1912-1994 .......... 4
Hawkinson, Lucy (Ozone) 1924-1971 ......... 21
Hawks, Robert 1961- .................................. 85
Hawley, Mabel C. ....................................... 67
  Earlier sketch in SATA 1
Hawthorne, Captain R. M.
  *See* Ellis, Edward S(ylvester)
Hawthorne, Nathaniel 1804-1864
  *See* YABC 2
  *See also* CLR 103

Hay, Jeff T. ..................................... *154*
Hay, John 1915- ................................ *13*
Hay, Timothy
    *See* Brown, Margaret Wise
Hayashi, Leslie Ann 1954- .................. *115*
Hayashi, Nancy 1939- ......................... *80*
Haycock, Kate 1962- ........................... *77*
Haycraft, Howard 1905-1991 ................. *6*
    Obituary ...................................... *70*
Haycraft, Molly Costain 1911- .............. *6*
Hayden, Gwendolen Lampshire 1904- ...... *35*
Hayden, Robert C(arter), Jr. 1937- ........ *47*
    Brief entry ................................... *28*
Hayden, Robert E(arl) 1913-1980 .......... *19*
    Obituary ...................................... *26*
Hayden, Torey L. 1951- ...................... *163*
    Earlier sketch in SATA 65
Hayden, Torey Lynn
    *See* Hayden, Torey L.
Hayes, Carlton J(oseph) H(untley) 1882-1964
    ................................................. *11*
Hayes, Daniel 1952- .......................... *109*
    Earlier sketch in SATA 73
Hayes, Geoffrey 1947- ........................ *91*
    Earlier sketch in SATA 26
Hayes, Joe 1945- .............................. *131*
    Earlier sketch in SATA 88
Hayes, John F. 1904-1980 ................... *11*
Hayes, Rosemary ............................. *158*
Hayes, Sheila 1937- ........................... *51*
    Brief entry ................................... *50*
Hayes, Will ...................................... *7*
Hayes, William D(imitt) 1913-1976 ......... *8*
Haynes, Betsy 1937- .......................... *94*
    Brief entry ................................... *37*
    Earlier sketch in SATA 48
    *See also* CLR 90
Haynes, David 1955- .......................... *97*
Haynes, Linda
    *See* Swinford, Betty (June Wells)
Haynes, Mary 1938- ........................... *65*
Haynes, Max 1956- ............................ *72*
Hays, H(offmann) R(eynolds) 1904-1980 ... *26*
Hays, Thomas Anthony 1957- ................ *84*
Hays, Tony
    *See* Hays, Thomas Anthony
Hays, Wilma Pitchford 1909- ................ *28*
    Earlier sketch in SATA 1
    *See also* CLR 59
    *See also* SAAS 3
Hayward, Linda 1943- ........................ *101*
    Brief entry ................................... *39*
Haywood, Carolyn 1898-1990 ............... *75*
    Obituary ...................................... *64*
    Earlier sketches in SATA 1, 29
    *See also* CLR 22
Hazell, Rebecca (Eileen) 1947- ............ *141*
Hazen, Barbara Shook 1930- ................ *90*
    Earlier sketch in SATA 27
Head, Gay
    *See* Hauser, Margaret L(ouise)
Head, Tom 1978- .............................. *167*
Headley, Elizabeth
    *See* Harrison, Elizabeth (Allen) Cavanna
Headley, Justina Chen 1968- ................ *176*
Headstrom, (Birger) Richard 1902-1985 ..... *8*
Heady, Eleanor B(utler) 1917-1979 ......... *8*
Heagy, William D. 1964- ..................... *76*
Heal, Edith 1903-1995 ........................ *7*
Heal, Gillian 1934- ............................ *89*
Heale, Jay (Jeremy Peter Wingfield) 1937-
    ................................................. *84*

Healey, Brooks
    *See* Albert, Burton
Healey, Larry 1927- ........................... *44*
    Brief entry ................................... *42*
Heap, Sue 1954- .............................. *150*
Heaps, Willard A(llison) 1908-1987 ......... *26*
Hearn, Diane Dawson 1952- ................. *79*
Hearn, Emily
    *See* Valleau, Emily

Hearn, Julie 1958- ............................ *152*
Hearn, Lian
    *See* Rubinstein, Gillian (Margaret)
Hearn, Sneed
    *See* Gregg, Andrew K.
Hearne, Betsy Gould 1942- .................. *146*
    Earlier sketches in SATA 38, 95
Heath, Charles D(ickinson) 1941- ........... *46*
Heath, Veronica
    *See* Blackett, Veronica Heath
Heaven, Constance (Christina) 1911- ...... *7*
Hebert-Collins, Sheila 1948- ................ *111*
Hecht, Henri Joseph 1922- .................. *9*
Hechtkopf, Henryk 1910- .................... *17*
Heck, Bessie (Mildred) Holland 1911-1995
    ................................................. *26*
Heck, Ed 1963- ............................... *173*
Heckert, Connie K(aye Delp) 1948- ........ *82*
Hedderwick, Mairi 1939- .................... *145*
    Earlier sketch in SATA 30, 77
Hedges, Sid(ney) G(eorge) 1897-1974 ..... *28*
Hedrick, Irene Hope 1920- .................. *175*
Heelan, Jamee Riggio 1965- ................ *146*
Heerboth, Sharon
    *See* Leon, Sharon
Heffernan, John 1949- ....................... *168*
    Earlier sketch in SATA 121
Heffron, Dorris 1944- ........................ *68*
Hefter, Richard 1942- ........................ *31*
Hegarty, Reginald Beaton 1906-1973 ...... *10*
Hehenberger, Shelly 1968- .................. *126*
Heidbreder, Robert K. 1947- ............... *130*
Heide, Florence Parry 1919- ................ *118*
    Earlier sketches in SATA 32, 69
    *See also* CLR 60
    *See also* SAAS 6
Heiderstadt, Dorothy 1907-2001 ............ *6*
Heidi Louise
    *See* Erdrich, Louise
Heidler, David S(tephen) 1955- ............. *132*
Heidler, Jeanne T. 1956- .................... *132*
Heilbroner, Joan Knapp 1922- .............. *63*
Heiligman, Deborah 1958- ................... *144*
    Earlier sketch in SATA 90
Heilman, Joan Rattner ....................... *50*
Heimann, Rolf 1940- .......................... *164*
    Earlier sketch in SATA 120
Hein, Lucille Eleanor 1915-1994 ............ *20*
Heine, Helme 1941- .......................... *135*
    Earlier sketch in SATA 67
    *See also* CLR 18
Heinlein, Robert A. 1907-1988 .............. *69*
    Obituary ...................................... *56*
    Earlier sketch in SATA 9
    *See also* CLR 75
Heinlein, Robert Anson
    *See* Heinlein, Robert A.
Heins, Ethel L(eah) 1918-1997 ............. *101*
Heins, Paul 1909- ............................. *13*
Heintze, Carl 1922- ........................... *26*
Heinz, Brian J(ames) 1946- ................. *95*
Heinz, W(ilfred) C(harles) 1915- ........... *26*
Heinzen, Mildred
    *See* Masters, Mildred
Heisel, Sharon E(laine) 1941- .............. *125*
    Earlier sketch in SATA 84
Heitzmann, William Ray 1948- .............. *73*
Heitzmann, Wm. Ray
    *See* Heitzmann, William Ray
Helberg, Shirley Adelaide Holden 1919- .. *138*
Helfer, Ralph ................................... *177*
Helfman, Elizabeth S(eaver) 1911-2001 ..... *3*
Helfman, Harry Carmozin 1910-1995 ...... *3*
Hellberg, Hans-Eric 1927- .................. *38*
Heller, Linda 1944- ........................... *46*
    Brief entry ................................... *40*
Heller, Mike
    *See* Hano, Arnold
Heller, Ruth M. 1924- ........................ *112*
    Earlier sketch in SATA 66

Hellman, Hal
    *See* Hellman, Harold
Hellman, Harold 1927- ........................ *4*
Helman, Andrea (Jean) 1946- ............... *160*
    Earlier sketch in SATA 107
Helmer, Diana Star 1962- .................... *86*
Helmer, Marilyn ............................... *160*
    Earlier sketch in SATA 112
Helps, Racey 1913-1971 ...................... *2*
    Obituary ...................................... *25*
Helquist, Brett ................................. *146*
Helweg, Hans H. 1917- ...................... *50*
    Brief entry ................................... *33*
Helyar, Jane Penelope Josephine 1933- .... *138*
    Autobiography Feature ...................... *138*
    Earlier sketch in SATA 82
    *See* Poole, Josephine
Hemmant, Lynette 1938- ..................... *69*
Hemming, Roy G. 1928-1995 ................ *11*
    Obituary ...................................... *86*
Hemphill, Kris (Harrison) 1963- ............ *118*
Hemphill, Martha Locke 1904-1973 ........ *37*
Henba, Bobbie 1926- ......................... *87*
Henbest, Nigel 1951- ......................... *55*
    Brief entry ................................... *52*
Henderley, Brooks ............................. *1*
Henderson, Aileen Mary
    *See* Fox, Aileen
Henderson, Gordon 1950- .................... *53*
Henderson, Kathy 1949- ..................... *155*
    Brief entry ................................... *53*
    Earlier sketches in SATA 55, 95
Henderson, LeGrand 1901-1965 ............. *9*
Henderson, Nancy Wallace 1916- .......... *22*
Henderson, Zenna (Chlarson) 1917-1983 ..... *5*
Hendrickson, Walter Brookfield, Jr. 1936- .... *9*
Hendry, Diana 1941- ......................... *106*
    Earlier sketch in SATA 68
Hendry, Frances Mary 1941- ................ *171*
    Earlier sketch in SATA 110
Hendry, Linda (Gail) 1961- .................. *83*
Heneghan, James 1930- ...................... *160*
    Earlier sketches in SATA 53, 97
Henkes, Kevin 1960- ......................... *154*
    Earlier sketches in SATA 43, 76, 108
    *See also* CLR 108
Hennessy, Barbara Gulbrandsen
    *See* Hennessy, B.G.
Hennessy, B.G. 1951- ........................ *175*
Henney, Carolee Wells 1928- ............... *102*
Henriod, Lorraine 1925- ..................... *26*
Henriquez, Emile F. 1937- .................. *170*
    Earlier sketch in SATA 89
Henry, April 1959- ............................ *174*
Henry, Ernest 1948- .......................... *107*
Henry, Joanne Landers 1927- ................ *6*
Henry, Maeve 1960- .......................... *75*
Henry, Marguerite 1902-1997 ............... *100*
    Obituary ...................................... *99*
    *See also* CLR 4
    *See also* SAAS 7
Henry, Marie H. 1935- ....................... *65*
Henry, Marilyn 1939- ......................... *117*
Henry, Marion
    *See* del Rey, Lester
Henry, O.
    *See* Porter, William Sydney
Henry, Oliver
    *See* Porter, William Sydney
Henry, T. E.
    *See* Rowland-Entwistle, (Arthur) Theodore
    (Henry)
Henschel, Elizabeth Georgie ................. *56*
Henson, James Maury
    *See* Henson, Jim
Henson, Jim 1936-1990 ...................... *43*
    Obituary ...................................... *65*
Henstra, Friso 1928- ......................... *73*
    Earlier sketch in SATA 8
    *See also* SAAS 14

Hentoff, Nat(han Irving) 1925- ................. *133*
  Brief entry ......................................... *27*
  Earlier sketches in SATA *42, 69*
  *See also* CLR *52*
Henty, G(eorge) A(lfred) 1832-1902 .......... *64*
  *See also* CLR *76*
Heo, Yumi 1964- .................................. *146*
  Earlier sketch in SATA *94*
Hepler, Heather ................................. *177*
Herald, Kathleen
  *See* Peyton, Kathleen Wendy (Herald)
Herb, Angela M. 1970- ........................... *92*
Herbert, Cecil
  *See* Hamilton, Charles (Harold St. John)
Herbert, Don(ald Jeffrey) 1917- ................. *2*
Herbert, Frank 1920-1986 ......................... *37*
  Obituary ......................................... *47*
  Earlier sketch in SATA *9*
Herbert, Frank Patrick
  *See* Herbert, Frank
Herbert, Helen (Jean) 1947- ..................... *57*
Herbert, Janis 1956- ............................ *139*
Herbert, Wally
  *See* Herbert, Walter William
Herbert, Walter William 1934- ................... *23*
Herbst, Judith 1947- ............................. *74*
Herda, D.J. 1948- ................................ *80*
Herge
  *See* CLR *114*
  *See* Remi, Georges
Heritage, Martin
  *See* Horler, Sydney
Herkimer, L(awrence) R(ussell) 1925(?)- ... *42*
Herlihy, Dirlie Anne 1935- ...................... *73*
Herman, Charlotte 1937- ......................... *99*
  Earlier sketch in SATA *20*
Hermanson, Dennis (Everett) 1947- ............ *10*
Hermes, Jules 1962- .............................. *92*
Hermes, Patricia (Mary) 1936- .................. *141*
  Earlier sketches in SATA *31, 78*
Hernandez, Natalie Nelson 1929- .............. *123*
Herndon, Ernest .................................. *91*
Herold, Ann Bixby 1937- ......................... *72*
Herrera, Juan Felipe 1948- ...................... *127*
Herrick, Steven 1958- ........................... *156*
  Earlier sketch in SATA *103*
Herriman, George (Joseph) 1880-1944 ..... *140*
Herriot, James 1916-1995 ........................ *135*
  Earlier sketch in SATA *86*
  *See also* CLR *80*
  *See* Wight, James Alfred
Herrmanns, Ralph 1933- ........................... *11*
Herrold, Tracey
  *See* Dils, Tracey E.
Herron, Edward A(lbert) 1912- .................... *4*
Herschler, Mildred Barger ....................... *130*
Hersey, John 1914-1993 ........................... *25*
  Obituary ......................................... *76*
Hersey, John Richard
  *See* Hersey, John
  and Hersey, John
Hershberger, Priscilla (Gorman) 1951- ....... *81*
Hershenhorn, Esther 1945- ....................... *151*
Hershey, Kathleen M. 1934- ...................... *80*
Hershey, Mary ................................... *173*
Hersom, Kathleen 1911- ........................... *73*
Hertz, Grete Janus 1915- ......................... *23*
Herzig, Alison Cragin 1935- ...................... *87*
Herzog, Brad 1968- .............................. *131*
Heslewood, Juliet 1951- ........................... *82*
Hess, Lilo 1916- .................................. *4*
Hess, Paul 1961- ................................. *134*
Hesse, Hermann 1877-1962 ......................... *50*
Hesse, Karen 1952- .............................. *158*
  Autobiography Feature ........................... *113*
  Earlier sketches in SATA *74, 103*
  *See also* CLR *54*
  *See also* SAAS *25*
Hest, Amy 1950- ................................. *129*
  Earlier sketches in SATA *55, 82*
Heuer, Kenneth John 1927- ........................ *44*

Heuman, William 1912-1971 ....................... *21*
Heuston, Kimberley 1960- ......................... *167*
Heuston, Kimberley Burton
  *See* Heuston, Kimberley
Hewes, Agnes Danforth 1874-1963 .............. *35*
Hewett, Anita 1918-1989 .......................... *13*
Hewett, Joan 1930- .............................. *140*
  Earlier sketch in SATA *81*
Hewett, Richard 1929- ............................ *81*
Hewitson, Jennifer 1961- ......................... *97*
Hewitt, Margaret 1961- ........................... *84*
Hewitt, Sally 1949- .............................. *127*
Hext, Harrington
  *See* Phillpotts, Eden
Hey, Nigel S(tewart) 1936- ....................... *20*
Heyduck-Huth, Hilde 1929- ......................... *8*
Heyer, Carol 1950- .............................. *130*
  Earlier sketch in SATA *74*
Heyer, Marilee 1942- ............................ *102*
  Earlier sketch in SATA *64*
Heyerdahl, Thor 1914-2002 ........................ *52*
  Earlier sketch in SATA *2*
Heyes, (Nancy) Eileen 1956- ..................... *150*
  Earlier sketch in SATA *80*
Heyliger, William 1884-1955
  *See* YABC *1*
Heyman, Ken(neth Louis) 1930- .................. *114*
  Earlier sketch in SATA *34*
Heyward, (Edwin) DuBose 1885-1940 ....... *21*
Heywood, Karen 1946- ............................. *48*
Hezlep, William (Earl) 1936- ..................... *88*
Hibbert, Christopher 1924- ........................ *4*
Hibbert, Eleanor Alice Burford 1906-1993 ... *2*
  Obituary ......................................... *74*
  *See* Holt, Victoria
Hickman, Estella (Lee) 1942- .................... *111*
Hickman, Janet 1940- ............................ *127*
  Earlier sketch in SATA *12*
Hickman, Martha Whitmore 1925- ............. *26*
Hickman, Pamela M. 1958- ........................ *128*
Hickock, Will
  *See* Harrison, C(hester) William
Hickok, Lorena A. 1893-1968 ..................... *20*
Hickox, Rebecca (Ayres) ......................... *116*
Hicks, Barbara Jean 1953- ....................... *165*
Hicks, Clifford B. 1920- ......................... *50*
Hicks, Eleanor B.
  *See* Coerr, Eleanor (Beatrice)
Hicks, Harvey
  *See* Stratemeyer, Edward L.
Hicks, Peter 1952- .............................. *111*
Hicyilmaz, Gaye 1947- ........................... *157*
  Earlier sketch in SATA *77*
Hieatt, Constance B(artlett) 1928- ............... *4*
Hiebert, Ray Eldon 1932- ......................... *13*
Higdon, Hal 1931- ................................. *4*
Higginbottom, David 1923- ........................ *87*
  *See* Fisk, Nicholas
Higginbottom, J(effrey) Winslow 1945- ...... *29*
Higgins, Joanna 1945- ........................... *125*
Higgins, Simon (Richard) 1958- .................. *105*
Higginsen, Vy .................................... *79*
High, Linda Oatman 1958- ........................ *145*
  Earlier sketch in SATA *94*
High, Philip E. 1914- ........................... *119*
High, Philip Empson
  *See* High, Philip E.
Higham, David (Michael) 1949- ................... *50*
Higham, Jon Atlas
  *See* Higham, Jonathan Huw
Higham, Jonathan Huw 1960- ...................... *59*
Highet, Helen
  *See* MacInnes, Helen (Clark)
Hightower, Florence Cole 1916-1981 ........... *4*
  Obituary ......................................... *27*
Highwater, Jamake (Mamake) 1942(?)-2001
  ................................................. *69*
  Brief entry ...................................... *30*
  Earlier sketch in SATA *32*
  *See also* CLR *17*

Hildebrandt, Greg 1939- ......................... *172*
  Brief entry ...................................... *33*
  Earlier sketch in SATA *55*
Hildebrandt, Tim 1939-2006 ...................... *55*
  Brief entry ...................................... *33*
Hildebrandt, Timothy
  *See* Hildebrandt, Tim
Hildebrandts, The
  *See* Hildebrandt, Greg
  and Hildebrandt, Tim
Hilder, Rowland 1905-1993 ........................ *36*
  Obituary ......................................... *77*
Hildick, E. W.
  *See* SAAS *6*
  *See* Hildick, (Edmund) Wallace
Hildick, (Edmund) Wallace 1925-2001 ....... *68*
  Earlier sketch in SATA *2*
  *See* Hildick, E. W.
Hilgartner, Beth 1957- ........................... *58*
Hill, Alexis
  *See* Craig, Mary (Francis) Shura
  and Glick, Ruth (Burtnick)
Hill, Anthony R. 1942- ........................... *164*
  Earlier sketch in SATA *91*
Hill, Anthony Robert
  *See* Hill, Anthony R.
Hill, David 1942- ............................... *152*
  Earlier sketch in SATA *103*
Hill, Donna (Marie) 1921- ....................... *124*
  Earlier sketch in SATA *24*
Hill, Douglas (Arthur) 1935- ..................... *78*
  Earlier sketch in SATA *39*
Hill, Elizabeth Starr 1925- ..................... *143*
  Earlier sketch in SATA *24*
Hill, Eric 1927- ................................ *133*
  Brief entry ...................................... *53*
  Earlier sketch in SATA *66*
  *See also* CLR *13*
Hill, Gordon
  *See* Eldin, Peter
Hill, Grace Brooks .............................. *67*
  Earlier sketch in SATA *1*
Hill, Grace Livingston 1865-1947
  *See* YABC *2*
Hill, Helen M(orey) 1915- ........................ *27*
Hill, John
  *See* Koontz, Dean R.
Hill, Johnson
  *See* Kunhardt, Edith
Hill, Judy I. R.
  *See* Roberts, Judy I.
Hill, Kathleen Louise 1917- ....................... *4*
Hill, Kay
  *See* Hill, Kathleen Louise
Hill, Kirkpatrick 1938- ......................... *126*
  Earlier sketch in SATA *72*
Hill, Laban Carrick .............................. *170*
Hill, Lee Sullivan 1958- ......................... *96*
Hill, Lorna 1902-1991 ............................ *12*
Hill, Margaret (Ohler) 1915- ..................... *36*
Hill, Meg
  *See* Hill, Margaret (Ohler)
Hill, Meredith
  *See* Craig, Mary (Francis) Shura
Hill, Monica
  *See* Watson, Jane Werner
Hill, Pamela Smith 1954- ........................ *112*
Hill, Ralph Nading 1917-1987 .................... *65*
Hill, Robert W(hite) 1919-1982 .................. *12*
  Obituary ......................................... *31*
Hill, Ruth A.
  *See* Viguers, Ruth Hill
Hill, Ruth Livingston
  *See* Munce, Ruth Hill
Hill, Thomas 1960- ............................... *82*
Hillcourt, William 1900-1992 .................... *27*
Hillenbrand, Will 1960- ......................... *147*
  Earlier sketch in SATA *84*
Hiller, Ilo (Ann) 1938- .......................... *59*
Hillerman, Tony 1925- ............................. *6*

Hillert, Margaret 1920- ............................ *91*
  Earlier sketch in SATA *8*
Hillman, Elizabeth 1942- ........................ *75*
Hillman, John 1952- ............................... *120*
Hillman, Martin
  *See* Hill, Douglas (Arthur)
Hillman, Priscilla 1940- ......................... *48*
  Brief entry ........................................... *39*
Hills, C.A.R. 1955- ................................. *39*
Hills, Charles Albert Reis
  *See* Hills, C.A.R.
Hills, Tad ............................................... *173*
Hilton, Irene Pothus -1979 ...................... *7*
Hilton, James 1900-1954 ......................... *34*
Hilton, Margaret Lynette 1946- ............... *105*
  Earlier sketch in SATA *68*
  *See* Hilton, Nette
Hilton, Nette
  *See* CLR *25*
  *See also* SAAS *21*
  *See* Hilton, Margaret Lynette
Hilton, Ralph 1907-1982 .......................... *8*
Hilton, Suzanne 1922- ............................. *4*
Hilton-Bruce, Anne
  *See* Hilton, Margaret Lynette
Himelstein, Shmuel 1940- ........................ *83*
Himler, Ann 1946- .................................. *8*
Himler, Ronald (Norbert) 1937- .............. *137*
  Earlier sketches in SATA *6, 92*
Himmelman, John C(arl) 1959- ............... *159*
  Earlier sketches in SATA *47, 94*
Hinckley, Helen
  *See* Jones, Helen Hinckley
Hind, Dolores (Ellen) 1931- ..................... *53*
  Brief entry ........................................... *49*
Hindin, Nathan
  *See* Bloch, Robert (Albert)
Hindley, Judy 1940- ................................ *120*
Hinds, P(atricia) Mignon ........................ *98*
Hines, Anna Grossnickle 1946- ............... *141*
  Brief entry ........................................... *45*
  Earlier sketches in SATA *51, 95*
  *See also* SAAS *16*
Hines, Gary (Roger) 1944- ...................... *136*
  Earlier sketch in SATA *74*
Hinojosa, Maria (de Lourdes) 1961- ......... *88*
Hinton, Nigel 1941- ................................ *166*
Hinton, Sam 1917- .................................. *43*
Hinton, S.E. 1950- .................................. *160*
  Earlier sketches in SATA *19, 58, 115*
  *See also* CLR *23*
Hinton, Susan Eloise
  *See* Hinton, S.E.
Hintz, Martin 1945- ................................ *128*
  Brief entry ........................................... *39*
  Earlier sketch in SATA *47*
Hintz, Stephen V. 1975- .......................... *129*
Hippopotamus, Eugene H.
  *See* Kraus, (Herman) Robert
Hirano, Cathy 1957- ............................... *68*
Hirsch, Karen 1941- ............................... *61*
Hirsch, Odo ............................................ *157*
  Earlier sketch in SATA *111*
Hirsch, Phil 1926- .................................. *35*
Hirsch, S. Carl 1913-1990 ....................... *2*
  *See also* SAAS *7*
Hirschfelder, Arlene B. 1943- ................. *138*
  Earlier sketch in SATA *80*
Hirschi, Ron 1948- ................................. *95*
  Earlier sketch in SATA *56*
Hirschmann, Linda (Ann) 1941- ............... *40*
Hirsh, Marilyn 1944-1988 ....................... *7*
  Obituary .............................................. *58*
Hirshberg, Al(bert Simon) 1909-1973 ...... *38*
Hiscock, Bruce 1940- .............................. *137*
  Earlier sketch in SATA *57*
Hiser, Constance 1950- ........................... *71*
Hiser, Iona Seibert -1998 ........................ *4*
Hislop, Julia Rose Catherine 1962- .......... *74*

Hissey, Jane 1952- .................................. *130*
  Autobiography Feature ......................... *130*
  Earlier sketch in SATA *58, 103*
Hissey, Jane Elizabeth
  *See* Hissey, Jane
Hitchcock, Alfred (Joseph) 1899-1980 ........ *27*
  Obituary .............................................. *24*
Hite, Sid 1954- ...................................... *175*
  Earlier sketch in SATA *75, 136*
Hitte, Kathryn 1919- .............................. *16*
Hitz, Demi 1942- .................................... *152*
  Earlier sketches in SATA *11, 66, 102*
  *See also* CLR *58*
  *See* Demi
Hitzeroth, Deborah L. 1961- .................... *78*
Hnizdovsky, Jacques 1915- ...................... *32*
Ho, Minfong 1951- .................................. *151*
  Earlier sketches in SATA *15, 94*
  *See also* CLR *28*
Hoagland, Edward (Morley) 1932- ............ *51*
Hoare, Robert J(ohn) 1921-1975 .............. *38*
Hoban, Lillian 1925-1998 ........................ *69*
  Obituary .............................................. *104*
  Earlier sketch in SATA *22*
  *See also* CLR *67*
Hoban, Russell 1925- ............................. *136*
  Earlier sketches in SATA *1, 40, 78*
  *See also* CLR *69*
Hoban, Russell Conwell
  *See* Hoban, Russell
Hoban, Tana 1917(?)-2006 ...................... *104*
  Obituary .............................................. *173*
  Earlier sketches in SATA *22, 70*
  *See also* CLR *76*
  *See also* SAAS *12*
Hobart, Lois (Elaine) .............................. *7*
Hobbie, Holly 1944-
  *See* CLR *88*
Hobbs, Leigh 1953- ................................. *166*
Hobbs, Valerie 1941- .............................. *145*
  Autobiography Feature ......................... *145*
  Earlier sketch in SATA *93*
Hobbs, Will 1947- .................................. *177*
  Autobiography Feature ......................... *127*
  Earlier sketches in SATA *72, 110*
  *See also* CLR *59*
Hobbs, William Carl
  *See* Hobbs, Will
Hoberman, Mary Ann 1930- ..................... *158*
  Earlier sketches in SATA *5, 72, 111*
  *See also* CLR *22*
  *See also* SAAS *18*
Hobson, Bruce 1950- .............................. *62*
Hobson, Burton (Harold) 1933- ............... *28*
Hobson, Laura Z(ametkin) 1900-1986 ...... *52*
Hobson, Sally 1967- ............................... *172*
  Earlier sketch in SATA *84*
Hoce, Charley E. ..................................... *174*
Hochschild, Arlie Russell 1940- ............... *11*
Hockaby, Stephen
  *See* Mitchell, Gladys (Maude Winifred)
Hockenberry, Hope
  *See* Newell, Hope Hockenberry
Hodge, Deborah 1954- ............................ *163*
  Earlier sketch in SATA *122*
Hodge, P. W.
  *See* Hodge, Paul W(illiam)
Hodge, Paul W(illiam) 1934- .................... *12*
Hodgell, P(atricia) C(hristine) 1951- ......... *42*
Hodges, C. Walter 1909-2004 .................. *2*
  Obituary .............................................. *158*
Hodges, Carl G. 1902-1964 ..................... *10*
Hodges, Cyril Walter
  *See* Hodges, C. Walter
Hodges, Elizabeth Jamison ....................... *1*
Hodges, Margaret
  *See* Hodges, Margaret Moore
Hodges, Margaret Moore 1911-2005 ......... *167*
  Obituary .............................................. *172*
  Earlier sketches in SATA *1, 33, 75, 117*
  *See also* SAAS *9*

Hodgetts, Blake Christopher 1967- ........... *43*
Hodgson, Harriet (W.) 1935- ................... *84*
Hoehne, Marcia 1951- ............................ *89*
Hoellwarth, Cathryn Clinton
  *See* Clinton, Cathryn
Hoestlandt, Jo 1948- .............................. *94*
Hoestlandt, Jocelyne
  *See* Hoestlandt, Jo
Hoexter, Corinne K. 1927- ...................... *6*
Hoeye, Michael 1947- ............................ *136*
Hoff, Carol 1900-1979 ............................ *11*
Hoff, Mary (King) 1956- ......................... *157*
  Earlier sketch in SATA *74*
Hoff, Syd(ney) 1912-2004 ....................... *138*
  Obituary .............................................. *154*
  Earlier sketches in SATA *9, 72*
  *See also* CLR *83*
  *See also* SAAS *4*
Hoffman, Edwin D. ................................. *49*
Hoffman, Mary (Margaret) 1945- ............. *144*
  Earlier sketches in SATA *59, 97*
  *See also* SAAS *24*
  *See* Lassiter, Mary
Hoffman, Mat 1972- ............................... *150*
Hoffman, Nina Kiriki 1955- ..................... *160*
Hoffman, Phyllis M(iriam) 1944- .............. *4*
Hoffman, Rosekrans 1926- ...................... *15*
Hoffmann, E(rnst) T(heodor) A(madeus)
  1776-1822 ........................................... *27*
Hoffmann, Felix 1911-1975 ..................... *9*
Hoffmann, Heinrich 1809-1894
  *See* CLR *122*
Hoffmann, Margaret Jones 1910- ............. *48*
Hoffmann, Peggy
  *See* Hoffmann, Margaret Jones
Hofher, Catherine Baxley 1954- ............... *130*
Hofher, Cathy
  *See* Hofher, Catherine Baxley
Hofmeyr, Dianne (Louise) ....................... *138*
Hofsepian, Sylvia A. 1932- ...................... *74*
Hofsinde, Robert 1902-1973 ................... *21*
Hogan, Bernice Harris 1929- ................... *12*
Hogan, Inez 1895-1973 ........................... *2*
Hogan, James P(atrick) 1941- .................. *81*
Hogan, Linda 1947- ................................ *132*
Hogarth, Burne 1911-1996 ...................... *89*
  Earlier sketch in SATA *63*
Hogarth, Grace (Weston Allen) 1905-1995 . *91*
Hogarth, Jr.
  *See* Kent, Rockwell
Hogarth, (Arthur) Paul 1917-2001 ........... *41*
Hogg, Garry 1902-1976 ........................... *2*
Hogg, Gary 1957- ................................... *172*
  Earlier sketch in SATA *105*
Hogner, Dorothy Childs ........................... *4*
Hogner, Nils 1893-1970 .......................... *25*
Hogrogian, Nonny 1932- ......................... *74*
  Autobiography Feature ......................... *127*
  Earlier sketch in SATA *7*
  *See also* CLR *95*
  *See also* SAAS *1*
Hoh, Diane 1937- ................................... *102*
  Brief entry ........................................... *48*
  Earlier sketch in SATA *52*
Hoke, John (Lindsay) 1925- ..................... *7*
Hol, Coby 1943- ..................................... *126*
Holabird, Katharine 1948- ....................... *135*
  Earlier sketch in SATA *62*
Holaday, Bobbie 1922- ............................ *153*
Holbeach, Henry
  *See* Rands, William Brighty
Holberg, Ruth L(angland) 1889-1984 ........ *1*
Holbrook, Kathy 1963- ............................ *107*
Holbrook, Peter
  *See* Glick, Carl (Cannon)
Holbrook, Sabra
  *See* Erickson, Sabra Rollins
Holbrook, Sara ...................................... *131*
Holbrook, Stewart Hall 1893-1964 ........... *2*
Holcomb, Jerry (Leona) Kimble 1927- ...... *113*

Holcomb, Nan
  *See* McPhee, Norma H.
Holden, Elizabeth Rhoda
  *See* Lawrence, Louise
Holding, James (Clark Carlisle, Jr.) 1907-1997
  ........................................................ *3*
Holeman, Linda 1949- .............................. *136*
  Autobiography Feature .......................... *136*
  Earlier sketch in SATA *102*
Holinger, William (Jacques) 1944- .............. *90*
Holisher, Desider 1901-1972 ........................ *6*
Holl, Adelaide Hinkle 1910- ........................ *8*
Holl, Kristi D(iane) 1951- ............................ *51*
Holland, Gay W. 1941- ............................... *128*
Holland, Isabelle (Christian) 1920-2002 ..... *70*
  Autobiography Feature .......................... *103*
  Obituary .............................................. *132*
  Earlier sketch in SATA *8*
  *See also* CLR *57*
Holland, Janice 1913-1962 ............................ *18*
Holland, John L(ewis) 1919- ........................ *20*
Holland, Joyce
  *See* Morice, Dave
Holland, Julia 1954- ................................... *106*
Holland, Lynda (H.) 1959- ............................ *77*
Holland, Lys
  *See* Gater, Dilys
Holland, Marion 1908-1989 .......................... *6*
  Obituary .............................................. *61*
Hollander, John 1929- ................................. *13*
Hollander, Nicole 1940(?)- ........................... *101*
Hollander, Paul
  *See* Silverberg, Robert
Hollander, Phyllis 1928- .............................. *39*
Hollander, Zander 1923- .............................. *63*
Holldobler, Turid 1939- ............................... *26*
Holliday, Joe
  *See* Holliday, Joseph
Holliday, Joseph 1910- ................................ *11*
Holling, Holling C(lancy) 1900-1973 ......... *15*
  Obituary .............................................. *26*
  *See also* CLR *50*
Hollingsworth, Alvin C(arl) 1930- .............. *39*
Hollingsworth, Mary 1947- ......................... *166*
  Earlier sketch in SATA *91*
Holloway, Teresa (Bragunier) 1906- .......... *26*
Holm, (Else) Anne (Lise) 1922-1998 .......... *1*
  *See also* CLR *75*
  *See also* SAAS *7*
Holm, Jennifer L. 1968(?)- ......................... *163*
  Earlier sketch in SATA *120*
Holm, Matthew 1974- ................................. *174*
Holm, Sharon Lane 1955- ............................ *114*
  Earlier sketch in SATA *78*
Holman, Felice 1919- .................................. *82*
  Earlier sketch in SATA *7*
  *See also* SAAS *17*
Holm and Hamel
  *See* Holm, Jennifer L.
Holme, Bryan 1913-1990 ............................. *26*
  Obituary .............................................. *66*
Holmes, Barbara Ware 1945- ....................... *127*
  Earlier sketch in SATA *65*
Holmes, John
  *See* Souster, (Holmes) Raymond
Holmes, Marjorie (Rose) 1910-2002 .......... *43*
Holmes, Martha 1961- ................................. *72*
Holmes, Mary Z(astrow) 1943- .................... *80*
Holmes, Oliver Wendell 1809-1894 ........... *34*
Holmes, Peggy 1898- .................................. *60*
Holmes, Raymond
  *See* Souster, (Holmes) Raymond
Holmes, Rick
  *See* Hardwick, Richard Holmes, Jr.
Holmgren, Helen Jean 1930- ....................... *45*
Holmgren, Sister George Ellen
  *See* Holmgren, Helen Jean
Holmgren, Virginia C(unningham) 1909- ... *26*
Holmquist, Eve 1921- ................................. *11*
Holt, Kimberly Willis 1960- ........................ *122*
Holt, Margaret 1937- .................................... *4*

Holt, Margaret Van Vechten (Saunders)
  1899-1963 .......................................... *32*
Holt, Michael (Paul) 1929- ......................... *13*
Holt, Rackham
  *See* Holt, Margaret Van Vechten (Saunders)
Holt, Rochelle L. .......................................... *41*
  *See* DuBois, Rochelle (Lynn) Holt
Holt, Stephen
  *See* Thompson, Harlan (Howard)
Holt, Victoria
  *See* Hibbert, Eleanor Alice Burford
Holton, Leonard
  *See* Wibberley, Leonard (Patrick O'Connor)
Holtze, Sally Holmes 1952- ......................... *64*
Holtzman, Jerome 1926- .............................. *57*
Holub, Joan 1956- ...................................... *149*
  Earlier sketch in SATA *99*
Holub, Josef 1926- ..................................... *175*
Holubitsky, Katherine 1955- ........................ *165*
  Earlier sketch in SATA *121*
Holyer, Erna Maria 1925- ............................ *22*
Holyer, Ernie
  *See* Holyer, Erna Maria
Holz, Loretta (Marie) 1943- ......................... *17*
Homel, David 1952- .................................... *97*
Homze, Alma C. 1932- ................................ *17*
Honey, Elizabeth 1947- ............................... *137*
  Autobiography Feature .......................... *137*
  Earlier sketch in SATA *112*
Honeycutt, Natalie 1945- ............................. *97*
Hong, Lily Toy 1958- .................................. *76*
Honig, Donald 1931- ................................... *18*
Honness, Elizabeth H. 1904- ......................... *2*
Hoobler, Dorothy 1941- ............................... *161*
  Earlier sketches in SATA *28, 109*
Hoobler, Thomas ......................................... *161*
  Earlier sketches in SATA *28, 109*
Hood, Joseph F. 1925- ................................... *4*
Hood, Robert E. 1926- ................................. *21*
Hood, Sarah
  *See* Killough, (Karen) Lee
Hook, Brendan 1963- ................................... *105*
Hook, Frances 1912-1983 ............................. *27*
Hook, Geoffrey R(aynor) 1928- ................... *103*
Hook, Jeff
  *See* Hook, Geoffrey R(aynor)
Hook, Martha 1936- .................................... *27*
Hooker, Richard
  *See* Heinz, W(ilfred) C(harles)
Hooker, Ruth 1920-1998 .............................. *21*
hooks, bell 1952(?)- .................................... *170*
  Earlier sketch in SATA *115*
Hooks, William H(arris) 1921- .................... *94*
  Earlier sketch in SATA *16*
Hoon, Patricia Easterly 1954- ...................... *90*
Hooper, Mary 1944- .................................... *160*
Hooper, Maureen Brett 1927- ...................... *76*
Hooper, Meredith (Jean) 1939- .................... *159*
  Earlier sketches in SATA *28, 101*
Hooper, Patricia 1941- ................................. *95*
Hoopes, Lyn Littlefield 1953- ...................... *49*
  Brief entry .......................................... *44*
Hoopes, Ned E(dward) 1932- ...................... *21*
Hoopes, Roy 1922- ...................................... *11*
Hoose, Phillip M. 1947- .............................. *137*
Hoover, H(elen) M(ary) 1935- ..................... *132*
  Brief entry .......................................... *33*
  Earlier sketches in SATA *44, 83*
  *See also* SAAS *8*
Hoover, Helen (Drusilla Blackburn) 1910-1984
  ........................................................ *12*
  Obituary .............................................. *39*
Hope, Christopher (David Tully) 1944- ...... *62*
Hope, Laura Lee .......................................... *67*
  Earlier sketch in SATA *1*
  *See* Goulart, Ron(ald Joseph)
  and Stanley, George Edward
Hope Simpson, Jacynth 1930- ...................... *12*
Hopf, Alice (Martha) L(ightner) 1904-1988 . *5*
  Obituary .............................................. *55*

Hopkins, C. M.
  *See* Hopkins, Cathy
Hopkins, Cathy 1953- .................................. *165*
Hopkins, Cathy M.
  *See* Hopkins, Cathy
Hopkins, Ellen L. 1955- ............................... *128*
Hopkins, Jackie (Mims) 1952- ..................... *92*
Hopkins, Joseph G(erard) E(dward) 1909- .. *11*
Hopkins, Lee Bennett 1938- ........................ *168*
  Earlier sketches in SATA *3, 68, 125*
  *See also* CLR *44*
  *See also* SAAS *4*
Hopkins, Lyman
  *See* Folsom, Franklin (Brewster)
Hopkins, Marjorie 1911-1999 ......................... *9*
Hopkins, Mary R(ice) 1956- ........................ *97*
Hopkinson, Amanda 1948- ............................ *84*
Hopkinson, Deborah 1952- ........................... *159*
  Earlier sketches in SATA *76, 108*
  *See also* CLR *118*
Hopman, Philip 1961- .................................. *177*
Hoppe, Joanne 1932- ................................... *42*
Hoppe, Matthias 1952- ................................. *76*
Hopper, Nancy J. 1937- ................................ *38*
  Brief entry .......................................... *35*
Hopping, Lorraine Jean
  *See* Egan, Lorraine Hopping
Horacek, Petr ............................................. *163*
Horenstein, Henry 1947- .............................. *108*
Horgan, Paul (George Vincent O'Shaughnessy)
  1903-1995 .......................................... *13*
  Obituary .............................................. *84*
Horlak, E. E.
  *See* Tepper, Sheri S.
Horler, Sydney 1888-1954 ............................ *102*
Horn, Sandra Ann 1944- .............................. *154*
Hornblow, Arthur, Jr. 1893-1976 ................. *15*
Hornblow, Leonora 1920-2005 ..................... *18*
  Obituary .............................................. *171*
Hornblow, Leonora Schinasi
  *See* Hornblow, Leonora
Horne, Constance 1927- ............................... *149*
Horne, Richard George Anthony
  *See* Horse, Harry
Horne, Richard Henry Hengist 1802(?)-1884
  ........................................................ *29*
Horner, Althea (Jane) 1926- ........................ *36*
Horner, Dave 1934- ..................................... *12*
Horner, Jack
  *See* Horner, John R(obert)
Horner, John R(obert) 1946- ........................ *106*
Hornik, Laurie Miller .................................. *159*
Horniman, Joanne 1951- .............................. *167*
  Earlier sketch in SATA *98*
Hornos, Axel 1907-1994 ............................... *20*
Hornstein, Reuben Aaron 1912- ................... *64*
Horowitz, Anthony 1955- ............................. *137*
Horowitz, Dave 1973(?)- .............................. *172*
Horowitz, Ruth 1957- .................................. *136*
Horrocks, Anita 1958- ................................. *169*
Horse, Harry 1960-2007 .............................. *169*
  Earlier sketch in SATA *111*
Horsfield, Alan 1939- .................................. *153*
Horton, James O. 1943- ............................... *173*
Horton, James Oliver
  *See* Horton, James O.
Horton, Madelyn (Stacey) 1962- .................. *77*
Horvath, Betty 1927- ..................................... *4*
Horvath, Polly 1957- ................................... *140*
  Earlier sketch in SATA *85*
  *See also* CLR *90*
Horwich, Frances R(appaport) 1908-2001 .. *11*
  Obituary .............................................. *130*
Horwitz, Elinor Lander ................................ *45*
  Brief entry .......................................... *33*
Horwood, William 1944- .............................. *85*
Hosford, Dorothy (Grant) 1900-1952 .......... *22*
Hosford, Jessie 1892-1990 ............................. *5*
Hoshi, Shin'ichi 1926- ................................. *101*
Hoskyns-Abrahall, Clare (Constance
  Drury) ................................................ *13*

Hossack, Sylvia 1939- ............................. 83
Hossack, Sylvie Adams
  See Hossack, Sylvia
Hosseini, Khaled 1965- ......................... 156
Hossell, Karen Price
  See Price, Karen
Hostetler, Marian 1932- .......................... 91
Houck, Carter 1924- ............................. 22
Hough, (Helen) Charlotte 1924- ................. 9
Hough, Judy Taylor 1932- ........................ 63
  Brief entry ..................................... 51
  Earlier sketch in SATA 56
Hough, Richard (Alexander) 1922-1999 ..... 17
Houghton, Eric 1930- ............................. 7
Houk, Randy 1944- ............................... 97
Houlehen, Robert J. 1918- ...................... 18
Household, Geoffrey (Edward West)
  1900-1988 ....................................... 14
  Obituary ....................................... 59
Housman, Laurence 1865-1959 ................. 25
Houston, Dick 1943- ............................. 74
Houston, Gloria ................................. 138
  Autobiography Feature ......................... 138
  Earlier sketch in SATA 81
Houston, James A(rchibald) 1921-2005 ...... 74
  Obituary ...................................... 163
  Earlier sketch in SATA 13
  See also CLR 3
  See also SAAS 17
Houston, James D. 1933- ......................... 78
Houston, Jeanne Toyo Wakatsuki
  See Houston, Jeanne Wakatsuki
Houston, Jeanne Wakatsuki 1934- ............. 168
  Autobiography Feature ......................... 168
  Earlier sketch in SATA 78
Houston, Juanita C. 1921- ...................... 129
Houton, Kathleen
  See Kilgore, Kathleen
Houts, Amy F. ................................... 164
Hovey, Kate .................................... 158
Howard, Alan 1922- .............................. 45
Howard, Alyssa
  See Buckholtz, Eileen (Garber)
  and Glick, Ruth (Burtnick)
  and Titchener, Louise
Howard, Arthur 1948- ........................... 165
Howard, Arthur Charles
  See Howard, Arthur
Howard, Elizabeth Fitzgerald 1927- .......... 119
  Earlier sketch in SATA 74
Howard, Ellen 1943- ............................. 99
  Earlier sketch in SATA 67
Howard, Jane R(uble) 1924- ..................... 87
Howard, Norman Barry 1949- .................... 90
Howard, P. M.
  See Howard, Pauline Rodriguez
Howard, Paul 1967- ............................. 118
Howard, Pauline Rodriguez 1951- ............. 124
Howard, Prosper
  See Hamilton, Charles (Harold St. John)
Howard, Robert West 1908-1988 ................. 5
Howard, Todd 1964- ............................. 135
Howard, Tristan
  See Currie, Stephen
Howard, Vernon (Linwood) 1918-1992 ...... 40
  Obituary ....................................... 73
Howard, Warren F.
  See Pohl, Frederik
Howarth, David (Armine) 1912-1991 .......... 6
  Obituary ....................................... 68
Howarth, Lesley 1952- ........................... 94
Howe, Deborah 1946-1978 ........................ 29
Howe, James 1946- .............................. 161
  Earlier sketches in SATA 29, 71, 111
  See also CLR 9
Howe, John F. 1957- ............................. 79
Howe, Norma 1930- .............................. 126
Howell, Pat 1947- ............................... 15
Howell, S.
  See Styles, (Frank) Showell

Howell, Virginia
  See Ellison, Virginia H(owell)
Howes, Barbara 1914-1996 ......................... 5
Howie, Diana (Melson) 1945- ................... 122
Howker, Janni 1957- ............................. 72
  Brief entry ..................................... 46
  See also CLR 14
  See also SAAS 13
Howland, Ethan 1963- ........................... 131
Hoy, Linda 1946- ................................. 65
Hoy, Nina
  See Roth, Arthur J(oseph)
Hoyle, Geoffrey 1942- ........................... 18
Hoyt, Edwin P(almer), Jr. 1923- ............... 28
Hoyt, Erich 1950- .............................. 140
  Earlier sketch in SATA 65
Hoyt, Olga
  See Gruhzit-Hoyt, Olga (Margaret)
Hrdlitschka, Shelley 1956- .................... 167
  Earlier sketch in SATA 111
Hrdlitschka, Shelley Joanne
  See Hrdlitschka, Shelley
Htin Aung, U.
  See Aung, (Maung) Htin
Hu, Ying-Hwa ................................... 173
Huang, Benrei 1959- ............................. 86
Hubalek, Linda K. 1954- ........................ 111
Hubbard, Michelle Calabro 1953- ............. 122
Hubbard, Patricia 1945- ........................ 124
Hubbard, Woodleigh Marx ...................... 160
  Earlier sketch in SATA 98
Hubbell, Patricia 1928- ........................ 132
  Earlier sketch in SATA 8
Hubley, Faith Elliot 1924-2001 ................. 48
  Obituary ...................................... 133
Hubley, John 1914-1977 .......................... 48
  Obituary ....................................... 24
Huck, Charlotte S. 1922- ....................... 136
  Earlier sketch in SATA 82
Hudak, Michal 1956- ............................ 143
Hudson, Cheryl Willis 1948- ................... 160
  Earlier sketch in SATA 81
Hudson, Jan 1954-1990 ........................... 77
  See also CLR 40
Hudson, Jeffrey
  See Crichton, Michael
Hudson, (Margaret) Kirsty 1947- ............... 32
Hudson, Margaret
  See Shuter, Jane (Margaret)
Hudson, W(illiam) H(enry) 1841-1922 ....... 35
Hudson, Wade 1946- ............................ 162
  Earlier sketch in SATA 74
Huelsmann, Eva 1928- ........................... 16
Huff, Barbara A. 1929- .......................... 67
Huff, Tanya 1957- .............................. 171
  Earlier sketch in SATA 85
Huff, Tanya Sue
  See Huff, Tanya
Huff, T.S.
  See Huff, Tanya
Huff, Vivian 1948- .............................. 59
Huffaker, Sandy 1943- .......................... 10
Huffman, Tom .................................... 24
Huggins, Nathan Irvin 1927-1989 .............. 63
Hughes, Carol 1955- ........................... 108
Hughes, Dean 1943- ............................ 139
  Earlier sketches in SATA 33, 77
  See also CLR 76
Hughes, Eden
  See Griffin, W.E.B.
Hughes, Edward James
  See Hughes, Ted
Hughes, (James Mercer) Langston 1902-1967
  ............................................... 33
  Earlier sketch in SATA 4
  See also CLR 17
Hughes, Libby ................................... 71
Hughes, Matilda
  See MacLeod, Charlotte (Matilda)

Hughes, Monica 1925-2003 ...................... 162
  Earlier sketches in SATA 15, 70, 119
  See also CLR 60
  See also SAAS 11
Hughes, Monica Ince
  See Hughes, Monica
Hughes, Richard (Arthur Warren) 1900-1976
  ................................................ 8
  Obituary ....................................... 25
Hughes, Sara
  See Saunders, Susan
Hughes, Shirley 1927- ......................... 159
  Earlier sketches in SATA 16, 70, 110
  See also CLR 15
Hughes, Ted 1930-1998 .......................... 49
  Brief entry ..................................... 27
  Obituary ...................................... 107
  See also CLR 3
  See Hughes, Edward James
Hughes, Thomas 1822-1896 ....................... 31
Hughes, Virginia
  See Campbell, Hope
Hughes, Walter (Llewellyn) 1910-1993 ...... 26
Hughey, Roberta 1942- .......................... 61
Hugo, Pierre Brackers de
  See Brackers de Hugo, Pierre
Hugo, Victor (Marie) 1802-1885 ................ 47
Huline-Dickens, Frank William 1931- ........ 34
Huling, Jan .................................... 172
Huliska-Beith, Laura ........................... 175
Hull, Eleanor (Means) 1913- .................... 21
Hull, Eric Traviss
  See Harnan, Terry
Hull, H. Braxton
  See Jacobs, Helen Hull
Hull, Jesse Redding
  See Hull, Jessie Redding
Hull, Jessie Redding 1932- ..................... 51
Hull, Katharine 1921-1977 ...................... 23
Hull, Lise (E.) 1954- .......................... 148
Hull, Maureen 1949- ........................... 142
Hulme, Joy N. 1922- ........................... 161
  Earlier sketches in SATA 74, 112
Hults, Dorothy Niebrugge 1898-2000 .......... 6
Humble, Richard 1945- .......................... 60
Hume, Lotta Carswell ............................ 7
Hume, Ruth Fox 1922-1980 ...................... 26
  Obituary ....................................... 22
Hume, Stephen Eaton 1947- .................... 136
Hummel, Berta 1909-1946 ....................... 43
Hummel, Sister Maria Innocentia
  See Hummel, Berta
Humphrey, Carol Sue 1956- .................... 167
Humphrey, Henry (III) 1930- .................... 16
Humphrey, Kate
  See Forsyth, Kate
Humphrey, Sandra McLeod 1936- .............. 95
Humphreys, Martha 1943- ....................... 71
Humphreys, Susan L.
  See Lowell, Susan
Hundal, Nancy 1957- ........................... 128
Huneck, Stephen 1949- ......................... 129
Hungerford, Hesba Fay
  See Brinsmead, H(esba) F(ay)
Hungerford, Pixie
  See Brinsmead, H(esba) F(ay)
Hunkin, Timothy Mark Trelawney 1950- ... 53
Hunt, Angela Elwell 1957- ..................... 159
  Earlier sketch in SATA 75
Hunt, Francesca
  See Holland, Isabelle (Christian)
Hunt, Irene 1907-2001 .......................... 91
  Earlier sketch in SATA 2
  See also CLR 1
Hunt, Janie Louise 1963- ...................... 102
Hunt, Jonathan 1966- ........................... 84
Hunt, Joyce 1927- .............................. 31
Hunt, Linda 1940- .............................. 39
Hunt, Lisa B(ehnke) 1967- ...................... 84
Hunt, Mabel Leigh 1892-1971 .................... 1
  Obituary ....................................... 26

Hunt, Morton M(agill) 1920- ...................... 22
Hunt, Nigel
    *See* Greenbank, Anthony Hunt
Hunt, Peter (Leonard) 1945- ...................... 76
Hunter, Anne B. 1966- ............................ 118
Hunter, Bernice Thurman 1922-2002 ......... 85
    Brief entry ...................................... 45
Hunter, Bobbi Dooley 1945- ..................... 89
Hunter, Captain Marcy
    *See* Ellis, Edward S(ylvester)
Hunter, Chris
    *See* Fluke, Joanne
Hunter, Clingham M.D.
    *See* Adams, William Taylor
Hunter, Edith Fisher 1919- ........................ 31
Hunter, Erin
    *See* Cary, Kate
Hunter, Evan 1926-2005 ........................... 25
    Obituary ........................................ 167
    *See* McBain, Ed
Hunter, George E.
    *See* Ellis, Edward S(ylvester)
Hunter, Hilda 1921- .................................. 7
Hunter, Jim 1939- .................................... 65
Hunter, Kristin
    *See* Lattany, Kristin (Elaine Eggleston) Hunter
Hunter, Leigh
    *See* Etchison, Birdie L(ee)
Hunter, Lieutenant Ned
    *See* Ellis, Edward S(ylvester)
Hunter, Mel 1927-2004 .............................. 39
Hunter, Mollie 1922- ............................... 139
    Autobiography Feature ...................... 139
    Earlier sketches in SATA *54, 106*
    *See also* CLR *25*
    *See also* SAAS *7*
    *See* McIlwraith, Maureen Mollie Hunter
Hunter, Ned
    *See* Ellis, Edward S(ylvester)
Hunter, Norman (George Lorimer) 1899-1995
    ..................................................... 84
    Earlier sketch in SATA *26*
Hunter, Ryan Ann
    *See* Greenwood, Pamela D.
    and Macalaster, Elizabeth G.
Hunter, Sara Hoagland 1954- ..................... 98
Hunter Blair, Pauline ................................. 3
    *See* Clarke, Pauline
Huntington, Amy 1956- ............................ 138
Huntington, Geoffrey .............................. 145
Huntington, Harriet E(lizabeth) 1909- ........... 1
Huntsberry, William E(mery) 1916- .............. 5
Hurd, Clement (G.) 1908-1988 ................... 64
    Obituary .......................................... 54
    Earlier sketch in SATA *2*
    *See also* CLR *49*
Hurd, Edith Thacher 1910-1997 ................. 64
    Obituary .......................................... 95
    Earlier sketch in SATA *2*
    *See also* CLR *49*
    *See also* SAAS *13*
Hurd, (John) Thacher 1949- ....................... 94
    Autobiography Feature ...................... 123
    Brief entry ...................................... 45
    Earlier sketch in SATA *46*
Hurlimann, Bettina ................................... 39
    Obituary .......................................... 34
    *See* Huerlimann, Bettina
Hurlimann, Ruth ..................................... 32
    Brief entry ...................................... 31
    *See* Huerlimann, Ruth
Hurmence, Belinda 1921- .......................... 77
    *See also* CLR *25*
    *See also* SAAS *20*
Hurst, Carol Otis 1933- ........................... 130
Hurt-Newton, Tania 1968- ........................ 84
Hurwitz, Johanna 1937- .......................... 175
    Earlier sketches in SATA *20, 71, 113*
    *See also* SAAS *18*
Hurwood, Bernhardt J. 1926-1987 .............. 12
    Obituary .......................................... 50

Husain, Shahrukh 1950- .......................... 108
Huser, Glen 1943- ................................. 151
Hutchens, Paul 1902-1977 ......................... 31
Hutchins, Carleen Maley 1911- .................... 9
Hutchins, Hazel J. 1952- ......................... 175
    Brief entry ...................................... 51
    Earlier sketches in SATA *81, 135*
    *See also* SAAS *24*
Hutchins, Pat 1942- ............................... 111
    Earlier sketches in SATA *15, 70*
    *See also* CLR *20*
    *See also* SAAS *16*
Hutchins, Ross Elliott 1906- ........................ 4
Hutchison, Linda 1942- ........................... 152
Huthmacher, J. Joseph 1929- ...................... 5
Hutto, Nelson (Allen) 1904-1985 ................. 20
Hutton, Kathryn 1915- ............................. 89
Hutton, Warwick 1939-1994 ...................... 20
    Obituary .......................................... 83
    *See also* SAAS *17*
Huxley, Aldous (Leonard) 1894-1963 ......... 63
Huxley, Elspeth (Josceline Grant) 1907-1997
    ..................................................... 62
    Obituary .......................................... 95
Hyde, Catherine R(yan) 1955- .................. 141
Hyde, Dayton O(gden) ............................... 9
Hyde, Hawk
    *See* Hyde, Dayton O(gden)
Hyde, Margaret O(ldroyd) 1917- ............... 139
    Earlier sketches in SATA *1, 42, 76*
    *See also* CLR *23*
    *See also* SAAS *8*
Hyde, Shelley
    *See* Reed, Kit
Hyde, Wayne Frederick 1922- ...................... 7
Hylander, Clarence J(ohn) 1897-1964 ............ 7
Hyman, Robin P(hilip) 1931- ...................... 12
Hyman, Trina Schart 1939-2004 ................. 95
    Obituary ........................................ 158
    Earlier sketches in SATA *7, 46*
    *See also* CLR *50*
Hymes, Lucia M(anley) 1907-1998 ................ 7
Hyndman, Jane Andrews Lee 1912-1978 ... 46
    Obituary .......................................... 23
    Earlier sketch in SATA *1*
Hyndman, Robert Utley 1906-1973 ............ 18
Hynes, Pat ........................................... 98

**I**

Iannone, Jeanne ...................................... 7
    *See* Balzano, Jeanne (Koppel)
Ibatoulline, Bagram 1965(?)- .................... 174
Ibbitson, John Perrie 1955- ...................... 102
Ibbotson, Eva 1925- ............................... 156
    Earlier sketches in SATA *13, 103*
Ibbotson, M. C(hristine) 1930- .................... 5
Icenoggle, Jodi 1967- ............................. 168
Icenoggle, Jodi O.
    *See* Icenoggle, Jodi
Ichikawa, Satomi 1949- ........................... 146
    Brief entry ...................................... 36
    Earlier sketches in SATA *47, 78*
    *See also* CLR *62*
Ignoffo, Matthew 1945- ............................ 92
Igus, Toyomi 1953- ............................... 112
    Earlier sketch in SATA *76*
Ihimaera, Witi (Tame) 1944- .................... 148
Ikeda, Daisaku 1928- ............................... 77
Ilowite, Sheldon A. 1931- ......................... 27
Ilsley, Velma (Elizabeth) 1918- .................. 12
Imai, Miko 1963- .................................... 90
Imershein, Betsy 1953- ............................ 62
Immel, Mary Blair 1930- ........................... 28
Immell, Myra H. 1941- ............................. 92
Impey, Rose 1947- ................................ 152
    Earlier sketch in SATA *69*
Ingelow, Jean 1820-1897 .......................... 33
Ingermanson, Randall 1958- .................... 134

Ingermanson, Randy
    *See* Ingermanson, Randall
Ingersoll, Norman 1928- ........................... 79
Ingham, Colonel Frederic
    *See* Hale, Edward Everett
Ingman, Bruce 1963- .............................. 134
Ingman, Nicholas 1948- ............................ 52
Ingold, Jeanette ................................... 128
Ingpen, Robert 1936- ............................. 166
    Earlier sketch in SATA *109*
Ingpen, Robert Roger
    *See* Ingpen, Robert
Ingraham, Erick 1950- ............................ 145
Ingraham, Leonard W(illiam) 1913-2003 ..... 4
Ingram, Scott 1948- .............................. 167
    Earlier sketch in SATA *92*
Ingram, W. Scott
    *See* Ingram, Scott
Ingrams, Doreen 1906-1997 ...................... 97
    Earlier sketch in SATA *20*
Ingrid, Charles
    *See* Salsitz, Rhondi Vilott
Ingves, Gunilla (Anna Maria Folkesdotter)
    1939- .......................................... 101
Inkpen, Mick 1952- ............................... 154
    Earlier sketch in SATA *99*
Innes, (Ralph) Hammond
    *See* Hammond Innes, Ralph
Innes, Ralph Hammond
    *See* Hammond Innes, Ralph
Innocenti, Roberto 1940- ......................... 159
    Earlier sketch in SATA *96*
    *See also* CLR *56*
Inyart, Gene ........................................... 6
    *See* Namovicz, Gene Inyart
Ionesco, Eugene 1912-1994 ........................ 7
    Obituary .......................................... 79
Ipcar, Dahlov (Zorach) 1917- .................. 147
    Autobiography Feature ...................... 147
    Earlier sketches in SATA *1, 49*
    *See also* SAAS *8*
Ireland, Karin ...................................... 151
    Earlier sketch in SATA *101*
Ironside, Jetske 1940- .............................. 60
Irvin, Fred 1914- ................................... 15
Irvine, Georgeanne 1955- ......................... 72
Irvine, Joan 1951- .................................. 80
Irving, Alexander
    *See* Hume, Ruth Fox
Irving, Robert
    *See* Adler, Irving
Irving, Washington 1783-1859
    *See* YABC *2*
    *See also* CLR *97*
Irwin, Ann(abelle Bowen) 1915-1998 ......... 89
    Brief entry ...................................... 38
    Obituary ........................................ 106
    Earlier sketch in SATA *44*
    *See also* CLR *40*
    *See* Irwin, Hadley
Irwin, Constance (H.) Frick 1913-1995 ........ 6
Irwin, Hadley
    *See* CLR *40*
    *See also* SAAS *14*
    *See* Hadley, Lee
    and Irwin, Ann(abelle Bowen)
Irwin, Keith Gordon 1885-1964 ................. 11
Isaac, Joanne 1934- ................................ 21
Isaacs, Anne 1949- ................................ 90
Isaacs, Jacob
    *See* Kranzler, George G(ershon)
Isaacson, Philip M(arshal) 1924- ............... 87
Isadora, Rachel 1953(?)- ......................... 165
    Brief entry ...................................... 32
    Earlier sketches in SATA *54, 79, 121*
    *See also* CLR *7*
Isbell, Rebecca T(emple) 1942- ................ 125
Isham, Charlotte H(ickock) 1912- ................ 21
Ishida, Jui ........................................... 176
Ish-Kishor, Judith 1892-1972 .................... 11
Ish-Kishor, Sulamith 1896-1977 ................ 17

Ishmael, Woodi 1914-1995 ............................ *31*
  Obituary ............................................ *109*
Isle, Sue 1963- ......................................... *105*
Israel, Elaine 1945- .................................... *12*
Iterson, S(iny) R(ose) Van
  *See* Van Iterson, S(iny) R(ose)
Ivanko, John D. 1966- ................................. *111*
Ivanko, John Duane
  *See* Ivanko, John D.
Iversen, Jeremy 1980(?)- ............................. *174*
Iversen, Jeremy Watt
  *See* Iversen, Jeremy
Iverson, Carol (L.) 1941- ............................ *145*
Iverson, Diane 1950- .................................. *122*
Iverson, Eric G.
  *See* Turtledove, Harry
Ivery, Martha M. 1948- ............................... *124*
Ives, David 1951- ...................................... *173*
Ives, Morgan
  *See* Bradley, Marion Zimmer
Iwamatsu, Jun Atsushi 1908-1994 ............... *81*
  Earlier sketch in SATA *14*
  *See* Yashima, Taro
Iwasaki (Matsumoto), Chihiro 1918-1974
  *See* CLR *18*

**J**

Jac, Lee
  *See* Morton, Lee Jack, Jr.
Jacka, Martin 1943- ..................................... *72*
Jackson, Alison 1953- ................................. *160*
  Earlier sketches in SATA *73, 108*
Jackson, C(aary) Paul 1902-1991 ................. *6*
Jackson, Caary
  *See* Jackson, C(aary) Paul
Jackson, Dave
  *See* Jackson, J. David
Jackson, Ellen B. 1943- .............................. *167*
  Earlier sketches in SATA *75, 115*
Jackson, Garnet Nelson 1944- ...................... *87*
Jackson, Gina
  *See* Fluke, Joanne
Jackson, Guida M. 1930- .............................. *71*
Jackson, J. David 1944- ................................ *91*
Jackson, Jacqueline 1928- ............................ *65*
Jackson, Jacqueline Dougan
  *See* Jackson, Jacqueline
Jackson, Jesse 1908-1983 ............................. *29*
  Obituary ............................................. *48*
  Earlier sketch in SATA *2*
  *See also* CLR *28*
Jackson, Marjorie 1928- .............................. *127*
Jackson, Melanie 1956- ............................... *141*
Jackson, Mike 1946- .................................... *91*
Jackson, Neta J. 1944- ................................. *91*
Jackson, O. B.
  *See* Jackson, C(aary) Paul
Jackson, Rob 1961- ..................................... *176*
Jackson, Robert B(lake) 1926- ...................... *8*
Jackson, Robert Bradley
  *See* Jackson, Rob
Jackson, Sally
  *See* Kellogg, Jean (Defrees)
Jackson, Shirley 1919-1965 ........................... *2*
Jackson, Woody 1948- .................................. *92*
Jacob, Helen Pierce 1927- ............................ *21*
Jacobin
  *See* Bisson, Terry
Jacobs, Flora Gill 1918-2006 .......................... *5*
Jacobs, Francine 1935- ................................ *150*
  Brief entry ........................................... *42*
  Earlier sketch in SATA *43*
Jacobs, Frank 1929- ..................................... *30*
Jacobs, Helen Hull 1908-1997 ...................... *12*
Jacobs, Joseph 1854-1916 ............................. *25*
Jacobs, Judy 1952- ...................................... *69*
Jacobs, Laurie A. 1956- ................................ *89*

Jacobs, Leah
  *See* Gellis, Roberta
Jacobs, Leland Blair 1907-1992 .................. *20*
  Obituary ............................................. *71*
Jacobs, Linda
  *See* Altman, Linda Jacobs
Jacobs, Lou(is), Jr. 1921- .............................. *2*
Jacobs, Shannon K. 1947- ............................ *77*
Jacobs, Susan ........................................... *30*
  *See* Quinn, Susan
Jacobs, William Jay 1933- ............................ *89*
  Earlier sketch in SATA *28*
Jacobsen, Laura ....................................... *177*
Jacobson, Daniel 1923- ................................ *12*
Jacobson, Jennifer
  *See* Jacobson, Jennifer Richard
Jacobson, Jennifer Richard 1958- ............... *170*
Jacobson, Morris K(arl) 1906- ..................... *21*
Jacobson, Rick ........................................ *170*
Jacopetti, Alexandra ................................... *14*
  *See* Hart, Alexandra
Jacques, Brian 1939- .................................. *176*
  Earlier sketches in SATA *62, 95, 138*
  *See also* CLR *21*
Jacques, Robin 1920-1995 ............................. *32*
  Brief entry ........................................... *30*
  Obituary ............................................. *86*
  *See also* SAAS *5*
Jaekel, Susan M. 1948- ................................ *89*
Jaffee, Al(lan) 1921- .................................... *66*
  Earlier sketch in SATA *37*
Jagendorf, Moritz (Adolf) 1888-1981 ........... *2*
  Obituary ............................................. *24*
Jahn, Michael
  *See* Jahn, (Joseph) Michael
Jahn, (Joseph) Michael 1943- ...................... *28*
Jahn, Mike
  *See* Jahn, (Joseph) Michael
Jahn-Clough, Lisa 1967- ............................. *152*
  Earlier sketch in SATA *88*
Jahsmann, Allan Hart 1916- ........................ *28*
Jakes, John 1932- ....................................... *62*
Jakes, John William
  *See* Jakes, John
  and Jakes, John
James, Andrew
  *See* Kirkup, James
James, Ann 1952- ....................................... *168*
  Earlier sketches in SATA *82, 117*
James, Brian 1976- ..................................... *140*
James, Bronte
  *See* Nash, Renea Denise
James, Captain Lew
  *See* Stratemeyer, Edward L.
James, Dynely
  *See* Mayne, William (James Carter)
James, Edwin
  *See* Gunn, James E(dwin)
James, Elizabeth 1942- ................................ *97*
  Earlier sketches in SATA *39, 45, 52*
James, Emily
  *See* Standiford, Natalie
James, Harry Clebourne 1896-1978 ............ *11*
James, J. Alison 1962- ................................. *146*
  Earlier sketch in SATA *83*
James, Josephine
  *See* Sterne, Emma Gelders
James, Mary
  *See* Meaker, Marijane
James, Philip
  *See* del Rey, Lester
  and Moorcock, Michael
James, Robin 1953- .................................... *50*
James, Robin Irene
  *See* James, Robin
James, Tegan
  *See* Odgers, Sally Farrell
James, Will(iam Roderick) 1892-1942 ........ *19*
Jameson, W. C. 1942- ................................. *93*
Jamieson, Ian R.
  *See* Goulart, Ron(ald Joseph)

Jamiolkowski, Raymond M. 1953- ............. *81*
Jane, Mary Childs 1909- ................................ *6*
Jane, Pamela ........................................... *158*
Janeczko, Paul B(ryan) 1945- ...................... *155*
  Earlier sketches in SATA *53, 98*
  *See also* CLR *47*
  *See also* SAAS *18*
Janes, Edward C. 1908- ................................ *25*
Janes, J(oseph) Robert 1935- ....................... *148*
  Brief entry ........................................... *50*
  Earlier sketch in SATA *101*
Janeway, Elizabeth (Hall) 1913-2005 ......... *19*
Janger, Kathleen N. 1940- ............................ *66*
Janice
  *See* Brustlein, Janice Tworkov
Janosch
  *See* CLR *26*
  *See* Eckert, Horst
Janover, Caroline (Davis) 1943- ............... *141*
  Earlier sketch in SATA *89*
Jansen, Jared
  *See* Cebulash, Mel
Janson, Dora Jane (Heineberg) 1916- ......... *31*
Janson, H(orst) W(oldemar) 1913-1982 ....... *9*
Jansson, Tove (Marika) 1914-2001 ............ *41*
  Earlier sketch in SATA *3*
  *See also* CLR *2*
Janus, Grete
  *See* Hertz, Grete Janus
Jaques, Faith 1923-1997 ............................... *97*
  Earlier sketches in SATA *21, 69*
Jaquith, Priscilla 1908- ................................ *51*
Jaramillo, Mari-Luci 1928- ........................ *139*
Jarman, Julia 1946- .................................... *133*
Jarman, Rosemary Hawley 1935- .................. *7*
Jarrell, Mary Von Schrader 1914- ................ *35*
Jarrell, Randall 1914-1965 ............................ *7*
  *See also* CLR *111*
Jarrett, Roxanne
  *See* Werner, Herma
Jarrow, Gail 1952- ...................................... *84*
Jarvis, E. K.
  *See* Ellison, Harlan
Jaskol, Julie 1958- ..................................... *127*
Jasner, W. K.
  *See* Watson, Jane Werner
Jassem, Kate
  *See* Oppenheim, Joanne
Jauss, Anne Marie 1902(?)-1991 ................. *10*
  Obituary ............................................. *69*
Javernick, Ellen 1938- ................................ *89*
Jayne, Lieutenant R. H.
  *See* Ellis, Edward S(ylvester)
Jaynes, Clare
  *See* Mayer, Jane Rothschild
Jeake, Samuel, Jr.
  *See* Aiken, Conrad (Potter)
Jean-Bart, Leslie 1954- .............................. *121*
Jeapes, Ben 1965- ..................................... *174*
Jefferds, Vincent H(arris) 1916- ................... *59*
  Brief entry ........................................... *49*
Jefferies, (John) Richard 1848-1887 ........... *16*
Jeffers, Oliver 1977- .................................. *175*
Jeffers, Susan 1942- ................................... *137*
  Earlier sketches in SATA *17, 70, 129*
  *See also* CLR *30*
Jefferson, Sarah
  *See* Farjeon, (Eve) Annabel
Jeffries, Roderic 1926- .................................. *4*
Jeffries, Roderic Graeme
  *See* Jeffries, Roderic
Jenkin-Pearce, Susie 1943- .......................... *80*
Jenkins, A.M. ........................................... *174*
Jenkins, Amanda McRaney
  *See* Jenkins, A.M.
Jenkins, Debra Reid
  *See* Reid Jenkins, Debra
Jenkins, Emily 1967- .................................. *174*
  Earlier sketch in SATA *144*
Jenkins, Jean ........................................... *98*
Jenkins, Jerry B. 1949- ............................... *149*

Jenkins, Jerry Bruce
  *See* Jenkins, Jerry B.
Jenkins, Marie M(agdalen) 1909- ................. 7
Jenkins, Patrick 1955- ................................. 72
Jenkins, Steve 1952- ................................... 154
Jenkins, William A(twell) 1922-1998 ........... 9
Jenkyns, Chris 1924- .................................... 51
Jennings, Coleman A(lonzo) 1933- ............. 64
Jennings, Dana Andrew 1957- ..................... 93
Jennings, Elizabeth (Joan) 1926-2001 ......... 66
Jennings, Gary (Gayne) 1928-1999 ............. 9
  Obituary ................................................. 117
Jennings, Patrick 1962- .............................. 160
  Earlier sketch in SATA 96
Jennings, Paul 1943- ................................... 165
  Earlier sketch in SATA 88
  *See also* CLR 40
Jennings, Richard (W.) 1945- ..................... 136
Jennings, Robert
  *See* Hamilton, Charles (Harold St. John)
Jennings, S. M.
  *See* Meyer, Jerome Sydney
Jennings, Sharon 1954- ................................ 95
Jennings, Sharon Elizabeth
  *See* Jennings, Sharon
Jennison, C. S.
  *See* Starbird, Kaye
Jennison, Keith Warren 1911-1995 .............. 14
Jensen, Kathryn 1949- ................................. 81
Jensen, Kristine Mary 1961- ....................... 78
Jensen, Niels 1927- ..................................... 25
Jensen, Vickie (Dee) 1946- ......................... 81
Jensen, Virginia Allen 1927- ........................ 8
Jenson-Elliott, Cynthia L(ouise) 1962- ..... 143
Jeram, Anita 1965- ..................................... 154
  Earlier sketches in SATA 71, 102
Jerman, Jerry 1949- ..................................... 89
Jernigan, E. Wesley 1940- ........................... 85
Jernigan, Gisela (Evelyn) 1948- ................. 85
Jeschke, Susan 1942- ................................... 42
  Brief entry ................................................ 27
Jessel, Camilla (Ruth) 1937- ..................... 143
  Earlier sketch in SATA 29
Jessell, Tim ................................................. 177
Jessey, Cornelia
  *See* Sussman, Cornelia Silver
Jewel
  *See* Kilcher, Jewel
Jewell, Nancy 1940- ................................... 109
  Brief entry ................................................ 41
Jewett, Eleanore Myers 1890-1967 ............... 5
Jewett, (Theodora) Sarah Orne 1849-1909 . 15
Jezard, Alison 1919- ..................................... 57
  Brief entry ................................................ 34
Jiang, Cheng An 1943- ............................... 109
Jiang, Ji-li 1954- ......................................... 101
Jiang, Zheng An
  *See* Jiang, Cheng An
Jiler, John 1946- ........................................... 42
  Brief entry ................................................ 35
Jimenez, Francisco 1943- ........................... 108
Jinks, Catherine 1963- ............................... 155
  Earlier sketch in SATA 94
Jobb, Jamie 1945- ........................................ 29
Jobling, Curtis ........................................... 131
Jocelyn, Ann Henning 1948- ....................... 92
Jocelyn, Marthe 1956- ................................ 163
  Earlier sketch in SATA 118
Joerns, Consuelo ........................................ 44
  Brief entry ................................................ 33
Joey D
  *See* Macaulay, Teresa (E.)
Johansen, K(rista) V(ictoria) 1968- .......... 129
Johansson, Philip ...................................... 163
John, Joyce .................................................. 59
Johns, Avery
  *See* Cousins, Margaret
Johns, Elizabeth 1943- ................................. 88
Johns, Janetta
  *See* Quin-Harkin, Janet
Johns, Linda 1945- ..................................... 173

Johns, W(illiam) E(arle) 1893-1968 ........... 55
Johns, Captain W. E.
  *See* Johns, W(illiam) E(arle)
Johnson, A.
  *See* Johnson, Annabell (Jones)
Johnson, A. E.
  *See* Johnson, Annabell (Jones)
  and Johnson, Edgar (Raymond)
Johnson, Angela 1961- ............................... 150
  Earlier sketches in SATA 69, 102
  *See also* CLR 33
Johnson, Annabel
  *See* Johnson, Annabell (Jones)
Johnson, Annabell (Jones) 1921- ................ 72
  Earlier sketch in SATA 2
  *See* Johnson, Annabel
Johnson, Art 1946- ..................................... 123
Johnson, Benjamin F., of Boone
  *See* Riley, James Whitcomb
Johnson, Bettye 1858-1919
  *See* Rogers, Bettye
Johnson, Caryn
  *See* Goldberg, Whoopi
Johnson, Caryn E.
  *See* Goldberg, Whoopi
Johnson, Charles R. 1925- ........................... 11
Johnson, Charlotte Buel ............................... 46
  *See* von Wodtke, Charlotte Buel Johnson
Johnson, Chuck
  *See* Johnson, Charles R.
Johnson, Crockett
  *See* CLR 98
  *See* Leisk, David (Johnson)
Johnson, D(onald) B. 1944- ....................... 146
Johnson, D(ana) William 1945- ................... 23
Johnson, Daniel Shahid 1954- ..................... 73
Johnson, Dinah 1954- ................................ 130
  *See* Johnson, Dianne
Johnson, Dolores 1949- ............................... 69
Johnson, Dorothy M(arie) 1905-1984 .......... 6
  Obituary ................................................... 40
Johnson, E(ugene) Harper ........................... 44
Johnson, Edgar (Raymond) 1912-1990 ....... 72
  Earlier sketch in SATA 2
Johnson, Elizabeth 1911-1984 ....................... 7
  Obituary ................................................... 39
Johnson, Eric W(arner) 1918-1994
  Obituary ................................................... 82
  Earlier sketch in SATA 8
Johnson, Evelyne 1922- ............................... 20
Johnson, Fred 19(?)-1982 ............................ 63
Johnson, Gaylord 1884-1972 ......................... 7
Johnson, Gerald White 1890-1980 ............... 19
  Obituary ................................................... 28
Johnson, Harper
  *See* Johnson, E(ugene) Harper
Johnson, James Ralph 1922- .......................... 1
Johnson, James Weldon 1871-1938 .............. 31
  *See also* CLR 32
Johnson, Jane 1951- ..................................... 48
Johnson, Joan J. 1942- ................................. 59
Johnson, John E(mil) 1929- ......................... 34
Johnson, Johnny 1901-1995
  *See* Johnson, (Walter) Ryerson
Johnson, La Verne B(ravo) 1925- ............... 13
Johnson, Lee Kaiser 1962- ........................... 78
Johnson, Lissa H(alls) 1955- ....................... 65
Johnson, Lois Smith 1894-1993 ..................... 6
Johnson, Lois Walfrid 1936- ...................... 130
  Earlier sketches in SATA 22, 91
Johnson, Margaret S(weet) 1893-1964 ........ 35
Johnson, Marguerite Annie
  *See* Angelou, Maya
Johnson, Meredith Merrell 1952- ............... 104
Johnson, Milton 1932- ................................. 31
Johnson, Neil 1954- ................................... 135
  Earlier sketch in SATA 73
Johnson, Pamela 1949- ................................ 71
Johnson, Patricia Polin 1956- ..................... 84
Johnson, Paul Brett 1947- .......................... 132
  Earlier sketch in SATA 83

Johnson, Rebecca L. 1956- ........................ 147
  Earlier sketch in SATA 67
Johnson, Rick L. 1954- ................................ 79
Johnson, (Walter) Ryerson 1901-1995 ........ 10
  Obituary ................................................. 106
  *See* Halliday, Brett
Johnson, Scott 1952- .................................. 119
  Earlier sketch in SATA 76
Johnson, Sherrie 1948- ................................ 87
Johnson, Shirley K(ing) 1927- ..................... 10
Johnson, Spencer 1938- ............................. 145
  Brief entry ................................................ 38
Johnson, Stephen T. 1964- ......................... 141
  Earlier sketch in SATA 84
Johnson, Steve 1960- .................................. 177
Johnson, Sue Kaiser 1963- ........................... 78
Johnson, Sylvia A. .................................... 166
  Brief entry ................................................ 52
  Earlier sketch in SATA 104
Johnson, William R. ..................................... 38
Johnson, William Weber 1909-1992 ............. 7
Johnston, Agnes Christine
  *See* Dazey, Agnes J(ohnston)
Johnston, Annie Fellows 1863-1931 ........... 37
Johnston, Dorothy Grunbock 1915-1979 .... 54
Johnston, Ginny 1946- ................................ 60
Johnston, H(ugh) A(nthony) S(tephen)
  1913-1967 ................................................ 14
Johnston, Janet 1944- .................................. 71
Johnston, Johanna 1914(?)-1982 ................. 12
  Obituary ................................................... 33
Johnston, Julie 1941- ................................. 110
  Autobiography Feature ............................ 128
  Earlier sketch in SATA 78
  *See also* CLR 41
  *See also* SAAS 24
Johnston, Lynn (Beverley) 1947- .............. 118
Johnston, Norma ........................................ 29
  *See* St. John, Nicole
Johnston, Portia
  *See* Takakjian, Portia
Johnston, Susan Taylor 1942- .................... 128
  Earlier sketch in SATA 83
  *See* Johnston, Tony
Johnston, Tim(othy Patrick) 1962- ........... 146
Johnston, Tony ............................................... 8
  *See* Johnston, Susan Taylor
Joinson, Carla ........................................... 160
Jonas, Ann 1932- ....................................... 135
  Brief entry ................................................ 42
  Earlier sketch in SATA 50
  *See also* CLR 74
Jonell, Lynne ............................................. 109
Jones, Adrienne 1915-2000 ......................... 82
  Earlier sketch in SATA 7
  *See also* SAAS 10
Jones, Annabel
  *See* Lewis, Mary (Christianna)
Jones, Betty Millsaps 1940- ........................ 54
Jones, Carol 1942- ..................................... 153
  Earlier sketch in SATA 79
Jones, Charles M(artin) 1912-2002 ............. 53
  Obituary ................................................. 133
  *See* Jones, Chuck
Jones, Charlotte Foltz 1945- ...................... 122
  Earlier sketch in SATA 77
Jones, Chuck
  *See* Jones, Charles M(artin)
Jones, Constance 1961- .............................. 112
Jones, Diana Wynne 1934- ........................ 160
  Earlier sketches in SATA 9, 70, 108
  *See also* CLR 120
  *See also* SAAS 7
Jones, Douglas C(lyde) 1924-1998 ............. 52
Jones, Elizabeth McDavid ......................... 155
Jones, Elizabeth Orton 1910-2005 ............. 18
  Obituary ................................................. 164
Jones, Evan 1915-1996 ................................. 3
Jones, Geraldine
  *See* McCaughrean, Geraldine

Jones, Gillingham
  *See* Hamilton, Charles (Harold St. John)
Jones, Gwyneth A(nn) 1952- ..................... *159*
Jones, Harold 1904-1992 .............. *14*
  Obituary ........................................ *72*
Jones, Helen Hinckley 1903-1991 .............. *26*
Jones, Hettie 1934- ........................... *42*
  Brief entry ..................................... *27*
Jones, Hortense P. 1918- ...................... *9*
Jones, J. Sydney 1948- ........................ *101*
Jones, Jasmine
  *See* Papademetriou, Lisa
Jones, Jennifer (Berry) 1947- ................... *90*
Jones, John R(obert) 1926- .................... *76*
Jones, Jon Sydney
  *See* Jones, J. Sydney
Jones, Marcia Thornton 1958- ................. *115*
  Earlier sketch in SATA *73*
Jones, Martha T(annery) 1931- ............... *130*
Jones, Mary Alice 1898(?)-1980 .............. *6*
Jones, McClure .................................. *34*
Jones, Patrick 1961- .......................... *136*
Jones, Penelope 1938- ......................... *31*
Jones, Rebecca C(astaldi) 1947- .............. *99*
  Earlier sketch in SATA *33*
Jones, Robin D(orothy) 1959- .................. *80*
Jones, Sanford W.
  *See* Thorn, John
Jones, Terence Graham Parry 1942- ......... *127*
  *See* Jones, Terry
  and Monty Python
Jones, Terry ...................................... *67*
  Brief entry ..................................... *51*
  *See* Jones, Terence Graham Parry
Jones, Tim(othy) Wynne
  *See* Wynne-Jones, Tim(othy)
Jones, V(ictoria) M(ary) 1958- ................. *147*
Jones, Veda Boyd 1948- ....................... *119*
Jones, Volcano
  *See* Mitchell, Adrian
Jones, Weyman (B.) 1928- ...................... *4*
  *See also* SAAS *11*
Jones, William Glynne
  *See* Glynne-Jones, William
Jonk, Clarence 1906-1987 ....................... *10*
Jonsberg, Barry 1951- .......................... *168*
Joos, Francoise 1956- ........................... *78*
Joos, Frederic 1953- ............................ *78*
Joosse, Barbara M. 1949- ...................... *164*
  Earlier sketches in SATA *52, 96*
Joosse, Barbara Monnot
  *See* Joosse, Barbara M.
Jordan, Alexis Hill
  *See* Glick, Ruth (Burtnick)
  and Titchener, Louise
Jordan, Anne Devereaux 1943- ................ *80*
Jordan, Chris
  *See* Philbrick, Rodman
Jordan, Don
  *See* Howard, Vernon (Linwood)
Jordan, Hope Dahle 1905-1995 ................ *15*
Jordan, Jael (Michal) 1949- ..................... *30*
Jordan, June 1936-2002 ........................ *136*
  Earlier sketch in SATA *4*
  *See also* CLR *10*
Jordan, June Meyer
  *See* Jordan, June
Jordan, Lee
  *See* Scholefield, Alan
Jordan, Martin George 1944- ................... *84*
Jordan, Robert 1948- ........................... *95*
  *See* Rigney, James Oliver, Jr.
Jordan, Sherryl 1949- ........................... *122*
  Earlier sketch in SATA *71*
  *See also* SAAS *23*
Jordan, Shirley 1930- ........................... *154*
Jordan, Tanis 1946- ............................. *84*
Jorgensen, Mary Venn -1995 .................... *36*
Jorgensen, Norman 1954- ...................... *157*
Jorgenson, Ivar
  *See* Silverberg, Robert

Joseph, Anne
  *See* Coates, Anna
Joseph, James (Herz) 1924- ..................... *53*
Joseph, Joan 1939- ............................. *34*
Joseph, Joseph M(aron) 1903-1979 ........ *22*
Joseph, Patrick
  *See* O'Malley, Kevin
Josephs, Rebecca
  *See* Talbot, Toby
Josh
  *See* Clemens, Samuel Langhorne
Joshua, Peter
  *See* Stone, Peter
Joslin, Mary 1953- .............................. *176*
Joslin, Sesyle .................................... *2*
  *See* Hine, Sesyle Joslin
Joyce, Bill
  *See* Joyce, William
Joyce, J(ames) Avery 1902-1987 ............... *11*
  Obituary ........................................ *50*
Joyce, Peter 1937- ............................. *127*
Joyce, William 1957- ........................... *118*
  Brief entry ..................................... *46*
  Earlier sketch in SATA *72*
  *See also* CLR *26*
Joyner, Jerry 1938- ............................. *34*
Juby, Susan 1969- .............................. *156*
Jucker, Sita 1921- .............................. *5*
Judah, Aaron 1923- ............................ *118*
Judd, Cyril
  *See* Kornbluth, C(yril) M.
  and Merril, Judith
  and Pohl, Frederik
Judd, Denis (O'Nan) 1938- ..................... *33*
Judd, Frances K. .................................. *1*
  *See* Benson, Mildred (Augustine Wirt)
Jude, Conny ..................................... *81*
Judson, Clara Ingram 1879-1960 ................ *38*
  Brief entry ..................................... *27*
Judy, Stephen
  *See* Tchudi, Stephen N.
Judy, Stephen N.
  *See* Tchudi, Stephen N.
Juhasz, Victor 1954- ........................... *177*
Jukes, Mavis 1947- ............................ *111*
  Brief entry ..................................... *43*
  Earlier sketch in SATA *72*
  *See also* SAAS *12*
Jules, Jacqueline 1956- ......................... *148*
Julian, Jane
  *See* Wiseman, David
Jumpp, Hugo
  *See* MacPeek, Walter G.
Jungman, Ann ................................... *165*
Jupo, Frank J. 1904-1981 ....................... *7*
Jurmain, Suzanne 1945- ....................... *169*
  Earlier sketch in SATA *72*
Jurmain, Suzanne Tripp
  *See* Jurmain, Suzanne
Juster, Norton 1929- ........................... *132*
  Earlier sketch in SATA *3*
  *See also* CLR *112*
Justus, May 1898-1989 .......................... *1*
  Obituary ........................................ *106*
Juvenilia
  *See* Taylor, Ann

**K**

Kaaberbol, Lene
  *See* Kaaberbol, Lene
Kaaberbol, Lene 1960- .......................... *159*
Kabdebo, Tamas
  *See* Kabdebo, Thomas
Kabdebo, Thomas 1934- ......................... *10*
Kabibble, Osh
  *See* Jobb, Jamie
Kacer, Kathy 1954- ............................. *142*
Kaczman, James ................................. *156*

Kadesch, Robert R(udstone) 1922- ........... *31*
Kadohata, Cynthia (Lynn) 1956(?)- .......... *155*
  *See also* CLR *121*
Kaempfert, Wade
  *See* del Rey, Lester
Kaestner, Erich 1899-1974 ...................... *14*
  *See also* CLR *4*
  *See* Kastner, Erich
Kahl, Jonathan (D.) 1959- ...................... *77*
Kahl, M(arvin) P(hilip) 1934- ................... *37*
Kahl, Virginia (Caroline) 1919-2004 ........... *48*
  Brief entry ..................................... *38*
  Obituary ........................................ *158*
Kahn, Joan 1914-1994 .......................... *48*
  Obituary ........................................ *82*
Kahn, Katherine Janus 1942- .................. *167*
  Earlier sketch in SATA *90*
Kahn, Peggy
  *See* Katz, Bobbi
Kahn, Roger 1927- ............................. *37*
Kahukiwa, Robyn 1940- ........................ *134*
Kains, Josephine
  *See* Goulart, Ron(ald Joseph)
Kaizuki, Kiyonori 1950- ........................ *72*
Kakimoto, Kozo 1915- .......................... *11*
Kalashnikoff, Nicholas 1888-1961 ............. *16*
Kalb, Jonah 1926- ............................. *23*
Kalbacken, Joan 1925- ......................... *96*
Kalechofsky, Roberta 1931- .................... *92*
Kaler, James Otis 1848-1912 ................... *15*
Kalish, Claire M. 1947- ......................... *92*
Kallen, Stuart A(rnold) 1955- .................. *126*
  Earlier sketch in SATA *86*
Kallevig, Christine Petrell 1955- .............. *164*
Kalman, Bobbie 1947- .......................... *63*
Kalman, Maira 1949- ........................... *137*
  Earlier sketch in SATA *96*
  *See also* CLR *32*
Kalnay, Francis 1899-1992 ...................... *7*
Kaloustian, Rosanne 1955- ..................... *93*
Kalow, Gisela 1946- ............................ *32*
Kalstein, Dave .................................. *175*
Kamen, Gloria 1923- ........................... *98*
  Earlier sketch in SATA *9*
Kamerman, Sylvia E.
  *See* Burack, Sylvia K.
Kamm, Josephine (Hart) 1905-1989 .......... *24*
Kammerman, Sylvia K.
  *See* Burack, Sylvia K.
Kandel, Michael 1941- .......................... *93*
Kandell, Alice S. 1938- .......................... *35*
Kane, Bob 1916-1998 ........................... *120*
Kane, Henry Bugbee 1902-1971 ................ *14*
Kane, L. A.
  *See* Mannetti, Lisa
Kane, Robert W. 1910- .......................... *18*
Kane, Wilson
  *See* Bloch, Robert (Albert)
Kanefield, Teri 1960- ........................... *135*
Kaner, Etta 1947- .............................. *126*
Kanetzke, Howard W(illiam) 1932- ........... *38*
Kanoza, Muriel Canfield
  *See* Canfield, Muriel
Kanzawa, Toshiko
  *See* Furukawa, Toshi
Kaplan, Andrew 1960- .......................... *78*
Kaplan, Anne Bernays
  *See* Bernays, Anne
Kaplan, Bess 1927- ............................. *22*
Kaplan, Boche 1926- ........................... *24*
Kaplan, Elizabeth 1956- ........................ *83*
Kaplan, Elizabeth A.
  *See* Kaplan, Elizabeth
Kaplan, Irma 1900- ............................. *10*
Kaplan, Jean Caryl Korn 1926- ................. *10*
Kaplow, Robert 1954- .......................... *70*
Karageorge, Michael
  *See* Anderson, Poul
Karen, Ruth 1922-1987 ......................... *9*
  Obituary ........................................ *54*

Kark, Nina Mary 1925- ............................ *132*
  Earlier sketch in SATA *4*
  *See* Bawden, Nina (Mary Mabey)
Karl, Herb 1938- ........................................ *73*
Karl, Jean E(dna) 1927-2000 ................ *122*
  Earlier sketch in SATA *34*
  *See also* SAAS *10*
Karlin, Bernie 1927- .................................. *68*
Karlin, Eugene 1918- .................................. *10*
Karlin, Nurit ........................................... *103*
  Earlier sketch in SATA *63*
Karnes, Frances A. 1937- ........................ *110*
Karp, Naomi J. 1926- ................................ *16*
Karpinski, J. Rick
  *See* Karpinski, John Eric
Karpinski, John Eric 1952- ........................ *81*
Karpinski, Rick
  *See* Karpinski, John Eric
Karr, Kathleen 1946- .............................. *127*
  Earlier sketch in SATA *82*
Karr, Phyllis Ann 1944- .......................... *119*
Karwoski, Gail 1949- .............................. *127*
Karwoski, Gail Langer
  *See* Karwoski, Gail
Kashiwagi, Isami 1925- .............................. *10*
Kassem, Lou 1931- .................................... *62*
  Brief entry .............................................. *51*
Kastel, Warren
  *See* Silverberg, Robert
Kastner, Erich
  *See* Kaestner, Erich
Kastner, Jill (Marie) 1964- ...................... *117*
  Earlier sketch in SATA *70*
Kasuya, Masahiro 1937- ............................ *51*
Kasza, Keiko 1951- ................................ *124*
Kataphusin
  *See* Ruskin, John
Katchen, Carole 1944- ................................ *9*
Kathryn
  *See* Searle, Kathryn Adrienne
Katona, Robert 1949- ................................ *21*
Katsarakis, Joan Harries
  *See* Harries, Joan
Katz, Avner 1939- .................................. *103*
Katz, Bobbi 1933- .................................... *12*
Katz, Fred(eric Phillip) 1938- ...................... *6*
Katz, Jane B(resler) 1934- .......................... *33*
Katz, Karen 1947- .................................. *158*
Katz, Marjorie P.
  *See* Weiser, Marjorie P(hillis) K(atz)
Katz, Susan 1945- .................................. *156*
Katz, Welwyn Wilton 1948- ........................ *96*
  Autobiography Feature .......................... *118*
  Earlier sketch in SATA *62*
  *See also* CLR *45*
Katz, William 1940- .................................. *98*
Katz, William Loren 1927- .......................... *13*
Kaufman, Bel ............................................ *57*
Kaufman, Jeff 1955- .................................. *84*
Kaufman, Joe 1911-2001 ............................ *33*
Kaufman, Joseph
  *See* Kaufman, Joe
Kaufman, Mervyn D. 1932- .......................... *4*
Kaufmann, Angelika 1935- .......................... *15*
Kaufmann, John 1931- ................................ *18*
Kaula, Edna Mason 1906-1987 .................... *13*
Kaur Khalsa, Dayal
  *See* Khalsa, Dayal Kaur
Kavaler, Lucy 1930- .................................. *23*
Kavanagh, Jack 1920- ................................ *85*
Kavanagh, P(atrick) J(oseph Gregory) 1931-
  .............................................................. *122*
Kavanaugh, Ian
  *See* Webb, Jean Francis (III)
Kay, Alan N. 1965- .................................. *144*
Kay, Elizabeth 1949- .............................. *165*
Kay, Guy Gavriel 1954- .......................... *167*
  Earlier sketch in SATA *121*
Kay, Helen
  *See* Goldfrank, Helen Colodny

Kay, Jackie 1961- .................................. *165*
  Earlier sketch in SATA *97*
Kay, Jacqueline Margaret
  *See* Kay, Jackie
Kay, Mara ...................................................... *13*
Kay, Verla 1946- .................................... *120*
Kaye, Geraldine (Hughesdon) 1925- .......... *85*
  Earlier sketch in SATA *10*
Kaye, Judy
  *See* Baer, Judy
Kaye, Marilyn 1949- .............................. *110*
  Earlier sketch in SATA *56*
Kaye, Mary Margaret
  *See* Kaye, M.M.
Kaye, M.M. 1908-2004 .............................. *62*
  Obituary ................................................ *152*
Kaye, Mollie
  *See* Kaye, M.M.
Kaye, Peggy 1948- .................................. *143*
Keach, James P. 1950- ............................ *125*
Keams, Geri 1951- .................................. *117*
Keane, Bil 1922- ........................................ *4*
Keaney, Brian 1954- .............................. *106*
Kearny, Jillian
  *See* Goulart, Ron(ald Joseph)
Keating, Bern
  *See* Keating, Leo Bernard
Keating, Frank 1944- .............................. *143*
Keating, Lawrence A. 1903-1966 ................ *23*
Keating, Leo Bernard 1915- ........................ *10*
Keats, Emma 1899(?)-1979(?) .................... *68*
Keats, Ezra Jack 1916-1983 ........................ *57*
  Obituary .................................................. *34*
  Earlier sketch in SATA *14*
  *See also* CLR *35*
Keefer, Catherine
  *See* Ogan, George F.
  and Ogan, Margaret E. (Nettles)
Keefer, Janice Kulyk ................................ *132*
  *See* Kulyk Keefer, Janice
Keegan, Marcia 1943- .............................. *104*
  Earlier sketch in SATA *9*
Keehn, Sally M. 1947- ............................ *165*
  Earlier sketch in SATA *87*
Keel, Frank
  *See* Keeler, Ronald F(ranklin)
Keeler, Ronald F(ranklin) 1913-1983 .......... *47*
Keely, Jack 1951- .................................. *119*
Keen, Martin L. 1913-1992 .......................... *4*
Keenan, Sheila 1953- ................................ *95*
Keene, Ann T(odd) 1940- .......................... *86*
Keene, Carolyn ...................................... *100*
  Earlier sketch in SATA *65*
  *See also* CLR *118*
  *See* Benson, Mildred (Augustine Wirt)
  and Goulart, Ron(ald Joseph)
  and Lerangis, Peter
  and McFarlane, Leslie (Charles)
  and Stanley, George Edward
  and Stratemeyer, Edward L.
Keens-Douglas, Richardo 1953- ................ *154*
  Earlier sketch in SATA *95*
Keep, Linda Lowery
  *See* Lowery, Linda
Keep, Richard 1949- .............................. *170*
Keep, Richard Cleminson
  *See* Keep, Richard
Keeping, Charles (William James) 1924-1988
  .............................................................. *69*
  Obituary .................................................. *56*
  Earlier sketch in SATA *9*
  *See also* CLR *34*
Keeshan, Robert J. 1927-2004 .................... *32*
  Obituary ................................................ *151*
Kehret, Peg 1936- .................................. *149*
  Autobiography Feature .......................... *149*
  Earlier sketches in SATA *73, 108*
Keillor, Garrison 1942- .............................. *58*
Keillor, Gary Edward
  *See* Keillor, Garrison

Keir, Christine
  *See* Pullein-Thompson, Christine
Keister, Douglas 1948- .............................. *88*
Keith, Doug 1952- .................................... *81*
Keith, Eros 1942- ...................................... *52*
Keith, Hal 1934- ........................................ *36*
Keith, Harold (Verne) 1903-1998 ................ *74*
  Earlier sketch in SATA *2*
Keith, Robert
  *See* Applebaum, Stan
Keleinikov, Andrei 1924- ............................ *65*
Kelemen, Julie 1959- ................................ *78*
Kelen, Emery 1896-1978 ............................ *13*
  Obituary .................................................. *26*
Kelleam, Joseph E(veridge) 1913-1975 ...... *31*
Kelleher, Anne 1959- ................................ *97*
Kelleher, Annette 1950- .......................... *122*
Kelleher, Daria Valerian 1955- .................... *79*
Kelleher, Victor (Michael Kitchener) 1939-
  .............................................................. *129*
  Brief entry .............................................. *52*
  Earlier sketch in SATA *75*
  *See also* CLR *36*
Keller, Beverly L(ou) ................................ *91*
  Earlier sketch in SATA *13*
Keller, Charles 1942- ................................ *82*
  Earlier sketch in SATA *8*
Keller, Debra 1958- .................................. *94*
Keller, Dick 1923- .................................... *36*
Keller, Emily .............................................. *96*
Keller, Gail Faithfull
  *See* Faithfull, Gail
Keller, Holly 1942- .................................. *157*
  Brief entry .............................................. *42*
  Earlier sketches in SATA *76, 108*
  *See also* CLR *45*
Keller, Irene (Barron) 1927-2002 ................ *36*
  Obituary ................................................ *139*
Kelley, Leo P(atrick) 1928- ........................ *32*
  Brief entry .............................................. *31*
Kelley, Patrick (G.) 1963- ........................ *129*
Kelley, Patte 1947- .................................... *93*
Kelley, True (Adelaide) 1946- .................... *130*
  Brief entry .............................................. *39*
  Earlier sketches in SATA *41, 92*
Kellin, Sally Moffet 1932- .......................... *9*
Kelling, Furn L. 1914-2000 ........................ *37*
Kellogg, Gene
  *See* Kellogg, Jean (Defrees)
Kellogg, Jean (Defrees) 1916-1978 ............ *10*
Kellogg, Steven 1941- .............................. *177*
  Earlier sketches in SATA *8, 57, 130*
  *See also* CLR *6*
Kellogg, Steven Castle
  *See* Kellogg, Steven
Kellow, Kathleen
  *See* Hibbert, Eleanor Alice Burford
Kelly, Clint 1950- .................................. *140*
Kelly, Eric P(hilbrook) 1884-1960
  *See* YABC *1*
Kelly, Fiona
  *See* Coleman, Michael (Lee)
  and Hendry, Frances Mary
  and Oldfield, Jenny
  and Welford, Sue
Kelly, Irene 1957- .................................. *147*
Kelly, Jeff
  *See* Kelly, Jeffrey
Kelly, Jeffrey 1946- .................................. *65*
Kelly, Joanne (W.) 1934- .......................... *87*
Kelly, Kate 1958- ...................................... *91*
Kelly, Kathleen M. 1964- .......................... *71*
Kelly, Katy 1955- .................................. *169*
Kelly, Lauren
  *See* Oates, Joyce Carol
Kelly, Laurene 1954- .............................. *123*
Kelly, Martha Rose 1914-1983 .................... *37*
Kelly, Marty
  *See* Kelly, Martha Rose
Kelly, Mij .............................................. *166*

Kelly, Ralph
 *See* Geis, Darlene Stern
Kelly, Regina Z(immerman) 1898-1986 ....... 5
Kelly, Rosalie (Ruth) ................................... 43
Kelly, Walt(er Crawford) 1913-1973 ........... 18
Kelsey, Alice Geer 1896-1982 ...................... 1
Kelsey, Elin ................................................ 159
Kemnitz, Thomas Milton, Jr. 1984- ......... 152
Kemnitz, Tom, Jr.
 *See* Kemnitz, Thomas Milton, Jr.
Kemp, Gene 1926- ....................................... 75
 Earlier sketch in SATA 25
 *See also* CLR 29
Kempner, Mary Jean 1913-1969 ................. 10
Kempton, Jean Welch 1914- ....................... 10
Kenda, Margaret 1942- ................................ 71
Kendall, Carol (Seeger) 1917- ................... 74
 Earlier sketch in SATA 11
 *See also* SAAS 7
Kendall, Katherine
 *See* Applegate, Katherine (Alice)
Kendall, Lace
 *See* Stoutenburg, Adrien (Pearl)
Kendall, Martha E. ..................................... 87
Kendall, Russ 1957- .................................... 83
Kenealy, James P. 1927- ............................. 52
 Brief entry ................................................ 29
Kenealy, Jim
 *See* Kenealy, James P.
Kennaway, Adrienne 1945- ....................... 171
 Earlier sketch in SATA 60
Kennedy, Brendan 1970- ............................. 57
Kennedy, Dana Forrest 1917- ..................... 74
Kennedy, Dorothy M(intzlaff) 1931- .......... 53
Kennedy, Doug(las) 1963- ......................... 122
Kennedy, John Fitzgerald 1917-1963 ......... 11
Kennedy, Joseph Charles 1929- ................. 130
 Autobiography Feature ........................... 130
 Earlier sketches in SATA 14, 86
 *See* Kennedy, X. J.
Kennedy, Pamela (J.) 1946- ........................ 87
Kennedy, Paul E(dward) 1929- ................. 113
 Earlier sketch in SATA 33
Kennedy, (Jerome) Richard 1932- .............. 22
Kennedy, Robert 1938- ................................ 63
Kennedy, T.A. 1953- ................................... 42
 Brief entry ................................................ 35
Kennedy, Teresa
 *See* Kennedy, T.A.
Kennedy, Teresa A.
 *See* Kennedy, T.A.
Kennedy, William 1928- .............................. 57
Kennedy, William Joseph
 *See* Kennedy, William
Kennedy, X. J.
 *See* CLR 27
 *See also* SAAS 22
 *See* Kennedy, Joseph Charles
Kennell, Ruth Epperson 1893-1977 ............. 6
 Obituary .................................................... 25
Kennemore, Tim 1957- .............................. 133
Kennett, David 1959- ................................ 121
Kenny, Herbert Andrew 1912-2002 ............ 13
Kenny, Jude
 *See* Daly, Jude
Kenny, Kathryn
 *See* Bowden, Joan Chase
 and Krull, Kathleen
 and Sanderlin, Owenita (Harrah)
 and Stack, Nicolete Meredith
Kenny, Kevin
 *See* Krull, Kathleen
Kensinger, George
 *See* Fichter, George S.
Kensington, Kathryn Wesley
 *See* Rusch, Kristine Kathryn
Kent, Alexander
 *See* Reeman, Douglas Edward
Kent, David
 *See* Lambert, David (Compton)

Kent, Deborah Ann 1948- ......................... 155
 Brief entry ................................................ 41
 Earlier sketches in SATA 47, 104
Kent, Jack
 *See* Kent, John Wellington
Kent, John Wellington 1920-1985 .............. 24
 Obituary .................................................... 45
Kent, Lisa 1942- .......................................... 90
Kent, Mallory
 *See* Lowndes, Robert A(ugustine) W(ard)
Kent, Margaret 1894- .................................... 2
Kent, Rockwell 1882-1971 ........................... 6
Kent, Sherman 1903-1986 .......................... 20
 Obituary .................................................... 47
Kenward, Jean 1920- .................................... 42
Kenworthy, Leonard S. 1912-1991 ............... 6
Kenyon, Karen (Smith) 1938- ................... 145
Kenyon, Kate
 *See* Adorjan, Carol (Madden)
 and Ransom, Candice F.
Kenyon, Ley 1913-1990 ................................ 6
Keown, Elizabeth ...................................... 78
Kepes, Juliet A(ppleby) 1919-1999 ............ 13
Kerby, Mona 1951- ..................................... 75
Kerigan, Florence 1896-1984 ..................... 12
Kerley, Barbara 1960- ............................... 138
Kerman, Gertrude
 *See* Furman, Gertrude Lerner Kerman
Kerns, Thelma 1929- ................................. 116
Kerr, Bob 1951- ......................................... 120
Kerr, Jessica 1901-1991 .............................. 13
Kerr, (Anne-)Judith 1923-1970 .................. 24
Kerr, M. E.
 *See* CLR 29
 *See also* SAAS 1
 *See* Meaker, Marijane
Kerr, P.B.
 *See* Kerr, Philip
Kerr, Philip 1956- ...................................... 168
Kerr, Phyllis Forbes 1942- .......................... 72
Kerr, Tom 1950- ......................................... 77
Kerrin, Jessica Scott ................................. 174
Kerry, Frances
 *See* Kerigan, Florence
Kerry, Lois
 *See* Duncan, Lois
Kershen, (L.) Michael 1982- ....................... 82
Kerven, Rosalind 1954- ............................... 83
Ker Wilson, Barbara 1929- ....................... 121
 Earlier sketches in SATA 20, 70
 *See also* SAAS 18
Keselman, Gabriela 1953- ......................... 128
Kesey, Ken 1935-2001 ................................ 66
 Obituary .................................................. 131
Kesey, Ken Elton
 *See* Kesey, Ken
Kesler, Jay 1935- ........................................ 65
Kessel, Joyce Karen 1937- .......................... 41
Kessler, Ethel 1922- .................................... 44
 Brief entry ................................................ 37
Kessler, Leonard P. 1921- ........................... 14
Kest, Kristin 1967- .................................... 168
 Earlier sketch in SATA 118
Kesteven, G. R.
 *See* Crosher, G. R.
Ketcham, Hank
 *See* Ketcham, Henry King
Ketcham, Henry King 1920-2001 ................ 28
 Brief entry ................................................ 27
 Obituary .................................................. 128
Ketcham, Sallie 1963- ............................... 124
Ketchum, Liza 1946- ................................. 132
 *See* Murrow, Liza Ketchum
Ketner, Mary Grace 1946- .......................... 75
Kettelkamp, Larry (Dale) 1933- ................... 2
 *See also* SAAS 3
Ketteman, Helen 1945- ............................. 167
 Earlier sketches in SATA 73, 115
Kettle, Peter
 *See* Glover, Denis (James Matthews)
Kevles, Bettyann Holtzmann 1938- ............ 23

Key, Alexander (Hill) 1904-1979 ................. 8
 Obituary .................................................... 23
Key, Samuel M.
 *See* de Lint, Charles
Keyes, Daniel 1927- .................................... 37
Keyes, Fenton 1915-1999 ............................ 34
Keyes, Greg
 *See* Keyes, J. Gregory
Keyes, J. Gregory 1963- ............................ 116
Keyser, Marcia 1933- .................................. 42
Keyser, Sarah
 *See* McGuire, Leslie (Sarah)
Khalsa, Dayal Kaur 1943-1989 ................... 62
 *See also* CLR 30
 *See* Kaur Khalsa, Dayal
Khan, Rukhsana 1962- .............................. 165
 Earlier sketch in SATA 118
Khanshendel, Chiron
 *See* Rose, Wendy
Kheirabadi, Masoud 1951- ........................ 158
Khemir, Sabiha ........................................... 87
Kherdian, David 1931- ................................ 74
 Autobiography Feature ........................... 125
 Earlier sketch in SATA 16
 *See also* CLR 24
Kibbe, Pat (Hosley) ..................................... 60
Kidd, Diana 1933-2000 .............................. 150
Kidd, Richard 1952- .................................. 152
Kidd, Ronald 1948- ................................... 173
 Earlier sketches in SATA 42, 92
Kiddell, John 1922- ...................................... 3
Kiddell-Monroe, Joan 1908-1972 ................ 55
Kidwell, Carl 1910- ..................................... 43
Kiefer, Irene 1926- ...................................... 21
Kiefer, Kathleen Balmes 1957- ................. 142
Kierstead, Vera M. 1913- .......................... 121
Kiesel, Stanley 1925- ................................... 35
Kiesler, Kate (A.) 1971- ............................ 152
 Earlier sketch in SATA 90
Kihn, Greg 1952- ...................................... 110
Kikukawa, Cecily H(arder) 1919- ............... 44
 Brief entry ................................................ 35
Kilcher, Jewel 1974- .................................. 109
Kile, Joan 1940- .......................................... 78
Kilgore, Kathleen 1946- .............................. 42
Kilian, Crawford 1941- ................................ 35
Killdeer, John
 *See* Mayhar, Ardath
Killien, Christi 1956- ................................... 73
Killilea, Marie (Lyons) 1913-1991 ............... 2
Killingback, Julia 1944- .............................. 63
Killough, (Karen) Lee 1942- ....................... 64
Kilreon, Beth
 *See* Walker, Barbara (Jeanne) K(erlin)
Kilworth, Garry 1941- ................................. 94
Kilworth, Garry D.
 *See* Kilworth, Garry
Kilworth, Garry Douglas
 *See* Kilworth, Garry
Kim, Helen 1899-1970 ................................. 98
Kimball, Gayle 1943- ................................... 90
Kimball, Violet T(ew) 1932- ..................... 126
Kimball, Yeffe 1914-1978 ........................... 37
Kimber, Murray 1964- .............................. 171
Kimble, Warren ......................................... 176
Kimbrough, Emily 1899-1989 ...................... 2
 Obituary .................................................... 59
Kimeldorf, Martin (R.) 1948- ................... 121
Kimenye, Barbara 1940(?)- ....................... 121
Kimmel, Elizabeth Cody ............................ 170
Kimmel, Eric A. 1946- .............................. 176
 Earlier sketches in SATA 13, 80, 125
Kimmel, Margaret Mary 1938- .................... 43
 Brief entry ................................................ 33
Kimmelman, Leslie (Grodinsky) 1958- ..... 156
 Earlier sketch in SATA 85
Kincaid, Jamaica 1949-
 *See* CLR 63
Kincher, Jonni 1949- ................................... 79
Kindl, Patrice 1951- .................................. 128
 Earlier sketch in SATA 82

Kindred, Wendy (Good) 1937- ..................... 7
Kines, Pat Decker 1937- .......................... 12
King, Adam
  *See* Hoare, Robert J(ohn)
King, Alison
  *See* Martini, Teri
King, (Maria) Anna 1964- ..................... 72
King, Billie Jean 1943- ......................... 12
King, Christopher (L.) 1945- ................... 84
King, (David) Clive 1924- ..................... 144
  Earlier sketch in SATA 28
King, Colin 1943- ............................... 76
King, Cynthia 1925- .............................. 7
King, Daniel (John) 1963- ..................... 130
King, Elizabeth 1953- ........................... 83
King, Frank R. 1904-1999 ..................... 127
King, Jane
  *See* Currie, Stephen
King, Jeanette (Margaret) 1959- .............. 105
King, Larry L. 1929- ............................ 66
King, Laurie R. 1952- ........................... 88
King, Marian 1900(?)-1986 ..................... 23
  Obituary ......................................... 47
King, Martin Luther, Jr. 1929-1968 .......... 14
King, Mary Ellen 1958- ......................... 93
King, Paul
  *See* Drackett, Phil(ip Arthur)
King, Paula
  *See* Downing, Paula E.
King, Stephen 1947- ............................ 161
  Earlier sketches in SATA 9, 55
King, Stephen Edwin
  *See* King, Stephen
King, Stephen Michael ......................... 157
King, Steve
  *See* King, Stephen
King, Thomas 1943- ............................. 96
King, Tony 1947- ................................ 39
Kingman, Dong (Moy Shu) 1911-2000 ...... 44
Kingman, Lee .................................... 67
  Earlier sketch in SATA 1
  *See also* SAAS 3
  *See* Natti, (Mary) Lee
Kingsland, Leslie William 1912- ............. 13
Kingsley, Charles 1819-1875
  *See* YABC 2
  *See also* CLR 77
Kingsley, Emily Perl 1940- .................... 33
King-Smith, Dick 1922- ....................... 135
  Brief entry ...................................... 38
  Earlier sketches in SATA 47, 80
  *See also* CLR 40
Kingston, Maxine Hong 1940- ................. 53
Kingston, Maxine Ting Ting Hong
  *See* Kingston, Maxine Hong
Kinney, C. Cle(land) 1915- ..................... 6
Kinney, Harrison 1921- ......................... 13
Kinney, Jean Stout 1912- ....................... 12
Kinsey, Elizabeth
  *See* Clymer, Eleanor
Kinsey, Helen 1948- ............................ 82
Kinsey-Warnock, Natalie 1956- .............. 167
  Earlier sketches in SATA 71, 116
Kinzel, Dorothy 1950- ........................... 57
Kinzel, Dottie
  *See* Kinzel, Dorothy
Kipling, (Joseph) Rudyard 1865-1936 ...... 100
  *See also* YABC 2
  *See also* CLR 65
Kippax, Frank
  *See* Needle, Jan
Kirby, David K. 1944- .......................... 78
Kirby, David Kirk
  *See* Kirby, David K.
Kirby, Margaret
  *See* Bingley, Margaret (Jane Kirby)
Kirby, Susan E. 1949- .......................... 62
Kirk, Connie Ann 1957- ....................... 167
Kirk, Daniel 1952- ............................. 153
  Earlier sketch in SATA 107

Kirk, David 1955- .............................. 161
  Earlier sketch in SATA 117
Kirk, Heather 1949- ........................... 166
Kirk, Ruth (Kratz) 1925- ........................ 5
Kirkham, Dinah
  *See* Card, Orson Scott
Kirkland, Will
  *See* Hale, Arlene
Kirkpatrick, Katherine (Anne) 1964- ......... 113
Kirkup, James 1918- ............................ 12
Kirkwood, Kathryn
  *See* Fluke, Joanne
Kirshenbaum, Binnie ........................... 79
Kirshner, David S. 1958- ....................... 123
Kish, Eleanor M(ary) 1924- .................... 73
Kish, Ely
  *See* Kish, Eleanor M(ary)
Kishida, Eriko 1929- ............................ 12
Kisinger, Grace Gelvin (Maze) 1913-1965 . 10
Kissin, Eva H. 1923- ............................ 10
Kissinger, Rosemary K.
  *See* Updyke, Rosemary K.
Kistler, John M. 1967- ......................... 160
Kitamura, Satoshi 1956- ....................... 143
  Earlier sketches in SATA 62, 98
  *See also* CLR 60
Kitchen, Bert
  *See* Kitchen, Herbert Thomas
Kitchen, Herbert Thomas 1940- ................ 70
Kite, (L.) Patricia ............................... 78
  *See* Kite, Pat
Kitt, Tamara
  *See* de Regniers, Beatrice Schenk (Freedman)
Kittinger, Jo S(usenbach) 1955- .............. 148
  Earlier sketch in SATA 96
Kituomba
  *See* Odaga, Asenath (Bole)
Kitzinger, Sheila 1929- ......................... 57
Kiwak, Barbara 1966- .......................... 103
Kjelgaard, James Arthur 1910-1959 .......... 17
  *See also* CLR 81
  *See* Kjelgaard, Jim
Kjelgaard, Jim
  *See* Kjelgaard, James Arthur
Kjelle, Marylou Morano 1954- ................ 146
Klagsbrun, Francine (Lifton) .................. 36
Klaits, Barrie 1944- ............................ 52
Klaperman, Gilbert 1921- ....................... 33
Klaperman, Libby Mindlin 1921-1982 ........ 33
  Obituary ......................................... 31
Klass, David 1960- ............................. 142
  Earlier sketch in SATA 88
Klass, Morton 1927-2001 ....................... 11
Klass, Sheila Solomon 1927- ................... 99
  Autobiography Feature ......................... 126
  Earlier sketch in SATA 45
  *See also* SAAS 26
Klause, Annette Curtis 1953- .................. 175
  Earlier sketch in SATA 79
  *See also* CLR 104
Klaveness, Jan O'Donnell 1939- ............... 86
Kleberger, Ilse 1921- ............................ 5
Kleeberg, Irene (Flitner) Cumming 1932- .. 65
Klein, Aaron E. 1930-1998 ..................... 45
  Brief entry ...................................... 28
Klein, Bill 1945- ............................... 89
Klein, David 1919-2001 ........................ 59
Klein, Frederick C. 1938- ..................... 154
Klein, Gerda Weissmann 1924- ................ 44
Klein, H(erbert) Arthur .......................... 8
Klein, James 1932- ............................ 115
Klein, Leonore (Glotzer) 1916- ................. 6
Klein, Mina C(ooper) 1906-1979 ............... 8
Klein, Norma 1938-1989 ........................ 57
  Earlier sketch in SATA 7
  *See also* CLR 19
  *See also* SAAS 1
Klein, Rachel S. 1953- ......................... 105

Klein, Robin 1936- ............................. 164
  Brief entry ...................................... 45
  Earlier sketches in SATA 55, 80
  *See also* CLR 21
Klemin, Diana .................................. 65
Klemm, Barry 1945- ........................... 104
Klemm, Edward G., Jr. 1910-2001 ............ 30
Klemm, Roberta K(ohnhorst) 1884-1975 ... 30
Kleven, Elisa 1958- ............................ 173
  Earlier sketch in SATA 76
  *See also* CLR 85
Klevin, Jill Ross 1935- .......................... 39
  Brief entry ...................................... 38
Kliban, B(ernard) 1935-1990 ................... 35
  Obituary ......................................... 66
Klimowicz, Barbara 1927- ...................... 10
Kline, Christina Baker 1964- .................. 101
Kline, James
  *See* Klein, James
Kline, Jim
  *See* Kline, Jim
Kline, Lisa Williams 1954- ..................... 143
Kline, Suzy 1943- ............................. 152
  Brief entry ...................................... 48
  Earlier sketches in SATA 67, 99
Kliros, Thea 1935- ............................. 106
Klise, M. Sarah 1961- .......................... 128
Klug, Ron(ald) 1939- ........................... 31
Knaak, Richard A. 1961- ....................... 166
  Earlier sketch in SATA 86
Knaak, Richard Allen
  *See* Knaak, Richard A.
Knapp, Edward
  *See* Kunhardt, Edith
Knapp, Ron 1952- .............................. 34
Knebel, Fletcher 1911-1993 ................... 36
  Obituary ......................................... 75
Kneeland, Linda Clarke 1947- ................. 94
Knickerbocker, Diedrich
  *See* Irving, Washington
Knifesmith
  *See* Cutler, Ivor
Knigge, Robert (R.) 1921(?)-1987 ............. 50
Knight, Anne (Katherine) 1946- ............... 34
Knight, Brenda .................................. 112
Knight, Christopher G. 1943- .................. 96
Knight, Damon (Francis) 1922-2002 ........... 9
  Obituary ........................................ 139
Knight, David C(arpenter) 1925-1984 ........ 14
  *See also* CLR 38
Knight, Eric 1897-1943 ........................ 18
Knight, Eric Mowbray
  *See* Knight, Eric
Knight, Francis Edgar 1905- ................... 14
Knight, Frank
  *See* Knight, Francis Edgar
Knight, Hilary 1926- ........................... 132
  Earlier sketches in SATA 15, 69
Knight, Joan (MacPhail) ....................... 159
  Earlier sketch in SATA 82
Knight, Joan
  *See* Knight, Joan (MacPhail)
Knight, Kathryn Lasky
  *See* Lasky, Kathryn
Knight, Mallory T.
  *See* Hurwood, Bernhardt J.
Knight, Theodore O. 1946- ..................... 77
Knobloch, Dorothea 1951- ...................... 88
Knoepfle, John (Ignatius) 1923- ............... 66
Knott, Bill
  *See* Knott, William C(ecil, Jr.)
Knott, William C(ecil, Jr.) 1927- ............... 3
  *See* Knott, Bill
  and Mitchum, Hank
  and Sharpe, Jon
Knotts, Howard (Clayton, Jr.) 1922- ......... 25
Knowles, Anne 1933- ........................... 37
Knowles, John 1926-2001 ...................... 89
  Obituary ........................................ 134
  Earlier sketch in SATA 8
  *See also* CLR 98

Knox, Calvin M.
  *See* Silverberg, Robert
Knox, (Mary) Eleanor Jessie 1909-2000 ..... *59*
  Earlier sketch in SATA *30*
Knox, Elizabeth 1959- ........................... *176*
Knox, Elizabeth Fiona
  *See* Knox, Elizabeth
Knox, James
  *See* Brittain, William (E.)
Knox, Jolyne 1937- ............................. *76*
Knudsen, James 1950- .......................... *42*
Knudsen, Michelle ............................... *171*
Knudson, R. R.
  *See* SAAS *18*
  *See* Knudson, Rozanne
Knudson, Richard L(ewis) 1930- ............ *34*
Knudson, Rozanne 1932- ...................... *79*
  Earlier sketch in SATA *7*
  *See* Knudson, R. R.
Knutson, Barbara 1959-2005 .................. *166*
Knutson, Kimberley ............................. *115*
Knye, Cassandra
  *See* Disch, Thomas M.
Koch, Dorothy Clarke 1924- ................... *6*
Koch, Kenneth 1925-2002 ...................... *65*
Koch, Kenneth Jay
  *See* Koch, Kenneth
Koch, Phyllis (Mae) McCallum 1911- ........ *10*
Kocsis, J. C.
  *See* Paul, James
Koda-Callan, Elizabeth 1944- ................. *140*
  Earlier sketch in SATA *67*
Koehler, Phoebe 1955- .......................... *85*
Koehler-Pentacoff, Elizabeth 1957- .......... *160*
  Earlier sketch in SATA *96*
Koehn, Ilse
  *See* Van Zwienen, Ilse Charlotte Koehn
Koenig, Viviane 1950- .......................... *80*
Koering, Ursula 1921-1976 ..................... *64*
Koerner, W(illiam) H(enry) D(avid) 1878-1938
  ........................................... *21*
Koertge, Ronald 1940- .......................... *131*
  Earlier sketches in SATA *53, 92*
Koestler-Grack, Rachel A. 1973- .............. *156*
Koff, Richard Myram 1926- .................... *62*
Koffinke, Carol 1949- ........................... *82*
Kogan, Deborah ................................... *50*
  *See* Kogan Ray, Deborah
Kogan Ray, Deborah 1940- ..................... *161*
  *See* Kogan, Deborah
  and Ray, Deborah
Kogawa, Joy Nozomi 1935- ..................... *99*
Kogler, Jennifer Anne 1982(?)- ............... *174*
Kohl, Herbert 1937- ............................. *47*
Kohl, Herbert R.
  *See* Kohl, Herbert
Kohl, MaryAnn F(aubion) 1947- .............. *144*
  Earlier sketch in SATA *74*
Kohn, Bernice .................................... *4*
  *See* Hunt, Bernice (Kohn)
Kohn, Rita (T.) 1933- ........................... *89*
Kohner, Frederick 1905-1986 .................. *10*
  Obituary ...................................... *48*
Koide, Tan 1938-1986 .......................... *50*
Koike, Kay 1940- ............................... *72*
Koja, Kathe 1960- .............................. *155*
Kolb, Larry J. 1953- ............................ *175*
Kolba, St. Tamara ............................... *22*
Kolibalova, Marketa
  *See* Kolibalova, Marketa
Kolibalova, Marketa 1953- ..................... *126*
Koller, Jackie French 1948- .................... *157*
  Earlier sketches in SATA *72, 109*
  *See also* CLR *68*
Kolodny, Nancy J. 1946- ....................... *76*
Komaiko, Leah 1954- ........................... *164*
  Earlier sketch in SATA *97*
Komisar, Lucy 1942- ........................... *9*
Komoda, Beverly 1939- ......................... *25*
Komoda, Kiyo 1937- ............................ *9*
Kompaneyets, Marc 1974- ...................... *169*

Komroff, Manuel 1890-1974 ................... *2*
  Obituary ...................................... *20*
Konigsburg, E. L. 1930- ........................ *126*
  Earlier sketches in SATA *4, 48, 94*
  *See also* CLR *81*
Konigsburg, Elaine Lobl
  *See* Konigsburg, E. L.
Koningsberger, Hans ........................... *5*
  *See* Koning, Hans
Konkle, Janet Everest 1917- ................... *12*
Kono, Erin Eitter 1973- ........................ *177*
Konzak, Burt 1946- ............................. *151*
Koob, Theodora (J. Foth) 1918- ............... *23*
Kooiker, Leonie
  *See* Kooyker-Romijn, Johanna Maria
Koons, James
  *See* Pernu, Dennis
Koontz, Dean R. 1945- ......................... *165*
  Earlier sketch in SATA *92*
Koontz, Dean Ray
  *See* Koontz, Dean R.
Koontz, Robin Michal 1954- ................... *136*
  Earlier sketch in SATA *70*
Kooyker, Leonie
  *See* Kooyker-Romijn, Johanna Maria
Kooyker-Romijn, Johanna Maria 1927- ...... *48*
  *See* Kooyker, Leonie
Kooyker-Romyn, Johanna Maria
  *See* Kooyker-Romijn, Johanna Maria
Kopelke, Lisa 1963- ............................ *154*
Kopper, Lisa (Esther) 1950- ................... *105*
  Brief entry ................................... *51*
Koppes, Steven N. 1957- ....................... *169*
Koppes, Steven Nelson
  *See* Koppes, Steven N.
Korach, Mimi 1922- ............................ *9*
Koralek, Jenny 1934- ........................... *140*
  Earlier sketch in SATA *71*
Korczak, Janusz ................................. *65*
  *See* Goldszmit, Henryk
Koren, Edward (Benjamin) 1935- ............. *148*
  Earlier sketch in SATA *5*
Korinets, Iurii Iosifovich
  *See* Korinetz, Yuri (Iosifovich)
Korinetz, Yuri (Iosifovich) 1923- ............. *9*
  *See also* CLR *4*
Korman, Bernice 1937- ......................... *78*
Korman, Gordon 1963- ......................... *167*
  Brief entry ................................... *41*
  Earlier sketches in SATA *49, 81, 119*
  *See also* CLR *25*
Korman, Gordon Richard
  *See* Korman, Gordon
Korman, Justine 1958- .......................... *70*
Kornblatt, Marc 1954- .......................... *147*
  Earlier sketch in SATA *84*
Kornprobst, Jacques 1937- ..................... *177*
Korte, Gene J. 1950- ........................... *74*
Korty, Carol 1937- ............................. *15*
Koscielniak, Bruce 1947- ...................... *153*
  Earlier sketches in SATA *67, 99*
Koshin, Alexander (A.) 1952- .................. *86*
Kositsky, Lynne 1947- .......................... *158*
Koskenmaki, Rosalie
  *See* Maggio, Rosalie
Koss, Amy Goldman 1954- ..................... *158*
  Earlier sketch in SATA *115*
Kossin, Sandy (Sanford) 1926- ................ *10*
Kossman, Nina 1959- ........................... *84*
Kotzwinkle, William 1938- ..................... *146*
  Earlier sketches in SATA *24, 70*
  *See also* CLR *6*
Kouhi, Elizabeth 1917- ......................... *54*
  Brief entry ................................... *49*
Kouts, Anne 1945- ............................. *8*
Koutsky, Jan Dale 1955- ....................... *146*
Kovacs, Deborah 1954- ......................... *132*
  Earlier sketch in SATA *79*

Kovalski, Maryann 1951- ....................... *175*
  Earlier sketches in SATA *58, 97*
  *See also* CLR *34*
  *See also* SAAS *21*
Kowalski, Kathiann M. 1955- .................. *151*
  Earlier sketch in SATA *96*
Kraft, Betsy Harvey 1937- ..................... *157*
Krahn, Fernando 1935- ......................... *49*
  Brief entry ................................... *31*
  *See also* CLR *3*
Krakauer, Hoong Yee Lee 1955- ............... *86*
Krakauer, Jon 1954- ............................ *108*
Kramer, George
  *See* Heuman, William
Kramer, Nora 1896(?)-1984 .................... *26*
  Obituary ...................................... *39*
Kramer, Remi (Thomas) 1935- ................. *90*
Krantz, Hazel (Newman) ........................ *12*
Kranzler, George G(ershon) 1916- ............ *28*
Kranzler, Gershon
  *See* Kranzler, George G(ershon)
Krasilovsky, Phyllis 1926- ..................... *38*
  Earlier sketch in SATA *1*
  *See also* CLR *83*
  *See also* SAAS *5*
Krasne, Betty
  *See* Levine, Betty K(rasne)
Krasner, Steven 1953- .......................... *154*
Krasno, Rena 1923- ............................. *104*
Kratman, Tom ................................... *175*
Kraus, Joanna Halpert 1937- ................... *87*
Kraus, (Herman) Robert 1925-2001 .......... *93*
  Obituary ...................................... *130*
  Earlier sketches in SATA *4, 65*
  *See also* SAAS *11*
Krauss, Ruth (Ida) 1911-1993 ................. *30*
  Obituary ...................................... *75*
  Earlier sketch in SATA *1*
  *See also* CLR *42*
Krautter, Elisa (Bialk) 1912(?)-1990 .......... *1*
  Obituary ...................................... *65*
Krautwurst, Terry 1946- ........................ *79*
Kray, Robert Clement 1930- ................... *82*
Kredel, Fritz 1900-1973 ........................ *17*
Kreikemeier, Gregory Scott 1965- ............ *85*
Krementz, Jill 1940- ............................ *134*
  Earlier sketches in SATA *17, 71*
  *See also* CLR *5*
  *See also* SAAS *8*
Kremer, Marcie
  *See* Sorenson, Margo
Krenina, Katya 1968- ........................... *101*
Krensky, Stephen 1953- ........................ *136*
  Brief entry ................................... *41*
  Earlier sketches in SATA *47, 93*
Krensky, Stephen Alan
  *See* Krensky, Stephen
Kresh, Paul 1919-1997 .......................... *61*
  Obituary ...................................... *94*
Kress, Nancy 1948- ............................. *147*
  Autobiography Feature ........................ *147*
  Earlier sketch in SATA *85*
Kricher, John C. 1944- ......................... *113*
Krieger, Melanie ............................... *96*
Kripke, Dorothy Karp ........................... *30*
Krisher, Trudy (B.) 1946- ...................... *160*
  Earlier sketch in SATA *86*
Krishnaswami, Uma 1956- ...................... *144*
Kristof, Jane 1932- ............................. *8*
Kroeber, Theodora (Kracaw) 1897-1979 ...... *1*
Kroeger, Mary Kay 1950- ....................... *92*
Krohn, Katherine E(lizabeth) 1961- .......... *125*
  Earlier sketch in SATA *84*
Kroll, Francis Lynde 1904-1973 ............... *10*
Kroll, Steven 1941- ............................. *135*
  Autobiography Feature ........................ *135*
  Earlier sketches in SATA *19, 66, 125*
  *See also* SAAS *7*
Kroll, Virginia L. 1948- ........................ *168*
  Earlier sketches in SATA *76, 114*

Kroll, Virginia Louisa
See Kroll, Virginia L.
Krommes, Beth 1956- .................................. 128
Kronenwetter, Michael 1943- ...................... 62
Kroniuk, Lisa
See Berton, Pierre (Francis de Marigny)
Kropp, Paul (Stephan) 1948- ........................ 38
Brief entry .................................................. 34
See also CLR 96
Krosoczka, Jarrett J. 1977- ........................ 155
Krovatin, Christopher 1985- ...................... 171
Kruess, James
See CLR 9
See Kruss, James
Krull, Kathleen 1952- ................................. 149
Autobiography Feature ............................. 106
Brief entry .................................................. 39
Earlier sketches in SATA 52, 80
See also CLR 44
Krumgold, Joseph (Quincy) 1908-1980 ...... 48
Obituary ..................................................... 23
Earlier sketch in SATA 1
Krupinski, Loretta 1940- ............................ 161
Earlier sketches in SATA 67, 102
Krupnick, Karen 1947- ................................. 89
Krupp, E(dwin) C(harles) 1944- ................. 123
Earlier sketch in SATA 53
Krupp, Robin Rector 1946- .......................... 53
Krush, Beth 1918- ........................................ 18
Krush, Joe 1918- .......................................... 18
See Krush, Joseph P.
Kruss, James 1926-1997 ................................ 8
See Kruess, James
Krykorka, Vladyana 1945- ............................ 96
Kubie, Eleanor Gottheil
See Kubie, Nora Gottheil Benjamin
Kubie, Nora Benjamin
See Kubie, Nora Gottheil Benjamin
Kubie, Nora Gottheil Benjamin 1899-1988
................................................................... 39
Obituary ..................................................... 59
Kubinyi, Laszlo 1937- ................................. 94
Earlier sketch in SATA 17
Kudlinski, Kathleen V. 1950- ..................... 150
Kuenstler, Morton 1927- .............................. 10
Kuharski, Janice 1947- ............................... 128
Kuklin, Susan 1941- ................................... 163
Earlier sketches in SATA 63, 95
See also CLR 51
Kulikov, Boris 1966- ................................... 170
Kulling, Monica 1952- .................................. 89
Kullman, Harry 1919-1982 ........................... 35
Kumin, Maxine 1925- ................................... 12
Kumin, Maxine Winokur
See Kumin, Maxine
Kunhardt, Dorothy (Meserve) 1901-1979 ... 53
Obituary ..................................................... 22
Kunhardt, Edith 1937- .................................. 67
Kunjufu, Jawanza 1953- ............................... 73
Kunstler, Morton
See Kuenstler, Morton
Kuntz, J(ohn) L. 1947- ................................. 91
Kuntz, Jerry 1956- ...................................... 133
Kupferberg, Herbert 1918-2001 ................... 19
Kuratomi, Chizuko 1939- ............................. 12
See also CLR 32
Kurczok, Belinda 1978- .............................. 121
Kurelek, William 1927-1977 ......................... 8
Obituary ..................................................... 27
See also CLR 2
Kurian, George 1928- ................................... 65
Kurjian, Judi(th M.) 1944- .......................... 127
Kurland, Gerald 1942- .................................. 13
Kurland, Michael 1938- .............................. 118
Earlier sketch in SATA 48
Kurland, Michael Joseph
See Kurland, Michael
Kuroi, Ken 1947- ........................................ 120
Kurokawa, Mitsuhiro 1954- .......................... 88
Kurten, Bjorn (Olof) 1924-1988 ................... 64

Kurtz, Jane 1952- ....................................... 139
Earlier sketch in SATA 91
See also CLR 123
Kurtz, Katherine (Irene) 1944- ................... 126
Earlier sketch in SATA 76
Kurz, Rudolf 1952- ....................................... 95
Kushner, Donn (J.) 1927- ............................. 52
See also CLR 55
Kushner, Ellen (Ruth) 1955- ....................... 98
Kushner, Jill Menkes 1951- .......................... 62
Kushner, Lawrence 1943- ............................ 169
Earlier sketch in SATA 83
Kushner, Tony 1956- ................................... 160
Kuskin, Karla 1932- ................................... 164
Earlier sketches in SATA 2, 68, 111
See also CLR 4
See also SAAS 3
Kuskin, Karla Seidman
See Kuskin, Karla
Kusugak, Michael (Arvaarluk) 1948- ......... 143
Kuttner, Paul 1922- ..................................... 18
Kuyper, Sjoerd 1952- ................................. 177
Kuzma, Kay 1941- ........................................ 39
Kvale, Velma R(uth) 1898-1979 .................... 8
Kvasnosky, Laura McGee 1951- ................. 142
Earlier sketch in SATA 93
Kwasney, Michelle D. 1960- ....................... 162
Kyle, Benjamin
See Gottfried, Theodore Mark
Kyle, Elisabeth
See Dunlop, Agnes M. R.
Kyte, Kathy S. 1946- .................................... 50
Brief entry .................................................. 44

**L**

L., Barry
See Longyear, Barry B(rookes)
L., Tommy
See Lorkowski, Thomas V(incent)
Lace, William W. 1942- .............................. 126
Lachner, Dorothea
See Knobloch, Dorothea
Lackey, Mercedes R. 1950- ......................... 127
Earlier sketch in SATA 81
Lackey, Mercedes Ritchie
See Lackey, Mercedes R.
Lacoe, Addie .............................................. 78
Lacome, Julie 1961- ................................... 174
Earlier sketch in SATA 80
Lacy, Leslie Alexander 1937- ......................... 6
Ladd, Cheryl (Jean) 1951- .......................... 113
Ladd, Louise 1943- ...................................... 97
Ladd, Veronica
See Miner, Jane Claypool
Laden, Nina 1962- ...................................... 148
Earlier sketch in SATA 85
Lader, Lawrence 1919-2006 ........................... 6
LaDoux, Rita C. 1951- ................................. 74
Lady, A
See Taylor, Ann
Lady of Quality, A
See Bagnold, Enid
La Farge, Oliver (Hazard Perry) 1901-1963
................................................................... 19
La Farge, Phyllis ........................................ 14
LaFaye, A. 1970- ........................................ 156
Earlier sketch in SATA 105
LaFaye, Alexandria R.T.
See LaFaye, A.
Laffin, John (Alfred Charles) 1922- ............. 31
LaFontaine, Bruce 1948- ............................ 176
Earlier sketch in SATA 114
La Fontaine, Jean de 1621-1695 .................. 18
Lager, Claude
See Lapp, Christiane (Germain)
Lager, Marilyn 1939- .................................... 52
Lagercrantz, Rose (Elsa) 1947- ................... 39

Lagerloef, Selma (Ottiliana Lovisa)
See Lagerlof, Selma (Ottiliana Lovisa)
Lagerlof, Selma (Ottiliana Lovisa) 1858-1940
................................................................... 15
See also CLR 7
See Lagerloef, Selma (Ottiliana Lovisa)
Laguna, Sofie 1968- ................................... 158
LaHaye, Tim F. 1926- ................................. 149
LaHaye, Timothy F.
See LaHaye, Tim F.
Laiken, Deirdre S(usan) 1948- ..................... 48
Brief entry .................................................. 40
Laimgruber, Monika 1946- ........................... 11
Lain, Anna
See Lamb, Nancy
Laing, Alexander (Kinnan) 1903-1976 ...... 117
Laing, Martha
See Celestino, Martha Laing
Laird, Christa 1944- ................................... 108
Autobiography Feature ............................. 120
See also SAAS 26
Laird, Elizabeth (Mary Risk) 1943- ........... 159
Earlier sketches in SATA 77, 114
See also CLR 65
Laird, Jean E(louise) 1930- .......................... 38
Laite, Gordon 1925- ..................................... 31
Lake, Harriet
See Taylor, Paula (Wright)
Laklan, Carli 1907-1988 ................................. 5
Laliberte, Louise-Andree 1958- ................. 169
Lalicki, Barbara ........................................... 61
Lally, Soinbhe 1945- ................................... 119
LaMarche, Jim ........................................... 162
Lamb, Beatrice Pitney 1904-1997 ............... 21
Lamb, Charles 1775-1834 ............................ 17
Lamb, Elizabeth Searle 1917- ...................... 31
Lamb, G(eoffrey) F(rederick) ....................... 10
Lamb, Harold (Albert) 1892-1962 ............... 53
Lamb, Lynton (Harold) 1907-1977 .............. 10
Lamb, Mary Ann 1764-1847 ........................ 17
Lamb, Nancy 1939- ...................................... 80
Lamb, Robert (Boyden) 1941- ...................... 13
Lambert, David (Compton) 1932- ............... 84
Brief entry .................................................. 49
Lambert, Janet 1895(?)-1973 ....................... 25
Lambert, Martha L. ................................... 113
Lambert, Saul 1928- ..................................... 23
Lambert, Stephen ....................................... 174
Lamburn, Richmal Crompton 1890-1969 ..... 5
See Crompton, Richmal
Lamensdorf, Len
See Lamensdorf, Leonard
Lamensdorf, Leonard 1930- ........................ 120
Laminack, Lester L. 1956- ......................... 163
Earlier sketch in SATA 120
Lamorisse, Albert (Emmanuel) 1922-1970 . 23
Lampert, Emily 1951- ................................... 52
Brief entry .................................................. 49
Lamplugh, Lois 1921- .................................. 17
Lampman, Evelyn Sibley 1907-1980 ........... 87
Obituary ..................................................... 23
Earlier sketch in SATA 4
Lamprey, Louise 1869-1951
See YABC 2
Lampton, Chris
See Lampton, Christopher F.
Lampton, Christopher
See Lampton, Christopher F.
Lampton, Christopher F. ............................... 67
Brief entry .................................................. 47
Lamstein, Sarah 1943- ............................... 174
Earlier sketch in SATA 126
Lamstein, Sarah Marwil
See Lamstein, Sarah
Lanagan, Margo 1960- ............................... 163
Lancaster, Bruce 1896-1963 .......................... 9
Lance, Kathryn 1943- ................................... 76
Land, Barbara (Neblett) 1923- ..................... 16
Land, Jane
See Borland, Kathryn Kilby
and Speicher, Helen Ross S(mith)

Land, Myrick (Ebben) 1922-1998 ............... *15*
Land, Ross
  *See* Borland, Kathryn Kilby
  and Speicher, Helen Ross S(mith)
Landau, Elaine 1948- ................................ *141*
  Earlier sketches in SATA *10, 94*
Landau, Jacob 1917- .................................. *38*
Landeck, Beatrice 1904-1978 ................... *15*
Landin, Les 1923- ........................................ *2*
Landis, J(ames) D(avid) 1942- .................. *60*
  Brief entry ............................................ *52*
Landis, James D.
  *See* Landis, J(ames) D(avid)
Landis, Jill Marie 1948- .......................... *101*
Landmann, Bimba 1968- .......................... *176*
Landon, Dena 1978(?)- ............................ *168*
Landon, Lucinda 1950- ............................. *56*
  Brief entry ............................................ *51*
Landon, Margaret (Dorothea Mortenson)
  1903-1993 ............................................. *50*
Landshoff, Ursula 1908-1989 ................... *13*
Landstrom, Lena 1943- ............................ *146*
Landstrom, Olof 1943- ............................. *146*
Lane, Carolyn 1926-1993 .......................... *10*
Lane, Connie
  *See* Laux, Constance
Lane, Dakota 1959- .................................. *166*
  Earlier sketch in SATA *105*
Lane, Jerry
  *See* Martin, Patricia Miles
Lane, John (Richard) 1932- ....................... *15*
Lane, Margaret 1907-1994 ........................ *65*
  Brief entry ............................................ *38*
  Obituary ................................................ *79*
Lane, Rose Wilder 1887-1968 ................... *29*
  Brief entry ............................................ *28*
Lanes, Selma Gordon 1929- ........................ *3*
Lanfredi, Judy 1964- ................................. *83*
Lang, Andrew 1844-1912 .......................... *16*
  *See also* CLR *101*
Lang, Aubrey .......................................... *169*
Lang, Paul 1948- ....................................... *83*
Lang, Susan S. 1950- ................................ *68*
Lang, T.T.
  *See* Taylor, Theodore
Langdo, Bryan 1973- ............................... *138*
Lange, John
  *See* Crichton, Michael
Lange, Suzanne 1945- .................................. *5*
Langley, Andrew 1949- ............................ *166*
  Earlier sketch in SATA *104*
Langley, Charles P(itman) III 1949- ......... *103*
Langley, Jonathan 1952- .......................... *122*
Langley, Wanda ....................................... *173*
Langner, Nola ............................................. *8*
  *See* Malone, Nola Langner
Langone, John (Michael) 1929- ................. *46*
  Brief entry ............................................ *38*
Langreuter, Jutta 1944- ........................... *122*
Langrish, Katherine ................................. *177*
Langsen, Richard C. 1953- ........................ *95*
Langstaff, John 1920-2005 ........................ *68*
  Obituary .............................................. *172*
  Earlier sketch in SATA *6*
  *See also* CLR *3*
Langstaff, John Meredith
  *See* Langstaff, John
Langstaff, Launcelot
  *See* Irving, Washington
Langton, Jane (Gillson) 1922- .................. *140*
  Autobiography Feature ......................... *140*
  Earlier sketches in SATA *3, 68, 129*
  *See also* CLR *33*
  *See also* SAAS *5*
Lanier, Sidney 1842-1881 ......................... *18*
Lanier, Sterling E(dmund) 1927- .............. *109*
Lanino, Deborah 1964- ............................ *123*
Lankford, Mary D. 1932- ......................... *112*
  Earlier sketch in SATA *77*
Lannin, Joanne (A.) 1951- ....................... *121*
Lansdale, Joe R. 1951- ............................ *116*

Lansdale, Joe Richard
  *See* Lansdale, Joe R.
Lansing, Alfred 1921-1975 ........................ *35*
Lansing, Karen E. 1954- ............................ *71*
Lansky, Vicki 1942- ................................. *177*
Lantier-Sampon, Patricia 1952- ................ *92*
Lantz, Fran
  *See* Lantz, Francess L(in)
Lantz, Francess L(in) 1952-2004 ............. *153*
  Autobiography Feature ......................... *153*
  Obituary .............................................. *159*
  Earlier sketches in SATA *63, 109*
  *See* Dixon, Franklin W.
Lantz, Paul 1908- ...................................... *45*
Lantz, Walter 1900-1994 ........................... *37*
  Obituary ................................................ *79*
Lanza, Barbara 1945- .............................. *101*
Lapp, Christiane (Germain) 1948- ............. *74*
Lappin, Peter 1911-1999 ........................... *32*
Lardy, Philippe 1963- .............................. *168*
Larkin, Amy
  *See* Burns, Olive Ann
Larkin, Maia
  *See* Wojciechowska, Maia (Teresa)
Laroche, Giles 1956- ............................... *126*
  Earlier sketch in SATA *71*
LaRochelle, David 1960- .......................... *171*
  Earlier sketch in SATA *115*
LaRose, Linda ........................................ *125*
Larrabee, Lisa 1947- .................................. *84*
Larrecq, John M(aurice) 1926-1980 .......... *44*
  Obituary ................................................ *25*
Larrick (Crosby), Nancy 1910-2004 ............ *4*
Larsen, Anita 1942- ................................... *78*
Larsen, Egon 1904- ................................... *14*
Larsen, Rebecca 1944- .............................. *54*
Larson, Eve
  *See* St. John, Wylly Folk
Larson, Gary 1950- ................................... *57*
Larson, Ingrid D(ana) 1965- ..................... *92*
Larson, Jean Russell 1930- ...................... *121*
Larson, Kirby 1954- .................................. *96*
Larson, Norita D(ittberner) 1944- ............. *29*
Larson, William H. 1938- .......................... *10*
Larsson, Carl (Olof) 1853-1919 ................. *35*
LaSalle, Charles A.
  *See* Ellis, Edward S(ylvester)
LaSalle, Charles E.
  *See* Ellis, Edward S(ylvester)
Lasell, Elinor H. 1929- .............................. *19*
Lasell, Fen H.
  *See* Lasell, Elinor H.
Lasenby, Jack 1931- ................................ *172*
  Earlier sketches in SATA *65, 103*
Laser, Michael 1954- ............................... *117*
Lash, Joseph P. 1909-1987 ........................ *43*
Lasher, Faith B. 1921- .............................. *12*
Lasker, David 1950- ................................... *38*
Lasker, Joe ........................................... *83*
  *See also* SAAS *17*
  *See* Lasker, Joseph Leon
Lasker, Joseph Leon 1919- .......................... *9*
  *See* Lasker, Joe
Laski, Marghanita 1915-1988 .................... *55*
Laskin, Pamela L. 1954- ........................... *75*
Lasky, Kathryn 1944- .............................. *157*
  Earlier sketches in SATA *13, 69, 112*
  *See also* CLR *11*
Lasky Knight, Kathryn
  *See* Lasky, Kathryn
Lass, Bonnie ........................................... *131*
Lassalle, C. E.
  *See* Ellis, Edward S(ylvester)
Lassiter, Mary ......................................... *59*
  *See* Hoffman, Mary (Margaret)
Lassiter, Rhiannon 1977- ......................... *157*
Latham, Barbara 1896- ............................. *16*
Latham, Frank B(rown) 1910-2000 ............. *6*
Latham, Jean Lee 1902-1995 ..................... *68*
  Earlier sketch in SATA *2*
  *See also* CLR *50*

Latham, Mavis
  *See* Clark, Mavis Thorpe
Latham, Philip
  *See* Richardson, Robert S(hirley)
Lathrop, Dorothy P(ulis) 1891-1980 .......... *14*
  Obituary ................................................ *24*
Lathrop, Francis
  *See* Leiber, Fritz (Reuter, Jr.)
Latimer, Jim 1943- .................................... *80*
Latta, Rich
  *See* Latta, Richard
Latta, Richard 1946- ............................... *113*
Latta, Sara L. 1960- ................................ *174*
Lattany, Kristin
  *See* Lattany, Kristin (Elaine Eggleston) Hunter
Lattany, Kristin (Eggleston) Hunter 1931-
  ................................................................ *154*
  Autobiography Feature ......................... *154*
  Earlier sketch in SATA *132*
Lattany, Kristin (Elaine Eggleston) Hunter
  1931- ..................................................... *132*
  Earlier sketch in SATA *12*
  *See also* CLR *3*
  *See also* SAAS *10*
  *See* Hunter, Kristin
Lattimore, Eleanor Frances 1904-1986 ........ *7*
  Obituary ................................................ *48*
Lattin, Ann
  *See* Cole, Lois Dwight
Lauber, Patricia (Grace) 1924- ................. *138*
  Earlier sketches in SATA *1, 33, 75*
  *See also* CLR *16*
Laugesen, Mary E(akin) 1906-1995 ............. *5*
Laughbaum, Steve 1945- ........................... *12*
Laughlin, Florence Young 1910-2001 .......... *3*
Laughlin, Rosemary 1941- ...................... *123*
Laure, Ettagale
  *See* Blauer, Ettagale
Laure, Jason 1940- ................................... *50*
  Brief entry ............................................ *44*
Laurence, Ester Hauser 1935- ..................... *7*
Laurie, Rona 1916- .................................... *55*
Laurin, Anne
  *See* McLaurin, Anne
Lauritzen, Jonreed 1902-1979 ................... *13*
Lauscher, Hermann
  *See* Hesse, Hermann
Lauture, Denize 1946- .............................. *86*
Laux, Connie
  *See* Laux, Constance
Laux, Constance 1952- .............................. *97*
Laux, Dorothy 1920- ................................. *49*
Lavallee, Barbara 1941- .......................... *166*
  Earlier sketch in SATA *74*
Lavender, David (Sievert) 1910-2003 ......... *97*
  Obituary .............................................. *145*
  Earlier sketch in SATA *64*
Lavender, William D. 1921- ..................... *143*
Laverne, Christine ................................... *175*
Lavert, Gwendolyn Battle 1951- .............. *131*
  *See* Battle-Lavert, Gwendolyn
Laverty, Donald
  *See* Blish, James (Benjamin)
  and Knight, Damon (Francis)
Lavigne, Louis-Dominique ........................ *107*
Lavine, David 1928- ................................... *31*
Lavine, Sigmund Arnold 1908-1986 ........... *82*
  Earlier sketch in SATA *3*
  *See also* CLR *35*
Lavond, Paul Dennis
  *See* Kornbluth, C(yril) M.
  and Lowndes, Robert A(ugustine) W(ard)
  and Pohl, Frederik
Lawhead, Stephen R. 1950- ..................... *109*
Lawhead, Steve
  *See* Lawhead, Stephen R.
Lawlor, Laurie 1953- .............................. *137*
  Earlier sketch in SATA *80*
Lawrence, Ann (Margaret) 1942-1987 ......... *41*
  Obituary ................................................ *54*
Lawrence, Iain 1955- .............................. *135*

Lawrence, J. T.
  See Rowland-Entwistle, (Arthur) Theodore (Henry)
Lawrence, Jerome 1915-2004 ...................... 65
Lawrence, John 1933- ................................. 30
Lawrence, Louise 1943- ............................. 119
  Earlier sketches in SATA 38, 78
Lawrence, Louise de Kiriline 1894-1992 .... 13
Lawrence, Lynn
  See Garland, Sherry
Lawrence, Margery H. 1889-1969 ............ 120
Lawrence, Michael 1943- .......................... 132
Lawrence, Mildred Elwood 1907-1997 ........ 3
Lawrence, R(onald) D(ouglas) 1921- .......... 55
Lawrinson, Julia 1969- ............................. 141
Lawson, Amy
  See Gordon, Amy
Lawson, Carol (Antell) 1946- .................... 42
Lawson, Don(ald Elmer) 1917-1990 ............ 9
Lawson, Joan 1906- ................................... 55
Lawson, Julie 1947- ................................. 126
  Earlier sketch in SATA 79
  See also CLR 89
Lawson, Marion Tubbs 1896-1994 ............. 22
Lawson, Robert 1892-1957 ....................... 100
  See also YABC 2
  See also CLR 73
Lawton, Clive A. 1951- ............................ 145
Laxdal, Vivienne 1962- ............................ 112
Laycock, George (Edwin) 1921- ................. 5
Layne, Laura
  See Knott, William C(ecil, Jr.)
Layne, Steven L. .................................... 171
Layton, Neal (Andrew) 1971- .................. 152
Lazare, Gerald John 1927- ........................ 44
Lazare, Jerry
  See Lazare, Gerald John
Lazarevich, Mila 1942- ............................. 17
Lazarus, Keo Felker 1913-1993 ................. 21
  Obituary ............................................ 129
Lea, Alec 1907- ....................................... 19
Lea, Joan
  See Neufeld, John (Arthur)
Leach, Maria 1892-1977 ............................ 39
  Brief entry .......................................... 28
Leacock, Elspeth 1946- ........................... 131
Leacroft, Helen (Mabel Beal) 1919- ........... 6
Leacroft, Richard (Vallance Becher) 1914- ... 6
Leaf, (Wilbur) Munro 1905-1976 .............. 20
  See also CLR 25
Leaf, VaDonna Jean 1929- ........................ 26
Leah, Devorah
  See Devorah-Leah
Leakey, Richard E(rskine Frere) 1944- ....... 42
Leander, Ed
  See Richelson, Geraldine
Lear, Edward 1812-1888 .......................... 100
  Earlier sketch in SATA 18
  See also CLR 75
Lears, Laurie 1955- ................................. 127
Leasor, (Thomas) James 1923- .................. 54
Leavitt, Jerome E(dward) 1916- ................ 23
Leavitt, Martine 1953- ............................ 170
LeBar, Mary E(velyn) 1910-1982 .............. 35
LeBlanc, Annette M. 1965- ...................... 68
LeBlanc, L(ee) 1913- ............................... 54
LeBox, Annette 1943- ............................. 145
Lebrun, Claude 1929- .............................. 66
Le Cain, Errol (John) 1941-1989 ............... 68
  Obituary ............................................. 60
  Earlier sketch in SATA 6
Lecourt, Nancy (Hoyt) 1951- .................... 73
Ledbetter, Suzann 1953- ......................... 119
Leder, Jane Mersky 1945- ........................ 61
  Brief entry .......................................... 51
Lederer, Muriel 1929- .............................. 48
Lederer, William J(ulius) 1912- ................ 62
Lee, Amanda
  See Baggett, Nancy
  and Buckholtz, Eileen (Garber)
  and Glick, Ruth (Burtnick)

Lee, Benjamin 1921- ................................ 27
Lee, Betsy 1949- ..................................... 37
Lee, Carol
  See Fletcher, Helen Jill
Lee, Cora
  See Anderson, Catherine Corley
Lee, Dennis (Beynon) 1939- .................... 102
  Earlier sketch in SATA 14
  See also CLR 3
Lee, Dom 1959- ..................................... 146
  Autobiography Feature ......................... 121
  Earlier sketch in SATA 83
  See also SAAS 26
Lee, Doris Emrick 1905-1983 .................... 44
  Obituary ............................................. 35
Lee, Elizabeth Rogers 1940- ..................... 90
Lee, Harper 1926- .................................... 11
Lee, Hector Viveros 1962- ....................... 115
Lee, Howard N.
  See Goulart, Ron(ald Joseph)
Lee, Huy Voun 1969- .............................. 129
Lee, J(oseph) Edward 1953- ..................... 130
Lee, Jeanne M. 1943- .............................. 138
Lee, John R(obert) 1923-1976 ................... 27
Lee, Jordan
  See Scholefield, Alan
Lee, Julian
  See Latham, Jean Lee
Lee, Liz
  See Lee, Elizabeth Rogers
Lee, Lucy
  See Talbot, Charlene Joy
Lee, Lyn 1953- ...................................... 128
Lee, Manning de Villeneuve 1894-1980 ..... 37
  Obituary ............................................. 22
Lee, Marian
  See Clish, (Lee) Marian
Lee, Marie G. 1964- ............................... 130
  Earlier sketch in SATA 81
Lee, Mary Price 1934- .............................. 82
  Earlier sketch in SATA 8
Lee, Mildred ............................................ 6
  See also SAAS 12
  See Scudder, Mildred Lee
Lee, Nelle Harper
  See Lee, Harper
Lee, Richard S. 1927- .............................. 82
Lee, Robert C. 1931- ............................... 20
Lee, Robert E(dwin) 1918-1994 ................ 65
  Obituary ............................................. 82
Lee, Robert J. 1921- ................................ 10
Lee, Sally 1943- ...................................... 67
Lee, Tammie
  See Townsend, Thomas L.
Lee, Tanith 1947- .................................. 134
  Earlier sketches in SATA 8, 88
Leech, Ben
  See Bowkett, Stephen
Leedy, Loreen 1959- .............................. 175
  Brief entry .......................................... 50
  Earlier sketches in SATA 54, 84, 128
Leedy, Loreen Janelle
  See Leedy, Loreen
Lee-Hostetler, Jeri 1940- ......................... 63
Leekley, Thomas B(riggs) 1910-2001 ........ 23
Leeming, Jo Ann
  See Leeming, Joseph
Leeming, Joseph 1897-1968 ...................... 26
Leemis, Ralph B. 1954- ............................ 72
Leese, Jennifer L.B. 1970- ...................... 163
Leeson, Muriel 1920- ............................... 54
Leeson, R. A.
  See Leeson, Robert (Arthur)
Leeson, Robert (Arthur) 1928- .................. 76
  Earlier sketch in SATA 42
Leffland, Ella 1931- ................................. 65
Lefler, Irene (Whitney) 1917- ................... 12
Le Gallienne, Eva 1899-1991 ..................... 9
  Obituary ............................................. 68
Legg, Gerald 1947- ................................ 143

LeGrand
  See Henderson, LeGrand
Le Guin, Ursula K. 1929- ....................... 149
  Earlier sketches in SATA 4, 52, 99
  See also CLR 91
Le Guin, Ursula Kroeber
  See Le Guin, Ursula K.
Legum, Colin 1919-2003 .......................... 10
Lehman, Barbara 1963- .......................... 170
  Earlier sketch in SATA 115
Lehman, Bob ........................................... 91
Lehman, Elaine ....................................... 91
Lehn, Cornelia 1920- ............................... 46
Lehne, Judith Logan 1947- ....................... 93
Lehr, Delores 1920- ................................. 10
Lehr, Norma 1930- .................................. 71
Leiber, Fritz (Reuter, Jr.) 1910-1992 .......... 45
  Obituary ............................................. 73
Leibold, Jay 1957- ................................... 57
  Brief entry .......................................... 52
Leichman, Seymour 1933- .......................... 5
Leigh, Nila K. 1981- ................................ 81
Leigh, Tom 1947- .................................... 46
Leigh-Pemberton, John 1911-1997 ............ 35
Leighton, Clare (Veronica Hope) 1899-1989 ... 37
Leighton, Margaret (Carver) 1896-1987 ....... 1
  Obituary ............................................. 52
Leiner, Al(an) 1938- ................................ 83
Leiner, Katherine 1949- ........................... 93
Leipold, L. Edmond 1902-1983 .................. 16
Leisk, David (Johnson) 1906-1975 ............. 30
  Obituary ............................................. 26
  Earlier sketch in SATA 1
  See also CLR 98
  See Johnson, Crockett
Leister, Mary 1917- ................................. 29
Leitch, Patricia 1933- ............................... 98
  Earlier sketch in SATA 11
Leitner, Isabella 1924- ............................. 86
Leland, Bob 1956- ................................... 92
Leland, Robert E.
  See Leland, Bob
Lematre, Pascal 1967- ............................ 176
Lember, Barbara Hirsch 1941- .................. 92
LeMieux, A.C. 1954- ............................. 125
  Earlier sketch in SATA 90
  See LeMieux, Anne
LeMieux, Anne
  See LeMieux, A.C.
LeMieux, Anne Connelly
  See LeMieux, A.C.
Lemieux, Michele 1955- .......................... 139
Lemke, Horst 1922- ................................. 38
Lenanton, Carola Mary Anima Oman
  See Oman, Carola (Mary Anima)
L'Engle, Madeleine 1918- ....................... 128
  Earlier sketches in SATA 1, 27, 75
  See also CLR 57
  See also SAAS 15
L'Engle, Madeleine Camp Franklin
  See L'Engle, Madeleine
Lengyel, Cornel Adam 1915- ..................... 27
Lengyel, Emil 1895-1985 ........................... 3
  Obituary ............................................. 42
Lennon, John (Ono) 1940-1980 ............... 114
Leno, Jay 1950- ..................................... 154
LeNoir, Janice 1941- ................................ 89
Lens, Sidney 1912-1986 ........................... 13
  Obituary ............................................. 48
Lenski, Lois 1893-1974 ........................... 100
  Earlier sketches in SATA 1, 26
  See also CLR 26
Lent, Blair ............................................ 133
  Earlier sketch in SATA 2
Lent, Henry Bolles 1901-1973 ................... 17
Lent, John 1948- ................................... 108
Leodhas, Sorche Nic
  See Alger, Leclaire (Gowans)
Leokum, Arkady 1916(?)- ......................... 45
Leon, Sharon 1959- ................................. 79

Leonard, Alison 1944- .............................. 70
Leonard, Constance (Brink) 1923- ............. 42
  Brief entry .......................................... 40
Leonard, Elmore 1925- ........................... 163
Leonard, Elmore John, Jr.
  See Leonard, Elmore
Leonard, Jonathan N(orton) 1903-1975 ...... 36
Leonard, Laura 1923- .............................. 75
Leong, Gor Yun
  See Ellison, Virginia H(owell)
Leonhardt, Alice 1950- ........................... 152
Lerangis, Peter 1955- ............................ 171
  Earlier sketch in SATA 72
  See Dixon, Franklin W.
  and Keene, Carolyn
Lerner, Aaron Bunsen 1920-2007 ............... 35
Lerner, Carol 1927- ................................ 86
  Earlier sketch in SATA 33
  See also CLR 34
  See also SAAS 12
Lerner, Gerda 1920- ................................ 65
Lerner, Harriet 1944- ............................. 101
Lerner, Marguerite Rush 1924-1987 ........... 11
  Obituary ............................................. 51
Lerner, Sharon (Ruth) 1938-1982 .............. 11
  Obituary ............................................. 29
Leroe, Ellen W(hitney) 1949- .................... 99
  Brief entry .......................................... 51
  Earlier sketch in SATA 61
Leroux, Gaston 1868-1927 ........................ 65
Leroux-Hugon, Helene 1955- .................... 132
LeRoy, Gen .......................................... 52
  Brief entry .......................................... 36
LeShan, Eda J(oan) 1922-2002 .................. 21
  See also CLR 6
LeSieg, Theo.
  See Dr. Seuss
  and Geisel, Theodor Seuss
  and Seuss, Dr.
  and Stone, Rosetta
Lesinski, Jeanne M. 1960- ....................... 120
Leslie, Robert Franklin 1911-1990 ............... 7
Leslie, Roger 1961- ............................... 168
Leslie, Roger James
  See Leslie, Roger
Leslie, Sarah
  See McGuire, Leslie (Sarah)
LeSourd, Catherine
  See Marshall, (Sarah) Catherine (Wood)
Lessac, Frane
  See Lessac, Frane
Lessac, Frane 1954- .............................. 148
  Earlier sketch in SATA 61
Lessem, Dino Don
  See Lessem, Don
Lessem, Don 1951- ................................ 155
  Earlier sketch in SATA 97
Lesser, Rika 1953- ................................. 53
Lester, Alison 1952- .............................. 129
  Earlier sketches in SATA 50, 90
Lester, Helen 1936- ............................... 145
  Earlier sketches in SATA 46, 92
Lester, Julius 1939- ............................... 157
  Earlier sketches in SATA 12, 74, 112
  See also CLR 41
Lester, Julius Bernard
  See Lester, Julius
Lester, Mike 1955- ................................ 131
Le Sueur, Meridel 1900-1996 ...................... 6
Le Tord, Bijou 1945- .............................. 95
  Earlier sketch in SATA 49
Letts, Billie 1938- ................................. 121
Leuck, Laura 1962- ................................ 146
  Earlier sketch in SATA 85
Leutscher, Alfred (George) 1913- ............... 23
Levai, Blaise 1919- ................................ 39
Levenkron, Steven 1941- .......................... 86
Leverich, Kathleen 1948- ......................... 103
LeVert, (William) John 1946- ..................... 55
Levete, Sarah 1961- ............................... 153

Levin, Betty 1927- ................................ 137
  Earlier sketches in SATA 19, 84
  See also SAAS 11
Levin, Ira 1929- .................................... 66
Levin, Marcia Obrasky 1918- ..................... 13
Levin, Meyer 1905-1981 ........................... 21
  Obituary ............................................. 27
Levin, Miriam (Ramsfelder) 1962- ............... 97
Levine, Abby 1943- ................................ 54
  Brief entry .......................................... 52
Levine, Betty K(rasne) 1933- ..................... 66
Levine, David 1926- ................................ 43
  Brief entry .......................................... 35
Levine, Edna S(imon) ............................. 35
Levine, Evan 1962- ................................ 77
  Earlier sketch in SATA 74
Levine, Gail Carson 1947- ........................ 161
  Earlier sketch in SATA 98
  See also CLR 85
Levine, I(srael) E. 1923-2003 .................... 12
  Obituary ............................................ 146
Levine, Joan Goldman .............................. 11
Levine, Joseph 1910- ............................... 33
Levine, Marge 1934- ................................ 81
Levine, Rhoda ....................................... 14
Levine, Sarah 1970- ................................ 57
Levine, Shar 1953- ................................ 131
Levine-Freidus, Gail
  See Provost, Gail Levine
Levinson, Nancy Smiler 1938- ................... 140
  Earlier sketches in SATA 33, 80
Levinson, Riki ...................................... 99
  Brief entry .......................................... 49
  Earlier sketch in SATA 52
Levithan, David 1972- ............................ 166
Levitin, Sonia (Wolff) 1934- ..................... 131
  Autobiography Feature ........................... 131
  Earlier sketches in SATA 4, 68, 119
  See also CLR 53
  See also SAAS 2
Levitt, Sidney (Mark) 1947- ...................... 68
Levon, O. U.
  See Kesey, Ken
Levoy, Myron ....................................... 49
  Brief entry .......................................... 37
Levy, Barrie ......................................... 112
Levy, Constance 1931- ............................ 140
  Earlier sketch in SATA 73
  See also SAAS 22
Levy, Elizabeth 1942- ............................. 169
  Earlier sketches in SATA 31, 69, 107
  See also SAAS 18
Levy, Janice ........................................ 172
Levy, Marilyn 1937- ................................ 67
Levy, Nathan 1945- ................................ 63
Levy, Robert 1945- ................................. 82
Lewees, John
  See Stockton, Francis Richard
Lewin, Betsy 1937- ................................ 169
  Autobiography Feature ........................... 115
  Earlier sketches in SATA 32, 90
Lewin, Hugh 1939- ................................. 72
  Brief entry .......................................... 40
  See also CLR 9
Lewin, Ted 1935- ................................... 165
  Autobiography Feature ........................... 115
  Earlier sketches in SATA 21, 76, 119
Lewis, Alice C. 1936- .............................. 46
Lewis, Amanda 1955- ............................... 80
Lewis, (Joseph) Anthony 1927- .................. 27
Lewis, Anthony 1966- ............................. 120
Lewis, Barbara A. 1943- ........................... 73
Lewis, Beverly 1949- .............................. 80
Lewis, Brenda Ralph 1932- ........................ 72
Lewis, Brian 1963- ................................ 128
Lewis, Claudia (Louise) 1907-2001 ............... 5
Lewis, Clive Staples
  See Lewis, C.S.
Lewis, C.S. 1898-1963 ............................ 100
  Earlier sketch in SATA 13
  See also CLR 109

Lewis, Cynthia Copeland 1960- ................. 111
Lewis, E. M. ....................................... 123
  Earlier sketch in SATA 20
Lewis, Earl Bradley
  See Lewis, E.B.
Lewis, E.B. 1956- ................................. 168
  Earlier sketches in SATA 93, 124
Lewis, Elizabeth Foreman 1892-1958 ......... 121
  See also YABC 2
Lewis, Francine
  See Wells, Helen
Lewis, J. Patrick 1942- ........................... 162
  Earlier sketches in SATA 69, 104
Lewis, Jack P(earl) 1919- ......................... 65
Lewis, Jean 1924- .................................. 61
Lewis, Julinda
  See Lewis-Ferguson, Julinda
Lewis, Kevin ....................................... 173
Lewis, Kim 1951- .................................. 136
  Earlier sketch in SATA 84
Lewis, Linda (Joy) 1946- .......................... 67
Lewis, Lucia Z.
  See Anderson, Lucia (Lewis)
Lewis, Marjorie 1929- ............................. 40
  Brief entry .......................................... 35
Lewis, Mary (Christianna) 1907(?)-1988 .... 64
  Obituary ............................................. 56
  See Brand, Christianna
Lewis, Mervyn
  See Frewer, Glyn (M.)
Lewis, Michael
  See Untermeyer, Louis
Lewis, Naomi ....................................... 144
  Earlier sketch in SATA 76
Lewis, Paeony 1960- .............................. 173
Lewis, Paul
  See Gerson, Noel Bertram
Lewis, Richard 1935- ................................ 3
Lewis, Rob 1962- ................................... 72
Lewis, Roger
  See Zarchy, Harry
Lewis, Shannon
  See Llywelyn, Morgan
Lewis, Shari 1934-1998 ........................... 35
  Brief entry .......................................... 30
  Obituary ............................................ 104
Lewis, Sylvan R.
  See Aronson, Virginia
Lewis, Thomas P(arker) 1936- .................... 27
Lewis, Wendy A. 1966- ........................... 150
Lewis-Ferguson, Julinda 1955- .................. 85
Lewison, Wendy Cheyette ........................ 177
Lewiton, Mina 1904-1970 .......................... 2
Lexau, Joan M. .................................... 130
  Earlier sketches in SATA 1, 36
Ley, Willy 1906-1969 ............................... 2
Leydon, Rita (Floden) 1949- ..................... 21
Leyland, Eric (Arthur) 1911- ..................... 37
Li, Xiao Jun 1952- ................................. 86
Liatsos, Sandra Olson 1942- ..................... 103
Libby, Barbara M. ................................. 153
Libby, Bill
  See Libby, William M.
Libby, William M. 1927-1984 ...................... 5
  Obituary ............................................. 39
Liberty, Gene 1924- ................................. 3
Lichtenheld, Tom .................................. 152
Liddell, Kenneth 1912-1975 ....................... 63
Lidz, Jane .......................................... 120
Lieberman, E(dwin) James 1934- ............... 62
Liebers, Arthur 1913-1984 ........................ 12
Lieblich, Irene 1923- .............................. 22
Liers, Emil E(rnest) 1890-1975 ................... 37
Lies, Brian 1963- .................................. 131
Liestman, Vicki 1961- .............................. 72
Lietz, Gerald S. 1918- ............................. 11
Life, Kay (Guinn) 1930- ........................... 83
Lifton, Betty Jean ................................. 118
  Earlier sketch in SATA 6
Lifton, Robert Jay 1926- .......................... 66
Lightburn, Ron 1954- .............................. 91

Lightburn, Sandra 1955- ............................. *91*
Lightner, A. M.
  *See* Hopf, Alice (Martha) L(ightner)
Lightner, Alice
  *See* Hopf, Alice (Martha) L(ightner)
Lignell, Lois 1911- ....................................... *37*
Liles, Maurine Walpole 1935- .................... *81*
Lilley, Stephen R. 1950- ............................. *97*
Lilley, Stephen Ray
  *See* Lilley, Stephen R.
Lillington, Kenneth (James) 1916-1998 ...... *39*
Lilly, Ray
  *See* Curtis, Richard (Alan)
Lim, John 1932- ........................................... *43*
Liman, Ellen (Fogelson) 1936- ................... *22*
Limb, Sue 1946- ......................................... *158*
Limburg, Peter R(ichard) 1929- ................. *13*
Lin, Grace 1974- ........................................ *162*
  Earlier sketch in SATA *111*
Lincoln, C(harles) Eric 1924-2000 ............... *5*
Lincoln, James
  *See* Bates, Katharine Lee
Lindbergh, Anne ................................................ *81*
  *See* Sapieyevski, Anne Lindbergh
Lindbergh, Anne Morrow 1906-2001 .......... *33*
  Obituary ..................................................... *125*
Lindbergh, Anne Spencer Morrow
  *See* Lindbergh, Anne Morrow
Lindbergh, Charles A(ugustus, Jr.) 1902-1974
  ..................................................................... *33*
Lindbergh, Reeve 1945- ............................. *163*
  Earlier sketch in SATA *116*
Lindblom, Steven (Winther) 1946- ............. *94*
  Brief entry .................................................... *39*
  Earlier sketch in SATA *42*
Linde, Gunnel 1924- ...................................... *5*
Lindenbaum, Pija 1955- ............................. *144*
  Earlier sketch in SATA *77*
Lindgren, Astrid (Anna Emilia Ericsson)
  1907-2002 ..................................................... *38*
  Obituary ..................................................... *128*
  Earlier sketch in SATA *2*
  *See also* CLR *119*
Lindgren, Barbro 1937- ............................. *120*
  Brief entry .................................................... *46*
  Earlier sketch in SATA *63*
  *See also* CLR *86*
Lindman, Maj (Jan) 1886-1972 ................... *43*
Lindop, Edmund 1925- ................................... *5*
Lindquist, Jennie Dorothea 1899-1977 ....... *13*
Lindquist, Rowena Cory 1958- ................... *98*
Lindquist, Willis 1908-1988 ........................ *20*
Lindsay, Norman Alfred William 1879-1969
  ..................................................................... *67*
  *See also* CLR *8*
Lindsay, (Nicholas) Vachel 1879-1931 ........ *40*
Lindsey, Kathleen D(orothy) 1949- ........... *153*
Line, David
  *See* Davidson, Lionel
Line, Les 1935- ............................................. *27*
Linfield, Esther ........................................... *40*
Lingard, Joan (Amelia) 1932- ................... *130*
  Autobiography Feature ............................... *130*
  Earlier sketches in SATA *8, 74, 114*
  *See also* CLR *89*
  *See also* SAAS *5*
Link, Martin 1934- ....................................... *28*
Linn, Margot
  *See* Ziefert, Harriet
Linnea, Sharon 1956- ................................... *82*
Lion, Melissa 1976- ................................... *176*
Lionni, Leo(nard) 1910-1999 ...................... *72*
  Obituary ..................................................... *118*
  Earlier sketch in SATA *8*
  *See also* CLR *71*
Lipinsky de Orlov, Lino S. 1908- ............... *22*
Lipkind, William 1904-1974 ........................ *15*
Lipman, David 1931- ................................... *21*
Lipman, Matthew 1923- ............................... *14*
Lippincott, Gary A. 1953- ......................... *119*
  Earlier sketch in SATA *73*

Lippincott, Joseph W(harton) 1887-1976 .... *17*
Lippincott, Sarah Lee 1920- ........................ *22*
Lippman, Peter J. 1936- ............................... *31*
Lipsyte, Robert 1938- ................................. *161*
  Earlier sketches in SATA *5, 68, 113*
  *See also* CLR *76*
Lipsyte, Robert Michael
  *See* Lipsyte, Robert
Lisandrelli, Elaine Slivinski 1951- ............. *94*
Lisker, Sonia O. 1933- ................................ *44*
Lisle, Holly 1960- ........................................ *98*
Lisle, Janet Taylor 1947- ........................... *150*
  Brief entry .................................................... *47*
  Earlier sketches in SATA *59, 96*
  *See also* SAAS *14*
Lisle, Rebecca ............................................ *162*
Lisle, Seward D.
  *See* Ellis, Edward S(ylvester)
Lisowski, Gabriel 1946- ............................... *47*
  Brief entry .................................................... *31*
Liss, Howard 1922-1995 ................................. *4*
  Obituary ........................................................ *84*
Lisson, Deborah 1941- ............................... *110*
  Earlier sketch in SATA *71*
List, Ilka Katherine 1935- ............................. *6*
Liston, Robert A. 1927- ................................. *5*
Litchfield, Ada B(assett) 1916-1999 ............. *5*
Litchfield, Jo 1973- ................................... *116*
Lithgow, John (Arthur) 1945- ................... *145*
Litowinsky, Olga (Jean) 1936- ................... *26*
Littke, Lael J. 1929- ................................... *140*
  Earlier sketches in SATA *51, 83*
Little, A. Edward
  *See* Klein, Aaron E.
Little, Douglas 1942- ................................... *96*
Little, (Flora) Jean 1932- ........................... *149*
  Earlier sketches in SATA *2, 68, 106*
  *See also* CLR *4*
  *See also* SAAS *17*
Little, Lessie Jones 1906-1986 ................... *60*
  Obituary ........................................................ *50*
Little, Mary E. 1912-1999 ........................... *28*
Littlechild, George 1958- ............................. *85*
Littledale, Freya (Lota) 1929-1992 ............. *74*
  Earlier sketch in SATA *2*
Littlefield, Bill 1948- ................................... *83*
Littlefield, Holly 1963- ................................. *97*
Littlesugar, Amy 1953- ............................... *176*
  Earlier sketch in SATA *122*
Littleton, Mark R. 1950- ............................. *142*
  Earlier sketch in SATA *89*
Littman, Sarah Darer ................................... *175*
Lively, Penelope 1933- ............................... *164*
  Earlier sketches in SATA *7, 60, 101*
  *See also* CLR *7*
Lively, Penelope Margaret
  *See* Lively, Penelope
Liversidge, (Henry) Douglas 1913- ............... *8*
Livesey, Claire (Warner) 1927- ................. *127*
Livingston, Carole 1941- ............................. *42*
Livingston, (M.) Irene 1932- ..................... *150*
Livingston, Myra Cohn 1926-1996 ............. *68*
  Obituary ........................................................ *92*
  Earlier sketch in SATA *5*
  *See also* CLR *7*
  *See also* SAAS *1*
Livingston, Richard R(oland) 1922- ............. *8*
Livo, Norma J. 1929- ................................... *76*
Llerena Aguirre, Carlos 1952- ..................... *19*
Llerena Aguirre, Carlos Antonio
  *See* Llerena Aguirre, Carlos
Llewellyn, Claire 1954- ............................. *143*
  Earlier sketch in SATA *77*
Llewellyn, Grace 1964- ............................. *110*
Llewellyn, Grace Katherine
  *See* Llewellyn, Grace
Llewellyn, Richard
  *See* Llewellyn Lloyd, Richard Dafydd Vivian
Llewellyn, Sam 1948- ................................... *95*

Llewellyn Lloyd, Richard Dafydd Vivian
  1906-1983 ..................................................... *11*
  Obituary ........................................................ *37*
  *See* Llewellyn, Richard
Llewelyn, T. Harcourt
  *See* Hamilton, Charles (Harold St. John)
Lloyd, Alan
  *See* Lloyd, A.R.
Lloyd, Alan Richard
  *See* Lloyd, A.R.
Lloyd, A.R. 1927- ....................................... *168*
  Earlier sketch in SATA *97*
Lloyd, David
  *See* Lloyd, David T.
Lloyd, David T. 1954- ............................... *167*
Lloyd, E. James
  *See* James, Elizabeth
Lloyd, Errol 1943- ....................................... *22*
Lloyd, Hugh
  *See* Fitzhugh, Percy Keese
Lloyd, James
  *See* James, Elizabeth
Lloyd, Megan 1958- ................................... *117*
  Earlier sketch in SATA *77*
Lloyd, (Mary) Norris 1908-1993 ................. *10*
  Obituary ........................................................ *75*
Lloyd Webber, Andrew 1948- ..................... *56*
  *See* Webber, Andrew Lloyd
Llywelyn, Morgan 1937- ........................... *109*
Lo, Ginnie ................................................... *165*
Lo, Virginia M.
  *See* Lo, Ginnie
Lobato, Jose Bento Monteiro 1882-1948 .. *114*
Lobel, Anita (Kempler) 1934- ................... *162*
  Earlier sketches in SATA *6, 55, 96*
Lobel, Arnold (Stark) 1933-1987 ............... *55*
  Obituary ........................................................ *54*
  Earlier sketch in SATA *6*
  *See also* CLR *5*
Lobsenz, Amelia ........................................... *12*
Lobsenz, Norman M(itchell) 1919- ............... *6*
Lochak, Michele 1936- ................................. *39*
Lochlons, Colin
  *See* Jackson, C(aary) Paul
Locke, Clinton W. ........................................... *1*
Locke, Elsie (Violet) 1912-2001 ................. *87*
Locke, Lucie 1904-1989 ............................... *10*
Locke, Robert 1944- ..................................... *63*
  *See* Bess, Clayton
Locker, Thomas 1937- ............................... *109*
  Earlier sketch in SATA *59*
  *See also* CLR *14*
Lockhart, E.
  *See* Jenkins, Emily
Lockridge, Hildegarde (Dolson) 1908-1981
  ..................................................................... *121*
  *See* Dolson, Hildegarde
Lockwood, Mary
  *See* Spelman, Mary
Lodge, Bernard 1933- ................................. *107*
  Earlier sketch in SATA *33*
Lodge, Jo 1966- ........................................... *173*
  Earlier sketch in SATA *112*
Loeb, Jeffrey 1946- ....................................... *57*
Loeb, Robert H., Jr. 1917- ........................... *21*
Loefgren, Ulf 1931- ........................................ *3*
Loehfelm, Bill 1969- ................................... *153*
Loeper, John J(oseph) 1929- ..................... *118*
  Earlier sketch in SATA *10*
Loescher, Ann Dull 1942- ............................. *20*
Loescher, Gil(burt Damian) 1945- ............. *20*
Loewer, Jean Jenkins
  *See* Jenkins, Jean
Loewer, (Henry) Peter 1934- ....................... *98*
LoFaro, Jerry 1959- ....................................... *77*
Lofo
  *See* Heimann, Rolf
Lofting, Hugh (John) 1886-1947 ............... *100*
  Earlier sketch in SATA *15*
  *See also* CLR *19*

Lofts, Norah (Robinson) 1904-1983 ............ *8*
  Obituary ........................................ *36*
Logan, Jake
  *See* Knott, William C(ecil, Jr.)
  and Krepps, Robert W(ilson)
  and Pearl, Jacques Bain
  and Riefe, Alan
  and Rifkin, Shepard
  and Smith, Martin Cruz
Logan, Mark
  *See* Nicole, Christopher (Robin)
Logan, Rochelle 1954- ............................. *169*
Logston, Anne 1962- ............................... *112*
Logue, Christopher 1926- ........................ *23*
Logue, Mary 1952- ................................. *161*
  Earlier sketch in SATA *112*
Loh, Morag 1935- .................................... *73*
Lohans, Alison 1949- .............................. *101*
Loken, Newton Clayton 1919- ................... *26*
Lomas, Steve
  *See* Brennan, Joseph Lomas
Lomask, Milton (Nachman) 1909-1991 ...... *20*
Lombino, Salvatore
  *See* Hunter, Evan
LoMonaco, Palmyra 1932- ........................ *102*
London, Jack 1876-1916 ........................... *18*
  *See also* CLR *108*
  *See* London, John Griffith
London, Jane
  *See* Geis, Darlene Stern
London, Jonathan (Paul) 1947- ................. *157*
  Earlier sketches in SATA *74, 113*
Lonergan, (Pauline) Joy (MacLean) 1909- . *10*
Lonette, Reisie (Dominee) 1924- ............... *43*
Long, Cathryn J. 1946- ............................. *89*
Long, Earlene (Roberta) 1938- .................. *50*
Long, Emmett
  *See* Leonard, Elmore
Long, Helen Beecher ................................. *1*
Long, Judith Elaine 1953- ......................... *20*
Long, Judy
  *See* Long, Judith Elaine
Long, Kim 1949- ...................................... *69*
Long, Loren 1966(?)- ................................ *151*
Long, Melinda 1960- ................................ *152*
Long, Sylvia 1948- ................................... *120*
Longbeard, Frederick
  *See* Longyear, Barry B(rookes)
Longfellow, Henry Wadsworth 1807-1882 . *19*
  *See also* CLR *99*
Longfellow, Layne (A.) 1937- ................... *102*
Longman, Harold S. 1919- ........................ *5*
Longsworth, Polly 1933- ........................... *28*
Longtemps, Kenneth 1933- ........................ *17*
Longway, A. Hugh
  *See* Lang, Andrew
Longyear, Barry B(rookes) 1942- .............. *117*
Loomans, Diane 1955- .............................. *90*
Loomis, Christine ................................... *160*
  Earlier sketch in SATA *113*
Loomis, Jennifer A. 1942- ......................... *101*
Loomis, Robert D. ..................................... *5*
Lopez, Angelo (Cayas) 1967- .................... *83*
Lopez, Barry (Holstun) 1945- ................... *67*
Lopshire, Robert M(artin) 1927- ............... *6*
Loraine, Connie
  *See* Reece, Colleen L.
Lorbiecki, Marybeth 1959- ....................... *172*
  Earlier sketch in SATA *121*
Lord, Athena V. 1932- .............................. *39*
Lord, Beman 1924-1991 ............................ *5*
  Obituary .......................................... *69*
Lord, Bette Bao 1938- .............................. *58*
Lord, (Doreen Mildred) Douglas 1904- ...... *12*
Lord, John Vernon 1939- ........................... *21*
Lord, Nancy
  *See* Titus, Eve
Lord, Walter 1917-2002 ............................ *3*
Lorde, Diana
  *See* Reno, Dawn E(laine)
Lorenz, Albert 1941- ................................ *115*

Lorenzini, Carlo 1826-1890 ...................... *100*
  Earlier sketch in SATA *29*
  *See* Collodi, Carlo
Lorimer, Janet 1941- ................................ *60*
Loring, Emilie (Baker) 1864(?)-1951 .......... *51*
Lorkowski, Thomas V(incent) 1950- ......... *92*
Lorkowski, Tom
  *See* Lorkowski, Thomas V(incent)
Lorraine, Walter (Henry) 1929- ................. *16*
Lorrimer, Claire
  *See* Clark, Patricia Denise
Loss, Joan 1933- ...................................... *11*
Lothrop, Harriet Mulford Stone 1844-1924
  ....................................................... *20*
Lottridge, Celia Barker 1936- ................... *157*
  Earlier sketch in SATA *112*
LoTurco, Laura 1963- .............................. *84*
Lotz, Wolfgang 1912-1981 ........................ *65*
Louie, Ai-Ling 1949- ............................... *40*
  Brief entry ....................................... *34*
Louis, Pat
  *See* Francis, Dorothy Brenner
Louisburgh, Sheila Burnford
  *See* Burnford, Sheila (Philip Cochrane Every)
Louise, Anita
  *See* Riggio, Anita
Lourie, Helen
  *See* Storr, Catherine (Cole)
Lourie, Peter (King) 1952- ........................ *142*
  Earlier sketch in SATA *82*
Love, Ann 1947- ...................................... *168*
  Earlier sketch in SATA *79*
Love, D. Anne 1949- ................................ *145*
  Earlier sketch in SATA *96*
Love, Douglas 1967- ................................ *92*
Love, Katherine (Isabel) 1907- .................. *3*
Love, Kathleen Ann
  *See* Love, Ann
Love, Sandra (Weller) 1940- ..................... *26*
Lovejoy, Jack 1937- ................................. *116*
Lovelace, Delos Wheeler 1894-1967 .......... *7*
Lovelace, Maud Hart 1892-1980 ................ *2*
  Obituary .......................................... *23*
Lovell, Ingraham
  *See* Bacon, Josephine Dodge (Daskam)
Loverseed, Amanda (Jane) 1965- ............... *75*
Lovett, Margaret (Rose) 1915- .................. *22*
Low, Alice 1926- ..................................... *156*
  Earlier sketches in SATA *11, 76*
Low, Elizabeth Hammond 1898-1991 ......... *5*
Low, Joseph 1911-2007 ............................ *14*
Low, William ......................................... *177*
Lowe, Jay, Jr.
  *See* Loeper, John J(oseph)
Lowell, Susan 1950- ................................. *127*
  Earlier sketch in SATA *81*
Lowenstein, Dyno 1914-1996 .................... *6*
Lowenstein, Sallie 1949- ........................... *116*
Lowery, Linda 1949- ................................ *151*
  Earlier sketch in SATA *74*
Lowitz, Anson C. 1901(?)-1978 ................. *18*
Lowitz, Sadyebeth Heath 1901-1969 .......... *17*
Lowndes, Robert A(ugustine) W(ard)
  1916-1998 ....................................... *117*
Lowrey, Janette Sebring 1892-1986 ........... *43*
Lowry, Lois 1937- .................................... *177*
  Autobiography Feature ....................... *127*
  Earlier sketches in SATA *23, 70, 111*
  *See also* CLR *72*
  *See also* SAAS *3*
Lowry, Lois Hammersberg
  *See* Lowry, Lois
Lowry, Peter 1953- ................................... *7*
Loyie, Larry 1933- ................................... *150*
Lozansky, Edward D. 1941- ....................... *62*
Lozier, Herbert 1915- .............................. *26*
Lubar, David 1954- ................................... *133*
Lubell, Cecil 1912-2000 ........................... *6*
Lubell, Winifred (A. Milius) 1914- ............ *6*
Lubin, Leonard
  *See* Lubin, Leonard B.

Lubin, Leonard B. 1943-1994 .................... *45*
  Brief entry ....................................... *37*
Lubka, S. Ruth 1948- ................................ *154*
Luby, Thia 1954- ..................................... *124*
Lucado, Max (Lee) 1955- .......................... *104*
Lucas, Cedric 1962- ................................. *101*
Lucas, E(dward) V(errall) 1868-1938 ......... *20*
Lucas, Eileen 1956- .................................. *113*
  Earlier sketch in SATA *76*
Lucas, George 1944- ................................. *56*
Lucas, Jerry 1940- .................................... *33*
Lucas, Victoria
  *See* Plath, Sylvia
Lucashenko, Melissa 1967- ....................... *104*
Luccarelli, Vincent 1923- ......................... *90*
Luce, Celia (Geneva Larsen) 1914- ............ *38*
Luce, Willard (Ray) 1914-1990 ................. *38*
Lucht, Irmgard 1937- ............................... *82*
Luckett, Dave 1951- ................................. *167*
  Earlier sketch in SATA *106*
Luckhardt, Mildred Corell 1898-1990 ........ *5*
Ludel, Jacqueline 1945- ............................ *64*
Ludlum, Mabel Cleland
  *See* Widdemer, Mabel Cleland
Ludwig, Helen ...................................... *33*
Ludwig, Lyndell 1923- ............................. *63*
Ludwig, Trudy 1959- ............................... *166*
Lueders, Edward (George) 1923- .............. *14*
Luenn, Nancy 1954- ................................. *79*
  Earlier sketch in SATA *51*
Lufkin, Raymond H. 1897- ....................... *38*
Lugard, Flora Louisa Shaw 1852-1929 ....... *21*
Luger, Harriett Mandelay 1914- ................ *23*
Luhrmann, Winifred B(ruce) 1934- ........... *11*
Luis, Earlene W. 1929- ............................. *11*
Lum, Peter
  *See* Crowe, (Bettina) Peter Lum
Lumry, Amanda (R.) .................................. *159*
Lund, Deb ............................................. *157*
Lund, Doris Herold 1919- ......................... *12*
Lung, Chang
  *See* Jordan, Robert
Lunge-Larsen, Lise 1955- .......................... *138*
Lunn, Carolyn (Kowalczyk) 1960- ............. *67*
Lunn, Janet (Louise Swoboda) 1928- ........ *110*
  Earlier sketches in SATA *4, 68*
  *See also* CLR *18*
  *See also* SAAS *12*
Lunsford, Cin Forshay
  *See* Forshay-Lunsford, Cin
Lupica, Mike .......................................... *177*
  *See* Lupica, Michael
Lupoff, Dick
  *See* Lupoff, Richard A(llen)
Lupoff, Richard A(llen) 1935- ................... *60*
Lurie, Alison 1926- .................................. *112*
  Earlier sketch in SATA *46*
Lurie, Morris 1938- .................................. *72*
Lussert, Anneliese 1929- ........................... *101*
Lusted, Marcia Amidon 1962- ................... *143*
Lustig, Arnost 1926- ................................. *56*
Lustig, Loretta 1944- ................................ *46*
Luthardt, Kevin 1973- .............................. *172*
Luther, Rebekah (Lyn) S(tiles) 1960- ........ *90*
Luttmann, Gail
  *See* Damerow, Gail
Luttrell, Guy L. 1938- .............................. *22*
Luttrell, Ida (Alleene) 1934- ..................... *91*
  Brief entry ....................................... *35*
  Earlier sketch in SATA *40*
Luttrell, William (J. III) 1954- .................. *149*
Lutz, Norma Jean 1943- ............................ *122*
Lutzeier, Elizabeth 1952- .......................... *72*
Lutzker, Edythe 1904-1991 ....................... *5*
Luxbacher, Irene M. 1970- ........................ *153*
Luzadder, Patrick 1954- ............................ *89*
Luzzati, Emanuele 1921-2007 ................... *7*
Luzzatto, Paola Caboara 1938- .................. *38*
Lybbert, Tyler 1970- ................................. *88*
Lydon, Michael 1942- .............................. *11*

Lyfick, Warren
  *See* Reeves, Lawrence F.
Lyle, Katie Letcher 1938- ............................ 8
Lynch, Chris 1962- ................................... *171*
  Earlier sketches in SATA *95, 131*
  *See also* CLR *58*
Lynch, Lorenzo 1932- ................................... 7
Lynch, Marietta 1947- ................................ 29
Lynch, P(atrick) J(ames) 1962- ............... *122*
  Earlier sketch in SATA *79*
Lynch, Patricia (Nora) 1898-1972 ............... 9
Lynds, Dennis 1924-2005 .......................... 47
  Brief entry ............................................. 37
Lyngseth, Joan
  *See* Davies, Joan
Lynn, Elizabeth A(nne) 1946- .................. 99
Lynn, Mary
  *See* Brokamp, Marilyn
Lynn, Patricia
  *See* Watts, Mabel Pizzey
Lynn, Tracy ................................................ *175*
Lyon, Elinor 1921- ...................................... 6
Lyon, George Ella 1949- ......................... *148*
  Autobiography Feature ........................ *148*
  Earlier sketches in SATA *68, 119*
Lyon, Lyman R.
  *See* de Camp, L(yon) Sprague
Lyons, Dorothy M(arawee) 1907-1997 ........ 3
Lyons, Grant 1941- .................................... 30
Lyons, Marcus
  *See* Blish, James (Benjamin)
Lyons, Mary E(velyn) 1947- ..................... *142*
  Earlier sketch in SATA *93*
Lystad, Mary (Hanemann) 1928- ............... *11*
Lytle, Elizabeth Stewart 1949- ................ 79
Lytle, Robert A. 1944- ............................. *119*
Lyttle, Richard B(ard) 1927- .................... 23
Lytton, Edward G(eorge) E(arle) L(ytton)
  Bulwer-Lytton Baron 1803-1873 ............ 23

**M**

Ma, Wenhai 1954- ..................................... *84*
Maar, Leonard (Frank, Jr.) 1927- ............. 30
Maartens, Maretha 1945- .......................... 73
Maas, Selve -1997 ...................................... 14
Mabie, Grace
  *See* Mattern, Joanne
Mac
  *See* MacManus, Seumas
  and Maccari, Ruggero
Macalaster, Elizabeth G. 1951- ............... *115*
MacAlister, Katie ...................................... *159*
MacAodhagain, Eamon
  *See* Egan, E(dward) W(elstead)
MacArthur-Onslow, Annette Rosemary 1933-
  ............................................................. 26
Macaulay, David (Alexander) 1946- ........ *137*
  Brief entry ............................................. 27
  Earlier sketches in SATA *46, 72*
  *See also* CLR *14*
Macaulay, Teresa (E.) 1947- ..................... 95
Macavinta, Courtney .................................. *176*
MacBeth, George (Mann) 1932-1992 ........ *4*
  Obituary ................................................. 70
MacBride, Roger Lea 1929-1995 ............... 85
MacCarter, Don 1944- ............................... 91
MacClintock, Dorcas 1932- ........................ 8
MacCullough, Carolyn ............................... *174*
MacDonald, Amy 1951- ............................ *156*
  Autobiography Feature ........................ *156*
  Earlier sketches in SATA *76, 136*
MacDonald, Anne Elizabeth Campbell Bard
  -1958
  *See* MacDonald, Betty
MacDonald, Anson
  *See* Heinlein, Robert A.

MacDonald, Betty 1908-1958
  *See* YABC *1*
  *See* MacDonald, Anne Elizabeth Campbell
  Bard
Macdonald, Blackie
  *See* Emrich, Duncan (Black Macdonald)
Macdonald, Caroline 1948- ....................... *86*
  Obituary ................................................. *111*
  *See also* CLR *60*
MacDonald, Dwight 1906-1982 ................. 29
  Obituary ................................................. 33
MacDonald, George 1824-1905 ............... *100*
  Earlier sketch in SATA *33*
  *See also* CLR *67*
MacDonald, Golden
  *See* Brown, Margaret Wise
Macdonald, James D. 1954- ..................... *165*
  Earlier sketches in SATA *81, 114*
  *See* Appleton, Victor
Macdonald, Marcia
  *See* Hill, Grace Livingston
MacDonald, Margaret Read 1940- ........... *164*
  Earlier sketch in SATA *94*
Macdonald, Marianne 1934- ...................... *113*
Macdonald, Mary
  *See* Gifford, Griselda
MacDonald, Maryann 1947- ....................... 72
Macdonald, Shelagh 1937- ........................ 25
MacDonald, Suse 1940- ............................ *109*
  Brief entry ............................................. 52
  Earlier sketch in SATA *54*
Macdonald, Zillah K(atherine) 1885-1979 .. *11*
MacDonnell, Megan
  *See* Stevens, Serita (Deborah)
MacDougal, John
  *See* Blish, James (Benjamin)
MacDougal, John
  *See* Blish, James (Benjamin)
  and Lowndes, Robert A(ugustine) W(ard)
Mace, Elisabeth 1933- ............................... 27
Mace, Varian 1938- ................................... 49
MacEwen, Gwendolyn (Margaret) 1941-1987
  ............................................................. 50
  Obituary ................................................. 55
Macfarlan, Allan A. 1892-1982 ................. 35
MacFarlane, Iris 1922- .............................. *11*
MacGill-Callahan, Sheila 1926-2000 ......... 78
MacGregor, Carol Lynn ............................. *153*
MacGregor, Ellen 1906-1954 .................... 39
  Brief entry ............................................. 27
MacGregor-Hastie, Roy (Alasdhair Niall)
  1929- ........................................................ 3
MacGrory, Yvonne 1948- .......................... *142*
Machado, Ana Maria 1941- ....................... *150*
MacHale, D.J. 1956- ................................. *175*
MacHale, Donald James
  *See* MacHale, D.J.
Machetanz, Frederick 1908- ...................... 34
Machin Goodall, Daphne (Edith) .............. 37
Macht, Norman L(ee) 1929- ..................... *122*
MacInnes, Helen (Clark) 1907-1985 ......... 22
  Obituary ................................................. 44
Macintosh, Brownie 1950- ......................... 98
MacIntyre, Elisabeth 1916- ....................... 17
Mack, Stan(ley) ......................................... 17
Mack, Todd ................................................ *168*
Mack, Tracy 1968- .................................... *128*
Mackall, Dandi Daley 1949- ..................... *177*
  Earlier sketch in SATA *118*
Mackay, Claire 1930- ................................ 97
  Autobiography Feature ........................ *124*
  Earlier sketch in SATA *40*
  *See also* CLR *43*
Mackay, Constance D'Arcy (?)-1966 ........ *125*
Mackay, Donald 1914-2005 ....................... *81*
  Obituary ................................................. *173*
Mackay, Donald Alexander
  *See* Mackay, Donald
MacKaye, Percy (Wallace) 1875-1956 ........ 32
Mackel, Kathryn 1950- .............................. *162*

Mackel, Kathy
  *See* Mackel, Kathryn
MacKellar, William 1914- ............................ *4*
Macken, Walter 1915-1967 ....................... 36
MacKenzie, Jill (Kelly) 1947- ................... 75
Mackey, Ernan
  *See* McInerny, Ralph
Mackie, Maron
  *See* McNeely, Jeannette
Mackin, Edward
  *See* McInerny, Ralph
MacKinnon, Bernie 1957- ......................... 69
MacKinnon Groomer, Vera 1915- .............. 57
MacKinstry, Elizabeth 1879-1956 ............. 42
Mackler, Carolyn 1973- ............................ *156*
MacLachlan, Patricia 1938- ....................... *168*
  Brief entry ............................................. 42
  Earlier sketches in SATA *62, 107*
  *See also* CLR *14*
MacLane, Jack
  *See* Crider, Bill
MacLean, Alistair (Stuart) 1922(?)-1987 .... 23
  Obituary ................................................. 50
Maclean, Art
  *See* Shirreffs, Gordon D(onald)
MacLean, Christine Kole ............................ *177*
MacLean, Glynne 1964- ............................ *150*
MacLeod, Beatrice 1910- ........................... *162*
  Earlier sketch in SATA *10*
MacLeod, Beatrice Beach
  *See* MacLeod, Beatrice
MacLeod, Charlotte (Matilda) 1922-2005 ... 28
  Obituary ................................................. *160*
MacLeod, Doug 1959- ................................ 60
MacLeod, Elizabeth ................................... *158*
MacLeod, Ellen Jane (Anderson) 1916- ..... 14
MacManus, James
  *See* MacManus, Seumas
MacManus, Seumas 1869-1960 ................. 25
MacMaster, Eve (Ruth) B(owers) 1942- ..... 46
MacMillan, Annabelle
  *See* Quick, Annabelle
MacMillan, Dianne M(arie) 1943- ............ *125*
  Earlier sketch in SATA *84*
Macneill, Janet
  *See* McNeely, Jeannette
MacPeek, Walter G. 1902-1973 .................. 4
  Obituary ................................................. 25
MacPhail, Catherine 1946- ....................... *130*
MacPherson, Margaret 1908-2001 ............... 9
  *See also* SAAS *4*
MacPherson, Winnie 1930- ........................ *107*
Macrae, Travis
  *See* Feagles, Anita M(acRae)
MacRaois, Cormac 1944- ........................... 72
Macumber, Mari
  *See* Sandoz, Mari(e Susette)
Macy, Sue 1954- ....................................... *134*
  Earlier sketch in SATA *88*
Madaras, Lynda 1947- ............................... *151*
Madden, Don 1927- ..................................... 3
Madden, Kerry 1961- ................................ *168*
Madden-Lunsford, Kerry
  *See* Madden, Kerry
Maddern, Eric 1950- .................................. *166*
Maddigan, Beth 1967- ............................... *174*
Maddison, Angela Mary 1923- ................... *10*
  *See* Banner, Angela
Maddock, Reginald (Bertram) 1912-1994 ... 15
Madenski, Melissa (Ann) 1949- ................ 77
Madian, Jon 1941- ....................................... 9
Madison, Arnold 1937- ................................ 6
Madison, Winifred ....................................... 5
Madonna 1958- .......................................... *149*
Madsen, Gunnar ........................................ *171*
Madsen, Ross Martin 1946- ...................... 82
Madsen, Susan A. 1954- ............................ 90
Madsen, Susan Arrington
  *See* Madsen, Susan A.

Maestro, Betsy (Crippen) 1944- ................ *106*
  Brief entry .................................. *30*
  Earlier sketch in SATA *59*
  *See also* CLR *45*
Maestro, Giulio 1942- ........................ *106*
  Earlier sketches in SATA *8, 59*
  *See also* CLR *45*
Maeterlinck, Maurice 1862-1949 ................ *66*
Magee, Doug 1947- ............................ *78*
Magee, Wes 1939- ............................. *64*
Maggio, Rosalie 1943- ........................ *69*
Magid, Ken(neth Marshall) .................... *65*
Magnus, Erica 1946- .......................... *77*
Magorian, James 1942- ........................ *92*
  Earlier sketch in SATA *32*
Magorian, Michelle 1947- ..................... *128*
  Earlier sketch in SATA *67*
Magorian, Michelle Jane
  *See* Magorian, Michelle
Magovern, Peg ................................ *103*
Maguire, Anne
  *See* Nearing, Penny
Maguire, Gregory 1954- ....................... *129*
  Earlier sketches in SATA *28, 84*
  *See also* SAAS *22*
Maguire, Gregory Peter
  *See* Maguire, Gregory
Maguire, Jack 1920-2000 ...................... *74*
Maguire, Jesse
  *See* Smith, Sherwood
Maguire, Jessie
  *See* Smith, Sherwood
Maher, Ramona 1934- .......................... *13*
Mahlqvist, (Karl) Stefan ..................... *30*
  *See* Maehlqvist, (Karl) Stefan
Mahon, Julia C(unha) 1916- ................... *11*
Mahood, Kenneth 1930- ........................ *24*
Mahy, Margaret 1936- ......................... *171*
  Earlier sketches in SATA *14, 69, 119*
  *See also* CLR *78*
Mahy, Margaret May
  *See* Mahy, Margaret
Maiden, Cecil (Edward) 1902-1981 ............. *52*
Maidoff, Ilka
  *See* List, Ilka Katherine
Maifair, Linda Lee 1947- ..................... *83*
Maik, Henri
  *See* Hecht, Henri Joseph
Maillu, David G(ian) 1939- ................... *111*
Maine, Trevor
  *See* Catherall, Arthur
Mains, Randolph P. 1946- ..................... *80*
Maiorano, Robert 1946- ....................... *43*
Maisner, Heather 1947- ....................... *89*
Maison, Della
  *See* Katz, Bobbi
Maitland, Antony Jasper 1935- ................ *25*
Maitland, Barbara ............................ *102*
Major, Kevin (Gerald) 1949- .................. *134*
  Earlier sketches in SATA *32, 82*
  *See also* CLR *11*
Majure, Janet 1954- .......................... *96*
Makie, Pam 1943- ............................. *37*
Makowski, Silk
  *See* Makowski, Silvia Ann
Makowski, Silvia Ann 1940- ................... *101*
Malam, John 1957- ............................ *152*
  Earlier sketch in SATA *89*
Malcolm, Dan
  *See* Silverberg, Robert
Malcolm, Jahnna N.
  *See* Beecham, Jahnna
Malcolmson, Anne
  *See* von Storch, Anne B.
Malcolmson, David 1899-1978 .................. *6*
Maletta, Dr. Arlene
  *See* Feltenstein, Arlene (H.)
Mali, Jane Lawrence 1937-1995 ................ *51*
  Brief entry .................................. *44*
  Obituary .................................... *86*
Mallett, Jerry J. 1939- ...................... *76*

Mallory, Kenneth 1945- ....................... *128*
Mallowan, Agatha Christie
  *See* Christie, Agatha (Mary Clarissa)
Malmberg, Carl 1904-1979 ..................... *9*
Malmgren, Dallin 1949- ....................... *65*
Malo, John W. 1911-2000 ...................... *4*
Malone, James Hiram 1930- .................... *84*
Malone, Patricia 1932- ....................... *155*
Maloney, Pat
  *See* Markun, Patricia Maloney
Malory, Sir Thomas 1410(?)-1471(?) ........... *59*
  Brief entry .................................. *33*
Malvasi, Meg Greene .......................... *143*
Malvern, Corinne 1905-1956 ................... *34*
Malvern, Gladys (?)-1962 ..................... *23*
Mama G.
  *See* Davis, Grania
Mammano, Julie (Lynn) 1962- .................. *107*
Mamonova, Tatyana 1943- ...................... *93*
Manchel, Frank 1935- ......................... *10*
Manchester, William (Raymond) 1922-2004
  .......................................... *65*
Mandel, Brett H. 1969- ....................... *108*
Mandel, Peter (Bevan) 1957-1998 .............. *87*
Mandel, Sally (Elizabeth) 1944- .............. *64*
Mandell, Muriel (Hortense Levin) 1921- ....... *63*
Manders, John 1957- .......................... *175*
Manes, Stephen 1949- ......................... *99*
  Brief entry .................................. *40*
  Earlier sketch in SATA *42*
Manfred, Frederick (Feikema) 1912-1994 .. *30*
Mangin, Marie France 1940- ................... *59*
Mangione, Jerre ............................... *6*
  Obituary .................................... *104*
  *See* Mangione, Gerlando
Mango, Karin N. 1936- ........................ *52*
Mangurian, David 1938- ....................... *14*
Mania, Cathy 1950- ........................... *102*
Mania, Robert 1952- .......................... *102*
Mania, Robert C., Jr.
  *See* Mania, Robert
Maniatty, Taramesha 1978- .................... *92*
Maniscalco, Joseph 1926- ..................... *10*
Manley, Deborah 1932- ........................ *28*
Manley, Seon 1921- ........................... *15*
  *See also* CLR *3*
  *See also* SAAS *2*
Mann, Elizabeth 1948- ........................ *153*
Mann, Josephine
  *See* Pullein-Thompson, Josephine (Mary
  Wedderburn)
Mann, Kenny 1946- ............................ *91*
Mann, Pamela 1946- ........................... *91*
Mann, Patrick
  *See* Waller, Leslie
Mann, Peggy .................................. *6*
  *See* Houlton, Peggy Mann
Mannetti, Lisa 1953- ......................... *57*
  Brief entry .................................. *51*
Mannheim, Grete (Salomon) 1909-1986 ..... *10*
Manniche, Lise 1943- ......................... *31*
Manning, Mick 1959- .......................... *176*
Manning, Rosemary (Joy) 1911-1988 ........ *10*
  *See* Davys, Sarah
  and Voyle, Mary
Manning, Sarra ............................... *162*
Manning-Sanders, Ruth (Vernon) 1895(?)-1988
  .......................................... *73*
  Obituary .................................... *57*
  Earlier sketch in SATA *15*
Mannion, Diane
  *See* Paterson, Diane
Mannis, Celeste Davidson ..................... *173*
Mansir, A. Richard 1932- ..................... *170*
Manson, Ainslie Kertland 1938- ............... *115*
Manson, Beverlie 1945- ....................... *57*
  Brief entry .................................. *44*
Manthorpe, Helen 1958- ....................... *122*
Mantinband, Gerda (B.) 1917- ................. *74*
Manton, Jo
  *See* Gittings, Jo (Grenville) Manton

Manuel, Lynn 1948- ........................... *99*
Manushkin, Fran 1942- ........................ *166*
  Earlier sketches in SATA *7, 54, 93*
Manushkin, Frances
  *See* Manushkin, Fran
Man Without a Spleen, A
  *See* Chekhov, Anton (Pavlovich)
Manzano, Sonia 1950- ......................... *167*
Mapes, Mary A.
  *See* Ellison, Virginia H(owell)
Maple, Marilyn 1931- ......................... *80*
Mappin, Strephyn 1956- ....................... *109*
Mara, Barney
  *See* Roth, Arthur J(oseph)
Mara, Jeanette
  *See* Cebulash, Mel
Marasmus, Seymour
  *See* Rivoli, Mario
Marbach, Ethel
  *See* Pochocki, Ethel (Frances)
Marcal, Annette B.
  *See* Callaway, Bernice (Anne)
Marcelino
  *See* Agnew, Edith J(osephine)
Marcellino, Fred 1939-2001 ................... *118*
  Obituary .................................... *127*
  Earlier sketch in SATA *68*
March, Carl
  *See* Fleischman, Sid
Marchant, Bessie 1862-1941
  *See* YABC *2*
Marchant, Catherine
  *See* Cookson, Catherine (McMullen)
Marcher, Marion Walden 1890-1987 ........... *10*
Marchesi, Stephen 1951- ...................... *114*
Marchesi, Steve
  *See* Marchesi, Stephen
  and Older, Effin
  and Older, Jules
Marchetta, Melina 1965- ...................... *170*
Marciano, John Bemelmans 1970- ............. *167*
Marciano, John Bemelmans 1970- ............. *118*
  *See also* CLR *93*
Marco, Lou
  *See* Gottfried, Theodore Mark
Marcus, Leonard S. 1950- ..................... *133*
Marcus, Paul 1953- ........................... *82*
Marcus, Rebecca B(rian) 1907- ................ *9*
Marcuse, Aida E. 1934- ....................... *89*
Margaret, Karla
  *See* Andersdatter, Karla M(argaret)
Margolin, Harriet
  *See* Ziefert, Harriet
Margolis, Jeffrey A. 1948- ................... *108*
Margolis, Richard J(ules) 1929-1991 ......... *86*
  Obituary .................................... *67*
  Earlier sketch in SATA *4*
Margolis, Vivienne 1922- ..................... *46*
Mariana
  *See* Foster, Marian Curtis
Marie, Geraldine 1949- ....................... *61*
Mariner, Scott
  *See* Pohl, Frederik
Marino, Dorothy Bronson 1912- ................ *14*
Marino, Jan 1936- ............................ *114*
Marino, Nick
  *See* Deming, Richard
Mario, Anna
  *See* Odgers, Sally Farrell
Marion, Henry
  *See* del Rey, Lester
Maris, Ron ................................... *71*
  Brief entry .................................. *45*
Mark, Jan 1943-2006 .......................... *164*
  Obituary .................................... *173*
  Earlier sketches in SATA *22, 69, 114*
  *See also* CLR *11*
Mark, Janet Marjorie
  *See* Mark, Jan
Mark, Joan T. 1937- .......................... *122*
Mark, Pauline (Dahlin) 1913-1997 ............ *14*

Mark, Polly
  *See* Mark, Pauline (Dahlin)
Mark, Ted
  *See* Gottfried, Theodore Mark
Markel, Michelle .............................. 169
Marker, Sherry 1941- .......................... 76
Markert, Jennifer 1965- ........................ 83
Markert, Jenny
  *See* Markert, Jennifer
Markham, Lynne 1947- ......................... 102
Markham, Marion M. 1929- ..................... 60
Markins, W. S.
  *See* Jenkins, Marie M(agdalen)
Markle, Sandra L. 1946- ....................... 148
  Brief entry ................................ 41
  Earlier sketches in SATA 57, 92
Markle, Sandra Lee
  *See* Markle, Sandra L.
Marko, Katherine D(olores) .................... 28
Markoosie
  *See* Patsauq, Markoosie
Marks, Alan 1957- ............................. 151
  Earlier sketch in SATA 77
Marks, Burton 1930- ........................... 47
  Brief entry ................................ 43
Marks, Graham ................................ 158
Marks, Hannah K.
  *See* Trivelpiece, Laurel
Marks, J.
  *See* Highwater, Jamake (Mamake)
Marks, J(ames) M(acdonald) 1921- .............. 13
Marks, Laurie J. 1957- ......................... 68
Marks, Mickey Klar -1986 ...................... 12
Marks, Peter
  *See* Smith, Robert Kimmel
Marks, Rita 1938- ............................. 47
Marks, Stan(ley) .............................. 14
Marks-Highwater, J.
  *See* Highwater, Jamake (Mamake)
Markun, Patricia Maloney 1924- ................ 15
Markusen, Bruce (Stanley Rodriguez) 1965-
  ............................................ 141
Marley, Louise 1952- .......................... 173
  Earlier sketch in SATA 120
Marlin, Hilda
  *See* Van Stockum, Hilda
Marlow, Max
  *See* Nicole, Christopher (Robin)
Marlowe, Amy Bell .............................. 67
  Earlier sketch in SATA 1
Marlowe, Jack
  *See* Deary, Terry
Marney, Dean 1952- ............................ 90
Marokvia, Artur 1909- ......................... 31
Marokvia, Mireille (Journet) 1918- ............. 5
Marol, Jean-Claude 1946- ..................... 125
Marr, John S(tuart) 1940- ..................... 48
Marric, J. J.
  *See* Butler, William (Arthur) Vivian
  and Creasey, John
Marrin, Albert 1936- ......................... 126
  Brief entry ................................ 43
  Earlier sketches in SATA 53, 90
  *See also* CLR 53
Marriott, Alice Lee 1910-1992 ................. 31
  Obituary .................................. 71
Marriott, Janice 1946- ....................... 134
Marriott, Pat(ricia) 1920- .................... 35
Marroquin, Patricio
  *See* Markun, Patricia Maloney
Mars, W. T.
  *See* Mars, Witold Tadeusz J.
Mars, Witold Tadeusz J. 1912-1985 .............. 3
Marsden, Carolyn 1950- ....................... 175
  Earlier sketch in SATA 140
Marsden, John 1950- .......................... 146
  Earlier sketches in SATA 66, 97
  *See also* CLR 34
  *See also* SAAS 22
Marsh, Carole 1946- .......................... 127
Marsh, Dave 1950- ............................. 66

Marsh, J. E.
  *See* Marshall, Evelyn
Marsh, James 1946- ............................ 73
Marsh, Jean
  *See* Marshall, Evelyn
Marsh, Joan F. 1923- .......................... 83
Marsh, Valerie 1954- .......................... 89
Marshall, Anthony D(ryden) 1924- .............. 18
Marshall, Bonnie C. 1941- .................... 141
  Earlier sketch in SATA 18
Marshall, Bridget M(ary) 1974- ............... 103
Marshall, (Sarah) Catherine (Wood) 1914-1983
  ............................................. 2
  Obituary .................................. 34
Marshall, Douglas
  *See* McClintock, Marshall
Marshall, Edward
  *See* Marshall, James
Marshall, Evelyn 1897-1991 .................... 11
Marshall, Felicity 1950- ..................... 116
Marshall, Garry 1934- ......................... 60
Marshall, H. H.
  *See* Jahn, (Joseph) Michael
Marshall, James 1942-1992 ..................... 75
  Earlier sketches in SATA 6, 51
  *See also* CLR 21
Marshall, James Edward
  *See* Marshall, James
Marshall, James Vance
  *See* Payne, Donald Gordon
Marshall, Janet (Perry) 1938- ................. 97
Marshall, Jeff
  *See* Laycock, George (Edwin)
Marshall, Kim
  *See* Marshall, Michael (Kimbrough)
Marshall, Michael (Kimbrough) 1948- ........... 37
Marshall, Percy
  *See* Young, Percy M(arshall)
Marshall, S(amuel) L(yman) A(twood)
  1900-1977 .................................. 21
Marsoli, Lisa Ann 1958- ...................... 101
  Brief entry ................................ 53
Marsten, Richard
  *See* Hunter, Evan
Marston, Elsa 1933- .......................... 156
Marston, Hope Irvin 1935- .................... 127
  Earlier sketch in SATA 31
Marszalek, John F. 1939- ..................... 167
Marszalek, John Francis, Jr.
  *See* Marszalek, John F.
Marszalek, John Francis 1939-
  *See* Marszalek, John F.
Martchenko, Michael 1942- .................... 154
  Earlier sketches in SATA 50, 95
Martel, Aimee
  *See* Thurlo, Aimee
  and Thurlo, David
Martel, Suzanne 1924- ......................... 99
Martin, Ann M(atthews) 1955- ................. 126
  Brief entry ................................ 41
  Earlier sketches in SATA 44, 70
  *See also* CLR 32
Martin, Bill, Jr. .............................. 67
  Brief entry ................................ 40
  *See also* CLR 97
  *See* Martin, William Ivan, Jr.
Martin, Charles E(lmer) ....................... 70
  Earlier sketch in SATA 69
  *See* Mastrangelo, Charles E(lmer)
Martin, Christopher
  *See* Hoyt, Edwin P(almer), Jr.
Martin, Claire 1933- .......................... 76
Martin, David Stone 1913-1992 ................. 39
Martin, Donald
  *See* Honig, Donald
Martin, Dorothy 1921- ......................... 47
Martin, Eugene ................................. 1
Martin, Eva M. 1939- .......................... 65
Martin, Frances M(cEntee) 1906-1998 ........... 36
Martin, Francesca 1947- ...................... 101
Martin, Fred 1948- ........................... 119

Martin, Fredric
  *See* Christopher, Matt(hew Frederick)
Martin, George Raymond Richard
  *See* Martin, George R.R.
Martin, George R.R. 1948- .................... 118
Martin, J(ohn) P(ercival) 1880(?)-1966 ........ 15
Martin, Jacqueline Briggs 1945- .............. 149
  Earlier sketch in SATA 98
Martin, Jane Read 1957- ....................... 84
Martin, Jeremy
  *See* Levin, Marcia Obrasky
Martin, Les
  *See* Schulman, L(ester) M(artin)
Martin, Linda 1961- ........................... 82
Martin, Lynne 1923- ........................... 21
Martin, Marcia
  *See* Levin, Marcia Obrasky
Martin, Marvin 1926- ......................... 126
Martin, Melanie
  *See* Pellowski, Michael (Joseph)
Martin, Nancy
  *See* Salmon, Annie Elizabeth
Martin, Patricia Miles 1899-1986 .............. 43
  Obituary .................................. 48
  Earlier sketch in SATA 1
Martin, Peter
  *See* Chaundler, Christine
Martin, Rafe 1946- ........................... 175
Martin, Rene 1891-1977 ........................ 42
  Obituary .................................. 20
Martin, Rupert (Claude) 1905- ................. 31
Martin, S. R.
  *See* Mappin, Strephyn
Martin, Stefan 1936- .......................... 32
Martin, Vicky
  *See* Storey, Victoria Carolyn
Martin, Webber
  *See* Silverberg, Robert
Martin, Wendy
  *See* Martini, Teri
Martin, William Ivan, Jr. 1916-2004 .......... 145
  Earlier sketch in SATA 40
  *See* Martin, Bill, Jr.
Martineau, Harriet 1802-1876
  *See* YABC 2
Martinet, Jeanne 1958- ........................ 80
Martinez, Agnes ............................. 167
Martinez, Ed(ward) 1954- ...................... 98
Martinez, Elizabeth Coonrod 1954- ............ 85
Martinez, Victor 1954- ........................ 95
Martini, Teri 1930- ............................ 3
Martini, Therese
  *See* Martini, Teri
Martino, Alfred C. 1964- ..................... 174
Martinson, Janis
  *See* Herbert, Janis
Marton, Jirina 1946- ......................... 144
  Earlier sketch in SATA 95
Marton, Pierre
  *See* Stone, Peter
Martson, Del
  *See* Lupoff, Richard A(llen)
Martyr, Paula (Jane) ........................... 57
  *See* Lawford, Paula Jane
Maruki, Toshi 1912-2000 ...................... 112
  *See also* CLR 19
Marvin, Isabel R(idout) 1924- ................. 84
Marx, Patricia Windschill 1948- .............. 160
  Earlier sketch in SATA 112
Marx, Robert F(rank) 1936- .................... 24
Marx, Trish
  *See* Marx, Patricia Windschill
Marzani, Carl (Aldo) 1912-1994 ................ 12
Marzollo, Jean 1942- ......................... 130
  Earlier sketches in SATA 29, 77
  *See also* SAAS 15
Masefield, John (Edward) 1878-1967 ............ 19
Masoff, Joy 1951- ............................ 118
Mason, Adrienne 1962- ........................ 163
Mason, Cherie ............................... 170

Mason, Ernst
  *See* Pohl, Frederik
Mason, F(rancis) van Wyck 1901-1978 ........ 3
  Obituary ................................................ 26
Mason, Frank W.
  *See* Mason, F(rancis) van Wyck
Mason, George Frederick 1904-2000 .......... 14
Mason, Miriam E(vangeline) 1900-1973 ...... 2
  Obituary ................................................ 26
Mason, Tally
  *See* Derleth, August (William)
Mason, Van Wyck
  *See* Mason, F(rancis) van Wyck
Mass, Wendy 1967- .................................... 158
Mass, William
  *See* Gibson, William
Masselman, George 1897-1971 ................. 19
Massie, Dianne Redfield 1938- ................. 125
  Earlier sketch in SATA 16
Massie, Elizabeth ..................................... 108
Masson, Sophie 1959- ............................... 133
Masters, Anthony (Richard) 1940-2003 .... 112
  Obituary ................................................ 145
Masters, Kelly R(ay) 1897-1987 ................. 3
Masters, Mildred 1932- ............................. 42
Masters, William
  *See* Cousins, Margaret
Masters, Zeke
  *See* Bensen, Donald R.
  and Goulart, Ron(ald Joseph)
Matas, Carol 1949- ..................................... 93
  Autobiography Feature ........................... 112
  *See also* CLR 52
Matchette, Katharine E. 1941- ................... 38
Math, Irwin 1940- ..................................... 42
Mathabane, Mark 1960- ........................... 123
Mather, Kirtley F(letcher) 1888-1978 ........ 65
Mathers, Petra 1945- ................................ 176
  Earlier sketch in SATA 119
  *See also* CLR 76
Matheson, Richard (Christian) 1953- ........ 119
Matheson, Shirlee Smith 1942- ................. 155
Mathews, Janet 1914-1992 ........................ 41
Mathews, Judith ..................................... 80
  *See* Goldberger, Judith M.
Mathews, Louise
  *See* Tooke, Louise Mathews
Mathieu, Joe 1949- ..................................... 94
  Brief entry ........................................... 36
  Earlier sketch in SATA 43
Mathieu, Joseph P.
  *See* Mathieu, Joe
Mathis, Sharon Bell 1937- ......................... 58
  Earlier sketch in SATA 7
  *See also* CLR 3
  *See also* SAAS 3
Matloff, Gregory 1945- ............................. 73
Matott, Justin 1961- ................................. 109
Matranga, Frances Carfi 1922- ................. 78
Matray, James I. 1948- ............................. 161
Matray, James Irving
  *See* Matray, James I.
Matson, Emerson N(els) 1926- ................... 12
Matsui, Tadashi 1926- ................................. 8
Matsuno, Masako ......................................... 6
  *See* Kobayashi, Masako Matsuno
Matte, (Encarnacion) L'Enc 1936- ............. 22
Mattern, Joanne 1963- ............................. 122
Matthews, Andrew 1948- ........................... 138
Matthews, Caitlin 1952- ........................... 122
Matthews, Downs 1925- ............................. 71
Matthews, Ellen
  *See* Bache, Ellyn
Matthews, Ellen 1950- ............................... 28
Matthews, Harold Downs
  *See* Matthews, Downs
Matthews, Jacklyn Meek
  *See* Meek, Jacklyn O'Hanlon
Matthews, John (Kentigern) 1948- ........... 116
Matthews, Liz
  *See* Pellowski, Michael (Joseph)

Matthews, Morgan
  *See* Pellowski, Michael (Joseph)
Matthews, Nicola
  *See* Browne, N.M.
Matthews, Patricia 1927-2006 ................... 28
Matthews, Patricia Anne
  *See* Matthews, Patricia
Matthews, William Henry III 1919- ........... 45
  Brief entry ........................................... 28
Matthiessen, Peter 1927- ........................... 27
Mattingley, Christobel (Rosemary) 1931- ... 85
  Earlier sketch in SATA 37
  *See also* CLR 24
  *See also* SAAS 18
Matulay, Laszlo 1912- ............................... 43
Matus, Greta 1938- ................................... 12
Maugham, W. S.
  *See* Maugham, W(illiam) Somerset
Maugham, W(illiam) Somerset 1874-1965 . 54
Maugham, William Somerset
  *See* Maugham, W(illiam) Somerset
Maurer, Diane Philippoff
  *See* Maurer-Mathison, Diane V(ogel)
Maurer, Diane Vogel
  *See* Maurer-Mathison, Diane V(ogel)
Maurer-Mathison, Diane V(ogel) 1944- ...... 89
Mauser, Pat Rhoads
  *See* McCord, Patricia
Mauser, Patricia Rhoads ........................... 37
  *See* McCord, Patricia
Maves, Mary Carolyn 1916- ....................... 10
Maves, Paul B(enjamin) 1913-1994 ........... 10
Mavor, Salley 1955- ................................. 125
Mawicke, Tran 1911- ................................. 15
Max, Peter 1939- ....................................... 45
Maxon, Anne
  *See* Best, (Evangel) Allena Champlin
Maxwell, Arthur S. 1896-1970 ................... 11
Maxwell, Edith 1923- ................................... 7
Maxwell, Gavin 1914-1969 ......................... 65
Maxwell, Katie
  *See* MacAlister, Katie
Maxwell-Hyslop, Miranda 1968- ............... 154
May, Charles Paul 1920- ............................. 4
May, Elaine Tyler 1947- ........................... 120
May, J. C.
  *See* May, Julian
May, Julian 1931- ..................................... 11
May, Robert Stephen 1929-1996 ............... 46
May, Robin
  *See* May, Robert Stephen
Mayall, Beth ......................................... 171
Mayberry, Florence V(irginia) Wilson ......... 10
Maybury, Richard J. 1946- ......................... 72
Maybury, Rick
  *See* Maybury, Richard J.
Mayer, Agatha
  *See* Maher, Ramona
Mayer, Ann M(argaret) 1938- ..................... 14
Mayer, Danuta 1958- ............................... 117
Mayer, Jane Rothschild 1903-2001 ........... 38
Mayer, Marianna 1945- ............................. 132
  Earlier sketches in SATA 32, 83
Mayer, Mercer 1943- ............................... 137
  Earlier sketches in SATA 16, 32, 73, 129
  *See also* CLR 11
Mayerson, Charlotte Leon ........................... 36
Mayerson, Evelyn Wilde 1935- ................... 55
Mayfield, Katherine 1958- ......................... 118
Mayfield, Sue 1963- ................................. 146
  Earlier sketch in SATA 72
Mayhar, Ardath 1930- ............................... 38
Mayhew, James (John) 1964- ..................... 149
  Earlier sketch in SATA 85
Maynard, Olga 1920- ................................. 40
Mayne, William (James Carter) 1928- ...... 122
  Earlier sketches in SATA 6, 68
  *See also* CLR 123
  *See also* SAAS 11
Maynes, J. O. Rocky, Jr.
  *See* Maynes, J. Oscar, Jr.

Maynes, J. Oscar, Jr. 1929- ....................... 38
Mayo, Gretchen Will 1936- ....................... 163
  Earlier sketch in SATA 84
Mayo, Margaret 1935- ............................. 165
  Earlier sketches in SATA 38, 96
Mayo, Margaret Mary
  *See* Mayo, Margaret
Mays, Lucinda L(a Bella) 1924- ................. 49
Mays, (Lewis) Victor (Jr.) 1927- ................. 5
Mazer, Anne 1953- ................................... 105
  Earlier sketch in SATA 67
Mazer, Harry 1925- ................................. 167
  Earlier sketches in SATA 31, 67, 105
  *See also* CLR 16
  *See also* SAAS 11
Mazer, Norma Fox 1931- ........................... 168
  Earlier sketches in SATA 24, 67, 105
  *See also* CLR 23
  *See also* SAAS 1
Mazille, Capucine 1953- ............................. 96
Mazza, Adriana 1928- ................................. 19
Mazzio, Joann 1926- ................................. 74
Mbugua, Kioi Wa 1962- ............................. 83
McAfee, Carol 1955- ................................. 81
McAllister, Amanda
  *See* Dowdell, Dorothy (Florence) Karns
  and Hager, Jean
  and Meaker, Eloise
McAllister, Margaret I. 1956- ..................... 169
  Earlier sketch in SATA 117
McAllister, M.I.
  *See* McAllister, Margaret I.
McArthur, Nancy ..................................... 96
McAvoy, Jim 1972- ................................... 142
McBain, Ed
  *See* Hunter, Evan
McBratney, Sam 1943- ............................. 164
  Earlier sketch in SATA 89
  *See also* CLR 44
McBrier, Michael
  *See* Older, Effin
  and Older, Jules
McCafferty, Jim 1954- ............................... 84
McCaffery, Janet 1936- ............................. 38
McCaffrey, Anne 1926- ............................. 152
  Autobiography Feature ........................... 152
  Earlier sketches in SATA 8, 70, 116
  *See also* CLR 49
  *See also* SAAS 11
McCaffrey, Anne Inez
  *See* McCaffrey, Anne
McCaffrey, Mary
  *See* Szudek, Agnes S(usan) P(hilomena)
McCain, Becky Ray 1954- ......................... 138
McCain, Murray (David, Jr.) 1926-1981 ....... 7
  Obituary ................................................ 29
McCall, Edith (Sansom) 1911- ..................... 6
McCall, Virginia Nielsen 1909-2000 .......... 13
McCall Smith, Alexander 1948- ................. 73
McCallum, Phyllis
  *See* Koch, Phyllis (Mae) McCallum
McCallum, Stephen 1960- ......................... 91
McCampbell, Darlene Z. 1942- ................... 83
McCann, Edson
  *See* del Rey, Lester
  and Pohl, Frederik
McCann, Gerald 1916- ............................... 41
McCann, Helen 1948- ............................... 75
McCannon, Dindga ................................... 41
McCants, William D. 1961- ....................... 82
McCarter, Neely Dixon 1929- ................... 47
McCarthy, Agnes 1933- ............................... 4
McCarthy, Colin (John) 1951- ................... 77
McCarthy, Meghan ................................... 168
McCarthy, Ralph F. 1950- ......................... 139
McCarthy-Tucker, Sherri N. 1958- ............. 83
McCarty, Rega Kramer 1904-1986 ........... 10
McCaslin, Nellie 1914-2005 ....................... 12
McCaughrean, Geraldine 1951- ................. 173
  Earlier sketches in SATA 87, 139
  *See also* CLR 38

McCaughren, Tom 1936- .................... 75
McCauley, Adam 1965- .................... 128
McCay, (Zenas) Winsor 1869-1934 .......... 134
    Earlier sketch in SATA 41
McClafferty, Carla Killough 1958- ............ 137
McCleery, Patsy R. 1925- .................... 133
    Earlier sketch in SATA 88
McClintock, Barbara 1955- .................... 146
    Earlier sketches in SATA 57, 95
McClintock, Marshall 1906-1967 ................ 3
McClintock, May Garelick
    See Garelick, May
McClintock, Mike
    See McClintock, Marshall
McClintock, Theodore 1902-1971 .............. 14
McClinton, Leon 1933- .................... 11
McCloskey, Kevin 1951- .................... 79
McCloskey, (John) Robert 1914-2003 ....... 100
    Obituary .................... 146
    Earlier sketches in SATA 2, 39
    See also CLR 7
McCloy, James F(loyd) 1941- .................... 59
McClung, Robert M(arshall) 1916- .......... 135
    Earlier sketches in SATA 2, 68
    See also CLR 11
    See also SAAS 15
McClure, Gillian Mary 1948- .................... 31
McColley, Kevin 1961- .................... 80
    See also SAAS 23
McConduit, Denise Walter 1950- .............. 89
McConnell, James Douglas Rutherford
    1915-1988 .................... 40
    Obituary .................... 56
McCord, Anne 1942- .................... 41
McCord, David (Thompson Watson)
    1897-1997 .................... 18
    Obituary .................... 96
    See also CLR 9
McCord, Jean 1924- .................... 34
McCord, Pat Mauser
    See McCord, Patricia
McCord, Patricia 1943- .................... 159
    See Mauser, Patricia Rhoads
McCord, Patricia Sue Rhoads Mauser
    See McCord, Patricia
McCormick, Brooks
    See Adams, William Taylor
McCormick, Dell J. 1892-1949 .................... 19
McCormick, (George) Donald (King)
    1911-1998 .................... 14
McCormick, Edith (Joan) 1934- .................... 30
McCormick, Kimberly A. 1960- .................... 153
McCormick, Patricia 1956- .................... 128
McCourt, Lisa 1964- .................... 159
    Earlier sketch in SATA 117
McCourt, Malachy 1931- .................... 126
McCoy, Iola Fuller .................... 3
McCoy, J(oseph) J(erome) 1917- .................... 8
McCoy, Karen Kawamoto 1953- .................... 82
McCoy, Lois (Rich) 1941- .................... 38
McCrady, Lady 1951- .................... 16
McCrea, James (Craig, Jr.) 1920- .................... 3
McCrea, Ruth (Pirman) 1921- .................... 3
McCreigh, James
    See Pohl, Frederik
McCrumb, Sharyn 1948- .................... 109
McCue, Lisa 1959- .................... 177
    Earlier sketch in SATA 65
McCue, Lisa Emiline
    See McCue, Lisa
McCullen, Andrew
    See Arthur, Robert, (Jr.)
McCullers, (Lula) Carson (Smith) 1917-1967
    .................... 27
McCulloch, John Tyler
    See Burroughs, Edgar Rice
McCulloch, Sarah
    See Ure, Jean
McCullough, David 1933- .................... 62
McCullough, David Gaub
    See McCullough, David

McCullough, Frances Monson 1938- ............ 8
McCullough, Sharon Pierce 1943- ............ 131
McCully, Emily Arnold .................... 134
    Autobiography Feature .................... 134
    Earlier sketches in SATA 5, 110
    See also CLR 46
    See also SAAS 7
    See Arnold, Emily
McCune, Dan
    See Haas, Dorothy F.
McCunn, Ruthanne Lum 1946- .................... 63
McCurdy, Michael (Charles) 1942- .......... 147
    Earlier sketches in SATA 13, 82
McCutcheon, Elsie (Mary Jackson) 1937- .. 60
McCutcheon, John 1952- .................... 97
McDaniel, Becky Bring 1953- .................... 61
McDaniel, Lurlene 1944- .................... 146
    Earlier sketch in SATA 71
McDaniels, Pellom III 1968- .................... 121
McDearmon, Kay .................... 20
McDermott, Beverly Brodsky 1941- .......... 11
McDermott, Eleni .................... 156
McDermott, Gerald (Edward) 1941- ......... 163
    Earlier sketches in SATA 16, 74
    See also CLR 9
McDermott, Michael 1962- .................... 76
McDevitt, John Charles .................... 155
    Earlier sketch in SATA 94
    See McDevitt, Jack
McDole, Carol
    See Farley, Carol (J.)
McDonald, Collin 1943- .................... 79
McDonald, Gerald D(oan) 1905-1970 .......... 3
McDonald, Jamie
    See Heide, Florence Parry
McDonald, Janet 1953- .................... 148
McDonald, Jill (Masefield) 1927-1982 ....... 13
    Obituary .................... 29
McDonald, Joyce 1946- .................... 164
    Earlier sketch in SATA 101
McDonald, Lucile Saunders 1898-1992 ...... 10
McDonald, Mary Ann 1956- .................... 84
McDonald, Megan 1959- .................... 151
    Autobiography Feature .................... 151
    Earlier sketches in SATA 67, 99, 148
    See also CLR 94
McDonald, Meme 1954- .................... 112
McDonald, Mercedes 1956- .................... 169
    Earlier sketch in SATA 97
McDonell, Chris 1960- .................... 138
McDonnell, Christine 1949- .................... 115
    Earlier sketch in SATA 34
McDonnell, Flora (Mary) 1963- .................... 146
    Earlier sketch in SATA 90
McDonnell, Lois Eddy 1914-2001 .............. 10
McDonough, Yona Zeldis 1957- .................... 73
McElligott, Matt(hew) 1968- .................... 135
McElmeel, Sharron L. 1942- .................... 128
McElmurry, Jill .................... 159
McElrath, William N. 1932- .................... 65
McElrath-Eslick, Lori 1960- .................... 96
McEntee, Dorothy (Layng) 1902- .................... 37
McFadden, Kevin Christopher 1961(?)- .... 156
    Earlier sketch in SATA 68
    See also CLR 29
    See Pike, Christopher
McFall, Christie 1918- .................... 12
McFarlan, Donald M(aitland) 1915- .......... 59
McFarland, Henry "Hammer"
    See McFarland, Henry O.
McFarland, Henry O. 1934- .................... 143
McFarland, Kenton D(ean) 1920- .............. 11
McFarland, Martha
    See Smith-Ankrom, M. E.
McFarlane, Leslie (Charles) 1902-1977 ...... 31
    See Dixon, Franklin W.
    and Ferris, James Cody
    and Keene, Carolyn
    and Rockwood, Roy
McFarlane, Peter (William) 1940- .............. 95
McFarlane, Sheryl P. 1954- .................... 86

McFarlane, Todd 1961- .................... 117
McGaw, Jessie Brewer 1913-1997 .............. 10
McGee, Barbara 1943- .................... 6
McGee, Marni .................... 163
McGiffin, (Lewis) Lee (Shaffer) 1908-1978 . 1
McGill, Alice .................... 159
McGill, Ormond 1913- .................... 92
McGinley, Jerry 1948- .................... 116
McGinley, Phyllis 1905-1978 .................... 44
    Obituary .................... 24
    Earlier sketch in SATA 2
McGinnis, Lila S(prague) 1924- .................... 44
McGinty, Alice B. 1963- .................... 134
McGivern, Justin 1985- .................... 129
McGivern, Maureen Daly
    See Daly, Maureen
McGivern, Maureen Patricia Daly
    See Daly, Maureen
McGough, Elizabeth (Hemmes) 1934- ........ 33
McGovern, Ann 1930- .................... 132
    Earlier sketches in SATA 8, 69, 70
    See also CLR 50
    See also SAAS 17
McGowen, Thomas E. 1927- .................... 109
    Earlier sketch in SATA 2
McGowen, Tom
    See McGowen, Thomas E.
McGrady, Mike 1933- .................... 6
McGrath, Barbara Barbieri 1953- .............. 169
    Earlier sketch in SATA 108
McGrath, Robin 1949- .................... 121
McGrath, Thomas (Matthew) 1916-1990 .... 41
    Obituary .................... 66
McGraw, Eloise Jarvis 1915-2000 .............. 67
    Obituary .................... 123
    Earlier sketch in SATA 1
    See also SAAS 6
McGraw, William Corbin 1916-1999 .......... 3
McGreal, Elizabeth
    See Yates, Elizabeth
McGregor, Barbara 1959- .................... 82
McGregor, Craig 1933- .................... 8
McGregor, Iona 1929- .................... 25
McGuffey, Alexander Hamilton 1816-1896
    .................... 60
McGuigan, Mary Ann 1949- .................... 106
McGuire, Edna 1899- .................... 13
McGuire, Leslie (Sarah) 1945- .................... 94
    Brief entry .................... 45
    Earlier sketch in SATA 52
McGuirk, Leslie (A.) 1960- .................... 152
McGurk, Slater
    See Roth, Arthur J(oseph)
McHargue, Georgess 1941- .................... 77
    Earlier sketch in SATA 4
    See also CLR 2
    See also SAAS 5
McHugh, (Berit) Elisabet 1941- .................... 55
    Brief entry .................... 44
McIlwraith, Maureen Mollie Hunter .............. 2
    See Hunter, Mollie
McInerney, Judith W(hitelock) 1945- .......... 49
    Brief entry .................... 46
McInerny, Ralph 1929- .................... 93
McInerny, Ralph Matthew
    See McInerny, Ralph
McKaughan, Larry (Scott) 1941- .................... 75
McKay, Donald 1895- .................... 45
McKay, Hilary (Jane) 1959- .................... 145
    Earlier sketch in SATA 92
    See also SAAS 23
McKay, Lawrence, Jr. 1948- .................... 114
McKay, Robert W. 1921- .................... 15
McKay, Sharon E. 1954- .................... 165
McKay, Simon
    See Nicole, Christopher (Robin)
McKeating, Eileen 1957- .................... 81
McKee, David (John) 1935- .................... 158
    Earlier sketches in SATA 70, 107
    See also CLR 38
McKee, Tim 1970- .................... 111

McKeever, Marcia
    *See* Laird, Jean E(louise)
McKelvey, Carole A. 1942- .......................... 78
McKelvy, Charles 1950- ............................. 124
McKendrick, Melveena (Christine) 1941- ... 55
McKendry, Joe 1972- ................................ 170
McKenna, Colleen O'Shaughnessy 1948- . 136
    Earlier sketch in SATA 76
McKenzie, Ellen Kindt 1928- ...................... 80
McKernan, Victoria 1957- .......................... 171
McKie, Robin ........................................... 112
McKillip, Patricia A. 1948- ........................ 174
    Earlier sketches in SATA 30, 80, 126
McKillip, Patricia Anne
    *See* McKillip, Patricia A.
McKillip, Patricia Anne
    *See* McKillip, Patricia A.
McKim, Audrey Margaret 1909-1999 ......... 47
McKinley, Jennifer Carolyn Robin
    *See* McKinley, Robin
McKinley, Robin 1952- .............................. 130
    Brief entry ........................................... 32
    Earlier sketches in SATA 50, 89
    *See also* CLR 81
McKinney, Barbara Shaw 1951- ................. 116
McKinney, Nadine 1938- ............................ 91
McKissack, Fredrick L. 1939- .................... 162
    Brief entry ........................................... 53
    Earlier sketches in SATA 73, 117
    *See also* CLR 55
McKissack, Fredrick Lemuel
    *See* McKissack, Fredrick L.
McKissack, Patricia C. 1944- ..................... 162
    Earlier sketches in SATA 51, 73, 117
    *See also* CLR 55
McKissack, Patricia L'Ann Carwell
    *See* McKissack, Patricia C.
McKissack and McKissack
    *See* McKissack, Fredrick L.
    and McKissack, Patricia C.
McKown, Robin (?)-1976 .............................. 6
McLaren, Clemence 1938- ......................... 158
    Earlier sketch in SATA 105
McLaughlin, Frank 1934- ............................ 73
McLaurin, Anne 1953- ............................... 27
McLean, Andrew 1946- .............................. 172
    Earlier sketch in SATA 113
McLean, J. Sloan
    *See* Gillette, Virginia M(ary)
    and Wunsch, Josephine (McLean)
McLean, Janet 1946- ................................. 113
McLean, Kathryn (Anderson) 1909-1966 ..... 9
McLean, Virginia Overton 1946- ................. 90
McLean-Carr, Carol 1948- ......................... 122
McLeish, Kenneth 1940-1997 ...................... 35
McLenighan, Valjean 1947- ......................... 46
    Brief entry ........................................... 40
McLennan, Connie ...................................... 171
McLennan, Will
    *See* Wisler, G(ary) Clifton
McLeod, Bob 1951- ................................... 173
McLeod, Chum 1955- ................................. 95
McLeod, Emilie Warren 1926-1982 ............. 23
    Obituary .............................................. 31
McLeod, Kirsty
    *See* Hudson, (Margaret) Kirsty
McLeod, Margaret Vail
    *See* Holloway, Teresa (Bragunier)
McLerran, Alice 1933- .............................. 137
    Earlier sketch in SATA 68
McLoughlin, John C. 1949- ......................... 47
McManus, Patrick F. 1933- ......................... 46
McManus, Patrick Francis
    *See* McManus, Patrick F.
McMeekin, Clark
    *See* McMeekin, Isabel McLennan
McMeekin, Isabel McLennan 1895-1973 ..... 3
McMenemy, Sarah 1965- ........................... 156
McMillan, Bruce 1947- .............................. 129
    Earlier sketches in SATA 22, 70
    *See also* CLR 47

McMillan, Naomi
    *See* Grimes, Nikki
McMorey, James L.
    *See* Moyer, Terry J.
McMorrow, Annalisa 1969- ........................ 104
McMullan, Jim 1934- ................................. 150
    Earlier sketch in SATA 87
McMullan, K. H.
    *See* McMullan, Kate
McMullan, Kate
    *See* McMullan, Kate
McMullan, Kate 1947- ............................... 132
    Brief entry ........................................... 48
    Earlier sketches in SATA 52, 87
McMullan, Kate Hall
    *See* McMullan, Kate
McMurtrey, Martin A(loysias) 1921- .......... 21
McNabb, Linda 1963- ................................ 147
McNair, Kate ............................................. 3
McNair, Sylvia 1924-2002 .......................... 74
McNaught, Harry ........................................ 32
McNaughton, Colin 1951- .......................... 134
    Earlier sketches in SATA 39, 92
    *See also* CLR 54
McNaughton, Janet 1953- ........................... 162
    Earlier sketch in SATA 110
McNeely, Jeannette 1918- ........................... 25
McNeer, May (Yonge) 1902-1994 ............... 81
    Earlier sketch in SATA 1
McNeese, Tim 1953- .................................. 139
McNeill, Janet ............................................ 97
    Earlier sketch in SATA 1
    *See* Alexander, Janet
McNicoll, Sylvia (Marilyn) 1954- ............... 113
    *See also* CLR 99
McNulty, Faith 1918-2005 .......................... 168
    Earlier sketches in SATA 12, 84, 139
McPhail, David M(ichael) 1940- ................. 140
    Brief entry ........................................... 32
    Earlier sketches in SATA 47, 81
McPhee, Norma H. 1928- ............................ 95
McPhee, Richard B(yron) 1934- .................. 41
McPherson, James M(unro) 1936- .............. 141
    Earlier sketch in SATA 16
McQueen, Lucinda 1950- ............................ 58
    Brief entry ........................................... 48
McQueen, Mildred Hark 1908-1978 ............ 12
McRae, Russell (William) 1934- .................. 63
McShean, Gordon 1936- ............................. 41
Mc Swigan, Marie 1907-1962 ..................... 24
McVeity, Jen ............................................ 148
McVey, Vicki 1946- ................................... 80
McVicker, Charles (Taggart) 1930- ............ 39
McVicker, Chuck
    *See* McVicker, Charles (Taggart)
McWhirter, A(lan) Ross 1925-1975 ............ 37
    Obituary .............................................. 31
McWhirter, Norris (Dewar) 1925-2004 ....... 37
McWilliams, Karen 1943- ........................... 65
Mdurvwa, Hajara E. 1962- ......................... 92
Meacham, Margaret 1952- .......................... 95
Meachum, Virginia 1918- ........................... 133
    Earlier sketch in SATA 87
Mead, Alice 1952- ..................................... 146
    Earlier sketch in SATA 94
Mead, Russell (M., Jr.) 1935- ..................... 10
Meade, Ellen ............................................. 5
    *See* Roddick, Ellen
Meade, Marion 1934- ................................. 127
    Earlier sketch in SATA 23
Meader, Stephen W(arren) 1892-1977 ......... 1
Meadmore, Susan
    *See* Sallis, Susan (Diana)
Meadow, Charles T(roub) 1929- ................. 23
Meadowcroft, Enid LaMonte
    *See* Wright, Enid Meadowcroft (LaMonte)
Meadows, Graham (W.) 1934- .................... 161
Meaker, M. J.
    *See* Meaker, Marijane

Meaker, Marijane 1927- ............................. 160
    Autobiography Feature ........................... 111
    Earlier sketches in SATA 20, 61, 99
    *See* Aldrich, Ann
    and James, Mary
    and Kerr, M. E.
    and Packer, Vin
Meaker, Marijane Agnes
    *See* Meaker, Marijane
Means, Florence Crannell 1891-1980 ........... 1
    Obituary .............................................. 25
    *See also* CLR 56
Mearian, Judy Frank 1936- ......................... 49
Mecca, Judy Truesdell 1955- ...................... 127
Medary, Marjorie 1890-1980 ....................... 14
Meddaugh, Susan 1944- .............................. 176
    Earlier sketches in SATA 29, 84, 125
Medearis, Angela Shelf 1956- ..................... 123
    Earlier sketch in SATA 72
Medearis, Mary 1915- ................................. 5
Medina, Jane 1953- .................................... 167
    Earlier sketch in SATA 122
Medlicott, Mary 1946- ................................ 88
Mee, Charles L., Jr. 1938- ........................... 72
    Earlier sketch in SATA 8
Meek, Jacklyn O'Hanlon 1933- .................... 51
    Brief entry ........................................... 34
Meeker, Clare Hodgson 1952- ..................... 96
Meeker, Oden 1919(?)-1976 ........................ 14
Meeker, Richard
    *See* Brown, Fornan
Meeks, Esther MacBain ................................ 1
Meggs, Libby Phillips 1943- ....................... 130
Mehdevi, Alexander (Sinclair) 1947- ........... 7
Mehdevi, Anne (Marie) Sinclair 1947- ......... 8
Meidell, Sherry 1951- ................................. 73
Meier, Minta 1906- ..................................... 55
Meighan, Donald Charles 1929- ................... 30
Meigs, Cornelia Lynde 1884-1973 ................ 6
    *See also* CLR 55
Meilach, Dona Z(weigoron) 1926- ................ 34
Meilman, Philip W(arren) 1951- ................... 79
Meinstereifel, Ronald L. 1960- .................... 134
Melcher, Marguerite Fellows 1879-1969 .... 10
Melendez, Francisco 1964- ........................... 72
Melin, Grace Hathaway 1892-1973 .............. 10
Mellersh, H(arold) E(dward) L(eslie) 1897-
    ........................................................... 10
Melmoth, Sebastian
    *See* Wilde, Oscar (Fingal O'Flahertie Wills)
Melnikoff, Pamela (Rita) .............................. 97
Meltzer, Milton 1915- ................................. 128
    Autobiography Feature ........................... 124
    Earlier sketches in SATA 1, 50, 80
    *See also* CLR 13
    *See also* SAAS 1
Melville, Anne
    *See* Potter, Margaret (Newman)
Melville, Herman 1819-1891 ....................... 59
Melwood, Mary
    *See* Lewis, E. M.
Melzack, Ronald 1929- ................................. 5
Memling, Carl 1918-1969 ............................. 6
Mendel, Jo
    *See* Bond, Gladys Baker
    and Gilbertson, Mildred Geiger
Mendelson, Steven T. 1958-1995 ................. 86
Mendes, Valerie 1939- ................................ 157
Mendez, Raymond A. 1947- ......................... 66
Mendonca, Susan
    Brief entry ........................................... 45
    *See* Smith, Susan Vernon
Mendoza, George 1934- .............................. 41
    Brief entry ........................................... 39
    *See also* SAAS 7
Menendez, Shirley (C.) 1937- ...................... 146
Meng, Heinz (Karl) 1924- ........................... 13
Mennen, Ingrid 1954- ................................. 85
Menotti, Gian Carlo 1911-2007 ................... 29
Menuhin, Sir Yehudi 1916-1999 .................. 40
    Obituary .............................................. 113

Menville, Douglas 1935- ............................ *64*
Menzel, Barbara Jean 1946- ...................... *63*
Mercati, Cynthia ...................................... *164*
Mercati, Cynthia J.
 *See* Mercati, Cynthia
Mercer, Charles (Edward) 1917-1988 ......... *16*
 Obituary ............................................... *61*
Meredith, David William
 *See* Miers, Earl Schenck
Meringoff, Laurene Krasny
 *See* Brown, Laurene Krasny
Meriwether, Louise 1923- ........................... *52*
 Brief entry ............................................ *31*
Merlin, Arthur
 *See* Blish, James (Benjamin)
Merlin, Christina
 *See* Heaven, Constance (Christina)
Merriam, Eve 1916-1992 ........................... *73*
 Earlier sketches in SATA *3, 40*
 *See also* CLR *14*
Merrill, Jane 1946- ................................... *42*
Merrill, Jean (Fairbanks) 1923- .................. *82*
 Earlier sketch in SATA *1*
 *See also* CLR *52*
Merriman, Alex
 *See* Silverberg, Robert
Merriman, Rachel 1971- ........................... *149*
 Earlier sketch in SATA *98*
Merrit, Elizabeth
 *See* Goudge, Eileen
Merski, Patricia K.
 *See* Merski, P.K.
Merski, P.K. ............................................ *172*
Mertz, Barbara 1927- ................................ *49*
Mertz, Barbara Gross
 *See* Mertz, Barbara
Meschel, Susan V. 1936- ........................... *83*
Messenger, Charles (Rynd Milles) 1942- .... *59*
Messick, Dale 1906-2005 .......................... *64*
 Brief entry ............................................ *48*
Messier, Claire 1956- ............................... *103*
Messieres, Nicole de
 *See* de Messieres, Nicole
Messmer, Otto 1892(?)-1983 ..................... *37*
Metcalf, Doris H(unter) .............................. *91*
Metcalf, Suzanne
 *See* Baum, L(yman) Frank
Metos, Thomas H(arry) 1932- ..................... *37*
Metter, Bert(ram Milton) 1927- ................... *56*
Metzenthen, David 1958- .......................... *167*
 Earlier sketch in SATA *106*
Meyer, Barbara 1939- ................................ *77*
Meyer, Carolyn (Mae) 1935- ...................... *142*
 Autobiography Feature ........................... *142*
 Earlier sketches in SATA *9, 70, 118*
 *See also* SAAS *9*
Meyer, Edith Patterson 1895-1993 ................ *5*
Meyer, F(ranklyn) E(dward) 1932- ................ *9*
Meyer, Jean Shepherd ................................. *11*
Meyer, Jerome Sydney 1895-1975 ................. *3*
 Obituary ............................................... *25*
Meyer, June
 *See* Jordan, June
Meyer, L. A.
 *See* Meyer, Louis A(lbert), Jr.
Meyer, Louis A(lbert), Jr. 1942- ................. *144*
 Earlier sketch in SATA *12*
Meyer, Renate 1930- .................................. *6*
Meyer, Susan E. 1940- .............................. *64*
Meyers, Susan 1942- ................................ *164*
 Earlier sketch in SATA *19, 108*
Meynier, Yvonne (Pollet) 1908- .................. *14*
Mezey, Robert 1935- ................................. *33*
Micale, Albert 1913- ................................. *22*
Michael, James
 *See* Scagnetti, Jack
Michael, Livi 1960- .................................. *172*
Michael, Manfred
 *See* Winterfeld, Henry
Michael, Olivia
 *See* Michael, Livi

Michaels, Barbara
 *See* Mertz, Barbara
Michaels, Joanne Louise
 *See* Teitelbaum, Michael
Michaels, Kristin
 *See* Williams, Jeanne
Michaels, Molly
 *See* Untermeyer, Louis
Michaels, Neal
 *See* Teitelbaum, Michael
Michaels, Ski
 *See* Pellowski, Michael (Joseph)
Michaels, Steve 1955- ............................... *71*
Michaels, William M. 1917- ....................... *77*
Michel, Anna 1943- .................................. *49*
 Brief entry ............................................ *40*
Michel, Francois 1948- .............................. *82*
Michelson, Richard ................................... *173*
Micich, Paul ............................................ *74*
Micklish, Rita 1931- ................................. *12*
Micklos, John, Jr. 1956- ........................... *173*
 Earlier sketch in SATA *129*
Micklos J., John, Jr. 1956-
 *See* Micklos, John, Jr.
Micucci, Charles (Patrick, Jr.) 1959- ......... *144*
 Earlier sketch in SATA *82*
Middleton, Haydn 1955- ........................... *152*
 Earlier sketch in SATA *85*
Miers, Earl Schenck 1910-1972 .................... *1*
 Obituary ............................................... *26*
Migdale, Lawrence 1951- .......................... *89*
Mikaelsen, Ben 1952- .............................. *173*
 Earlier sketches in SATA *73, 107*
Mikaelsen, Benjamin John
 *See* Mikaelsen, Ben
Miklowitz, Gloria D. 1927- ....................... *129*
 Earlier sketches in SATA *4, 68*
 *See also* SAAS *17*
Mikolaycak, Charles 1937-1993 .................. *78*
 Obituary ............................................... *75*
 Earlier sketch in SATA *9*
 *See also* SAAS *4*
Mild, Warren (Paul) 1922- .......................... *41*
Milelli, Pascal 1965- ................................ *135*
Miles, Betty 1928- ................................... *78*
 Earlier sketch in SATA *8*
 *See also* SAAS *9*
Miles, Miska
 *See* Martin, Patricia Miles
Miles, (Mary) Patricia 1930- ...................... *29*
Miles, Patricia A.
 *See* Martin, Patricia Miles
Milgrim, David ....................................... *158*
Milgrom, Harry 1912-1978 ........................ *25*
Milhous, Katherine 1894-1977 .................... *15*
Milich, Zoran ......................................... *174*
Milios, Rita 1949- ................................... *79*
Militant
 *See* Sandburg, Carl (August)
Millais, Raoul 1901- ................................. *77*
Millar, Barbara F. 1924- ............................ *12*
Millar, Margaret (Ellis Sturm) 1915-1994 .. *61*
 Obituary ............................................... *79*
Millbank, Captain H. R.
 *See* Ellis, Edward S(ylvester)
Millen, C(ynthia) M. 1955- ....................... *114*
Miller, Albert G(riffith) 1905-1982 .............. *12*
 Obituary ............................................... *31*
Miller, Alice Ann 1958- ........................... *150*
Miller, Alice P(atricia McCarthy) ................. *22*
Miller, Debbie 1951- ............................... *160*
 Earlier sketch in SATA *103*
Miller, Debbie S.
 *See* Miller, Debbie
Miller, Deborah Uchill 1944- ...................... *61*
Miller, Don 1923- .................................... *15*
Miller, Doris R.
 *See* Mosesson, Gloria R(ubin)
Miller, Eddie
 *See* Miller, Edward
Miller, Edna Anita 1920- ........................... *29*

Miller, Edward 1905-1974 ........................... *8*
Miller, Elizabeth 1933- ............................. *41*
Miller, Ellanita 1957- ............................... *87*
Miller, Eugene 1925- ................................ *33*
Miller, Frances A. 1937- ............................ *52*
 Brief entry ............................................ *46*
Miller, Helen M(arkley) -1984 ...................... *5*
Miller, Jane (Judith) 1925-1989 .................. *15*
Miller, Jewel 1956- .................................. *73*
Miller, John
 *See* Samachson, Joseph
Miller, Judi ........................................... *117*
Miller, Louise (Rolfe) 1940- ....................... *76*
Miller, M. L. ........................................... *85*
Miller, Madge 1918- ................................. *63*
Miller, Margaret J.
 *See* Dale, Margaret J(essy) Miller
Miller, Marilyn (Jean) 1925- ...................... *33*
Miller, Marvin ........................................ *65*
Miller, Mary Beth 1942- .............................. *9*
Miller, Maryann 1943- .............................. *73*
Miller, Natalie 1917-1976 .......................... *35*
Miller, Robert H. 1944- ............................. *91*
Miller, Ruth White
 *See* White, Ruth C.
Miller, Sandra
 *See* Miller, Sandy
Miller, Sandra Peden
 *See* Miller, Sandy
Miller, Sandy 1948- .................................. *41*
 Brief entry ............................................ *35*
Miller, Sarah 1969- .................................. *175*
Miller, Virginia
 *See* Austin, Virginia
Miller, William R. 1959- ........................... *116*
Milligan, Bryce 1953- .............................. *170*
Milligan, Spike
 *See* CLR *92*
 *See* Milligan, Terence Alan
Milligan, Terence Alan 1918-2002 .............. *29*
 Obituary ............................................... *134*
 *See* Milligan, Spike
Millington, Ada
 *See* Deyneka, Anita
Millman, Isaac 1933- ............................... *140*
Mills, Adam
 *See* Stanley, George Edward
Mills, Claudia 1954- ................................ *145*
 Brief entry ............................................ *41*
 Earlier sketches in SATA *44, 89*
Mills, Elaine (Rosemary) 1941- ................... *72*
Mills, Joyce C. 1944- .............................. *102*
Mills, Judith Christine 1956- ..................... *130*
Mills, Yaroslava Surmach 1925- ................. *35*
Millspaugh, Ben P. 1936- .......................... *77*
Millstead, Thomas E. ............................... *30*
Milne, A. A. 1882-1956 ............................ *100*
 *See also* YABC *1*
 *See also* CLR *108*
Milne, Alan Alexander
 *See* Milne, A. A.
Milne, Lorus J. ........................................ *5*
 *See also* CLR *22*
 *See also* SAAS *18*
Milne, Margery ......................................... *5*
 *See also* CLR *22*
 *See also* SAAS *18*
Milne, Terry
 *See* Milne, Theresa Ann
Milne, Theresa Ann 1964- .......................... *84*
Milnes, Irma McDonough 1924- ................. *101*
Milonas, Rolf
 *See* Myller, Rolf
Milord, Susan 1954- ................................ *147*
 Earlier sketch in SATA *74*
Milotte, Alfred G(eorge) 1904-1989 .............. *11*
 Obituary ............................................... *62*
Milstein, Linda 1954- ............................... *80*
Milton, Ann ........................................... *134*
Milton, Hilary (Herbert) 1920- ................... *23*
Milton, John R(onald) 1924- ...................... *24*

Milton, Joyce 1946- .......................... *101*
   Brief entry .................................. *41*
   Earlier sketch in SATA *52*
Milverton, Charles A.
   *See* Penzler, Otto
Minahan, John A. 1956- ...................... *92*
Minar, Barbra (Goodyear) 1940- ......... *79*
Minard, Rosemary 1939- ...................... *63*
Minarik, Else Holmelund 1920- ......... *127*
   Earlier sketch in SATA *15*
   *See also* CLR *33*
Miner, Jane Claypool 1933- ................ *38*
   Brief entry .................................. *37*
   *See* Claypool, Jane
Miner, Lewis S. 1909-1971 ................. *11*
Mines, Jeanette 1948- ......................... *61*
Mines, Jeanette Marie
   *See* Mines, Jeanette
Minier, Nelson
   *See* Stoutenburg, Adrien (Pearl)
Minnitt, Ronda Jacqueline
   *See* Armitage, David
Minor, Wendell G. 1944- ................... *164*
   Earlier sketches in SATA *78, 109*
Minter, Daniel 1961- ......................... *176*
Mintonye, Grace ................................. *4*
Miranda, Anne 1954- ......................... *109*
   Earlier sketch in SATA *71*
Mirsky, Jeannette 1903-1987 ............... *8*
   Obituary ...................................... *51*
Mirsky, Reba Paeff 1902-1966 ............. *1*
Mishica, Clare 1960- .......................... *91*
Miskovits, Christine 1939- .................. *10*
Miss Frances
   *See* Horwich, Frances R(appaport)
Miss Read
   *See* Saint, Dora Jessie
Mister Rogers
   *See* Rogers, Fred McFeely
Mitchard, Jacquelyn 1953- ................. *168*
   Earlier sketch in SATA *98*
Mitchell, Adrian 1932- ...................... *166*
   Earlier sketch in SATA *104*
Mitchell, Allison
   *See* Griffin, W.E.B.
Mitchell, B(etty) J(o) 1931- ............... *120*
Mitchell, Clyde
   *See* Ellison, Harlan
Mitchell, Cynthia 1922- ..................... *29*
Mitchell, (Sibyl) Elyne (Keith) 1913- ... *10*
Mitchell, Gladys (Maude Winifred) 1901-1983
   .................................................. *46*
   Obituary ...................................... *35*
Mitchell, Jay
   *See* Roberson, Jennifer
Mitchell, Joyce Slayton 1933- ............. *142*
   Brief entry .................................. *43*
   Earlier sketch in SATA *46*
Mitchell, K. L.
   *See* Lamb, Elizabeth Searle
Mitchell, Kathy 1948- ........................ *59*
Mitchell, Lori 1961- .......................... *128*
Mitchell, Margaree King 1953- ............ *84*
Mitchell, Marianne 1947- ................... *145*
Mitchell, Rhonda ............................... *89*
Mitchelson, Mitch
   *See* Mitchelson, Peter Richard
Mitchelson, Peter Richard 1950- .......... *104*
Mitchison, Naomi (Margaret Haldane)
   1897-1999 .................................. *24*
   Obituary ...................................... *112*
Mitchnik, Helen 1901-1982 ................. *41*
   Brief entry .................................. *35*
Mitchum, Hank
   *See* Knott, William C(ecil, Jr.)
   and Murray, Stuart A. P.
   and Newton, D(wight) B(ennett)
   and Sherman, Jory (Tecumseh)
Mitgutsch, Ali 1935- ......................... *76*
Mitsuhashi, Yoko .............................. *45*
   Brief entry .................................. *33*

Mitton, Jacqueline 1948- ................... *162*
   Earlier sketches in SATA *66, 115*
Mitton, Simon 1946- .......................... *66*
Mitton, Tony 1951- ........................... *149*
   Earlier sketch in SATA *104*
Mizner, Elizabeth Howard 1907- .......... *27*
Mizumura, Kazue .............................. *18*
Mobin-Uddin, Asma ........................... *172*
Mobley, Joe A. 1945- ........................ *91*
Moche, Dinah (Rachel) L(evine) 1936- ... *44*
   Brief entry .................................. *40*
Mochi, Ugo (A.) 1889-1977 ................ *38*
Mochizuki, Ken 1954- ....................... *146*
   Earlier sketch in SATA *81*
   *See also* SAAS *22*
Modarressi, Mitra 1967- ..................... *126*
Modell, Frank B. 1917- ...................... *39*
   Brief entry .................................. *36*
Modesitt, Jeanne 1953- ...................... *143*
   Earlier sketch in SATA *92*
Modesitt, L.E., Jr. 1943- .................... *164*
   Earlier sketch in SATA *91*
Modesitt, Leland Exton, Jr.
   *See* Modesitt, L.E., Jr.
Modrell, Dolores 1933- ...................... *72*
Moe, Barbara 1937- ........................... *20*
Moe, Jorgen (Ingebretsen) 1813-1882
   *See* CLR *104*
   *See* Asbjornsen and Moe
Moed-Kass, Pnina .............................. *169*
Moerbeek, Kees 1955- ........................ *98*
Moeri, Louise 1924- .......................... *93*
   Earlier sketch in SATA *24*
   *See also* SAAS *10*
Moffett, Jami 1952- ........................... *84*
Moffett, Martha (Leatherwood) 1934- ... *8*
Mogensen, Suzanne A(ncher) 1946- ...... *129*
Mohn, Peter B(urnet) 1934- ................ *28*
Mohn, Viola Kohl 1914- ..................... *8*
Mohr, Nicholasa 1938- ...................... *97*
   Autobiography Feature ................. *113*
   Earlier sketch in SATA *8*
   *See also* CLR *22*
   *See also* SAAS *8*
Mok, Esther 1953- ............................ *93*
Molan, Christine 1943- ...................... *84*
Molarsky, Osmond 1909- .................... *16*
Moldon, Peter L(eonard) 1937- ............ *49*
Mole, John 1941- .............................. *103*
   Earlier sketch in SATA *36*
   *See also* CLR *61*
Molesworth, Mary Louisa 1839-1921 ...... *98*
Molin, Charles
   *See* Mayne, William (James Carter)
Molina, Silvia 1946- .......................... *97*
Molk, Laurel 1957- ........................... *162*
   Earlier sketch in SATA *92*
Mollel, Tololwa M. 1952- ................... *88*
Molloy, Anne Baker 1907-1999 ............ *32*
Molloy, Michael (John) 1940- .............. *162*
Molloy, Paul (George) 1924- ................ *5*
Moloney, James 1954- ........................ *144*
   Autobiography Feature ................. *144*
   Earlier sketch in SATA *94*
Momaday, N. Scott 1934- .................... *48*
   Brief entry .................................. *30*
Momaday, Navarre Scott
   *See* Momaday, N. Scott
Monaco, Octavia 1963- ...................... *169*
Monagle, Bernie 1957- ....................... *121*
Moncure, Jane Belk 1926- ................... *23*
Monjo, F(erdinand) N(icholas III) 1924-1978
   .................................................. *16*
   *See also* CLR *2*
Monk, Isabell 1952- ........................... *136*
Monroe, Lyle
   *See* Heinlein, Robert A.
Monsell, Helen Albee 1895-1971 .......... *24*
Monson-Burton, Marianne 1975- .......... *139*
Montecalvo, Janet ............................. *177*
Montenegro, Laura Nyman 1953- ......... *95*

Montero, Gloria 1933- ....................... *109*
Montes, Marisa 1951- ........................ *144*
Montgomerie, Norah (Mary) 1913- ........ *26*
Montgomery, Constance
   *See* Cappel, Constance
Montgomery, Elizabeth Rider .............. *34*
   Obituary ...................................... *41*
   Earlier sketch in SATA *3*
   *See* Julesberg, Elizabeth Rider Montgomery
Montgomery, Hugh (Edward) 1962- ....... *146*
Montgomery, L(ucy) M(aud) 1874-1942 .. *100*
   *See also* YABC *1*
   *See also* CLR *91*
Montgomery, Raymond A. (Jr.) 1936- ..... *39*
Montgomery, Rutherford George 1894-1985
   .................................................. *3*
Montgomery, Sy 1958- ....................... *132*
   Autobiography Feature ................. *132*
   Earlier sketch in SATA *114*
Montgomery, Vivian ........................... *36*
Montpetit, Charles 1958- .................... *101*
Montresor, Beni 1926-2001 ................. *38*
   Earlier sketch in SATA *3*
   *See also* SAAS *4*
Monty Python
   *See* Chapman, Graham
   and Cleese, John (Marwood)
   and Gilliam, Terry
   and Idle, Eric
   and Jones, Terence Graham Parry
   and Palin, Michael (Edward)
Moodie, Craig 1956- .......................... *172*
Moodie, Fiona 1952- .......................... *133*
Moody, Minerva
   *See* Alcott, Louisa May
Moody, Ralph Owen 1898-1982 ............ *1*
Moon, Carl 1879(?)-1948 .................... *25*
Moon, Grace (Purdie) 1877(?)-1947 ...... *25*
Moon, Lily
   *See* Warnes, Tim
Moon, Nicola 1952- ........................... *147*
   Earlier sketch in SATA *96*
Moon, Pat 1946- ............................... *113*
Moon, Sheila (Elizabeth) 1910-1991 ...... *5*
   Obituary ...................................... *114*
Mooney, Bel 1946- ............................ *95*
Mooney, Bill ................................... *122*
   *See* Mooney, William F.
Moor, Emily
   *See* Deming, Richard
Moorcock, Michael 1939- .................... *166*
   Earlier sketch in SATA *93*
   *See* Bradbury, Edward P.
Moore, Anne Carroll 1871-1961 ........... *13*
Moore, Cheri
   *See* Ladd, Cheryl (Jean)
Moore, Clement Clarke 1779-1863 ........ *18*
Moore, Cyd 1957- ............................. *133*
   Earlier sketch in SATA *83*
Moore, Elaine 1944- .......................... *86*
Moore, Eva 1942- ............................. *103*
   Earlier sketch in SATA *20*
Moore, Ishbel (Lindsay) 1954- ............. *140*
Moore, Jack (William) 1941- ............... *46*
   Brief entry .................................. *32*
Moore, Janet Gaylord 1905-1992 ......... *18*
Moore, Jim 1946- ............................. *42*
Moore, John Travers 1908- ................. *12*
Moore, Lilian 1909-2004 .................... *137*
   Obituary ...................................... *155*
   Earlier sketch in SATA *52*
   *See also* CLR *15*
Moore, Liz
   *See* Moore, M. Elizabeth
Moore, M. Elizabeth 1959- .................. *156*
Moore, Margaret R(umberger) 1903- ...... *12*
Moore, Margie ................................. *176*
Moore, Marianne (Craig) 1887-1972 ...... *20*
Moore, Patrick (Alfred Caldwell) 1923- ... *49*
   Brief entry .................................. *39*
   *See also* SAAS *8*

Moore, Peter 1963- ............................................. *175*
Moore, Regina
    *See* Dunne, Mary Collins
Moore, Ruth (Ellen) 1908-1989 .................. 23
Moore, Ruth Nulton 1923- ......................... 38
Moore, S(arah) E. .......................................... 23
Moore, Sarah Margaret
    *See* Hodges, Margaret Moore
Moore, Tara 1950- ......................................... 61
Moore, Yvette 1958- .................................... *154*
    Earlier sketches in SATA *69, 70*
Mooser, Stephen 1941- ................................. 75
    Earlier sketch in SATA *28*
Mora, Francisco X(avier) 1952- .................. 90
Mora, Pat 1942- ........................................... *134*
    Earlier sketch in SATA *92*
    *See also* CLR *58*
Mora, Patricia
    *See* Mora, Pat
Morales, Yuyi ................................................ *154*
Moran, Tom 1943- ......................................... 60
Moranville, Sharelle Byars ........................ *152*
Moray Williams, Ursula 1911-2006 ......... *142*
    Obituary .................................................... *177*
    Earlier sketch in SATA *73*
    *See also* SAAS *9*
    *See* Williams, Ursula Moray
Mordvinoff, Nicolas 1911-1973 ................. 17
More, Caroline
    *See* Cone, Molly (Lamken)
    and Strachan, Margaret Pitcairn
Moreton, Andrew Esq.
    *See* Defoe, Daniel
Morey, Charles
    *See* Fletcher, Helen Jill
Morey, Walt(er Nelson) 1907-1992 ............. *51*
    Obituary .................................................... *70*
    Earlier sketch in SATA *3*
    *See also* SAAS *9*
Morgan, Alfred P(owell) 1889-1972 ........... 33
Morgan, Alison (Mary) 1930- ..................... 85
    Earlier sketch in SATA *30*
Morgan, Anne 1954- .................................. *121*
Morgan, Douglas
    *See* Macdonald, James D.
Morgan, Ellen
    *See* Bumstead, Kathleen Mary
Morgan, Geoffrey 1916- ............................... 46
Morgan, Helen (Gertrude Louise) 1921-1990
    ................................................................ 29
Morgan, Jane
    *See* Cooper, James Fenimore
    and Franklin, Jane (Morgan)
    and Moren, Sally M(oore)
Morgan, Lenore H. 1908-1976 .................... 8
Morgan, Mary 1957- .................................. *114*
    Earlier sketch in SATA *81*
Morgan, Nicola 1961- ................................ *161*
Morgan, Nina 1953- ................................... *110*
Morgan, Pierr 1952- ................................... *122*
    Earlier sketch in SATA *77*
Morgan, Robin (Evonne) 1941- .................. 80
Morgan, Roxanne
    *See* Gentle, Mary
Morgan, Sarah (Nicola) 1959- .................... 68
Morgan, Shirley ............................................. 10
    *See* Kiepper, Shirley Morgan
Morgan, Stacy T(owle) 1959- .................... *104*
Morgan, Stevie
    *See* Davies, Nicola
Morgan, Tom 1942- ...................................... 42
Morgan, Wendy
    *See* Staub, Wendy Corsi
Morgan-Vanroyen, Mary
    *See* Morgan, Mary
Morgenstern, Susie Hoch 1945- ................ *133*
Mori, Hana 1909-1990(?) ........................... 88
Mori, Kyoko 1957- .................................... *122*
    Autobiography Feature ........................... *126*
    *See also* CLR *64*
    *See also* SAAS *26*

Moriarty, Jaclyn ......................................... *162*
Moriarty, William J. 1930- ......................... *127*
Morice, Dave 1946- ...................................... 93
Morin, Isobel V. 1928- ............................... *110*
Morley, Wilfred Owen
    *See* Lowndes, Robert A(ugustine) W(ard)
Morningstar, Mildred (Whaley) 1912-1997
    ................................................................ *61*
    Obituary .................................................. *114*
Morozumi, Atsuko ...................................... *110*
Morpurgo, Michael 1943- ........................ *143*
    Earlier sketch in SATA *93*
    *See also* CLR *51*
Morrah, Dave
    *See* Morrah, David Wardlaw, Jr.
Morrah, David Wardlaw, Jr. 1914-1991 ...... 10
Morreale-de la Garza, Phyllis
    *See* De la Garza, Phyllis
Morressy, John 1930-2006 ......................... 23
Morrill, Leslie H(olt) 1934-2003 ............... 48
    Brief entry ................................................ 33
    Obituary .................................................. *148*
    *See also* SAAS *22*
Morris, Chris(topher Crosby) 1946- ......... 66
Morris, Deborah 1956- ............................... 91
Morris, Desmond 1928- ............................... 14
Morris, Desmond John
    *See* Morris, Desmond
Morris, Don 1954- ........................................ 83
Morris, Gerald (Paul) 1963- ..................... *150*
    Earlier sketch in SATA *107*
Morris, Gilbert (Leslie) 1929- ................... *104*
Morris, Jackie .............................................. *151*
Morris, Janet (Ellen) 1946- ......................... 66
Morris, Jay
    *See* Tatham, Julie Campbell
Morris, (Margaret) Jean 1924- .................... 98
Morris, Jeffrey B(randon) 1941- ................. 92
Morris, Jill 1936- ...................................... *165*
    Earlier sketch in SATA *119*
Morris, Juddi ............................................... 85
Morris, Judy K. 1936- .................................. 61
Morris, Oradel Nolen .................................. *128*
Morris, Robert A(da) 1933- .......................... 7
Morris, William 1913-1994 ......................... 29
Morrison, Bill 1935- ..................................... 66
    Brief entry ................................................ 37
Morrison, Chloe Anthony Wofford
    *See* Morrison, Toni
Morrison, Dorothy Nafus ........................... 29
Morrison, Gordon 1944- ........................... *128*
    Earlier sketch in SATA *87*
Morrison, Joan 1922- ................................... 65
Morrison, Lillian 1917- ............................. *108*
    Earlier sketch in SATA *3*
Morrison, Lucile Phillips 1896- ................. 17
Morrison, Martha A. 1948- ......................... 77
Morrison, Meighan 1966- ........................... 90
Morrison, Richard
    *See* Lowndes, Robert A(ugustine) W(ard)
Morrison, Robert
    *See* Lowndes, Robert A(ugustine) W(ard)
Morrison, Roberta
    *See* Webb, Jean Francis (III)
Morrison, Susan Dudley
    *See* Gold, Susan Dudley
Morrison, Taylor 1971- ............................. *159*
    Earlier sketch in SATA *95*
Morrison, Toni 1931- ................................ *144*
    Earlier sketch in SATA *57*
    *See also* CLR *99*
Morrison, Velma Ford 1909- ....................... 21
Morrison, Wilbur Howard 1915- ............... 64
Morrison, William
    *See* Samachson, Joseph
Morriss, James E(dward) 1932- .................... 8
Morrow, Barbara Olenyik 1952- ............... *167*
Morrow, Betty
    *See* Bacon, Elizabeth
Morse, Carol
    *See* Yeakley, Marjory Hall

Morse, Flo 1921- ........................................... 30
Morse, Tony 1953- .................................... *129*
Mort, Vivian
    *See* Cromie, Alice Hamilton
Mortimer, Anne 1958- .............................. *116*
Morton, Alexandra (Hubbard) 1957- ........ *144*
Morton, Anthony
    *See* Arthur, Robert, (Jr.)
Morton, Jane 1931- ...................................... 50
Morton, Joseph C. 1932- .......................... *156*
Morton, Lee Jack, Jr. 1928- ........................ 32
Morton, Miriam 1918(?)-1985 .................... 9
    Obituary .................................................... 46
Mosatche, Harriet (S.) 1949- .................... *122*
Moscow, Alvin 1925- ..................................... 3
Mosel, Arlene (Tichy) 1921-1996 ............... 7
Moseley, James W(illett) 1931- ................ *139*
Moseng, Elisabeth 1967- ............................. 90
Moser, Barry (A.) 1940- ............................ *138*
    Earlier sketches in SATA *56, 79*
    *See also* CLR *49*
    *See also* SAAS *15*
Moser, Don(ald Bruce) 1932- ..................... 31
Moses, Sheila P. 1961- ............................... *168*
Moses, Will 1956- ....................................... *120*
Mosesson, Gloria R(ubin) ........................... 24
Mosher, Richard 1949- .............................. *120*
Moskin, Marietta D(unston) 1928- ........... 23
Moskof, Martin Stephen 1930- .................. 27
Mosley, Francis 1957- .................................. 57
Moss, Don(ald) 1920- .................................. 11
Moss, Elaine (Dora) 1924- ........................... 57
    Brief entry ................................................ 31
Moss, Jeff(rey) 1942-1998 ........................... 73
    Obituary .................................................. *106*
Moss, Marissa 1959- .................................. *163*
    Earlier sketches in SATA *71, 104*
Moss, Miriam 1955- ................................... *140*
    Earlier sketch in SATA *76*
Moss, Thylias 1954- ................................... *108*
Moss, Thylias Rebecca Brasier
    *See* Moss, Thylias
Most, Bernard 1937- .................................. *134*
    Brief entry ................................................ 40
    Earlier sketches in SATA *48, 91*
Mott, Evelyn Clarke 1962- ....................... *133*
    Earlier sketch in SATA *75*
Motz, Lloyd 1909- ........................................ 20
Mould, Edwin
    *See* Whitlock, Ralph
Mouly, Francoise ........................................ *155*
Mountain, Robert
    *See* Montgomery, Raymond A. (Jr.)
Mountfield, David
    *See* Grant, Neil
Moussard, Jacqueline 1924- ........................ 24
Mowat, Claire (Angel Wheeler) 1933- ...... *123*
Mowat, Farley 1921- .................................... 55
    Earlier sketch in SATA *3*
    *See also* CLR *20*
Mowat, Farley McGill
    *See* Mowat, Farley
Mowry, Jess 1960- ..................................... *131*
    Autobiography Feature ........................... *131*
    Earlier sketch in SATA *109*
    *See also* CLR *65*
Moxley, Sheila 1966- .................................... 96
Moyer, Terry J. 1937- ................................... 94
Moyes, Patricia ............................................. 63
    *See* Haszard, Patricia Moyes
Moyler, Alan (Frank Powell) 1926- ........... 36
Mozley, Charles 1915- ................................. 43
    Brief entry ................................................ 32
Mphahlele, Es'kia
    *See* Mphahlele, Ezekiel
Mphahlele, Ezekiel 1919- ......................... *119*
    *See* Mphahlele, Es'kia
Mr. McGillicuddy
    *See* Abisch, Roslyn Kroop
Mr. Sniff
    *See* Abisch, Roslyn Kroop

Mr. Tivil
See Lorkowski, Thomas V(incent)
Mr. Wizard
See Herbert, Don(ald Jeffrey)
Mrs. Fairstar
See Horne, Richard Henry Hengist
Muchamore, Robert 1972- ......................... *175*
Muchmore, Jo Ann 1937- ......................... *103*
Mude, O.
See Gorey, Edward (St. John)
Mudgeon, Apeman
See Mitchell, Adrian
Mueller, Jorg 1942- ................................. *67*
See also CLR 43
Mueller, Virginia 1924- ............................. *28*
Muggs
See Watkins, Lois
Muir, Diana
See Appelbaum, Diana Muir Karter
Muir, Frank (Herbert) 1920-1998 ............... *30*
Muir, Helen 1937- .................................. *65*
Mukerji, Dhan Gopal 1890-1936 ................. *40*
See also CLR 10
Mulcahy, Lucille Burnett ............................. *12*
Mulford, Philippa G. 1948- ........................ *112*
Earlier sketch in SATA 43
Mulford, Philippa Greene
See Mulford, Philippa G.
Mulila, Vigad G.
See Maillu, David G(ian)
Mullen, Michael 1937- ............................. *122*
Muller, Billex
See Ellis, Edward S(ylvester)
Muller, Jorg
See Mueller, Jorg
Muller, (Lester) Robin 1953- ...................... *86*
Mullin, Caryl Cude 1969- ......................... *130*
Mullins, Edward S(wift) 1922- .................... *10*
Mullins, Hilary 1962- ............................... *84*
Mulock, Dinah Maria
See Craik, Dinah Maria (Mulock)
Mulvihill, William Patrick 1923- .................. *8*
Mumford, Ruth 1919- ............................... *86*
See Dallas, Ruth
Mumy, Bill 1954- .................................... *112*
Mun
See Leaf, (Wilbur) Munro
Munari, Bruno 1907-1998 ........................... *15*
See also CLR 9
Munce, Ruth Hill 1898- ............................. *12*
Mundy, Simon 1954- ................................. *64*
Mundy, Simon Andrew James Hainault
See Mundy, Simon
Munger, Nancy ........................................ *170*
Munowitz, Ken 1935-1977 ........................... *14*
Munoz, William 1949- ................................ *92*
Earlier sketch in SATA 42
Munro, Alice 1931- .................................. *29*
Munro, Alice Anne
See Munro, Alice
Munro, Eleanor 1928- ................................ *37*
Munro, Roxie 1945- .................................. *136*
Earlier sketch in SATA 58
Munsch, Bob
See Munsch, Robert (Norman)
Munsch, Robert (Norman) 1945- ................... *120*
Brief entry ........................................... *48*
Earlier sketches in SATA 50, 83
See also CLR 19
Munsinger, Lynn 1951- .............................. *177*
Earlier sketches in SATA 33, 94
Munson, Derek 1970- ................................ *139*
Munson, R. W.
See Karl, Jean E(dna)
Munson-Benson, Tunie 1946- ....................... *15*
Munsterberg, Peggy 1921- ........................... *102*
Munthe, Nelly 1947- ................................. *53*
Munves, James (Albert) 1922- ....................... *30*
Munzer, Martha E. 1899-1999 ....................... *4*
Murch, Mel
See Manes, Stephen

Murdoch, David H(amilton) 1937- ............... *96*
Murhall, J(acqueline) J(ane) 1964- ............ *143*
Murphy, Barbara Beasley 1933- ................. *130*
Earlier sketch in SATA 5
Murphy, Claire Rudolf 1951- .................... *137*
Earlier sketch in SATA 76
Murphy, E(mmett) Jefferson 1926- .............. *4*
Murphy, Jill (Frances) 1949- .................... *142*
Earlier sketches in SATA 37, 70
See also CLR 39
Murphy, Jim 1947- ................................ *124*
Brief entry .......................................... *32*
Earlier sketches in SATA 37, 77
See also CLR 53
Murphy, Joseph E., Jr. 1930- ...................... *65*
Murphy, Kelly 1977- ............................... *143*
Murphy, Louise 1943- .............................. *155*
Murphy, Pat
See Murphy, E(mmett) Jefferson
Murphy, Patricia J. 1963- ......................... *132*
Murphy, Robert (William) 1902-1971 ......... *10*
Murphy, Shirley Rousseau 1928- ................ *126*
Earlier sketches in SATA 36, 71
See also SAAS 18
Murphy, Stuart J. 1942- ........................... *157*
Earlier sketch in SATA 115
Murphy, Tim
See Murphy, Jim
Murray, John 1923- ................................. *39*
Murray, Kirsty 1960- ............................... *165*
Earlier sketch in SATA 108
Murray, Marguerite 1917- .......................... *63*
Murray, Marian ...................................... *5*
Murray, Martine 1965- ............................. *125*
Murray, (Judith) Michele (Freedman)
1933-1974 ......................................... *7*
Murray, Ossie 1938- ................................ *43*
Murray, Peter
See Hautman, Pete
Murrow, Liza Ketchum 1946- ...................... *78*
See Ketchum, Liza
Musgrave, Florence 1902-1999 .................... *3*
Musgrove, Margaret W(ynkoop) 1943- ....... *124*
Earlier sketch in SATA 26
Mussey, Virginia Howell
See Ellison, Virginia H(owell)
Mussey, Virginia T.H.
See Ellison, Virginia H(owell)
Mutel, Cornelia F. 1947- ........................... *74*
Muth, Jon J. ........................................ *165*
Mutz
See Kuenstler, Morton
Mwangi, Meja 1948- ................................ *174*
My Brother's Brother
See Chekhov, Anton (Pavlovich)
Myers, Anna ......................................... *160*
Myers, Arthur 1917- ................................ *91*
Earlier sketch in SATA 35
Myers, Bernice ...................................... *81*
Earlier sketch in SATA 9
Myers, Caroline Elizabeth Clark 1887-1980
.................................................... *28*
Myers, Christopher 1975-
See CLR 97
Myers, Edward 1950- .............................. *172*
Earlier sketch in SATA 96
Myers, Elisabeth P(erkins) 1918- ................. *36*
Myers, (Mary) Hortense (Powner) 1913-1987
.................................................... *10*
Myers, Jack 1913-2006 ............................ *83*
Myers, Jack Edgar
See Myers, Jack
Myers, Lou 1915-2005 ............................. *81*
Obituary ........................................... *171*
Myers, Louis
See Myers, Lou
Myers, R.E. 1924- .................................. *119*
Myers, Robert Eugene
See Myers, R.E.
Myers, Tim 1953- ................................... *176*
Earlier sketch in SATA 147

Myers, Timothy Joseph
See Myers, Tim
Myers, Walter Dean 1937- ........................ *157*
Brief entry .......................................... *27*
Earlier sketches in SATA 41, 71, 109
See also CLR 110
See also SAAS 2
See Myers, Walter M.
Myers, Walter M.
See Myers, Walter Dean
Myller, Rolf 1926-2006 ............................ *27*
Obituary ........................................... *175*
Myra, Harold L(awrence) 1939- .................. *46*
Brief entry .......................................... *42*
Myracle, Lauren 1969- ............................. *162*
Myrus, Donald (Richard) 1927- ................... *23*
Mysterious Traveler, The
See Arthur, Robert, (Jr.)

N

Na, An .............................................. *149*
Naaslund, Goorel Kristina 1940- ................ *170*
Nadel, Laurie 1948- ................................ *74*
Naden, Corinne J. 1930- .......................... *166*
Earlier sketch in SATA 79
Nagel, Andreas Fischer
See Fischer-Nagel, Andreas
Nagel, Heiderose Fischer
See Fischer-Nagel, Heiderose
Nagle, Shane ....................................... *176*
Naidoo, Beverley 1943- ........................... *135*
Earlier sketch in SATA 63
See also CLR 29
Naipaul, Shivadhar Srinivasa
See Naipaul, Shiva
Nakae, Noriko 1940- ............................... *59*
Nakatani, Chiyoko 1930-1981 ..................... *55*
Brief entry .......................................... *40*
See also CLR 30
Nally, Susan W. 1947- ............................. *90*
Namioka, Lensey 1929- ............................ *157*
Autobiography Feature ............................. *116*
Earlier sketches in SATA 27, 89
See also CLR 48
See also SAAS 24
Nanji, Shenaaz 1954- .............................. *131*
Nanogak Agnes 1925- ............................. *61*
Napier, Mark
See Laffin, John (Alfred Charles)
Napoli, Donna Jo 1948- ........................... *137*
Earlier sketch in SATA 92
See also CLR 51
See also SAAS 23
Narahashi, Keiko 1959- ........................... *115*
Earlier sketch in SATA 79
Narayan, Rasipuram Krishnaswami
See Narayan, R.K.
Narayan, R.K. 1906-2001 ......................... *62*
Nascimbene, Yan 1949- ............................ *173*
Earlier sketch in SATA 133
Nash, Bruce M(itchell) 1947- ..................... *34*
Nash, Linell
See Smith, Linell Nash
Nash, Mary (Hughes) 1925- ....................... *41*
Nash, (Frediric) Ogden 1902-1971 ............. *46*
Earlier sketch in SATA 2
Nash, Renea Denise 1963- ......................... *81*
Nast, Elsa Ruth
See Watson, Jane Werner
Nast, Thomas 1840-1902 .......................... *51*
Brief entry .......................................... *33*
Nastick, Sharon 1954- ............................. *41*
Nathan, Amy ........................................ *155*
Earlier sketch in SATA 104
Nathan, Dorothy (Goldeen) (?)-1966 .......... *15*
Nathan, Robert (Gruntal) 1894-1985 .......... *6*
Obituary ........................................... *43*
Nathanson, Laura Walther 1941- ................. *57*

Natti, Susanna 1948- ............................... *125*
  Earlier sketch in SATA *32*
Naughtie, Eleanor
  *See* Updale, Eleanor
Naughton, Bill
  *See* Naughton, William John (Francis)
Naughton, James Franklin 1957- ............. *85*
Naughton, Jim
  *See* Naughton, James Franklin
Naughton, William John (Francis) 1910-1992
  ........................................................ *86*
  *See* Naughton, Bill
Navarra, John Gabriel 1927- ..................... *8*
Naylor, Penelope 1941- ........................... *10*
Naylor, Phyllis 1933-
  *See* Naylor, Phyllis Reynolds
Naylor, Phyllis Reynolds 1933- ............... *152*
  Autobiography Feature ........................ *152*
  Earlier sketches in SATA *12, 66, 102*
  *See also* CLR *17*
  *See also* SAAS *10*
  *See* Naylor, Phyllis
Nazarian, Nikki
  *See* Nichols, Cecilia Fawn
Nazaroff, Alexander I(vanovich) 1898-1981 . *4*
Neal, Harry Edward 1906-1993 ................. *5*
  Obituary ............................................. *76*
Neal, Michael
  *See* Teitelbaum, Michael
Nearing, Penny 1916- ............................. *47*
  Brief entry .......................................... *42*
Nebel, Gustave E. ................................... *45*
  Brief entry .......................................... *33*
Nebel, Mimouca
  *See* Nebel, Gustave E.
Nee, Kay Bonner ..................................... *10*
Needham, Kate 1962- ............................. *95*
Needle, Jan 1943- ................................... *98*
  Earlier sketch in SATA *30*
  *See also* CLR *43*
  *See also* SAAS *23*
Needleman, Jacob 1934- ........................... *6*
Neel, David 1960- ................................... *82*
Neel, Preston 1959- ................................. *93*
Negri, Rocco 1932- ................................. *12*
Neier, Aryeh 1937- ................................. *59*
Neigoff, Anne ......................................... *13*
Neigoff, Mike 1920- ............................... *13*
Neilson, Frances Fullerton (Jones) 1910-2001
  ........................................................ *14*
Neimark, Anne E. 1935- ........................... *145*
  Earlier sketch in SATA *4*
Neimark, Paul G. 1934- ........................... *80*
  Brief entry .......................................... *37*
Neitzel, Shirley 1941- ............................. *134*
  Earlier sketch in SATA *77*
Nell
  *See* Hanna, Nell(ie L.)
Nelson, Blake 1960- ............................... *177*
Nelson, Catherine Chadwick 1926- ........... *87*
Nelson, Cordner (Bruce) 1918- ................. *54*
  Brief entry .......................................... *29*
Nelson, Drew 1952- ............................... *77*
Nelson, Esther L. 1928- ........................... *13*
Nelson, Jim A.
  *See* Stotter, Mike
Nelson, Julie L. 1970- ............................. *117*
Nelson, Kadir ....................................... *154*
Nelson, Kris
  *See* Rusch, Kristine Kathryn
Nelson, Marilyn 1946- ........................... *151*
  *See* Waniek, Marilyn Nelson
Nelson, Mary Carroll 1929- ..................... *23*
Nelson, O. Terry 1941- ........................... *62*
Nelson, Peter N. 1953- ........................... *73*
Nelson, Richard K(ing) 1941- ................... *65*
Nelson, Robin Laura 1971- ....................... *141*
Nelson, Roy Paul 1923- ........................... *59*
Nelson, Sharlene (P.) 1933- ..................... *96*
Nelson, Ted (W.) 1931- ........................... *96*

Nelson, Theresa 1948- ........................... *143*
  Autobiography Feature ........................ *143*
  Earlier sketch in SATA *79*
Nerlove, Miriam 1959- ........................... *53*
  Brief entry .......................................... *49*
Nesbit, E(dith) 1858-1924 ....................... *100*
  *See also* YABC *1*
  *See also* CLR *70*
Nesbit, Troy
  *See* Folsom, Franklin (Brewster)
Nespojohn, Katherine V(eronica) 1912-1975
  ........................................................ *7*
Ness, Evaline (Michelow) 1911-1986 ......... *26*
  Obituary ............................................. *49*
  Earlier sketch in SATA *1*
  *See also* CLR *6*
  *See also* SAAS *1*
Nestor, Larry 1940- ............................... *149*
Nestor, William P(rodromos) 1947- ........... *49*
Nethery, Mary ....................................... *93*
Neubecker, Robert ................................. *170*
Neuberger, Julia (Babette Sarah) 1950- .... *142*
  Earlier sketch in SATA *78*
Neufeld, John (Arthur) 1938- ................... *131*
  Autobiography Feature ........................ *131*
  Earlier sketches in SATA *6, 81*
  *See also* CLR *52*
  *See also* SAAS *3*
Neuhaus, David 1958- ............................. *83*
Neumeyer, Peter F(lorian) 1929- ............... *13*
Neurath, Marie (Reidemeister) 1898-1986 .... *1*
Neuschwander, Cindy 1953- ..................... *157*
  Earlier sketch in SATA *107*
Neusner, Jacob 1932- ............................. *38*
Neville, Charles
  *See* Bodsworth, (Charles) Fred(erick)
Neville, Emily Cheney 1919- ..................... *1*
  *See also* SAAS *2*
Neville, Mary
  *See* Woodrich, Mary Neville
Nevins, Albert (Francis) J(erome) 1915-1997
  ........................................................ *20*
Newberger, Devra
  *See* Speregen, Devra Newberger
Newberry, Clare Turlay 1903-1970 ............. *1*
  Obituary ............................................. *26*
Newbery, John 1713-1767 ......................... *20*
Newbery, Linda 1952- ............................. *142*
Newcombe, Jack ..................................... *45*
  Brief entry .......................................... *33*
  *See* Newcombe, Eugene A.
Newcome, Robert 1955- ........................... *91*
Newcome, Zita 1959- ............................. *88*
Newell, Crosby
  *See* Bonsall, Crosby Barbara (Newell)
Newell, Edythe W(eatherford) 1910-1989 .. *11*
Newell, Hope Hockenberry 1896-1965 ....... *24*
Newfeld, Frank 1928- ............................. *26*
Newlon, (Frank) Clarke 1905(?)-1982 ......... *6*
  Obituary ............................................. *33*
Newman, Daisy 1904-1994 ....................... *27*
  Obituary ............................................. *78*
Newman, Gerald 1939- ........................... *46*
  Brief entry .......................................... *42*
Newman, Jerry 1935- ............................. *82*
Newman, Leslea 1955- ........................... *134*
  Earlier sketches in SATA *71, 128*
Newman, Margaret
  *See* Potter, Margaret (Newman)
Newman, Marjorie ................................. *146*
Newman, Matthew (Harrison) 1955- ........... *56*
Newman, Nanette 1934- ........................... *162*
Newman, Robert (Howard) 1909-1988 ....... *87*
  Obituary ............................................. *60*
  Earlier sketch in SATA *4*
Newman, Shirlee P(etkin) ......................... *144*
  Earlier sketches in SATA *10, 90*
Newsom, Carol 1948- ............................. *92*
  Earlier sketch in SATA *40*
Newsom, Tom 1944- ............................... *80*
Newth, Mette 1942- ............................... *140*

Newton, David E(dward) 1933- ................. *67*
Newton, James R(obert) 1935- ................. *23*
Newton, Suzanne 1936- ........................... *77*
  Earlier sketch in SATA *5*
Ney, John 1923- ..................................... *43*
  Brief entry .......................................... *33*
Nez, John ............................................. *155*
Ng, Franklin ......................................... *82*
Nichol, B(arrie) P(hillip) 1944-1988 ........... *66*
Nicholas, Louise D.
  *See* Watkins, Dawn L.
Nicholls, Judith (Ann) 1941- ................... *61*
Nichols, Cecilia Fawn 1906-1987 ............. *12*
Nichols, Grace 1950- ............................. *164*
  Earlier sketch in SATA *98*
Nichols, Janet (Louise) 1952- ................... *67*
Nichols, Judy 1947- ............................... *124*
Nichols, Leigh
  *See* Koontz, Dean R.
Nichols, Paul
  *See* Hawks, Robert
Nichols, Peter
  *See* Youd, (Christopher) Samuel
Nichols, (Joanna) Ruth 1948- ................... *15*
Nicholson, C. R.
  *See* Nicole, Christopher (Robin)
Nicholson, Christina
  *See* Nicole, Christopher (Robin)
Nicholson, Joyce Thorpe 1919- ................. *35*
Nicholson, Lois P. 1949- ......................... *88*
Nicholson, Robin
  *See* Nicole, Christopher (Robin)
Nicholson, William 1872-1949
  *See* CLR *76*
Nickell, Joe 1944- ................................. *167*
  Earlier sketch in SATA *73*
Nickelsburg, Janet 1893-1983 ................... *11*
Nickerson, Elizabeth ............................. *14*
  *See* Nickerson, Betty
Nickl, Barbara (Elisabeth) 1939- ............... *56*
Nicklaus, Carol ..................................... *62*
  Brief entry .......................................... *33*
Nickless, Will 1902-1979(?) ..................... *66*
Nic Leodhas, Sorche
  *See* Alger, Leclaire (Gowans)
Nicol, Ann
  *See* Turnbull, Ann (Christine)
Nicolas
  *See* Mordvinoff, Nicolas
Nicolay, Helen 1866-1954
  *See* YABC *1*
Nicole, Christopher (Robin) 1930- ............. *5*
Nicoll, Helen 1937- ............................... *87*
Nicolson, Cynthia Pratt 1949- ................. *141*
Ni Dhuibhne, Eilis 1954- ......................... *91*
Niehaus, Paddy Bouma
  *See* Bouma, Paddy
Nields, Nerissa 1967- ............................. *166*
Nielsen, Kay (Rasmus) 1886-1957 ............. *16*
  *See also* CLR *16*
Nielsen, Laura F(arnsworth) 1960- ........... *93*
Nielsen, Nancy J. 1951- ......................... *77*
Nielsen, Virginia
  *See* McCall, Virginia Nielsen
Nieuwsma, Milton J(ohn) 1941- ............... *142*
Nightingale, Sandy 1953- ......................... *76*
Nikolajeva, Maria 1952- ......................... *127*
Nikola-Lisa, W. 1951- ............................. *71*
Niland, Deborah 1951- ........................... *172*
  Earlier sketch in SATA *27*
Niland, Kilmeny ..................................... *75*
Nilsen, Anna 1948- ................................. *174*
  Earlier sketch in SATA *96*
Nilsson, Eleanor 1939- ........................... *117*
  Earlier sketch in SATA *81*
  *See also* SAAS *23*
Nilsson, Per 1954- ................................. *159*
Nimmo, Jenny 1944- ............................... *144*
  Earlier sketch in SATA *87*
  *See also* CLR *44*

Niven, Larry 1938- ..................................... *171*
  Earlier sketch in SATA *95*
  *See* Niven, Laurence VanCott
Niven, Laurence VanCott
  *See* Niven, Larry
Nivola, Claire A. 1947- ............................... *140*
  Earlier sketch in SATA *84*
Nix, Garth 1963- ........................................ *143*
  Earlier sketch in SATA *97*
  *See also* CLR *68*
Nixon, Hershell Howard 1923- ................. *42*
Nixon, Joan Lowery 1927-2003 ............... *115*
  Obituary ............................................... *146*
  Earlier sketches in SATA *8, 44, 78*
  *See also* CLR *24*
  *See also* SAAS *9*
Nixon, K.
  *See* Nixon, Kathleen Irene (Blundell)
Nixon, Kathleen Irene (Blundell) 1894-1988(?)
  ................................................................ *14*
  Obituary ................................................. *59*
Nobisso, Josephine 1953- .......................... *121*
  Earlier sketch in SATA *78*
Noble, Iris (Davis) 1922-1986 ...................... *5*
  Obituary ................................................. *49*
Noble, Marty 1947- .................................... *125*
  Earlier sketch in SATA *97*
Noble, Trinka Hakes ................................... *123*
  Brief entry ............................................. *37*
Noda, Takayo 1961- .................................... *168*
Nodelman, Perry 1942- .............................. *101*
Nodset, Joan L.
  *See* Lexau, Joan M.
Noel Hume, Ivor 1927- ................................. *65*
Noestlinger, Christine
  *See* Nostlinger, Christine
Noguere, Suzanne 1947- ............................... *34*
Nolan, Dennis 1945- ................................... *166*
  Brief entry ............................................. *34*
  Earlier sketches in SATA *42, 92*
Nolan, Han 1956- ....................................... *157*
  Earlier sketch in SATA *109*
Nolan, Janet 1956- ..................................... *145*
Nolan, Jeannette Covert 1897-1974 .............. *2*
  Obituary ................................................. *27*
Nolan, Paul T(homas) 1919- ........................ *48*
Nolan, William F(rancis) 1928- .................... *88*
  Brief entry ............................................. *28*
Nolen, Jerdine 1953- ................................... *157*
  Earlier sketch in SATA *105*
Noll, Sally 1946- .......................................... *82*
Noonan, Diana 1960- .................................. *146*
Noonan, Julia 1946- ................................... *148*
  Earlier sketches in SATA *4, 95*
Norac, Carl 1960- ....................................... *166*
Nordan, Robert W(arren) 1934-2004 ........ *133*
Nordhoff, Charles Bernard 1887-1947 ........ *23*
Nordlicht, Lillian ........................................ *29*
Nordstrom, Ursula 1910-1988 ....................... *3*
  Obituary ................................................. *57*
Nordtvedt, Matilda 1926- ............................ *67*
Norling, Beth 1969- .................................... *149*
Norman, Charles 1904-1996 ......................... *38*
  Obituary ................................................. *92*
Norman, Howard
  *See* Norman, Howard A.
Norman, Howard A. 1949- ............................ *81*
Norman, James
  *See* Schmidt, James Norman
Norman, Jay
  *See* Arthur, Robert, (Jr.)
Norman, Lilith 1927- .................................. *120*
  Earlier sketch in SATA *86*
Norman, Mary 1931- .................................... *36*
Norman, Steve
  *See* Pashko, Stanley
Norment, Lisa 1966- ..................................... *91*
Norris, Gunilla Brodde 1939- ...................... *20*
North, Andrew
  *See* Norton, Andre

North, Anthony
  *See* Koontz, Dean R.
North, Captain George
  *See* Stevenson, Robert Louis (Balfour)
North, Captain George
  *See* Stevenson, Robert Louis (Balfour)
North, Howard
  *See* Trevor, Elleston
North, Joan 1920- ......................................... *16*
North, Milou
  *See* Erdrich, Louise
North, Robert
  *See* Withers, Carl A.
North, Sara
  *See* Bonham, Barbara Thomas
  and Hager, Jean
North, Sterling 1906-1974 ............................ *45*
  Obituary ................................................. *26*
  Earlier sketch in SATA *1*
Northeast, Brenda V(ictoria) 1948- ........... *106*
Northmore, Elizabeth Florence 1906-1974
  ................................................................ *122*
Norton, Alice Mary .................................... *43*
  Earlier sketch in SATA *1*
  *See* Norton, Andre
Norton, Andre 1912-2005 ............................. *91*
  *See also* CLR *50*
  *See* Norton, Alice Mary
Norton, Browning
  *See* Norton, Frank R. B(rowning)
Norton, Frank R. B(rowning) 1909-1989 .... *10*
Norton, Mary 1903-1992 .............................. *60*
  Obituary ................................................. *72*
  Earlier sketch in SATA *18*
  *See also* CLR *6*
Nosredna, Trebor
  *See* Anderson, Bob
Nostlinger, Christine 1936- ......................... *162*
  Brief entry ............................................. *37*
  Earlier sketch in SATA *64*
  *See also* CLR *12*
Nourse, Alan E(dward) 1928-1992 .............. *48*
  *See also* CLR *33*
Novak, Matt 1962- ...................................... *165*
  Brief entry ............................................. *52*
  Earlier sketches in SATA *60, 104*
Novelli, Luca 1947- ...................................... *61*
Nowell, Elizabeth Cameron ......................... *12*
Noyes, Deborah
  *See* Wayshak, Deborah Noyes
Nugent, Nicholas 1949- ................................ *73*
Numeroff, Laura Joffe 1953- ...................... *142*
  Earlier sketches in SATA *28, 90*
  *See also* CLR *85*
Nunes, Lygia Bojunga 1932- ...................... *154*
  Earlier sketch in SATA *75*
  *See* Bojunga, Lygia
Nunn, Laura (Donna) Silverstein 1968- .... *124*
Nurnberg, Maxwell 1897-1984 .................... *27*
  Obituary ................................................. *41*
Nussbaumer, Paul (Edmund) 1934- ............ *16*
Nutt, Ken 1951- ........................................... *163*
  Earlier sketch in SATA *97*
Nuygen, Mathieu 1967- ................................. *80*
Nyberg, (Everett Wayne) Morgan 1944- ..... *87*
Nyce, (Nellie) Helene von Strecker 1885-1969
  ................................................................ *19*
Nyce, Vera 1862-1925 ................................. *19*
Nye, Naomi Shihab 1952- .......................... *147*
  Earlier sketch in SATA *86*
  *See also* CLR *59*
Nye, Robert 1939- .......................................... *6*
Nyikos, Stacy A. 1969- ............................... *164*
Nystrom, Carolyn 1940- ............................. *130*
  Earlier sketch in SATA *67*

## O

Oakes, Elizabeth H. 1964- .......................... *132*
Oakes, Vanya 1909-1983 ............................... *6*
  Obituary ................................................. *37*
Oakley, Don(ald G.) 1927- ............................ *8*
Oakley, Graham 1929- ................................. *84*
  Earlier sketch in SATA *30*
  *See also* CLR *7*
Oakley, Helen (McKelvey) 1906- ................. *10*
Oana, Katherine 1929- ................................. *53*
  Brief entry ............................................. *37*
Oates, Eddie H. 1943- ................................. *88*
Oates, Joyce Carol 1938- ............................ *159*
Oates, Stephen B(aery) 1936- ...................... *59*
Obed, Ellen Bryan 1944- .............................. *74*
Oberle, Joseph 1958- .................................... *69*
Oberman, Sheldon 1949-2004 ....................... *85*
  Autobiography Feature ........................... *114*
  Obituary ............................................... *153*
  *See also* CLR *54*
  *See also* SAAS *26*
Obligado, Lilian (Isabel) 1931- .................... *61*
  Brief entry ............................................. *45*
Obrant, Susan 1946- ..................................... *11*
O'Brian, E. G.
  *See* Clarke, Arthur C.
O'Brien, Anne Sibley 1952- .......................... *80*
  Brief entry ............................................. *48*
  Earlier sketch in SATA *53*
O'Brien, Robert C.
  *See* CLR *2*
  *See* Conly, Robert Leslie
O'Brien, Thomas C(lement) 1938- ............... *29*
O'Callaghan, Julie 1954- ............................. *113*
O'Callahan, Jay 1938- ................................. *88*
O'Carroll, Ryan
  *See* Markun, Patricia Maloney
Ochiltree, Dianne 1953- .............................. *117*
Ockham, Joan Price
  *See* Price, Joan
O'Connell, Margaret F(orster) 1935-1977 .. *30*
  Obituary ................................................. *30*
O'Connell, Peg
  *See* Ahern, Margaret McCrohan
O'Connell, Rebecca 1968- ........................... *130*
O'Connor, Barbara 1950- ............................. *154*
O'Connor, Francine M(arie) 1930- .............. *90*
O'Connor, Genevieve A. 1914- .................... *75*
O'Connor, Jane 1947- ................................. *150*
  Brief entry ............................................. *47*
  Earlier sketches in SATA *59, 103*
O'Connor, Karen 1938- ............................... *89*
  Earlier sketch in SATA *34*
O'Connor, Patrick
  *See* Wibberley, Leonard (Patrick O'Connor)
O'Conor, Jane 1958- ................................... *78*
Odaga, Asenath (Bole) 1937- ...................... *130*
  Earlier sketch in SATA *67*
  *See also* SAAS *19*
O Danachair, Caoimhin
  *See* Danaher, Kevin
Odanaka, Barbara ....................................... *159*
O'Daniel, Janet 1921- ................................. *24*
O'Day, Cathy
  *See* Crane, Barbara (Joyce)
O'Dell, Scott 1898-1989 ............................. *134*
  Earlier sketches in SATA *12, 60*
  *See also* CLR *16*
Odenwald, Robert P(aul) 1899-1965 ........... *11*
Odgers, Sally
  *See* Odgers, Sally Farrell
Odgers, Sally Farrell 1957- ........................ *139*
  Earlier sketch in SATA *72*
O'Donnell, Dick
  *See* Lupoff, Richard A(llen)
  and Thompson, Don(ald Arthur)
Oechsli, Kelly 1918-1999 .............................. *5*
Oesterle, Virginia Rorby
  *See* Rorby, Ginny

Ofek, Uriel 1926- ........................................ _36_
  _See also_ CLR 28
Offenbacher, Ami 1958- .............................. _91_
Offit, Sidney 1928- ...................................... _10_
Ofosu-Appiah, L(awrence) H(enry) 1920- .. _13_
Ogan, George F. 1912-1983 ........................ _13_
Ogan, M. G.
  _See_ Ogan, George F.
  and Ogan, Margaret E. (Nettles)
Ogan, Margaret E. (Nettles) 1923-1979 ...... _13_
Ogburn, Charlton (Jr.) 1911-1998 ................ _3_
  Obituary ................................................ _109_
Ogburn, Jacqueline K. .............................. _162_
Ogilvie, Elisabeth May 1917-2006 .............. _40_
  Brief entry ............................................ _29_
  Obituary ................................................ _176_
Ogilvy, Gavin
  _See_ Barrie, J(ames) M(atthew)
Ogilvy, Ian 1943- ...................................... _177_
Ogilvy, Ian Raymond
  _See_ Ogilvy, Ian
Ogletree, Charles J. 1952- ........................ _175_
O'Green, Jennifer
  _See_ Roberson, Jennifer
O'Green, Jennifer Roberson
  _See_ Roberson, Jennifer
O'Hagan, Caroline 1946- ............................ _38_
O'Hanlon, Jacklyn
  _See_ Meek, Jacklyn O'Hanlon
O'Hara, Elizabeth
  _See_ Ni Dhuibhne, Eilis
O'Hara, Kenneth
  _See_ Morris, (Margaret) Jean
O'Hara, Mary
  _See_ Alsop, Mary O'Hara
O'Hara (Alsop), Mary
  _See_ Alsop, Mary O'Hara
O'Hare, Jeff(rey A.) 1958- ........................ _105_
Ohi, Ruth 1964- ........................................ _95_
Ohiyesa
  _See_ Eastman, Charles A(lexander)
Ohlsson, Ib 1935- ........................................ _7_
Ohmi, Ayano 1959- .................................. _115_
Ohtomo, Yasuo 1946- ................................ _37_
o huigin, sean 1942- ................................ _138_
  _See also_ CLR 75
Oiseau
  _See_ Moseley, James W(illett)
Oke, Janette 1935- .................................... _97_
O'Keefe, Susan Heyboer .......................... _176_
  Earlier sketch in SATA _133_
O'Keeffe, Frank 1938- ................................ _99_
O'Kelley, Mattie Lou 1908-1997 ................ _97_
  Earlier sketch in SATA 36
Okimoto, Jean Davies 1942- .................... _103_
  Earlier sketch in SATA 34
Okomfo, Amasewa
  _See_ Cousins, Linda
Olaleye, Isaac O. 1941- .............................. _96_
  _See also_ SAAS 23
Olcott, Frances Jenkins 1872(?)-1963 ........ _19_
Old, Wendie C(orbin) 1943- .................... _154_
Old Boy
  _See_ Hughes, Thomas
Oldenburg, E(gbert) William 1936-1974 ..... _35_
Older, Effin 1942- .................................... _114_
Older, Jules 1940- .................................... _156_
  Earlier sketch in SATA _114_
Oldfield, Jenny 1949- .............................. _140_
Oldfield, Margaret J(ean) 1932- .................. _56_
Oldfield, Pamela 1931- .............................. _86_
Oldham, June .......................................... _70_
Oldham, Mary 1944- .................................. _65_
Olds, Elizabeth 1896-1991 .......................... _3_
  Obituary ................................................ _66_
Olds, Helen Diehl 1895-1981 ...................... _9_
  Obituary ................................................ _25_
Oldstyle, Jonathan
  _See_ Irving, Washington
O'Leary, Brian (Todd) 1940- ........................ _6_
O'Leary, Patsy B(aker) 1937- ...................... _97_

Oliphant, B. J.
  _See_ Tepper, Sheri S.
Oliver, Burton
  _See_ Burt, Olive Woolley
Oliver, Chad
  _See_ Oliver, Symmes C(hadwick)
Oliver, John Edward 1933- ........................ _21_
Oliver, Marilyn Tower 1935- ...................... _89_
Oliver, Narelle 1960- ................................ _152_
Oliver, Shirley (Louise Dawkins) 1958- .... _74_
Oliver, Symmes C(hadwick) 1928-1993 ... _101_
  _See_ Oliver, Chad
Oliviero, Jamie 1950- ................................ _84_
Olmsted, Lorena Ann 1890-1989 .............. _13_
Olney, Ross R. 1929- ................................ _13_
Olschewski, Alfred (Erich) 1920- ................ _7_
Olsen, Barbara ...................................... _148_
Olsen, Carol 1945- .................................... _89_
Olsen, Ib Spang 1921- .............................. _81_
  Earlier sketch in SATA 6
Olsen, Violet (Mae) 1922-1991 .................. _58_
Olson, Arielle North 1932- ........................ _67_
Olson, Gene 1922- .................................... _32_
Olson, Helen Kronberg .............................. _48_
Olson, Kay Melchisedech 1948- .............. _175_
Olson, Marianne
  _See_ Mitchell, Marianne
Olugebefola, Ademole 1941- ...................... _15_
Oluonye, Mary N(kechi) 1955- ................ _111_
Om
  _See_ Gorey, Edward (St. John)
O'Malley, Kevin 1961- .............................. _157_
Oman, Carola (Mary Anima) 1897-1978 .... _35_
O'Mara, Carmel 1965- .............................. _166_
O'Mara-Horwitz, Carmel
  _See_ O'Mara, Carmel
O'Meara, Walter (Andrew) 1897-1989 ....... _65_
Ommanney, F(rancis) D(ownes) 1903-1980
  ............................................................ _23_
O Mude
  _See_ Gorey, Edward (St. John)
Oneal, Elizabeth 1934- .............................. _82_
  Earlier sketch in SATA 30
  _See_ Oneal, Zibby
O'Neal, Reagan
  _See_ Jordan, Robert
Oneal, Zibby
  _See_ CLR 13
  _See_ Oneal, Elizabeth
O'Neill, Amanda 1951- ............................ _111_
O'Neill, Gerard K(itchen) 1927-1992 ........ _65_
O'Neill, Judith (Beatrice) 1930- ................ _34_
O'Neill, Mary L(e Duc) 1908(?)-1990 ........ _2_
  Obituary ................................................ _64_
Onslow, Annette Rosemary MacArthur
  _See_ MacArthur-Onslow, Annette Rosemary
Onyefulu, Ifeoma 1959- ............................ _157_
  Earlier sketches in SATA _81, 115_
Opie, Iona (Margaret Balfour) 1923- ........ _118_
  Earlier sketches in SATA _3, 63_
  _See also_ SAAS 6
Opie, Peter (Mason) 1918-1982 ................ _118_
  Obituary ................................................ _28_
  Earlier sketches in SATA _3, 63_
Oppel, Kenneth 1967- .............................. _153_
  Earlier sketch in SATA _99_
Oppenheim, Joanne 1934- ........................ _174_
  Earlier sketches in SATA _5, 82, 136_
Oppenheim, Shulamith Levey 1928- ........ _177_
Oppenheimer, Joan L(etson) 1925- ............ _28_
Oppong, Joseph Ransford 1953- .............. _160_
Optic, Oliver
  _See_ Adams, William Taylor
  and Stratemeyer, Edward L.
Oram, Hiawyn 1946- ................................ _101_
  Earlier sketch in SATA _56_
Orbach, Ruth Gary 1941- .......................... _21_
Orczy, Emma
  _See_ Orczy, Baroness Emmuska
Orczy, Emma Magdalena Rosalia Maria Josefa
  _See_ Orczy, Baroness Emmuska

Orczy, Emmuska
  _See_ Orczy, Baroness Emmuska
Orczy, Baroness Emmuska 1865-1947 ........ _40_
  _See_ Orczy, Emma
Orde, A. J.
  _See_ Tepper, Sheri S.
O'Reilly, Jackson
  _See_ Jordan, Robert
Orenstein, Denise Gosliner 1950- ............ _157_
Orgel, Doris 1929- .................................. _148_
  Earlier sketches in SATA _7, 85_
  _See also_ CLR 48
  _See also_ SAAS 19
Orleans, Ilo 1897-1962 .............................. _10_
Orlev, Uri 1931- ...................................... _135_
  Earlier sketch in SATA 58
  _See also_ CLR 30
  _See also_ SAAS 19
Ormai, Stella .......................................... _57_
  Brief entry ............................................ _48_
Ormerod, Jan 1946- ................................ _132_
  Brief entry ............................................ _44_
  Earlier sketches in SATA _55, 70_
  _See also_ CLR 20
Ormondroyd, Edward 1925- ...................... _14_
Ormsby, Virginia H(aire) 1906-1990 .......... _11_
Orr, Katherine S(helley) 1950- .................. _72_
Orr, Wendy 1953- .................................... _141_
  Earlier sketch in SATA 90
Orris
  _See_ Ingelow, Jean
Orth, Richard
  _See_ Gardner, Richard (M.)
Ortiz Cofer, Judith
  _See_ Cofer, Judith Ortiz
Orwell, George
  _See_ CLR 68
  _See_ Blair, Eric (Arthur)
Orwin, Joanna 1944- ................................ _141_
Osborn, Elinor 1939- ................................ _145_
Osborn, Lois D(orothy) 1915- .................... _61_
Osborne, Charles 1927- .............................. _59_
Osborne, Chester G(orham) 1915-1987 ....... _11_
Osborne, David
  _See_ Silverberg, Robert
Osborne, George
  _See_ Silverberg, Robert
Osborne, Leone Neal 1914-1996 .................. _2_
Osborne, Mary Pope 1949- ...................... _144_
  Earlier sketches in SATA _41, 55, 98_
  _See also_ CLR 88
Osceola
  _See_ Blixen, Karen (Christentze Dinesen)
Osgood, William E(dward) 1926- .............. _37_
O'Shaughnessy, Darren
  _See_ Shan, Darren
O'Shaughnessy, Ellen Cassels 1937- .......... _78_
O'Shea, Catherine Patricia Shiels
  _See_ O'Shea, Pat
O'Shea, Pat 1931- .................................... _87_
  _See also_ CLR 18
Osmond, Edward 1900- ............................ _10_
Ossoli, Sarah Margaret (Fuller) 1810-1850
  ............................................................ _25_
  _See_ Fuller, Margaret
  and Fuller, Sarah Margaret
Ostendorf, (Arthur) Lloyd, (Jr.) 1921-2000
  ............................................................ _65_
  Obituary .............................................. _125_
Ostow, Micol 1976- .................................. _170_
Otfinoski, Steven 1949- ............................ _116_
  Earlier sketch in SATA 56
Otis, James
  _See_ Kaler, James Otis
O'Toole, Thomas 1941- .............................. _71_
O'Trigger, Sir Lucius
  _See_ Horne, Richard Henry Hengist
Otten, Charlotte F(ennema) 1926- .............. _98_
Ottley, Matt 1962- .................................. _171_
  Earlier sketch in SATA _102_

Ottley, Reginald Leslie 1909-1985 .............. *26*
  *See also CLR 16*
Otto, Svend
  *See* Soerensen, Svend Otto
Oughton, Jerrie (Preston) 1937- .............. *131*
  Earlier sketch in SATA *76*
Oughton, (William) Taylor 1925- .............. *104*
Ouida
  *See* De La Ramee, Marie Louise
Ousley, Odille 1896-1976 ........................... *10*
Outcalt, Todd 1960- ................................... *123*
Overmyer, James E. 1946- .......................... *88*
Overton, Jenny (Margaret Mary) 1942- ...... *52*
  Brief entry ............................................... *36*
Owen, Ann
  *See* Qualey, Marsha
Owen, Annie 1949- ...................................... *75*
Owen, Caroline Dale
  *See* Snedeker, Caroline Dale (Parke)
Owen, Clifford
  *See* Hamilton, Charles (Harold St. John)
Owen, Dilys
  *See* Gater, Dilys
Owen, (Benjamin) Evan 1918-1984 ............ *38*
Owen, (John) Gareth 1936-2002 .............. *162*
  Earlier sketch in SATA *83*
  *See also CLR 31*
  *See also SAAS 14*
Owens, Bryant 1968- ................................. *116*
Owens, Gail 1939- ....................................... *54*
Owens, Thomas S(heldon) 1960- ................. *86*
Owens, Tom
  *See* Owens, Thomas S(heldon)
Oxenbury, Helen 1938- ............................. *149*
  Earlier sketches in SATA *3, 68*
  *See also CLR 70*
Oxendine, Bess Holland 1933- ................... *90*
Oz, Frank (Richard) 1944- .......................... *60*
Ozer, Jerome S. 1927- ................................ *59*

**P**

Pace, Lorenzo 1943- ................................. *131*
Pace, Mildred Mastin 1907- ........................ *46*
  Brief entry ............................................... *29*
Pachter, Hedwig (?)-1988 ........................... *63*
Pack, Janet 1952- ....................................... *77*
Pack, Robert 1929- ................................... *118*
Packard, Edward 1931- ............................. *148*
  Earlier sketches in SATA *47, 90*
Packer, Kenneth L. 1946- .......................... *116*
Packer, Vin
  *See* Meaker, Marijane
Pad, Peter
  *See* Stratemeyer, Edward L.
Page, Eileen
  *See* Heal, Edith
Page, Eleanor
  *See* Coerr, Eleanor (Beatrice)
Page, Jake 1936- ......................................... *81*
Page, James Keena, Jr.
  *See* Page, Jake
Page, Lou Williams 1912-1997 ................... *38*
Page, Mary
  *See* Heal, Edith
Page, Robin 1943- ..................................... *154*
Pagnucci, Susan 1944- ................................ *90*
Pahz, Cheryl
  *See* Pahz, Cheryl Suzanne
Pahz, Cheryl Suzanne 1949- ........................ *11*
Pahz, James Alon 1943- .............................. *11*
Paice, Margaret 1920- ................................ *10*
Paige, Harry W(orthington) 1922- .............. *41*
  Brief entry ............................................... *35*
Paige, Richard
  *See* Koontz, Dean R.
Paige, Robin
  *See* Albert, Susan Wittig
Paine, Penelope Colville 1946- ................... *87*

Paine, Roberta M. 1925- ............................. *13*
Paisley, Tom 1932- ...................................... *78*
  *See* Bethancourt, T. Ernesto
Palatini, Margie ............................................ *174*
  Earlier sketch in SATA *134*
Palazzo, Anthony D.
  *See* Palazzo, Tony
Palazzo, Tony 1905-1970 ............................... *3*
Palder, Edward L. 1922- ................................ *5*
Palecek, Josef 1932- ..................................... *56*
Palecek, Libuse 1937- .................................. *89*
Palin, Michael (Edward) 1943- ..................... *67*
  *See* Monty Python
Palladini, David (Mario) 1946- ..................... *40*
  Brief entry ............................................... *32*
Pallas, Norvin 1918-1983 ............................. *23*
Pallotta-Chiarolli, Maria 1960- ................... *117*
Palmer, Bernard (Alvin) 1914-1998 ............ *26*
Palmer, C. Everard 1930- .............................. *14*
Palmer, (Ruth) Candida 1926- ...................... *11*
Palmer, Cyril Everard
  *See* Palmer, C. Everard
Palmer, Don
  *See* Benson, Mildred (Augustine Wirt)
Palmer, Hap 1942- ....................................... *68*
Palmer, Heidi 1948- ...................................... *15*
Palmer, Helen Marion
  *See* Geisel, Helen
Palmer, Jessica 1953- .................................. *120*
Palmer, Judd 1972- ..................................... *153*
Palmer, Juliette 1930- ................................... *15*
Palmer, Kate Salley 1946- ............................ *97*
Palmer, Maria
  *See* Brennan, J(ames) H(erbert)
  and Strachan, Ian
Palmer, Robin 1909-2000 ............................. *43*
Paltrowitz, Donna 1950- ............................... *61*
  Brief entry ............................................... *50*
Paltrowitz, Donna Milman
  *See* Paltrowitz, Donna
Paltrowitz, Stuart 1946- ............................... *61*
  Brief entry ............................................... *50*
Panagopoulos, Janie Lynn ............................. *149*
Panati, Charles 1943- .................................. *65*
Panchyk, Richard 1970- .............................. *138*
Panetta, George 1915-1969 ........................... *15*
Panetta, Joseph N. 1953- ............................. *96*
Panik, Sharon 1952- ..................................... *82*
Panowski, Eileen Thompson 1920- .............. *49*
Pansy
  *See* Alden, Isabella (Macdonald)
Pantell, Dora (Fuchs) ................................... *39*
Panter, Carol 1936- ........................................ *9*
Paolini, Christopher 1983- .......................... *157*
  *See also CLR 102*
Papademetriou, Lisa .................................... *175*
Papas, Bill
  *See* Papas, William
Papas, William 1927-2000 ............................ *50*
Papashvily, George 1898-1978 ...................... *17*
Papashvily, Helen (Waite) 1906-1996 ......... *17*
Pape, D. L.
  *See* Pape, Donna (Lugg)
Pape, Donna (Lugg) 1930- ............................ *82*
  Earlier sketch in SATA *2*
Paperny, Myra (Green) 1932- ....................... *51*
  Brief entry ............................................... *33*
Paradis, Adrian A(lexis) 1912- ..................... *67*
  Earlier sketch in SATA *1*
  *See also SAAS 8*
Paradis, Marjorie Bartholomew 1886(?)-1970
  ........................................................... *17*
Paradiz, Valerie 1963- ................................ *176*
Parenteau, Shirley Laurolyn 1935- .............. *47*
  Brief entry ............................................... *40*
Parish, Margaret (Cecile) 1927-1988 ......... *73*
  *See* Parish, Peggy
Parish, Margaret Holt
  *See* Holt, Margaret

Parish, Peggy ............................................... *17*
  Obituary ................................................... *59*
  *See also CLR 22*
  *See* Parish, Margaret (Cecile)
Park, Barbara 1947- ................................... *123*
  Brief entry ............................................... *35*
  Earlier sketches in SATA *40, 78*
  *See also CLR 34*
Park, Bill
  *See* Park, W(illiam) B(ryan)
Park, Frances 1955- ................................... *171*
Park, Ginger ............................................... *173*
Park, Janie Jaehyun ................................... *150*
Park, Jordan
  *See* Kornbluth, C(yril) M.
  and Pohl, Frederik
Park, Linda Sue 1960- ................................. *173*
  Earlier sketch in SATA *127*
  *See also CLR 84*
Park, Nick 1958- ......................................... *113*
Park, (Rosina) Ruth (Lucia) 1923(?)- ......... *93*
  Earlier sketch in SATA *25*
  *See also CLR 51*
Park, W(illiam) B(ryan) 1936- ..................... *22*
Parke, Marilyn 1928- ................................... *82*
Parker, Barbara Keevil 1938- ..................... *157*
Parker, Elinor Milnor 1906- ........................... *3*
Parker, Julie F. 1961- ................................... *92*
Parker, Kim 1963- ...................................... *174*
Parker, Kristy 1957- ..................................... *59*
Parker, Lois M(ay) 1912-1996 ..................... *30*
Parker, Margot M. 1937- .............................. *52*
Parker, Marjorie Blain 1960- ...................... *145*
Parker, Mary Jessie 1948- ............................ *71*
Parker, Nancy Winslow 1930- ..................... *132*
  Earlier sketches in SATA *10, 69*
  *See also SAAS 20*
Parker, Richard 1915-1990 .......................... *14*
Parker, Robert
  *See* Boyd, Waldo T.
Parker, Toni Trent 1947-2005 ..................... *142*
  Obituary ................................................... *169*
Parkes, Lucas
  *See* Harris, John (Wyndham Parkes Lucas)
  Beynon
Parkhill, John
  *See* Cox, William R(obert)
Parkins, David 1955- ................................... *176*
Parkinson, Ethelyn M(inerva) 1906-1999 ... *11*
Parkinson, Kathy ........................................... *71*
  *See* Parkinson, Kathryn N.
Parks, Deborah A. 1948- ............................. *133*
  Earlier sketch in SATA *91*
Parks, Edd Winfield 1906-1968 ................... *10*
Parks, Gordon 1912-2006 .......................... *108*
  Obituary ................................................... *175*
  Earlier sketch in SATA *8*
Parks, Gordon Roger Alexander
  *See* Parks, Gordon
Parks, Peggy J. 1951- ................................. *143*
Parks, PJ
  *See* Parks, Peggy J.
Parks, Rosa 1913-2005 ................................ *83*
  Obituary ................................................... *169*
Parks, Rosa Louise Lee
  *See* Parks, Rosa
Parks, Van Dyke 1943- ................................. *62*
Parley, Peter
  *See* Goodrich, Samuel Griswold
Parlin, John
  *See* Graves, Charles Parlin
Parnall, Peter 1936- ..................................... *69*
  Earlier sketch in SATA *16*
  *See also SAAS 11*
Parotti, Phillip (Elliott) 1941- ..................... *109*
Parr, Ann 1943- .......................................... *144*
Parr, Danny
  *See* Parr, Ann
Parr, Letitia (Evelyn) 1906-1985(?) ............ *37*
Parr, Lucy 1924- .......................................... *10*
Parr, Todd ................................................... *134*

Parrish, Anne 1888-1957 .............................. 27
Parrish, Mary
See Cousins, Margaret
Parrish, Maxfield
See Parrish, (Frederick) Maxfield
Parrish, (Frederick) Maxfield 1870-1966 .... 14
Parry, Marian 1924- ................................. 13
Parson Lot
See Kingsley, Charles
Parsons, Alexandra 1947- ........................... 92
Parsons, Ellen
See Dragonwagon, Crescent
Parsons, Martin (Leslie) 1951- ................ 116
Parsons-Yazzi, Evangeline ......................... 172
Partch, Virgil Franklin II 1916-1984 .......... 39
Obituary ............................................... 39
Parton, Dolly 1946- .................................. 94
Parton, Dolly Rebecca
See Parton, Dolly
Partridge, Benjamin W., Jr. 1915-2005 ....... 28
Obituary ............................................. 163
Partridge, Benjamin Waring, Jr.
See Partridge, Benjamin W., Jr.
Partridge, Cora Cheney
See Cheney, Cora
Partridge, Elizabeth .............................. 134
Partridge, Jenny (Lilian) 1947- ................. 52
Brief entry ........................................... 37
Pasachoff, Naomi 1947- ........................... 147
Pascal, David 1918- ................................. 14
Pascal, Francine 1938- ............................ 143
Brief entry ........................................... 37
Earlier sketches in SATA 51, 80
See also CLR 25
Paschal, Nancy
See Trotter, Grace V(iolet)
Paschkis, Julie 1957- .............................. 177
Pascudniak, Pascal
See Lupoff, Richard A(llen)
Pashko, Stanley 1913-1982 ....................... 29
Passailaigue, Thomas E.
See Paisley, Tom
Pateman, Robert 1954- ............................. 84
Patent, Dorothy Hinshaw 1940- ................ 162
Autobiography Feature ........................... 162
Earlier sketches in SATA 22, 69, 120
See also CLR 19
See also SAAS 13
Paterson, A(ndrew) B(arton) 1864-1941 ..... 97
Paterson, Banjo
See Paterson, A(ndrew) B(arton)
Paterson, Diane 1946- ............................. 177
Brief entry ........................................... 33
Earlier sketch in SATA 59
Paterson, John (Barstow) 1932- ................ 114
Paterson, Katherine 1932- ........................ 133
Earlier sketches in SATA 13, 53, 92
See also CLR 50
Paterson, Katherine Womeldorf
See Paterson, Katherine
Patience, John 1949- ................................ 90
Patneaude, David 1944- ........................... 159
Earlier sketch in SATA 85
Paton, Alan 1903-1988 .............................. 11
Obituary ............................................... 56
Paton, Alan Stewart
See Paton, Alan
Paton, Jane (Elizabeth) 1934- ................... 35
Paton, Priscilla 1952- .............................. 98
Paton Walsh, Gillian
See Paton Walsh, Jill
Paton Walsh, Jill 1937- ........................... 109
Earlier sketches in SATA 4, 72
See also CLR 65
See also SAAS 3
See Paton Walsh, Gillian
and Walsh, Jill Paton
Patrick, Susan
See Clark, Patricia Denise
Patron, Susan 1948- ................................. 76

Patsauq, Markoosie 1942-
See CLR 23
Patschke, Steve 1955- ............................. 125
Patten, Brian 1946- ................................. 152
Earlier sketch in SATA 29
Patterson, Charles 1935- ........................... 59
Patterson, Geoffrey 1943- .......................... 54
Brief entry ........................................... 44
Patterson, James 1947- ............................ 164
Patterson, James B.
See Patterson, James
Patterson, Lillie G. -1999 ......................... 88
Earlier sketch in SATA 14
Patterson, Nancy Ruth 1944- ..................... 148
Earlier sketch in SATA 72
Pattison, Darcy (S.) 1954- ........................ 126
Earlier sketch in SATA 72
Pattou, Edith ....................................... 164
Patz (Blaustein), Nancy ........................... 154
Paul, Aileen 1917- .................................. 12
Paul, Ann Whitford 1941- ......................... 168
Earlier sketches in SATA 76, 110
Paul, Elizabeth
See Crow, Donna Fletcher
Paul, Hamish Vigne Christie 1951- ............ 151
See also CLR 87
Paul, James 1936- ................................... 23
Paul, Korky
See Paul, Hamish Vigne Christie
Paul, Robert
See Roberts, John G(aither)
Paul, Tessa 1944- ................................... 103
Pauli, Hertha (Ernestine) 1909-1973 ............ 3
Obituary ............................................... 26
Paull, Grace A. 1898- .............................. 24
Paulsen, Gary 1939- ............................... 158
Earlier sketches in SATA 22, 50, 54, 79, 111
See also CLR 82
Paulson, Jack
See Jackson, C(aary) Paul
Pauquet, Gina Ruck
See Ruck-Pauquet, Gina
Pausacker, Jenny 1948- ............................ 72
See also SAAS 23
Pausewang, Gudrun 1928- ......................... 165
Earlier sketch in SATA 104
Pavel, Frances 1907- ................................ 10
Paver, Michelle ..................................... 170
Paxton, Tom .......................................... 70
See Paxton, Thomas R.
Payne, Alan
See Jakes, John
Payne, Bernal C., Jr. 1941- ....................... 60
Payne, C. D. 1949- ................................. 133
Payne, Donald Gordon 1924- ...................... 37
Payne, Emmy
See West, Emily Govan
Payne, Nina ........................................... 135
Payne, Rachel Ann
See Jakes, John
Payson, Dale 1943- .................................... 9
Payzant, Charles ..................................... 18
Paz, A.
See Pahz, James Alon
Paz, Zan
See Pahz, Cheryl Suzanne
Peace, Mary
See Finley, Mary Peace
Peake, Mervyn 1911-1968 .......................... 23
Peale, Norman Vincent 1898-1993 ............... 20
Obituary ............................................... 78
Pearce, Jacqueline 1962- .......................... 146
Pearce, Margaret ................................... 104
Peare, Catherine Owens 1911- ..................... 9
Pearson, Gayle 1947- .............................. 119
Earlier sketch in SATA 53
Pearson, Kit 1947- ................................... 77
Autobiography Feature ........................... 117
See also CLR 26
Pearson, Mary E. 1955- ........................... 134

Pearson, Susan 1946- .............................. 166
Brief entry ........................................... 27
Earlier sketches in SATA 39, 91
Pearson, Tracey Campbell 1956- ............... 155
Earlier sketch in SATA 64
Pease, (Clarence) Howard 1894-1974 ........... 2
Obituary ............................................... 25
Peavy, Linda 1943- .................................. 54
Peck, Anne Merriman 1884-1976 ................ 18
Peck, Beth 1957- ..................................... 79
Peck, Jan ............................................ 159
Peck, Jeanie J. 1967- .............................. 147
Peck, Marshall III 1951- ........................... 92
Peck, Richard 1934- ................................ 158
Autobiography Feature ........................... 110
Earlier sketches in SATA 18, 55, 97, 110
See also CLR 15
See also SAAS 2
Peck, Richard Wayne
See Peck, Richard
Peck, Robert Newton 1928- ....................... 156
Autobiography Feature ........................... 108
Earlier sketches in SATA 21, 62, 111
See also CLR 45
See also SAAS 1
Peck, Sylvia 1953- .................................. 133
Peck-Whiting, Jeanie J.
See Peck, Jeanie J.
Pederson, Sharleen
See Collicott, Sharleen
Peebles, Anne
See Galloway, Priscilla
Peek, Merle 1938- ................................... 39
Peel, John 1954- ...................................... 79
Peel, Norman Lemon
See Hirsch, Phil
Peeples, Edwin A(ugustus, Jr.) 1915-1994 .... 6
Peers, Judi 1956- ................................... 119
Peers, Judith May West
See Peers, Judi
Peet, Bill
See CLR 12
See Peet, William Bartlett
Peet, Creighton B. 1899-1977 ..................... 30
Peet, Mal ............................................ 171
Peet, Malcolm
See Peet, Mal
Peet, William Bartlett 1915-2002 ............... 78
Obituary ............................................. 137
Earlier sketches in SATA 2, 41
See Peet, Bill
Peguero, Leone ..................................... 116
Pelaez, Jill 1924- ................................... 12
Pelham, David 1938- ................................ 70
Pell, Ed(ward) 1950- .............................. 157
Pellowski, Anne 1933- .............................. 20
Pellowski, Michael (Joseph) 1949- ............ 151
Brief entry ........................................... 48
Earlier sketch in SATA 88
Pellowski, Michael Morgan
See Pellowski, Michael (Joseph)
Pelta, Kathy 1928- ................................... 18
Peltier, Leslie C(opus) 1900-1980 ............... 13
Pemberton, John Leigh
See Leigh-Pemberton, John
Pembury, Bill
See Groom, Arthur William
Pemsteen, Hans
See Manes, Stephen
Pendennis, Arthur Esquir
See Thackeray, William Makepeace
Pender, Lydia Podger 1907- ....................... 61
Pendery, Rosemary (Schmitz) ...................... 7
Pendle, Alexy 1943- ................................. 29
Pendleton, Don
See Cunningham, Chet
and Garside, (Clifford) Jack
and Jagninski, Tom
and Krauzer, Steven M(ark)
and Obstfeld, Raymond
Pendziwol, Jean E. 1965- ......................... 177

Pene du Bois, William (Sherman) 1916-1993
..................................................... *68*
  Obituary ...................................... *74*
  Earlier sketch in SATA *4*
  *See also* CLR *1*
Penn, Ruth Bonn
  *See* Rosenberg, Eth(el) Clifford
Pennac, Daniel 1944- ................................. *155*
Pennage, E. M.
  *See* Finkel, George (Irvine)
Penner, Fred 1946- ................................. *169*
  Earlier sketch in SATA *67*
Penner, Frederick Ralph Cornelius
  *See* Penner, Fred
Penney, Grace Jackson 1904-2000 .............. *35*
Penney, Ian 1960- ............................... *76*
Penney, Sue 1957- ............................... *152*
  Earlier sketch in SATA *102*
Pennington, Eunice 1923- ..................... *27*
Pennington, Lillian Boyer 1904- ............. *45*
Penrose, Gordon 1925- ........................ *66*
Penson, Mary E. 1917- ......................... *78*
Penzler, Otto 1942- ............................. *38*
Pepe, Phil 1935- ................................. *20*
Pepe, Philip
  *See* Pepe, Phil
Peppe, Rodney (Darrell) 1934- .................. *74*
  Earlier sketch in SATA *4*
  *See also* SAAS *10*
Percy, Charles Henry
  *See* Smith, Dorothy Gladys
Percy, Rachel 1930- ............................ *63*
Perdrizet, Marie-Pierre 1952- ................. *79*
Perenyi, Constance 1954- ..................... *93*
Perenyi, Constance Marie
  *See* Perenyi, Constance
Perera, Hilda 1926- ............................ *105*
Perera, Thomas Biddle 1938- ................. *13*
Peretti, Frank E. 1951- ......................... *141*
  Earlier sketch in SATA *80*
Perez, Lana
  *See* Perez, Marlene
Perez, Marlene ................................... *170*
Perkins, Al(bert Rogers) 1904-1975 .......... *30*
Perkins, Lucy Fitch 1865-1937 ............... *72*
Perkins, Lynne Rae ............................. *172*
  Earlier sketch in SATA *131*
Perkins, (Richard) Marlin 1905-1986 ........ *21*
  Obituary ....................................... *48*
Perkins, Mitali 1963- .......................... *88*
Perks, Anne-Marie 1955- ..................... *122*
Perl, Lila ......................................... *72*
  Earlier sketch in SATA *6*
Perl, Susan 1922-1983 ......................... *22*
  Obituary ....................................... *34*
Perlmutter, O(scar) William 1920-1975 ....... *8*
Pernu, Dennis 1970- ........................... *87*
Perrault, Charles 1628-1703 ................... *25*
  *See also* CLR *79*
Perret, Gene (Richard) 1937- ................. *76*
Perrine, Mary 1913-1976 ...................... *2*
Perrins, Lesley 1953- .......................... *56*
Perrow, Angeli 1954- .......................... *121*
Perry, Andrea 1956- ........................... *148*
Perry, Barbara Fisher
  *See* Fisher, Barbara
Perry, Elizabeth 1959- ........................ *174*
Perry, Elizabeth Goodwin
  *See* Perry, Elizabeth
Perry, Marie Fritz ............................. *165*
Perry, Patricia 1949- .......................... *30*
Perry, Phyllis J(ean) 1933- .................. *152*
  Earlier sketches in SATA *60, 101*
Perry, Ritchie (John Allen) 1942- ............ *105*
Perry, Roger 1933- ............................ *27*
Perry, Steve(n Carl) 1947- ................... *76*
Pershall, Mary K. 1951- ...................... *172*
  Earlier sketch in SATA *70*
Pershing, Marie
  *See* Schultz, Pearle Henriksen
Perske, Robert 1927- ......................... *57*

Persun, Morgan Reed
  *See* Watkins, Dawn L.
Petach, Heidi ................................... *149*
Peter
  *See* Stratemeyer, Edward L.
Peters, Alexander
  *See* Hollander, Zander
Peters, Andrew Fusek 1965- .................. *169*
  Earlier sketch in SATA *107*
Peters, Caroline
  *See* Betz, Eva Kelly
Peters, David 1954- ........................... *72*
Peters, Elizabeth
  *See* Mertz, Barbara
Peters, Emma
  *See* Price, Karen
Peters, Gabriel
  *See* Matott, Justin
Peters, Julie Anne 1952- ..................... *128*
  Earlier sketch in SATA *82*
Peters, Linda
  *See* Catherall, Arthur
Peters, Lisa Westberg 1951- ................. *161*
  Earlier sketches in SATA *74, 115*
Peters, Patricia 1953- ........................ *84*
Peters, Russell M. 1929- ..................... *78*
Peters, S. H.
  *See* Porter, William Sydney
  and Proffitt, Nicholas
Petersen, David 1946- ........................ *109*
  Earlier sketch in SATA *62*
Petersen, Gwenn Boardman 1924- ......... *61*
  *See* Boardman, Gwenn R.
Petersen, P(eter) J(ames) 1941- ............. *118*
  Brief entry ................................... *43*
  Earlier sketches in SATA *48, 83*
Petersen, Palle 1943- ......................... *85*
Petersham, Maud (Sylvia Fuller) 1890-1971
..................................................... *17*
  *See also* CLR *24*
Petersham, Miska 1888-1960 ................. *17*
  *See also* CLR *24*
Peterson, Cris 1952- .......................... *174*
  Earlier sketches in SATA *84, 145*
Peterson, Dawn 1934- ........................ *86*
Peterson, Esther (Allen) 1934- .............. *35*
Peterson, Hans 1922- ......................... *8*
Peterson, Harold L(eslie) 1922-1978 ....... *8*
Peterson, Helen Stone 1910- ................. *8*
Peterson, Jean Sunde 1941- ................. *108*
Peterson, Jeanne Whitehouse 1939- ........ *159*
  *See* Whitehouse, Jeanne
Peterson, Kathleen B. 1951- ................. *119*
Peterson, Lorraine 1940- ..................... *56*
  Brief entry ................................... *44*
Peterson, Shelley 1952- ...................... *146*
Petie, Haris ................................... *10*
  *See* Petty, Roberta
Petricic, Dusan 1946- ........................ *176*
Petrides, Heidrun 1944- ...................... *19*
Petrie, Catherine 1947- ...................... *52*
  Brief entry ................................... *41*
Petroski, Catherine (Ann Groom) 1939- ..... *48*
Petrovich, Michael B(oro) 1922- ............ *40*
Petrovskaya, Kyra
  *See* Wayne, Kyra Petrovskaya
Petruccio, Steven James 1961- .............. *67*
Petry, Ann (Lane) 1908-1997 ................. *5*
  Obituary ...................................... *94*
  *See also* CLR *12*
Pettit, Jayne 1932- ........................... *108*
Pevsner, Stella ............................... *131*
  Earlier sketches in SATA *8, 77*
  *See also* SAAS *14*
Peyo
  *See* Culliford, Pierre
Peyton, K. M.
  *See* CLR *3*
  *See also* SAAS *17*
  *See* Peyton, Kathleen Wendy (Herald)

Peyton, Kathleen Wendy (Herald) 1929- .. *157*
  Earlier sketches in SATA *15, 62*
  *See* Peyton, K. M.
Pfanner, (Anne) Louise 1955- ............... *68*
Pfeffer, Susan Beth 1948- .................... *83*
  Earlier sketch in SATA *4*
  *See also* CLR *11*
  *See also* SAAS *17*
Pfeffer, Wendy 1929- ......................... *142*
  Earlier sketch in SATA *78*
Pfeiffer, Janet (B.) 1949- .................... *96*
Pfister, Marcus ............................... *150*
  Earlier sketch in SATA *83*
  *See also* CLR *42*
Pfitsch, Patricia Curtis 1948- ............... *148*
Pflieger, Pat 1955- ........................... *84*
Pham, LeUyen 1973- .......................... *175*
Phelan, Mary Kay 1914- ...................... *3*
Phelan, Matt 1970- ........................... *172*
Phelan, Terry Wolfe 1941- ................... *56*
Phelps, Ethel Johnston 1914-1984 .......... *35*
Philbrick, Rodman 1951- ..................... *163*
  Earlier sketch in SATA *122*
  *See* Philbrick, W. R.
Philbrick, W. R. ............................... *163*
  *See* Philbrick, Rodman
Philbrick, W. Rodman
  *See* Philbrick, Rodman
Philbrook, Clem(ent E.) 1917- ............... *24*
Phillips, Aileen Paul
  *See* Paul, Aileen
Phillips, Betty Lou
  *See* Phillips, Elizabeth Louise
Phillips, Bob 1940- ........................... *95*
Phillips, Douglas A. 1949- ................... *161*
Phillips, Elizabeth Louise ................... *58*
  Brief entry ................................... *48*
Phillips, Irv(ing W.) 1905-2000 ............. *11*
  Obituary ...................................... *125*
Phillips, Jack
  *See* Sandburg, Carl (August)
Phillips, Leon
  *See* Gerson, Noel Bertram
Phillips, Loretta (Hosey) 1893-1987 ......... *10*
Phillips, Louis 1942- ......................... *102*
  Earlier sketch in SATA *8*
Phillips, Mary Geisler 1881-1964 ........... *10*
Phillips, Michael
  *See* Nolan, William F(rancis)
Phillips, (Woodward) Prentice 1894-1981 .. *10*
Phillpotts, Eden 1862-1960 .................. *24*
Phin
  *See* Thayer, Ernest Lawrence
Phipson, Joan
  *See* CLR *5*
  *See also* SAAS *3*
  *See* Fitzhardinge, Joan Margaret
Phiz
  *See* Browne, Hablot Knight
Phleger, Fred B. 1909-1993 .................. *34*
Phleger, Marjorie Temple 1908(?)-1986 ....... *1*
  Obituary ...................................... *47*
Piatti, Celestino 1922- ....................... *16*
Picard, Barbara Leonie 1917- ................ *89*
  Earlier sketch in SATA *2*
  *See also* SAAS *10*
Pichon, Liz ................................... *174*
Pickard, Charles 1932- ....................... *36*
Pickering, James Sayre 1897-1969 .......... *36*
  Obituary ...................................... *28*
Pickering, Robert B. 1950- ................... *93*
Pielichaty, Helena 1955- ..................... *142*
Pienkowski, Jan (Michal) 1936- ............. *131*
  Earlier sketches in SATA *6, 58*
  *See also* CLR *6*
Pierce, Edith Gray 1893-1977 ............... *45*
Pierce, Katherine
  *See* St. John, Wylly Folk

Pierce, Meredith Ann 1958- ..................... 127
  Brief entry .................................. 48
  Earlier sketch in SATA 67
  See also CLR 20
Pierce, Ruth (Ireland) 1936- ..................... 5
Pierce, Sharon
  See McCullough, Sharon Pierce
Pierce, Tamora 1954- ............................ 153
  Brief entry .................................. 49
  Earlier sketches in SATA 51, 96
Pierik, Robert 1921- ............................. 13
Piers, Robert
  See Anthony, Piers
Pig, Edward
  See Gorey, Edward (St. John)
Pike, Bob
  See Pike, Robert W(ilson)
Pike, Christopher
  See McFadden, Kevin Christopher
Pike, Deborah 1951- .............................. 89
Pike, E(dgar) Royston 1896-1980 ............... 22
  Obituary ..................................... 56
Pike, R. William 1956- ........................... 92
Pike, Robert W(ilson) 1931- ..................... 102
Pilarski, Laura 1926- ............................ 13
Pilgrim, Anne
  See Allan, Mabel Esther
Pilkey, Dav 1966- ............................... 166
  Earlier sketches in SATA 68, 115
  See also CLR 48
Pilkey, David Murray, Jr.
  See Pilkey, Dav
Pilkington, Francis Meredyth 1907- ............. 4
Pilkington, Roger (Windle) 1915-2003 ....... 10
  Obituary .................................... 144
Pincus, Harriet 1938- ............................ 27
Pinczes, Elinor J(ane) 1940- ..................... 81
Pine, Nicholas 1951- ............................. 91
Pine, Tillie S(chloss) 1896-1999 ................. 13
Pini, Richard (Alan) 1950- ....................... 89
Pini, Wendy 1951- ................................ 89
Pinkett, Jada
  See Smith, Jada Pinkett
Pinkney, Andrea Davis 1963- .................... 160
  Earlier sketch in SATA 113
Pinkney, (Jerry) Brian 1961- .................... 148
  Earlier sketch in SATA 74
  See also CLR 54
Pinkney, Gloria Jean 1941- ....................... 85
Pinkney, J. Brian
  See Pinkney, (Jerry) Brian
Pinkney, Jerry 1939- ............................ 151
  Brief entry .................................. 32
  Earlier sketches in SATA 41, 71, 107
  See also CLR 43
  See also SAAS 12
Pinkney, John ............................... 97
Pinkney, Sandra L. .......................... 128
Pinkwater, D. Manus
  See Pinkwater, Daniel Manus
Pinkwater, Daniel
  See Pinkwater, Daniel Manus
Pinkwater, Daniel M.
  See Pinkwater, Daniel Manus
Pinkwater, Daniel Manus 1941- ............. 158
  Earlier sketches in SATA 8, 46, 76, 114
  See also CLR 4
  See also SAAS 3
Pinkwater, Manus
  See Pinkwater, Daniel Manus
Pinner, Joma
  See Werner, Herma
Pioneer
  See Yates, Raymond F(rancis)
Piowaty, Kim Kennelly 1957- .................... 49
Piper, Roger
  See Fisher, John (Oswald Hamilton)
Pirner, Connie White 1955- ...................... 72
Piro, Richard 1934- .............................. 7
Pirot, Alison Lohans
  See Lohans, Alison

Pirsig, Robert M(aynard) 1928- ................. 39
Pita
  See Rendon, Maria
Pitcher, Caroline (Nell) 1948- .................. 128
Pitre, Felix 1949- ............................... 84
Pitrone, Jean Maddern 1920- ..................... 4
Pittman, Helena Clare 1945- ..................... 71
Pitz, Henry C(larence) 1895-1976 ............... 4
  Obituary ..................................... 24
Piven, Hanoch 1963- ............................ 173
Pizer, Vernon 1918- ............................. 21
Place, Marian T(empleton) 1910- ................. 3
Place, Robin (Mary) 1926- ....................... 71
Plaidy, Jean
  See Hibbert, Eleanor Alice Burford
Plain, Belva 1919- ............................... 62
Plath, Sylvia 1932-1963 .......................... 96
Platt, Kin 1911- ................................. 86
  Earlier sketch in SATA 21
  See also SAAS 17
Platt, Randall 1948- ............................. 95
Platt, Randall Beth
  See Platt, Randall
Platt, Richard 1953- ............................ 166
  Earlier sketch in SATA 120
Playfellow, Robin
  See Ellis, Edward S(ylvester)
Playsted, James
  See Wood, James Playsted
Plecas, Jennifer 1966- .......................... 149
  Earlier sketch in SATA 84
Plimpton, George 1927-2003 ..................... 10
  Obituary .................................... 150
Plimpton, George Ames
  See Plimpton, George
Plomer, William Charles Franklin 1903-1973
  .............................................. 24
Plotz, Helen Ratnoff 1913-2000 ................. 38
Plourde, Lynn 1955- ............................ 168
  Earlier sketch in SATA 122
Plowden, David 1932- ............................ 52
Plowden, Martha Ward 1948- ..................... 98
Plowhead, Ruth Gipson 1877-1967 ............... 43
Plowman, Stephanie 1922- ......................... 6
Pluckrose, Henry (Arthur) 1931- ............... 141
  Earlier sketch in SATA 13
Plum, J.
  See Wodehouse, P(elham) G(renville)
Plum, Jennifer
  See Kurland, Michael
Plume, Ilse .................................... 170
  Brief entry .................................. 43
Plumme, Don E.
  See Katz, Bobbi
Plummer, Margaret 1911- .......................... 2
Pochocki, Ethel (Frances) 1925- ................. 76
Podendorf, Illa (E.) 1903(?)-1983 ............... 18
  Obituary ..................................... 35
Podwal, Mark 1945- ............................. 160
  Earlier sketch in SATA 101
Poe, Edgar Allan 1809-1849 ..................... 23
Poe, Ty (Christopher) 1975- ..................... 94
Pogany, William Andrew 1882-1955 ........... 44
  See Pogany, Willy
Pogany, Willy
  Brief entry .................................. 30
  See Pogany, William Andrew
Pohl, Frederik 1919- ............................ 24
Pohlmann, Lillian (Grenfell) 1902-1997 ..... 11
Pohrt, Tom 1953- ............................... 152
  Earlier sketch in SATA 67
Pointon, Robert
  See Rooke, Daphne (Marie)
Points, Larry G. 1945- ......................... 177
  Earlier sketch in SATA 133
Points, Larry Gene
  See Points, Larry G.
Pokeberry, P. J.
  See Mitchell, B(etty) J(o)
POLA
  See Watson, Pauline

Polacco, Patricia Ann 1944- .................... 123
  Earlier sketch in SATA 74
  See also CLR 40
Polatnick, Florence T. 1923- ..................... 5
Polder, Markus
  See Kruss, James
Polese, Carolyn 1947- ........................... 58
Polese, James 1914- ............................. 87
Polette, Nancy (Jane) 1930- ..................... 42
Polhamus, Jean Burt 1928- ....................... 21
Policoff, Stephen Phillip 1948- .................. 77
Polikoff, Barbara G. 1929- ...................... 162
  Earlier sketch in SATA 77
Polikoff, Barbara Garland
  See Polikoff, Barbara G.
Polisar, Barry Louis 1954- ...................... 134
  Earlier sketch in SATA 77
Politi, Leo 1908-1996 ............................ 47
  Obituary ..................................... 88
  Earlier sketch in SATA 1
  See also CLR 29
Polking, Kirk 1925- .............................. 5
Pollack, Jill S. 1963- ............................ 88
Polland, Barbara K(ay) 1939- .................... 44
Polland, Madeleine A(ngela Cahill) 1918- .. 68
  Earlier sketch in SATA 6
  See also SAAS 8
Pollema-Cahill, Phyllis 1958- ................... 123
Pollock, Bruce 1945- ............................ 46
Pollock, Mary
  See Blyton, Enid (Mary)
Pollock, Penny 1935- ........................... 137
  Brief entry .................................. 42
  Earlier sketch in SATA 44
Pollowitz, Melinda Kilborn 1944- ............... 26
Polner, Murray 1928- ............................ 64
Polonsky, Arthur 1925- .......................... 34
Polseno, Jo .................................... 17
Pomaska, Anna 1946- ........................... 117
Pomerantz, Charlotte 1930- ..................... 177
  Earlier sketches in SATA 20, 80
Pomeroy, Pete
  See Roth, Arthur J(oseph)
Pond, Alonzo W(illiam) 1894-1986 ............... 5
Pontiflet, Ted 1932- ............................ 32
Poole, Gray Johnson 1906- ....................... 1
Poole, Josephine .................................. 5
  See also SAAS 2
  See Helyar, Jane Penelope Josephine
Poole, (Jane Penelope) Josephine
  See Helyar, Jane Penelope Josephine
Poole, Lynn 1910-1969 ............................ 1
Poole, Peggy 1925- .............................. 39
Poortvliet, Rien 1932- ........................... 65
  Brief entry .................................. 37
Pope, Elizabeth Marie 1917- ..................... 38
  Brief entry .................................. 36
Popescu, Christine
  See Pullein-Thompson, Christine
Poploff, Michelle 1956- .......................... 67
Popp, K. Wendy ................................. 91
Poppel, Hans 1942- .............................. 71
Portal, Colette 1936- ............................. 6
Porte, Barbara Ann 1943- ....................... 152
  Brief entry .................................. 45
  Earlier sketches in SATA 57, 93
Porter, A(nthony) P(eyton) 1945- ............... 68
Porter, Connie (Rose) 1959(?)- ................. 129
  Earlier sketch in SATA 81
Porter, Donald Clayton
  See Gerson, Noel Bertram
Porter, Eleanor H(odgman) 1868-1920
  See CLR 110
Porter, Gene(va Grace) Stratton
  See Stratton-Porter, Gene(va Grace)
Porter, Janice Lee 1953- ....................... 108
  Earlier sketch in SATA 68
Porter, Katherine Anne 1890-1980 ............... 39
  Obituary ..................................... 23
Porter, Kathryn
  See Swinford, Betty (June Wells)

Porter, Sheena 1935- ..................... 24
See also SAAS 10
Porter, Sue
See Limb, Sue
Porter, Sue 1951- ............................. 76
Porter, William Sydney 1862-1910
See YABC 2
See Henry, O.
Porto, Tony 1960- ............................. 153
Posell, Elsa Z(eigerman) -1995 .............. 3
Posten, Margaret L(ois) 1915- ............... 10
Posthuma, Sieb 1960- ......................... 150
Potok, Chaim 1929-2002 ...................... 106
Obituary ..................................... 134
Earlier sketch in SATA 33
See also CLR 92
Potok, Herbert Harold -2002
See Potok, Chaim
Potok, Herman Harold
See Potok, Chaim
Potter, Beatrix 1866-1943 ................... 132
Earlier sketch in SATA 100
See also YABC 1
See also CLR 73
Potter, Giselle ............................... 150
Potter, Helen Beatrix
See Potter, Beatrix
Potter, Margaret (Newman) 1926-1998 ....... 21
Obituary ..................................... 104
See Betteridge, Anne
Potter, Marian 1915- .......................... 9
Potter, Miriam Clark 1886-1965 ............... 3
Poulin, Stephane 1961- ....................... 98
See also CLR 28
Poulton, Kimberly 1957(?)- ................... 136
Pournelle, Jerry (Eugene) 1933- .............. 161
Earlier sketches in SATA 26, 91
Povelite, Kay 1955- .......................... 102
Pow, Tom 1950- ................................ 163
Powe-Allred, Alexandra
See Allred, Alexandra Powe
Powell, A. M.
See Morgan, Alfred P(owell)
Powell, Consie ................................ 174
Powell, E. Sandy 1947- ........................ 72
Powell, E.S.
See Powell, E. Sandy
Powell, Pamela 1960- .......................... 78
Powell, Patricia Hruby 1966- ................. 136
Powell, Randy 1956- ........................... 118
Powell, Richard Stillman
See Barbour, Ralph Henry
Powell, Robert (Stephenson Smyth) Baden
See Baden-Powell, Robert (Stephenson Smyth)
Powell, Stephanie 1953- ....................... 93
Power, Margaret (M.) 1945- ................... 125
Earlier sketch in SATA 75
Powers, Anne
See Schwartz, Anne Powers
Powers, Bill 1931- ............................ 52
Brief entry ................................... 31
Powers, Daniel 1959- .......................... 164
Powers, Margaret
See Heal, Edith
Powers, Tim 1952- ............................. 107
Powers, Timothy Thomas
See Powers, Tim
Powledge, Fred 1935- .......................... 37
Poynter, Margaret 1927- ....................... 27
Prachaticka, Marketa
See Kolibalova, Marketa
Prachatika, Marketa
See Kolibalova, Marketa
Prager, Arthur ............................... 44
Prager, Ellen J. 1962- ....................... 136
Prange, Beckie ............................... 172
Prap, Lila 1955- ............................. 177
Pratchett, Terry 1948- ....................... 139
Earlier sketch in SATA 82
See also CLR 64

Prater, John 1947- ............................ 149
Earlier sketches in SATA 72, 103
Pratt, (Murray) Fletcher 1897-1956 .......... 102
Pratt, Kristin Joy 1976- ...................... 87
Pratt, Pierre 1962- ........................... 166
Earlier sketch in SATA 95
Preiss, Byron 1953-2005 ...................... 166
Brief entry ................................... 42
Earlier sketch in SATA 47
Preiss, Byron Cary
See Preiss, Byron
Preller, James 1961- .......................... 88
Prelutsky, Jack 1940- ......................... 171
Earlier sketches in SATA 22, 66, 118
See also CLR 115
Prentice, Amy
See Kaler, James Otis
Prescott, Casey
See Morris, Chris(topher Crosby)
Presnall, Judith (Ann) Janda 1943- .......... 96
Pressler, Mirjam 1940- ....................... 155
Preston, Douglas 1956- ....................... 113
Preston, Edna Mitchell ....................... 40
Preston, Lillian Elvira 1918- ................ 47
Preussler, Otfried 1923- ...................... 24
Price, Beverley Joan 1931- ................... 98
Price, Christine (Hilda) 1928-1980 ........... 3
Obituary ..................................... 23
Price, Jennifer
See Hoover, Helen (Drusilla Blackburn)
Price, Joan 1931- ............................. 124
Price, Jonathan (Reeve) 1941- ................. 46
Price, Karen 1957- ........................... 125
Price, Kathy Z. 1957- ......................... 172
Price, Lucie Locke
See Locke, Lucie
Price, Olive 1903-1991 ......................... 8
Price, Susan 1955- ........................... 128
Earlier sketches in SATA 25, 85
Price, Willard 1887-1983 ...................... 48
Brief entry ................................... 38
Price-Groff, Claire .......................... 127
Priceman, Marjorie 1958- ..................... 168
Earlier sketches in SATA 81, 120
Prichard, Katharine Susannah 1883-1969 ... 66
Prideaux, Tom 1908-1993 ....................... 37
Obituary ..................................... 76
Priestley, Alice 1962- ........................ 95
Priestley, Lee (Shore) 1904-1999 ............. 27
Priestly, Doug 1954- .......................... 122
Priestly, Douglas Michael
See Priestly, Doug
Prieto, Mariana Beeching 1912-1999 ........... 8
Primavera, Elise 1954- ....................... 109
Brief entry ................................... 48
Earlier sketch in SATA 58
Prime, Derek (James) 1931- .................... 34
Prince, Alison (Mary) 1931- ................... 86
Earlier sketch in SATA 28
Prince, J(ack) H(arvey) 1908- ................. 17
Prince, Maggie ............................... 102
Pringle, Eric ................................ 138
Pringle, Laurence P(atrick) 1935- ............ 154
Earlier sketches in SATA 4, 68, 104
See also CLR 57
See also SAAS 6
Prinz, Yvonne 1960- ........................... 175
Prior, Natalie Jane 1963- .................... 106
Pritchett, Elaine H(illyer) 1920- ............. 36
Pritts, Kim Derek 1953- ....................... 83
Prochazkova, Iva 1953- ........................ 68
Proctor, Everitt
See Montgomery, Rutherford George
Proeysen, Alf 1914-1970
See CLR 24
See Proysen, Alf
Professor Scribbler
See Hollingsworth, Mary
Proimos, James 1955- ......................... 173
Prose, Francine 1947- ......................... 149
Earlier sketch in SATA 101

Provensen, Alice 1918- ....................... 147
Earlier sketches in SATA 9, 70
See also CLR 11
Provensen, Martin (Elias) 1916-1987 ......... 70
Obituary ..................................... 51
Earlier sketch in SATA 9
See also CLR 11
Provenzo, Eugene (F., Jr.) 1949- ............. 142
Earlier sketch in SATA 78
Provost, Gail Levine 1944- .................... 65
Provost, Gary (Richard) 1944-1995 ............ 66
Proysen, Alf ................................. 67
See Proeysen, Alf
Pruett, Candace (J.) 1968- ................... 157
Pryor, Bonnie H. 1942- ....................... 69
Pryor, Boori (Monty) 1950- .................. 112
Pryor, Helen Brenton 1897-1972 ............... 4
Pryor, Michael 1957- ......................... 153
Pucci, Albert John 1920- ..................... 44
Pudney, John (Sleigh) 1909-1977 ............. 24
Pugh, Ellen (Tiffany) 1920- ................... 7
Pullein-Thompson, Christine 1925-2005 ..... 82
Obituary ..................................... 172
Earlier sketch in SATA 3
Pullein-Thompson, Diana ....................... 3
See Farr, Diana (Pullein-Thompson)
Pullein-Thompson, Josephine (Mary
Wedderburn) .................................. 82
Earlier sketch in SATA 3
Pullman, Philip 1946- ........................ 150
Earlier sketches in SATA 65, 103
See also CLR 84
See also SAAS 17
Pullman, Philip Nicholas
See Pullman, Philip
Pulver, Harry, Jr. 1960- ..................... 129
Pulver, Robin 1945- .......................... 133
Earlier sketch in SATA 76
Puner, Helen W(alker) 1915-1989 .............. 37
Obituary ..................................... 63
Purdy, Carol 1943- ........................... 120
Earlier sketch in SATA 66
Purdy, Susan G(old) 1939- ..................... 8
Purmell, Ann 1953- ........................... 147
Purnell, Idella 1901-1982 .................... 120
Purscell, Phyllis 1934- ....................... 7
Purtill, Richard L. 1931- ..................... 53
Pushker, Gloria 1927- ........................ 162
Earlier sketch in SATA 75
Pushker, Gloria Teles
See Pushker, Gloria
Pushkin, Aleksandr Sergeevich
See Pushkin, Alexander (Sergeyevich)
Pushkin, Alexander (Sergeyevich) 1799-1837
............................................. 61
See Pushkin, Aleksandr Sergeevich
Putnam, Alice 1916- .......................... 61
Putnam, Arthur Lee
See Alger, Horatio, Jr.
Putnam, Peter B(rock) 1920-1998 .............. 30
Obituary ..................................... 106
Pyle, Howard 1853-1911 ....................... 100
Earlier sketch in SATA 16
See also CLR 117
Pyle, Katharine 1863-1938 .................... 66
Pyne, Mable Mandeville 1903-1969 ............. 9
Pyrnelle, Louise-Clarke 1850-1907 ........... 114

# Q

Quackenbush, Robert M(ead) 1929- ......... 133
Autobiography Feature ....................... 133
Earlier sketches in SATA 7, 70
See also CLR 122
See also SAAS 7
Qualey, Marsha 1953- ......................... 124
Earlier sketch in SATA 79
Qualls, Sean ................................. 177
Quammen, David 1948- .......................... 7

Quark, Jason
    See Eldin, Peter
Quarles, Benjamin (Arthur) 1904-1996 ....... *12*
Quatermass, Martin
    See Carpenter, John (Howard)
Quattlebaum, Mary 1958- ......................... *134*
    Earlier sketch in SATA *88*
Quay, Emma ............................................. *173*
    Earlier sketch in SATA *119*
Queen, Ellery
    See Deming, Richard
    and Dannay, Frederic
    and Davidson, Avram (James)
    and Fairman, Paul W.
    and Flora, Fletcher
    and Hoch, Edward D(entinger)
    and Kane, Henry
    and Lee, Manfred B.
    and Marlowe, Stephen
    and Powell, (Oval) Talmage
    and Sheldon, Walter J(ames)
    and Sturgeon, Theodore (Hamilton)
    and Tracy, Don(ald Fiske)
    and Vance, Jack
Queen, Ellery, Jr.
    See Dannay, Frederic
    and Holding, James (Clark Carlisle, Jr.)
    and Lee, Manfred B.
Quennell, Marjorie Courtney 1884-1972 .... *29*
Quentin, Brad
    See Bisson, Terry
Quest, (Edna) Olga W(ilbourne) Hall
    See Hall-Quest, (Edna) Olga W(ilbourne)
Quick, Annabelle 1922-1986 ........................ *2*
Quill, Monica
    See McInerny, Ralph
Quin-Harkin, Janet 1941- ......................... *165*
    Earlier sketches in SATA *18, 90, 119*
Quin-Harkin, Janet Elizabeth
    See Quin-Harkin, Janet
Quinlan, Susan E. 1954- ............................. *88*
Quinlan, Susan Elizabeth
    See Quinlan, Susan E.
Quinn, Elisabeth 1881-1962 ....................... *22*
Quinn, Pat 1947- ..................................... *130*
Quinn, Patrick 1950- ................................. *73*
Quinn, Rob 1972- ..................................... *138*
Quinn, Theodora K.
    See Kroeber, Theodora (Kracaw)
Quinn, Vernon
    See Quinn, Elisabeth
Quirk, Anne (E.) 1956- ............................... *99*
Quixley, Jim 1931- ..................................... *56*
Quyth, Gabriel
    See Jennings, Gary (Gayne)

**R**

Ra, Carol F. 1939- ..................................... *76*
Raab, Evelyn 1951- ................................... *129*
Rabe, Berniece (Louise) 1928- ................. *148*
    Autobiography Feature ........................... *148*
    Earlier sketches in SATA *7, 77*
    See also SAAS *10*
Rabe, Olive H(anson) (?)-1968 ................... *13*
Rabin, Staton 1958- ................................... *162*
    Earlier sketch in SATA *84*
Rabinowich, Ellen 1946- ............................. *29*
Rabinowitz, Sandy 1954- ............................. *52*
    Brief entry ............................................. *39*
Rachlin, Carol K(ing) 1919- ....................... *64*
Rachlin, Harvey 1951- ............................... *47*
Rachlin, Harvey Brant
    See Rachlin, Harvey
Rachlin, Nahid ......................................... *64*
Rackham, Arthur 1867-1939 ..................... *100*
    Earlier sketch in SATA *15*
    See also CLR *57*
Raczka, Bob 1963- ..................................... *163*

Radencich, Marguerite C. 1952-1998 .......... *79*
Radford, Ruby L(orraine) 1891-1971 ............ *6*
Radin, Ruth Yaffe 1938- ........................... *107*
    Brief entry ............................................. *52*
    Earlier sketch in SATA *56*
Radlauer, David 1952- ................................. *28*
Radlauer, Edward 1921- ............................. *15*
Radlauer, Ruth Shaw 1926- ......................... *98*
    Earlier sketch in SATA *15*
Radley, Gail 1951- ................................... *112*
    Earlier sketch in SATA *25*
Radunsky, Vladimir ................................... *177*
Rae, Gwynedd 1892-1977 ............................. *37*
Raebeck, Lois 1921- ..................................... *5*
Rael, Elsa Okon 1927-
    See CLR *84*
Raffi
    See Cavoukian, Raffi
Raftery, Gerald (Bransfield) 1905-1986 ...... *11*
Ragan-Reid, Gale 1956- ............................. *90*
Rahaman, Vashanti 1953- ........................... *98*
Rahn, Joan Elma 1929- ............................... *27*
Rai, Bali 1971- ....................................... *152*
Raible, Alton (Robert) 1918- ....................... *35*
Raiff, Stan 1930- ....................................... *11*
Raines, Shirley C(arol) 1945- ..................... *128*
Rainey, W. B.
    See Blassingame, Wyatt Rainey
Rake, Jody 1961- ....................................... *157*
Ralston, Jan
    See Dunlop, Agnes M. R.
Ramal, Walter
    See de la Mare, Walter (John)
Ramanujan, A(ttipat) K(rishnaswami)
    1929-1993 ............................................. *86*
Ramstad, Ralph L. 1919- ........................... *115*
Rana, Indi
    See Rana, Indira Higham
Rana, Indira Higham 1944- ......................... *82*
Ranadive, Gail 1944- ................................. *10*
Rand, Ann (Binkley) ................................... *30*
Rand, Gloria 1925- ................................... *156*
    Earlier sketch in SATA *101*
Rand, Paul 1914-1996 ................................. *6*
Randall, Carrie
    See Ransom, Candice F.
Randall, David 1972- ................................. *167*
Randall, Florence Engel 1917-1997 ............... *5*
Randall, Janet
    See Young, Janet Randall
    and Young, Robert W(illiam)
Randall, Robert
    See Garrett, (Gordon) Randall (Phillip)
    and Silverberg, Robert
Randall, Ruth (Elaine) Painter 1892-1971 .... *3*
Randell, Beverley
    See Price, Beverley Joan
Randle, Kristen D. 1952- ............................. *92*
    Autobiography Feature ........................... *119*
    See also SAAS *24*
Randle, Kristen Downey
    See Randle, Kristen D.
Randolph, Boynton M.D.
    See Ellis, Edward S(ylvester)
Randolph, Ellen
    See Rawn, Melanie
Randolph, Geoffrey
    See Ellis, Edward S(ylvester)
Randolph, J. H.
    See Ellis, Edward S(ylvester)
Randolph, Lieutenant J. H.
    See Ellis, Edward S(ylvester)
Rands, William Brighty 1823-1882 ............. *17*
Raney, Ken 1953- ..................................... *74*
Rankin, Joan 1940- ................................... *148*
    Earlier sketch in SATA *88*
Rankin, Laura 1953(?)- ............................... *176*
Ranney, Agnes V. 1916-1985 ......................... *6*
Ransom, Candice F. 1952- ........................... *135*
    Brief entry ............................................. *49*
    Earlier sketches in SATA *52, 89*

Ransome, Arthur (Michell) 1884-1967 ....... *22*
    See also CLR *8*
Ransome, James E. 1961- ........................... *123*
    Earlier sketch in SATA *76*
    See also CLR *86*
Rant, Tol E.
    See Longyear, Barry B(rookes)
Raphael, Elaine ........................................... *23*
    See Bolognese, Elaine (Raphael Chionchio)
Rapp, Adam 1968(?)- ................................. *148*
Rappaport, Doreen ..................................... *151*
Rappaport, Eva 1924- ................................... *6*
Rappoport, Ken 1935- ............................... *167*
    Earlier sketch in SATA *89*
Rarick, Carrie 1911-2002 ........................... *41*
Raschka, Chris 1959- ................................. *166*
    Earlier sketches in SATA *80, 117*
Raschka, Christopher
    See Raschka, Chris
Rascol, Sabina I. ....................................... *159*
Rash, Andy ............................................... *162*
Raskin, Edith Lefkowitz 1908-1987 ............... *9*
Raskin, Ellen 1928-1984 ........................... *139*
    Earlier sketches in SATA *2, 38*
    See also CLR *12*
Raskin, Joseph 1897-1982 ........................... *12*
    Obituary ............................................. *29*
Rathjen, Carl Henry 1909-1984 ................... *11*
Rathmann, Peggy 1953- ............................. *157*
    Earlier sketch in SATA *94*
    See Crosby, Margaret
Ratliff, Thomas M. 1948- ........................... *118*
Rattigan, Jama Kim 1951- ......................... *99*
Ratto, Linda Lee 1952- ............................... *79*
Rattray, Simon
    See Trevor, Elleston
Ratz de Tagyos, Paul 1958- ......................... *76*
Rau, Dana Meachen 1971- ......................... *167*
    Earlier sketch in SATA *94*
Rau, Margaret 1913- ................................. *168*
    Earlier sketch in SATA *9*
    See also CLR *8*
Raucher, Herman 1928- ............................... *8*
Raum, Elizabeth 1949- ............................... *155*
RavenWolf, Silver 1956- ............................. *155*
Ravielli, Anthony 1916-1997 ......................... *3*
    Obituary ............................................. *95*
Ravilious, Robin 1944- ............................... *77*
Rawding, F(rederick) W(illiam) 1930- ........ *55*
Rawlings, Marjorie Kinnan 1896-1953 ..... *100*
    See also YABC *1*
    See also CLR *63*
Rawlinson, Julia ....................................... *175*
Rawls, (Woodrow) Wilson 1913-1984 ......... *22*
    See also CLR *81*
Rawlyk, George Alexander 1935- ............... *64*
Rawn, Melanie 1954- ................................. *98*
Rawn, Melanie Robin
    See Rawn, Melanie
Ray, Carl 1943-1978 ................................... *63*
Ray, Deborah ................................................. *8*
    See Kogan Ray, Deborah
Ray, Delia 1963- ....................................... *70*
Ray, Irene
    See Sutton, Margaret Beebe
Ray, Jane 1960- ....................................... *152*
    Earlier sketch in SATA *72*
Ray, JoAnne 1935- ....................................... *9*
Ray, Mary (Eva Pedder) 1932- ................... *127*
    Earlier sketch in SATA *2*
Ray, Mary Lyn 1946- ................................. *154*
    Earlier sketch in SATA *90*
Rayban, Chloe 1944- ................................. *167*
Rayevsky, Robert 1955- ............................. *81*
Raymond, Robert
    See Alter, Robert Edmond
Rayner, Hugh ........................................... *151*
Rayner, Mary 1933- ................................... *87*
    Earlier sketch in SATA *22*
    See also CLR *41*

Rayner, Shoo
   *See* Rayner, Hugh
Rayner, William 1929- ............................. 55
   Brief entry ........................................... 36
Raynor, Dorka ......................................... 28
Rayson, Steven 1932- ............................. 30
Razzell, Arthur (George) 1925- ................ 11
Razzell, Mary (Catherine) 1930- ............. 102
Razzi, James 1931- ................................. 10
Read, Elfreida 1920- ................................. 2
Read, Nicholas 1956- ............................. 146
Read, Piers Paul 1941- ............................. 21
Reade, Deborah 1949- ............................. 69
Reader, Dennis 1929- ............................... 71
Reading, Richard P(atrick) 1962- ............. 161
Readman, Jo 1958- ................................. 89
Ready, Kirk L(ewis) 1943- ....................... 39
Reaney, James 1926- ............................... 43
Reaver, Chap 1935-1993 ......................... 69
   Obituary ............................................. 77
Reaver, Herbert R.
   *See* Reaver, Chap
Reaves, J. Michael
   *See* Reaves, (James) Michael
Reaves, (James) Michael 1950- ................. 99
Redding, Robert Hull 1919- ....................... 2
Redekopp, Elsa ....................................... 61
Redway, Ralph
   *See* Hamilton, Charles (Harold St. John)
Redway, Ridley
   *See* Hamilton, Charles (Harold St. John)
Reece, Colleen L. 1935- ......................... 116
Reece, Gabrielle 1970- ........................... 108
Reed, Betty Jane 1921- ............................. 4
Reed, E.
   *See* Evans, Mari
Reed, Gwendolyn E(lizabeth) 1932- ........... 21
Reed, Kit 1932- ..................................... 116
   Earlier sketch in SATA *34*
Reed, Lynn Rowe ................................... 171
Reed, Neil 1961- ..................................... 99
Reed, Talbot Baines 1852-1893
   *See* CLR *76*
Reed, Thomas (James) 1947- ..................... 34
Reed, William Maxwell 1871-1962 ............. 15
Reeder, Carolyn 1937- ............................. 97
   Earlier sketch in SATA *66*
   *See also* CLR *69*
Reeder, Colonel Red
   *See* Reeder, Russell P(otter), Jr.
Reeder, Russell P(otter), Jr. 1902-1998 ........ 4
   Obituary ............................................. 101
Reeder, Stephanie Owen 1951- ................. 102
Reed-Jones, Carol 1955- ......................... 112
Reef, Catherine 1951- ............................. 128
   Earlier sketch in SATA *73*
Reekie, Jocelyn (Margaret) 1947- ............. 145
Reeman, Douglas Edward 1924- ................ 63
   Brief entry ........................................... 28
Rees, Celia 1949- ................................... 124
Rees, David (Bartlett) 1936-1993 .............. 69
   Obituary ............................................. 76
   Earlier sketch in SATA *36*
   *See also* SAAS *5*
Rees, Douglas 1947- ............................. 169
Rees, Ennis (Samuel, Jr.) 1925- .................. 3
Rees, (George) Leslie (Clarence) 1905-2000
   ......................................................... 105
   Obituary ............................................. 135
Reese, Bob
   *See* Reese, Robert A.
Reese, Della 1931(?)- ............................. 114
Reese, Lyn ..................................................... 64
   *See* Reese, Carolyn Johnson
Reese, Robert A. 1938- ............................. 60
   Brief entry ........................................... 53
Reese, (John) Terence 1913-1996 ............. 59
Reeve, Joel
   *See* Cox, William R(obert)
Reeve, Kirk 1934- ................................... 117

Reeve, Philip ......................................... 170
Reeves, Faye Couch 1953- ....................... 76
Reeves, James ......................................... 15
   *See* Reeves, John Morris
Reeves, Jeni 1947- ................................. 111
Reeves, John Morris 1909-1978 ................ 87
   *See* Reeves, James
Reeves, Joyce 1911- ............................... 17
Reeves, Lawrence F. 1926- ....................... 29
Reeves, Ruth Ellen
   *See* Ranney, Agnes V.
Regan, Dian Curtis 1950- ......................... 149
   Autobiography Feature ........................... 149
   Earlier sketches in SATA *75, 133*
Regehr, Lydia 1903-1991 ......................... 37
Reger, James P. 1952- ............................. 106
Reggiani, Renee 1925- ............................. 18
Rehm, Karl M. 1935- ............................... 72
Reich, Ali
   *See* Katz, Bobbi
Reich, Susanna 1954- ............................. 113
Reiche, Dietlof 1941- ............................. 159
Reichert, Mickey Zucker
   *See* Reichert, Miriam Zucker
Reichert, Miriam Zucker 1962- ................. 85
Reichert, Renee ..................................... 172
Reichhold, Jane(t E.) 1937- ..................... 147
Reid, Alastair 1926- ............................... 46
Reid, Barbara 1922- ............................... 21
Reid, Barbara (Jane) 1957- ....................... 93
   *See also* CLR *64*
Reid, Desmond
   *See* Moorcock, Michael
   and McNeilly, Wilfred (Glassford)
Reid, Eugenie Chazal 1924- ..................... 12
Reid, John Calvin ..................................... 21
Reid, (Thomas) Mayne 1818-1883 ............. 24
Reid, Meta Mayne 1905-1991 ................... 58
   Brief entry ........................................... 36
Reid, Robin (Nicole) 1969- ....................... 145
Reid Banks, Lynne 1929- ......................... 165
   Earlier sketches in SATA *22, 75, 111*
   *See also* CLR *24*
   *See* Banks, Lynne Reid
Reider, Katja 1960- ............................... 126
Reid Jenkins, Debra 1955- ....................... 87
Reiff, Stephanie Ann 1948- ....................... 47
   Brief entry ........................................... 28
Reig, June 1933- ..................................... 30
Reigot, Betty Polisar 1924- ....................... 55
   Brief entry ........................................... 41
Reim, Melanie (K.) 1956- ......................... 104
Reinach, Jacquelyn (Krasne) 1930-2000 ..... 28
Reiner, Carl 1922- ................................. 151
Reiner, William B(uck) 1910-1976 ............. 46
   Obituary ............................................. 30
Reinfeld, Fred 1910-1964 .......................... 3
Reinhardt, Dana 1971- ........................... 175
Reinhart, Matthew ................................. 161
Reiniger, Lotte 1899-1981 ....................... 40
   Obituary ............................................. 33
Reinsma, Carol 1949- ............................. 91
Reinstedt, Randall A. 1935- ..................... 101
Reinstedt, Randy
   *See* Reinstedt, Randall A.
Reisberg, Mira 1955- ............................... 82
Reisberg, Veg
   *See* Reisberg, Mira
Reiser, Lynn (Whisnant) 1944- ................. 138
   Earlier sketch in SATA *81*
Reisgies, Teresa (Maria) 1966- ................. 74
Reiss, Johanna (de Leeuw) 1929(?)- .......... 18
   *See also* CLR *19*
Reiss, John J. ......................................... 23
Reiss, Kathryn 1957- ............................. 144
   Earlier sketch in SATA *76*
Reit, Seymour Victory 1918-2001 ............. 21
   Obituary ............................................. 133
Reit, Sy
   *See* Reit, Seymour Victory

Relf, Patricia 1954- ............................... 134
   Earlier sketch in SATA *71*
Remi, Georges 1907-1983 ....................... 13
   Obituary ............................................. 32
   *See* Herge
Remington, Frederic S(ackrider) 1861-1909
   ......................................................... 41
Remkiewicz, Frank 1939- ......................... 152
   Earlier sketch in SATA *77*
Remy, Georges
   *See* Remi, Georges
Renaud, Bernadette 1945- ....................... 66
Renault, Mary
   *See* Challans, Mary
Rendell, Joan ......................................... 28
Rendina, Laura (Jones) Cooper 1902- ........ 10
Rendon, Marcie R. 1952- ......................... 97
Rendon, Maria 1965- ............................. 116
Renee, Janina 1956- ............................... 140
Renfro, Ed 1924- ................................... 79
Renick, Marion (Lewis) 1905-1983 .............. 1
Renken, Aleda 1907- ............................... 27
Renlie, Frank H. 1936- ............................. 11
Rennert, Richard Scott 1956- ................... 67
Rennison, Louise 1951- ........................... 149
Reno, Dawn E(laine) 1953- ....................... 130
Rensie, Willis
   *See* Eisner, Will
Renton, Cam
   *See* Armstrong, Richard
Renvoize, Jean ......................................... 5
Resciniti, Angelo G. 1952- ....................... 75
Resnick, Michael David
   *See* Resnick, Mike
Resnick, Mike 1942- ............................... 159
   Earlier sketches in SATA *38, 106*
Resnick, Seymour 1920- ........................... 23
Retla, Robert
   *See* Alter, Robert Edmond
Reuter, Bjarne (B.) 1950- ......................... 142
   Earlier sketch in SATA *68*
Reuter, Carol (Joan) 1931- ........................ 2
Revena
   *See* Wright, Betty Ren
Revsbech, Vicki
   *See* Liestman, Vicki
Rey, H(ans) A(ugusto) 1898-1977 ............. 100
   Earlier sketches in SATA *1, 26, 69*
   *See also* CLR *93*
Rey, Margret (Elisabeth) 1906-1996 .......... 86
   Obituary ............................................. 93
   Earlier sketch in SATA *26*
   *See also* CLR *93*
Reyher, Becky
   *See* Reyher, Rebecca Hourwich
Reyher, Rebecca Hourwich 1897-1987 ....... 18
   Obituary ............................................. 50
Reynolds, C. Buck 1957- ......................... 107
Reynolds, John
   *See* Whitlock, Ralph
Reynolds, Madge
   *See* Whitlock, Ralph
Reynolds, Malvina 1900-1978 ................... 44
   Obituary ............................................. 24
Reynolds, Marilyn (M.) 1935- ................... 121
   *See also* SAAS *23*
Reynolds, Marilynn 1940- ......................... 141
   Earlier sketch in SATA *80*
Reynolds, Pamela 1923- ........................... 34
Reynolds, Peter H. 1961- ......................... 128
Rhine, Richard
   *See* Silverstein, Alvin
   and Silverstein, Virginia B(arbara Opshelor)
Rhoades, Diane 1952- ............................. 90
Rhodes, Bennie (Loran) 1927- ................... 35
Rhodes, Donna McKee 1962- ................... 87
Rhodes, Frank Harold Trevor 1926- ........... 37
Rhue, Morton
   *See* Strasser, Todd
Rhyne, Nancy 1926- ............................... 66
Rhynes, Martha E. 1939- ......................... 141

Ribbons, Ian 1924- ........................................ *37*
    Brief entry ................................................ *30*
    *See also* SAAS *3*
Ricciuti, Edward R(aphael) 1938- .............. *10*
Rice, Alice (Caldwell) Hegan 1870-1942 ... *63*
Rice, Bebe Faas 1932- ................................... *89*
Rice, Dale R. 1948- ...................................... *42*
Rice, Dale Richard
    *See* Rice, Dale R.
Rice, Dick
    *See* Rice, R. Hugh
Rice, Earle (Wilmont), Jr. 1928- .............. *151*
    Earlier sketch in SATA *92*
Rice, Edward 1918-2001 .............................. *47*
    Brief entry ................................................ *42*
Rice, Elizabeth 1913-1976 .............................. *2*
Rice, Eve 1951- ............................................. *91*
    Earlier sketch in SATA *34*
Rice, Eve Hart
    *See* Rice, Eve
Rice, Inez 1907- ............................................. *13*
Rice, James 1934- ......................................... *93*
    Earlier sketch in SATA *22*
Rice, John F. 1958- ........................................ *82*
Rice, R. Hugh 1929- ..................................... *115*
Rice, Richard H.
    *See* Rice, R. Hugh
Rich, Barbara
    *See* Graves, Robert
Rich, Elaine Sommers 1926- ............................. *6*
Rich, Josephine Bouchard 1912- ................ *10*
Rich, Louise Dickinson 1903-1991 ............ *54*
    Obituary .................................................... *67*
Richard, Adrienne 1921- .................................. *5*
    *See also* SAAS *9*
Richard, James Robert
    *See* Bowen, Robert Sydney
Richards, Chuck 1957- ................................ *170*
Richards, Frank
    *See* Hamilton, Charles (Harold St. John)
Richards, Hilda
    *See* Hamilton, Charles (Harold St. John)
Richards, Jackie 1925- ................................ *102*
Richards, Jean 1940- ................................... *135*
Richards, Justin ........................................... *169*
Richards, Kay
    *See* Baker, Susan (Catherine)
Richards, Laura E(lizabeth Howe) 1850-1943
    *See* YABC *1*
    *See also* CLR *54*
Richards, Norman 1932- ............................... *48*
Richards, R(onald) C(harles) W(illiam) 1923-
    ................................................................. *59*
    Brief entry ................................................ *43*
Richardson, Andrew (William) 1986- ....... *120*
Richardson, Carol 1932- ............................... *58*
Richardson, Grace Lee
    *See* Dickson, Naida
Richardson, Jean (Mary) ............................... *59*
Richardson, Judith Benet 1941- ................ *77*
Richardson, Robert S(hirley) 1902-1981 ...... *8*
Richardson, Sandy 1949- ............................ *116*
Richardson, Willis 1889-1977 ...................... *60*
Richelson, Geraldine 1922- ........................... *29*
Richemont, Enid 1940- .................................. *82*
Richler, Mordecai 1931-2001 ...................... *98*
    Brief entry ................................................ *27*
    Earlier sketch in SATA *44*
    *See also* CLR *17*
Richman, Sophia 1941- ............................... *142*
Rich-McCoy, Lois
    *See* McCoy, Lois (Rich)
Richmond, Robin 1951- ................................ *75*
Richoux, Pat(ricia) 1927- ................................ *7*
Richter, Alice 1941- ...................................... *30*
Richter, Conrad (Michael) 1890-1968 .......... *3*
Richter, Hans Peter 1925-1993 ...................... *6*
    *See also* CLR *21*
    *See also* SAAS *11*
Rickard, Graham 1949- ................................. *71*

Riddell, Chris 1962- .................................... *166*
    Earlier sketch in SATA *114*
Riddell, Christopher Barry
    *See* Riddell, Chris
Riddell, Edwina 1955- .................................. *82*
Ridden, Brian (John) 1934- ........................ *123*
Riddle, Tohby 1965- .................................... *151*
    Earlier sketch in SATA *74*
Riddles, Libby 1956- ................................... *140*
Ridge, Antonia (Florence) (?)-1981 .............. *7*
    Obituary .................................................... *27*
Ridge, Martin 1923-2003 .............................. *43*
Ridley, Philip ............................................... *171*
    Earlier sketch in SATA *88*
Ridlon, Marci ............................................... *22*
    *See* Balterman, Marcia Ridlon
Riedman, Sarah R(egal) 1902-1995 ................ *1*
Riehecky, Janet 1953- ................................. *164*
Riesenberg, Felix, Jr. 1913-1962 ................ *23*
Rieu, E(mile) V(ictor) 1887-1972 ................ *46*
    Obituary .................................................... *26*
Riffenburgh, Beau 1955- ............................. *175*
Rigg, Sharon
    *See* Creech, Sharon
Riggio, Anita 1952- ..................................... *148*
    Earlier sketch in SATA *73*
Riggs, Stephanie 1964- ................................ *138*
Rigney, James Oliver, Jr.
    *See* Jordan, Robert
Rikhoff, Jean 1928- ......................................... *9*
Rikki
    *See* Ducornet, Erica
Riley, James A. 1939- .................................. *97*
Riley, James Whitcomb 1849-1916 ............ *17*
Riley, Jocelyn 1949- .................................... *60*
    Brief entry ................................................ *50*
Riley, Jocelyn Carol
    *See* Riley, Jocelyn
Riley, Linda Capus 1950- ............................. *85*
Riley, Martin 1948- ...................................... *81*
Rimes, (Margaret) LeAnn 1982- ................ *154*
Rinaldi, Ann 1934- ...................................... *161*
    Brief entry ................................................ *50*
    Earlier sketches in SATA *51, 78, 117*
    *See also* CLR *46*
Rinard, Judith E(llen) 1947- ...................... *140*
    Earlier sketch in SATA *44*
Rinder, Lenore 1949- .................................... *92*
Ring, Elizabeth 1920- ................................... *79*
Ringdahl, Mark
    *See* Longyear, Barry B(rookes)
Ringgold, Faith 1930- ................................. *114*
    Earlier sketch in SATA *71*
    *See also* CLR *30*
Ringi, Kjell (Arne Soerensen) 1939- .......... *12*
Rinkoff, Barbara Jean (Rich) 1923-1975 ...... *4*
    Obituary .................................................... *27*
Rinn, Miriam 1946- ..................................... *127*
Riordan, James 1936- ................................... *95*
Riordan, Rick ............................................... *174*
Rios, Tere
    *See* Versace, Marie Teresa Rios
Ripken, Cal, Jr. 1960- .................................. *114*
Ripken, Calvin Edward, Jr.
    *See* Ripken, Cal, Jr.
Ripley, Catherine 1957- ............................... *82*
Ripley, Elizabeth Blake 1906-1969 ............... *5*
Ripper, Charles L(ewis) 1929- ........................ *3*
Ripper, Chuck
    *See* Ripper, Charles L(ewis)
Riq
    *See* Atwater, Richard (Tupper)
Rish, David 1955- ........................................ *110*
Riskind, Mary 1944- .................................... *60*
Rissinger, Matt 1956- ................................... *93*
Rissman, Art
    *See* Sussman, Susan
Rissman, Susan
    *See* Sussman, Susan
Ritchie, Barbara Gibbons ............................. *14*

Ritter, Felix
    *See* Kruss, James
Ritter, John H. 1951- .................................. *137*
    Earlier sketch in SATA *129*
Ritter, Lawrence S(tanley) 1922-2004 ........ *58*
    Obituary .................................................. *152*
Ritthaler, Shelly 1955- .................................. *91*
Ritz, Karen 1957- ......................................... *80*
Rivera, Geraldo (Miguel) 1943- .................. *54*
    Brief entry ................................................ *28*
Rivers, Elfrida
    *See* Bradley, Marion Zimmer
Rivers, Karen 1970- .................................... *131*
Riverside, John
    *See* Heinlein, Robert A.
Rivkin, Ann 1920- ........................................ *41*
Rivoli, Mario 1943- ...................................... *10*
Roach, Marilynne K. 1946- ............................. *9*
Roach, Marilynne Kathleen
    *See* Roach, Marilynne K.
Roach, Portia
    *See* Takakjian, Portia
Robb, Laura 1937- ........................................ *95*
Robbins, Frank 1917-1994(?) ....................... *42*
    Brief entry ................................................ *32*
Robbins, Ken 1945- .................................... *147*
    Brief entry ................................................ *53*
    Earlier sketch in SATA *94*
Robbins, Raleigh
    *See* Hamilton, Charles (Harold St. John)
Robbins, Ruth 1917(?)- ................................. *14*
Robbins, Tony
    *See* Pashko, Stanley
Robbins, Wayne
    *See* Cox, William R(obert)
Robel, S. L.
    *See* Fraustino, Lisa Rowe
Roberson, Jennifer 1953- ............................. *72*
Roberson, John R(oyster) 1930- .................. *53*
Robert, Adrian
    *See* St. John, Nicole
Roberts, Bethany ........................................ *133*
Roberts, Bruce (Stuart) 1930- ...................... *47*
    Brief entry ................................................ *39*
Roberts, Charles G(eorge) D(ouglas)
    1860-1943 ................................................. *88*
    Brief entry ................................................ *29*
    *See also* CLR *33*
Roberts, David
    *See* Cox, John Roberts
Roberts, Elizabeth 1944- .............................. *80*
Roberts, Elizabeth Madox 1886-1941 ......... *33*
    Brief entry ................................................ *27*
    *See also* CLR *100*
Roberts, Jim
    *See* Bates, Barbara S(nedeker)
Roberts, John G(aither) 1913-1993 ............. *27*
Roberts, Judy I. 1957- .................................. *93*
Roberts, Katherine 1962- ............................ *152*
Roberts, M. L.
    *See* Mattern, Joanne
Roberts, Nancy Correll 1924- ...................... *52*
    Brief entry ................................................ *28*
Roberts, Terence
    *See* Sanderson, Ivan T(erence)
Roberts, Willo Davis 1928-2004 ................ *150*
    Autobiography Feature ............................ *150*
    Obituary .................................................. *160*
    Earlier sketches in SATA *21, 70, 133*
    *See also* CLR *95*
    *See also* SAAS *8*
Robertson, Barbara (Anne) 1931- ................ *12*
Robertson, Don 1929-1999 ............................. *8*
    Obituary .................................................. *113*
Robertson, Dorothy Lewis 1912- .................. *12*
Robertson, Ellis
    *See* Ellison, Harlan
    and Silverberg, Robert
Robertson, Janet (E.) 1935- .......................... *68*
Robertson, Jennifer Sinclair 1942-1998 ...... *12*

Robertson, Jenny
See Robertson, Jennifer Sinclair
Robertson, Keith (Carlton) 1914-1991 ........ 85
Obituary ............................................................ 69
Earlier sketch in SATA 1
See also SAAS 15
Robertson, Stephen
See Walker, Robert W(ayne)
Robertus, Polly M. 1948- ............................. 73
Robeson, Kenneth
See Dent, Lester
and Goulart, Ron(ald Joseph)
Robeson, Kenneth
See Johnson, (Walter) Ryerson
Robinet, Harriette Gillem 1931- ................ 104
Earlier sketch in SATA 27
See also CLR 64
Robins, Deri 1958- ...................................... 166
Earlier sketch in SATA 117
Robins, Patricia
See Clark, Patricia Denise
Robins, Rollo, Jr.
See Ellis, Edward S(ylvester)
Robins, Seelin
See Ellis, Edward S(ylvester)
Robinson, Adjai 1932- ..................................... 8
Robinson, Aminah Brenda Lynn 1940- ..... 159
Earlier sketch in SATA 77
Robinson, Barbara (Webb) 1927- ................ 84
Earlier sketch in SATA 8
Robinson, C(harles) A(lexander), Jr. 1900-1965
.......................................................................... 36
Robinson, Charles 1870-1937 ...................... 17
Robinson, Charles 1931- ................................. 6
Robinson, Dorothy W. 1929- ........................ 54
Robinson, Eve
See Tanselle, Eve
Robinson, Glen 1953- ................................... 92
Robinson, Glendal P.
See Robinson, Glen
Robinson, Jan M. 1933- ................................. 6
Robinson, Jean O. 1934- ................................ 7
Robinson, Joan (Mary) G(ale Thomas)
1910-1988 ...................................................... 7
Robinson, Kim Stanley 1952- ................... 109
Robinson, Lee 1948- ................................... 110
Robinson, Lloyd
See Silverberg, Robert
Robinson, Lynda S(uzanne) 1951- ........... 107
Robinson, Marileta 1942- ............................. 32
Robinson, Maudie Millian Oller 1914- ....... 11
Robinson, Nancy K(onheim) 1942-1994 ..... 91
Brief entry ..................................................... 31
Obituary ......................................................... 79
Earlier sketch in SATA 32
Robinson, Ray(mond Kenneth) 1920- ......... 23
Robinson, Shari
See McGuire, Leslie (Sarah)
Robinson, Sharon 1950- .............................. 162
Robinson, Spider 1948- .............................. 118
Robinson, Sue
See Robinson, Susan Maria
Robinson, Susan Maria 1955- ................... 105
Robinson, Suzanne
See Robinson, Lynda S(uzanne)
Robinson, T(homas) H(eath) 1869-1950 ..... 17
Robinson, (Wanda) Veronica 1926- ............. 30
Robinson, W(illiam) Heath 1872-1944 ....... 17
Robison, Bonnie 1924- ................................. 12
Robison, Nancy L(ouise) 1934- ................... 32
Robles, Harold E. 1948- ............................... 87
Robottom, John 1934- ..................................... 7
Robson, Eric 1939- ....................................... 82
Roche, A. K.
See Abisch, Roslyn Kroop
and Kaplan, Boche
Roche, Denis (Mary) 1967- .......................... 99
Roche, Luane 1937- .................................... 170
Roche, P(atricia) K. 1935- ........................... 57
Brief entry ..................................................... 34

Roche, Terry
See Poole, Peggy
Rochman, Hazel 1938- ................................ 105
Rock, Lois
See Joslin, Mary
Rock, Maxine 1940- .................................... 108
Rocker, Fermin 1907- .................................... 40
Rocklin, Joanne 1946- ................................ 134
Earlier sketch in SATA 86
Rockwell, Anne F(oote) 1934- ................... 162
Earlier sketches in SATA 33, 71, 114
See also SAAS 19
Rockwell, Bart
See Pellowski, Michael (Joseph)
Rockwell, Harlow 1910-1988 ....................... 33
Obituary ......................................................... 56
Rockwell, Norman (Percevel) 1894-1978 ... 23
Rockwell, Thomas 1933- .............................. 70
Earlier sketch in SATA 7
See also CLR 6
Rockwood, Joyce 1947- ................................ 39
Rockwood, Roy ....................................................... 67
Earlier sketch in SATA 1
See McFarlane, Leslie (Charles)
and Stratemeyer, Edward L.
Rodanas, Kristina 1952- ............................. 155
Rodari, Gianni 1920-1980
See CLR 24
Rodd, Kathleen Tennant ............................... 57
Obituary ......................................................... 55
See Rodd, Kylie Tennant
Rodda, Emily 1948- .................................... 146
Earlier sketch in SATA 97
See also CLR 32
Roddenberry, Eugene Wesley 1921-1991 .... 45
Obituary ......................................................... 69
See Roddenberry, Gene
Roddenberry, Gene
Obituary ......................................................... 69
See Roddenberry, Eugene Wesley
Roddie, Shen ............................................... 153
Roddy, Lee 1921- .......................................... 57
Rodenas, Paula .............................................. 73
Rodgers, Frank 1944- ................................... 69
Rodgers, Mary 1931- .................................. 130
Earlier sketch in SATA 8
See also CLR 20
Rodman, Emerson
See Ellis, Edward S(ylvester)
Rodman, Eric
See Silverberg, Robert
Rodman, Maia
See Wojciechowska, Maia (Teresa)
Rodman, (Cary) Selden 1909-2002 ............... 9
Rodowsky, Colby 1932- .............................. 164
Earlier sketches in SATA 21, 77, 120
See also SAAS 22
Rodowsky, Colby F.
See Rodowsky, Colby
Rodriguez, Alejo 1941- ................................. 83
Rodriguez, Christina 1981- ........................ 177
Rodriguez, Luis J. 1954- ............................. 125
Roeder, Virginia Marsh 1926- ..................... 98
Roehrig, Catharine H. 1949- ........................ 67
Roennfeldt, Robert 1953- ............................. 78
Roessel-Waugh, C. C.
See Waugh, Carol-Lynn Rossel
and Waugh, Charles G(ordon)
Roets, Lois F. 1937- ..................................... 91
Roever, J(oan) M(arilyn) 1935- ................... 26
Rofes, Eric 1954-2006 .................................. 52
Rofes, Eric Edward 1954-2006
See Rofes, Eric
Roffey, Maureen 1936- ................................. 33
Rogak, Lisa 1962- ......................................... 80
Rogak, Lisa Angowski
See Rogak, Lisa
Rogasky, Barbara 1933- .............................. 144
Earlier sketch in SATA 86

Rogers, (Thomas) Alan (Stinchcombe) 1937-
.......................................................................... 81
Earlier sketch in SATA 2
Rogers, Bettye 1858-1919 .......................... 103
Rogers, Cindy 1950- ..................................... 89
Rogers, Emma 1951- ..................................... 74
Rogers, Frances 1888-1974 .......................... 10
Rogers, Fred McFeely 1928-2003 ............... 33
Obituary ....................................................... 138
Rogers, Hal
See Sirimarco, Elizabeth
Rogers, Jean 1919- ....................................... 55
Brief entry ..................................................... 47
Rogers, Matilda 1894-1976 ............................ 5
Obituary ......................................................... 34
Rogers, Pamela 1927- ..................................... 9
Rogers, Paul 1950- ........................................ 98
Earlier sketch in SATA 54
Rogers, Robert
See Hamilton, Charles (Harold St. John)
Rogers, W(illiam) G(arland) 1896-1978 ..... 23
Rohan, M. S.
See Rohan, Michael Scott
Rohan, Michael Scott 1951- ......................... 98
Rohan, Mike Scott
See Rohan, Michael Scott
Rohmann, Eric 1957- .................................. 171
See also CLR 100
Rohmer, Harriet 1938- .................................. 56
Rohrer, Doug 1962- ....................................... 89
Rojan
See Rojankovsky, Feodor (Stepanovich)
Rojankovsky, Feodor (Stepanovich) 1891-1970
.......................................................................... 21
Rojany, Lisa ................................................... 94
Rokeby-Thomas, Anna E(lma) 1911- .......... 15
Roland, Albert 1925-2002 ............................ 11
Roland, Mary
See Lewis, Mary (Christianna)
Roleff, Tamara L. 1959- ............................. 143
Rolerson, Darrell A(llen) 1946- ..................... 8
Roll, Winifred 1909-1998 .............................. 6
Rollins, Charlemae Hill 1897-1979 ............... 3
Obituary ......................................................... 26
Rollock, Barbara T(herese) 1924- ............... 64
Romack, Janice Reed
See LeNoir, Janice
Romain, Trevor ........................................... 134
Romanenko, Vitaliy 1962- .......................... 101
Romano, Louis G. 1921- ............................... 35
Romano, Melora A. 1966- .......................... 118
Romano, Ray 1957- ..................................... 170
Romano, Raymond
See Romano, Ray
Romijn, Johanna Maria Kooyker
See Kooyker-Romijn, Johanna Maria
Romyn, Johanna Maria Kooyker
See Kooyker-Romijn, Johanna Maria
Rong, Yu 1970- ........................................... 174
Rongen, Bjoern 1906- ................................... 10
Rongen, Bjorn
See Rongen, Bjoern
Ronson, Mark
See Alexander, Marc
Rood, Ronald (N.) 1920- ............................... 12
Rook, Sebastian
See Jeapes, Ben
Rooke, Daphne (Marie) 1914- ..................... 12
Roop, Connie 1951- .................................... 167
Brief entry ..................................................... 49
Earlier sketches in SATA 54, 116
Roop, Constance Betzer
See Roop, Connie
Roop, Peter 1951- ....................................... 167
Brief entry ..................................................... 49
Earlier sketches in SATA 54, 116
Roop, Peter G.
See Roop, Peter
Roop, Peter Geiger
See Roop, Peter

Roos, Stephen 1945- .................................. *128*
   Brief entry .......................................... *41*
   Earlier sketches in SATA *47, 77*
Roose-Evans, James 1927- ......................... *65*
Roosevelt, (Anna) Eleanor 1884-1962 ........ *50*
Root, Betty ............................................... *84*
Root, Phyllis 1949- ................................... *145*
   Brief entry .......................................... *48*
   Earlier sketches in SATA *55, 94*
Roper, Laura (Newbold) Wood 1911-2003 . *34*
   Obituary ............................................. *150*
Roper, Robert 1946- ................................. *142*
   Earlier sketch in SATA *78*
Roraback, Robin (Ellan) 1964- ................... *111*
Rorby, Ginny 1944- ................................... *94*
Rorer, Abigail 1949- .................................. *85*
Roscoe, D(onald) T(homas) 1934- ............. *42*
Rose, Anne ............................................... *8*
Rose, Deborah Lee 1955- .......................... *124*
   Earlier sketch in SATA *71*
Rose, Elizabeth (Jane Pretty) 1933- ........... *68*
   Brief entry .......................................... *28*
Rose, Florella
   *See* Carlson, Vada F.
Rose, Gerald (Hembdon Seymour) 1935- ... *68*
   Brief entry .......................................... *30*
Rose, Malcolm 1953- ................................. *168*
   Earlier sketch in SATA *107*
Rose, Nancy A.
   *See* Sweetland, Nancy A(nn)
Rose, Ted 1940- ........................................ *93*
Rose, Wendy 1948- ................................... *12*
Rosen, Lillian (Diamond) 1928- ................. *63*
Rosen, Marvin 1933- ................................. *161*
Rosen, Michael (Wayne) 1946- .................. *137*
   Brief entry .......................................... *40*
   Earlier sketches in SATA *48, 84*
   *See also* CLR *45*
Rosen, Michael J(oel) 1954- ...................... *86*
Rosen, Sidney 1916- .................................. *1*
Rosen, Winifred 1943- ............................... *8*
Rosenbaum, Maurice 1907- ........................ *6*
Rosenberg, Amye 1950- ............................. *74*
Rosenberg, Dorothy 1906- ......................... *40*
Rosenberg, Eth(el) Clifford 1915- .............. *3*
   *See* Clifford, Eth
Rosenberg, Jane 1949- ............................... *58*
Rosenberg, Liz 1958- ................................. *129*
   Earlier sketch in SATA *75*
Rosenberg, Maxine B(erta) 1939- ............... *93*
   Brief entry .......................................... *47*
   Earlier sketch in SATA *55*
Rosenberg, Nancy (Sherman) 1931- ........... *4*
Rosenberg, Sharon 1942- ........................... *8*
Rosenberry, Vera 1948- ............................. *144*
   Earlier sketch in SATA *83*
Rosenblatt, Arthur
   *See* Rosenblatt, Arthur S.
Rosenblatt, Arthur S. 1938- ....................... *68*
   Brief entry .......................................... *45*
Rosenblatt, Lily 1956- ............................... *90*
Rosenbloom, Joseph 1928- ......................... *21*
Rosenblum, Richard 1928- ......................... *11*
Rosenburg, John M. 1918- ......................... *6*
Rosenfeld, Dina 1962- ............................... *99*
Rosenthal, Amy Krouse 1965- .................... *177*
Rosenthal, Harold 1914-1999 ..................... *35*
Rosenthal, M(acha) L(ouis) 1917-1996 ...... *59*
Rosenthal, Mark A(lan) 1946- .................... *64*
Rosman, Steven M 1956- ........................... *81*
Rosman, Steven Michael
   *See* Rosman, Steven M
Rosoff, Meg 1956- .................................... *160*
Ross, Alan
   *See* Warwick, Alan R(oss)
Ross, Christine 1950- ................................. *172*
   Earlier sketch in SATA *83*
Ross, Clare ............................................... *111*
   Earlier sketch in SATA *48*
   *See* Romano, Clare

Ross, Dana Fuller
   *See* Cockrell, Amanda
   and Gerson, Noel Bertram
Ross, Dave ............................................... *32*
   *See* Ross, David
Ross, David 1896-1975 .............................. *49*
   Obituary ............................................. *20*
Ross, David 1949- ..................................... *133*
   *See* Ross, Dave
Ross, Diana
   *See* Denney, Diana
Ross, Edward S(hearman) 1915- ................. *85*
Ross, Eileen 1950- .................................... *115*
Ross, Frank (Xavier), Jr. 1914- .................. *28*
Ross, Jane 1961- ....................................... *79*
Ross, John 1921- ....................................... *45*
Ross, Judy 1942- ....................................... *54*
Ross, Katharine Reynolds
   *See* Ross, Kathy
Ross, Kathy 1948- ..................................... *169*
   Earlier sketch in SATA *89*
Ross, Kent 1956- ....................................... *91*
Ross, Lillian Hammer 1925- ....................... *72*
Ross, Michael Elsohn 1952- ....................... *170*
   Earlier sketches in SATA *80, 127*
Ross, Pat(ricia Kienzle) 1943- .................... *53*
   Brief entry .......................................... *48*
Ross, Ramon R(oyal) 1930- ....................... *62*
Ross, Stewart 1947- ................................... *134*
   Earlier sketch in SATA *92*
   *See also* SAAS *23*
Ross, Tom 1958- ....................................... *84*
Ross, Tony 1938- ....................................... *176*
   Earlier sketches in SATA *17, 65, 130*
Ross, Wilda 1915- ..................................... *51*
   Brief entry .......................................... *39*
Rossel, Seymour 1945- .............................. *28*
Rossel-Waugh, C. C.
   *See* Waugh, Carol-Lynn Rossel
Rossetti, Christina 1830-1894 ..................... *20*
   *See also* CLR *115*
Rossetti, Christina Georgina
   *See* Rossetti, Christina
Rossi, Joyce 1943- .................................... *116*
Rossotti, Hazel Swaine 1930- ..................... *95*
Rostkowski, Margaret I. 1945- .................... *59*
Roth, Arnold 1929- .................................... *21*
Roth, Arthur J(oseph) 1925-1993 ............... *43*
   Brief entry .......................................... *28*
   Obituary ............................................. *75*
   *See also* SAAS *11*
Roth, David 1940- ..................................... *36*
Roth, Matthue 1978(?)- .............................. *174*
Roth, Susan L. ........................................... *134*
Rothberg, Abraham 1922- .......................... *59*
Roth-Hano, Renee 1931- ............................ *85*
Rothkopf, Carol Z. 1929- ........................... *4*
Rothman, Joel 1938- .................................. *7*
Rotner, Shelley 1951- ................................ *169*
   Earlier sketch in SATA *76*
Rottman, S(usan) L(ynn) 1970- .................. *157*
   Earlier sketch in SATA *106*
Roueche, Berton 1911-1994 ....................... *28*
Roughsey, Dick 1921(?)-1985 .................... *35*
   *See also* CLR *41*
Roughsey, Goobalathaldin
   *See* Roughsey, Dick
Rounds, Glen (Harold) 1906-2002 ............. *112*
   Obituary ............................................. *141*
   Earlier sketches in SATA *8, 70*
Rourke, Constance Mayfield 1885-1941
   *See* YABC *1*
Rowan, Deirdre
   *See* Williams, Jeanne
Rowe, Jennifer
   *See* Rodda, Emily
Rowe, John A. 1949- .................................. *146*
Rowh, Mark 1952- ..................................... *90*
Rowland, Florence Wightman 1900-1997 ..... *8*
   Obituary ............................................. *108*

Rowland-Entwistle, (Arthur) Theodore (Henry)
   1925- ................................................. *94*
   Earlier sketch in SATA *31*
Rowling, J.K. 1965- ................................... *174*
   Earlier sketch in SATA *109*
   *See also* CLR *112*
Rowling, Joanne Kathleen
   *See* Rowling, J.K.
Rowsome, Frank (Howard), Jr. 1914-1983 . *36*
Roy, Gabrielle 1909-1983 .......................... *104*
Roy, Jacqueline 1954- ................................ *74*
Roy, Liam
   *See* Scarry, Patricia (Murphy)
Roy, Ron(ald) 1940- .................................. *110*
   Brief entry .......................................... *35*
   Earlier sketch in SATA *40*
Roybal, Laura 1956- ................................... *85*
Roybal, Laura Husby
   *See* Roybal, Laura
Royds, Caroline 1953- ............................... *55*
Royston, Angela 1945- ............................... *169*
   Earlier sketch in SATA *120*
Rozakis, Laurie E. 1952- ............................ *84*
Rubel, Nicole 1953- ................................... *135*
   Earlier sketches in SATA *18, 95*
Rubin, Eva Johanna 1925- ......................... *38*
Rubin, Susan Goldman 1939- ..................... *132*
   Earlier sketch in SATA *84*
Rubinetti, Donald 1947- ............................. *92*
Rubinstein, Gillian (Margaret) 1942- .......... *158*
   Autobiography Feature ......................... *116*
   Earlier sketches in SATA *68, 105*
   *See also* CLR *35*
   *See also* SAAS *25*
Rubinstein, Patricia (Giulia Caulfield Kate)
   -2003 ................................................ *29*
   Obituary ............................................. *149*
   *See* Forest, Antonia
Rubinstein, Robert E(dward) 1943- ............ *49*
Rublowsky, John M(artin) 1928- ................ *62*
Rubright, Lynn 1936- ................................. *171*
Ruby, Laura ............................................... *155*
Ruby, Lois (F.) 1942- ................................ *95*
   Autobiography Feature ......................... *105*
   Brief entry .......................................... *34*
   Earlier sketch in SATA *35*
Ruchlis, Hy(man) 1913-1992 ...................... *3*
   Obituary ............................................. *72*
Rucker, Mike 1940- .................................... *91*
Ruckman, Ivy 1931- .................................. *93*
   Earlier sketch in SATA *37*
Ruck-Pauquet, Gina 1931- ......................... *40*
   Brief entry .......................................... *37*
Rudley, Stephen 1946- ............................... *30*
Rudolph, Marguerita 1908- ........................ *21*
Rudomin, Esther
   *See* Hautzig, Esther Rudomin
Rue, Leonard Lee III 1926- ........................ *142*
   Earlier sketch in SATA *37*
Ruedi, Norma Paul
   *See* Ainsworth, Norma
Ruelle, Karen Gray 1957- ........................... *126*
   Earlier sketch in SATA *84*
Ruemmler, John D(avid) 1948- ................... *78*
Ruepp, Krista 1947- ................................... *143*
Ruffell, Ann 1941- ..................................... *30*
Ruffins, Reynold 1930- .............................. *125*
   Earlier sketch in SATA *41*
Rugoff, Milton 1913- ................................. *30*
Ruhen, Olaf 1911-1989 .............................. *17*
Rumbaut, Hendle 1949- ............................. *84*
Rumford, James 1948- ............................... *116*
Rumsey, Marian (Barritt) 1928- ................. *16*
Rumstuckle, Cornelius
   *See* Brennan, J(ames) H(erbert)
Runnerstroem, Bengt Arne 1944- ............... *75*
Runyan, John
   *See* Palmer, Bernard (Alvin)
Runyon, Catherine 1947- ........................... *62*
Ruoff, A. LaVonne Brown 1930- ................ *76*

Rusch, Kris
  *See* Rusch, Kristine Kathryn
Rusch, Kristine Kathryn 1960- ................. *113*
Rush, Alison 1951- ...................................... *41*
Rush, Peter 1937- ......................................... *32*
Rushford, Patricia H(elen) 1943- .............. *134*
Rushmore, Helen 1898-1994 ........................ *3*
Rushmore, Robert (William) 1926-1986 ....... *8*
  Obituary ................................................. *49*
Ruskin, Ariane
  *See* Batterberry, Ariane Ruskin
Ruskin, John 1819-1900 ............................. *24*
Russ, Lavinia (Faxon) 1904-1992 .............. *74*
Russell, Charlotte
  *See* Rathjen, Carl Henry
Russell, Ching Yeung 1946- ...................... *107*
Russell, Franklin (Alexander) 1926- ........... *11*
Russell, Gertrude Barrer
  *See* Barrer-Russell, Gertrude
Russell, Helen Ross 1915- ........................... *8*
Russell, James 1933- .................................. *53*
Russell, Jim
  *See* Russell, James
Russell, Joan Plummer 1930- ..................... *139*
Russell, P(hilip) Craig 1951- .................... *162*
  Earlier sketch in SATA *80*
Russell, Patrick
  *See* Sammis, John
Russell, Paul (Gary) 1942- ......................... *57*
Russell, Sarah
  *See* Laski, Marghanita
Russell, Sharman Apt 1954- ...................... *123*
Russell, Solveig Paulson 1904-1985 ............. *3*
Russo, Marisabina 1950- ........................... *151*
  Earlier sketch in SATA *106*
Russo, Monica J. 1950- ............................... *83*
Russo, Susan 1947- ..................................... *30*
Rutgers van der Loeff, An
  *See* Rutgers van der Loeff-Basenau, An(na)
  Maria Margaretha
Rutgers van der Loeff-Basenau, An(na) Maria
  Margaretha 1910- ................................... *22*
Ruth, Rod 1912-1987 .................................... *9*
Rutherford, Douglas
  *See* McConnell, James Douglas Rutherford
Rutherford, Meg 1932- ................................ *34*
Ruthin, Margaret ............................................ *4*
  *See* Catherall, Arthur
Rutledge, Jill Zimmerman 1951- ............... *155*
Rutz, Viola Larkin 1932- ............................ *12*
Ruurs, Margriet 1952- ............................... *147*
  Earlier sketch in SATA *97*
Ruzzier, Sergio 1966- ............................... *159*
Ryan, Betsy
  *See* Ryan, Elizabeth (Anne)
Ryan, Cheli Duran ...................................... *20*
Ryan, Darlene 1958- .................................. *176*
Ryan, Elizabeth (Anne) 1943- ..................... *30*
Ryan, Jeanette
  *See* Mines, Jeanette
Ryan, John (Gerald Christopher) 1921- ...... *22*
Ryan, Margaret 1950- ................................ *166*
  Earlier sketch in SATA *78*
Ryan, Mary E. 1953- ................................... *61*
Ryan, Mary Elizabeth
  *See* Ryan, Mary E.
Ryan, Pam(ela) Munoz ................................ *134*
Ryan, Patrick 1957- ................................... *138*
Ryan, Peter (Charles) 1939- ......................... *15*
Ryan-Lush, Geraldine 1949- ........................ *89*
Rybakov, Anatoli (Naumovich) 1911-1998 . *79*
  Obituary ............................................... *108*
  *See* Rybakov, Anatolii (Naumovich)
Rybakov, Anatolii (Naumovich)
  *See* Rybakov, Anatoli (Naumovich)
Rybolt, Thomas R(oy) 1954- ....................... *62*
Rydberg, Ernest E(mil) 1901-1993 ............. *21*
Rydberg, Lou(isa Hampton) 1908- ............. *27*
Rydell, Katy 1942- ....................................... *91*
Rydell, Wendell
  *See* Rydell, Wendy

Rydell, Wendy ............................................... *4*
Ryden, Hope ................................................. *91*
  Earlier sketch in SATA *8*
Ryder, Joanne (Rose) 1946- ....................... *163*
  Brief entry ............................................. *34*
  Earlier sketches in SATA *65, 122*
  *See also* CLR *37*
Ryder, Pamela
  *See* Lamb, Nancy
Rye, Anthony
  *See* Youd, (Christopher) Samuel
Rylant, Cynthia 1954- ............................... *160*
  Brief entry ............................................. *44*
  Earlier sketches in SATA *50, 76, 112*
  *See also* CLR *86*
  *See also* SAAS *13*
Rymer, Alta May 1925- ................................ *34*

**S**

S. L. C.
  *See* Clemens, Samuel Langhorne
S., Svend Otto
  *See* Soerensen, Svend Otto
Saaf, Donald W(illiam) 1961- .................... *124*
Saal, Jocelyn
  *See* Sachs, Judith
Sabbeth, Carol (Landstrom) 1957- ............ *125*
Saberhagen, Fred 1930- ............................... *89*
  Earlier sketch in SATA *37*
Saberhagen, Fred Thomas
  *See* Saberhagen, Fred
Sabin, Edwin L(egrand) 1870-1952
  *See* YABC *2*
Sabin, Francene ......................................... *27*
Sabin, Lou
  *See* Sabin, Louis
Sabin, Louis 1930- ..................................... *27*
Sabre, Dirk
  *See* Laffin, John (Alfred Charles)
Sabuda, Robert 1965- ................................ *170*
Sabuda, Robert (James) 1965- ................... *120*
  Earlier sketch in SATA *81*
Sabuda, Robert James
  *See* Sabuda, Robert
Sachar, Louis 1954- ................................... *154*
  Brief entry ............................................. *50*
  Earlier sketches in SATA *63, 104*
  *See also* CLR *79*
Sachs, Elizabeth-Ann 1946- ......................... *48*
Sachs, Judith 1947- ..................................... *52*
  Brief entry ............................................. *51*
Sachs, Marilyn 1927- ................................. *164*
  Autobiography Feature ........................... *110*
  Earlier sketches in SATA *3, 68*
  *See also* CLR *2*
  *See also* SAAS *2*
Sachs, Marilyn Stickle
  *See* Sachs, Marilyn
Sackett, S(amuel) J(ohn) 1928- ................... *12*
Sackson, Sid 1920- ...................................... *16*
Sacre, Antonio 1968- .................................. *152*
Saddler, Allen
  *See* Richards, R(onald) C(harles) W(illiam)
Saddler, K. Allen
  *See* Richards, R(onald) C(harles) W(illiam)
Sadie, Stanley (John) 1930-2005 ................. *14*
Sadiq, Nazneen 1944- ................................ *101*
Sadler, Catherine Edwards 1952- ................ *60*
  Brief entry ............................................. *45*
Sadler, Marilyn (June) 1950- ....................... *79*
Sadler, Mark
  *See* Lynds, Dennis
Saffer, Barbara ......................................... *144*
Sagan, Carl 1934-1996 ................................ *58*
  Obituary ................................................. *94*
Sagan, Carl Edward
  *See* Sagan, Carl

Sage, Juniper
  *See* Brown, Margaret Wise
  and Hurd, Edith Thacher
Sagsoorian, Paul 1923- ............................... *12*
Said, S.F. 1967- ....................................... *174*
Saidman, Anne 1952- ................................... *75*
Saint, Dora Jessie 1913- ............................. *10*
St. Anthony, Jane ...................................... *175*
St. Antoine, Sara L. 1966- ............................ *84*
Saint-Exupery, Antoine de 1900-1944 .......... *20*
  *See also* CLR *10*
Saint-Exupery, Antoine Jean Baptiste Marie
  Roger de
  *See* Saint-Exupery, Antoine de
St. George, Judith 1931- ........................... *161*
  Earlier sketches in SATA *13, 99*
  *See also* CLR *57*
  *See also* SAAS *12*
St. James, Blakely
  *See* Gottfried, Theodore Mark
  and Platt, Charles
St. James, Blakely
  *See* Griffin, W.E.B.
Saint James, Synthia 1949- ........................ *152*
  Earlier sketch in SATA *84*
St. John, Nicole ........................................ *143*
  Autobiography Feature ........................... *143*
  Earlier sketch in SATA *89*
  *See also* CLR *46*
  *See also* SAAS *7*
  *See* Johnston, Norma
St. John, Philip
  *See* del Rey, Lester
St. John, Wylly Folk 1908-1985 .................. *10*
  Obituary ................................................. *45*
St. Max, E. S.
  *See* Ellis, Edward S(ylvester)
St. Meyer, Ned
  *See* Stratemeyer, Edward L.
St. Mox, E. A.
  *See* Ellis, Edward S(ylvester)
St. Myer, Ned
  *See* Stratemeyer, Edward L.
St. Tamara
  *See* Kolba, St. Tamara
Saito, Michiko
  *See* Fujiwara, Michiko
Sakers, Don 1958- ....................................... *72*
Sakharnov, S.
  *See* Sakharnov, Svyatoslav
Sakharnov, Svyatoslav 1923- ........................ *65*
Sakharnov, Svyatoslav Vladimirovich
  *See* Sakharnov, Svyatoslav
Saksena, Kate ........................................... *148*
Sakurai, Gail 1952- ................................... *153*
  Earlier sketch in SATA *87*
Salassi, Otto R(ussell) 1939-1993 ............... *38*
  Obituary ................................................. *77*
Salat, Cristina ............................................ *82*
Saldutti, Denise 1953- ................................. *39*
Sale, Tim 1956- ........................................ *153*
Salem, Kay 1952- ........................................ *92*
Salerno, Steven ........................................ *176*
Salinger, J.D. 1919- .................................... *67*
  *See also* CLR *18*
Salinger, Jerome David
  *See* Salinger, J.D.
Salisbury, Graham 1944- ........................... *161*
  Earlier sketches in SATA *76, 108*
Salisbury, Joyce E(llen) 1944- ................... *138*
Salkey, (Felix) Andrew (Alexander) 1928-1995
  .............................................................. *118*

  Earlier sketch in SATA *35*
Salley, Coleen .......................................... *166*
Sallis, Susan (Diana) 1929- ......................... *55*
Salmon, Annie Elizabeth 1899- .................... *13*
Salsi, Lynn 1947- ...................................... *130*
Salsitz, R. A. V.
  *See* Salsitz, Rhondi Vilott
Salsitz, Rhondi Vilott ................................. *115*
  *See* Salsitz, R. A. V.

Salten, Felix
  *See* Salzmann, Siegmund
Salter, Cedric
  *See* Knight, Francis Edgar
Saltman, Judith 1947- .................................. *64*
Saltzberg, Barney 1955- ......................... *135*
Saltzman, David (Charles Laertes) 1967-1990
  ........................................................... *86*
Salvadori, Mario (George) 1907-1997 ........ *97*
  Earlier sketch in SATA *40*
Salwood, F. K.
  *See* Kilworth, Garry
Salzer, L. E.
  *See* Wilson, Lionel
Salzman, Marian 1959- ............................. *77*
Salzmann, Siegmund 1869-1945 ................ *25*
  *See* Salten, Felix
Samachson, Dorothy (Mirkin) 1914-1997 ..... *3*
Samachson, Joseph 1906-1980 .................... *3*
  Obituary ................................................. *52*
Sammis, John 1942- ..................................... *4*
Sampson, Emma (Keats) Speed 1868-1947
  ........................................................... *68*
Sampson, Fay (Elizabeth) 1935- ............. *151*
  Brief entry ............................................. *40*
  Earlier sketch in SATA *42*
Sampson, Michael 1952- ......................... *143*
  Earlier sketch in SATA *95*
Samson, Anne S(tringer) 1933- .................... *2*
Samson, Joan 1937-1976 ............................ *13*
Samson, Suzanne M. 1959- ....................... *91*
Samuels, Charles 1902-1982 ...................... *12*
Samuels, Cynthia K(alish) 1946- ............... *79*
Samuels, Gertrude 1910(?)-2003 ............... *17*
  Obituary ............................................... *147*
Sanborn, Duane 1914-1996 ....................... *38*
Sancha, Sheila 1924- ................................. *38*
Sanchez, Alex 1957- ................................ *151*
Sanchez, Sonia 1934- .............................. *136*
  Earlier sketch in SATA *22*
  *See also* CLR *18*
Sanchez-Silva, Jose Maria 1911- ............. *132*
  Earlier sketch in SATA *16*
  *See also* CLR *12*
Sand, George X. ........................................ *45*
Sandak, Cass R(obert) 1950-2001 ............. *51*
  Brief entry ............................................. *37*
Sandberg, (Karin) Inger 1930- ................... *15*
Sandberg, Karl C. 1931- ............................ *35*
Sandberg, Lasse (E. M.) 1924- .................. *15*
Sandburg, Carl (August) 1878-1967 ............ *8*
  *See also* CLR *67*
Sandburg, Charles
  *See* Sandburg, Carl (August)
Sandburg, Charles A.
  *See* Sandburg, Carl (August)
Sandburg, Helga 1918- ............................... *3*
  *See also* SAAS *10*
Sandell, Lisa Ann 1977- .......................... *175*
Sander, Heather L. 1947- ......................... *157*
Sanderlin, George 1915- ............................. *4*
Sanderlin, Owenita (Harrah) 1916- ............ *11*
Sanders, Nancy I. 1960- ........................... *141*
  Earlier sketch in SATA *90*
Sanders, Scott Russell 1945- .................... *109*
  Earlier sketch in SATA *56*
Sanders, Winston P.
  *See* Anderson, Poul
Sanderson, Irma 1912- ............................... *66*
Sanderson, Ivan T(erence) 1911-1973 .......... *6*
Sanderson, Margaret Love
  *See* Keats, Emma
  and Sampson, Emma (Keats) Speed
Sanderson, Ruth 1951- ............................. *172*
  Earlier sketches in SATA *41, 109*
Sanderson, Ruth L.
  *See* Sanderson, Ruth
Sandin, Joan 1942- .................................. *153*
  Earlier sketches in SATA *12, 94*
Sandison, Janet
  *See* Cameron, Elizabeth Jane

Sandler, Martin W. ................................... *160*
Sandoz, Mari(e Susette) 1900-1966 ............. *5*
Sanford, Agnes (White) 1897-1976 ............ *61*
Sanford, Doris 1937- ................................. *69*
Sanger, Marjory Bartlett 1920- .................... *8*
San Jose, Christine 1929- ........................ *167*
Sankey, Alice (Ann-Susan) 1910- ............... *27*
San Souci, Daniel ..................................... *96*
San Souci, Robert D. 1946- ..................... *158*
  Earlier sketches in SATA *40, 81, 117*
  *See also* CLR *43*
Santiago, Esmeralda 1948- ....................... *129*
Santos, Helen
  *See* Griffiths, Helen
Santrey, Louis
  *See* Sabin, Louis
Santucci, Barbara 1948- ........................... *130*
Sapieyevski, Anne Lindbergh 1940-1993 ... *78*
  Earlier sketch in SATA *35*
  *See* Feydy, Anne Lindbergh
  and Lindbergh, Anne
Saport, Linda 1954- ................................. *123*
Sapp, Allen 1929- .................................... *151*
Sarac, Roger
  *See* Caras, Roger A(ndrew)
Sarah, Duchess of York
  *See* Ferguson, Sarah
Sarasin, Jennifer
  *See* Sachs, Judith
Sarg, Anthony Frederick
  *See* Sarg, Tony
Sarg, Tony 1882-1942
  *See* YABC *1*
Sargent, Pamela 1948- ............................... *78*
  Earlier sketch in SATA *29*
Sargent, Robert 1933- ................................. *2*
Sargent, Sarah 1937- ................................. *44*
  Brief entry ............................................. *41*
Sargent, Shirley 1927-2004 ....................... *11*
Sarnoff, Jane 1937- ................................... *10*
Saroyan, William 1908-1981 ..................... *23*
  Obituary ................................................. *24*
Sarton, Eleanor May
  *See* Sarton, May
Sarton, May 1912-1995 ............................. *36*
  Obituary ................................................. *86*
Saseen, Sharon (Dillon) 1949- .................. *59*
Sasek, Miroslav 1916-1980 ....................... *16*
  Obituary ................................................. *23*
  *See also* CLR *4*
Sasso, Sandy Eisenberg 1947- .................. *162*
  Earlier sketches in SATA *86, 116*
Sathre, Vivian 1952- ................................ *133*
  Earlier sketch in SATA *79*
Satterfield, Charles
  *See* del Rey, Lester
  and Pohl, Frederik
Sattgast, L. J.
  *See* Sattgast, Linda J.
Sattgast, Linda J. 1953- ............................. *91*
Sattler, Helen Roney 1921-1992 ................ *74*
  Earlier sketch in SATA *4*
  *See also* CLR *24*
Sauer, Julia Lina 1891-1983 ..................... *32*
  Obituary ................................................. *36*
Sauerwein, Leigh 1944- ........................... *155*
Saul, Carol P. 1947- ................................ *117*
  Earlier sketch in SATA *78*
Saul, John (W. III) 1942- ........................... *98*
Saul, (Ellen) Wendy 1946- ........................ *42*
Saulnier, Karen Luczak 1940- .................... *80*
Saunders, Caleb
  *See* Heinlein, Robert A.
Saunders, Dave 1939- ............................... *85*
Saunders, Julie 1939- ............................... *85*
Saunders, (William) Keith 1910-1994 ........ *12*
Saunders, Rubie (Agnes) 1929- ................. *21*
Saunders, Susan 1945- .............................. *96*
  Brief entry ............................................. *41*
  Earlier sketch in SATA *46*
Saunders-Smith, Gail 1952- ..................... *169*

Sauvain, Philip Arthur 1933- .................... *111*
Savadier, Elivia 1950- ............................. *164*
  Earlier sketch in SATA *79*
Savage, Alan
  *See* Nicole, Christopher (Robin)
Savage, Blake
  *See* Goodwin, Harold L(eland)
Savage, Candace (M.) 1949- .................... *142*
Savage, Deborah 1955- ............................. *76*
Savage, Jeff 1961- ..................................... *97*
Savageau, Cheryl 1950- ............................. *96*
Savery, Constance (Winifred) 1897-1999 ..... *1*
Saville, Andrew
  *See* Taylor, Andrew
Saville, (Leonard) Malcolm 1901-1982 ...... *23*
  Obituary ................................................. *31*
Saviozzi, Adriana
  *See* Mazza, Adriana
Savitt, Sam 1917(?)-2000 ............................ *8*
  Obituary ............................................... *126*
Savitz, Harriet May 1933- ......................... *72*
  Earlier sketch in SATA *5*
  *See also* SAAS *26*
Sawicki, Mary 1950- .................................. *90*
Sawyer, (Frederick) Don(ald) 1947- ........... *72*
Sawyer, Kem Knapp 1953- ........................ *84*
Sawyer, Robert J. 1960- .......................... *149*
  Earlier sketch in SATA *81*
Sawyer, Robert James
  *See* Sawyer, Robert J.
Sawyer, Ruth 1880-1970 ........................... *17*
  *See also* CLR *36*
Saxby, H. M.
  *See* Saxby, (Henry) Maurice
Saxby, (Henry) Maurice 1924- ................... *71*
Saxon, Andrew
  *See* Arthur, Robert, (Jr.)
Saxon, Antonia
  *See* Sachs, Judith
Say, Allen 1937- ..................................... *161*
  Earlier sketches in SATA *28, 69, 110*
  *See also* CLR *22*
Sayers, Frances Clarke 1897-1989 ............... *3*
  Obituary ................................................. *62*
Sayles, Elizabeth 1956- ........................... *163*
  Earlier sketch in SATA *108*
Saylor-Marchant, Linda 1963- ................... *82*
Sayre, April Pulley 1966- ......................... *131*
  Earlier sketch in SATA *88*
Sazer, Nina 1949- ..................................... *13*
Scabrini, Janet 1953- ................................. *13*
Scagell, Robin 1946- ............................... *107*
Scagnetti, Jack 1924- .................................. *7*
Scamander, Newt
  *See* Rowling, J.K.
Scamell, Ragnhild 1940- ............................ *77*
Scanlon, Marion Stephany .......................... *11*
Scannell, Vernon 1922- ............................. *59*
Scarborough, Elizabeth ........................... *171*
  *See* Scarborough, Elizabeth Ann
Scarborough, Elizabeth Ann 1947- ........... *171*
  Earlier sketch in SATA *98*
  *See* Scarborough, Elizabeth
Scarf, Maggi
  *See* Scarf, Maggie
Scarf, Maggie 1932- ..................................... *5*
Scariano, Margaret M. 1924- ..................... *86*
Scarlett, Susan
  *See* Streatfeild, (Mary) Noel
Scarry, Huck
  *See* Scarry, Richard McClure, Jr.
Scarry, Patricia (Murphy) 1924- ................... *2*
Scarry, Patsy
  *See* Scarry, Patricia (Murphy)
Scarry, Richard (McClure) 1919-1994 ........ *75*
  Obituary ................................................. *90*
  Earlier sketches in SATA *2, 35*
  *See also* CLR *41*
Scarry, Richard McClure, Jr. 1953- ........... *35*
Schachner, Judith Byron 1951- .................. *88*
Schachtel, Roger 1949- ............................. *38*

Schachtel, Roger Bernard
  See Schachtel, Roger
Schaedler, Sally .......................................... 116
Schaefer, Carole Lexa .................................. 173
Schaefer, Jack (Warner) 1907-1991 ............. 66
  Obituary ................................................. 65
  Earlier sketch in SATA 3
Schaefer, Lola M. 1950- ............................. 144
  Earlier sketch in SATA 91
Schaeffer, Mead 1898- ................................ 21
Schaeffer, Susan Fromberg 1941- ............... 22
Schaer, Brigitte 1958- ................................ 112
Schaller, George B(eals) 1933- ................... 30
Schanzer, Rosalyn (Good) 1942- ............... 138
  Earlier sketch in SATA 77
Schatell, Brian ........................................... 66
  Brief entry ............................................. 47
Schechter, Betty (Goodstein) 1921- ............. 5
Schecter, Ellen 1944- ................................. 85
Scheeder, Louis 1946- ............................... 141
Scheer, Julian (Weisel) 1926-2001 ............... 8
Scheffer, Victor B(lanchard) 1906- .............. 6
Scheffler, Ursel 1938- ................................ 81
Scheffrin-Falk, Gladys 1928- ..................... 76
Scheidl, Gerda Marie 1913- ....................... 85
Scheier, Michael 1943- ............................... 40
  Brief entry ............................................. 36
Schell, Mildred 1922- ................................. 41
Schell, Orville (Hickok) 1940- .................... 10
Scheller, Melanie 1953- .............................. 77
Schellie, Don 1932- ................................... 29
Schembri, Jim 1962- .................................. 124
Schemm, Mildred Walker 1905-1998 .......... 21
  Obituary ............................................... 103
  See Walker, Mildred
Schenker, Dona 1947- ............................... 133
  Earlier sketch in SATA 68
Scher, Paula 1948- .................................... 47
Scherf, Margaret 1908-1979 ....................... 10
Schermer, Judith (Denise) 1941- ................. 30
Schertle, Alice 1941- ................................ 145
  Earlier sketches in SATA 36, 90
Schick, Alice 1946- .................................... 27
Schick, Eleanor 1942- ............................... 144
  Earlier sketches in SATA 9, 82
Schick, Joel 1945- ..................................... 31
  Brief entry ............................................. 30
Schields, Gretchen 1948- ............................ 75
Schiff, Ken(neth Roy) 1942- ......................... 7
Schiller, Andrew 1919- ............................... 21
Schiller, Barbara (Heyman) 1928- ................ 21
Schiller, Pamela (Byrne) ............................ 127
Schindel, John 1955- ................................ 115
  Earlier sketch in SATA 77
Schindelman, Joseph 1923- .......................... 67
  Brief entry ............................................. 32
Schindler, S.D. 1952- ............................... 171
  Brief entry ............................................. 50
  Earlier sketches in SATA 75, 118
Schindler, Steven D.
  See Schindler, S.D.
Schinto, Jeanne 1951- ................................. 93
Schisgall, Oscar 1901-1984 ........................ 12
  Obituary ................................................. 38
Schlaepfer, Gloria G. 1931- ....................... 154
Schlee, Ann 1934- ...................................... 44
  Brief entry ............................................. 36
Schleichert, Elizabeth 1945- ........................ 77
Schlein, Miriam 1926-2004 ....................... 130
  Obituary ............................................... 159
  Earlier sketches in SATA 2, 87
  See also CLR 41
Schlesinger, Arthur M., Jr. 1917-2007 ........ 61
Schlesinger, Arthur Meier, Jr.
  See Schlesinger, Arthur M., Jr.
Schlessinger, Laura (Catherine) 1947- ....... 160
  Earlier sketch in SATA 110
Schloat, G. Warren, Jr. 1914-2000 ................ 4
Schmid, Eleonore 1939- ............................ 126
  Earlier sketches in SATA 12, 84
Schmiderer, Dorothy 1940- .......................... 19

Schmidt, Annie M. G. 1911-1995 ............... 67
  Obituary ................................................. 91
  See also CLR 22
Schmidt, Diane 1953- .................................. 70
Schmidt, Elizabeth 1915- ............................ 15
Schmidt, Gary D. 1957- ............................. 135
  Earlier sketch in SATA 93
Schmidt, James Norman 1912-1983 ............. 21
Schmidt, Karen Lee 1953- ........................... 94
Schmidt, Lynette 1952- ............................... 76
Schneider, Antonie 1954- .......................... 167
  Earlier sketch in SATA 89
Schneider, Christine M. 1972(?)- ............... 171
  Earlier sketch in SATA 120
Schneider, Dick
  See Schneider, Richard H.
Schneider, Elisa
  See Kleven, Elisa
Schneider, Herman 1905-2003 ...................... 7
  Obituary ............................................... 148
Schneider, Laurie
  See Adams, Laurie
Schneider, Nina 1913- .................................. 2
Schneider, Rex 1937- .................................. 44
Schneider, Richard H. 1922- ...................... 171
Schneider, Richard Henry
  See Schneider, Richard H.
Schnirel, James R. 1931- ............................ 14
Schnitter, Jane T. 1958- .............................. 88
Schnitzlein, Danny ................................... 134
Schnur, Steven 1952- ................................ 144
  Earlier sketch in SATA 95
Schoberle, Cecile 1949- .............................. 80
Schock, Pauline 1928- ................................ 45
Schoell, William 1951- .............................. 160
Schoen, Barbara (Taylor) 1924-1993 ............ 13
Schoenherr, Ian ...................................... 177
Schoenherr, John (Carl) 1935- .................... 66
  Earlier sketch in SATA 37
  See also SAAS 13
Schofield, Sandy
  See Rusch, Kristine Kathryn
Scholastica, Sister Mary
  See Jenkins, Marie M(agdalen)
Scholefield, A. T.
  See Scholefield, Alan
Scholefield, Alan 1931- .............................. 66
Scholefield, Edmund O.
  See Griffin, W.E.B.
Scholey, Arthur 1932- ................................ 28
Schone, Virginia ....................................... 22
Schongut, Emanuel 1936- ........................... 52
  Brief entry ............................................. 36
Schoonover, Frank (Earle) 1877-1972 ........ 24
Schoor, Gene 1921- ...................................... 3
Schories, Pat 1952- .................................. 164
  Earlier sketch in SATA 116
Schott, Jane A. 1946- ............................... 172
Schotter, Roni ......................................... 149
  Earlier sketch in SATA 105
Schraff, Anne E(laine) 1939- ....................... 92
  Earlier sketch in SATA 27
Schram, Peninnah 1934- ........................... 119
Schrecengost, Maity 1938- ........................ 118
Schrecengost, S. Maitland
  See Schrecengost, Maity
Schrecker, Judie 1954- ............................... 90
Schreiber, Elizabeth Anne (Ferguson) 1947-
  ............................................................. 13
Schreiber, Ralph W(alter) 1942- ................. 13
Schreiner, Samuel A(gnew), Jr. 1921- ......... 70
Schroeder, Alan 1961- ............................... 98
  Earlier sketch in SATA 66
Schroeder, Binette
  See Nickl, Barbara (Elisabeth)
Schroeder, Russell (K.) 1943- ................... 146
Schubert, Dieter 1947- ............................. 101
  Earlier sketch in SATA 62
Schubert-Gabrys, Ingrid 1953- ................. 101
  Earlier sketch in SATA 62
Schuerger, Michele R. ............................... 110

Schuett, Stacey 1960- ............................... 168
  Earlier sketch in SATA 75
Schulke, Flip Phelps Graeme 1930- ............. 57
Schulman, Arlene 1961- ............................ 105
Schulman, Janet 1933- ............................. 137
  Earlier sketch in SATA 22
Schulman, L(ester) M(artin) 1934- ............. 13
Schulte, Elaine L(ouise) 1934- .................... 36
Schultz, Betty K(epka) 1932- ..................... 125
Schultz, Gwendolyn .................................. 21
Schultz, James Willard 1859-1947
  See YABC 1
Schultz, Pearle Henriksen 1918- ................. 21
Schulz, Charles M. 1922-2000 .................... 10
  Obituary ............................................... 118
Schulz, Charles Monroe
  See Schulz, Charles M.
Schumaker, Ward 1943- ............................. 96
Schuman, Michael A. 1953- ...................... 134
  Earlier sketch in SATA 85
Schur, Maxine
  See Schur, Maxine Rose
Schur, Maxine Rose 1948- ........................ 135
  Autobiography Feature ............................ 135
  Brief entry ............................................. 49
  Earlier sketches in SATA 53, 98
Schurfranz, Vivian 1925- ............................ 13
Schutzer, A. I. 1922- .................................. 13
Schuyler, Pamela R. 1948- .......................... 30
Schwager, Tina 1964- ............................... 110
Schwandt, Stephen (William) 1947- ............. 61
Schwark, Mary Beth 1954- .......................... 51
Schwartz, Alvin 1927-1992 .......................... 56
  Obituary ................................................. 71
  Earlier sketch in SATA 4
  See also CLR 89
Schwartz, Amy 1954- ............................... 131
  Brief entry ............................................. 41
  Earlier sketches in SATA 47, 83
  See also CLR 25
  See also SAAS 18
Schwartz, Anne Powers 1913-1987 ............. 10
Schwartz, Carol 1954- ................................ 77
Schwartz, Charles W(alsh) 1914- .................. 8
Schwartz, David M. 1951- ......................... 110
  Earlier sketch in SATA 59
Schwartz, David Martin
  See Schwartz, David M.
Schwartz, Elizabeth Reeder 1912- ................. 8
Schwartz, Ellen 1949- .............................. 117
Schwartz, Jerome L.
  See Lawrence, Jerome
Schwartz, Joel L. 1940- .............................. 54
  Brief entry ............................................. 51
Schwartz, Joyce R. 1950- ............................ 93
Schwartz, Julius 1907-2004 ........................ 45
Schwartz, Perry 1942- ................................ 75
Schwartz, Sheila (Ruth) 1929- ..................... 27
Schwartz, Stephen (Lawrence) 1948- ........... 19
Schwartz, Virginia Frances 1950- .............. 131
Schwarz, (Silvia Tessa) Viviane 1977- ...... 141
Schweitzer, Byrd Baylor
  See Baylor, Byrd
Schweitzer, Iris ........................................ 59
  Brief entry ............................................. 36
Schweninger, Ann 1951- ........................... 168
  Earlier sketches in SATA 29, 98
Schwerin, Doris H(alpern) 1922- ................. 64
Scieszka, Jon 1954- ................................. 160
  Earlier sketches in SATA 68, 105
  See also CLR 107
Scillian, Devin ....................................... 128
Scioscia, Mary (Hershey) 1926- .................. 63
Scofield, Penrod 1933- ............................... 62
  Obituary ................................................. 78
Scoggin, Margaret C(lara) 1905-1968 ......... 47
  Brief entry ............................................. 28
Scoltock, Jack 1942- ................................ 141
  Earlier sketch in SATA 72

Scoppettone, Sandra 1936- .......................... 92
  Earlier sketch in SATA 9
  *See* Early, Jack
Scot, Michael
  *See* Rohan, Michael Scott
Scotland, Jay
  *See* Jakes, John
Scott, Alastair
  *See* Allen, Kenneth S.
Scott, Ann Herbert 1926- .......................... 140
  Autobiography Feature ........................... 140
  Brief entry ....................................... 29
  Earlier sketches in SATA 56, 94
Scott, Bill
  *See* Scott, William N(eville)
Scott, Cora Annett (Pipitone) 1931- ............ 11
Scott, Dan
  *See* Barker, S(quire) Omar
Scott, Elaine 1940- .............................. 164
  Earlier sketches in SATA 36, 90
Scott, Jack Denton 1915-1995 ................... 83
  Earlier sketch in SATA 31
  *See also* CLR 20
  *See also* SAAS 14
Scott, Jane (Harrington) 1931- .................. 55
Scott, John 1912-1976 ........................... 14
Scott, John Anthony 1916- ....................... 23
Scott, John M(artin) 1913- ...................... 12
Scott, Mary
  *See* Mattern, Joanne
Scott, Melissa 1960- ............................ 109
Scott, Richard
  *See* Rennert, Richard Scott
Scott, Roney
  *See* Gault, William Campbell
Scott, Sally 1909-1978 ........................... 43
Scott, Sally 1948- ............................... 44
Scott, Sally Elisabeth
  *See* Scott, Sally
Scott, W. N.
  *See* Scott, William N(eville)
Scott, Sir Walter 1771-1832
  *See* YABC 2
Scott, Warwick
  *See* Trevor, Elleston
Scott, William N(eville) 1923- .................. 87
Scotti, Anna
  *See* Coates, Anna
Scotton, Rob 1960- .............................. 177
Scribner, Charles, Jr. 1921-1995 ................ 13
  Obituary ......................................... 87
Scribner, Joanne L. 1949- ....................... 33
Scribner, Kimball 1917- ......................... 63
Scrimger, Richard 1957- ......................... 164
  Earlier sketch in SATA 119
Scroder, Walter K. 1928- ........................ 82
Scruggs, Sandy 1961- ............................ 89
Scudder, Brooke 1959- ........................... 154
Scull, Marie-Louise 1943-1993 .................. 77
Scuro, Vincent 1951- ............................ 21
Seabrooke, Brenda 1941- ......................... 148
  Earlier sketches in SATA 30, 88
Seaman, Augusta Huiell 1879-1950 ............... 31
Seamands, Ruth 1916- ............................. 9
Searcy, Margaret Zehmer 1926- ................... 54
  Brief entry ....................................... 39
Searight, Mary W(illiams) 1918- ................ 17
Searle, Kathryn Adrienne 1942- ................. 10
Searle, Ronald (William Fordham) 1920- ...... 70
  Earlier sketch in SATA 42
Sears, Stephen W. 1932- .......................... 4
Sebastian, Lee
  *See* Silverberg, Robert
Sebestyen, Igen
  *See* Sebestyen, Ouida
Sebestyen, Ouida 1924- .......................... 140
  Earlier sketch in SATA 39
  *See also* CLR 17
  *See also* SAAS 10
Sebrey, Mary Ann 1951- .......................... 62
Sechrist, Elizabeth Hough 1903-1991 ........... 2

Sedges, John
  *See* Buck, Pearl S(ydenstricker)
Sedgwick, Marcus 1968- .......................... 160
Seed, Cecile Eugenie 1930- ...................... 86
  *See* Seed, Jenny
Seed, Jenny ......................................... 8
  *See also* CLR 76
  *See* Seed, Cecile Eugenie
Seeger, Laura Vaccaro ........................... 172
Seeger, Pete 1919- .............................. 139
  Earlier sketch in SATA 13
Seeger, Peter R.
  *See* Seeger, Pete
Seeley, Laura L. 1958- ........................... 71
Seever, R.
  *See* Reeves, Lawrence F.
Sefozo, Mary 1925- ............................... 82
Sefton, Catherine
  *See* Waddell, Martin
Segal, Joyce 1940- ............................... 35
Segal, Lore 1928- ............................... 163
  Earlier sketches in SATA 4, 66
  *See also* SAAS 11
Segal, Lore Groszmann
  *See* Segal, Lore
Segar, E(lzie) C(risler) 1894-1938 ............. 61
Seguin, Marilyn W(eymouth) 1951- .............. 91
Seguin-Fontes, Marthe 1924- .................... 109
Seibold, J. Otto 1960- .......................... 149
  Earlier sketch in SATA 83
  *See also* SAAS 22
Seidel, Ross ....................................... 95
Seidelman, James Edward 1926- ................... 6
Seiden, Art(hur) ................................. 107
  Brief entry ....................................... 42
Seidler, Ann (G.) 1925- ......................... 131
Seidler, Tor 1952- .............................. 149
  Brief entry ....................................... 46
  Earlier sketches in SATA 52, 98
Seidman, Laurence Ivan 1925- ................... 15
Seigel, Kalman 1917-1998 ........................ 12
  Obituary ......................................... 103
Seignobosc, Françoise 1897-1961 ................ 21
Seinfeld, Jerry 1954- ........................... 146
Seitz, Jacqueline 1931- .......................... 50
Seixas, Judith S. 1922- .......................... 17
Sejima, Yoshimasa 1913- ........................... 8
Selberg, Ingrid (Maria) 1950- ................... 68
Selden, George
  *See* CLR 8
  *See* Thompson, George Selden
Selden, Neil R(oy) 1931- ......................... 61
Self, Margaret Cabell 1902-1996 ................ 24
Selig, Sylvie 1942- ............................. 13
Sellers, Naomi
  *See* Flack, Naomi John White
Selman, LaRue W. 1927- ........................... 55
Selsam, Millicent E(llis) 1912-1996 ............ 29
  Obituary ......................................... 92
  Earlier sketch in SATA 1
  *See also* CLR 1
Seltzer, Meyer 1932- ............................. 17
Seltzer, Richard 1946- ........................... 41
Seltzer, Richard Warren, Jr.
  *See* Seltzer, Richard
Selvadurai, Shyam 1965(?)- ..................... 171
Selway, Martina 1940- ........................... 169
  Earlier sketch in SATA 74
Selznick, Brian 1966- ........................... 171
  Earlier sketches in SATA 79, 117
Semel, Nava 1954- ............................... 107
Semloh
  *See* Holmes, Peggy
Sendak, Jack 1924(?)-1995 ....................... 28
Sendak, Maurice 1928- ........................... 165
  Earlier sketches in SATA 1, 27, 113
  *See also* CLR 74
Sendak, Maurice Bernard
  *See* Sendak, Maurice
Sender, Ruth M(insky) 1926- ..................... 62
Sengler, Johanna 1924- ........................... 18

Senisi, Ellen B. 1951- .......................... 116
Senisi, Ellen Babinec
  *See* Senisi, Ellen B.
Senn, J(oyce) A(nn) 1941- ....................... 115
Senn, Steve 1950- ................................ 60
  Brief entry ....................................... 48
Serage, Nancy 1924- .............................. 10
Seredy, Kate 1899-1975 ............................ 1
  Obituary ......................................... 24
  *See also* CLR 10
Seroff, Victor I(ilyitch) 1902-1979 ............ 12
  Obituary ......................................... 26
Serraillier, Ian (Lucien) 1912-1994 ............ 73
  Obituary ......................................... 83
  Earlier sketch in SATA 1
  *See also* CLR 2
  *See also* SAAS 3
Serros, Michele ................................. 175
Serros, Michele M.
  *See* Serros, Michele
Servello, Joe 1932- .............................. 10
Service, Pamela F. 1945- ......................... 64
Service, Robert
  *See* Service, Robert W(illiam)
Service, Robert W(illiam) 1874(?)-1958 ..... 20
  *See* Service, Robert
Serwadda, W(illiam) Moses 1931- ............... 27
Serwer-Bernstein, Blanche L(uria) 1910-1997
  ................................................. 10
Sescoe, Vincent E. 1938- ........................ 123
Seth, Mary
  *See* Lexau, Joan M.
Seton, Anya 1904(?)-1990 .......................... 3
  Obituary ......................................... 66
Seton, Ernest (Evan) Thompson 1860-1946
  ................................................. 18
  *See also* CLR 59
Seton-Thompson, Ernest
  *See* Seton, Ernest (Evan) Thompson
Seuling, Barbara 1937- .......................... 145
  Earlier sketches in SATA 10, 98
  *See also* SAAS 24
Seuss, Dr.
  *See* Dr. Seuss
  and Geisel, Theodor Seuss
  and LeSieg, Theo.
  and Stone, Rosetta
Severn, Bill
  *See* Severn, William Irving
Severn, David
  *See* Unwin, David S(torr)
Severn, William Irving 1914- ..................... 1
Sewall, Marcia 1935- ............................ 119
  Earlier sketches in SATA 37, 69
Seward, Prudence 1926- ........................... 16
Sewell, Anna 1820-1878 .......................... 100
  Earlier sketch in SATA 24
  *See also* CLR 17
Sewell, Helen (Moore) 1896-1957 ................ 38
Sexton, Anne (Harvey) 1928-1974 ............... 10
Seymour, Alta Halverson .......................... 10
Seymour, Jane 1951- ............................. 139
Seymour, Tres 1966- ............................. 164
  Earlier sketch in SATA 82
Shachtman, Tom 1942- ............................. 49
Shackleton, C. C.
  *See* Aldiss, Brian W.
Shader, Rachel
  *See* Sofer, Barbara
Shadow, Jak
  *See* Sutherland, Jon
Shadyland, Sal
  *See* Cooper, Louise
Shafer, Robert E(ugene) 1925- .................... 9
Shaffer, Terea 1968- ............................. 79
Shahan, Sherry 1949- ............................ 134
  Earlier sketch in SATA 92
Shahn, Bernarda Bryson
  *See* Bryson, Bernarda
Shaik, Fatima ................................... 114
Shalant, Phyllis 1949- .......................... 150

Shan, Darren 1972- ............................ *168*
  Earlier sketch in SATA *129*
Shanberg, Karen
  *See* Shragg, Karen (I.)
Shane, Harold Gray 1914-1993 ............ *36*
  Obituary ...................................... *76*
Shange, Ntozake 1948- ...................... *157*
Shanks, Ann Zane (Kushner) ............... *10*
Shannon, David 1959- ........................ *152*
  Earlier sketch in SATA *107*
  *See also* CLR *87*
Shannon, George (William Bones) 1952- . *143*
  Earlier sketches in SATA *35, 94*
Shannon, Jacqueline ............................ *63*
Shannon, Margaret
  *See* Silverwood, Margaret Shannon
Shannon, Monica 1905(?)-1965 ............ *28*
Shannon, Terry ................................... *21*
  *See* Mercer, Jessie
Shannon, Terry Miller 1951- ................ *148*
Shapiro, Irwin 1911-1981 ................... *32*
Shapiro, Milton J. 1926- ..................... *32*
Shapiro, Tricia
  *See* Andryszewski, Tricia
Shapp, Martha Glauber 1910- .............. *3*
Sharfman, Amalie ............................... *14*
Sharma, Partap 1939- ......................... *15*
Sharma, Rashmi
  *See* Singh, Rashmi Sharma
Sharman, Alison
  *See* Leonard, Alison
Sharmat, Marjorie Weinman 1928- ...... *133*
  Earlier sketches in SATA *4, 33, 74*
Sharmat, Mitchell 1927- ..................... *127*
  Earlier sketch in SATA *33*
Sharp, Anne Wallace 1947- ................. *144*
Sharp, Luke
  *See* Alkiviades, Alkis
Sharp, Margery 1905-1991 .................. *29*
  Obituary ...................................... *67*
  Earlier sketch in SATA *1*
  *See also* CLR *27*
Sharpe, Jon
  *See* Duncan, Alice
  and Knott, William C(ecil, Jr.)
  and Messman, Jon
Sharpe, Mitchell R(aymond) 1924- ....... *12*
Sharpe, Susan 1946- .......................... *71*
Sharratt, Nick 1962- .......................... *153*
  Earlier sketch in SATA *104*
Shasha, Mark 1961- ........................... *80*
Shattuck, Roger 1923-2005 ................. *64*
  Obituary ...................................... *174*
Shattuck, Roger Whitney
  *See* Shattuck, Roger
Shaw, Arnold 1909-1989 ..................... *4*
  Obituary ...................................... *63*
Shaw, Carolyn V. 1934- ...................... *91*
Shaw, Charles (Green) 1892-1974 ........ *13*
Shaw, Evelyn S. 1927- ........................ *28*
Shaw, Flora Louisa
  *See* Lugard, Flora Louisa Shaw
Shaw, Janet 1937- .............................. *146*
  Earlier sketch in SATA *61*
  *See also* CLR *96*
Shaw, Janet Beeler
  *See* Shaw, Janet
Shaw, Lisa
  *See* Rogak, Lisa
Shaw, Margret 1940- .......................... *68*
Shaw, Nancy 1946- ............................ *162*
  Earlier sketch in SATA *71*
Shaw, Ray ........................................ *7*
Shaw, Richard 1923- .......................... *12*
Shawn, Frank S.
  *See* Goulart, Ron(ald Joseph)
Shay, Art
  *See* Shay, Arthur
Shay, Arthur 1922- ............................. *4*
Shay, Lacey
  *See* Shebar, Sharon Sigmond

Shea, George 1940- ............................ *54*
  Brief entry ................................... *42*
Shea, Pegi Deitz 1960- ....................... *172*
  Earlier sketches in SATA *77, 137*
Shearer, John 1947- ........................... *43*
  Brief entry ................................... *27*
  *See also* CLR *34*
Shearer, Ted 1919- ............................ *43*
Shebar, Sharon Sigmond 1945- ........... *36*
Shecter, Ben 1935- ............................ *16*
Shedd, Warner 1934- .......................... *147*
  Earlier sketch in SATA *87*
Sheedy, Alexandra Elizabeth 1962- ...... *39*
  Earlier sketch in SATA *19*
Sheehan, Ethna 1908-2000 .................. *9*
Sheehan, Patty 1945- ......................... *77*
Sheehan, Sean 1951- .......................... *154*
  Earlier sketch in SATA *86*
Sheen, Barbara 1949- ......................... *143*
Shefelman, Janice Jordan 1930- ........... *129*
  Earlier sketch in SATA *58*
Shefelman, Tom (Whitehead) 1927- ...... *58*
Sheffer, H. R.
  *See* Abels, Harriette S(heffer)
Sheffield, Charles 1935-2002 .............. *109*
Sheffield, Janet N. 1926- .................... *26*
Sheikh, Nazneen
  *See* Sadiq, Nazneen
Shekerjian, Regina Tor ....................... *16*
Shelby, Anne 1948- ............................ *85*
  Autobiography Feature ..................... *121*
  *See also* SAAS *26*
Sheldon, Ann .................................... *67*
  Earlier sketch in SATA *1*
Sheldon, Ann
  *See* Antle, Nancy
Sheldon, Aure 1917-1976 .................... *12*
Sheldon, John
  *See* Bloch, Robert (Albert)
Sheldon, Muriel 1926- ........................ *45*
  Brief entry ................................... *39*
Shell, Barry 1951- ............................. *176*
Shelley, Frances
  *See* Wees, Frances Shelley
Shelley, Mary Wollstonecraft (Godwin)
    1797-1851 .................................. *29*
Shelton, William Roy 1919-1995 ......... *5*
  Obituary ...................................... *129*
Shemie, Bonnie (Jean Brenner) 1949- ... *96*
Shemin, Margaretha (Hoeneveld) 1928- . *4*
Shen, Michele 1953- .......................... *173*
Shenker, Michele
  *See* Shen, Michele
Shenton, Edward 1895-1977 ............... *45*
Shepard, Aaron 1950- ........................ *113*
  Earlier sketch in SATA *75*
Shepard, Ernest Howard 1879-1976 ..... *100*
  Obituary ...................................... *24*
  Earlier sketches in SATA *3, 33*
  *See also* CLR *27*
Shepard, James R.
  *See* Shepard, Jim
Shepard, Jim 1956- ............................ *164*
  Earlier sketch in SATA *90*
Shepard, Mary
  *See* Knox, (Mary) Eleanor Jessie
Shephard, Esther 1891-1975 ............... *5*
  Obituary ...................................... *26*
Shepherd, Donna Walsh
  *See* Walsh Shepherd, Donna
Shepherd, Elizabeth .......................... *4*
Shepherd, Irana ............................... *173*
Shepherd, Roni
  *See* Shepherd, Irana
Sherburne, Zoa (Lillian Morin) 1912-1995 ... *3*
  *See also* SAAS *18*
Sherlock, Patti ................................. *71*
Sherman, D(enis) R(onald) 1934- ......... *48*
  Brief entry ................................... *29*
Sherman, Diane (Finn) 1928- .............. *12*

Sherman, Elizabeth
  *See* Friskey, Margaret (Richards)
Sherman, Harold (Morrow) 1898-1987 ....... *37*
  Obituary ...................................... *137*
Sherman, Josepha .............................. *163*
  Earlier sketch in SATA *75*
Sherman, Michael
  *See* Lowndes, Robert A(ugustine) W(ard)
Sherman, Nancy
  *See* Rosenberg, Nancy (Sherman)
Sherman, Pat .................................... *174*
Sherman, Peter Michael
  *See* Lowndes, Robert A(ugustine) W(ard)
Sherrard, Valerie (Anne) 1957- ............ *141*
Sherrod, Jane
  *See* Singer, Jane Sherrod
Sherry, Clifford J. 1943- ..................... *84*
Sherry, (Dulcie) Sylvia 1932- ............... *122*
  Earlier sketch in SATA *8*
Sherwan, Earl 1917- ........................... *3*
Sherwood, Jonathan
  *See* London, Jonathan (Paul)
Shetterly, Will 1955- .......................... *78*
  Autobiography Feature ..................... *106*
Shetterly, William Howard
  *See* Shetterly, Will
Shiefman, Vicky 1942- ........................ *22*
Shields, Brenda Desmond (Armstrong) 1914- ........................................... *37*
Shields, Carol Diggory ....................... *174*
Shields, Charles 1944- ........................ *10*
Shiels, Barbara
  *See* Adams, Barbara Johnston
Shiffman, Lena 1957- .......................... *101*
Shiina, Makoto 1944- ......................... *83*
Shimin, Symeon 1902-1984 ................. *13*
Shine, Andrea 1955- ........................... *104*
Shine, Deborah 1932- ......................... *71*
Shinn, Everett 1876-1953 .................... *21*
Shinn, Sharon 1957- ........................... *164*
  Earlier sketch in SATA *110*
Shippen, Katherine B(inney) 1892-1980 ....... *1*
  Obituary ...................................... *23*
  *See also* CLR *36*
Shippey, T(homas) A(lan) 1943- ........... *143*
Shipton, Eric Earle 1907-1977 ............ *10*
Shiraz, Yasmin ................................. *173*
Shirer, William L(awrence) 1904-1993 .. *45*
  Obituary ...................................... *78*
Shirley, Gayle C 1955- ....................... *96*
Shirley, Gayle Corbett
  *See* Shirley, Gayle C
Shirley, Jean 1919- ............................ *70*
Shirreffs, Gordon D(onald) 1914-1996 ...... *11*
Shirts, Morris A(lpine) 1922- .............. *63*
Shlichta, Joe 1968- ............................ *84*
Shmurak, Carole B. 1944- ................... *118*
Shore, June Lewis ............................. *30*
Shore, Nancy 1960- ........................... *124*
Shore, Robert 1924- ........................... *39*
Short, Michael 1937- .......................... *65*
Short, Roger
  *See* Arkin, Alan
Shortall, Leonard W. .......................... *19*
Shortt, Tim(othy Donald) 1961- ........... *96*
Shotwell, Louisa Rossiter 1902-1993 .... *3*
Shoup, Barbara 1947- ........................ *156*
  Earlier sketch in SATA *86*
  *See also* SAAS *24*
Showalter, Jean B(reckinridge) ............ *12*
Showell, Ellen Harvey 1934- ............... *33*
Showers, Paul C. 1910-1999 ............... *92*
  Obituary ...................................... *114*
  Earlier sketch in SATA *21*
  *See also* CLR *6*
  *See also* SAAS *7*
Shpakow, Tanya 1959(?)- .................... *94*
Shpitalnik, Vladimir 1964- ................. *83*
Shragg, Karen (I.) 1954- ..................... *142*
Shreeve, Elizabeth 1956- .................... *156*

Shreve, Susan
    *See* Shreve, Susan Richards
Shreve, Susan Richards 1939- .................. *152*
    Brief entry ....................................... *41*
    Earlier sketches in SATA *46, 95*
Shriver, Jean Adair 1932- ....................... *75*
Shriver, Maria 1955- ............................ *134*
Shriver, Maria Owings
    *See* Shriver, Maria
Shrode, Mary
    *See* Hollingsworth, Mary
Shtainmets, Leon .................................. *32*
Shub, Elizabeth 1915(?)-2004 ..................... *5*
Shuken, Julia 1948- .............................. *84*
Shulevitz, Uri 1935- ............................ *165*
    Earlier sketches in SATA *3, 50, 106*
    *See also* CLR *61*
Shulman, Alix Kates 1932- ......................... *7*
Shulman, Dee 1957- .............................. *146*
Shulman, Irving 1913-1995 ........................ *13*
Shulman, Neil B(arnett) 1945- .................... *89*
Shumsky, Zena
    *See* Collier, Zena
Shura, Mary Francis
    *See* Craig, Mary (Francis) Shura
Shusterman, Neal 1962- .......................... *140*
    Autobiography Feature .......................... *140*
    Earlier sketches in SATA *85, 121*
Shuter, Jane (Margaret) 1955- ................... *151*
    Earlier sketch in SATA *90*
Shuttlesworth, Dorothy Edwards ..................... *3*
Shwartz, Susan (Martha) 1949- .................... *94*
Shyer, Christopher 1961- ......................... *98*
Shyer, Marlene Fanta ............................. *13*
Siberell, Anne ................................... *29*
Sibley, Don 1922- ................................ *12*
Siburt, Ruth 1951- .............................. *121*
Siculan, Daniel 1922- ............................ *12*
Sidgwick, Ethel 1877-1970 ....................... *116*
Sidjakov, Nicolas 1924- .......................... *18*
Sidman, Joyce 1956- ............................. *145*
Sidney, Frank
    *See* Warwick, Alan R(oss)
Sidney, Margaret
    *See* Lothrop, Harriet Mulford Stone
Siegal, Aranka 1930- ............................. *88*
    Brief entry ....................................... *37*
Siegel, Beatrice ................................. *36*
Siegel, Helen
    *See* Siegl, Helen
Siegel, Robert (Harold) 1939- .................... *39*
Siegelson, Kim L. 1962- ......................... *114*
Siegl, Helen 1924- ............................... *34*
Siepmann, Mary Aline
    *See* Wesley, Mary (Aline)
Sierra, Judy 1945- .............................. *162*
    Earlier sketch in SATA *104*
Sieswerda, Paul L. 1942- ........................ *147*
Sievert, Terri
    *See* Dougherty, Terri (L.)
Silas
    *See* McCay, (Zenas) Winsor
Silcock, Sara Lesley 1947- ....................... *12*
Sill, Cathryn 1953- ............................. *141*
    Earlier sketch in SATA *74*
Sill, John 1947- ................................ *140*
    Earlier sketch in SATA *74*
Sillitoe, Alan 1928- ............................. *61*
Sills, Leslie (Elka) 1948- ...................... *129*
Silly, E. S.
    *See* Kraus, (Herman) Robert
Silsbe, Brenda 1953- ............................. *73*
Silva, Joseph
    *See* Goulart, Ron(ald Joseph)
Silver, Ruth
    *See* Chew, Ruth
Silverberg, Robert 1935- ......................... *91*
    Autobiography Feature .......................... *104*
    Earlier sketch in SATA *13*
    *See also* CLR *59*

Silverman, Erica 1955- .......................... *165*
    Earlier sketches in SATA *78, 112*
Silverman, Janis L. 1946- ....................... *127*
Silverman, Mel(vin Frank) 1931-1966 .......... *9*
Silverman, Robin L. 1954- ........................ *96*
Silverman, Robin Landew
    *See* Silverman, Robin L.
Silverstein, Alvin 1933- ........................ *124*
    Earlier sketches in SATA *8, 69*
    *See also* CLR *25*
Silverstein, Herma 1945- ........................ *106*
Silverstein, Robert Alan 1959- .................. *124*
    Earlier sketch in SATA *77*
Silverstein, Shel 1932-1999 ...................... *92*
    Brief entry ....................................... *27*
    Obituary ......................................... *116*
    Earlier sketch in SATA *33*
    *See also* CLR *96*
Silverstein, Sheldon Allan
    *See* Silverstein, Shel
Silverstein, Virginia B(arbara Opshelor) 1937-
    ................................................. *124*
    Earlier sketches in SATA *8, 69*
    *See also* CLR *25*
Silverthorne, Elizabeth 1930- .................... *35*
Silverwood, Margaret Shannon 1966- ....... *137*
    Earlier sketch in SATA *83*
Silvey, Diane F. 1946- .......................... *135*
Sim, David 1953- ................................ *162*
Sim, Dorrith M. 1931- ............................ *96*
Simard, Remy 1959- .............................. *168*
Simmie, Lois (Ann) 1932- ........................ *106*
Simmonds, Posy 1945- ............................ *130*
    *See also* CLR *23*
Simmons, Andra 1939- ............................ *141*
Simmons, Elly 1955- ............................. *134*
Simms, Laura 1947- .............................. *117*
Simner, Janni Lee ............................... *113*
Simon, Charlie May
    *See* Fletcher, Charlie May Hogue
Simon, Francesca 1955- .......................... *111*
Simon, Gabriel 1972- ............................ *118*
Simon, Hilda Rita 1921- .......................... *28*
    *See also* CLR *39*
Simon, Howard 1903-1979 .......................... *32*
    Obituary ......................................... *21*
Simon, Joe
    *See* Simon, Joseph H.
Simon, Joseph H. 1913- ............................ *7*
Simon, Martin P(aul William) 1903-1969 ... *12*
Simon, Mina Lewiton
    *See* Lewiton, Mina
Simon, Norma (Feldstein) 1927- .............. *129*
    Earlier sketches in SATA *3, 68*
Simon, Seymour 1931- ............................ *138*
    Earlier sketches in SATA *4, 73*
    *See also* CLR *63*
Simon, Shirley (Schwartz) 1921- ................. *11*
Simon, Solomon 1895-1970 ......................... *40*
Simonetta, Linda 1948- ........................... *14*
Simonetta, Sam 1936- ............................. *14*
Simons, Barbara B(rooks) 1934- ................... *41*
Simont, Marc 1915- .............................. *126*
    Earlier sketches in SATA *9, 73*
Simpson, Colin 1908-1983 ......................... *14*
Simpson, Harriette
    *See* Arnow, Harriette (Louisa) Simpson
Simpson, Jacynth Hope
    *See* Hope Simpson, Jacynth
Simpson, Lesley 1963- ........................... *150*
Simpson, Margaret 1943- ......................... *128*
Simpson, Myrtle L(illias) 1931- .................. *14*
Sims, Blanche .................................... *168*
    Earlier sketch in SATA *75*
Sims, Blanche L.
    *See* Sims, Blanche
Simundsson, Elva 1950- ........................... *63*
Sinclair, Clover
    *See* Gater, Dilys
Sinclair, Emil
    *See* Hesse, Hermann

Sinclair, Jeff 1958- ............................. *77*
Sinclair, Olga 1923- ............................ *121*
Sinclair, Rose
    *See* Smith, Susan Vernon
Sinclair, Upton 1878-1968 ......................... *9*
Sinclair, Upton Beall
    *See* Sinclair, Upton
Singer, A.L.
    *See* Lerangis, Peter
Singer, Arthur 1917-1990 ......................... *64*
Singer, Isaac
    *See* Singer, Isaac Bashevis
Singer, Isaac Bashevis 1904-1991 ............. *27*
    Obituary ......................................... *68*
    Earlier sketch in SATA *3*
    *See also* CLR *1*
Singer, Jane Sherrod 1917-1985 ................... *4*
    Obituary ......................................... *42*
Singer, Julia 1917- .............................. *28*
Singer, Kurt D. 1911-2005 ........................ *38*
    Obituary ......................................... *172*
Singer, Marilyn 1948- ........................... *158*
    Autobiography Feature .......................... *158*
    Brief entry ....................................... *38*
    Earlier sketches in SATA *48, 80, 125*
    *See also* CLR *48*
    *See also* SAAS *13*
Singer, Muff 1942-2005 .......................... *104*
    Obituary ......................................... *160*
Singer, Susan (Mahler) 1941- ...................... *9*
Singh, Rashmi Sharma 1952- ....................... *90*
Singleton, Linda Joy 1957- ...................... *166*
    Earlier sketch in SATA *88*
Singleton, L.J.
    *See* Singleton, Linda Joy
Sinykin, Sheri(l Terri) Cooper 1950- ........ *142*
    Autobiography Feature .......................... *142*
    Earlier sketches in SATA *72, 133*
Sipiera, Paul P., (Jr.) 1948- .................... *144*
    Earlier sketch in SATA *89*
Siracusa, Catherine (Jane) 1947- ................. *82*
Sirett, Dawn (Karen) 1966- ....................... *88*
Sirimarco, Elizabeth 1966- ...................... *158*
Sirof, Harriet 1930- ............................. *94*
    Earlier sketch in SATA *37*
Sirois, Allen L. 1950- ........................... *76*
Sirvaitis (Chernyaev), Karen (Ann) 1961- .. *79*
Sis, Peter 1949- ................................ *106*
    Earlier sketch in SATA *67*
    *See also* CLR *110*
    *See* Sis, Peter
Sis, Peter 1949- ................................ *149*
    *See also* CLR *110*
    *See* Sis, Peter
Sisson, Rosemary Anne 1923- ...................... *11*
Sister Mary Terese
    *See* Donze, Mary Terese
Sita, Lisa 1962- ................................. *87*
Sitomer, Alan Lawrence .......................... *174*
Sitomer, Harry 1903-1985 ......................... *31*
Sitomer, Mindel 1903-1987 ........................ *31*
Sittenfeld, Curtis 1976(?)- ..................... *164*
Sive, Helen R(obinson) 1951- ..................... *30*
Sivulich, Sandra (Jeanne) Stroner 1941- ....... *9*
Skarmeta, Antonio 1940- .......................... *57*
Skelly, James R(ichard) 1927- .................... *17*
Skinner, Constance Lindsay 1877-1939
    *See* YABC *1*
Skinner, Cornelia Otis 1901-1979 ................. *2*
Skipper, G. C. 1939- ............................. *46*
    Brief entry ....................................... *38*
Sklansky, Amy E(dgar) 1971- ..................... *145*
Skofield, James .................................. *95*
    Brief entry ....................................... *44*
Skold, Betty Westrom 1923- ....................... *41*
Skorpen, Liesel Moak 1935- ........................ *3*
Skott, Maria
    *See* Nikolajeva, Maria
Skrypuch, Marsha Forchuk 1954- .............. *134*
Skultety, Nancy Laney 1960- ..................... *175*

Skurzynski, Gloria 1930- ............................ 145
   Autobiography Feature ............................ 145
   Earlier sketches in SATA *8, 74, 122*
   *See also* SAAS *9*
Skurzynski, Gloria Joan
   *See* Skurzynski, Gloria
Skutch, Robert 1925- .................................... 89
Skye, Maggie
   *See* Werner, Herma
Skye, Obert ............................................... 170
Slackman, Charles B. 1934- ........................... 12
Slade, Arthur G(regory) 1967- ..................... 149
   Earlier sketch in SATA *106*
Slade, Richard 1910-1971 ................................ 9
Slangerup, Erik Jon 1969- ........................... 130
Slate, Joseph 1928- ................................... 174
   Earlier sketches in SATA *38, 122*
Slate, Joseph Frank
   *See* Slate, Joseph
Slater, Ray
   *See* Lansdale, Joe R.
Slaughter, Hope 1940- ................................... 84
Slaughter, Jean
   *See* Doty, Jean Slaughter
Slaughter, Tom 1955- .................................. 152
Slavicek, Louise Chipley 1956- ..................... 144
Slavin, Bill 1959- ...................................... 148
   Earlier sketch in SATA *76*
Slaymaker, Melissa Eskridge 1958- ............... 158
Sleator, William (Warner III) 1945- ............... 161
   Earlier sketches in SATA *3, 68, 118*
   *See also* CLR *29*
Slegers, Liesbet 1975- ................................. 154
Sleigh, Barbara 1906-1982 ............................. 86
   Obituary .............................................. 30
   Earlier sketch in SATA *3*
Slepian, Jan 1921- ....................................... 85
   Brief entry ........................................... 45
   Earlier sketch in SATA *51*
   *See also* SAAS *8*
Slepian, Janice B.
   *See* Slepian, Jan
Slicer, Margaret O. 1920- ................................ 4
Slier, Debby
   *See* Shine, Deborah
Sloan, Brian 1966- ..................................... 172
Sloan, Carolyn 1937- .................................. 116
   Earlier sketch in SATA *58*
Sloan, Glenna (Davis) 1930- ......................... 120
Sloane, Eric 1910(?)-1985 .............................. 52
   Obituary .............................................. 42
Sloane, Todd 1955- ...................................... 88
Sloat, Teri 1948- ....................................... 164
   Earlier sketches in SATA *70, 106*
Slobodkin, Florence Gersh 1905-1994 ................ 5
   Obituary ............................................. 107
Slobodkin, Louis 1903-1975 ........................... 26
   Earlier sketch in SATA *1*
Slobodkina, Esphyr 1908-2002 .......................... 1
   Obituary ............................................. 135
   *See also* SAAS *8*
Sloggett, Nellie 1851-1923 ............................. 44
Sloss, Lesley Lord 1965- ................................ 72
Slote, Alfred 1926- ...................................... 72
   Earlier sketch in SATA *8*
   *See also* CLR *4*
   *See also* SAAS *21*
Slote, Elizabeth 1956- ................................... 80
Small, David 1945- .................................... 126
   Brief entry ........................................... 46
   Earlier sketches in SATA *50, 95*
   *See also* CLR *53*
Small, Ernest
   *See* Lent, Blair
Small, Mary 1932- ..................................... 165
Small, Terry 1942- ...................................... 75
Smallcomb, Pam 1954- ................................ 159
Smalls, Irene
   *See* Smalls-Hector, Irene

Smalls-Hector, Irene 1950- ........................... 146
   Earlier sketch in SATA *73*
   *See also* CLR *103*
Smaridge, Norah (Antoinette) 1903-1994 ........... 6
Smee, Nicola 1948- .................................... 167
   Earlier sketch in SATA *76*
Smiley, Virginia Kester 1923- .......................... 2
Smith, Anne Warren 1938- ............................. 41
   Brief entry ........................................... 34
Smith, Barry (Edward Jervis) 1943- ................. 75
Smith, Beatrice S(chillinger) ........................... 12
Smith, Betsy Covington 1937- ......................... 55
   Earlier sketch in SATA *43*
Smith, Betty (Wehner) 1904-1972 ..................... 6
Smith, Bradford 1909-1964 .............................. 5
Smith, Brenda 1946- ..................................... 82
Smith, C. Pritchard
   *See* Hoyt, Edwin P(almer), Jr.
Smith, Caesar
   *See* Trevor, Elleston
Smith, Charles R., (Jr.) 1969- ....................... 159
Smith, Craig 1955- ..................................... 172
   Earlier sketches in SATA *81, 117*
Smith, Cynthia Leitich 1967- ......................... 152
Smith, D. James 1955- ................................. 176
Smith, Datus C(lifford), Jr. 1907-1999 .............. 13
   Obituary ............................................. 116
Smith, Debra 1955- ...................................... 89
Smith, Derek 1943- .................................... 141
Smith, Dick King
   *See* King-Smith, Dick
Smith, Dodie
   *See* Smith, Dorothy Gladys
Smith, Doris Buchanan 1934-2002 .................... 75
   Obituary ............................................. 140
   Earlier sketch in SATA *28*
   *See also* SAAS *10*
Smith, Dorothy Gladys 1896-1990 .................... 82
   Obituary .............................................. 65
   *See* Smith, Dodie
Smith, Dorothy Stafford 1905- .......................... 6
Smith, E(lmer) Boyd 1860-1943
   *See* YABC *1*
Smith, E(dric) Brooks 1917- ........................... 40
Smith, Emma 1923- ...................................... 52
   Brief entry ........................................... 36
Smith, (Katherine) Eunice (Young) 1902-1993
   ......................................................... 5
Smith, Frances C(hristine) 1904-1986 ................. 3
Smith, Gary R. 1932- .................................... 14
Smith, Geof 1969- ...................................... 102
Smith, George Harmon 1920- ........................... 5
Smith, Greg Leitich ..................................... 152
Smith, Helene 1937- ................................... 142
Smith, Howard E(verett), Jr. 1927- ................... 12
Smith, Hugh L(etcher) 1921-1968 ...................... 5
Smith, Imogene Henderson 1922- ..................... 12
Smith, Jacqueline B. 1937- ............................. 39
Smith, Jada Pinkett 1971- ............................ 161
Smith, Janet (Buchanan) Adam
   *See* Adam Smith, Janet (Buchanan)
Smith, Janice Lee 1949- ............................... 155
   Earlier sketch in SATA *54*
Smith, Jean
   *See* Smith, Frances C(hristine)
Smith, Jean Pajot 1945- ................................. 10
Smith, Jeff(rey Alan) 1960- ........................... 161
   Earlier sketch in SATA *93*
Smith, Jeff Allen
   *See* Smith, Jeff(rey Alan)
Smith, Jenny 1963- ...................................... 90
Smith, Jessie
   *See* Kunhardt, Edith
Smith, Jessie Willcox 1863-1935 ...................... 21
   *See also* CLR *59*
Smith, Joan (Mary) 1933- ............................... 54
   Brief entry ........................................... 46
Smith, Johnston
   *See* Crane, Stephen (Townley)
Smith, Jos(eph) A. 1936- ............................. 120
   Earlier sketch in SATA *73*

Smith, Judie R. 1936- ................................... 80
Smith, Lafayette
   *See* Higdon, Hal
Smith, Lane 1959- ...................................... 131
   Earlier sketch in SATA *76*
   *See also* CLR *47*
Smith, Lee
   *See* Albion, Lee Smith
Smith, Lendon H(oward) 1921- ......................... 64
Smith, Linda 1949- .................................... 177
Smith, Linell Nash 1932- ................................. 2
Smith, Lucia B. 1943- ................................... 30
Smith, Marion Hagens 1913- ........................... 12
Smith, Marion Jaques 1899-1987 ...................... 13
Smith, Mary Ellen ....................................... 10
Smith, Marya 1945- ...................................... 78
Smith, Mike
   *See* Smith, Mary Ellen
Smith, Nancy Covert 1935- ............................. 12
Smith, Norman F. 1920- ................................. 70
   Earlier sketch in SATA *5*
Smith, Patricia Clark 1943- ............................. 96
Smith, Pauline C.
   *See* Arthur, Robert, (Jr.)
Smith, Pauline C(oggeshall) 1908-1994 ............. 27
Smith, Philip Warren 1936- ............................. 46
Smith, Rebecca 1946- ................................. 123
Smith, Robert Kimmel 1930- ........................... 77
   Earlier sketch in SATA *12*
Smith, Robert Paul 1915-1977 ......................... 52
   Obituary .............................................. 30
Smith, Roland 1951- ................................... 161
   Earlier sketch in SATA *115*
Smith, Rosamond
   *See* Oates, Joyce Carol
Smith, Ruth Leslie 1902- ................................. 2
Smith, Sandra Lee 1945- ................................ 75
Smith, Sarah Stafford
   *See* Smith, Dorothy Stafford
Smith, Sharon 1947- ..................................... 82
Smith, Sherri L. 1971- ................................. 156
Smith, Sherwood 1951- ................................ 140
   Earlier sketch in SATA *82*
Smith, Shirley Raines
   *See* Raines, Shirley C(arol)
Smith, Susan Carlton 1923- ............................. 12
Smith, Susan Mathias 1950- ............................ 43
   Brief entry ........................................... 35
Smith, Susan Vernon 1950- ............................. 48
Smith, Susan
   *See* Mendonca, Susan
Smith, Tim(othy R.) 1945- ............................ 151
Smith, Ursula 1934- ..................................... 54
Smith, Vian (Crocker) 1920-1969 ...................... 11
Smith, Wanda VanHoy 1926- ........................... 65
Smith, Ward
   *See* Goldsmith, Howard
Smith, William A. 1918- ................................. 10
Smith, William Jay 1918- .............................. 154
   Autobiography Feature .............................. 154
   Earlier sketches in SATA *2, 68*
   *See also* SAAS *22*
Smith, Winsome 1935- ................................... 45
Smith, Z.Z.
   *See* Westheimer, David
Smith-Ankrom, M. E. 1942- ........................... 130
Smith-Griswold, Wendy 1955- .......................... 88
Smith-Rex, Susan J. 1950- ............................. 94
Smithsen, Richard
   *See* Pellowski, Michael (Joseph)
Smits, Teo
   *See* Smits, Theodore R(ichard)
Smits, Theodore R(ichard) 1905-1996 ................ 45
   Brief entry ........................................... 28
Smolinski, Dick 1932- ................................... 86
Smothers, Ethel Footman 1944- ...................... 149
   Earlier sketch in SATA *76*
Smucker, Barbara (Claassen) 1915- .................. 130
   Earlier sketches in SATA *29, 76*
   *See also* CLR *10*
   *See also* SAAS *11*
Smyth, Iain 1959- ...................................... 105

Snedeker, Caroline Dale (Parke) 1871-1956
  *See* YABC 2
Snell, Nigel (Edward Creagh) 1936- .......... 57
  Brief entry ............................................. 40
Snellgrove, L(aurence) E(rnest) 1928- ...... 53
Snelling, Dennis (Wayne) 1958- ................ 84
Sneve, Virginia Driving Hawk 1933- ......... 95
  Earlier sketch in SATA 8
  *See also* CLR 2
Snicket, Lemony 1970- ............................ 126
  *See also* CLR 79
  *See* Handler, Daniel
Snodgrass, Mary Ellen 1944- ..................... 75
Snodgrass, Quentin Curtius
  *See* Clemens, Samuel Langhorne
Snodgrass, Thomas Jefferson
  *See* Clemens, Samuel Langhorne
Snook, Barbara (Lillian) 1913-1976 .......... 34
Snow, Donald Clifford 1917-1979 .............. 16
Snow, Dorothea J(ohnston) 1909- ................ 9
Snow, Richard F(olger) 1947- .................... 52
  Brief entry ............................................. 37
Snyder, Anne 1922-2001 ............................. 4
  Obituary ............................................... 125
Snyder, Bernadette McCarver 1930- ........... 97
Snyder, Carol 1941- .................................... 35
Snyder, Gerald S(eymour) 1933- ................ 48
  Brief entry ............................................. 34
Snyder, Midori 1954- ............................... 106
Snyder, Paul A. 1946- ............................... 125
Snyder, Zilpha Keatley 1927- ................... 163
  Autobiography Feature .......................... 163
  Earlier sketches in SATA 1, 28, 75, 110
  *See also* CLR 121
  *See also* SAAS 2
Snyderman, Reuven K. 1922- ....................... 5
So, Meilo ................................................. 162
Sobel, June 1950- ..................................... 149
Soble, Jennie
  *See* Cavin, Ruth (Brodie)
Sobol, Donald J. 1924- .............................. 132
  Earlier sketches in SATA 1, 31, 73
  *See also* CLR 4
Sobol, Harriet Langsam 1936- .................... 47
  Brief entry ............................................. 34
Sobol, Rose 1931- ...................................... 76
Sobott-Mogwe, Gaele 1956- ...................... 97
Soderlind, Arthur E(dwin) 1920- ............... 14
Soentpiet, Chris K. 1970- ......................... 159
  Earlier sketch in SATA 97
Soerensen, Svend Otto 1916- ...................... 67
Sofer, Barbara 1949- ................................ 109
Sofer, Rachel
  *See* Sofer, Barbara
Softly, Barbara Frewin 1924- ..................... 12
Sohl, Frederic J(ohn) 1916- ......................... 10
Sokol, Bill
  *See* Sokol, William
Sokol, William 1923- ................................. 37
Sokolov, Kirill 1930- .................................. 34
Solbert, Romaine G. 1925- ........................... 2
Solbert, Ronni
  *See* Solbert, Romaine G.
Solheim, James ................................... 133
Solomon, Joan 1930- .................................. 51
  Brief entry ............................................. 40
Solomons, Ikey Esquir
  *See* Thackeray, William Makepeace
Solonevich, George 1915-2003 ................... 15
Solot, Mary Lynn 1939- ............................. 12
Somerlott, Robert 1928-2001 ..................... 62
Somervill, Barbara A(nn) 1948- ............... 140
Sommer, Angela
  *See* Sommer-Bodenburg, Angela
Sommer, Carl 1930- ................................. 175
  Earlier sketch in SATA 126
Sommer, Elyse 1929- .................................... 7
Sommer, Robert 1929- ................................ 12
Sommer-Bodenburg, Angela 1948- ............. 63
Sommer-Bodenburg, Angela 1948- ........... 113
Sommerdorf, Norma (Jean) 1926- ............. 131

Sommerfelt, Aimee 1892-1975 ..................... 5
Son, John ................................................ 160
Sones, Sonya ............................................ 131
Sonneborn, Ruth (Cantor) 1899-1974 .......... 4
  Obituary ................................................. 27
Sonnenmark, Laura A. 1958- ...................... 73
Sopko, Eugen 1949- .................................... 58
Sorel, Edward 1929- ................................. 126
  Brief entry ............................................. 37
  Earlier sketch in SATA 65
Sorensen, Henri 1950- ............................... 115
  Earlier sketch in SATA 77
Sorensen, Svend Otto
  *See* Soerensen, Svend Otto
Sorensen, Virginia 1912-1991 ...................... 2
  Obituary ................................................. 72
  *See also* SAAS 15
Sorenson, Jane 1926- .................................. 63
Sorenson, Margo 1946- ............................... 96
Sorley Walker, Kathrine ............................ 41
Sorrells, Walter ...................................... 177
Sorrentino, Joseph N. 1937- ......................... 6
Sortor, June Elizabeth 1939- ....................... 12
Sortor, Toni
  *See* Sortor, June Elizabeth
Soskin, V. H.
  *See* Ellison, Virginia H(owell)
Soto, Gary 1952- ..................................... 174
  Earlier sketches in SATA 80, 120
  *See also* CLR 38
Sotomayor, Antonio 1902-1985 ................... 11
Souci, Robert D. San
  *See* San Souci, Robert D.
Soudley, Henry
  *See* Wood, James Playsted
Souhami, Jessica ..................................... 176
Soule, Gardner (Bosworth) 1913-2000 ....... 14
Soule, Jean Conder 1919- ........................... 10
Souster, (Holmes) Raymond 1921- ............. 63
South, Sheri Cobb 1959- ............................ 82
Southall, Ivan (Francis) 1921- .................. 134
  Autobiography Feature .......................... 134
  Earlier sketches in SATA 3, 68
  *See also* CLR 2
  *See also* SAAS 3
Southey, Robert 1774-1843 ........................ 54
Southgate, Vera ......................................... 54
Sovak, Jan 1953- ...................................... 115
Sowden, Celeste
  *See* Walters, Celeste
Sowter, Nita .............................................. 69
Spafford, Suzy 1945- ................................ 160
Spagnoli, Cathy 1950- ............................. 134
  Earlier sketch in SATA 79
Spain, Sahara Sunday 1991- ..................... 133
Spalding, Andrea 1944- ............................ 150
  Earlier sketch in SATA 101
Spanfeller, James J(ohn) 1930- ................... 19
  *See* Spanfeller, Jim
Spanfeller, Jim
  *See* SAAS 8
  *See* Spanfeller, James J(ohn)
Spangenberg, Judith Dunn 1942- .................. 5
Spanyol, Jessica 1965- .............................. 137
Spar, Jerome 1918- .................................... 10
Sparks, Barbara 1942- ................................ 78
Sparks, Beatrice (Mathews) 1918- .............. 44
  Brief entry ............................................. 28
Sparks, Mary W. 1920- .............................. 15
Spaulding, Douglas
  *See* Bradbury, Ray
Spaulding, Leonard
  *See* Bradbury, Ray
Spaulding, Norma .................................... 107
Speare, Elizabeth George 1908-1994 .......... 62
  Obituary ................................................. 83
  Earlier sketch in SATA 5
  *See also* CLR 8
Spearing, Judith (Mary Harlow) 1922- ......... 9
Speck, Nancy 1959- ................................. 104
Specking, Inez 1890-1960(?) ...................... 11

Speed, Nell
  *See* Keats, Emma
  and Sampson, Emma (Keats) Speed
Speed, Nell (Ewing) 1878-1913 ................. 68
Speer, Bonnie Stahlman 1929- .................. 113
Speer-Lyon, Tammie L. 1965- ..................... 89
Speicher, Helen Ross S(mith) 1915- ............. 8
Speir, Nancy 1958- ................................... 81
Spellman, John W(illard) 1934- .................. 14
Spellman, Roger G.
  *See* Cox, William R(obert)
Spelman, Cornelia Maude 1946- ............... 144
  Earlier sketch in SATA 96
Spelman, Mary 1934- ................................. 28
Spelvin, George
  *See* Lerangis, Peter
  and Phillips, David Atlee
Spence, Cynthia
  *See* Eble, Diane
Spence, Eleanor (Rachel) 1928- ................. 21
  *See also* CLR 26
Spence, Geraldine 1931- ............................. 47
Spencer, Ann 1918- .................................... 10
Spencer, Cornelia
  *See* Yaukey, Grace S(ydenstricker)
Spencer, Donald D(ean) 1931- .................... 41
Spencer, Elizabeth 1921- ............................ 14
Spencer, Leonard G.
  *See* Garrett, (Gordon) Randall (Phillip)
  and Silverberg, Robert
Spencer, William 1922- ................................ 9
Spencer, Zane A(nn) 1935- ......................... 35
Sper, Emily 1957- .................................... 142
Speregen, Devra Newberger 1964- ............. 84
Sperling, Dan(iel Lee) 1949- ...................... 65
Sperry, Armstrong W. 1897-1976 .................. 1
  Obituary ................................................. 27
Sperry, Raymond
  *See* Garis, Howard R(oger)
Sperry, Raymond, Jr. ................................... 1
Spetter, Jung-Hee 1969- ........................... 134
Spicer, Dorothy Gladys -1975 ..................... 32
Spiegelman, Art 1948- ............................. 158
  Earlier sketch in SATA 109
Spiegelman, Judith M. ................................. 5
Spielberg, Steven 1947- .............................. 32
Spier, Peter (Edward) 1927- ....................... 54
  Earlier sketch in SATA 4
  *See also* CLR 5
Spilhaus, Athelstan (Frederick) 1911-1998 . 13
  Obituary ............................................... 102
Spilka, Arnold 1917- .................................... 6
Spillane, Frank Morrison
  *See* Spillane, Mickey
Spillane, Mickey 1918-2006 ....................... 66
  Obituary ............................................... 176
  *See* Spillane, Frank Morrison
Spinelli, Eileen 1942- ............................... 150
  Earlier sketches in SATA 38, 101
Spinelli, Jerry 1941- ................................. 158
  Earlier sketches in SATA 39, 71, 110
  *See also* CLR 82
Spink, Reginald (William) 1905-1994 ......... 11
Spinka, Penina Keen 1945- ......................... 72
Spinner, Stephanie 1943- .......................... 132
  Earlier sketches in SATA 38, 91
Spinossimus
  *See* White, William, Jr.
Spiotta-DiMare, Loren ............................. 173
Spires, Elizabeth 1952- ............................. 111
  Earlier sketch in SATA 71
Spirin, Gennadii
  *See* Spirin, Gennady
Spirin, Gennadij
  *See* Spirin, Gennady
Spirin, Gennady 1948- .............................. 134
  Earlier sketch in SATA 95
  *See also* CLR 88
Spivak, Dawnine ...................................... 101
Spohn, David 1948- .................................... 72

Spohn, Kate 1962- ................................. 147
Earlier sketch in SATA 87
Spollen, Christopher 1952- ....................... 12
Spooner, Michael (Tim) 1954- .................. 92
Spowart, Robin 1947- ............................. 177
Earlier sketch in SATA 82
Sprague, Gretchen 1926-2003 .................. 27
Sprengel, Artie
See Lerangis, Peter
Sprigge, Elizabeth (Miriam Squire) 1900-1974
.......................................................... 10
Spring, (Robert) Howard 1889-1965 ......... 28
Springer, Margaret 1941- ........................ 78
Springer, Marilyn Harris 1931- ................ 47
Springer, Nancy 1948- ............................ 172
Earlier sketches in SATA 65, 110
Springstubb, Tricia 1950- ......................... 78
Brief entry ......................................... 40
Earlier sketch in SATA 46
Spudvilas, Anne 1951- ............................. 94
Spurll, Barbara 1952- .............................. 78
Spurr, Elizabeth ................................... 172
Spykman, E(lizabeth) C(hoate) 1896-1965 . 10
See also CLR 35
Spyri, Johanna (Heusser) 1827-1901 ......... 100
Earlier sketch in SATA 19
See also CLR 115
Squires, Phil
See Barker, S(quire) Omar
Srba, Lynne ................................. 98
Sreenivasan, Jyotsna 1964- ....................... 101
S-Ringi, Kjell
See Ringi, Kjell (Arne Soerensen)
Stacey, Cherylyn 1945- ............................ 96
Stacy, Donald
See Pohl, Frederik
Stadtler, Bea 1921- ................................. 17
Stafford, Liliana 1950- ............................. 141
Stafford, Paul 1966- ................................ 116
Stahl, Ben(jamin) 1910-1987 ................... 5
Obituary ............................................ 54
Stahl, Hilda 1938-1993 ............................ 48
Obituary ............................................ 77
Stahler, David, Jr. .................................. 162
Stair, Gobin (John) 1912- ....................... 35
Stalder, Valerie .................................... 27
Stamaty, Mark Alan 1947- ....................... 12
Stambler, Irwin 1924- ............................. 5
Standiford, Natalie 1961- ......................... 169
Earlier sketch in SATA 81
Stanek, Lou Willett 1931- ........................ 63
Stang, Judit 1921-1977 ............................ 29
Stang, Judy
See Stang, Judit
Stangl, (Mary) Jean 1928- ....................... 67
Stanhope, Eric
See Hamilton, Charles (Harold St. John)
Stankevich, Boris 1928- ........................... 2
Stanley, Diane 1943- ............................... 164
Brief entry ......................................... 32
Earlier sketches in SATA 37, 80, 115
See also CLR 46
See also SAAS 15
Stanley, George Edward 1942- .................. 157
Earlier sketches in SATA 53, 111
See Dixon, Franklin W.
and Hope, Laura Lee
and Keene, Carolyn
Stanley, Jerry 1941- ................................ 127
Earlier sketch in SATA 79
Stanley, Mandy ..................................... 165
Stanley, Robert
See Hamilton, Charles (Harold St. John)
Stanley, Sanna 1962- ............................... 145
Stanli, Sue
See Meilach, Dona Z(weigoron)
Stanstead, John
See Groom, Arthur William
Stanton, Schuyler
See Baum, L(yman) Frank

Staples, Suzanne Fisher 1945- .................. 151
Earlier sketches in SATA 70, 105
See also CLR 60
Stapleton, Marjorie (Winifred) 1932- ......... 28
Stapp, Arthur D(onald) 1906-1972 ............ 4
Starbird, Kaye 1916- .............................. 6
See also CLR 60
Stark, Evan 1942- .................................. 78
Stark, James
See Goldston, Robert (Conroy)
Stark, Ulf 1944- .................................... 124
Starke, Ruth (Elaine) 1946- ..................... 129
Starkey, Marion L(ena) 1901-1991 ........... 13
Starr, Ward
See Manes, Stephen
Starret, William
See McClintock, Marshall
Starr Taylor, Bridget 1959- ....................... 99
Stasiak, Krystyna .................................. 49
Staub, Frank 1949- ................................. 116
Staub, Frank Jacob
See Staub, Frank
Staub, Wendy Corsi 1964- ....................... 114
Stauffacher, Sue 1961- ............................ 155
Staunton, Schuyler
See Baum, L(yman) Frank
Staunton, Ted 1956- ............................... 167
Earlier sketch in SATA 112
Steadman, Ralph (Idris) 1936- .................. 123
Earlier sketch in SATA 32
Stearman, Kaye 1951- ............................. 118
Stearns, Monroe (Mather) 1913-1987 ........ 5
Obituary ............................................ 55
Steckler, Arthur 1921-1985 ..................... 65
Steding, Laurie 1953- ............................. 119
Steel, Danielle 1947- .............................. 66
Steel, Danielle Fernande
See Steel, Danielle
Steele, Addison II
See Lupoff, Richard A(llen)
Steele, Alexander 1958- ........................... 116
Steele, Henry Maxwell
See Steele, Max
Steele, Mary 1930- ................................. 94
Steele, Mary Q(uintard Govan) 1922-1992 . 51
Obituary ............................................ 72
Earlier sketch in SATA 3
Steele, Max 1922-2005 ............................ 168
Earlier sketch in SATA 10
Steele, Philip 1948- ................................ 140
Earlier sketch in SATA 81
Steele, William O(wen) 1917-1979 ............ 51
Obituary ............................................ 27
Earlier sketch in SATA 1
Steelhammer, Ilona 1952- ........................ 98
Steelsmith, Shari 1962- ........................... 72
Stefanik, Alfred T. 1939- ......................... 55
Steffanson, Con
See Cassiday, Bruce (Bingham)
and Goulart, Ron(ald Joseph)
Steffens, Bradley 1955- ........................... 166
Earlier sketch in SATA 77
Stegeman, Janet Allais 1923- .................... 53
Brief entry ......................................... 49
See Britton, Kate
Steig, William 1907-2003 ........................ 111
Obituary ............................................ 149
Earlier sketches in SATA 18, 70
See also CLR 103
Steig, William H.
See Steig, William
Stein, M(eyer) L(ewis) 1920- ................... 6
Stein, Mini ........................................ 2
Stein, R(ichard) Conrad 1937- .................. 154
Earlier sketches in SATA 31, 82
Stein, Wendy 1951- ............................... 77
Steinbeck, John (Ernst) 1902-1968 ........... 9
Steinberg, Alfred 1917-1995 ..................... 9
Steinberg, Fannie 1899-1990 .................... 43
Steinberg, Fred J. 1933- ........................... 4
Steinberg, Phillip Orso 1921- .................... 34

Steinberg, Rafael (Mark) 1927- ................. 45
Steinberg, Saul 1914-1999 ....................... 67
Steincrohn, Maggie
See Davis, Maggie S.
Steiner, Barbara A(nnette) 1934- ............... 83
Earlier sketch in SATA 13
See also SAAS 13
Steiner, Charlotte 1900-1981 .................... 45
Steiner, George 1929- ............................. 62
Steiner, Joan ....................................... 110
Steiner, Jorg
See Steiner, Jorg
Steiner, Jorg 1930- ................................. 35
Steiner, K. Leslie
See Delany, Samuel R., Jr.
Steiner, Stan(ley) 1925-1987 .................... 14
Obituary ............................................ 50
Steins, Richard 1942- ............................. 79
Stem, Jacqueline 1931- ............................ 110
Steneman, Shep 1945- ............................. 132
Stengel, Joyce A. 1938- ........................... 158
Stephanie, Gordon
See Gordon, Stephanie Jacob
Stephens, Alice Barber 1858-1932 ............ 66
Stephens, Casey
See Wagner, Sharon B.
Stephens, J.B.
See Lynn, Tracy
Stephens, Mary Jo 1935- ......................... 8
Stephens, Rebecca 1961- .......................... 141
Stephens, Reed
See Donaldson, Stephen R(eeder)
Stephens, Suzanne
See Kirby, Susan E.
Stephens, William M(cLain) 1925- ............ 21
Stephensen, A. M.
See Manes, Stephen
Stepp, Ann 1935- .................................. 29
Stepto, Michele 1946- ............................. 61
Steptoe, Javaka 1971- ............................. 151
Steptoe, John (Lewis) 1950-1989 .............. 63
Earlier sketch in SATA 8
See also CLR 12
Sterling, Brett
See Bradbury, Ray
and Hamilton, Edmond
and Samachson, Joseph
Sterling, Dorothy 1913- ........................... 83
Autobiography Feature ........................... 127
Earlier sketch in SATA 1
See also CLR 1
See also SAAS 2
Sterling, Philip 1907-1989 ....................... 8
Obituary ............................................ 63
Sterling, Shirley (Anne) 1948- .................. 101
Stern, Ellen Norman 1927- ....................... 26
Stern, Judith M. 1951- ............................. 75
Stern, Madeleine B(ettina) 1912- .............. 14
Stern, Maggie 1953- ............................... 156
Stern, Philip Van Doren 1900-1984 ........... 13
Obituary ............................................ 39
Stern, Simon 1943- ................................ 15
Sterne, Emma Gelders 1894- .................... 6
Steurt, Marjorie Rankin 1888-1978 ........... 10
Stevens, Bryna 1924- .............................. 65
Stevens, Carla M(cBride) 1928- ................ 13
Stevens, Chambers 1968- ......................... 128
Stevens, Diane 1939- .............................. 94
Stevens, Franklin 1933- ........................... 6
Stevens, Greg
See Cook, Glen
Stevens, Gwendolyn 1944- ....................... 33
Stevens, Jan Romero 1953- ....................... 95
Stevens, Janet 1953- ............................... 148
Earlier sketch in SATA 90
Stevens, Kathleen 1936- .......................... 49
Stevens, Leonard A. 1920- ....................... 67
Stevens, Lucile Vernon 1899-1994 ............ 59
Stevens, Margaret Dean
See Aldrich, Bess Streeter
Stevens, Patricia Bunning 1931- ............... 27

Stevens, Peter
　See Geis, Darlene Stern
Stevens, Serita (Deborah) 1949- ................. *70*
Stevens, Shira
　See Stevens, Serita (Deborah)
Stevenson, Anna (M.) 1905- ....................... *12*
Stevenson, Augusta 1869(?)-1976 ............... *2*
　Obituary .................................................. *26*
Stevenson, Burton Egbert 1872-1962 ......... *25*
Stevenson, Drew 1947- ............................... *60*
Stevenson, Harvey 1960- ........................... *148*
　Earlier sketch in SATA *80*
Stevenson, James 1929- ............................. *161*
　Brief entry ............................................... *34*
　Earlier sketches in SATA *42, 71, 113*
　See also CLR *17*
Stevenson, Janet 1913- ................................. *8*
Stevenson, Robert Louis (Balfour) 1850-1894
　.............................................................. *100*
　See also YABC *2*
　See also CLR *107*
Stevenson, Susie 1956- ............................. *104*
Stewart, A(gnes) C(harlotte) ....................... *15*
Stewart, Chantal 1945- ............................. *173*
　Earlier sketch in SATA *121*
Stewart, Charles
　See Zurhorst, Charles (Stewart, Jr.)
Stewart, Eleanor
　See Porter, Eleanor H(odgman)
Stewart, Elisabeth J(ane) 1927- ................. *93*
Stewart, Elizabeth Laing 1907- ..................... *6*
Stewart, Gail B. 1949- ............................... *141*
Stewart, George Rippey 1895-1980 ............. *3*
　Obituary .................................................. *23*
Stewart, Jennifer J(enkins) 1960- ............. *128*
Stewart, Joel .............................................. *151*
Stewart, John (William) 1920- ..................... *14*
　See Cole, Jack
Stewart, Mary (Florence Elinor) 1916- ....... *12*
Stewart, Mary Rainbow
　See Stewart, Mary (Florence Elinor)
Stewart, Melissa 1968- ............................. *167*
　Earlier sketch in SATA *111*
Stewart, Paul 1955- ................................... *163*
　Earlier sketch in SATA *114*
Stewart, Robert Neil 1891-1972 ................... *7*
Stewart, Sarah .......................................... *143*
Stewart, Scott
　See Zaffo, George J.
Stewart, W(alter) P. 1924- ........................... *53*
Stewart, Whitney 1959- ............................. *167*
　Earlier sketch in SATA *92*
Stewig, John Warren 1937- ....................... *162*
　Earlier sketches in SATA *26, 110*
Stickler, Soma Han 1942- ......................... *128*
Stidworthy, John 1943- ............................... *63*
Stiles, Martha Bennett ............................... *108*
　Earlier sketch in SATA *6*
Still, James 1906-2001 ................................. *29*
　Obituary ................................................. *127*
Stille, Darlene R. 1942- ............................. *170*
　Earlier sketch in SATA *126*
Stille, Darlene Ruth
　See Stille, Darlene R.
Stillerman, Marci ...................................... *104*
Stillerman, Robbie 1947- ............................. *12*
Stilley, Frank 1918- ..................................... *29*
Stilton, Geronimo ..................................... *158*
Stimpson, Gerald
　See Mitchell, Adrian
Stine, Catherine ........................................ *165*
Stine, G(eorge) Harry 1928-1997 ............. *136*
　Earlier sketch in SATA *10*
Stine, Jovial Bob
　See Stine, R.L.
Stine, R.L. 1943- ...................................... *129*
　Earlier sketches in SATA *31, 76*
　See also CLR *111*
Stine, Robert Lawrence
　See Stine, R.L.
Stinetorf, Louise (Allender) 1900-1992 ...... *10*

Stinson, Kathy 1952- ................................... *98*
Stirling, Arthur
　See Sinclair, Upton
Stirling, Ian 1941- ....................................... *77*
Stirling, Nora B(romley) 1900-1997 ............. *3*
Stirnweis, Shannon 1931- ........................... *10*
Stobbs, William 1914-2000 ......................... *17*
　Obituary ................................................. *120*
Stock, Carolmarie 1951- ............................. *75*
Stock, Catherine 1952- ............................. *158*
　Earlier sketches in SATA *65, 114*
Stockdale, Susan 1954- ............................... *98*
Stockham, Peter (Alan) 1928- ..................... *57*
Stockton, Francis Richard 1834-1902 ......... *44*
　See Stockton, Frank R.
Stockton, Frank R.
　Brief entry ............................................... *32*
　See Stockton, Francis Richard
Stockwell-Moniz, Marc J. 1954- ............... *164*
Stoddard, Edward G. 1923- ......................... *10*
Stoddard, Hope 1900-1987 ........................... *6*
Stoddard, Sandol 1927- ............................... *98*
　See Warburg, Sandol Stoddard
Stoehr, Shelley 1969- ................................. *107*
Stoeke, Janet Morgan 1957- ....................... *136*
　Earlier sketch in SATA *90*
Stoiko, Michael 1919- ................................. *14*
Stojic, Manya 1967- ................................... *156*
Stoker, Abraham 1847-1912 ....................... *29*
　See Stoker, Bram
Stoker, Bram
　See Stoker, Abraham
Stokes, Cedric
　See Beardmore, George
Stokes, Jack (Tilden) 1923- ......................... *13*
Stokes, Olivia Pearl 1916- ........................... *32*
Stolz, Mary 1920-2006 ............................... *133*
　Earlier sketches in SATA *10, 71*
　See also SAAS *3*
Stolz, Mary Slattery
　See Stolz, Mary
Stone, Alan
　See Svenson, Andrew E(dward)
Stone, David K(arl) 1922- ............................. *9*
Stone, David Lee 1978- ............................. *166*
Stone, Eugenia 1879-1971 ........................... *7*
Stone, Gene
　See Stone, Eugenia
Stone, Helen V(irginia) ................................. *6*
Stone, Idella Purnell
　See Purnell, Idella
Stone, Ikey
　See Purnell, Idella
Stone, Irving 1903-1989 ............................... *3*
　Obituary ................................................... *64*
Stone, Jon 1931-1997 ................................. *39*
　Obituary ................................................... *95*
Stone, Josephine Rector
　See Dixon, Jeanne
Stone, Lesley
　See Trevor, Elleston
Stone, Peter 1930-2003 ............................... *65*
　Obituary ................................................. *143*
Stone, Phoebe .......................................... *134*
Stone, Raymond ............................................ *1*
Stone, Rosetta
　See Dr. Seuss
　and Geisel, Theodor Seuss
　and LeSieg, Theo.
　and Seuss, Dr.
Stonehouse, Bernard 1926- ....................... *140*
　Earlier sketches in SATA *13, 80*
Stones, (Cyril) Anthony 1934- ..................... *72*
Stong, Phil(ip Duffield) 1899-1957 ............. *32*
Stoops, Erik D(aniel) 1966- ....................... *142*
　Earlier sketch in SATA *78*
Stoppelmoore, Cheryl Jean
　See Ladd, Cheryl (Jean)
Stops, Sue 1936- ......................................... *86*
Storad, Conrad J. 1957- ............................. *119*
Storey, Margaret 1926- ................................. *9*

Storey, Victoria Carolyn 1945- ................... *16*
Storme, Peter
　See Stern, Philip Van Doren
Storr, Catherine (Cole) 1913-2001 ............. *87*
　Obituary ................................................. *122*
　Earlier sketch in SATA *9*
Story, Josephine
　See Loring, Emilie (Baker)
Stotko, Mary-Ann 1960- ........................... *154*
Stott, Dorothy (M.) 1958- ........................... *99*
　Earlier sketch in SATA *67*
Stott, Dot
　See Stott, Dorothy (M.)
Stotter, Mike 1957- ................................... *108*
Stout, William 1949- ................................. *132*
Stoutenburg, Adrien (Pearl) 1916-1982 ....... *3*
Stoutland, Allison 1963- ........................... *130*
Stover, Allan C(arl) 1938- ........................... *14*
Stover, Jill (Griffin) 1958- ........................... *82*
Stover, Marjorie Filley 1914- ....................... *9*
Stowe, Harriet (Elizabeth) Beecher 1811-1896
　See YABC *1*
Stowe, Leland 1899-1994 ............................. *60*
　Obituary ................................................... *78*
Stowe, Rosetta
　See Ogan, George F.
　and Ogan, Margaret E. (Nettles)
Strachan, Ian 1938- ..................................... *85*
Strachan, Linda .......................................... *167*
Strachan, Margaret Pitcairn 1908-1998 ....... *14*
Strahinich, H. C.
　See Strahinich, Helen C.
Strahinich, Helen C. 1949- ......................... *78*
Strait, Treva Adams 1909- ........................... *35*
Strand, Mark 1934- ..................................... *41*
Stranger, Joyce
　See SAAS *24*
　See Wilson, Joyce M(uriel Judson)
Strangis, Joel 1948- ................................... *124*
Strannigan, Shawn 1956- ............................. *93*
Strannigan, Shawn Alyne
　See Strannigan, Shawn
Strasser, Todd 1950- ................................. *153*
　Earlier sketches in SATA *41, 45, 71, 107*
　See also CLR *11*
Stratemeyer, Edward L. 1862-1930 ........... *100*
　Earlier sketches in SATA *1, 67*
　See Adams, Harrison
　and Appleton, Victor
　and Dixon, Franklin W.
　and Keene, Carolyn
　and Rockwood, Roy
　and Young, Clarence
Stratford, Philip 1927- ................................. *47*
Stratton, J. M.
　See Whitlock, Ralph
Stratton, Thomas
　See Coulson, Robert S(tratton)
　and DeWeese, Thomas Eugene
Stratton-Porter, Gene(va Grace) 1863-1924
　.............................................................. *15*
　See also CLR *87*
　See Porter, Gene(va Grace) Stratton
Strauss, Gwen 1963- ................................... *77*
Strauss, Joyce 1936- ................................... *53*
Strauss, Linda Leopold 1942- ................... *127*
Strauss, Susan (Elizabeth) 1954- ............... *75*
Strayer, E. Ward
　See Stratemeyer, Edward L.
Streano, Vince(nt Catello) 1945- ................. *20*
Streatfeild, (Mary) Noel 1897(?)-1986 ........ *20*
　Obituary ................................................... *48*
　See also CLR *83*
Street, Janet Travell 1959- ........................... *84*
Street, Julia Montgomery 1898-1993 ........... *11*
Streissguth, Thomas 1958- ......................... *116*
Strelkoff, Tatiana 1957- ............................... *89*
Stren, Patti 1949- ......................................... *88*
　Brief entry ............................................... *41*
　See also CLR *5*

Strete, Craig Kee 1950- ............................ 96
    Earlier sketch in SATA 44
Stretton, Barbara (Humphrey) 1936- .......... 43
    Brief entry ........................................... 35
Strickland, (William) Brad(ley) 1947- ...... 142
    Earlier sketches in SATA 83, 137
Strickland, Craig (A.) 1956- ..................... 102
Strickland, Dorothy S(alley) 1933- ............ 89
Strickland, Michael R. 1965- .................... 144
    Earlier sketch in SATA 83
Strickland, Tessa ..................................... 173
Striegel, Jana 1955- ................................. 140
Striegel-Wilson, Jana
    See Striegel, Jana
Striker, Lee
    See Clark, Margaret (D.)
Striker, Susan 1942- .................................. 63
Stringer, Lauren 1957- ............................. 129
Stroeyer, Poul 1923- .................................. 13
Stromoski, Rick 1958- .............................. 111
Strong, Charles
    See Epstein, Beryl (M. Williams)
    and Epstein, Samuel
Strong, David
    See McGuire, Leslie (Sarah)
Strong, Jeremy 1949- ............................... 175
    Earlier sketches in SATA 36, 105
Strong, J.J.
    See Strong, Jeremy
Strong, Pat
    See Hough, Richard (Alexander)
Strong, Stacie 1965- .................................. 74
Stroud, Bettye 1939- ................................ 165
    Earlier sketch in SATA 96
Stroud, Jonathan 1970- ............................ 159
    Earlier sketch in SATA 102
Stroyer, Poul
    See Stroeyer, Poul
Strug, Kerri 1977- ................................... 108
Stryker, Daniel
    See Morris, Chris(topher Crosby)
    and Stump, Jane Barr
Stuart, David
    See Hoyt, Edwin P(almer), Jr.
Stuart, Derek
    See Foster, John L(ouis)
Stuart, Forbes 1924- .................................. 13
Stuart, Ian
    See MacLean, Alistair (Stuart)
Stuart, Jesse (Hilton) 1906-1984 .................. 2
    Obituary ................................................ 36
Stuart, Ruth McEnery 1849(?)-1917 ......... 116
Stuart, Sheila
    See Baker, Mary Gladys Steel
Stuart-Clark, Christopher (Anthony) 1940- . 32
Stubis, Talivaldis 1926- ............................... 5
Stubley, Trevor (Hugh) 1932- ..................... 22
Stucky, Naomi R. 1922- ............................. 72
Stucley, Elizabeth
    See Northmore, Elizabeth Florence
Stultifer, Morton
    See Curtis, Richard (Alan)
Sture-Vasa, Mary
    See Alsop, Mary O'Hara
Sturges, Philemon ................................... 174
Sturtevant, Katherine 1950- ..................... 130
Sturton, Hugh
    See Johnston, H(ugh) A(nthony) S(tephen)
Sturtzel, Howard A(llison) 1894-1985 .......... 1
Sturtzel, Jane Levington 1903-1996 .............. 1
Stutley, D(oris) J(ean) 1959- ..................... 142
Stutson, Caroline 1940- ............................ 104
Stuve-Bodeen, Stephanie 1965- ................. 158
    Earlier sketch in SATA 114
Stux, Erica 1929- ..................................... 140
Styles, (Frank) Showell 1908- ...................... 10
Stynes, Barbara White .............................. 133
Suba, Susanne ........................................... 4
Subond, Valerie
    See Grayland, Valerie (Merle Spanner)
Sudbery, Rodie 1943- ................................ 42

Suen, Anastasia 1956(?)- ........................... 157
Sufrin, Mark 1925- .................................... 76
Sugarman, Joan G. 1917- ........................... 64
Sugarman, Tracy 1921- ............................... 37
Sugita, Yutaka 1930- .................................. 36
Suhl, Yuri (Menachem) 1908-1986 ................. 8
    Obituary ................................................ 50
    See also CLR 2
    See also SAAS 1
Suhr, Joanne ......................................... 129
Suid, Murray 1942- .................................... 27
Sullivan, George (Edward) 1927- ............... 147
    Earlier sketches in SATA 4, 89
Sullivan, Jody
    See Rake, Jody
Sullivan, Kathryn A. 1954- ........................ 141
Sullivan, Mary Ann 1954- ........................... 63
Sullivan, Mary W(ilson) 1907- ..................... 13
Sullivan, Pat
    See Messmer, Otto
Sullivan, Paul 1939- ................................. 106
Sullivan, Silky
    See Makowski, Silvia Ann
Sullivan, Sue
    See Sullivan, Susan E.
Sullivan, Susan E. 1962- ........................... 123
Sullivan, Thomas Joseph, Jr. 1947- ............. 16
Sullivan, Tom
    See Sullivan, Thomas Joseph, Jr.
Sully, Tom 1959- ..................................... 104
Sumichrast, Jozef 1948- ............................. 29
Sumiko
    See Davies, Sumiko
Summerforest, Ivy B.
    See Kirkup, James
Summers, James L(evingston) 1910-1973 .. 57
    Brief entry ........................................... 28
Summertree, Katonah
    See Windsor, Patricia
Sun, Chyng Feng 1959- ............................. 90
Sunderlin, Sylvia (S.) 1911-1997 ................. 28
    Obituary ................................................ 99
Sung, Betty Lee ........................................ 26
Supeene, Shelagh Lynne 1952- ................... 153
Supraner, Robyn 1930- ............................. 101
    Earlier sketch in SATA 20
Supree, Burt(on) 1941-1992 ....................... 73
Surface, Mary Hall 1958- .......................... 126
Surge, Frank 1931- .................................... 13
Susac, Andrew 1929- ................................... 5
Susi, Geraldine Lee 1942- ........................... 98
Sussman, Cornelia Silver 1914-1999 ............ 59
Sussman, Irving 1908-1996 ......................... 59
Sussman, Susan 1942- ................................ 48
Sutcliff, Rosemary 1920-1992 ..................... 78
    Obituary ................................................ 73
    Earlier sketches in SATA 6, 44
    See also CLR 37
Sutcliffe, Jane 1957- ................................ 138
Sutherland, Colleen 1944- ........................... 79
Sutherland, Efua (Theodora Morgue)
    1924-1996 ............................................ 25
Sutherland, Jon 1958- .............................. 167
Sutherland, Jonathan D.
    See Sutherland, Jon
Sutherland, Margaret 1941- ......................... 15
Sutherland, Zena Bailey 1915-2002 .............. 37
    Obituary .............................................. 137
Suttles, Shirley (Smith) 1922- ..................... 21
Sutton, Ann (Livesay) 1923- ....................... 31
Sutton, Eve(lyn Mary) 1906-1992 ................ 26
Sutton, Felix 1910(?)-1973 ......................... 31
Sutton, Jane 1950- .................................... 52
    Brief entry ........................................... 43
Sutton, Larry M(atthew) 1931- ................... 29
Sutton, Margaret Beebe 1903-2001 ............... 1
    Obituary .............................................. 131
Sutton, Myron Daniel 1925- ........................ 31
Sutton, Roger 1956- .................................. 93

Suzanne, Jamie
    See Hawes, Louise
    and Lantz, Francess L(in)
    and Singleton, Linda Joy
    and Zach, Cheryl (Byrd)
Suzuki, David T(akayoshi) 1936- .............. 138
Svendsen, Mark (Nestor) 1962- ................ 120
Svenson, Andrew E(dward) 1910-1975 ........ 2
    Obituary ................................................ 26
Swain, Carol 1962- .................................. 172
Swain, Gwenyth 1961- .............................. 134
    Earlier sketch in SATA 84
Swain, Ruth
    See Swain, Ruth Freeman
Swain, Ruth Freeman 1951- ...................... 161
    Earlier sketch in SATA 119
Swain, Su Zan (Noguchi) 1916- ................... 21
Swamp, Jake 1941- .................................... 98
Swan, Susan 1944- ................................... 108
    Earlier sketch in SATA 22
Swann, Brian (Stanley Frank) 1940- ......... 116
Swann, E. L.
    See Lasky, Kathryn
Swann, Ruth Rice 1920- .............................. 84
Swanson, Helen M(cKendry) 1919- .............. 94
Swanson, June 1931- .................................. 76
Swanson, Wayne 1942- ............................. 167
Swarthout, Glendon (Fred) 1918-1992 ......... 26
Swarthout, Kathryn 1919- ............................. 7
Swayne, Sam(uel F.) 1907- ......................... 53
Swayne, Zoa (Lourana) 1905- ...................... 53
Sweat, Lynn 1934- ................................... 168
    Earlier sketch in SATA 57
Swede, George 1940- .................................. 67
Sweeney, James B(artholomew) 1910-1999
    ........................................................... 21
Sweeney, Joyce 1955- .............................. 167
    Earlier sketches in SATA 65, 68, 108
Sweeney, Joyce Kay
    See Sweeney, Joyce
Sweeney, Karen O'Connor
    See O'Connor, Karen
Sweeney, Matthew (Gerard) 1952- ............ 156
Sweet, Melissa 1956- ............................... 172
Sweet, Sarah C.
    See Jewett, (Theodora) Sarah Orne
Sweetland, Nancy A(nn) 1934- ..................... 48
Swenson, Allan A(rmstrong) 1933- .............. 21
Swenson, May 1919-1989 ............................ 15
Swentzell, Rina 1939- ................................. 79
Swift, Bryan
    See Knott, William C(ecil, Jr.)
Swift, David
    See Kaufmann, John
Swift, Jonathan 1667-1745 .......................... 19
    See also CLR 53
Swift, Merlin
    See Leeming, Joseph
Swiger, Elinor Porter 1927- .......................... 8
Swinburne, Laurence (Joseph) 1924- ............. 9
Swinburne, Stephen R. 1952- ..................... 150
Swinburne, Steve
    See Swinburne, Stephen R.
Swindells, Robert (Edward) 1939- ............. 150
    Brief entry ........................................... 34
    Earlier sketches in SATA 50, 80
    See also SAAS 14
Swinford, Betty (June Wells) 1927- ............. 58
Swinford, Bob
    See Swinford, Betty (June Wells)
Swithen, John
    See King, Stephen
Switzer, Ellen 1923- .................................. 48
Swope, Sam ........................................... 156
Swope, Samuel
    See Swope, Sam
Sybesma, Jetske
    See Ironside, Jetske
Sydney, Frank
    See Warwick, Alan R(oss)
Sylvester, Natalie G(abry) 1922- ................. 22

Syme, (Neville) Ronald 1913-1992 ............. 87
  Earlier sketch in SATA 2
Symes, R. F. .................................................. 77
Symons, (Dorothy) Geraldine 1909- .......... 33
Symons, Stuart
  *See* Stanley, George Edward
Symynkywicz, Jeffrey B. 1954- ................. 87
Symynkywicz, Jeffrey Bruce
  *See* Symynkywicz, Jeffrey B.
Synge, (Phyllis) Ursula 1930- ...................... 9
Sypher, Lucy Johnston 1907- ...................... 7
Szasz, Suzanne (Shorr) 1915-1997 ............ 13
  Obituary ................................................... 99
Szekeres, Cyndy 1933- ............................. 157
  Autobiography Feature ........................... 157
  Earlier sketches in SATA 5, 60, 131
  *See also* SAAS 13
Szekessy, Tanja ........................................... 98
Szpura, Beata 1961- .................................... 93
Szudek, Agnes S(usan) P(hilomena) ............ 57
  Brief entry ............................................... 49
Szulc, Tad 1926-2001 ................................. 26
Szydlow, Jarl
  *See* Szydlowski, Mary Vigliante
Szydlowski, Mary Vigliante 1946- ............. 94
Szymanski, Lois 1957- ............................... 91

## T

Taback, Simms 1932- ................................ 170
  Brief entry ............................................... 36
  Earlier sketches in SATA 40, 104
  *See also* CLR 100
Tabor, Nancy Maria Grande 1949- ............ 161
  Earlier sketch in SATA 89
Tabrah, Ruth Milander 1921- ...................... 14
Tackach, James 1953- ............................... 123
Tadgell, Nicole 1969- ............................... 177
Tafuri, Nancy (E.) 1946- ........................... 130
  Earlier sketches in SATA 39, 75
  *See also* CLR 74
  *See also* SAAS 14
Tagg, Christine Elizabeth 1962- ............... 138
Tagliaferro, Linda ....................................... 173
Taha, Karen T(erry) 1942- ........................ 156
  Earlier sketch in SATA 71
Tai, Sharon O. 1963- ................................ 153
Tait, Douglas 1944- .................................... 12
Takabayashi, Mari 1960- ........................... 156
  Earlier sketch in SATA 115
Takahashi, Rumiko 1957- .......................... 163
Takakjian, Portia 1930- .............................. 15
Takashima, Shizuye 1928- .......................... 13
Takayama, Sandi 1962- ............................. 106
Takeda, Pete(r M.) 1964- ......................... 148
Tal, Eve 1947- .......................................... 176
Talbert, Marc (Alan) 1953- ...................... 154
  Autobiography Feature ........................... 154
  Earlier sketches in SATA 68, 99
Talbot, Charlene Joy 1928- ........................ 10
Talbot, Toby 1928- ..................................... 14
Talbott, Hudson 1949- .............................. 131
  Earlier sketch in SATA 84
Talifero, Gerald 1950- ................................ 75
Talker, T.
  *See* Rands, William Brighty
Tallarico, Tony 1933- ............................... 116
Tallcott, Emogene ....................................... 10
Tallis, Robyn
  *See* Coville, Bruce
  and Doyle, Debra
  and Macdonald, James D.
  and Smith, Sherwood
  and Zambreno, Mary Frances
Tallon, Robert 1939- .................................. 43
  Brief entry ............................................... 28
Talmadge, Marian ....................................... 14
Tamar, Erika 1934- ................................... 150
  Earlier sketches in SATA 62, 101

Tamarin, Alfred H. 1913-1980 ................... 13
Tamburine, Jean 1930- ............................... 12
Tames, Richard (Lawrence) 1946- ........... 102
  Earlier sketch in SATA 67
Tamminga, Frederick W(illiam) 1934- ........ 66
Tan, Amy 1952- .......................................... 75
Tan, Amy Ruth
  *See* Tan, Amy
Tanaka, Beatrice 1932- ............................... 76
Tanaka, Shelley ........................................ 136
Tang, Charles 1948- .................................... 81
Tang, Greg ............................................... 172
Tang, You-Shan 1946- ................................ 53
Tania B.
  *See* Blixen, Karen (Christentze Dinesen)
Tannen, Mary 1943- .................................... 37
Tannenbaum, Beulah Goldstein 1916- ......... 3
Tannenbaum, D(onald) Leb 1948- .............. 42
Tanner, Jane 1946- ..................................... 74
Tanner, Louise S(tickney) 1922-2000 ........... 9
Tanobe, Miyuki 1937- ................................ 23
Tanselle, Eve 1933- .................................. 125
Tapio, Pat Decker
  *See* Kines, Pat Decker
Tapp, Kathy Kennedy 1949- ....................... 88
  Brief entry ............................................... 50
Tarbescu, Edith 1939- .............................. 107
Tarkington, (Newton) Booth 1869-1946 ..... 17
Tarpley, Natasha A(nastasia) 1971- .......... 147
Tarr, Judith 1955- .................................... 149
  Earlier sketch in SATA 64
Tarry, Ellen 1906- ...................................... 16
  *See also* CLR 26
  *See also* SAAS 16
Tarshis, Jerome 1936- .................................. 9
Tarsky, Sue 1946- ...................................... 41
Tashjian, Janet 1956- ............................... 151
  Earlier sketch in SATA 102
Tashjian, Virginia A. 1921- .......................... 3
Tasker, James 1908- .................................... 9
Tate, Don(ald E.) ...................................... 159
Tate, Eleanora E(laine) 1948- .................... 94
  Earlier sketch in SATA 38
  *See also* CLR 37
Tate, Ellalice
  *See* Hibbert, Eleanor Alice Burford
Tate, Joan 1922- ......................................... 86
  Earlier sketch in SATA 9
  *See also* SAAS 20
Tate, Mary Anne
  *See* Hale, Arlene
Tate, Nikki .............................................. 134
Tate, Richard
  *See* Masters, Anthony (Richard)
Tate, Suzanne 1930- .................................... 91
Tatham, Betty .......................................... 142
Tatham, Campbell
  *See* Elting, Mary
Tatham, Julie
  *See* Tatham, Julie Campbell
Tatham, Julie Campbell 1908-1999 ............. 80
Tavares, Matt ........................................... 159
Tavares, Victor 1971- ............................... 176
Taves, Isabella 1915- .................................. 27
Taylor, Alastair 1959- ............................... 130
Taylor, Andrew 1951- ................................. 70
Taylor, Andrew John Robert
  *See* Taylor, Andrew
Taylor, Ann 1782-1866 ............................... 41
  Brief entry ............................................... 35
Taylor, Audilee Boyd 1931- ........................ 59
Taylor, Barbara J. 1927- ............................. 10
Taylor, Ben
  *See* Strachan, Ian
Taylor, Carl 1937- ...................................... 14
Taylor, Cheryl Munro 1957- ....................... 96
Taylor, Cora (Lorraine) 1936- ................... 103
  Earlier sketch in SATA 64
  *See also* CLR 63
Taylor, Dave 1948- ..................................... 78

Taylor, David
  *See* Taylor, Dave
Taylor, David 1900-1965 ............................. 10
Taylor, Debbie A. 1955- ............................ 169
Taylor, Elizabeth 1912-1975 ...................... 13
Taylor, Florance Walton ............................... 9
Taylor, Florence M(arian Tompkins) 1892-1983
  ................................................................... 9
Taylor, G(raham) P(eter) 1959(?)- ............ 156
Taylor, Gage 1942-2000 ............................. 87
Taylor, Graham
  *See* Taylor, G(raham) P(eter)
Taylor, Herb(ert Norman, Jr.) 1942-1987 .... 22
  Obituary ................................................... 54
Taylor, J. David
  *See* Taylor, Dave
Taylor, Jane 1783-1824 .............................. 41
  Brief entry ............................................... 35
Taylor, Jerry D(uncan) 1938- ..................... 47
Taylor, John Robert
  *See* Taylor, Andrew
Taylor, Judy
  *See* Hough, Judy Taylor
Taylor, Kenneth N. 1917-2005 ................... 26
Taylor, Kenneth Nathaniel
  *See* Taylor, Kenneth N.
Taylor, L(ester) B(arbour), Jr. 1932- .......... 27
Taylor, Lois Dwight Cole
  *See* Cole, Lois Dwight
Taylor, Louise Todd 1939- .......................... 47
Taylor, Margaret 1950- ............................. 106
Taylor, Mark 1927- ..................................... 32
  Brief entry ............................................... 28
Taylor, Mildred D. 1943- .......................... 135
  *See also* CLR 90
  *See also* SAAS 5
Taylor, Mildred Delois
  *See* Taylor, Mildred D.
Taylor, Paula (Wright) 1942- ...................... 48
  Brief entry ............................................... 33
Taylor, Robert Lewis 1912-1998 ................. 10
Taylor, Sydney (Brenner) 1904(?)-1978 ...... 28
  Obituary ................................................... 26
  Earlier sketch in SATA 1
Taylor, Theodore 1921-2006 ..................... 128
  Obituary ................................................. 177
  Earlier sketches in SATA 5, 54, 83
  *See also* CLR 30
  *See also* SAAS 4
Taylor, William 1938- ............................... 164
  Earlier sketches in SATA 78, 113
  *See also* CLR 63
Tazewell, Charles 1900-1972 ...................... 74
Tchana, Katrin Hyman 1963- ..................... 177
  Earlier sketch in SATA 125
Tchekhov, Anton
  *See* Chekhov, Anton (Pavlovich)
Tchen, Richard ......................................... 120
Tchudi, Stephen N. 1942- ........................... 55
Teague, Bob
  *See* Teague, Robert
Teague, Mark 1963- .................................. 170
  Earlier sketches in SATA 68, 99
Teague, Mark Christopher
  *See* Teague, Mark
Teague, Robert 1929- .................................. 32
  Brief entry ............................................... 31
Teal, Val(entine M.) 1902-1997 .................. 10
  Obituary ................................................. 114
Teale, Edwin Way 1899-1980 ...................... 7
  Obituary ................................................... 25
Teasdale, Sara 1884-1933 ........................... 32
Tebbel, John (William) 1912-2004 ............. 26
Teensma, Lynne Bertrand
  *See* Bertrand, Lynne
Tee-Van, Helen Damrosch 1893-1976 ......... 10
  Obituary ................................................... 27
Tegner, Bruce 1928- ................................... 62
Teitelbaum, Michael 1953- ....................... 116
  Earlier sketch in SATA 59

Tejima
  *See* Tejima, Keizaburo
Tejima, Keizaburo 1931- ............................ *139*
  *See also* CLR *20*
Telander, Todd (G.) 1967- .......................... *88*
Teleki, Geza 1943- ..................................... *45*
Telemaque, Eleanor Wong 1934- ................ *43*
Telescope, Tom
  *See* Newbery, John
Temkin, Sara Anne Schlossberg 1913-1996
  ........................................................... *26*
Temko, Florence ........................................ *13*
Templar, Maurice
  *See* Groom, Arthur William
Temple, Charles 1947- ............................... *79*
Temple, Frances (Nolting) 1945-1995 ........ *85*
Temple, Herbert 1919- ............................... *45*
Temple, Paul
  *See* McConnell, James Douglas Rutherford
Temple, William F(rederick) 1914-1989 ... *107*
Tenggren, Gustaf 1896-1970 ...................... *18*
  Obituary .............................................. *26*
Tennant, Kylie ............................................ *6*
  *See* Rodd, Kylie Tennant
Tennant, Veronica 1947- ............................ *36*
Tenneshaw, S. M.
  *See* Beaumont, Charles
  and Garrett, (Gordon) Randall (Phillip)
  and Silverberg, Robert
Tenniel, John 1820-1914 ............................ *74*
  Brief entry ........................................... *27*
  *See also* CLR *18*
Tepper, Sheri S. 1929- .............................. *113*
Terada, Alice M. 1928- ............................... *90*
Terban, Marvin 1940- ................................. *54*
  Brief entry ........................................... *45*
ter Haar, Jaap 1922- .................................... *6*
  *See* Haar, Jaap ter
Terhune, Albert Payson 1872-1942 ............ *15*
Terkel, Susan N(eiburg) 1948- ................. *103*
  Earlier sketch in SATA *59*
Terlouw, Jan (Cornelis) 1931- .................... *30*
Terris, Susan 1937- .................................... *77*
  Earlier sketch in SATA *3*
Terry, Luther L(eonidas) 1911-1985 ............ *11*
  Obituary .............................................. *42*
Terry, Margaret
  *See* Dunnahoo, Terry Janson
Terry, Walter 1913-1982 ............................ *14*
Terzian, James P. 1915- ............................. *14*
Tessendorf, K(enneth) C(harles) 1925-2003
  ........................................................... *75*
  Obituary ............................................ *142*
Tessler, Stephanie Gordon
  *See* Gordon, Stephanie Jacob
Tester, Sylvia Root 1939- .......................... *64*
  Brief entry ........................................... *37*
Tether, (Cynthia) Graham 1950- ................. *46*
  Brief entry ........................................... *36*
Tetzner, Lisa 1894-1963 ........................... *169*
Thacher, Mary McGrath 1933- ...................... *9*
Thackeray, William Makepeace 1811-1863
  ........................................................... *23*
Thaler, Michael C.
  *See* Thaler, Mike
Thaler, Mike 1936- .................................... *93*
  Brief entry ........................................... *47*
  Earlier sketch in SATA *56*
Thaler, Shmuel 1958- ............................... *126*
  Earlier sketch in SATA *72*
Thamer, Katie 1955- .................................. *42*
Thane, Elswyth 1900-1984(?) ..................... *32*
Tharp, Louise (Marshall) Hall 1898-1992 .... *3*
  Obituary ............................................ *129*
Thayer, Ernest Lawrence 1863-1940 .......... *60*
Thayer, Jane
  *See* Woolley, Catherine
Thayer, Marjorie 1908-1992 ....................... *74*
  Brief entry ........................................... *37*
Thayer, Peter
  *See* Wyler, Rose

Thelwell, Norman 1923-2004 ...................... *14*
Themerson, Stefan 1910-1988 ..................... *65*
Thermes, Jennifer 1966- ............................ *155*
Theroux, Paul 1941- ................................. *109*
  Earlier sketch in SATA *44*
Theroux, Paul Edward
  *See* Theroux, Paul
Thesman, Jean ........................................ *124*
  Earlier sketch in SATA *74*
Thieda, Shirley Ann 1943- .......................... *13*
Thiele, Colin 1920-2006 ........................... *125*
  Earlier sketches in SATA *14, 72*
  *See also* CLR *27*
  *See also* SAAS *2*
Thiele, Colin Milton
  *See* Thiele, Colin
Thiesing, Lisa 1958- ................................. *159*
  Earlier sketch in SATA *95*
Thiry, Joan (Marie) 1926- .......................... *45*
Thistlethwaite, Miles 1945- ......................... *12*
Thollander, Earl 1922- ............................... *22*
Thomas, Abigail 1941- .............................. *112*
Thomas, Andrea
  *See* Hill, Margaret (Ohler)
Thomas, Art(hur Lawrence) 1952- ............... *48*
  Brief entry ........................................... *38*
Thomas, Carroll
  *See* Ratliff, Thomas M.
  and Shmurak, Carole B.
Thomas, Dylan (Marlais) 1914-1953 .......... *60*
Thomas, Egbert S.
  *See* Ellis, Edward S(ylvester)
Thomas, Estelle Webb 1899-1982 .............. *26*
Thomas, Frances 1943- ............................. *171*
  Earlier sketch in SATA *92*
Thomas, H. C.
  *See* Keating, Lawrence A.
Thomas, Ianthe 1951- ............................... *139*
  Brief entry ........................................... *42*
  *See also* CLR *8*
Thomas, Jane Resh 1936- .......................... *171*
  Earlier sketches in SATA *38, 90*
Thomas, Jerry D. 1959- .............................. *91*
Thomas, Joan Gale
  *See* Robinson, Joan (Mary) G(ale Thomas)
Thomas, Joyce Carol 1938- ....................... *137*
  Autobiography Feature .......................... *137*
  Earlier sketches in SATA *40, 78, 123*
  *See also* CLR *19*
  *See also* SAAS *7*
Thomas, Lowell Jackson, Jr. 1923- .............. *15*
Thomas, Margaret
  *See* Thomas, Peggy
Thomas, Meredith 1963- ............................ *119*
Thomas, Michael
  *See* Wilks, Michael Thomas
Thomas, Patricia J. 1934- ........................... *51*
Thomas, Peggy ........................................ *174*
Thomas, Rob 1965- ..................................... *97*
Thomas, Scott 1959- ................................. *147*
Thomas, Velma Maia 1955- ....................... *171*
Thomas, Vernon (Arthur) 1934- ................... *56*
Thomas, Victoria
  *See* DeWeese, Thomas Eugene
  and Kugi, Constance Todd
Thomasma, Kenneth R. 1930- ...................... *90*
Thomassie, Tynia 1959- .............................. *92*
Thompson, Brenda 1935- ............................ *34*
Thompson, Carol 1951- .............................. *85*
Thompson, China
  *See* Lewis, Mary (Christianna)
Thompson, Colin (Edward) 1942- .............. *163*
  Earlier sketch in SATA *95*
Thompson, David H(ugh) 1941- .................. *17*
Thompson, Eileen
  *See* Panowski, Eileen Thompson
Thompson, George Selden 1929-1989 ........ *73*
  Obituary .............................................. *63*
  Earlier sketch in SATA *4*
  *See* Selden, George

Thompson, Harlan (Howard) 1894-1987 .... *10*
  Obituary .............................................. *53*
  *See* Holt, Stephen
Thompson, Hilary 1943- ............................. *56*
  Brief entry ........................................... *49*
Thompson, Julian F(rancis) 1927- ............. *155*
  Brief entry ........................................... *40*
  Earlier sketches in SATA *55, 99*
  *See also* CLR *24*
  *See also* SAAS *13*
Thompson, K(athryn Carolyn) Dyble 1952-
  ........................................................... *82*
Thompson, Kay 1912(?)-1998 ..................... *16*
  *See also* CLR *22*
Thompson, Lauren 1962- ........................... *174*
  Earlier sketch in SATA *132*
Thompson, Lauren Stevens
  *See* Thompson, Lauren
Thompson, Ruth Plumly 1891-1976 ........... *66*
Thompson, Sharon (Elaine) 1952- ............. *119*
Thompson, Stith 1885-1976 ........................ *57*
  Obituary .............................................. *20*
Thompson, Vivian L(aubach) 1911- .............. *3*
Thomson, Celia
  *See* Lynn, Tracy
Thomson, David (Robert Alexander)
  1914-1988 ........................................... *40*
  Obituary .............................................. *55*
Thomson, Pat 1939- .................................. *122*
  Earlier sketch in SATA *77*
Thomson, Peggy 1922- ............................... *31*
Thon, Melanie Rae 1957- .......................... *132*
Thong, Roseanne ...................................... *174*
Thorn, John 1947- ...................................... *59*
Thorndyke, Helen Louise ............................ *67*
  Earlier sketch in SATA *1*
  *See* Benson, Mildred (Augustine Wirt)
Thorne, Ian
  *See* May, Julian
Thorne, Jean Wright
  *See* May, Julian
Thornhill, Jan 1955- ................................. *148*
  Earlier sketch in SATA *77*
Thornton, Hall
  *See* Silverberg, Robert
Thornton, W. B.
  *See* Burgess, Thornton Waldo
Thornton, Yvonne S(hirley) 1947- ............... *96*
Thorpe, E(ustace) G(eorge) 1916- .............. *21*
Thorpe, J. K.
  *See* Nathanson, Laura Walther
Thorvall, Kerstin 1925- .............................. *13*
Thorvall-Falk, Kerstin
  *See* Thorvall, Kerstin
Thrasher, Crystal (Faye) 1921- ................... *27*
Threadgall, Colin 1941- .............................. *77*
Three Little Pigs
  *See* Lantz, Francess L(in)
Thum, Gladys 1920- ................................... *26*
Thum, Marcella ........................................ *28*
  Earlier sketch in SATA *3*
Thundercloud, Katherine
  *See* Witt, Shirley Hill
Thurber, James (Grover) 1894-1961 .......... *13*
Thurlo, Aimee .......................................... *161*
Thurlo, David .......................................... *161*
Thurman, Judith 1946- ............................... *33*
Thurman, Mark (Gordon Ian) 1948- ........... *63*
Thwaite, Ann (Barbara Harrop) 1932- ......... *14*
Tibbetts, Peggy ....................................... *127*
Tibbles, Jean-Paul 1958- .......................... *115*
Tibo, Gilles 1951- .................................... *107*
  Earlier sketch in SATA *67*
Tiburzi, Bonnie 1948- ................................ *65*
Ticheburn, Cheviot
  *See* Ainsworth, William Harrison
Tichenor, Tom 1923-1992 .......................... *14*
Tichnor, Richard 1959- ............................... *90*
Tichy, William 1924- ................................. *31*
Tickle, Jack
  *See* Chapman, Jane

Tiegreen, Alan F. 1935- .............................. 94
    Brief entry ........................................ 36
Tierney, Frank M. 1930- ......................... 54
Tierney, Tom 1928- ............................... 113
Tiffault, Benette W. 1955- .................... 77
Tiller, Ruth L. 1949- ............................ 83
Tilly, Nancy 1935- ............................... 62
Tilton, Madonna Elaine 1929- ............. 41
Tilton, Rafael
    *See* Tilton, Madonna Elaine
Timberlake, Amy ......................... 156
Timberlake, Carolyn
    *See* Dresang, Eliza (Carolyn Timberlake)
Timmins, William F(rederick) ................ 10
Tiner, John Hudson 1944- ................. 32
Tingle, Dolli (?)-
    *See* Brackett, Dolli Tingle
Tingle, Rebecca ........................... 174
Tingum, Janice 1958- ..................... 91
Tinkelman, Murray 1933- ................ 12
Tinkle, (Julien) Lon 1906-1980 ............ 36
Tinling, Marion (Rose) 1904- ........... 140
Tipene, Tim 1972- .......................... 141
Tippett, James S(terling) 1885-1958 .......... 66
Tirone Smith, Mary-Ann 1944- ......... 143
Titler, Dale M(ilton) 1926- ............... 35
    Brief entry ....................................... 28
Titmarsh, Michael Angelo
    *See* Thackeray, William Makepeace
Titus, Eve 1922- ................................ 2
Tjong Khing, The 1933- ..................... 76
Tobias, Katherine
    *See* Gottfried, Theodore Mark
Tobias, Tobi 1938- ............................ 82
    Earlier sketch in SATA 5
    *See also* CLR 4
Todd, Anne Ophelia
    *See* Dowden, Anne Ophelia
Todd, Barbara 1961- ....................... 173
Todd, Barbara K(eith) 1917- ................ 10
Todd, H(erbert) E(atton) 1908-1988 .......... 84
    Earlier sketch in SATA 11
Todd, Loreto 1942- ............................ 30
Todd, Pamela 1950- ....................... 124
Todd, Peter
    *See* Hamilton, Charles (Harold St. John)
Toews, Miriam 1964- .................... 165
Tofel, Richard J. 1957- ................... 140
Toft, Kim Michelle 1960- ................ 170
Tolan, Stephanie S. 1942- ............... 142
    Earlier sketches in SATA 38, 78
Toland, John (Willard) 1912-2004 ........... 38
Tolbert, Steve 1944- ...................... 143
Tolkien, J(ohn) R(onald) R(euel) 1892-1973

    ...................................................... 100
    Obituary ........................................ 24
    Earlier sketches in SATA 2, 32
    *See also* CLR 56
Toll, Emily
    *See* Cannon, Eileen E(mily)
Toll, Nelly S. 1935- ......................... 78
Tolland, W. R.
    *See* Heitzmann, William Ray
Tolles, Martha 1921- ....................... 76
    Earlier sketch in SATA 8
Tolliver, Ruby C(hangos) 1922- ......... 110
    Brief entry ....................................... 41
    Earlier sketch in SATA 55
Tolmie, Kenneth Donald 1941- ........... 15
Tolstoi, Lev
    *See* Tolstoy, Leo (Nikolaevich)
Tolstoy, Leo (Nikolaevich) 1828-1910 ........ 26
    *See* Tolstoi, Lev
Tolstoy, Count Leo
    *See* Tolstoy, Leo (Nikolaevich)
Tomalin, Ruth ............................... 29
Tomaselli, Rosa
    *See* Pausacker, Jenny
Tomecek, Steve ............................ 172

Tomes, Margot (Ladd) 1917-1991 .............. 70
    Brief entry ....................................... 27
    Obituary ........................................ 69
    Earlier sketch in SATA 36
Tomey, Ingrid 1943- ....................... 77
Tomfool
    *See* Farjeon, Eleanor
Tomkins, Jasper
    *See* Batey, Tom
Tomline, F. Latour
    *See* Gilbert, W(illiam) S(chwenck)
Tomlinson, Jill 1931-1976 ..................... 3
    Obituary ........................................ 24
Tomlinson, Theresa 1946- ................ 165
    Earlier sketch in SATA 103
    *See also* CLR 60
Tompert, Ann 1918- ........................ 139
    Earlier sketches in SATA 14, 89
Toner, Raymond John 1908-1986 .............. 10
Tong, Gary S. 1942- ......................... 66
Took, Belladonna
    *See* Chapman, Vera (Ivy May)
Tooke, Louise Mathews 1950- ............. 38
Tooke, Susan ................................ 173
Toonder, Martin
    *See* Groom, Arthur William
Toothaker, Roy Eugene 1928- ............. 18
Tooze, Ruth (Anderson) 1892-1972 ............ 4
Topek, Susan Remick 1955- ............... 78
Topping, Audrey R(onning) 1928- ............ 14
Tor, Regina
    *See* Shekerjian, Regina Tor
Torbert, Floyd James 1922- ................ 22
Torgersen, Don Arthur 1934- ............. 55
    Brief entry ....................................... 41
Torley, Luke
    *See* Blish, James (Benjamin)
Torres, Daniel 1958- ...................... 102
Torres, John A. 1965- ..................... 163
    Earlier sketch in SATA 94
Torres, John Albert
    *See* Torres, John A.
Torres, Laura 1967- ....................... 146
    Earlier sketch in SATA 87
Torres, Leyla 1960- ....................... 155
Torrie, Malcolm
    *See* Mitchell, Gladys (Maude Winifred)
Toten, Teresa 1955- ......................... 99
Totham, Mary
    *See* Breinburg, Petronella
Touponce, William F. 1948- ............... 114
Tournier, Michel 1924- .................... 23
Tournier, Michel Edouard
    *See* Tournier, Michel
Towle, Wendy 1963- ........................ 79
Towne, Mary
    *See* Spelman, Mary
Townley, Rod
    *See* Townley, Roderick
Townley, Roderick 1942- ................. 177
Townsend, Brad W. 1962- ................. 91
Townsend, John Rowe 1922- ............. 132
    Autobiography Feature ................. 132
    Earlier sketches in SATA 4, 68
    *See also* CLR 2
    *See also* SAAS 2
Townsend, Sue ............................... 93
    Brief entry ....................................... 48
    Earlier sketch in SATA 55
    *See* Townsend, Susan Lilian
Townsend, Thomas L. 1944- .............. 59
Townsend, Tom
    *See* Townsend, Thomas L.
Townson, Hazel ............................ 134
Toye, William Eldred 1926- ................ 8
Traherne, Michael
    *See* Watkins-Pitchford, Denys James
Trahey, Jane 1923-2000 ...................... 36
    Obituary ....................................... 120
Trapani, Iza 1954- ......................... 116
    Earlier sketch in SATA 80

Trapp, Maria Augusta von ..................... 16
    *See* von Trapp, Maria Augusta
Travers, P(amela) L(yndon) 1899-1996 .... 100
    Obituary ........................................ 90
    Earlier sketches in SATA 4, 54
    *See also* CLR 93
    *See also* SAAS 2
Travis, Lucille ............................. 133
    Earlier sketch in SATA 88
Treadgold, Mary 1910- ..................... 49
Trease, (Robert) Geoffrey 1909-1998 ......... 60
    Obituary ....................................... 101
    Earlier sketch in SATA 2
    *See also* CLR 42
    *See also* SAAS 6
Treat, Lawrence 1903-1998 .................. 59
Tredez, Alain 1926- ......................... 17
Tredez, Denise 1930- ....................... 50
Treece, Henry 1912-1966 ..................... 2
    *See also* CLR 2
Tregarthen, Enys
    *See* Sloggett, Nellie
Tregaskis, Richard 1916-1973 ................. 3
    Obituary ........................................ 26
Treherne, Katie Thamer 1955- ............. 76
Trell, Max 1900-1996 ....................... 14
    Obituary ....................................... 108
Tremain, Ruthven 1922- .................... 17
Trembath, Don 1963- ...................... 168
    Earlier sketch in SATA 96
Tremens, Del
    *See* MacDonald, Amy
Trent, Robbie 1894-1988 ................... 26
Trent, Timothy
    *See* Malmberg, Carl
Treseder, Terry Walton 1956- .............. 68
Tresilian, (Cecil) Stuart 1891-(?) ............. 40
Tresselt, Alvin 1916-2000 ..................... 7
    *See also* CLR 30
Trevino, Elizabeth B(orton) de 1904- ......... 29
    Earlier sketch in SATA 1
    *See also* SAAS 5
Trevor, Elleston 1920-1995 ................. 28
    *See* Hall, Adam
Trevor, Frances
    *See* Teasdale, Sara
Trevor, Glen
    *See* Hilton, James
Trevor, (Lucy) Meriol 1919-2000 ............. 113
    Obituary ....................................... 122
    Earlier sketch in SATA 10
Trez, Alain
    *See* Tredez, Alain
Trez, Denise
    *See* Tredez, Denise
Trezise, Percy (James) 1923-
    *See* CLR 41
Triggs, Tony D. 1946- ...................... 70
Trimble, Marshall I(ra) 1939- .............. 93
Trimby, Elisa 1948- ......................... 47
    Brief entry ....................................... 40
Tripp, Eleanor B(aldwin) 1936- ............. 4
Tripp, Janet 1942- ......................... 108
Tripp, John
    *See* Moore, John Travers
Tripp, Nathaniel 1944- .................... 101
Tripp, Paul 1916-2002 ........................ 8
    Obituary ....................................... 139
Tripp, Valerie 1951- ...................... 168
    Earlier sketch in SATA 78
Tripp, Wallace (Whitney) 1940- ............. 31
Trivelpiece, Laurel 1926- ................. 56
    Brief entry ....................................... 46
Trivett, Daphne Harwood 1940- ........... 22
Trivizas, Eugene 1946- ..................... 84
Trnka, Jiri 1912-1969 ...................... 43
    Brief entry ....................................... 32
Trollope, Anthony 1815-1882 .............. 22
Trost, Lucille W(ood) 1938- ............... 149
    Earlier sketch in SATA 12
Trott, Betty 1933- .......................... 91

Trotter, Grace V(iolet) 1900-1991 .............. *10*
Trottier, Maxine 1950- ............................ *175*
    Earlier sketch in SATA *131*
Troughton, Joanna (Margaret) 1947- .......... *37*
Trout, Kilgore
    *See* Farmer, Philip Jose
Trout, Richard E. .................................... *123*
Trudeau, Garretson Beekman
    *See* Trudeau, G.B.
Trudeau, Garry
    *See* Trudeau, G.B.
Trudeau, Garry B.
    *See* Trudeau, G.B.
Trudeau, G.B. 1948- .............................. *168*
    Earlier sketch in SATA *35*
    *See* Trudeau, Garry B.
Trueman, Terry 1947- ............................. *132*
Truesdell, Judy
    *See* Mecca, Judy Truesdell
Truesdell, Sue
    *See* Truesdell, Susan G.
Truesdell, Susan G. .............................. *108*
    Brief entry ...................................... *45*
Trumbauer, Lisa (Trutkoff) 1963- ............ *149*
Truss, Jan 1925- .................................... *35*
Tryon, Leslie ........................................ *139*
Tubb, Jonathan N. 1951- .......................... *78*
Tubby, I. M.
    *See* Kraus, (Herman) Robert
Tucker, Caroline
    *See* Nolan, Jeannette Covert
Tudor, Tasha 1915- ................................ *160*
    Earlier sketches in SATA *20, 69*
    *See also* CLR *13*
Tuerk, Hanne 1951- ................................. *71*
Tulloch, Richard (George) 1949- ................ *76*
Tulloch, Shirley .................................... *169*
Tully, John (Kimberley) 1923- .................... *14*
Tumanov, Vladimir A. 1961- ...................... *138*
Tung, Angela 1972- ................................ *109*
Tunis, Edwin (Burdett) 1897-1973 .............. *28*
    Obituary .......................................... *24*
    Earlier sketch in SATA *1*
    *See also* CLR *2*
Tunis, John R(oberts) 1889-1975 ................ *37*
    Brief entry ...................................... *30*
Tunnell, Michael
    *See* Tunnell, Michael O('Grady)
Tunnell, Michael O('Grady) 1950- ............ *157*
    Earlier sketch in SATA *103*
Tunnicliffe, C(harles) F(rederick) 1901-1979
    ...................................................... *62*
Turck, Mary C. 1950- .............................. *144*
Turk, Hanne
    *See* Tuerk, Hanne
Turk, Ruth 1917- .................................... *82*
Turkle, Brinton 1915- .............................. *79*
    Earlier sketch in SATA *2*
Turlington, Bayly 1919-1977 ...................... *5*
    Obituary .......................................... *52*
Turnbull, Agnes Sligh 1888-1982 ................ *14*
Turnbull, Ann (Christine) 1943- ................ *160*
    Earlier sketch in SATA *18*
Turner, Alice K. 1940- .............................. *10*
Turner, Ann W(arren) 1945- ...................... *113*
    Earlier sketches in SATA *14, 77*
Turner, Bonnie 1932- .............................. *75*
Turner, Elizabeth 1774-1846
    *See* YABC *2*
Turner, Glennette Tilley 1933- .................... *71*
Turner, Josie
    *See* Crawford, Phyllis
Turner, Megan Whalen 1965- .................... *174*
    Earlier sketch in SATA *94*
Turner, Philip (William) 1925- .................... *83*
    Earlier sketch in SATA *11*
    *See also* CLR *89*
    *See also* SAAS *6*
Turner, Robyn 1947- ................................ *77*
Turngren, Ellen (?)-1964 ............................ *3*

Turska, Krystyna (Zofia) 1933- .................... *31*
    Brief entry ...................................... *27*
Turteltaub, H.N.
    *See* Turtledove, Harry
Turtledove, Harry 1949- .......................... *166*
    Earlier sketch in SATA *116*
Turtledove, Harry Norman
    *See* Turtledove, Harry
Tusa, Tricia 1960- .................................. *111*
    Earlier sketch in SATA *72*
Tusiani, Joseph 1924- .............................. *45*
Twain, Mark
    *See* CLR *66*
    *See* Clemens, Samuel Langhorne
Tweit, Susan J 1956- ................................ *94*
Tweit, Susan Joan
    *See* Tweit, Susan J
Tweton, D. Jerome 1933- .......................... *48*
Twinem, Neecy 1958- .............................. *92*
Tworkov, Jack 1900-1982 .......................... *47*
    Obituary .......................................... *31*
Tyche
    *See* Papademetriou, Lisa
Tyers, Jenny 1969- .................................. *89*
Tyers, Kathy 1952- .................................. *82*
Tyler, Anne 1941- .................................. *173*
    Earlier sketches in SATA *7, 90*
Tyler, Linda
    *See* Tyler, Linda W(agner)
Tyler, Linda W(agner) 1952- ...................... *65*
Tyler, Vicki 1952- .................................... *64*
Tyne, Joel
    *See* Schembri, Jim
Tyrrell, Frances 1959- ............................ *107*

### U

Ubell, Earl 1926- .................................... *4*
Uchida, Yoshiko 1921-1992 ........................ *53*
    Obituary .......................................... *72*
    Earlier sketch in SATA *1*
    *See also* CLR *56*
    *See also* SAAS *1*
Udall, Jan Beaney 1938- .......................... *10*
Uden, (Bernard Gilbert) Grant 1910- .......... *26*
Uderzo, Albert 1927-
    *See* CLR *37*
Udry, Janice May 1928- ............................ *152*
    Earlier sketch in SATA *4*
Uegaki, Chieri 1969- .............................. *153*
Ueno, Noriko
    *See* Nakae, Noriko
Uhlberg, Myron .................................... *174*
Uhlig, Susan 1955- ................................ *129*
Ulam, S(tanislaw) M(arcin) 1909-1984 ........ *51*
Ullman, James Ramsey 1907-1971 .............. *7*
Ulm, Robert 1934-1977 ............................ *17*
Ulmer, Louise 1943- ................................ *53*
Ulyatt, Kenneth 1920- .............................. *14*
Umansky, Kaye 1946- .............................. *158*
Unada
    *See* Gliewe, Unada (Grace)
Uncle Carter
    *See* Boucher, (Clarence) Carter
Uncle Eric
    *See* Maybury, Richard J.
Uncle Gus
    *See* Rey, H(ans) A(ugusto)
Uncle Ray
    *See* Coffman, Ramon Peyton
Uncle Shelby
    *See* Silverstein, Shel
Underhill, Alice Mertie (Waterman) 1900-1971
    ...................................................... *10*
Underhill, Liz 1948- ................................ *53*
    Brief entry ...................................... *49*
Unger, Harlow G. 1931- .......................... *75*
Unger, Jim 1937- .................................... *67*

Ungerer, (Jean) Thomas 1931- .................... *106*
    Earlier sketches in SATA *5, 33*
    *See* Ungerer, Tomi
Ungerer, Tomi 1931-
    *See* CLR *77*
    *See* Ungerer, (Jean) Thomas
Unkelbach, Kurt 1913-1992 ........................ *4*
Unnerstad, Edith (Totterman) 1900-1982 ...... *3*
    *See also* CLR *36*
Unobagha, Uzo .................................... *139*
Unrau, Ruth 1922- .................................... *9*
Unstead, R(obert) J(ohn) 1915-1988 .......... *12*
    Obituary .......................................... *56*
Unsworth, Walt(er) 1928- .......................... *4*
Untermeyer, Bryna Ivens 1909-1985 .......... *61*
Untermeyer, Louis 1885-1977 .................... *37*
    Obituary .......................................... *26*
    Earlier sketch in SATA *2*
Unwin, David S(torr) 1918- ...................... *14*
Unwin, Nora S(picer) 1907-1982 ................ *3*
    Obituary .......................................... *49*
Unzner, Christa 1958- ............................ *141*
    Earlier sketch in SATA *80*
Unzner-Fischer, Christa
    *See* Unzner, Christa
Updale, Eleanor 1953- ............................ *175*
Updyke, Rosemary K. 1924- ...................... *103*
Upitis, Alvis ........................................ *109*
Urban, Helle (Denise) 1957- ...................... *149*
Ure, Jean 1943- .................................... *129*
    Earlier sketches in SATA *48, 78*
    *See also* CLR *34*
    *See also* SAAS *14*
U'Ren, Andrea 1968- .............................. *142*
Uris, Leon 1924-2003 .............................. *49*
    Obituary .......................................... *146*
Uris, Leon Marcus
    *See* Uris, Leon
Ursu, Anne .......................................... *177*
Ury, Allen B. 1954- ................................ *98*
Uschan, Michael V. 1948- ........................ *129*
Usher, Margo Scegge
    *See* McHargue, Georgess
Uslan, Michael E. 1951- .......................... *169*
Uston, Ken(neth Senzo) 1935-1987 ............ *65*
Uttley, Alice Jane (Taylor) 1884-1976 ........ *88*
    Obituary .......................................... *26*
    Earlier sketch in SATA *3*
    *See* Uttley, Alison
Uttley, Alison
    *See* Uttley, Alice Jane (Taylor)
Utz, Lois (Marie) 1932-1986 ...................... *5*
    Obituary .......................................... *50*

### V

Vaeth, J(oseph) Gordon 1921- .................... *17*
Vagin, Vladimir (Vasilevich) 1937- .......... *142*
Vail, Rachel 1966- ................................ *163*
    Earlier sketch in SATA *94*
Vainio, Pirkko 1957- .............................. *123*
    Earlier sketch in SATA *76*
Valen, Nanine 1950- ................................ *21*
Valencak, Hannelore .............................. *42*
    *See* Mayer, Hannelore Valencak
Valens, Amy 1946- .................................. *70*
Valens, E(vans) G(ladstone), Jr. 1920-1992 .. *1*
Valentine, Johnny .................................... *72*
Valgardson, W(illiam) D(empsey) 1939- .. *151*
    Earlier sketch in SATA *101*
Valleau, Emily 1925- .............................. *51*
Van Abbe, Salaman 1883-1955 .................... *18*
Van Allsburg, Chris 1949- ...................... *156*
    Earlier sketches in SATA *37, 53, 105*
    *See also* CLR *113*
Van Anrooy, Francine 1924- ...................... *2*
Van Anrooy, Frans
    *See* Van Anrooy, Francine
Vanasse, Deb 1957- .............................. *170*

Vance, Eleanor Graham 1908-1985 ............ *11*
Vance, Gerald
　*See* Garrett, (Gordon) Randall (Phillip)
　and Silverberg, Robert
Vance, Marguerite 1889-1965 ..................... *29*
VanCleave, Janice 1942- ........................... *116*
　Autobiography Feature ......................... *123*
　Earlier sketch in SATA *75*
Vandenburg, Mary Lou 1943- ..................... *17*
Vander Boom, Mae M. ............................... *14*
Vander-Els, Betty 1936- ............................. *63*
van der Linde, Laurel 1952- ....................... *78*
van der Meer, Ron 1945- ........................... *98*
Van der Veer, Judy 1912-1982 ..................... *4*
　Obituary ............................................. *33*
Vanderwerff, Corrine 1939- ....................... *117*
Vander Zee, Ruth ..................................... *159*
Vande Velde, Vivian 1951- ......................... *141*
　Earlier sketches in SATA *62, 95*
Vandivert, Rita (Andre) 1905-1986 ............ *21*
Van Draanen, Wendelin .............................. *122*
Van Dusen, Chris ..................................... *173*
Van Duyn, Janet 1910- .............................. *18*
Van Dyne, Edith
　*See* Baum, L(yman) Frank
　and Sampson, Emma (Keats) Speed
　and van Zantwijk, Rudolf (Alexander
　Marinus)
Vane, Mitch
　*See* Vane, Mitchelle
Vane, Mitchelle ....................................... *176*
van Frankenhuyzen, Gijsbert 1951- ........... *132*
Van Genechten, Guido 1957- ..................... *165*
Van Hook, Beverly H. 1941- ...................... *99*
Van Horn, William 1939- ........................... *43*
Van Iterson, S(iny) R(ose) ......................... *26*
Van Kampen, Vlasta 1943- ......................... *163*
　Earlier sketch in SATA *54*
Van Laan, Nancy 1939- ............................. *105*
van Lawick-Goodall, Jane
　*See* Goodall, Jane
Van Leeuwen, Jean 1937- .......................... *141*
　Autobiography Feature ......................... *141*
　Earlier sketches in SATA *6, 82, 132*
　*See also* SAAS *8*
van Lhin, Erik
　*See* del Rey, Lester
Van Loon, Hendrik Willem 1882-1944 ....... *18*
VanOosting, James 1951- .......................... *170*
Van Orden, M(erton) D(ick) 1921- .............. *4*
Van Rensselaer, Alexander (Taylor Mason)
　1892-1962 ........................................... *14*
Van Riper, Guernsey, Jr. 1909-1995 ............ *3*
van Rossum, Heleen 1962- ......................... *174*
Van Rynbach, Iris 1952- ............................ *102*
Vansant, Rhonda Joy Edwards 1950- .......... *92*
Van Steenwyk, Elizabeth (Ann) 1928- ........ *89*
　Earlier sketch in SATA *34*
Van Stockum, Hilda 1908-2006 ................... *5*
Van Tuyl, Barbara 1940- ............................ *11*
van Vogt, A(lfred) E(lton) 1912-2000 ......... *14*
　Obituary ............................................. *124*
Van Woerkom, Dorothy (O'Brien) 1924-1996
　.......................................................... *21*
Van Wormer, Joe
　*See* Van Wormer, Joseph Edward
Van Wormer, Joseph Edward 1913-1998 .... *35*
Van Wright, Cornelius ............................... *173*
Van Zwienen, Ilse Charlotte Koehn 1929-1991
　.......................................................... *34*
　Brief entry .......................................... *28*
　Obituary ............................................. *67*
Van Zyle, Jon 1942- ................................. *176*
　Earlier sketch in SATA *84*
Varga, Judy
　*See* Stang, Judit
Varley, Dimitry V. 1906-1984 ..................... *10*
Varley, Susan 1961- ................................. *134*
　Earlier sketch in SATA *63*
Vasileva, Tatiana
　*See* Wassiljewa, Tatjana

Vasiliev, Valery 1949- .............................. *80*
Vasilieva, Tatiana
　*See* Wassiljewa, Tatjana
Vasiliu, Mircea 1920- .................................. *2*
Vass, George 1927- .................................. *57*
　Brief entry .......................................... *31*
Vaughan, Carter A.
　*See* Gerson, Noel Bertram
Vaughan, Harold Cecil 1923- ..................... *14*
Vaughan, Marcia (K.) 1951- ...................... *159*
　Earlier sketches in SATA *60, 95*
Vaughan, Richard 1947- ............................ *87*
Vaughan, Sam(uel) 1928- .......................... *14*
Vaughn, Ruth 1935- .................................. *14*
Vautier, Ghislaine 1932- ........................... *53*
Vavra, Robert James 1935- .......................... *8*
Vecsey, George Spencer 1939- ..................... *9*
Vedral, Joyce L(auretta) 1943- ................... *65*
Vega, Denise B. ...................................... *174*
　*See* Vega, Denise
Veglahn, Nancy (Crary) 1937- ...................... *5*
Velasquez, Gloria (Louise) 1949- .............. *113*
　*See* Velasquez(-Trevino), Gloria (Louise)
Velthuijs, Max 1923-2005 .......................... *110*
　Obituary ............................................. *160*
　Earlier sketch in SATA *53*
Venable, Alan (Hudson) 1944- ...................... *8*
Venezia, Mike 1945- ................................ *150*
Ventura, Anthony
　*See* Pellowski, Michael (Joseph)
Ventura, Piero (Luigi) 1937- ....................... *61*
　Brief entry .......................................... *43*
　*See also* CLR *16*
Vequin, Capini
　*See* Quinn, Elisabeth
Verba, Joan Marie 1953- ........................... *78*
Verboven, Agnes 1951- ............................. *103*
verDorn, Bethea (Stewart) 1952- ................ *76*
Verissimo, Erico (Lopes) 1905-1975 ......... *113*
Verne, Jules (Gabriel) 1828-1905 ............... *21*
　*See also* CLR *88*
Verney, John 1913-1993 ............................ *14*
　Obituary ............................................. *75*
Vernon, (Elda) Louise A(nderson) 1914- .... *14*
Vernon, Rosemary
　*See* Smith, Susan Vernon
Vernor, D.
　*See* Casewit, Curtis W(erner)
Verr, Harry Coe
　*See* Kunhardt, Edith
Verral, Charles Spain 1904-1990 ................ *11*
　Obituary ............................................. *65*
Versace, Marie Teresa Rios 1917- ................. *2*
Vertreace, Martha M(odena) 1945- ............. *78*
Vesey, A(manda) 1939- ............................. *62*
Vesey, Mark (David) 1958- ....................... *123*
Vesey, Paul
　*See* Allen, Samuel W(ashington)
Vestly, Anne-Cath(arina) 1920- .................. *14*
　*See also* CLR *99*
Vevers, (Henry) Gwynne 1916-1988 ........... *45*
　Obituary ............................................. *57*
Viator, Vacuus
　*See* Hughes, Thomas
Vicar, Henry
　*See* Felsen, Henry Gregor
Vick, Helen Hughes 1950- ........................... *88*
Vicker, Angus
　*See* Felsen, Henry Gregor
Vickers, Sheena 1960- .............................. *94*
Vickery, Kate
　*See* Kennedy, T.A.
Victor, Edward 1914- ................................. *3*
Victor, Joan Berg 1942- ............................ *30*
Vidrine, Beverly Barras 1938- ................... *103*
Viereck, Ellen K. 1928- ............................ *14*
Viereck, Phillip 1925- ................................ *3*
Viertel, Janet 1915- .................................. *10*
Vigliante, Mary
　*See* Szydlowski, Mary Vigliante

Vigna, Judith 1936- ................................. *102*
　Earlier sketch in SATA *15*
Viguers, Ruth Hill 1903-1971 ...................... *6*
Villasenor, Edmundo
　*See* Villasenor, Victor
Villasenor, Victor 1940- ........................... *171*
Villasenor, Victor E. 1940-
　*See* Villasenor, Victor
Villasenor, Victor Edmundo
　*See* Villasenor, Victor
Villiard, Paul 1910-1974 ........................... *51*
　Obituary ............................................. *20*
Villiers, Alan (John) 1903-1982 ................. *10*
Vilott, Rhondi
　*See* Salsitz, Rhondi Vilott
Vincent, Eric Douglas 1953- ...................... *40*
Vincent, Felix 1946- ................................. *41*
Vincent, Gabrielle 1928-2000 .................... *121*
　Earlier sketch in SATA *61*
　*See also* CLR *13*
Vincent, Mary Keith
　*See* St. John, Wylly Folk
Vincent, William R.
　*See* Heitzmann, William Ray
Vinegar, Tom
　*See* Gregg, Andrew K.
Vinest, Shaw
　*See* Longyear, Barry B(rookes)
Vinge, Joan (Carol) D(ennison) 1948- ...... *113*
　Earlier sketch in SATA *36*
Vining, Elizabeth Gray 1902-1999 ............... *6*
　Obituary ............................................. *117*
　*See* Gray, Elizabeth Janet
Vinson, Kathryn 1911-1995 ....................... *21*
Vinton, Iris 1906(?)-1988 ......................... *24*
　Obituary ............................................. *55*
Viola, Herman J(oseph) 1938- ................... *126*
Viorst, Judith 1931- ................................. *172*
　Earlier sketches in SATA *7, 70, 123*
　*See also* CLR *90*
Vip
　*See* Partch, Virgil Franklin II
Vipont, Charles
　*See* Foulds, Elfrida Vipont
Vipont, Elfrida
　*See* Foulds, Elfrida Vipont
Viscott, David S(teven) 1938-1996 ............ *65*
Visser, W(illem) F(rederik) H(endrik)
　1900-1968 ........................................... *10*
Vitale, Stefano 1958- ............................... *114*
Vivas, Julie 1947- .................................... *96*
Vivelo, Jackie 1943- ................................. *63*
Vivelo, Jacqueline J.
　*See* Vivelo, Jackie
Vivelo, Jacqueline Jean
　*See* Vivelo, Jackie
Vizzini, Ned 1981- ................................... *125*
Vlahos, Olivia 1924- .................................. *31*
Vlasic, Bob
　*See* Hirsch, Phil
Voake, Charlotte ...................................... *114*
Vo-Dinh, Mai 1933- .................................. *16*
Vogel, Carole Garbuny 1951- ................... *105*
　Earlier sketch in SATA *70*
Vogel, Ilse-Margret 1918- ......................... *14*
Vogel, John H., Jr. 1950- ........................... *18*
Vogt, Esther Loewen 1915-1999 ................ *14*
Vogt, Gregory L. .................................... *94*
Vogt, Marie Bollinger 1921- ...................... *45*
Voight, Virginia Frances 1909-1989 ............. *8*
Voigt, Cynthia 1942- ............................... *160*
　Brief entry .......................................... *33*
　Earlier sketches in SATA *48, 79, 116*
　*See also* CLR *48*
Voigt, Erna 1925- .................................... *35*
Voigt-Rother, Erna
　*See* Voigt, Erna
Vojtech, Anna 1946- ................................ *108*
　Earlier sketch in SATA *42*
Vollstadt, Elizabeth Weiss 1942- ............... *121*
Volponi, Paul ......................................... *175*

Volting, Dr. R.E.
    *See* Lerangis, Peter
Von Ahnen, Katherine 1922- ....................... *93*
Vondra, Josef (Gert) 1941- ........................ *121*
Von Gunden, Kenneth 1946- ..................... *113*
Von Hagen, Victor Wolfgang 1908-1985 .... *29*
von Klopp, Vahrah
    *See* Malvern, Gladys
von Schmidt, Eric 1931-2007 ..................... *50*
    Brief entry ......................................... *36*
von Storch, Anne B. 1910- ........................... *1*
von Ziegesar, Cecily 1970- ....................... *161*
Vos, Ida 1931- ........................................ *121*
    Earlier sketch in SATA *69*
    *See also* CLR *85*
Vosburgh, Leonard (W.) 1912- ................... *15*
Voyle, Mary
    *See* Manning, Rosemary (Joy)
Vriens, Jacques 1946- ............................. *151*
Vugteveen, Verna Aardema ...................... *107*
    Obituary ........................................... *119*
    Earlier sketches in SATA *4, 68*
    *See also* CLR *17*
    *See also* SAAS *8*
    *See* Aardema, Verna
Vulture, Elizabeth T.
    *See* Gilbert, Suzie
Vuong, Lynette Dyer 1938- ...................... *110*
    Earlier sketch in SATA *60*

## W

Waas, Uli
    *See* Waas-Pommer, Ulrike
Waas-Pommer, Ulrike 1949- ...................... *85*
Waber, Bernard 1924- ............................. *155*
    Brief entry ......................................... *40*
    Earlier sketches in SATA *47, 95*
    *See also* CLR *55*
Wachtel, Shirley Russak 1951- ................... *88*
Wachter, Oralee (Roberts) 1935- ............... *61*
    Brief entry ......................................... *51*
Waddell, Evelyn Margaret 1918- ................ *10*
Waddell, Martin 1941- ............................. *129*
    Autobiography Feature .......................... *129*
    Earlier sketches in SATA *43, 81, 127*
    *See also* CLR *31*
    *See also* SAAS *15*
Waddy, Lawrence (Heber) 1914- ................. *91*
Wade, Mary Dodson 1930- ....................... *151*
    Earlier sketch in SATA *79*
Wade, Suzanne
    *See* Kirby, Susan E.
Wade, Theodore E., Jr. 1936- ..................... *37*
Wademan, Peter John 1946- ..................... *122*
Wademan, Spike
    *See* Wademan, Peter John
Wadsworth, Ginger 1945- ........................ *157*
    Earlier sketch in SATA *103*
Wagenheim, Kal 1935- .............................. *21*
Wagner, Michele R. 1975- ........................ *157*
Wagner, Sharon B. 1936- ........................... *4*
Wagoner, David (Russell) 1926- ................ *14*
Wahl, Jan (Boyer) 1933- ......................... *132*
    Earlier sketches in SATA *2, 34, 73*
    *See also* SAAS *3*
Waide, Jan 1952- .................................... *29*
Wainscott, John Milton 1910-1981 ............. *53*
Wainwright, Richard M. 1935- ................... *91*
Wait, Lea 1946- ..................................... *137*
Waite, Judy ........................................... *174*
Waite, Michael P(hillip) 1960- .................. *101*
Waite, P(eter) B(usby) 1922- ..................... *64*
Waitley, Douglas 1927- ............................ *30*
Wakefield, Jean L.
    *See* Laird, Jean E(louise)
Wakin, Daniel (Joseph) 1961- .................... *84*
Wakin, Edward 1927- ............................... *37*
Walden, Amelia Elizabeth ........................... *3*

Waldherr, Kris 1963- ................................ *76*
Waldman, Bruce 1949- .............................. *15*
Waldman, Neil 1947- ............................... *142*
    Earlier sketches in SATA *51, 94*
Waldron, Ann Wood 1924- ......................... *16*
Waldron, Kathleen Cook ........................... *176*
Walgren, Judy 1963- ............................... *118*
Walker, Addison
    *See* Walker, (Addison) Mort
Walker, Alice 1944- .................................. *31*
Walker, Alice Malsenior
    *See* Walker, Alice
Walker, Barbara (Jeanne) K(erlin) 1921- .... *80*
    Earlier sketch in SATA *4*
Walker, Barbara M(uhs) 1928- .................... *57*
Walker, (James) Braz(elton) 1934-1983 ...... *45*
Walker, David G(ordon) 1926- .................... *60*
Walker, David Harry 1911-1992 ................... *8*
    Obituary ............................................. *71*
Walker, Diana 1925- .................................. *9*
Walker, Diane Marie Catherine
    *See* Walker, Kate
Walker, Dick
    *See* Pellowski, Michael (Joseph)
Walker, Frank 1931-2000 ........................... *36*
Walker, Holly Beth
    *See* Bond, Gladys Baker
Walker, Kate 1950- ................................. *165*
    Earlier sketch in SATA *82*
Walker, Kathrine Sorley
    *See* Sorley Walker, Kathrine
Walker, Lou Ann 1952- ............................. *66*
    Brief entry ......................................... *53*
Walker, Mary Alexander 1927- .................... *61*
Walker, Mildred
    *See* Schemm, Mildred Walker
Walker, (Addison) Mort 1923- ...................... *8*
Walker, Pamela 1948- ............................. *142*
    Earlier sketch in SATA *24*
Walker, Paul Robert 1953- ....................... *154*
Walker, Robert W(ayne) 1948- .................... *66*
Walker, Sally M(acArt) 1954- .................... *135*
Walker, Stephen J. 1951- ........................... *12*
Walker-Blondell, Becky 1951- ..................... *89*
Wallace, Barbara Brooks 1922- .................. *136*
    Earlier sketches in SATA *4, 78*
    *See also* SAAS *17*
Wallace, Beverly Dobrin 1921- .................... *19*
Wallace, Bill 1947- ................................. *169*
    Brief entry ......................................... *47*
    Earlier sketches in SATA *53, 101*
Wallace, Daisy
    *See* Cuyler, Margery S(tuyvesant)
Wallace, Ian 1950- ................................. *141*
    Earlier sketches in SATA *53, 56*
    *See also* CLR *37*
Wallace, John 1966- ............................... *155*
    Earlier sketch in SATA *105*
Wallace, John A(dam) 1915-2004 .................. *3*
    Obituary ........................................... *155*
Wallace, Karen 1951- .............................. *139*
    Earlier sketch in SATA *83*
Wallace, Nancy Elizabeth 1948- ................ *141*
Wallace, Nigel
    *See* Hamilton, Charles (Harold St. John)
Wallace, Paula S. ................................... *153*
Wallace, Rich 1957- ............................... *158*
    Earlier sketch in SATA *117*
Wallace, Robert 1932-1999 ........................ *47*
    Brief entry ......................................... *37*
Wallace, William Keith
    *See* Wallace, Bill
Wallace-Brodeur, Ruth 1941- .................... *169*
    Brief entry ......................................... *41*
    Earlier sketches in SATA *51, 88*
Wallenta, Adam 1974- ............................. *123*
Waller, Leslie 1923-2007 ........................... *20*
Walley, Byron
    *See* Card, Orson Scott
Wallis, Diz 1949- ..................................... *77*

Wallis, G. McDonald
    *See* Campbell, Hope
Wallner, Alexandra 1946- ........................ *156*
    Brief entry ......................................... *41*
    Earlier sketches in SATA *51, 98*
Wallner, John C. 1945- ............................ *133*
    Earlier sketches in SATA *10, 51*
Wallower, Lucille ................................... *11*
Walsh, Ann 1942- .................................. *176*
    Earlier sketch in SATA *62*
Walsh, Ellen Stoll 1942- .......................... *147*
    Earlier sketches in SATA *49, 99*
Walsh, George Johnston 1889-1981 ............ *53*
Walsh, Gillian Paton
    *See* Paton Walsh, Jill
Walsh, Jill Paton
    *See* CLR *65*
    *See* Paton Walsh, Jill
Walsh, Lawrence 1942- ............................ *170*
Walsh, Mary Caswell 1949- ....................... *118*
Walsh, Suella ....................................... *170*
Walsh, V. L.
    *See* Walsh, Vivian
Walsh, Vivian 1960- ................................ *120*
Walsh Shepherd, Donna 1948- ................... *78*
Walter, Frances V. 1923- ........................... *71*
Walter, Mildred Pitts 1922- ....................... *133*
    Brief entry ......................................... *45*
    Earlier sketch in SATA *69*
    *See also* CLR *61*
    *See also* SAAS *12*
Walter, Villiam Christian
    *See* Andersen, Hans Christian
Walter, Virginia ................................... *134*
    *See* Walter, Virginia A.
Walters, Audrey 1929- .............................. *18*
Walters, Celeste 1938- ............................ *126*
Walters, Eric (Robert) 1957- ..................... *155*
    Earlier sketch in SATA *99*
Walters, Hugh
    *See* Hughes, Walter (Llewellyn)
Walther, Thomas A. 1950- .......................... *31*
Walther, Tom
    *See* Walther, Thomas A.
Waltner, Elma 1912-1987 ........................... *40*
Waltner, Willard H. 1909- ......................... *40*
Walton, Darwin McBeth 1926- .................. *119*
Walton, Fiona L. M. 1959- ......................... *89*
Walton, Richard J. 1928- ............................ *4*
Walton, Rick 1957- ................................. *151*
    Earlier sketch in SATA *101*
Waltrip, Lela (Kingston) 1904-1995 .............. *9*
Waltrip, Mildred 1911- ............................. *37*
Waltrip, Rufus (Charles) 1898-1988 ............. *9*
Walworth, Nancy Zinsser 1917- .................. *14*
Wangerin, Walter, Jr. 1944- ....................... *98*
    Brief entry ......................................... *37*
    Earlier sketch in SATA *45*
Waniek, Marilyn Nelson 1946- ................... *60*
    *See* Nelson, Marilyn
Wannamaker, Bruce
    *See* Moncure, Jane Belk
Warbler, J. M.
    *See* Cocagnac, Augustin Maurice(-Jean)
Warburg, Sandol Stoddard .......................... *14*
    *See* Stoddard, Sandol
Ward, E. D.
    *See* Gorey, Edward (St. John)
    and Lucas, E(dward) V(errall)
Ward, Ed
    *See* Stratemeyer, Edward L.
Ward, Helen 1962- .................................. *144*
    Earlier sketch in SATA *72*
Ward, Jennifer 1963- .............................. *146*
Ward, John (Stanton) 1917- ....................... *42*
Ward, Jonas
    *See* Ard, William (Thomas)
    and Cox, William R(obert)
    and Garfield, Brian (Francis Wynne)

Ward, Lynd (Kendall) 1905-1985 ............ 36
    Obituary ................................ 42
    Earlier sketch in SATA 2
Ward, Martha (Eads) ........................ 5
Ward, Melanie
    See Curtis, Richard (Alan)
    and Lynch, Marilyn
Ward, Tom
    See Stratemeyer, Edward L.
Wardell, Dean
    See Prince, J(ack) H(arvey)
Wardlaw, Lee 1955- ........................ 115
    Earlier sketch in SATA 79
Ware, Cheryl 1963- ........................ 101
Ware, Chris 1967- ........................ 140
Ware, Leon (Vernon) 1909-1976 ............ 4
Wargin, Kathy-jo 1965- .................... 145
Warner, Frank A. ........................... 67
    Earlier sketch in SATA 1
Warner, Gertrude Chandler 1890-1979 ........ 9
    Obituary ................................ 73
Warner, J(ohn) F. 1929- .................... 75
Warner, Lucille Schulberg .................. 30
Warner, Matt
    See Fichter, George S.
Warner, Oliver (Martin Wilson) 1903-1976
    ..................................... 29
Warner, Sally 1946- ...................... 131
Warner, Sunny (B.) 1931- .................. 108
Warnes, Tim 1971- ........................ 166
    Earlier sketch in SATA 116
Warnes, Timothy
    See Warnes, Tim
Warnick, Elsa 1942- ...................... 113
Warren, Andrea 1946- ...................... 98
Warren, Betsy
    See Warren, Elizabeth Avery
Warren, Billy
    See Warren, William Stephen
Warren, Cathy 1951- ....................... 62
    Brief entry ............................. 46
Warren, Elizabeth
    See Supraner, Robyn
Warren, Elizabeth Avery 1916- ............. 46
    Brief entry ............................. 38
Warren, Jackie M. 1953- .................. 135
Warren, Joshua P(aul) 1976- .............. 107
Warren, Joyce W(illiams) 1935- ............ 18
Warren, Mary Phraner 1929- ................ 10
Warren, Robert Penn 1905-1989 ............ 46
    Obituary ................................ 63
Warren, Scott S. 1957- .................... 79
Warren, William Stephen 1882-1968 .......... 9
Warrick, Patricia Scott 1925- ............. 35
Warsh
    See Warshaw, Jerry
Warshaw, Jerry 1929- ...................... 30
Warshaw, Mary 1931- ....................... 89
Warshofsky, Fred 1931- .................... 24
Warshofsky, Isaac
    See Singer, Isaac Bashevis
Wartski, Maureen (Ann Crane) 1940- ........ 50
    Brief entry ............................. 37
Warwick, Alan R(oss) 1900-1973 ............ 42
Wa-sha-quon-asin
    See Belaney, Archibald Stansfeld
Wa-Sha-Quon-Asin
    See Belaney, Archibald Stansfeld
Washburn, Bradford 1910-2007 .............. 38
Washburn, Henry Bradford, Jr.
    See Washburn, Bradford
Washburn, Jan(ice) 1926- .................. 63
Washburne, Carolyn Kott 1944- ............. 86
Washburne, Heluiz Chandler 1892-1970 ..... 10
    Obituary ................................ 26
Washington, Booker T(aliaferro) 1856-1915
    ..................................... 28
Washington, Donna L. 1967- ............... 159
    Earlier sketch in SATA 98
Wasserstein, Wendy 1950-2006 .............. 94
    Obituary ............................... 174

Wassiljewa, Tatjana 1928- ................ 106
Watanabe, Shigeo 1928- ................... 131
    Brief entry ............................. 32
    Earlier sketch in SATA 39
    See also CLR 8
Waters, John F(rederick) 1930- ............. 4
Waters, Tony 1958- ........................ 75
Waterton, Betty (Marie) 1923- ............. 99
    Brief entry ............................. 34
    Earlier sketch in SATA 37
Watkins, Dawn L. ......................... 126
Watkins, Gloria Jean
    See hooks, bell
Watkins, Lois 1930- ....................... 88
Watkins, Peter 1934- ...................... 66
Watkins, Yoko Kawashima 1933- ............. 93
Watkins-Pitchford, Denys James 1905-1990
    ..................................... 87
    Obituary ................................ 66
    Earlier sketch in SATA 6
    See also SAAS 4
Watling, James 1933- ..................... 117
    Earlier sketch in SATA 67
Watson, Aldren A(uld) 1917- ............... 42
    Brief entry ............................. 36
Watson, Amy Zakrzewski 1965- .............. 76
Watson, B. S.
    See Teitelbaum, Michael
Watson, Carol 1949- ....................... 78
Watson, Clyde 1947- ....................... 68
    Earlier sketch in SATA 5
    See also CLR 3
Watson, James 1936- ...................... 106
    Earlier sketch in SATA 10
Watson, Jane Werner 1915- ................. 54
    Earlier sketch in SATA 3
Watson, John H.
    See Farmer, Philip Jose
Watson, Mary 1953- ....................... 117
Watson, N. Cameron 1955- .................. 81
Watson, Nancy Dingman ..................... 32
Watson, Pauline 1925- ..................... 14
Watson, Richard F.
    See Silverberg, Robert
Watson, Richard Jesse 1951- ............... 62
Watson, Sally (Lou) 1924- .................. 3
Watson, Wendy (McLeod) 1942- ............. 142
    Earlier sketches in SATA 5, 74
Watson Taylor, Elizabeth 1915- ............ 41
Watt, Melanie 1975- ...................... 136
Watt, Thomas 1935- ......................... 4
Wattenberg, Jane ......................... 174
Watterson, Bill 1958- ..................... 66
Watt-Evans, Lawrence 1954- ............... 121
    See Evans, Lawrence Watt
Watts, (Anna) Bernadette 1942- ........... 103
    Earlier sketch in SATA 4
Watts, Ephraim
    See Horne, Richard Henry Hengist
Watts, Franklin (Mowry) 1904-1978 ......... 46
    Obituary ................................ 21
Watts, Irene N(aemi) 1931- ............... 111
    Earlier sketch in SATA 56
Watts, Isaac 1674-1748 .................... 52
Watts, James K(ennedy) M(offitt) 1955- ..... 59
Watts, Jeri Hanel 1957- .................. 170
Watts, Julia 1969- ....................... 103
Watts, Leander 1956- ..................... 146
Watts, Leslie Elizabeth 1961- ............ 168
Watts, Mabel Pizzey 1906-1994 ............. 11
Watts, Nigel 1957-1999 ................... 121
Waugh, C. C. Roessel
    See Waugh, Carol-Lynn Rossel
    and Waugh, Charles G(ordon)
Waugh, Carol-Lynn Rossel 1947- ............ 41
Waugh, Dorothy -1996 ...................... 11
Waugh, Sylvia 1935- ...................... 169
Waugh, Virginia
    See Sorensen, Virginia
Wax, Wendy A. 1963- ...................... 163
    Earlier sketch in SATA 73

Wayland, April Halprin 1954- ............. 143
    Earlier sketch in SATA 78
    See also SAAS 26
Wayne, (Anne) Jenifer 1917-1982 ........... 32
Wayne, Kyra Petrovskaya 1918- .............. 8
Wayne, Richard
    See Decker, Duane
Wayshak, Deborah Noyes 1965- ............. 145
Waystaff, Simon
    See Swift, Jonathan
Weales, Gerald (Clifford) 1925- ........... 11
Weary, Ogdred
    See Gorey, Edward (St. John)
Weatherford, Carole Boston 1956- ......... 138
Weatherly, Myra (S.) 1926- ............... 130
Weaver, Harriett E. 1908-1993 ............. 65
Weaver, John L. 1949- ..................... 42
Weaver, Robyn
    See Conley-Weaver, Robyn
Weaver, Robyn M.
    See Conley-Weaver, Robyn
Weaver, Ward
    See Mason, F(rancis) van Wyck
Weaver, Will 1950- ....................... 161
    Earlier sketches in SATA 88, 109
Weaver, William Weller
    See Weaver, Will
Weaver-Gelzer, Charlotte 1950- ............ 79
Webb, Christopher
    See Wibberley, Leonard (Patrick O'Connor)
Webb, Jacqueline
    See Pearce, Margaret
Webb, Jacquelyn
    See Pearce, Margaret
    and Pearce, Margaret
Webb, Jean Francis (III) 1910-1991 ........ 35
Webb, Kaye 1914- .......................... 60
Webb, Lois Sinaiko 1922- .................. 82
Webb, Margot 1934- ........................ 67
Webb, Sharon 1936- ........................ 41
Webb, Sophie 1958- ....................... 135
Webber, Andrew Lloyd
    See Lloyd Webber, Andrew
Webber, Desiree Morrison 1956- ........... 170
Webber, Irma E(leanor Schmidt) 1904-1995
    ..................................... 14
Weber, Alfons 1921- ........................ 8
Weber, Bruce 1942- ....................... 120
    Earlier sketch in SATA 73
Weber, Debora 1955- ....................... 58
Weber, EdNah New Rider 1919(?)- .......... 168
Weber, Jill 1950- ........................ 127
Weber, Judith E(ichler) 1938- ............. 64
Weber, Ken(neth J.) 1940- ................. 90
Weber, Lenora Mattingly 1895-1971 .......... 2
    Obituary ................................ 26
Weber, Michael 1945- ...................... 87
Weber, Sandra 1961- ...................... 158
Weber, William J(ohn) 1927- ............... 14
Webster, Alice Jane Chandler 1876-1916 ... 17
Webster, David 1930- ...................... 11
Webster, Frank V. ......................... 67
    Earlier sketch in SATA 1
Webster, Gary
    See Garrison, Webb B(lack)
Webster, James 1925-1981 ................. 17
    Obituary ................................ 27
Webster, Jean
    See Webster, Alice Jane Chandler
Wechter, Nell (Carolyn) Wise 1913-1989 . 127
    Earlier sketch in SATA 60
Weck, Thomas L. 1942- ..................... 62
Wedd, Kate
    See Gregory, Philippa
Weddle, Ethel Harshbarger 1897-1996 ....... 11
Weeks, Sarah ............................. 158
Weems, David B(urnola) 1922- .............. 80
Wees, Frances Shelley 1902-1982 ........... 58
Weevers, Peter 1944- ...................... 59
Wegen, Ronald 1946-1985 .................. 99

Wegman, William (George) 1943- ............ 135
  Earlier sketches in SATA *78, 129*
Wegner, Fritz 1924- ........................... 20
Weidhorn, Manfred 1931- ..................... 60
Weidt, Maryann N. 1944- ..................... 85
Weigel, Jeff 1958- ............................ 170
Weigelt, Udo 1960- ........................... 168
Weihs, Erika 1917- ........................... 107
  Earlier sketch in SATA *15*
Weik, Mary Hays 1898(?)-1979 ................. 3
  Obituary ..................................... 23
Weil, Ann Yezner 1908-1969 ................... 9
Weil, Lisl 1910- .............................. 7
Weilerstein, Sadie Rose 1894-1993 ............ 3
  Obituary ..................................... 75
Weill, Cynthia 1959- ......................... 167
Wein, Elizabeth E(ve) 1964- .................. 151
  Earlier sketch in SATA *82*
Weinberg, Larry
  *See* Weinberg, Lawrence (E.)
Weinberg, Lawrence (E.) ...................... 92
  Brief entry ................................. 48
Weinberger, Tanya 1939- ...................... 84
Weiner, Sandra 1922- ......................... 14
Weingarten, Violet (Brown) 1915-1976 ........ 3
  Obituary ..................................... 27
Weingartner, Charles 1922- ................... 5
Weinstein, Nina 1951- ........................ 73
Weir, Bob 1947- .............................. 76
Weir, Diana (R.) Loiewski 1958- .............. 111
Weir, Joan S(herman) 1928- ................... 99
Weir, LaVada .................................. 2
Weir, Rosemary (Green) 1905-1994 ............. 21
Weir, Wendy 1949- ............................ 76
Weis, Margaret 1948- ......................... 164
  Earlier sketches in SATA *38, 92*
Weisberger, Bernard A(llen) 1922- ............ 21
Weiser, Marjorie P(hillis) K(atz) 1934- ...... 33
Weisgard, Leonard (Joseph) 1916-2000 ......... 85
  Obituary ..................................... 122
  Earlier sketches in SATA *2, 30*
  *See also* SAAS *19*
Weiss, Adelle 1920- .......................... 18
Weiss, Ann E(dwards) 1943- ................... 69
  Earlier sketch in SATA *30*
  *See also* SAAS *13*
Weiss, Edna
  *See* Barth, Edna
Weiss, Ellen 1953- ........................... 44
Weiss, Harvey 1922- .......................... 76
  Earlier sketches in SATA *1, 27*
  *See also* CLR *4*
  *See also* SAAS *19*
Weiss, Jaqueline Shachter 1926- .............. 65
Weiss, Malcolm E. 1928- ...................... 3
Weiss, Margaret Edith
  *See* Weis, Margaret
Weiss, Miriam
  *See* Schlein, Miriam
Weiss, Mitch 1951- ........................... 123
Weiss, Nicki 1954- ........................... 86
  Earlier sketch in SATA *33*
Weiss, Renee Karol 1923- ..................... 5
Weitzman, David L. 1936- ..................... 172
  Earlier sketch in SATA *122*
Wekesser, Carol A. 1963- ..................... 76
Welber, Robert ............................... 26
Welch, Amanda (Jane) 1945- ................... 75
Welch, Jean-Louise
  *See* Kempton, Jean Welch
Welch, Pauline
  *See* Bodenham, Hilda Morris
Welch, Ronald
  *See* Felton, Ronald Oliver
Welch, Sheila Kelly 1945- .................... 130
Welch, Willy 1952- ........................... 93
Welford, Sue 1942- ........................... 75
Weller, George (Anthony) 1907-2002 ........... 31
  Obituary ..................................... 140
Welling, Peter J. 1947- ...................... 135

Wellington, Monica 1957- ..................... 157
  Earlier sketches in SATA *67, 99*
Wellman, Alice 1900-1984 ..................... 51
  Brief entry ................................. 36
Wellman, Manly Wade 1903-1986 ................ 6
  Obituary ..................................... 47
Wellman, Paul I(selin) 1898-1966 ............. 3
Wellman, Sam(uel) 1939- ...................... 122
Wells, H(erbert) G(eorge) 1866-1946 .......... 20
  *See also* CLR *64*
Wells, Helen
  *See* Campbell, Hope
Wells, Helen 1910-1986 ....................... 49
  Earlier sketch in SATA *2*
Wells, J. Wellington
  *See* de Camp, L(yon) Sprague
Wells, June
  *See* Swinford, Betty (June Wells)
Wells, Robert
  *See* Welsch, Roger L(ee)
Wells, Rosemary 1943- ........................ 156
  Earlier sketches in SATA *18, 69, 114*
  *See also* CLR *69*
  *See also* SAAS *1*
Wells, Susan (Mary) 1951- .................... 78
Wels, Byron G(erald) 1924-1993 ............... 9
Welsbacher, Anne 1955- ....................... 89
Welsch, Roger L(ee) 1936- .................... 82
Welsh, David
  *See* Hills, C.A.R.
Weltner, Linda R(iverly) 1938- ............... 38
Welton, Jude 1955- ........................... 143
  Earlier sketch in SATA *79*
Welty, S. F.
  *See* Welty, Susan F.
Welty, Susan F. 1905- ........................ 9
Wendelin, Rudolph 1910-2000 .................. 23
Wentworth, Robert
  *See* Hamilton, Edmond
Werlin, Nancy 1961- .......................... 161
  Earlier sketches in SATA *87, 119*
Werner, Elsa Jane
  *See* Watson, Jane Werner
Werner, Herma 1926- .......................... 47
  Brief entry ................................. 41
Werner, Jane
  *See* Watson, Jane Werner
Werner, K.
  *See* Casewit, Curtis W(erner)
Wersba, Barbara 1932- ........................ 58
  Autobiography Feature ....................... 103
  Earlier sketch in SATA *1*
  *See also* CLR *78*
  *See also* SAAS *2*
Werstein, Irving 1914(?)-1971 ................ 14
Werth, Kurt 1896-1983 ........................ 20
Wesley, Alison
  *See* Barnes, Michael
Wesley, Mary (Aline) 1912-2002 ............... 66
Wesley, Valerie Wilson 1947- ................. 168
  Earlier sketch in SATA *106*
West, Andrew
  *See* Arthur, Robert, (Jr.)
West, Anna 1938- ............................. 40
West, Barbara
  *See* Price, Olive
West, Betty 1921- ............................ 11
West, Bruce 1951- ............................ 63
West, C. P.
  *See* Wodehouse, P(elham) G(renville)
West, Dorothy
  *See* Benson, Mildred (Augustine Wirt)
West, Emily Govan 1919- ...................... 38
West, Emmy
  *See* West, Emily Govan
West, James
  *See* Withers, Carl A.
West, Jerry
  *See* Svenson, Andrew E(dward)
West, John
  *See* Arthur, Robert, (Jr.)

West, Owen
  *See* Koontz, Dean R.
Westall, Robert (Atkinson) 1929-1993 ......... 69
  Obituary ..................................... 75
  Earlier sketch in SATA *23*
  *See also* CLR *13*
  *See also* SAAS *2*
Westaway, Jane 1948- ......................... 121
Westcott, Nadine Bernard 1949- ............... 130
Westerberg, Christine 1950- .................. 29
Westerduin, Anne 1945- ....................... 105
Westerfeld, Scott ............................ 161
Westervelt, Virginia Veeder 1914-2005 ........ 10
Westheimer, David 1917-2005 .................. 14
  Obituary ..................................... 170
Westheimer, David Kaplan
  *See* Westheimer, David
Westmacott, Mary
  *See* Christie, Agatha (Mary Clarissa)
Westman, Barbara ............................. 70
Westman, Paul (Wendell) 1956- ................ 39
Westmoreland, William C. 1914-2005 ........... 63
Westmoreland, William Childs
  *See* Westmoreland, William C.
Weston, Allen
  *See* Hogarth, Grace (Weston Allen)
  and Norton, Andre
Weston, Carol 1956- .......................... 135
Weston, John (Harrison) 1932- ................ 21
Weston, Martha 1947- ......................... 119
  Earlier sketch in SATA *53*
Westphal, Arnold Carl 1897- .................. 57
Westrup, Hugh ................................ 102
Westwood, Jennifer 1940- ..................... 10
Wexler, Jerome (LeRoy) 1923- ................. 14
Weyland, Jack 1940- .......................... 81
Weyn, Suzanne 1955- .......................... 164
  Earlier sketches in SATA *63, 101*
Weyr, Garret
  *See* Freymann-Weyr, (Rhoda) Garret (Michaela)
Wezyk, Joanna 1966- .......................... 82
Whaley, Joyce Irene 1923- .................... 61
Whalin, W. Terry 1953- ....................... 93
Wharf, Michael
  *See* Weller, George (Anthony)
Wharmby, Margot .............................. 63
Whatley, Bruce 1954- ......................... 177
Wheatley, Arabelle 1921- ..................... 16
Wheatley, Nadia 1949- ........................ 147
Wheeler, Cindy 1955- ......................... 49
  Brief entry ................................. 40
Wheeler, Deborah (Jean Ross) 1947- ........... 83
Wheeler, Janet D. ............................ 1
Wheeler, Jill C. 1964- ....................... 136
  Earlier sketch in SATA *86*
Wheeler, Jody 1952- .......................... 148
  Earlier sketch in SATA *84*
Wheeler, Lisa 1963- .......................... 162
Wheeler, Opal 1898- .......................... 23
Whelan, Elizabeth M(urphy) 1943- ............. 14
Whelan, Gloria 1923- ......................... 128
  Earlier sketch in SATA *85*
  *See also* CLR *90*
Whelan, Gloria Ann
  *See* Whelan, Gloria
Whipple, A(ddison) B(eecher) C(olvin) 1918- ... 64
Whipple, Cal
  *See* Whipple, A(ddison) B(eecher) C(olvin)
Whisp, Kennilworthy
  *See* Rowling, J.K.
Whistler, Reginald John 1905-1944 ............ 30
Whistler, Rex
  *See* Whistler, Reginald John
Whitcher, Susan (Godsil) 1952- ............... 96
Whitcomb, Jon 1906-1988 ...................... 10
  Obituary ..................................... 56
Whitcomb, Laura .............................. 171
White, Anne Terry 1896-1980 .................. 2
White, Carolyn 1948- ......................... 130

White, Dale
  *See* Place, Marian T(empleton)
White, Dori 1919- ............................................ *10*
White, E. B. 1899-1985 ............................ *100*
  Obituary ................................................ *44*
  Earlier sketches in SATA *2, 29*
  *See also* CLR *107*
White, Eliza Orne 1856-1947
  *See* YABC *2*
White, Elwyn Brooks
  *See* White, E. B.
White, Florence M(eiman) 1910- ............... *14*
White, Laurence B(arton), Jr. 1935- ........... *10*
White, Lee ...................................................... *176*
White, Martin 1943- ....................................... *51*
White, Nancy 1942- ..................................... *126*
White, Ramy Allison ...................................... *67*
  Earlier sketch in SATA *1*
White, Robb 1909-1990 ................................. *83*
  Earlier sketch in SATA *1*
  *See also* CLR *3*
  *See also* SAAS *1*
White, Ruth C. 1942- ................................... *165*
  Earlier sketches in SATA *39, 117*
White, T(erence) H(anbury) 1906-1964 ...... *12*
White, Tekla N. 1934- ................................. *115*
White, Timothy (Thomas Anthony) 1952-2002
  .......................................................... *60*
White, Tom 1923- ......................................... *148*
White, William, Jr. 1934- ............................... *16*
Whitehead, Don(ald) F. 1908-1981 .............. *4*
Whitehead, Kathy 1957- ............................... *176*
Whitehouse, Arch
  *See* Whitehouse, Arthur George Joseph
Whitehouse, Arthur George Joseph 1895-1979
  .......................................................... *14*
  Obituary ................................................ *23*
Whitehouse, Elizabeth S(cott) 1893-1968 ... *35*
Whitehouse, Jeanne ..................................... *29*
  *See* Peterson, Jeanne Whitehouse
Whitelaw, Nancy 1933- ............................... *166*
  Earlier sketch in SATA *76*
Whitesel, Cheryl Aylward .......................... *162*
Whitinger, R. D.
  *See* Place, Marian T(empleton)
Whitley, Mary Ann
  *See* Sebrey, Mary Ann
Whitley, Peggy 1938- ................................... *140*
Whitlock, Ralph 1914-1995 .......................... *35*
Whitman, Alice
  *See* Marker, Sherry
Whitman, Sylvia (Choate) 1961- ............... *135*
  Earlier sketch in SATA *85*
Whitman, Walt(er) 1819-1892 ..................... *20*
Whitmore, Arvella 1922- ............................. *125*
Whitney, Alex(andra) 1922- ......................... *14*
Whitney, David C(harles) 1921- ................. *48*
  Brief entry ............................................. *29*
Whitney, Kim Ablon ................................... *162*
Whitney, Phyllis A(yame) 1903- ................. *30*
  Earlier sketch in SATA *1*
  *See also* CLR *59*
Whitney, Sharon 1937- ................................. *63*
Whitney, Thomas P(orter) 1917- ................. *25*
Whittington, Mary K(athrine) 1941- ........... *75*
Whitworth, John 1945- ............................... *123*
Whybrow, Ian ............................................. *132*
Whyte, Mal(colm Kenneth, Jr.) 1933- ........ *62*
Whyte, Mary 1953- ..................................... *148*
  Earlier sketch in SATA *94*
Whytock, Cherry ......................................... *177*
Wiater, Stanley 1953- ................................... *84*
Wibbelsman, Charles J(oseph) 1945- ......... *59*
Wibberley, Leonard (Patrick O'Connor)
  1915-1983 ................................................ *45*
  Obituary ................................................ *36*
  Earlier sketch in SATA *2*
  *See also* CLR *3*
  *See* Holton, Leonard
Wiberg, Harald (Albin) 1908- ..................... *93*
  Brief entry ............................................. *40*

Wick, Walter 1953- ..................................... *148*
Wickens, Elaine ........................................... *86*
Wickstrom, Sylvie 1960- ............................. *169*
Widdemer, Mabel Cleland 1902-1964 ........... *5*
Widener, Terry 1950- ................................. *105*
Widerberg, Siv 1931- ................................... *10*
Wiebe, Rudy 1934- ..................................... *156*
Wiebe, Rudy Henry
  *See* Wiebe, Rudy
Wieler, Diana (Jean) 1961- ......................... *109*
Wiener, Lori 1956- ....................................... *84*
Wier, Ester (Alberti) 1910-2000 .................... *3*
Wiese, Kurt 1887-1974 ................................. *36*
  Obituary ................................................ *24*
  Earlier sketch in SATA *3*
  *See also* CLR *86*
Wiesel, Elie 1928- ......................................... *56*
Wiesel, Eliezer
  *See* Wiesel, Elie
Wiesner, David 1956- ................................. *139*
  Earlier sketches in SATA *72, 117*
  *See also* CLR *84*
Wiesner, Portia
  *See* Takakjian, Portia
Wiesner, William 1899-1984 .......................... *5*
Wiggers, Raymond 1952- ............................. *82*
Wiggin, Eric E. 1939- ................................. *167*
  Earlier sketch in SATA *88*
Wiggin, Eric Ellsworth 1939-
  *See* Wiggin, Eric E.
Wiggin (Riggs), Kate Douglas (Smith)
  1856-1923
  *See* YABC *1*
  *See also* CLR *52*
Wiggins, VeraLee (Chesnut) 1928-1995 ..... *89*
Wight, James Alfred 1916-1995 ................... *55*
  Brief entry ............................................. *44*
  *See* Herriot, James
Wignell, Edel 1936- ..................................... *69*
Wijnberg, Ellen ........................................... *85*
Wikland, Ilon 1930- ..................................... *93*
  Brief entry ............................................. *32*
Wikler, Madeline 1943- ............................... *114*
Wilber, Donald N(ewton) 1907-1997 ......... *35*
Wilbur, C. Keith 1923- ............................... *27*
Wilbur, Frances 1921- ................................. *107*
Wilbur, Richard 1921- ................................. *108*
  Earlier sketch in SATA *9*
Wilbur, Richard Purdy
  *See* Wilbur, Richard
Wilburn, Kathy 1948- ................................... *68*
Wilcox, Charlotte 1948- ............................... *72*
Wilcox, R(uth) Turner 1888-1970 .............. *36*
Wilcox, Roger
  *See* Collins, Paul
Wild, Jocelyn 1941- ..................................... *46*
Wild, Margaret 1948- ................................. *151*
Wild, Robin (Evans) 1936- ......................... *46*
Wild, Robyn 1947- ..................................... *117*
Wilde, D. Gunther
  *See* Hurwood, Bernhardt J.
Wilde, Oscar (Fingal O'Flahertie Wills)
  1854(?)-1900 ........................................... *24*
  *See also* CLR *114*
Wilder, Buck
  *See* Smith, Tim(othy R.)
Wilder, Laura (Elizabeth) Ingalls 1867-1957
  .......................................................... *100*
  Earlier sketches in SATA *15, 29*
  *See also* CLR *111*
Wildsmith, Brian 1930- ............................... *124*
  Earlier sketches in SATA *16, 69*
  *See also* CLR *52*
  *See also* SAAS *5*
Wiles, Deborah ........................................... *171*
Wilhelm, Hans 1945- ................................. *135*
  Earlier sketch in SATA *58*
  *See also* CLR *46*
  *See also* SAAS *21*
Wilkie, Katharine E(lliott) 1904-1980 ......... *31*

Wilkin, Eloise 1904-1987 ............................. *49*
  Obituary ................................................ *54*
Wilkins, Frances 1923- ................................. *14*
Wilkins, Kim ............................................... *147*
Wilkins, Marilyn (Ruth) 1926- ................... *30*
Wilkins, Marne
  *See* Wilkins, Marilyn (Ruth)
Wilkins, Mary Huiskamp 1926- ............... *139*
  Earlier sketch in SATA *84*
  *See* Calhoun, Mary
Wilkins, Mary Huiskamp Calhoun
  *See* Wilkins, Mary Huiskamp
Wilkinson, (Thomas) Barry 1923- ............. *50*
  Brief entry ............................................. *32*
Wilkinson, Beth 1925- ................................. *80*
Wilkinson, Brenda 1946- ............................. *91*
  Earlier sketch in SATA *14*
  *See also* CLR *20*
Wilkinson, (John) Burke 1913-2000 ............ *4*
Wilkinson, Sylvia 1940- ............................. *56*
  Brief entry ............................................. *39*
Wilkon, Jozef 1930- ................................... *133*
  Earlier sketches in SATA *31, 71*
Wilks, Michael Thomas 1947- ................... *44*
  *See* Thomas, Michael
Wilks, Mike
  *See* Wilks, Michael Thomas
Will
  *See* Lipkind, William
Willard, Barbara (Mary) 1909-1994 ........... *74*
  Earlier sketch in SATA *17*
  *See also* CLR *2*
  *See also* SAAS *5*
Willard, Mildred Wilds 1911-1978 ............. *14*
Willard, Nancy 1936- ................................. *127*
  Brief entry ............................................. *30*
  Earlier sketches in SATA *37, 71*
  *See also* CLR *5*
Willcox, Isobel 1907-1996 ........................... *42*
Willems, Mo ............................................... *154*
  *See also* CLR *114*
Willett, Edward (C.) 1959- ......................... *115*
Willey, Margaret 1950- ................................. *86*
Willey, Robert
  *See* Ley, Willy
Willhoite, Michael A. 1946- ......................... *71*
William, Kate
  *See* Armstrong, Jennifer
Williams, Arlene ......................................... *171*
Williams, Barbara 1925- ............................. *107*
  Earlier sketch in SATA *11*
  *See also* CLR *48*
  *See also* SAAS *16*
Williams, Barbara 1937- ............................... *62*
Williams, Beryl
  *See* Epstein, Beryl (M. Williams)
Williams, Brian (Peter) 1943- ..................... *54*
Williams, Carol Lynch 1959- ..................... *110*
Williams, Charles
  *See* Collier, James Lincoln
Williams, Clyde C. 1881-1974 ...................... *8*
  Obituary ................................................ *27*
Williams, Coe
  *See* Harrison, C(hester) William
Williams, Colleen Madonna Flood 1963- . *156*
Williams, Cynthia G. 1958- ....................... *123*
Williams, Dar 1967- ................................... *168*
Williams, Donna Reilly 1945- ..................... *83*
Williams, (Marcia) Dorothy ........................ *71*
  *See* Williams, Marcia (Dorothy)
Williams, Dorothy
  *See* Williams, Marcia (Dorothy)
Williams, Dorothy Snowden
  *See* Williams, Dar
Williams, Eric (Ernest) 1911-1983 ............. *14*
  Obituary ................................................ *38*
Williams, Ferelith Eccles ............................. *22*
  *See* Eccles Williams, Ferelith
Williams, Frances B.
  *See* Browin, Frances Williams

Williams, Garth (Montgomery) 1912-1996 . *66*
    Obituary ........................................... *90*
    Earlier sketch in SATA *18*
    *See also* CLR *57*
    *See also* SAAS *7*
Williams, Guy R(ichard) 1920- ................. *11*
Williams, Hawley
    *See* Heyliger, William
Williams, Helen 1948- ............................. *77*
Williams, J. R.
    *See* Williams, Jeanne
Williams, J. Walker
    *See* Wodehouse, P(elham) G(renville)
Williams, Jay 1914-1978 ........................ *41*
    Obituary ........................................... *24*
    Earlier sketch in SATA *3*
    *See also* CLR *8*
Williams, Jeanne 1930- ............................. *5*
Williams, Jenny 1939- ............................. *60*
Williams, Karen Lynn 1952- ..................... *99*
    Earlier sketch in SATA *66*
Williams, Kit 1946(?)- ............................ *44*
    *See also* CLR *4*
Williams, Leslie 1941- ............................ *42*
Williams, Linda 1948- ............................ *59*
Williams, Lynn
    *See* Hale, Arlene
Williams, Marcia (Dorothy) 1945- ............ *159*
    Earlier sketch in SATA *97*
    *See* Williams, (Marcia) Dorothy
Williams, Margery
    *See* Bianco, Margery Williams
Williams, Mark
    *See* Arthur, Robert, (Jr.)
Williams, Mark London 1959- ................. *140*
Williams, Maureen 1951- ........................ *12*
Williams, Michael
    *See* St. John, Wylly Folk
Williams, Patrick J.
    *See* Griffin, W.E.B.
Williams, Pete
    *See* Faulknor, Cliff(ord Vernon)
Williams, S. P.
    *See* Hart, Virginia
Williams, Sam ................................... *177*
    Earlier sketch in SATA *124*
Williams, Selma R(uth) 1925- ................. *14*
Williams, Sherley Anne 1944-1999 ............ *78*
    Obituary ......................................... *116*
Williams, Sheron 1955- .......................... *77*
Williams, Shirley
    *See* Williams, Sherley Anne
Williams, Slim
    *See* Williams, Clyde C.
Williams, Sophy 1965- .......................... *135*
Williams, Suzanne (Bullock) 1953- ............ *71*
Williams, Ursula Moray ............................. *3*
    *See* Moray Williams, Ursula
Williams, Vera B(aker) 1927- .................. *102*
    Brief entry ....................................... *33*
    Earlier sketch in SATA *53*
    *See also* CLR *9*
Williams-Andriani, Renee 1963- ............... *98*
Williams-Ellis, (Mary) Amabel (Nassau
    Strachey) 1894-1984 ......................... *29*
    Obituary ......................................... *41*
Williams-Garcia, Rita 1957- ................... *160*
    Earlier sketch in SATA *98*
    *See also* CLR *36*
Williamson, Gwyneth 1965- ................... *109*
Williamson, Henry (William) 1895-1977 .... *37*
    Obituary ......................................... *30*
Williamson, Joanne S(mall) 1926- ............ *122*
    Earlier sketch in SATA *3*
Willis, Charles
    *See* Clarke, Arthur C.
Willis, Connie 1945- ............................ *110*
    *See also* CLR *66*
Willis, Jeanne 1959- ............................ *123*
    Earlier sketch in SATA *61*

Willis, Jeanne Mary
    *See* Willis, Jeanne
Willis, Meredith Sue 1946- ..................... *101*
Willis, Nancy Carol 1952- ..................... *139*
    Earlier sketch in SATA *93*
Willis, Paul J. 1955- ............................ *113*
Willms, Russ ................................... *95*
Willoughby, Lee Davis
    *See* Avallone, Michael (Angelo, Jr.)
    and Brandner, Gary (Phil)
    and Deming, Richard
    and DeAndrea, William L(ouis)
    and Laymon, Richard (Carl)
    and Streib, Dan(iel Thomas)
    and Toombs, John
    and Webb, Jean Francis (III)
Willson, Robina Beckles ....................... *27*
    *See* Beckles Willson, Robina (Elizabeth)
Wilma, Dana
    *See* Faralla, Dana
Wilson, April ................................... *80*
Wilson, Barbara Ker
    *See* Ker Wilson, Barbara
Wilson, Beth P(ierre) ............................. *8*
Wilson, Budge 1927- ............................ *55*
    *See* Wilson, Marjorie
Wilson, Carletta 1951- .......................... *81*
Wilson, Carter 1941- ............................. *6*
Wilson, Charles Morrow 1905-1977 .......... *30*
Wilson, Darryl B(abe) 1939- .................. *90*
Wilson, Diane Lee ............................. *172*
Wilson, Dirk
    *See* Pohl, Frederik
Wilson, Dorothy Clarke 1904-2003 .......... *16*
Wilson, Edward A(rthur) 1886-1970 .......... *38*
Wilson, Ellen (Janet Cameron) (?)-1976 ...... *9*
    Obituary ......................................... *26*
Wilson, Eric (H.) 1940- ........................ *34*
    Brief entry ....................................... *32*
Wilson, Erica ................................... *51*
Wilson, Forrest 1918- ............................ *27*
Wilson, Gahan 1930- ............................ *35*
    Brief entry ....................................... *27*
Wilson, Gina 1943- ............................. *85*
    Brief entry ....................................... *34*
    Earlier sketch in SATA *36*
Wilson, (Leslie) Granville 1912- ............... *14*
Wilson, Hazel (Hutchins) 1898-1992 .......... *3*
    Obituary ......................................... *73*
Wilson, J(erry) M. 1964- ....................... *121*
Wilson, Jacqueline 1945- ..................... *153*
    Brief entry ....................................... *52*
    Earlier sketches in SATA *61, 102*
Wilson, John 1922- .............................. *22*
Wilson, Johnniece Marshall 1944- ............ *75*
Wilson, Joyce M(uriel Judson) ................ *84*
    Earlier sketch in SATA *21*
    *See* Stranger, Joyce
Wilson, Karma ................................. *174*
Wilson, Leslie 1952- ............................ *166*
Wilson, Linda Miller 1936- ................... *116*
Wilson, Lionel 1924-2003 ...................... *33*
    Brief entry ....................................... *31*
    Obituary ......................................... *144*
Wilson, Marjorie
    Brief entry ....................................... *51*
    *See* Wilson, Budge
Wilson, Maurice (Charles John) 1914- ....... *46*
Wilson, Nancy Hope 1947- .................... *138*
    Earlier sketch in SATA *81*
Wilson, Nick
    *See* Ellis, Edward S(ylvester)
Wilson, Ron(ald William) 1941- ............... *38*
Wilson, Sarah 1934- ............................ *142*
    Earlier sketch in SATA *50*
Wilson, Tom 1931- ............................. *33*
    Brief entry ....................................... *30*
Wilson, Troy 1970- ............................. *169*
Wilson, Walt(er N.) 1939- ...................... *14*
Wilson-Max, Ken 1965- ........................ *170*
    Earlier sketch in SATA *93*

Wilton, Elizabeth 1937- ........................ *14*
Wilwerding, Walter Joseph 1891-1966 ......... *9*
Wimmer, Mike 1961- ............................ *70*
Winborn, Marsha (Lynn) 1947- ............... *75*
Winch, John 1944- ............................. *165*
    Earlier sketch in SATA *117*
Winchester, James H(ugh) 1917-1985 ......... *30*
    Obituary ......................................... *45*
Winchester, Stanley
    *See* Youd, (Christopher) Samuel
Windawi, Thura al- 1983(?)- .................. *165*
Winders, Gertrude Hecker -1987 ................ *3*
Windham, Basil
    *See* Wodehouse, P(elham) G(renville)
Windham, Kathryn T(ucker) 1918- ........... *14*
Windling, Terri 1958- .......................... *151*
Windrow, Martin
    *See* Windrow, Martin Clive
Windrow, Martin C.
    *See* Windrow, Martin Clive
Windrow, Martin Clive 1944- .................. *68*
Windsor, Claire
    *See* Hamerstrom, Frances
Windsor, Linda 1950- .......................... *124*
Windsor, Patricia 1938- ........................ *78*
    Earlier sketch in SATA *30*
    *See also* SAAS *19*
Wineman-Marcus, Irene 1952- ................. *81*
Winer, Yvonne 1934- .......................... *120*
Winerip, Michael ............................. *175*
Winfield, Arthur M.
    *See* Stratemeyer, Edward L.
Winfield, Edna
    *See* Stratemeyer, Edward L.
Winfield, Julia
    *See* Armstrong, Jennifer
Wing, Natasha (Lazutin) 1960- ................ *82*
Winick, Judd 1970- ............................ *124*
Winks, Robin William 1930-2003 ............. *61*
Winn, Alison
    *See* Wharmby, Margot
Winn, Chris 1952- .............................. *42*
Winn, Janet Bruce 1928- ........................ *43*
Winn, Marie 1936(?)- ........................... *38*
Winnick, Karen B(eth) B(inkoff) 1946- ...... *51*
Winslow, Barbara 1947- ........................ *91*
Winston, Clara 1921-1983 ...................... *54*
    Obituary ......................................... *39*
Winston, Richard 1917-1979 ................... *54*
Winter, Janet 1926- ............................ *126*
Winter, Jeanette 1939- ......................... *151*
Winter, Milo (Kendall) 1888-1956 ............ *21*
Winter, Paula Cecelia 1929- ................... *48*
Winter, R. R.
    *See* Winterbotham, R(ussell) R(obert)
Winterbotham, R(ussell) R(obert) 1904-1971
    ................................................... *10*
Winterbotham, Russ
    *See* Winterbotham, R(ussell) R(obert)
Winterfeld, Henry 1901-1990 .................. *55*
Winters, J. C.
    *See* Cross, Gilbert B.
Winters, Jon
    *See* Cross, Gilbert B.
Winters, Katherine 1936- ...................... *153*
    Earlier sketch in SATA *103*
Winters, Kay
    *See* Winters, Katherine
Winters, Nina 1944- ............................ *62*
Winters, Paul A. 1965- ......................... *106*
Winterton, Gayle
    *See* Adams, William Taylor
Winthrop, Elizabeth ............................ *164*
    Autobiography Feature ........................ *116*
    Earlier sketches in SATA *8, 76*
    *See also* CLR *89*
    *See* Mahony, Elizabeth Winthrop
Winton, Ian (Kenneth) 1960- ................... *76*
Winton, Tim 1960- ............................. *98*
Wirt, Ann
    *See* Benson, Mildred (Augustine Wirt)

Wirt, Mildred A.
See Benson, Mildred (Augustine Wirt)
Wirtenberg, Patricia Z(arrella) 1932- .......... 10
Wirth, Beverly 1938- ................................. 63
Wirths, Claudine (Turner) G(ibson) 1926-2000
.................................................................. 104
Earlier sketch in SATA 64
Wise, Lenny
See Wise, Leonard
Wise, Leonard 1940- ................................ 167
Wise, Leonard A.
See Wise, Leonard
Wise, Leonard Allan
See Wise, Leonard
Wise, William 1923- ................................. 163
Earlier sketch in SATA 4
Wise, Winifred E. ........................................ 2
Wiseman, Ann (Sayre) 1926- ....................... 31
Wiseman, B(ernard) 1922-1995 .................... 4
Wiseman, David 1916- ................................ 43
Brief entry ............................................ 40
Wishinsky, Frieda 1948- ............................ 166
Earlier sketches in SATA 70, 112
Wisler, G(ary) Clifton 1950- ...................... 103
Brief entry ............................................ 46
Earlier sketch in SATA 58
Wismer, Donald (Richard) 1946- ................. 59
Wisner, Bill
See Wisner, William L.
Wisner, William L. 1914(?)-1983 ................ 42
Wisnewski, David 1953-2002
See Wisniewski, David
Wisniewski, David 1953-2002 ...................... 95
Obituary ............................................... 139
See also CLR 51
Wister, Owen 1860-1938 ............................. 62
Witham, (Phillip) Ross 1917- ....................... 37
Withers, Carl A. 1900-1970 ......................... 14
Withrow, Sarah 1966- ............................... 124
Witt, Dick 1948- ....................................... 80
Witt, Shirley Hill 1934- ............................... 17
Wittanen, Etolin 1907- ............................... 55
Wittels, Harriet Joan 1938- .......................... 31
Wittig, Susan
See Albert, Susan Wittig
Wittlinger, Ellen 1948- .............................. 122
Autobiography Feature ............................ 128
Earlier sketch in SATA 83
Wittman, Sally (Anne Christensen) 1941- .. 30
Witty, Paul 1898-1976 ................................ 50
Obituary ................................................ 30
Wodehouse, P(elham) G(renville) 1881-1975
.................................................................. 22
Wodge, Dreary
See Gorey, Edward (St. John)
Woelfle, Gretchen 1945- ............................ 145
Wohlberg, Meg 1905-1990 .......................... 41
Obituary ................................................ 66
Wohlrabe, Raymond A. 1900-1977 ................ 4
Wojciechowska, Maia (Teresa) 1927-2002 . 83
Autobiography Feature ............................ 104
Obituary ................................................ 134
Earlier sketches in SATA 1, 28
See also CLR 1
See also SAAS 1
Wojciechowski, Susan ................................ 126
Earlier sketch in SATA 78
Wolcott, Patty 1929- ................................... 14
Wold, Allen L. 1943- ................................... 64
Wold, Jo Anne 1938- ................................... 30
Woldin, Beth Weiner 1955- .......................... 34
Wolf, Bernard 1930- ................................. 102
Brief entry ............................................ 37
Wolf, Erica (Van Varick) 1978- ................. 156
Wolf, Gita 1956- ...................................... 101
Wolf, Janet 1957- ....................................... 78
Wolf, Sallie 1950- ...................................... 80
Wolfe, Art 1952- ........................................ 76
Wolfe, Burton H. 1932- ................................ 5
Wolfe, Gene 1931- ................................... 165
Earlier sketch in SATA 118

Wolfe, Gene Rodman
See Wolfe, Gene
Wolfe, Louis 1905-1985 ................................ 8
Obituary ............................................... 133
Wolfe, Rinna (Evelyn) 1925- ........................ 38
Wolfenden, George
See Beardmore, George
Wolfer, Dianne 1961- ................................ 167
Autobiography Feature ............................ 117
Earlier sketch in SATA 104
Wolff, Alexander (Nikolaus) 1957- .......... 137
Earlier sketch in SATA 63
Wolff, Ashley 1956- .................................. 155
Earlier sketches in SATA 50, 81
Wolff, Diane 1945- ..................................... 27
Wolff, Ferida 1946- .................................. 164
Earlier sketch in SATA 79
Wolff, Jennifer Ashley
See Wolff, Ashley
Wolff, Robert Jay 1905-1977 ....................... 10
Wolff, Sonia
See Levitin, Sonia (Wolff)
Wolff, Virginia Euwer 1937- ...................... 137
Earlier sketch in SATA 78
See also CLR 62
Wolfman, Judy 1933- ................................ 138
Wolfson, Evelyn 1937- ................................ 62
Wolitzer, Hilma 1930- ................................. 31
Wolkoff, Judie (Edwards) ............................ 93
Brief entry ............................................ 37
Wolkstein, Diane 1942- ............................. 138
Earlier sketches in SATA 7, 82
Wolny, P.
See Janeczko, Paul B(ryan)
Wolters, Richard A. 1920-1993 ..................... 35
Wondriska, William 1931- ............................. 6
Wong, Jade Snow 1922-2006 ...................... 112
Obituary ............................................... 175
Wong, Janet S. 1962- ................................ 148
Earlier sketch in SATA 98
See also CLR 94
Wood, Anne (Savage) 1937- ........................ 64
Wood, Audrey ........................................... 139
Brief entry ............................................ 44
Earlier sketches in SATA 50, 81
See also CLR 26
Wood, Catherine
See Etchison, Birdie L(ee)
Wood, David 1944- ..................................... 87
Wood, Don 1945- ....................................... 50
Brief entry ............................................ 44
See also CLR 26
Wood, Douglas (Eric) 1951- ...................... 132
Earlier sketch in SATA 81
Wood, Edgar A(llardyce) 1907-1998 ............. 14
Wood, Esther
See Brady, Esther Wood
Wood, Frances Elizabeth .............................. 34
Wood, Frances M. 1951- .............................. 97
Wood, James Playsted 1905- .......................... 1
Wood, Jenny 1955- ..................................... 88
Wood, John Norris 1930- ............................. 85
Wood, June Rae 1946- ............................... 120
Earlier sketch in SATA 79
See also CLR 82
Wood, Kerry
See Wood, Edgar A(llardyce)
Wood, Kim Marie ...................................... 134
Wood, Laura N.
See Roper, Laura (Newbold) Wood
Wood, Linda C(arol) 1945- ........................... 59
Wood, Marcia 1956- ................................... 80
Wood, Marcia Mae
See Wood, Marcia
Wood, Nancy 1936- ...................................... 6
Wood, Nuria
See Nobisso, Josephine
Wood, Owen 1929- ..................................... 64
Wood, Phyllis Anderson 1923- ...................... 33
Brief entry ............................................ 30
Wood, Richard 1949- ................................ 110

Wood, Tim(othy William Russell) 1946- .... 88
Woodard, Carol 1929- ................................. 14
Woodburn, John Henry 1914- ....................... 11
Woodbury, David Oakes 1896-1981 ............. 62
Woodford, Peggy 1937- ............................... 25
Woodhouse, Barbara (Blackburn) 1910-1988
.................................................................. 63
Wooding, Chris 1977- ............................... 166
Wooding, Sharon
See Wooding, Sharon L(ouise)
Wooding, Sharon L(ouise) 1943- ................. 66
Woodman, Allen 1954- ................................ 76
Woodrich, Mary Neville 1915- ....................... 2
Woodruff, Elvira 1951- .............................. 162
Earlier sketches in SATA 70, 106
Woodruff, Joan Leslie 1953- ...................... 104
Woodruff, Marian
See Goudge, Eileen
Woodruff, Noah 1977- ................................ 86
Woods, George A(llan) 1926-1988 ................ 30
Obituary ................................................ 57
Woods, Geraldine 1948- ............................ 111
Brief entry ............................................ 42
Earlier sketch in SATA 56
Woods, Harold 1945- ................................. 56
Brief entry ............................................ 42
Woods, Lawrence
See Lowndes, Robert A(ugustine) W(ard)
Woods, Margaret 1921- ................................. 2
Woods, Nat
See Stratemeyer, Edward L.
Woodson, Jack
See Woodson, John Waddie Jr.
Woodson, Jacqueline 1964- ....................... 139
Earlier sketch in SATA 94
See also CLR 49
Woodson, Jacqueline Amanda
See Woodson, Jacqueline
Woodson, John Waddie Jr. 1913- ................. 10
Woodtor, Dee
See Woodtor, Delores Parmer
Woodtor, Dee Parmer 1945(?)-2002
See Woodtor, Delores Parmer
Woodtor, Delores Parmer 1945-2002 .......... 93
Wood-Trost, Lucille
See Trost, Lucille W(ood)
Woodward, (Landon) Cleveland 1900-1986
.................................................................. 10
Obituary ................................................ 48
Woodworth, Chris 1957- ............................ 168
Woodworth, Viki 1952- .............................. 127
Woody, Regina Jones 1894-1983 .................... 3
Woog, Adam 1953- ................................... 125
Earlier sketch in SATA 84
Wooldridge, Connie Nordhielm 1950- ...... 143
Earlier sketch in SATA 92
Wooldridge, Frosty 1947- ........................... 140
Wooldridge, Rhoda 1906-1988 ..................... 22
Wooley, Susan Frelick 1945- ...................... 113
Woolf, Paula 1950- ................................... 104
Woolfe, Angela 1976- ................................ 169
Woolley, Catherine 1904-2005 ....................... 3
Obituary ............................................... 166
Woolman, Steven 1969-2004 ...................... 163
Earlier sketch in SATA 90
Woolsey, Janette 1904-1989 .......................... 3
Obituary ............................................... 131
Worcester, Donald E(mmet) 1915- ............. 18
Word, Reagan 1944- ................................. 103
Work, Virginia 1946- ................................... 57
Brief entry ............................................ 45
Worline, Bonnie Bess 1914- ......................... 14
Wormell, Christopher 1955- ...................... 154
Earlier sketch in SATA 103
Wormell, Mary 1959- .................................. 96
Wormser, Richard 1933- ............................ 106
Autobiography Feature ............................ 118
See also SAAS 26
Wormser, Sophie 1897-1979 ......................... 22
Worth, Richard 1945- ................................. 59
Brief entry ............................................ 46

Worth, Valerie -1994 .................................. 70
  Earlier sketch in SATA 8
  *See also* CLR 21
  *See* Bahlke, Valerie Worth
Wortis, Avi 1937- ................................... 14
  *See* Avi
  and Wortis, Edward (Irving)
Wortis, Edward (Irving) .......................... 156
  *See* Wortis, Avi
Wosmek, Frances 1917- ............................ 29
Woychuk, Denis 1953- ............................. 71
Wrede, Patricia C(ollins) 1953- ............... 146
  Earlier sketch in SATA 67
Wriggins, Sally Hovey 1922- .................... 17
Wright, Alexandra 1979- ......................... 103
Wright, Betty Ren .................................. 109
  Brief entry ...................................... 48
  Earlier sketch in SATA 63
Wright, Cliff 1963- ............................... 168
  Earlier sketch in SATA 76
Wright, Courtni
  *See* Wright, Courtni C(rump)
Wright, Courtni C(rump) 1950- ................. 84
Wright, Courtni Crump
  *See* Wright, Courtni C(rump)
Wright, Dare 1914(?)-2001 ...................... 21
  Obituary .......................................... 124
Wright, David K. 1943- .......................... 112
  Earlier sketch in SATA 73
Wright, Enid Meadowcroft (LaMonte)
  1898-1966 ......................................... 3
Wright, Esmond 1915-2003 ...................... 10
Wright, Frances Fitzpatrick 1897-1982 ....... 10
Wright, J. B.
  *See* Barkan, Joanne
Wright, Judith 1915-2000 ........................ 14
  Obituary .......................................... 121
Wright, Judith Arundell
  *See* Wright, Judith
Wright, Katrina
  *See* Gater, Dilys
Wright, Kenneth
  *See* del Rey, Lester
Wright, Kit 1944- ................................. 87
Wright, Leslie B(ailey) 1959- .................. 91
Wright, Nancy Means ............................. 38
Wright, R(obert) H(amilton) 1906- ............. 6
Wright, Rachel .................................... 134
Wright, Susan Kimmel 1950- .................... 97
Wrightfrierson
  *See* Wright-Frierson, Virginia (Marguerite)
Wright-Frierson, Virginia (Marguerite) 1949-
  ..................................................... 110
  Earlier sketch in SATA 58
Wrightson, (Alice) Patricia 1921- ............. 112
  Earlier sketches in SATA 8, 66
  *See also* CLR 14
  *See also* SAAS 4
Wroble, Lisa A. 1963- ........................... 134
Wronker, Lili
  *See* Wronker, Lili Cassel
Wronker, Lili Cassel 1924- ..................... 10
Wryde, Dogear
  *See* Gorey, Edward (St. John)
Wu, Norbert 1961- ............................... 155
  Earlier sketch in SATA 101
Wulffson, Don (L.) 1943- ....................... 155
  Earlier sketches in SATA 32, 88
Wunderli, Stephen 1958- ......................... 79
Wunsch, Josephine (McLean) 1914- ............ 64
Wuorio, Eva-Lis 1918- ........................... 34
  Brief entry ...................................... 28
Wurts, Janny 1953- .............................. 98
Wyatt, B. D.
  *See* Robinson, Spider
Wyatt, Jane
  *See* Bradbury, Bianca (Ryley)
Wyatt, Melissa 1963- ............................ 177
Wyeth, Betsy James 1921- ....................... 41
Wyeth, N(ewell) C(onvers) 1882-1945 ........ 17
  *See also* CLR 106

Wyler, Rose 1909-2000 ........................... 18
  Obituary .......................................... 121
Wylie, Betty Jane ................................ 48
Wylie, Laura
  *See* Matthews, Patricia
Wylie, Laurie
  *See* Matthews, Patricia
Wyllie, Stephen .................................. 86
Wyman, Andrea .................................... 75
Wyman, Carolyn 1956- ............................ 83
Wymer, Norman (George) 1911- .................. 25
Wynard, Talbot
  *See* Hamilton, Charles (Harold St. John)
Wyndham, John
  *See* Harris, John (Wyndham Parkes Lucas)
  Beynon
Wyndham, Lee
  *See* Hyndman, Jane Andrews Lee
Wyndham, Robert
  *See* Hyndman, Robert Utley
Wynne-Jones, Tim(othy) 1948- .................. 136
  Autobiography Feature ........................... 136
  Earlier sketches in SATA 67, 96
  *See also* CLR 58
Wynter, Edward (John) 1914- .................... 14
Wynyard, Talbot
  *See* Hamilton, Charles (Harold St. John)
Wyss, Johann David Von 1743-1818 ........... 29
  Brief entry ...................................... 27
  *See also* CLR 92
Wyss, Thelma Hatch 1934- ...................... 140
  Earlier sketch in SATA 10

**X**

Xavier, Father
  *See* Hurwood, Bernhardt J.
Xuan, YongSheng 1952- .......................... 116
  Autobiography Feature ........................... 119

**Y**

Yaccarino, Dan ................................... 141
Yadin, (Rav-Aloof) Yigael 1917-1984 ........ 55
Yaffe, Alan
  *See* Yorinks, Arthur
Yagher, Kevin 1962- ............................. 143
Yakovetic, (Joseph Sandy) 1952- ............... 59
Yakovetic, Joe
  *See* Yakovetic, (Joseph Sandy)
Yamaguchi, Marianne (Illenberger) 1936- .... 7
Yamaka, Sara 1978- ............................... 92
Yamanaka, Lois-Ann 1961- ...................... 166
Yancey, Diane 1951- ............................. 138
  Earlier sketch in SATA 81
Yang, Belle 1960- ............................... 170
Yang, Jay 1941- .................................. 12
Yang, Mingyi 1943- .............................. 72
Yarbrough, Camille 1938- ....................... 79
  *See also* CLR 29
Yaroslava
  *See* Mills, Yaroslava Surmach
Yashima, Taro
  *See* CLR 4
  *See* Iwamatsu, Jun Atsushi
Yates, Elizabeth 1905-2001 ..................... 68
  Obituary .......................................... 128
  Earlier sketch in SATA 4
  *See also* SAAS 6
Yates, Janelle K(aye) 1957- .................... 77
Yates, John 1939- ................................ 74
Yates, Philip 1958- ............................. 149
  Earlier sketch in SATA 92
Yates, Raymond F(rancis) 1895-1966 .......... 31
Yaukey, Grace S(ydenstricker) 1899-1994 .. 80
  Earlier sketch in SATA 5
Ye, Ting-xing 1952- ............................. 106
Yeakley, Marjory Hall 1908- .................... 21

Yeatman, Linda 1938- ............................ 42
Yee, Brenda Shannon ............................ 133
Yee, Lisa 1959- .................................. 160
Yee, Paul (R.) 1956- ............................. 143
  Earlier sketches in SATA 67, 96
  *See also* CLR 44
Yee, Wong Herbert 1953- ......................... 172
  Earlier sketches in SATA 78, 115
Yeh, Chun-Chan 1914- ............................ 79
  *See* Ye Junjian
Ye Junjian
  *See* Yeh, Chun-Chan
Yenawine, Philip 1942- .......................... 85
Yensid, Retlaw
  *See* Disney, Walt(er Elias)
Yeo, Wilma (Lethem) 1918-1994 ............... 81
  Earlier sketch in SATA 24
Yeoman, John 1934- .............................. 80
  Earlier sketch in SATA 28
  *See also* CLR 46
Yep, Laurence 1948- ............................. 176
  Earlier sketches in SATA 7, 69, 123
  *See also* CLR 54
Yep, Laurence Michael
  *See* Yep, Laurence
Yepsen, Roger B(ennet), Jr. 1947- ............. 59
Yerian, Cameron John ........................... 21
Yerian, Margaret A. ............................. 21
Yetska
  *See* Ironside, Jetske
Ylvisaker, Anne 1965(?)- ....................... 172
Yoder, Carolyn P(atricia) 1953- ............... 149
Yoder, Dorothy Meenen 1921- ................... 96
Yoder, Dot
  *See* Yoder, Dorothy Meenen
Yoder, Walter D. 1933- .......................... 88
Yolen, Jane 1939- ............................... 158
  Autobiography Feature ........................... 111
  Earlier sketches in SATA 4, 40, 75, 112
  *See also* CLR 44
  *See also* SAAS 1
Yolen, Jane Hyatt
  *See* Yolen, Jane
Yonge, Charlotte (Mary) 1823-1901 .......... 17
Yoo, Paula 1969(?)- ............................. 174
Yorinks, Adrienne 1956- ........................ 171
Yorinks, Arthur 1953- ........................... 144
  Earlier sketches in SATA 33, 49, 85
  *See also* CLR 20
York, Alison
  *See* Nicole, Christopher (Robin)
York, Andrew
  *See* Nicole, Christopher (Robin)
York, Carol Beach 1928- ........................ 77
  Earlier sketch in SATA 6
York, Rebecca
  *See* Buckholtz, Eileen (Garber)
  and Glick, Ruth (Burtnick)
York, Simon
  *See* Heinlein, Robert A.
Yoshida, Toshi 1911- ............................ 77
Youd, C. S.
  *See* SAAS 6
  *See* Youd, (Christopher) Samuel
Youd, (Christopher) Samuel 1922- ............. 135
  Brief entry ...................................... 30
  Earlier sketch in SATA 47
  *See* Christopher, John
  and Youd, C. S.
Young, Bob
  *See* Young, Robert W(illiam)
  and Young, James Robert
Young, Carol 1945- .............................. 102
Young, Catherine
  *See* Olds, Helen Diehl
Young, Clarence ................................. 67
  Earlier sketch in SATA 1
  *See* Stratemeyer, Edward L.
Young, Collier
  *See* Bloch, Robert (Albert)
Young, Dan 1952- ................................ 126

Young, Dianne 1959- ...................................... 88
Young, Dorothea Bennett 1924- .................... 31
Young, Ed 1931- ........................................ 173
　Earlier sketches in SATA 10, 74, 122
　See also CLR 27
Young, Ed Tse-chun
　See Young, Ed
Young, Edward
　See Reinfeld, Fred
Young, Elaine L.
　See Schulte, Elaine L(ouise)
Young, James
　See Graham, Ian
Young, Jan
　See Young, Janet Randall
Young, Janet Randall 1919-1994 .................. 3
Young, Jeff C. 1948- ................................. 132
Young, John
　See Macintosh, Brownie
Young, Judy 1956- ..................................... 155
Young, Judy (Elaine) Dockrey 1949- .......... 72
Young, Karen Romano 1959- ..................... 168
　Earlier sketch in SATA 116
Young, Ken 1956- ........................................ 86
Young, Lois Horton 1911-1981 .................... 26
Young, Louisa .......................................... 161
Young, Louise B. 1919- .............................. 64
Young, Margaret B(uckner) 1922- ................ 2
Young, Mary 1940- ..................................... 89
Young, Miriam 1913-1974 ........................... 7
Young, Noela 1930- ..................................... 89
Young, (Rodney Lee) Patrick (Jr.) 1937- .... 22
Young, Percy M(arshall) 1912-2004 .......... 31
　Obituary ................................................ 154
Young, Richard Alan 1946- .......................... 72
Young, Robert W(illiam) 1916-1969 ............ 3
Young, Ross B. 1955- ................................ 150
Young, Ruth 1946- ....................................... 67
Young, Scott A. 1918-2005 ............................ 5
Young, Scott Alexander
　See Young, Scott A.
Young, Vivien
　See Gater, Dilys
Younger, Barbara 1954- ............................ 108
Youngs, Betty 1934-1985 ............................ 53
　Obituary .................................................. 42
Younkin, Paula 1942- .................................. 77
Yount, Lisa (Ann) 1944- ............................ 124
　Earlier sketch in SATA 74
Yuditskaya, Tatyana 1964- .......................... 75
Yumoto, Kazumi 1959- .............................. 153

# Z

Zach, Cheryl (Byrd) 1947- .......................... 98
　Brief entry .............................................. 51
　Earlier sketch in SATA 58
　See also SAAS 24
Zacharias, Gary L. 1946- .......................... 153
Zaffo, George J. (?)-1984 ............................ 42
Zagwyn, Deborah Turney 1953- ................ 138
　Earlier sketch in SATA 78
Zahn, Timothy 1951- ................................ 156
　Earlier sketch in SATA 91
Zaid, Barry 1938- ....................................... 51
Zaidenberg, Arthur 1908(?)-1990 .............. 34
　Obituary .................................................. 66
Zalben, Jane Breskin 1950- ...................... 170
　Earlier sketches in SATA 7, 79, 120
　See also CLR 84
Zallinger, Jean (Day) 1918- ...................... 115
　Earlier sketches in SATA 14, 80
Zallinger, Peter Franz 1943- ........................ 49

Zambreno, Mary Frances 1954- ................ 140
　Earlier sketch in SATA 75
Zanderbergen, George
　See May, Julian
Zappler, Lisbeth 1930- ................................ 10
Zarchy, Harry 1912-1987 ............................ 34
Zarin, Cynthia 1959- ................................ 108
Zaring, Jane (Thomas) 1936- ...................... 40
Zarins, Joyce Audy ...................................... 57
　See dos Santos, Joyce Audy
Zaslavsky, Claudia 1917- ............................ 36
Zaugg, Sandra L. 1938- ............................ 118
Zaugg, Sandy
　See Zaugg, Sandra L.
Zaunders, Bo 1939- .................................. 137
Zawadzki, Marek 1958- .............................. 97
Zebra, A.
　See Scoltock, Jack
Zebrowski, George 1945- ............................ 67
Zebrowski, George T.
　See Zebrowski, George
Zeck, Gerald Anthony 1939- ...................... 40
Zeck, Gerry
　See Zeck, Gerald Anthony
Zed, Dr.
　See Penrose, Gordon
Zei, Alki 1925- .......................................... 24
　See also CLR 6
Zeier, Joan T(heresa) 1931- ........................ 81
Zeinert, Karen 1942-2002 ........................ 137
　Earlier sketch in SATA 79
Zeises, Lara M. 1976- .............................. 145
Zelazny, Roger 1937-1995 .......................... 57
　Brief entry .............................................. 39
Zelazny, Roger Joseph
　See Zelazny, Roger
Zeldis, Malcah 1931- ................................ 146
　Earlier sketch in SATA 86
Zelinsky, Paul O. 1953- ............................ 154
　Brief entry .............................................. 33
　Earlier sketches in SATA 49, 102
　See also CLR 55
Zellan, Audrey Penn .................................... 22
　See Penn, Audrey
Zemach, Harve ............................................. 3
　See Fischtrom, Harvey
Zemach, Kaethe 1958- .............................. 149
　Brief entry .............................................. 39
　Earlier sketch in SATA 49
Zemach, Margot 1931-1989 ........................ 70
　Obituary .................................................. 59
　Earlier sketch in SATA 21
Zemach-Bersin, Kaethe
　See Zemach, Kaethe
Zeman, Ludmila 1947- .............................. 153
Zephaniah, Benjamin 1958- ...................... 140
　Earlier sketch in SATA 86
Zephaniah, Benjamin Obadiah Iqbal
　See Zephaniah, Benjamin
Zerman, Melvyn Bernard 1930- .................. 46
Zettner, Pat 1940- ....................................... 70
Zevin, Gabrielle ........................................ 176
Zhang, Christopher Zhong-Yuan 1954- ....... 91
Zhang, Song Nan 1942- ............................ 170
　Earlier sketch in SATA 85
Ziefert, Harriet 1941- .............................. 154
　Earlier sketch in SATA 101
Ziegler, Jack (Denmore) 1942- .................... 60
Ziemienski, Dennis (Theodore) 1947- ......... 10
Ziliox, Marc
　See Fichter, George S.
Zillah
　See Macdonald, Zillah K(atherine)

Zim, Herbert S(pencer) 1909-1994 ............ 30
　Obituary .................................................. 85
　Earlier sketch in SATA 1
　See also CLR 2
　See also SAAS 2
Zima, Gordon 1920- .................................... 90
Zimelman, Nathan 1921- ............................ 65
　Brief entry .............................................. 37
Zimmer, Dirk 1943- .................................. 147
　Earlier sketch in SATA 65
Zimmer, Tracie Vaughn ............................ 169
Zimmerman, Andrea Griffing 1950- .......... 123
Zimmerman, H. Werner 1951- .................. 101
Zimmerman, Heinz Werner
　See Zimmerman, H. Werner
Zimmerman, Naoma 1914-2004 .................. 10
Zimmermann, Arnold E. 1909- .................... 58
Zimmett, Debbie
　See Becker, Deborah Zimmett
Zimmy
　See Stratemeyer, Edward L.
Zimnik, Reiner 1930- .................................. 36
　See also CLR 3
Zindel, Bonnie 1943- .................................. 34
Zindel, Paul 1936-2003 ............................ 102
　Obituary ................................................ 142
　Earlier sketches in SATA 16, 58
　See also CLR 85
Ziner, Feenie
　See Ziner, Florence
Ziner, Florence 1921- ................................... 5
Zingara, Professor
　See Leeming, Joseph
Zinger, Yitskhok
　See Singer, Isaac Bashevis
Zion, Eugene 1913-1975 ............................ 18
Zion, Gene
　See Zion, Eugene
Zohorsky, Janet R. 1958- .......................... 148
Zolkower, Edie Stoltz ................................ 171
Zolkowski, Cathy (A.) 1969- ...................... 121
Zolotow, Charlotte (Gertrude) S(hapiro) 1915-
　............................................................ 138
　Earlier sketches in SATA 1, 35, 78
　See also CLR 77
Zonderman, Jon 1957- ................................ 92
Zonia, Dhimitri 1921- ................................. 20
Zonta, Pat 1951- ....................................... 143
Zubrowski, Bernard 1939- .......................... 90
　Earlier sketch in SATA 35
Zubrowski, Bernie
　See Zubrowski, Bernard
Zucker, Miriam S.
　See Reichert, Miriam Zucker
Zudeck, Darryl 1961- .................................. 61
Zupa, G. Anthony
　See Zeck, Gerald Anthony
Zupancic, Lilijana Praprotnik
　See Prap, Lila
Zurbo, Matt(hew) 1967- .............................. 98
Zurhorst, Charles (Stewart, Jr.) 1913-1989 . 12
Zurlo, Tony 1941- .................................... 145
Zuromskis, Diane
　See Stanley, Diane
Zuromskis, Diane Stanley
　See Stanley, Diane
Zusak, Markus 1975- ................................ 149
Zwahlen, Diana 1947- ................................. 88
Zweifel, Frances W. 1931- .......................... 14
Zwerger, Lisbeth 1954- ............................ 130
　Earlier sketch in SATA 66
　See also CLR 46
　See also SAAS 13
Zwinger, Ann (H.) 1925- ............................ 46
Zymet, Cathy Alter 1965- .......................... 121